Street by Street

SURREY

GW00580018

Enlarged areas CROYDON, FARNHAM, GUILDFORD, KINGSTON UPON THAMES, WOKING

Plus Aldershot, Biggin Hill, Bracknell, Crawley, East Grinstead, Farnborough, Gatwick Airport, Heathrow Airport, Horley, Horsham, Liphook, Richmond, Sutton

3rd edition February 2007
© Automobile Association Developments Limited 2007

Original edition printed May 2001

 This product includes map data licensed from Ordnance Survey® with the permission of the Controller of Her Majesty's Stationery Office. © Crown copyright 2007. All rights reserved. Licence number 100021153.

The copyright in all PAF is owned by Royal Mail Group plc.

Published by AA Publishing (a trading name of Automobile Association Developments Limited, whose registered office is Fanum House, Basing View, Basingstoke, Hampshire RG21 4EA. Registered number 1878835).

Produced by the Mapping Services Department of The Automobile Association. (A02664)

A CIP Catalogue record for this book is available from the British Library.

Printed by Leo, China

The contents of this atlas are believed to be correct at the time of the latest revision. However, the publishers cannot be held responsible or liable for any loss or damage occasioned to any person acting or refraining from action as a result of any use or reliance on any material in this atlas, nor for any errors, omissions or changes in such material. This does not affect your statutory rights. The publishers would welcome information to correct any errors or omissions and to keep this atlas up to date. Please write to Publishing, The Automobile Association, Fanum House (FH12), Basing View, Basingstoke, Hampshire, RG21 4EA.
E-mail: *streetbystreet@theaa.com*

Ref: MX118y

Key to map pages	ii-iii
Key to map symbols	iv-1
Map pages - 1:10,000	2-11
Map pages - 1:17,500	12-167
Map pages - 1:25,000	168-205
Index – towns & villages	206-207
Index – streets	208-259
Index – featured places	259-268
Acknowledgements	268

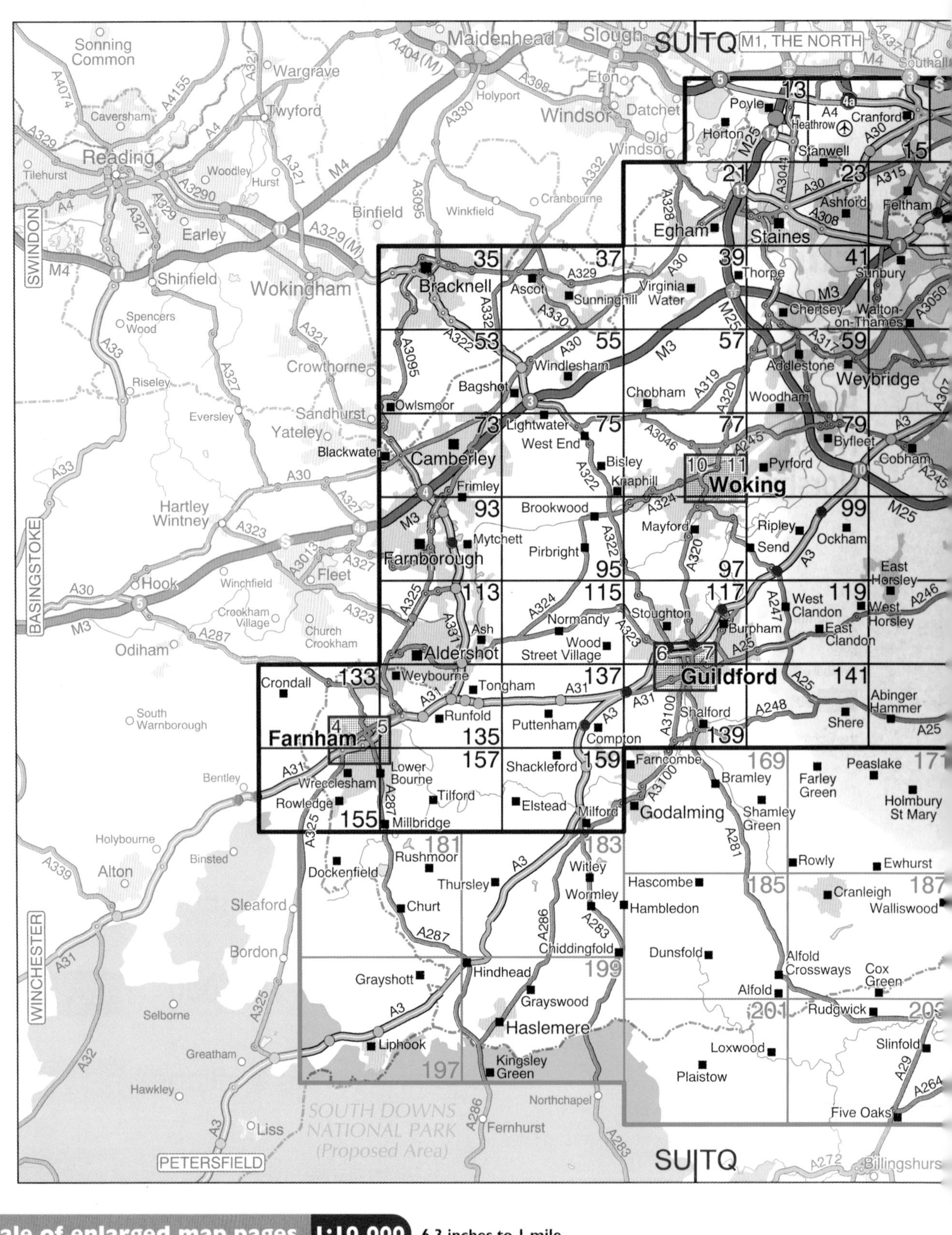

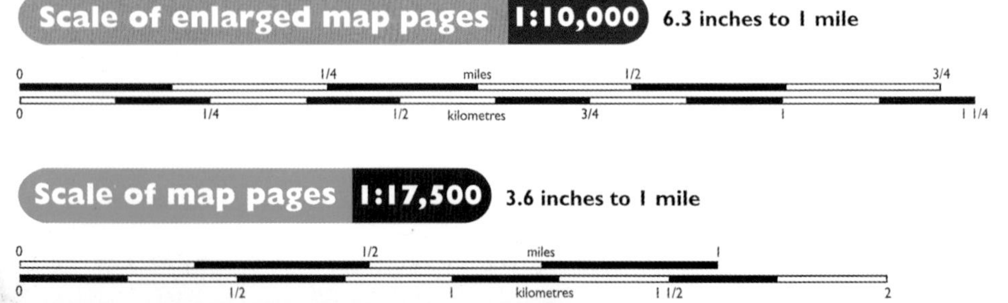

Scale of enlarged map pages | **1:10,000** 6.3 inches to 1 mile

| 0 | | 1/4 | miles | 1/2 | | 3/4 | |
| 0 | 1/4 | | 1/2 | kilometres | 3/4 | 1 | 1 1/4 |

Scale of map pages | **1:17,500** 3.6 inches to 1 mile

| 0 | | 1/2 | miles | | 1 |
| 0 | 1/2 | | 1 | kilometres | 1 1/2 | 2 |

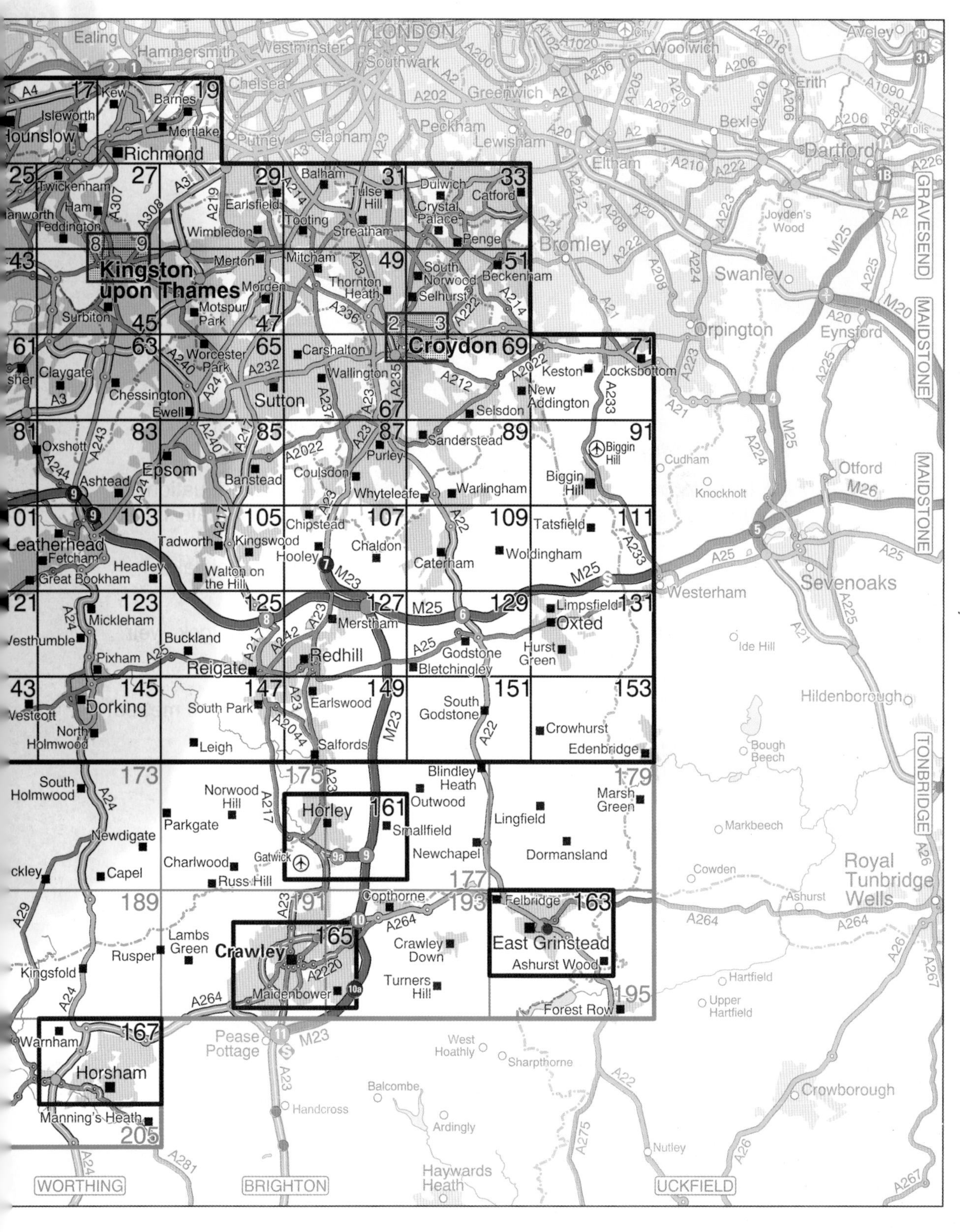

National Grid references are shown on the map frame of each page.
Red figures denote the 100 km square and the blue figures the 1km square.

Example, page 16 : Hounslow Station 514 175

The reference can also be written using the National Grid two-letter prefix
shown on this page, where 5 and 1 are replaced by TQ to give TQ1475

2.5 inches to 1 mile   Scale of map pages   1:25,000

0   1/2   miles   1   1 1/2

0   1/2   kilometres   1 1/2   2

iv

Junction 9	Motorway & junction	*LC*	Level crossing
Services	Motorway service area	•—•—•—•—•	Tramway
	Primary road single/dual carriageway	- - - - - - -	Ferry route
Services	Primary road service area	....	Airport runway
	A road single/dual carriageway	—·—·—·—·	County, administrative boundary
	B road single/dual carriageway	◄168	Page continuation 1:25,000
	Other road single/dual carriageway	◄93	Page continuation 1:17,500
	Minor/private road, access may be restricted	◄7	Page continuation to enlarged scale 1:10,000
← ←	One-way street		River/canal, lake
	Pedestrian area		Aqueduct, lock, weir
- - - - - - -	Track or footpath	465 ▲ Winter Hill	Peak (with height in metres)
▮▮▮▮▮▮▮	Road under construction		Beach
[- - - - -]	Road tunnel		Woodland
P	Parking		Park
P+🚌	Park & Ride		Cemetery
🚌	Bus/coach station		Built-up area
	Railway & main railway station		Industrial/business building
	Railway & minor railway station		Leisure building
⊖	Underground station		Retail building
⊖	Light railway & station		Other building
+++++++++	Preserved private railway	IKEA	IKEA store

City wall		Castle
A&E	Hospital with 24-hour A&E department		Historic house or building
PO	Post Office	Wakehurst Place NT	National Trust property
	Public library	M	Museum or art gallery
i	Tourist Information Centre		Roman antiquity
i	Seasonal Tourist Information Centre		Ancient site, battlefield or monument
	Petrol station, 24 hour Major suppliers only		Industrial interest
†	Church/chapel		Garden
	Public toilets		Garden Centre Garden Centre Association Member
	Toilet with disabled facilities		Garden Centre Wyevale Garden Centre
PH	Public house AA recommended		Arboretum
	Restaurant AA inspected		Farm or animal centre
Madeira Hotel	Hotel AA inspected		Zoological or wildlife collection
	Theatre or performing arts centre		Bird collection
	Cinema		Nature reserve
	Golf course		Aquarium
▲	Camping AA inspected	V	Visitor or heritage centre
	Caravan site AA inspected		Country park
	Camping & caravan site AA inspected		Cave
	Theme park		Windmill
	Abbey, cathedral or priory		Distillery, brewery or vineyard

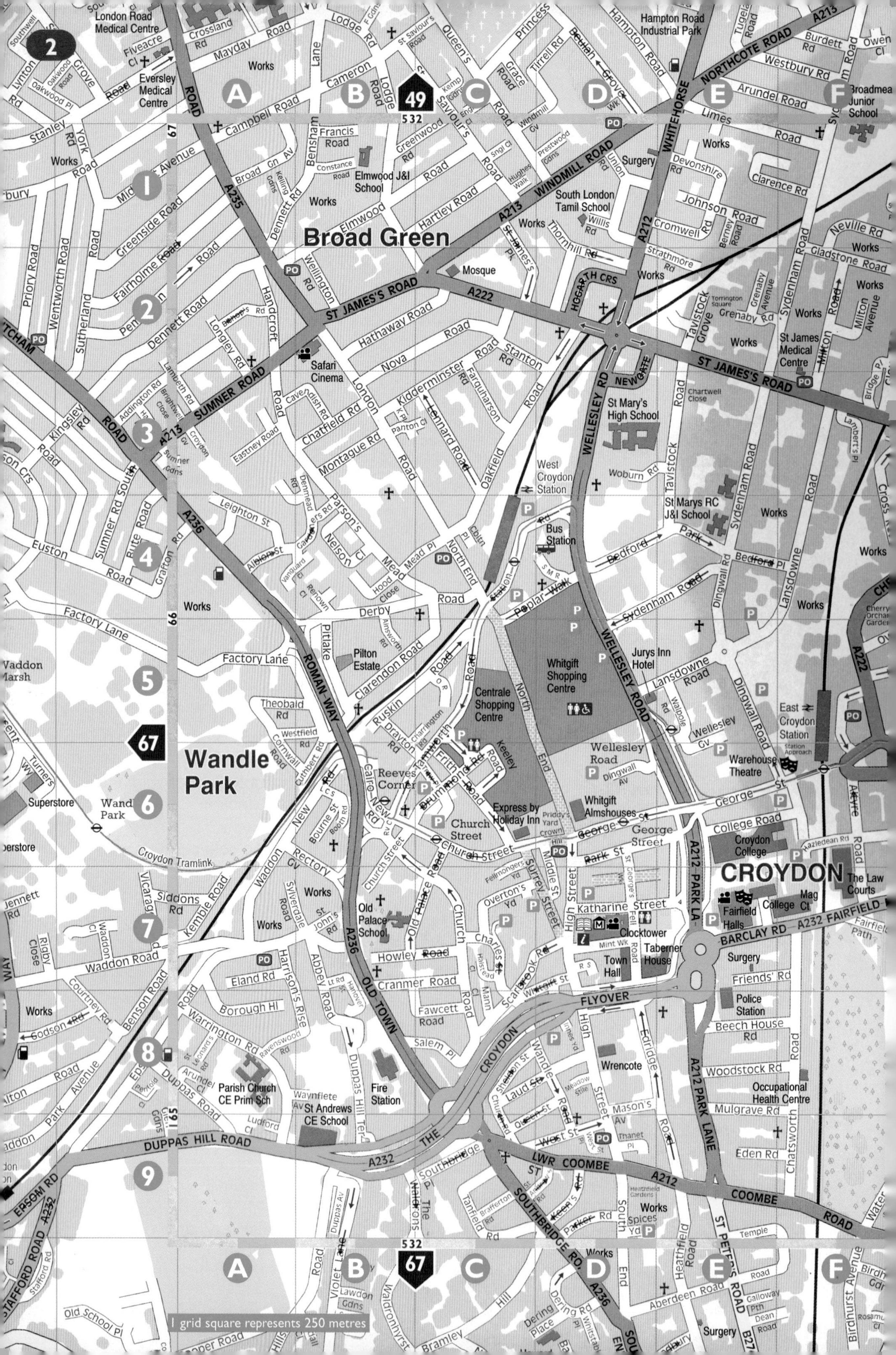
2
Broad Green
Wandle Park
CROYDON
Whitgift Shopping Centre
Centrale Shopping Centre
West Croydon Station
East Croydon Station
St Mary's High School
St Marys RC J&I School
Elmwood J&I School
South London Tamil School
Safari Cinema
Mosque
Pilton Estate
Bus Station
Jurys Inn Hotel
Warehouse Theatre
Croydon College
Fairfield Halls
The Law Courts
Clocktower
Town Hall
Taberner House
Police Station
Occupational Health Centre
Whitgift Almshouses
Express by Holiday Inn
Reeves Corner
Church Street
Old Palace School
Parish Church CE Prim Sch
St Andrews CE School
Fire Station
Wrencote
St James Medical Centre
Broadmead Junior School
Hampton Road Industrial Park
London Road Medical Centre
Eversley Medical Centre
Superstore
Waddon Marsh
Croydon Tramlink
ST JAMES'S ROAD
WELLESLEY ROAD
ROMAN WAY
OLD TOWN
DUPPAS HILL ROAD
CROYDON FLYOVER
A212 PARK LANE
COOMBE ROAD
SOUTHBRIDGE RD
BARCLAY RD
A232 FAIRFIELD
WINDMILL ROAD
WHITEHORSE
NORTHCOTE ROAD
SUMNER ROAD
ST PETER'S ROAD
49
67
532
1 grid square represents 250 metres

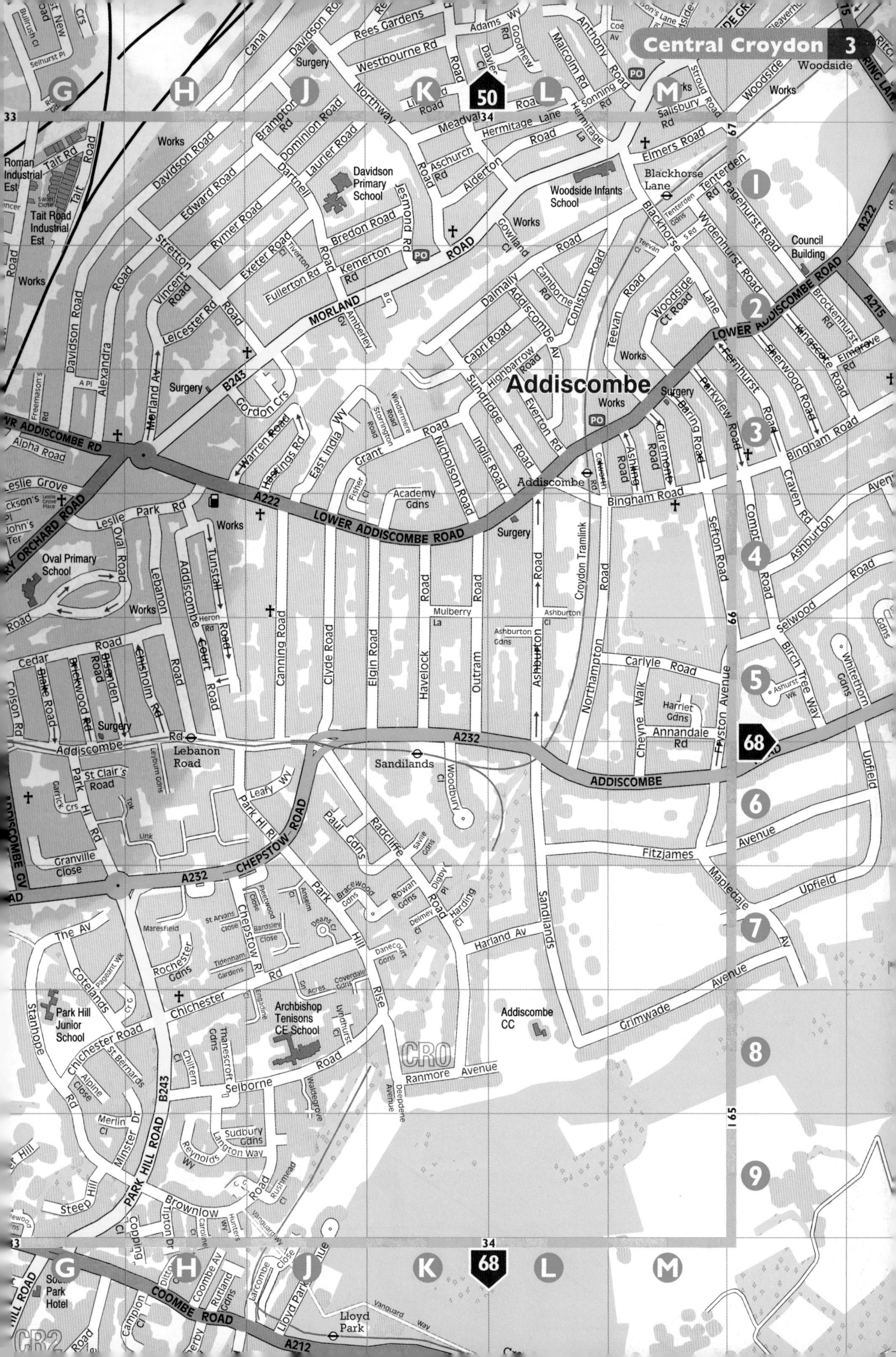
Addiscombe
Lower Addiscombe Road
Morland Road
Chepstow Road
Park Hill Road
Coombe Road
Addiscombe Road
Davidson Primary School
Woodside Infants School
Oval Primary School
Park Hill Junior School
Archbishop Tenisons CE School
Addiscombe CC
Council Building
Lloyd Park
Sandilands
Blackhorse Lane
Lebanon Road
Croydon Tramlink
Tait Road Industrial Est
Roman Industrial Est
Sefton Road
Ashburton Road
Grimwade Avenue
Fitzjames Avenue
Bingham Road
Woodside

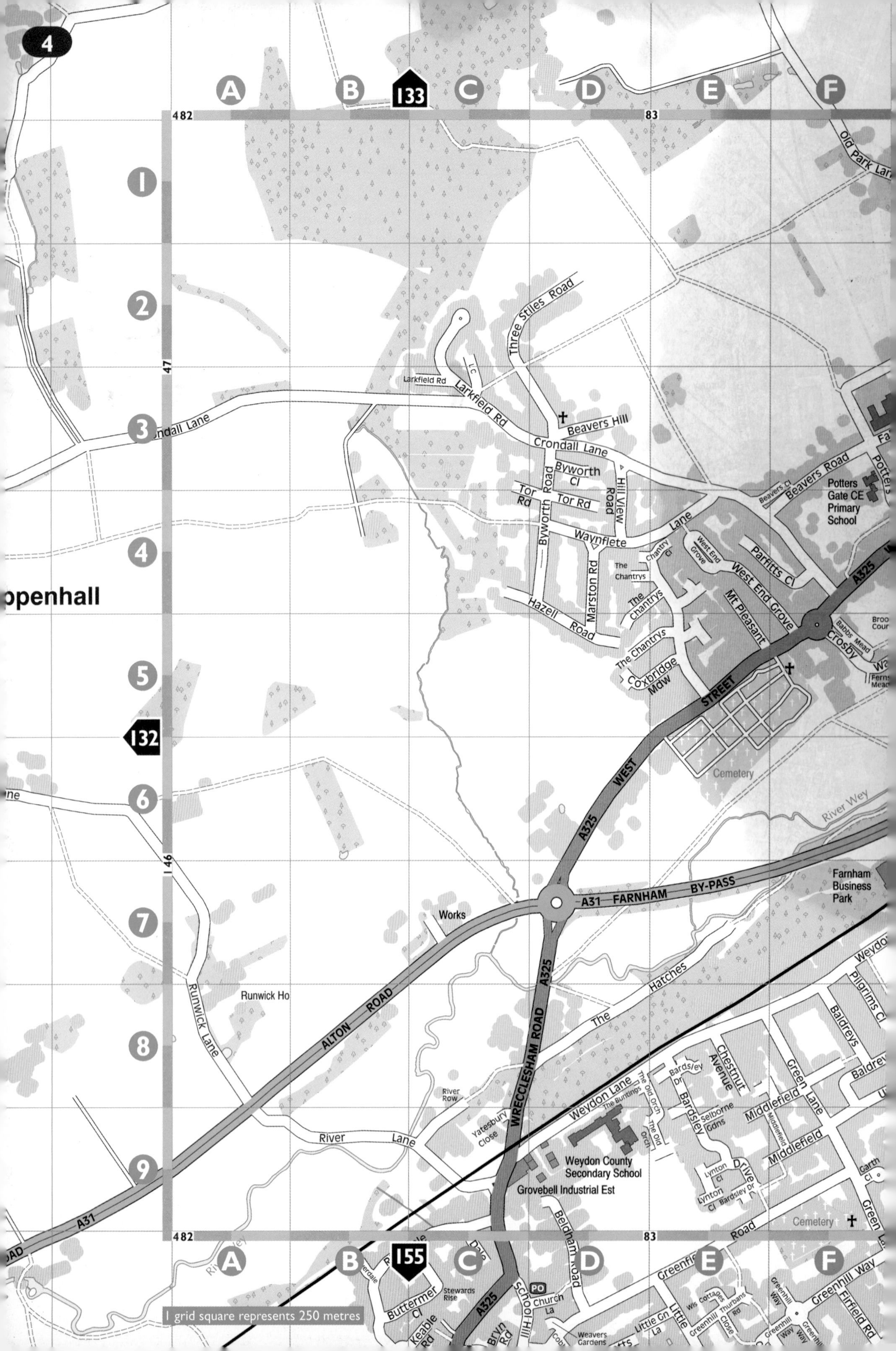

133
155
132
Old Park Lane
Three Stiles Road
Larkfield Rd
Crondall Lane
Beavers Hill
Byworth Cl
Tor Rd
Byworth Road
Hill View Road
Waynflete Lane
Beavers Road
Beavers Cl
Potters Gate CE Primary School
Marston Rd
Hazell Road
The Chantrys
Chantry Cl
West End Grove
Parfitts Cl
Mt Pleasant
Coxbridge Mdw
A325
WEST STREET
Cemetery
River Wey
Farnham Business Park
A31 FARNHAM BY-PASS
Works
Runwick Ho
Runwick Lane
ALTON ROAD
A31
WRECCLESHAM ROAD
The Hatches
River Row
River Lane
Yatesbury Close
Weydon Lane
The Buntings
The Old Orch
Bardsley Dr
Chestnut Avenue
Selborne Gdns
Bardsley Drive
Lynton Cl
Weydon County Secondary School
Grovebell Industrial Est
Beldham Road
Middlefield
Green Lane
Baldreys
Pilgrims Cl
Garth Cl
Greenhill Way
Firfield Rd
Greenhill Close
Thurbans Rd
Little Gn La
Church La
Weavers Gardens
School Hill
Bryn Rd
Keable Rd
Buttermer Cl
Stewards Rise
Crosby Way
Babbs Mead
Ferns Mead
Grid labels: A B C D E F; 1 2 3 4 5 6 7 8 9; 482 83 47 146
1 grid square represents 250 metres

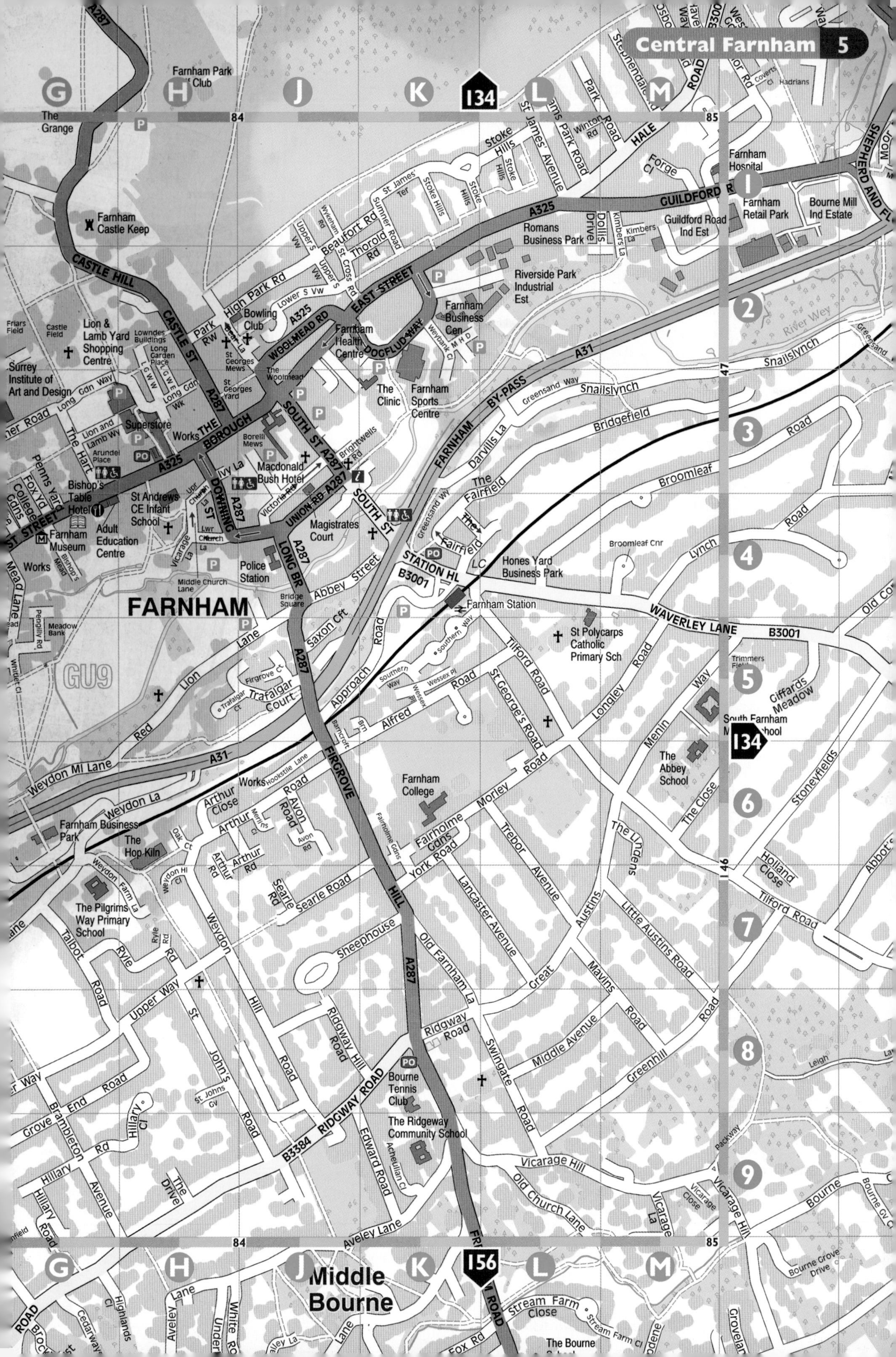
FARNHAM
Middle Bourne
The Grange
Farnham Park Golf Club
Farnham Castle Keep
Castle Hill
Castle St
Lion & Lamb Yard Shopping Centre
Surrey Institute of Art and Design
Superstore
The Borough
Bishop's Table Hotel
Farnham Museum
Adult Education Centre
St Andrews CE Infant School
Police Station
Macdonald Bush Hotel
Magistrates Court
Bowling Club
Farnham Health Centre
The Clinic
Farnham Sports Centre
Farnham Business Cen
Riverside Park Industrial Est
Romans Business Park
Guildford Road Ind Est
Farnham Hospital
Farnham Retail Park
Bourne Mill Ind Estate
River Wey
Farnham By-Pass
Station Hl
Farnham Station
Hones Yard Business Park
Waverley Lane
St Polycarps Catholic Primary Sch
South Farnham School
The Abbey School
Farnham College
Farnham Business Park
The Hop Kiln
The Pilgrims Way Primary School
Bourne Tennis Club
The Ridgeway Community School
Firgrove Hill
Ridgway Road
Vicarage Hill
Tilford Road
Guildford Rd
East Street
Woolmead Rd
Dogflud Way
South St
Union Rd
Long Br
Downing St
Abbey Street
Weydon Hill Road
Upper Way
Lion Lane
Red Lion Lane
Weydon Ml Lane
Weydon La
Longley Road
Bridgefield
Broomleaf Road
Snailslynch
GU9
134
156

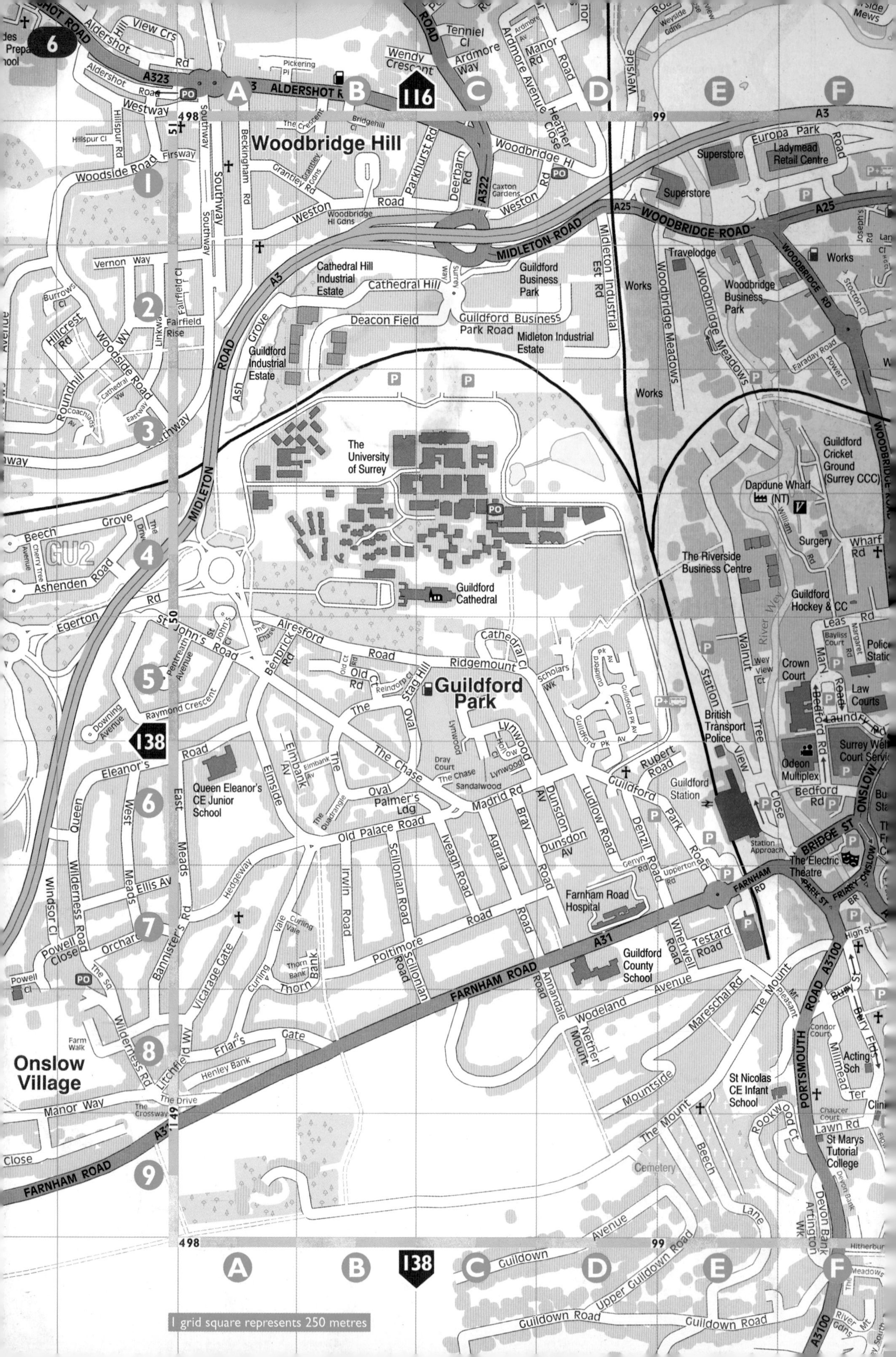

6
116
138
Woodbridge Hill
Guildford Park
Onslow Village
GU2
The University of Surrey
Guildford Cathedral
Cathedral Hill Industrial Estate
Guildford Industrial Estate
Guildford Business Park
Midleton Industrial Estate
Woodbridge Business Park
Ladymead Retail Centre
Superstore
Travelodge
Works
Guildford Cricket Ground (Surrey CCC)
Dapdune Wharf (NT)
The Riverside Business Centre
Guildford Hockey & CC
Crown Court
Law Courts
Surgery
Odeon Multiplex
British Transport Police
Guildford Station
Station Approach
The Electric Theatre
Farnham Road Hospital
Guildford County School
Queen Eleanor's CE Junior School
St Nicolas CE Infant School
St Marys Tutorial College
Acting Sch
Cemetery
ALDERSHOT ROAD
MIDLETON ROAD
WOODBRIDGE ROAD
FARNHAM ROAD
PORTSMOUTH ROAD
BRIDGE ST
A3
A25
A31
A322
A323
A3100
498
99
1 grid square represents 250 metres

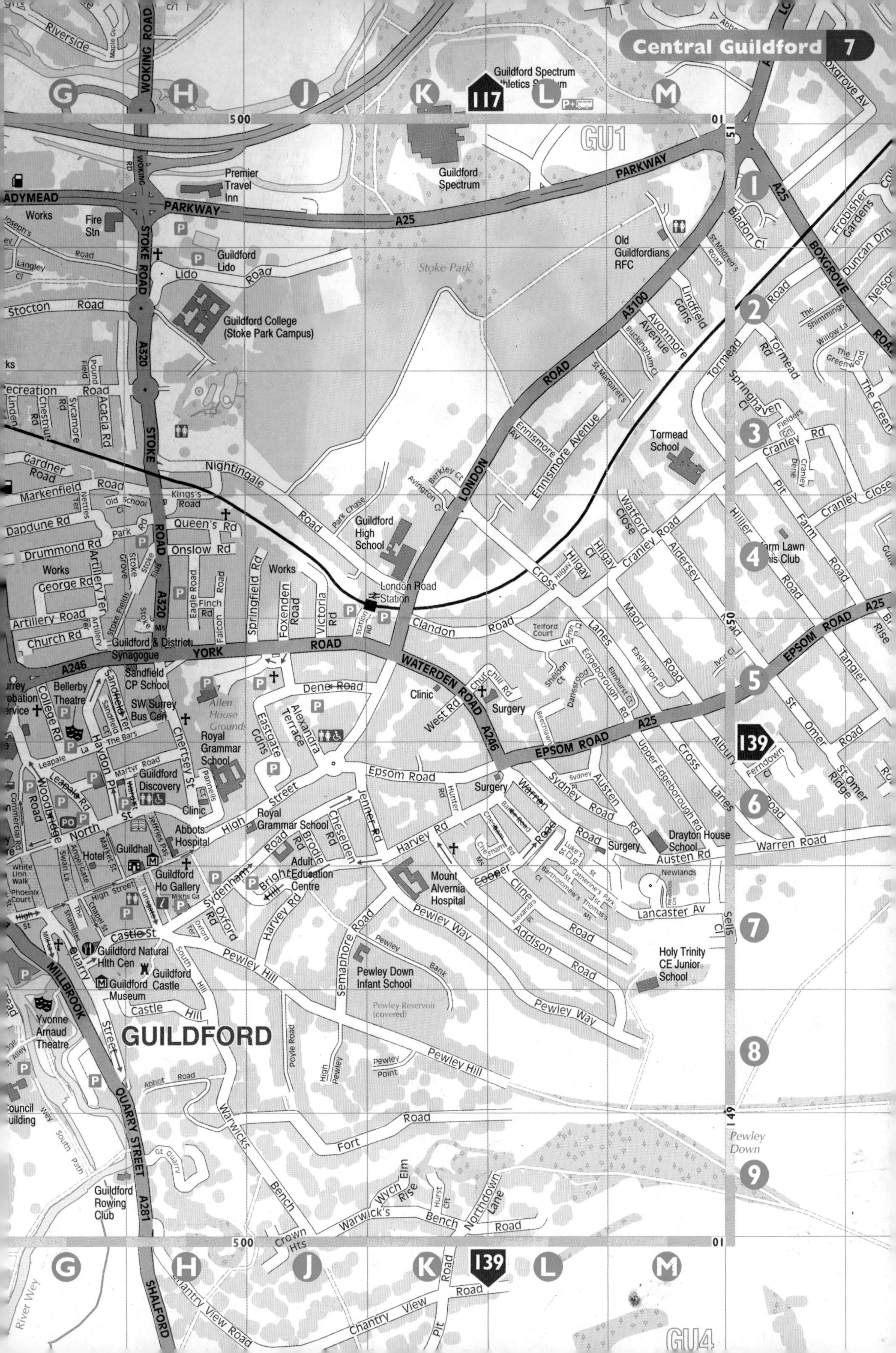

Guildford Spectrum
117
GU1
PARKWAY
A25
Premier Travel Inn
Guildford Spectrum
Fire Stn
Works
STOKE ROAD
Guildford Lido
Lido Road
Stoke Park
Old Guildfordians RFC
Stocton Road
Guildford College (Stoke Park Campus)
A320
A3100
LONDON ROAD
BOXGROVE ROAD
Tormead Rd
Tormead School
Recreation Road
Gardner Road
Markenfield Road
Nightingale Road
Guildford High School
Queen's Rd
Onslow Rd
Drummond Rd
Dapdune Rd
Works
George Rd
Artillery Road
Church Rd
London Road Station
YORK ROAD
A246
Guildford & District Synagogue
Sandfield CP School
Bellerby Theatre
SW Surrey Bus Cen
Allen House Grounds
Royal Grammar School
Dene Road
Clinic
Surgery
WATERDEN ROAD
EPSOM ROAD
Epsom Road
Guildford Discovery
Clinic
Abbots Hospital
High Street
Royal Grammar School
Guildhall
Hotel
Guildford Ho Gallery
Adult Education Centre
Mount Alvernia Hospital
Harvey Rd
Warren Road
Drayton House School
Surgery
Austen Rd
Lancaster Av
Holy Trinity CE Junior School
Castle St
Guildford Natural Hlth Cen
Guildford Castle
Guildford Museum
Pewley Down Infant School
Pewley Reservoir (covered)
Pewley Way
Pewley Hill
GUILDFORD
Yvonne Arnaud Theatre
MILLBROOK
QUARRY STREET
Council Building
Fort Road
Warwicks Bench
Guildford Rowing Club
A281
Pewley Down
Warwick's Bench Road
Northdown Lane
Chantry View Road
SHALFORD
River Wey
139
GU4
G H J K L M
1 2 3 4 5 6 7 8 9
500
01
51
50
49

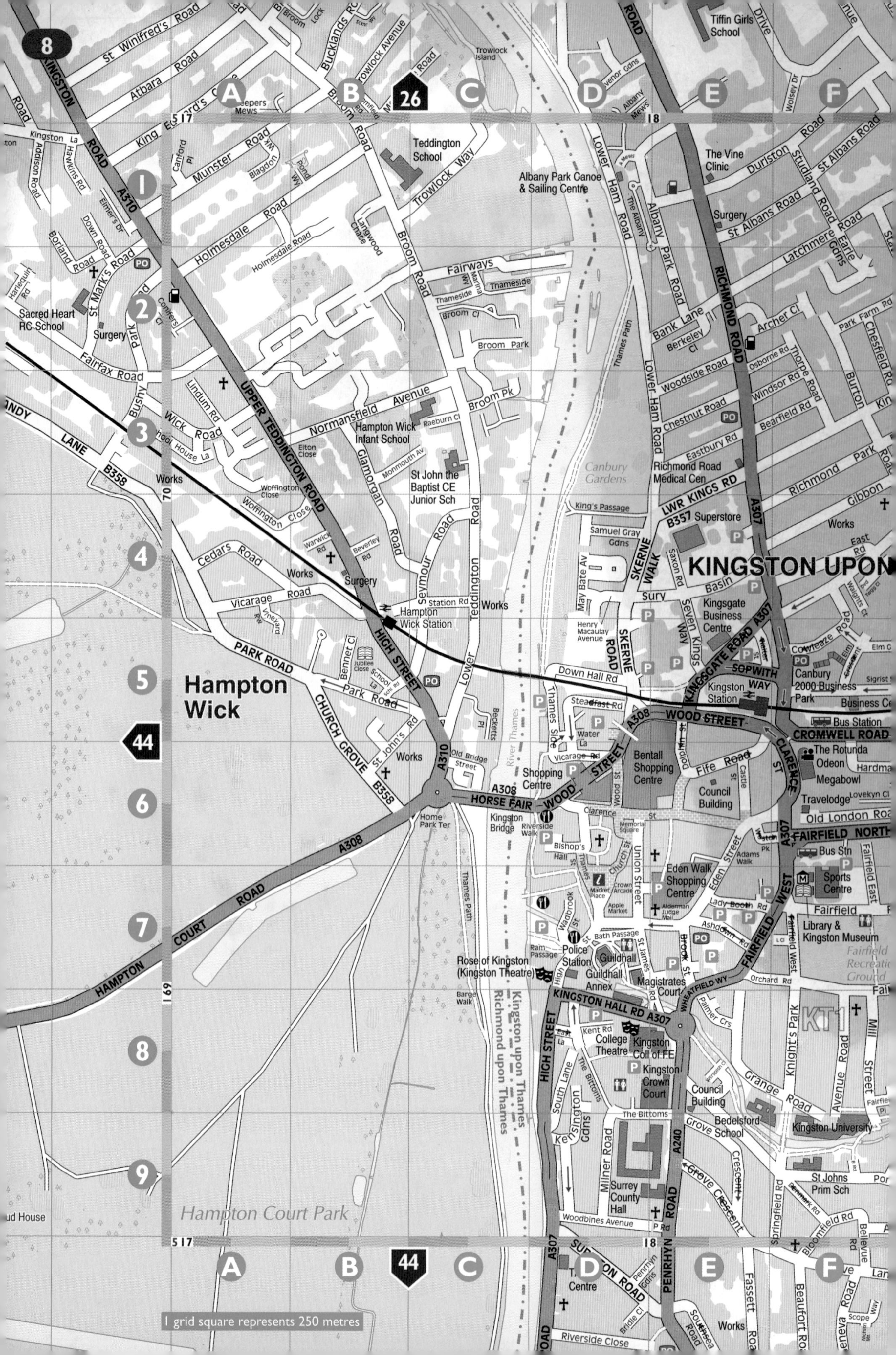
26
44
Hampton Wick
KINGSTON UPON
Hampton Court Park
Teddington School
Hampton Wick Infant School
St John the Baptist CE Junior Sch
Hampton Wick Station
Kingston Station
Bentall Shopping Centre
Eden Walk Shopping Centre
Guildhall
Rose of Kingston (Kingston Theatre)
Kingston Coll of FE
Kingston Crown Court
Surrey County Hall
Kingston University
Library & Kingston Museum
Canbury Gardens
River Thames
Albany Park Canoe & Sailing Centre
Tiffin Girls School
Sacred Heart RC School
1 grid square represents 250 metres

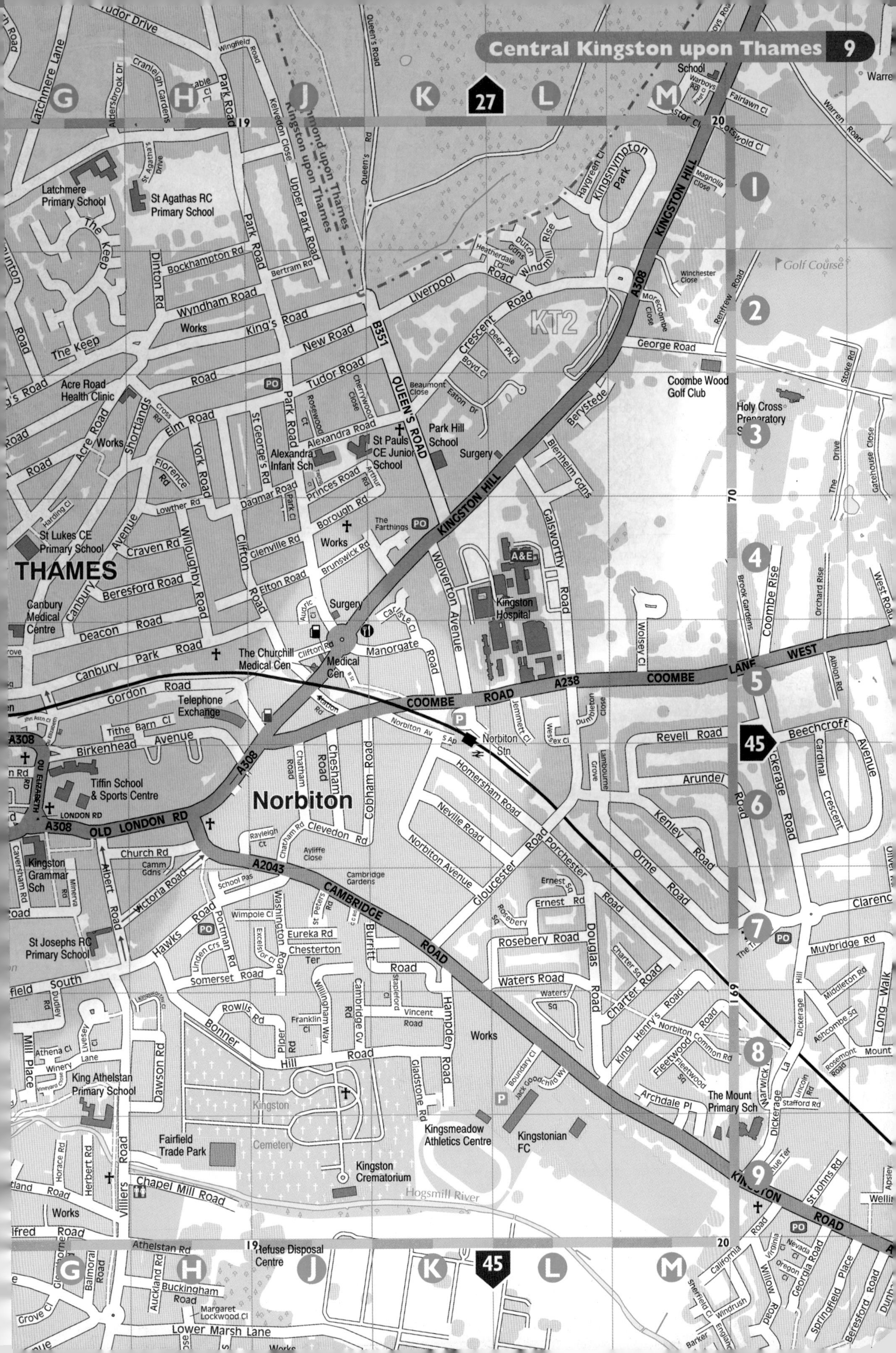

Tudor Drive
Latchmere Lane
Aldersbrook Dr
Cranleigh Gardens
Park Road
Wingfield Road
Kelvedon Close
Kingston upon Thames
Upper Park Road
Queen's Road
Fairlawn Cl
Warren Road
Cotswold Cl
Kingsnympton Park
Haygreen Cl
Magnolia Close
Latchmere Primary School
St Agathas RC Primary School
St Agatha's Drive
The Keep
Bockhampton Rd
Bertram Rd
Dutch Gdns
Heatherdale Cl
Windmill Rise
Kingston Hill
Golf Course
Winchester Close
Renfrew Road
Dinton Rd
Wyndham Road
Liverpool Road
Morecoombe Close
KT2
Works
King's Road
New Road
B351
Crescent Road
Deer Pk Cl
George Road
Stoke Rd
Tudor Road
Boyd Cl
Coombe Wood Golf Club
Acre Road Health Clinic
Cherrywood Close
Beaumont Close
Eaton Dr
Holy Cross Preparatory
Shortlands
Cross Rd
Elm Road
Rosewood Ct
Queen's Road
Berystede
Acre Road
Works
York Road
St George's Rd
Park Road
Alexandra Road
St Pauls CE Junior School
Park Hill School
The Drive
Gatehouse Close
Florence Rd
Alexandra Infant Sch
Surgery
Blenheim Gdns
Princes Road
Arthur Rd
Dagmar Road
Lowther Rd
Park Cl
Borough Rd
Harding Cl
St Lukes CE Primary School
Avenue
Craven Rd
Willoughby Road
Clifton Road
Glenville Rd
The Farthings
Works
Galsworthy Road
A&E
THAMES
Beresford Road
Brunswick Rd
Wolverton Avenue
Kingston Hospital
Brook Gardens
Coombe Rise
Orchard Rise
West Road
Canbury Medical Centre
Canbury
Elton Road
Deacon Road
Surgery
Carlisle Cl
Wolsey Cl
Canbury Park Road
The Churchill Medical Cen
Clifton Rd
Manorgate Road
Medical Cen
Coombe Lane West
Albion Rd
Gordon Road
A238
Coombe Road
Telephone Exchange
Jemmett Cl
Dumbleton Close
Tithe Barn Cl
Norbiton Av
Norbiton Stn
Wessex Cl
Revell Road
Beechcroft Avenue
A308
Birkenhead Avenue
Chatham Road
Chesham Road
Cobham Road
Homersham Road
Lambourne Grove
Arundel Road
Dickerage Road
Cardinal Crescent
Tiffin School & Sports Centre
Norbiton
Neville Road
Kenley Road
London Rd
A308 Old London Rd
Rayleigh Ct
Chatham Rd
Clevedon Rd
Norbiton Avenue
Porchester Road
Orme Road
Church Rd
Aylifffe Close
Gloucester Road
Kingston Grammar Sch
Camm Gdns
Victoria Road
A2043
Cambridge Gardens
Ernest Sq
Caversham Rd
Minerva Rd
Albert Road
School Pas
Cambridge Road
Ernest Rd
Clarence
Wimpole Cl
Washington Road
St Peters Rd
Burritt Road
Rosebery Sq
Portman Rd
Eureka Rd
Rosebery Road
Douglas Road
Muybridge Rd
St Josephs RC Primary School
Hawks Road
Excelsior Cl
Chesterton Ter
Charter Sq
Linden Crs
Waters Road
Middleton Rd
Somerset Road
Charter Road
Long Walk
South
Staplerford Cl
Waters Sq
Dudley Rd
Willingham Way
Cambridge Gv
Vincent Road
Hampden Road
Rowlls Rd
Franklin Cl
King Henry's Road
Norbiton Common Rd
Ashcombe Sq
Bonner
Piper Rd
Works
Mount
Mill Place
Athena Cl
Livesey Cl
Dawson Rd
Hill Road
Fleetwood Ct
Fleetwood Sq
Rosemont Road
Winery Lane
Vineyard Close
Gladstone Rd
Boundary Cl
Jack Goodchild Wy
Dickerage La
Warwick
Lincoln Rd
King Athelstan Primary School
Archdale Pl
The Mount Primary Sch
Stafford Rd
Kingston
Kingsmeadow Athletics Centre
Kingstonian FC
Fairfield Trade Park
Cemetery
Kingston Crematorium
Horace Rd
Herbert Rd
Villiers Road
Kingston Road
St Johns Rd
Chapel Mill Road
Hogsmill River
Works
Road
Alfred Road
Athelstan Rd
Refuse Disposal Centre
Glenthorne
Balmoral Road
Auckland Rd
California Road
Virginia Cl
Nevada Cl
Oregon Cl
Georgia Road
Springfield Place
Beresford Road
Willow Road
Buckingham Road
Sherfield Cl
Windrush
Grove Cl
Margaret Lockwood Cl
Lower Marsh Lane
Barker
Works
G
H
J
K
L
M
27
45
19
20
70
69
1
2
3
4
5
6
7
8
9

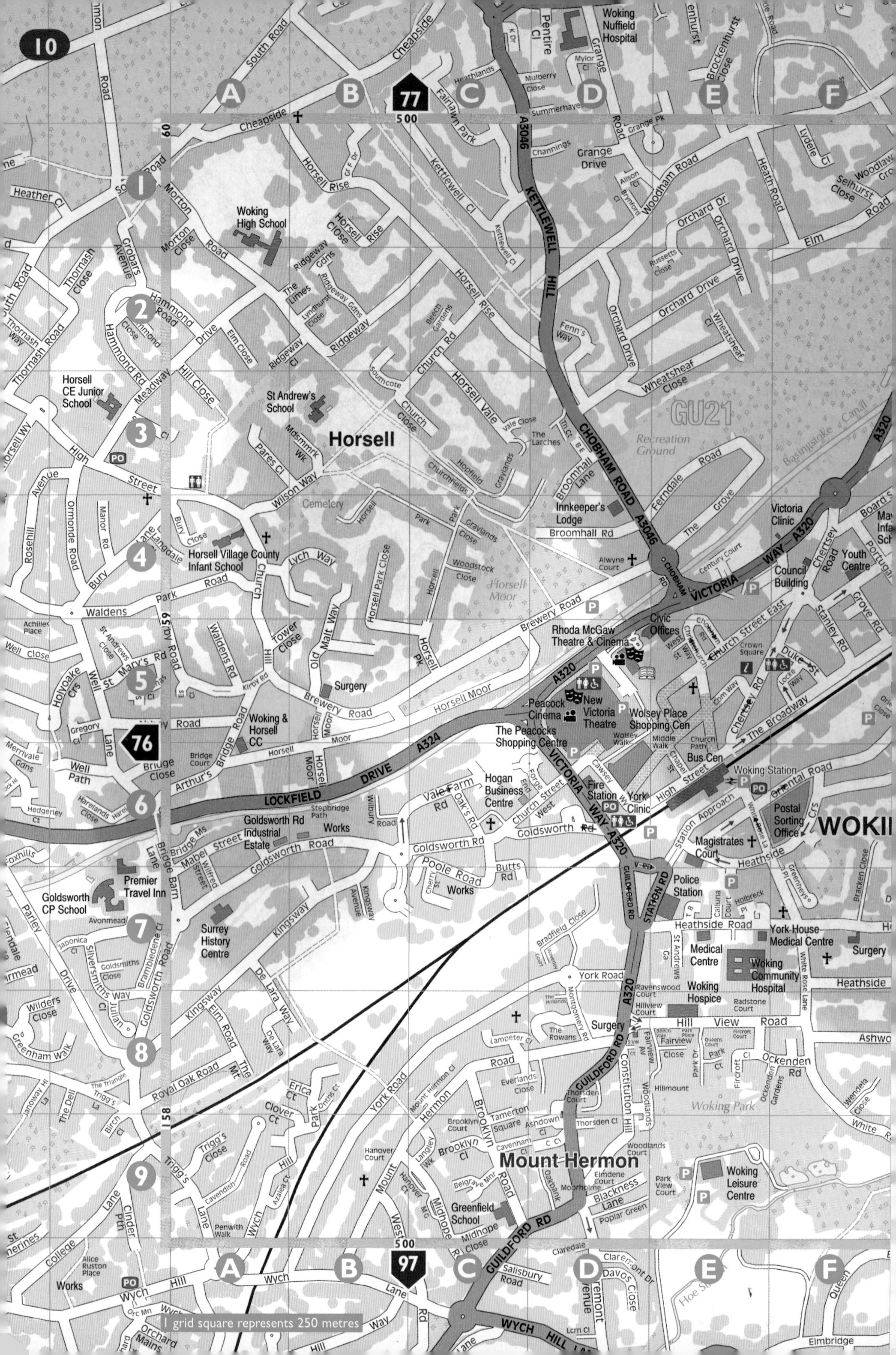

10
77
76
97
500
A
B
C
D
E
F
1
2
3
4
5
6
7
8
9
60
59
58
Horsell
Mount Hermon
WOKI
GU21
South Road
Cheapside
Woking Nuffield Hospital
Pentire Cl
Grange Road
Mylor Cl
Mulberry Close
Heathlands
Summerhayes
Fairlawn Park
Brockenhurst Close
Grange Pk
Grange Drive
Channings
Heather Cl
Morton Road
Morton Close
Woking High School
Horsell Rise
Horsell Close
Kettlewell Cl
Kettlewell Hill
A3046
Woodham Road
Heath Road
Lyndele Cl
Selhurst Close
Elm Road
Orchard Dr
Orchard Drive
Russetts Close
Wheatsheaf Cl
Wheatsheaf Close
Grobars Avenue
Thornash Close
Thornash Road
Thornash Way
Hammond Road
Hammond Close
Hammond Rd
Ridgeway
Ridgeway Gdns
Ridgeway Cl
The Limes
Lyndhurst Close
Beech Gardens
Church Rd
Horsell Vale
Fenn's Way
Elm Close
Hill Close
Meadway
Drive
Horsell CE Junior School
St Andrew's School
Church Close
Vale Close
The Larches
Chobham Road
Recreation Ground
Basingstoke Canal
A320
High Street
PO
Avenue
Rosehill Avenue
Ormonde Road
Manor Rd
Pares Cl
Wilson Way
Cemetery
Hopfield
Churchfields
Gravlands
Broomhall Lane
Ferndale Road
The Grove
Innkeeper's Lodge
Broomhall Rd
Victoria Clinic
Board School
Youth Centre
Chertsey Road
Portugal Road
Bury Close
Horsell Village County Infant School
Lych Way
Gravlands Close
Woodstock Close
Horsell Park Close
Horsell Moor
Alwyne Court
Century Court
Victoria Way
Council Building
Waldens Park Road
Achilles Place
St Andrews Close
Waldens Rd
Tower Close
Old Malt Way
Horsell Pk
Brewery Road
Rhoda McGaw Theatre & Cinema
Civic Offices
Church Street East
Stanley Rd
Grove Rd
Crown Square
Duke St
Locke Way
Well Close
St Mary's Rd
Holyoake Crs
Well Lane
Kirby Rd
Surgery
Peacock Cinema
New Victoria Theatre
Wolsey Place Shopping Cen
Wolsey Walk
Middle Walk
Chapel St
Church Path
Chertsey Rd
The Broadway
Gregory Cl
Merrivale Gdns
Well Path
Bridge Close
Arthur's Bridge Road
Woking & Horsell CC
Bridge Court
The Peacocks Shopping Centre
Lockfield Drive
A324
Forge End
Cawsey Way
Bus Cen
Woking Station
Oriental Road
Postal Sorting Office
Harelands Close
Hedgerley Ct
Goldsworth Rd Industrial Estate
Stepbridge Path
Works
Wilbury Road
Vale Farm Rd
Oak's Rd
Hogan Business Centre
Church Street West
Fire Station
York Clinic
High Street
Station Approach
Whitehouse La
Magistrates Court
Heathside
Crs
Foxhills
Bridge Barn Lane
Bridge Ms
Mabel Street
Wilfred Street
Goldsworth Road
Goldsworth Rd
Poole Road
Cherry St
Butts Rd
Guildford Rd
Station Rd
Police Station
Calluna Court
Holbreck Pl
Greenheys Pl
Bracken Close
Premier Travel Inn
Goldsworth CP School
Avonmead
Kingsway
Kingsway Avenue
Surrey History Centre
Bradfield Close
Heathside Road
St Andrews Ga
Medical Centre
York House Medical Centre
Woking Community Hospital
White Rose Lane
Parley Drive
Japonica Cl
Goldsmiths Close
Silversmiths Way
Brambledene Cl
Goldsworth Road
Julian Cl
De Lara Way
York Road
Montgomery Rd
Ravenswood Court
Woking Hospice
Radstone Court
Hillview Court
Hill View Road
Ashwood
Wilders Close
Greenham Walk
Elm Road
The Mount
Royal Oak Road
Lampeter Cl
The Rowans
Fairview Close
Park Dr
Queens Court
Park Ct
Fircroft Cl
Fircroft Court
Ockenden Rd
Ockenden Gardens
Wendela Close
Woking Park
White Rose
The Triangle
Trigg's La
The Dell
Birch Cl
Erica Ct
Clover Ct
Park Dr
York Road
Mount Hermon Cl
Everlands Close
Brooklyn Road
Tamerton Square
Brooklyn Court
Ashdown Cl
Thorsden Court
Thorsden Cl
Constitution Hill
Woodlands Court
Hillmount
Trigg's Close
Trigg's Lane
Cavendish Road
Hill
Azalea Ct
Wych Hill
Hanover Court
Hanover Ct
Mount Hermon
Langley Wk
Brooklyn Cl
Cavenham Cl
Belgrave Mnr
Oakbank
Moorholme
Elmdene Court
Blackness Lane
Poplar Green
Park View Court
Woking Leisure Centre
Cinder Pth
College Lane
Alice Ruston Place
Penwith Walk
Midhope Rd
Midhope Close
Greenfield School
Guildford Rd
Claredale
Claremont Dr
Davos Close
Salisbury Road
Hoe Stream
Queen's
Works
Wych Hill
Orchard Mains
Wych Hill Lane
Lane
Rd
Way
Lcrn Cl
Avenue
Claremont
Elmbridge
1 grid square represents 250 metres

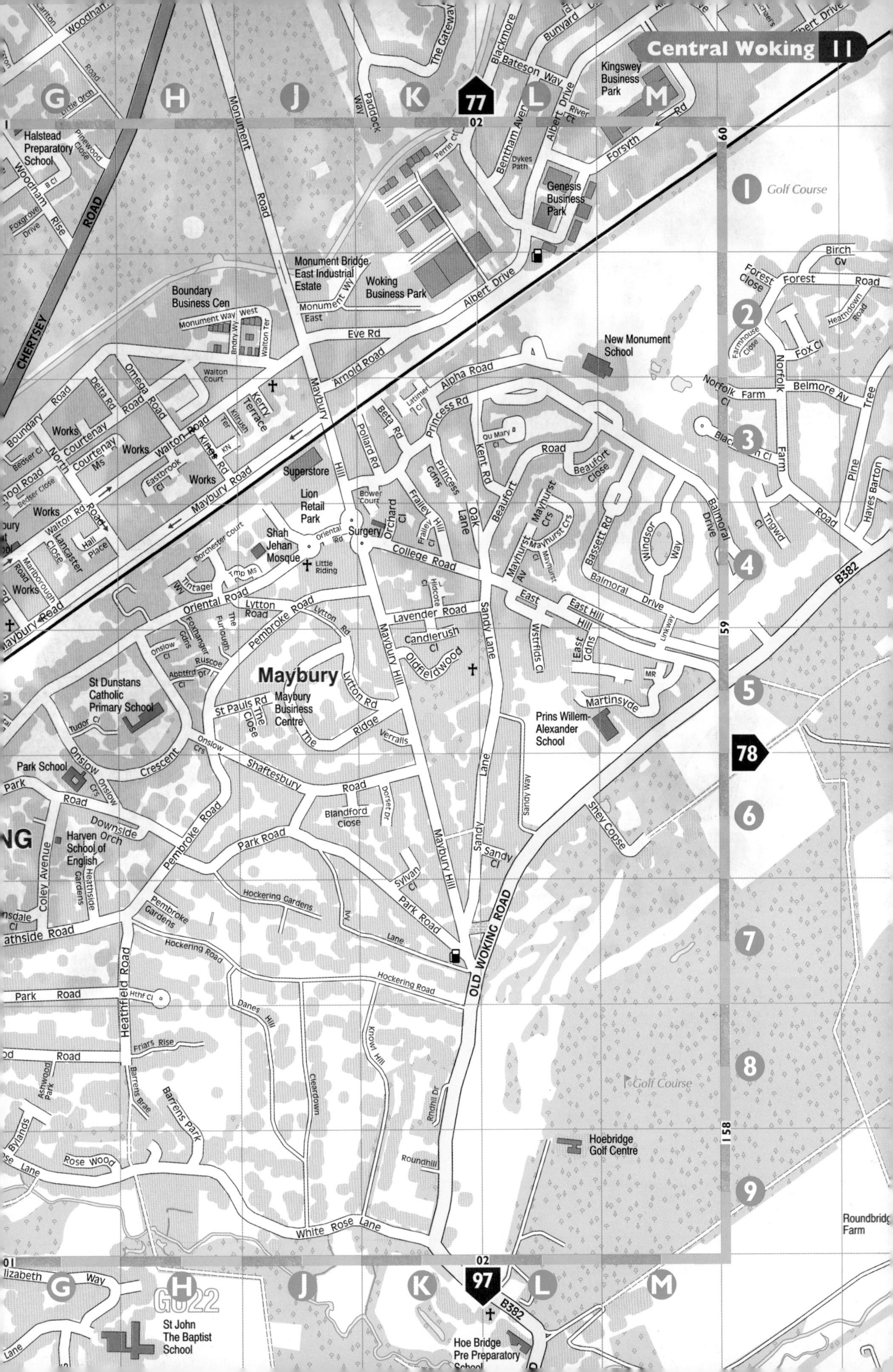
Maybury
Monument Road
Chertsey Road
Maybury Hill
Old Woking Road
Sandy Lane
Albert Drive
Walton Road
Maybury Road
Oriental Road
College Road
Pembroke Road
Park Road
Heathfield Road
White Rose Lane
Hockering Road
Shaftesbury Road
Onslow Crescent
Beaufort Road
Balmoral Drive
East Hill
Forest Road
Farm Road
Golf Course
Kingswey Business Park
Genesis Business Park
Monument Bridge East Industrial Estate
Woking Business Park
Boundary Business Cen
New Monument School
Superstore
Lion Retail Park
Surgery
Shah Jehan Mosque
Maybury Business Centre
St Dunstans Catholic Primary School
Park School
Harven School of English
Prins Willem-Alexander School
Hoebridge Golf Centre
St John The Baptist School
Hoe Bridge Pre Preparatory School
Halstead Preparatory School
Roundbridge Farm
GU22
B382
77
78
97

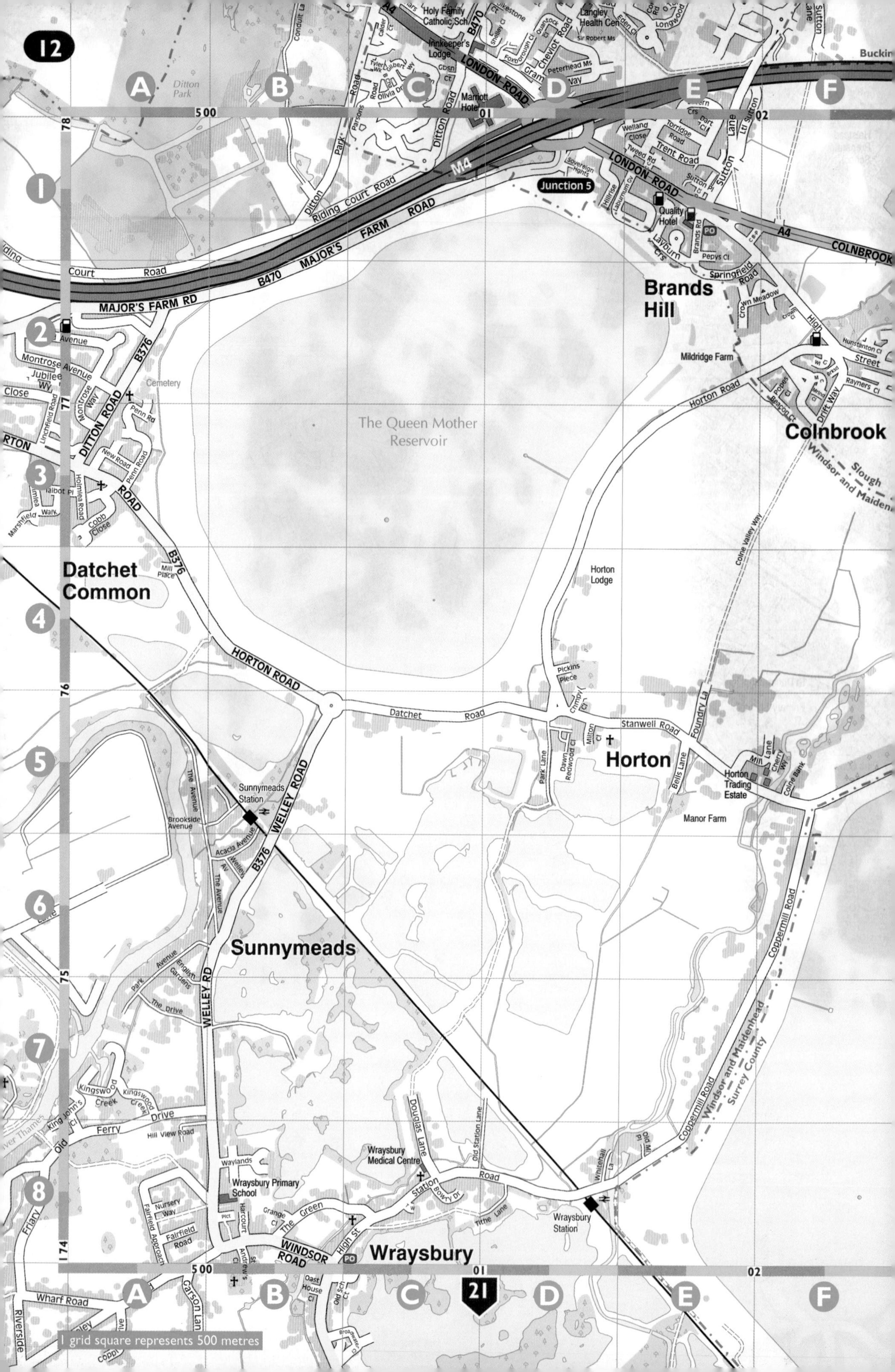

Brands Hill
Colnbrook
Datchet Common
Horton
Sunnymeads
Wraysbury
The Queen Mother Reservoir
Junction 5
M4
LONDON ROAD
MAJOR'S FARM ROAD
HORTON ROAD
WELLEY ROAD
Datchet Road
Stanwell Road
Coppermill Road
WINDSOR ROAD
Horton Road
Riding Court Road
Ditton Park
Cemetery
Horton Lodge
Mildridge Farm
Manor Farm
Horton Trading Estate
Sunnymeads Station
Wraysbury Station
Wraysbury Medical Centre
Wraysbury Primary School
Quality Hotel
Marriott Hotel
Holy Family Catholic Sch
Langley Health Cen
Innkeeper's Lodge
Windsor and Maidenhead
Surrey County
Slough
1 grid square represents 500 metres

21

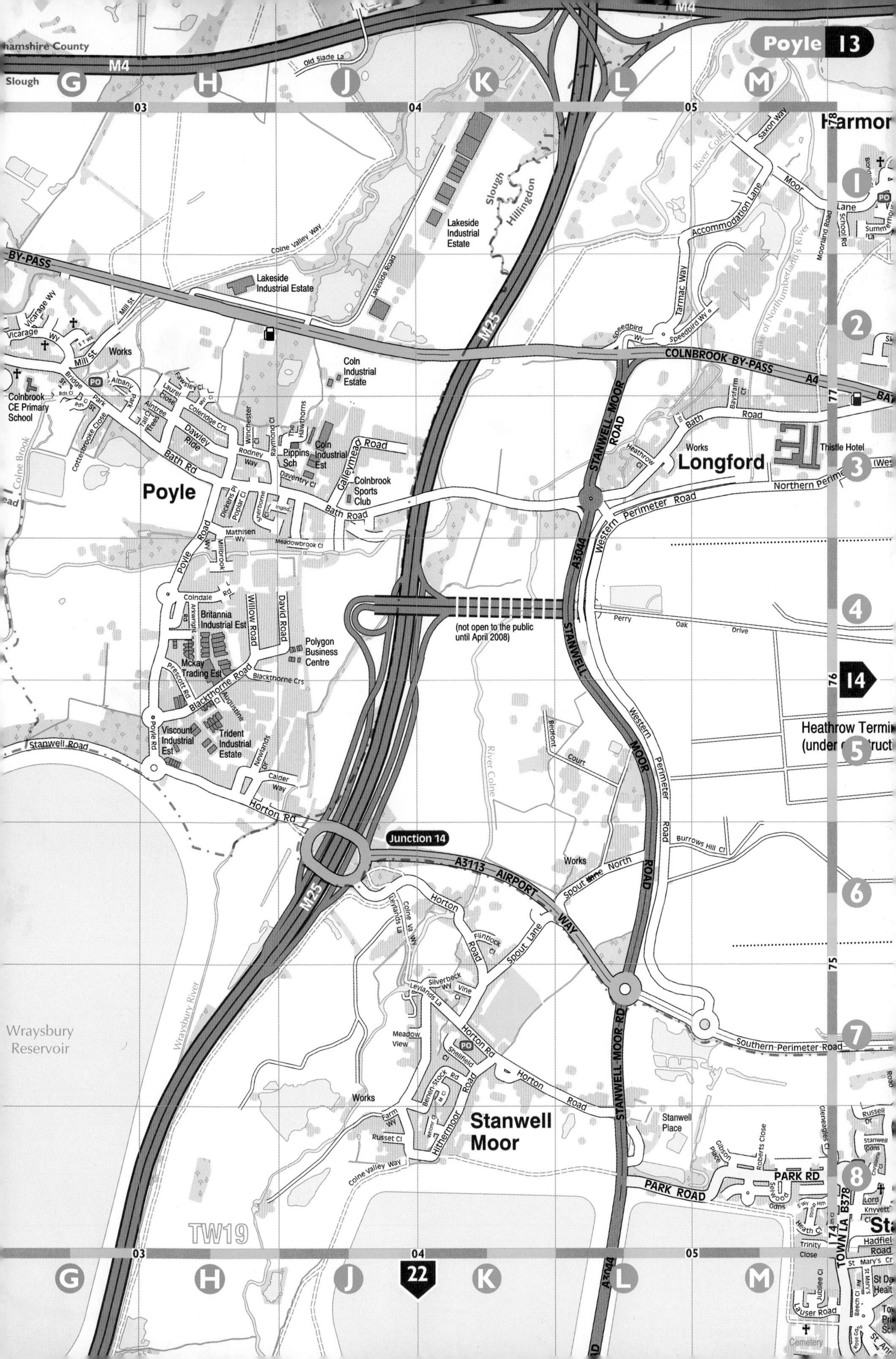

M4

hamshire County

Slough

G M4 **H** **J** **K** **L** **M**

03 04 05

Harmor

Old Slade La

River Colne

Saxon Way

Accommodation Lane

Moorland Road

School Lane

Bronte Close

PO

Summer La

1

BY-PASS

Colne Valley Way

Lakeside Road

Slough Hillingdon

Lakeside Industrial Estate

Duke of Northumberland's River

Tarmac Way

Speedbird Wy

Speedbird Wy

2

COLNBROOK BY-PASS A4

BY-PASS

Lakeside Industrial Estate

M25

Coln Industrial Estate

Baystern

Bath

Road

Works

Thistle Hotel

BA

77

78

(West)

Vicarage

Mill St

S W

Vicarage Wy

Works

Albany

PO

Park

Ra

Bridge

Rds Cl

Rawsley Cl

Laurel Close

Aintree

Colne Brook

Colnbrook CE Primary School

Cottesbrooke Close

Bath Rd

Dawley Ride

Fairey

Tait

Aintree

Poplar Cl

Dickens Pl

Coleridge Crs

Rodney Way

Winchester

Raymond Cl

The Hawthorns

The Pippins Sch

Daventry Cl

Coln Industrial Est

Galleymead Road

Colnbrook Sports Club

STANWELL MOOR ROAD

Heathrow Cl

Longford

A304

Western Perimeter Road

Northern Perimeter

3

Poyle

Poyle Road

Mathisen Wy

Millbrook Rd

Sherborne

Meadowbrook Cl

Bath Road

Ingles

Perry

Oak

Drive

4

Coindale

Arkwright Wy

Britannia Industrial Est

Willow Road

David Road

Polygon Business Centre

Mckay Trading Est

Prescott Rd

Blackthorne Road

Augustine

Blackthorne Crs

STANWELL

MOOR

Western

Perimeter

Road

76

75

(not open to the public until April 2008)

14

Heathrow Termin (under c struct

5

Viscount Industrial Est

Poyle Rd

Trident Industrial Estate

Newlands

Calder Way

Bedfont

court

6

Stanwell Road

Horton Rd

M25

Junction 14

A3113 AIRPORT

Spout Lane North

Works

Burrows Hill Cl

Wraysbury River

River Colne

WAY

A304

STANWELL MOOR RD

7

Southern Perimeter Road

Wraysbury Reservoir

Colne Va Wy

Leyland's La

Horton

Flintlock Cl

Spout Lane

Silverbeck Wy

Vine

Leyland's La

Meadow View

PO

Shelfield Rd

Horton Rd

Horton Road

Stanwell Place

Stanwell Gdns

Russet Dr

Gibson Place

Roberts Close

stanwell Gdns

Russell Dr

8

Works

Farm Wy

Russet Cl

Hithermoor

Benn Stock Rd

Horton Road

Stanwell Moor

PARK RD

Senior Gdns

Gleadon

TOWN LA

B378

Sta

Hadfiel Road

Lord Knyvett

Colne Valley Way

PARK ROAD

Heath Cl

S W Cl

Trinity Close

St D

Pri

TW19

Beech Cl

Jubilee Cl

Lauser Road

St Mary's Cr

To

Pri

Cemetery

St AN

G **H** **J** **K** **L** **M**

03 04 05

22

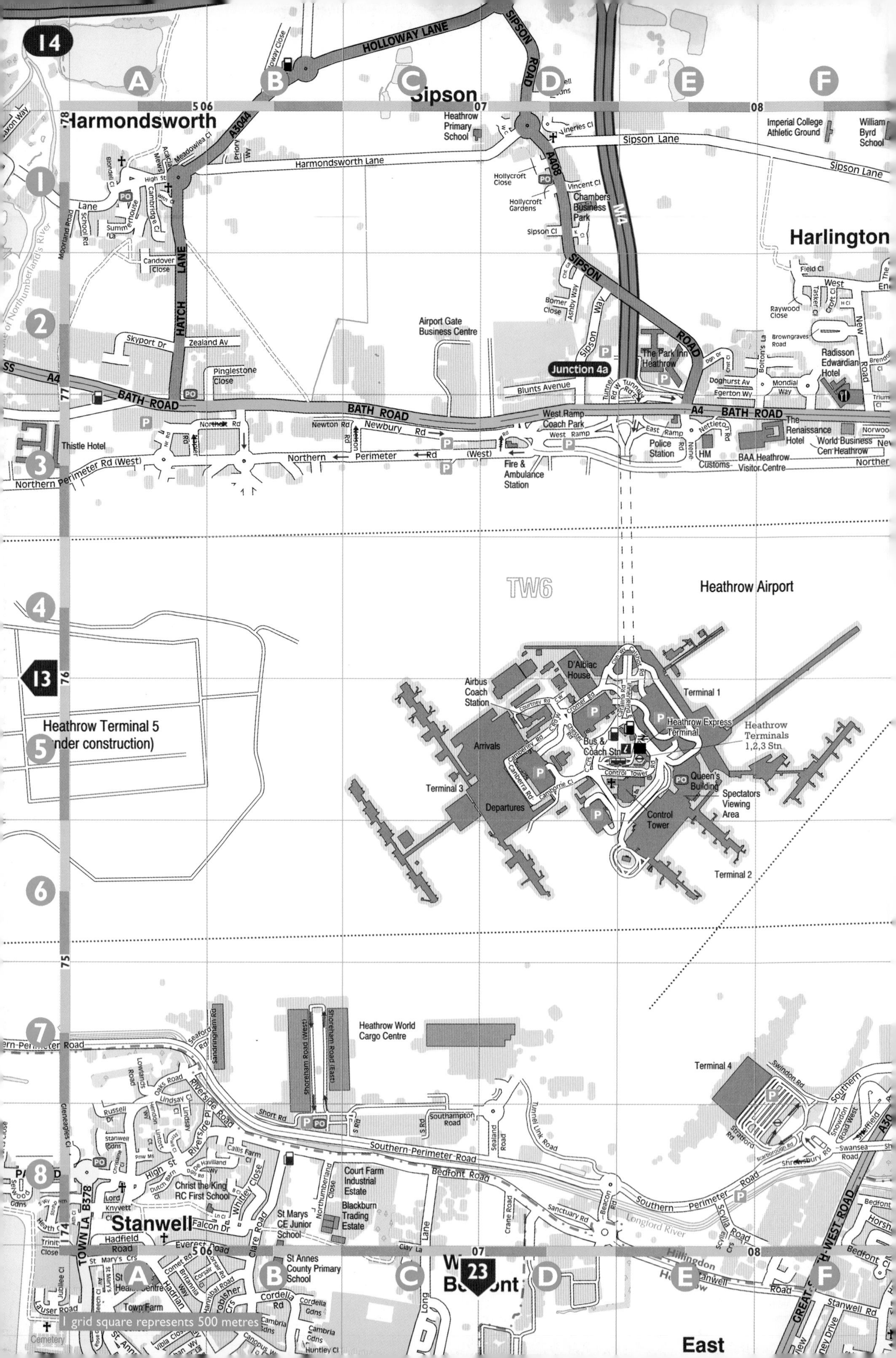
A
B
C
D
E
F
506
07
08
78
77
76
75
74
1
2
3
4
5
6
7
8
Harmondsworth
Sipson
Harlington
HOLLOWAY LANE
SIPSON ROAD
A3044
A408
M4
Heathrow Primary School
Imperial College Athletic Ground
William Byrd School
Sipson Lane
Harmondsworth Lane
Meadowlea Cl
Vineries Cl
Hollycroft Close
Hollycroft Gardens
Vincent Cl
Chambers Business Park
Sipson Cl
Moorland Road
School Rd
Candover Close
HATCH LANE
Field Cl
West End
Raywood Close
Tasker Cl
Croft Cl
New Road
Browngraves Road
Radisson Edwardian Hotel
Bomer Close
Ashby Way
Sipson Way
Airport Gate Business Centre
Skyport Dr
Zealand Av
Pinglestone Close
Junction 4a
The Park Inn Heathrow
Doghurst Av
Egerton Wy
Bolton's La
Mondial Way
Blunts Avenue
A4
BATH ROAD
Thistle Hotel
Northolt Rd
Newton Rd
Newbury Rd
West Ramp Coach Park
East Ramp
Police Station
HM Customs
The Renaissance Hotel
World Business Cen Heathrow
BAA Heathrow Visitor Centre
Northern Perimeter Rd (West)
Northern Perimeter Rd (West)
Fire & Ambulance Station
TW6
Heathrow Airport
13
Heathrow Terminal 5
(under construction)
D'Albiac House
Airbus Coach Station
Terminal 1
Heathrow Express Terminal
Heathrow Terminals 1,2,3 Stn
Arrivals
Bus & Coach Stn
Queen's Building
Terminal 3
Departures
Control Tower
Spectators Viewing Area
Terminal 2
Heathrow World Cargo Center
Shoreham Road (West)
Shoreham Road (East)
Terminal 4
Swindon Rd
Southern Perimeter Road
Short Rd
Southampton Road
Sealand Road
Tunnel Link Road
Stanwell
Christ the King RC First School
Court Farm Industrial Estate
Blackburn Trading Estate
St Marys CE Junior School
Bedfont Road
Crane Road
Sanctuary Rd
Longford River
Scylla Road
Shrewsbury Rd
Stratford Rd
Swansea Road
GREAT SOUTH-WEST ROAD
A30
TOWN LA B378
Falcon Dr
Hadfield Road
Everest Road
Clare Road
Whitley Close
Riverside Road
Lowlands Road
Oaks Road
Lindsay Cl
Russell Dr
High St
Lord Knyvett Cl
St Annes County Primary School
Cordelia Rd
Town Farm
Lauser Road
Cemetery
Clay La
Long Lane
23
East
Stanwell Rd
Bedfont
1 grid square represents 500 metres

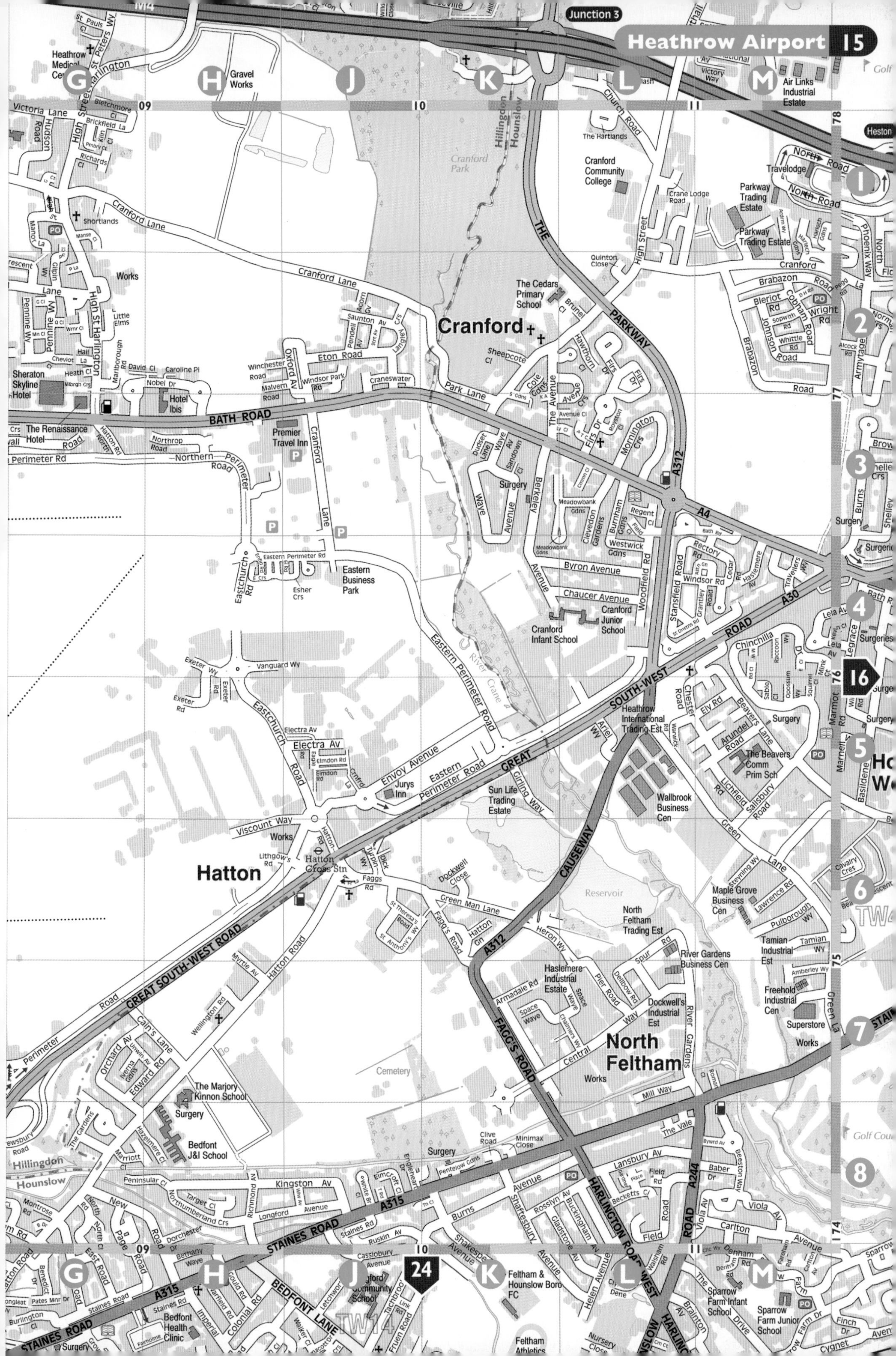
Cranford
Hatton
North Feltham
Cranford Park
Bath Road
A4
Great South-West Road
A30
The Parkway
A312
Causeway
Faggs Road
Harlington Road West
Staines Road
A315
A244
Bedfont Lane
Eastern Perimeter Road
Northern Perimeter Road
Cranford Lane
High Street
Hatton Road
Eastchurch Road
Hatton Cross Stn
Heathrow International Trading Est
Wallbrook Business Cen
Sun Life Trading Estate
North Feltham Trading Est
Haslemere Industrial Estate
Dockwell's Industrial Est
Maple Grove Business Cen
Tamian Industrial Est
Freehold Industrial Cen
River Gardens Business Cen
Parkway Trading Estate
Air Links Industrial Estate
Eastern Business Park
Cranford Community College
The Cedars Primary School
Cranford Infant School
Cranford Junior School
The Beavers Comm Prim Sch
The Marjory Kinnon School
Bedfont J&I School
Sheraton Skyline Hotel
The Renaissance Hotel
Hotel Ibis
Premier Travel Inn
Jurys Inn
Travelodge
Reservoir
Cemetery
River Crane
Gravel Works
Works
Surgery
Superstore
Junction 3
M4
TW14
Feltham & Hounslow Boro FC
Sparrow Farm Infant School
Sparrow Farm Junior School
Bedfont Health Clinic
Hillingdon
Hounslow
Heathrow Medical Cen
Golf Course

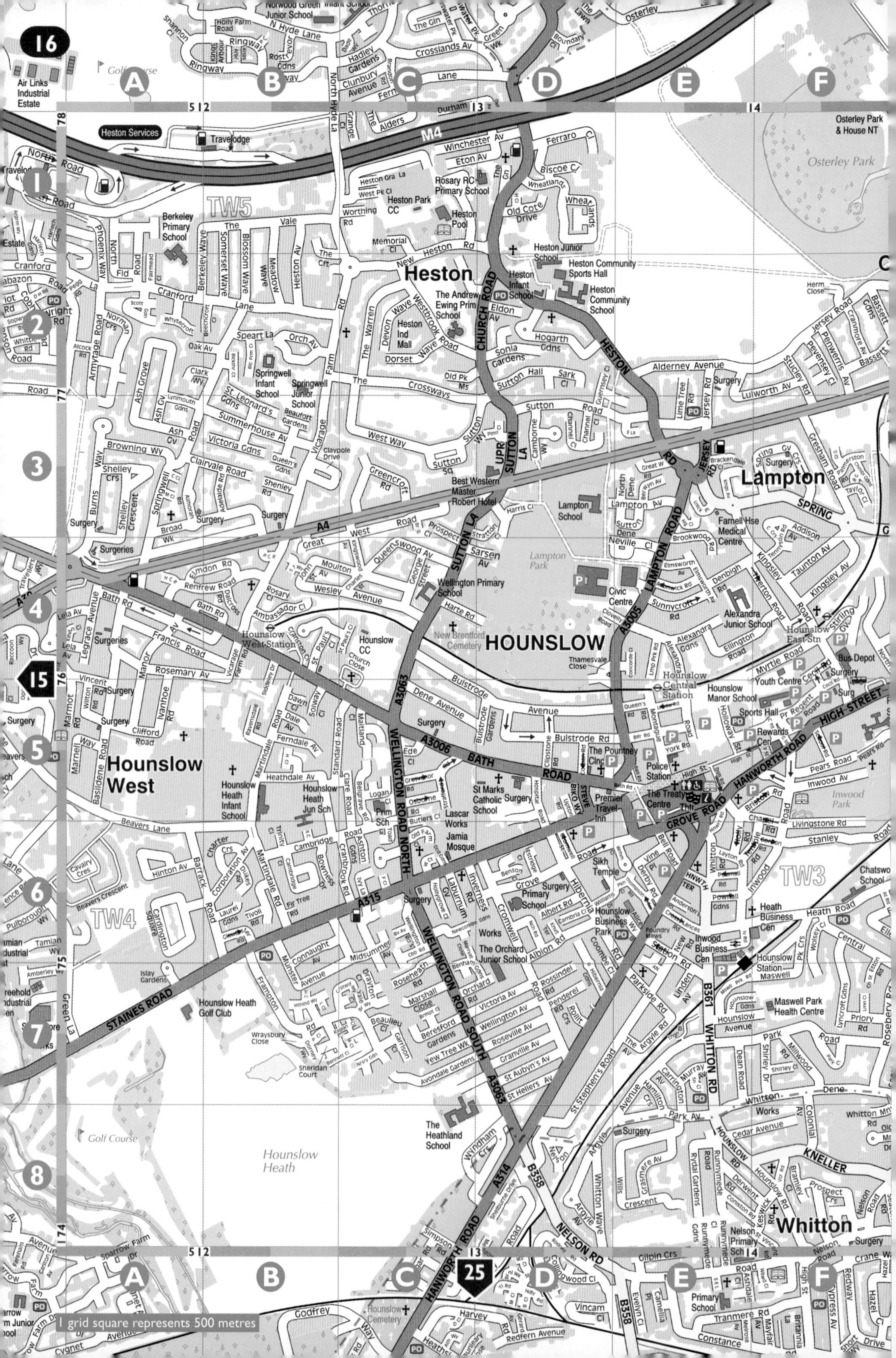
16
15
25
Heston
HOUNSLOW
Hounslow West
Lampton
Whitton
Osterley Park
Osterley Park & House NT
Hounslow Heath
Heston Services
M4
A4
A3006 BATH ROAD
A315
STAINES ROAD
A3063
WELLINGTON ROAD NORTH
WELLINGTON ROAD SOUTH
HANWORTH ROAD
A314
A3005
LAMPTON ROAD
CHURCH ROAD
HESTON RD
SUTTON LA
HIGH STREET
GROVE ROAD
WHITTON RD
B358
B361
NELSON RD
TW3
TW4
TW5
1 grid square represents 500 metres

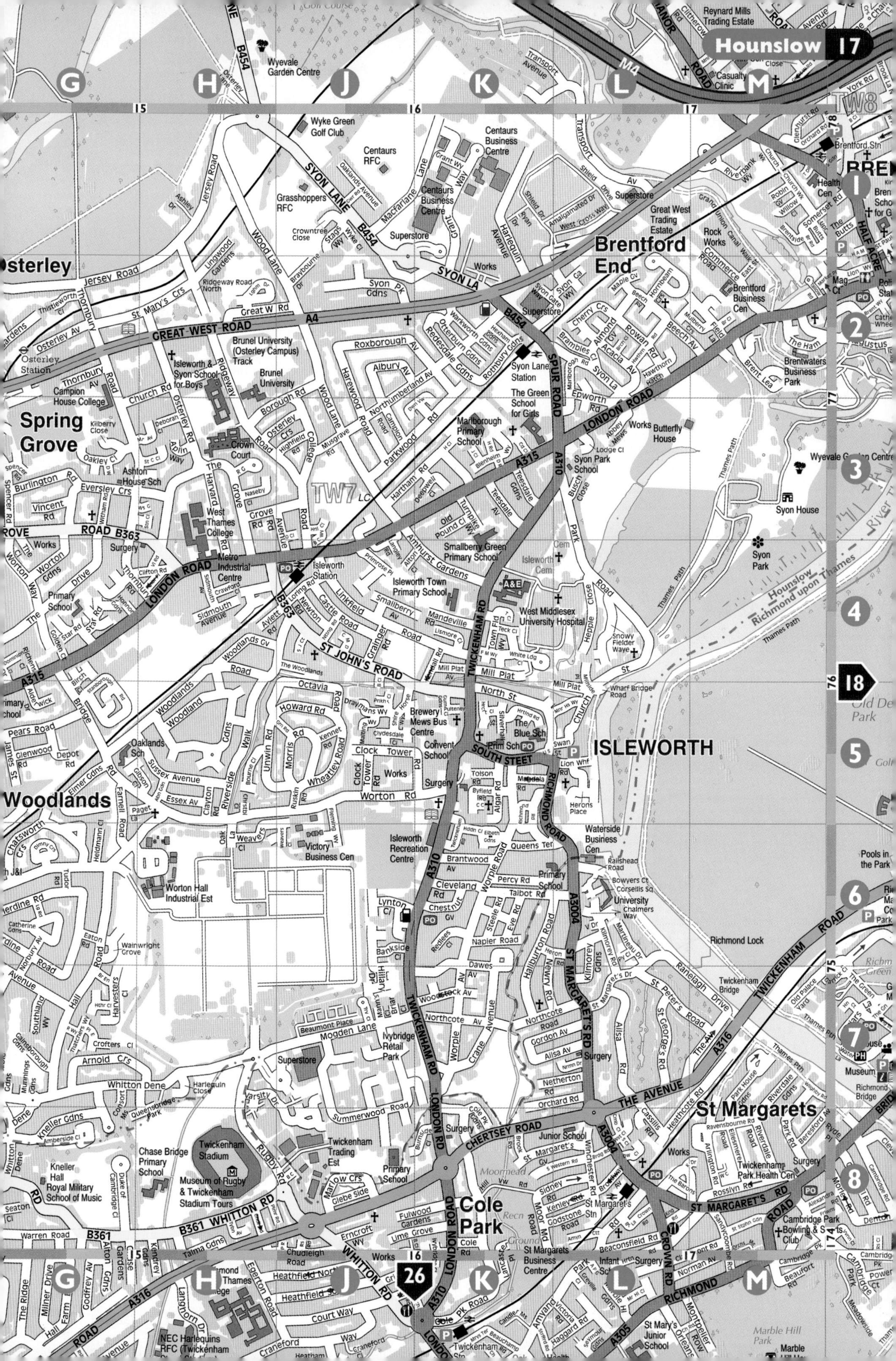
Wyevale Garden Centre
Reynard Mills Trading Estate
Casualty Clinic
Transport Avenue
Wyke Green Golf Club
Centaurs RFC
Centaurs Business Centre
Grasshoppers RFC
SYON LANE
B454
Superstore
Great West Trading Estate
Brentford End
Osterley
Jersey Road
GREAT WEST ROAD
A4
Brunel University (Osterley Campus) Track
Brunel University
Isleworth & Syon School for Boys
Osterley Station
Campion House College
Spring Grove
Crown Court
Syon Lane Station
The Green School for Girls
SPUR ROAD
LONDON ROAD
A315
Marlborough Primary School
Syon Park School
Butterfly House
Syon House
Syon Park
Wyevale Garden Centre
Thames Path
Ashton House Sch
West Thames College
Metro Industrial Centre
Isleworth Station
TW7
Smallberry Green Primary School
Isleworth Cem
Isleworth Town Primary School
West Middlesex University Hospital
Hounslow
Richmond upon Thames
ST JOHN'S ROAD
TWICKENHAM RD
A310
Brewery Mews Bus Centre
Convent School
ISLEWORTH
SOUTH STEET
RICHMOND ROAD
Woodlands
Oaklands Sch
Victory Business Cen
Isleworth Recreation Centre
Worton Hall Industrial Est
Waterside Business Cen
Primary School
University
Richmond Lock
Twickenham Bridge
ST MARGARET'S RD
A3004
Ivybridge Retail Park
Superstore
THE AVENUE
A316
TWICKENHAM ROAD
St Margarets
Twickenham Park Health Cen
Chase Bridge Primary School
Twickenham Stadium
Museum of Rugby & Twickenham Stadium Tours
Kneller Hall Royal Military School of Music
Twickenham Trading Est
CHERTSEY ROAD
Junior School
St Margarets Stn
Cole Park
B361 WHITTON RD
WHITTON RD
LONDON ROAD
CROWN RD
St Margarets Business Centre
Infant Sch
Cambridge Park Bowling & Sports Club
RICHMOND
A305
St Mary's Junior School
Marble Hill Park
Twickenham Stn
NEC Harlequins RFC (Twickenham
Richmond Bridge
Museum
Pools in the Park
18
26

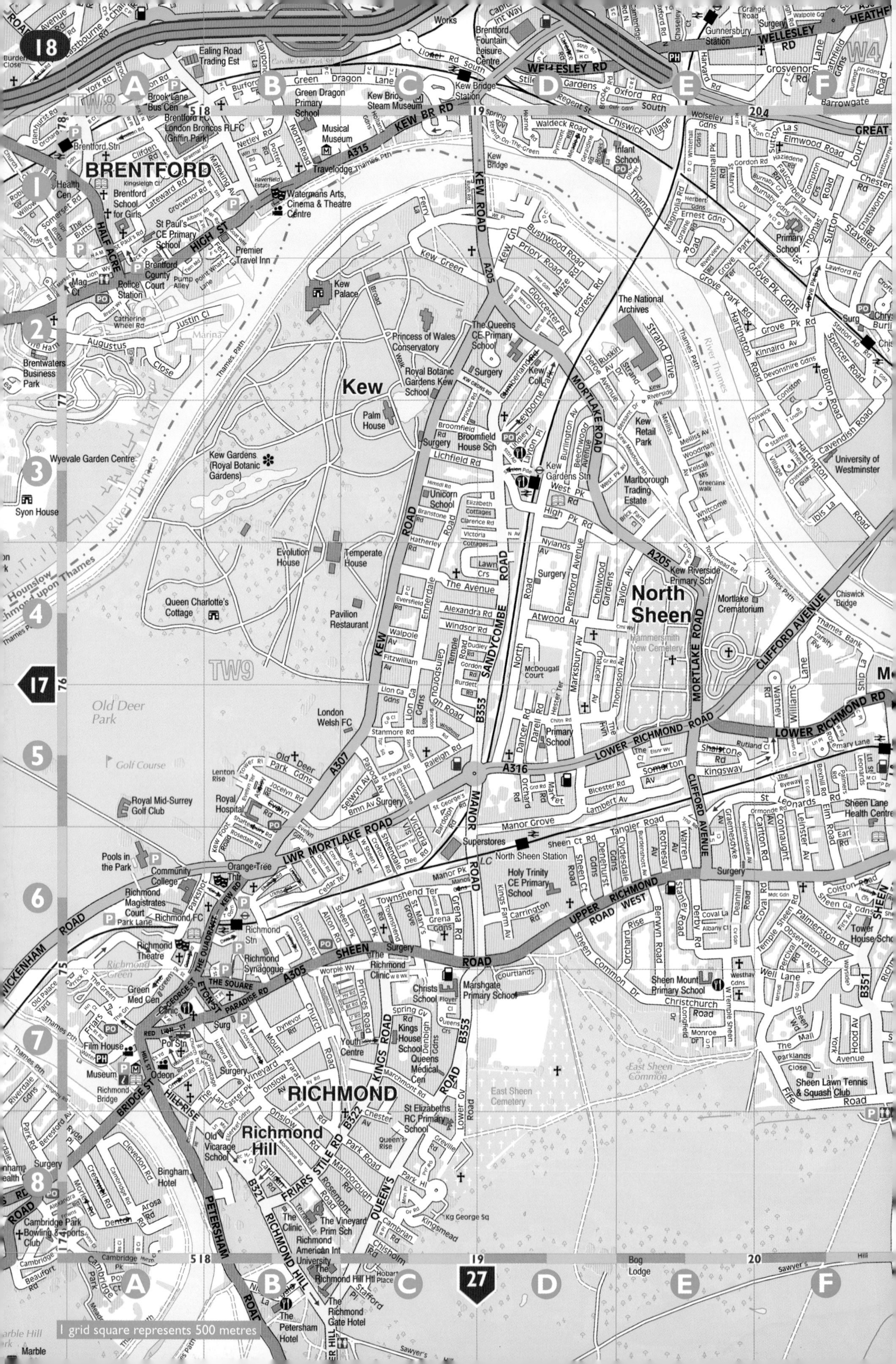

18
A
B
C
D
E
F
TW8
518
19
204
BRENTFORD
Brentford Stn
Health Cen
Brentford School for Girls
St Paul's CE Primary School
Brentford County Court
Police Station
Catherine Wheel Rd
Brentwaters Business Park
Brook Lane Bus Cen
Brentford FC London Broncos RLFC (Griffin Park)
Ealing Road Trading Est
Green Dragon Primary School
Green Dragon Lane
Kew Bridge Steam Museum
Musical Museum
Kew Bridge Station
KEW BR RD
A315
HIGH ST
HALF ACRE
Travelodge
Watermans Arts, Cinema & Theatre Centre
Premier Travel Inn
Augustus Close
Justin Cl
Marina
Thames Path
River Thames
Syon House
Wyevale Garden Centre
Brentford Fountain Leisure Centre
Works
Lionel Rd South
WELLESLEY RD
Gunnersbury Station
WELLESLEY RD
HEATHFIELD
W4
Grosvenor Rd
Barrowgate
Oxford Rd South
Chiswick Village
Waldeck Road
Strand-On-The-Green
Infant School
Kew Bridge
KEW ROAD
A205
Kew Green
Kew Palace
Bushwood Road
Priory Road
Gloucester Rd
Forest Rd
The National Archives
Strand Drive
Thames Path
River Thames
The Queens CE Primary School
Princess of Wales Conservatory
Royal Botanic Gardens Kew School
Kew
Palm House
Kew Gardens (Royal Botanic Gardens)
Surgery
Broomfield House Sch
Lichfield Rd
Kew Gardens Stn
West Pk
High Pk Rd
MORTLAKE ROAD
Kew Retail Park
Marlborough Trading Estate
Unicorn School
Evolution House
Temperate House
Queen Charlotte's Cottage
Pavilion Restaurant
TW9
Old Deer Park
Golf Course
Royal Mid-Surrey Golf Club
London Welsh FC
Kew Riverside Primary Sch
North Sheen
Mortlake Crematorium
Hammersmith New Cemetery
McDougall Court
Primary School
SANDYCOMBE ROAD
B353
MANOR ROAD
A316
A307
LOWER RICHMOND ROAD
CLIFFORD AVENUE
Chiswick Bridge
University of Westminster
Primary School
Grove Park Rd
Hartington Road
Cavendish Road
Bolton Road
Spencer Road
Royal Hospital
Pools in the Park
Community College
Richmond Magistrates Court
Park Lane
Richmond FC
Orange Tree Thtr
LWR MORTLAKE ROAD
Superstores
North Sheen Station
Manor Grove
Holy Trinity CE Primary School
UPPER RICHMOND ROAD WEST
Sheen Lane Health Centre
Tower House Sch
Sheen Mount Primary School
Christchurch Road
Richmond Stn
Richmond Theatre
Richmond Synagogue
THE QUADRANT
KEW RD
TWICKENHAM ROAD
Richmond Green
Green Med Cen
THE SQUARE
PARADISE RD
A305
SHEEN ROAD
The Richmond Clinic
Christs School
Marshgate Primary School
Courtlands
Youth Centre
Kings House School
Queens Medical Cen
RICHMOND
Richmond Hill
Old Vicarage School
St Elizabeths RC Primary School
Film House
Museum
Richmond Bridge
Odeon
BRIDGE ST
HILL RISE
PETERSHAM
RICHMOND HILL
FRIARS STILE RD
B321
B322
QUEEN'S ROAD
Bingham Hotel
Cambridge Park Bowling & Sports Club
The Clinic
The Vineyard Prim Sch
Richmond American Int University
The Richmond Hill Htl
The Richmond Gate Hotel
The Petersham Hotel
East Sheen Cemetery
East Sheen Common
Sheen Lawn Tennis & Squash Club
Bog Lodge
Kg George Sq
Sawyer's Hill
17
27
1
2
3
4
5
6
7
8
75
76
77
78
20
1 grid square represents 500 metres

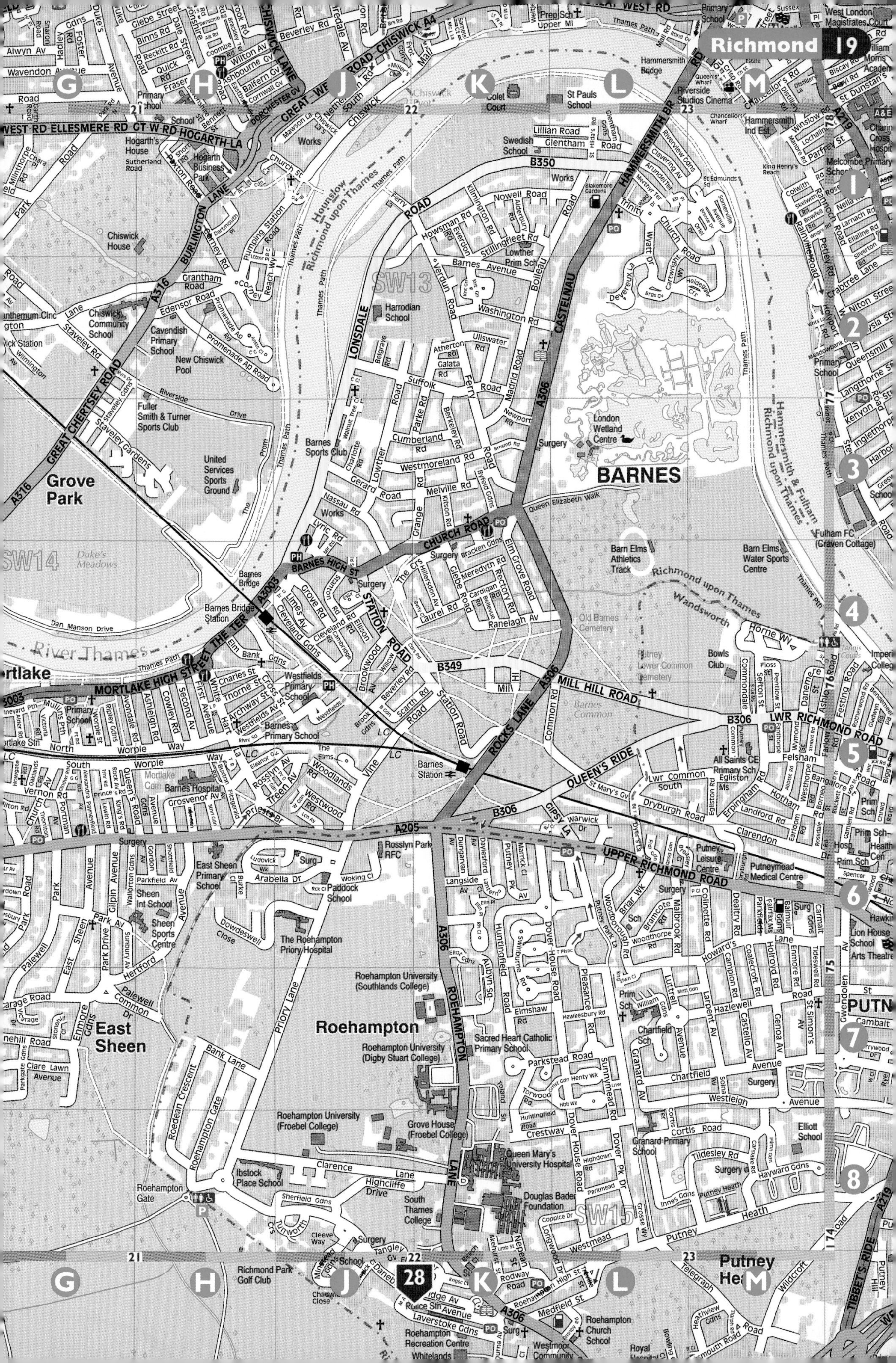
G
H
J
K
L
M
21
22
23
Chiswick Lane
Great West Road
Chiswick A4
Hammersmith Bridge
Riverside Studios Cinema
Hammersmith Ind Est
Colet Court
St Pauls School
Lillian Road
Glentham Road
Swedish School
B350
Hogarth's House
Hogarth Business Park
Burlington Lane
A316
Chiswick House
Grantham Road
Edensor Road
Chiswick Community School
Cavendish Primary School
New Chiswick Pool
Promenade Ap Road
Riverside Drive
Fuller Smith & Turner Sports Club
United Services Sports Ground
Great Chertsey Road
Staveley Rd
Staveley Gardens
Grove Park
SW14
Duke's Meadows
Dan Manson Drive
River Thames
Thames Path
Hounslow
Richmond upon Thames
Lonsdale Road
Harrodian School
SW13
Castelnau
A306
Hammersmith Br Rd
Nowell Road
Howsman Rd
Lowther Prim Sch
Barnes Avenue
Washington Rd
Ullswater Rd
Suffolk Road
Madrid Road
Barnes Sports Club
Cumberland
Westmoreland Rd
Gerard Road
Melville Rd
London Wetland Centre
BARNES
Queen Elizabeth Walk
Church Road
Barnes High St
Barn Elms Athletics Track
Barn Elms Water Sports Centre
Fulham FC (Craven Cottage)
Hammersmith & Fulham
Wandsworth
Station Road
Elm Grove Road
Ranelagh Av
Old Barnes Cemetery
Putney Lower Common Cemetery
Bowls Club
Barnes Bridge
Barnes Bridge Station
Mortlake High Street
The Terrace
A3003
Mill Hill Road
Rocks Lane
B349
B306
Barnes Common
Lwr Richmond Road
Westfields Primary School
Barnes Primary School
Barnes Station
Queen's Ride
Lwr Common South
All Saints CE Primary Sch
Dryburgh Road
Mortlake Cem
Barnes Hospital
Grosvenor Av
North Worple Way
South Worple Way
A205
Upper Richmond Road
Rosslyn Park RFC
Putney Leisure Centre
Putneymead Medical Centre
East Sheen Primary School
Sheen Int School
Sheen Sports Centre
Paddock School
The Roehampton Priory Hospital
Roehampton University (Southlands College)
Roehampton
Roehampton Lane
East Sheen
Palewell Common
Priory Lane
Roehampton University (Digby Stuart College)
Sacred Heart Catholic Primary School
Parkstead Road
Dover House Road
Chartfield Avenue
Westleigh Avenue
Roehampton University (Froebel College)
Grove House (Froebel College)
Queen Mary's University Hospital
Douglas Bader Foundation
Clarence Lane
Ibstock Place School
Highcliffe Drive
South Thames College
Roehampton Gate
Roedean Crescent
Roehampton Gate
Bank Lane
Granard Primary School
Elliott School
Putney Heath
SW15
Putney Heath
Richmond Park Golf Club
Roehampton Recreation Centre
Roehampton Church School
Tibbet's Ride
A219
PUTN
1
2
3
4
5
6
7
8
74
75
76
77
78

28

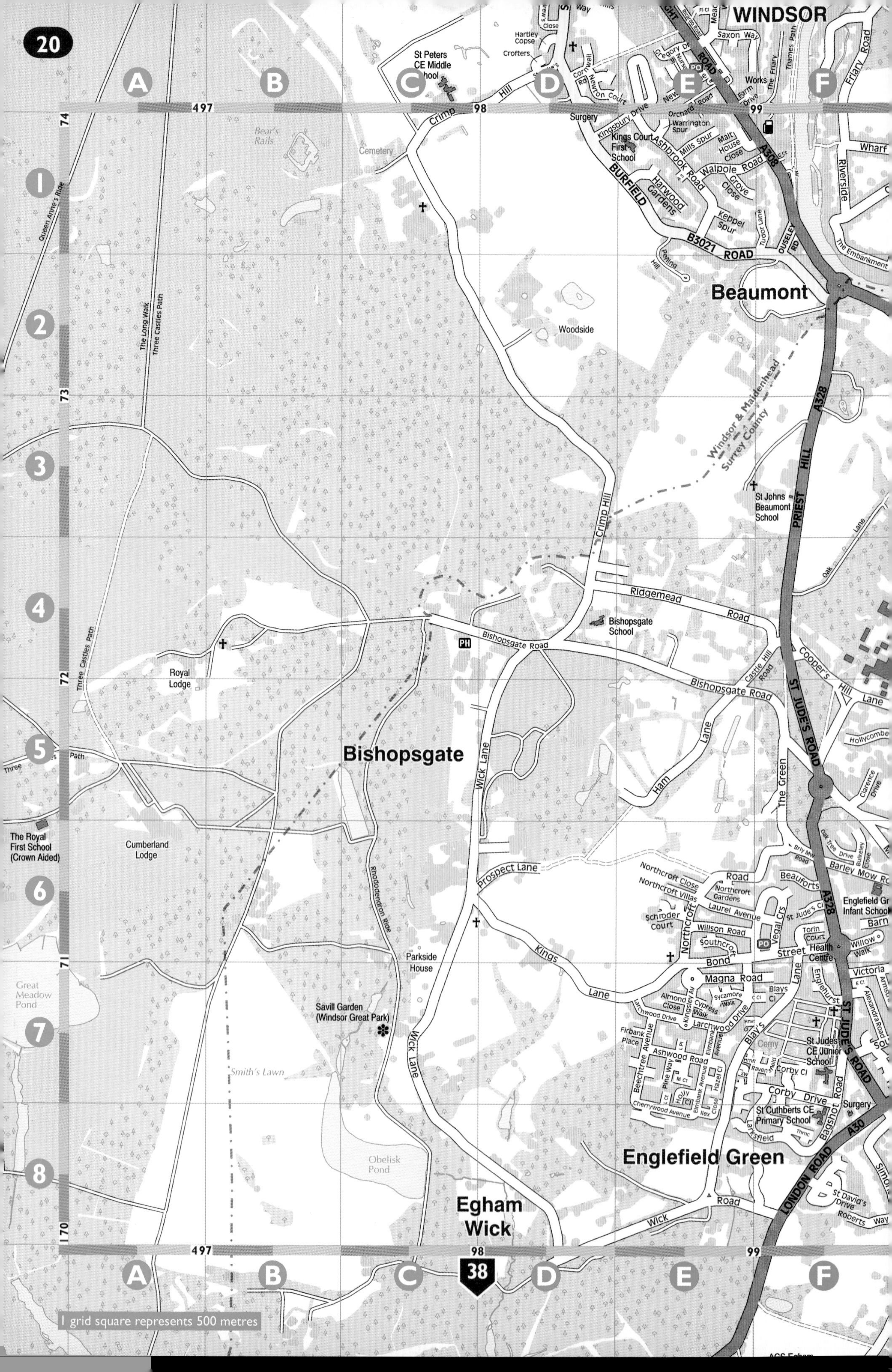

WINDSOR

Saxon Way

St Peters
CE Middle
School

Crimp Hill

Hartley
Copse
Crofters

Surgery

Kingsbury Drive

Kings Court
First
School

Ashbrook Road

Orchard
Road

Warrington
Spur

Mills Spur

New

BURFIELD

Harwood
Gardens

Walpole
Grove

Malt
House
Close

Keppel
Spur

Works

Wharf

Riverside

The Embankment

B3021 ROAD

OUSELEY RD

The Friary

Friary Road

A308

Bear's
Rails

Cemetery

Beaumont

A B C D E F

497

98

99

I

2

Queen Anne's Ride

The Long Walk

Three Castles Path

74

73

Woodside

Windsor & Maidenhead
Surrey County

St Johns
Beaumont
School

PRIEST HILL

A308

3

72

Three Castles Path

Crimp Hill

Ridgemead
Road

Bishopsgate
School

Bishopsgate Road

Castle Hill Road

Bishopsgate Road

Cooper's
Hill Lane

Hollycombe

4

PH

Royal
Lodge

The Royal
First School
(Crown Aided)

Three
Path

Cumberland
Lodge

Bishopsgate

Wick Lane

Ham Lane

Lane

The Green

Clarence

ST JUDE'S ROAD

5

71

Rhododendron Ride

Parkside
House

Prospect Lane

Kings Lane

Northcroft Close

Northcroft Villas

Schroder
Court

Willson Road

Southcroft

Bond

Northcroft Gardens

Laurel Avenue

Northcroft

Road

St Jude's Drive

Beauforts

PO

Street

Magna Road

Torin
Court

Brly Mkt
Road

Oak Tree Drive

Blakeley

Vegal Crs

A328

Health
Centre

Barley Mow Rd

Englefield Gn
Infant School

Barn

Willow
Walk

Victoria

Englehurst

Alexandra Road

Victoria Road

6

7

Great
Meadow
Pond

Savill Garden
(Windsor Great Park)

Smith's Lawn

Almond Ave

Kingsley Av

Cypress
Walk

Sycamore
Walk

Firbank
Place

Beechtree
Avenue

Larchwood
Drive

Pine Way

Ashwood
Road

Larchwood Drive

Elmbank Avenue

Blays La

Blays
Cl

Cherrywood Avenue

Hazel Cl

M Ct

Ilex

Raven

Corby Cl

St Judes
CE Junior
School

Cemy

St Cuthberts CE
Primary School

Corby Drive

Surgery

Larksfield

Bagshot Road

8

Egham
Wick

Englefield Green

Wick Road

LONDON ROAD

St David's
Drive

Roberts Way

A30

A B C D E F

497

98

38

99

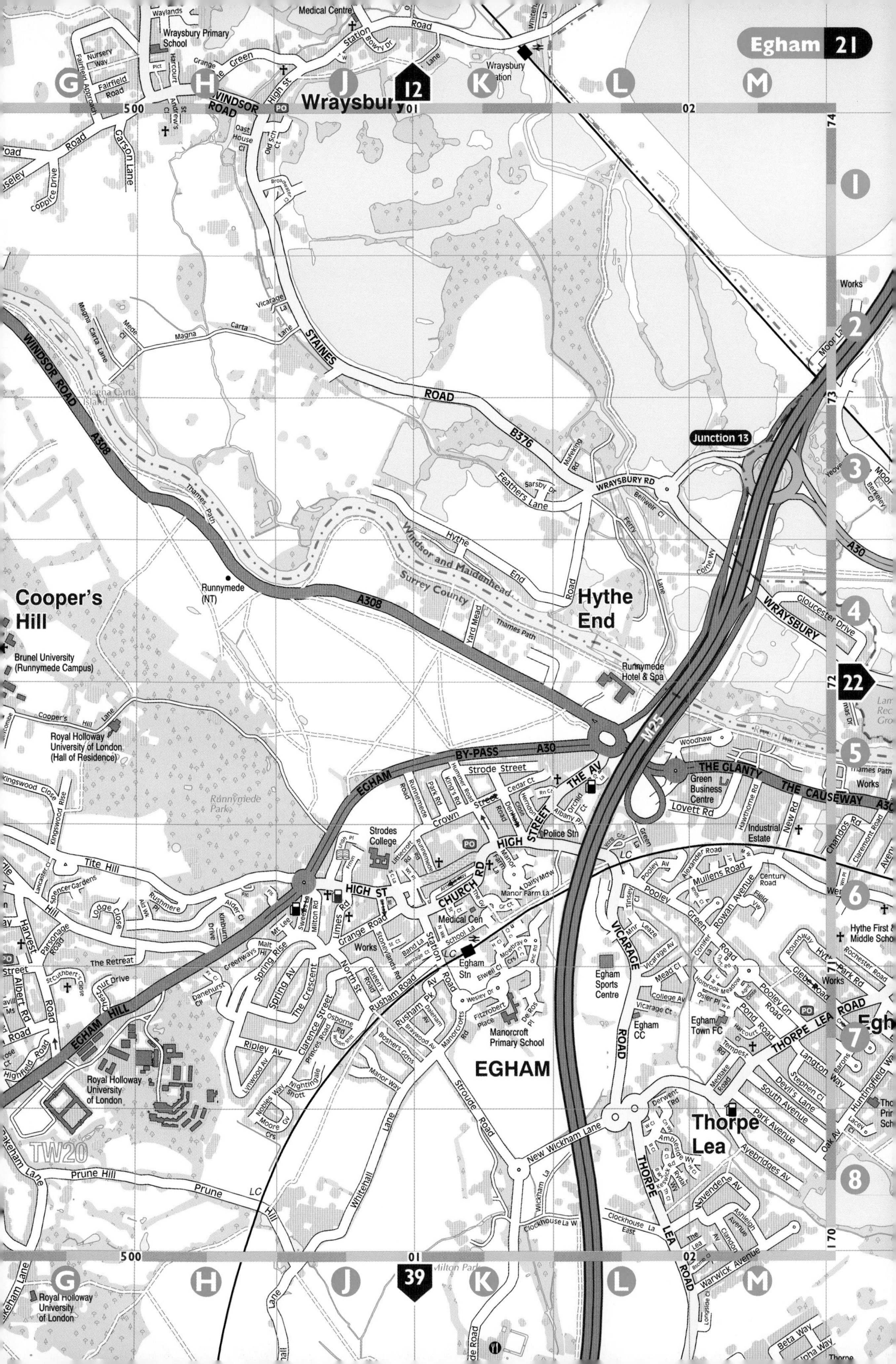
Wraysbury
Wraysbury Primary School
Wraysbury Station
Medical Centre
Cooper's Hill
Brunel University (Runnymede Campus)
Royal Holloway University of London (Hall of Residence)
Runnymede (NT)
Runnymede Park
Magna Carta Island
Hythe End
Runnymede Hotel & Spa
Junction 13
Green Business Centre
Industrial Estate
Strodes College
Police Stn
Medical Cen
Egham Stn
Egham Sports Centre
Egham CC
Egham Town FC
Manorcroft Primary School
EGHAM
Thorpe Lea
Royal Holloway University of London
Hythe First & Middle School
TW20
WINDSOR ROAD
STAINES ROAD
B376
A308
EGHAM BY-PASS A30
HIGH STREET
HIGH ST
CHURCH RD
THE AV
THE GLANTY
THE CAUSEWAY
WRAYSBURY RD
VICARAGE ROAD
THORPE LEA ROAD
EGHAM HILL
M25
Thames Path
Windsor and Maidenhead
Surrey County
Prune Hill
New Wickham Lane
Stroude Road
Whitehall Lane
Rusham Road
Grange Road
Station Road
Pooley Green Road
Rowan Avenue
Mullens Road
South Avenue
Park Avenue
Avebridges Av
Warwick Avenue
Tite Hill
Cooper's Hill Lane
Kingswood Rise
Harvest Road
Parsonage Road
Albert Rd
Highfield Road
Spring Rise
Clarence Street
North St
Manor Way
Lovett Rd
Hawthorne Rd
New Rd
Gloucester Drive
Coppice Drive
Carson Lane
Featherss Lane
Hythe End Road
Yard Mead
Ferry Lane
Strode Street
Crown Street
Runnemede Road
Limes Rd
Milton Rd
Clockhouse La
12
22
39
500
01
02
74
73
72
71
170
G H J K L M
1 2 3 4 5 6 7 8

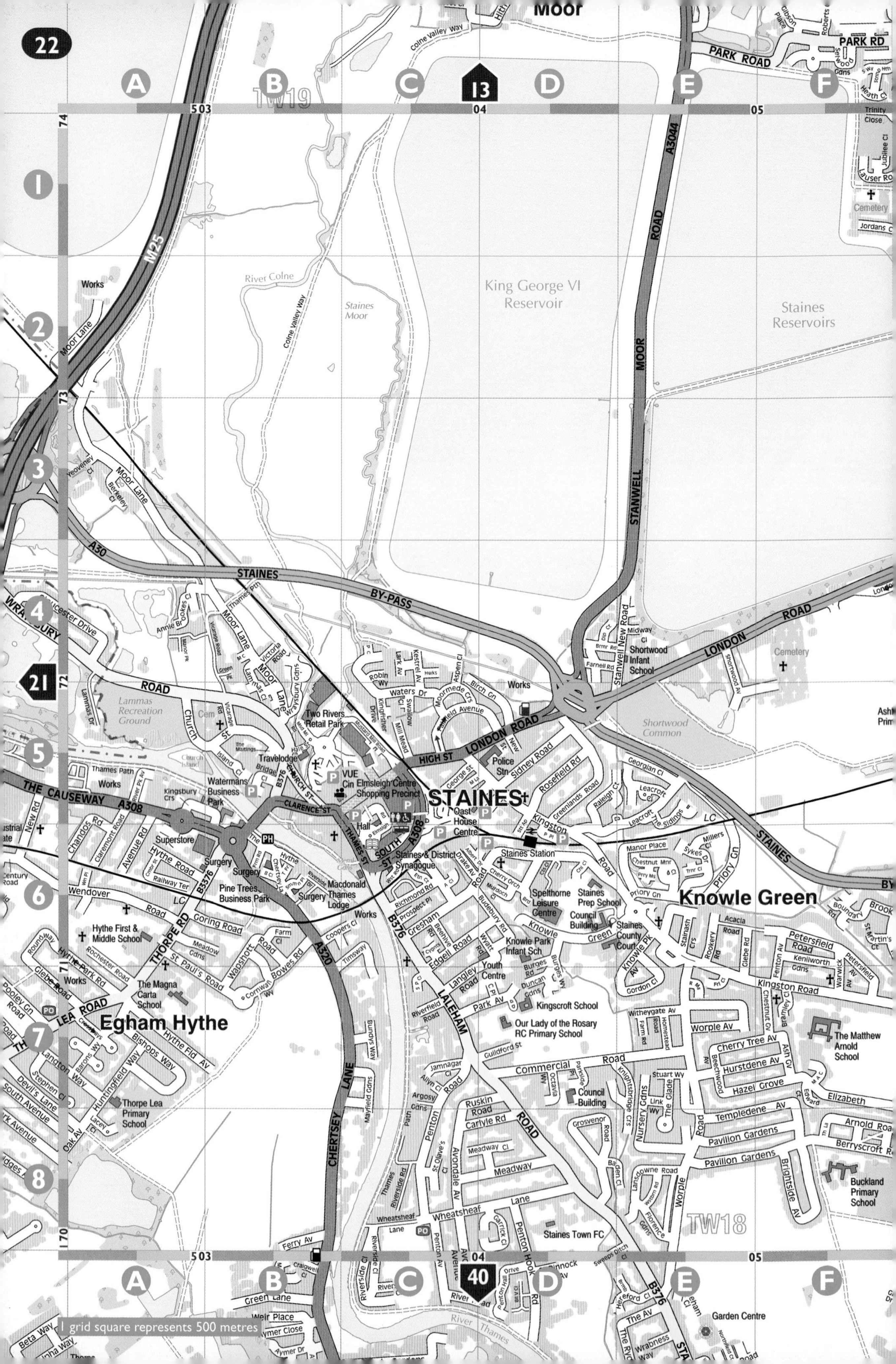

Moor
Colne Valley Way
PARK RD
PARK ROAD
13
TW19
A B C D E F
503 04 05
74 73 72 71 70
1 2 3 4 5 6 7 8
M25
A3044
ROAD
MOOR
STANWELL
River Colne
Colne Valley Way
Staines Moor
King George VI Reservoir
Staines Reservoirs
Cemetery
Jordans Cl
Works
Moor Lane
Yeoveney Cl
Berkeley Cl
A30
STAINES BY-PASS
LONDON ROAD
Thames Pth
Wraysbury Road
Gloucester Drive
21
Lammas Recreation Ground
Lammas Dr
Church Island
Thames Path
Works
THE CAUSEWAY A308
Kingsbury Crs
Watermans Business Park
Travelodge
Two Rivers Retail Park
VUE Cin
Elmsleigh Centre Shopping Precinct
STAINES
HIGH ST
LONDON ROAD
Police Stn
Sidney Road
Rosefield Rd
Greenlands Road
Shortwood Common
Shortwood Infant School
Stanwell New Road
Midway Cl
Farnell Rd
Shortwood Av
Robin Wy
Kingfisher Drive
Waters Dr
Moormede Crs
Fairfield Avenue
Birch Gn
Mill Mead
CLARENCE ST
THAMES ST
SOUTH ST A308
Hall
Oast House Centre
Staines Station
Kingston Road
Staines & District Synagogue
Superstore
Surgery
Pine Trees Business Park
Macdonald Thames Lodge
Works
Hythe Road
Railway Ter
Wendover Road
Goring Road
THORPE RD
B3376
Hythe First & Middle School
Rochester Road
St Paul's Road
Wapshott Road
Bowes Rd
Coopers Cl
Timsway
A320
CHERTSEY LANE
The Magna Carta School
Egham Hythe
LEA ROAD
Bishops Way
Hythe Fld Av
Huntingfield Way
Thorpe Lea Primary School
Devil's Lane
South Avenue
Oak Av
Richmond Rd
Prospect Pl
Gresham Rd
Edgell Road
Langley Road
Youth Centre
Park Av
Riverfield Road
LALEHAM ROAD
B376
Spelthorne Leisure Centre
Staines Prep School
Council Building
Staines County Court
Knowle Park Infant Sch
Kingscroft School
Our Lady of the Rosary RC Primary School
Knowle Green
Priory Gn
Manor Place
Acacia Road
Petersfield Road
Kenilworth Gdns
Kingston Road
The Matthew Arnold School
Worple Av
Cherry Tree Av
Hurstdene Av
Hazel Grove
Elizabeth
Templedene Av
Pavilion Gardens
Arnold Road
Berryscroft Rd
Buckland Primary School
Brightside Av
Commercial Road
Council Building
Guildford St
Ruskin Road
Carlyle Rd
Meadway Cl
Meadway
Avondale Av
Penton Road
Wheatsheaf Lane
Penton Hook Rd
Staines Town FC
Lansdowne Road
Worple Road
TW18
Grosvenor Road
Nursery Gdns
The Glade
Thames Side
Riverside Rd
Ferry Av
Green Lane
Weir Place
River Thames
40
Hereford Cl
Garden Centre
B376
1 grid square represents 500 metres

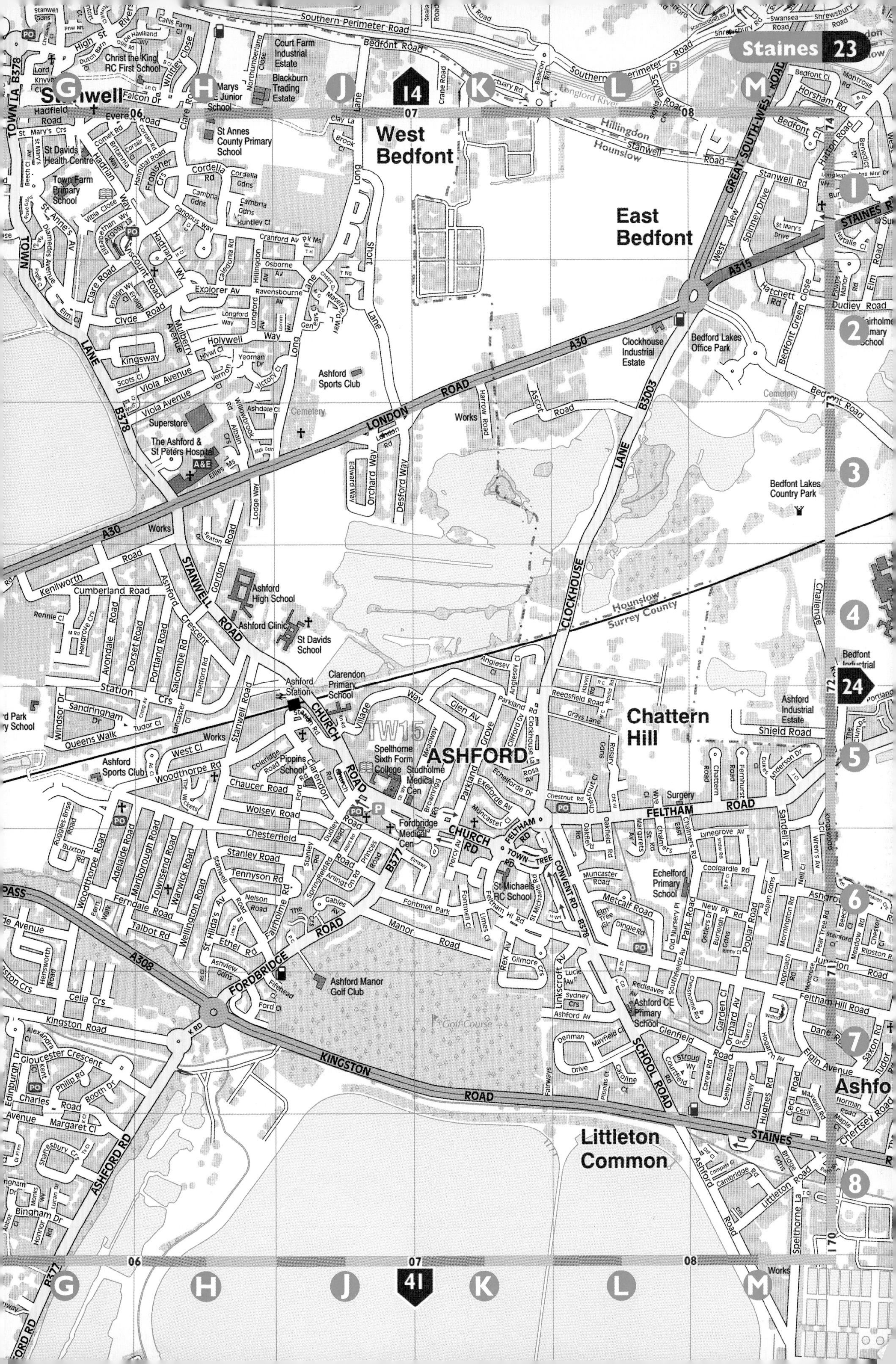

Stanwell
West Bedfont
East Bedfont
Chattern Hill
ASHFORD
TW15
Littleton Common
Southern Perimeter Road
Bedfont Road
London Road
A30
Kingston Road
Staines Road
Clockhouse Lane
Feltham Road
Church Road
Stanwell Road
Fordbridge Road
School Road
Ashford Road
Great South-West Road
A315
A308
B378
B3003
B377
Court Farm Industrial Estate
Blackburn Trading Estate
St Annes County Primary School
Town Farm Primary School
St Davids Health Centre
The Ashford & St Peters Hospital
Superstore
Ashford Sports Club
Cemetery
Works
Clockhouse Industrial Estate
Bedford Lakes Office Park
Bedfont Lakes Country Park
Ashford High School
Ashford Clinic
St Davids School
Ashford Station
Clarendon Primary School
Spelthorne Sixth Form College
Studholme Medical Cen
Fordbridge Medical Cen
Pippins School
St Michaels RC School
Echelford Primary School
Ashford CE Primary School
Ashford Manor Golf Club
Golf Course
Ashford Industrial Estate
Bedfont Industrial
Surgery
Hounslow
Surrey County
Longford River
14
24
41
G H J K L M
06 07 08
1 2 3 4 5 6 7 8

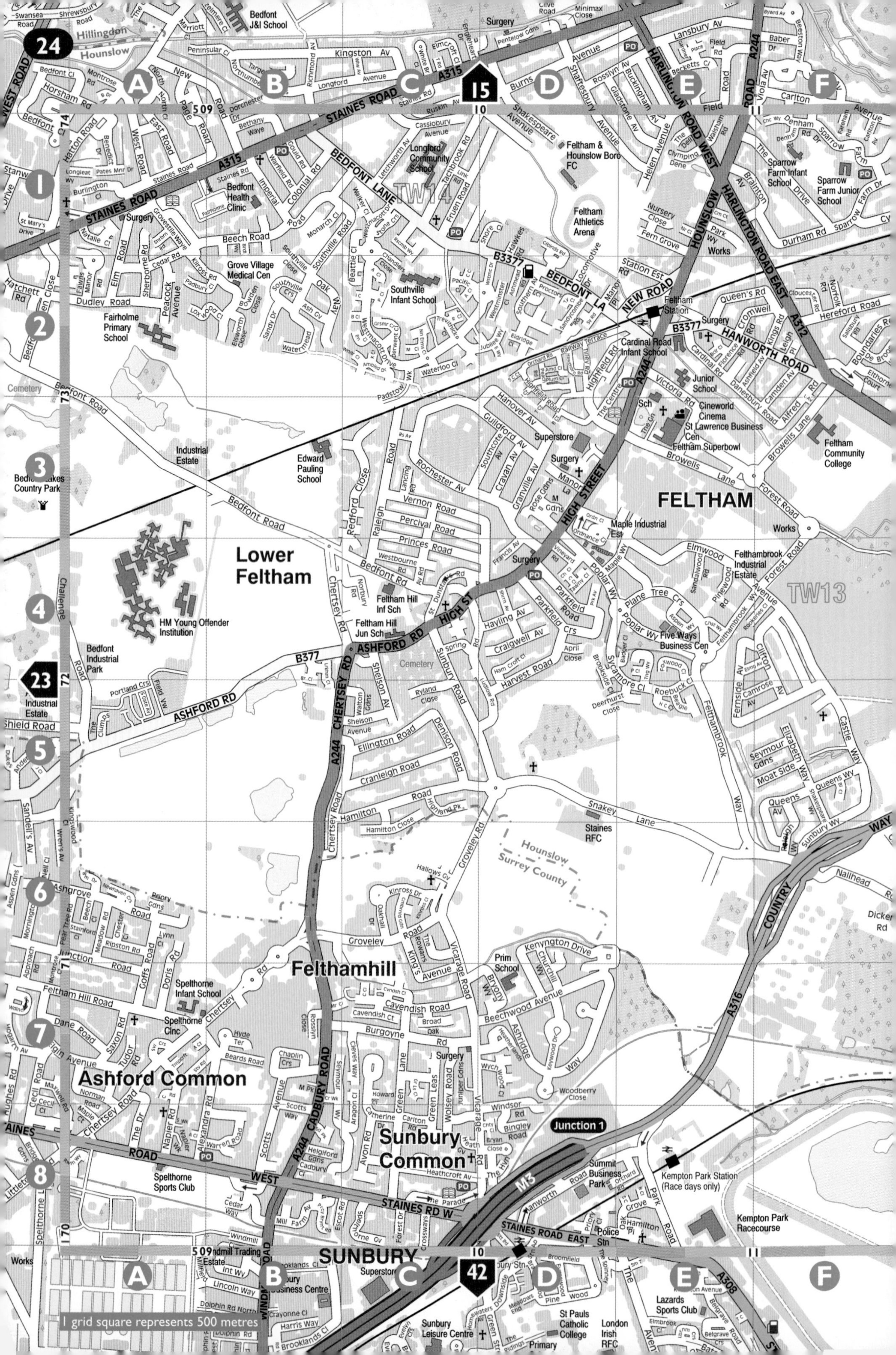

24
15
23
42
Hillingdon
Hounslow
Bedfont J&I School
Staines Road
A315
Bedfont Lane
TW14
Longford Community School
Bedfont Health Clinic
Surgery
Grove Village Medical Cen
Fairholme Primary School
Southville Infant School
Feltham & Hounslow Boro FC
Feltham Athletics Arena
Bedfont La
B3377
New Road
Feltham Station
Hanworth Road
Harlington Road West
Harlington Road East
Hounslow Road
A244
A312
Sparrow Farm Infant School
Sparrow Farm Junior School
Cardinal Road Infant School
Junior School
Cineworld Cinema
St Lawrence Business Cen
Feltham Superbowl
Feltham Community College
FELTHAM
Superstore
High Street
Maple Industrial Est
Felthambrook Industrial Estate
TW13
Five Ways Business Cen
Cemetery
Bedfont Road
Industrial Estate
Bedfont Lakes Country Park
Edward Pauling School
Lower Feltham
HM Young Offender Institution
Bedfont Industrial Park
Feltham Hill Inf Sch
Feltham Hill Jun Sch
Ashford Rd
B377
Chertsey Rd
Sunbury Road
Snakey Lane
Staines RFC
Hounslow
Surrey County
Country Way
A316
Felthamhill
Prim School
Spelthorne Infant School
Spelthorne Clnc
Ashford Common
Cadbury Road
Sunbury Common
Junction 1
M3
Summit Business Park
Kempton Park Station (Race days only)
Kempton Park Racecourse
Spelthorne Sports Club
Staines Road West
Staines Road East
Windmill Trading Estate
Sunbury Business Centre
SUNBURY
Superstore
Sunbury Leisure Centre
St Pauls Catholic College
London Irish RFC
Lazards Sports Club
A308
1 grid square represents 500 metres

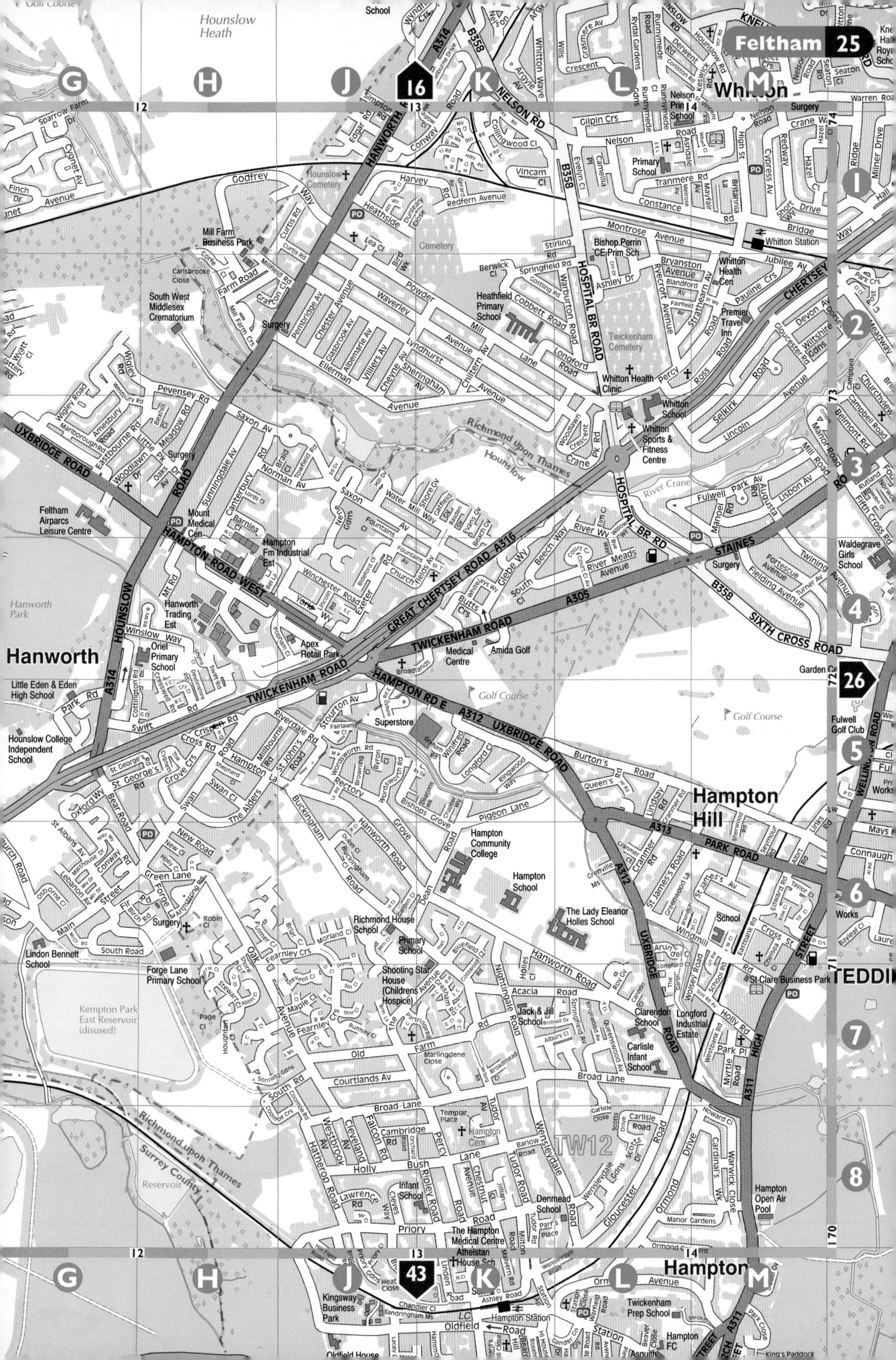

Hounslow Heath
G
H
J
K
L
M
16
Whitton
12
13
14
Hounslow Cemetery
Cemetery
Mill Farm Business Park
South West Middlesex Crematorium
Surgery
HANWORTH ROAD
Heathside
Harvey
Redfern Avenue
Powder Mill Lane
Waverley
Chester Avenue
Pembridge Av
Glasbrook Av
Albemarle Av
Villiers Av
Cheyne Av
Sheringham Av
Lyndhurst Avenue
Ellerman Avenue
Chiltern Av
Heathfield Primary School
Twickenham Cemetery
Whitton Health Clinic
Whitton School
Whitton Sports & Fitness Centre
Bishop Perrin CE Prim Sch
HOSPITAL BR ROAD
Montrose Avenue
Constance
Tranmere Rd
Nelson Prim School
NELSON RD
Primary School
Whitton Station
Whitton Health Cen
Premier Travel Inn
CHERTSEY
Percy
Ross Road
Selkirk
Lincoln
Godfrey Way
Finch Dr
Cygnet Av
Sparrow Farm Dr
Avenue
UXBRIDGE ROAD
Feltham Airparcs Leisure Centre
Mount Medical Cen
HAMPTON ROAD WEST
Hampton Fm Industrial Est
Hanworth Trading Est
Hanworth Park
Hanworth
HOUNSLOW
A314
Oriel Primary School
Little Eden & Eden High School
Hounslow College Independent School
Richmond upon Thames
Hounslow
River Crane
GREAT CHERTSEY ROAD A316
TWICKENHAM ROAD
A305
STAINES
Apex Retail Park
Medical Centre
Amida Golf
Golf Course
SIXTH CROSS ROAD
Waldegrave Girls School
Surgery
Fortescue Avenue
Fielding Avenue
B358
Fulwell Park Av
Garden Ce
26
Fulwell Golf Club
HAMPTON RD E
A312
UXBRIDGE ROAD
Superstore
Burton's Road
Queen's Rd
Hampton Hill
A313
PARK ROAD
Pigeon Lane
Hampton Community College
Hampton School
The Lady Eleanor Holles School
Richmond House School
Primary School
Shooting Star House (Childrens Hospice)
Jack & Jill School
Clarendon School
Longford Industrial Estate
Carlisle Infant School
St Clare Business Park
TEDDI
HIGH STREET
A311
Works
Kempton Park East Reservoir (disused)
Forge Lane Primary School
Lindon Bennett School
Surgery
Main Street
South Road
New Road
Green Lane
Oak Avenue
Old Farm Rd
Courtlands Av
Broad Lane
Hampton Cem
TW12
Wensleydale Road
Gloucester Road
Ormond Drive
Hampton Open Air Pool
Reservoir
Surrey County
Richmond upon Thames
Infant School
Denmead School
The Hampton Medical Centre
Athelstan House Sch
Priory
Hampton
43
Kingsway Business Park
Hampton Station
Twickenham Prep School
Hampton FC
Oldfield Road
Station
Avenue
1
2
3
4
5
6
7
8
74
73
72
71
170

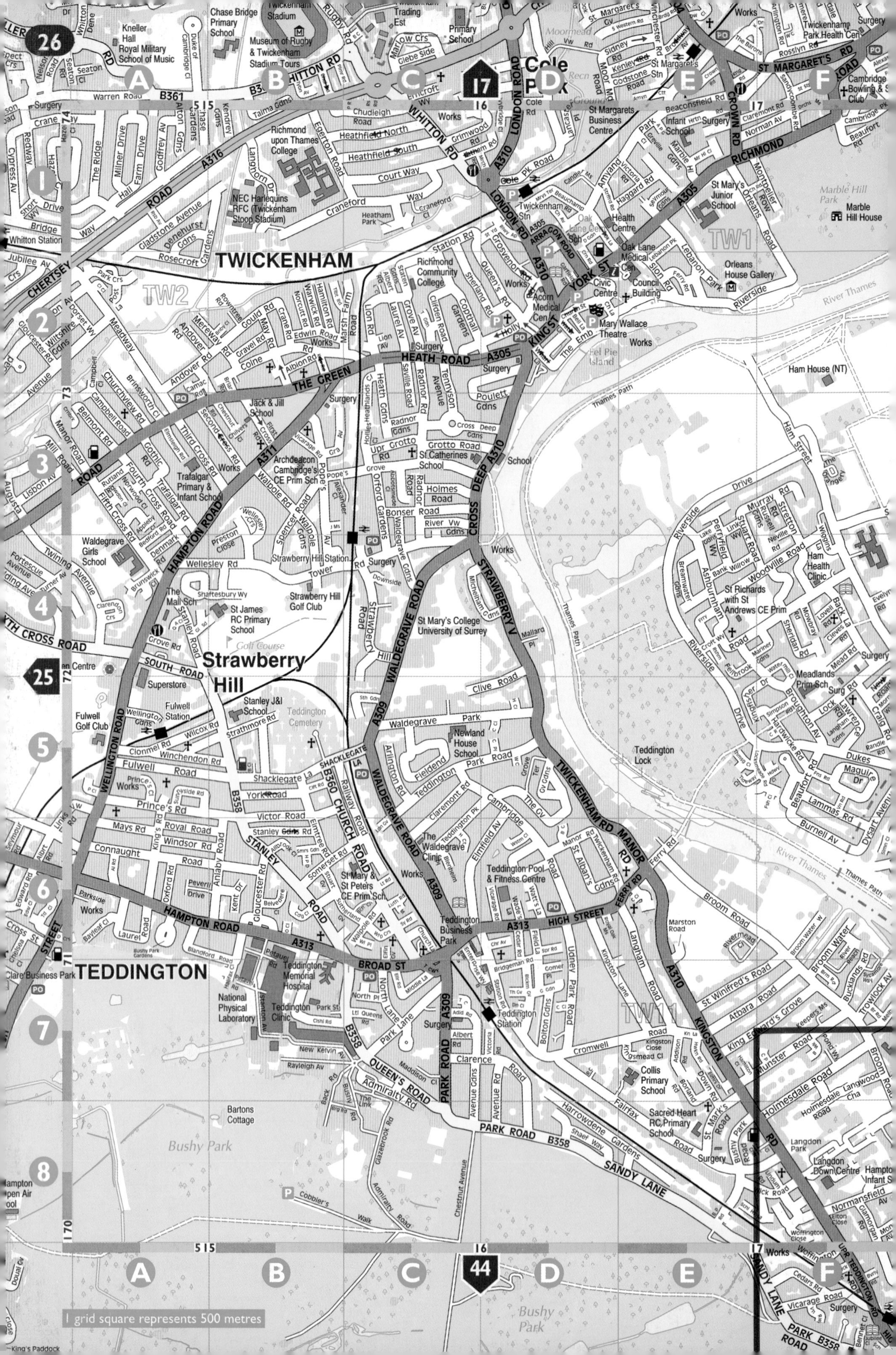

26
Kneller Hall Royal Military School of Music
Chase Bridge Primary School
Twickenham Stadium
Museum of Rugby & Twickenham Stadium Tours
Trading Est
Primary School
Moormead
Cole Park
St Margarets
St Margaret's Stn
Works
Twickenham Park Health Cen
Surgery
A
B
C
D
E
F
17
Warren Road
B361
WHITTON RD
Talma Gdns
Chudleigh Road
Heathfield North
Heathfield South
Court Way
Craneford Way
WHITTON RD
Egerton Road
Richmond upon Thames College
LONDON ROAD
A310
St Margarets Business Centre
Beaconsfield Rd
Infant School
CROWN RD
ST MARGARET'S RD
Cambridge Bowling & Sports Club
RICHMOND ROAD
A305
St Mary's Junior School
Marble Hill Park
Marble Hill House
TW1
Orleans House Gallery
River Thames
Riverside
Ham House (NT)
1
Chertsey Road
A316
Whitton Station
Gladstone Avenue
Denehurst Gdns
Rosecroft Gardens
NEC Harlequins RFC (Twickenham Stoop Stadium)
Heatham Park
TWICKENHAM
Twickenham Stn
Station Rd
Richmond Community College
Queen's Rd
Grosvenor Rd
ARRAGON ROAD
YORK ST
Civic Centre
Council Building
Health Centre
Oak Lane Medical Cen
Acorn Medical Cen
KING ST
The Emb
Mary Wallace Theatre
Eel Pie Island
TW2
2
The Green
HEATH ROAD
A305
Andover Rd
Gould Rd
Edwin Road
Jack & Jill School
Surgery
Heath Gdns
Saville Road
Radnor Rd
Tennyson Avenue
Poulett Gdns
Cross Deep Gdns
Grotto Road
St Catherines School
Thames Path
Ham Street
3
Manor Road
Mill Road
Lisbon Av
Gothic Rd
Trafalgar Primary & Infant School
Archdeacon Cambridge's CE Prim Sch
Pope's Grove
Orford Gardens
Holmes Road
Bonser Road
River Vw Gdns
CROSS DEEP
A310
School
Waldegrave Girls School
HAMPTON ROAD
A311
Preston Close
Strawberry Hill Station
Tower Rd
Surgery
Works
STRAWBERRY V
Riverside Drive
Ham Health Clinic
4
Fortescue Avenue
Twining Avenue
Wellesley Rd
The Mall Sch
Shaftesbury Wy
St James RC Primary School
Strawberry Hill Golf Club
WALDEGRAVE ROAD
St Mary's College University of Surrey
St Richards with St Andrews CE Prim
Grove Rd
Golf Course
SOUTH ROAD
Strawberry Hill
Mallard Pl
Meadlands Prim Sch
25
Superstore
Fulwell Station
Stanley J&I School
Teddington Cemetery
Clive Road
Fulwell Golf Club
5
WELLINGTON ROAD
Wilcox Rd
Strathmore Rd
Clonmel Rd
Winchendon Rd
Fulwell Road
Shacklegate La
SHACKLEGATE LA
B360 CHURCH ROAD
Waldegrave Park
Newland House School
Teddington Lock
Fieldend
Teddington Park Road
TWICKENHAM RD
Prince's Rd
York Road
Victor Road
Royal Road
Windsor Rd
Mays Rd
Connaught Road
STANLEY ROAD
Claremont Rd
Cambridge
The Gv
Elmfield Av
MANOR RD
Ferry Rd
6
Parkside
Works
Peverill Drive
Kent Dr
Somerset Rd
St Mary & St Peters CE Prim Sch
The Waldegrave Clinic
Teddington Pool & Fitness Centre
St Alban's Gdns
FERRY RD
HAMPTON ROAD
A313
Laurel Road
Blandford Road
Teddington Memorial Hospital
BROAD ST
Teddington Business Park
HIGH STREET
A313
Langham Road
Broom Road
Marston Road
Rivermead Cl
Broom Water
TEDDINGTON
Clare Business Park
National Physical Laboratory
Teddington Clinic
North La
Park Lane
PARK ROAD
A309
Teddington Station
Cromwell Road
Udney Park Road
Bolton Gdns
Kingston Lane
St Winifred's Road
Atbara Road
King Edward's Grove
TW11
KINGSTON RD
A310
7
New Kelvin Av
Rayleigh Av
B358
QUEEN'S ROAD
Admiralty Rd
Clarence Road
Avenue Gdns
Avenue Rd
Collis Primary School
Sacred Heart RC Primary School
Munster Road
Holmesdale Road
Bartons Cottage
Bushy Park
PARK ROAD B358
Harrowdene Gardens
SANDY LANE
Langdon Park
Langdon Down Centre
8
Hampton Open Air Pool
Cobbler's Walk
Chestnut Avenue
Glazebrook Rd
Normansfield
515
16
44
Bushy Park
Cedars Rd
Vicarage Road
Surgery
UPR TEDDINGTON RD
1 grid square represents 500 metres
King's Paddock

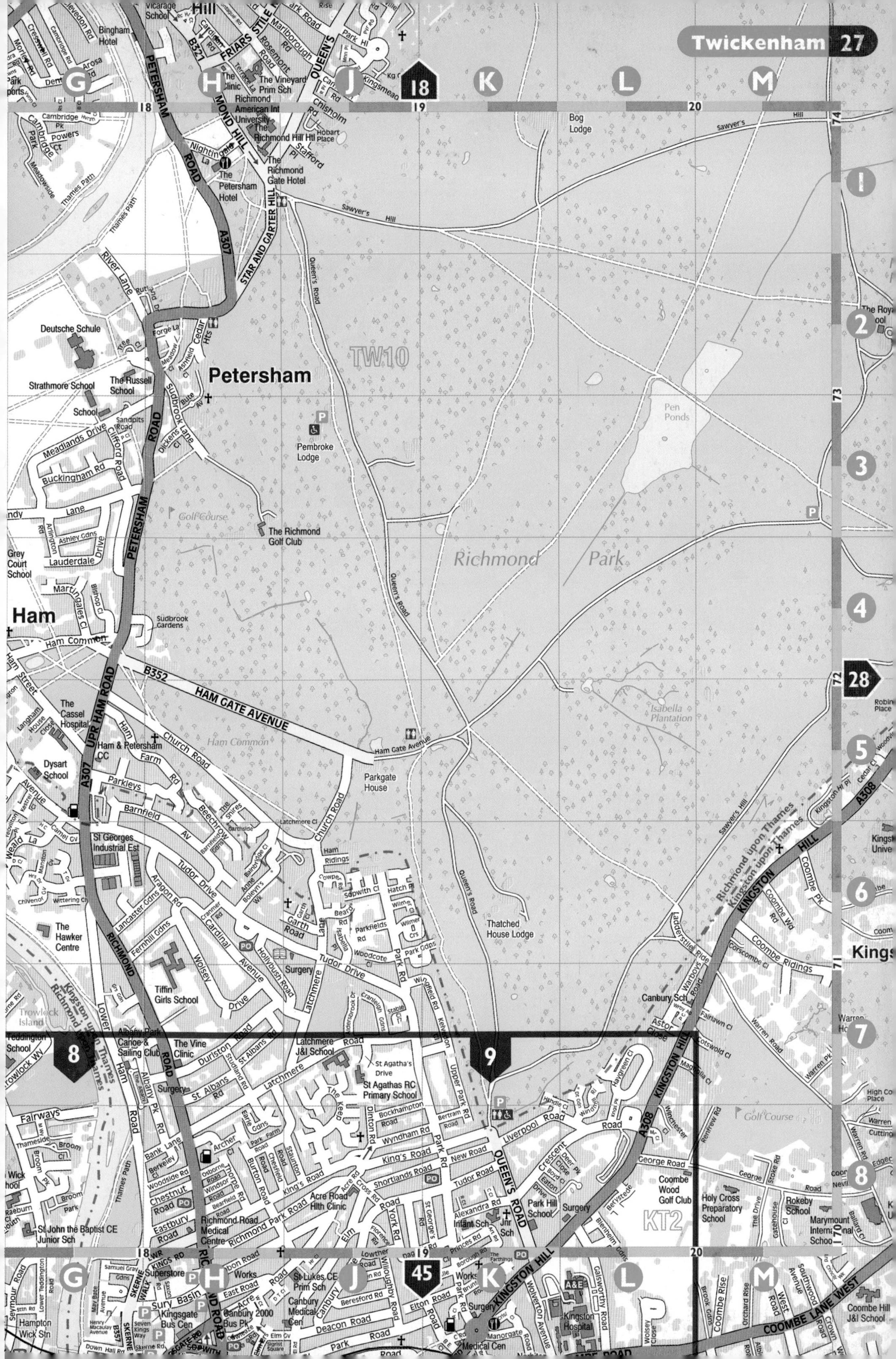
Petersham
Ham
Richmond Park
TW10
KT2
Pen Ponds
Isabella Plantation
Pembroke Lodge
Thatched House Lodge
Bog Lodge
Parkgate House
The Richmond Golf Club
Golf Course
Ham Common
Sudbrook Gardens
Deutsche Schule
Strathmore School
The Russell School
Grey Court School
The Cassel Hospital
Ham & Petersham CC
Dysart School
St Georges Industrial Est
The Hawker Centre
Tiffin Girls School
Trowlock Island
Teddington School
Albany Park Canoe & Sailing Club
The Vine Clinic
Latchmere J&I School
St Agathas RC Primary School
Canbury Sch
Coombe Wood Golf Club
Holy Cross Preparatory School
Rokeby School
Marymount International School
Park Hill School
Alexandra Rd Infant Sch
Richmond Road Medical Centre
St John the Baptist CE Junior Sch
St Lukes CE Prim Sch
Canbury Medical Cen
Kingston Hospital
Coombe Hill J&I School
Kingsgate Bus Cen
Canbury 2000 Bus Pk
Hampton Wick Stn
The Richmond Gate Hotel
The Richmond Hill Htl
The Petersham Hotel
Richmond American Int University
The Vineyard Prim Sch
Bingham Hotel
PETERSHAM ROAD
A307
STAR AND GARTER HILL
Sawyer's Hill
Queen's Road
B352 HAM GATE AVENUE
UPR HAM ROAD
RICHMOND ROAD
KINGSTON HILL
A308
COOMBE LANE WEST
Richmond upon Thames
Kingston upon Thames
Ham Street
Church Road
Tudor Drive
Latchmere Road
Park Rd
King's Road
Liverpool Road
George Road
Coombe Ridings
Warren Road
Ladderstile Ride
Lower Ham Road
Thames Path
River Lane
Meadlands Drive
Buckingham Rd
Lauderdale Drive
Sudbrook Lane
Cardinal Avenue
Wolsey Drive
Elton Road
Deacon Road
Park Road
Galsworthy Road
Wolverton Avenue
G H J K L M
18 19 20
1 2 3 4 5 6 7 8
74 73 72 71 70
8 9 18 28 45

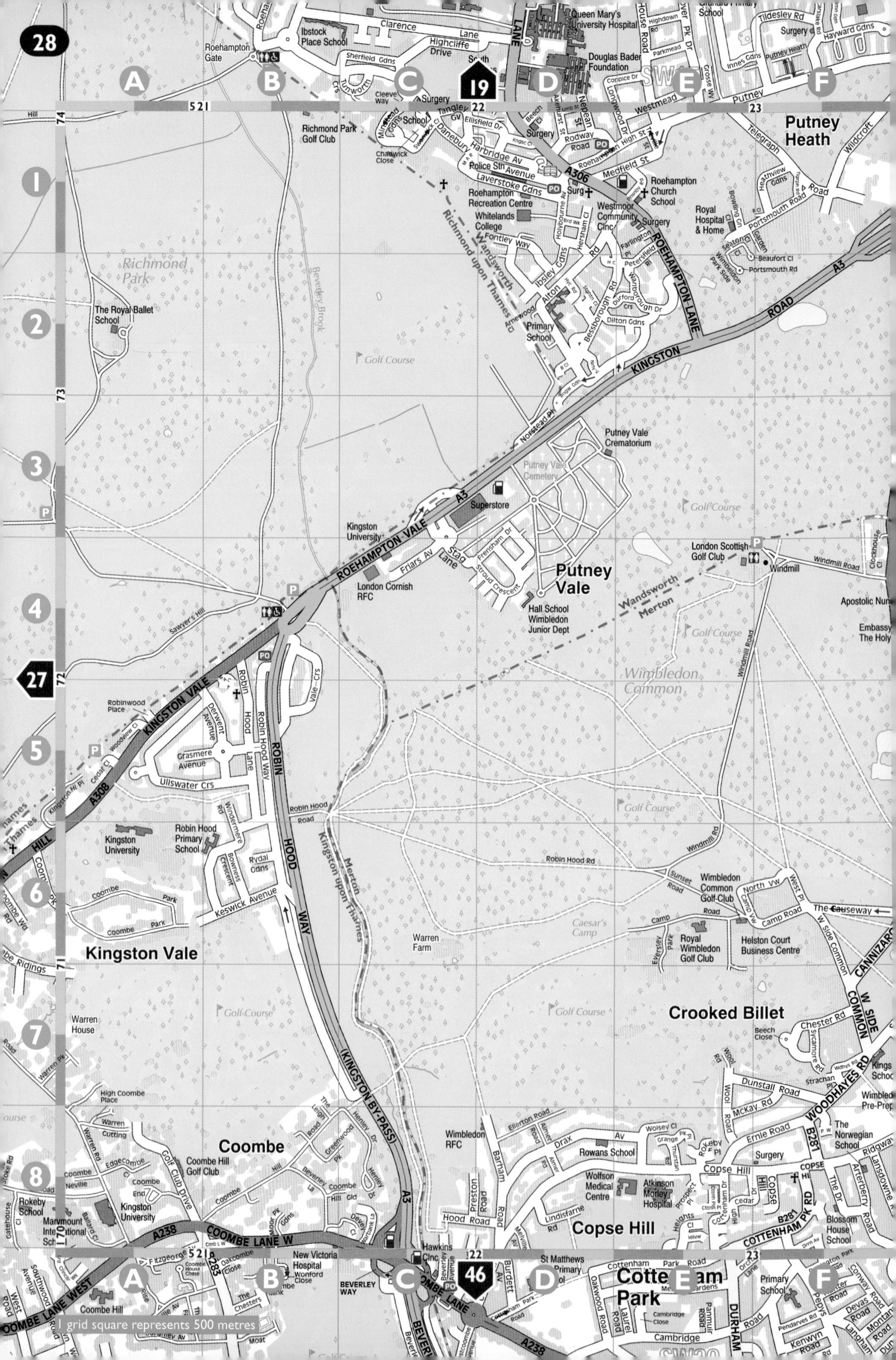

A
B
C
D
E
F
19
27
46
521
22
23
74
73
72
71
170
1
2
3
4
5
6
7
8
Roehampton Gate
Clarence Lane
Ibstock Place School
Highcliffe Drive
Sherfield Gdns
Tunworth Crs
Cleeve Way
Surgery
Queen Mary's University Hospital
Douglas Bader Foundation
Highdown Rd
Parkmead
Coppice Dr
Longwood Dr
Nepean St
Alderhurst St
Westmead
Putney
Tildesley Rd
Hayward Gdns
Innes Gdns
Putney Heath
Putney Heath
Telegraph Road
Wildcroft
Richmond Park Golf Club
Minstead Gdns
School
Tangley Gv
Ellisfield Dr
Danebury Av
Harbridge Av
Chadwick Close
Police Stn
Avenue
Laverstoke Gdns
Beech
Surgery
Rodway Road
Roehampton High St
Medfield St
A306
Roehampton Church School
Roehampton Recreation Centre
Whitelands College
Fontley Way
Holybourne Av
Hersham Cl
Westmoor Community Clinic
Surgery
Farlington Pl
Petersfield Ri
Royal Hospital & Home
Heathview Gdns
Portsmouth Road
Bowling Gn Cl
Seaton Cl
Beaufort Cl
Portsmouth Rd
Wimbledon Park Side
Richmond upon Thames
Wandsworth
Richmond Park
The Royal Ballet School
Beverley Brook
Ibsley Gdns
Alton Rd
Bessborough Rd
Wanborough Dr
Dilton Gdns
Arnewood Cl
Primary School
ROEHAMPTON LANE
KINGSTON ROAD
A3
Golf Course
Norstead Pl
Putney Vale Crematorium
Putney Vale Cemetery
Superstore
ROEHAMPTON VALE
Kingston University
Friars Av
Stag Lane
Frensham Dr
Stroud Crescent
London Cornish RFC
Putney Vale
Hall School Wimbledon Junior Dept
London Scottish Golf Club
Windmill
Windmill Road
Clockhouse Cl
Apostolic Nu
Embassy The Holy
Wandsworth
Merton
Wimbledon Common
Sawyer's Hill
KINGSTON VALE
Robinwood Place
Woodview Cl
Derwent Avenue
Robin Hood Lane
Robin Hood Way
Vale Crs
ROBIN HOOD WAY
Grasmere Avenue
Ullswater Crs
Cedar Cl
Kingston Hill Pl
A308
HILL
Thames
Windermere Rd
Robin Hood Primary School
Kingston University
Bowness Crescent
Rydal Gdns
Keswick Avenue
Robin Hood Road
Kingston upon Thames
Merton
Windmill Rd
Robin Hood Rd
Sunset Road
Wimbledon Common Golf Club
North Vw
West Pl
Camp Vw
Camp Road
The Causeway
Coombe Park
Coombe Park
Kingston Vale
Coombe Ridings
Warren Farm
Caesar's Camp
Camp Road
Royal Wimbledon Golf Club
Eversley Pk
Helston Court Business Centre
W Side Common
CANNIZARO
Warren House
Warren Pk
Crooked Billet
Beech Close
Chester Rd
Sycamore Rd
W SIDE COMMON
WOODHAYES RD
Strachan Pl
Wool Rd
Dunstall Road
McKay Rd
High Coombe Place
Warren Cutting
Warren Rd
Coombe
The Leigh
Henley Dr
Greenwood Pk
(KINGSTON BY-PASS)
Wimbledon RFC
Ellerton Road
Almer Road
Drax Av
Woisey Cl
Grange Pk Pl
Rokeby Pl
Ernie Road
B281
The Norwegian School
Edgecombe
Coombe Hill Golf Club
Coombe Hill Rd
Beverley La
Coombe Hill Gld
Henley Dr
Barham Road
Rowans School
Thurstan Rd
Surgery
Copse Hill
Wolfson Medical Centre
Atkinson Morley Hospital
Lindisfarne Rd
Copse Hill
Cottenham Dr
Cedar Dr
Preston Road
Hood Road
Melville Av
Rokeby School
Marymount International School
Coombe End
Kingston University
Devey Cl
Vernam La
Blossom House School
COTTENHAM PK RD
A238
COOMBE LANE W
Fitzgerald
Oakcombe Close
The Chesters
New Victoria Hospital
Wonford Close
BEVERLEY WAY
Hawkins Clinic
Beverley Avenue
Burdett Av
St Matthews Primary School
Cottenham Park Road
Cotte ham Park
Oakwood Road
Laurel Road
Cambridge Close
Panmuir Road
Cambridge Road
DURHAM
Primary School
Pendarves Rd
Kenwyn Road
Conway Road
Devas Road
Pepys Road
COOMBE LANE WEST
Coombe Hill
West Road
Southwood Avenue
1 grid square represents 500 metres

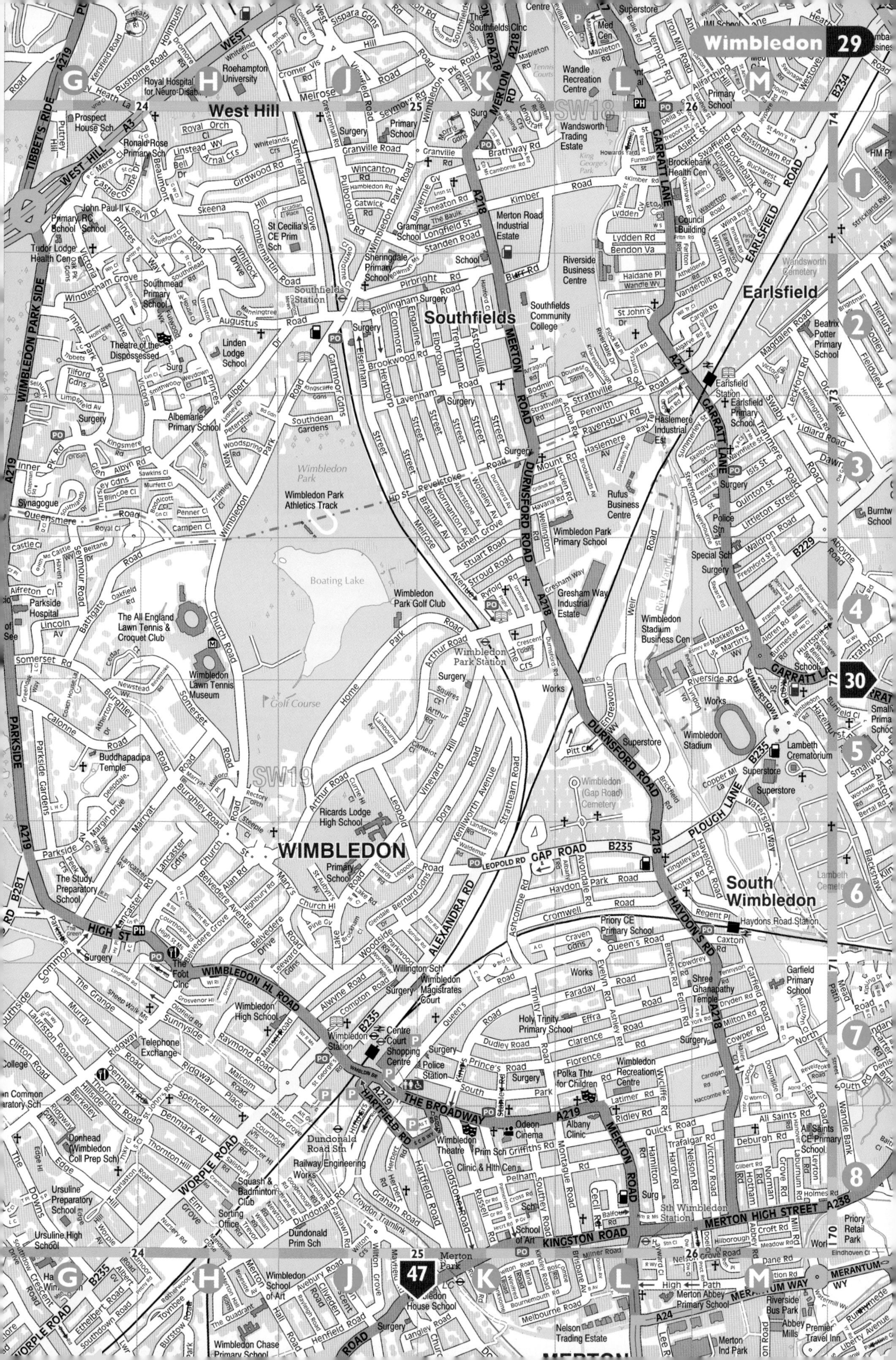
West Hill
Southfields
Earlsfield
WIMBLEDON
South Wimbledon
SW18
SW19
Roehampton University
Royal Hospital for Neuro-Disability
Prospect House Sch
Wandle Recreation Centre
Wandsworth Trading Estate
King George's Park
Brocklebank Health Cen
Council Building
Merton Road Industrial Estate
Riverside Business Centre
Southfields Community College
Southfields Station
Sheringdale Primary School
St Cecilia's CE Prim Sch
Southmead Primary School
Theatre of the Dispossessed
Linden Lodge School
Albemarle Primary School
Tudor Lodge Health Cen
Synagogue
Wimbledon Park
Wimbledon Park Athletics Track
Boating Lake
Wimbledon Park Golf Club
Golf Course
Wimbledon Park Station
The All England Lawn Tennis & Croquet Club
Wimbledon Lawn Tennis Museum
Parkside Hospital
Buddhapadipa Temple
Ricards Lodge High School
Wimbledon Park Primary School
Gresham Way Industrial Estate
Rufus Business Centre
Haslemere Industrial Est
Earlsfield Station
Earlsfield Primary School
Beatrix Potter Primary School
Wandsworth Cemetery
Wimbledon Stadium Business Cen
Wimbledon Stadium
Lambeth Crematorium
Wimbledon (Gap Road) Cemetery
Superstore
Haydons Road Station
Priory CE Primary School
Shree Ghanapathy Temple
Garfield Primary School
Holy Trinity Primary School
Wimbledon High School
Wimbledon Station
Centre Court Shopping Centre
Police Station
Wimbledon Magistrates Court
Telephone Exchange
The Study Preparatory School
Donhead (Wimbledon Coll Prep Sch)
Ursuline Preparatory School
Ursuline High School
Dundonald Road Stn
Railway Engineering Works
Dundonald Prim Sch
Squash & Badminton Club
Sorting Office
Wimbledon Theatre
Odeon Cinema
Polka Thtr for Children
Wimbledon Recreation Centre
Albany Clinic
All Saints CE Primary School
Sth Wimbledon Station
Merton Park
Wimbledon School of Art
Wimbledon Chase Primary School
Merton Abbey Primary School
Riverside Bus Park
Abbey Mills
Premier Travel Inn
Priory Retail Park
Nelson Trading Estate
Merton Ind Park
WIMBLEDON PARK SIDE
PARKSIDE
WEST HILL
MERTON ROAD
DURNSFORD ROAD
GARRATT LANE
EARLSFIELD ROAD
PLOUGH LANE
GAP ROAD
HAYDON'S RD
ALEXANDRA RD
WIMBLEDON HL ROAD
HIGH ST
THE BROADWAY
HARTFIELD RD
WORPLE ROAD
KINGSTON ROAD
MERTON HIGH STREET
MERANTUM WAY
A219
A218
A217
A3
B235
B229
B281
A238
A24
30
47

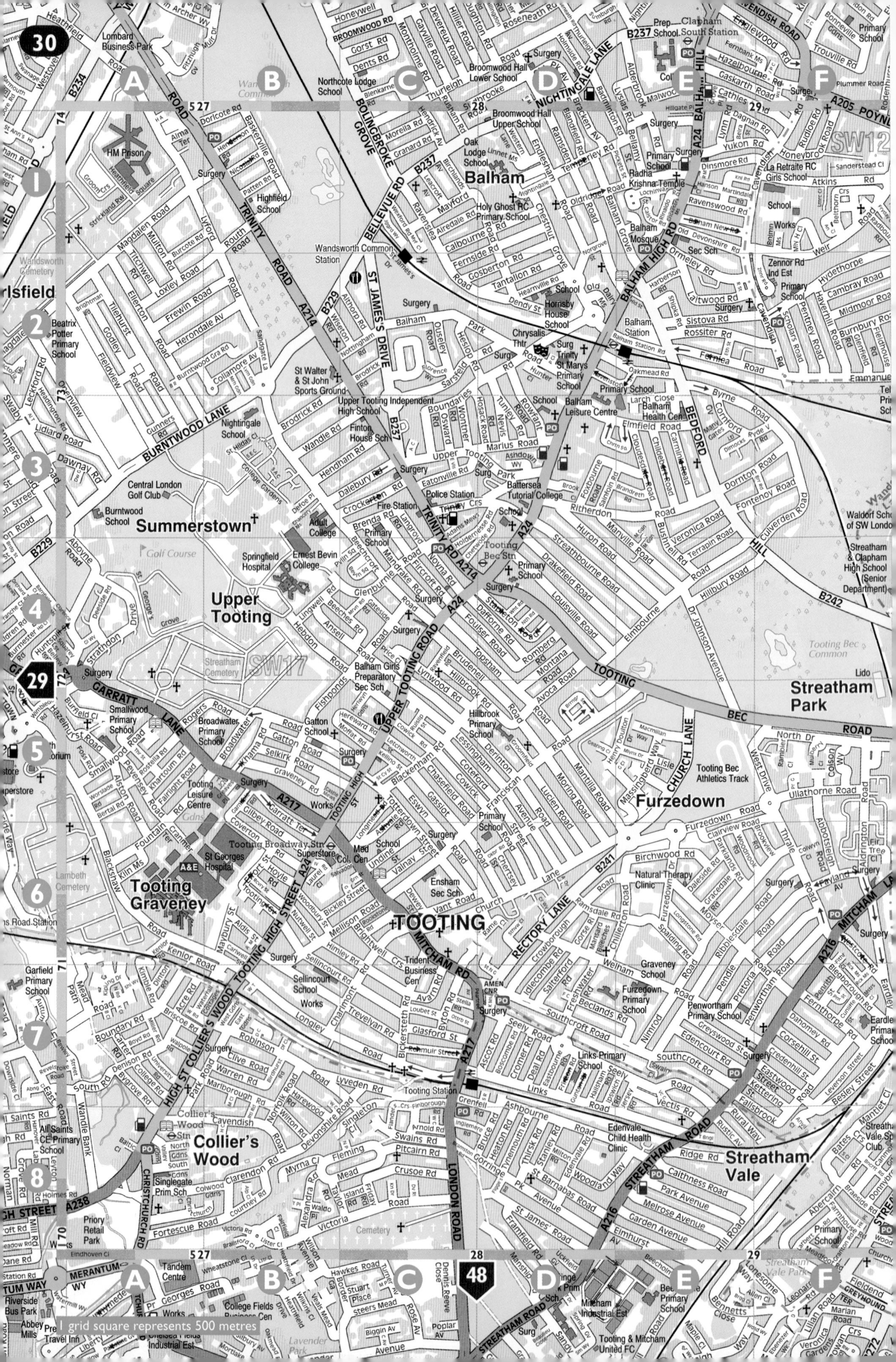

30
29
48
A
B
C
D
E
F
1
2
3
4
5
6
7
8
527
28
29
Balham
Summerstown
Upper Tooting
Tooting Graveney
TOOTING
Furzedown
Streatham Park
Streatham Vale
Collier's Wood
SW12
SW17
HM Prison
Lombard Business Park
Wandsworth Common Station
Balham Station
Tooting Bec Stn
Tooting Broadway Stn
Tooting Station
Clapham South Station
Collier's Wood Stn
St Georges Hospital
Springfield Hospital
Ernest Bevin College
Central London Golf Club
Burntwood School
Lambeth Cemetery
Streatham Cemetery
Tooting Bec Common
Tooting Bec Athletics Track
Balham Leisure Centre
Tooting Leisure Centre
Balham Mosque
Radha Krishna Temple
Holy Ghost RC Primary School
Broomwood Hall Upper School
Broomwood Hall Lower School
Northcote Lodge School
Upper Tooting Independent High School
Balham Girls Preparatory Sec Sch
Ensham Sec Sch
Graveney School
Furzedown Primary School
Links Primary School
Penwortham Primary School
Streatham & Clapham High School (Senior Department)
Waldorf School of SW London
Priory Retail Park
Tandem Centre
College Fields Business Cen
Mitcham Industrial Est
Tooting & Mitcham United FC
TRINITY ROAD A214
UPPER TOOTING ROAD A24
BALHAM HIGH RD A24
TOOTING HIGH ST
MITCHAM RD
LONDON ROAD A217
GARRATT LANE A217
TOOTING BEC ROAD
BURNTWOOD LANE
STREATHAM ROAD A216
MITCHAM LANE A216
RECTORY LANE B241
CHURCH LANE
BEDFORD HILL
NIGHTINGALE LANE
HIGH ST COLLIER'S WOOD
CHRISTCHURCH RD
MERANTUM WY
1 grid square represents 500 metres

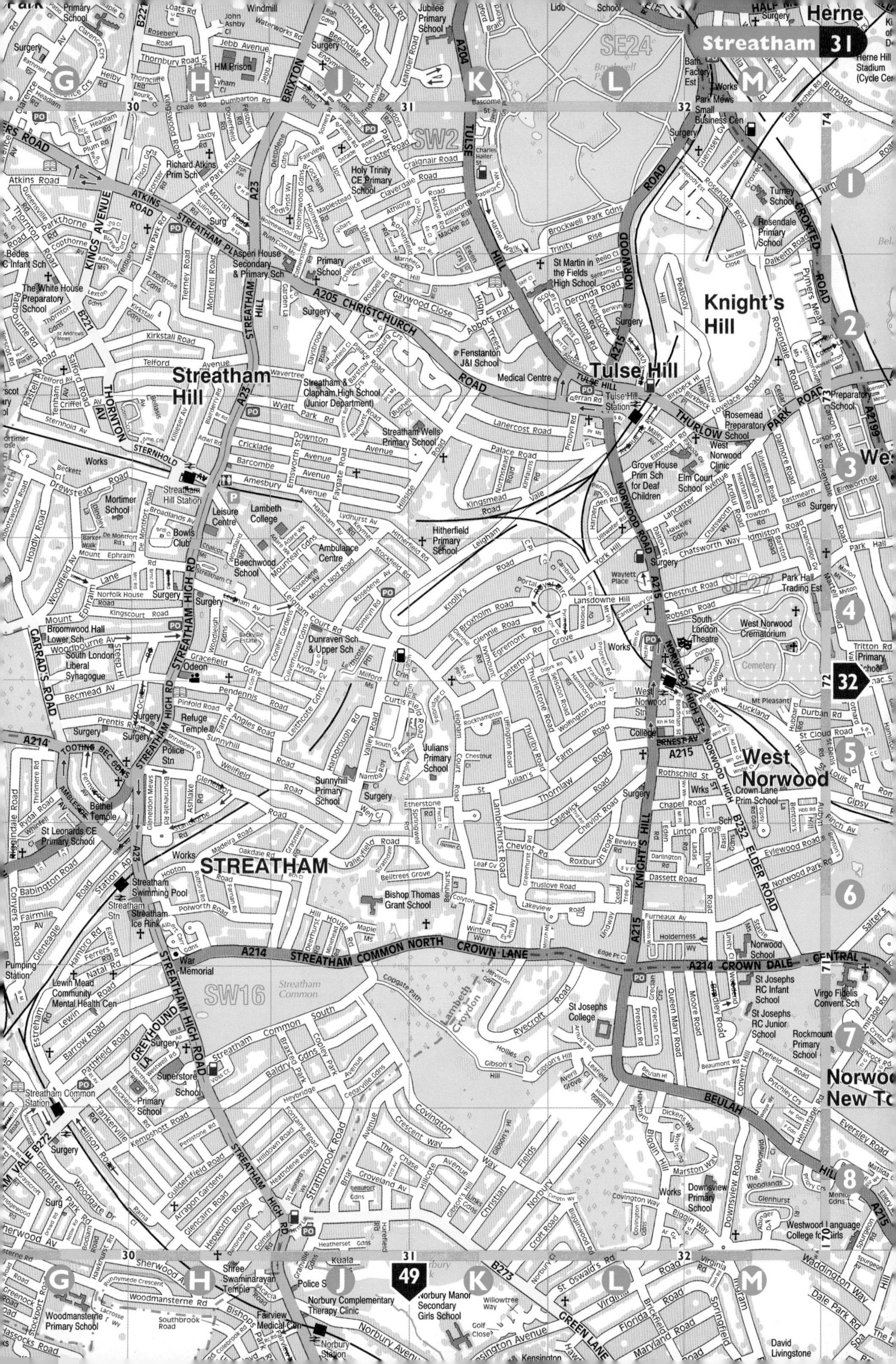
Herne Hill
SE24
Brockwell Park
SW2
Tulse Hill
Knight's Hill
Streatham Hill
West Norwood
STREATHAM
SW16
Streatham Common
SE27
Norwood New Town
HM Prison
Jebb Avenue
Thornbury Road
Atkins Road
Kings Avenue
Streatham Place
Christchurch Road
A205 Christchurch Road
Brixton Hill
Tulse Hill
Norwood Road
Croxted Road
Rosendale Road
Thurlow Park Road
Lancaster Avenue
Leigham Court Road
Knolly's Road
Streatham High Road
Streatham Common North
Crown Lane
A214 Crown Dale
Knight's Hill
Elder Road
Norwood High Street
Beulah Hill
Greyhound Lane
Tooting Bec Gardens
Garrad's Road
Sternhold Avenue
Sunnyhill Road
Valley Road
Lambeth College
Streatham Hill Station
Tulse Hill Station
West Norwood Station
Streatham Station
Streatham Common Station
Norbury Station
Streatham Swimming Pool
Streatham Ice Rink
West Norwood Crematorium
South London Theatre
Bishop Thomas Grant School
St Josephs College
Virgo Fidelis Convent Sch
Norbury Manor Secondary Girls School
Woodmansterne Primary School
Norwood School
Rosemead Preparatory School
St Martin in the Fields High School
Dunraven Sch & Upper Sch
Streatham & Clapham High School (Junior Department)
Streatham Wells Primary School
War Memorial
Odeon
Leisure Centre
Police Stn
Norbury Complementary Therapy Clinic
Fairview Medical Cen
Shree Swaminarayan Temple
G
H
J
K
L
M
30
31
32
49
32
I
2
3
4
5
6
7
8
74
73
72
71
70

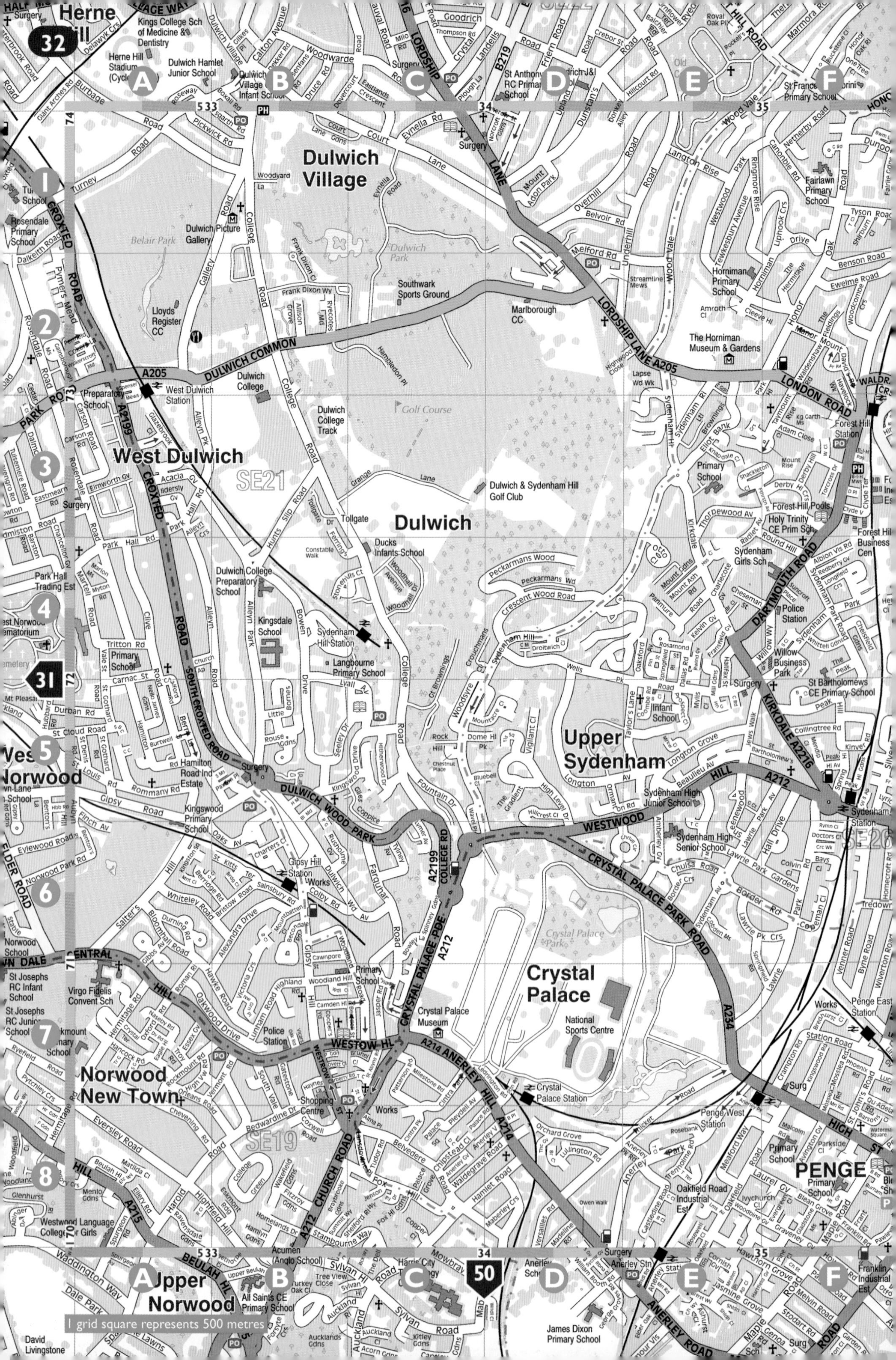
32
Herne Hill
Kings College Sch of Medicine & Dentistry
Herne Hill Stadium (Cycle)
Dulwich Hamlet Junior School
Dulwich Village Infant School
A
B
C
D
E
F
Dulwich Village
Dulwich Picture Gallery
Belair Park
Dulwich Park
Southwark Sports Ground
Lloyds Register CC
DULWICH COMMON
A205
West Dulwich Station
Dulwich College
Marlborough CC
LORDSHIP LANE A205
LONDON ROAD
The Horniman Museum & Gardens
Horniman Primary School
Fairlawn Primary School
Forest Hill Station
Golf Course
Dulwich College Track
West Dulwich
SE21
CROXTED ROAD
A2199
Dulwich & Sydenham Hill Golf Club
Dulwich
Tollgate
Ducks Infants School
Dulwich College Preparatory School
Kingsdale School
Sydenham Hill Station
Langbourne Primary School
Peckarmans Wood
Crescent Wood Road
Sydenham Hill
Sydenham Girls Sch
DARTMOUTH ROAD
Forest Hill Pools
Holy Trinity CE Prim Sch
Police Station
Willow Business Park
St Bartholomews CE Primary School
KIRKDALE A2216
Upper Sydenham
Sydenham High Junior School
Sydenham High Senior School
Sydenham Station
SE26
Park Hall Trading Est
West Norwood Crematorium
31
West Norwood
Hamilton Road Ind Estate
SOUTH CROXTED ROAD
DULWICH WOOD PARK
Kingswood Primary School
Gipsy Hill Station
COLLEGE RD
A212
WESTWOOD HILL
CRYSTAL PALACE PARK ROAD
Crystal Palace Park
Crystal Palace
National Sports Centre
A234
Virgo Fidelis Convent Sch
St Josephs RC Infant School
St Josephs RC Junior School
Norwood New Town
Police Station
WESTOW HL
A214 ANERLEY HILL
Crystal Palace Museum
CRYSTAL PALACE PDE
Crystal Palace Station
Penge West Station
Penge East Station
SE19
Shopping Centre
CHURCH ROAD
A215
BEULAH HILL
Westwood Language College for Girls
Oakfield Road Industrial Est
PENGE
HIGH ST
Anerley Stn
50
Upper Norwood
All Saints CE Primary School
James Dixon Primary School
ANERLEY ROAD
Franklin Industrial Est
1 grid square represents 500 metres
David Livingstone

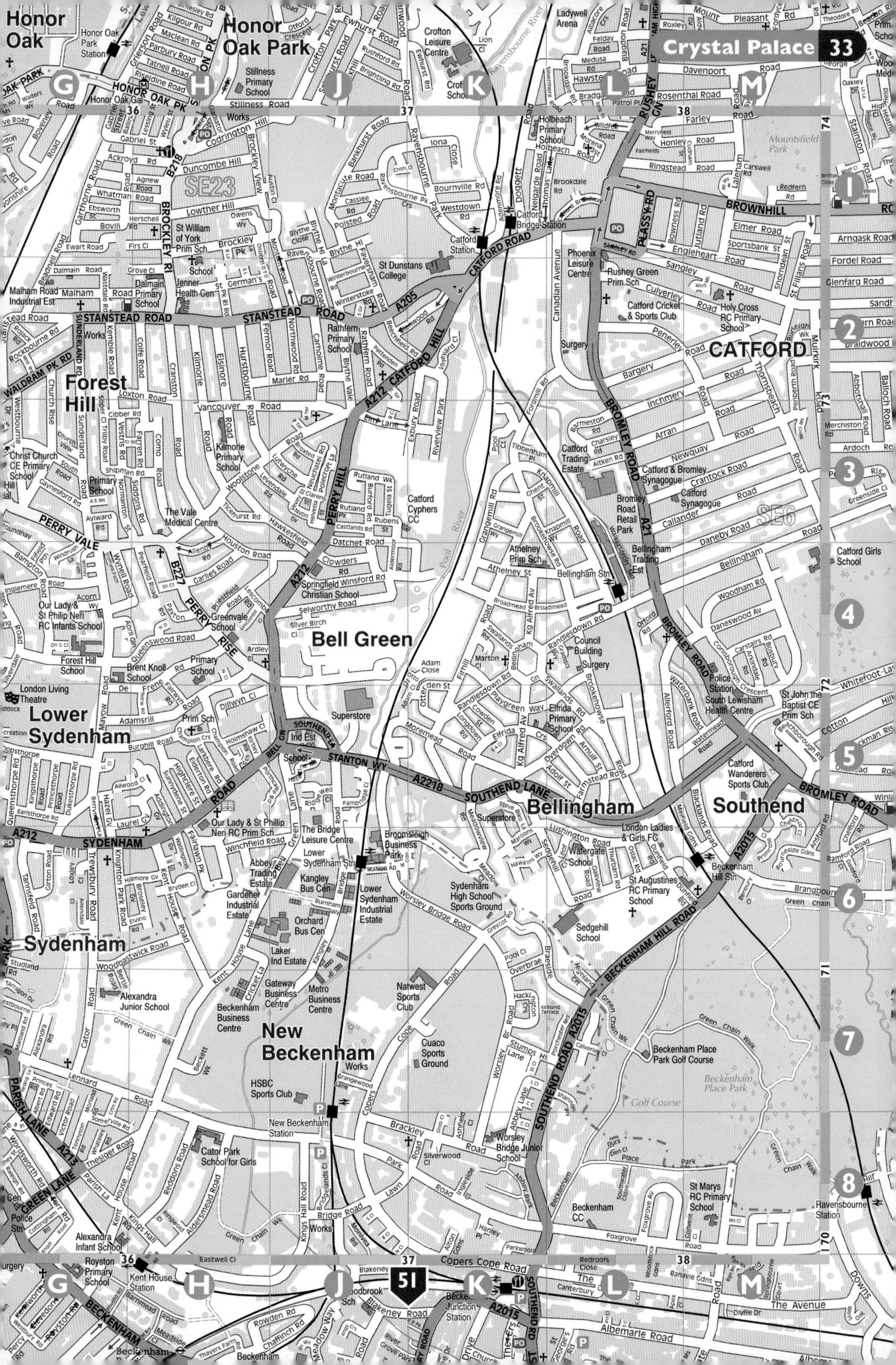

Crystal Palace 33
Honor Oak
Honor Oak Park Station
Honor Oak Park
Stillness Primary School
Stillness Road
Crofton Leisure Centre
Ladywell Arena
Mount Pleasant Rd
Davenport Road
Rosenthal Road
Holbeach Primary School
Mountsfield Park
Brownhill Rd
Ringstead Road
SE23
Duncombe Hill
Codrington Hill
Brockley View
Lowther Hill
Bournville Rd
Westdown Rd
Catford Bridge Station
Catford Station
Catford Road
Rushey Green
Plassy Rd
Phoenix Leisure Centre
Rushey Green Prim Sch
St Dunstans College
St William of York Prim Sch
Jenner Health Cen
Dalmain Road Primary School
Malham Road Industrial Est
Stanstead Road
A205
Rathfern Primary School
Catford Hill
Catford Cricket & Sports Club
Holy Cross RC Primary School
CATFORD
Forest Hill
Perry Hill
Perry Vale
Perry Rise
Kilmorie Primary School
Christ Church CE Primary School
The Vale Medical Centre
Catford Cyphers CC
Catford Trading Estate
Bromley Road Retail Park
Catford & Bromley Synagogue
Catford Synagogue
SE6
Catford Girls School
Bellingham Trading Est
Bellingham Stn
Athelney Prim Sch
Springfield Christian School
Our Lady & St Philip Neri RC Infants School
Greenvale School
Bell Green
Forest Hill School
Brent Knoll School
London Living Theatre
Lower Sydenham
Council Building
Surgery
Police Station
South Lewisham Health Centre
St John the Baptist CE Prim Sch
Elfrida Primary School
Superstore
Stanton Wy
A2218
Southend Lane
Bellingham
Southend
Catford Wanderers Sports Club
Bromley Road
Sydenham
A212
Our Lady & St Phillip Neri RC Prim Sch
The Bridge Leisure Centre
Lower Sydenham Stn
Broomsleigh Business Park
Lower Sydenham Industrial Estate
Abbey Trading Estate
Kangley Bus Cen
Gardener Industrial Estate
Orchard Bus Cen
Laker Ind Estate
Sydenham High School Sports Ground
Watergate School
London Ladies & Girls FC
St Augustines RC Primary School
Beckenham Hill Stn
Beckenham Hill Road
Sedgehill School
A2015
Alexandra Junior School
Gateway Business Centre
Metro Business Centre
Beckenham Business Centre
Natwest Sports Club
New Beckenham
Cuaco Sports Ground
Southend Road A2015
Beckenham Place Park Golf Course
Beckenham Place Park
Golf Course
Green Chain Walk
HSBC Sports Club
New Beckenham Station
Cator Park School for Girls
Worsley Bridge Junior School
St Marys RC Primary School
Ravensbourne Station
Beckenham CC
Parish Lane
A213
Green Lane
Police Stn
Alexandra Infant School
Royston Primary School
Kent House Station
Beckenham Junction Station
Copers Cope Road
The Avenue
Albemarle Road
Beckenham
51

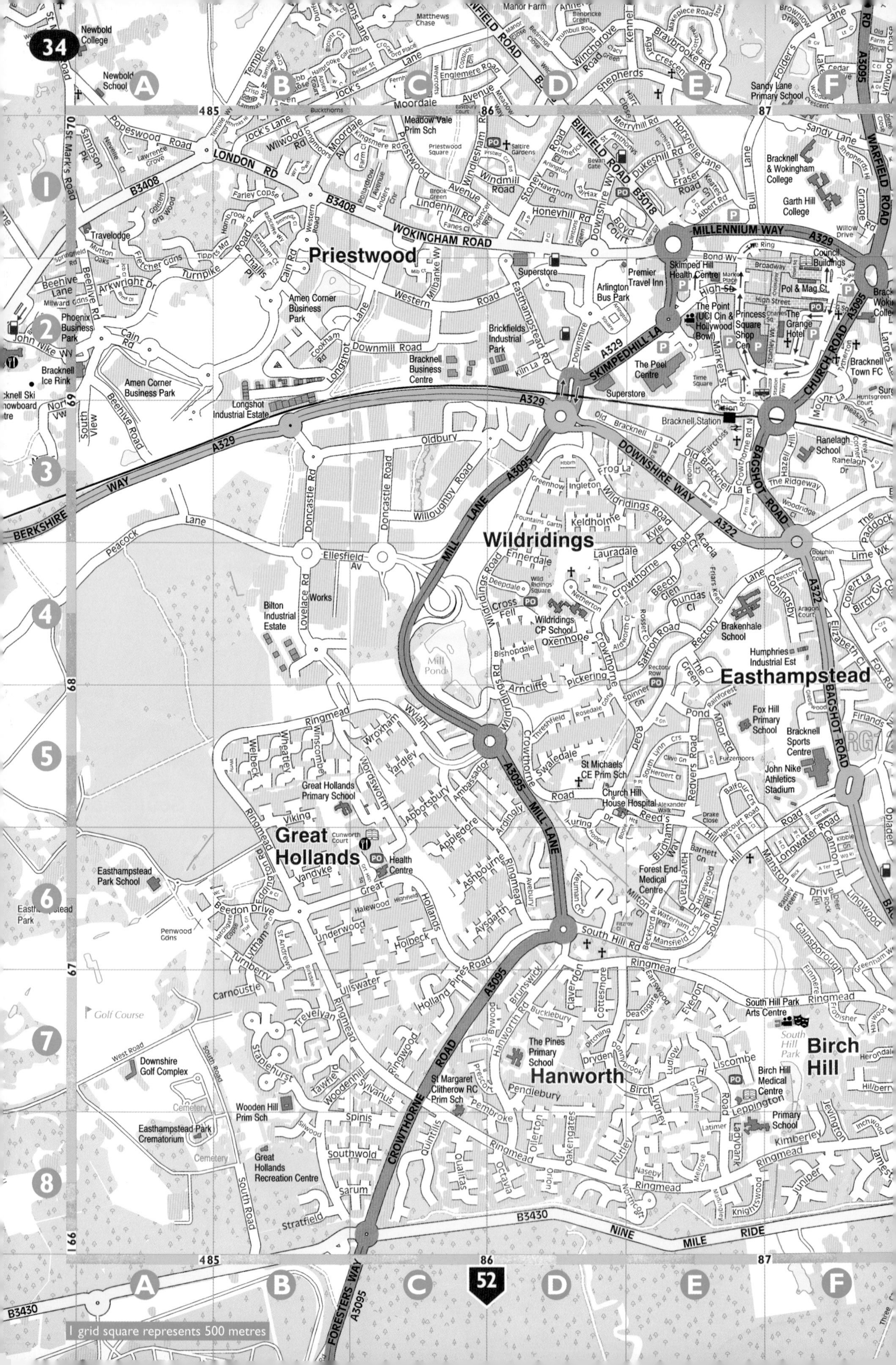
A
B
C
D
E
F
1
2
3
4
5
6
7
8
485
86
87
70
69
68
67
66
Newbold College
Newbold School
Matthews Chase
Manor Farm
BINFIELD ROAD
Winchgrove Road
Kennel
Braybrooke Rd
Agar Crescent
Shepherds
Brownlow Drive
Folder's Lane
Sandy Lane Primary School
Cedar
A3095
WARFIELD ROAD
Temple Wy
Jock's Lane
Englemere Road
Moordale
Buckthorns
Meadow Vale Prim Sch
Priestwood Square
Saltire Gardens
Merryhill Rd
Dukeshill Rd
Horsneile Lane
Sandy Lane
Bracknell & Wokingham College
Garth Hill College
Grange Rd
Sampson Pk
Popeswood Road
Lawrence Grove
LONDON RD
B3408
Wilwood Rd
Kingsmere Rd
Priestwood Avenue
Windlesham Rd
Windmill Road
Stoney Road
BINFIELD ROAD
B3018
Fraser Road
Albert Rd
Bull Lane
Farley Copse
Lindenhill Rd
Honeyhill Rd
Hawthorn Cl
Downshire Wy
Boyd Court
MILLENNIUM WAY
A329
St Mark's Road
Travelodge
WOKINGHAM ROAD
Priestwood
Superstore
Skimped Hill Health Centre
Council Buildings
Bond Wy
Broadway
High St
Pol & Mag Ct
Springfield Rd
Mutton Oaks
Fletcher Gdns
Turnpike
Challis Pl
Cain Rd
Western Road
Milbanke Wy
Easthampstead Rd
Premier Travel Inn
Arlington Bus Park
High Street
The Point (UCI Cin & Hollywood Bowl)
Princess Square Shop Cen
The Grange Hotel
Beehive Lane
Arkwright Dr
Amen Corner Business Park
Phoenix Business Park
John Nike Wy
Cain Rd
Downmill Road
Longshot Lane
Cookham Rd
Bracknell Business Centre
Brickfields Industrial Park
Kiln La
SKIMPEDHILL LA
The Peel Centre
Market St
CHURCH ROAD
Bracknell Town FC
Bracknell Ice Rink
Amen Corner Business Park
Beehive Road
Longshot Industrial Estate
Superstore
Time Square
Bracknell Station
Mount La
South View
A329
Oldbury
Old Bracknell La W
DOWNSHIRE WAY
Ranelagh School
Ranelagh Dr
BERKSHIRE WAY
Doncastle Rd
Doncastle Road
Willoughby Road
Frog La
Ingleton
Wildridings Road
Old Bracknell La E
The Ridgeway
BAGSHOT ROAD
Woodridge Cl
Peacock Lane
Fountains Garth
Keldholme
A322
Wildridings
Kyle Cl
Acacia
Ellesfield Av
MILL LANE
A3095
Ennerdale
Lauradale
Lime Wk
Dolphin Court
Deepdale
Wild Ridings Square
Crowthorne
Beech Glen
Dundas Cl
Coningsby
Covert La
Birch Gv
Lovelace Rd
Works
Bilton Industrial Estate
Cross Fell
Wildridings CP School
Netherton
Oxenhope
Rectory Lane
Brakenhale School
Aragon Court
Elizabeth Cl
Fox Hill
Mill Pond
Bishopdale
Saffron Road
Humphries Industrial Est
Easthampstead
Arncliffe
Pickering
Rectory Row
Spinner Gn
The Green
Rainforest Wk
Fox Hill Primary School
Bracknell Sports Centre
Firlands
Ringmead
Wylam
Wroxham
Threshfield
Rosedale Gdns
Pond Moor Rd
Furzemoors
Welbeck
Wheatley
Winscombe
Yardley
Wordsworth
Swaledale
South Lynn Crs
Clive Gn
Herbert Cl
Redvers Road
John Nike Athletics Stadium
St Michaels CE Prim Sch
Church Hill House Hospital
Great Hollands Primary School
Abbotsbury
Ambassador
Road
Reed's Hill
Balfour Crs
Drake Close
Viking
Appledore
Ardingly
Luring Dr
Hopper
Alexander Walk
Harcourt Road
Longwater Road
Cannon Hl
Great Hollands
Cunworth Court
Health Centre
Ringmead
Ashbourne
Bugham Way
Barnett Gn
Manston Dr
Easthampstead Park School
Vandyke
Great Hollands
Forest End Medical Centre
Haversham Drive
Horewood Rd
Lingwood
Beedon Drive
Halewood
Highfield
Holbeck
Underwood
Aysgarth
Neuman Crs
Milton Cl
Waterham Rd
Mansfield Crs
South Hill Rd
Gainsborough
Penwood Gdns
Lytham
St Andrews
Turnberry
Holland Pines Road
Claverdon
Cottesmore
Easthampstead Park
Carnoustie
Ullswater
Ringmead
Evedon
Frobisher
Greenham Wd
South Hill Park Arts Centre
Golf Course
West Road
Downshire Golf Complex
Trevelyan
Staplehurst
Tawfield
Woodenhill
Sylvanus
Ringwood
CROWTHORNE ROAD
Bywood
Prescott
Hanworth Rd
Brunswick
Bucklebury
Deansgate
Ditchling
Dryden
Donnybrook
Ludlow
Liscombe
South Hill Park
Birch Hill
Herondale
The Pines Primary School
Hanworth
Pendlebury
Birch Hill Medical Centre
Leppington
Cemetery
Easthampstead Park Crematorium
Wooden Hill Prim Sch
Spinis
Silwood
St Margaret Clitherow RC Prim Sch
Pembroke
Quintilis
Ollerton
Oakengates
Nutley
Lydney
Latimer
Ladybank
Primary School
Kimberley
Jevington
Inchwood
Southwold
Great Hollands Recreation Centre
Sarum
Qualitas
Octavia
Orion
Ringmead
Naseby
Melrose
Northcott
Knightswood
Juniper
Stratfield
South Road
Cemetery
B3430
NINE MILE RIDE
FORESTERS WAY
A3095
B3430
Three
1 grid square represents 500 metres

52

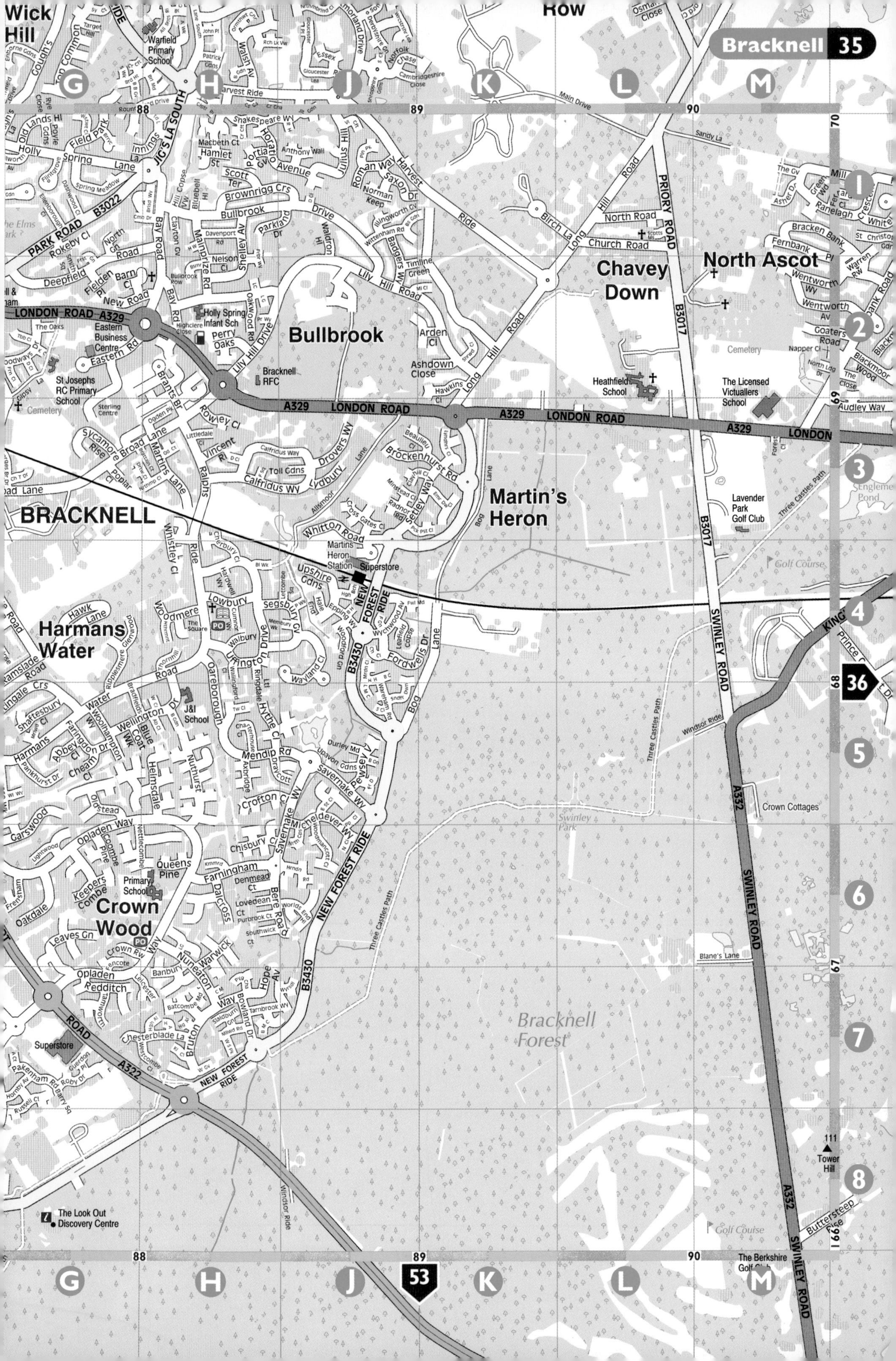
Wick Hill
Bullbrook
BRACKNELL
Harmans Water
Crown Wood
Martin's Heron
Chavey Down
North Ascot
Bracknell Forest
LONDON ROAD A329
A329 LONDON ROAD
PARK ROAD B3022
JIG'S LA SOUTH
PRIORY ROAD B3017
SWINLEY ROAD
A332
NEW FOREST RIDE
B3430
A322
Harvest Ride
Long Hill Road
Lily Hill Road
Lily Hill Drive
Bullbrook Drive
Church Road
North Road
Birch La
Main Drive
Sandy La
Bog Lane
Three Castles Path
Windsor Ride
Blane's Lane
Crown Cottages
Swinley Park
Lavender Park Golf Club
Golf Course
The Berkshire Golf Club
Heathfield School
The Licensed Victuallers School
Cemetery
Bracknell RFC
Holly Spring Infant Sch
Warfield Primary School
St Josephs RC Primary School
Eastern Business Centre
Martins Heron Station
Superstore
J&I School
Primary School
The Look Out Discovery Centre
Tower Hill
111
Broad Lane
Martins Lane
Ralphs Ride
Whitton Road
Upshire Gdns
Lowbury
Uffington Drive
Mendip Rd
Savernake Wy
Opladen Way
Leaves Gn
Crown Rw
Nuneaton
Warwick
Farningham
Garswood
Oakdale
Frensham
Keepers Combe
Queens Pine
Coombe Pine
Helmsdale
Nuthurst
Woodmere
Hawk Lane
Ramslade Road
Shaftesbury
Harmans
Abbey Cl
Cheam Cl
Wellington Dr
Blue Coat Wk
Oareborough
Ringdale
Hythe Cl
Crofton Cl
Chisbury
Michelde ver Wy
Pewsey V
Dalcross
Bere Road
Hope Av
Bowland Dr
Bruton
Chesterblade La
Pakenham Rd
Roby Dr
Redditch
Opladen
Banbury
Leicester
Spring Lane
Holly
Field Park
Old Lands Hl
Innings La
Bay Road
Rokeby Cl
Deepfield
Fielden Pl
Barn Cl
New Road
North Gn Road
Clayton Gv
Mainprize Rd
Shelley Av
Bullbrook
Brownrigg Crs
Scott Ter
Hamlet St
Macbeth Ct
Portia Gv
Horatio Avenue
Anthony Wall
Shakespeare Wy
Roman Way
Saxon Dr
Norman Keep
Julius Hill
Parkland Dr
Waldron Hl
Timline Green
Arden Cl
Ashdown Close
Rowley Cl
Vincent Rl
Calfridus Wy
Toll Gdns
Lydbury
Drovers Wy
Brockenhurst Rd
Setley Way
Segsbury Gv
Wayland Cl
Fordwells Dr
Wychwood Av
Sycamore Rise
Poplar
Whistley Cl
Cherbury Cl
Perry Oaks
Eastern Rd
Essex
Gloucester
Norfolk Chase
Oakwood Rd
Mill Ride
Ranelagh Crescent
Bracken Bank
Fernbank
Wentworth Wy
Wentworth Av
Goaters Road
Blackmoor Wood
Audley Way
Warren
Buttersteep Rise
Prince
G
H
J
K
L
M
88
89
90
70
69
68
67
1
2
3
4
5
6
7
8
36
53

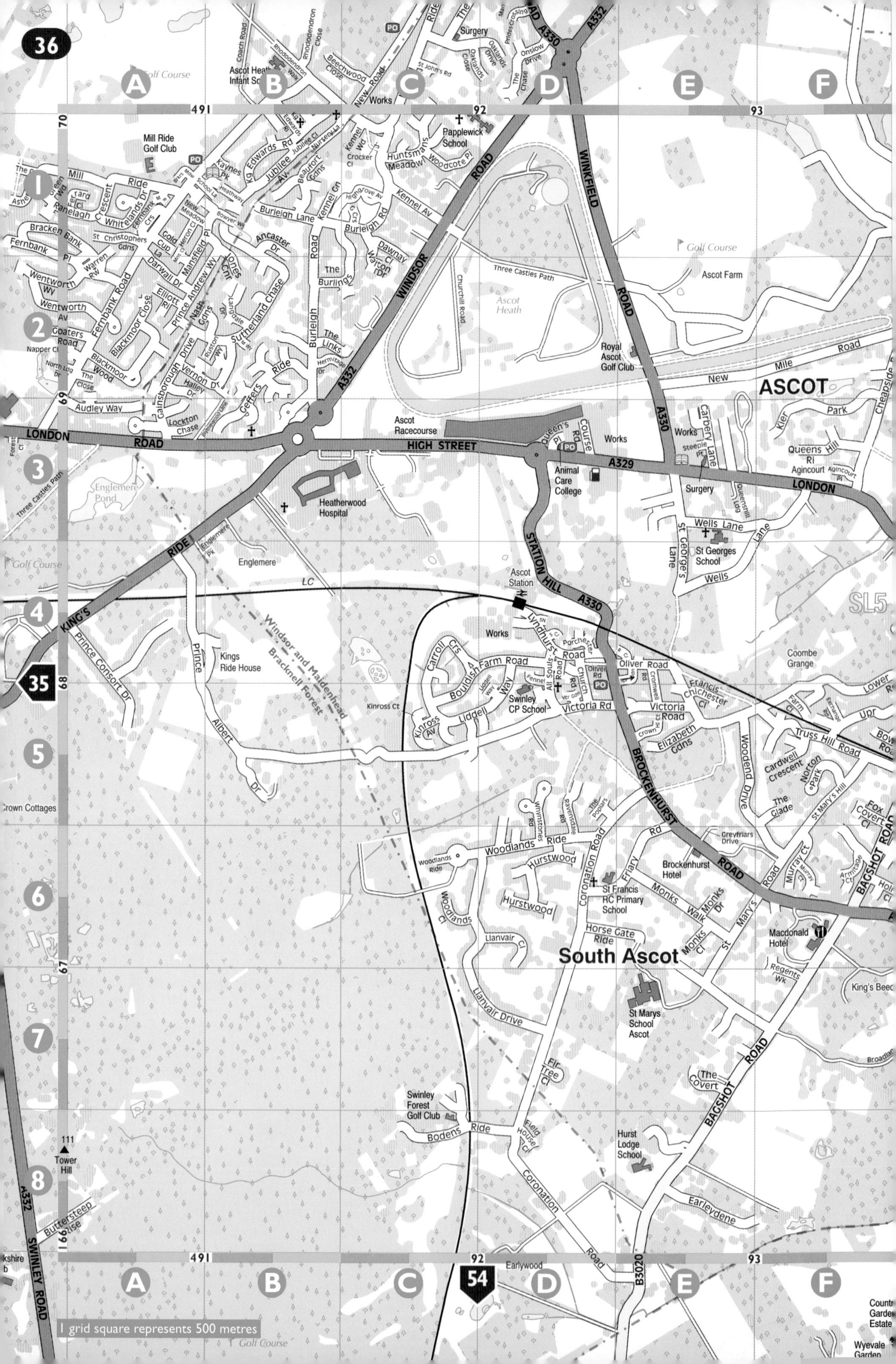

ASCOT
South Ascot
SL5
WINDSOR ROAD
WINKFIELD ROAD
LONDON ROAD
HIGH STREET
KING'S RIDE
STATION HILL
BROCKENHURST ROAD
BAGSHOT ROAD
SWINLEY ROAD
Ascot Racecourse
Ascot Heath
Ascot Station
Royal Ascot Golf Club
Mill Ride Golf Club
Swinley Forest Golf Club
Heatherwood Hospital
Papplewick School
Ascot Heath Infant School
Animal Care College
St Georges School
Swinley CP School
St Francis RC Primary School
St Marys School Ascot
Hurst Lodge School
Macdonald Hotel
Brockenhurst Hotel
Kings Ride House
Ascot Farm
Coombe Grange
Englemere
Englemere Pond
Windsor and Maidenhead
Bracknell Forest
Crown Cottages
Tower Hill
Three Castles Path
New Mile Road
Lyndhurst Road
Bouldish Farm Road
Victoria Road
Coronation Road
Woodlands Ride
Llanvair Drive
Bodens Ride
Earlydene
Earlywood
Prince Consort Dr
Prince Albert Dr
Buttersteep Rise
Audley Way
Burleigh Road
Kennel Av
Fernbank Road
Sutherland Chase
Truss Hill Road
Woodend Drive
Wells Lane
1 grid square represents 500 metres

35
54

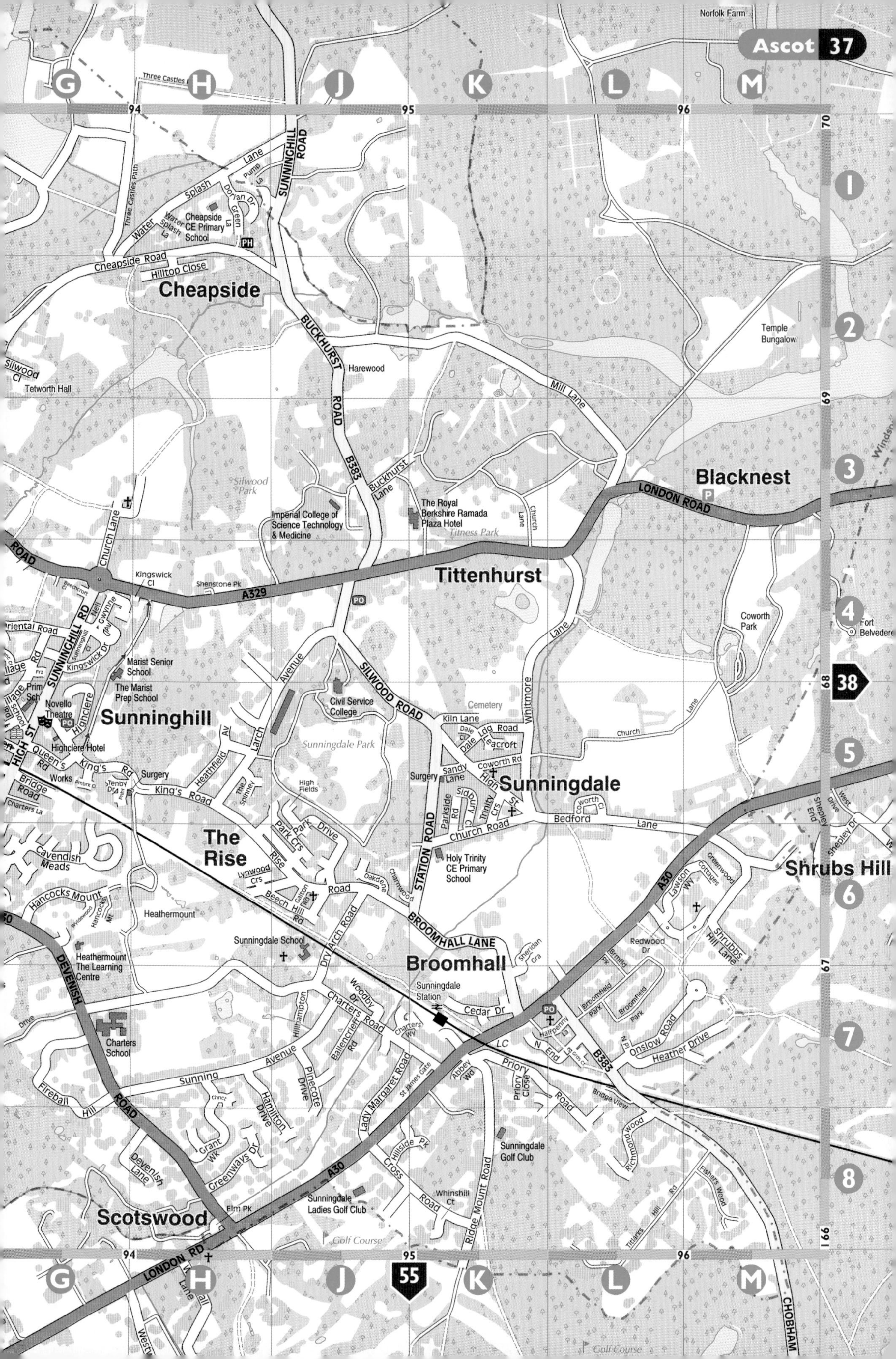

G H J K L M

Norfolk Farm

I

Three Castles Path

Cheapside CE Primary School

PH

Splash Lane
Dorian Dr
Green

SUNNINGHILL ROAD

Water Splash La
Water Splash La

Cheapside Road

Hilltop Close

Cheapside

Temple Bungalow

2

Silwood Cl
Tetworth Hall

Harewood

Mill Lane

BUCKHURST ROAD

B383

Silwood Park

Buckhurst Lane

The Royal Berkshire Ramada Plaza Hotel

LONDON ROAD

P

Blacknest

3

Church Lane

Imperial College of Science Technology & Medicine

Titness Park

Windso

Kingswick Cl

Shenstone Pk

A329

PO

Tittenhurst

Coworth Park

Fort Belvedere

4

ROAD

Church Lane

Oriental Road

SUNNINGHILL RD
Nell Gwynne
Kingswick Dr

Marist Senior School

The Marist Prep School

Highclere
Novello Theatre PO

Sunninghill

AVENUE

Civil Service College

SILWOOD ROAD

Cemetery

Whitmore

Kiln Lane

Church

38

5

Village
Village
Prim Sch

Highclere Hotel

Larch

Sunningdale Park

Dale Ldg
Dale La
Seacroft Road

Sandy Lane

Coworth Rd

High St

Sunningdale

HIGH ST

Queen's Rd
King's Rd
Surgery
Works
Tenby Rd
Pmbk Cl

King's Road

The Spinney
Heathfield Av

High Fields

Surgery

Parkside Rd
Sidn Rd
Trinity Crs

Church Road

coworth
Bedford
Lane

Shrubs Hill Lane

Shrubs Hill

6

Bridge Road
Charters La

The Rise

Park Crs
Park Drive
Rise
Lynwood Crs

Garden Rd
Beech Hill Rd

Oakdene
Charnwood

STATION ROAD

Holy Trinity CE Primary School

A30
Lawson Ww
Greenwood Cottages

Redwood Dr

Cavendish Meads

Hancocks Mount

Heathermount

Sunningdale School

Dry Arch Road

BROOMHALL LANE

Broomhall

Sheridan Cres

Broomfield Park

Broomhall Park

Onslow Road

7

DEVENISH

Heathermount The Learning Centre

Hillhampton
Charters Road
Ballencrieff Rd
Woodby Dr

Sunningdale Station

Charters Ww

LC

Cedar Dr

N End
Halfpenny La
Abbey Ww

PO

B383

Heather Drive

Richmond Wood
Bridge View

Drive

Charters School

Sunning Avenue
Pinecote Drive
Hamilton Drive

Christ

St James Gate

Priory Close
Priory Road

Sunningdale Golf Club

8

Fireball Hill
ROAD

Grant Ww
Greenways Dr
Devenish Lane

A30

Elm Pk

Sunningdale Ladies Golf Club

Cross Road

Hillside Pk

Whinshill Ct

Ridge Mount Road

Intakes Hill Rd

Fishers Wood

Scotswood

LONDON RD

Golf Course

Golf Course

CHOBHAM

G H J **55** K L M

94 95 96

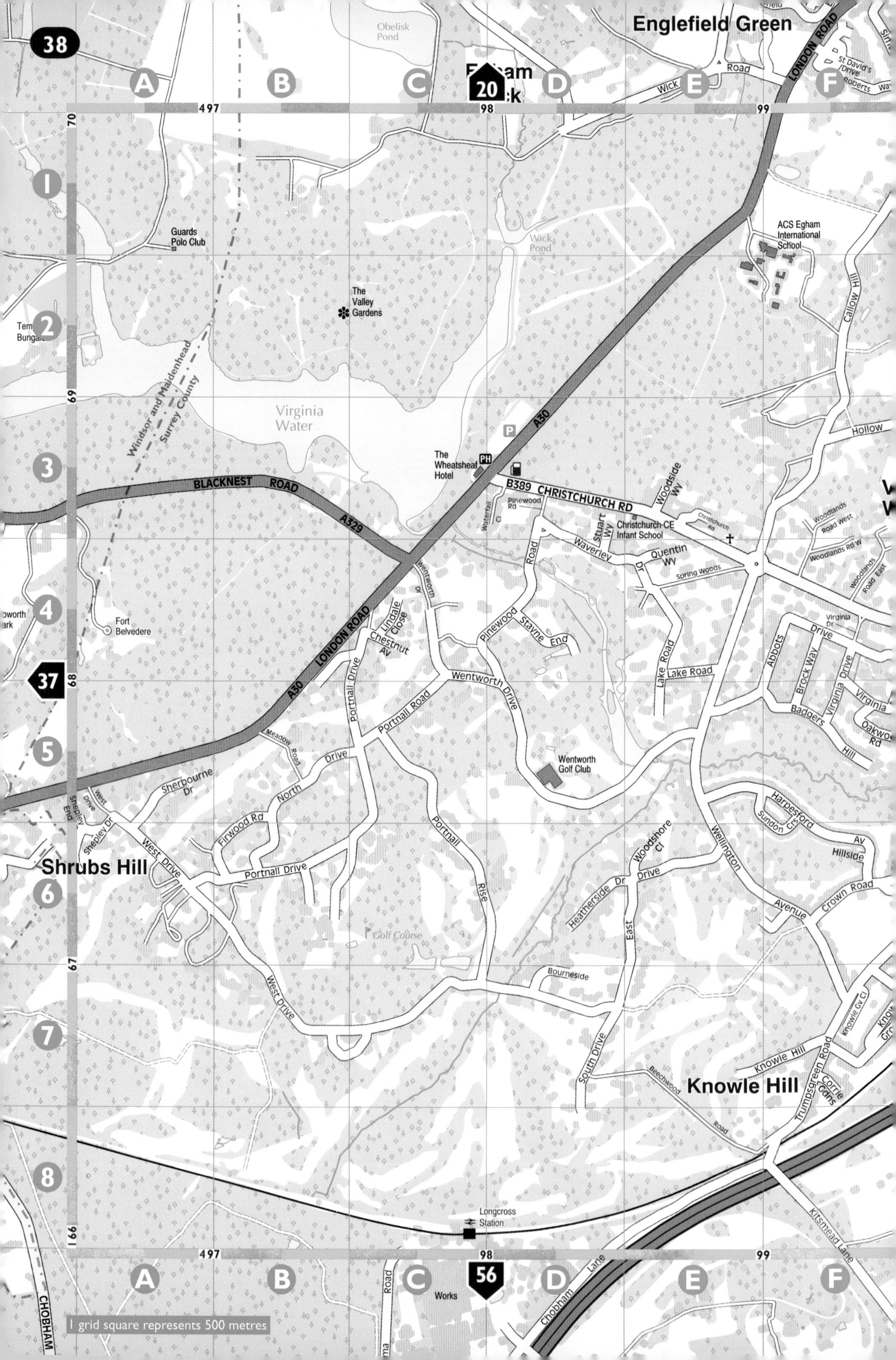

Englefield Green

A   B   C   20   D   E   F
497   98   99

70

1

Obelisk Pond

St David's /Drive
Roberts Way

Egham Park

Wick Road

LONDON ROAD

2

Tem Bungal

Guards Polo Club

Wick Pond

ACS Egham International School

Callow Hill

Hollow

69

3

Virginia Water

The Valley Gardens

A30

P

The Wheatsheaf Hotel

PH

B389 CHRISTCHURCH RD

Pinewood Rd

Woodside Wy

Christchurch Rd

Woodlands Road West

Woodlands Rd W

Windsor and Maidenhead
Surrey County

BLACKNEST   ROAD

A329

Waterfall

Road

Christchurch CE Infant School

Stuart Wy

Waverley

Quentin Wy

Spring Woods

Woodlands Road East

4

worth Park

Fort Belvedere

LONDON ROAD

A30

Wentworth

Undale Close

Chestnut Av

Portnall Drive

Pinewood

Stayne End

Pinewood Road

Lake Road

Lake Road

Abbots Drive

Virginia Dr

Brock Way

Virginia Drive

Virginia Drive

68

37

Wentworth Drive

Badgers Hill

Oakwo Rd

5

Meadow Road

North Drive

Portnall Road

Wentworth Golf Club

Harpesford Av

Sundon

Hillside

Sherbourne Dr

West Drive

Snepley End

Firwood Rd

Portnall Rise

Woodshore Cl

Wellington Avenue

Crown Road

Shrubs Hill

6

Portnall Drive

Heatherside Dr

East Drive

Knowle Gv Cl

67

Golf Course

Bourneside

7

West Drive

South Drive

Beechwood

Knowle Hill

Trumpsgreen Road

Corrie Gdns

Knowle Hill

Knowle

66

8

Longcross Station

Kitsmead Lane

CHOBHAM

A   B   C   56   D   E   F
497   98   99

Road

Works

Chobham Lane

1 grid square represents 500 metres

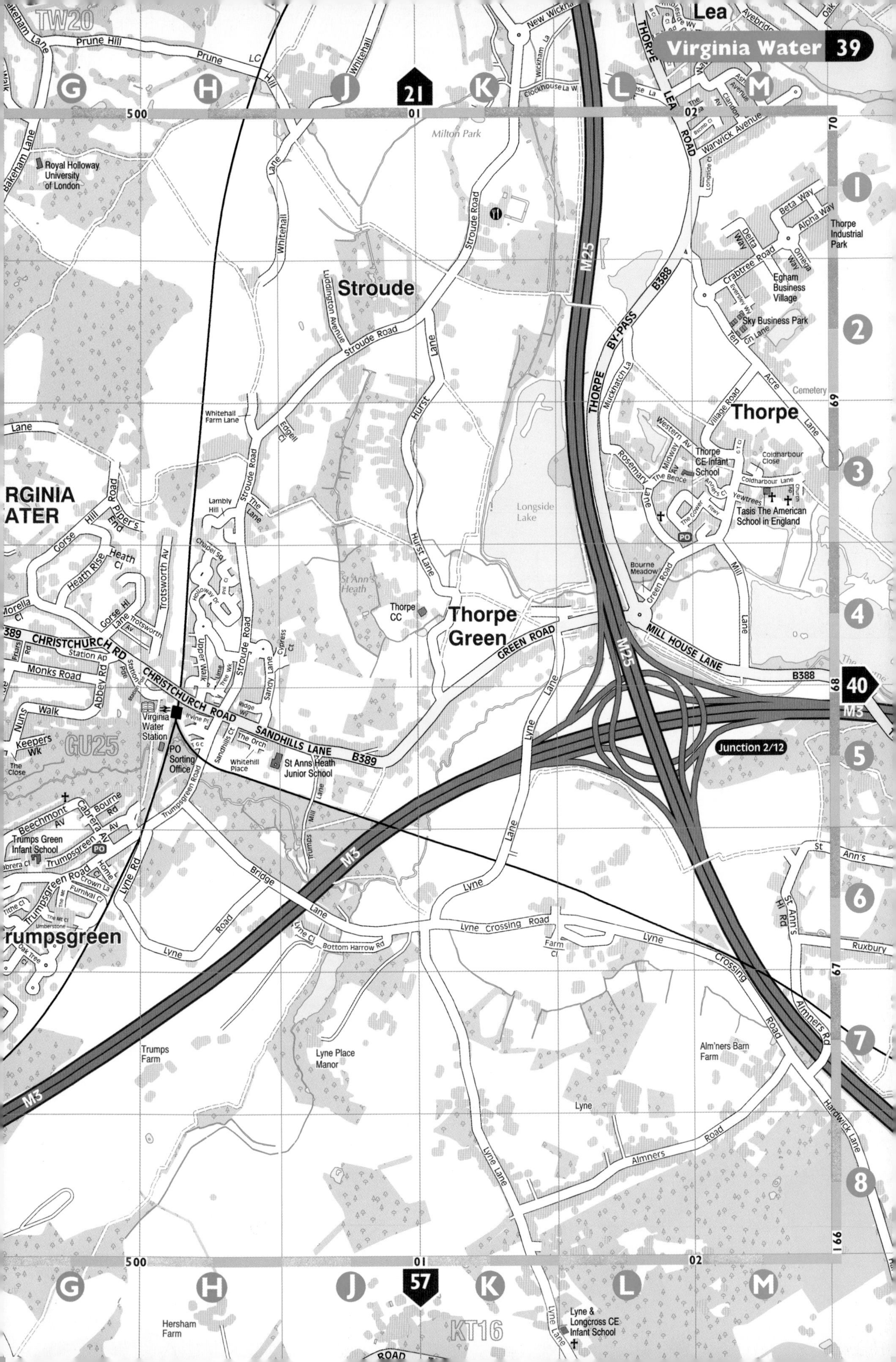

TW20
Pashham Lane
Prune Hill
Prune Hill LC
New Wickh
New Wickham La
Lea
Thorpe

G   H   J   21   K   L   M
500   01   02   70

Milton Park

Royal Holloway University of London

Bakeham Lane

Whitehall
Whitehall Lane

Stroude

Stroude Road
Luddington Avenue
Hurst Lane
Edgell
Stroude Road

Whitehall Farm Lane

Thorpe Industrial Park

Beta Way
Alpha Way
Delta Way
Crabtree Road
Omega Way

Egham Business Village

Sky Business Park

Cemetery

Thorpe

Mucklatch La
Western Av
Rosemary Lane
The Bence
Village Road
Acre Lane

Thorpe CE Infant School

Coldharbour Close
Coldharbour Lane

The Covert
PO

Yewtrees

Tasis The American School in England

RGINIA ATER

Gorse Hill
Piper's End
Heath Rise
Heath Cl
Morella
Gorse Hill
Trotsworth Av
Lane
Lambly Hill
Chapel Sq
The Lane
St Ann's Heath

Thorpe CC

Thorpe Green

Green Road

Longside Lake

Bourne Meadow
Green Road
Mill Lane

CHRISTCHURCH RD
Station Ap
CHRISTCHURCH ROAD
Monks Road
Abbey Rd
Nuns Walk
Keepers Wk
The Close
GU25

Virginia Water Station
Irvine Pl
PO Sorting Office

Upper Walk
Tree Wk
Sancy Lane
Cypress Ct
Stroude Road
Ridge Wf
The Orch
Sandhills Ct
Whitehill Place

SANDHILLS LANE
B389

St Anns Heath Junior School

Lyne Lane

MILL HOUSE LANE
B388

40
M3

Junction 2/12

Beechmont Av
Cabrera Av
Bourne Rd
Trumps Green Infant School
Cabrera Cl
Trumpsgreen Road
PO
Crown La
Home Pk
Furnival Cl
The Mt Cl
Trithe Cl
Oak Tree

rumpsgreen

Lyne Road
Bridge Lane
Lyne Cl
Bottom Harrow Rd

Trumpsgreen Road
Mill Lane
Trumps La
M3

Lyne Crossing Road
Farm Cl
Lyne Crossing Road
Lyne Crossing Road

St Ann's Hl Rd
St Ann's
Ruxbury
Almners Rd

Trumps Farm

Lyne Place Manor

Lyne Lane

Alm'ners Barn Farm

Lyne
Almners Road
Almners Road

Hardwick Lane

M3

500   01   02

G   H   J   57   K   L   M

Hersham Farm

KT16

Lyne & Longcross CE Infant School

Lyne Lane

ROAD

I 2 3 4 5 6 7 8
70 69 68 67 66

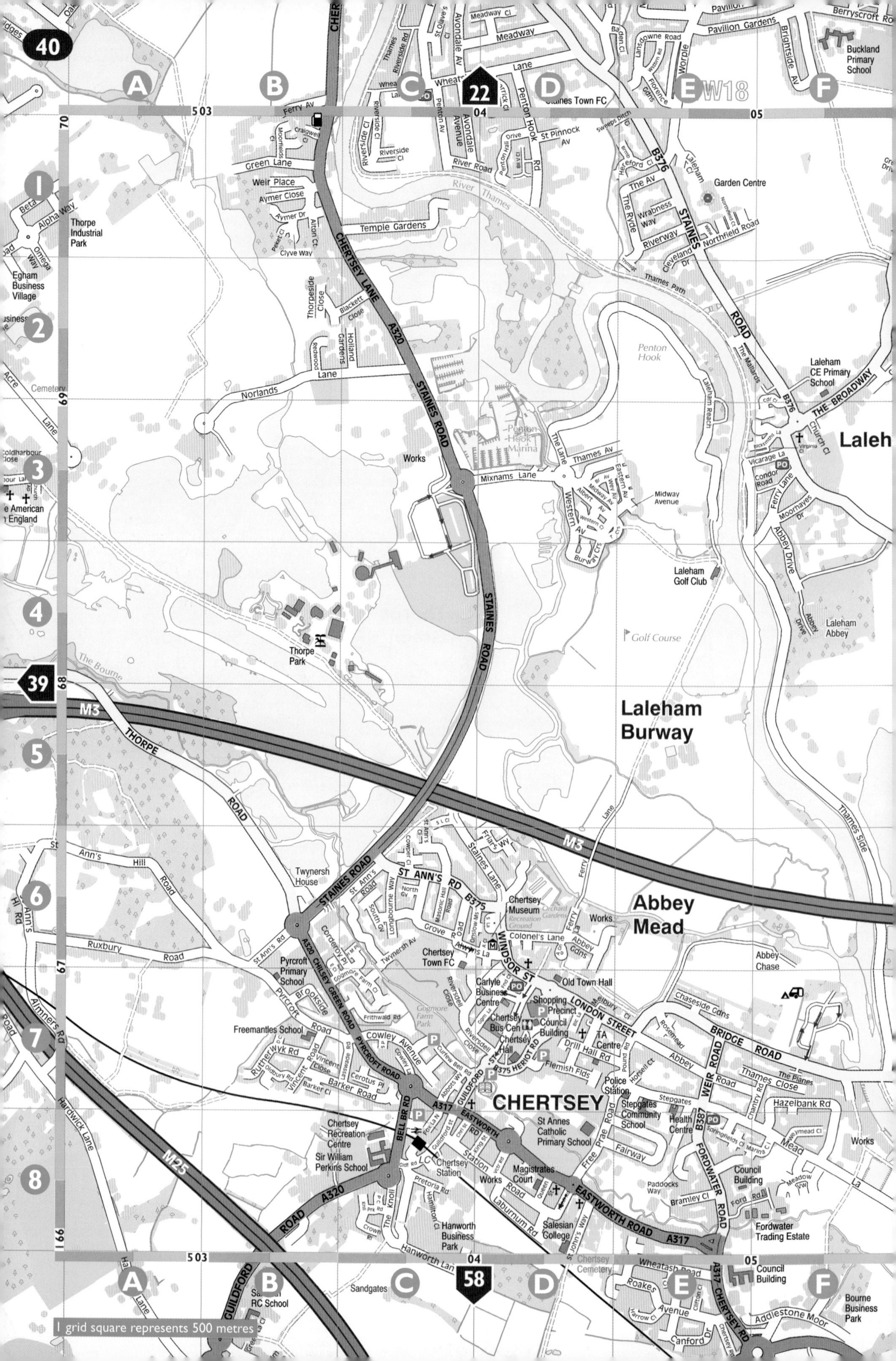

40
22
39
58
TW18
Buckland Primary School
Staines Town FC
Thorpe Industrial Park
Egham Business Village
Garden Centre
River Thames
Thames Path
Penton Hook
Penton Hook Marina
Laleham CE Primary School
Laleham
Works
Midway Avenue
Laleham Golf Club
Laleham Abbey
Golf Course
Thorpe Park
The Bourne
M3
Laleham Burway
Abbey Mead
Twynersh House
Chertsey Museum
Chertsey Town FC
Pyrcroft Primary School
Carlyle Business Centre
Old Town Hall
Shopping Precinct
Council Building
Chertsey Bus Cen
Chertsey Hall
TA Centre
Freemantles School
Gogmore Farm Park
CHERTSEY
Police Station
Stepgates Community School
Health Centre
St Annes Catholic Primary School
Chertsey Recreation Centre
Sir William Perkins School
Chertsey Station
Magistrates Court
Salesian College
Hanworth Business Park
Fordwater Trading Estate
Chertsey Cemetery
Sandgates
Bourne Business Park
M25
CHERTSEY LANE
STAINES ROAD
A320
THORPE ROAD
ST ANN'S RD
WINDSOR ST
LONDON STREET
BRIDGE ROAD
GUILDFORD ST
EASTWORTH ROAD
A317
PYRCROFT ROAD
CHILSEY GREEN ROAD
BELL BR RD
FORDWATER ROAD
WEIR ROAD
THE BROADWAY
B376
1 grid square represents 500 metres

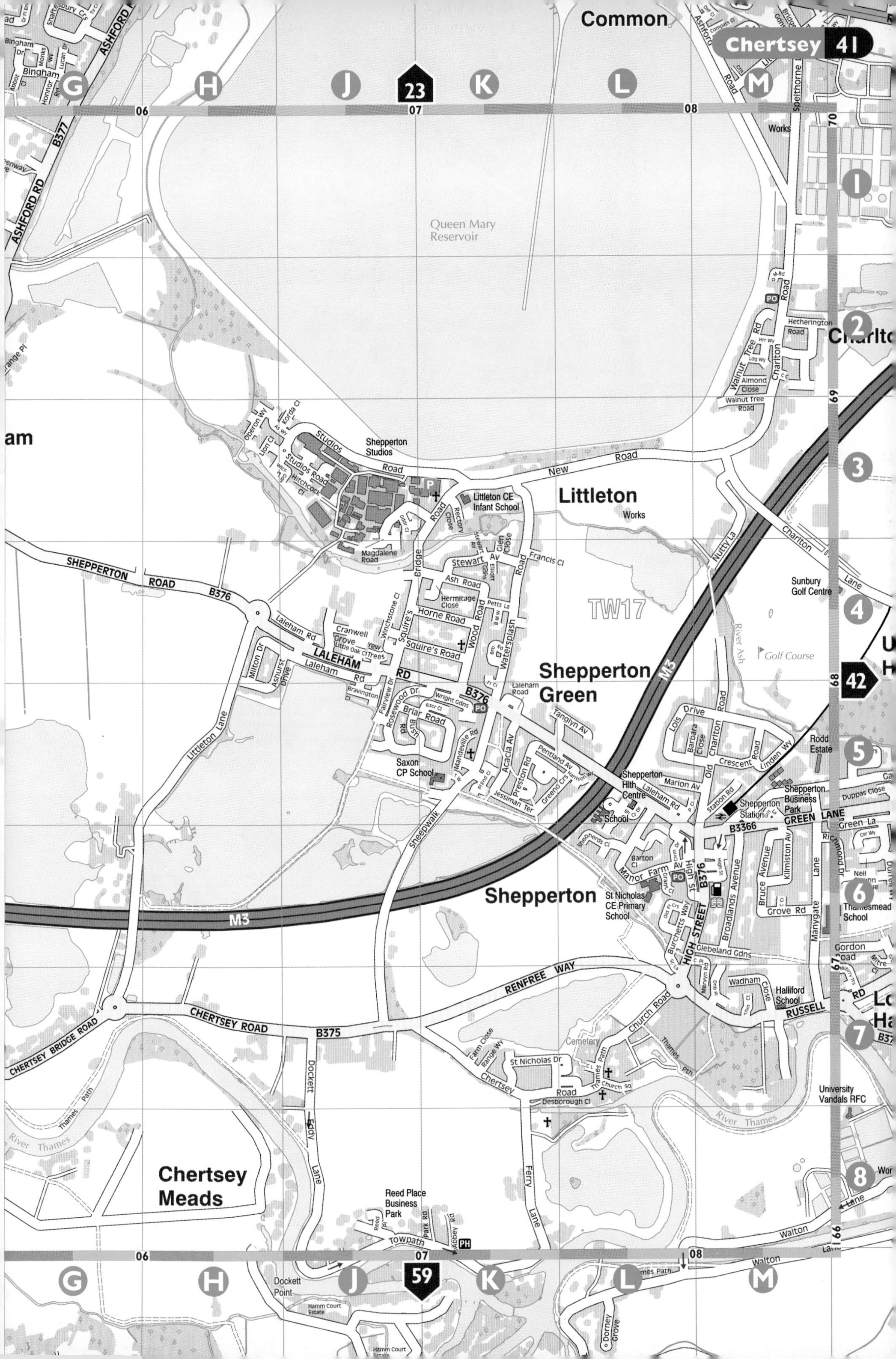

G **06** **H** **J** **23** **07** **K** **L** **08** **M** **70**

1

Works

Queen Mary
Reservoir

2 Charlto

Hetherington
Road

Walnut Tree Rd

Almond
Close

Walnut Tree
Road

3

New Road

Charlton

Studios Road

Shepperton
Studios

Littleton CE
Infant School

Littleton

Works

M3

River Ash

Charlton Lane

SHEPPERTON ROAD B376

Magdalene
Road

Rectory

Bridge Road

Glen Close

Stewart

Francis Cl

Sunbury
Golf Centre

4

Laleham Rd

Winchstone Cl

Horne Road

Ash Road

Hermitage
Close

Petts La

WOOD ROAD

Watersplash

TW17

Golf Course

42

U
H

Milton Dr

Ashurst
Drive

Cranwell
Grove

Little Oak Cl

Yew
Trees

Squire's

Squire's Road

LALEHAM
Laleham

Laleham
Rd

Fairview Rd

Rosewood Dr

Briar Rd

Busy

Bravington

LALEHAM RD

Wright Gdns

B376

PO

B376 Road

Laleham
Road

Mandeville Rd

Shepperton
Green

Tanglyn Av

Lois Drive

Barbara
Close

Old Charlton Road

Crescent

Linden Wy

Rodd
Estate

Shepperton
Business
Park

5

Duppas Close

Littleton Lane

Saxon
CP School

Acacia Av

Preston Rd

Reed Cl

Jessiman Ter

Greeno Crs

Denton

Pentland Av

Marion Av

Shepperton
Hlth
Centre

Laleham Rd

Station Rd

Shepperton
Station

B3366 **GREEN LANE**

Kilmiston Av

Richmond Dr

Green-La

Csr Wy

Nell
Cl

6

Thames mead
School

Sheepwalk

School

Shepherds Cl

Barton
Cl

Manor
Farm

PO

B375

Bruce Avenue

Broadlands Avenue

Manygate Lane

Gordon
Road

Shepperton

St Nicholas
CE Primary
School

Bucheits Way

Grove Rd

Grove Rd

Halliford
School

RD **Lo**
Ha

RUSSELL

7

RENFREE WAY

CHERTSEY ROAD B375

Church Road

Farm Close

Range Wy

St Nicholas Dr

Cemetery

Thames Pth

Wadham

Mervyn Rd

Glebeland Gdns

RUSSELL

University
Vandals RFC

CHERTSEY BRIDGE ROAD

Thames Path

Dockett
Lane

Eddy Lane

Chertsey

Road

Desborough Cl

Church Sq

Thames Path

River Thames

8 Wor

Chertsey
Meads

Reed Place
Business
Park

Park Rd

PH

Towpath

Ferry
Lane

Walton Lane

River Thames

Dockett
Point

Hamm Court
Estate

Dorney
Grove

Hamm Court

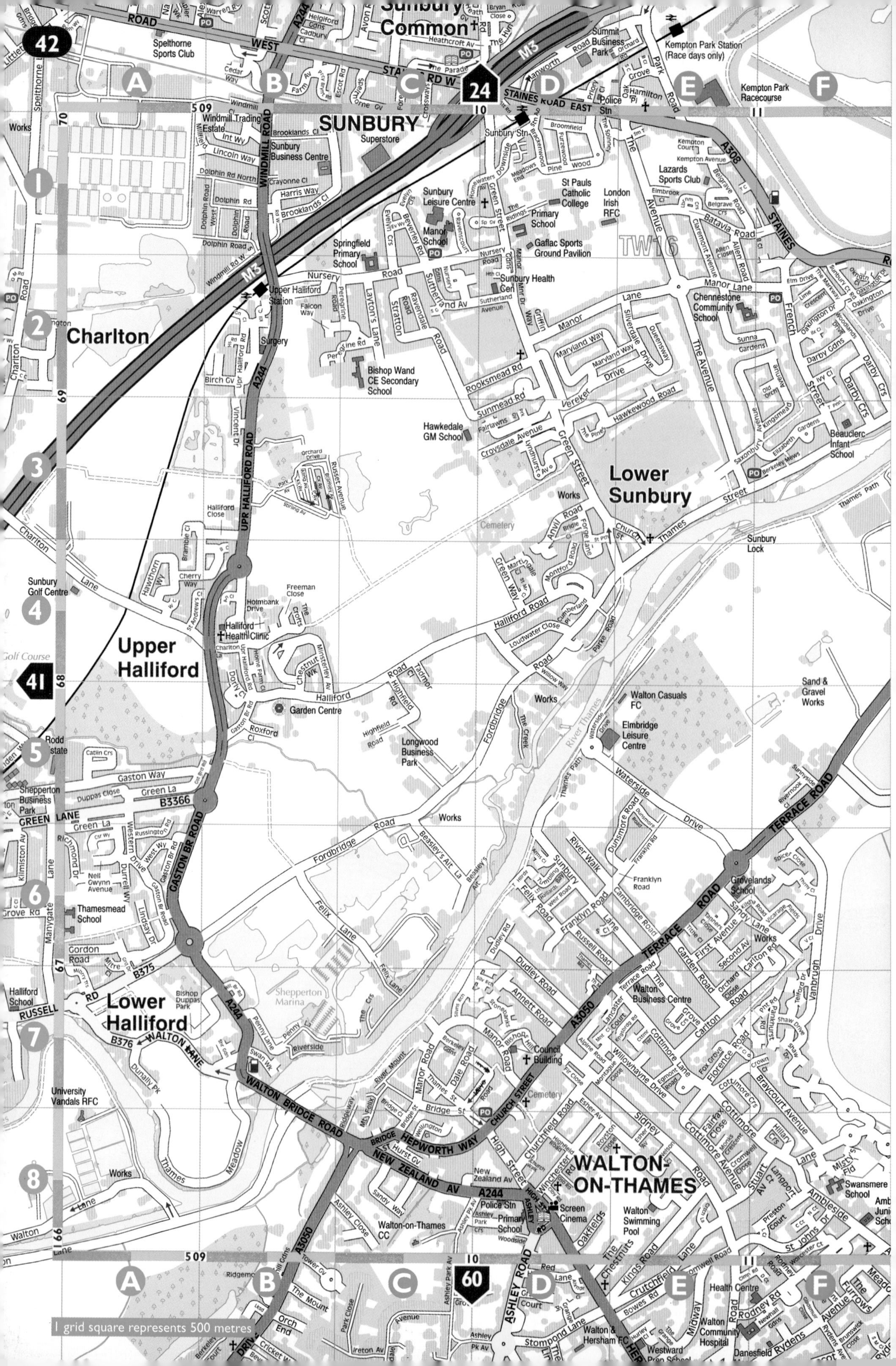

42
24
41
60
A
B
C
D
E
F
1
2
3
4
5
6
7
8
509
10
11
70
69
68
67
66
Sunbury Common
SUNBURY
Lower Sunbury
Charlton
Upper Halliford
Lower Halliford
WALTON-ON-THAMES
TW16
M3
A244
A308
A3050
B3366
B375
B376
STAINES ROAD WEST
STAINES ROAD EAST
STAINES RD
Spelthorne Sports Club
Kempton Park Station (Race days only)
Kempton Park Racecourse
Summit Business Park
Heathcroft Av
The Parade
Sunbury Stn
Superstore
Windmill Trading Estate
WINDMILL ROAD
Sunbury Business Centre
Brooklands Cl
Brooklands Rd
Lincoln Way
Dolphin Rd North
Dolphin Rd
Dolphin Road West
Harris Way
Crayonne Cl
Windmill Rd W
Upper Halliford Station
Sunbury Leisure Centre
Manor School
Springfield Primary School
St Pauls Catholic College
London Irish RFC
Primary School
Gaflac Sports Ground Pavilion
Lazards Sports Club
Kempton Court
Kempton Avenue
Batavia Road
Belgrave Road
Manor Lane
Nursery Road
Sunbury Health Cen
Chennestone Community School
Sutherland Av
Stratton Road
Ravendale Road
Layton's Lane
Peregrine Rd
Falcon Way
Bishop Wand CE Secondary School
Surgery
Manor Lane
Maryland Way
Silverdale Drive
Queensway
The Avenue
French Street
Darby Gdns
Darby Crs
Sunna Gardens
Kingsmead
Saxonbury Avenue
Beauclerc Infant School
Rooksmead Rd
Sunmead Rd
Vereker Drive
Hawkewood Road
Croysdale Avenue
Fairlawns
Hawkedale GM School
Green Street
Works
Cemetery
Thames Street
Thames Path
Church St
Sunbury Lock
Anvil Road
Forge Lane
Montford Road
Green Way
Halliford Road
Loudwater Close
Parke Road
UPR HALLIFORD ROAD
Russet Avenue
Orchard Drive
Stirling Av
Halliford Close
Charlton Lane
Sunbury Golf Centre
Golf Course
Hawthorn Wy
Cherry Way
Bramble Cl
Holmbank Drive
Freeman Close
The Crofts
Halliford Health Clinic
Chestnut Wk
Minsterley Av
Tadmor Cl
Highfield Rd
Highfield Road
Garden Centre
Roxford Cl
Longwood Business Park
Fordbridge Road
Willow Way
The Creek
Walton Casuals FC
Elmbridge Leisure Centre
River Thames
Waterside Drive
Sand & Gravel Works
Rodd Estate
Catlin Crs
Gaston Way
Green La
Duppas Close
Shepperton Business Park
GREEN LANE
Russington Rd
Western Drive
West Wy
Durrell Wy
Nell Gwynn Avenue
Richmond Dr
Kilmiston Av
Manygate Lane
Thamesmead School
Lindsay Dr
Gordon Road
GASTON BR ROAD
Halliford School
RUSSELL RD
Bishop Duppas Park
Shepperton Marina
Felix Lane
Penny Lane
Riverside
Swan Wk
WALTON LANE
Dunally Pk
University Vandals RFC
Thames Meadow
Works
Walton Lane
Beasley's Ait La
Dunsmore Road
Franklyn Road
River Walk
Cambridge Road
Russell Road
Felix Road
Dudley Road
Annett Road
TERRACE ROAD
Grovelands School
Sandy Lane
First Avenue
Second Av
Garden Road
Carlton Road
Vicarage Fields
Spicer Close
Vanbrugh Drive
Walton Business Centre
Terrace Road
Cottimore Lane
Cottimore Avenue
Cottimore Crs
Florence Road
Fox Grove
Braycourt Avenue
Hillary Crs
Misty's Fld
Swansmere School
Ambleside Av
Langport Ct
Preston Court
St Johns Dr
Manor Road
Dale Road
Bishops Hill
Council Building
Cemetery
Willowhayne Drive
Egmont Road
Sidney Road
River Mount
Bridge St
Thames St
WALTON BRIDGE ROAD
BRIDGE ST
HEPWORTH WAY
CHURCH STREET
NEW ZEALAND AV
New Zealand Av
High Street
Churchfield Road
Esher Av
Hurst Gv
Sandy Way
Ashley Close
Walton-on-Thames CC
Police Stn
Primary School
Screen Cinema
Oakfields
Walton Swimming Pool
The Chestnuts
Kings Road
Crutchfield Lane
Bowes Rd
Midway
Cromwell Road
Health Centre
Walton Community Hospital
Rodney Rd
Danesfield
Rydens Avenue
The Furrows
Walton & Hersham FC
Westward Prep School
Stompond Lane
ASHLEY ROAD
Ashley Park Av
Park Close
The Mount
Tower Gv
Orch End
Cricket Way
Ridgemount
Ireton Av
1 grid square represents 500 metres

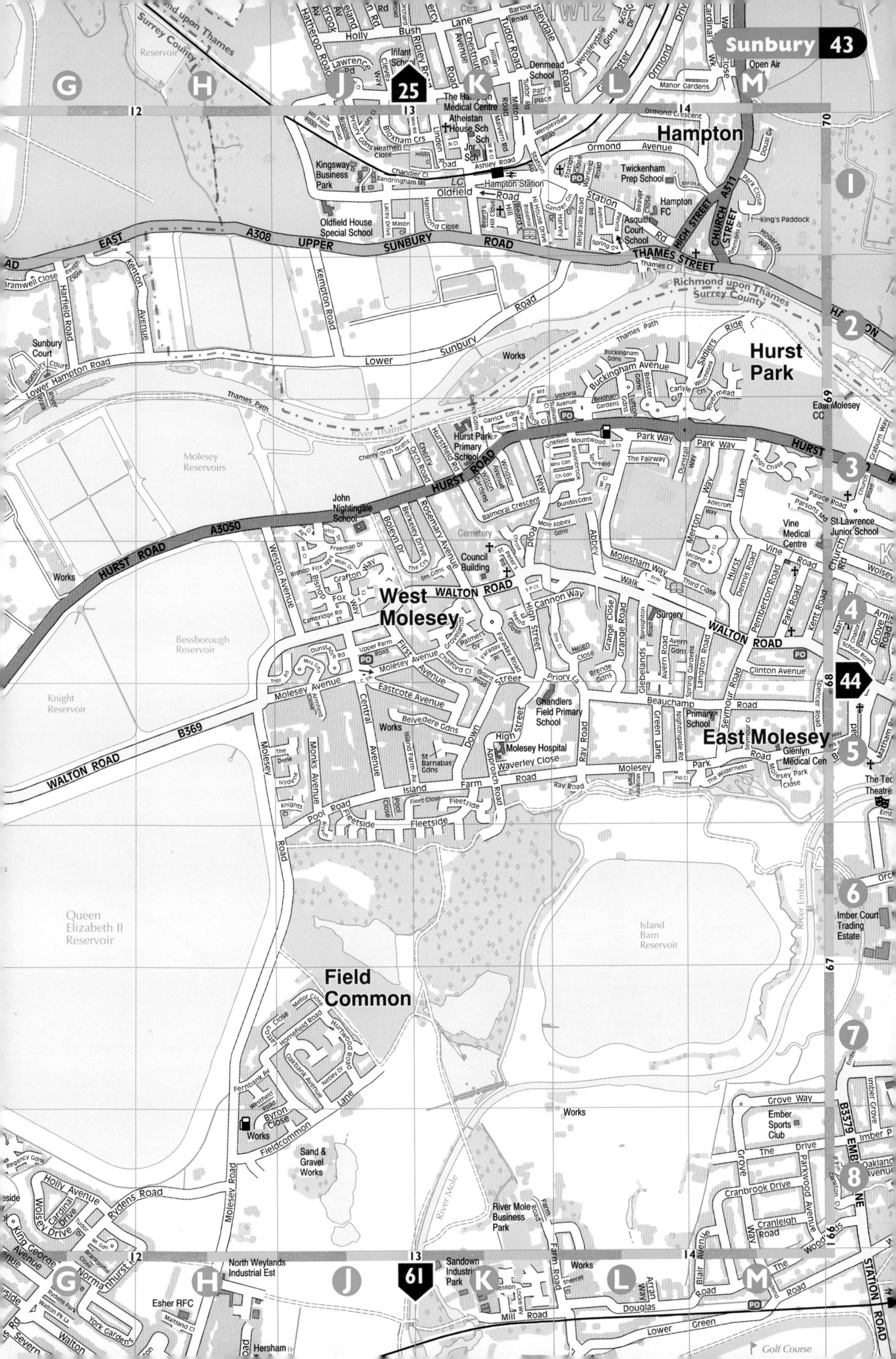

Sunbury 43
Hampton
Hurst Park
West Molesey
East Molesey
Field Common
Hampton Station
Twickenham Prep School
Hampton FC
Asquith Court School
Kingsway Business Park
Oldfield House Special School
The Hampton Medical Centre
Atheistan House Sch
Infant School
Denmead School
Open Air
Manor Gardens
Ormond Crescent
Ormond Avenue
King's Paddock
Upper Sunbury Road
A308
Thames Street
High Street
Church Street
A311
Richmond upon Thames
Surrey County
Thames Path
River Thames
Lower Sunbury Road
Kempton Road
Kenton Avenue
Harfield Road
Sunbury Court
Lower Hampton Road
Molesey Reservoirs
Bessborough Reservoir
Knight Reservoir
Queen Elizabeth II Reservoir
Island Barn Reservoir
Hurst Road
A3050
John Nightingale School
Hurst Park Primary School
Buckingham Avenue
East Molesey CC
Vine Medical Centre
St Lawrence Junior School
Palace Road
Walton Road
Molesham Way
Council Building
Cemetery
Surgery
Weston Avenue
Rosemary Avenue
Chandlers Field Primary School
Molesey Hospital
Primary School
Glenlyn Medical Cen
Beauchamp Road
Seymour Road
Spencer Road
Molesey Avenue
Central Avenue
Molesey Road
Island Farm Road
Pool Road
Fleetside
B369
Walton Road
Works
Sand & Gravel Works
River Mole
River Mole Business Park
River Ember
Imber Court Trading Estate
The Ted Theatre
Ember Sports Club
Grove Way
The Drive
Cranbrook Drive
Parkwood Avenue
B3379
Fieldcommon Lane
Rydens Road
North Weylands Industrial Est
Sandown Industrial Park
Esher RFC
Hersham
Douglas Road
Mill Road
Lower Green Road
Station Road
Golf Course
Farm Road
Blair Avenue
25
44
61
G H J K L M
12 13 14
2 3 4 5 6 7 8
67 68 69 70

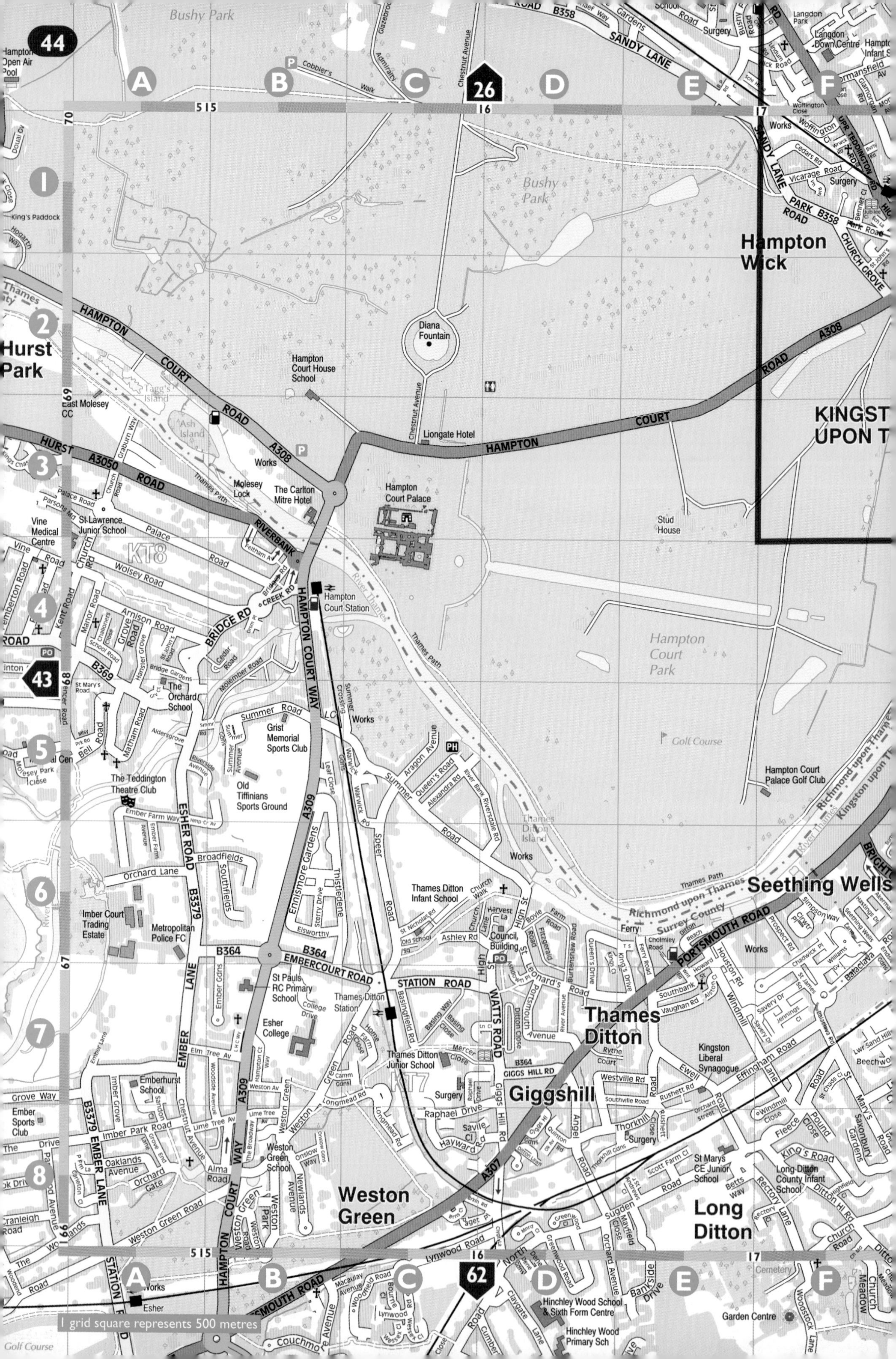
44
26
43
62
Bushy Park
Hampton Open Air Pool
Hurst Park
Hampton Wick
KINGSTON UPON T
Diana Fountain
Hampton Court House School
Liongate Hotel
Hampton Court Palace
Hampton Court Station
The Carlton Mitre Hotel
Molesey Lock
Tagg's Island
Ash Island
East Molesey CC
Hampton Court Park
Stud House
Golf Course
Hampton Court Palace Golf Club
Thames Ditton Island
Grist Memorial Sports Club
Old Tiffinians Sports Ground
The Teddington Theatre Club
The Orchard School
St Lawrence Junior School
Vine Medical Centre
Imber Court Trading Estate
Metropolitan Police FC
St Pauls RC Primary School
Esher College
Thames Ditton Station
Thames Ditton Infant School
Thames Ditton Junior School
Council Building
Emberhurst School
Ember Sports Club
Weston Green School
Weston Green
Thames Ditton
Giggshill
Seething Wells
Kingston Liberal Synagogue
St Marys CE Junior School
Long Ditton County Infant School
Long Ditton
Hinchley Wood School & Sixth Form Centre
Hinchley Wood Primary Sch
Garden Centre
Cemetery
Esher
HAMPTON COURT ROAD
HAMPTON COURT WAY
HURST ROAD
PORTSMOUTH ROAD
EMBER LANE
ESHER ROAD
EMBERCOURT ROAD
STATION ROAD
WATTS ROAD
SANDY LANE
GIGGS HILL RD
1 grid square represents 500 metres

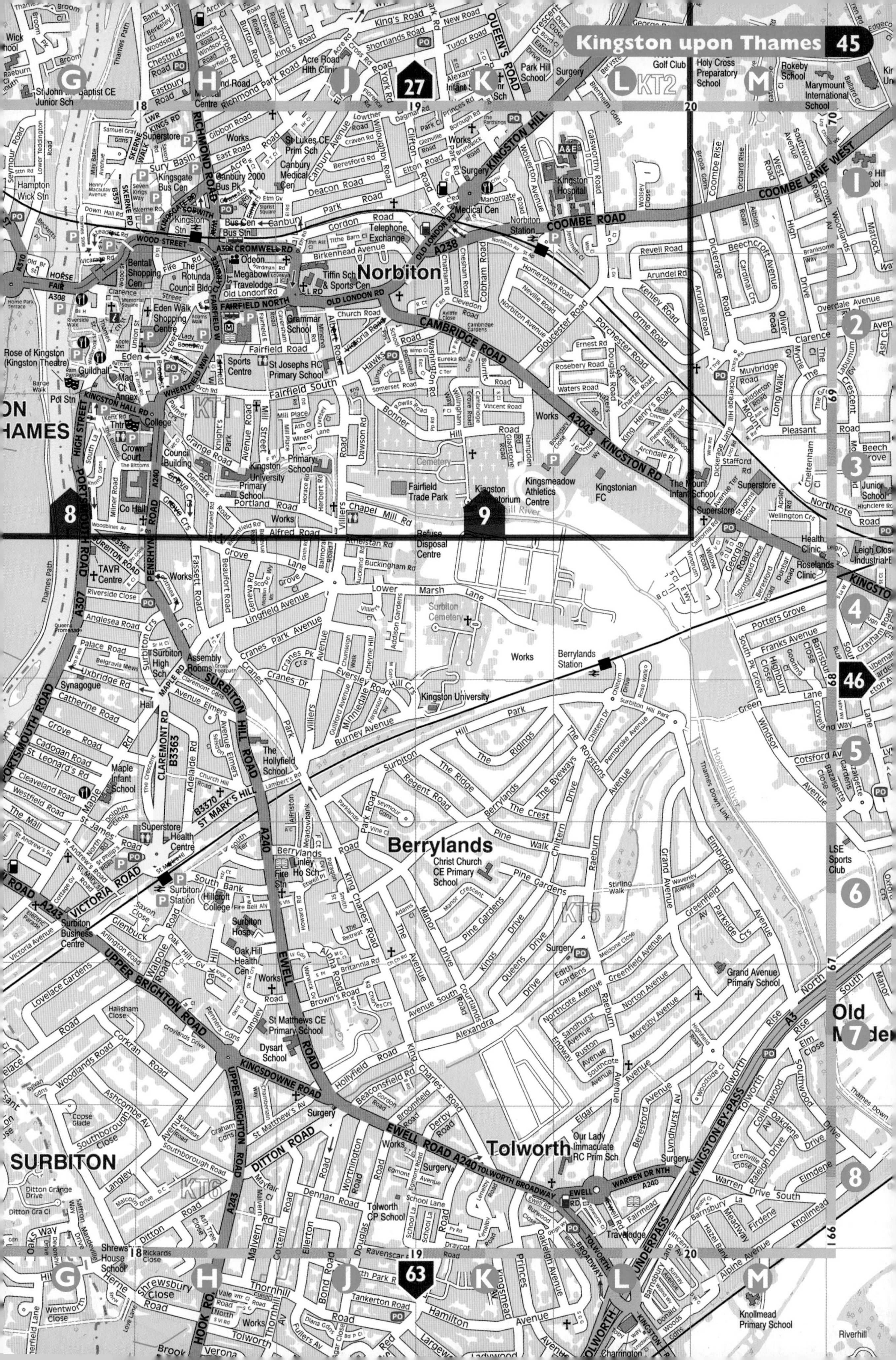
Norbiton
Berrylands
Tolworth
SURBITON
KINGSTON UPON THAMES
Old Malden
KT1
KT2
KT5
KT6
27
8
9
46
63
G
H
J
K
L
M
18
19
20
1
2
3
4
5
6
7
8
RICHMOND ROAD
KINGSTON HILL
QUEEN'S ROAD
COOMBE ROAD
COOMBE LANE WEST
CAMBRIDGE ROAD
KINGSTON RD
A2043
A238
OLD LONDON RD
FAIRFIELD NORTH
WOOD STREET
CROMWELL RD
KINGSTON HALL RD
HIGH STREET
PORTSMOUTH ROAD
PENRHYN ROAD
SURBITON HILL ROAD
EWELL ROAD
VICTORIA ROAD
UPPER BRIGHTON ROAD
KINGSDOWNE ROAD
DITTON ROAD
TOLWORTH BROADWAY
KINGSTON BY-PASS
WARREN DR NTH
CLAREMONT RD
ST MARK'S HILL
HOOK RD
Kingston Stn
Norbiton Station
Berrylands Station
Surbiton Station
Hampton Wick Stn
Kingston Hospital
Tiffin Sch & Sports Cen
Grammar School
St Josephs RC Primary School
Kingston University
Kingsmeadow Athletics Centre
Kingstonian FC
Fairfield Trade Park
Kingston Crematorium
Surbiton Cemetery
Refuse Disposal Centre
Hogsmill River
Thames Path
Guildhall
Rose of Kingston (Kingston Theatre)
Bentall Shopping Cen
Eden Walk Shopping Centre
The Rotunda
Council Bldg
Odeon
Crown Court
Co Hall
Sports Centre
The Hollyfield School
Christ Church CE Primary School
Surbiton Hosp
Oak Hill Health Cen
St Matthews CE Primary School
Dysart School
Hillcroft College
Surbiton Business Centre
Maple Infant School
Grand Avenue Primary School
Our Lady Immaculate RC Prim Sch
Tolworth CP School
Knollmead Primary School
Shrewsbury House School
LSE Sports Club
Holy Cross Preparatory School
Rokeby School
Marymount International School
Park Hill School
Golf Club
Superstore
Surgery
Works
Travelodge
Leigh Close Industrial Est
Roselands Clinic
Health Clinic
The Mount Infant School
St John the Baptist CE Junior Sch
Canbury 2000 Bus Pk
Kingsgate Bus Cen
Acre Road Hlth Clinic
Megabowl
Travelodge
TAVR Centre
Assembly Rooms
Synagogue
Surbiton High Sch
Health Centre

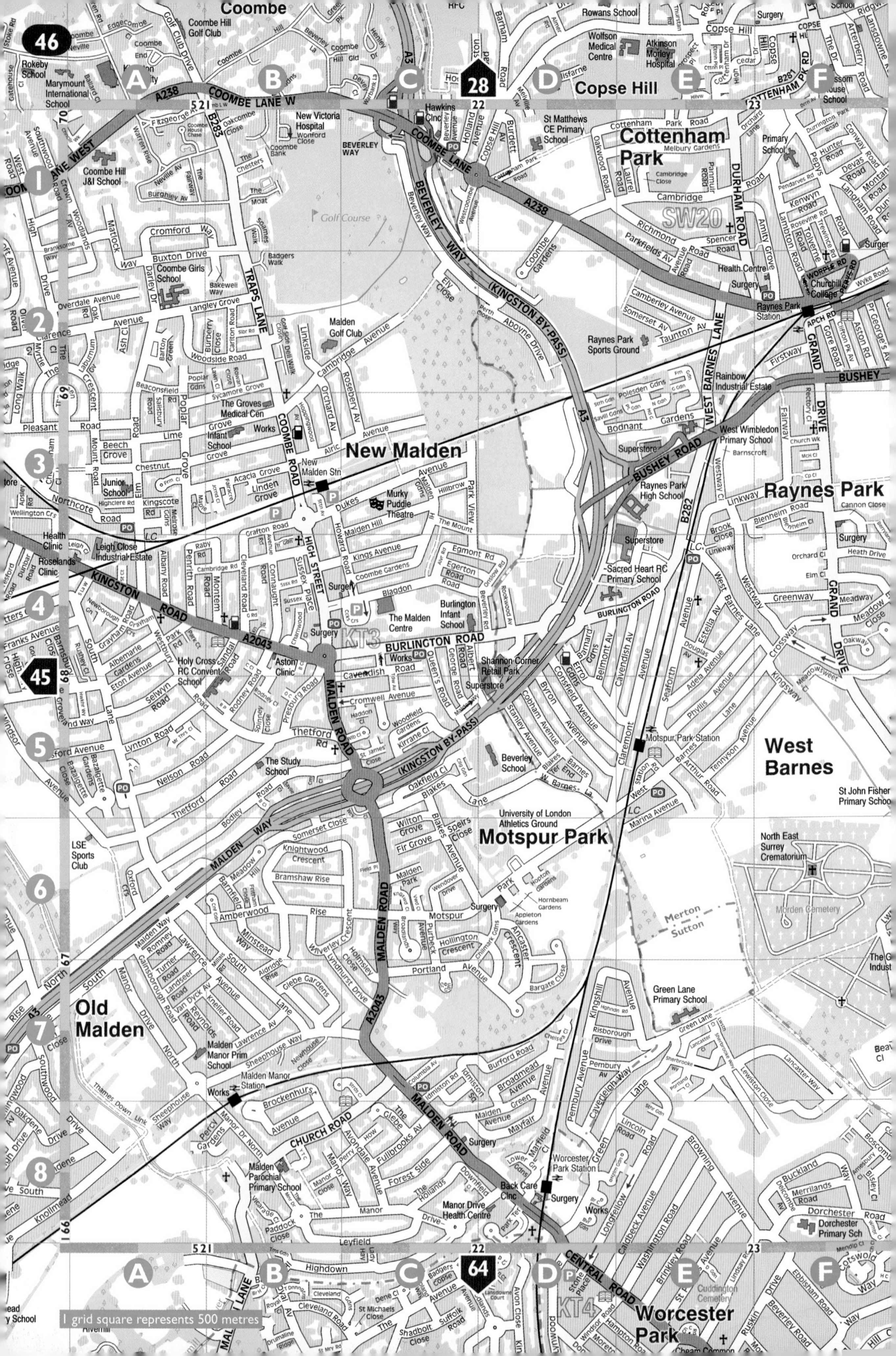

Coombe
Coombe Hill Golf Club
Rokeby School
Marymount International School
COOMBE LANE W
A238
B283
Coombe Hill J&I School
New Victoria Hospital
Hawkins Clnc
Copse Hill
Rowans School
Wolfson Medical Centre
Atkinson Morley Hospital
St Matthews CE Primary School
Cottenham Park
SW20
Golf Course
Coombe Girls School
Malden Golf Club
TRAPS LANE
BEVERLEY WAY
KINGSTON BY-PASS
A3
COOMBE LANE
DURHAM ROAD
Raynes Park Station
Raynes Park Sports Ground
Rainbow Industrial Estate
West Wimbledon Primary School
BUSHEY ROAD
WEST BARNES LANE
B282
Raynes Park
Raynes Park High School
New Malden
New Malden Stn
COOMBE ROAD
The Groves Medical Cen
Grove Infant School
Murky Puddle Theatre
HIGH STREET
Leigh Close Industrial Estate
Roselands Clinic
Health Clinic
KINGSTON ROAD
A2043
Holy Cross RC Convent School
Aston Clinic
The Malden Centre
KT3
BURLINGTON ROAD
Burlington Infant School
Shannon Corner Retail Park
Sacred Heart RC Primary School
MALDEN ROAD
Beverley School
Motspur Park Station
West Barnes
St John Fisher Primary School
The Study School
LSE Sports Club
MALDEN WAY
University of London Athletics Ground
Motspur Park
North East Surrey Crematorium
Morden Cemetery
Merton
Sutton
Green Lane Primary School
Old Malden
Malden Manor Prim School
Malden Manor Station
CHURCH ROAD
Malden Parochial Primary School
Manor Drive Health Centre
Back Care Clnc
Worcester Park Station
CENTRAL ROAD
Dorchester Primary Sch
Cuddington Cemetery
KT4
Worcester Park
28
45
64
1 grid square represents 500 metres

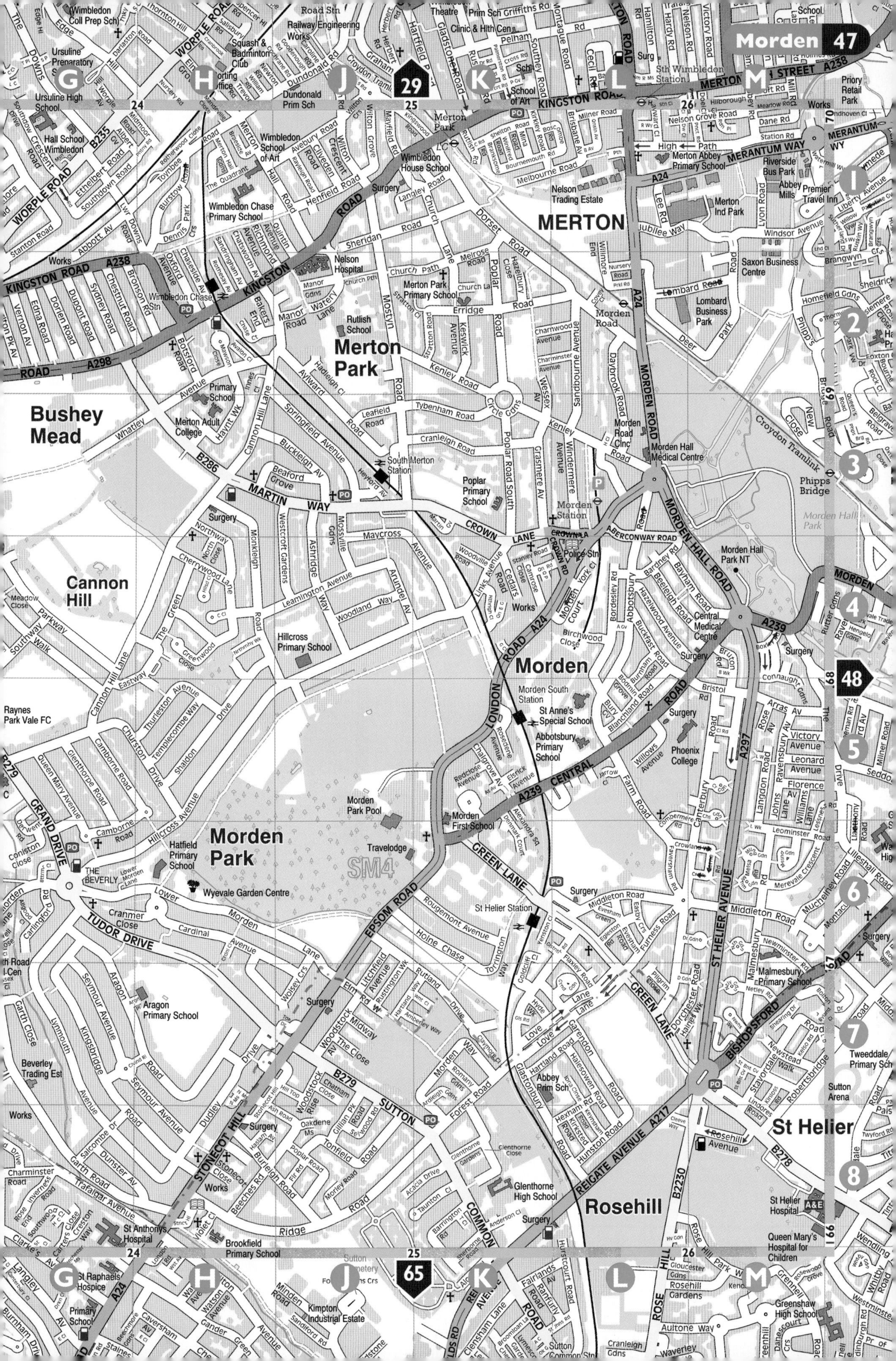
29
48
65
G
H
J
K
L
M
24
25
26
70
69
68
67
66
1
2
3
4
5
6
7
8
MERTON
Merton Park
Bushey Mead
Cannon Hill
Morden
Morden Park
Rosehill
St Helier
SM4
KINGSTON ROAD
A238
A298
WORPLE ROAD
B235
MERTON HIGH STREET
MERANTUM WAY
A24
MORDEN ROAD
MORDEN HALL ROAD
LONDON ROAD
A239 CENTRAL ROAD
EPSOM ROAD
MARTIN WAY
B286
CROWN LANE
GREEN LANE
ST HELIER AVENUE
A297
REIGATE AVENUE
A217
BISHOPSFORD ROAD
STONECOT HILL
SUTTON COMMON ROAD
B279
B278
B2230
TUDOR DRIVE
GRAND DRIVE
Croydon Tramlink
Sth Wimbledon Station
Wimbledon Chase Stn
South Merton Station
Morden Station
Morden South Station
St Helier Station
Morden Road
Phipps Bridge
Merton Park
Nelson Hospital
Wimbledon School of Art
Wimbledon Chase Primary School
Merton Park Primary School
Rutlish School
Merton Adult College
Hillcross Primary School
Poplar Primary School
Morden Hall Medical Centre
Morden Hall Park NT
Police Stn
St Anne's Special School
Abbotsbury Primary School
Phoenix College
Morden First School
Morden Park Pool
Travelodge
Wyevale Garden Centre
Hatfield Primary School
Aragon Primary School
Beverley Trading Est
St Anthony's Hospital
Brookfield Primary School
Glenthorne High School
Abbey Prim Sch
Malmesbury Primary School
St Helier Hospital
Queen Mary's Hospital for Children
Sutton Arena
Tweeddale Primary Sch
Greenshaw High School
St Raphaels Hospice
Kimpton Industrial Estate
Nelson Trading Estate
Merton Ind Park
Saxon Business Centre
Lombard Business Park
Riverside Bus Park
Abbey Mills
Premier Travel Inn
Priory Retail Park
Merton Abbey Primary School
Raynes Park Vale FC
Ursuline High School
Ursuline Preparatory School
Hall School Wimbledon
Wimbledon House School
Dundonald Prim Sch
Squash & Badminton Club
Railway Engineering Works
THE BEVERLY

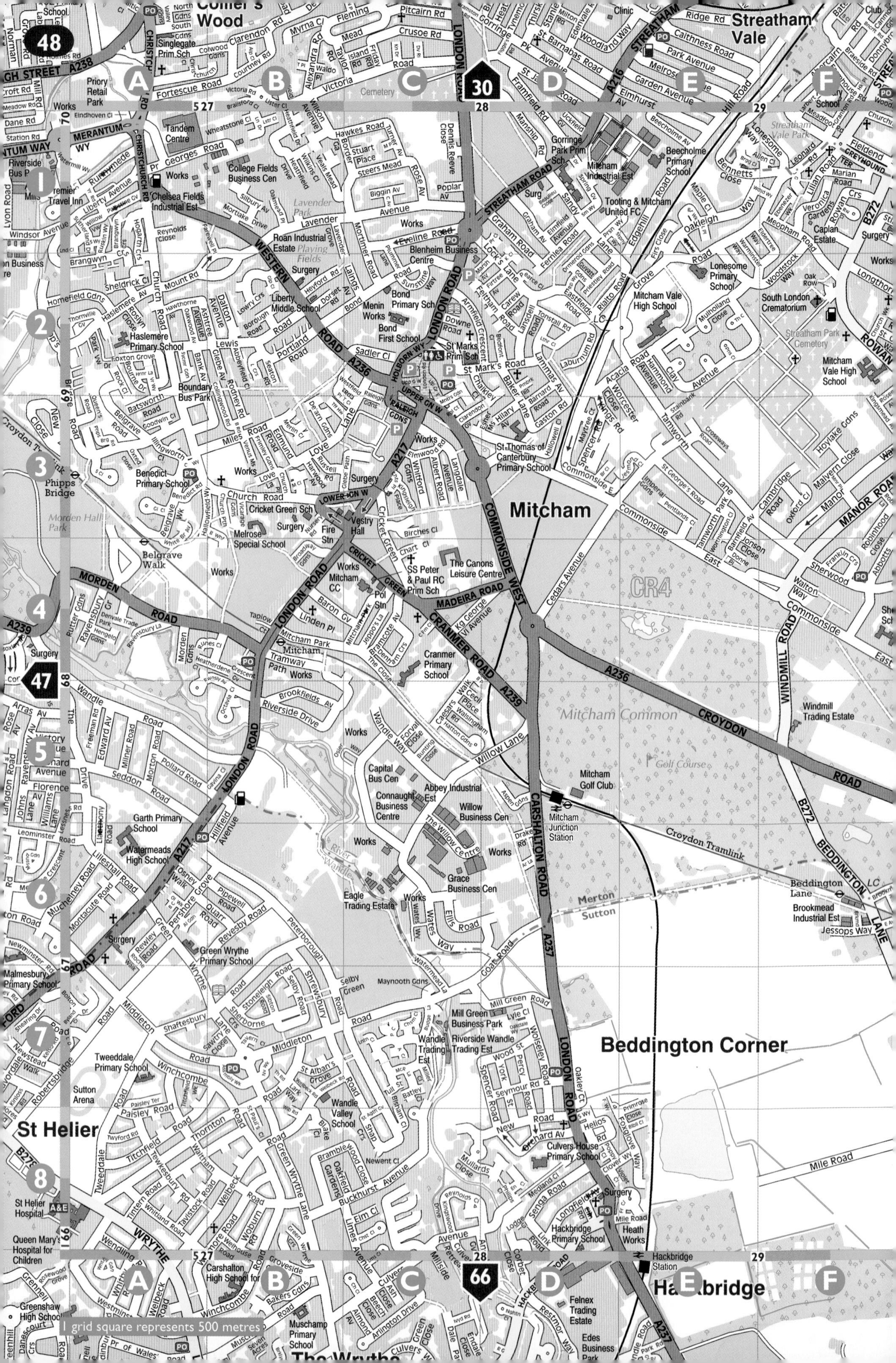
48
30
47
66
Colliers Wood
Streatham Vale
Mitcham
Beddington Corner
St Helier
Hackbridge
The Wrythe
Mitcham Common
CR4
A
B
C
D
E
F
1
2
3
4
5
6
7
8
527
28
29
70
69
68
67
166
A238
A216
A236
A217
A239
A237
B272
B276
Priory Retail Park
Tandem Centre
College Fields Business Cen
Chelsea Fields Industrial Est
Singlegate Prim Sch
Merantum Way
Riverside Bus Pk
Premier Travel Inn
Christchurch Rd
Western Road
Streatham Road
London Road
Lavender Park
Playing Fields
Roan Industrial Estate
Liberty Middle School
Haslemere Primary School
Boundary Bus Park
Benedict Primary School
Phipps Bridge
Morden Hall Park
Belgrave Walk
Melrose Special School
Cricket Green Sch
Vestry Hall
Fire Stn
Mitcham CC
Pol Stn
SS Peter & Paul RC Prim Sch
The Canons Leisure Centre
Madeira Road
Commonside West
Commonside East
Cranmer Road
Cranmer Primary School
Morden Road
Mitcham Tramway Path
Riverside Drive
Capital Bus Cen
Connaught Business Centre
Abbey Industrial Est
Willow Business Cen
The Willow Centre
Grace Business Cen
Eagle Trading Estate
River Wandle
Garth Primary School
Watermeads High School
Green Wrythe Primary School
Tweeddale Primary School
Sutton Arena
Wandle Valley School
St Helier Hospital
A&E
Queen Mary's Hospital for Children
Carshalton High School for
Muschamp Primary School
Greenshaw High School
Mill Green Business Park
Riverside Wandle Trading Est
Wandle Trading Est
Culvers House Primary School
Hackbridge Primary School
Hackbridge Station
Heath Works
Felnex Trading Estate
Edes Business Park
Carshalton Road
Mitcham Golf Club
Mitcham Junction Station
Golf Course
Croydon Tramlink
Croydon Road
Merton
Sutton
Windmill Road
Windmill Trading Estate
Beddington Lane
Brookmead Industrial Est
Jessops Way
Mile Road
Mitcham Industrial Est
Tooting & Mitcham United FC
Gorringe Park Prim Sch
Beecholme Primary School
Mitcham Vale High School
Lonesome Primary School
South London Crematorium
Streatham Park Cemetery
Streatham Vale Park
Caplan Estate
Manor Road
St Thomas of Canterbury Primary School
St Marks Prim Sch
Bond Primary Sch
Bond First School
Menin Works
Blenheim Business Centre
Cemetery
Works
Surgery
1 grid square represents 500 metres

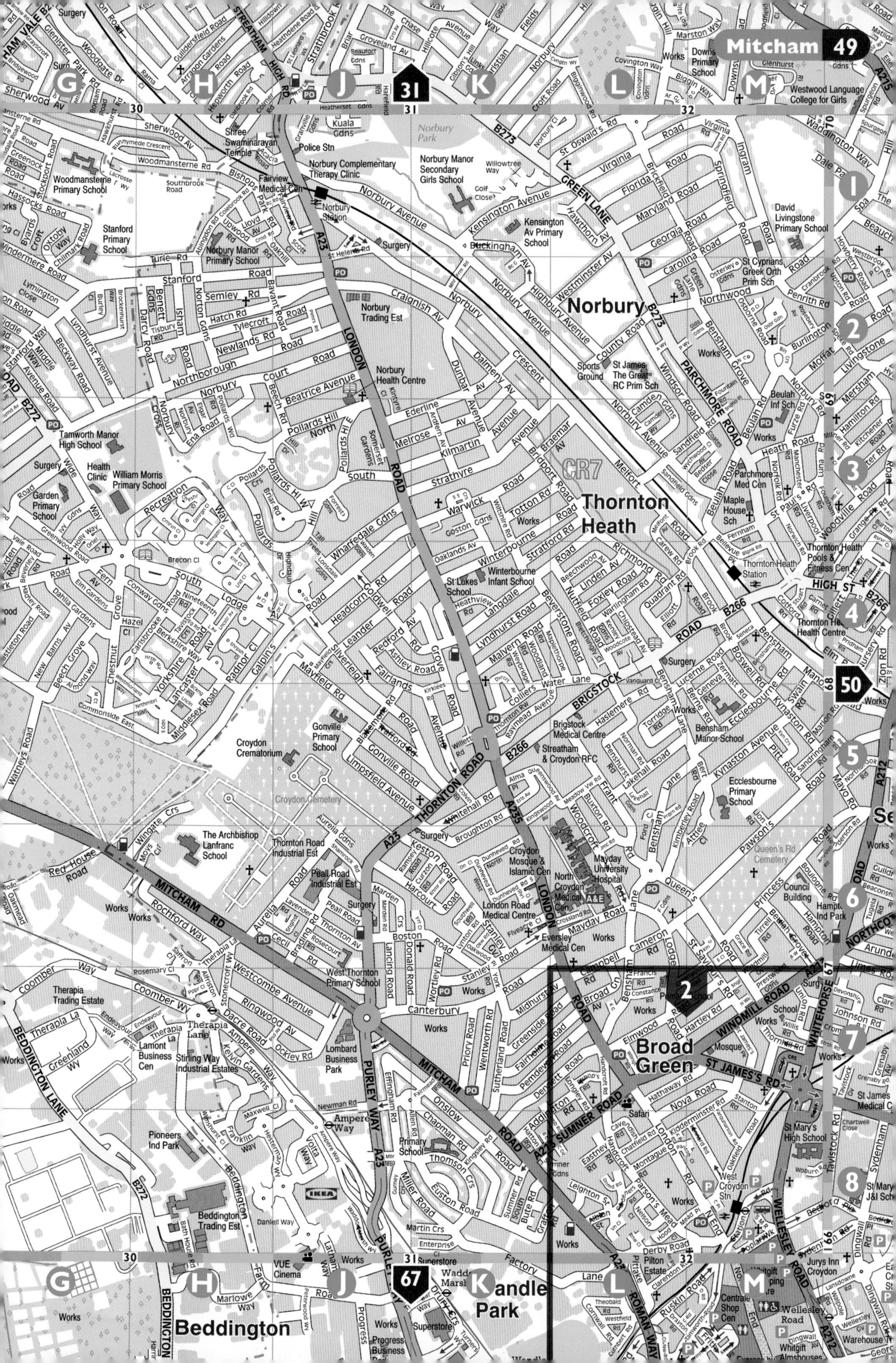

Mitcham 49
31
50
67
2
Norbury
Thornton Heath
Broad Green
Beddington
Kandle Park
CR7
Norbury Station
Thornton Heath Station
West Croydon Stn
Norbury Park
Norbury Manor Secondary Girls School
Kensington Av Primary School
Norbury Trading Est
Norbury Health Centre
Norbury Complementary Therapy Clinic
Fairview Medical Cen
Police Stn
Shree Swaminarayan Temple
Woodmansterne Primary School
Stanford Primary School
Norbury Manor Primary School
Tamworth Manor High School
Health Clinic
William Morris Primary School
Garden Primary School
Croydon Crematorium
Croydon Cemetery
Gonville Primary School
St Lukes School
Winterbourne Infant School
Brigstock Medical Centre
Streatham & Croydon RFC
Bensham Manor School
Ecclesbourne Primary School
Queen's Rd Cemetery
Council Building
Hampton Ind Park
The Archbishop Lanfranc School
Thornton Road Industrial Est
Peall Road Industrial Est
West Thornton Primary School
Croydon Mosque & Islamic Cen
Mayday University Hospital
North Croydon Medical Cen
London Road Medical Centre
Eversley Medical Cen
Therapia Trading Estate
Lamont Business Cen
Stirling Way Industrial Estates
Lombard Business Park
Pioneers Ind Park
Beddington Trading Est
VUE Cinema
Superstore
Progress Business
Centrale Shop Cen
Whitgift Almshouses
Jurys Inn Croydon
St Mary's High School
Westwood Language College for Girls
David Livingstone Primary School
St Cyprians Greek Orth Prim Sch
St James The Great RC Prim Sch
Sports Ground
Beulah Inf Sch
Parchmore Med Cen
Maple House Sch
Thornton Heath Pools & Fitness Cen
Thornton Heath Health Centre
Downs Primary School
LONDON ROAD
A23
A235
A236
A212
A215
B266
B272
B273
MITCHAM RD
PURLEY WAY
GREEN LANE
PARCHMORE ROAD
BRIGSTOCK ROAD
THORNTON ROAD
WINDMILL ROAD
WHITEHORSE ROAD
SUMNER ROAD
ROMAN WAY
WELLESLEY ROAD
STREATHAM HIGH RD
HIGH ST
BEDDINGTON LANE
Norbury Avenue
Craignish Av
Northborough Road
Pollards Hill North
Pollards Hill South
Mayfield Rd
Limpsfield Avenue
Westcombe Avenue
Coomber Way
Canterbury Road
Queen's Road
St James's Rd

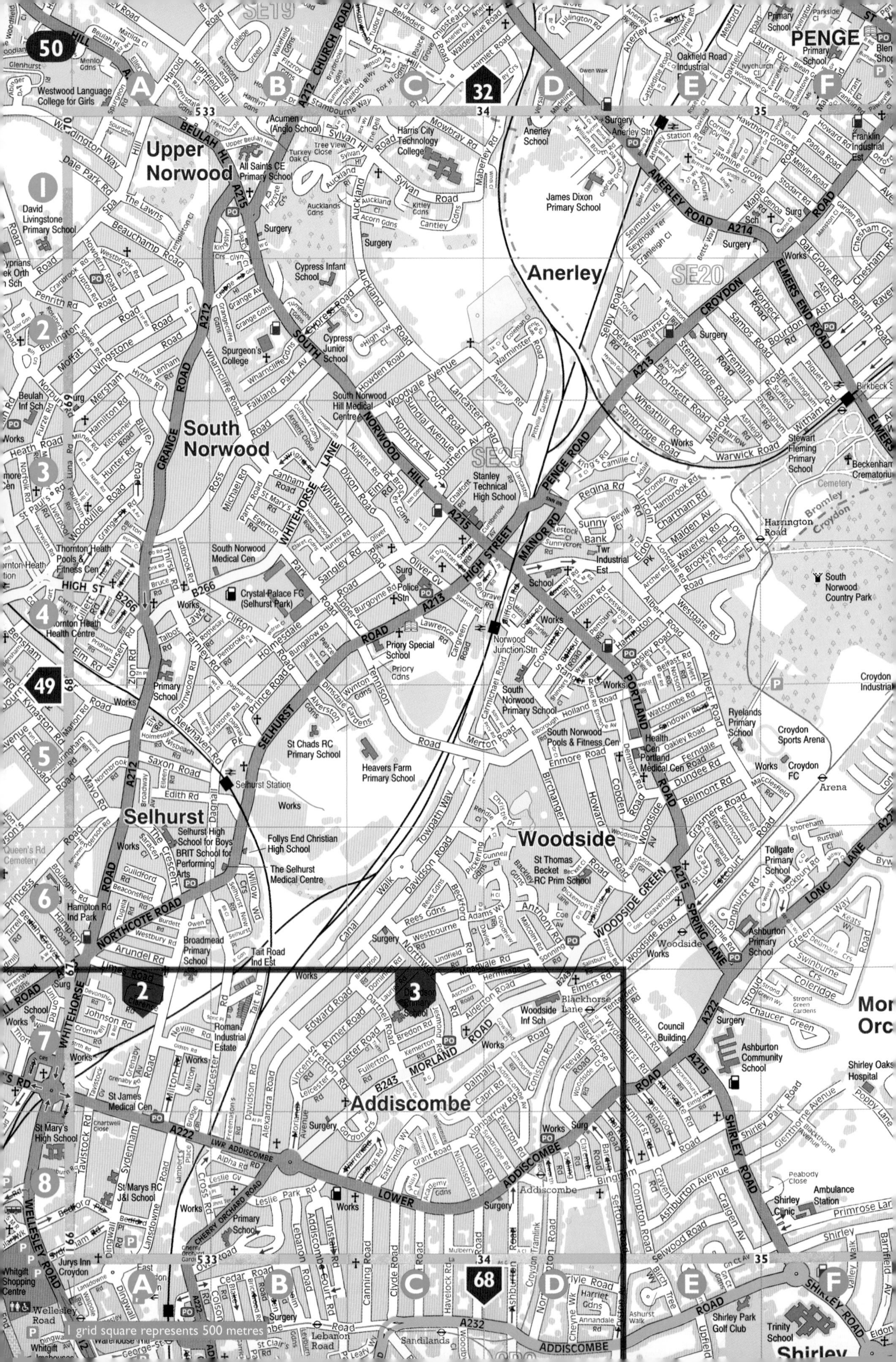
50
32
49
68
2
3
A
B
C
D
E
F
1
2
3
4
5
6
7
8
33
34
35
SE19
SE20
SE25
PENGE
Upper Norwood
South Norwood
Anerley
Selhurst
Woodside
Addiscombe
Shirley
Westwood Language College for Girls
David Livingstone Primary School
Beulah Inf Sch
Acumen (Anglo School)
Harris City Technology College
All Saints CE Primary School
Cypress Infant School
Cypress Junior School
Spurgeon's College
Anerley School
James Dixon Primary School
Oakfield Road Industrial
Anerley Stn
Anerley Station
Franklin Industrial Est
South Norwood Hill Medical Centre
Stanley Technical High School
Stewart Fleming Primary School
Beckenham Crematorium
Cemetery
Birkbeck Stn
Harrington Road
South Norwood Country Park
Thornton Heath Pools & Fitness Cen
Thornton Heath Health Centre
South Norwood Medical Cen
Crystal Palace FC (Selhurst Park)
Priory Special School
Priory Gdns
Norwood Junction Stn
Twr Industrial Est
South Norwood Primary School
South Norwood Pools & Fitness Cen
Health Cen
Portland Medical Cen
Ryelands Primary School
Croydon Sports Arena
Croydon FC
Arena
Croydon Industrial
St Chads RC Primary School
Heavers Farm Primary School
Selhurst Station
Selhurst High School for Boys
BRIT School for Performing Arts
Follys End Christian High School
The Selhurst Medical Centre
Hampton Rd Ind Park
Broadmead Primary School
Tait Road Ind Est
Queen's Rd Cemetery
St Thomas Becket RC Prim School
Woodside
Tollgate Primary School
Ashburton Primary School
Council Building
Ashburton Community School
Shirley Oaks Hospital
Woodside Inf Sch
Blackhorse Lane
Roman Industrial Estate
St James Medical Cen
St Mary's High School
St Marys RC J&I School
Primary School
Addiscombe
Shirley Clinic
Ambulance Station
Peabody Close
Shirley Park Golf Club
Trinity School
Whitgift Shopping Centre
Jurys Inn Croydon
Sandilands
Lebanon Road
Works
Surgery
Surg
PO
A212
A213
A214
A215
A222
A232
B243
B266
BEULAH HL
CHURCH ROAD
GRANGE ROAD
SOUTH NORWOOD HILL
WHITEHORSE LANE
HIGH STREET
PENGE ROAD
MANOR RD
PORTLAND ROAD
SELHURST ROAD
NORTHCOTE ROAD
WHITEHORSE ROAD
CROYDON ROAD
ANERLEY ROAD
ELMERS END ROAD
WOODSIDE GREEN
SPRING LANE
LONG LANE
SHIRLEY ROAD
LOWER ADDISCOMBE ROAD
MORLAND ROAD
CHERRY ORCHARD ROAD
WELLESLEY ROAD
ADDISCOMBE ROAD
1 grid square represents 500 metres

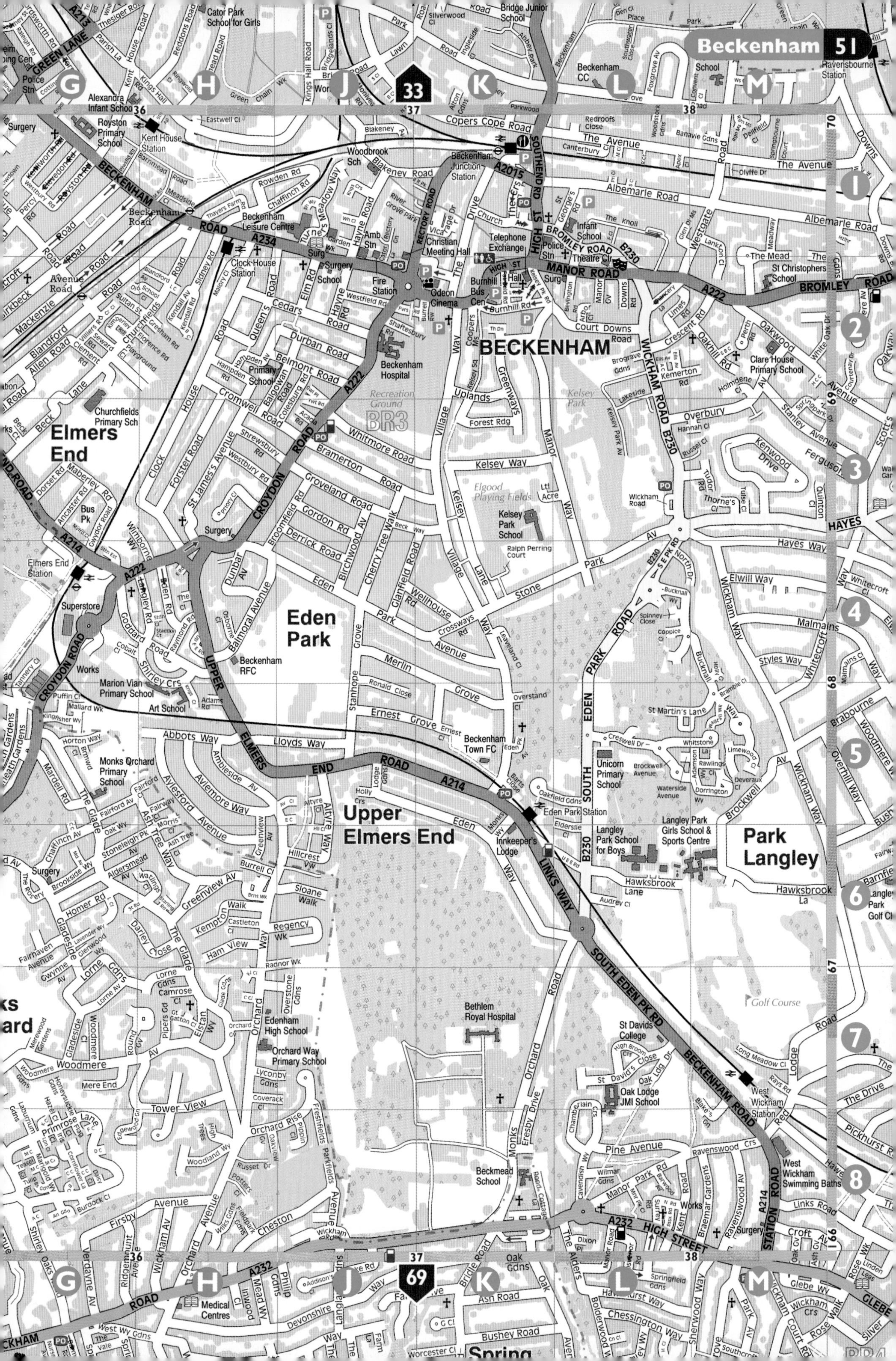
BECKENHAM
Elmers End
Eden Park
Upper Elmers End
Park Langley
BECKENHAM ROAD
CROYDON ROAD
UPPER ELMERS END ROAD
SOUTH EDEN PARK ROAD
SOUTH EDEN PK RD
WICKHAM ROAD
BROMLEY ROAD
MANOR ROAD
HIGH ST
SOUTHEND RD
RECTORY ROAD
HIGH STREET
STATION ROAD
LINKS WAY
GREEN LANE
A213
A234
A222
A214
A2015
B230
A232
Copers Cope Road
The Avenue
Albemarle Road
Kelsey Park
Kelsey Park School
Elgood Playing Fields
Recreation Ground
BR3
Beckenham Hospital
Beckenham Junction Station
Clock House Station
Kent House Station
Elmers End Station
Eden Park Station
West Wickham Station
Ravensbourne Station
Beckenham Leisure Centre
Odeon Cinema
Fire Station
Amb Stn
Police Stn
Theatre Ctr
Telephone Exchange
Christian Meeting Hall
Cator Park School for Girls
Bridge Junior School
Alexandra Infant School
Royston Primary School
Churchfields Primary Sch
Marion Vian Primary School
Art School
Beckenham RFC
Beckenham Town FC
Monks Orchard Primary School
Unicorn Primary School
Langley Park School for Boys
Langley Park Girls School & Sports Centre
Clare House Primary School
St Christophers School
Bethlem Royal Hospital
St Davids College
Oak Lodge JMI School
Beckmead School
Edenham High School
Orchard Way Primary School
West Wickham Swimming Baths
Innkeeper's Lodge
Superstore
Golf Course
Medical Centres
Beckenham CC
Woodbrook Sch
Ralph Perring Court
Burnhill Bus Cen
Surgery
Works
G
H
J
K
L
M
33
69
36
37
38
1
2
3
4
5
6
7
8
66
67
68
69
70

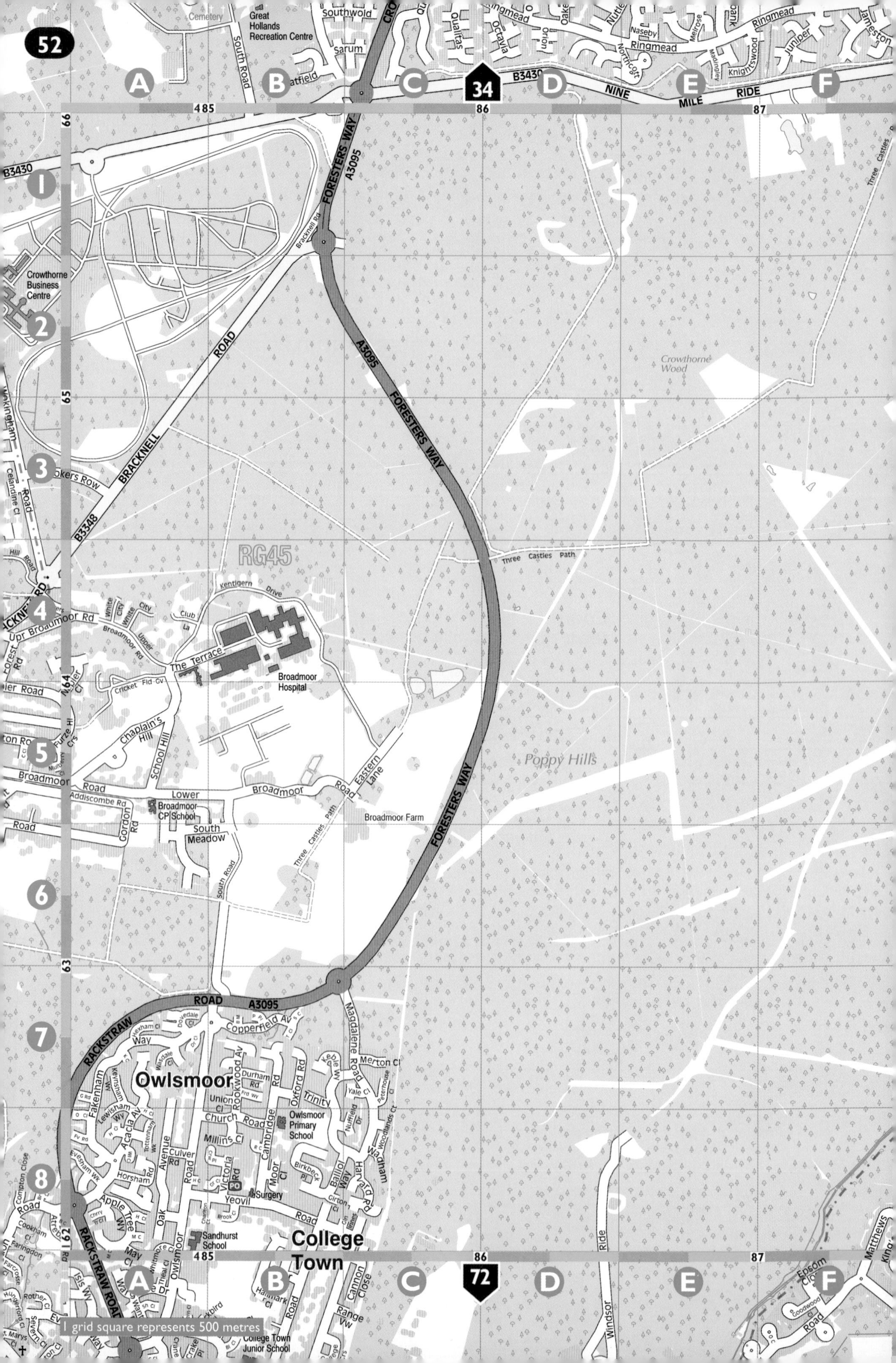
34
72
Crowthorne Business Centre
Great Hollands Recreation Centre
Crowthorne Wood
Poppy Hills
RG45
Broadmoor Hospital
Broadmoor CP School
Broadmoor Farm
Owlsmoor
Owlsmoor Primary School
Sandhurst School
College Town
College Town Junior School
Surgery
FORESTERS WAY
A3095
BRACKNELL ROAD
B3348
B3430
NINE MILE RIDE
RACKSTRAW ROAD
Three Castles Path
Lower Broadmoor Road
Eastern Lane
South Road
Kentigern Drive
The Terrace
Chaplain's Hill
School Hill
South Meadow
Copperfield Av
Magdalene Road
Merton Cl
Church Road
Rookwood Av
Oxford Rd
Cambridge Rd
Victoria Rd
Yeovil Road
Windsor Ride
1 grid square represents 500 metres

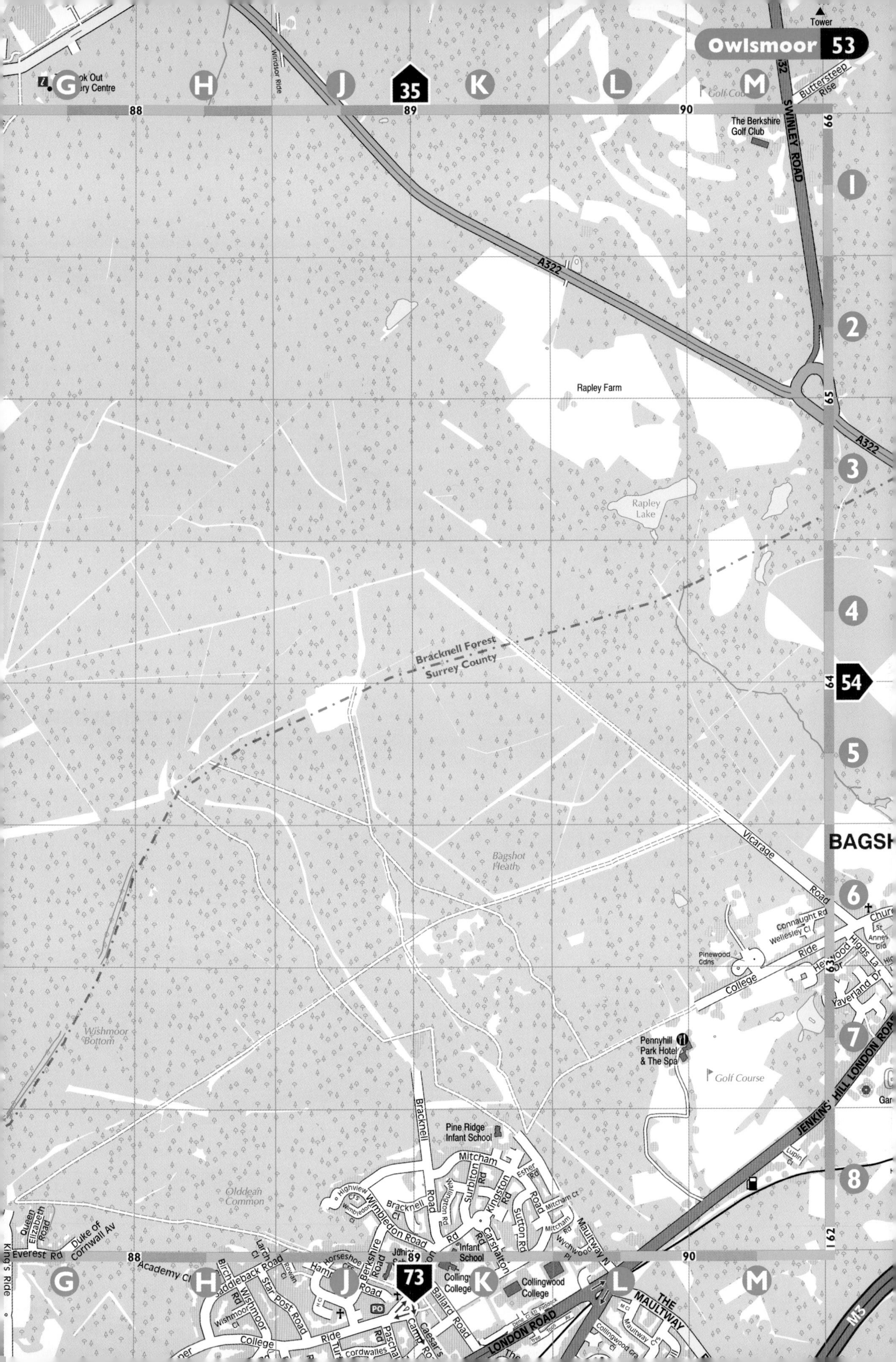

G H J 35 K L M

88 89 90

Tower

Look Out Discovery Centre

Windsor Ride

Golf Co...

Butterstee... Rise

The Berkshire Golf Club

SWINLEY ROAD

1

2

A322

Rapley Farm

3

Rapley Lake

4

Bracknell Forest
Surrey County

54

5

Bagshot Heath

BAGSH

Vicarage Road

6

Connaught Rd
Wellesley Cl
College Ride

Pinewood Gdns

Heywood Dr

Church St
Annes Dr

Yaverland Dr

7

Pennyhill Park Hotel & The Spa

Golf Course

JENKINS HILL LONDON ROAD

Wishmoor Bottom

Bracknell Road

Pine Ridge Infant School

Mitcham

Sturbiton Rd

Kingston Rd

Esher Rd

Carshalton Rd

Mitcham Ct.

Maultway N

Wychwood Pl

8

Olddean Common

Highview
Windlesham
Bracknell Cl
Wimbledon Road
Larch Cl
Horseshoe Rd
Hamlet
Berkshire Road
73
Walburton Rd
Junior
Infant School
Sutton Rd
Sutton Rd
Mitcham Rd

Queen Elizabeth Road
Duke of Cornwall Av
King's Ride

Academy Cl

Birch Rd
Saddleback Rd
Star Post Road
Wishmoor Rd
College Ride
Rowan
Turf
Cordwalles
Paschal
Caesar's Rd
Ballard Rd

Collingwood College
Collingwood College

LONDON ROAD

THE MAULTWAY

M3

G H J 35 K L M

88 89 90

73

PO

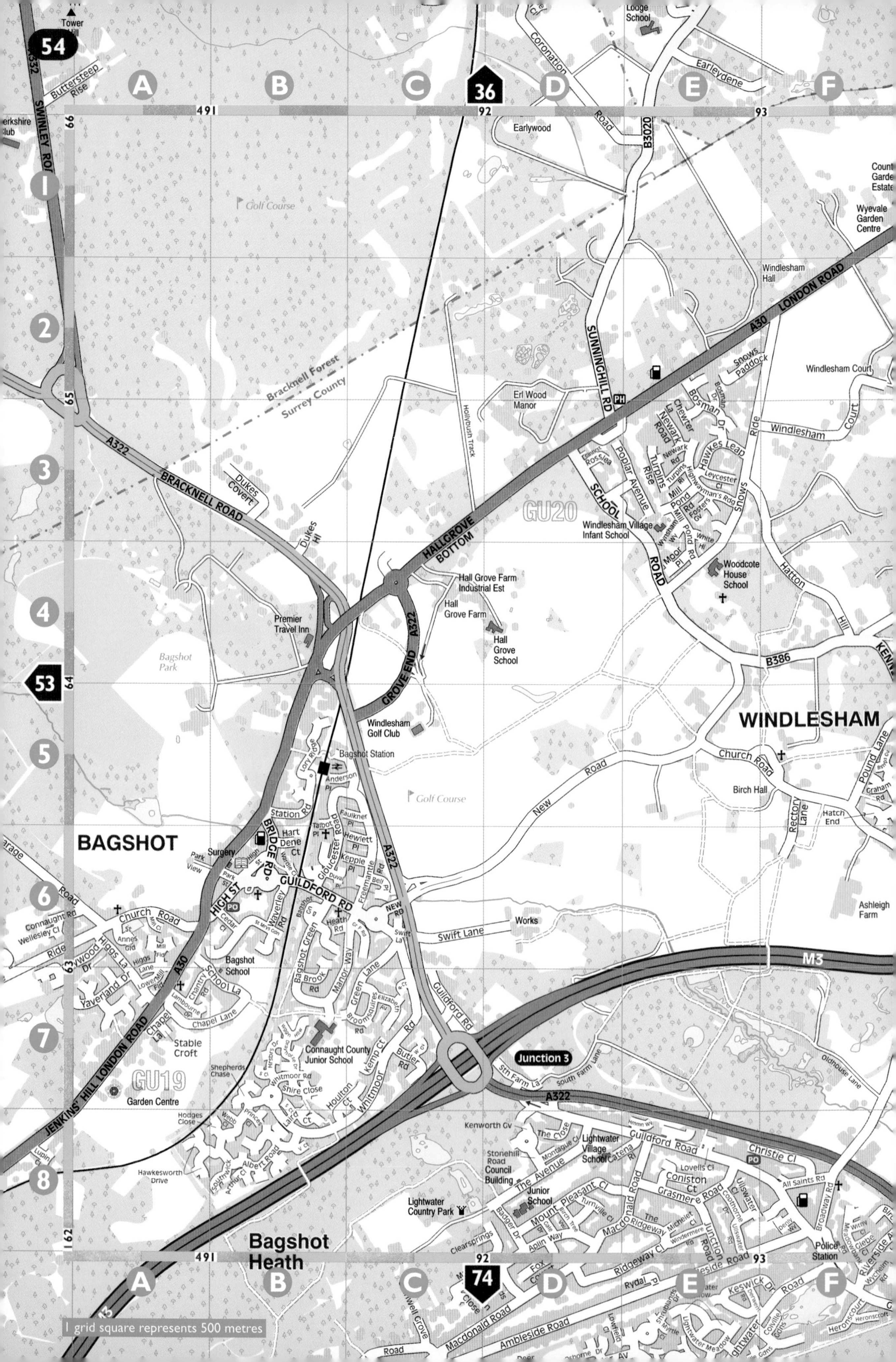

54
36
53
74
A
B
C
D
E
F
1
2
3
4
5
6
7
8
BAGSHOT
WINDLESHAM
Bagshot Heath
GU19
GU20
Brackwell Forest
Surrey County
A322
BRACKNELL ROAD
HALLGROVE BOTTOM
A30 LONDON ROAD
GROVE END
SUNNINGHILL RD
B3020
B386
M3
Junction 3
JENKINS' HILL LONDON ROAD
GUILDFORD RD
HIGH ST
BRIDGE RD
Bagshot Station
Bagshot School
Connaught County Junior School
Windlesham Golf Club
Golf Course
Hall Grove Farm Industrial Est
Hall Grove Farm
Hall Grove School
Premier Travel Inn
Bagshot Park
Erl Wood Manor
Windlesham Village Infant School
Woodcote House School
Windlesham Hall
Windlesham Court
Wyevale Garden Centre
Birch Hall
Hatch End
Ashleigh Farm
Works
Swift Lane
New Road
Church Road
Rectory Lane
Pound Lane
Snows Ride
Hatton Hill
Earlywood
Coronation Road
Earleydene
Lightwater Village School
Lightwater Country Park
Stonehill Road Council Building
Junior School
Guildford Road
Christie Cl
Police Station
Garden Centre
Stable Croft
Hawkesworth Drive
Shepherds Chase
Hodges Close
Dukes Covert
Dukes Hl
Hollybush Track
Surgery
Lightwater Meadow
Macdonald Road
Ambleside Road
Ridgeway Cl
1 grid square represents 500 metres

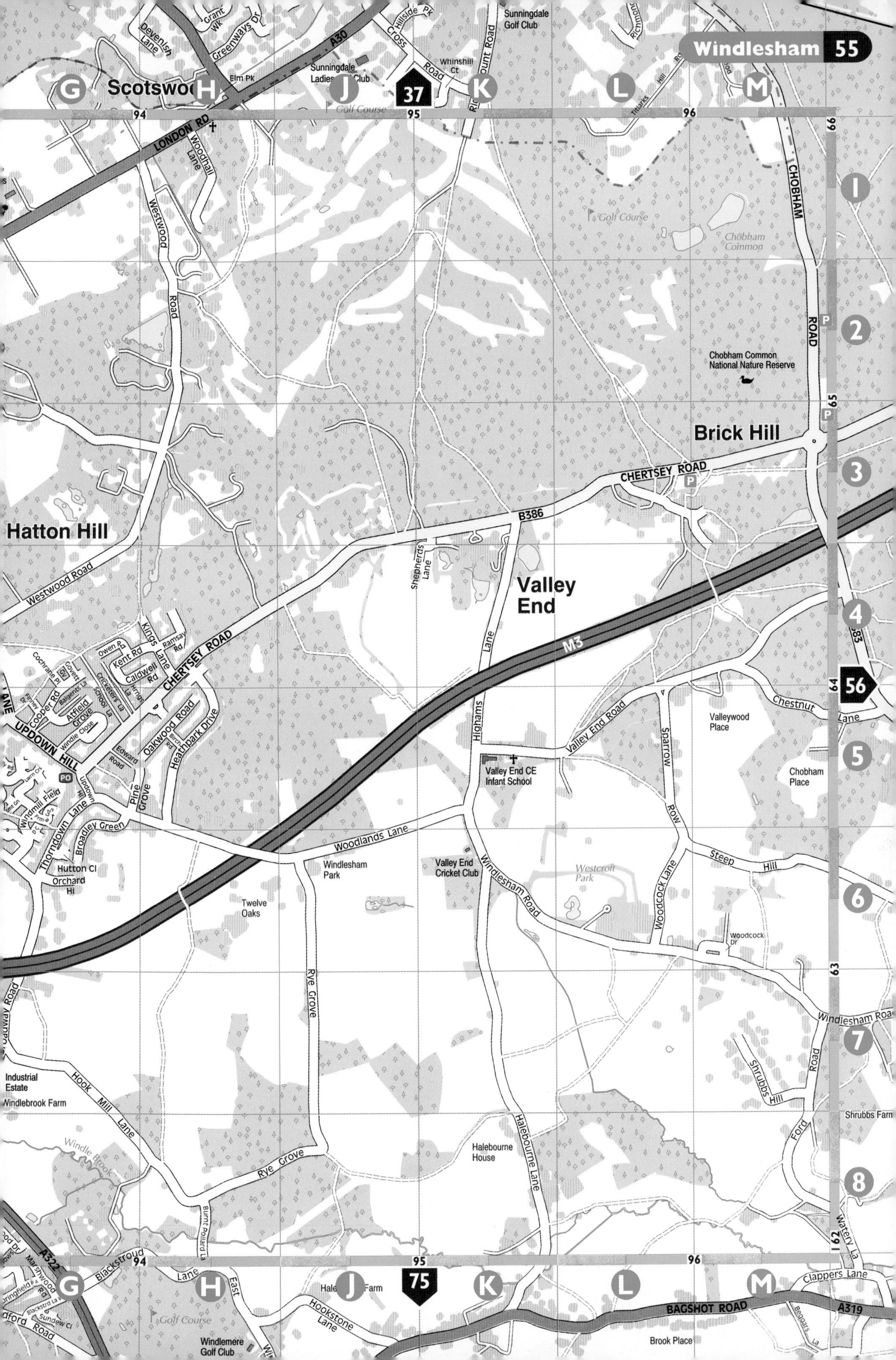
Scotswood
Hatton Hill
Brick Hill
Valley End
Sunningdale Golf Club
Sunningdale Ladies Golf Club
Golf Course
Chobham Common
Chobham Common National Nature Reserve
CHERTSEY ROAD
B386
M3
LONDON RD
A30
CHOBHAM ROAD
Westwood Road
Woodhall Lane
Devenish Lane
Greenways Dr
Cross Road
Hillside Pk
Whinshill Ct
Elm Pk
Kings Lane
Ramsay Rd
Kent Rd
Owen Rd
Caldwell Rd
Cochrane Pl
Cooper Rd
Baigents La
Attfield Grove
Windle Close
Cricketers La
School La
Oakwood Road
Heathpark Drive
Edward Road
Pine Grove
Updown Hill
UPDOWN HILL
Windmill Field
Thorndown Lane
Broadley Green
Hutton Cl
Orchard Hi
Woodlands Lane
Windlesham Park
Twelve Oaks
Shepherds Lane
Highams Lane
Valley End CE Infant School
Valley End Road
Valley End Cricket Club
Windlesham Road
Westcroft Park
Sparrow Row
Woodcock Lane
Woodcock Dr
Steep Hill
Chestnut Lane
Valleywood Place
Chobham Place
Windlesham Road
Shrubbs Hill
Ford Road
Shrubbs Farm
Watery La
Rye Grove
Hook Mill Lane
Industrial Estate
Windlebrook Farm
Windle Brook
Burnt Pollard La
Halebourne Lane
Halebourne House
Blackstroud
A322
Blackstrd La
Sundew Cl
Lane
East
Hale Farm
Hookstone Lane
Windlemere Golf Club
BAGSHOT ROAD
A319
Clappers Lane
Brook Place
Beggars La
37
56
75

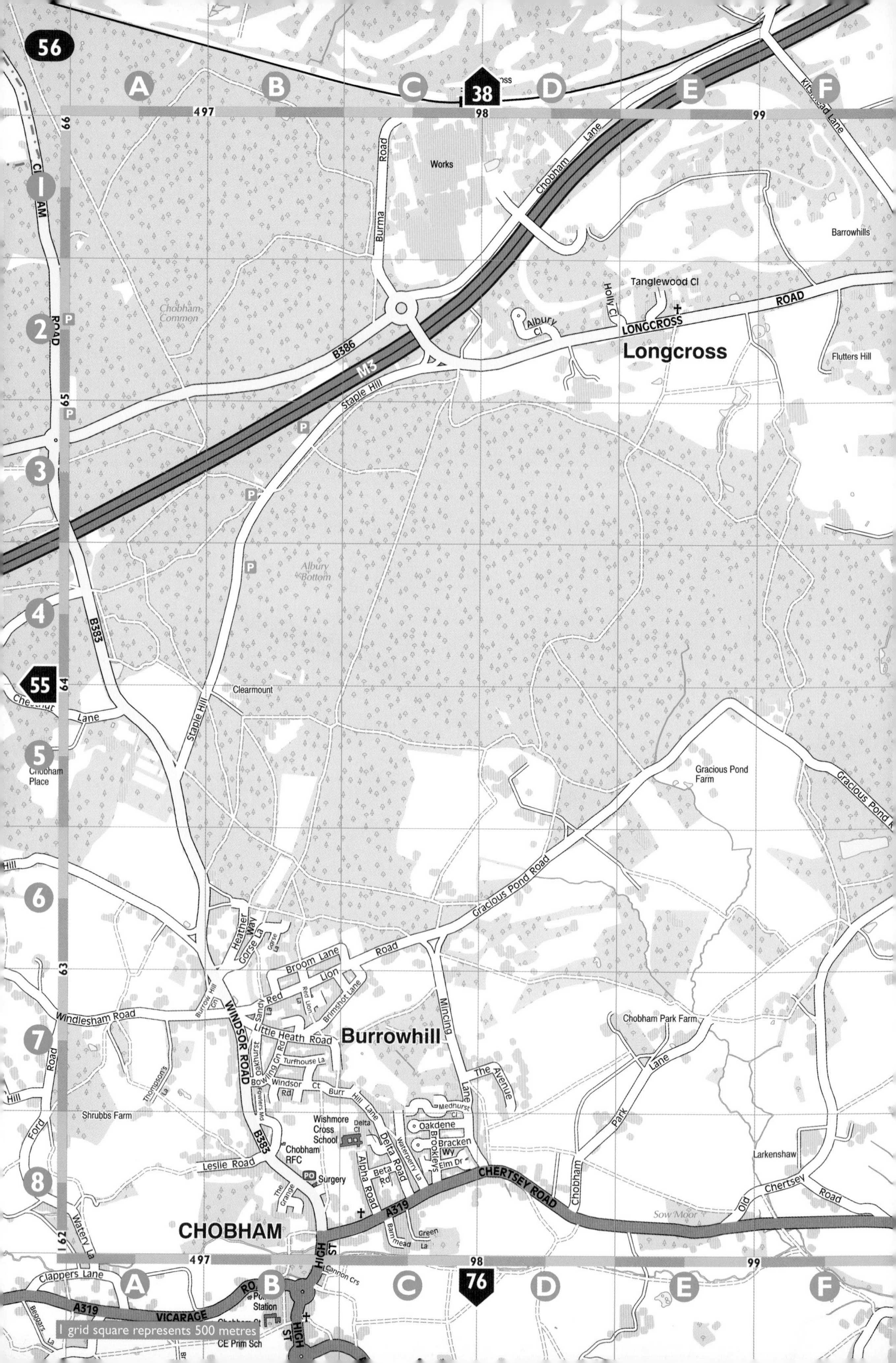

A
B
C
D
E
F
38
497
98
99
1
2
3
4
5
6
7
8
55
76
Works
Burma Road
Chobham Lane
Kitsmead Lane
Barrowhills
Tanglewood Cl
Holly Cl
Albury Cl
LONGCROSS ROAD
Longcross
Flutters Hill
Chobham Common
B386
M3
Staple Hill
Albury Bottom
B383
Clearmount
Chestnut Lane
Chobham Place
Gracious Pond Farm
Gracious Pond Road
Heather Way
Gorse La
Broom Lane
Road
Red Lion
Brimshot Lane
Sandy La
Windlesham Road
WINDSOR ROAD
Burrow Hill Grn
Little Heath Road
Burrowhill
Mincing Lane
The Avenue
Chobham Park Farm
Park Lane
Bowling Gn Rd
Turfhouse La
Windsor Ct Rd
Burr Hill Lane
Thompson's La
Fowlers Md
Shrubbs Farm
Ford Road
Wishmore Cross School
Delta Cl
Delta Road
Waterperry La
Mednurst Cl
Oakdene
Brookleys
Bracken Wy
Elm Dr
Chobham RFC
Leslie Road
Surgery
Alpha Road
Beta Rd
The Grange
CHERTSEY ROAD
A319
Chobham
Larkenshaw
Old Chertsey Road
Sow Moor
Barrmead
Green La
CHOBHAM
HIGH ST
Watery La
Clappers Lane
Cannon Crs
VICARAGE ROAD
Police Station
Chobham St Lawrence CE Prim Sch
Beggars La

1 grid square represents 500 metres

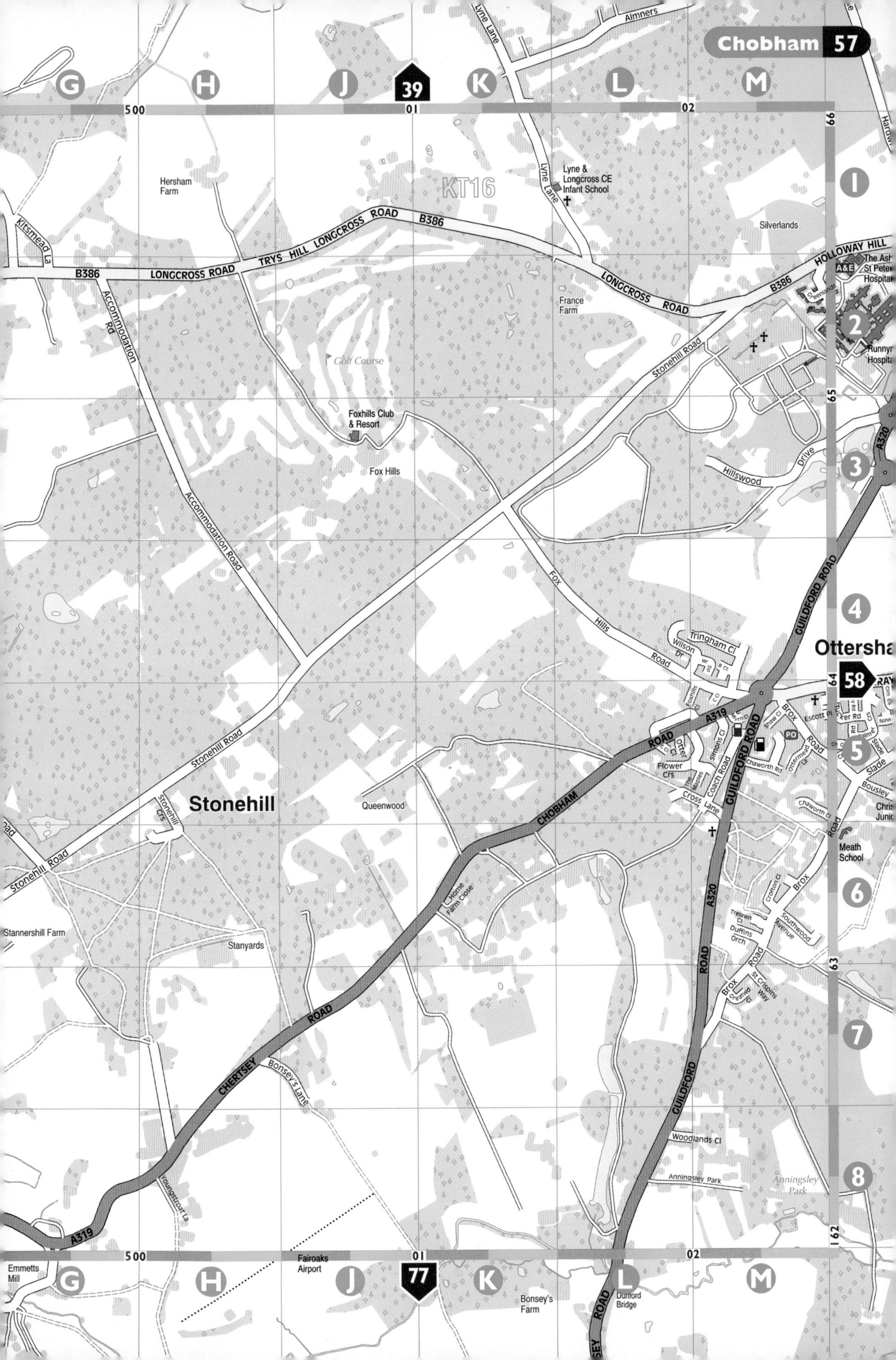

Lyne Lane
Almners
39
G
H
J
K
L
M
500
01
02
66
Hersham Farm
KT16
Lyne & Longcross CE Infant School
Silverlands
I
Kitsmead La
B386
LONGCROSS ROAD
TRYS HILL LONGCROSS ROAD
HOLLOWAY HILL
Accommodation Rd
France Farm
Golf Course
Stonehill Road
2
Foxhills Club & Resort
Fox Hills
65
Hillswood Drive
A320
3
Accommodation Road
Fox Hills Road
GUILDFORD ROAD
4
Tringham Cl
Wilson Dr
Ottersha
58
64
A319
CHOBHAM ROAD
Brox Road
Escott Pl
Flower Crs
Simons Cl
Coach Road
Chaworth Rd
Ottermead La
5
Slade
Stonehill Road
Stonehill Crs
Stonehill
Queenwood
Cross Lane
Bousley
Chaworth Cl
Meath School
6
Home Farm Close
Crofton Cl
Trelawn Cl
Duffins Orch
Southwood Avenue
Stannershill Farm
Stanyards
63
St Crispins Way
7
CHERTSEY ROAD
Bonsey's Lane
GUILDFORD ROAD
Woodlands Cl
Anningsley Park
8
Youngstroat La
A319
62
Emmetts Mill
Fairoaks Airport
77
Bonsey's Farm
Dunford Bridge

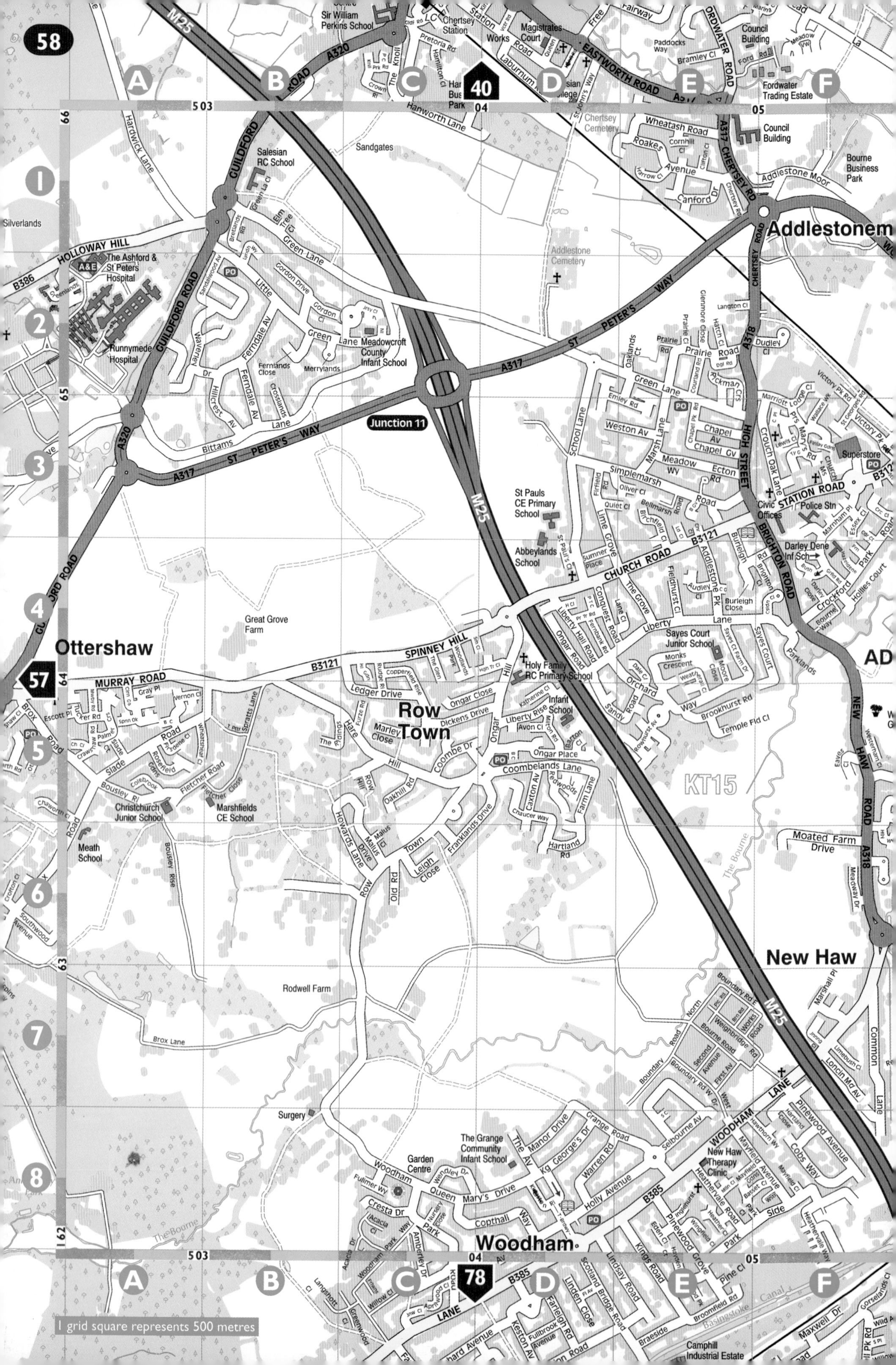

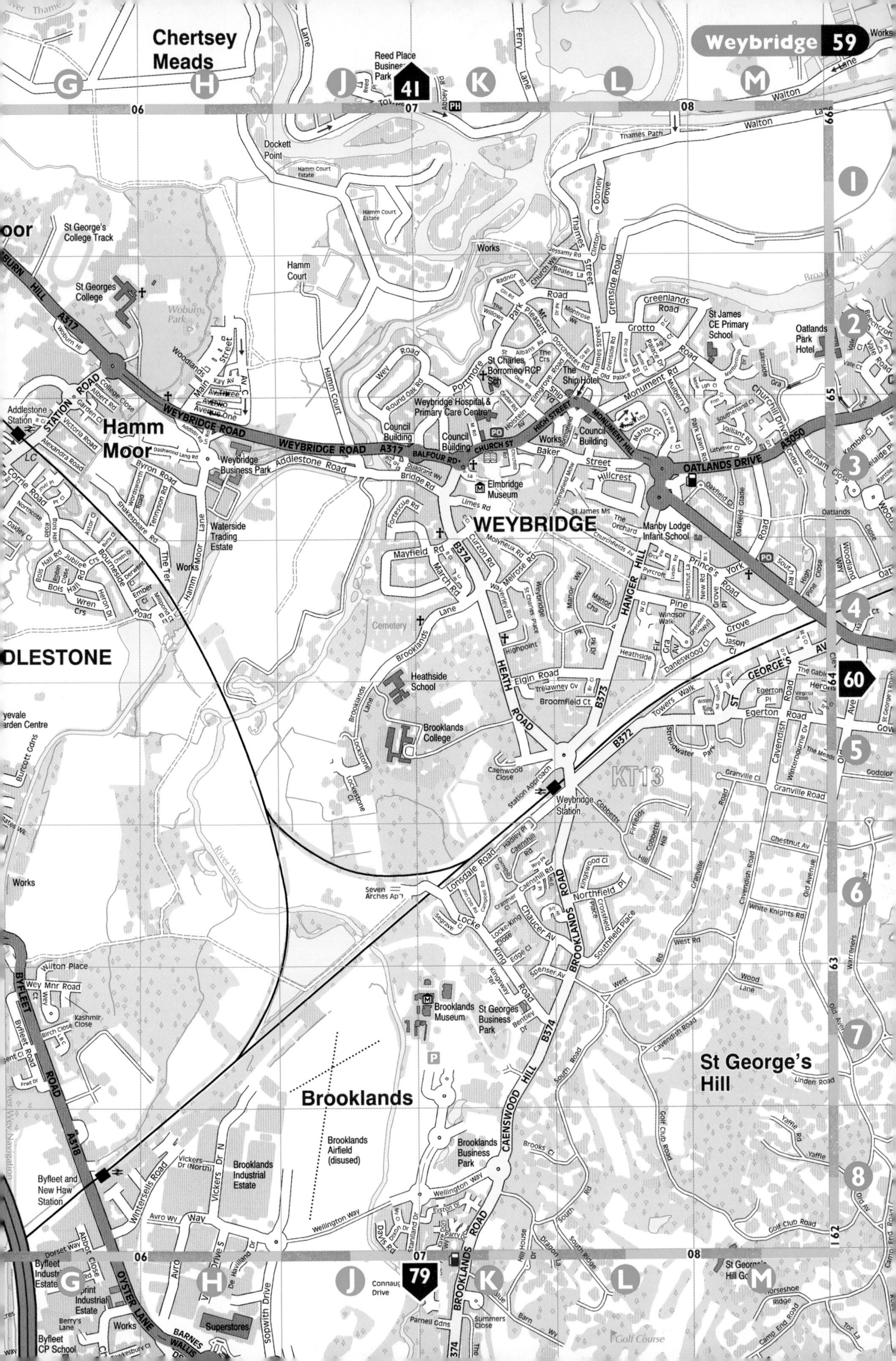
Chertsey Meads
Reed Place Business Park
41
Dockett Point
Hamm Court Estate
St George's College Track
Hamm Court
St Georges College
Woburn Park
Addlestone Station
Hamm Moor
Weybridge Road
Weybridge Business Park
Waterside Trading Estate
Works
DLESTONE
Weybridge Hospital & Primary Care Centre
St Charles Borromeo RCP Sch
Council Building
Elmbridge Museum
WEYBRIDGE
The Ship Hotel
Monument Hill
Oatlands Drive
St James CE Primary School
Oatlands Park Hotel
Manby Lodge Infant School
Heathside School
Brooklands College
Cemetery
Weybridge Station
KT13
Seven Arches Ap
Brooklands Museum
St Georges Business Park
Brooklands
Brooklands Airfield (disused)
Brooklands Business Park
Brooklands Industrial Estate
Byfleet and New Haw Station
St George's Hill
Caenswood Hill
Heath Road
Hanger Hill
St George's Av
Byfleet Road
Oyster Lane
Superstores
Byfleet CP School
60
79
Golf Course

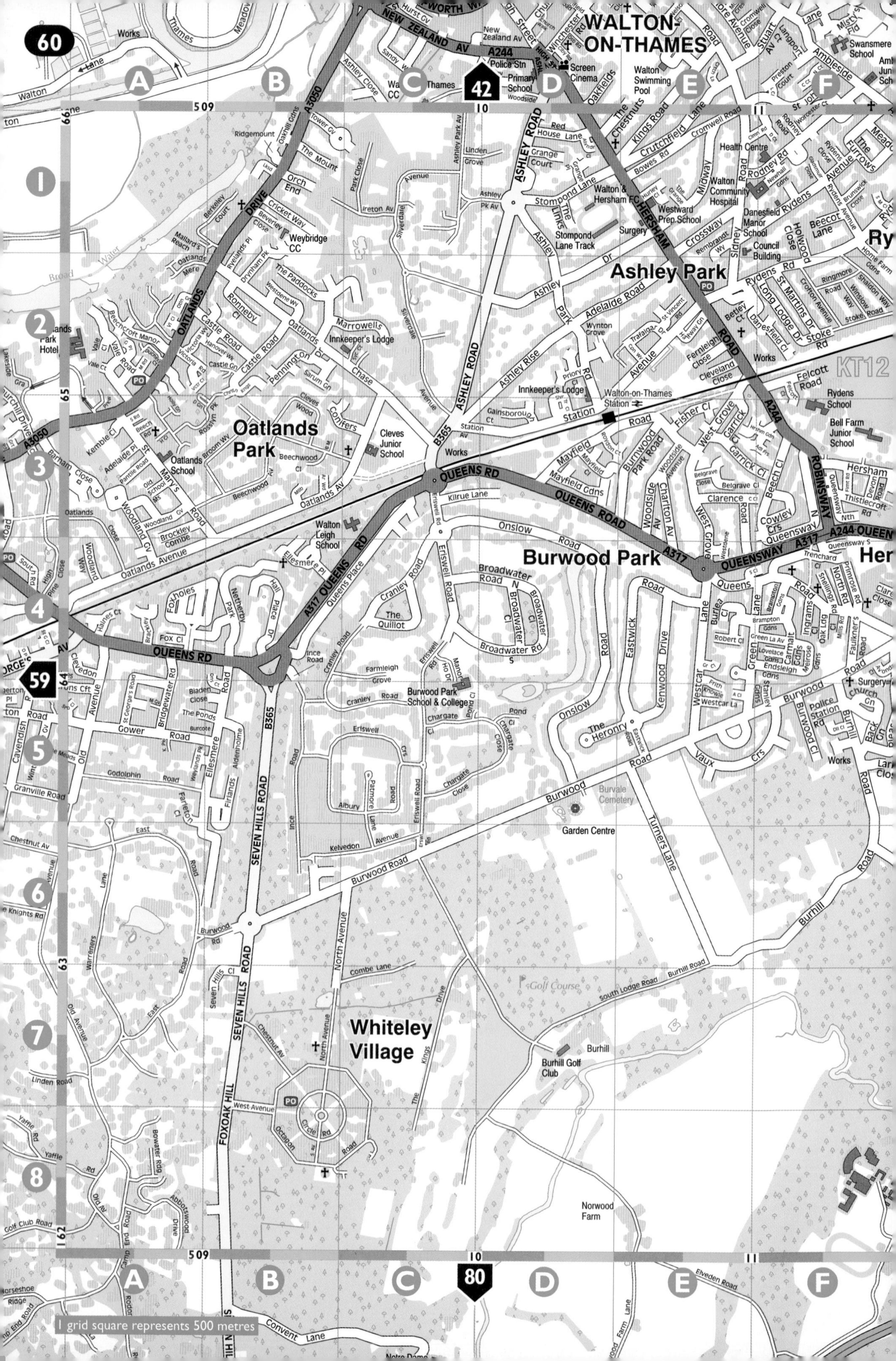

60
WALTON-
ON-THAMES
Walton Swimming Pool
Screen Cinema
Police Stn
Primary School
New Zealand Av
NEW ZEALAND AV
A244
42
Swansmere School
Oakhill Gdns
Ridgemount
Tower Gv
The Mount
Orch End
Cricket Way
Beverley Close
Weybridge CC
Berkeley Court
Mallard's Reach
Oatlands Mere
OATLANDS DRIVE
A3050
Broad Water
Ronneby Cl
Drynham Pk
Ryelands Pl
The Paddocks
Westdene Wy
Marrowells
Innkeeper's Lodge
Oatlands Chase
Castle Road
Beechcroft Manor
Vale Road
Oatlands Park Hotel
Victoria Wy
Hanover Wk
Castle Gn
Pennington Dr
Sarum Gn
Rossyln Pk
Oatlands Park
Oatlands School
Kemble Cl
Adelaide Pl
Pantile Road
Old School Ms
St Mary's Road
Woodland Gv
Woodland Way
Oatlands Close
Brockley Combe
Oatlands Avenue
Barham Close
Beechwood Cl
Beechwood Av
Conifers
Cleves Wood
Cleves Junior School
Oatlands Av
Park Close
Ireton Av
Silverdale Avenue
Silverdale
Linden Grove
Ashley Park Av
Ashley Pk Av
ASHLEY ROAD
Red House Lane
Grange Court
Stompond Lane
The Links
Stompond Lane Track
Walton & Hersham FC
Westward Prep School
Surgery
HERSHAM ROAD
Ashley Park
Ashley Dr
Ashley Park
Adelaide Road
Wynton Grove
Ashley Rise
Priory Rd
Innkeeper's Lodge
Gainsborough Ct
Station Av
Station Road
Walton-on-Thames Station
B365
Works
Crutchfield Lane
Kings Road
Bowes Rd
Cromwell Road
Midway
Crossway
Walton Community Hospital
Health Centre
Rodney Rd
Danesfield Manor School
Council Building
Rydens Rd
Rydens Avenue
Holwood Close
Beecot Lane
Long Lodge Dr
St Martins Dr
Crofton Avenue
Ringmore Road
Stoke Rd
Fernleigh Close
Cleveland Close
Felcott Road
KT12
Rydens School
Bell Farm Junior School
Hersham
A244
ROBINSWAY
Queensway
Thistlecroft
QUEENS RD
QUEENS ROAD
A317
Kilrue Lane
Onslow Road
Mayfield Gdns
Burwood Park Road
Woodside Av
Charlton Av
West Grove
Fisher Cl
Garrick Cl
Belgrave Cl
Clarence Road
Beech Cl
Cowley Crs
QUEENSWAY
Burwood Park
Walton Leigh School
Ellesmere Pl
QUEENS RD
Queens Place
Craniey Road
The Quillot
Erswell Road
Broadwater Road
Broadwater Cl
Broadwater Rd
Foxholes
Netherby Park
Hall Place Dr
Haines Ct
Fox Cl
59
Clevedon
Old Avenue
Bridgewater Rd
Gower Road
Bladen Close
The Ponds
Ellesmere Road
Aldenholme
Firlands
Godolphin Road
Granville Road
Cavendish Road
Farleton Cl
Ince Road
Farmleigh Grove
Cranley Road
Burwood Park School & College
Chargate Cl
Chargate Close
Pond Cl
Erriswell Crs
Albury
Patmore Lane
Kelvedon Avenue
Onslow Road
The Heronry
Eastwick Road
Kenwood Drive
Westcar Lane
Westcar La
Burlea Cl
Green Lane
Robert Cl
Lovelace Gdns
Endsleigh Gdns
Ingrams Cl
Faulkner's Road
Surgery
Church Gn
Police Station
Burwood Cl
Burhill Road
Vaux Crs
Burwood Road
Burvale Cemetery
Garden Centre
Turners Lane
Works
Chestnut Av
East Road
Knights Rd
Burwood Rd
Warreners Lane
SEVEN HILLS ROAD
Seven Hills Cl
North Avenue
Combe Lane
Golf Course
Burhill Road
South Lodge Road
Burhill
Burhill Golf Club
Whiteley Village
Chestnut Av
The Kings Drive
FOXOAK HILL
West Avenue
Circle Rd
Octagon Road
Linden Road
Yaffle Rd
Yaffle Rd
Bowater Rdg
Abbotswood Drive
Old Av
Golf Club Road
Camp End Road
Norwood Farm
Horseshoe Ridge
509
10
11
66
65
64
63
62
A
B
C
D
E
F
1
2
3
4
5
6
7
8
80
Elveden Road
Convent Lane
Notre Dame
1 grid square represents 500 metres

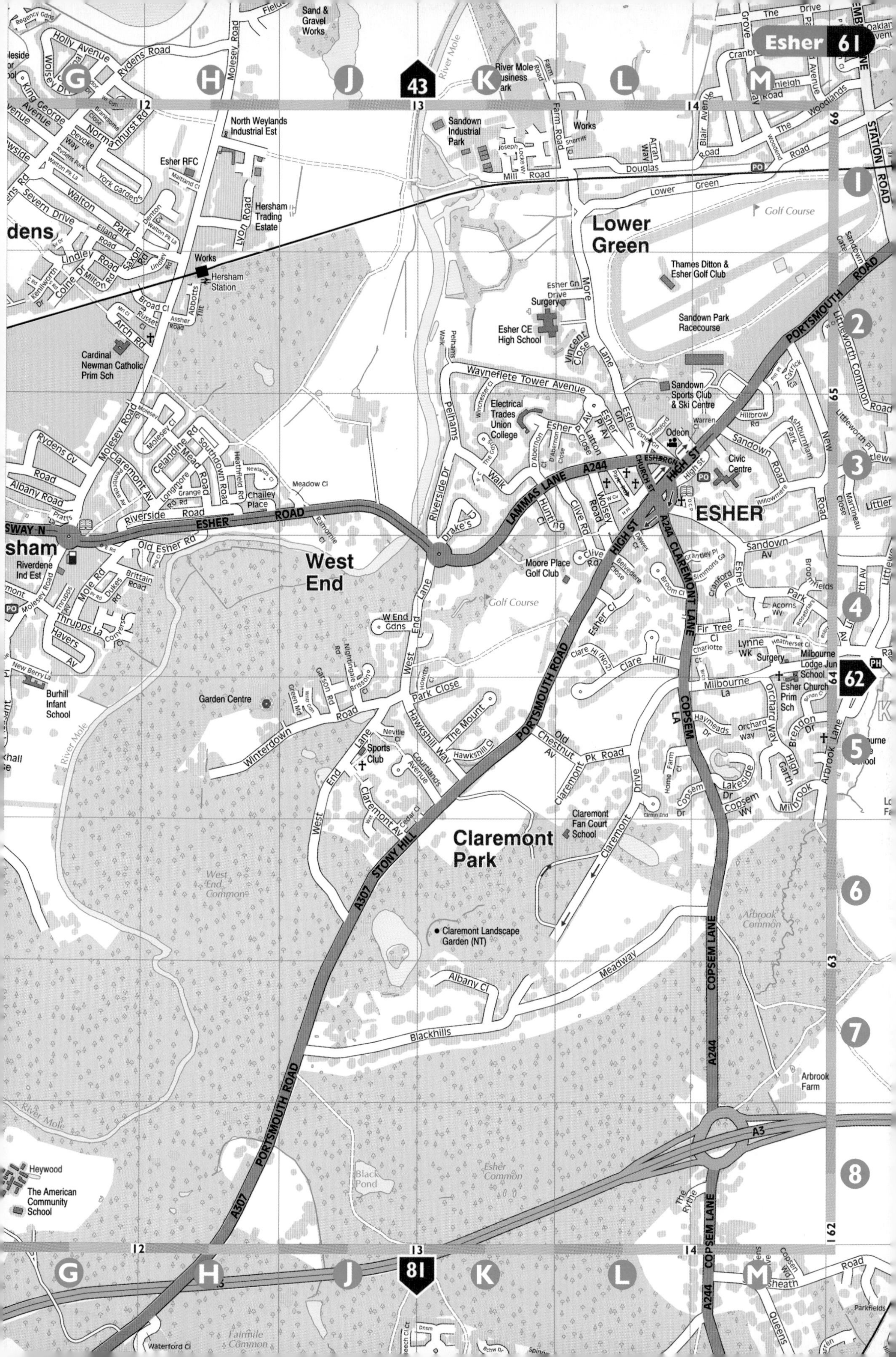
Sand & Gravel Works
River Mole
River Mole Business Park
North Weylands Industrial Est
Sandown Industrial Park
Works
Esher RFC
Hersham Trading Estate
Lower Green
Golf Course
Thames Ditton & Esher Golf Club
Sandown Park Racecourse
Works
Hersham Station
Cardinal Newman Catholic Prim Sch
Surgery
Esher CE High School
Sandown Sports Club & Ski Centre
Electrical Trades Union College
Odeon
Civic Centre
ESHER
Riverdene Ind Est
West End
Moore Place Golf Club
Golf Course
Burhill Infant School
Garden Centre
Sports Club
Surgery
Milbourne Lodge Jun School
Esher Church Prim Sch
Claremont Fan Court School
Claremont Park
West End Common
Claremont Landscape Garden (NT)
Arbrook Common
Arbrook Farm
Heywood
The American Community School
Black Pond
Esher Common
Fairmile Common
Holly Avenue
Rydens Road
Molesey Road
Lyon Road
Mill Road
Douglas Road
Lower Green Road
Station Road
Portsmouth Road
Wayneflete Tower Avenue
Lammas Lane
A244
High St
Church St
Claremont Lane
Esher Road
Riverside Road
Old Esher Rd
Winterdown Road
West End Lane
Hawkshill Way
Park Close
The Mount
Stony Hill
A307
Copsem Lane
Clare Hill
Milbourne La
Blackhills
Meadway
Albany Cl
Claremont Drive
Old Chestnut Av
Sandown Road
Sandown Av
Esher Park Av
Fir Tree Cl
Orchard Way
Arbrook Lane
Littleworth Common Road
A3
43
62
81
G H J K L M
1 2 3 4 5 6 7 8

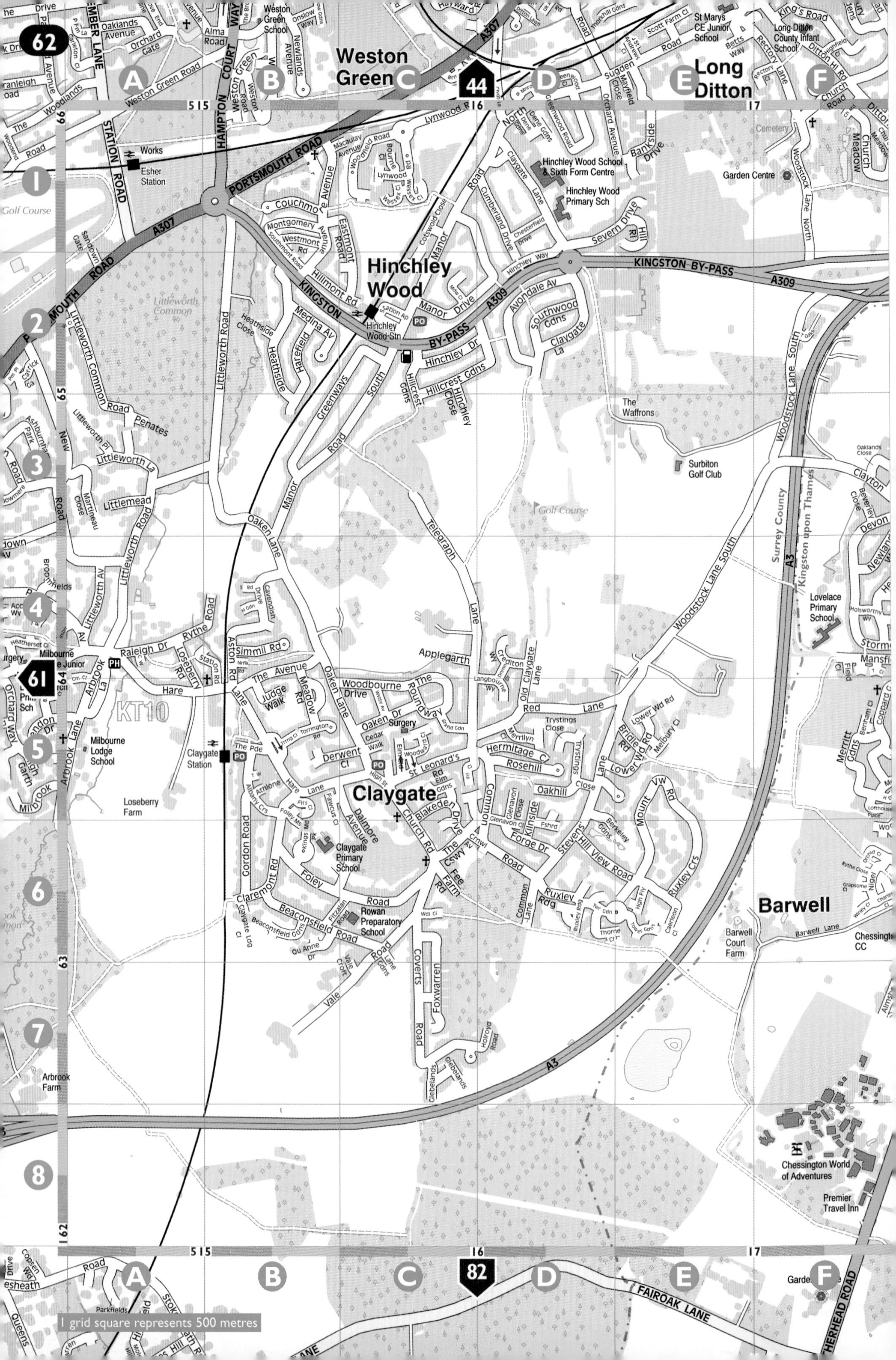
62
Weston Green
Long Ditton
44
Hinchley Wood
Claygate
Barwell
KT10
61
82
Esher Station
Works
Golf Course
Littleworth Common
PORTSMOUTH ROAD
HAMPTON COURT WAY
STATION ROAD
KINGSTON BY-PASS
A307
A309
A3
Weston Green Road
Weston Green School
St Marys CE Junior School
Long Ditton County Infant School
Hinchley Wood School & Sixth Form Centre
Hinchley Wood Primary Sch
Hinchley Wood Stn
Garden Centre
Cemetery
The Waffrons
Surbiton Golf Club
Surrey County
Kingston upon Thames
Woodstock Lane South
Woodstock Lane North
Lovelace Primary School
Littleworth Road
Littleworth Common Road
Oaken Lane
Telegraph Lane
Manor Road
Greenways
Milbourne Lodge School
Claygate Station
Loseberry Farm
Claygate Primary School
Rowan Preparatory School
Barwell Court Farm
Barwell Lane
Chessington CC
Chessington World of Adventures
Premier Travel Inn
Arbrook Farm
Arbrook Lane
Red Lane
Hare Lane
Foley Road
Beaconsfield Road
Gordon Road
Claremont Rd
Coverts Road
Foxwarren
Holroyd Road
Common Road
Ruxley Crs
Hill View Road
Fee Farm Rd
FAIROAK LANE
HERHEAD ROAD
1 grid square represents 500 metres

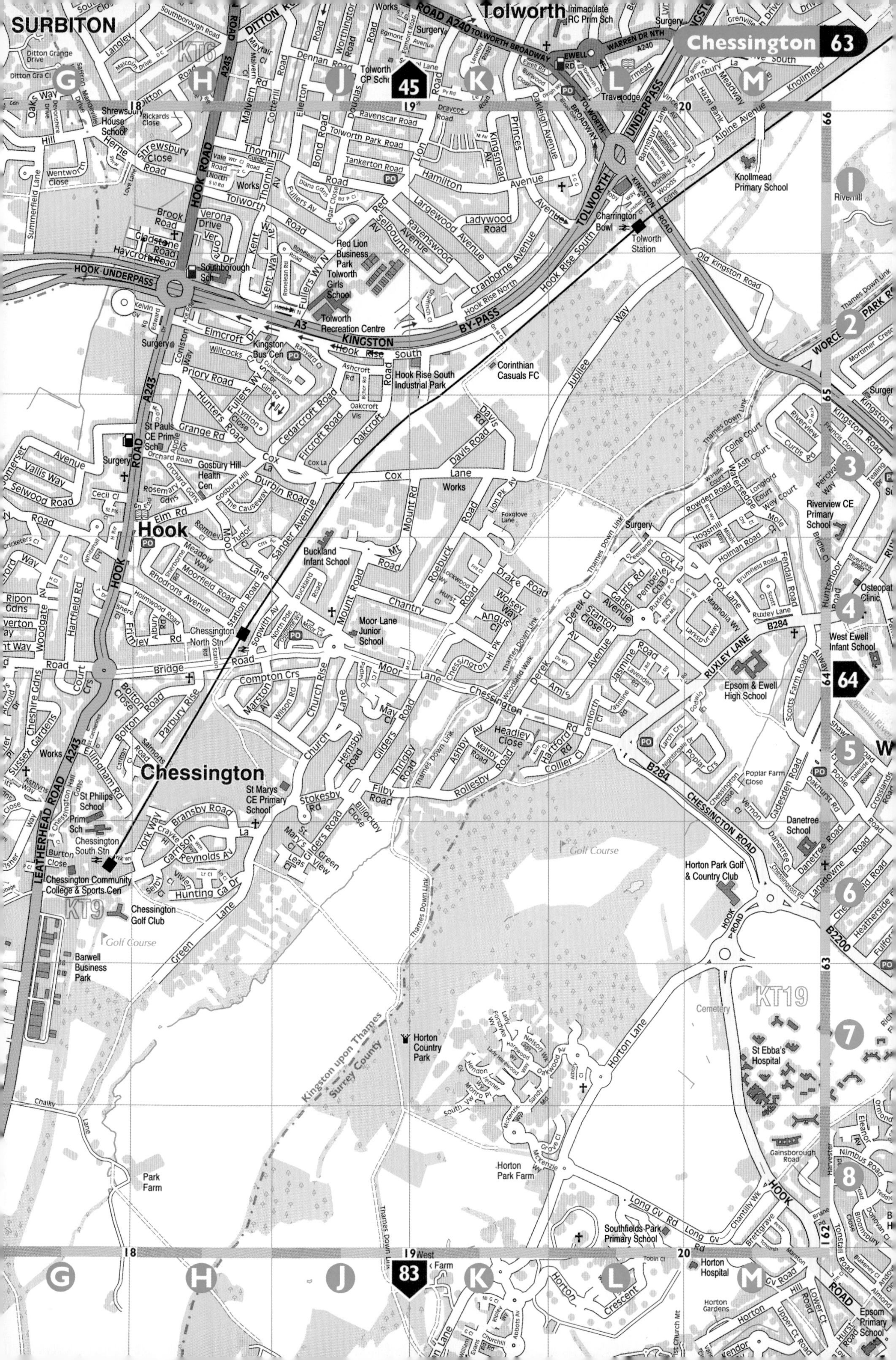
SURBITON
Tolworth
Hook
Chessington
KT6
KT9
KT19
45
64
83
HOOK ROAD
HOOK UNDERPASS
KINGSTON BY-PASS
TOLWORTH BROADWAY
TOLWORTH UNDERPASS
LEATHERHEAD ROAD
CHESSINGTON ROAD
RUXLEY LANE
Tolworth Station
Chessington North Stn
Chessington South Stn
Horton Country Park
Golf Course
Horton Park Golf & Country Club
St Ebba's Hospital
Epsom & Ewell High School
Chessington Community College & Sports Cen
Chessington Golf Club
Barwell Business Park
Kingston upon Thames
Surrey County
Thames Down Link

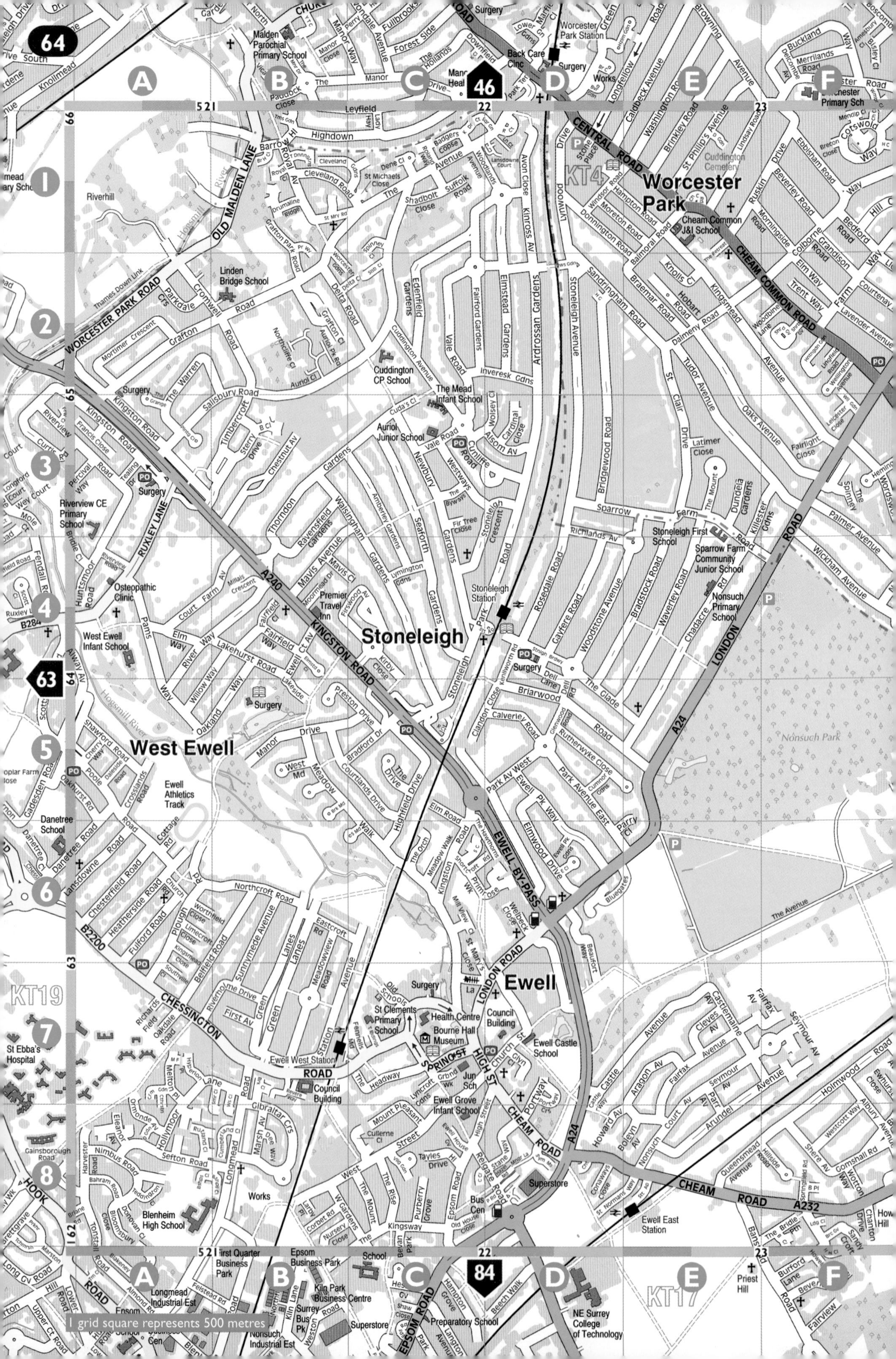
64
46
63
84
A
B
C
D
E
F
1
2
3
4
5
6
7
8
521
22
23
66
65
64
63
62
Worcester Park
Stoneleigh
West Ewell
Ewell
KT4
KT19
KT17
Malden Parochial Primary School
Worcester Park Station
Back Care Clinic
Surgery
Cheam Common J&I School
Cuddington Cemetery
Linden Bridge School
Cuddington CP School
The Mead Infant School
Auriol Junior School
Riverview CE Primary School
Osteopathic Clinic
West Ewell Infant School
Premier Travel Inn
Stoneleigh Station
Stoneleigh First School
Sparrow Farm Community Junior School
Nonsuch Primary School
Nonsuch Park
Ewell Athletics Track
Danetree School
St Ebba's Hospital
Ewell West Station
Council Building
St Clements Primary School
Health Centre
Bourne Hall Museum
Ewell Castle School
Ewell Grove Infant School
Superstore
Bus Cen
Ewell East Station
Blenheim High School
First Quarter Business Park
Epsom Business Park
Kiln Park Business Centre
Longmead Industrial Est
Nonsuch Industrial Est
Surrey Bus Pk
Preparatory School
NE Surrey College of Technology
Priest Hill
Cheam Common Road
Central Road
Worcester Park Road
Old Malden Lane
Kingston Road
A240
Ruxley Lane
London Road
A24
Ewell-By-Pass
Chessington Road
B2200
B284
Cheam Road
A232
High St
Spring St
Epsom Road
Hook Road
1 grid square represents 500 metres

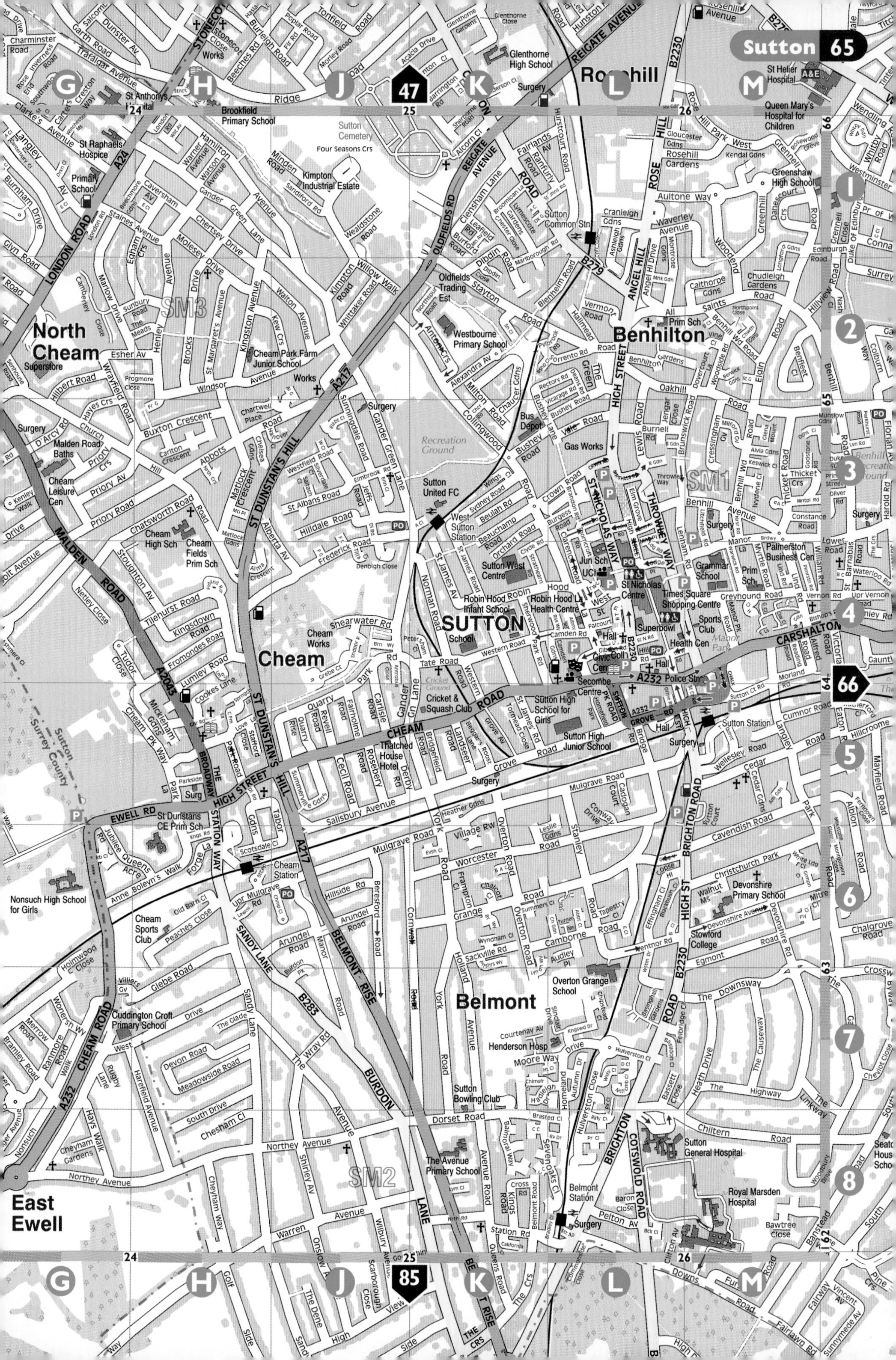
North Cheam
Cheam
SUTTON
Benhilton
Rosehill
Belmont
East Ewell
SM1
SM2
SM3
47
66
85

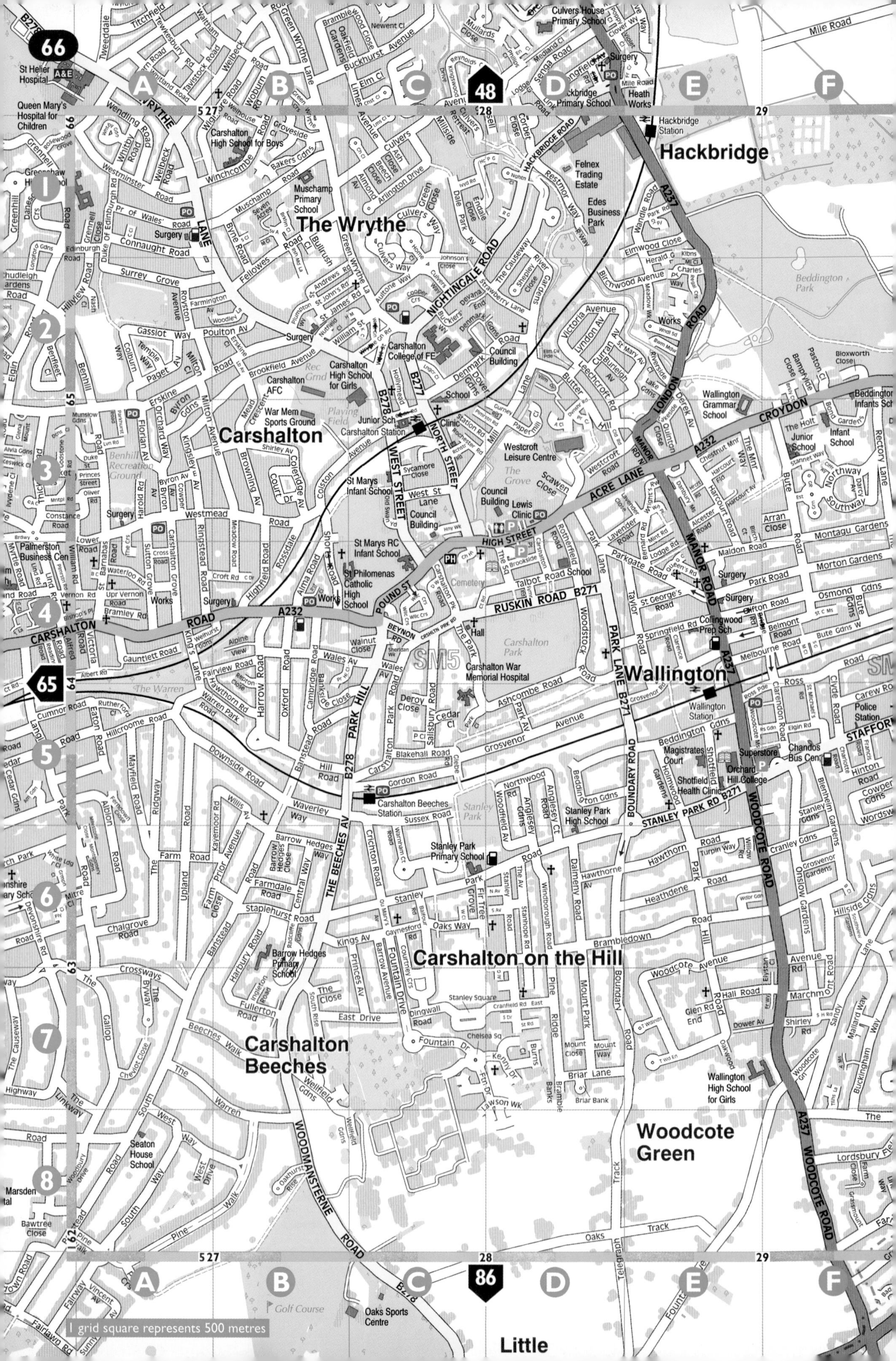

66
48
65
86
A
B
C
D
E
F
1
2
3
4
5
6
7
8
527
28
29
63
64
65
66
St Helier Hospital
A&E
Queen Mary's Hospital for Children
Culvers House Primary School
Hackbridge Primary School
Hackbridge Station
Hackbridge
Mile Road
Heath Works
Surgery
Felnex Trading Estate
Edes Business Park
Carshalton High School for Boys
Muschamp Primary School
The Wrythe
Wrythe Lane
Green Wrythe Lane
Nightingale Road
Hackbridge Road
London Road
A237
Beddington Park
Wallington Grammar School
Beddington Infants School
The Holt Junior School
Infant School
Croydon Road
A232
Acre Lane
Manor Road
Carshalton College of FE
Carshalton High School for Girls
Carshalton AFC
War Mem Sports Ground
Playing Field
Rec Grnd
Carshalton
Junior Sch
Carshalton Station
North Street
West Street
B277
B278
Clinic
Westcroft Leisure Centre
The Grove
Council Building
Lewis Clinic
High Street
St Marys Infant School
St Marys RC Infant School
St Philomenas Catholic High School
Benhill Recreation Ground
Palmerston Business Cen
Carshalton Road
Pound St
Beynon Rd
Ruskin Road B271
Talbot Road School
Cemetery
Carshalton Park
Carshalton War Memorial Hospital
SM5
Hall
Collingwood Prep Sch
Wallington
Wallington Station
Park Lane B271
Police Station
Chandos Bus Cen
Superstore
Magistrates Court
Orchard Hill College
Shotfield Health Clinic
Stanley Park Rd B271
Stanley Park High School
Boundary Road
Woodcote Road
The Warren
Park Hill
Carshalton Beeches Station
Stanley Park
Stanley Park Primary School
The Beeches Av
Barrow Hedges Primary School
Carshalton on the Hill
Carshalton Beeches
Seaton House School
Woodmansterne Road
Wallington High School for Girls
Woodcote Green
Briar Bank
Track
Oaks Track
Telegraph Track
Golf Course
Oaks Sports Centre
Little
Marsden
Bawtree Close
1 grid square represents 500 metres

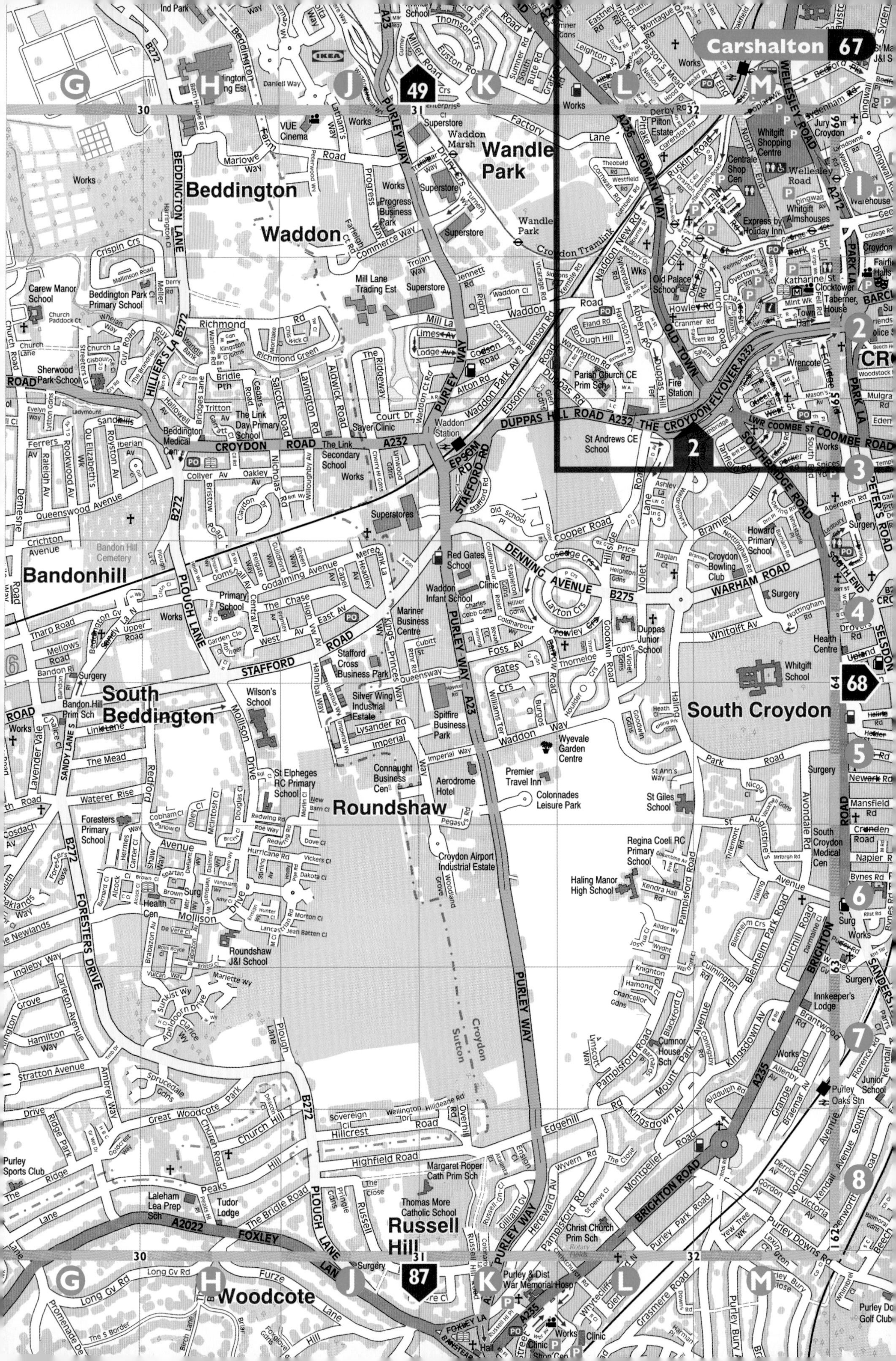

Carshalton
67
49
68
87
2
G
H
J
K
L
M
30
31
32
Beddington
Waddon
Wandle Park
Bandonhill
South Beddington
Roundshaw
South Croydon
Russell Hill
Woodcote
Beddington Lane
Purley Way
Croydon Road
Stafford Road
Plough Lane
Foresters Drive
Duppas Hill Road A232
The Croydon Flyover A232
Roman Way
Old Town
Denning Avenue
Warham Road
Brighton Road
Southbridge Road
Foxley Lane
A2022
A23
A232
A235
A236
B272
B275
Croydon Tramlink
Waddon Marsh
Waddon Station
Wandle Park
VUE Cinema
IKEA
Superstore
Progress Business Park
Mill Lane Trading Est
Commerce Way
Carew Manor School
Beddington Park Primary School
Sherwood Park School
Bandon Hill Cemetery
Beddington Medical Cen
The Link Day Primary School
The Link Secondary School
Sayer Clinic
Red Gates School
Waddon Infant School
Mariner Business Centre
Stafford Cross Business Park
Silver Wing Industrial Estate
Spitfire Business Park
Connaught Business Cen
Aerodrome Hotel
Croydon Airport Industrial Estate
Premier Travel Inn
Colonnades Leisure Park
Wyevale Garden Centre
Wilson's School
St Elpheges RC Primary School
Roundshaw J&I School
Foresters Primary School
Bandon Hill Prim Sch
Whitgift Shopping Centre
Centrale Shop Cen
Whitgift Almshouses
Express by Holiday Inn
Old Palace School
Parish Church CE Prim Sch
Fire Station
St Andrews CE School
Howard Primary School
Croydon Bowling Club
Duppas Junior School
Whitgift School
St Giles School
Regina Coeli RC Primary School
Haling Manor High School
Cumnor House Sch
South Croydon Medical Cen
Innkeeper's Lodge
Purley Oaks Stn
Margaret Roper Cath Prim Sch
Thomas More Catholic School
Christ Church Prim Sch
Purley & Dist War Memorial Hosp
Laleham Lea Prep Sch
Tudor Lodge
Purley Sports Club
Purley Downs Golf Club
Croydon
Sutton

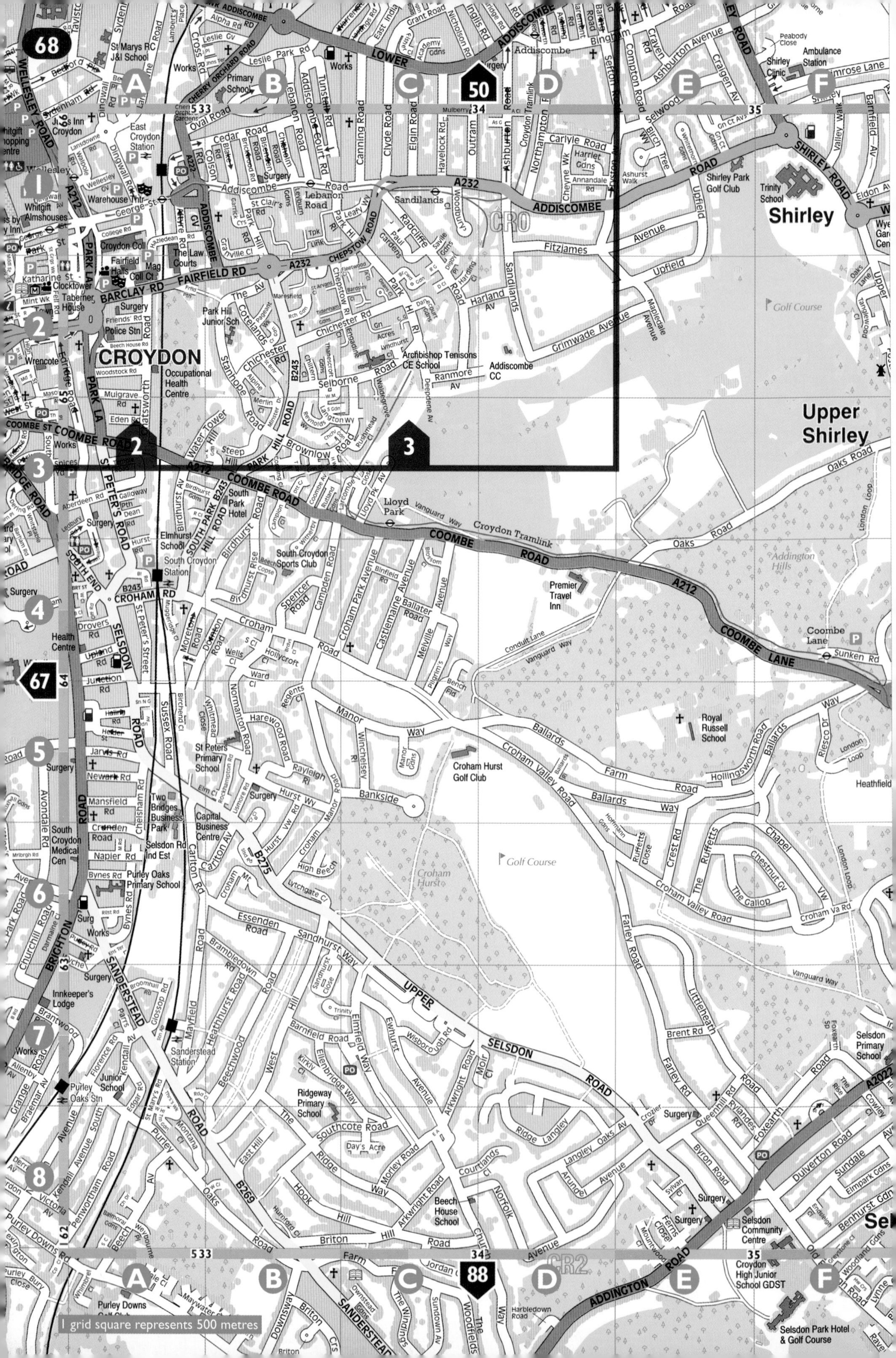
68
50
67
88
2
3
A
B
C
D
E
F
1
2
3
4
5
6
7
8
533
34
35
CROYDON
Shirley
Upper Shirley
Addiscombe
CR0
CR2
LOWER ADDISCOMBE ROAD
ADDISCOMBE ROAD
A232
A212
A222
B243
B275
B269
A2022
WELLESLEY ROAD
CHERRY ORCHARD ROAD
FAIRFIELD RD
BARCLAY RD
PARK LANE
COOMBE ROAD
COOMBE LANE
SHIRLEY ROAD
CHEPSTOW ROAD
PARK HILL ROAD
SOUTH PARK HILL ROAD
ST PETER'S ROAD
SOUTH END
SELSDON ROAD
BRIGHTON ROAD
SANDERSTEAD ROAD
UPPER SELSDON ROAD
ADDINGTON ROAD
Croham Valley Road
Ballards Way
Ballards Farm Road
Oaks Road
Croydon Tramlink
Vanguard Way
Conduit Lane
Farley Road
Littleheath
East Croydon Station
South Croydon Station
Sanderstead Station
Purley Oaks Stn
Lloyd Park
Sandilands
Lebanon Road
Coombe Lane
St Marys RC J&I School
Primary School
Works
Warehouse Thtr
Croydon Coll
Fairfield Halls
The Law Courts
Mag Coll Ct
Clocktower
Taberner House
Friends' Rd
Police Stn
Whitgift Almshouses
Whitgift Shopping Centre
Wrencote
Park Hill Junior Sch
Occupational Health Centre
Archbishop Tenisons CE School
Addiscombe CC
Shirley Park Golf Club
Trinity School
Peabody Close
Ambulance Station
Shirley Clinic
Golf Course
Addington Hills
Premier Travel Inn
Royal Russell School
Heathfield
South Park Hotel
Elmhurst School
South Croydon Sports Club
Croham Hurst Golf Club
Croham Hurst
St Peters Primary School
Two Bridges Business Park
Capital Business Centre
Selsdon Rd Ind Est
South Croydon Medical Cen
Health Centre
Purley Oaks Primary School
Innkeeper's Lodge
Junior School
Ridgeway Primary School
Beech House School
Selsdon Primary School
Selsdon Community Centre
Croydon High Junior School GDST
Selsdon Park Hotel & Golf Course
Purley Downs Golf Club
Surgery
1 grid square represents 500 metres

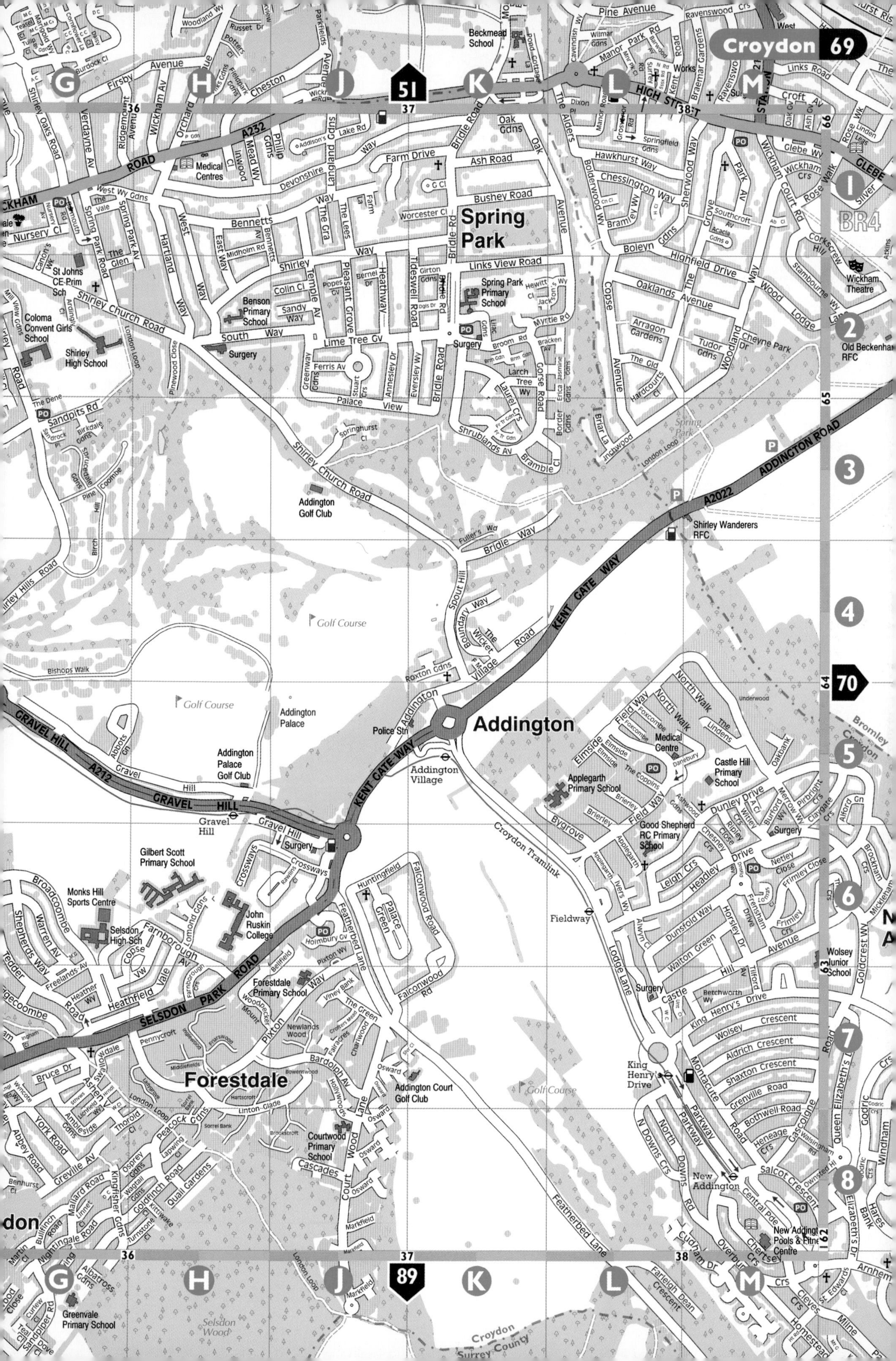
Croydon 69
51
70
89
Spring Park
Addington
Forestdale
Beckmead School
HIGH STREET
A232
ROAD
Shirley Church Road
Bridle Road
Bridle Way
Links View Road
Bushey Road
Ash Road
Farm Drive
Oak Gdns
Oak Avenue
Medical Centres
Benson Primary School
Spring Park Primary School
St Johns CE Prim Sch
Coloma Convent Girls School
Shirley High School
Surgery
Addington Golf Club
Golf Course
Addington Palace
Addington Palace Golf Club
Shirley Wanderers RFC
A2022
ADDINGTON ROAD
KENT GATE WAY
Village Road
Spout Hill
Boundary Way
The Wicket
Roxton Gdns
Police Stn
Addington Village
GRAVEL HILL
A212
Gravel Hill
Bishops Walk
Gilbert Scott Primary School
Monks Hill Sports Centre
Selsdon High Sch
John Ruskin College
SELSDON PARK ROAD
Forestdale Primary School
Featherbed Lane
Falconwood Road
Palace Green
Addington Court Golf Club
Courtwood Primary School
Croydon Tramlink
Fieldway
Lodge Lane
Applegarth Primary School
Good Shepherd RC Primary School
Castle Hill Primary School
Medical Centre
King Henry's Drive
King Henry Drive
New Addington
Parkway
Central Pde
Wolsey Crescent
Aldrich Crescent
Shaxton Crescent
Grenville Road
Bothwell Road
Salcot Crescent
Queen Elizabeth's Dr
Wolsey Junior School
New Addington Pools & Fitness Centre
Greenvale Primary School
Selsdon Wood
Croydon
Surrey County
Bromley
Wickham Theatre
Old Beckenham RFC
Spring Park
London Loop
BR4
G H J K L M
36 37 38
62 63 64 65 66
1 2 3 4 5 6 7 8

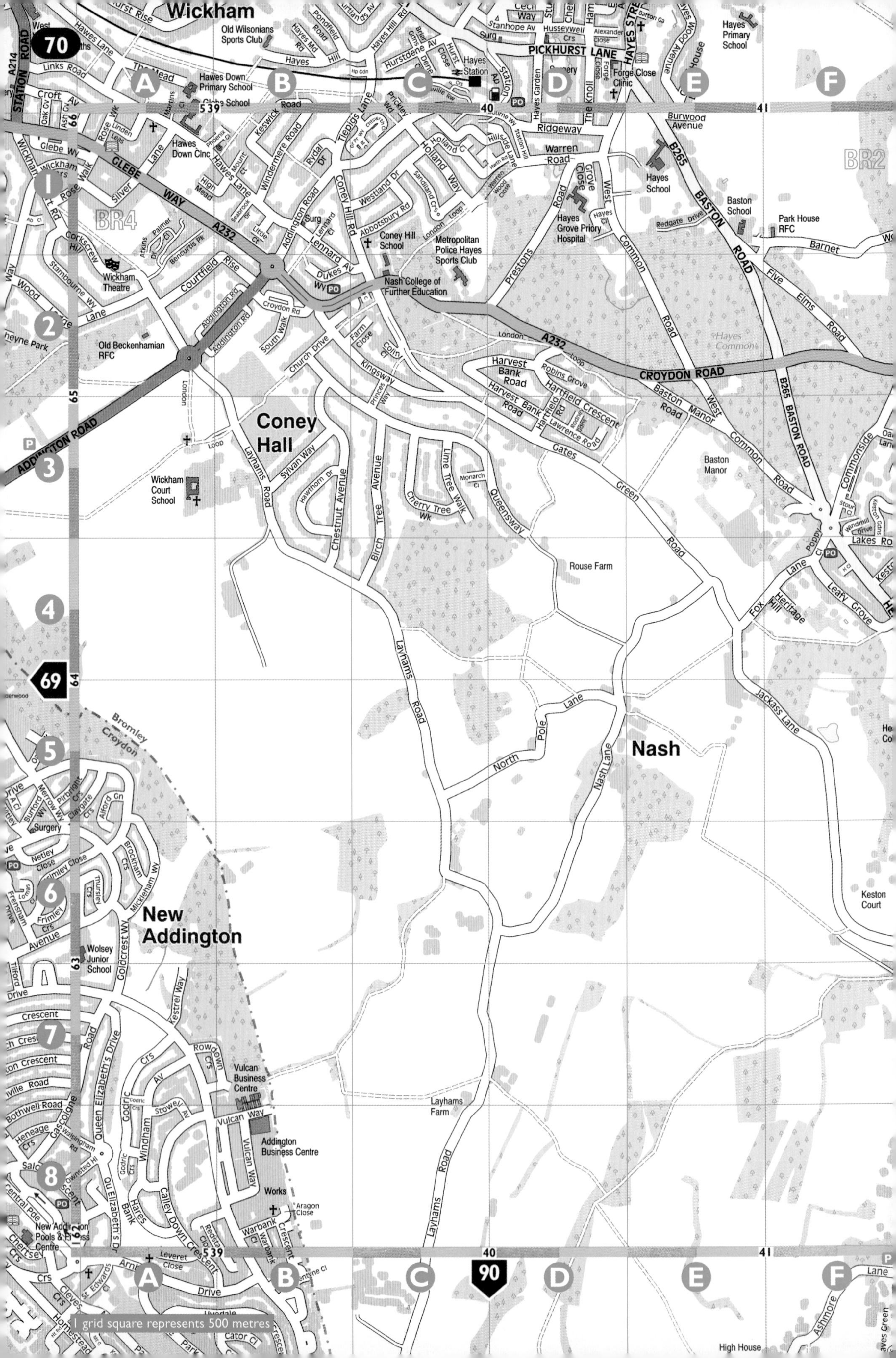
Wickham
Old Wilsonians Sports Club
Hawes Down Primary School
Hayes Station
PICKHURST LANE
HAYES STREET
Forge Close
Hayes Primary School
Ridgeway
Warren Road
Hayes School
BASTON ROAD
Baston School
Park House RFC
GLEBE WAY
A232
Coney Hill School
Metropolitan Police Hayes Sports Club
Hayes Grove Priory Hospital
Nash College of Further Education
Wickham Theatre
Old Beckenhamian RFC
ADDINGTON ROAD
CROYDON ROAD
Hayes Common
Coney Hall
Wickham Court School
Baston Manor
Rouse Farm
Layhams Road
Nash
Nash Lane
Jackass Lane
Keston Court
New Addington
Wolsey Junior School
Vulcan Business Centre
Addington Business Centre
Layhams Farm
New Addington Pools & Fitness Centre
High House
Bromley
Croydon
BR2
BR4
1 grid square represents 500 metres

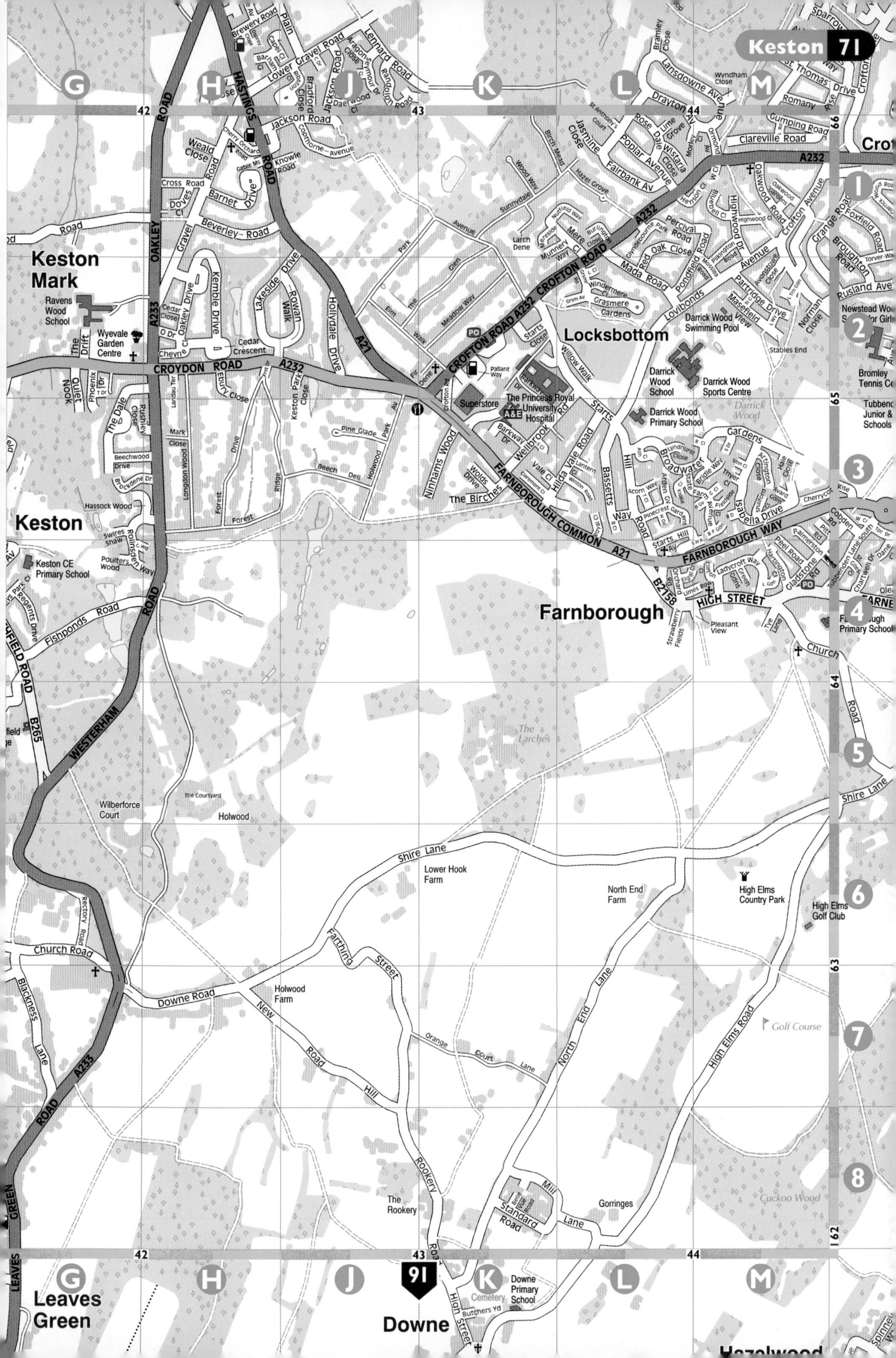
Keston Mark
Keston
Locksbottom
Farnborough
Leaves Green
Downe
Ravens Wood School
Wyevale Garden Centre
Keston CE Primary School
Darrick Wood School
Darrick Wood Sports Centre
Darrick Wood Swimming Pool
Darrick Wood Primary School
The Princess Royal University Hospital
Superstore
Newstead Wood School for Girls
Bromley Tennis Centre
Tubbenden Junior & Infant Schools
Farnborough Primary School
High Elms Country Park
High Elms Golf Club
Golf Course
Cuckoo Wood
The Larches
Holwood
Holwood Farm
Lower Hook Farm
North End Farm
Wilberforce Court
The Courtyard
The Rookery
Gorringes
Downe Primary School
Cemetery
CROYDON ROAD
OAKLEY ROAD
HASTINGS ROAD
WESTERHAM ROAD
FARNBOROUGH COMMON
FARNBOROUGH WAY
CROFTON ROAD
HIGH STREET
LEAVES GREEN ROAD
Shire Lane
Downe Road
Church Road
High Elms Road
North End Lane
New Road Hill
Rookery Road
Farthing Street
Orange Court Lane
Mill Lane
Standard Road
Blackness Lane
Rectory Road
Fishponds Road
Lower Gravel Road
Jackson Road
Lansdowne Avenue
Clareville Road
Crofton Avenue
Lovibonds Avenue
Starts Hill Road
Bassetts Way
Broadwater Gardens
Isabella Drive
Hilda Vale Road
Ninhams Wood
Holwood Park Av
Beech Dell
Kemble Drive
Lakeside Drive
Hollydale Drive
Cedar Crescent
Beverley Road
Barnet Drive
Cross Road
A21
A232
A233
B265
B2158
91

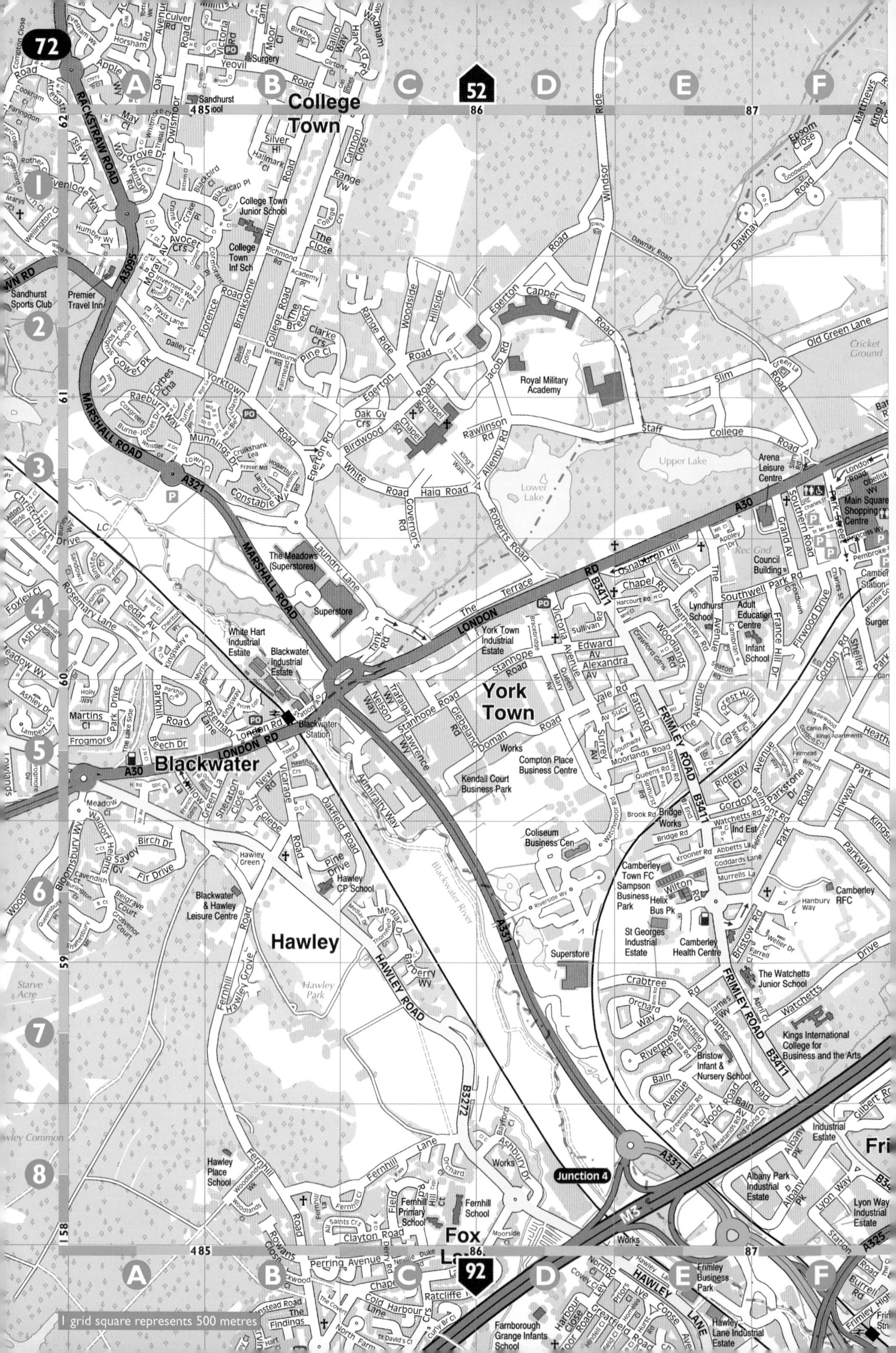
72
52
92
A
B
C
D
E
F
1
2
3
4
5
6
7
8
485
86
87
62
61
60
59
158
College Town
College Town Junior School
College Town Inf Sch
Sandhurst Sports Club
Premier Travel Inn
RACKSTRAW ROAD
MARSHALL ROAD
A3095
A321
Yorktown
Royal Military Academy
Upper Lake
Lower Lake
Old Green Lane
Cricket Ground
Staff College Road
Arena Leisure Centre
Main Square Shopping Centre
Council Building
Adult Education Centre
Lyndhurst School
Infant School
A30
LONDON RD
B3411
FRIMLEY ROAD
The Meadows (Superstores)
Superstore
White Hart Industrial Estate
Blackwater Industrial Estate
Blackwater Station
Blackwater
York Town
York Town Industrial Estate
Compton Place Business Centre
Kendall Court Business Park
Coliseum Business Cen
Camberley Town FC
Sampson Business Park
Helix Bus Pk
St Georges Industrial Estate
Camberley Health Centre
Camberley RFC
The Watchetts Junior School
Kings International College for Business and the Arts
Bristow Infant & Nursery School
Hawley
Hawley Park
HAWLEY ROAD
Blackwater & Hawley Leisure Centre
Hawley CP School
Blackwater River
A331
B3272
Hawley Place School
Fernhill Primary School
Fernhill School
Fox Lane
Junction 4
M3
Albany Park Industrial Estate
Lyon Way Industrial Estate
Industrial Estate
Frimley Business Park
Hawley Lane Industrial Estate
HAWLEY LANE
Farnborough Grange Infants School
Starve Acre
Hawley Common
1 grid square represents 500 metres

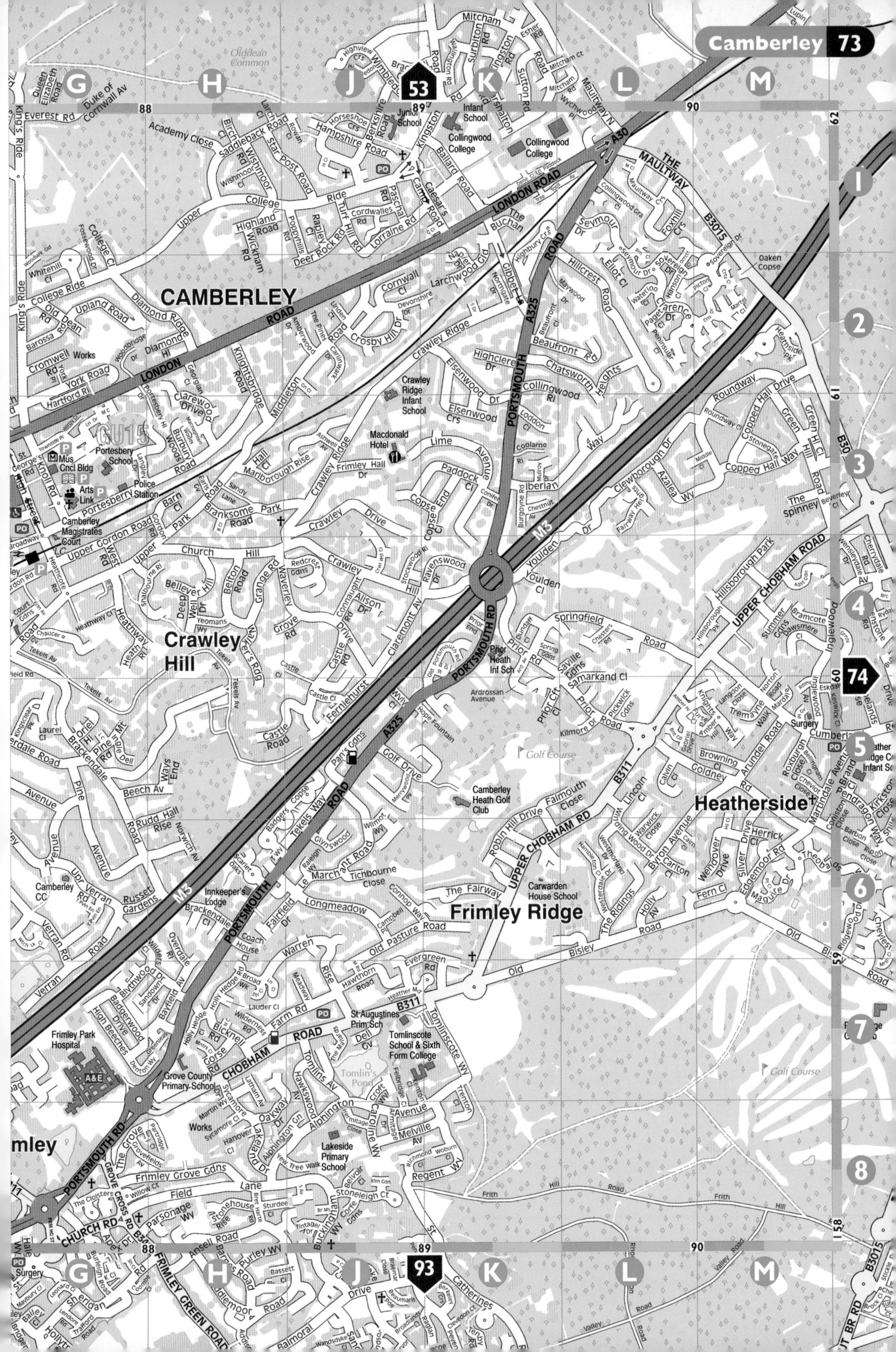
CAMBERLEY
Crawley Hill
Frimley Ridge
Heatherside
Frimley
LONDON ROAD
PORTSMOUTH ROAD
A325
M3
A30
B3015
B311
UPPER CHOBHAM ROAD
CHOBHAM ROAD
THE MAULTWAY
FRIMLEY GREEN ROAD
CHURCH RD
PORTSMOUTH RD
GU15
Collingwood College
Infant School
Junior School
Crawley Ridge Infant School
Macdonald Hotel
Portesbery School
Police Station
Mus
Cncl Bldg
Arts Link
Camberley Magistrates Court
Prior Heath Inf Sch
Camberley Heath Golf Club
Golf Course
Carwarden House School
Innkeeper's Lodge
Camberley CC
Frimley Park Hospital
A&E
Grove County Primary School
St Augustines Prim Sch
Tomlinscote School & Sixth Form College
Lakeside Primary School
Tomlin's Pond
Works
Surgery
Oaken Copse
Olddean Common
College Ride
Upper College Ride
Academy Close
Crawley Ridge
Crawley Drive
Church Hill
Upper Gordon Road
Portesbery Rd
Knightsbridge Road
Middleton Rd
Branksome Park Road
Chatsworth Heights
Collingwood Ri
Elsenwood Dr
Hillcrest Road
Beaufront Rd
Highclere Dr
Youlden Dr
Springfield Road
Prior Road
Golf Drive
Old Pasture Road
Old Bisley Road
Bisley Road
Copped Hall Drive
Copped Hall Way
Hillsborough Park
Roundway
Clewborough Dr
Longmeadow
Tekels Way
Tekels Av
Brackendale Road
Beech Av
Rudd Hall Rise
Russet Gardens
Verran Road
Frimley Grove Gdns
Field Lane
Frith Hill Road
Valley Road
Regent Wy
Melville Av
Ansell Road
Balmoral
Camberley 73
53
74
93
88
89
90
58
59
60
61
62
G
H
J
K
L
M
1
2
3
4
5
6
7
8

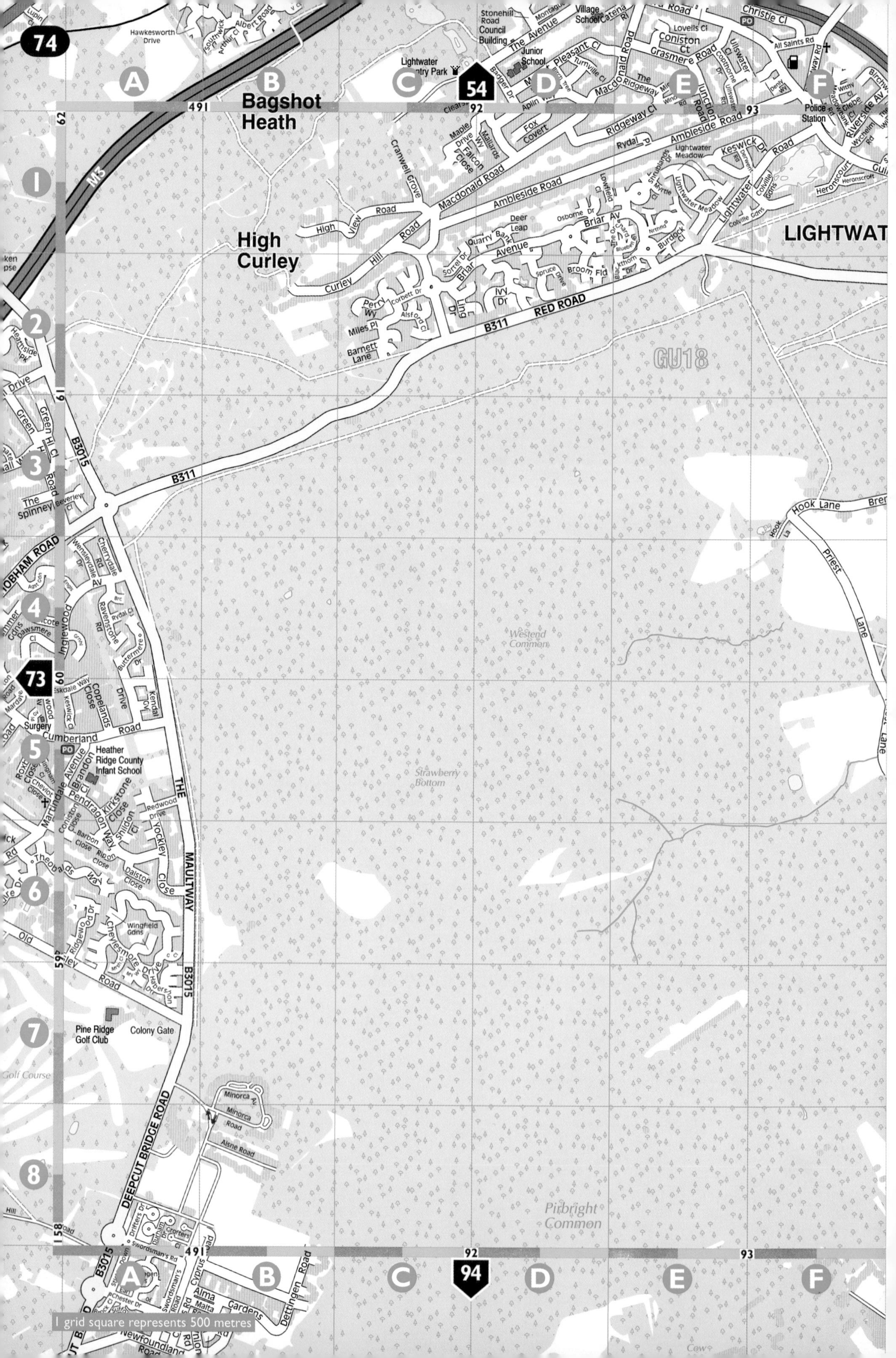

74
54
73
94
A
B
C
D
E
F
1
2
3
4
5
6
7
8
491
92
93
62
61
60
59
158
M3
Bagshot Heath
High Curley
LIGHTWAT
GU18
B311
B311 RED ROAD
B3015
THE MAULTWAY
DEEPCUT BRIDGE ROAD
Hawkesworth Drive
Lightwater Country Park
Stonehill Road Council Building
The Avenue
Village School
Junior School
Christie Cl
All Saints Rd
Police Station
Coniston Ct
Lovells Cl
Grasmere Road
Ridgeway Cl
Ambleside Road
Macdonald Road
Cranwell Grove
Curley Hill Road
High View Road
Lightwater Meadow
Keswick Dr
Briar Av
Briar Avenue
Deer Leap
Quarry Bank
Broom Fld
Ling Dr
Ivy Dr
Perry Wy
Miles Pl
Barnett Lane
Alsford Cl
Hook Lane
Priest Lane
Westend Common
Strawberry Bottom
Pirbright Common
Cumberland Road
Heather Ridge County Infant School
Surgery
Inglewood
Copelands Close
Kendal Gv
Kirkstone Close
Pendragon Way
Martindale Avenue
Theobalds Way
Wingfield Gdns
Cheylesmore Drive
Old Bisley Road
Pine Ridge Golf Club
Colony Gate
Golf Course
Minorca Av
Minorca Road
Aisne Road
Dettingen Road
Alma Gardens
Newfoundland Road
Cyprus Road
Swordsman's Rd
The Spinney
COBHAM ROAD
1 grid square represents 500 metres

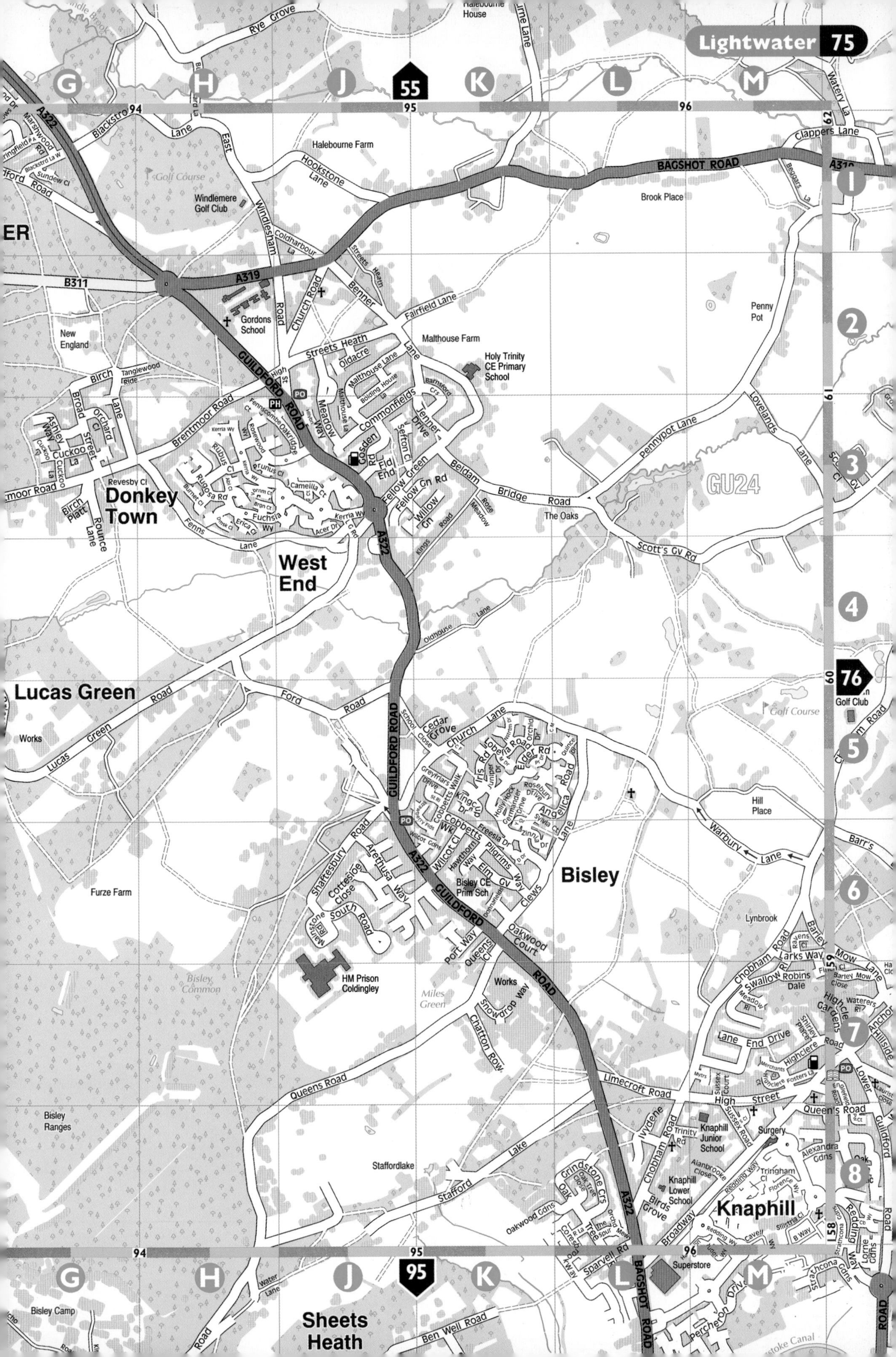
55
76
95
Donkey Town
West End
Lucas Green
Bisley
Knaphill
Sheets Heath
New England
Halebourne Farm
Windlemere Golf Club
Golf Course
Gordons School
Malthouse Farm
Holy Trinity CE Primary School
Brook Place
Penny Pot
GU24
The Oaks
Hill Place
Lynbrook
Furze Farm
Works
HM Prison Coldingley
Bisley Common
Miles Green
Bisley Ranges
Staffordlake
Bisley CE Prim Sch
Knaphill Junior School
Knaphill Lower School
Superstore
Bisley Camp
Golf Club
GUILDFORD ROAD
BAGSHOT ROAD
A322
A319
B311
Guildford Road
Bagshot Road
Brentmoor Road
Bridge Road
Pennypot Lane
Scott's Gv Rd
Lucas Green Road
Ford Road
Queens Road
Limecroft Road
High Street
Chobham Road
Warbury Lane
Church Lane
Streets Heath
Benner Lane
Fairfield Lane
Hookstone Lane
Coldharbour La
Windlesham Road
Church Road
Fenns Lane
Rounce Lane
Broad Street
Orchard Cl
Birch Platt
Cuckoo La
Donkey Town
Stafford Lake
Oakwood Court
Clews Lane
Shaftesbury Road
South Road
Arethusa Way
Snowdrop Way
Chatton Row
Lane End Drive
Highcliere Road
Ben Well Road
Sparvell Rd
Grindstone Crs
Broadway
Alexandra Gdns
Barley Mow Lane
Clappers Lane
Lovelands Lane
Oldhouse Lane
Kings Road
Commonfields
Jenner Drive
Meadow Way
Sefton Cl
Fellow Green
Willow Gn
Rose Meadow
Fuchsia Wy
Rugosa Rd
Angelica Road
Elder Rd
Iris Rd
Cobbetts Walk
Pilgrims Way
Cedar Grove
School Close
Greyfriars Drive
Ivydene
Birds Grove
Oakwood Gdns
Reading Way
Tringham Cl
Perchern Drive
Queen's Road
Larks Way
Robins Dale
Swallow Ri
Highcle Gardens
Knaphill
G
H
J
K
L
M
1
2
3
4
5
6
7
8
94
95
96
62
61
60
59
58

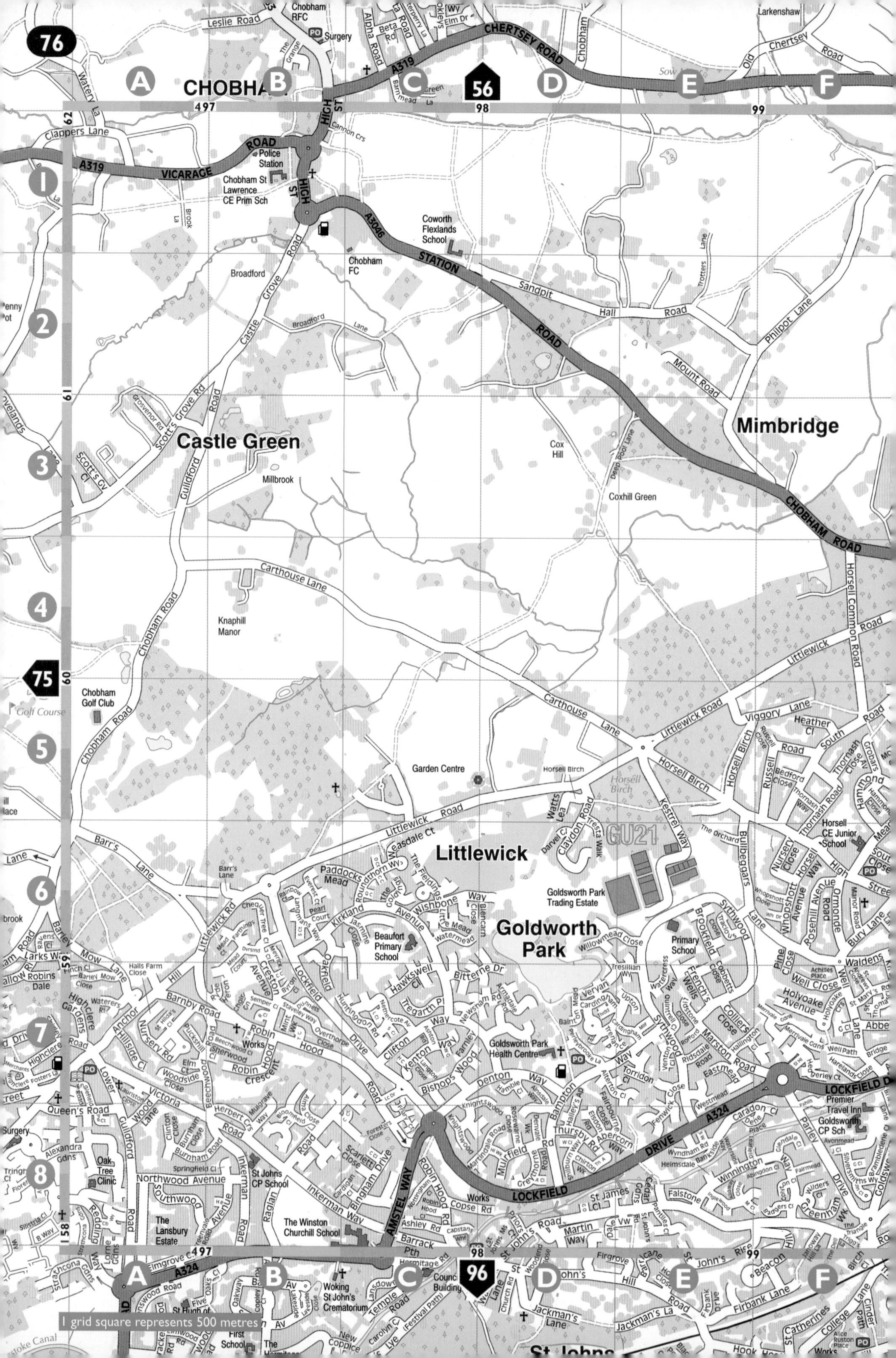
76
56
75
96
CHOBHAM
Castle Green
Mimbridge
Littlewick
Goldworth Park
GU21
A319
A3046
A324
CHERTSEY ROAD
VICARAGE ROAD
STATION ROAD
CHOBHAM ROAD
LOCKFIELD DRIVE
AMSTEL WAY
HIGH ST
Chobham RFC
Surgery
Police Station
Chobham St Lawrence CE Prim Sch
Coworth Flexlands School
Chobham FC
Broadford
Millbrook
Knaphill Manor
Cox Hill
Coxhill Green
Chobham Golf Club
Golf Course
Garden Centre
Horsell Birch
Goldsworth Park Trading Estate
Beaufort Primary School
Primary School
Horsell CE Junior School
Goldsworth Park Health Centre
Works
St Johns CP School
The Winston Churchill School
Oak Tree Clinic
The Lansbury Estate
Woking St John's Crematorium
Council Building
Premier Travel Inn
Goldsworth CP Sch
Leslie Road
Clappers Lane
Sandpit Hall Road
Mount Road
Philpot Lane
Carthouse Lane
Littlewick Road
Horsell Common Road
Horsell Birch
Bullbeggars Lane
Guildford Road
Castle Grove Road
Scott's Grove Rd
Deep Pool Lane
Barr's Lane
Kestrel Way
Kirkland Avenue
Robin Hood Crescent
Inkerman Road
Queen's Road
Northwood Avenue
Marston Road
Chertsey Road
Larkenshaw
1 grid square represents 500 metres

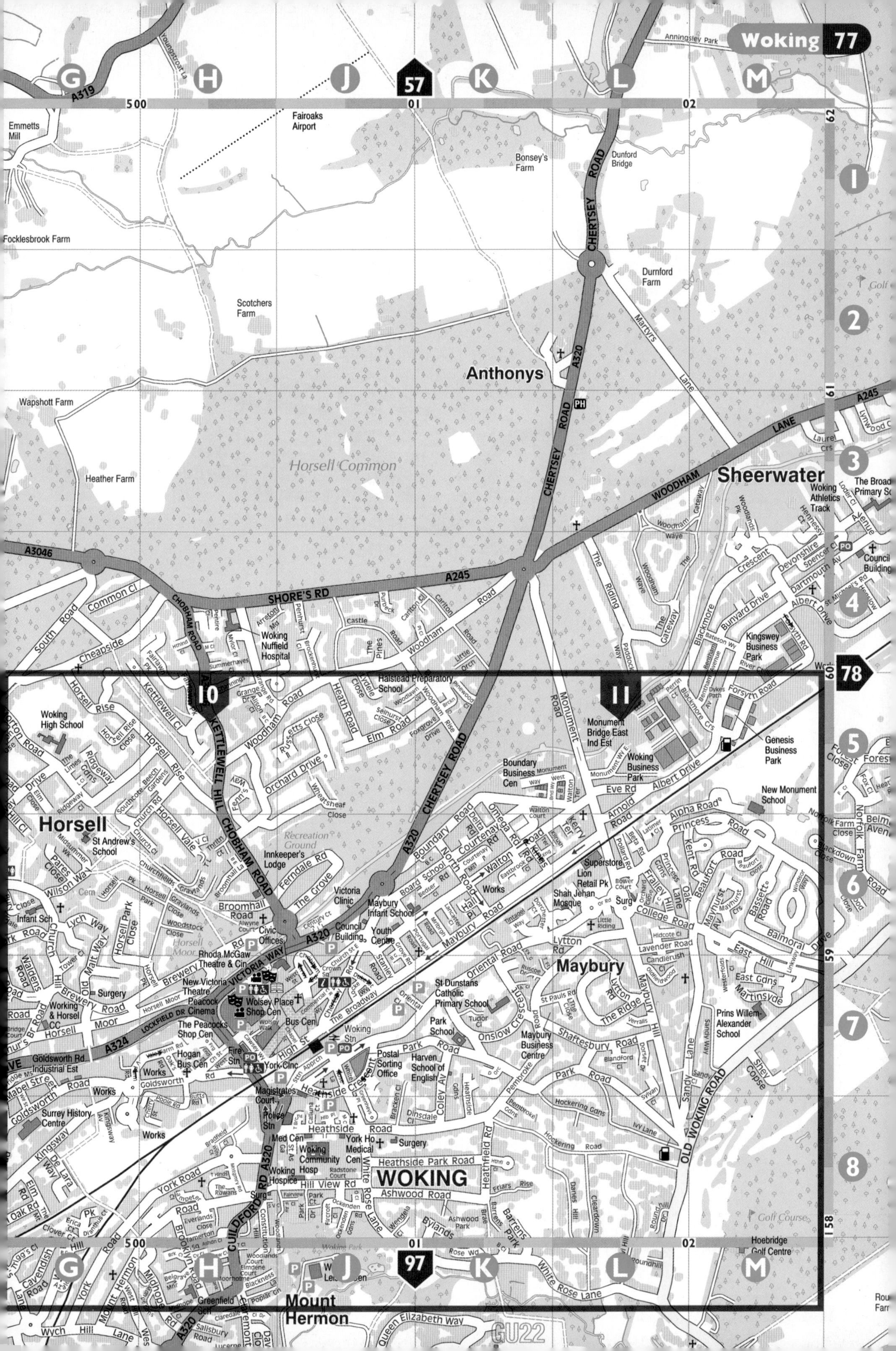
57
97
78
Fairoaks Airport
Emmetts Mill
Focklesbrook Farm
Bonsey's Farm
Dunford Bridge
Durnford Farm
Scotchers Farm
Anthonys
Wapshott Farm
Heather Farm
Horsell Common
Sheerwater
Woking Athletics Track
CHERTSEY ROAD
WOODHAM LANE
SHORE'S RD
Woking Nuffield Hospital
Halstead Preparatory School
Woking High School
Horsell
St Andrew's School
Monument Bridge East Ind Est
Woking Business Park
Boundary Business Cen
Genesis Business Park
New Monument School
Kingswey Business Park
Recreation Ground
Innkeeper's Lodge
Victoria Clinic
Maybury Infant School
Youth Centre
Council Building
Civic Offices
Rhoda McGaw Theatre & Cin
New Victoria Theatre
Peacock Cinema
Wolsey Place Shop Cen
The Peacocks Shop Cen
Bus Cen
Woking Stn
Hogan Bus Cen
Fire Stn
York Clnc
Goldsworth Rd Industrial Est
Surrey History Centre
Magistrates Court
Police Stn
Postal Sorting Office
Harven School of English
Superstore
Lion Retail Pk
Shah Jehan Mosque
Maybury
St Dunstans Catholic Primary School
Park School
Maybury Business Centre
Prins Willem-Alexander School
Med Cen
Woking Community Hosp
York Ho Medical Cen
Surgery
Woking Hospice
WOKING
Hoebridge Golf Centre
Golf Course
Mount Hermon
Heathside Road
OLD WOKING ROAD
VICTORIA WAY
KETTLEWELL HILL
CHOBHAM ROAD
GUILDFORD RD
GU22

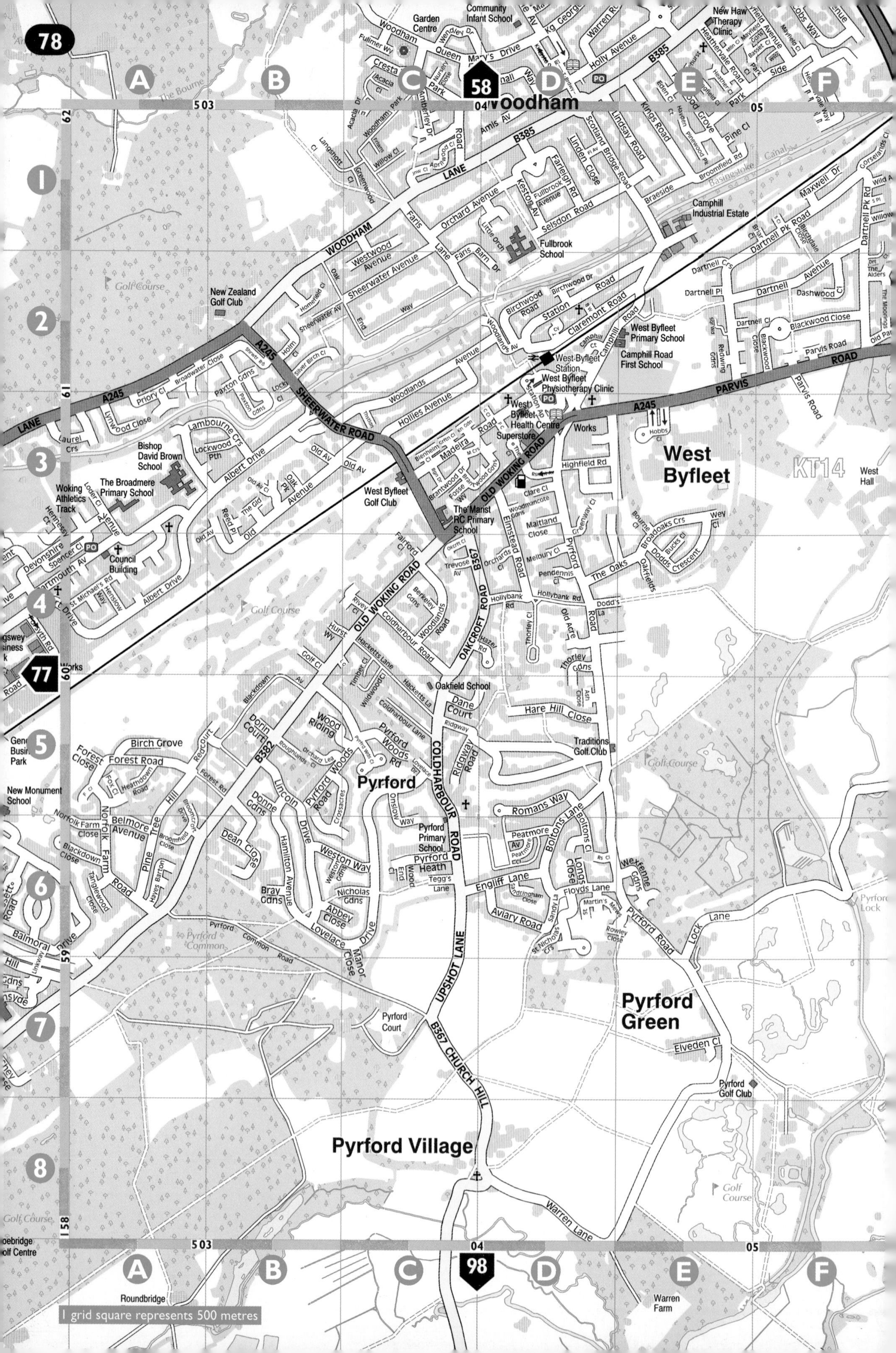

78
Woodham
58
98
77
West Byfleet
Pyrford
Pyrford Green
Pyrford Village
KT14
West Hall
Garden Centre
Community Infant School
New Haw Therapy Clinic
Queen Mary's Drive
Holly Avenue
Warren Rd
Woodham Lane
B385
A245
Sheerwater Road
Parvis Road
Old Woking Road
B367
B382
Coldharbour Road
Oakcroft Road
Upshot Lane
B367 Church Hill
Pyrford Road
Basingstoke Canal
Camphill Industrial Estate
Fullbrook School
New Zealand Golf Club
Golf Course
West Byfleet Primary School
Camphill Road First School
West Byfleet Station
West Byfleet Physiotherapy Clinic
West Byfleet Health Centre
Superstore
Works
Bishop David Brown School
The Broadmeere Primary School
Woking Athletics Track
Council Building
West Byfleet Golf Club
The Marist RC Primary School
Oakfield School
Traditions Golf Club
Pyrford Primary School
Pyrford Common
Pyrford Court
Pyrford Golf Club
Pyrford Lock
Roundbridge
Warren Farm
Warren Lane
Lock Lane
Elveden Cl
New Monument School
Orchard Avenue
Sheerwater Avenue
Westwood Avenue
Scotland Bridge Road
Lindsay Road
Kings Road
Dartnell Avenue
Dartnell Pk Road
Maxwell Dr
Blackwood Close
Station Road
Claremont Road
Madeira Road
Highfield Rd
Elmstead Road
Hollybank Rd
Hare Hill Close
Romans Way
Boltons Lane
Floyds Lane
Engliff Lane
Aviary Road
Weston Way
Hamilton Avenue
Lincoln Drive
Forest Road
Birch Grove
Norfolk Farm Road
Albert Drive
Lambourne Crs
Woodlands Avenue
Hollies Avenue
A
B
C
D
E
F
1
2
3
4
5
6
7
8
503
04
05
62
61
60
59
158
1 grid square represents 500 metres

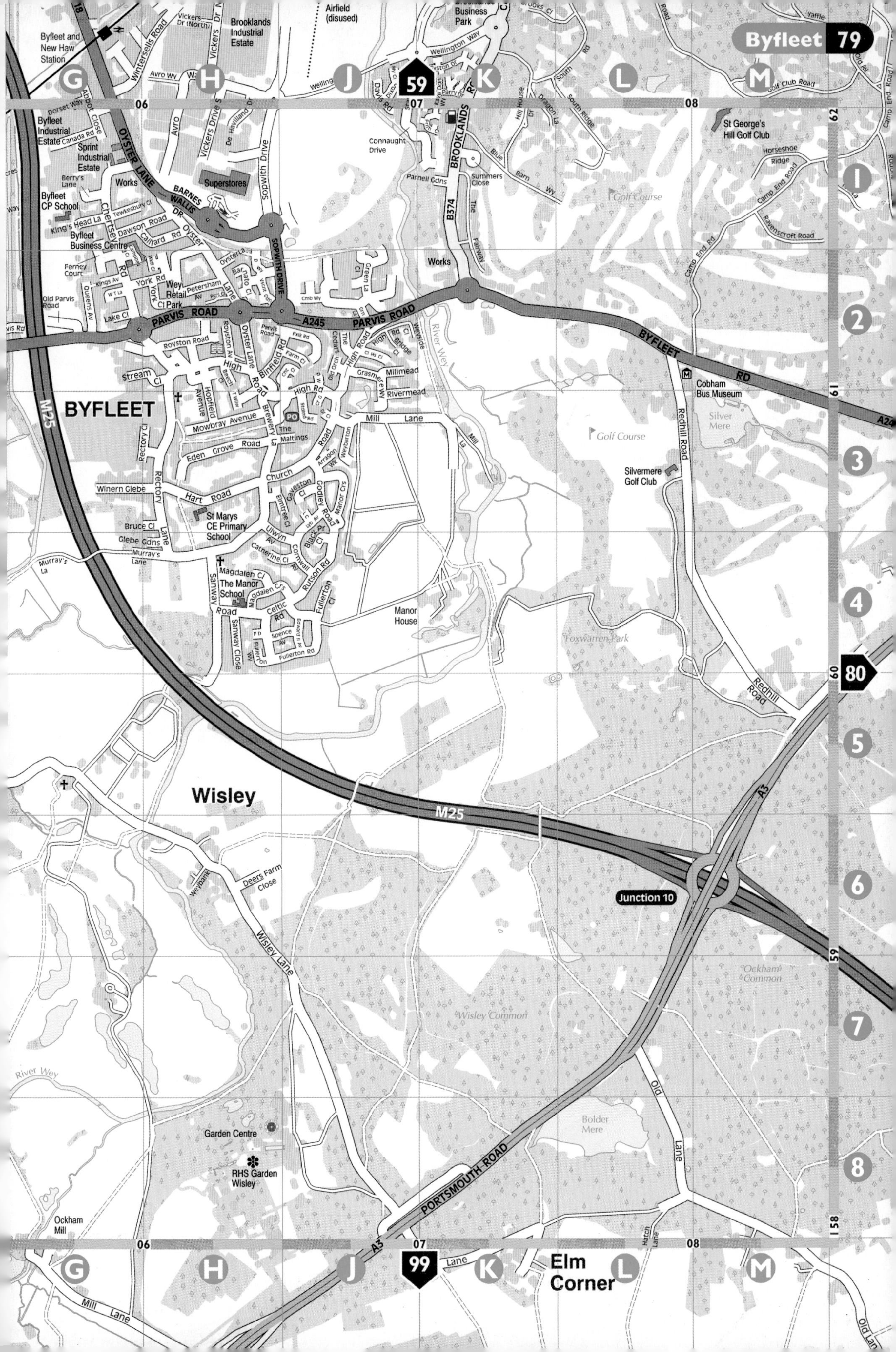
Byfleet and New Haw Station
Brooklands Industrial Estate
Airfield (disused)
Business Park
Byfleet Industrial Estate
Sprint Industrial Estate
Berry's Lane
Works
Superstores
Byfleet CP School
Byfleet Business Centre
Ferney Court
Wey Retail Park
Old Parvis Road
Connaught Drive
Parnell Gdns
Summers Close
St George's Hill Golf Club
Horseshoe Ridge
Camp End Road
Ravenscroft Road
Golf Course
OYSTER LANE
BARNES WALLIS DR
SOPWITH DRIVE
BROOKLANDS RD
B374
PARVIS ROAD
A245
BYFLEET RD
BYFLEET
Stream Cl
Royston Road
High Road
Mowbray Avenue
Eden Grove Road
Church Road
Mill Lane
Rivermead
Millmead
Grasmere Wy
River Wey
Cobham Bus Museum
Silver Mere
Golf Course
Redhill Road
Silvermere Golf Club
Winern Glebe
Rectory Lane
Hart Road
St Marys CE Primary School
Bruce Cl
Glebe Gdns
Murray's Lane
The Manor School
Sanway Road
Sanway Close
Manor House
Foxwarren Park
M25
Wisley
Deers Farm Close
Weybank
Wisley Lane
Junction 10
A3
Ockham Common
Wisley Common
River Wey
Garden Centre
RHS Garden Wisley
Bolder Mere
Old Lane
PORTSMOUTH ROAD
Ockham Mill
Mill Lane
Hatch Lane
Elm Corner
59
80
99
G H J K L M
06 07 08
62 61 60 59 58
1 2 3 4 5 6 7 8

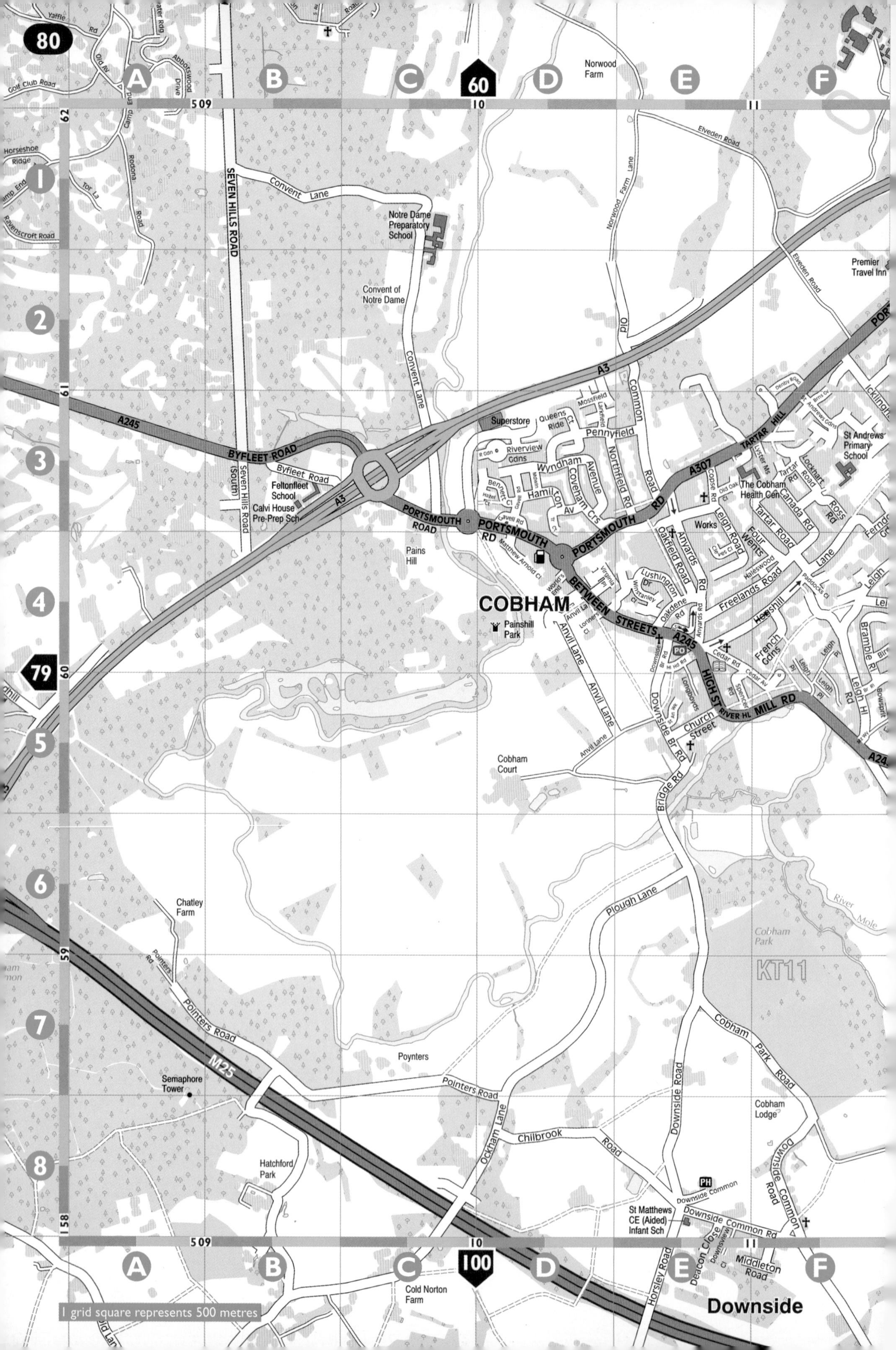

I grid square represents 500 metres

COBHAM

Downside

KT11

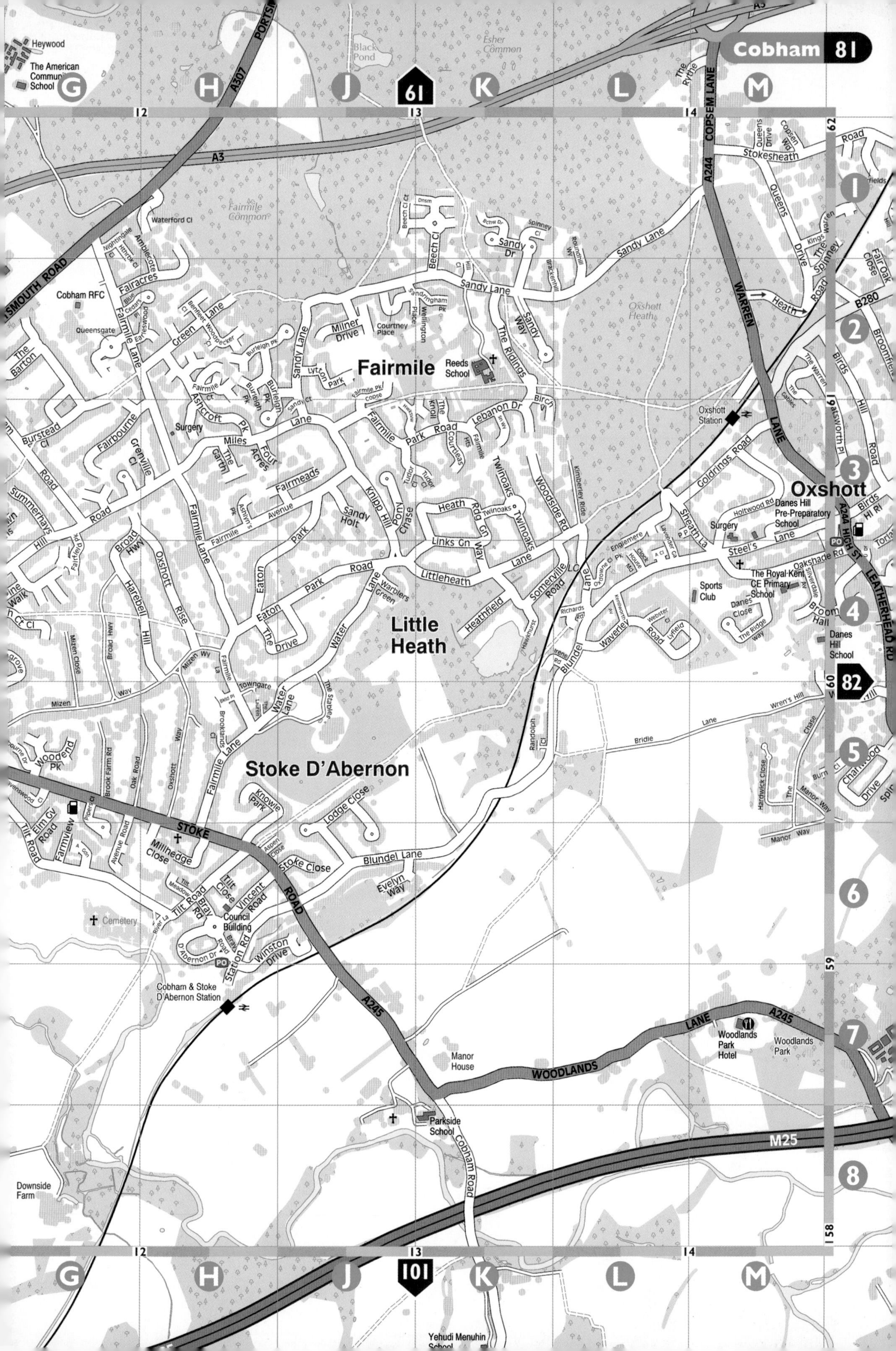
Fairmile
Little Heath
Stoke D'Abernon
Oxshott
Fairmile Common
Esher Common
Oxshott Heath
Black Pond
Heywood
The American Community School
Cobham RFC
Reeds School
Oxshott Station
Danes Hill Pre-Preparatory School
The Royal Kent CE Primary School
Sports Club
Danes Hill School
Surgery
Council Building
Cemetery
Cobham & Stoke D'Abernon Station
Manor House
Parkside School
Woodlands Park Hotel
Woodlands Park
Downside Farm
Yehudi Menuhin School
A3
A307
PORTSMOUTH ROAD
A244
COPSEM LANE
WARREN LANE
B280
LEATHERHEAD RD
A244 HIGH ST
A245
STOKE ROAD
WOODLANDS LANE
M25
Sandy Lane
Fairmile Lane
Fairmile Park Road
Miles Lane
Miles Road
Eaton Park Road
Littleheath Lane
Blundel Lane
Water Lane
Knipp Hill
Oxshott Rise
Oxshott Way
Mizen Way
Bridle Lane
Wren's Hill
Steel's Lane
Goldrings Road
Sheath La
Woodside Rd
Kimberley Ride
Somerville Road
Heathfield
Twinoaks
Pony Chase
Links Gn Way
Heath Rdg Gn
Lebanon Dr
Courtleas
The Knoll
Beech Cl
Sandy Dr
Sandy Way
The Ridings
Birch Cl
Stokesheath Road
Queens Drive
Heath Road
Birds Hill Road
Broomfield
Chatsworth Pl
Fair Oak Close
The Spinney
The Warren
Milner Drive
Courtney Place
Wellington
Sandringham Pk
Lytton Park
Burleigh Pk
Ashcroft Pk
Four Acres
The Garth
Fairmeads
Fairmile Avenue
Sandy Holt
Green Lane
Fairacres
Amblecote
Waterford Cl
Queensgate
The Barton
Burstead Cl
Fairbourne
Grenville Cl
Summerhays
Broad Hwy
Harebell Hill
Mizen Close
Brook Farm Rd
Oak Road
Woodend Pk
Elm Gv Road
Tilt Road
Farmview
Avenue Road
Millnedge Close
Tilt Close
Vincent Road
Bray Rd
Station Rd
Winston Drive
D'Abernon Dr
Aspen Close
Stoke Close
Blundel Lane
Evelyn Way
Lodge Close
Knowle Park
Brooklands Cl
Towngate
Warblers Green
The Drive
The Stables
Randolph Cl
Hawkhurst
Richards Rd
Irene Rd
Waverley Road
Lynfield
Danes Close
The Ridge Way
Broom Hall
Oakshade Rd
Holtwood Rd
Chartwood Drive
Manor Way
Hardwick Close
Cobham Road
12
13
14
62
61
60
59
58
G
H
J
K
L
M
1
2
3
4
5
6
7
8
61
82
101

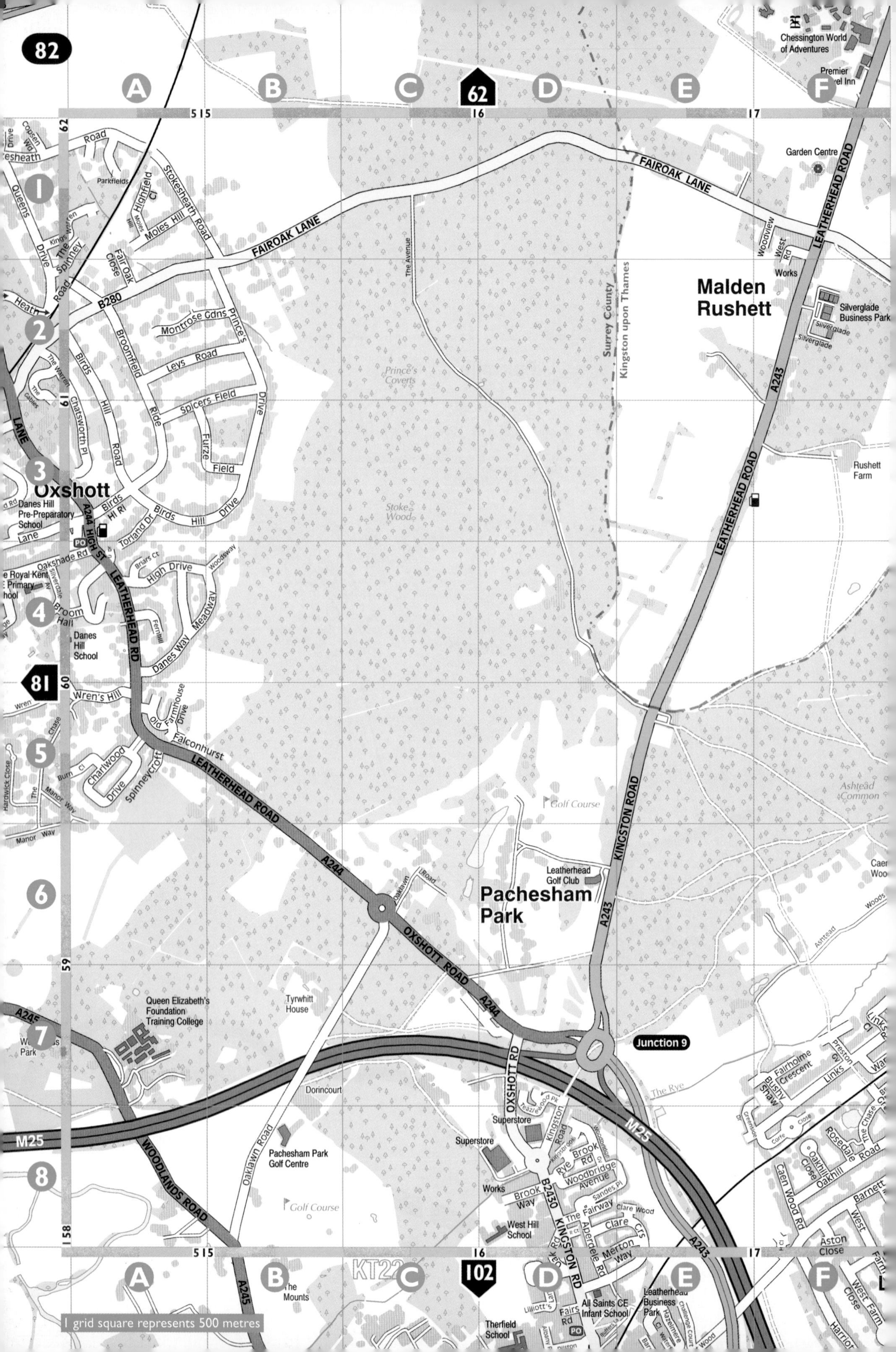
62
A
B
C
D
E
F
Chessington World of Adventures
Premier Travel Inn
Garden Centre
FAIROAK LANE
LEATHERHEAD ROAD
Malden Rushett
Silverglade Business Park
Silverglade
Works
Woodview
West Rd
Surrey County
Kingston upon Thames
Prince's Coverts
The Avenue
Stoke Wood
Rushett Farm
A243
Oxshott
Stokesheath Road
Highfield Cl
Moles Hill
Parkfields
Fair Oak Close
B280
Montrose Gdns
Princes Drive
Broomfield Ride
Leys Road
Spicers Field
Furze Field
Birds Hill Road
Birds Hill Drive
Chatsworth Pl
Queens Drive
The Spinney
Danes Hill Pre-Preparatory School
A244 HIGH ST
Torland Dr
Oakshade Rd
High Drive
Woodsway
Meadway
Danes Way
Danes Hill School
Broom Hall
81
Wren's Hill
Farmhouse Drive
Falconhurst
Charlwood Drive
Spinneycroft
Burn Cl
Manor Way
LEATHERHEAD ROAD
A244
Golf Course
Leatherhead Golf Club
Pachesham Park
KINGSTON ROAD
Ashtead Common
OXSHOTT ROAD
Oaklawn Road
Queen Elizabeth's Foundation Training College
Tyrwhitt House
Junction 9
M25
Dorincourt
Pachesham Park Golf Centre
WOODLANDS ROAD
A245
OXSHOTT RD
Superstore
Superstore
Kingston Road
Rye Brook Rd
Woodbridge Avenue
Works
Brook Way
B2430 KINGSTON RD
The Fairway
Clare Crs
Merton Way
West Hill School
The Rye
Fairholme Crescent
Bushy Shaw
Links
Rosedale
Oakhill Close
Caen Wood Rd
Barnett
Aston Close
West Farm Close
KT22
102
The Mounts
All Saints CE Infant School
Leatherhead Business Park
Therfield School
Fairs Rd
PO
1 grid square represents 500 metres

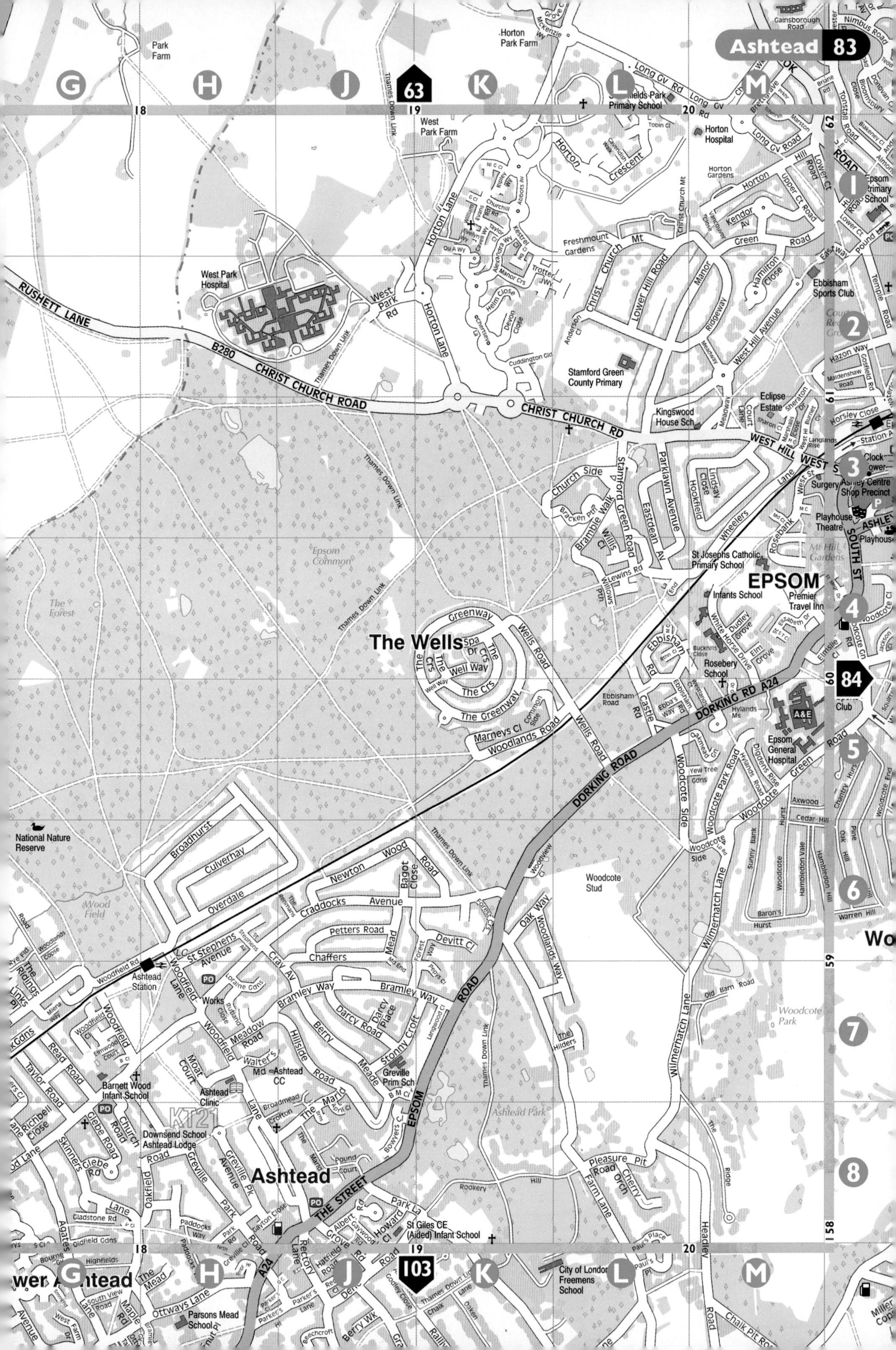

G 18 H J 63 19 K L 20 M

I
2
3
4
84 60
5
6
7
8

RUSHETT LANE

B280 CHRIST CHURCH ROAD

West Park Farm

Horton Park Farm

West Park Hospital

Long Gv Rd

Sheffields Park Primary School

Horton Hospital

Horton Crescent

Horton Gardens

Stamford Green County Primary

CHRIST CHURCH RD

Kingswood House Sch

Epsom Primary School

Ebbisham Sports Club

WEST HILL

WEST ST

Station A

Clock-tower

Ashley Centre Shop Precinct

Surgery

Playhouse Theatre

Playhouse

SOUTH ST

St Josephs Catholic Primary School

EPSOM

Infants School

Premier Travel Inn

ASHLE

Mt Hill Gardens

Epsom Common

The Wells

Greenway

Wells Road

The Crs

Spa Dr Crs

The Well Way

The Crs

The Greenway

Marneys Cl

Woodlands Road

Roseberry School

DORKING RD A24

A&E

Epsom General Hospital

Woodcote Green

Club

The Forest

Wood Field

National Nature Reserve

Broadhurst

Culverhay

Overdale

Newton

Wood Road

Bagot Close

Craddocks Avenue

Petters Road

Devitt Cl

Oak Way

Woodcote Stud

Woodcote Park Road

Woodcote Side

Wilmerhatch Lane

Woodcote Park

Wo

St Stephens Avenue

Crav Av

Chaffers

Mead

Bramley Way

Ashtead Station

Works

Woodfield

Meadow Road

Darcy Road

Darcy Place

Berry

Stonny Croft

EPSOM ROAD

Greville Prim Sch

The Hilders

Taylor Road

Read Road

Barnett Wood Infant School

Ashtead Clinic

KT21

Downsend School Ashtead Lodge

Moat Court

Walter's Md

Ashtead CC

Broadmead

Crofton

The Marld

Ashtead Park

Church Road

Glebe Road

Skinners

Greville Park

Greville Avenue

Ashtead

THE STREET

Park La

St Giles CE (Aided) Infant School

Pleasure Pit Road

Cherry Orch

Rookery

Paw's Place

Oakfield Road

Ottways Lane

Parsons Mead School

City of London Freemens School

St Paul's

G 18 H J 103 19 K L 20 M

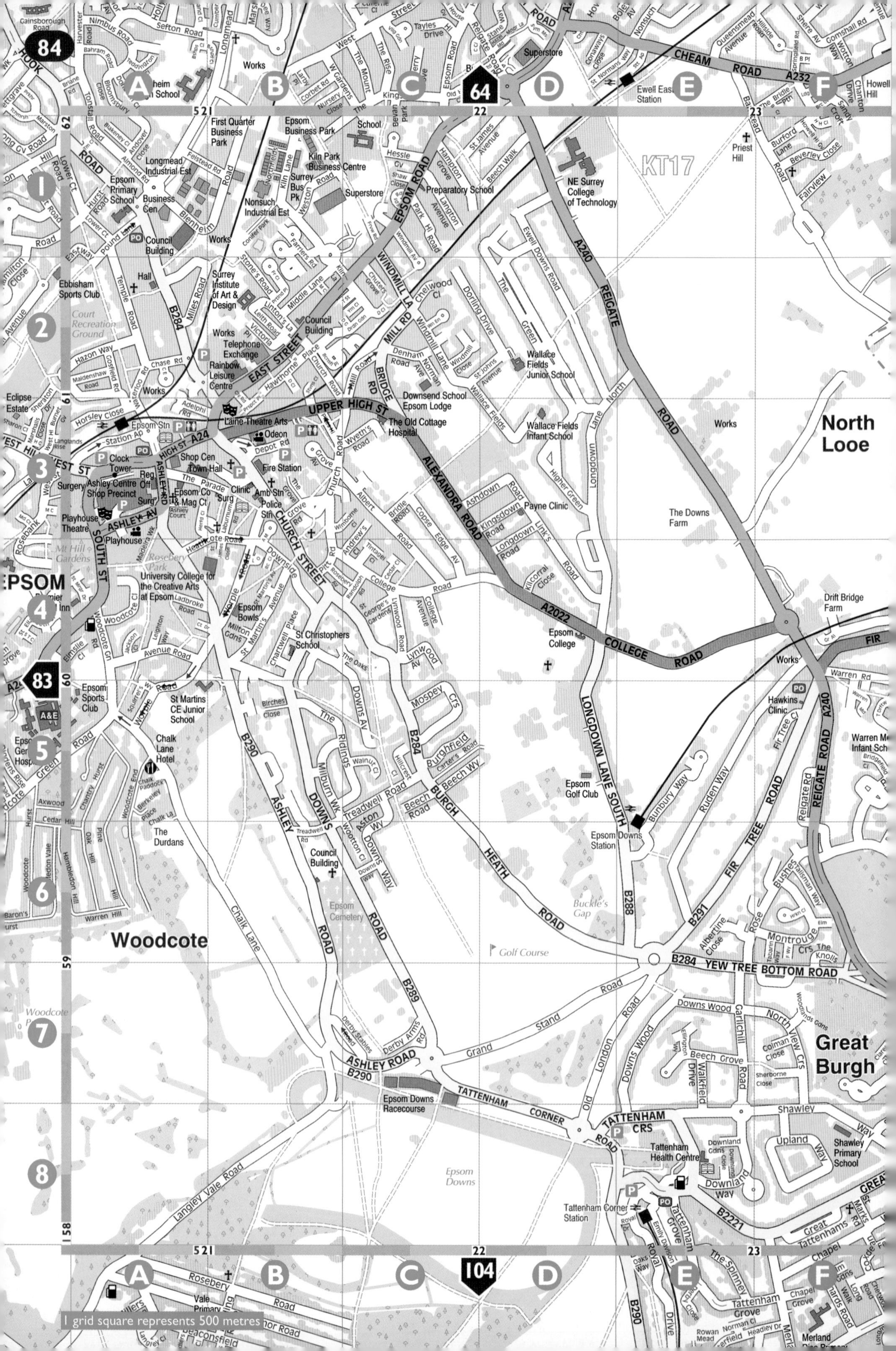

84
64
83
104
A
B
C
D
E
F
1
2
3
4
5
6
7
8
521
22
23
62
61
60
59
58
Gainsborough Road
HOOK
Nimbus Road
Sefton Road
Longmead
Works
West Street
Tayles Drive
Epsom Road
Reigate Road
Superstore
Ewell East Station
CHEAM ROAD
A232
Queensmead Avenue
Hillside Road
Nonsuch
Conaways Close
Shere Av
Gomshall Rd
Wotton Way
Howell Hill
Chanton Drive
Sandy Croft
First Quarter Business Park
Epsom Business Park
School
Hessle Gv
Hampton Grove
St James Avenue
Beech Walk
Kiln Park Business Centre
Longmead Industrial Est
Epsom Primary School
Business Cen
Nonsuch Industrial Est
Surrey Bus Pk
Superstore
Preparatory School
EPSOM ROAD
Langton Avenue
Park Hl Road
KT17
NE Surrey College of Technology
Priest Hill
Burford Lane
Beverley Close
Fairview
Bramble Road
Ebbisham Sports Club
Court Recreation Ground
Temple Road
Hall
Council Building
Blenheim Road
Surrey Institute of Art & Design
Miles Road
B284
Stone's Road
Middle Lane
Linton's La
Leith Road
Victoria Pl
Works
Telephone Exchange
Rainbow Leisure Centre
Council Building
EAST STREET
WINDMILL LA
MILL RD
Chelwood Cl
Windmill Lane
Dorling Drive
The Green
Ewell Downs Road
A240
REIGATE ROAD
Wallace Fields Junior School
Wallace Fields
Wallace Fields Infant School
Denham Road
Norman Ave
Downsend School Epsom Lodge
The Old Cottage Hospital
Hazon Way
Cosfield Rd
Maidenshaw Road
Chase Rd
Eclipse Estate
Horsley Close
Epsom Stn
Station Ap
Laine Theatre Arts
UPPER HIGH ST
BRIDGE RD
Odeon
Depot Rd
Fire Station
HIGH ST
A24
WEST ST
Clock Tower
Shop Cen
Town Hall
Reg Off
ASHLEY RD
The Parade
Clinic
Amb Stn
Police Stn
Surgery
Ashley Centre Shop Precinct
Epsom Co & Mag Ct
Surg
Playhouse Theatre
ASHLEY AV
Playhouse
SOUTH ST
Rosebank
Mt Hill Gardens
Rosebery Park
University College for the Creative Arts at Epsom
Heathcote Road
Ladbroke Road
CHURCH STREET
Church Road
The Grove
Albert Road
Bridle Road
Copse Edge Av
ALEXANDRA ROAD
Ashdown Road
Kingsdown Road
Longdown Road
Payne Clinic
Link's Road
Higher Green
Longdown Lane North
North Looe
Works
The Downs Farm
EPSOM
Woodcote Cl
Woodcote Gn
Worple Road
Epsom Bowls
Milton Gdns
St Martin's Avenue
Downside
St George's Gardens
College Road
Lynwood Road
College Avenue
Kilcorral Close
A2022
COLLEGE ROAD
Epsom College
Drift Bridge Farm
FIR
Works
Warren Rd
Hawkins Clinic
Avenue Road
Leighton Way
Epsom Sports Club
A&E
St Martins CE Junior School
Chalk Lane Hotel
St Christophers School
Chartwell Place
The Oaks
Lynwood Av
Birches Close
The Ridings
Downs Av
Mospey Crs
Burghfield
Carter's Road
Beech Wy
B290
ASHLEY
DOWNS
Milburn Wk
Walnut Cl
Treadwell Road
Aston Wy
Beech Road
BURGH HEATH ROAD
B284
LONGDOWN LANE SOUTH
Epsom Golf Club
Epsom Downs Station
Bunbury Way
Ruden Way
FIR TREE ROAD
Fir Tree Cl
REIGATE ROAD
A240
Reigate Rd
Warren Me Infant Sch
Axwood
Cedar Hill
Hambledon Hill
Oak Hill
Pine Hill
Woodcote End
Chantry Hurst
Chalk Paddock
Berkeley Place
Chalk La
The Durdans
Council Building
Wootton Cl
Downs Way
Epsom Cemetery
Woodcote
Warren Hill
Chalk Lane
ROAD
B289
B288
Buckle's Gap
Golf Course
B291
Albertine Close
Rose Bushes
Talisman Way
Montrouge Crs
The Knolls
B284
YEW TREE BOTTOM ROAD
Woodcote Park
Derby Stables Road
Derby Arms Rd
ASHLEY ROAD
B290
Grand Stand Road
Old London Road
Downs Wood
Downs Wood
Garlichill Road
North View Crs
Colman Close
Great Burgh
Beech Grove
Walkfield Drive
Sherborne Close
Epsom Downs Racecourse
TATTENHAM CORNER ROAD
TATTENHAM CRS
Shawley Way
Upland Way
Shawley Primary School
Tattenham Health Centre
Downland Gdns
Downland Way
Langley Vale Road
Epsom Downs
Tattenham Corner Station
Tattenham Grove
B2221
Great Tattenhams
Marks Rd
Chapel Way
Rosebery Road
Vale Primary
Oaks Way
B290
Royal Drive
The Spinney
Tattenham Grove
Chapel Grove
Merland
1 grid square represents 500 metres

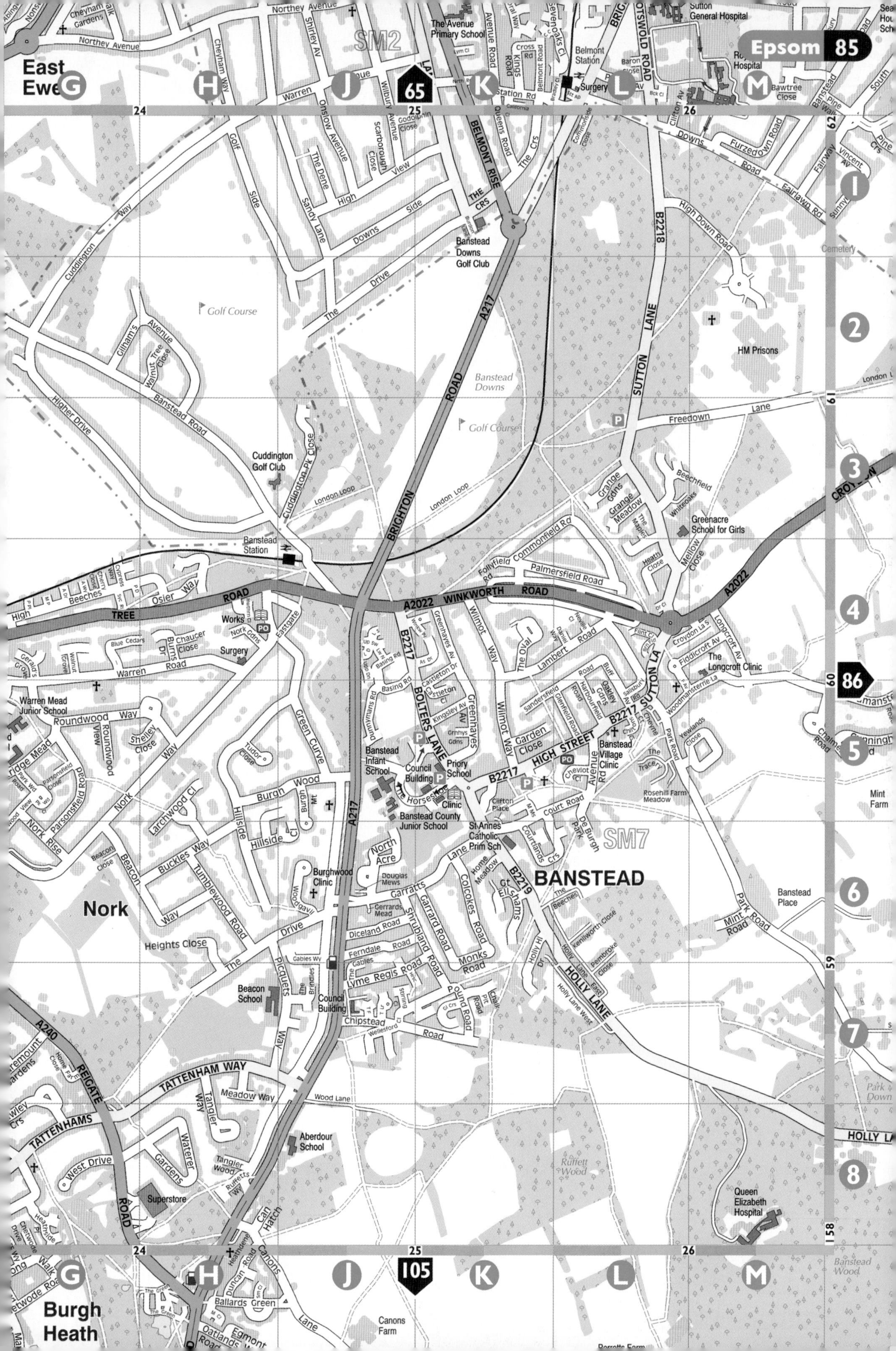
East Ewell
Nork
BANSTEAD
Burgh Heath
SM2
SM7
BRIGHTON ROAD
A217
A2022 WINKWORTH ROAD
TREE ROAD
SUTTON LANE
B2218
HIGH STREET
B2217
BOLTERS LANE
B2219
HOLLY LANE
REIGATE ROAD
A240
TATTENHAM WAY
TATTENHAMS
BELMONT RISE
Banstead Station
Belmont Station
Banstead Downs
Banstead Downs Golf Club
Cuddington Golf Club
Golf Course
HM Prisons
Greenacre School for Girls
The Longcroft Clinic
Banstead Village Clinic
Priory School
Banstead Infant School
Banstead County Junior School
St Annes Catholic Prim Sch
Burghwood Clinic
Beacon School
Aberdour School
Warren Mead Junior School
Queen Elizabeth Hospital
Sutton General Hospital
The Avenue Primary School
Superstore
Banstead Place
Mint Farm
Ruffett Wood
Banstead Wood
Canons Farm
Park Downs
Freedown Lane
London Loop
65
86
105

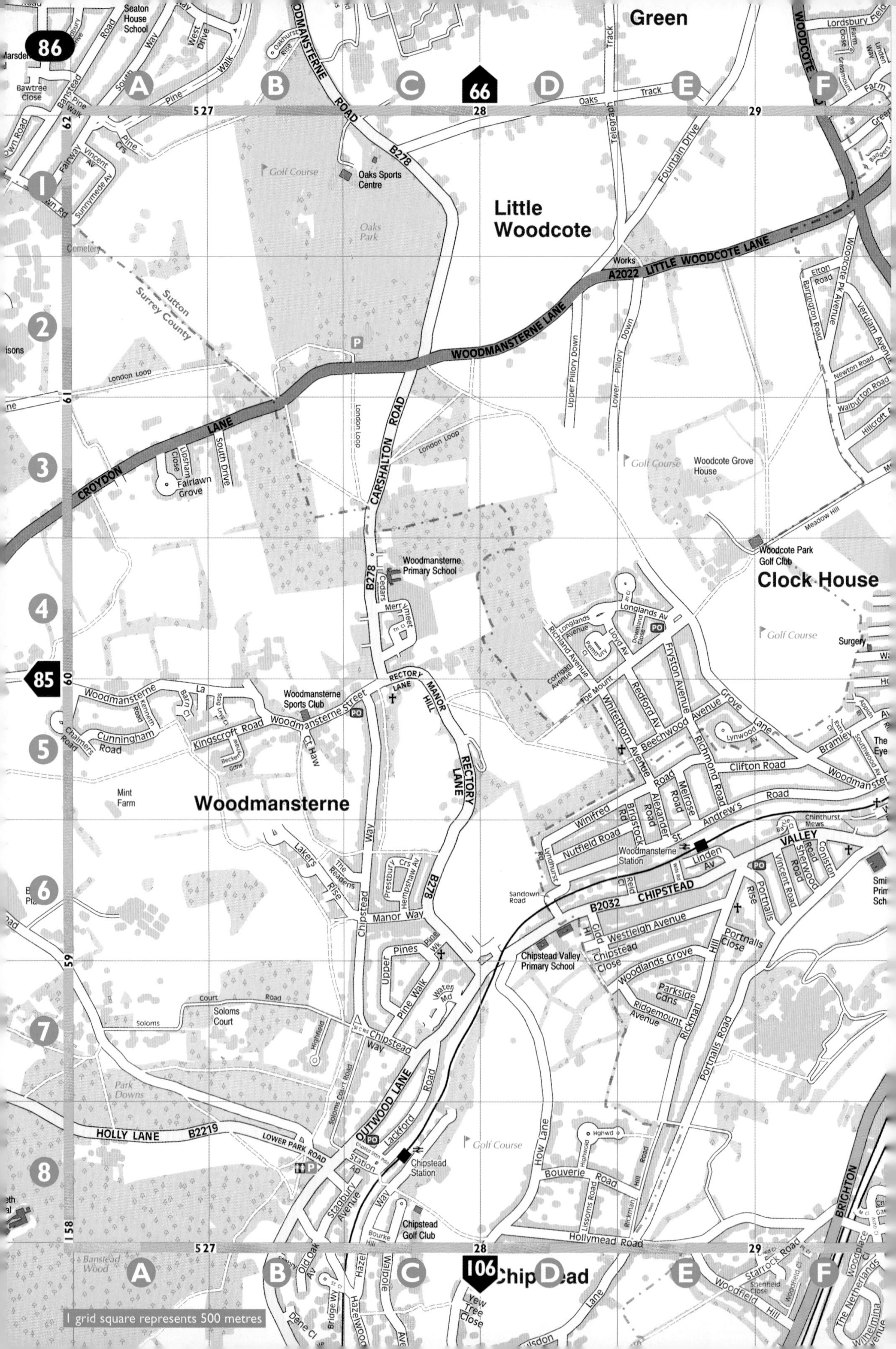
86
85
66
106
Green
Little Woodcote
Clock House
Woodmansterne
Chipstead
Oaks Sports Centre
Oaks Park
Golf Course
A2022 LITTLE WOODCOTE LANE
WOODMANSTERNE LANE
CROYDON LANE
CARSHALTON ROAD
B278
RECTORY LANE
Woodmansterne Primary School
Woodmansterne Sports Club
Woodcote Park Golf Club
Woodcote Grove House
Woodmansterne Station
B2032 CHIPSTEAD VALLEY
Chipstead Valley Primary School
OUTWOOD LANE
Chipstead Station
Chipstead Golf Club
HOLLY LANE B2219
LOWER PARK ROAD
Park Downs
Banstead Wood
Solom's Court
Mint Farm
Surrey County
Sutton
Cemetery
Works
Surgery
BRIGHTON
1 grid square represents 500 metres

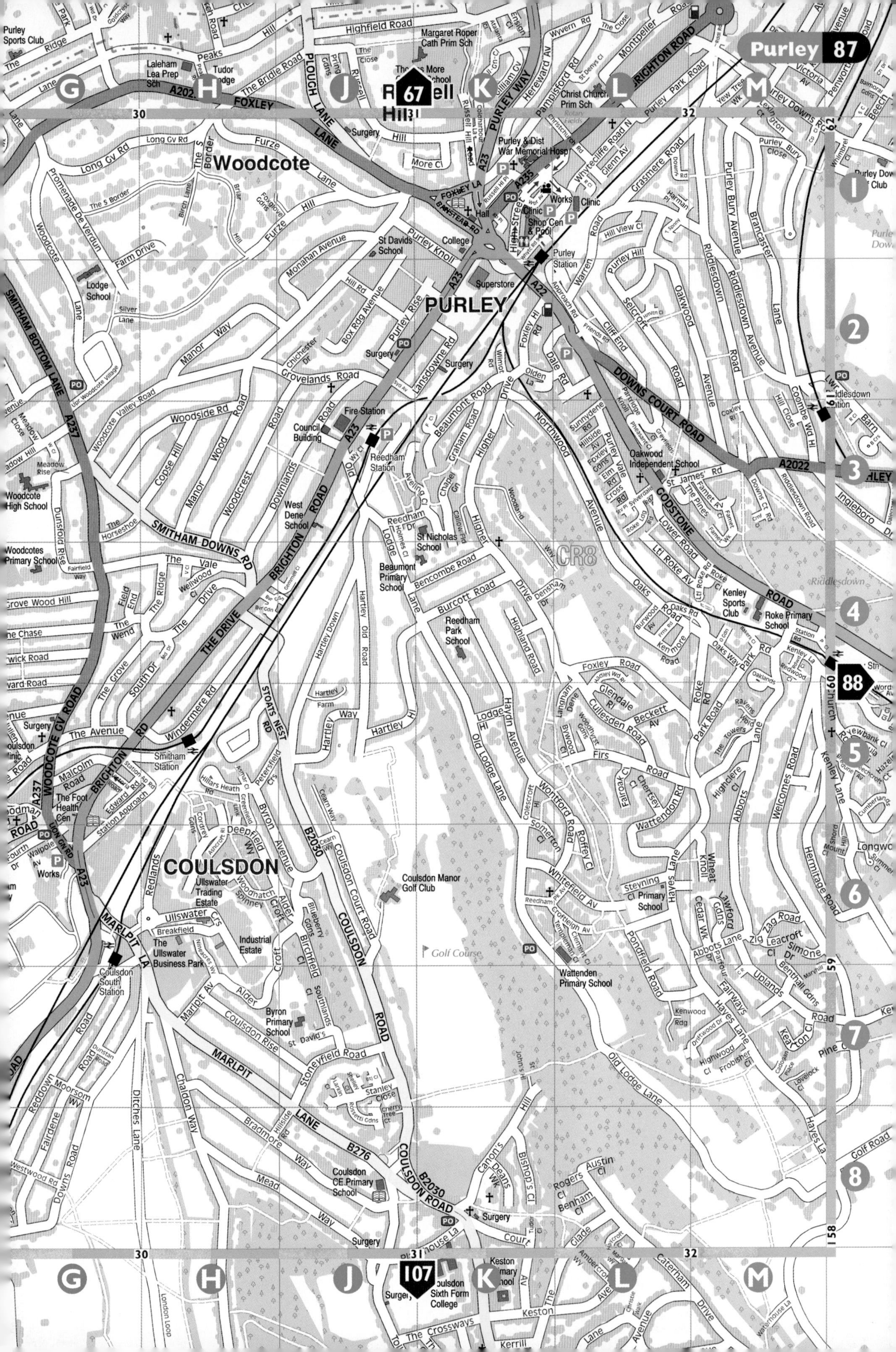

Purley 87
67
88
107
G
H
J
K
L
M
30
31
32
2
3
4
5
6
7
8
Woodcote
PURLEY
COULSDON
CR8
Purley Sports Club
Laleham Lea Prep Sch
Tudor Lodge
Highfield Road
Margaret Roper Cath Prim Sch
FOXLEY LANE
A2022
PLOUGH LANE
PURLEY WAY
BRIGHTON ROAD
Christ Church Prim Sch
Purley & Dist War Memorial Hosp
Shop Cen & Pool
Works
Clinic
Purley Station
Superstore
College
St Davids School
Lodge School
Woodcote High School
Woodcotes Primary School
SMITHAM BOTTOM LANE
A237
SMITHAM DOWNS RD
Woodcote Valley Road
Grovelands Road
Fire Station
Council Building
Reedham Station
West Dene School
St Nicholas School
Beaumont Primary School
Reedham Park School
Oakwood Independent School
DOWNS COURT ROAD
GODSTONE ROAD
A22
A23
Kenley Sports Club
Roke Primary School
Riddlesdown Avenue
Purley Bury Avenue
Brancaster Lane
Purley Downs Rd
Purley Downs Golf Club
THE DRIVE
WOODCOTE GV ROAD
Smitham Station
The Foot Health Cen
Coulsdon South Station
MARLPIT LA
Ullswater Trading Estate
Industrial Estate
The Ullswater Business Park
STOATS NEST RD
B2030
COULSDON ROAD
Coulsdon Court Road
Coulsdon Manor Golf Club
Golf Course
Old Lodge Lane
Stevning Cl Primary School
Wattenden Primary School
Byron Primary School
Coulsdon CE Primary School
Coulsdon Sixth Form College
B276
Chaldon Way
Ditches Lane
Hermitage Road
Hayes Lane
Kenley Lane
Welcomes Road
The Crossways
Keston
Caterham Drive

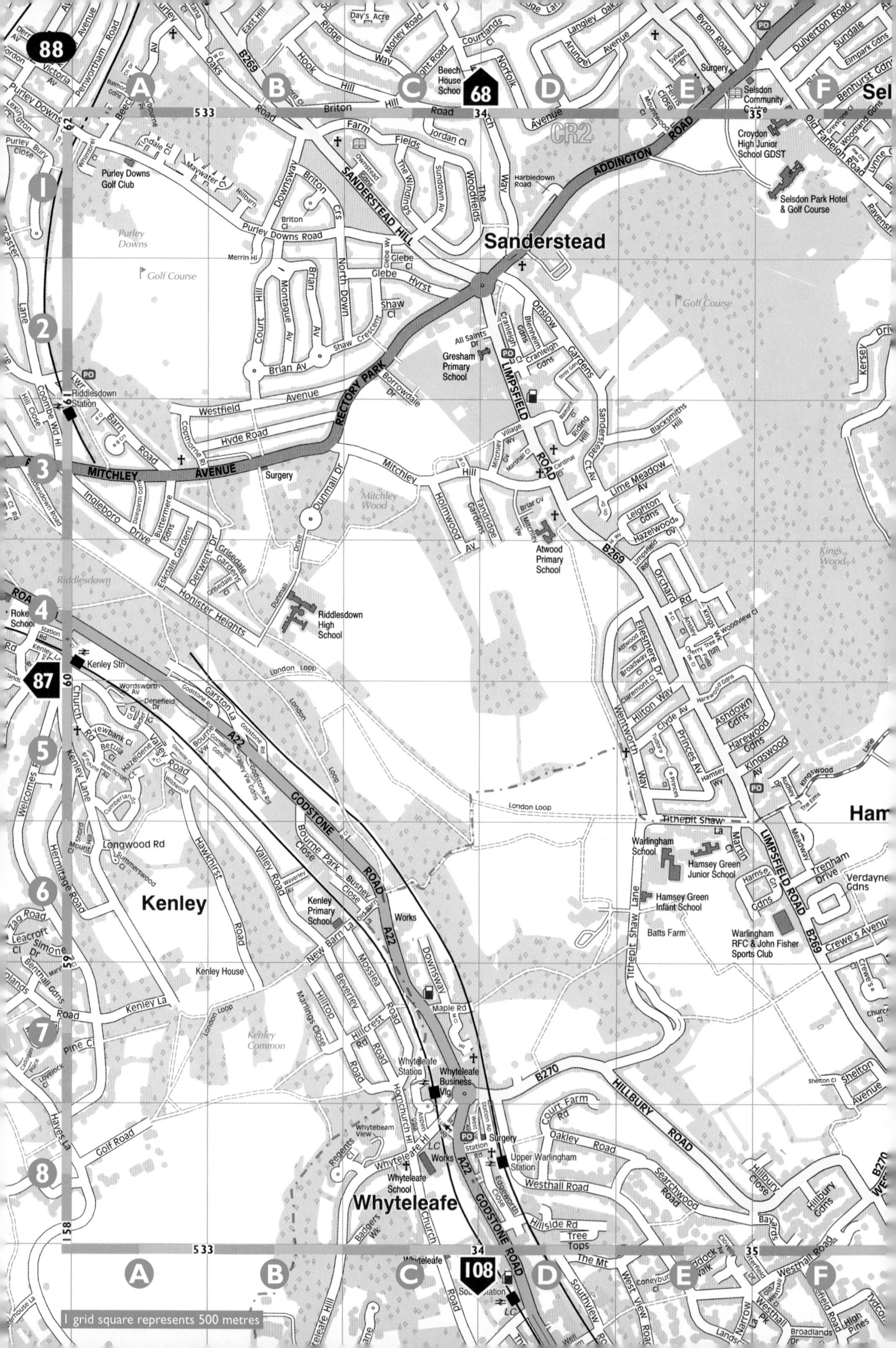

88
68
87
108
A
B
C
D
E
F
1
2
3
4
5
6
7
8
533
34
35
62
61
60
59
158
CR2
Sanderstead
Kenley
Whyteleafe
Purley Downs Golf Club
Purley Downs
Golf Course
Riddlesdown Station
Riddlesdown
Roke School
Kenley Stn
Kenley House
Kenley Common
Kenley Primary School
Riddlesdown High School
Mitchley Wood
Gresham Primary School
Atwood Primary School
Beech House School
Selsdon Community Centre
Croydon High Junior School GDST
Selsdon Park Hotel & Golf Course
Kings Wood
Warlingham School
Hamsey Green Junior School
Hamsey Green Infant School
Batts Farm
Warlingham RFC & John Fisher Sports Club
Whyteleafe Station
Whyteleafe Business Vlg
Whyteleafe School
Upper Warlingham Station
Works
Surgery
London Loop
ADDINGTON ROAD
SANDERSTEAD HILL
RECTORY PARK
MITCHLEY AVENUE
LIMPSFIELD ROAD
GODSTONE ROAD
HILLBURY ROAD
A22
B269
B270
Purley Downs Road
Briton Hill Road
Farm Fields
Westfield Avenue
Hyde Road
Mitchley Hill
Ingleboro Drive
Honister Heights
Valley Road
Hawkhirst Road
Kenley Lane
Hermitage Road
Golf Road
Tithepit Shaw Lane
Wentworth Way
Westhall Road
Oakley Road
Searchwood Road
Court Farm Rd
Hillside Rd
The Mt
Southview
Downsway
Church Rd
Longwood Rd
Kenley La
Welcomes Rd
Haves La
1 grid square represents 500 metres

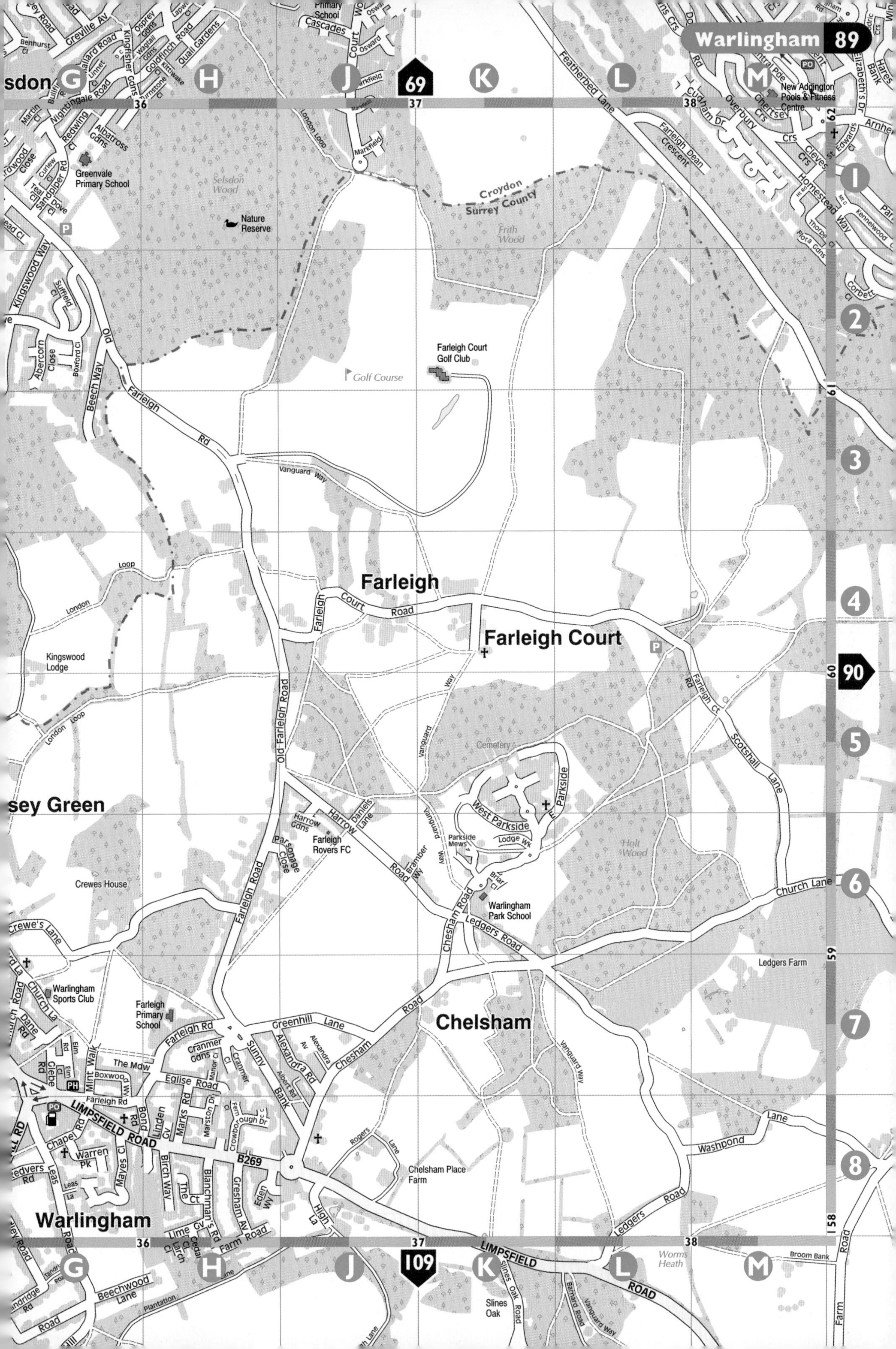
Farleigh
Farleigh Court
Chelsham
Warlingham
sey Green
sdon
Farleigh Court Golf Club
Golf Course
Selsdon Wood
Nature Reserve
Frith Wood
Croydon
Surrey County
Greenvale Primary School
New Addington Pools & Fitness Centre
Kingswood Lodge
Crewes House
Farleigh Rovers FC
Warlingham Park School
Cemetery
Holt Wood
Ledgers Farm
Warlingham Sports Club
Farleigh Primary School
Chelsham Place Farm
Worms Heath
Slines Oak
Farleigh Court Road
Old Farleigh Road
Farleigh Road
Farleigh Rd
Featherbed Lane
Farleigh Dean Crescent
Harrow Road
Chesham Road
Ledgers Road
Church Lane
Scotshall Lane
Washpond Lane
Limpsfield Road
B269
Greenhill Lane
Vanguard Way
London Loop
West Parkside
E Parkside
Lodge Wk
Parkside Mews
Sunny Bank
Alexandra Rd
Eglise Road
Crewe's Lane
Beech Way
Kingswood Way
Abercorn Close
Boxford Cl
Daniels Lane
Parsonage Close
Harrow Gdns
Bramber Wy
Briar Cl
Mint Walk
The Mdw
Birch Way
Marks Rd
Blanchman's Rd
Gresham Av
Farm Road
Eden Wy
High La
Beechwood Lane
Plantation
Slines Oak Road
Barnard Road
Broom Bank
Farm Road
Ledgers Road
Overbury Crs
Homestead Way
Cleves Crs
Cudham Dr
Greville Av
Quail Gardens
Goldfinch Road
Kingfisher Gdns
Nightingale Road
Redwing Cl
Albatross Gdns
Sandpiper Rd
Markfield
Cascades
Primary School
Warren Pk
Chapel Rd
Mayes Cl
Linden Gv
Cranmer Gdns
Cranmer Cl
Marston Dr
Crowborough Dr
Glebe Rd
Church La
Dane Rd
69
109
90
G H J K L M
1 2 3 4 5 6 7 8
36 37 38
58 59 60 61 62

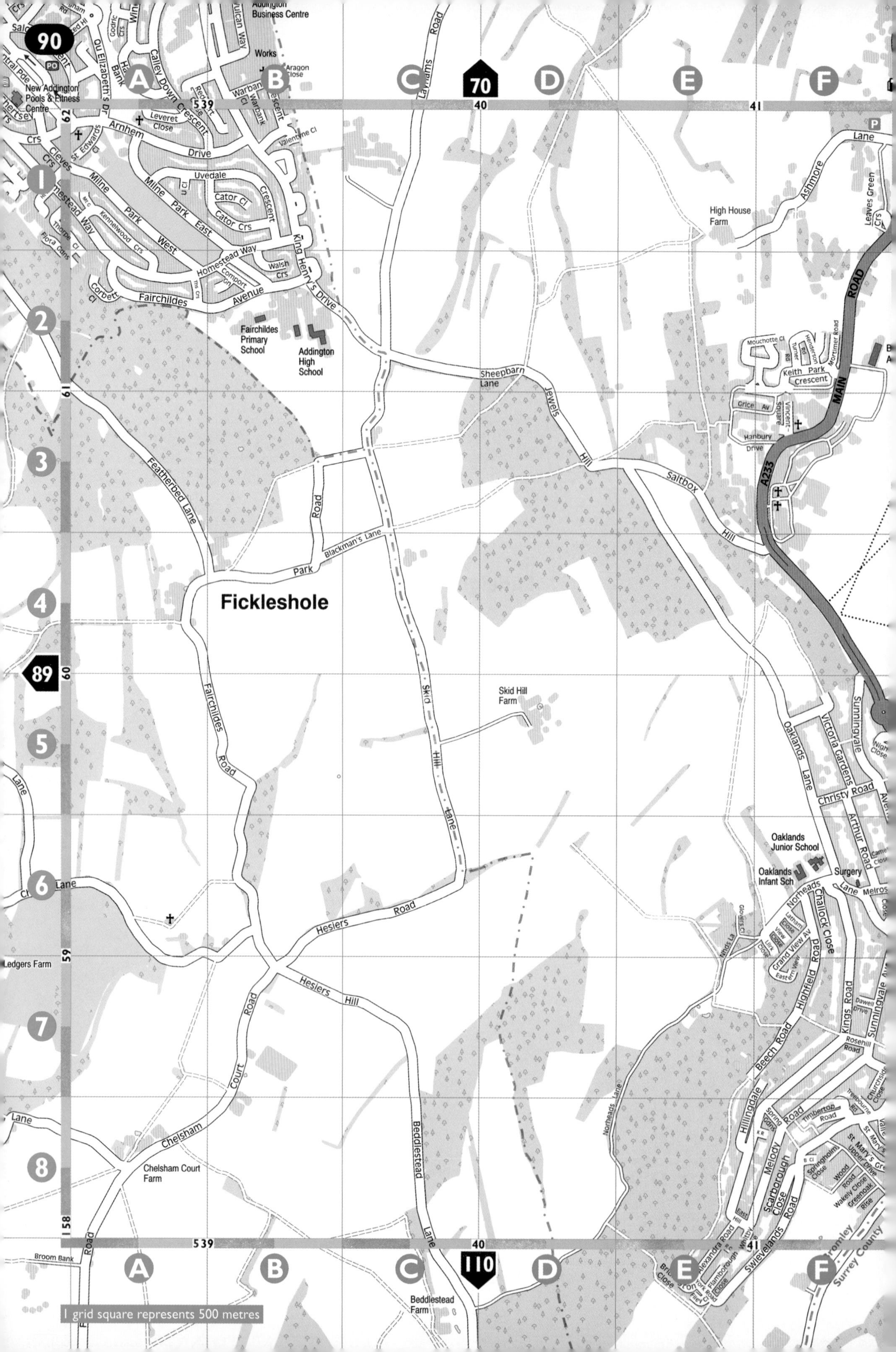

90
70
89
110
A
B
C
D
E
F
1
2
3
4
5
6
7
8
539
40
41
62
61
60
59
158
Fickleshole
New Addington Pools & Fitness Centre
Addington Business Centre
Works
Aragon Close
Calley Down Crescent
Leveret Close
Arnhem Drive
Cleves Crs
Homestead Way
Milne Park West
Milne Park East
Uvedale Crescent
Cator Cl
Cator Crs
Kennelwood Crs
Fairchildes Avenue
Corbett Cl
King Henry's Drive
Walsh Crs
Comport Gn
Valentyne Cl
Warbank Crescent
Fairchildes Primary School
Addington High School
Featherbed Lane
Sheepbarn Lane
Jewels Hill
Saltbox Hill
Blackman's Lane
Park Road
Skid Hill Lane
Skid Hill Farm
High House Farm
Ashmore Lane
Leaves Green Crs
MAIN ROAD
A233
Keith Park Crescent
Mouchotte Cl
Henderson Rd
Turner Rd
Mortimer Road
Grice Av
Vincent Square
Hanbury Drive
Fairchildes Road
Hesiers Road
Hesiers Hill
Chelsham Court Road
Chelsham Court Farm
Beddlestead Lane
Beddlestead Farm
Ledgers Farm
Broom Bank
Oaklands Lane
Victoria Gardens
Sunningvale
Christy Road
Arthur Road
Oaklands Junior School
Oaklands Infant Sch
Surgery
Norheads Lane
Challock Close
Highfield Road
Grand View Av
Beech Road
Hillingdale
Kings Road
Rosehill Road
Dawell Drive
Sunningvale Av
Melody Road
Scarborough Close
Swievelands Road
Alexandra Road
Northeads Lane
Timberton Road
Upper Drive
Wood Road
Wakely Close
Greenoak Rise
Bromley
Surrey County
1 grid square represents 500 metres

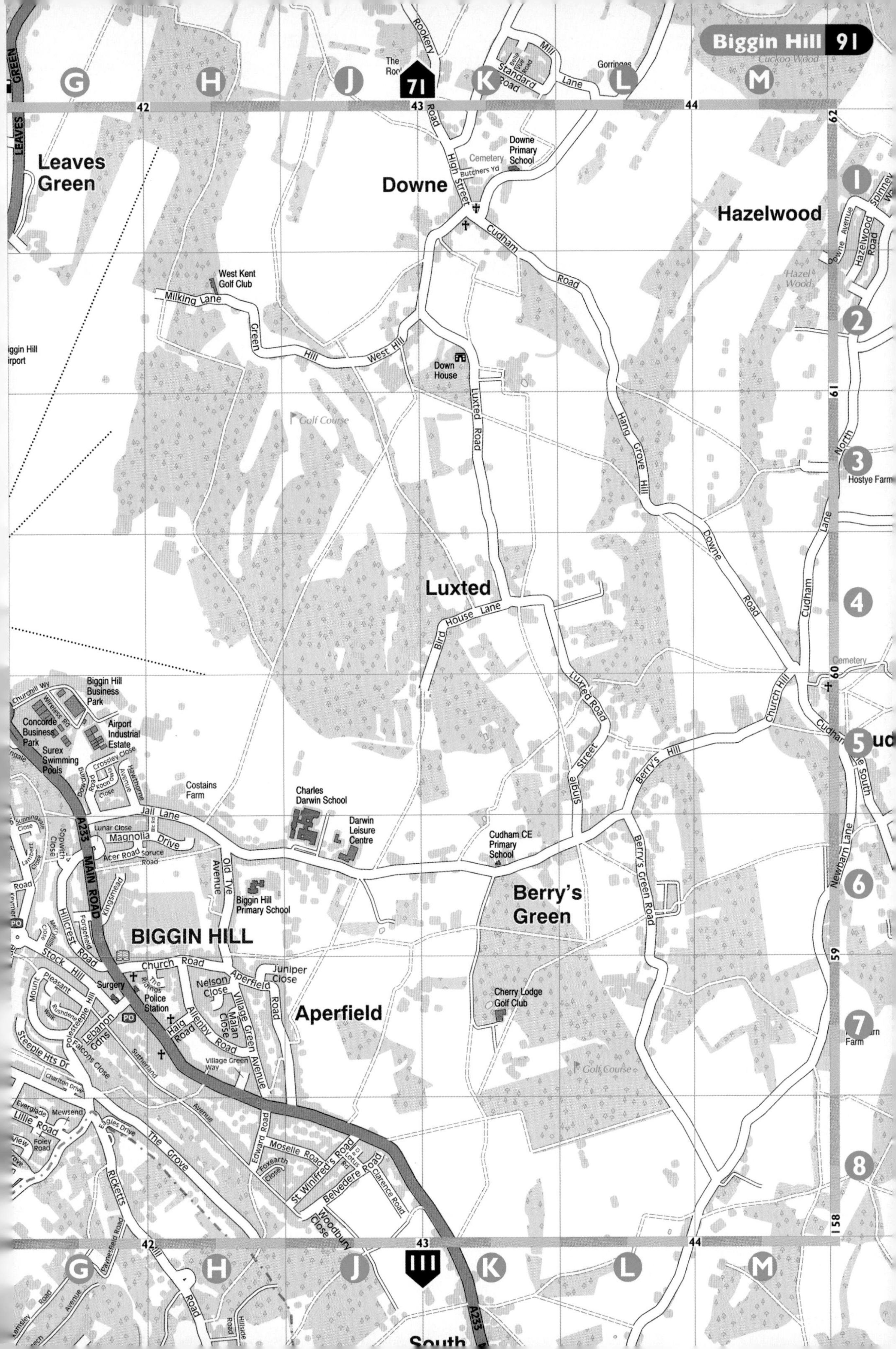

G 42 H J **71** 43 K 44 L M

Leaves Green

Downe

Hazelwood

Cuckoo Wood

I

Downe Avenue

Hazelwood Road

Spinney Wy

62

The Rookery

Rookery Road

Blue Violet Road

Standard Road

Mill Lane

Gorringes

Cemetery

Downe Primary School

Butchers Yd

High Street

Hazel Woods

1

2

West Kent Golf Club

Milking Lane

Green Hill

West Hill

Down House

Cudham Road

Luxted Road

Hang Grove Hill

Downe Road

Cudham Lane North

61

Biggin Hill Airport

Golf Course

3

Hostye Farm

Luxted

Bird House Lane

4

Cemetery

60

Cudham South

Church Hill

Cudham Lane South

5

Cud

Biggin Hill Business Park

Concorde Business Park

Airport Industrial Estate

Surex Swimming Pools

Churchill Wy

Wirelss Rd

Koon Road

Crossley Close

Hawthorne Avenue

Costains Farm

Charles Darwin School

Darwin Leisure Centre

Luxted Road

Shaws Street

Berry's Hill

Cudham CE Primary School

Berry's Green Road

Newbarn Lane

59

5

6

Jail Lane

Lunar Close

Magnolia Drive

Acer Road

Spruce Road

Kingsmead

Old Tye Avenue

Biggin Hill Primary School

Berry's Green

A233

MAIN ROAD

Sopwith Close

Sunningvale Avenue

Lambert

Lebanon Close

7

Farm

BIGGIN HILL

Church Road

Aperfield Road

Nelson Close

Malan Close

Juniper Close

Surgery

The Kings Police Station

Haig Road

Allenby Avenue

Village Green Road

Aperfield

Cherry Lodge Golf Club

PO

Mount Pleasant

Hillcrest Road

Ryshdene Close

Polesteeple Hill

Falcons Close

Village Green Way

Sutherland Avenue

7

Steeple Hts Dr

Charlton Drive

8

Everglade Mewsend

Lillie Road

Eagles Drive

The Grove

Avenue

Edward Road

Moselle Road

St Winifred's Road

Belvedere Road

Foxearth Close

Clarence Road

Woodbury Close

158

A233

South

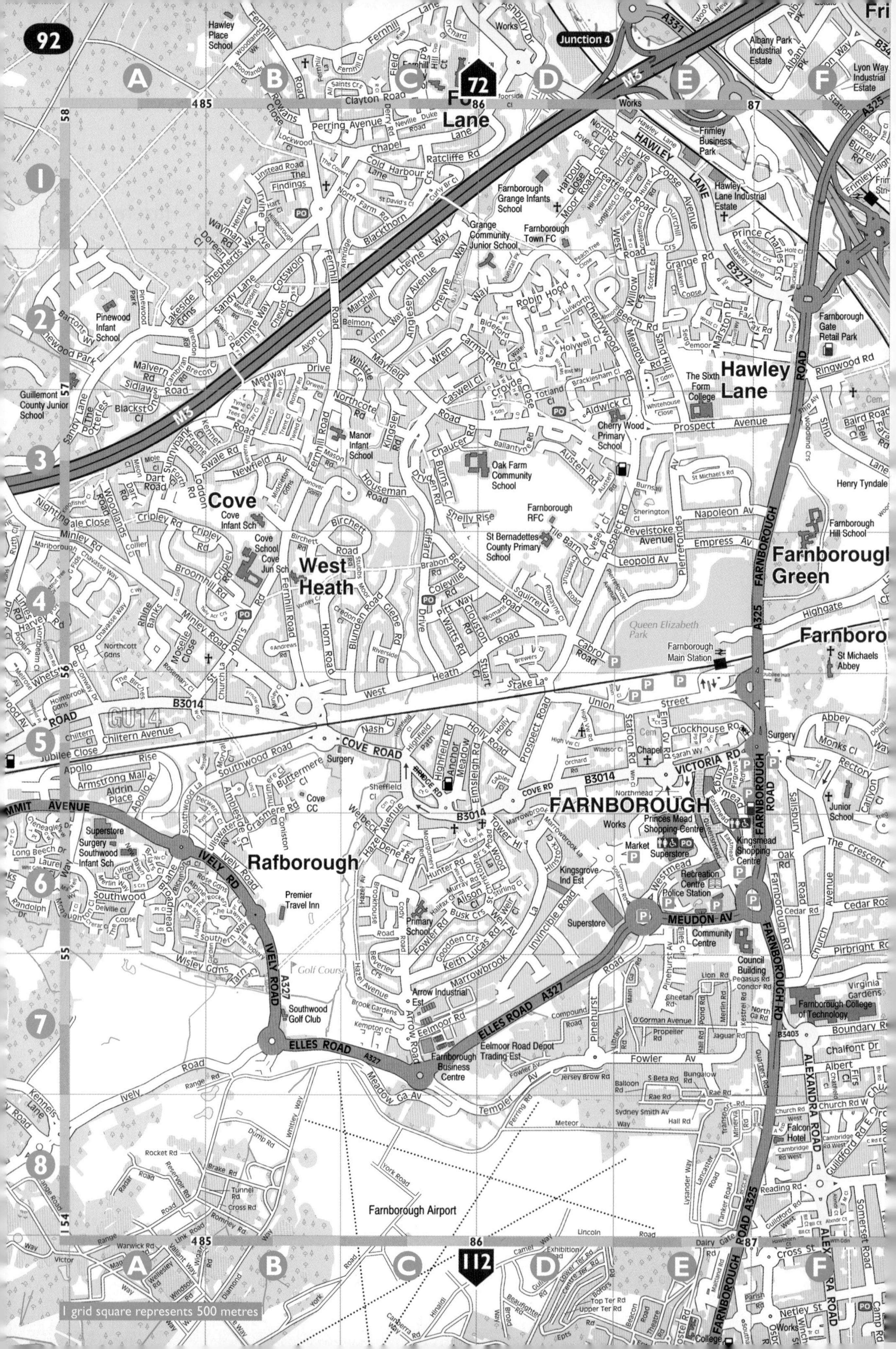
92
Hawley Place School
Junction 4
Fernhill Lane
Frimley Business Park
Albany Park Industrial Estate
Lyon Way Industrial Estate
Hawley Lane Industrial Estate
Perring Avenue
Clayton Road
Chapel Lane
Cold Harbour Lane
Ratcliffe Rd
Blackthorn Crs
The Findings
Hawley Lane
Farnborough Grange Infants School
Farnborough Town FC
Grange Community Junior School
Prince Charles Crs
Pinewood Infant School
Guillemont County Junior School
Sandy Lane
Shepherds Wk
Sidlaws Road
Malvern Rd
Pennine Way
Cotswold Cl
Fernhill Road
Anglesey Avenue
Cheyne Way
Robin Hood Cl
Cherrywood Rd
Sand Hill
Beech Rd
Farnborough Gate Retail Park
Ringwood Rd
The Sixth Form College
Hawley Lane
Prospect Avenue
Cherry Wood Primary School
Oak Farm Community School
Manor Infant School
Houseman Road
Newfield Av
Swale Rd
Cove
Cove Infant Sch
Cove School
Cove Jun Sch
West Heath
Birchett Road
Fernhill Road
Minley Road
Cripley Rd
Broomhill Rd
Nightingale Close
Farnborough RFC
St Bernadettes County Primary School
Napoleon Av
Revelstoke Avenue
Empress Av
Leopold Av
Farnborough Hill School
Farnborough Green
Henry Tyndale
Queen Elizabeth Park
Farnborough Main Station
Farnborough
St Michaels Abbey
Highgate
Farnborough Road
A325
West Heath Rd
Cabrol Road
Stake La
B3014
Union Street
Station Rd
Clockhouse Rd
Victoria Rd
Cove Road
Southwood Road
Chiltern Avenue
Jubilee Close
Apollo Rise
Armstrong Mall
Aldrin Place
Summit Avenue
Superstore
Surgery
Southwood Infant Sch
Ively Road
Rafborough
Premier Travel Inn
Golf Course
Southwood Golf Club
A327
Elles Road
FARNBOROUGH
Princes Mead Shopping Centre
Kingsmead Shopping Centre
Market
Works
Kingsgrove Ind Est
Invincible Road
Recreation Centre
Police Station
Meudon Av
Community Centre
Council Building
Farnborough College of Technology
Primary School
Arrow Industrial Est
Eelmoor Rd
Farnborough Business Centre
Eelmoor Road Depot Trading Est
Fowler Av
O'Gorman Avenue
Pinehurst Av
Boundary Rd
Chalfont Dr
Alexandra Road
Church Rd W
Falcon Hotel
Guildford Rd E
Reading Rd
Somerset Road
Junior School
The Crescent
Cedar Rd
Pirbright Road
Virginia Gardens
Farnborough Airport
Meteor Way
Templer Av
Lincoln
Rocket Rd
Reservoir Rd
Dump Rd
Tunnel Rd
Cross Rd
Romney Rd
Kennels Lane
Cross St
Camp Rd
Netley St
GU14
485
86
87
58
57
56
55
154
A
B
C
D
E
F
1
2
3
4
5
6
7
8
72
112
1 grid square represents 500 metres

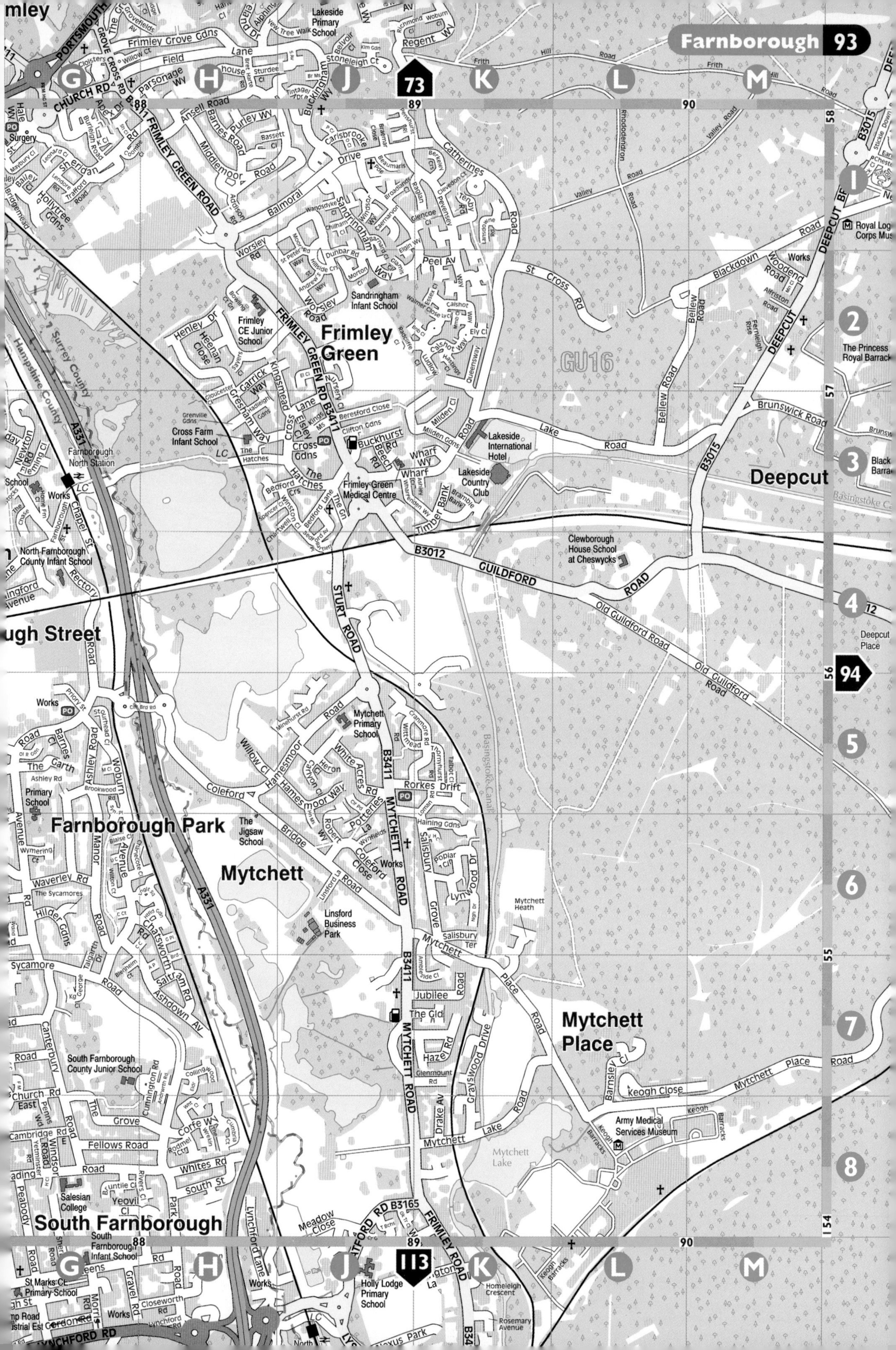

Farnborough 93
73
94
113
G
H
J
K
L
M
88
89
90
58
57
56
55
54
1
2
3
4
5
6
7
8
Frimley Green
Deepcut
Mytchett
Mytchett Place
Farnborough Park
South Farnborough
ugh Street
GU16
FRIMLEY GREEN ROAD
FRIMLEY GREEN RD B3411
CHURCH RD
PORTSMOUTH
Frimley Grove Gdns
Field
Lane
Regent Wy
Frith Hill Road
Valley Road
Rhododendron Road
Balmoral
Drive
Catherines Road
St Cross Rd
Blackdown Road
Woodend Road
DEEPCUT BR
DEEPCUT
B3015
Bellew Road
Lake Road
Brunswick Road
B3012
GUILDFORD ROAD
Old Guildford Road
STURT ROAD
B3411
MYTCHETT ROAD
Coleford Bridge Road
Hamesmoor Way
Rorkes Drift
Salisbury Grove
Mytchett Place Road
Mytchett Lake Road
Grayswood Drive
Keogh Close
Keogh Barracks
A331
Surrey County
Hampshire County
Basingstoke Canal
Lakeside Primary School
Sandringham Infant School
Frimley CE Junior School
Cross Farm Infant School
Farnborough North Station
North Farnborough County Infant School
Lakeside International Hotel
Lakeside Country Club
Frimley Green Medical Centre
Clewborough House School at Cheswycks
The Princess Royal Barracks
Royal Logistic Corps Museum
Mytchett Primary School
The Jigsaw School
Linsford Business Park
Mytchett Heath
Mytchett Lake
Army Medical Services Museum
South Farnborough County Junior School
Salesian College
South Farnborough Infant School
St Marks CE Primary School
Holly Lodge Primary School
Deepcut Place
Works
Surgery

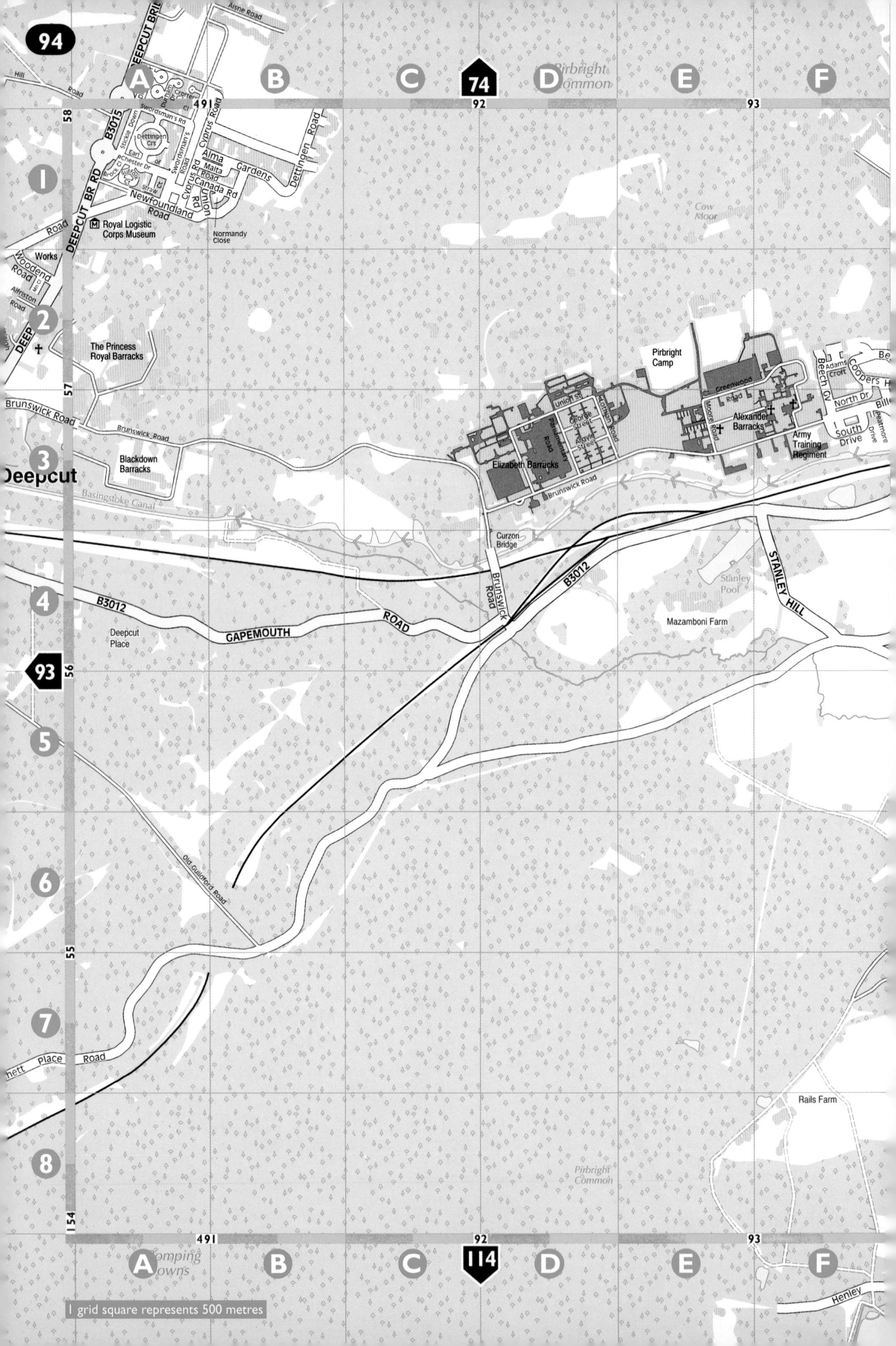

A   B   C   74   D   E   F
92

I

58

491

DEEPCUT BRID
B3015
DEEPCUT BR RD
Ticks Down
Dr
Earl
Chester Dr
Swordsman's Rd
Dettingen Crs
Swordsman's Rd
Strat
Newfoundland
Road
Alma   Gardens
Dettingen Road
Alsne Road
Aisne Road

Pirbright
Common

Cow
Moor

M Royal Logistic
Corps Museum

Normandy
Close

Malta
Road
Canada Rd
Union   Rd

Hill

Road

Works
Woodend

57

Alfriston
Road

DEEP
✝

2

The Princess
Royal Barracks

Pirbright
Camp

Greenwood
Road

Beech Dv
Adams
Croft
Coopers H
North Dr
Bill
South
Drive
Peatmore
Drive
Be

Brunswick Road

Brunswick Road

Union St
George
Street
Gotham Road
Moore Road

✝
Alexander
Barracks

3

Deepcut

Blackdown
Barracks

Elizabeth Barracks

Brunswick Road
Movie
Street
✝

Army
Training
Regiment

Basingstoke Canal

Curzon
Bridge

Brunswick
Road

B3012

STANLEY HILL

Stanley
Pool

4

B3012

GAPEMOUTH   ROAD

Deepcut
Place

Mazamboni Farm

56

93

5

Old Guildford Road

6

55

Rails Farm

7

hett Place Road

8

Pirbright
Common

154

491   92   93
A   B   C   114   D   E   F

Henley

1 grid square represents 500 metres

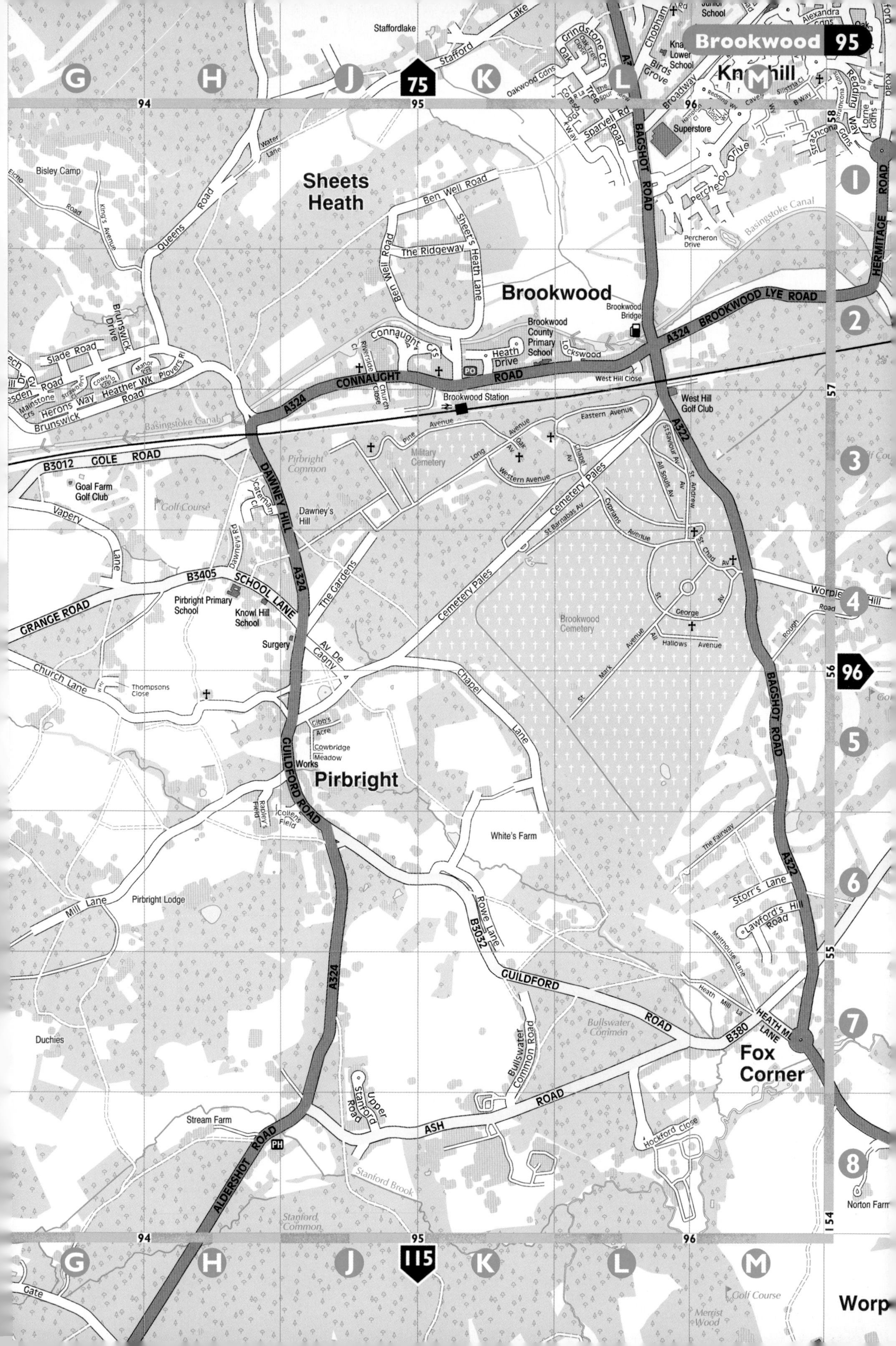

Staffordlake
Stafford Lake
75
Sheets Heath
Bisley Camp
Queens Road
Water Lane
Ben Well Road
The Ridgeway
Sheet's Heath Lane
Brookwood
Brookwood Bridge
Bagshot Road
A322
Superstore
Percheron Drive
Basingstoke Canal
Brookwood Lye Road
A324
Hermitage Road
Knaphill
Chobham Rd
Knaphill Lower School
Birch Grove
Broadway
Grindstone Crs
Oak Tree Close
Oakwood Gdns
Sparvell Rd
Anchor Crs
Strathcona Gdns
Redding Way
Lorne Gdns
Alexandra Gdns
Brunswick Drive
Slade Road
Manor Crs
Heather Wk
Plovers Rd
Herons Way
Brunswick Road
Mainstone Crs
Connaught Crs
Riverside Cl
Heath Drive
Brookwood County Primary School
Lockswood
Connaught Road
Church Close
West Hill Close
Brookwood Station
West Hill Golf Club
B3012 Gole Road
Goal Farm Golf Club
Golf Course
Pirbright Common
Military Cemetery
Pine Avenue
Long Avenue
Oak Av
Western Avenue
Eastern Avenue
Chapel Av
Cemetery Pales
St Saviour Av
All Souls Av
St Andrew
Cyprians Avenue
St Barnabas Av
St Chad Av
Dawney Hill
Dawney's Hill
Caterham Cl
Vapery Lane
Dawneys Rd
B3405 School Lane
Grange Road
Pirbright Primary School
Knowl Hill School
Surgery
The Gardens
Av De Cagny
Brookwood Cemetery
St George Av
All Hallows Avenue
St Mark Avenue
Worplesdon Hill Road
Rough
Church Lane
Thompsons Close
Chapel Lane
Gibbs Acre
Cowbridge Meadow
Works
Pirbright
Guildford Road
Rapley's Field
Collens Field
White's Farm
The Fairway
Storr's Lane
Lawford's Hill Road
Malthouse Lane
Mill Lane
Pirbright Lodge
Rowe Lane
B3032
Guildford Road
Bullswater Common Road
Bullswater Common
Heath Mill La
Heath Mill Lane
B380
Fox Corner
Duchies
Upper Stanford Road
Ash Road
Stream Farm
Aldershot Road
PH
PO
Hockford Close
Stanford Brook
Stanford Common
Norton Farm
Gate
Golf Course
Merrist Wood
Worp
115
96
G H J K L M
94 95 96
1 2 3 4 5 6 7 8
54 55 56 57 58

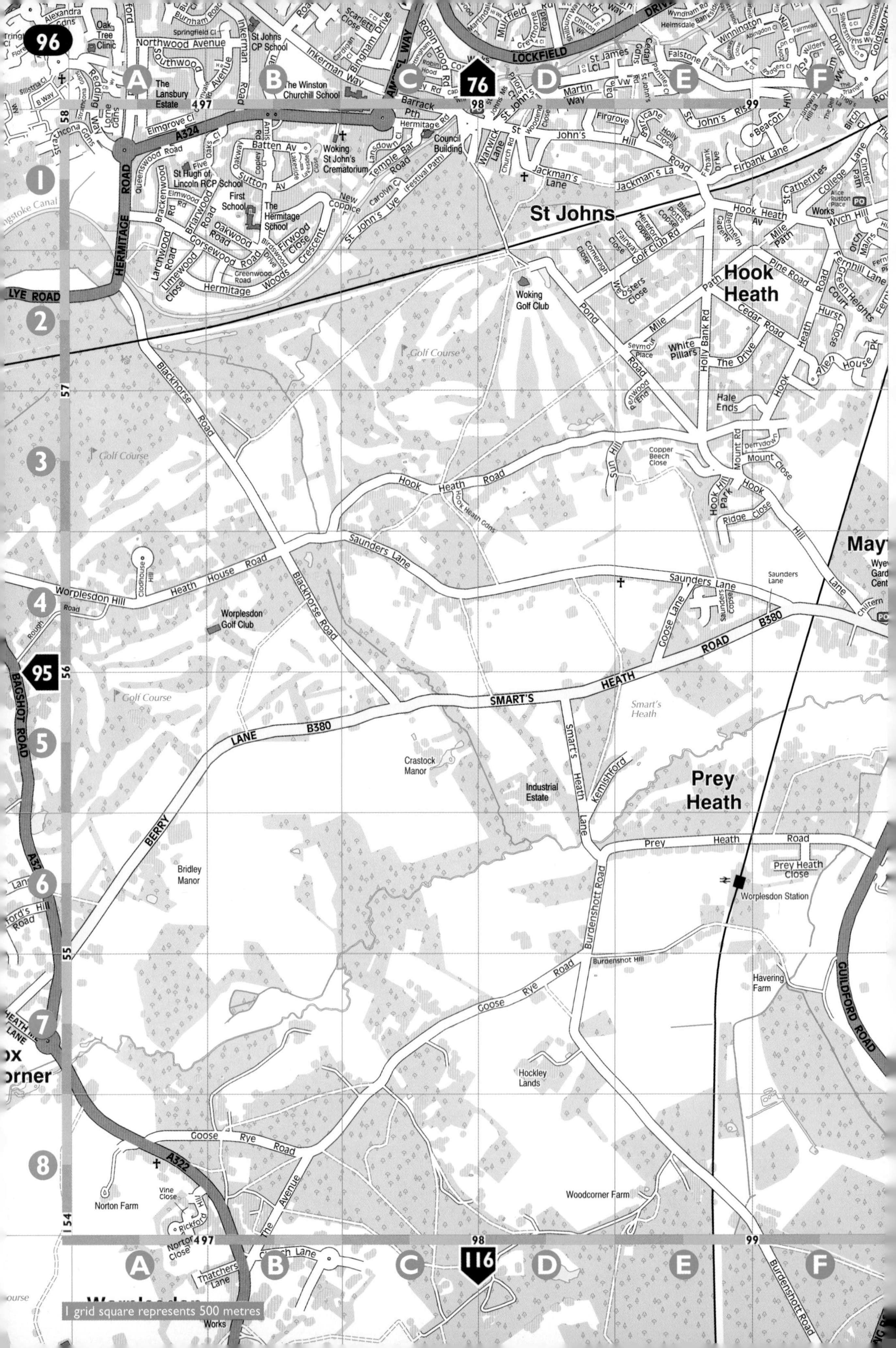

96
76
95
116
St Johns
Hook Heath
Prey Heath
Woking Golf Club
Worplesdon Golf Club
Golf Course
Crastock Manor
Industrial Estate
Bridley Manor
Hockley Lands
Woodcorner Farm
Havering Farm
Norton Farm
Worplesdon Station
Smart's Heath
The Lansbury Estate
The Winston Churchill School
St Johns CP School
St Hugh of Lincoln RCP School
First School
The Hermitage School
Woking St John's Crematorium
Council Building
Oak Tree Clinic
HERMITAGE ROAD
SMART'S HEATH ROAD B380
BERRY LANE B380
BAGSHOT ROAD
GUILDFORD ROAD
A322
A324
Blackhorse Road
Hook Heath Road
Saunders Lane
Heath House Road
Worplesdon Hill
Goose Rye Road
Burdenshott Road
Burdenshot Hill
Prey Heath Road
Prey Heath Close
Smart's Heath Lane
Kemishford
Goose Lane
Pond Road
Mile Path
Holly Bank Rd
Cedar Road
Hook Hill
Hook Hill Park
Ridge Close
Mount Close
Copper Beech Close
Sun Hill
White Pillars
The Drive
Hale Ends
Golf Club Rd
Websters Close
Jackman's Lane
St John's Hill Road
Firbank Lane
Hook Heath Av
Wych Hill
Pine Road
St John's Lye (Festival Path)
Hermitage Woods Crescent
Corsewood Road
Oakwood Road
Briarwood Road
Larchwood Road
Limewood Close
Batten Av
Sutton Av
Temple Bar Road
Inkerman Way
Inkerman Road
Northwood Avenue
Southwood Avenue
Lockfield Drive
Robin Hood Rd
Bingham Drive
Martin Way
Elmgrove Cl
Queenswood Road
Thatchers Lane
Church Lane
The Avenue
Rickford Hill
Vine Close
Norton Close
Worplesdon
1 grid square represents 500 metres

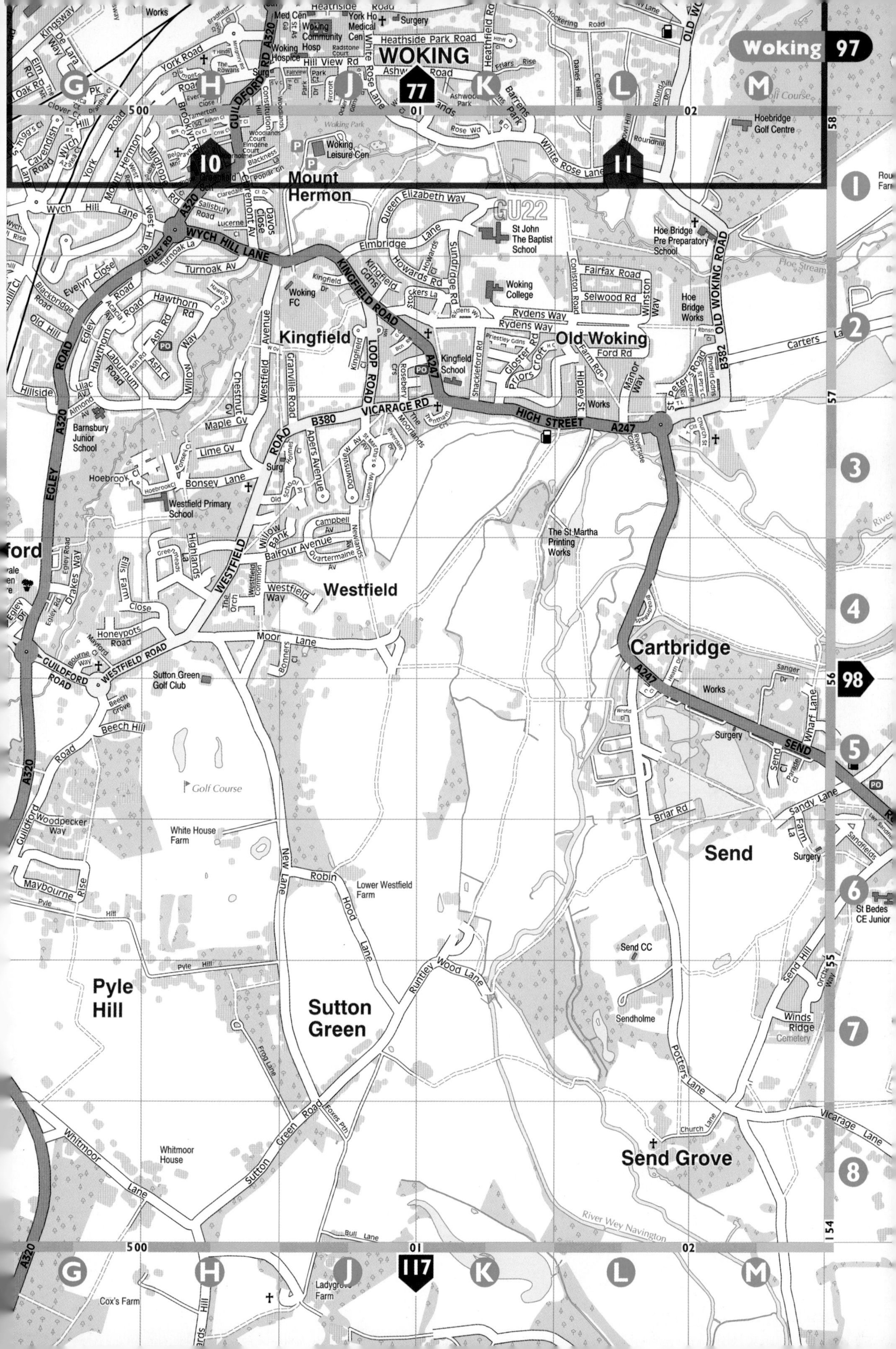
WOKING
Mount Hermon
Kingfield
Old Woking
Westfield
Cartbridge
Send
Pyle Hill
Sutton Green
Send Grove
GU22
WYCH HILL LANE
KINGFIELD ROAD
HIGH STREET
VICARAGE RD
LOOP ROAD
WESTFIELD ROAD
GUILDFORD ROAD
EGLEY ROAD
OLD WOKING ROAD
GUILDFORD RD A320
A320
A247
B380
B382
Woking Community Hosp
Woking Hospice
Woking Leisure Cen
Woking FC
St John The Baptist School
Woking College
Kingfield School
Barnsbury Junior School
Westfield Primary School
Hoe Bridge Pre Preparatory School
Hoebridge Golf Centre
Sutton Green Golf Club
Golf Course
White House Farm
Lower Westfield Farm
Whitmoor House
The St Martha Printing Works
Hoe Bridge Works
Sendholme
Send CC
Winds Ridge Cemetery
St Bedes CE Junior
River Wey Navigation
Cox's Farm
Ladygrove Farm
10
11
77
98
117
G H J K L M
500 01 02
58 57 56 55 154
1 2 3 4 5 6 7 8

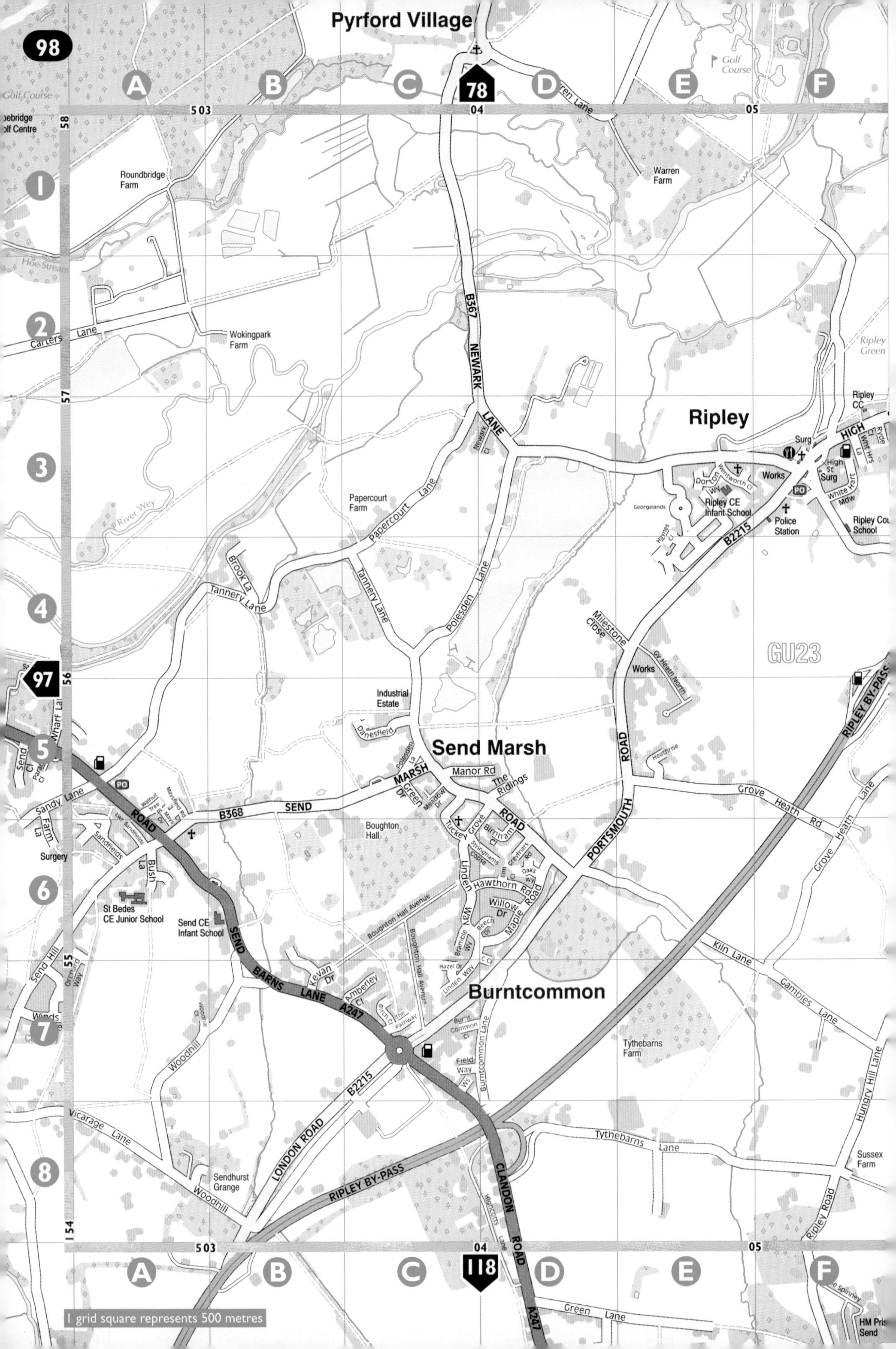
98
Pyrford Village
78
97
118
Ripley
Send Marsh
Burntcommon
Roundbridge Farm
Wokingpark Farm
Warren Farm
Papercourt Farm
Industrial Estate
Boughton Hall
St Bedes CE Junior School
Send CE Infant School
Ripley CE Infant School
Police Station
Tythebarns Farm
Sendhurst Grange
Sussex Farm
GU23
Carters Lane
Newark Lane
Papercourt Lane
Tannery Lane
Polesden Lane
Send Marsh Road
Send Road
Send Barns Lane
London Road
Ripley By-Pass
Clandon Road
Portsmouth Road
Grove Heath Rd
Kiln Lane
Gambles Lane
Hungry Hill Lane
Tythebarns Lane
Vicarage Lane
Woodhill
Green Lane
Ripley Road
1 grid square represents 500 metres

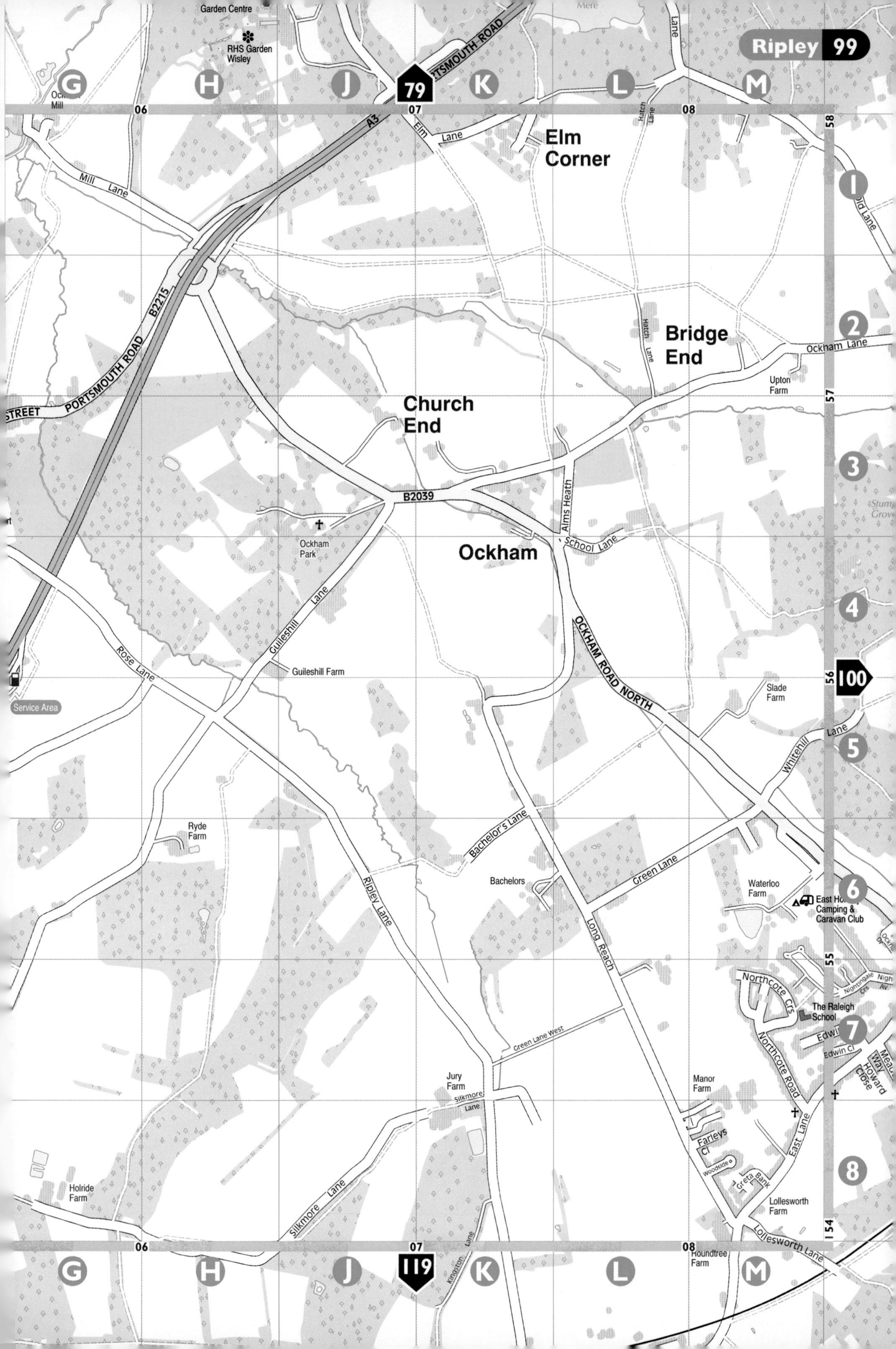
Garden Centre
RHS Garden Wisley
PORTSMOUTH ROAD
79
Mere
Lane
G
H
J
K
L
M
06
07
08
A3
Elm Lane
Elm Corner
Hatch Lane
Mill Lane
58
1
Old Lane
B2215
PORTSMOUTH ROAD
STREET
Bridge End
Hatch Lane
Ockham Lane
Upton Farm
2
57
Church End
B2039
3
Alms Heath
School Lane
Ockham Park
Ockham
Guileshill Lane
4
OCKHAM ROAD NORTH
Rose Lane
Guileshill Farm
Service Area
56
100
Slade Farm
Whitehill Lane
5
Ryde Farm
Bachelor's Lane
Green Lane
Bachelors
Waterloo Farm
6
East Horsley Camping & Caravan Club
Ripley Lane
Long Reach
55
Northcote Crs
The Raleigh School
Nightingale Av
7
Edwin Cl
Howard Close
Green Lane West
Jury Farm
Silkmore Lane
Manor Farm
Northcote Road
Farleys Cl
Woodside
Greta Bank
East Lane
8
Holride Farm
Silkmore Lane
Lollesworth Farm
54
Kingston Lane
Roundtree Farm
Lollesworth Lane
119

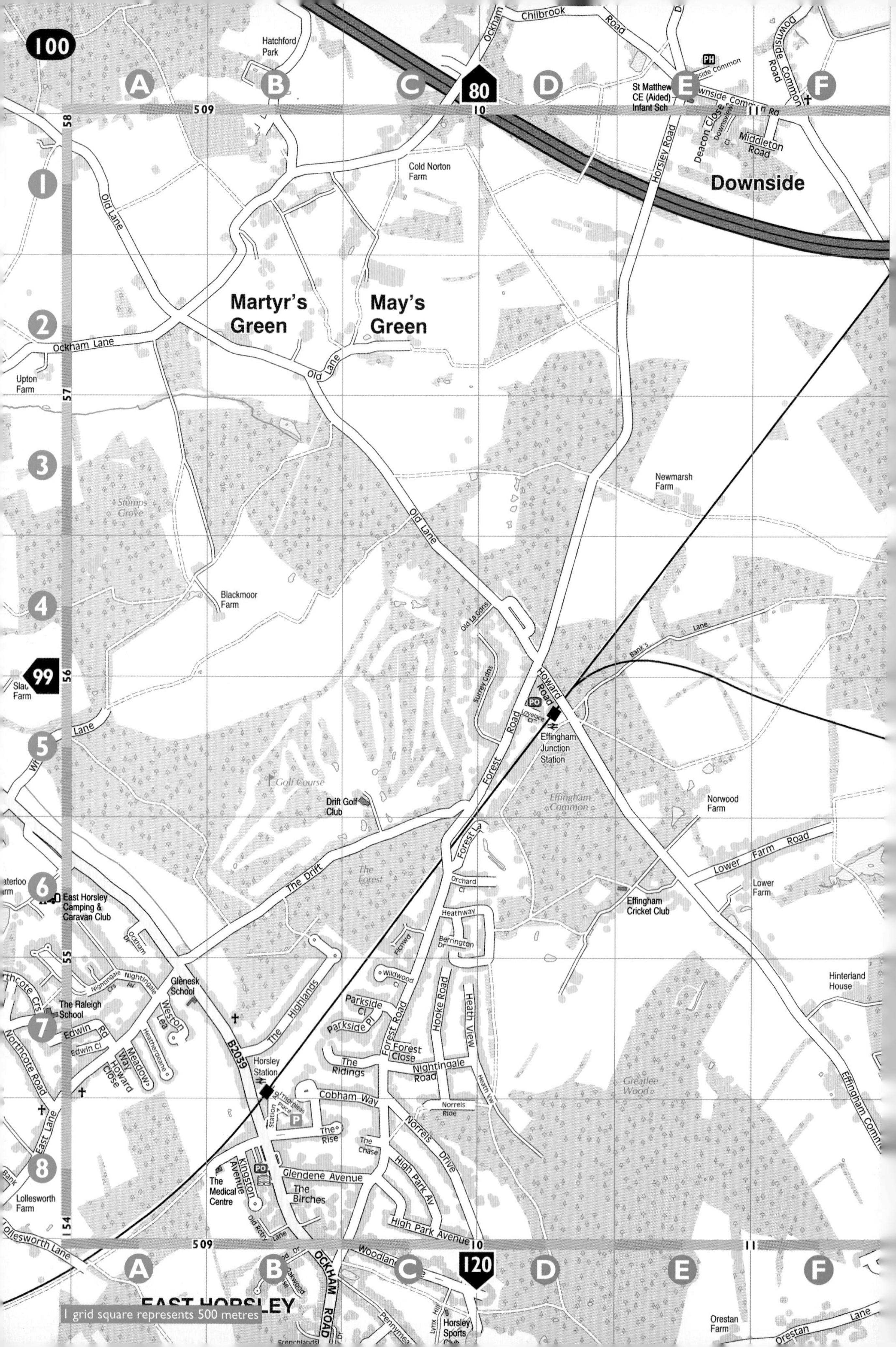

100

A   509   B   C   **80** 10   D   E   F

58

Hatchford Park

Cold Norton Farm

St Matthew CE (Aided) Infant Sch

Downside common PH

Deacon Close

Middleton Road

Downside

1

57

Ockham Lane

Upton Farm

Martyr's Green

May's Green

Old Lane

Newmarsh Farm

2

3

Stumps Grove

Blackmoor Farm

Old Lane

99 Slad Farm

Old La Gdns

Surrey Gdns

56

4

Golf Course

Drift Golf Club

Howard Road

Forest Road

Bank's Lane

Effingham Junction Station

PO

Loveland Ct

Effingham Common

Norwood Farm

5

Lane

6 East Horsley Camping & Caravan Club

The Drift

The Forest

Orchard Cl

Heathway

Berrington Dr

Lower Farm Road

Effingham Cricket Club

Lower Farm

Hinterland House

55

Northcote Crs

Glenesk School

The Raleigh School

Nightingale Av Nightingale

Weston Lea

Heathervale

The Highlands

Wildwood Cl

Parkside Cl

Parkside Pl

Hooke Road

Forest Road

Forest Close

Heath View

Greatlee Wood

7

Edwin Rd

Edwin Cl

Meadow Close

Howard Close

B2039

Horsley Station

The Ridings

Cobham Way

Nightingale Road

Norrels Ride

Norrels Drive

Heath Vw

8

54

Tollesworth Lane

Lollesworth Farm

East Lane

The Medical Centre

Kingston Avenue

PO

St Martins place

Station place P

The Rise

Glendene Avenue

The Birches

The Chase

High Park Av

Effingham Comm

Effingham Common Road

EAST HORSLEY

A   509   B   OCKHAM ROAD   Woodlan   C   **120** 10   D   E   F

High Park Avenue

Pennymea

Lynx Hill

Horsley Sports Club

Orestan Farm

Orestan Lane

1 grid square represents 500 metres

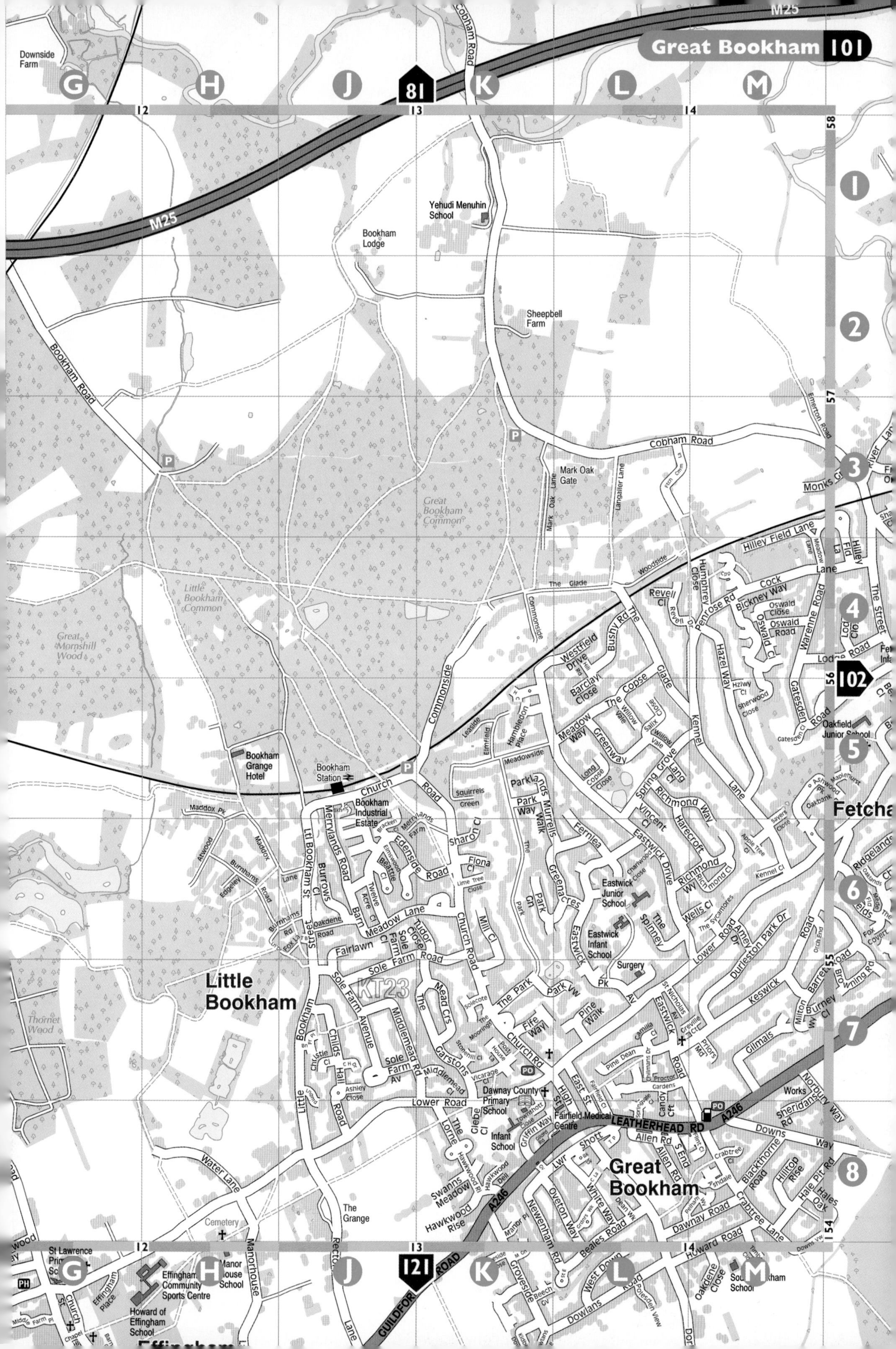
M25
Downside Farm
G
H
J
81
K
L
M
12
13
14
58
57
56
55
54
1
2
3
4
5
6
7
8
Cobham Road
Yehudi Menuhin School
Bookham Lodge
Sheepbell Farm
Bookham Road
Cobham Road
Emerton Road
Mark Oak Gate
Mark Oak Lane
Langaller Lane
Great Bookham Common
Little Bookham Common
Great Mornshill Wood
Hilley Field Lane
Humphrey Close
Revell Cl
Revell Dr
Penrose Rd
Bickney Way
Cock Lane
Oswald Close
Oswald Road
Oswald Cl
Warenne Road
The Street
Lodge Road
102
Hazel Way
Hzlwy Cl
Sherwood Close
Gatesden Road
Gatesden Cl
Oakfield Junior School
Woodside
The Glade
Commonside
Westfield Drive
Bushy Rd
Barclay Close
The Copse
Meadow Way
Greenway
Willow Vale
Salix Close
Glade
Kennel Lane
Spring Grove
Lang Cl
Richmond Way
Long Copse Close
Hambledon Place
Elmfield
Leaside
Meadowside
Bookham Grange Hotel
Bookham Station
Church Road
Bookham Industrial Estate
Merrylands Road
Merrylands Farm
Edenside Road
Sharon Cl
Fiona Cl
Lime Tree Close
Squirrels Green
Parklands
Park Way
Murrells Walk
Fernlea
Vincent Cl
Harecroft
Eastwick Drive
Charnwood Close
Eastwick Junior School
Eastwick Infant School
Surgery
Richmond Wy
Richmond Cl
Wells Cl
The Sycamores
Lower Road
Apple Tree Cl
Kennel Cl
Fetcham
Ridgelands
Maddox Pk
Atwood
Maddox Lane
Burnhams Road
Edgeley
Burnhams Rd
Fox La
Ltl Bookham St
Burrows Cl
Barn Cl
Twelve Acre Cl
Beattie Cl
Oakdene Road
Meadow Lane
Tudor Close
Sole Farm Cl
Fairlawn
Sole Farm Road
Church Road
Mill Cl
Park Gn
Greenacres
The Park
Park Vw
Eastwick Pk Av
Little Bookham
KT23
Sole Farm Avenue
Middlemead Rd
The Mead Crs
Solecote
The Moorings
Fife Way
Pine Walk
Church Rd
Durleston Park Dr
Keswick
Barrett Rd
Burney Cl
Milton Wy
Browning Rd
Gilmais
Childs Hall Road
Christie Cl
Ashley Close
Little Bookham
Sole Farm Av
Garstons
Middlemead Cl
Vicarage Cl
Dawnay County Primary School
Infant School
High St
East St
Fairfield Medical Centre
Pine Dean
Camilla
Proctor Gardens
Candy Cft
Eastwick Road
St Nicholas Av
Greville Cl
Priors Md
Lower Road
Glebe Cl
The Lorne
Hawkwood Dell
Griffin Way
LEATHERHEAD RD
A246
Works
Norbury Way
Sheridans Rd
Downs Way
Thornet Wood
Water Lane
Allen Rd
Shott Cl
White Way
Great Bookham
St End
Crabtree Cl
Ashdale
Blackthorne Road
Hilltop Rise
Hale Pit Rd
Hales Oak
Swanns Meadow
Hawkwood Rise
Manor Pl
Newenham Rd
Overton Way
Dean Wk
Dawnay Road
Crabtree Lane
Beales Road
The Grange
Cemetery
Manorhouse
Rectory Lane
GUILDFORD ROAD
121
Howard Road
West Down
Dowlans
Polesden View
Oakdene Close
St Lawrence Primary School
PH
Church St
Effingham Place
Effingham Community Sports Centre
Manor House School
Howard of Effingham School
Middle Farm Pl
Chapel Hill
Groveside
Beech Gv
Downs Vw
Effingham

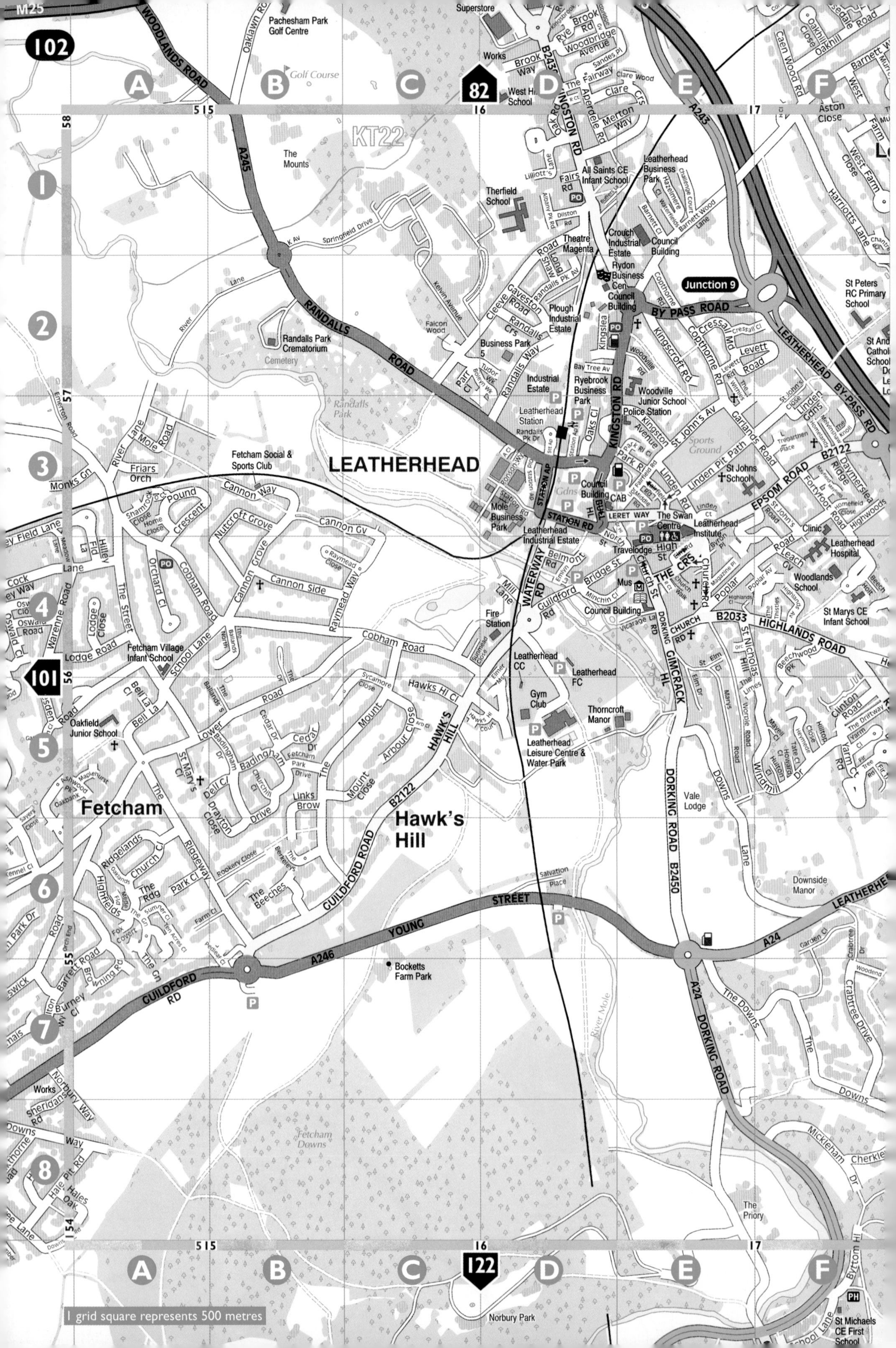

Woodlands Road

Pachesham Park
Golf Centre

Golf Course

82

West Hill
School

Superstore

Rye Brook
Rd

Woodbridge
Avenue

B243

Brook
Way

Sandes Pl

The Fairway

Clare Wood

Clare Crs

A B C D E F

515 16 17

KT22

The Mounts

K AV

Springfield Drive

Kelvin Avenue

Falcon
Wood

Therfield
School

All Saints CE
Infant School

Fairs
Rd

Theatre
Magenta

Plough
Industrial
Estate

Leatherhead
Business
Park

Council
Building

Rydon
Business
Cen-
Council
Building

Crouch
Industrial
Estate

Hazelmere

Barnett Wood
Lane

St Peters
RC Primary
School

Junction 9

I

2

RANDALLS

River

ROAD

Randalls Park
Crematorium

Cemetery

Randalls
Park

LEATHERHEAD

Fetcham Social &
Sports Club

Business Park
5

Randalls
Crs

Randalls
Way

Park
Ct

Tudor
Wk

Robyn Wk

Industrial
Estate

Ryebrook
Business
Park

Leatherhead
Station

Randalls
Pk Dr

Kingslea

Woodville
Junior School

Police Station

Bay Tree Av

Woodville Rd

Kingscroft Rd

Cressall Rd

Copthorne

BY PASS ROAD

Cressall Rd

Cressall Cl

Levett
Road

Levett
Rd

LEATHERHEAD BY-PASS RD

St Andr
Catholic
School

2

Monks Gn

River

Friars
Orch

Mole

Road

Pound
Crescent

Cannon Way

Nutcroft Grove

Cannon Gv

Raymead
Close

Council
Building

CAB

Mole
Business
Park

Leatherhead
Industrial Estate

Park Rise

North

Leret Way

The Swan
Centre

PO

Leatherhead
Institute

Travelodge

High St

St John's Av

Linden Road

Linden Pit Path

St Johns
School

Sports
Ground

Garlands Road

St John's

Tregowan
Place

EPSOM ROAD

Ridge

B2122

Fortyfoot
Road

Homefield
Road

Highwoods

Clinic

Leatherhead
Hospital

3

River Lane

Hilley
Fld

Lane

Cobham Road

Cannon Grove

Cannon Side

Shamrock
Close

Orchard Cl

Home
Close

Raymead Way

Sycamore
Close

The Street

Belmont

Bridge St

Fire
Station

Mus

Council
Building

Leach
Gv

Poplar

Poplar Av

Woodlands
School

St Marys CE
Infant School

HIGHLANDS ROAD

The
Thistles

Beechwood

4

101

Oswald
Road

Warenne Road

The Street

Lodge
Close

Lodge Road

Fetcham Village
Infant School

School Lane

Cedar Cl

Guildford
Rd

Minchin Cl

Leatherhead
CC

Leatherhead
FC

THE CRES

Church Rd

CHURCH

Elm Rd

CHURCH ROAD

B2033

St Nicholas
Hill

St Marys

The Limes

Beechwood
Pk

Clinton
Road

5

Oakfield
Junior School

Bell La

Bell La

St Mary's
Cl

Lower
Badingham

Badingham

Drayton
Close

Dell Cl

The
Fetcham
Park
Drive

Mount
Close

Arbour Close

Sycamore
Close

Hawks Hi Cl

Hawks
Court

HAWK'S HILL

Gym
Club

Leatherhead
Leisure Centre &
Water Park

Thorncroft
Manor

DORKING ROAD

Downs

Mayell Cl

Windmill

The Driftway

Yarm

Fetcham

Ridgelands

Highfields

Church Cl

Park Cl

Ridgeway

The Rdg

The Beeches

Farm Cl

Rookery Close

Links
Brow

B2122

Cedar
Dr

Hawk's
Hill

B2450

Vale
Lodge

Downside
Manor

6

Kennel La

Fox
Covert

Burney Rd

The Grn

GUILDFORD ROAD

Salvation
Place

Young STREET

A246

DORKING ROAD

LEATHERHE

7

Works

Norbury Way

Sheridan
Rd

Barrett Road

Browning Rd

GUILDFORD RD

A246

Bocketts
Farm Park

River Mole

A24

Garden Cl

Woodena

Crabtree Drive

8

Hale
Oak

Hale Pit Rd

Hales
Oak

54

Fetcham
Downs

The Priory

Mickleham Dr

The Downs

Cherkle

Norbury Park

PH

St Michaels
CE First
School

1 grid square represents 500 metres

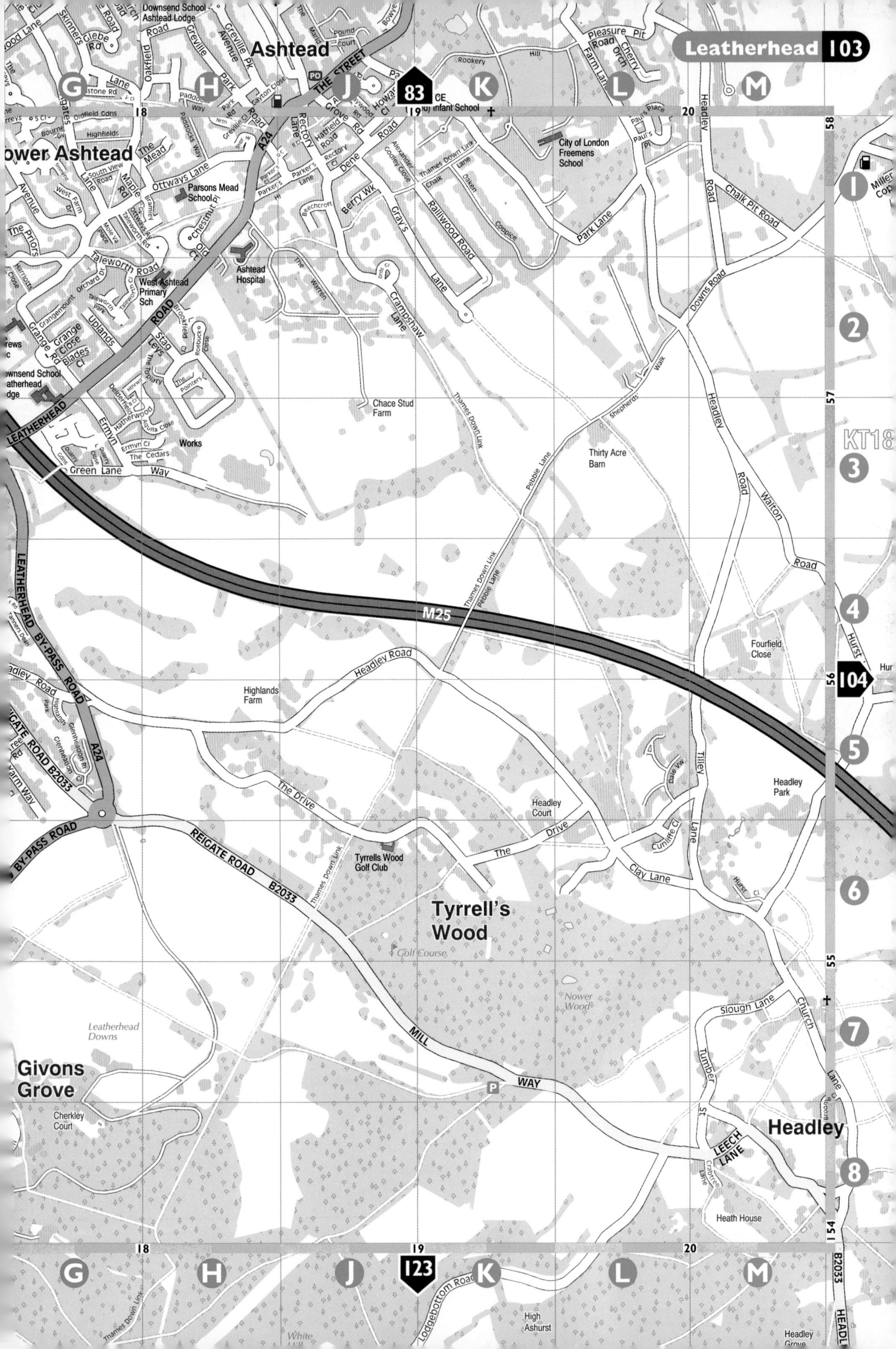
Ashtead
Lower Ashtead
Tyrrell's Wood
Givons Grove
Headley
M25
A24
Leatherhead By-Pass Road
Reigate Road B2033
Mill Way
Headley Road
The Drive
Headley Lane
Tilley Lane
Clay Lane
Thames Down Link
Pebble Lane
Shepherds Walk
Downs Road
Chalk Pit Road
Park Lane
Rookery Hill
Cramphaw Lane
Grays Lane
Railwood Road
Ashtead Hospital
Parsons Mead School
West Ashtead Primary Sch
City of London Freemens School
Chace Stud Farm
Thirty Acre Barn
Highlands Farm
Headley Court
Tyrrells Wood Golf Club
Fourfield Close
Headley Park
Leatherhead Downs
Nower Wood
Cherkley Court
Heath House
High Ashurst
Slough Lane
Church Lane
Tumber St
Leech Lane
Lodgebottom Road
Walton Road
KT18
83
104
123

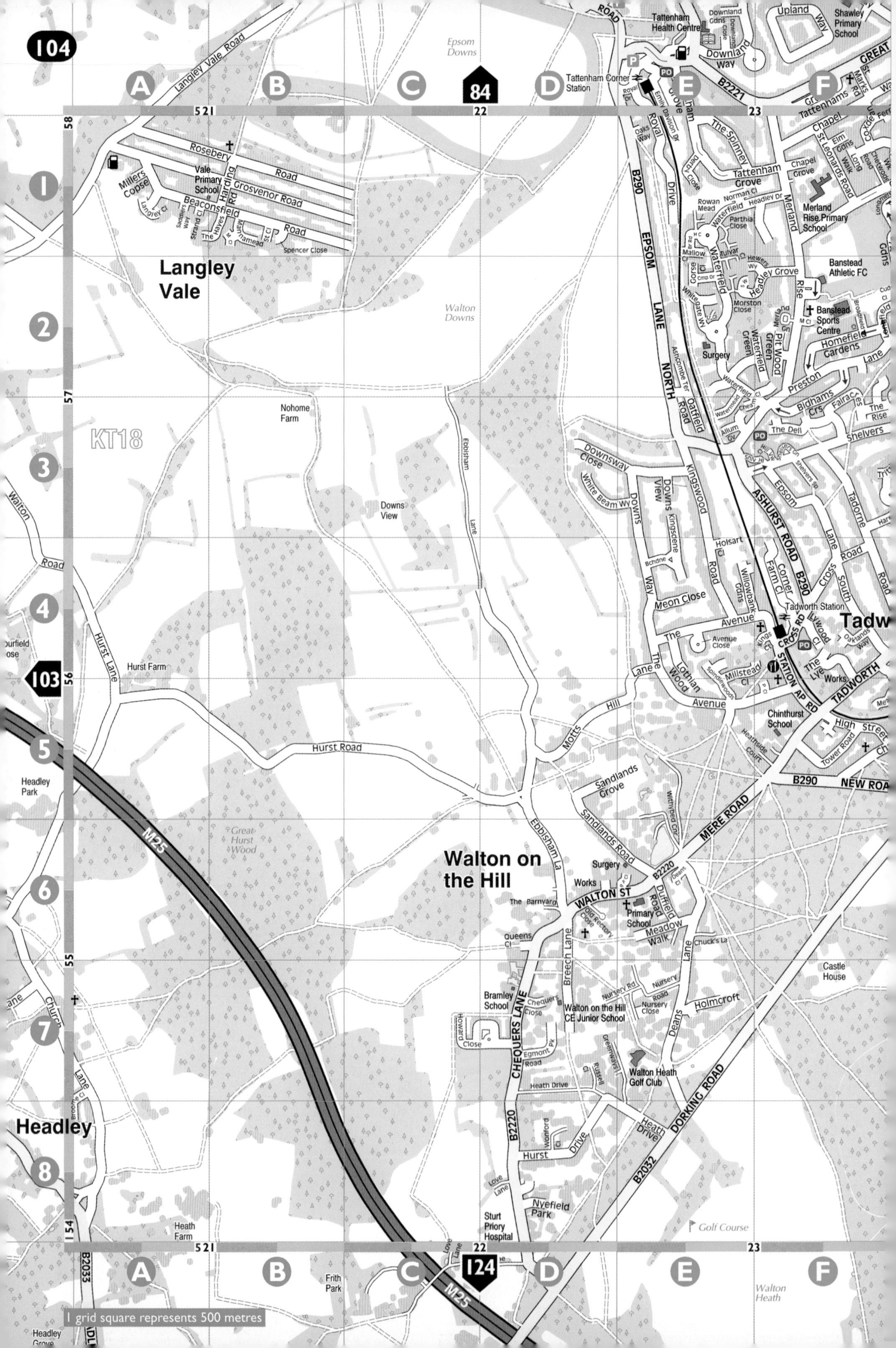

84
A
B
C
D
E
F
1
2
3
4
5
6
7
8
103
124
Langley Vale
Walton on the Hill
Headley
Tadw
Epsom Downs
Walton Downs
Tattenham Corner Station
Tattenham Health Centre
Shawley Primary School
Vale Primary School
Merland Rise Primary School
Banstead Athletic FC
Banstead Sports Centre
Nohome Farm
Downs View
Hurst Farm
Headley Park
Great Hurst Wood
Tadworth Station
Chinthurst School
Walton Heath Golf Club
Walton on the Hill CE Junior School
Bramley School
Castle House
Sturt Priory Hospital
Heath Farm
Frith Park
Walton Heath
Golf Course
KT18
Langley Vale Road
Rosebery Road
Grosvenor Road
Beaconsfield Road
Hurst Lane
Hurst Road
Ebbisham Lane
Motts Hill Lane
Sandlands Grove
Sandlands Road
Mere Road
Walton St
Chequers Lane
Dorking Road
Epsom Lane North
Ashurst Road
New Road
M25
B290
B2220
B2221
B2032
B2033
1 grid square represents 500 metres

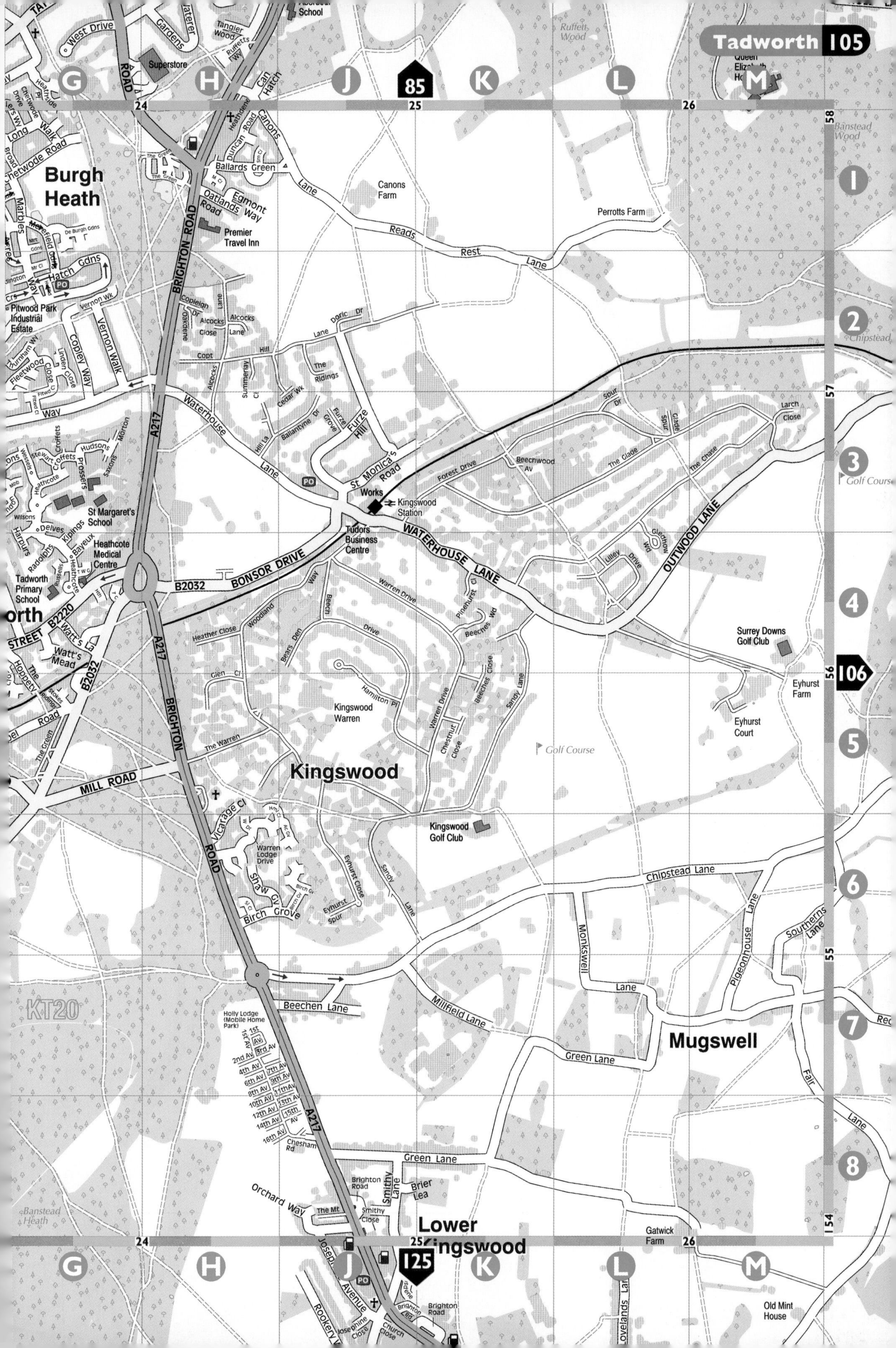

G H J **85** K L M
24 25 26 58

Banstead
Wood

1

Queen
Elizabeth
Ho

Burgh
Heath

West Drive
Gardens
Tangier
Wood
Ruffetts Wy
Can Hatch
Canons

Superstore

The Green

Duncan Road
Heathedge

Canons
Lane

Canons
Farm

Reads Lane

Perrotts Farm

Ballards Green

Egmont
Way

Oatlands
Road

Premier
Travel Inn

Rest Lane

2
Chipstead

BRIGHTON ROAD

Copley Way
Vernon Walk
Hatch Gdns
De Burgh Gdns

PO

Pitwood Park
Industrial
Estate

Fleetwood
Close
Linden Close
Way
Way
Vernon Walk

Copeland
Alcocks
Close
Alcocks
Lane
Copt

Summeray Cl
Cedar Wk
Alcocks Lane

Doric Dr

Hill
The
Ridings

57

3
Golf Course

Waterhouse
Lane

Ballantyne Dr
Furze Grove
St Monica's Road
Furze Hill

PO

Works

Spur
Dr

Spur

Larch
Close

Forest Drive

Beechwood
Av

The Glade

Cistel
Spur

The Chase

Heathcote
Medical
Centre

Hill La

Kingswood
Station

OUTWOOD LANE

St Margaret's
School

A217

BONSOR DRIVE
B2032

WATERHOUSE LANE

Lilley
Drive

Glenthorn
Wd

4

Tadworth
Primary
School

Heather Close
Woodland
Beech
Way
Bears Den
Warren Drive
Drive

Pinehurst
Beeches Wd

Beeches Close
Sandy Lane

Surrey Downs
Golf Club

Eyhurst
Farm

56 **106**

orth
STREET
B2220
Watt's
Watt's
Mead
B2032

Hoppety

Glen Cl

Hamilton Pl

Warren Drive

Chestnut
Close

Eyhurst
Court

5

Kingswood
Warren

Golf Course

Road

The Warren

Vicarage Cl

Kingswood

Warren
Lodge
Drive

BRIGHTON ROAD

Shaw Cl
Birch Grove
Birch Cl

Ephurst Close
Eyhurst
Spur

Sandy
Lane

Chipstead Lane

6

MILL ROAD

A217

Kingswood
Golf Club

Monkswell
Lane
Pigeonhouse Lane
Southerns Lane

55

KT20

Holly Lodge
(Mobile Home
Park)
1st Av 1st
Av
2nd Av 3rd Av
4th Av 5th Av
6th Av 11th Av
12th Av 13th Av
14th Av 15th
16th Av
Chesham
Rd

Beechen Lane

Millfield Lane

Green Lane

Mugswell

Fall
Lane

7

54

Banstead
Heath

Road
el

Orchard Way

Green Lane

Brighton
Road
Smithy Lane
Brier
Lea

Gatwick
Farm

8

Lower
Kingswood

The Mt
Smithy
Close

Old Mint
House

Joseph
Avenue
Josephine
Close
Church
Close
Rookery Wy
Brighton Road

G H J **125** K L M
24 25 25 26
PO

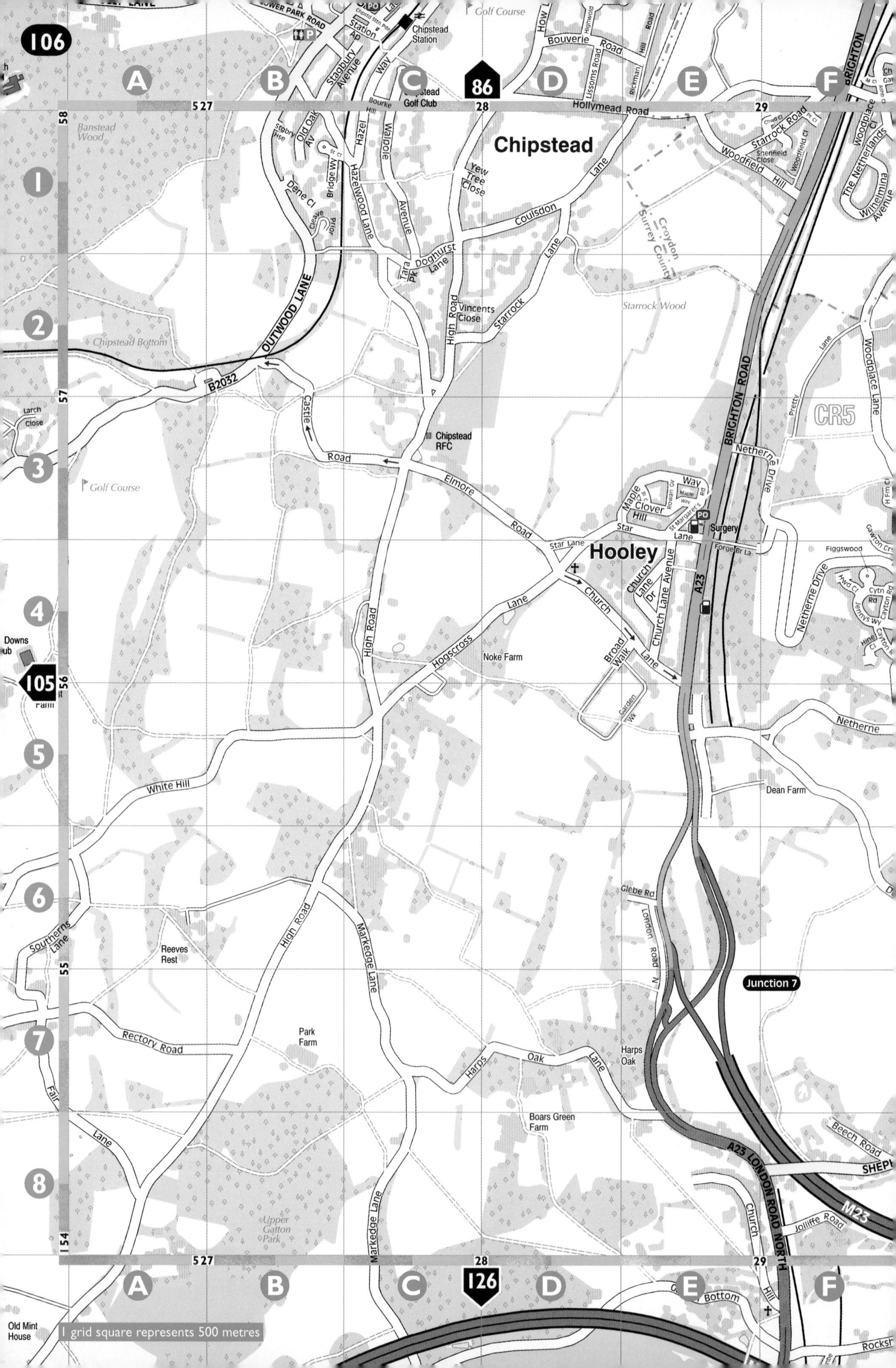
106
86
105
126
Chipstead
Hooley
Chipstead Station
Chipstead Golf Club
Golf Course
Hollymead Road
Bouverie Road
Banstead Wood
Chipstead Bottom
OUTWOOD LANE
B2032
Castle Road
Elmore Road
Chipstead RFC
High Road
Hazelwood Lane
Walpole Avenue
Doghurst Lane
Coulsdon Lane
Starrock Lane
Vincents Close
Yew Tree Close
Dene Cl
Starrock Wood
Croydon
Surrey County
BRIGHTON ROAD
A23
CR5
Netherne Drive
Woodplace Lane
Star Lane
Church Lane
Church Lane Avenue
Hogscross Lane
Noke Farm
Broad Walk
Garden Wk
Surgery
Netherne Lane
Dean Farm
White Hill
Southerns Lane
Reeves Rest
Rectory Road
Park Farm
Markedge Lane
Harps Oak Lane
Harps Oak
Boars Green Farm
Glebe Rd
London Road N
Junction 7
A23 LONDON ROAD NORTH
M23
Beech Road
Jolliffe Road
Upper Gatton Park
Fair Lane
Larch Close
Downs
Old Mint House
Figgswood
Woodfield Hill
Starrock Road
The Netherlands
Wilhelmina Avenue
Maple Way
Clover Hill
1 grid square represents 500 metres

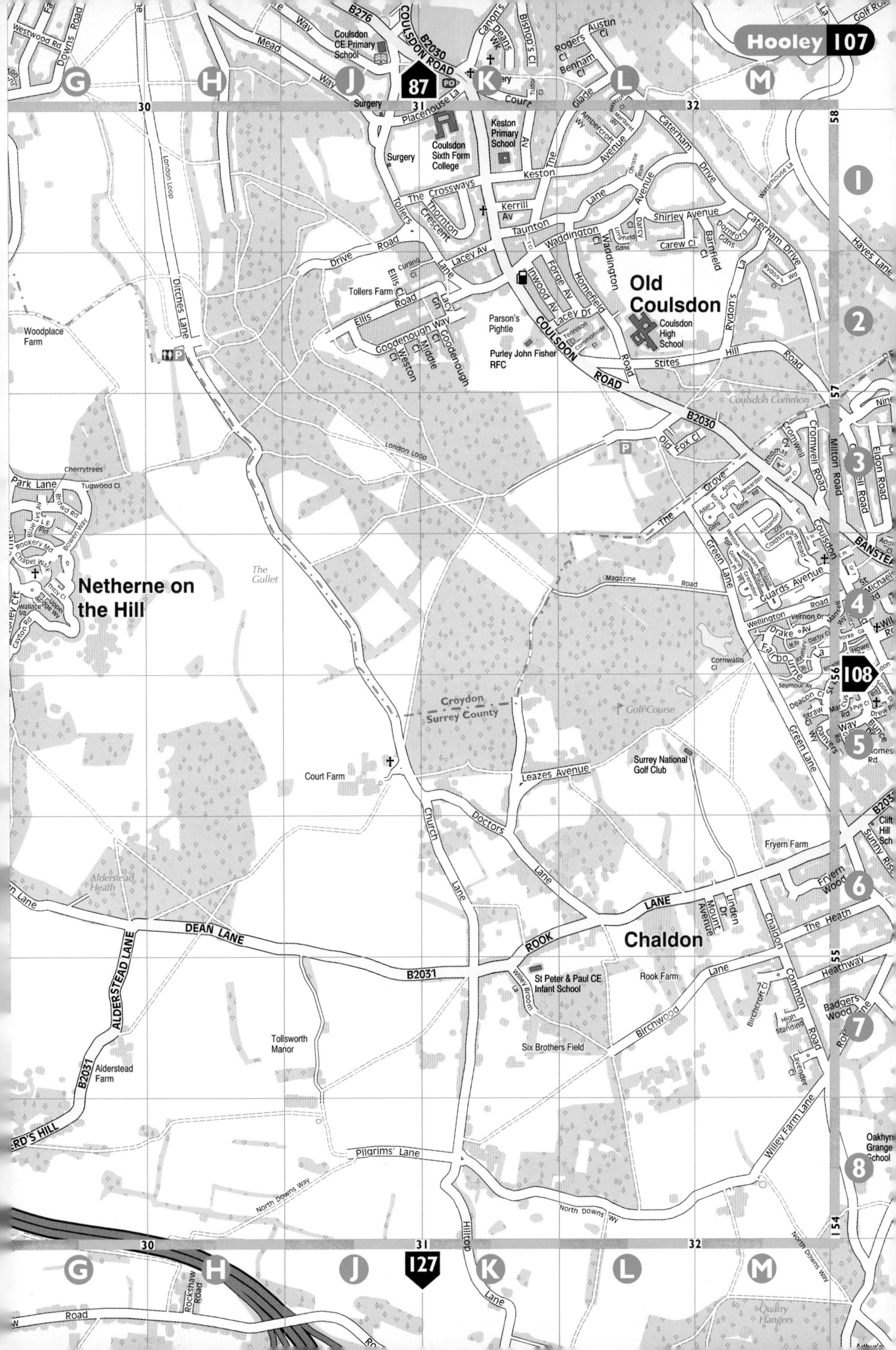

G H J **87** K L M

30 31 32 58 57

I

2

Netherne on
the Hill

3

BANSTE

4

Old Coulsdon

108

5

6

Chaldon

7

8

G H J **127** K L M

30 31 32 154

Westwood Rd Downs Road Mead Way B276 COULSDON ROAD B2030 Canons Wk Deans Wk Bishop's Cl Rogers Cl Benham Cl Austin Cl GOLF R

Coulsdon CE Primary School Placenouse La PO Keston Court Glade

Surgery Hayes Lane

Surgery Coulsdon Sixth Form College Keston Primary School Keston

The Crossways Taunton Waddington Shirley Avenue Caterham Drive

Tollers Road Thornton Crescent Lacey Av Forge Av Lacey Dr Homefield Waddington Lane Darcy Carew Cl Barnfield Caterham Drive Rydon's

Drive Road Curling Lacey Gn Inwood Av Parson's Pightle Coulsdon High School Stites Hill Coulsdon Road

Tollers Farm Ellis Cl Weston Cl Middle Goodenough Tennison Coulsdon High School

Woodplace Farm P Ellis Goodenough Way Purley John Fisher RFC COULSDON ROAD B2030 P The Grove Old Fox Cl Cromwell Road Milton Road Eldon Road

Coulsdon Common Nine

London Loop The Gullet London Loop Green Lane Guards Avenue

Park Lane Cherrytrees Tugwood Cl Magazine Road Wellington Vernon Dr Fairbourne BANSTE

Cookery Md Chapel Wk Wallace Rd Drake Av Howe

Netherne on the Hill Croydon Surrey County Golf Course Cornwallis Cl Seymour Av 108 Way Bunce Homes Rd

Court Farm Surrey National Golf Club Deacon Straw Danvers Marcus Pyc Cl Drew 5

Leazes Avenue Fryern Farm B203

Church Lane Doctors Lane Clift Hill Sch Sunny Bk

Fryern Wood 6

ROOK LANE Linden Mount Avenue Chaldon Common Road The Heath Heathway

Alderstead Heath DEAN LANE **Chaldon** Birchcroft Cl High Standing Badgers Wood 7

Alderstead Lane B2031 St Peter & Paul CE Infant School Rook Farm Birchwood Lavender Willey Farm Lane

Alderstead Farm Tollsworth Manor Six Brothers Field Oakhyrst Grange School 8

RD'S HILL Pilgrims' Lane North Downs Way Hilltop North Downs Wy North Downs Way Quarry Hangers

Rockshaw Road

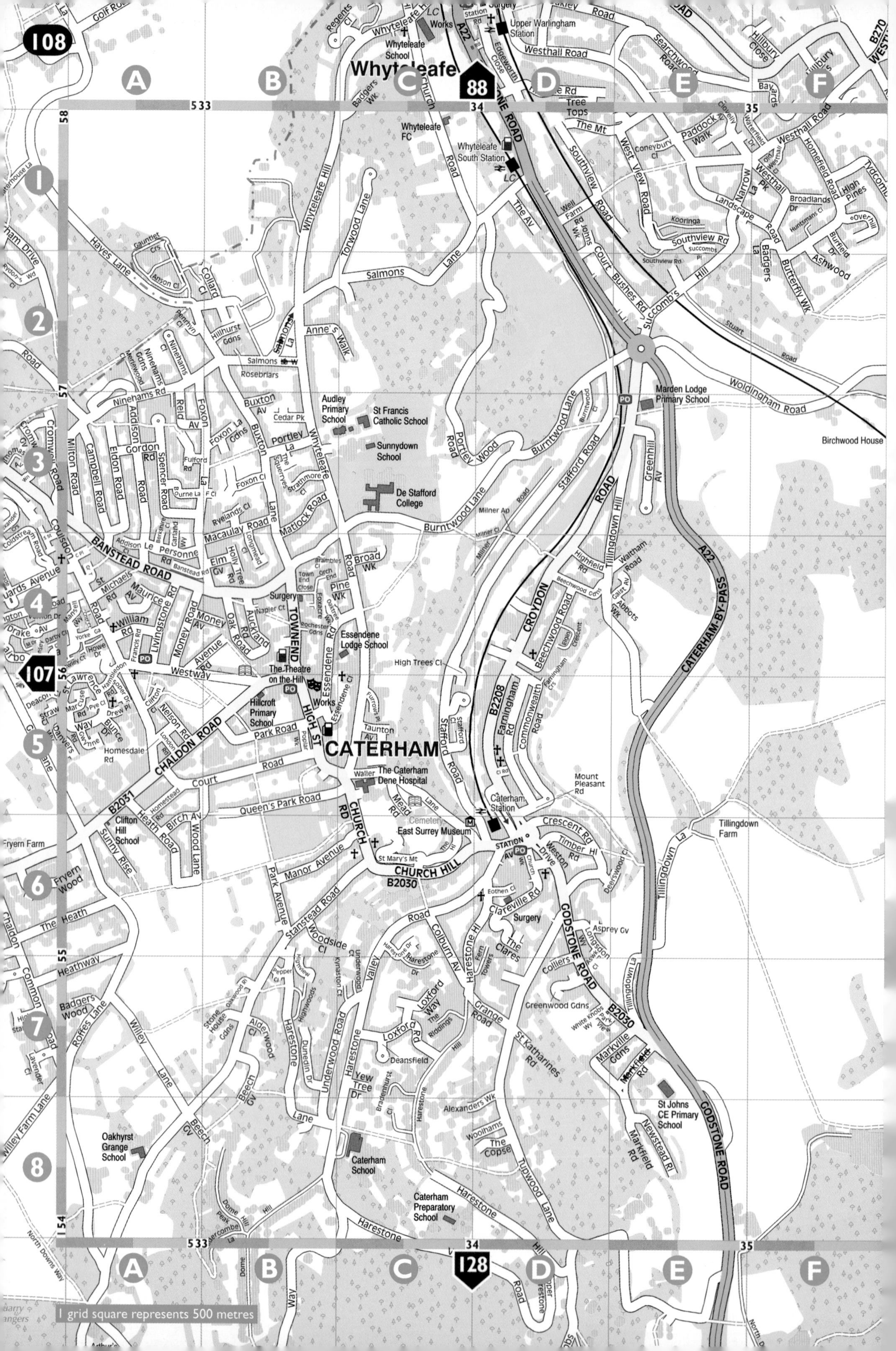

108
88
107
128
Whyteleafe
CATERHAM
Upper Warlingham Station
Whyteleafe School
Whyteleafe FC
Whyteleafe South Station
Westhall Road
Searchwood Road
Hillbury Close
Paddock Walk
Coneybury Cl
West View Road
Southview Road
Landscape Road
Broadlands Dr
High Pines
Ashwood
Butterfly Wk
Badgers La
Succomb's Hill
Southview Rd
Court Bushes Rd
Stuart Road
Woldingham Road
Marden Lodge Primary School
Birchwood House
Salmons Lane
Torwood Lane
Whyteleafe Hill
Hayes Lane
Anne's Walk
Audley Primary School
St Francis Catholic School
Sunnydown School
De Stafford College
Burntwood Lane
Portley Wood Road
Stafford Road
Croydon Road
Greenhill Av
Tillingdown Hill
Caterham-By-Pass
A22
B2208
B2031
B2030
Banstead Road
Ninehams Rd
Milton Road
Campbell Road
Eldon Road
Gordon Rd
Spencer Road
Macaulay Road
Buxton Lane
Portley La
Matlock Road
Townend
High St
Essendene Lodge School
Essendene Road
The Theatre on the Hill
Hillcroft Primary School
Westway
Chaldon Road
Park Road
Court Road
Queen's Park Road
Clifton Hill School
Heath Road
Birch Av
Wood Lane
The Caterham Dene Hospital
East Surrey Museum
Cemetery
Caterham Station
Church Rd
Church Hill
Manor Avenue
Park Avenue
Stanstead Road
Godstone Road
Farningham Rd
Commonwealth Road
Beechwood Road
Mount Pleasant Rd
Tillingdown Farm
Tillingdown La
Crescent Rd
Timber Hl
Weston Drive
Surgery
Harestone Hill
Colburn Av
Grange Road
Loxford Way
Underwood Road
Harestone Lane
Yew Tree Dr
Alexanders Wk
Tupwood Lane
St Katharines Rd
Greenwood Gdns
Markville Gdns
St Johns CE Primary School
Newstead Ri
Markfield Rd
Fryern Farm
Fryern Wood
The Heath
Heathway
Chaldon Common Road
Badgers Wood
Roffes Lane
Willey Lane
Willey Farm Lane
Oakhyrst Grange School
Beech Gv
Alderwood Cl
Stone House Gdns
Caterham School
Caterham Preparatory School
Harestone Valley
North Downs Way
1 grid square represents 500 metres

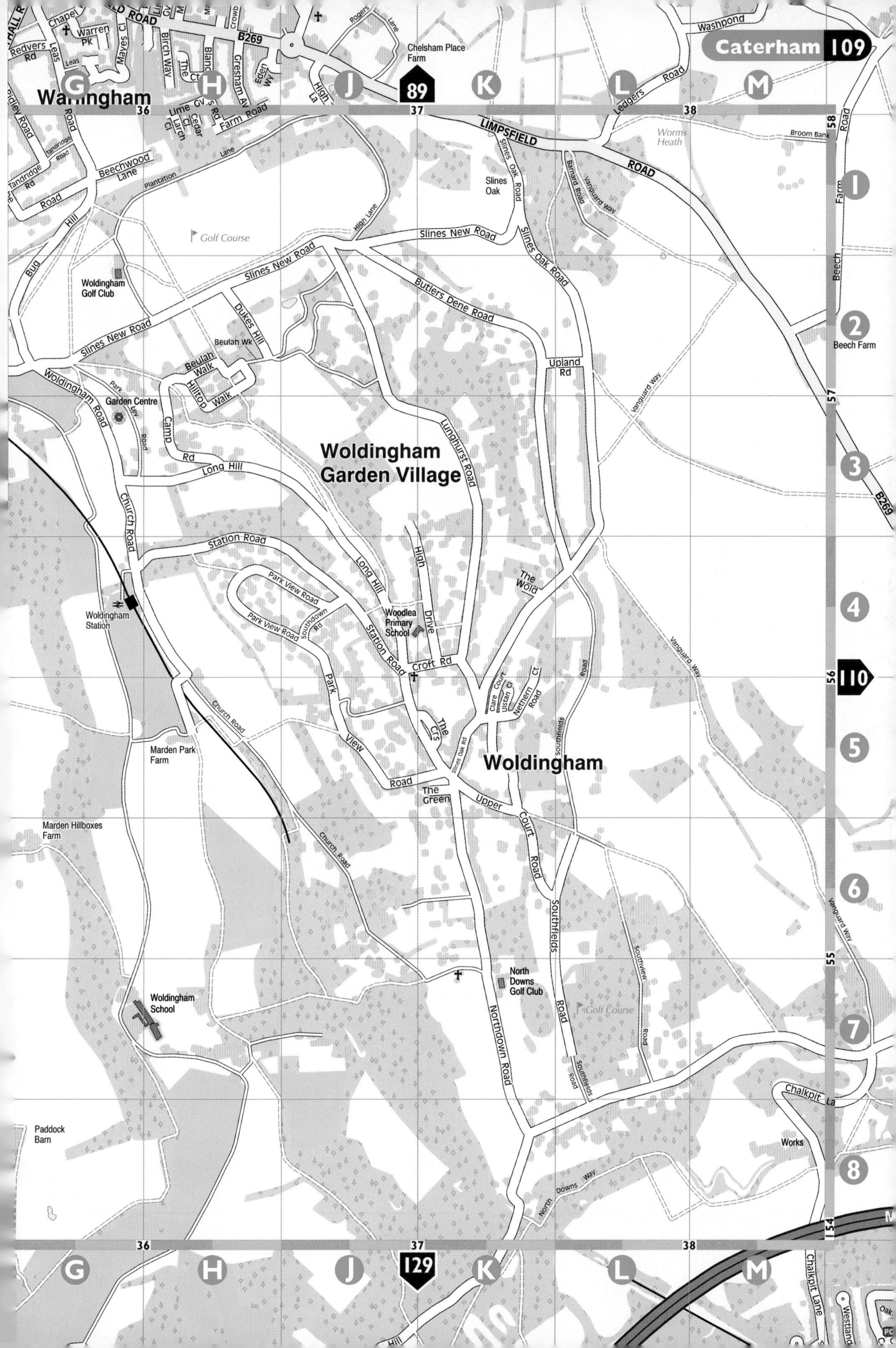
Woldingham Garden Village
Woldingham
Warlingham
Chelsham Place Farm
Worms Heath
Slines Oak
Golf Course
Woldingham Golf Club
Garden Centre
Woldingham Station
Woodlea Primary School
Marden Park Farm
Marden Hillboxes Farm
Woldingham School
Paddock Barn
North Downs Golf Club
Beech Farm
Works
LIMPSFIELD ROAD
B269
Slines New Road
Slines Oak Road
Butlers Dene Road
Lunghurst Road
Long Hill
Station Road
Park View Road
Church Road
Northdown Road
Southfields Road
Upper Court Road
Vanguard Way
North Downs Way
Chalkpit Lane
89
110
129

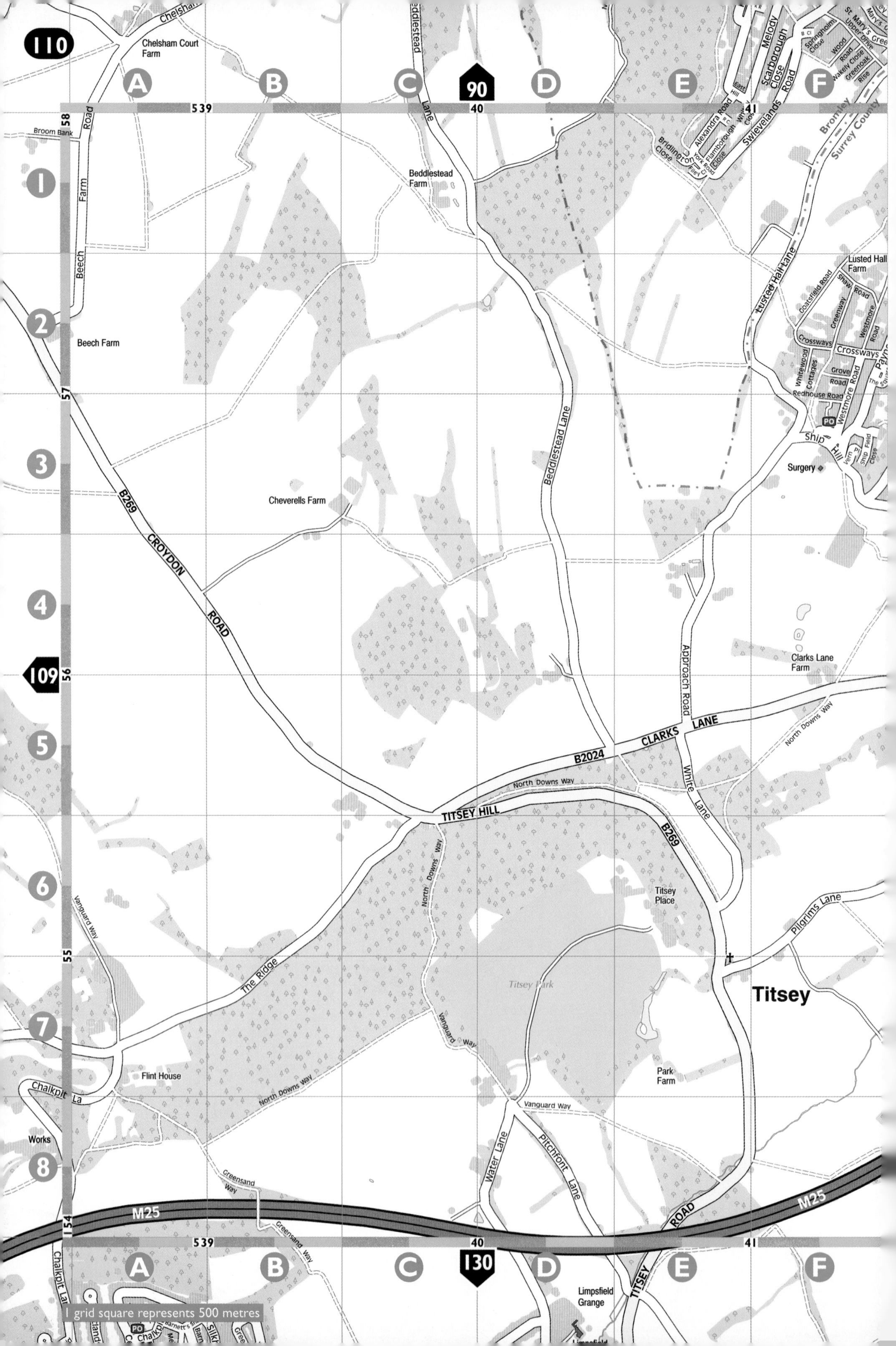

90
130
109
Chelsham Court Farm
Broom Bank
Beech Farm Road
Beech Farm
Beddlestead Farm
Beddlestead Lane
Cheverells Farm
B269
CROYDON ROAD
Lusted Hall Lane
Lusted Hall Farm
Bromley
Surrey County
Scarborough Close
Melody
Swievelands Road
Alexandra Road
Bridlington Close
Flamborough Close
Springholm Close
Wood Road
Greenoak Rise
Coatsfield Road
Shaw Road
Greenway
Westmore Road
Crossways
Whitewood Cottages
Grove Road
Redhouse Road
PO
Ship Hill
Ship Field Close
Surgery
Approach Road
Clarks Lane Farm
B2024
CLARKS LANE
North Downs Way
White Lane
TITSEY HILL
Titsey Place
Pilgrims Lane
Titsey
Titsey Park
Park Farm
Vanguard Way
The Ridge
Flint House
Chalkpit La
Works
Water Lane
Pitchfront Lane
Greensand Way
M25
TITSEY ROAD
Limpsfield Grange
1 grid square represents 500 metres

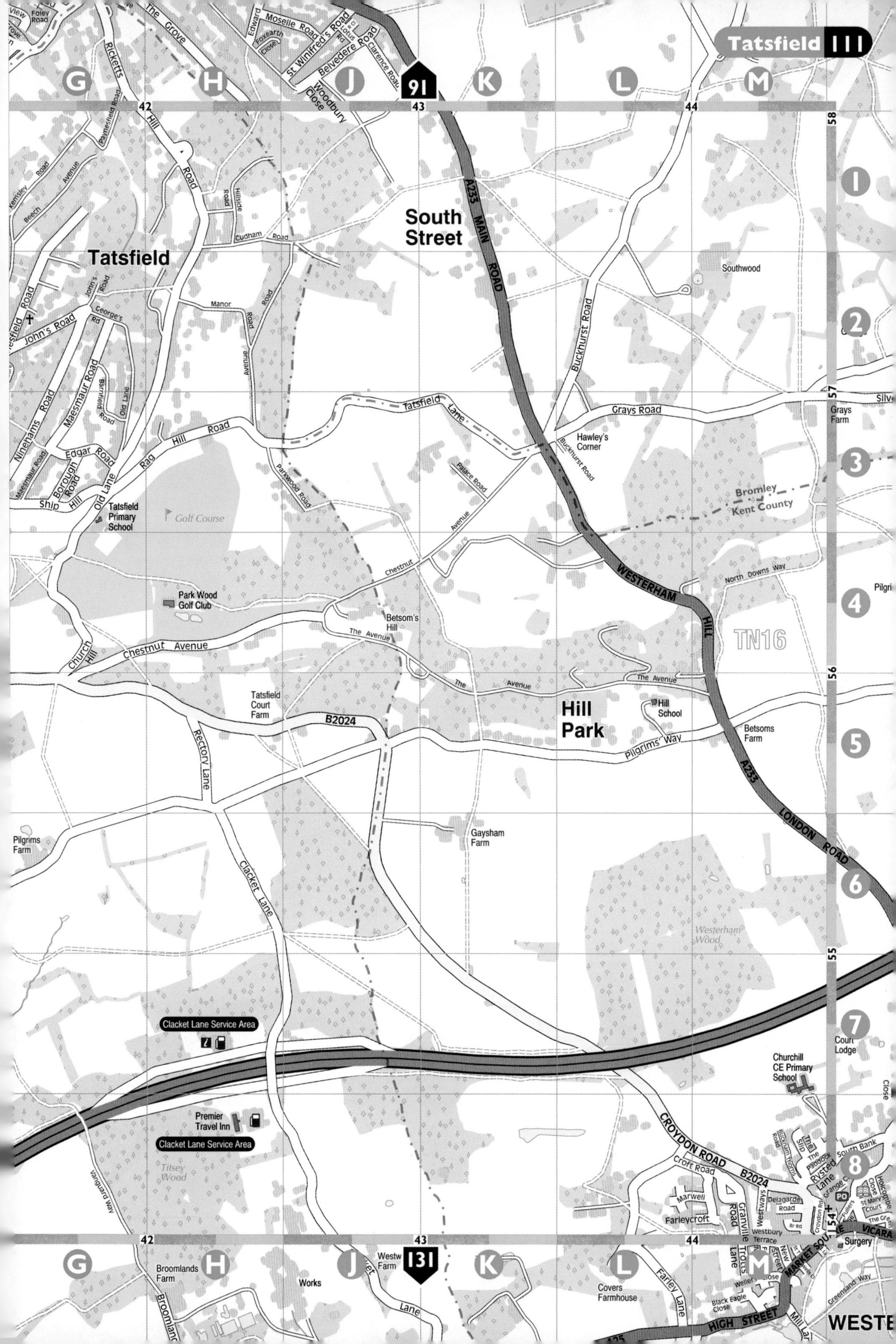
Tatsfield
South Street
Hill Park
A233 MAIN ROAD
WESTERHAM HILL
A233 LONDON ROAD
CROYDON ROAD B2024
B2024
Chestnut Avenue
The Avenue
Pilgrims' Way
Rectory Lane
Clacket Lane
Tatsfield Lane
Grays Road
Buckhurst Road
Rag Hill Road
Cudham Road
Manor Road
Hillside Road
Ricketts Hill Road
The Grove
Moselle Road
St Winifred's Road
Belvedere Road
Clarence Road
Woodbury Close
Edward Road
Foxearth Close
Paynesfield Road
Kemsley Road
Beech Avenue
John's Road
St John's Road
George's Rd
Maesmaur Road
Ninehams Road
Edgar Road
Borough Road
Barnfield Road
Old Lane
Ship Hill
Church Hill
Parkwood Road
Palace Road
Hawley's Corner
Tatsfield Primary School
Golf Course
Park Wood Golf Club
Betsom's Hill
Tatsfield Court Farm
Hill School
Betsoms Farm
Grays Farm
Southwood
Bromley
Kent County
North Downs Way
TN16
Gaysham Farm
Pilgrims Farm
Westerham Wood
Clacket Lane Service Area
Premier Travel Inn
Titsey Wood
Vanguard Way
Court Lodge
Churchill CE Primary School
Croft Road
Farleycroft
Granville Road
Westways
Delagarde Road
Westbury Terrace
Market Square
Surgery
Greensand Way
Broomlands Farm
Works
Covers Farmhouse
Farley Lane
High Street
Black Eagle Close
Trotts Lane
New Street
Rysted Lane
The Paddock
Grange Close
South Bank
Holcombe Close
St Mary's Court
The Green
Vicarage
Westerham
42
43
44
55
56
57
58
91
131
G
H
J
K
L
M
1
2
3
4
5
6
7
8

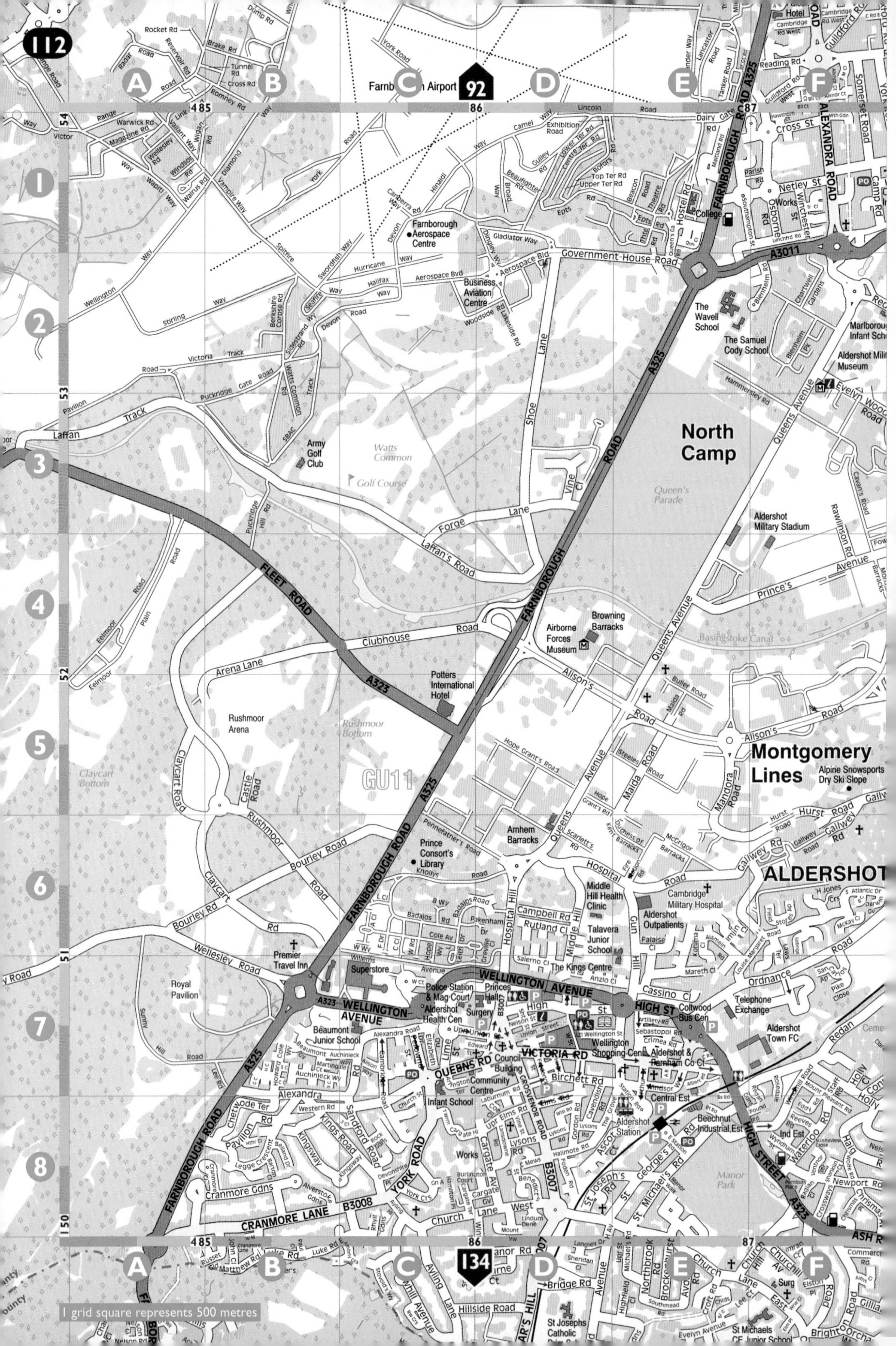

92
134
Farnborough Airport
Farnborough Aerospace Centre
Business Aviation Centre
North Camp
Queen's Parade
Aldershot Military Stadium
The Wavell School
The Samuel Cody School
Aldershot Military Museum
Army Golf Club
Watts Common
Golf Course
FARNBOROUGH ROAD
FLEET ROAD
A325
A323
A3011
Airborne Forces Museum
Browning Barracks
Basingstoke Canal
Potters International Hotel
Rushmoor Arena
Rushmoor Bottom
Claycart Bottom
GU11
Montgomery Lines
Alpine Snowsports Dry Ski Slope
Arnhem Barracks
Prince Consort's Library
ALDERSHOT
Cambridge Military Hospital
Aldershot Outpatients
Middle Hill Health Clinic
Talavera Junior School
The Kings Centre
Premier Travel Inn
Superstore
Royal Pavilion
WELLINGTON AVENUE
Police Station & Mag Court
Aldershot Health Cen
Princes Hall
Beaumont Junior School
QUEENS RD
VICTORIA RD
Wellington Shopping Cen
Aldershot & Farnham Co Cl
Council Building
Community Centre
Infant School
Coltwood Bus Cen
Telephone Exchange
Aldershot Town FC
Central Est
Beechnut Industrial Est
Aldershot Station
Manor Park
HIGH STREET
Ind Est
CRANMORE LANE B3008
YORK ROAD
Works
St Josephs Catholic
St Michaels CE Junior School
1 grid square represents 500 metres

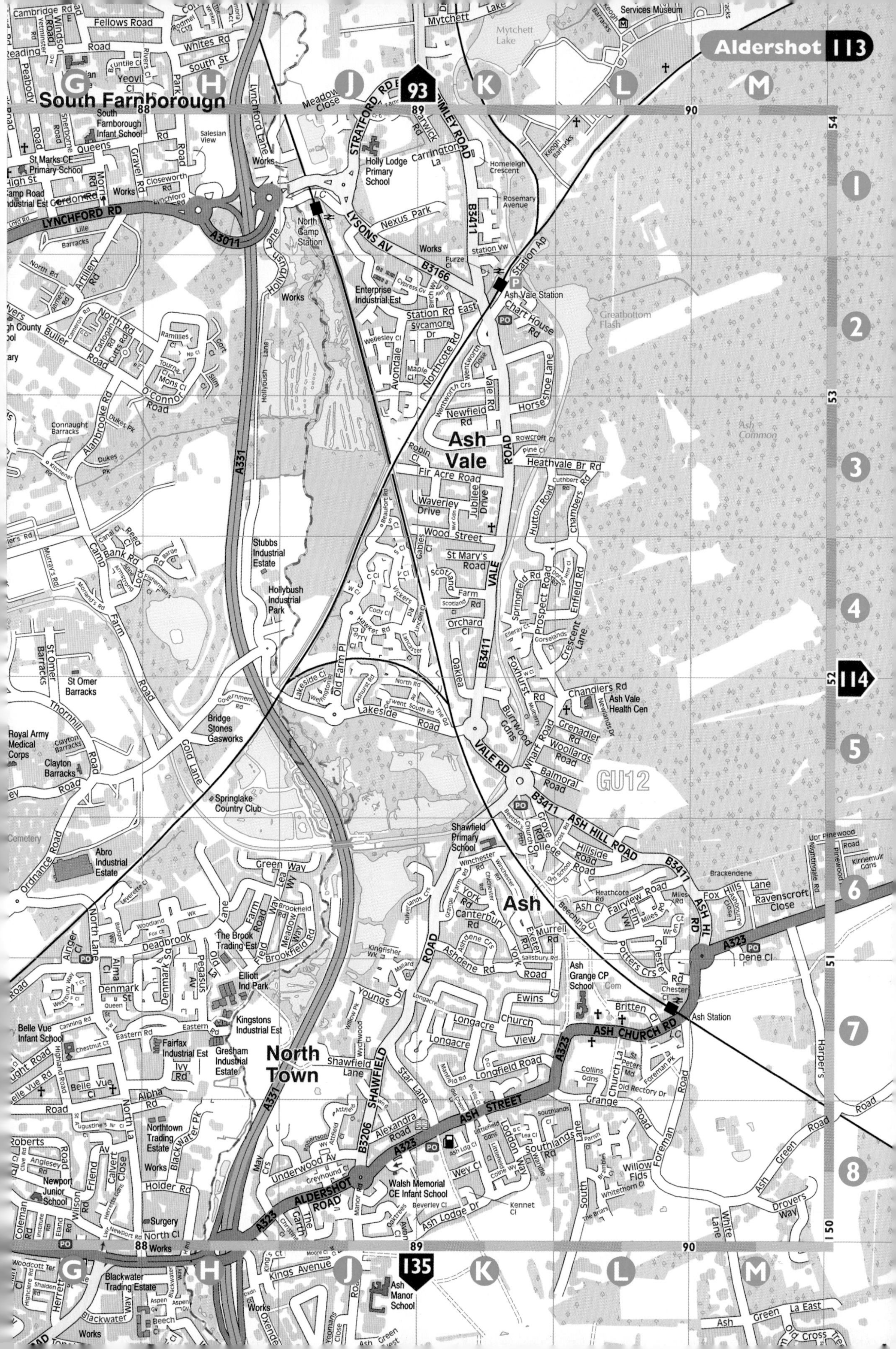
South Farnborough
Ash Vale
Ash
North Town
GU12
Mytchett
Mytchett Lake
Services Museum
Keogh Barracks
Holly Lodge Primary School
North Camp Station
Ash Vale Station
Greatbottom Flash
Ash Common
Enterprise Industrial Est
Stubbs Industrial Estate
Hollybush Industrial Park
Bridge Stones Gasworks
Springlake Country Club
Connaught Barracks
St Omer Barracks
Royal Army Medical Corps
Clayton Barracks
Abro Industrial Estate
Cemetery
Shawfield Primary School
Ash Vale Health Cen
Ash Grange CP School
Ash Station
The Brook Trading Est
Elliott Ind Park
Kingstons Industrial Est
Fairfax Industrial Est
Gresham Industrial Estate
Northtown Trading Estate
Belle Vue Infant School
Newport Junior School
Walsh Memorial CE Infant School
Blackwater Trading Estate
Ash Manor School
South Farnborough Infant School
St Marks CE Primary School
Lynchford Rd
A3011
A331
B3411
B3166
A323
B3206
Lysons Av
Vale Road
Ash Hill Road
Ash Church Rd
Ash Street
Aldershot Road
Shawfield Road
Lakeside Road
Camp Farm Road
Ordnance Road
North Lane
Ash Green Road
93
113
114
135
G
H
J
K
L
M
88
89
90
1
2
3
4
5
6
7
8
54
53
52
51
150

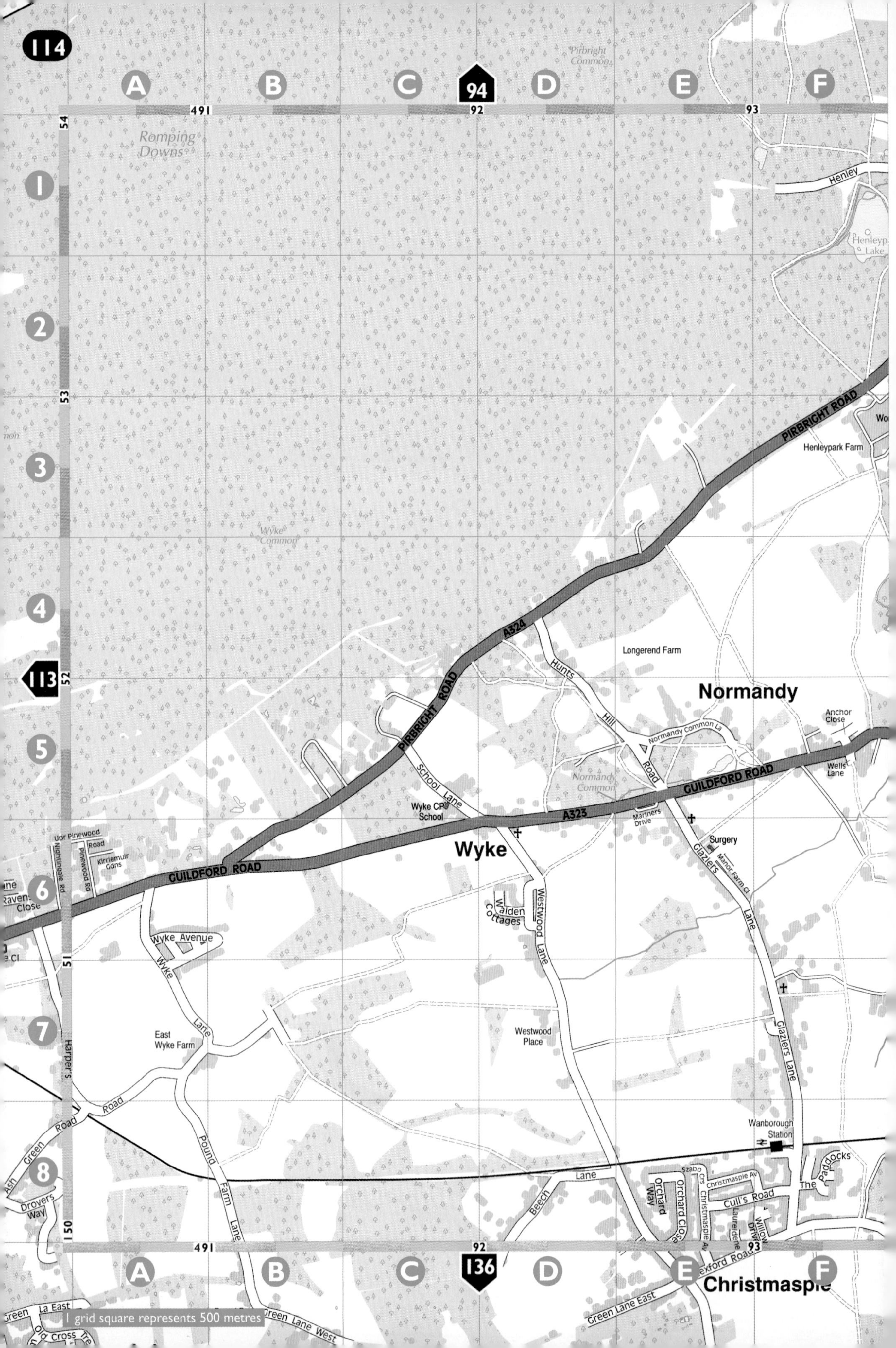
A
B
C
D
E
F
94
92
491
93
54
53
52
51
150
Pirbright Common
Romping Downs
Henley
Henleypark Lake
PIRBRIGHT ROAD
Henleypark Farm
Wyke Common
A324
Longerend Farm
Hunts Hill Road
Normandy
Anchor Close
Normandy Common La
Wells Lane
GUILDFORD ROAD
Normandy Common
School Lane
Wyke CP School
A323
Mariners Drive
Surgery
Glazlers
Manor Farm Cl
Upr Pinewood Road
Nightingale Rd
Pinewood Rd
Kirriemuir Gdns
Wyke
Ravens Close
Walden Cottages
Westwood Lane
Wyke Avenue
Wyke Lane
East Wyke Farm
Westwood Place
Glazlers Lane
Harper's Road
Ash Green Road
Pound Farm Lane
Wanborough Station
The Paddocks
Drovers Way
Beech Lane
Orchard Way
Orchard Close
Christmaspie Av
Cull's Road
Laurel Crs
Willow Drive
Flexford Road
113
136
Christmaspie
Green La East
Green Lane West
Green Lane East
Old Cross Tree
1 grid square represents 500 metres

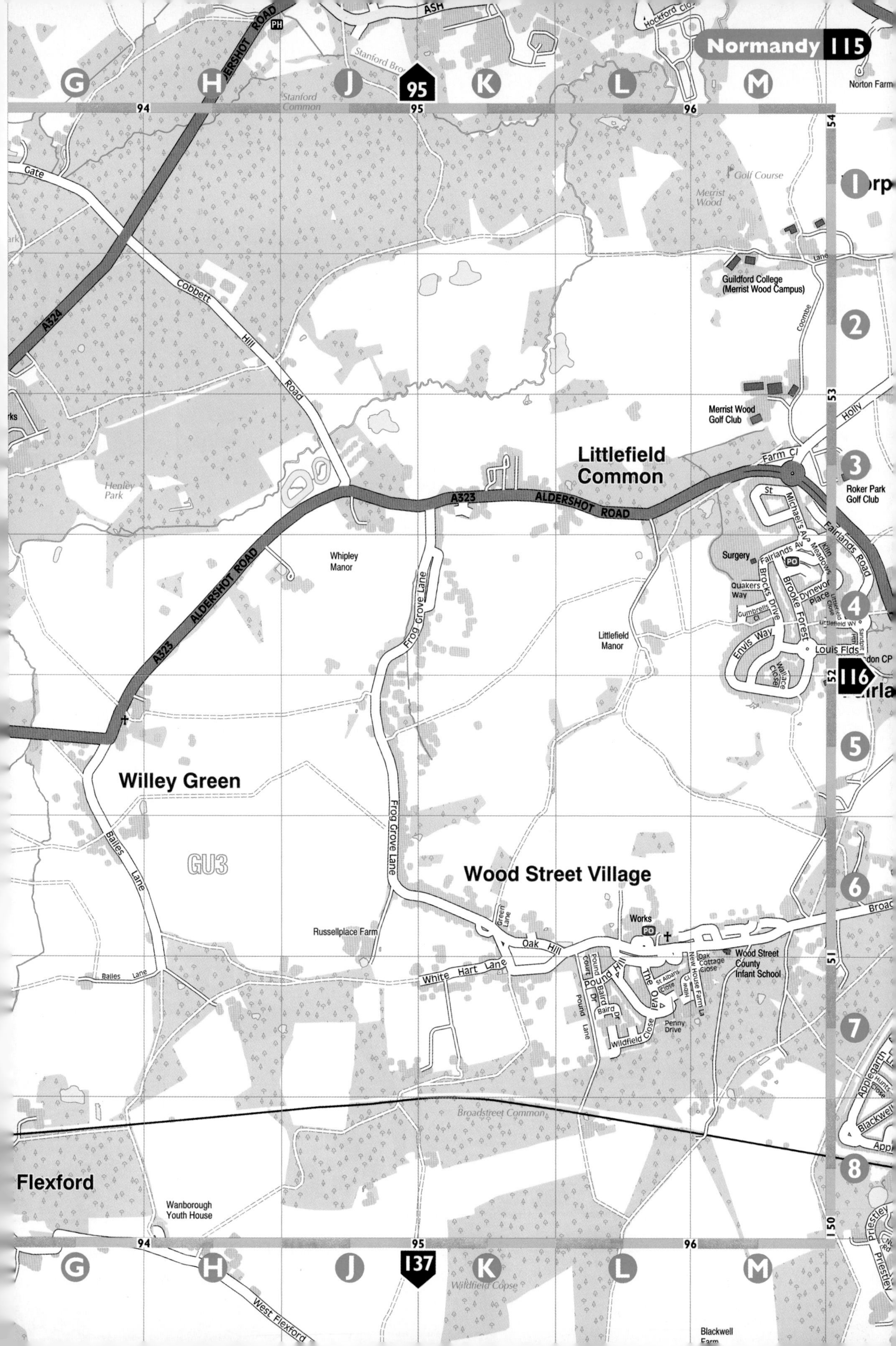

G   H   J   **95**   K   L   M

94   95   96   54

PH

ASH

Stanford Brook

Stanford Common

Hockford Clo

Norton Farm

I rp

Gate

Cobbett

A324

Hill

Road

Golf Course

Merrist Wood

2

Guildford College (Merrist Wood Campus)

Lane

Coombe

Henley Park

Merrist Wood Golf Club

Holly

3

Farm Cl

Roker Park Golf Club

A323   ALDERSHOT ROAD

Littlefield Common

St Michael's Av

Fairlands Road

ALDERSHOT ROAD

Whipley Manor

Surgery

Fairlands Av

Kiln Meadows

Brocke Forest

PO

A323

Quakers Way

Brocks Drive

Dynevor Place

Littlefield WN

4

Frog Grove Lane

Cumbrells Cl

Littlefield Manor

Envis Way

Louis Flds

don CP

Wallace Close

52 **116**

†

5

Willey Green

Bailes Lane

Frog Grove Lane

GU3

6

Broad

Russellplace Farm

Green Lane

Oak Hill

Wood Street Village

Works

PO

†

Wood Street County Infant School

51

Bailes Lane

White Hart Lane

Pound Court Dr

Oak Cottage Close

New House Farm La

St Albans Cl

Baird Dr

7

Pound Hill

The Oval

Pound Lane

Penny Drive

Wildfield Close

Appledarth

Blackwe

App

8

Broadstreet Common

Flexford

Wanborough Youth House

50

Priestley

Priestley

G   H   J   **137**   K   L   M

94   95   96

West Flexford

Wildfield Copse

Blackwell Farm

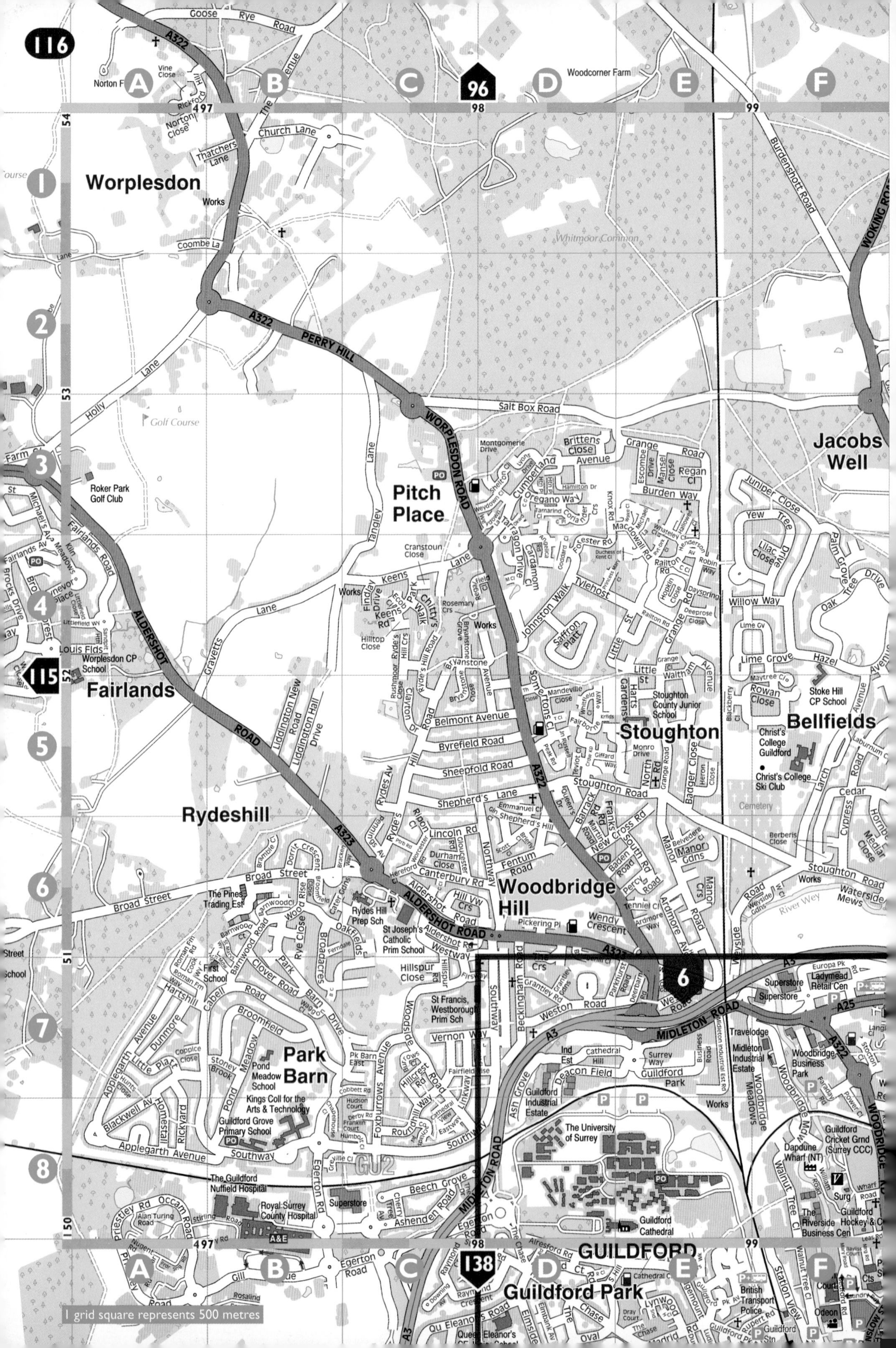

96
115
138
6
A
B
C
D
E
F
1
2
3
4
5
6
7
8
497
98
99
54
53
52
51
150
Worplesdon
Works
Goose Rye Road
A322
Vine Close
Norton F
Rickford
Norton Close
Church Lane
Thatchers Lane
Coombe La
Woodcorner Farm
Burdenshott Road
Whitmoor Common
WOKING ROAD
PERRY HILL
Holly Lane
Golf Course
Salt Box Road
WORPLESDON ROAD
Montgomerie Drive
Brittens Close
Grange Road
Avenue
Cumberland
Hamilton Dr
Burden Way
Oregano Way
Tarragon Drive
Cardamom
Knox Rd
Macdowall Rd
Escombe Drive
Mansel Close
Regan Cl
Jacobs Well
Juniper Close
Yew Tree Drive
Lilac Close
Palm Grove
Oak Tree Drive
Willow Way
Lime Gv
Lime Grove
Hazel Avenue
Pitch Place
Roker Park Golf Club
Farm
Michaels
Fairlands Av
Fairlands Road
Meadows
Brocks Drive
Littlefield Wy
Louis Flds
Worplesdon CP School
Fairlands
ALDERSHOT ROAD
Tangley Lane
Cranstoun Close
Keens Lane
Findlay Drive
Keens Rd
Park Walk
Chitty's
Rosemary Crs
Bryanstone Grove
Works
Hilltop Close
Ryde's Hill Crs
Ryde's Hill Road
Vanstone
Johnston Walk
Saffron Platt
Tylehost
Railton Rd
Grange Rd
Daysprings
Deeprose Close
Little St
Harts Gardens
Waltham Avenue
Stoughton County Junior School
Stoughton
Stoke Hill CP School
Bellfields
Christ's College Guildford
Christ's College Ski Club
Laburnum Cl
Cedar
Cemetery
Berberis Close
Stoughton Road
Waterside Mews
River Wey
Weyside Gdns
Gravetts Lane
Liddington New Road
Liddington Hall Drive
Rydeshill
Belmont Avenue
Byrefield Road
Sheepfold Road
Shepherd's Lane
Emmanuel Cl
Shepherd's Hill
Somertons Cl
Mandeville Close
Monro Drive
North Rd
Grange Road
Badger Close
Heron Close
Barrack Road
Franks Rd
New Cross Rd
South Rd
Manor Road
Belvedere Cl
Manor Gdns
Manor Crs
Ardmore Av
Rydes Av
Ryde's Av
Ripon Cl
Lincoln Rd
Durham Close
Canterbury Rd
Northway
Fentum Road
Woodbridge Hill
Broad Street
The Pines Trading Est
Dorrit Crescent
Bramble Cl
Wood Rise
Rydes Hill Prep Sch
St Joseph's Catholic Prim School
Aldershot Road
Hill Vw Crs
Westway
Pickering Pl
Wendy Crescent
A323
Barnwood Road
Rye Close
Broadacres
Oakfields
Clover Road
Park Barn Drive
First School
Hillspur Close
St Francis, Westborough Prim Sch
Vernon Way
Southway
Beckingham Road
Grantley Rd
Weston Road
Parkhurst Road
MIDLETON ROAD
A3
Midleton Industrial Est Rd
Europa Pk
Ladymead Retail Cen
Superstore
A25
Travelodge
Midleton Industrial Estate
Woodbridge Meadows
Woodbridge Business Park
Roman Fm
Hartshill
Cabell Road
Broomfield
Applegarth Avenue
Dunmore
Little Platt
Coppice Close
Stoney Brook
Pond Meadow
Pond Meadow School
Park Barn
Pk Barn East
Foxburrows Avenue
Hillcrest Rd
Woodside Road
Cathedral Hill
Ind Est
Deacon Field
Surrey Way
Guildford Park
Business Road
Works
Ash Grove
Guildford Industrial Estate
Kings Coll for the Arts & Technology
Guildford Grove Primary School
Blackwell Av
Homestall
Rickyard
Hudson Court
Roundhill Way
Cathedral View
Eastway
Linkway
The University of Surrey
Guildford Cricket Grnd (Surrey CCC)
Dapdune Wharf (NT)
Walnut Tree Close
Woodbridge Mdw
GU2
Egerton Rd
Beech Grove
The Guildford Nuffield Hospital
Royal Surrey County Hospital
A&E
Superstore
Ashenden Road
Cherry Tree Av
MIDLETON ROAD
Guildford Cathedral
The Riverside Business Cen
Guildford Hockey & C
Priestley Rd
Occam Road
Alan Turing Road
Stirling Road
Gill
Egerton Road
Rosalind
Alresford Rd
GUILDFORD
Guildford Park
Cathedral Cl
British Transport Police
Station View
Odeon
Queen Eleanor's Road
Elmside
Oval
Dray Court
The Chase
Madrid Rd
Guildford Stn
1 grid square represents 500 metres

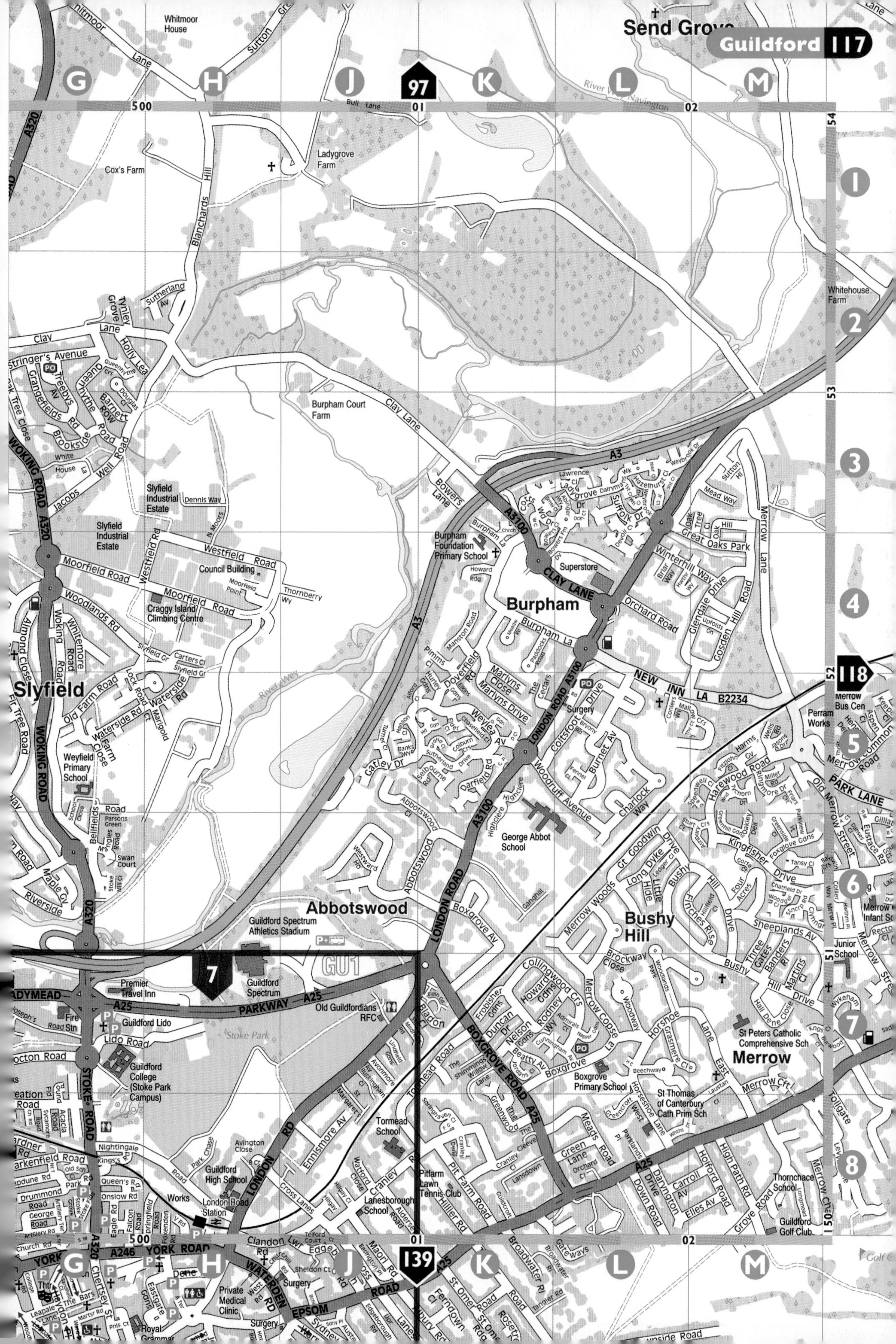

Guildford 117
Send Grove
Whitmoor House
Sutton Green
Lane
97
118
7
139
River Wey Navigation
Bull Lane
Ladygrove Farm
Cox's Farm
Blanchards Hill
Whitehouse Farm
Sutherland Av
Tyrley Grove
Clay Lane
Holly Lea
Stringer's Avenue
Grangefields Rd
Treebys Av
Queen Eleanors Road
Queenhythe Road
Barnett Row
Brookside
Well Road
White House La
Jacobs
Burpham Court Farm
Oak Tree Close
WOKING ROAD A320
Slyfield Industrial Estate
Dennis Way
Westfield Rd
Westfield Road
Council Building
Moorfield Road
Moorfield Point
Thornberry Wy
Craggy Island Climbing Centre
Woodlands Rd
Whitmore Road
Almond Close
Slyfield Gn
Carters Cl
Slyfield
Old Farm Road
Lock Road
Waterside Rd
Waterside Ct
Marigold Ct
Farm Close
Weyfield Primary School
Fir Tree Road
Bellfields Road
Parsons Green
Swan Court
Stoke Mill Cl
Maple Gv
Riverside
River Wey
A3
A3100
Bowers Lane
Burpham Foundation Primary School
Burpham La
Howard Rdg
Lawrence
Ladygrove Dr
Dairyma
Hazelhurst Cl
Suffolk Dr
Weybrook Dr
Sutton Hl
Mead Way
Oak Tree Cl
Oak Hill
Great Oaks Park
Merrow Lane
Superstore
CLAY LANE
Burpham
Orchard Road
Winterhill Way
Glendale Drive
Gosden Hill Road
Manston Road
Pimms Cl
Doverfield Rd
Marlyns Close
Marlyns Drive
The Cedars
Paddocks Road
Weylea Av
NEW INN LA B2234
LONDON ROAD A3100
Surgery
Coltsfoot Drive
Burnet Av
Gatley Dr
Selbourne Rd
Sutherland Drive
Colburn Crs
Darfield Rd
Woodruff Avenue
Charlock Way
Highclere
George Abbot School
Abbotswood
Abbotswood Cl
Westward Ho
Merrow Bus Cen
Perram Works
Merrow Common Road
PARK LANE
Harms Gv
Harewood Road
Rhymmore Dr
Old Merrow Street
Eustace Rd
Kingfisher Drive
Foxglove Gdns
Gt Goodwin Drive
Long Dyke
Little Hide
Bushy Hill Drive
Merrow Woods
Finches Rise
Four Acres
Sheeplands Av
Merrow Infant Sch
Junior School
Bushy Hill
Three Gates
Banders Ri
Martins Cl
Hall Dene Close
Wykeham
Guildford Spectrum Athletics Stadium
GU1
Boxgrove Av
Brockway Close
Collingwood Crs
Howard Gdns
Frobisher Gdns
Duncan Dr
Nelson Gdns
Rodney Wy
Merrow Copse
Woodway
Woodlands Park
St Peters Catholic Comprehensive Sch
Merrow
Premier Travel Inn
Guildford Spectrum
PARKWAY A25
A25
Old Guildfordians RFC
Bladon
ADYMEAD
Fire Stn
Guildford Lido
Lido Road
Stoke Park
Guildford College (Stoke Park Campus)
STOKE ROAD
BOXGROVE ROAD A25
Boxgrove La
Beatty Av
Boxgrove Primary School
Horseshoe Lane
Grasmere Cl
St Thomas of Canterbury Cath Prim Sch
East Lane
Merrow Cft
Tollgate
Tormead Road
Tormead School
Ennismore Av
Cranley Rd
Pit Farm Road
Hillier Rd
Greenwood
Green Lane
Orchard Ct
Meads Road
Down Road
Drive
Daryngton
Carroll Av
Holford Road
High Path Rd
Grove Road
Thornchace School
Guildford Golf Club
Elles Av
Nightingale
Avington Close
Guildford High School
London Road Station
Works
Cross Lanes
Lanesborough School
Pitfarm Lawn Tennis Club
Merrow Ch
Queen's Rd
Onslow Rd
Drummond Rd
George Road
Falcon Rd
Eagle Rd
YORK ROAD
A246
A320
Chertsey St
WATERDEN RD
EPSOM ROAD
Private Medical Clinic
Surgery
Clandon Rd
Maori Rd
Ferndown
St Omer Road
Broadwater Rl
Gateways
Tangier Rd
Royal Grammar
The Bars
Artillery Rd
Church Rd
Leapale
Dene
Eastgate Gdns
500
01
02
50
51
52
53
54
G
H
J
K
L
M

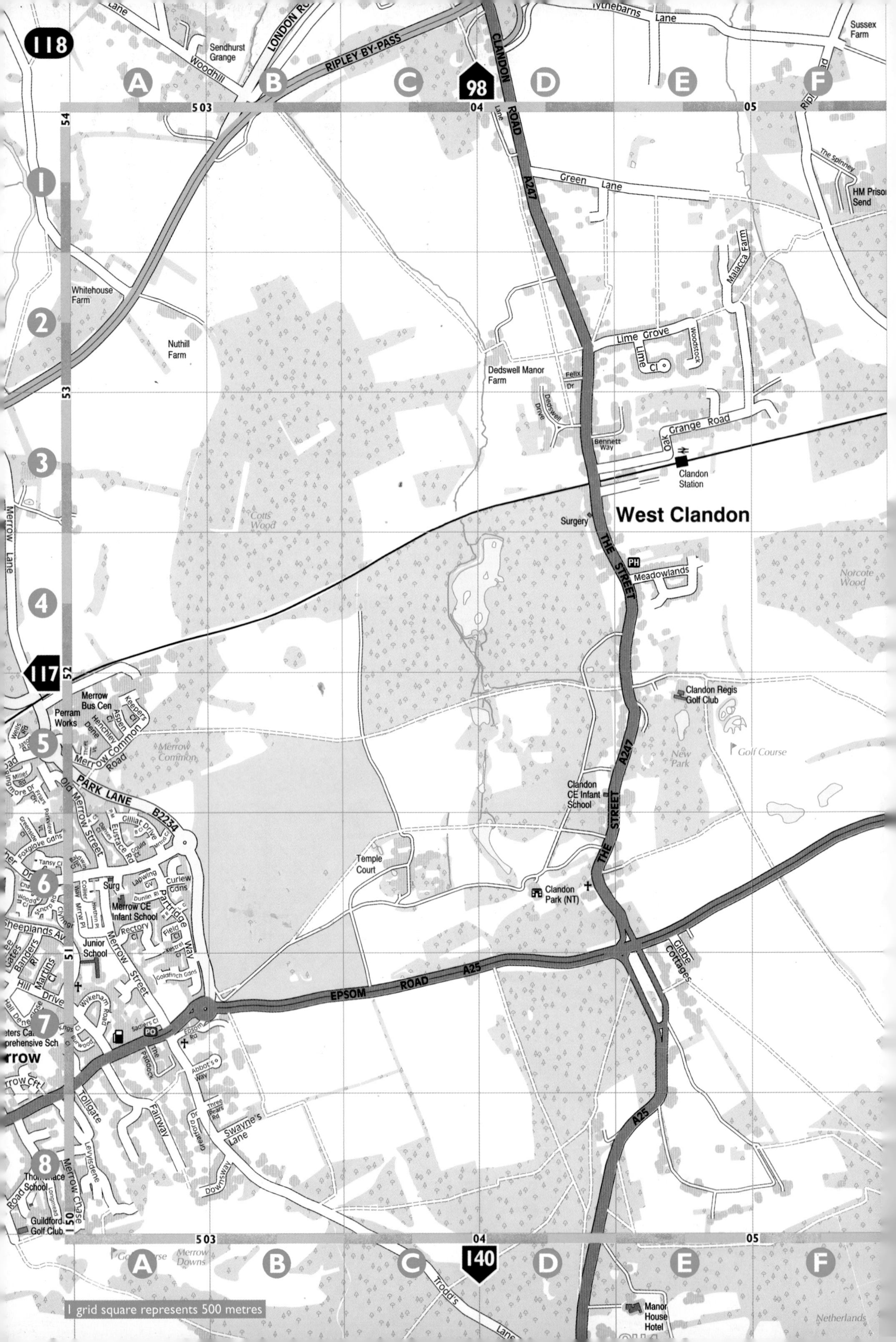

118

503

54

53

52

51

50

A

B

C

D

E

F

1

2

3

4

5

6

7

8

98
04

140
04

117

Woodhill Lane

LONDON ROAD

RIPLEY BY-PASS

Sendhurst Grange

Tythebarns Lane

Sussex Farm

Ripley Rd

The Spinney

HM Prison Send

CLANDON ROAD

A247

Green Lane

Malacca Farm

Whitehouse Farm

Nuthill Farm

Dedswell Manor Farm

Dedswell Drive

Felix Dr

Bennett Way

Lime Grove

Lime Cl

Woodstock

Grange Road

Clandon Station

Cotts Wood

Surgery

West Clandon

THE STREET

PH

Meadowlands

Norcote Wood

Merrow Lane

Merrow Bus Cen

Perram Works

Keepers

Aspen

Henchley Dene

Merrow Common Road

Merrow Common

Clandon Regis Golf Club

Golf Course

New Park

A247

Clandon CE Infant School

PARK LANE B2234

Old Merrow Street

Gilliat Drive

Eustace Rd

Collyer Ct

Temple Court

Clandon Park (NT)

THE STREET

Merrow

Surg

Lapwing

Curlew Gdns

Dunlin La

Merrow CE Infant School

Rectory Cl

Field Cl

Kestrel Cl

Junior School

Partridge Way

Merrow Street

Sheeplands Av

Banders Rise

Martins Cl

Hill Drive

Goldfinch Gdns

Foxglove Gdns

Greystoke Ct

Pinkview

Tansy Cl

EPSOM ROAD A25

Clebe Cottages

A25

Wykeham Road

Sadlers Cl

PO

Paddock Way

Abbot's Way

Three Pears Rd

Tollgate

Fairway

Swayne's Lane

Downs Way

Levylsdene

Merrow Chase

Thornmeace School

Guildford Golf Club

Manor House Hotel

Golf Course

Merrow Downs

Netherlands

Todd's Lane

1 grid square represents 500 metres

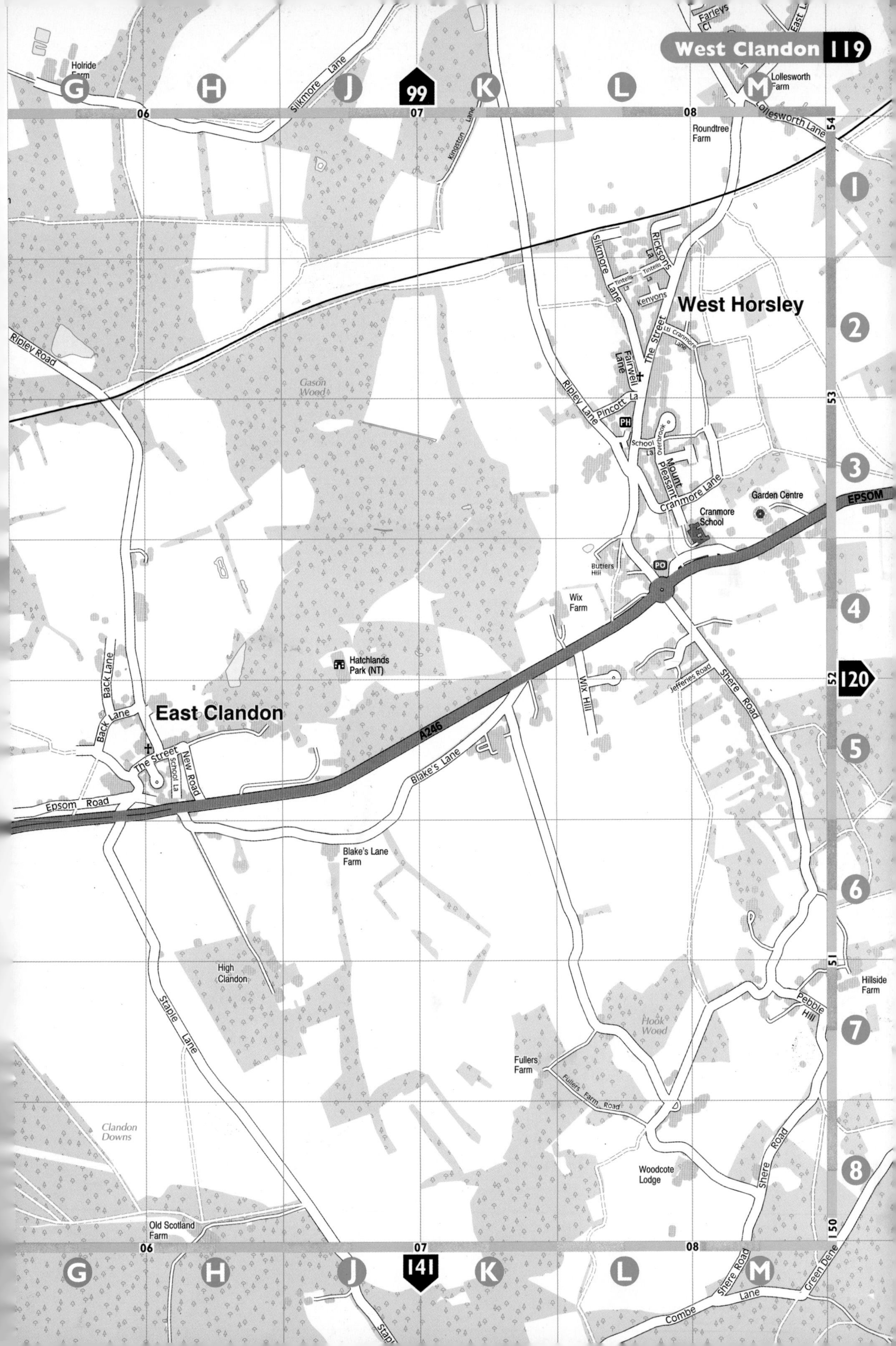

G 06
H
Silkmore Lane
J
99 07
K
L 08
M 54

Holride Farm

Lollesworth Farm

Roundtree Farm

Lollesworth Lane

1

Ripley Road

Gason Wood

Silkmore Lane
Ricksons La
Tintells La
Kenvons
Tintells La
The Street
Cranmore La

West Horsley

53

2

Fairwell Lane
Ripley Lane
Pincott La
PH
School La
Overbrook La
Cranmore Lane
Mount Pleasant

Garden Centre

EPSOM

3

Butlers Hill
PO
Cranmore School

52 120

Wix Farm

4

East Clandon

Hatchlands Park (NT)

Wix Hill

Jefferies Road
Shere Road

5

Back Lane
The Street
School La
New Road
A246
Blake's Lane

Epsom Road

51

6

Blake's Lane Farm

High Clandon

Hook Wood

7

Stable Lane

Fullers Farm

Hillside Farm
Pebble Hill

Clandon Downs

Fullers Farm Road

Woodcote Lodge

Shere Road

8

Old Scotland Farm

50

Stable
Combe
Shere Road
Green Dene Lane

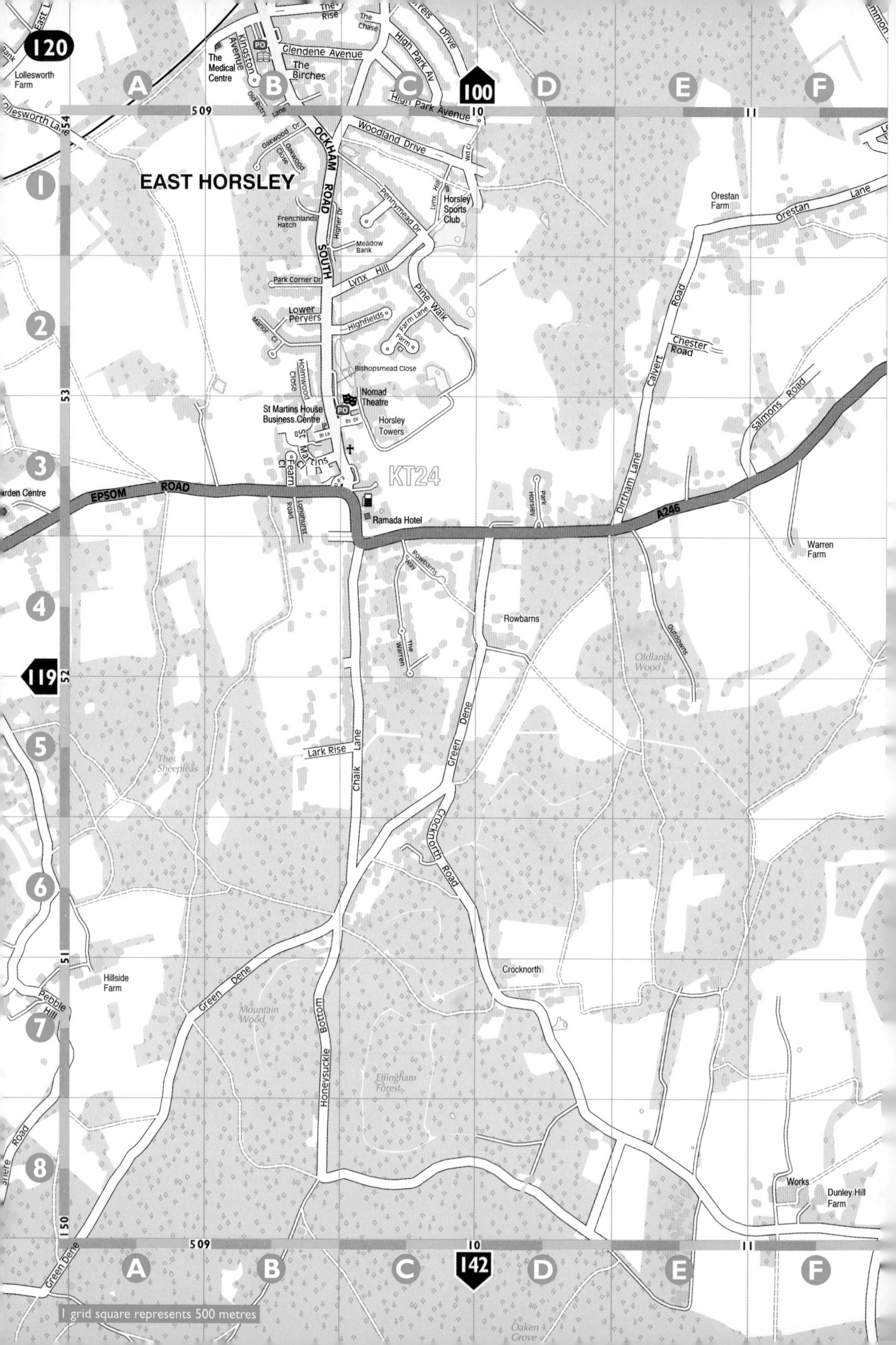

EAST HORSLEY

Lollesworth Farm

Kingston Avenue

The Medical Centre

Glendene Avenue

The Birches

High Park Av

High Park Avenue

100

Oakwood Dr

Oakwood Close

Woodland Drive

OCKHAM ROAD SOUTH

Pennymead Dr

Higher Dr

Horsley Sports Club

Orestan Farm

Orestan Lane

Frenchlands Hatch

Meadow Bank

Lynx Hill

Lynx Hill

Park Corner Dr

Manor Cl

Lower Peryers

Highfields

Farm Lane

Pine Walk

Farm Cl

Calvert Road

Chester Road

Holmwood Close

Bishopsmead Close

St Martins House Business Centre

Nomad Theatre

Horsley Towers

PO

Salmons Road

KT24

Horsley

Park

Fearn Cl

Longhurst

St Martins

Dirtham Lane

A246

Warren Farm

Garden Centre

EPSOM ROAD

Ramada Hotel

Rowbarns Way

Rowbarns

Oldlands Wood

119

The Warren

The Sheepleas

Lark Rise

Chalk Lane

Green Dene

Crocknorth Road

Crocknorth

Hillside Farm

Green Dene

Mountain Wood

Honeysuckle Bottom

Effingham Forest

Pebble Hill

Works

Dunley Hill Farm

Green Dene

I grid square represents 500 metres

Oaken Grove

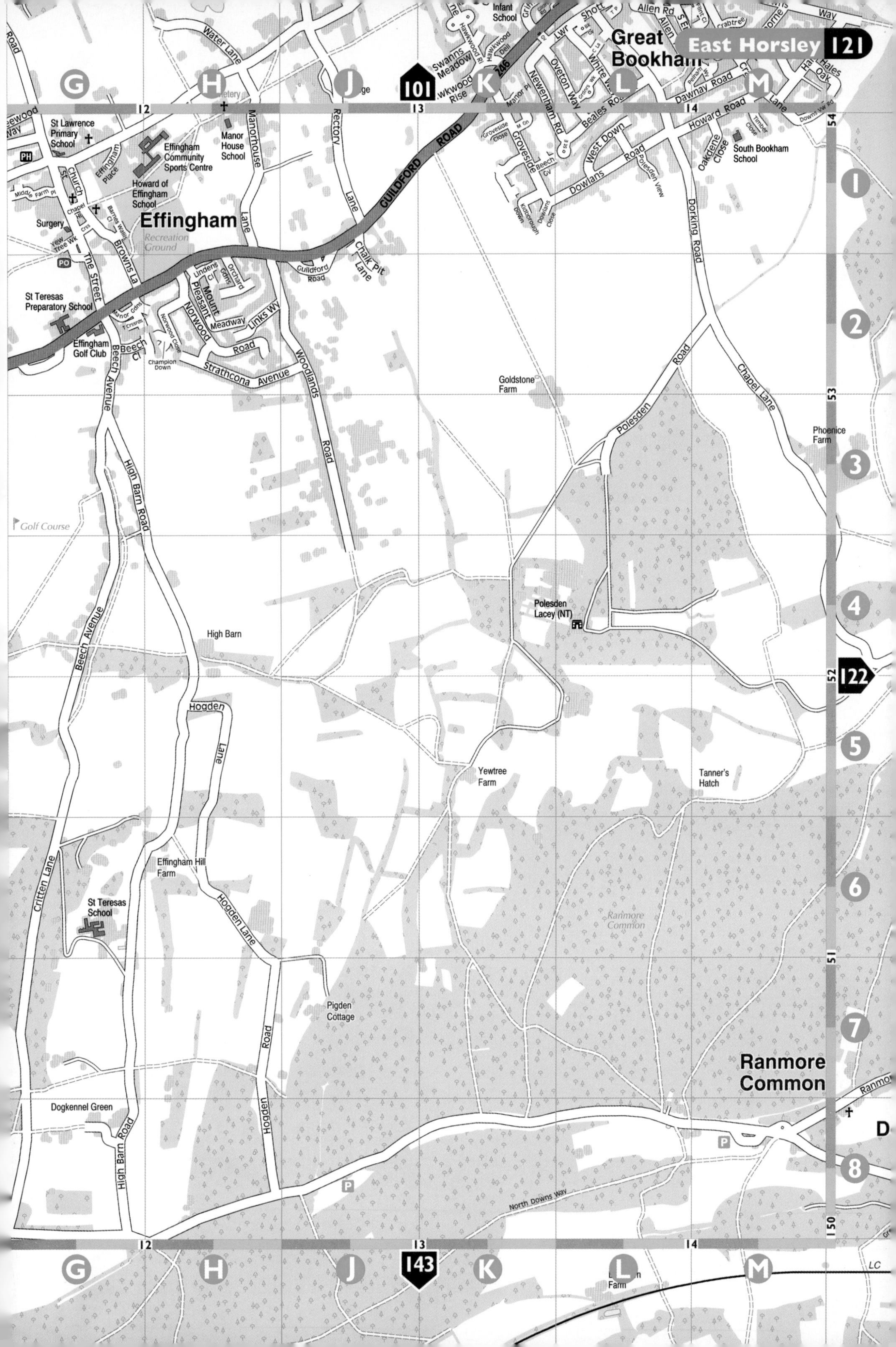
Great Bookham
Effingham
Ranmore Common
St Lawrence Primary School
Effingham Community Sports Centre
Howard of Effingham School
Manor House School
St Teresas Preparatory School
Effingham Golf Club
Recreation Ground
Surgery
South Bookham School
Goldstone Farm
Phoenice Farm
Polesden Lacey (NT)
High Barn
Yewtree Farm
Tanner's Hatch
Effingham Hill Farm
St Teresas School
Ranmore Common
Pigden Cottage
Dogkennel Green
Golf Course
North Downs Way
GUILDFORD ROAD
Dorking Road
Polesden Road
Chapel Lane
Beech Avenue
High Barn Road
Hogden Lane
Hogden Road
Critten Lane
Woodlands Road
Strathcona Avenue
Rectory Lane
Chalk Pit Lane
Manorhouse Lane
Water Lane
The Street
Browns La
Dowlans Road
Howard Road
Dawnay Road
West Down
Groveside
Newenham Rd
Oveton Way
Beales Rd
Oakdene Close
Norwood Road
Mount Pleasant
Meadway
Links Wy
Champion Down
101
122
143
G H J K L M
12 13 14
50 51 52 53 54
1 2 3 4 5 6 7 8

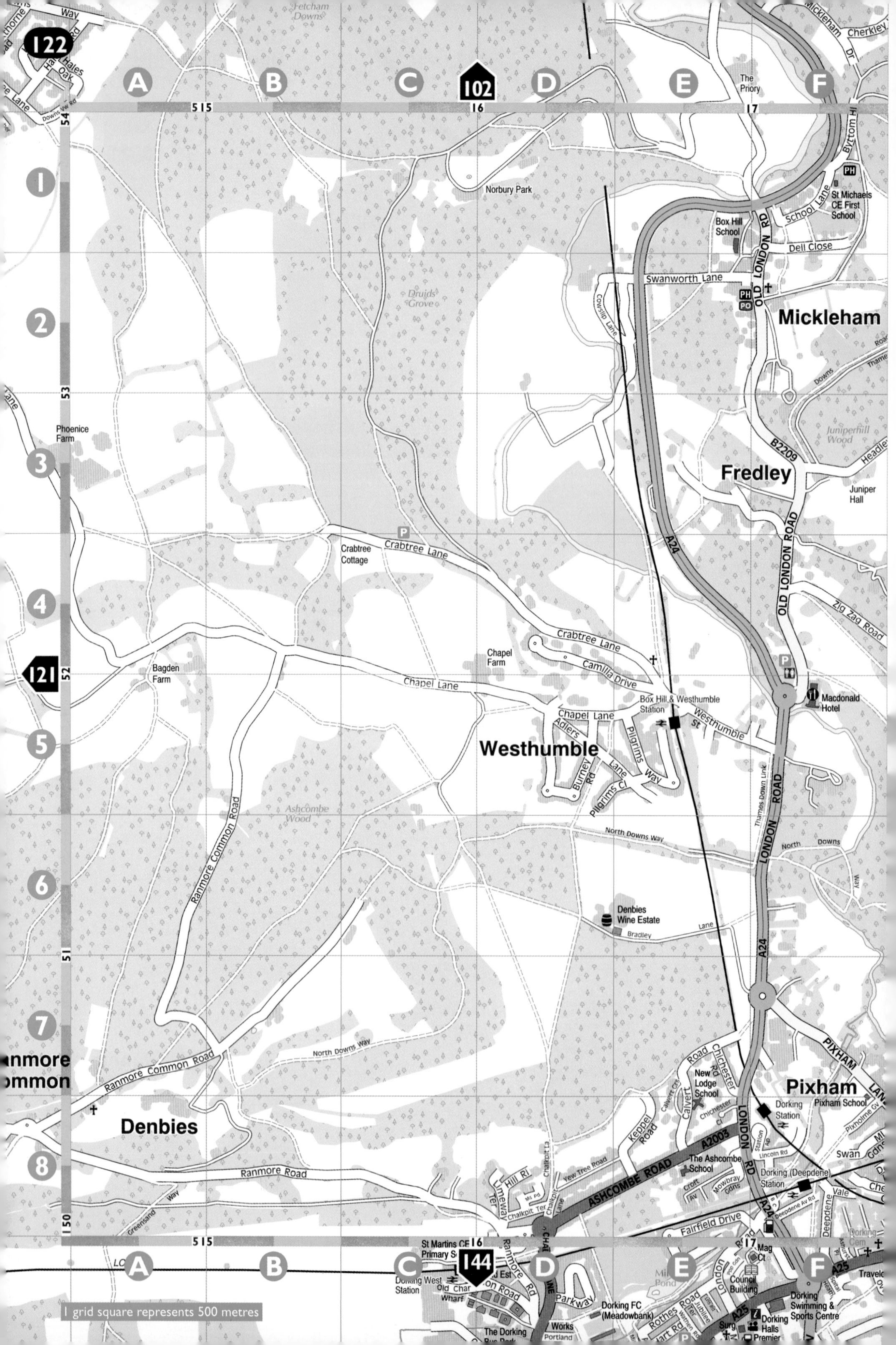
122
102
121
144
Fetcham Downs
Norbury Park
Druids Grove
The Priory
Box Hill School
St Michaels CE First School
School Lane
Dell Close
Swanworth Lane
Cowslip Lane
OLD LONDON RD
Mickleham
Phoenice Farm
Juniperhill Wood
B2209
Fredley
Juniper Hall
Crabtree Cottage
Crabtree Lane
OLD LONDON ROAD
Zig Zag Road
A24
Chapel Farm
Camilla Drive
Bagden Farm
Chapel Lane
Box Hill & Westhumble Station
Macdonald Hotel
Westhumble St
Westhumble
Adlers Lane
Pilgrims Way
Burney Rd
Pilgrims Cl
Thames Down Link
LONDON ROAD
Ashcombe Wood
North Downs Way
Ranmore Common Road
Denbies Wine Estate
Bradley Lane
North Downs Way
Ranmore Common Road
Pixham
Pixham School
PIXHAM LANE
New Lodge School
Chichester Road
Calvert Rd
Keppel Road
Dorking Station
Denbies
Ranmore Road
Greensand Way
Hill Rl
Yew Tree Road
ASHCOMBE ROAD
A2003
The Ashcombe School
LONDON RD
Dorking (Deepdene) Station
Fairfield Drive
St Martins CE Primary S
Dorking West Station
Ranmore Rd
Parkway
Dorking FC (Meadowbank)
Rothes Road
Council Building
Dorking Swimming & Sports Centre
Dorking Halls
A25
1 grid square represents 500 metres

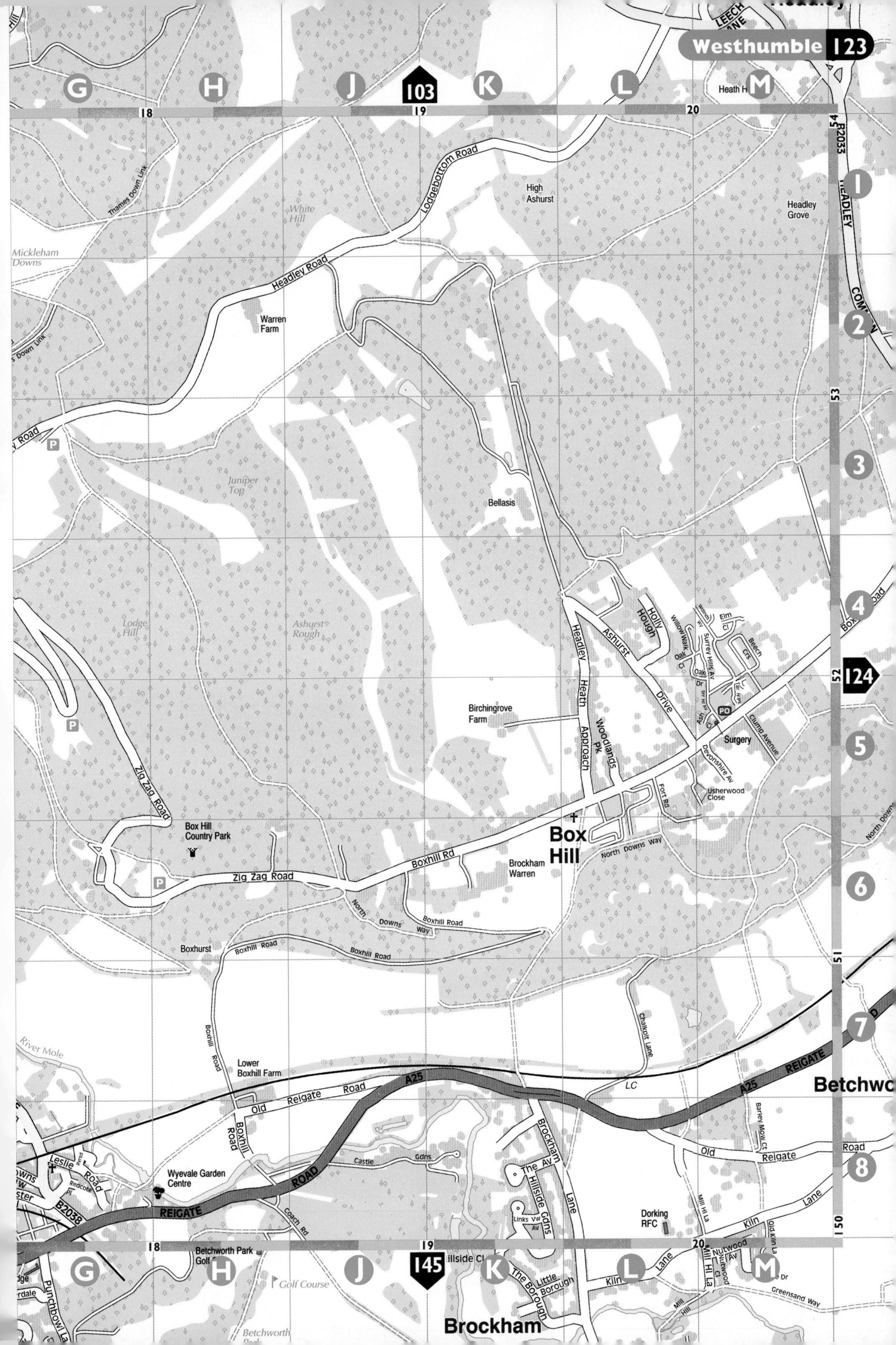

G
H
J
103
K
L
M
18
19
20
Heath H
Leech Lane
B2033
Headley
Common
54
53
52
51
150
1
2
3
4
5
6
7
8
124
Lodgebottom Road
Thames Down Link
White Hill
High Ashurst
Headley Grove
Mickleham Downs
Headley Road
Warren Farm
Juniper Top
Bellasis
Lodge Hill
Ashurst Rough
Headley Heath Approach
Ashurst Drive
Holly Hough
Willow Walk
Oak Cl
Oak Dr
Surrey Hills Av
Elm Cl
Beech Crs
Woodlands Pk
Birchingrove Farm
Ash Cl
PO
Surgery
Clump Avenue
Devonshire Av
Usherwood Close
Fort Rd
Box Hill
Box Hill Country Park
Zig Zag Road
Boxhill Rd
Brockham Warren
North Downs Way
Boxhill Road
Boxhurst
Chalkpit Lane
River Mole
Lower Boxhill Farm
Old Reigate Road
A25
Reigate Road
LC
Betchwo
Barley Mow Ct
Old Reigate Road
Brockham Lane
The Av
Hillside Gdns
Links Vw Av
Castle Gdns
Coach Rd
Wyevale Garden Centre
Leslie Road
Redcote Pl
B2038
Dorking RFC
Mill Hl La
Kiln Lane
Old Kiln La
Nutwood Av
Nutwood Cl
Betchworth Park Golf
Golf Course
145
Hillside Cl
The Borough
Little Borough
Greensand Way
Mill Hill
Punchbowl La
Betchworth
Brockham
P

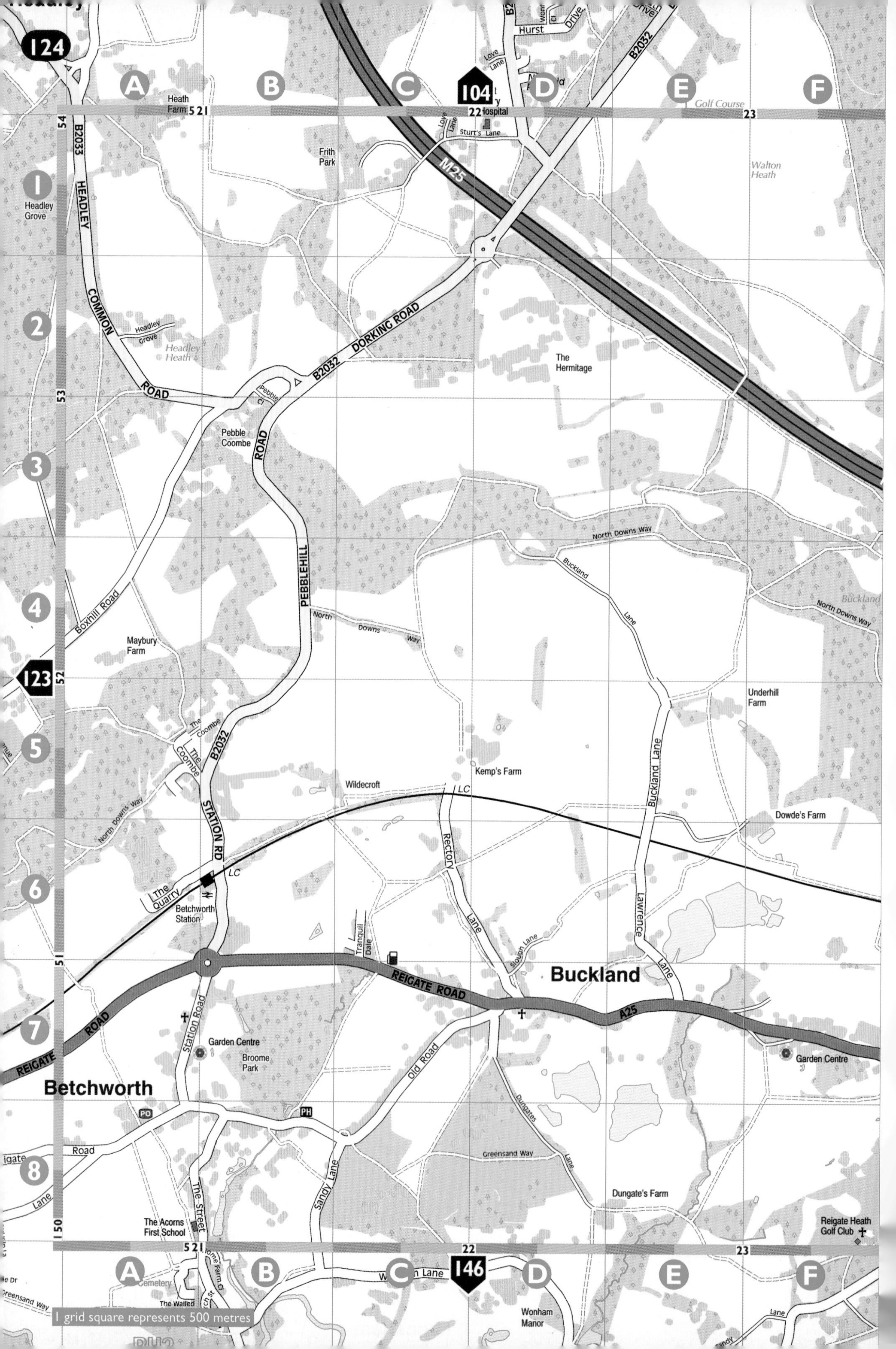
124
104
123
146
A
B
C
D
E
F
1
2
3
4
5
6
7
8
54
53
52
51
50
521
22
23
Heath Farm
Golf Course
Hospital
Hurst
Drive
Love Lane
Sturt's Lane
B2032
B2033
M25
Frith Park
Walton Heath
Headley Grove
HEADLEY COMMON ROAD
Headley Grove
Headley Heath
DORKING ROAD
Pebble Cl
The Hermitage
Pebble Coombe
PEBBLEHILL ROAD
North Downs Way
Buckland Lane
Buckland
Boxhill Road
Maybury Farm
Underhill Farm
The Coombe
Kemp's Farm
Wildecroft
LC
STATION RD
Dowde's Farm
Rectory Lane
The Quarry
Betchworth Station
Lawrence Lane
Tranquil Dale
Slough Lane
Buckland
REIGATE ROAD
A25
Station Road
Garden Centre
Broome Park
Old Road
Betchworth
Dungates Lane
PO
PH
Road
Lane
Greensand Way
Sandy Lane
The Street
Dungate's Farm
The Acorns First School
Reigate Heath Golf Club
Cemetery
Lane
Wonham Manor
Greensand Way
The Walled
1 grid square represents 500 metres

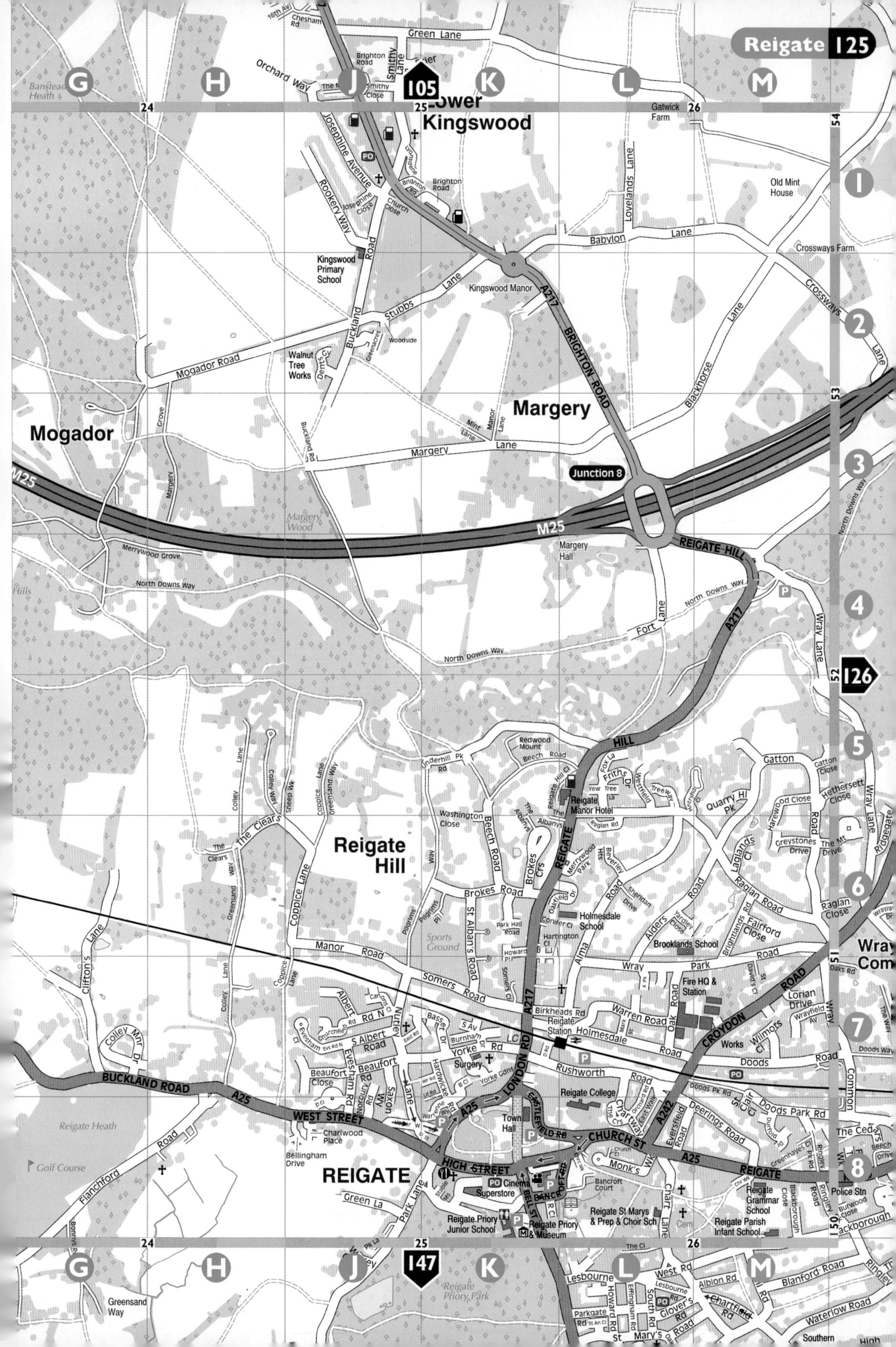
Lower Kingswood
Mogador
Margery
Reigate Hill
REIGATE
Junction 8
M25
A217
BRIGHTON ROAD
REIGATE HILL
A25
A242
BUCKLAND ROAD
WEST STREET
HIGH STREET
CHURCH ST
CROYDON ROAD
LONDON RD
Green Lane
Orchard Way
Brighton Road
Smithy Lane
Josephine Avenue
Rookery Way
Kingswood Primary School
Buckland Road
Stubbs Lane
Kingswood Manor
Mogador Road
Walnut Tree Works
Margery Lane
Babylon Lane
Lovelands Lane
Old Mint House
Crossways Farm
Blackhorse Lane
Gatwick Farm
Margery Wood
Margery Hall
Merrywood Grove
North Downs Way
Fort Lane
Wray Lane
Coppice Lane
Colley Lane
The Clears
Manor Road
Somers Road
Reigate Manor Hotel
Holmesdale School
Brooklands School
Fire HQ & Station
Wray Park Road
Reigate Station
Holmesdale Road
Rushworth Road
Reigate College
Town Hall
Doods Road
Reigate Heath
Golf Course
Flanchford Road
Charlwood Place
Bellingham Drive
Cinema
Superstore
Reigate Priory Junior School
Reigate Priory & Museum
Reigate St Marys & Prep & Choir Sch
Reigate Grammar School
Reigate Parish Infant School
Police Stn
Reigate Priory Park
Greensand Way
Blanford Road
Waterlow Road
105
126
147

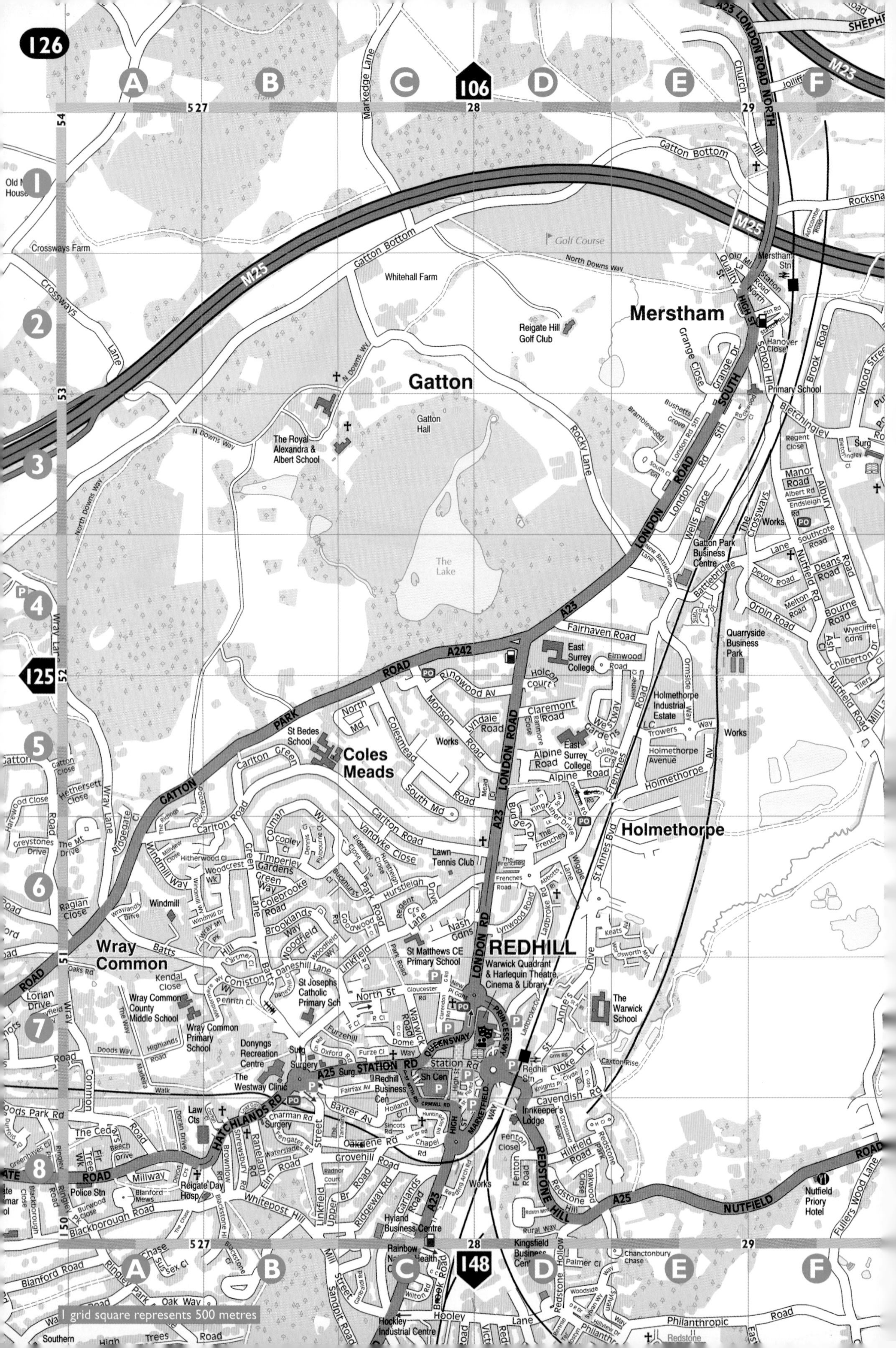

106
Gatton
Gatton Hall
The Lake
Merstham
Merstham Stn
Reigate Hill Golf Club
Golf Course
Whitehall Farm
Crossways Farm
The Royal Alexandra & Albert School
Gatton Park Business Centre
Quarryside Business Park
Holmethorpe Industrial Estate
East Surrey College
St Bedes School
Coles Meads
Holmethorpe
REDHILL
Warwick Quadrant & Harlequin Theatre, Cinema & Library
St Matthews CE Primary School
St Josephs Catholic Primary Sch
The Warwick School
Wray Common
Wray Common County Middle School
Wray Common Primary School
Donyngs Recreation Centre
The Westway Clinic
Redhill Business Cen
Redhill Stn
Innkeeper's Lodge
Reigate Day Hosp
Police Stn
Hyland Business Centre
Rainbow Health Centre
Kingsfield Business Centre
Hockley Industrial Centre
Nutfield Priory Hotel
M25
M23
A23 LONDON ROAD NORTH
A242 PARK ROAD
GATTON PARK ROAD
A25 STATION RD
HATCHLANDS RD
REDSTONE HILL
A25 NUTFIELD ROAD
Lawn Tennis Club
Windmill
148
125
1 grid square represents 500 metres

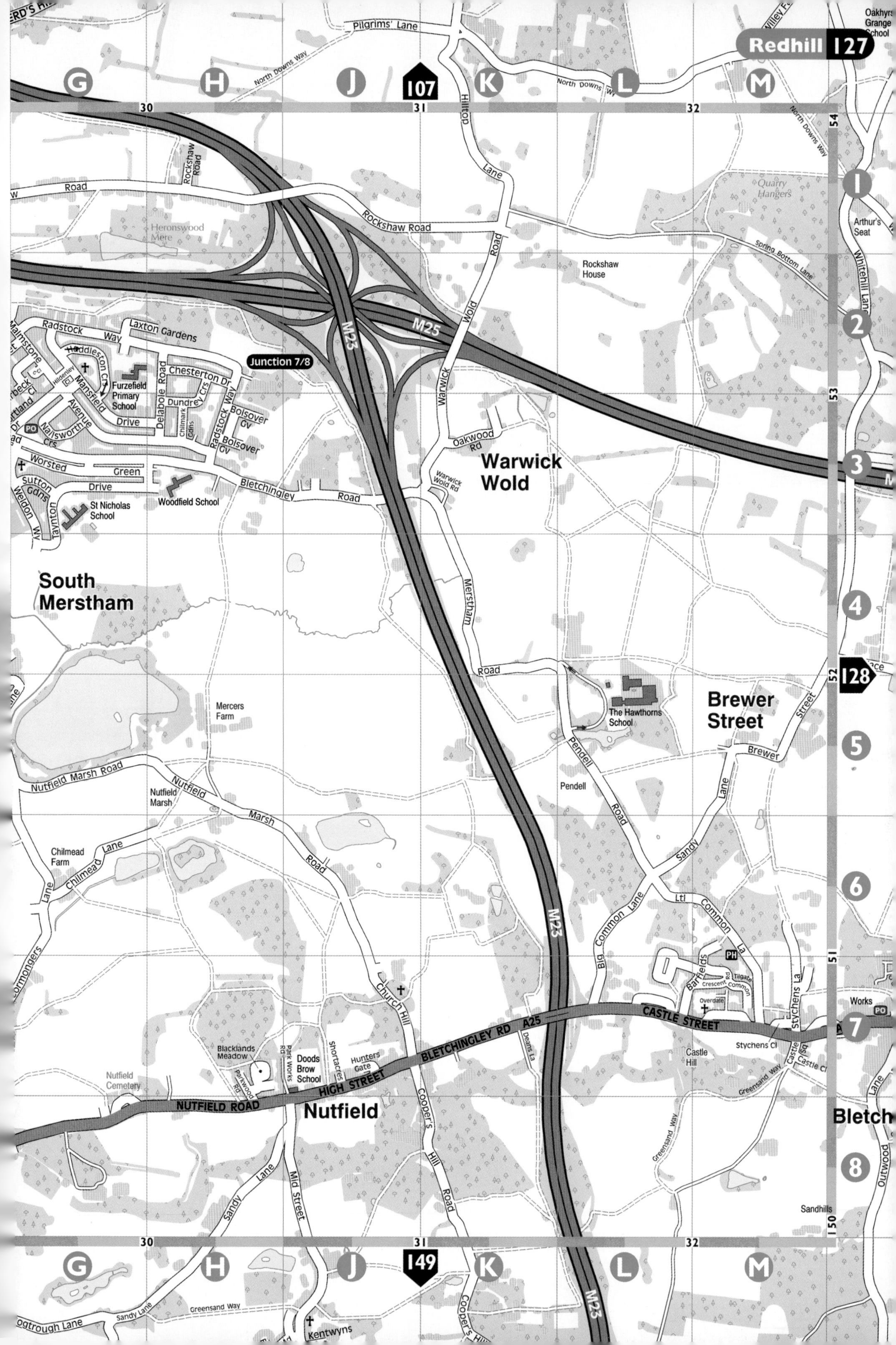

Redhill 127
107
128
149
Junction 7/8
M25
M23
South Merstham
Warwick Wold
Brewer Street
Nutfield
Pendell
Rockshaw House
The Hawthorns School
Mercers Farm
Nutfield Marsh
Chilmead Farm
Furzefield Primary School
Woodfield School
St Nicholas School
Doods Brow School
Nutfield Cemetery
Castle Hill
Sandhills
Quarry Hangers
Arthur's Seat
Heronswood Mere
Pilgrims' Lane
North Downs Way
Rockshaw Road
Hilltop Lane
Warwick Wold Road
Oakwood Rd
Bletchingley Road
Merstham Road
Pendell Road
Brewer Street
Sandy Lane
Big Common Lane
Ltl Common La
Castle Street
Bletchingley Rd A25
High Street
Nutfield Road
Nutfield Marsh Road
Chilmead Lane
Church Hill
Cooper's Hill Road
Mid Street
Spring Bottom Lane
Whitehill Lane
Radstock Way
Laxton Gardens
Chesterton Dr
Mansfield
Delabole Road
Nailsworth Crs
Worsted Green
Sutton Gdns
Tayton Wy
Weldon Wy
Greensand Way
Stychens La
Stychens Cl
Deans La
Blacklands Meadow
Hunters Gate
Shortacres
Works
Bletch
Outwood Lane
Kentwyns
Hogtrough Lane

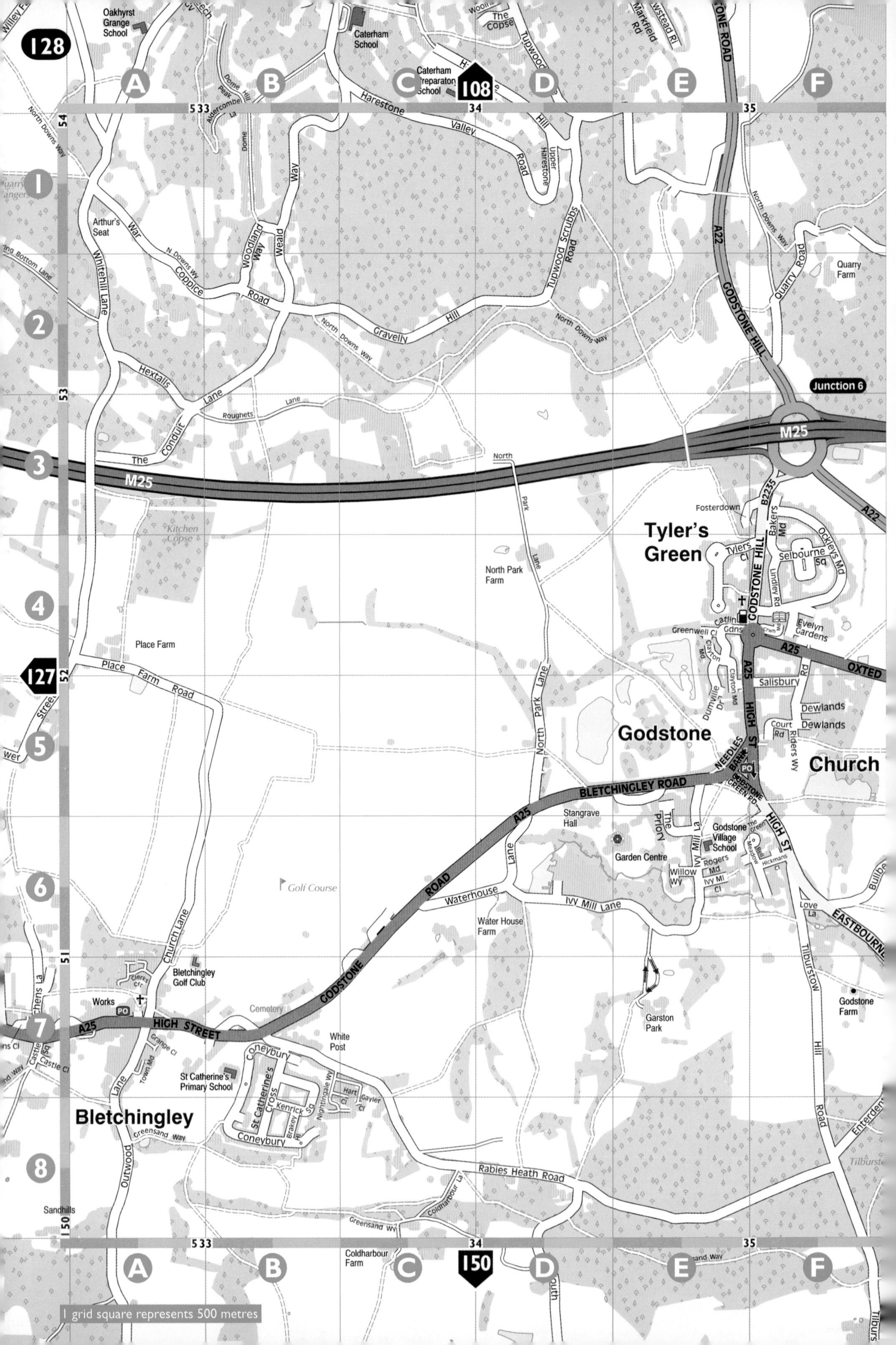
Oakhyrst Grange School
Caterham School
Caterham Preparatory School
108
Harestone Valley Road
Tupwood Scrubbs Road
Arthur's Seat
War Coppice Road
Woodland Way
Weald Way
Whitehill Lane
Gravelly Hill
North Downs Way
Hextalls Lane
Roughets Lane
The Conduit
M25
A22
GODSTONE HILL
Quarry Road
Quarry Farm
Junction 6
Kitchen Copse
North Park Lane
North Park Farm
Fosterdown
B2235
Tyler's Green
Tylers Cl
Bakers Md
Ockleys Md
Selbourne Sq
Lindley Rd
Evelyn Gardens
Catlin Gdns
Greenwell Cl
Clayton Md
Dumville Dr
A25
OXTED
Salisbury Rd
Dewlands
Court Rd
Riders Wy
Godstone
Church
NEEDLES BANK
GODSTONE GREEN RD
BLETCHINGLEY ROAD
HIGH ST
Stangrave Hall
The Priory
Ivy Mill La
Godstone Village School
Garden Centre
Willow Wy
Rogers Md
Ivy Ml Cl
Hickmans Cl
Love La
EASTBOURNE
Place Farm
127
Place Farm Road
Golf Course
Waterhouse Lane
Ivy Mill Lane
Water House Farm
Church Lane
Bletchingley Golf Club
GODSTONE ROAD
Garston Park
Tilburstow Hill Road
Godstone Farm
Works
PO
HIGH STREET
Cemetery
White Post
Grange Cl
Town Md
Castle Cl
Coneybury
St Catherine's Primary School
St Catherine's Cross
Kenrick Sq
Nightingale Wy
Hart
Gayler Cl
Brakey Hl
Bletchingley
Greensand Way
Outwood Lane
Rabies Heath Road
Coldharbour La
Sandhills
Coldharbour Farm
150
A B C D E F
1 2 3 4 5 6 7 8
533 34 35
54 53 52 51 150
1 grid square represents 500 metres

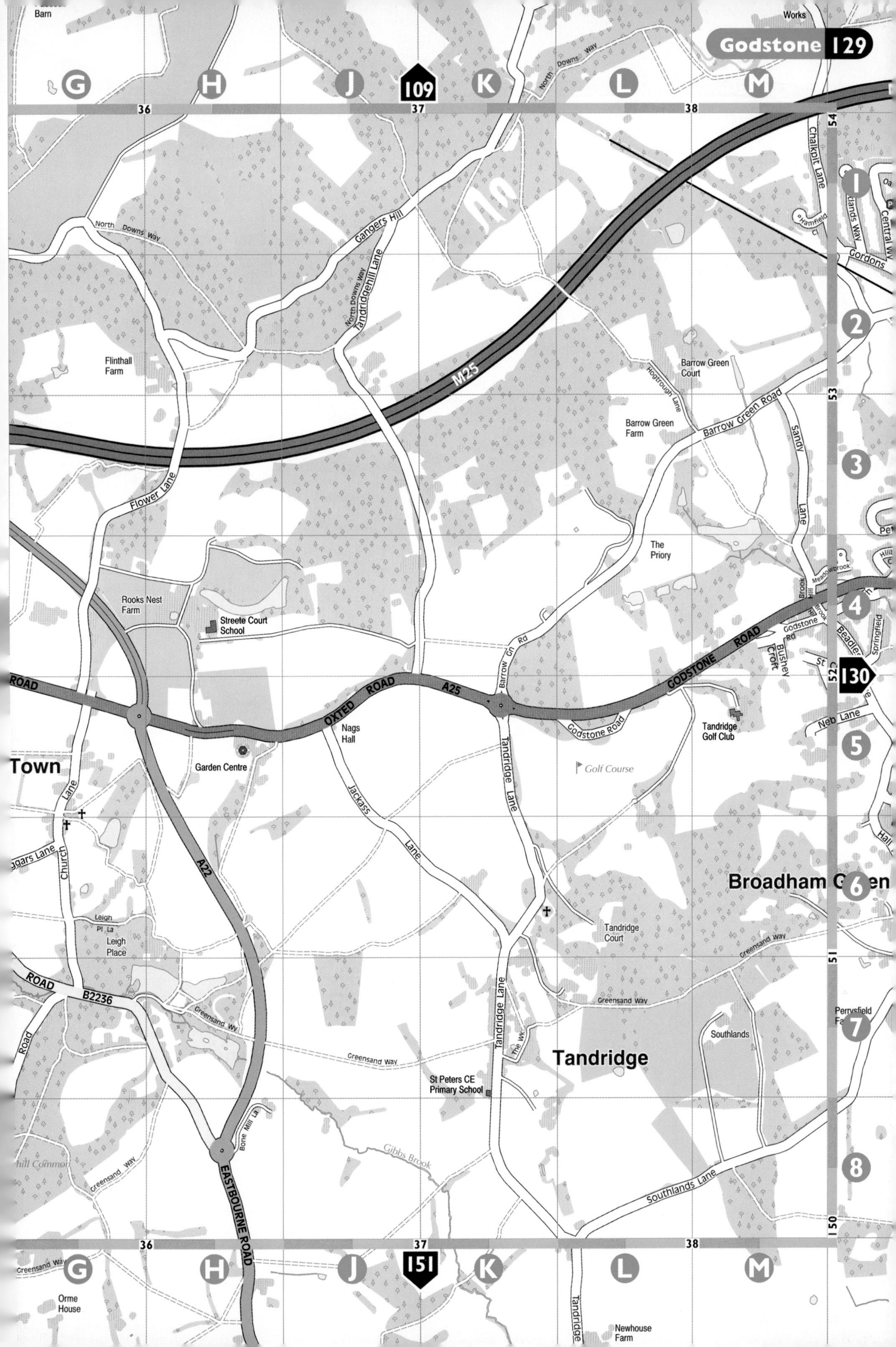

Barn
Works
G
H
J
109
K
North Downs Way
L
M
36
37
38
54
Chalkpit Lane
Hamfield Cl
Gordons
Central Wy
North Downs Way
Gangers Hill
North Downs Way
Tandridgehill Lane
2
Flinthall Farm
Barrow Green Court
Hogtrough Lane
M25
53
Barrow Green Farm
Barrow Green Road
Sandy Lane
3
Flower Lane
The Priory
Meadowbrook
Rooks Nest Farm
Streete Court School
Brook Hill
4
Godstone Rd
Beadles
Springfield
Barrow Gn Rd
Bushey Croft
52
130
ROAD
OXTED ROAD
A25
GODSTONE ROAD
Nags Hall
Godstone Road
Tandridge Golf Club
Neb Lane
5
Town
Garden Centre
Tandridge Lane
Golf Course
Church Lane
Jackass Lane
ggars Lane
A22
Broadham Green
6
Leigh Pl La
Leigh Place
Tandridge Court
Greensand Way
51
ROAD
B2236
Greensand Way
Tandridge Lane
Perrysfield Fa
7
Road
Greensand Wy
The Wk
Southlands
Greensand Way
Tandridge
St Peters CE Primary School
Bone Mill La
Gibbs Brook
8
hill Common
Greensand Way
EASTBOURNE ROAD
Southlands Lane
150
36
37
38
Greensand Way
G
H
J
151
K
L
M
Orme House
Tandridge
Newhouse Farm

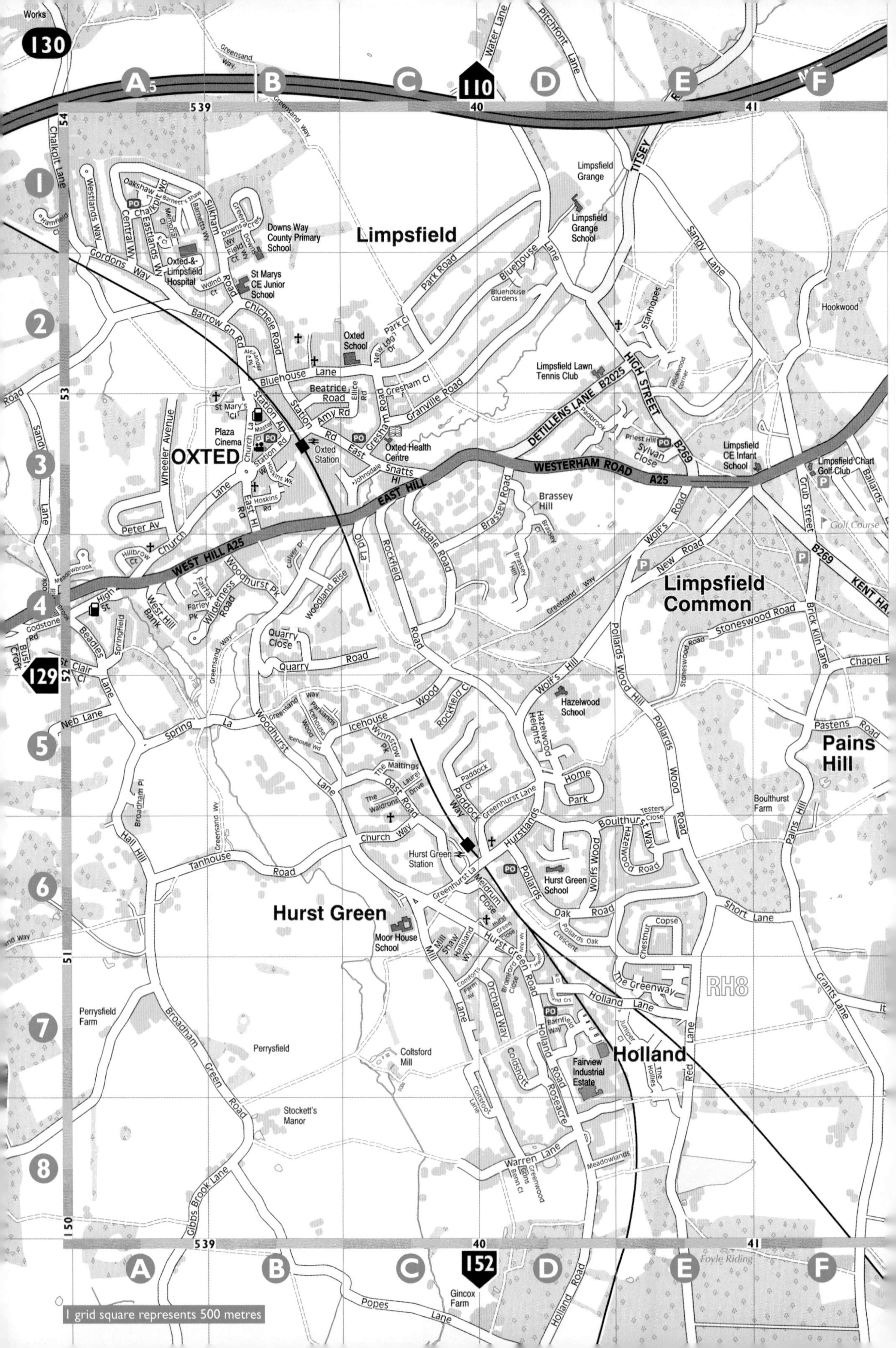
130
110
129
152
A
B
C
D
E
F
1
2
3
4
5
6
7
8
539
40
41
54
53
52
51
150
Works
Limpsfield
OXTED
Limpsfield Common
Pains Hill
Hurst Green
Holland
RH8
Limpsfield Grange
Limpsfield Grange School
Downs Way County Primary School
Oxted-&-Limpsfield Hospital
St Marys CE Junior School
Oxted School
Limpsfield Lawn Tennis Club
Plaza Cinema
Oxted Station
Oxted Health Centre
Limpsfield CE Infant School
Limpsfield Chart Golf Club
Golf Course
Hookwood
Hazelwood School
Hurst Green Station
Hurst Green School
Moor House School
Boulthurst Farm
Perrysfield Farm
Perrysfield
Coltsford Mill
Stockett's Manor
Fairview Industrial Estate
Gincox Farm
Foyle Riding
Brassey Hill
Bluehouse Gardens
WESTERHAM ROAD A25
EAST HILL
WEST HILL A25
DETILLENS LANE B2025
HIGH STREET
TITSEY
B269
KENT HA
Chalkpit Lane
Westlands Way
Central Wy
Eastlands Wy
Gordons Way
Silkham Road
Barrow Gn Rd
Chichele Road
Bluehouse Lane
Park Road
Granville Road
Gresham Road
Station Rd East
Beatrice Road
Amy Rd
Wheeler Avenue
Peter Av
Church Lane
Uvedale Road
Brassey Road
Rockfield Road
Old La
Woodland Rise
Quarry Close
Quarry Road
Woodhurst Pk
Wilderness Road
West Hill Bank
Beadles Lane
Springfield
Spring La
Neb Lane
Icehouse Wood
Wynnstow Pk
The Maltings
Oast Road
Laurel Drive
Church Way
Tanhouse Road
Hall Hill
Broadham Green Road
Gibbs Brook Lane
Paddock Way
Greenhurst Lane
Hurstlands
Pollards Oak Road
Pollards Crescent
Wolfs Wood
Boulthurst Way
Hazelwood Road
Hazelwood Heights
Home Park
Wolf's Hill
Wolf's Road
New Road
Pollards Wood Hill
Pollards Wood Road
Stoneswood Road
Brick Kiln Lane
Chapel Rd
Pastens Road
Pains Hill
Short Lane
Grants Lane
Copse
Chestnut
The Greenway
Holland Lane
Red Lane
Holland Road
Roseacre
Coldshott
Orchard Way
Mill Lane
Hurst Green Road
Warren Lane
Meadowlands
Popes Lane
Sandy Lane
Stanhopes
Padbrook
Sylvan Close
Grub Street
Ballards
Water Lane
Pitchfont Lane
Greensand Way
Godstone Rd
Hillbrow Ct
Meadowbrook
Woodhurst Lane
Coltsfoot Lane
1 grid square represents 500 metres

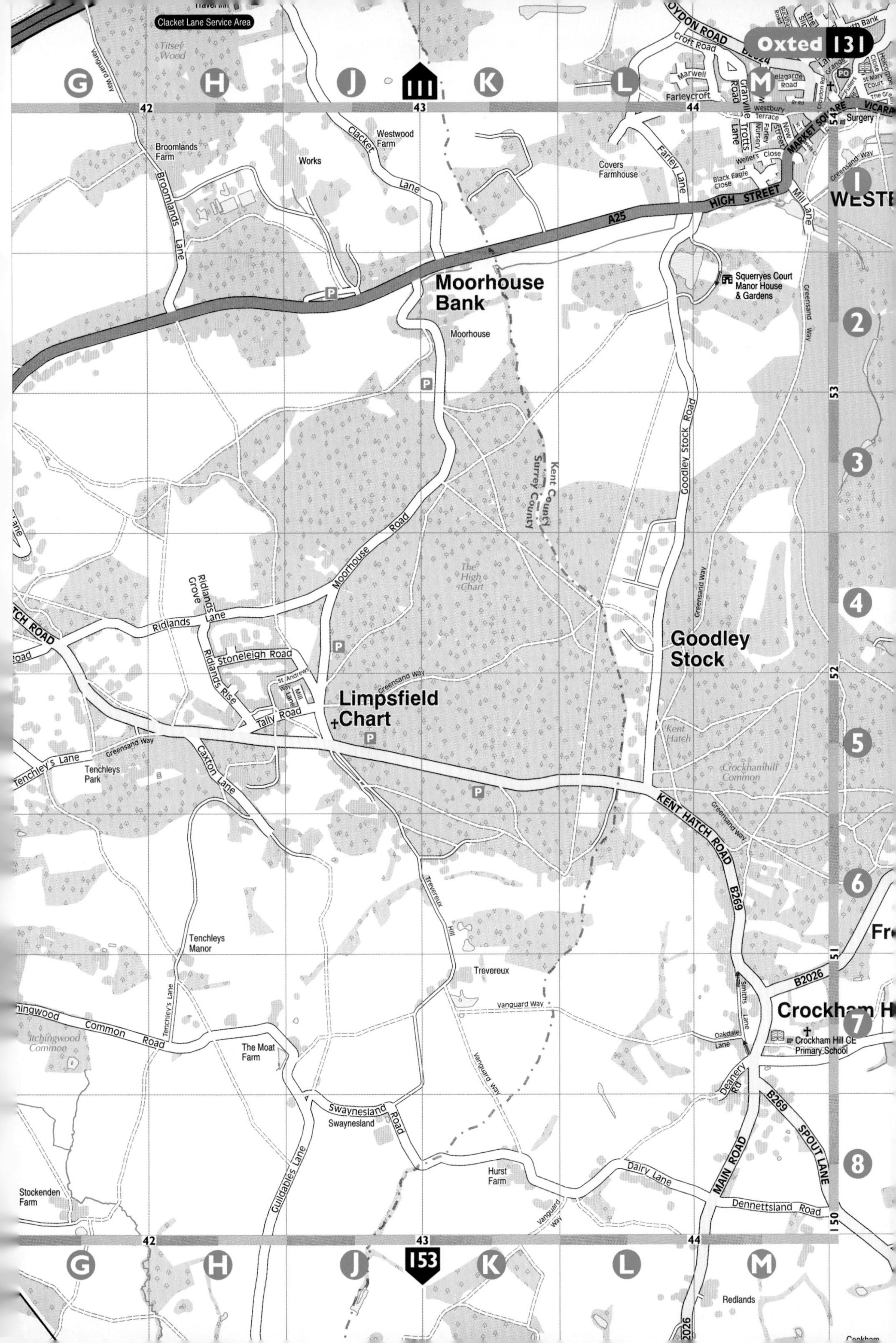

Clacket Lane Service Area

Titsey Wood

Vanguard Way

Broomlands Farm

Westwood Farm

Works

Clacket Lane

Broomlands Lane

Moorhouse Bank

Moorhouse

A25

HIGH STREET

Covers Farmhouse

Black Eagle Close

Farley Lane

Mill Lane

WESTE...

Squerryes Court Manor House & Gardens

Greensand Way

Croft Road

B2024

Marwell

Granville Road

Farleycroft

Westbury Terrace

New Street

Trotts Lane

MARKET SQUARE

VICARA...

Surgery

The High Chart

Kent County

Surrey County

Goodley Stock Road

Greensand Way

Goodley Stock

Ridlands Grove

Ridlands Lane

Ridlands

TCH ROAD

Road

Stoneleigh Road

Ridlands Rise

St. Andrew's Way

Mill Lane

Tally Road

Limpsfield Chart

Greensand Way

Moorhouse Road

Kent Hatch

Crockhamhill Common

Tenchley's Lane

Tenchleys Park

Greensand Way

Caxton Lane

Tenchleys Manor

KENT HATCH ROAD

Greensand Way

B269

Fre...

Trevereux Hill

Trevereux

Vanguard Way

Smiths Lane

B2026

Crockham H...

Oakdale Lane

Crockham Hill CE Primary School

ingwood Common Road

Itchingwood Common

The Moat Farm

Vanguard Way

Swaynesland Road

Swaynesland

Guildables Lane

Hurst Farm

Dairy Lane

Deanery Rd

MAIN ROAD

B269

SPOUT LANE

Dennettsland Road

B2026

Stockenden Farm

Redlands

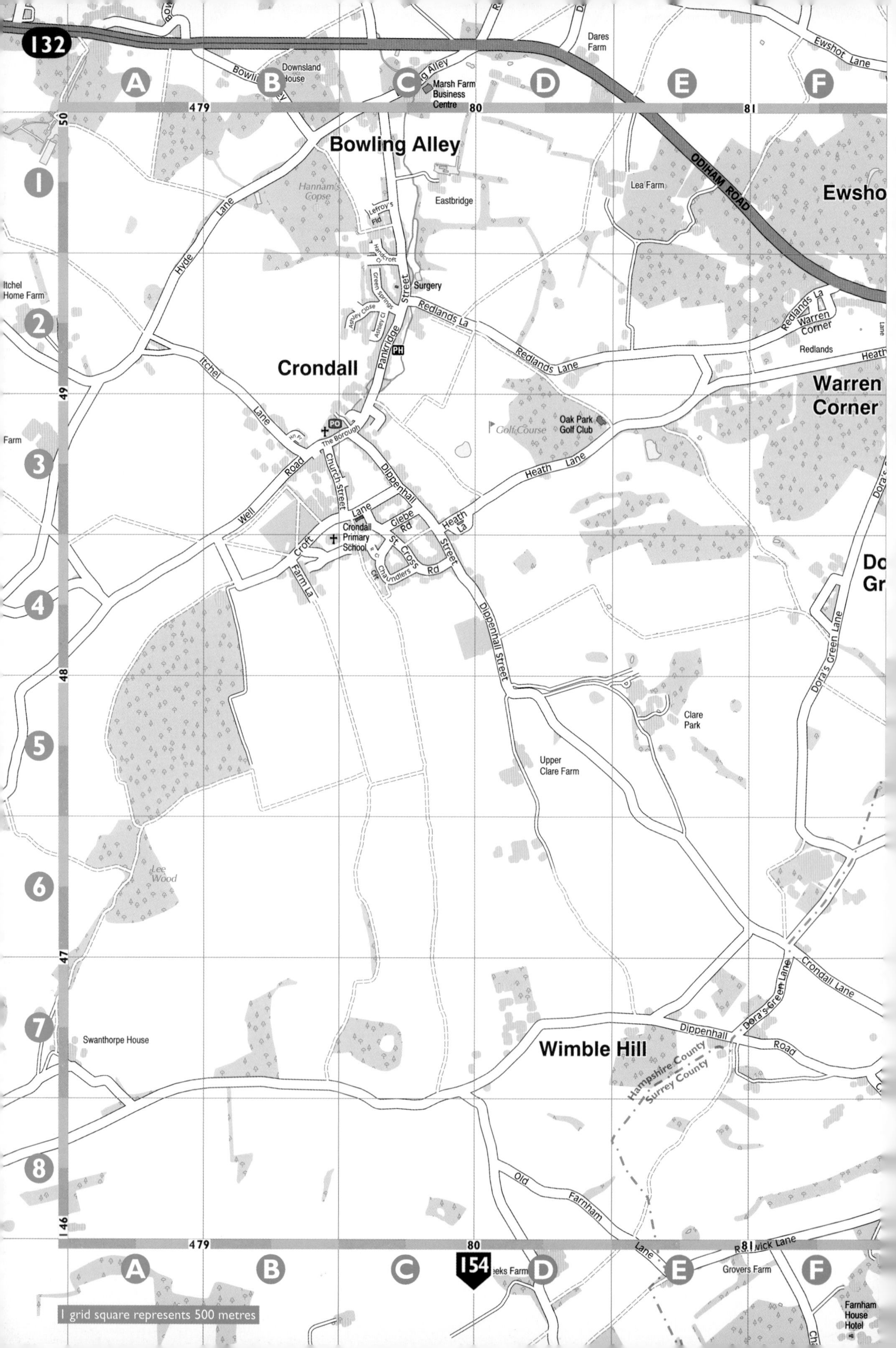

132
Downsland House
Marsh Farm Business Centre
Dares Farm
Ewshot Lane
Bowling Alley
Hannam's Copse
Eastbridge
Lea Farm
ODIHAM ROAD
Ewsho
Surgery
Redlands La
Warren Corner
Redlands
Crondall
Redlands Lane
Hyde Lane
Itchel Lane
Pankridge Street
Itchel Home Farm
Farm
Golf Course
Oak Park Golf Club
Heath Lane
The Borough
Church Street
Dippenhall Street
Well Road
Glebe Rd
Heath La
Crondall Primary School
Croft
Farm La
Cross Rd
Chaundlers Croft
Dippenhall Street
Clare Park
Upper Clare Farm
Dora's Green Lane
Lee Wood
Crondall Lane
Wimble Hill
Dippenhall Road
Dora's Green Lane
Hampshire County
Surrey County
Swanthorpe House
Old Farnham Lane
Grovers Farm
Farnham House Hotel
154
1 grid square represents 500 metres

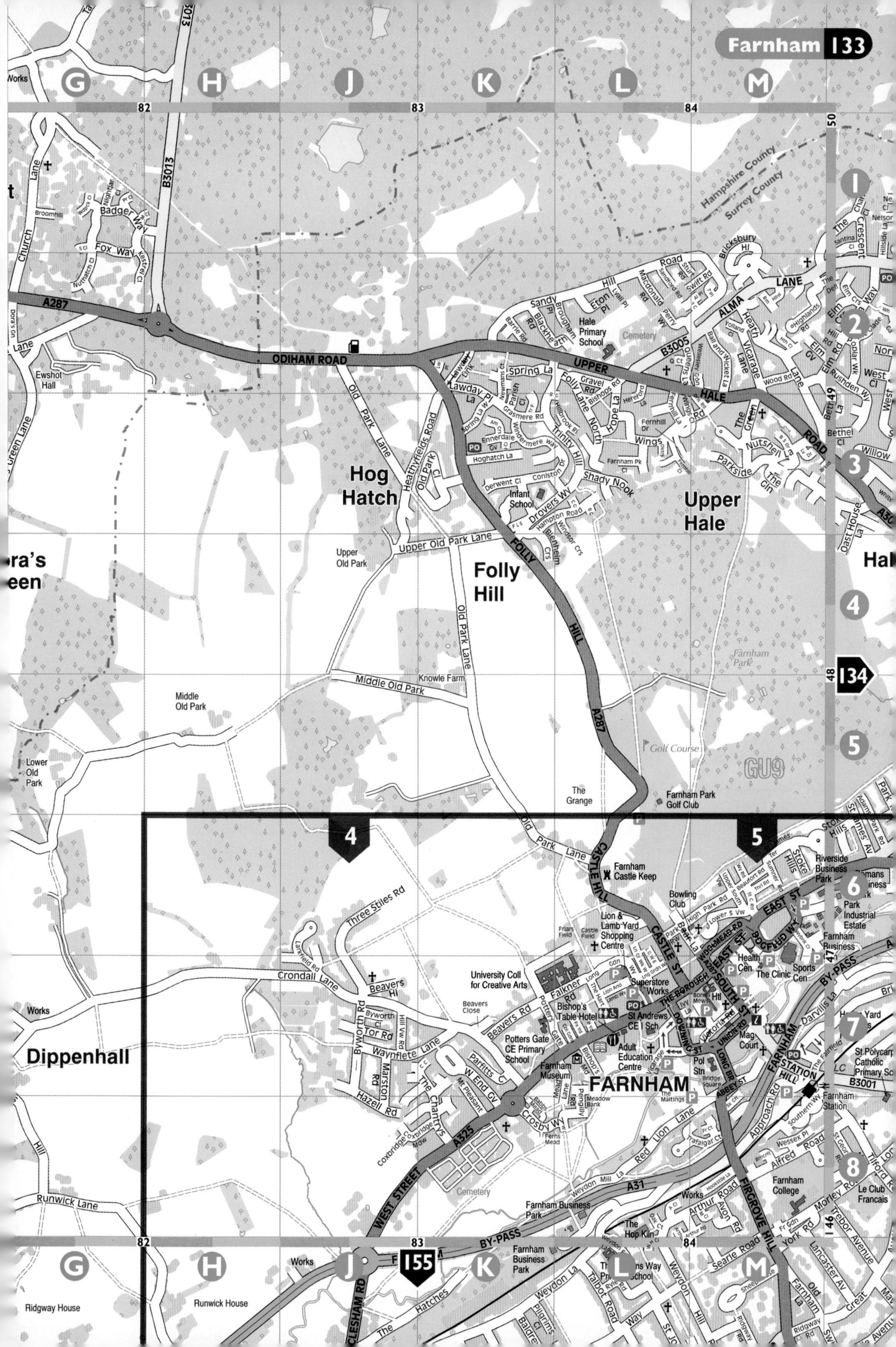
G
H
J
K
L
M
82
83
84
Hog Hatch
Folly Hill
Upper Hale
Upper Old Park
Middle Old Park
Lower Old Park
Ewshot Hall
Dippenhall
FARNHAM
Hampshire County
Surrey County
ODIHAM ROAD
UPPER HALE ROAD
FOLLY HILL
CASTLE HILL
CASTLE ST
WEST STREET
A287
A325
A31
B3005
B3013
B3001
Farnham Castle Keep
Farnham Park Golf Club
Golf Course
Farnham Park
The Grange
Knowle Farm
Hale Primary School
Infant School
University Coll for Creative Arts
Potters Gate CE Primary School
Farnham Museum
Farnham Station
Farnham College
Farnham Business Park
Riverside Business Park
Park Industrial Estate
Lion & Lamb Yard Shopping Centre
Bishop's Table Hotel
St Andrews CE I Sch
Adult Education Centre
Bowling Club
Cemetery
Works
Runwick Lane
Runwick House
Ridgway House
Crondall Lane
Three Stiles Rd
Old Park Lane
Middle Old Park
Upper Old Park Lane
Heathyfields Road
GU9
134
155
4
5
1
2
3
6
7
8

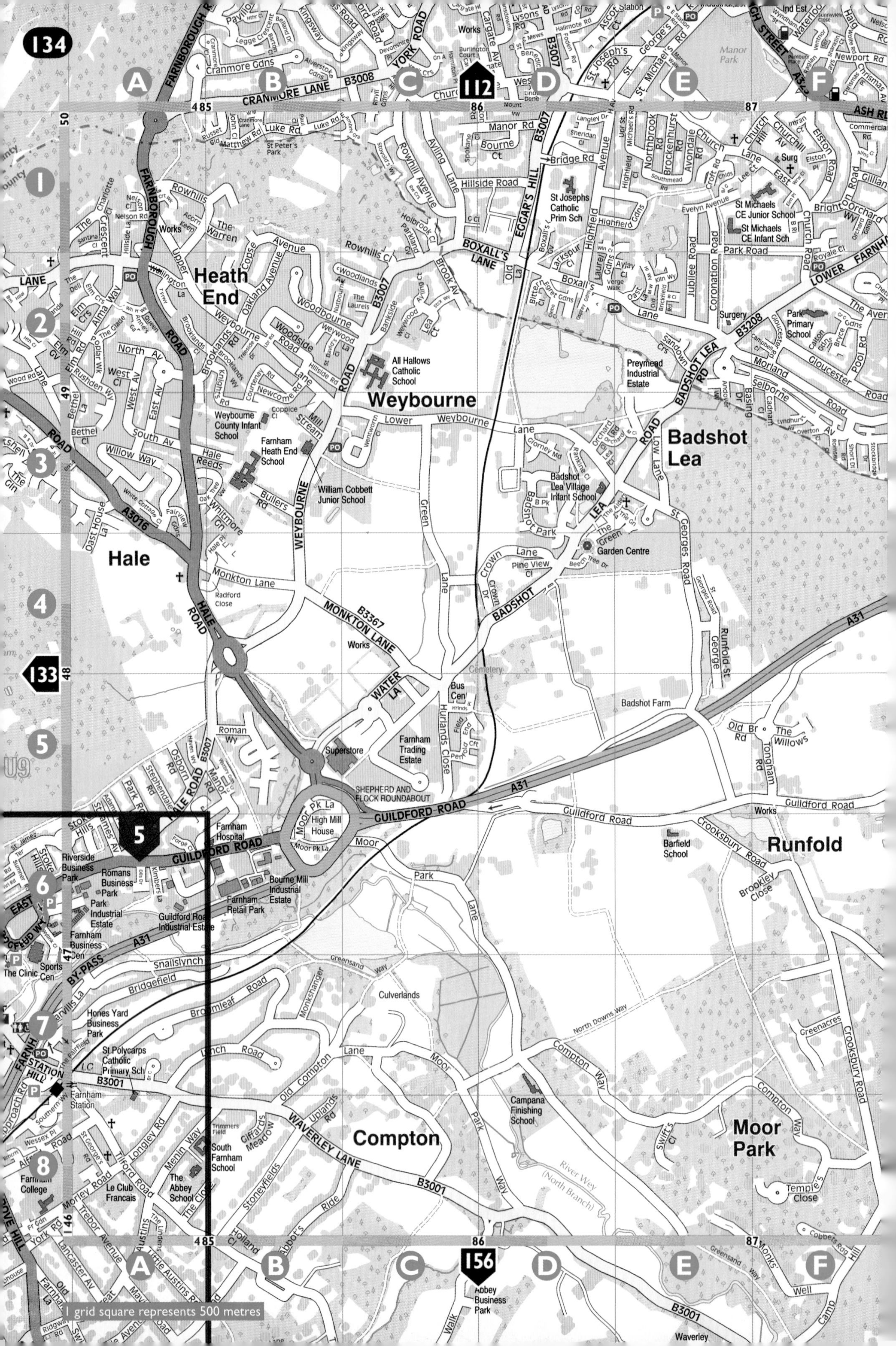
134
112
133
5
156
Heath End
Weybourne
Badshot Lea
Hale
Runfold
Compton
Moor Park
FARNBOROUGH ROAD
HALE ROAD
WEYBOURNE ROAD
MONKTON LANE
GUILDFORD ROAD
WAVERLEY LANE
CRANMORE LANE
BOXALL'S LANE
EGGAR'S HILL
BADSHOT LEA RD
LOWER FARNHAM
All Hallows Catholic School
St Josephs Catholic Prim Sch
St Michaels CE Junior School
St Michaels CE Infant Sch
Park Primary School
Preymead Industrial Estate
Weybourne County Infant School
Farnham Heath End School
William Cobbett Junior School
Badshot Lea Village Infant School
Garden Centre
Badshot Farm
Superstore
Farnham Trading Estate
SHEPHERD AND FLOCK ROUNDABOUT
High Mill House
Farnham Hospital
Riverside Business Park
Romans Business Park
Park Industrial Estate
Bourne Mill Industrial Estate
Farnham Retail Park
Guildford Road Industrial Estate
Farnham Business Cen
Sports Cen
The Clinic
Hones Yard Business Park
St Polycarps Catholic Primary Sch
Farnham Station
Farnham College
Le Club Francais
The Abbey School
South Farnham School
Campana Finishing School
Barfield School
Culverlands
Abbey Business Park
Waverley
1 grid square represents 500 metres

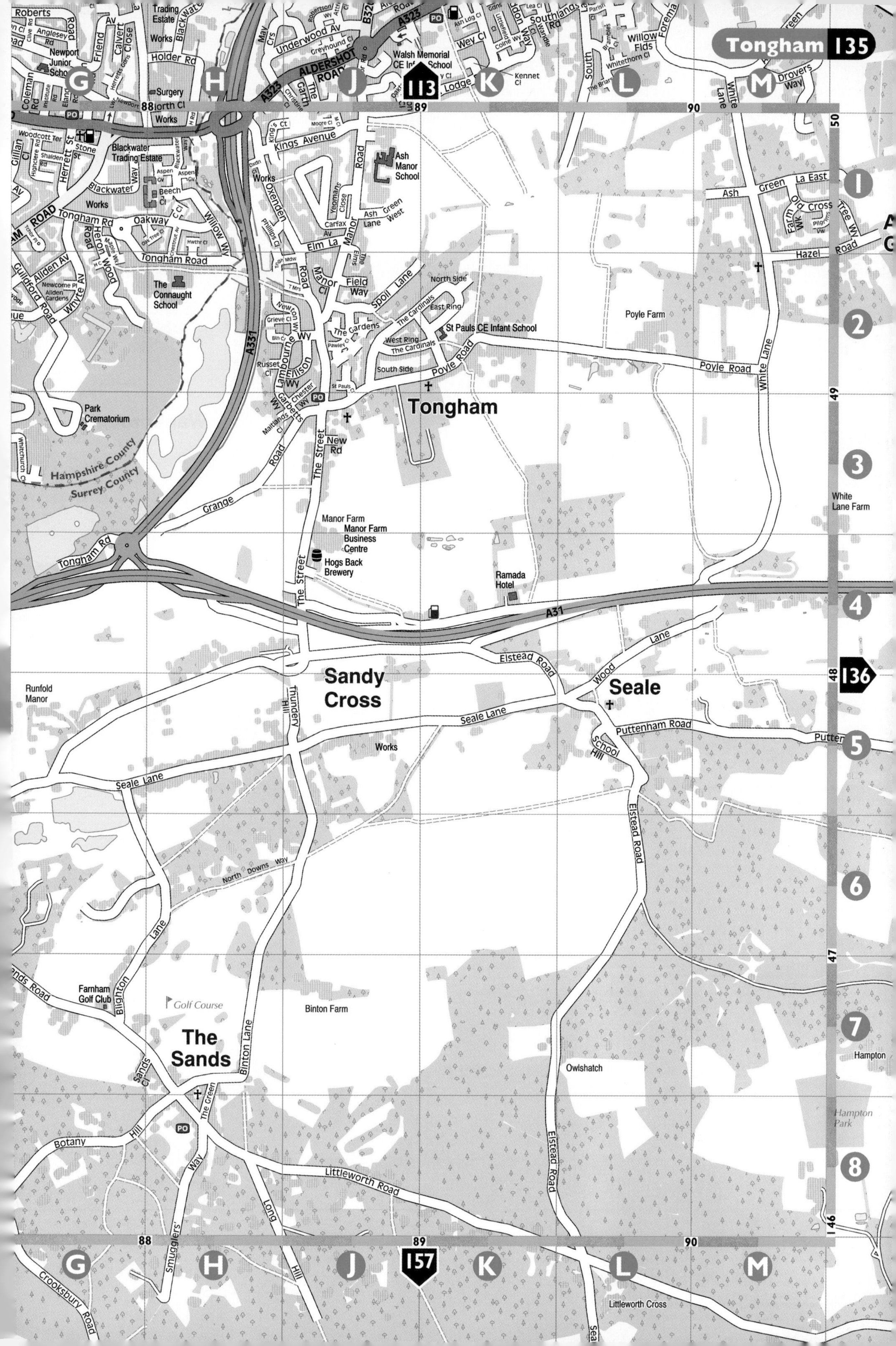
Tongham
Sandy Cross
Seale
The Sands
Poyle Farm
Poyle Road
White Lane
White Lane Farm
Ash Green La East
Hazel Road
St Pauls CE Infant School
Ash Manor School
Kings Avenue
Oxenden Road
Manor Farm
Manor Farm Business Centre
Hogs Back Brewery
Ramada Hotel
A31
A331
A323
ALDERSHOT ROAD
Tongham Road
Grange Road
The Street
The Connaught School
Park Crematorium
Hampshire County
Surrey County
Blackwater Trading Estate
Elstead Road
Wood Lane
Puttenham Road
School Hill
Seale Lane
Thundery Hill
Works
Runfold Manor
North Downs Way
Binton Farm
Binton Lane
Farnham Golf Club
Golf Course
Blighton Lane
Sands Road
Botany Hill
The Green
Smugglers' Way
Littleworth Road
Long Hill
Owlshatch
Hampton
Hampton Park
Littleworth Cross
Crooksbury Road
Walsh Memorial CE Inf School
113
136
157
G H J K L M
88 89 90
50 49 48 47 46
1 2 3 4 5 6 7 8

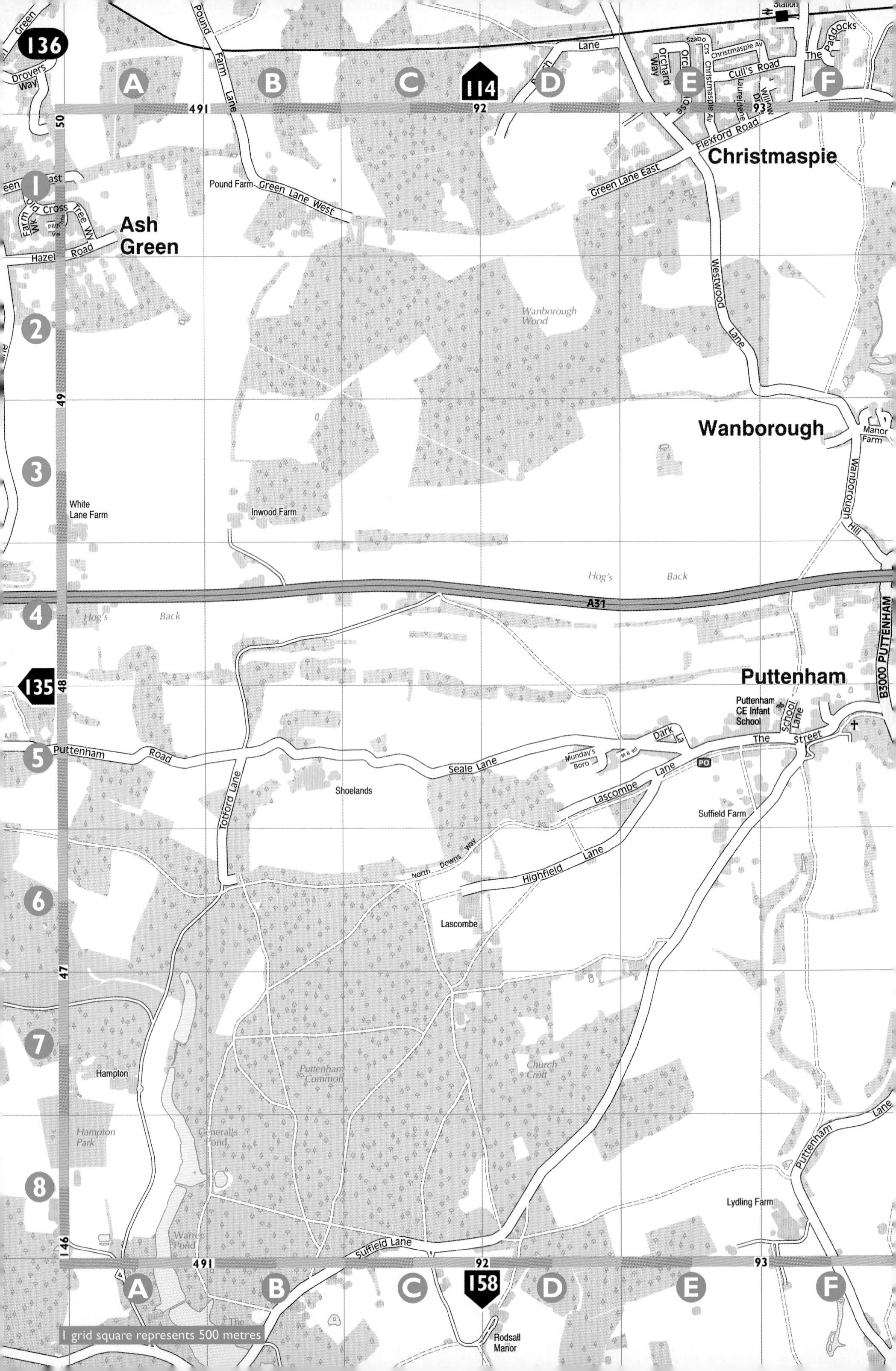

136
114
135
158
A
B
C
D
E
F
1
2
3
4
5
6
7
8
491
92
93
50
49
48
47
46
Christmaspie
Ash Green
Wanborough
Puttenham
Station
The Paddocks
Christmaspie Av
Cull's Road
Orchard Way
Flexford Road
Green Lane East
Green Lane West
Pound Farm Lane
Pound Farm
Drovers Way
Hazel Road
Westwood Lane
Wanborough Wood
Manor Farm
Wanborough Hill
White Lane Farm
Inwood Farm
Hog's Back
A31
B3000 PUTTENHAM
Puttenham CE Infant School
School Lane
The Street
Dark La
Munday's Boro
Puttenham Road
Seale Lane
Lascombe Lane
Shoelands
Totford Lane
Suffield Farm
North Downs Way
Highfield Lane
Lascombe
Hampton
Puttenham Common
Church Croft
Hampton Park
General's Pond
Warren Pond
Puttenham Lane
Lydling Farm
Suffield Lane
Rodsall Manor
1 grid square represents 500 metres

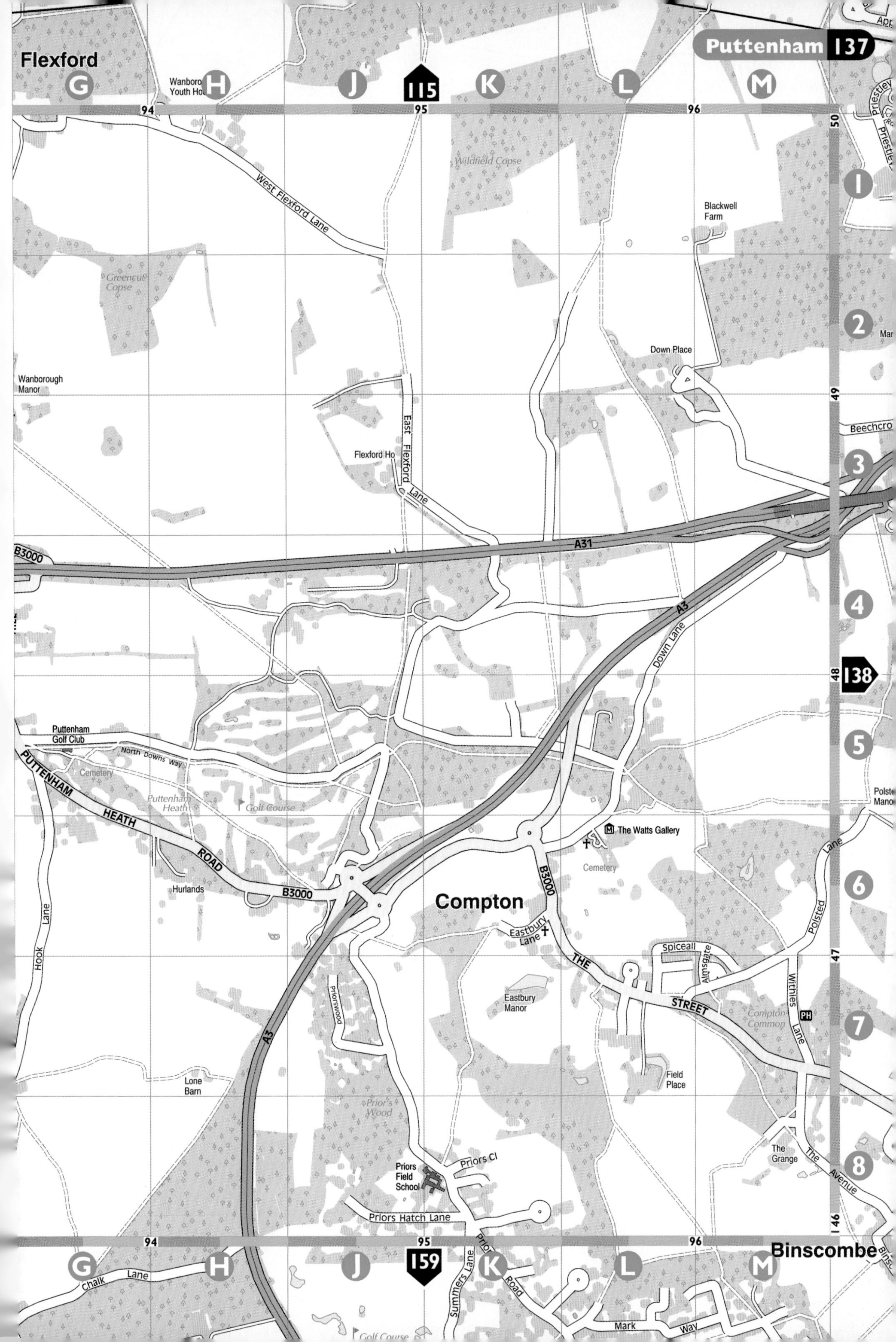
Flexford
Wanborough Youth Ho
115
94
95
96
West Flexford Lane
Wildfield Copse
Blackwell Farm
Greencut Copse
Down Place
Wanborough Manor
East Flexford Lane
Flexford Ho
Beechcro
A31
B3000
A3
Down Lane
138
Puttenham Golf Club
North Downs Way
Cemetery
Puttenham Heath
Golf Course
PUTTENHAM HEATH ROAD
The Watts Gallery
Polsted Manor
Polsted Lane
Hurlands
B3000
Compton
Cemetery
Eastbury Lane
Hook Lane
THE STREET
Spiceall
Almsgate
Priorswood
Eastbury Manor
Withies Lane
PH
Compton Common
Field Place
Lone Barn
Prior's Wood
The Grange
The Avenue
Priors Cl
Priors Field School
Priors Hatch Lane
159
Binscombe
Chalk Lane
Summers Lane
Priors Road
Mark Way
Golf Course
G
H
J
K
L
M
1
2
3
4
5
6
7
8
50
49
48
47
46

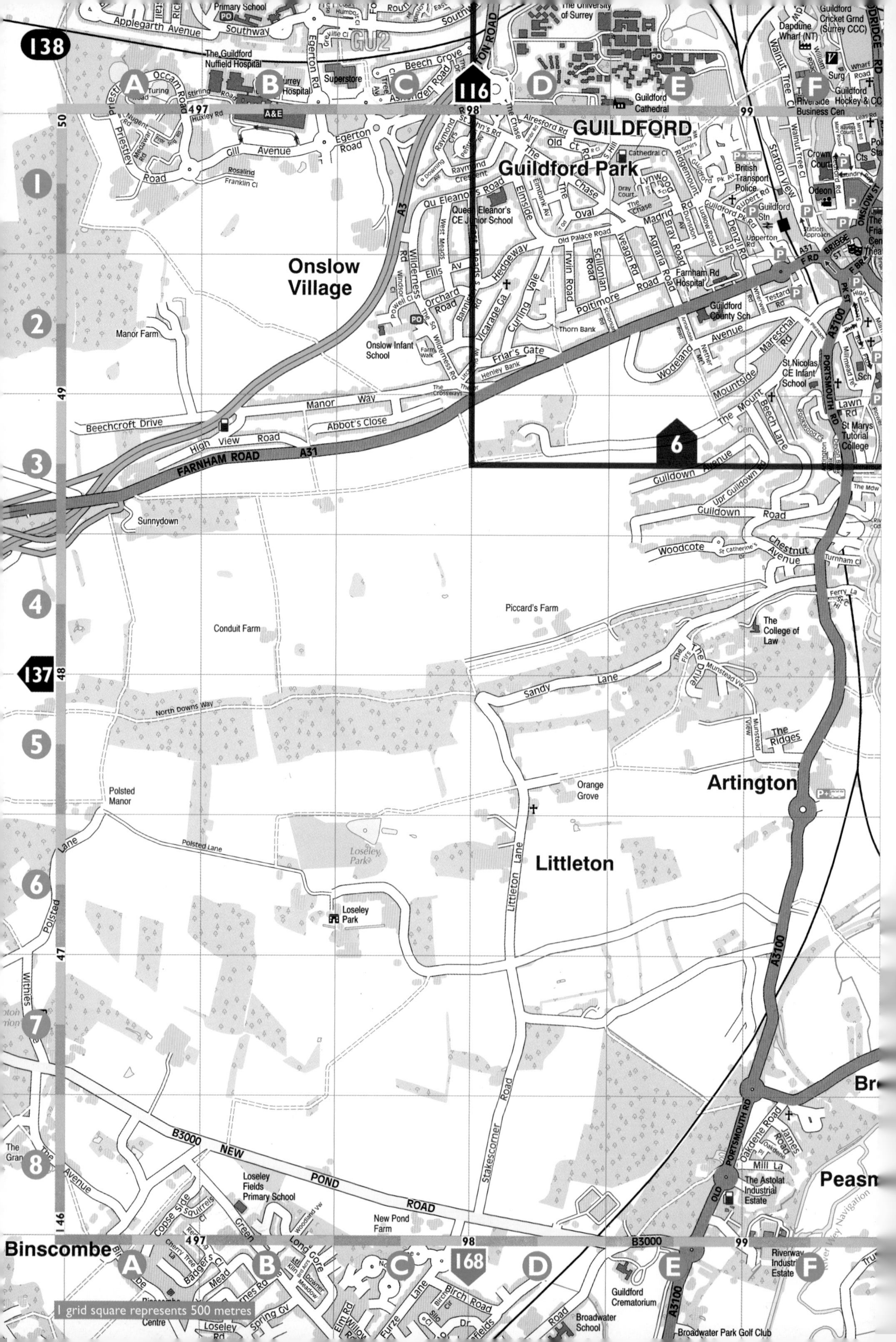

138
137
116
168
6
GUILDFORD
Guildford Park
Onslow Village
Artington
Littleton
Binscombe
Peasm
Br
Applegarth Avenue
Southway
Primary School
GU2
The Guildford Nuffield Hospital
Surrey Hospital
Superstore
Egerton Rd
Beech Grove
Occam Road
Turing
Stirling Road
Huxley Rd
A&E
Priestley Road
Nugent
Gill Avenue
Egerton Road
Rosalind
Franklin Cl
The University of Surrey
Guildford Cathedral
Cathedral Cl
Guildford Cricket Grnd (Surrey CCC)
Dapdune Wharf (NT)
Walnut Tree Cl
Riverside Business Cen
Guildford Hockey & CC
Station View
British Transport Police
Guildford Stn
Odeon
Crown Court
Alresford Rd
Old Ct Rd
The Chase
The Oval
Raymond Crescent
Qu Eleanor's Road
Queen Eleanor's CE Junior School
Elmside
West Meads
Wilderness Rd
Ellis Av
Hedgeway
Old Palace Road
Irwin Road
Scillonian Road
Agraria Road
Bray Road
Madrid Rd
Dunsdon
Ludlow Road
Denzil Rd
Ridgemount
Farnham Rd Hospital
Guildford County Sch.
Poltimore Road
Curling Vale
Vicarage Ga
Orchard Road
Bannister's Rd
Friar's Gate
Henley Bank
Thorn Bank
Onslow Infant School
Powell Cl
Windsor Cl
The Crossways
Manor Farm
Manor Way
Abbot's Close
Beechcroft Drive
High View Road
FARNHAM ROAD
A31
A3
Sunnydown
Wodeland Avenue
Mareschal Rd
Mountside
The Mount
Beech Lane
Cem
St Nicolas CE Infant School
PORTSMOUTH RD
A3100
Millmead Ter
Lawn Rd
St Marys Tutorial College
Guildown Avenue
Upr Guildown Rd
Guildown Road
Woodcote
Chestnut Avenue
Turnham Cl
Ferry La
Piccard's Farm
Conduit Farm
The College of Law
Sandy Lane
The Drive
The Firs
Munstead Vw
Munstead View
The Ridges
North Downs Way
Polsted Manor
Polsted Lane
Polsted Lane
Loseley Park
Orange Grove
Littleton Lane
Stakescorner Road
Withies
B3000 NEW POND ROAD
New Pond Farm
Loseley Fields Primary School
Copse Side
Squirrels
Green
Long Gore
Woodland Vw
The Avenue
OLD PORTSMOUTH RD
Oakdene Road
James Road
Mill La
The Astolat Industrial Estate
Riverway Industrial Estate
Guildford Crematorium
Broadwater School
Broadwater Park Golf Club
B3000
Badger's Cl
Cherry Tree La
Birch Road
Furze Lane
Elm Rd
Spring Gv
Loseley Rd
497
98
99
50
49
48
47
46
A
B
C
D
E
F
1
2
3
4
5
6
7
8
1 grid square represents 500 metres

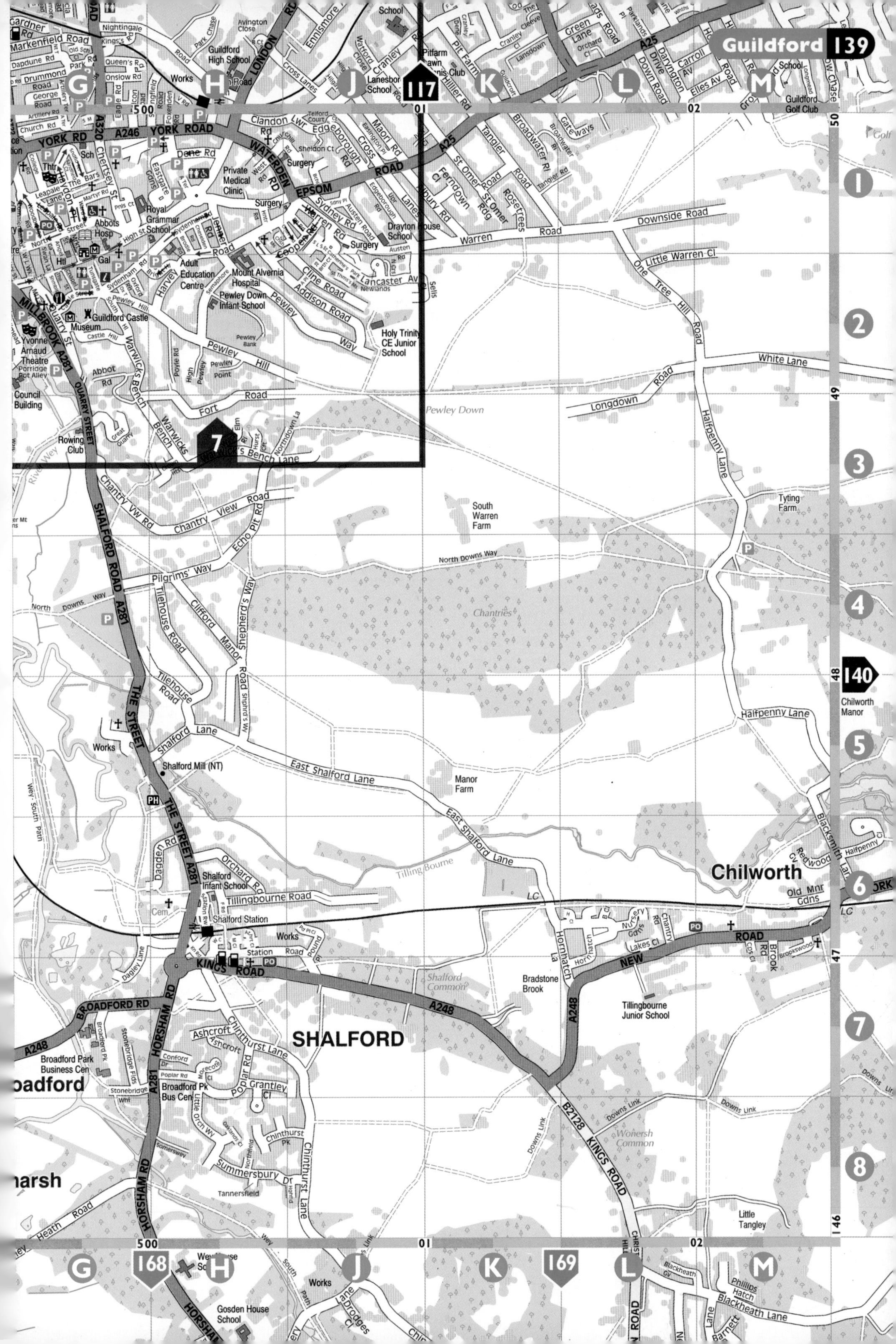

Guildford 139
117
7
140
Chilworth Manor
168
169
G
H
J
K
L
M
1
2
3
4
5
6
7
8
500
01
02
50
49
48
47
46
Markenfield Road
Dapdune Rd
Drummond Road
George Road
Artillery Rd
Church Rd
Nightingale Rd
Queen's Rd
Onslow Rd
Park Chase
Guildford High School
Works
Avington Close
Ennismore Av
Cross Lanes
Watford Close
Cranley Rd
Lanesborough School
Pitfarm Lawn Tennis Club
Pit Farm Rd
Hillier Rd
Cranley Cl
Guildford Golf Club
Green Lane
Orchard Cl
Down Road
Darvington Drive
Carroll Av
Elles Av
School
YORK RD
YORK ROAD
A320
A246
A25
A281
A248
B2128
Chertsey St
Sch
Thtr
Dene Rd
Clandon Rd
Edgeborough Rd
Maori Rd
Cross Rd
Surgery
Private Medical Clinic
WATERDEN RD
EPSOM ROAD
St Omer Rd
Tangier Road
Broadwater Ri
Gateways
Ferndown Cl
St Omer Rdg
Rosetrees
Warren Road
Downside Road
Royal Grammar School
Abbots Hosp
High St
Sydenham Rd
Adult Education Centre
Mount Alvernia Hospital
Pewley Down Infant School
Harvey Rd
Jenner Rd
Austen Road
Cline Road
Addison Road
Lancaster Av
Drayton House School
Little Warren Cl
One Tree Hill Road
Guildford Castle
Museum
Yvonne Arnaud Theatre
Council Building
Pewley Hill
Pewley Way
Holy Trinity CE Junior School
White Lane
Longdown Road
Pewley Down
Halfpenny Lane
MILLBROOK
QUARRY STREET
Abbot Rd
Fort Road
Warwicks Bench
Warwick's Bench Lane
Northdown La
Rowing Club
River Wey
Chantry Vw Rd
Chantry View Road
Echo Pit Rd
South Warren Farm
Tyting Farm
North Downs Way
SHALFORD ROAD
Pilgrims' Way
Tilehouse Road
Clifford Manor Road
Shepherd's Way
Chantries
Halfpenny Lane
Works
THE STREET
Shalford Lane
Shalford Mill (NT)
East Shalford Lane
Manor Farm
PH
Dagden Rd
Orchard Rd
Shalford Infant School
Tilling Bourne
Tillingbourne Road
Chilworth
Redwood Gv
Blacksmith Lane
Old Mnr Gdns
LC
Cem
Shalford Station
Works
Station Road
KINGS ROAD
PO
Hornhatch La
Nursery Gdns
Chantry Rd
Lakes Cl
NEW ROAD
Brook Rd
Dagley Lane
Shalford Common
Bradstone Brook
Tillingbourne Junior School
BROADFORD RD
HORSHAM RD
Ashcroft
Chinthurst Lane
SHALFORD
Broadford Park Business Cen
Stonebridge Flds
Broadford Pk Bus Cen
Poplar Rd
Grantley Cl
Downs Link
Wonersh Common
KINGS ROAD
Broadford
Chinthurst Pk
Summersbury Dr
Tannersfield
Little Tangley
Heath Road
Wey South Path
Works
Gosden House School
Blackheath Gv
Phillips Hatch
Blackheath Lane

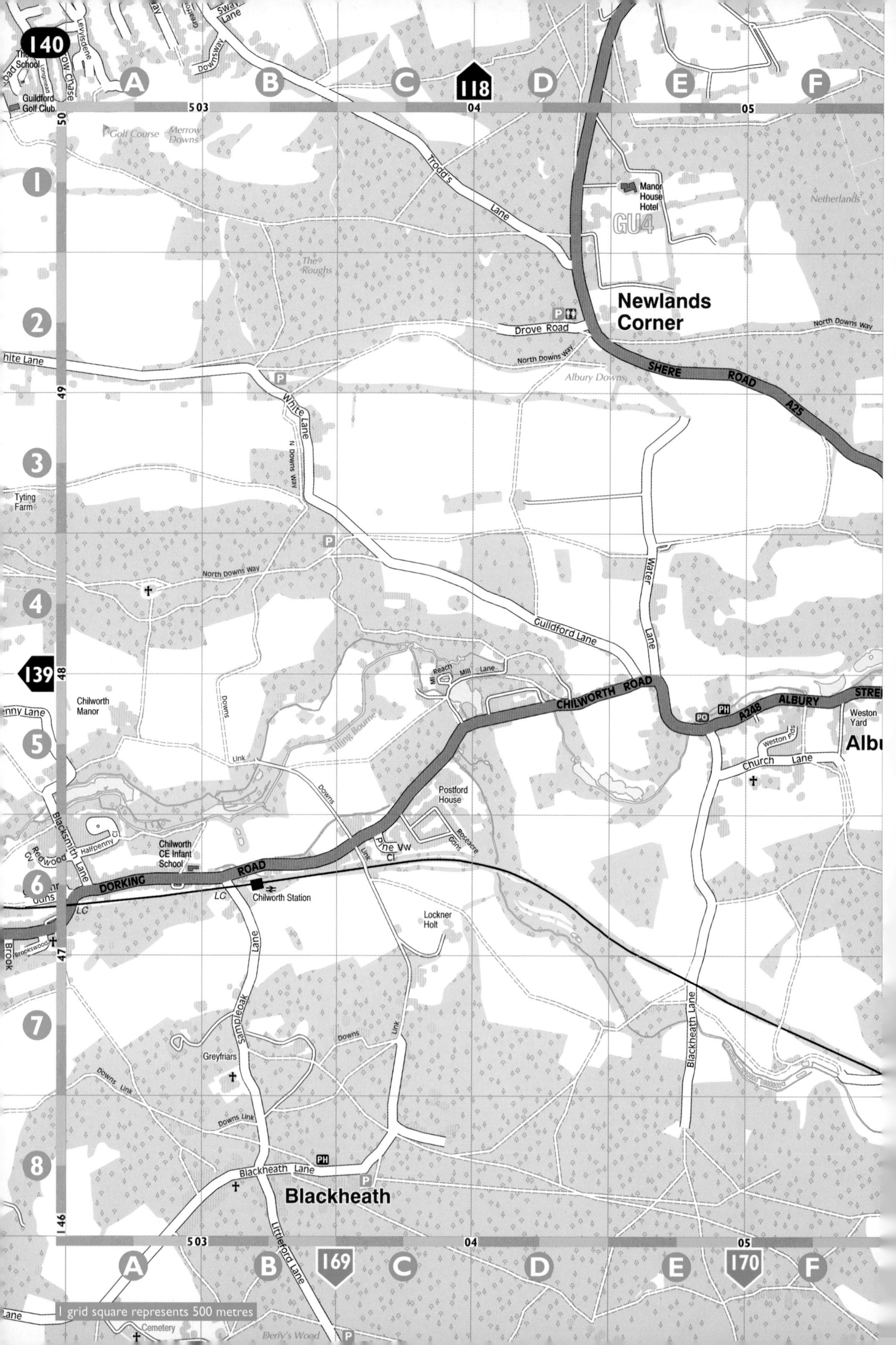

A   B   C   **118** 04   D   E   05   F

1

2

3

4

5

6

7

8

Guildford
Golf Club

Golf Course
Merrow
Downs

The
Roughs

Trodd's
Lane

Manor
House
Hotel

Netherlands

GU4

**Newlands
Corner**

Drove Road

North Downs Way

North Downs Way

Albury Downs

SHERE   ROAD

A25

White Lane

N Downs Way

White Lane

Tyting
Farm

North Downs Way

Water Lane

Guildford Lane

Mi Reach

Mill Lane

CHILWORTH   ROAD

ALBURY   **STREET**

PO PH   **A248**

Weston
Yard

Albu

Weston PO's

Church Lane

Chilworth
Manor

Downs

Tilling Bourne

Postford
House

Roseacre Gdns

Church Lane

enny Lane

Link

Blacksmith Lane

Redwood
Cv

Halfpenny

Chilworth
CE Infant
School

DORKING   ROAD

Lane

Pine Vw
Cl

LC

LC

Chilworth Station

Lockner
Holt

Blackheath Lane

Brook

Brookswood

Samplecak Lane

Downs   Link

Greyfriars

Downs Link

Downs   Link

PH

Blackheath Lane

Blackheath

Littleford Lane

A   B   **169**   C   04   D   E   05   **170**   F

1 grid square represents 500 metres

Cemetery

Derry's Wood

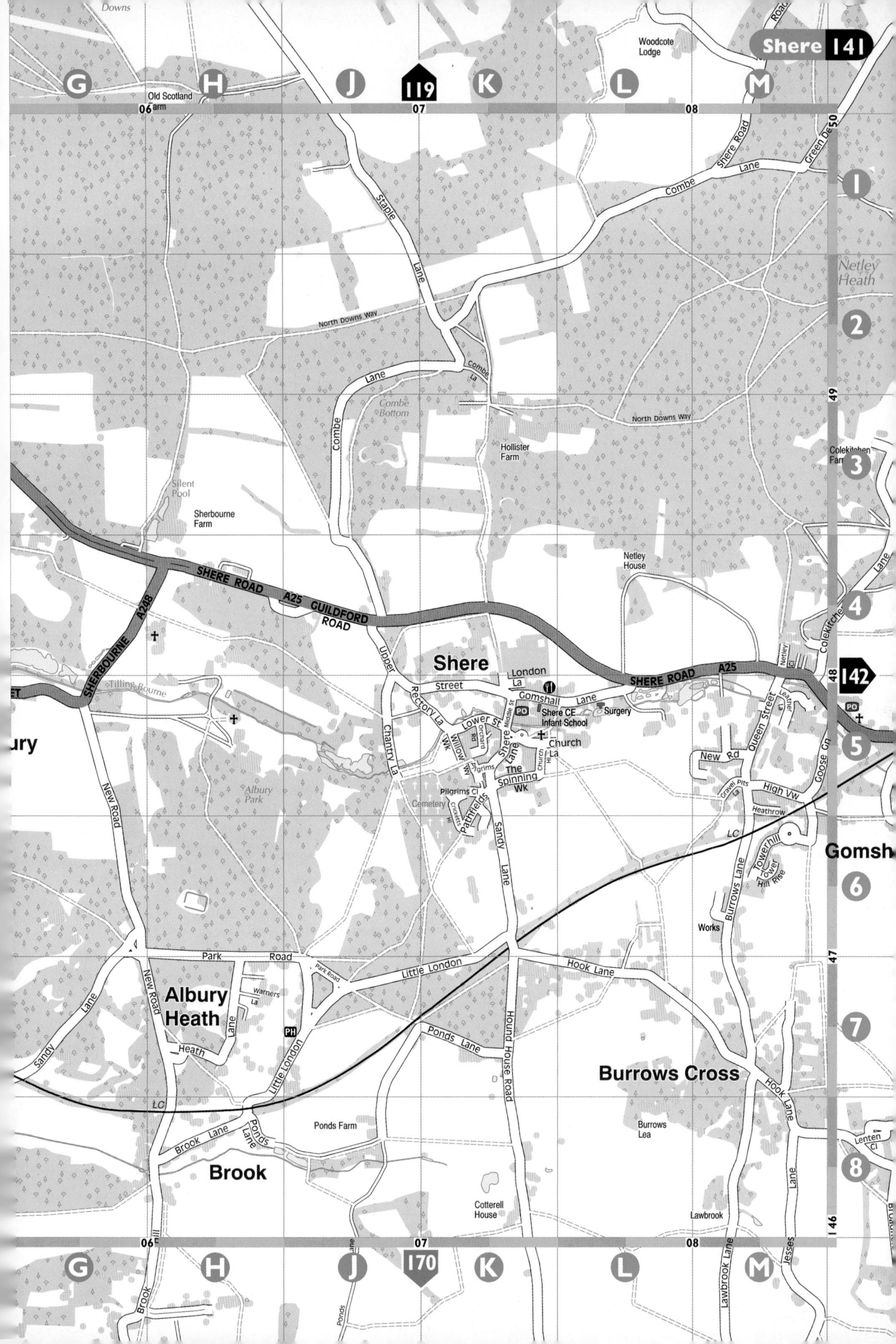
Shere 141
Downs
Woodcote Lodge
G
H
J
119
K
L
M
Old Scotland Farm
06
07
08
50
Shere Road
Green Dene
Combe Lane
Staple Lane
Netley Heath
North Downs Way
Combe La
Combe Lane
Combe Bottom
49
North Downs Way
Colekitchen Farm
Hollister Farm
Combe
Silent Pool
Sherbourne Farm
Netley House
SHERE ROAD
A25
GUILDFORD ROAD
A248
SHERBOURNE
Lane
Colekitchen
Upper
Shere
London La
Street
Gomshall Lane
SHERE ROAD
A25
Netley Cl
Leather
142
48
Tilling Bourne
Rectory La
Middle St
PO
Shere CE Infant School
Surgery
Lower St
Orchard Rd
Willow Wk
Chantry La
Shere Lane
Church Hill
Church La
Queen Street
New Rd
Goose Gn
Pilgrims Wy
The Spinning Wk
Gravel Pits La
High Vw
Albury Park
Pilgrims Cl
Cemetery
Crocketts Hl
Pathfields
Heathrow
New Road
Sandy Lane
LC
Towerhill
Tower Hill Rise
Gomsh
Burrows Lane
Works
Park Road
Park Road
Little London
Hook Lane
47
Warners La
Albury Heath
New Road
Lane
PH
Ponds Lane
Hound House Road
Heath
Sandy Lane
Little London
Burrows Cross
Hook Lane
LC
Ponds Farm
Burrows Lea
Lenten Cl
Brook Lane
Ponds Lane
Brook
Cotterell House
Lane
Lawbrook
46
06
07
08
G
H
J
170
K
L
M
Brook Hill
Ponds Lane
Lawbrook Lane
Jesses Lane

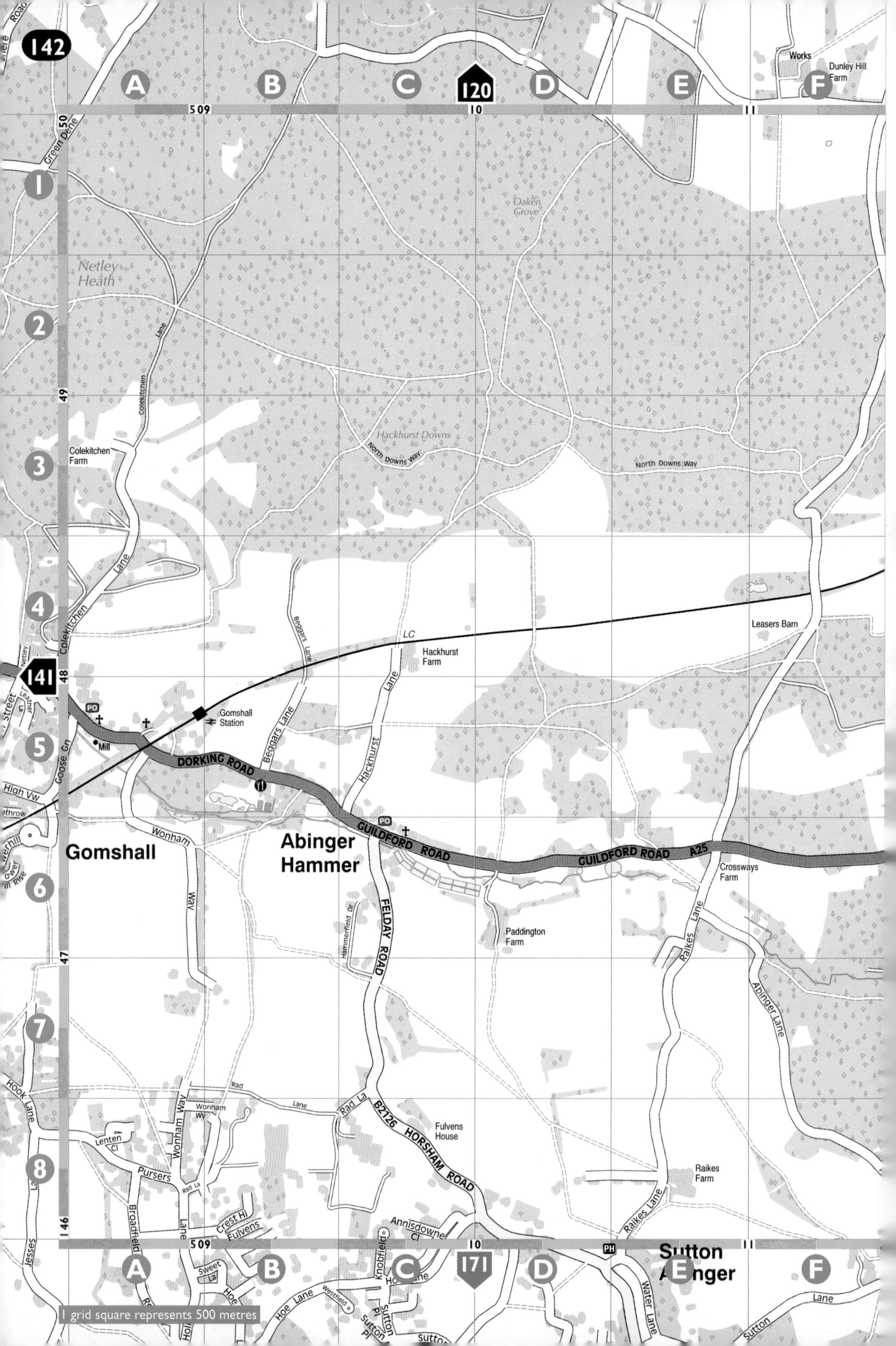

A
B
C
120
D
E
F
509
10
11
Works
Dunley Hill Farm
Green Dene
50
Oaken Grove
Netley Heath
Colekitchen Lane
49
Hackhurst Downs
North Downs Way
North Downs Way
Colekitchen Farm
Leasers Barn
Beggars Lane
LC
Hackhurst Farm
141
48
PO
Gomshall Station
Mill
Goose Gn
DORKING ROAD
Beggars Lane
Hackhurst Lane
High Vw
PO
Wonham
GUILDFORD ROAD
GUILDFORD ROAD
A25
Gomshall
Abinger Hammer
Crossways Farm
Way
FELDAY ROAD
Hammerfield Dr
Paddington Farm
Raikes Lane
47
Abinger Lane
Hook Lane
Rad
Lane
Rad La
Wonham Way
Wonham Wy
B2126 HORSHAM ROAD
Fulvens House
Lenten Cl
Pursers
Rad La
Raikes Farm
Broadfield
Lane
Crest Hl
Fulvens
Annisdowne Cl
Raikes Lane
146
Jesses
PH
Sutton Abinger
171
Knobfield
Sweet La
Hoe
Hoe Lane
Westfield
Sutton Pl
Water Lane
Lane
Sutton
1 grid square represents 500 metres

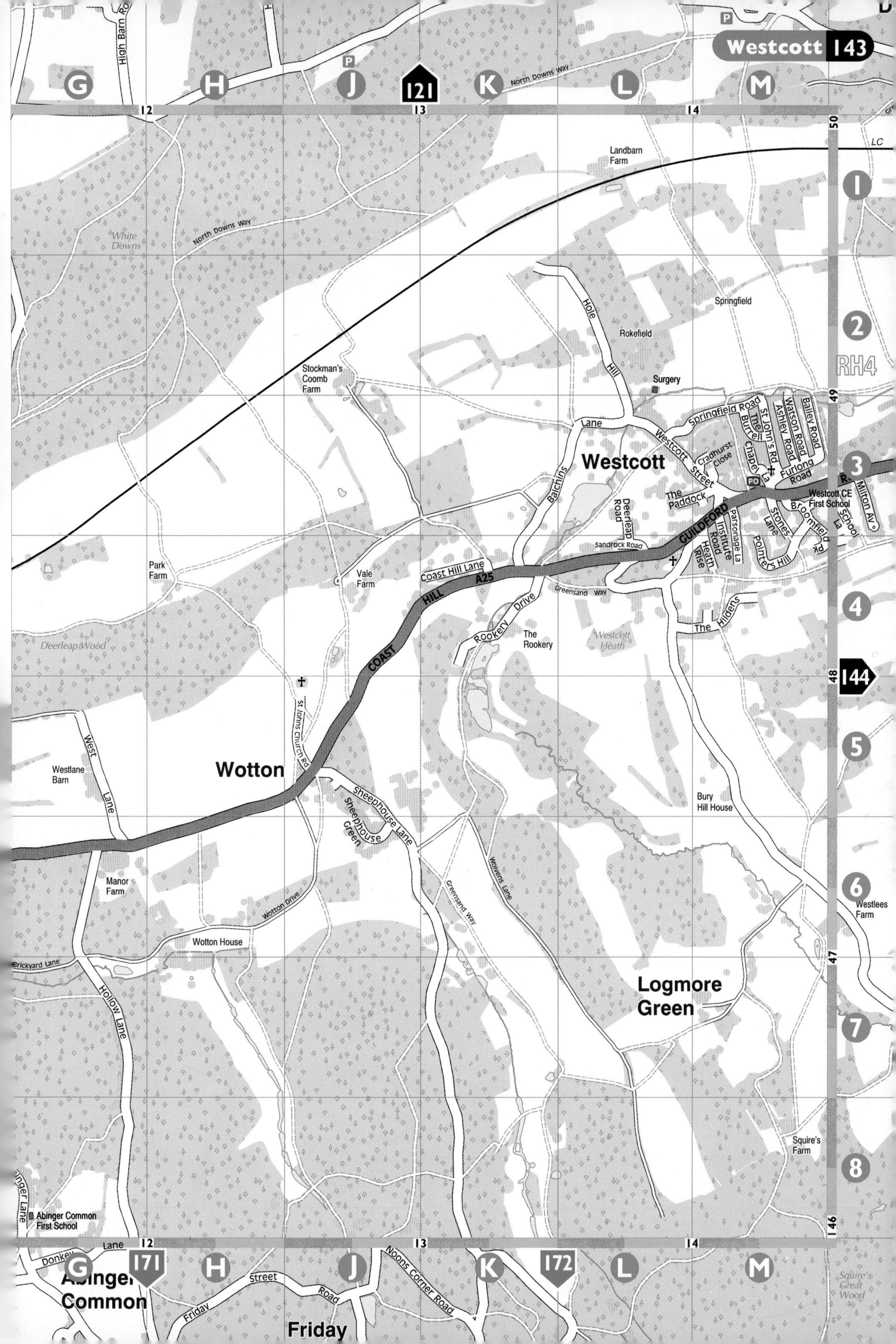
Westcott
Wotton
Logmore Green
Friday
Abinger Common
Landbarn Farm
Springfield
Rokefield
Surgery
Stockman's Coomb Farm
White Downs
North Downs Way
Hole Hill
Lane
Westcott Street
Springfield Road
The Burrell
St John's Rd
Ashley Road
Watson Road
Bailey Road
Cradhurst Close
Chapel La
Furlong Road
Milton Av
Westcott CE First School
School La
Broomfield Pk
Stones Lane
Pointers Hill
Balchins
The Paddock
Deerleap Road
Sandrock Road
GUILDFORD RD
Parsonage La
Institute Road
Heath Rise
Park Farm
Vale Farm
Coast Hill Lane
COAST HILL A25
Greensand Way
Rookery Drive
The Rookery
Westcott Heath
The Hildens
Deerleap Wood
St Johns Church Rd
West Lane
Westlane Barn
Sheephouse Lane
Sheephouse Green
Bury Hill House
Manor Farm
Wotton Drive
Wotton House
Wolvens Lane
Westlees Farm
Brickyard Lane
Hollow Lane
Squire's Farm
Abinger Common First School
Donkey Lane
Friday Street
Noons Corner Road
Squire's Great Wood
RH4
LC

121 171 172 144

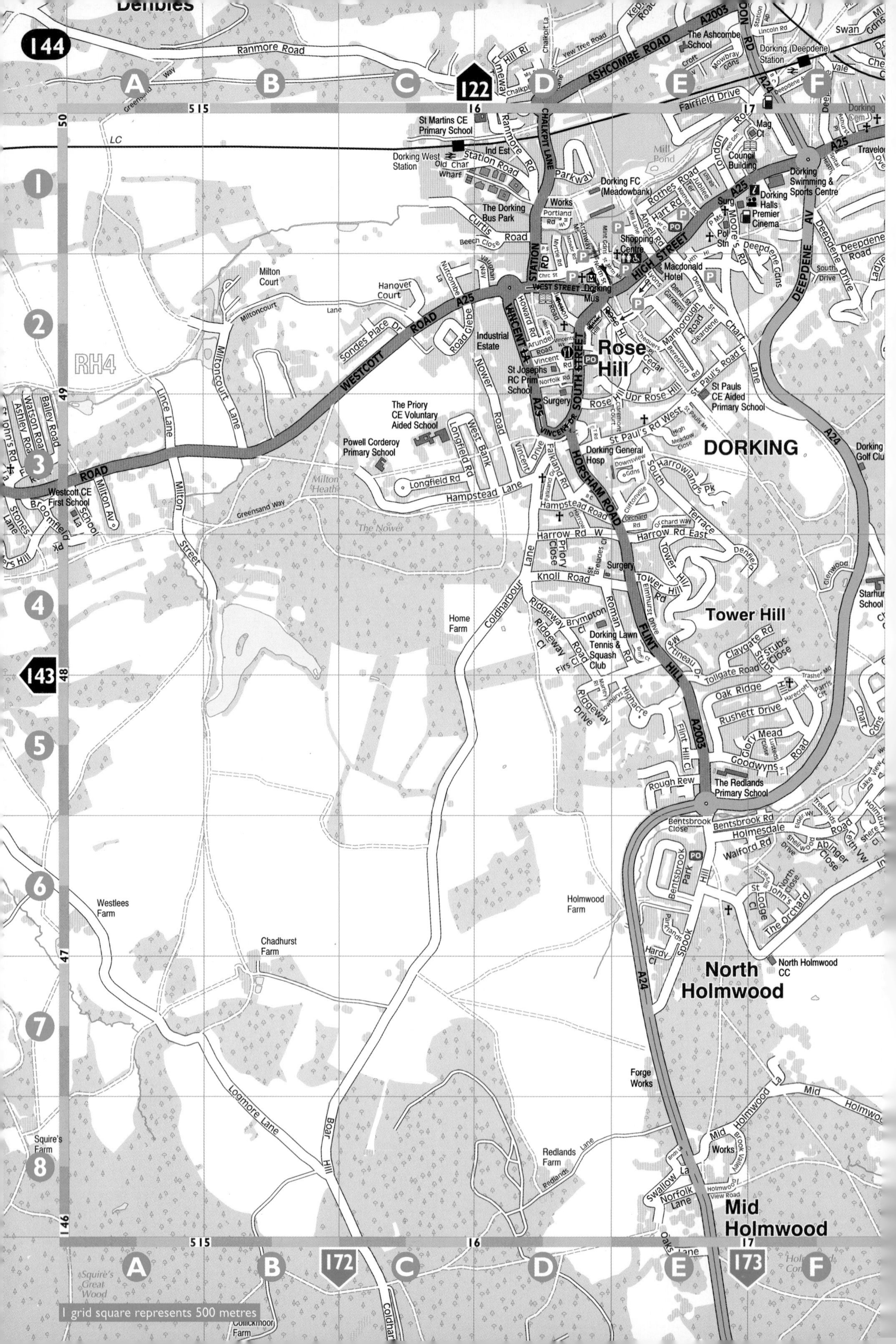

144
122
143
172
173
DORKING
Rose Hill
Tower Hill
North Holmwood
Mid Holmwood
RH4
Ranmore Road
Ashcombe Road
Westcott Road
High Street
West Street
South Street
Horsham Road
Flint Hill
Deepdene Av
Chalkpit Lane
Station Rd
Vincent La
Coldharbour Lane
Logmore Lane
Boar Hill
Milton Street
Miltoncourt Lane
Lince Lane
Hampstead Lane
Hampstead Road
Harrow Rd East
Knoll Road
Tollgate Road
Rushett Drive
Goodwyns Road
Bentsbrook Rd
Holmesdale
Spook Hill
Dorking West Station
Dorking (Deepdene) Station
Dorking General Hosp
Dorking Halls
Premier Cinema
Dorking Swimming & Sports Centre
Dorking FC (Meadowbank)
The Dorking Bus Park
Shopping Centre
Dorking Mus
Macdonald Hotel
Council Building
Industrial Estate
St Martins CE Primary School
The Ashcombe School
St Josephs RC Prim School
St Pauls CE Aided Primary School
The Priory CE Voluntary Aided School
Powell Corderoy Primary School
Westcott CE First School
The Redlands Primary School
Dorking Lawn Tennis & Squash Club
North Holmwood CC
Milton Court
Hanover Court
Milton Heath
The Nower
Home Farm
Westlees Farm
Chadhurst Farm
Holmwood Farm
Redlands Farm
Squire's Farm
Squire's Great Wood
Forge Works
Greensand Way
1 grid square represents 500 metres

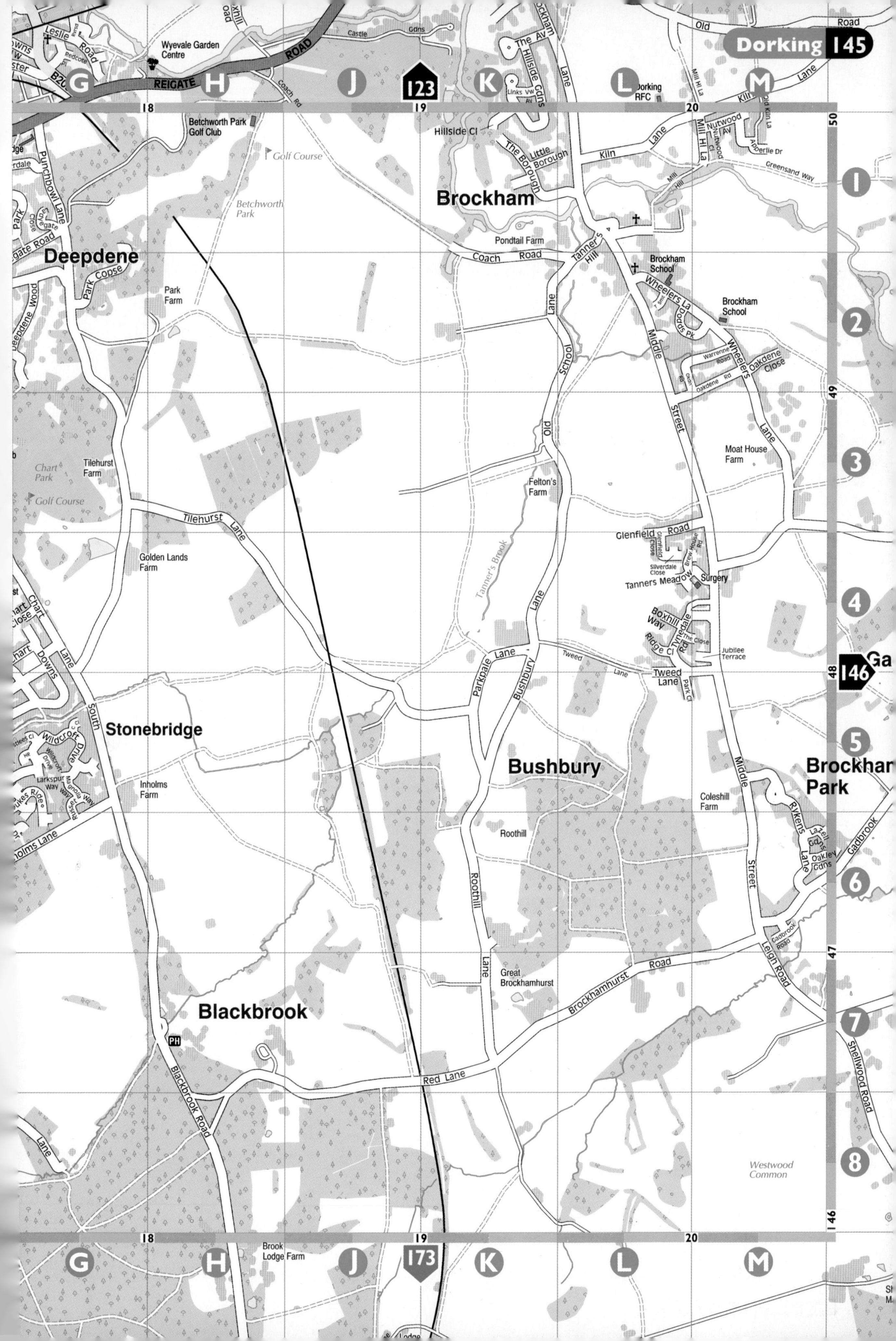

G   H   J   **123**   K   L   M

18   19   20   50

Leslie Road

Wyevale Garden Centre

REIGATE   ROAD

Coach Rd

Castle Gdns

Hillside Cl

Old Road

Dorking RFC

Kiln Lane

Nutwood Av

Greensand Way

Aperlie Dr

I

Betchworth Park Golf Club

Golf Course

Betchworth Park

The Borough

Little Borough

Links Vw Av

Hillside Gdns

The Av

Kiln Lane

Mill Hill La

Brockham

Pondtail Farm

Coach Road

Tanner's Hill

Brockham School

Wheelers La

Brockham School

Warrenne Rd

Oakdene Close

Wheelers Lane

2

49

Deepdene

Park Copse

Deepdene Wood

Park Farm

School Lane

Old School Lane

Oakdene Rd

Moat House Farm

3

Chart Park

Tilehurst Farm

Golf Course

Felton's Farm

Tanner's Brook

Glenfield Road

Glenfield Close

Brookhouse Rd

Tanners Meadow

Silverdale Close

Surgery

4

48

Tilehurst Lane

Golden Lands Farm

Parkgale Lane

Bushbury Lane

Tweed Lane

Boxhill Way

Tynedale Rd

Tynedale Close

Ridge Cl

Jubilee Terrace

Park Cl

Tweed Lane

146   Ga

Chart Downs

South Drive

Wildcroft Dr

Wildcroft Way

Larkspur Way

Magnolia Way

Stonebridge

Inholms Farm

Bushbury

Roothill

Coleshill Farm

Middle Street

Rikens Lane

Oakley Gdns

Gadbrook

Brockham Park

5

6

47

Inholms Lane

Roothill Lane

Great Brockhamhurst

Brockhamhurst Road

Leigh Road

Gadbrook Road

Shellwood Road

7

Blackbrook

PH

Blackbrook Road

Red Lane

Westwood Common

8

46

G   H   J   **173**   K   L   M

18   19   20

Brook Lodge Farm

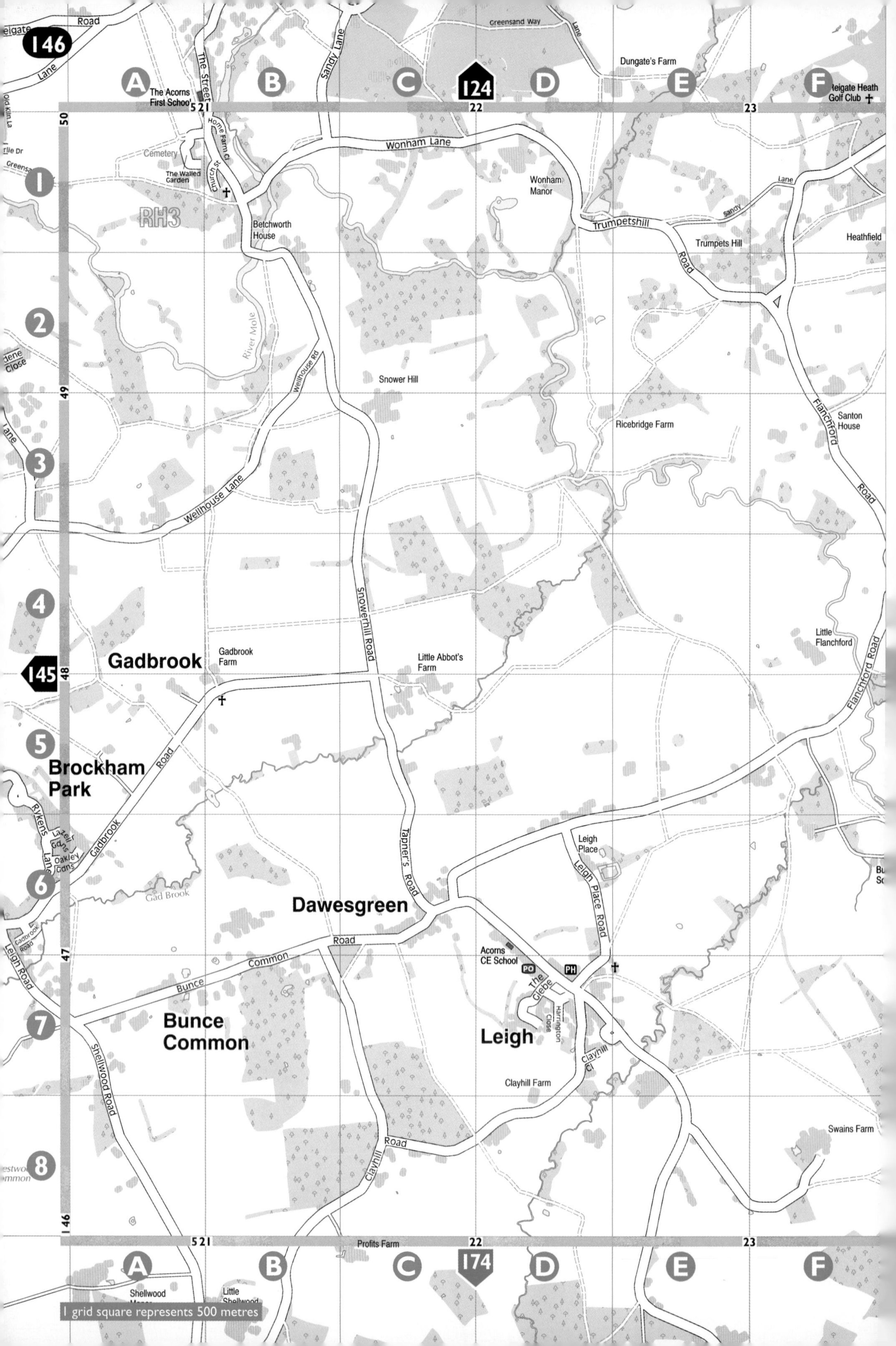

146
124
145
174
A
B
C
D
E
F
1
2
3
4
5
6
7
8
521
22
23
50
49
48
47
146
Reigate Road
Lane
The Acorns First School
The Street
Home Farm Cl
Church St
Cemetery
The Walled Garden
RH3
Betchworth House
River Mole
Wellhouse Rd
Wellhouse Lane
Sandy Lane
Greensand Way
Lane
Dungate's Farm
Reigate Heath Golf Club
Wonham Lane
Wonham Manor
Trumpetshill Road
Sandy Lane
Trumpets Hill
Heathfield
Snower Hill
Ricebridge Farm
Flanchford Road
Santon House
Little Flanchford
Snowerhill Road
Gadbrook
Gadbrook Farm
Little Abbot's Farm
Brockham Park
Gadbrook Road
Rykens Lane
Oakley Gdns
Gad Brook
Tapner's Road
Dawesgreen
Leigh Place
Leigh Place Road
Road
Common
Bunce
Bunce Common
Acorns CE School
PO
PH
The Glebe
Harrington Close
Leigh
Clayhill Cl
Clayhill Farm
Shellwood Road
Clayhill Road
Leigh Road
Swains Farm
Profits Farm
Shellwood Manor
Little Shellwood
1 grid square represents 500 metres

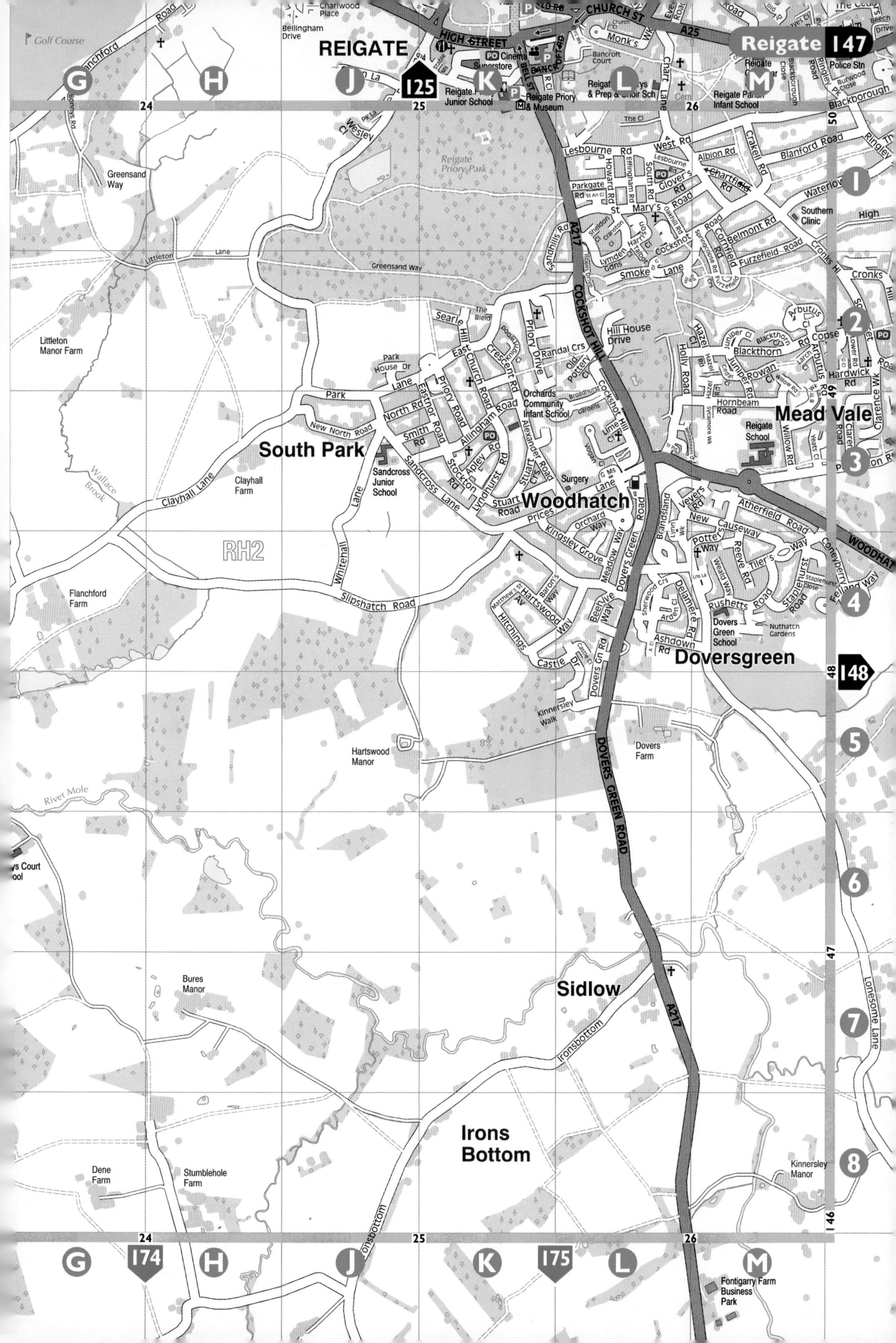

REIGATE
Reigate 147
HIGH STREET
CHURCH ST
A25
Golf Course
Bellingham Drive
Cinema
Superstore
Reigate Priory Junior School
Reigate Priory & Museum
Bancroft Court
Chart Lane
Reigate Parish Infant School
Police Stn
Blackborough
125
G
H
J
K
L
M
24
25
26
Wesley Cl
Greensand Way
Reigate Priory Park
Littleton Lane
Littleton Manor Farm
Lesbourne Rd
West Rd
Albion Rd
Blanford Road
Crakell Rd
Effingham Rd
Howard Rd
South Rd
Glover's Rd
Chartfield Rd
Parkgate Rd
St Mary's Road
Southern Clinic
Belmont Rd
Cornfield Road
Furzefield Road
Cronks Hill
Sandhills Rd
Smoke Lane
Cockshot
A217
COCKSHOT HILL
Searle Hill
The Bield
East Hill
Church Road
Crescent Rd
Priory Drive
Randal Crs
Old Pottery Cl
Hill House Drive
Holly Road
Blackthorn Rd
Arbutus Cl
Copse
Juniper Rd
Rowan Cl
Hardwick Rd
Hornbeam Road
Mead Vale
Reigate School
Park House Dr
Park Lane
North Rd
Eastnor Road
Priory Road
Allingham Road
Alexander Road
Orchards Community Infant School
Cockshot Hill
Lime Cl
New North Road
South Park
Smith Rd
Apley Rd
Lyndhurst Rd
Stuart Cl
Sandcross Junior School
Sandcross Lane
Stockton Rd
Stuart Road
Surgery
Woodhatch
Prices Lane
Clayhall Lane
Clayhall Farm
Wallace Brook
Whitehall Lane
RH2
Kingsley Grove
Orchard Way
Meadow Way
Dovers Green Road
Brandsland
Vevers Rd
New Causeway
Atherfield Road
Potters Way
Reeve Rd
Tiler's Way
Weald Way
Staplehurst Road
Felland Way
WOODHATCH
Flanchford Farm
Slipshatch Road
Hartswood Av
Baron's Way
Hitchings Way
Beehive Way
Sherwood Crs
Arden Cl
Delamere Rd
Rushetts Road
Dovers Green School
Nuthatch Gardens
Ashdown Rd
Castle Dr
Dovers Gn Rd
Doversgreen
148
Kinnersley Walk
Hartswood Manor
DOVERS GREEN ROAD
Dovers Farm
River Mole
Sidlow
Bures Manor
Ironsbottom
Irons Bottom
Dene Farm
Stumblehole Farm
Kinnersley Manor
Lonesome Lane
174
175
Fontigarry Farm Business Park
50
49
48
47
46
1
2
3
4
5
6
7
8

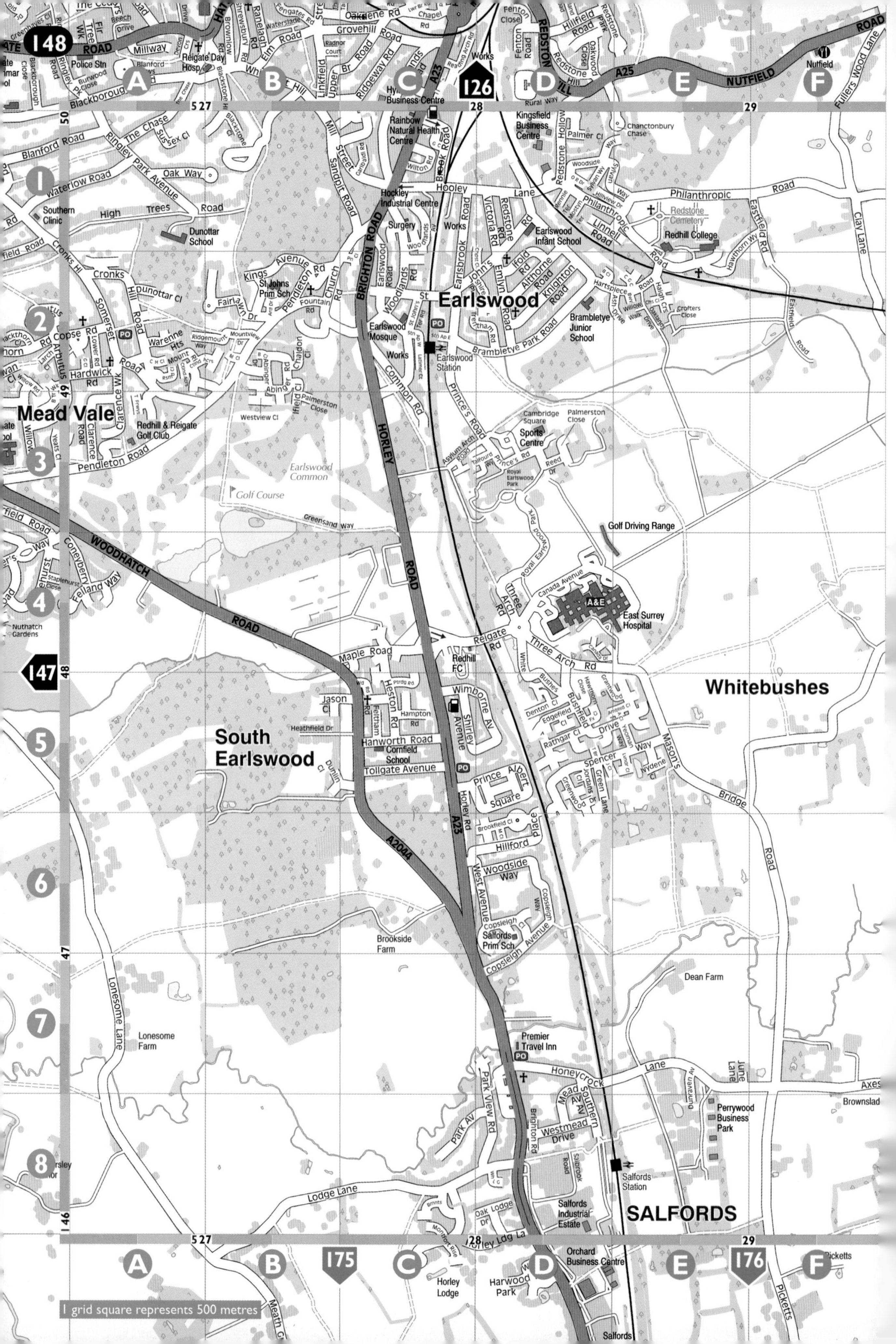

148
126
147
175
176
Earlswood
Mead Vale
South Earlswood
Whitebushes
SALFORDS
Earlswood Common
Golf Course
East Surrey Hospital
Golf Driving Range
Redhill College
Earlswood Station
Salfords Station
BRIGHTON ROAD
HORLEY ROAD
WOODHATCH ROAD
NUTFIELD ROAD
Lonesome Lane
Lonesome Farm
Brookside Farm
Dean Farm
Perrywood Business Park
Salfords Industrial Estate
Orchard Business Centre
Premier Travel Inn
Redhill FC
Dunottar School
Redhill & Reigate Golf Club
Hooley Lane
Philanthropic Road
Honeycrock Lane
Lodge Lane
Mason's Bridge Road
Three Arch Rd
Reigate Rd
1 grid square represents 500 metres

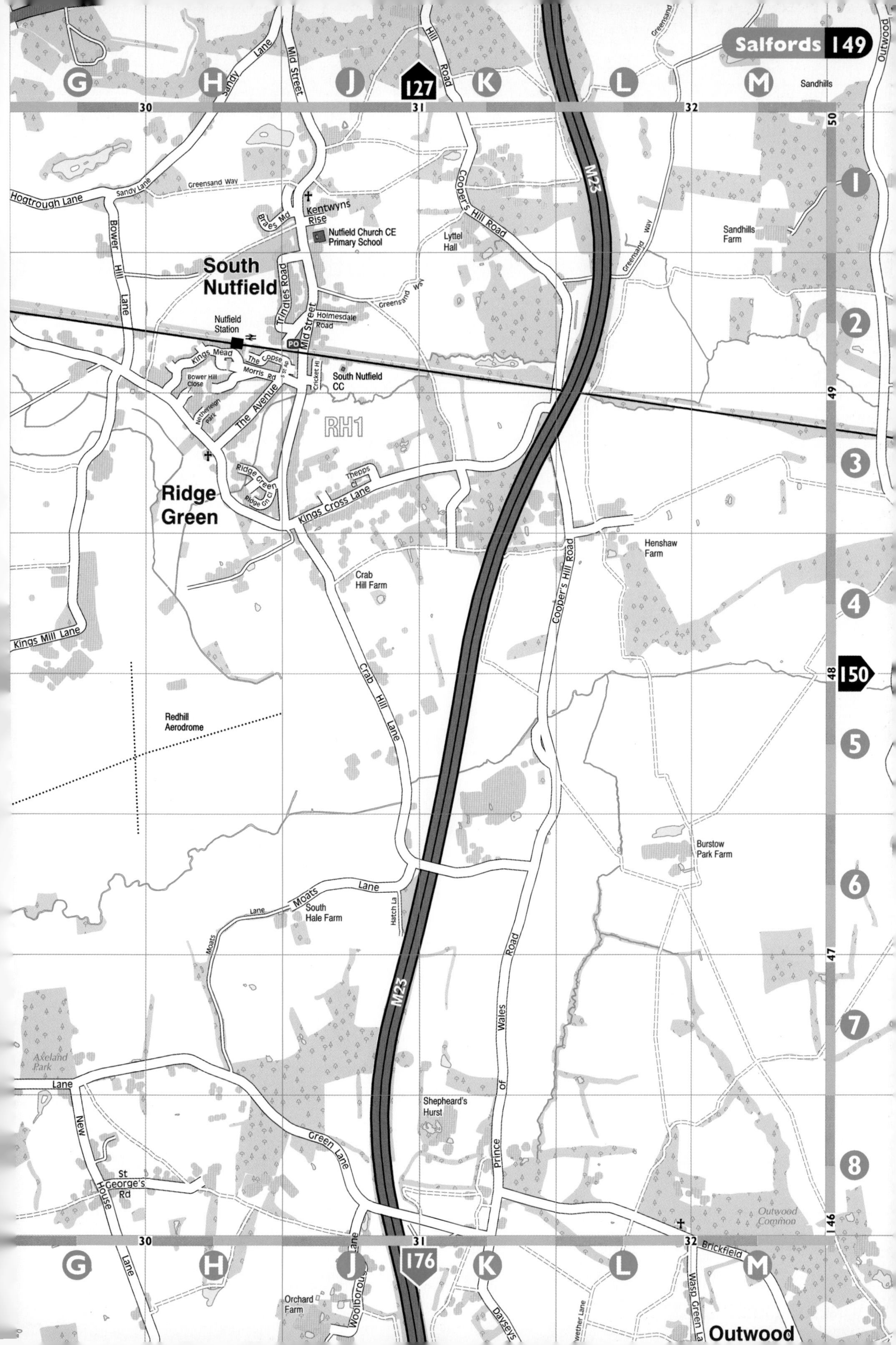

G H Mid Street J 127 31 K L M Sandhills

30 31 32 50

Sandy Lane Greensand Way Hill Road Cooper's Hill Road M23 Greensand Way

Hogtrough Lane Sandy Lane Kentwyns Rise Lyttel Hall Sandhills Farm

Braes Md Nutfield Church CE Primary School

Bower Hill Lane **South Nutfield** Greensand Way

Trindles Road Mid Street Holmesdale Road

Nutfield Station PO South Nutfield CC

Kings Mead The Copse St Rd Cricket Hl Morris Rd Bower Hill Close Netherleigh Park The Avenue **RH1**

Ridge Green Thepps Cl Henshaw Farm

Ridge Green Ridge Grn Kings Cross Lane

Crab Hill Farm Cooper's Hill Road

Kings Mill Lane Crab Hill Lane

Redhill Aerodrome 150 48

Burstow Park Farm

Moats Lane Lane Hatch La

Moats Lane South Hale Farm 47

Axeland Park Lane

New St George's Rd Green Lane Shepheard's Hurst Prince of Wales Road Outwood Common 146

St House Rd M23

G H J 176 K L M Brickfield

30 31 32

Orchard Farm Woolborough Daysers wether Lane Wasp Green Lane **Outwood**

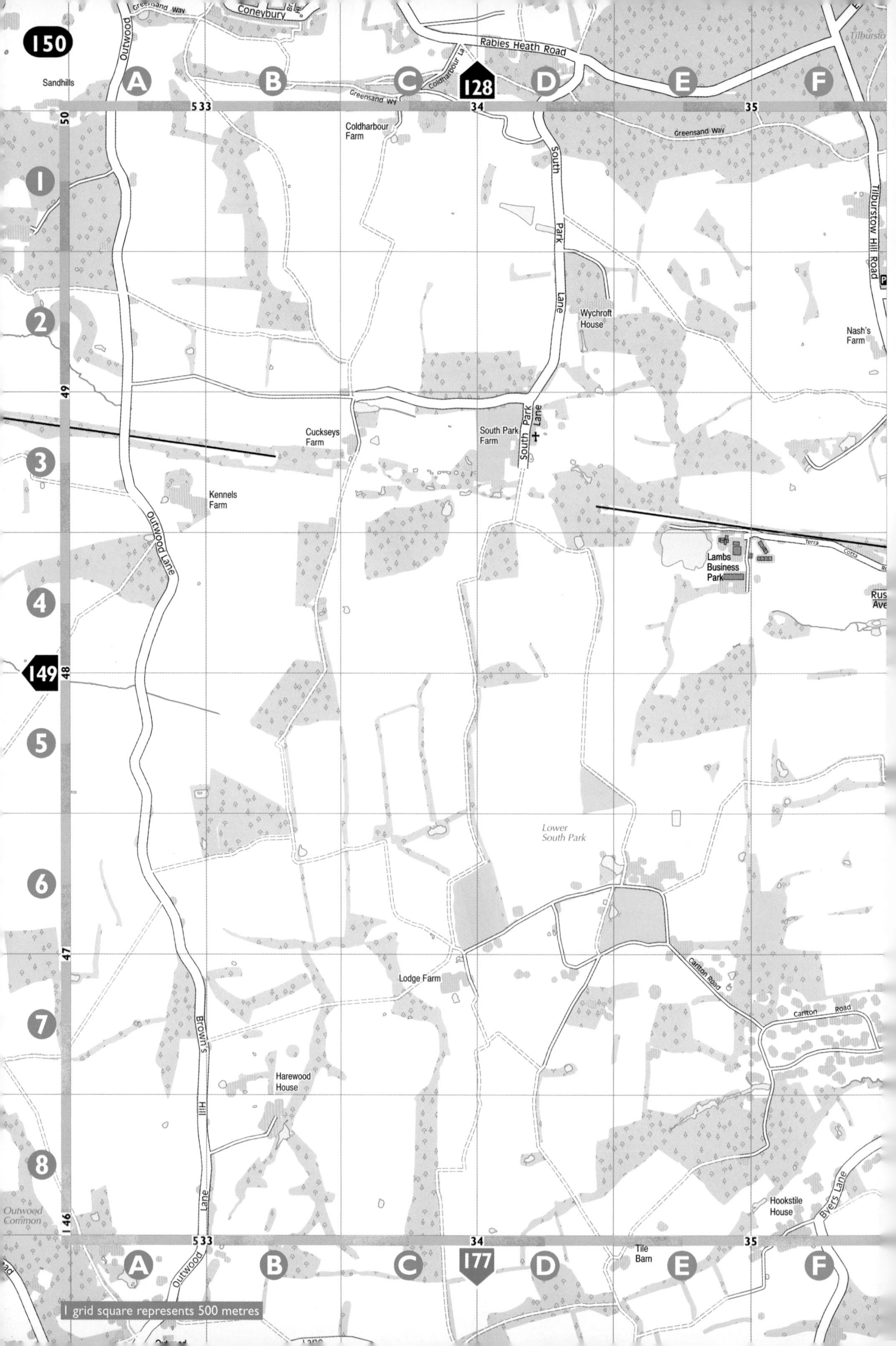

Sandhills

A   B   C   128   D   E   F

Coneybury

Rabies Heath Road

Tilburstone

Greensand Way

Coldharbour La

Greensand Wy

5 33   34   35

50

I

Coldharbour Farm

Greensand Way

South Park Lane

Tilburstow Hill Road

2

Wychroft House

Nash's Farm

49

Cuckseys Farm

South Park Farm

South Park Lane

3

Kennels Farm

Terra Cotta

Lambs Business Park

Rus Ave

Outwood Lane

4

149 48

5

Lower South Park

6

47

Carlton Road

Lodge Farm

7

Carlton Road

Brown's Hill Lane

Harewood House

Byers Lane

8

Hookstile House

Outwood Common

146

5 33   34   35

A   Outwood   B   C   177   D   Tile Barn E   F

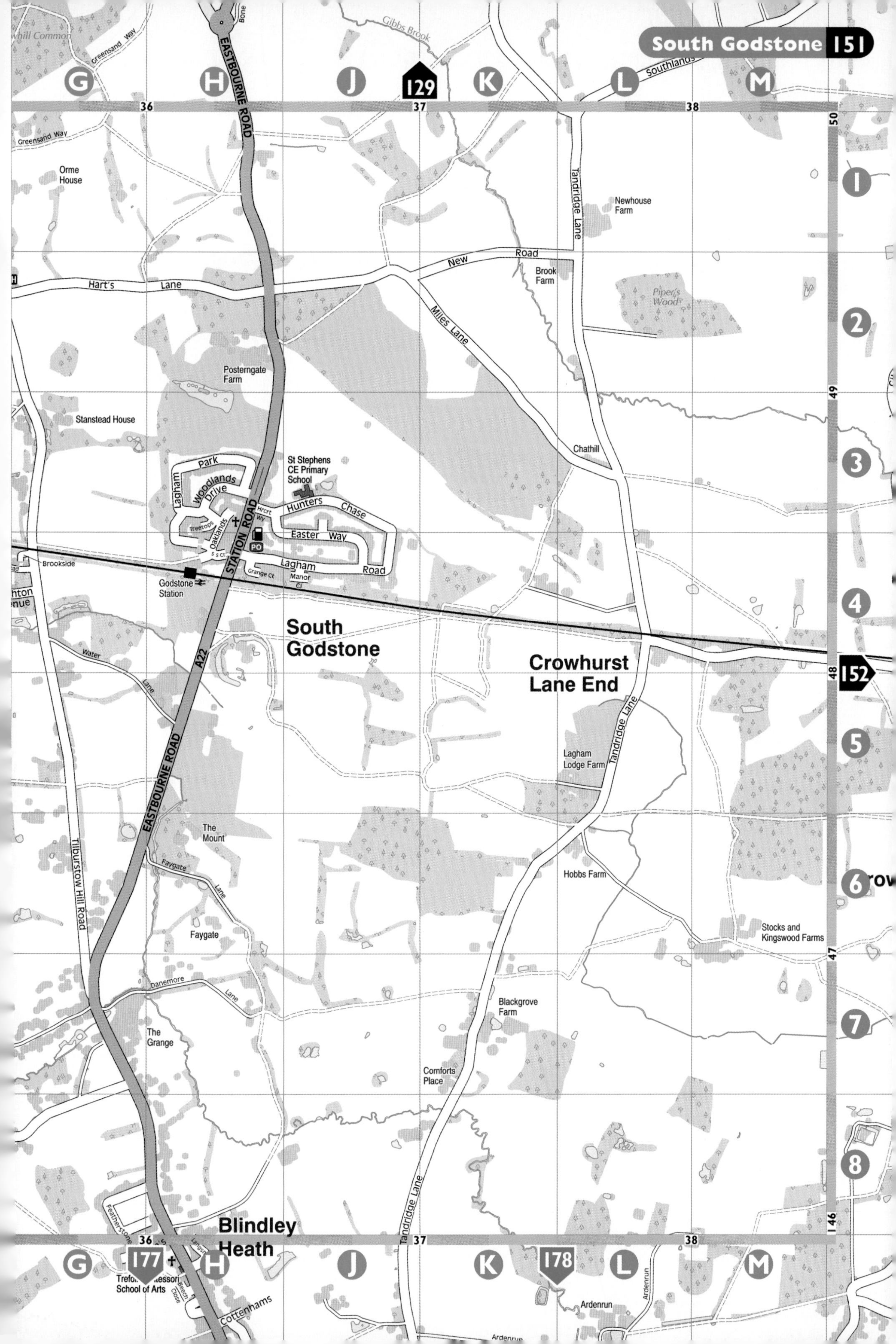

EASTBOURNE ROAD
Gibbs Brook
Southlands
Greensand Way
Orme House
Tandridge Lane
Newhouse Farm
New Road
Brook Farm
Hart's Lane
Piper's Wood
Miles Lane
Posterngate Farm
Stanstead House
Chathill
St Stephens CE Primary School
Lagham Park
Woodlands Drive
Hunters Chase
Easter Way
STATION ROAD
Treetops
Oaklands
Lagham Road
Grange Ct
Manor Ct
Brookside
Godstone Station
South Godstone
Crowhurst Lane End
Water Lane
A22
Lagham Lodge Farm
The Mount
Faygate Lane
Hobbs Farm
Tilburstow Hill Road
Faygate
Stocks and Kingswood Farms
Danemore Lane
Blackgrove Farm
The Grange
Comforts Place
Featherstone
Blindley Heath
Cottenhams
Ardenrun

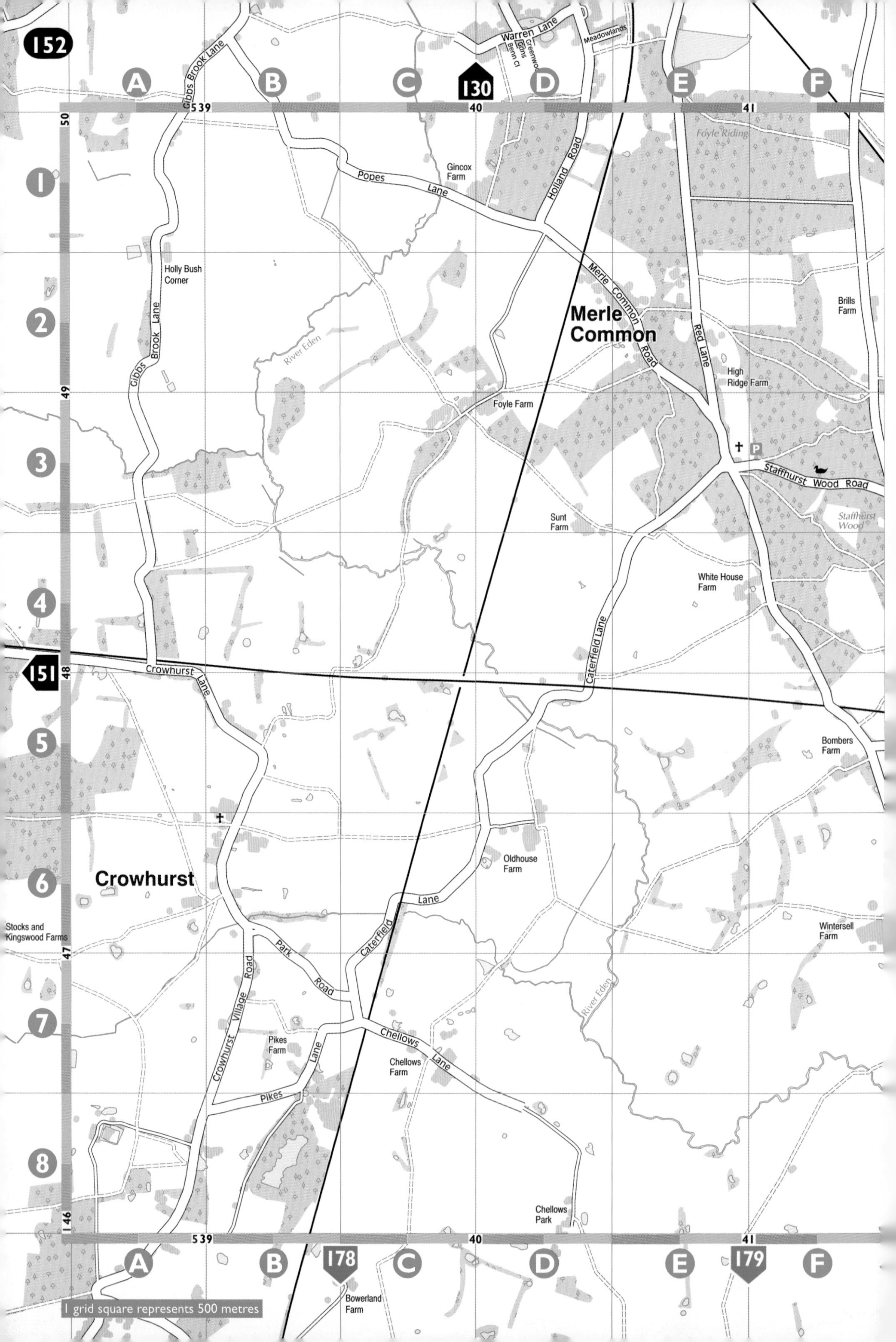

A
B
C
130
D
E
F
539
40
41
50
1
2
3
4
49
48
151
5
6
47
7
8
146
Gibbs Brook Lane
Warren Lane
Glebe
Benn Cl
Greenwood
Meadowlands
Foyle Riding
Gincox Farm
Popes Lane
Holland Road
Holly Bush Corner
Merle Common Road
Merle Common
Brills Farm
Red Lane
High Ridge Farm
River Eden
Foyle Farm
Staffhurst Wood Road
Staffhurst Wood
Sunt Farm
White House Farm
Caterfield Lane
Crowhurst Lane
Bombers Farm
Oldhouse Farm
Crowhurst
Stocks and Kingswood Farms
Lane
Wintersell Farm
Caterfield
Park Road
Crowhurst Village Road
Chellows Lane
Pikes Farm
Chellows Farm
Pikes Lane
Chellows Park
178
179
Bowerland Farm
1 grid square represents 500 metres

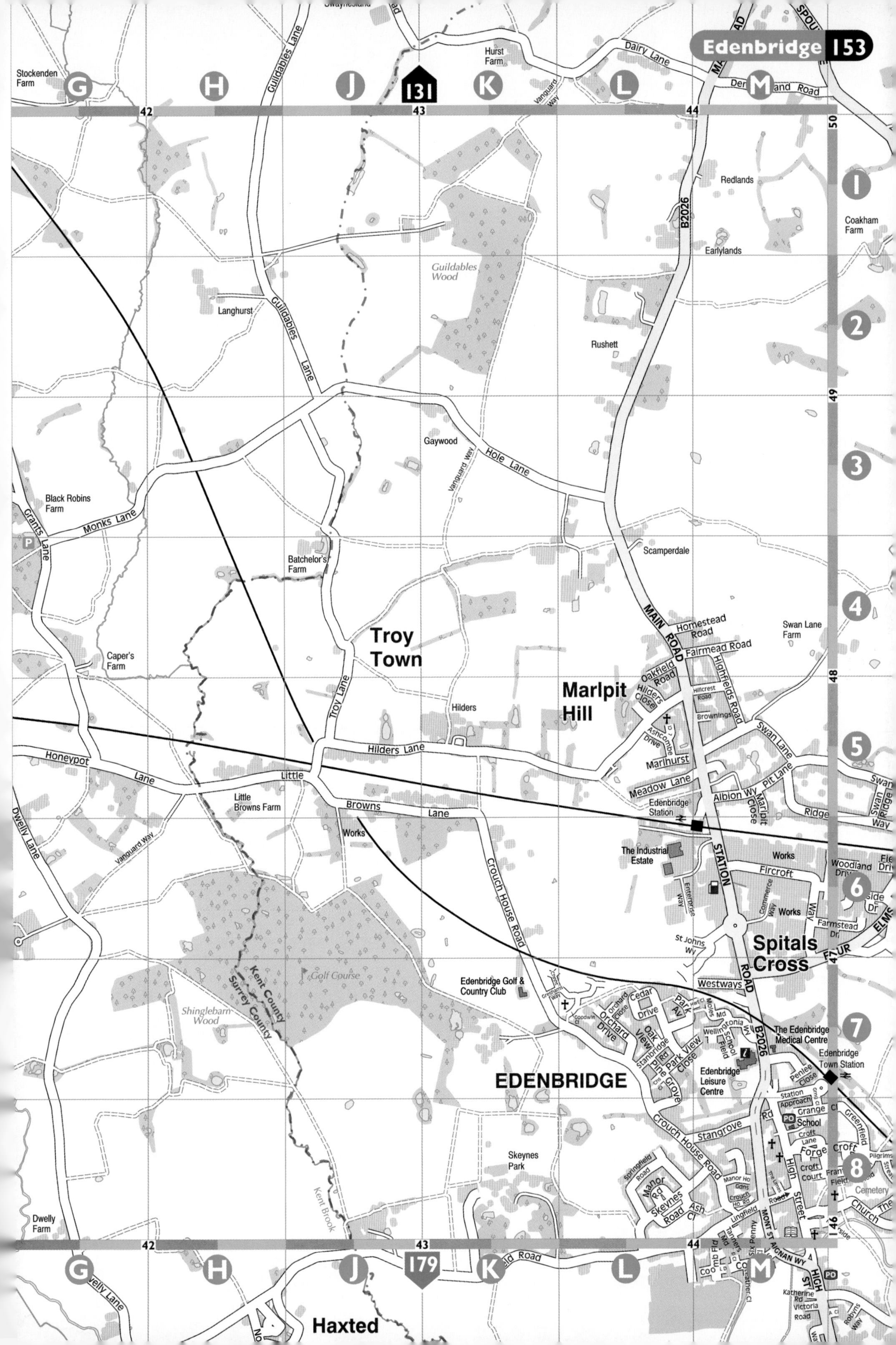
Stockenden Farm
Hurst Farm
Dairy Lane
Guildables Lane
Redlands
Coakham Farm
Earlylands
B2026
Guildables Wood
Langhurst
Rushett
Gaywood
Hole Lane
Vanguard Way
Black Robins Farm
Monks Lane
Grants Lane
Batchelor's Farm
Scamperdale
Troy Town
Marlpit Hill
Homestead Road
Fairmead Road
Swan Lane Farm
Caper's Farm
Hilders
Troy Lane
Hilders Lane
Honeypot Lane
Little Browns Farm
Browns Lane
Meadow Lane
Edenbridge Station
Albion Wy
Works
The Industrial Estate
Crouch House Road
Fircroft
Spitals Cross
Golf Course
Kent County
Surrey County
Shinglebarn Wood
Edenbridge Golf & Country Club
Westways
Orchard Drive
Cedar Drive
The Edenbridge Medical Centre
Edenbridge Town Station
EDENBRIDGE
Edenbridge Leisure Centre
Station Approach
School
Skeynes Park
Stangrove
Manor Rd
Skeynes Road
High Street
Kent Brook
Dwelly Lane
Dwelly Farm
Haxted
Cemetery
MAIN ROAD
STATION ROAD

131
179

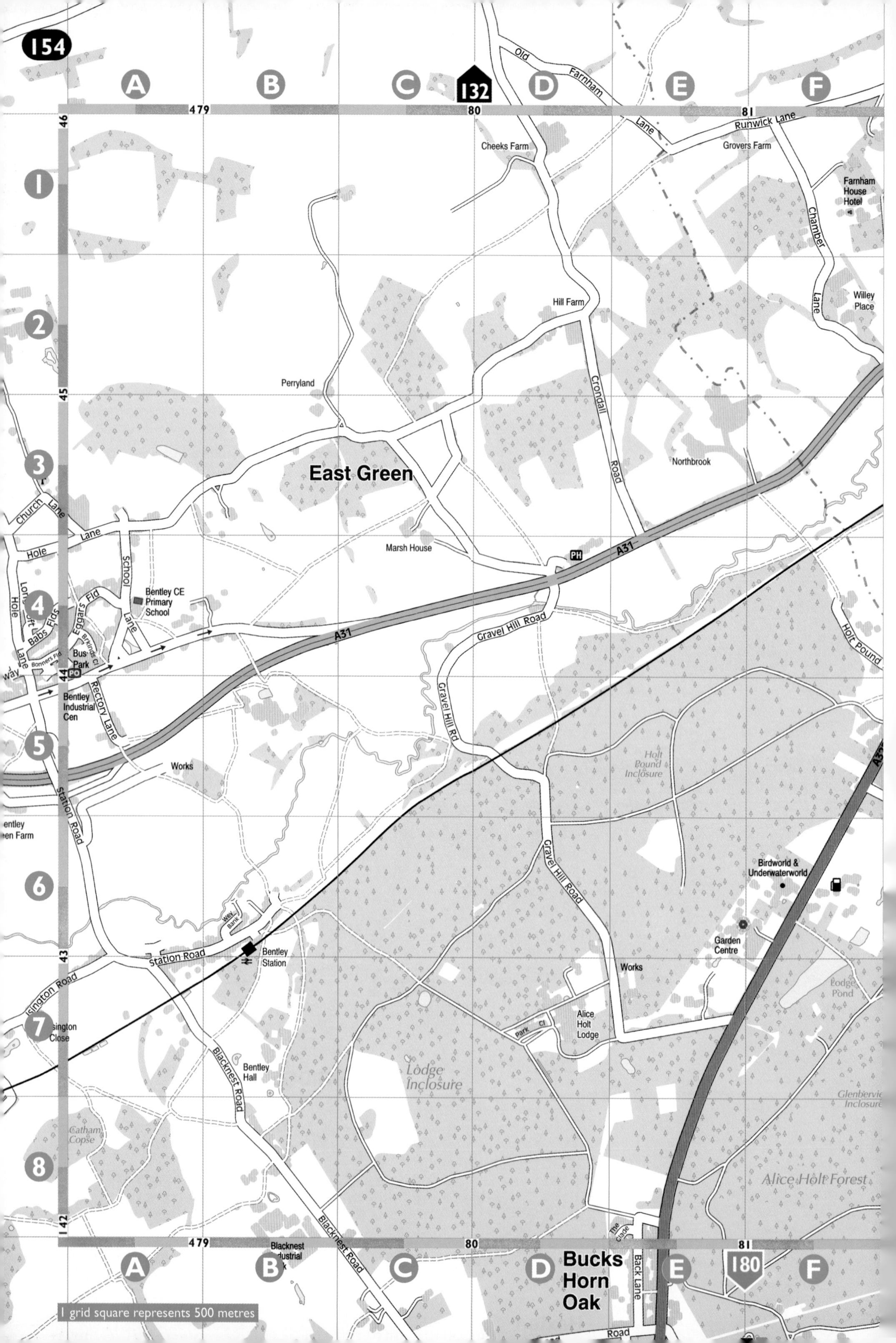

A   B   C   D   E   F

479   80   81

Old Farnham Lane
Runwick Lane

I

Cheeks Farm

Grovers Farm

132

Chamber Lane

Farnham House Hotel

2

Hill Farm

Willey Place

Perryland

Crondall Road

Northbrook

3

East Green

Marsh House

PH   A31

4

Bentley CE Primary School

Church Lane

Hole Lane

Gravel Hill Road

Holt Pound

Eggar's Fld

School Lane

Longcroft

Bades Flds

Bonners Fld

Bus Park

PO

Bentley Industrial Cen

A31

5

Works

Gravel Hill Rd

Holt Pound Inclosure

Station Road

Bentley Green Farm

6

Rectory Lane

Gravel Hill Road

Birdworld & Underwaterworld

Garden Centre

Lodge Pond

Works

7

Station Road

Way Barn

Bentley Station

Park Cl

Alice Holt Lodge

Kensington Road

sington Close

Blacknest Road

Bentley Hall

Lodge Inclosure

Glenbervie Inclosure

8

Catham Copse

Alice Holt Forest

The Chase

A   B   C   D   E   F

479   80   81

Bucks Horn Oak

180

Back Lane

Road

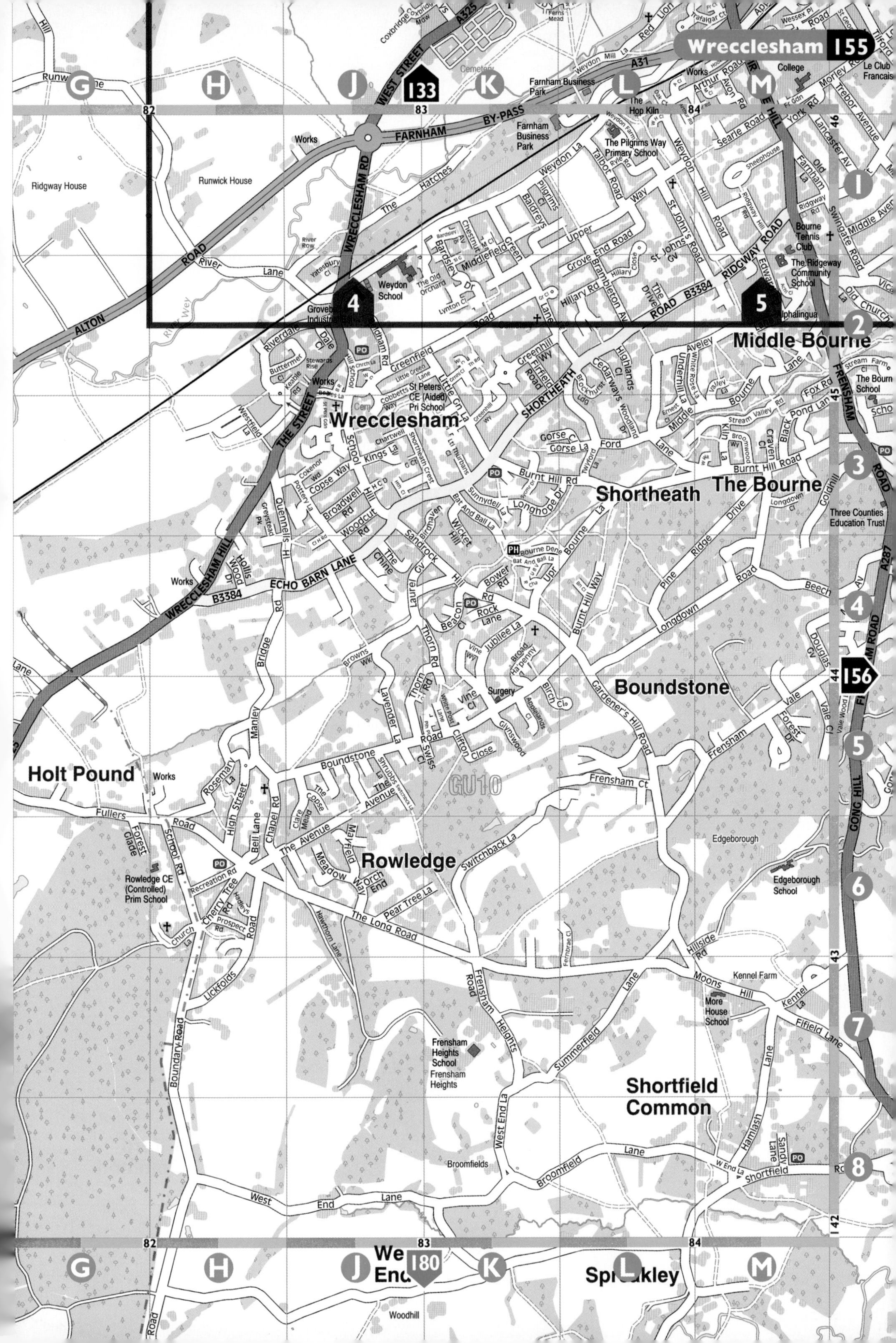
Wrecclesham
Middle Bourne
Shortheath
The Bourne
Boundstone
Holt Pound
Rowledge
Shortfield Common
GU10
Ridgway House
Runwick House
Farnham Business Park
The Hop Kiln
The Pilgrims Way Primary School
Weydon School
Grovebell Industrial Estate
St Peters CE (Aided) Pri School
Rowledge CE (Controlled) Prim School
Bourne Tennis Club
The Ridgeway Community School
Three Counties Education Trust
Edgeborough School
Edgeborough
Kennel Farm
More House School
Frensham Heights School
Frensham Heights
Broomfields
Woodhill
College
Le Club Francais
Surgery
ALTON ROAD
FARNHAM BY-PASS
WEST STREET
WRECCLESHAM RD
WRECCLESHAM HILL
THE STREET
ECHO BARN LANE
SHORTHEATH
RIDGWAY ROAD
FRENSHAM ROAD
GONG HILL
The Long Road
Boundstone Road
Gardener's Hill Road
Longdown Road
Burnt Hill Road
Frensham Road
Boundary Road
West End Lane
Broomfield Lane
Moons Hill
Fifield Lane
A31
A325
A287
B3384
133
156
180
Spreakley
G
H
J
K
L
M
82
83
84
1
2
3
4
5
6
7
8
46
45
44
43
142

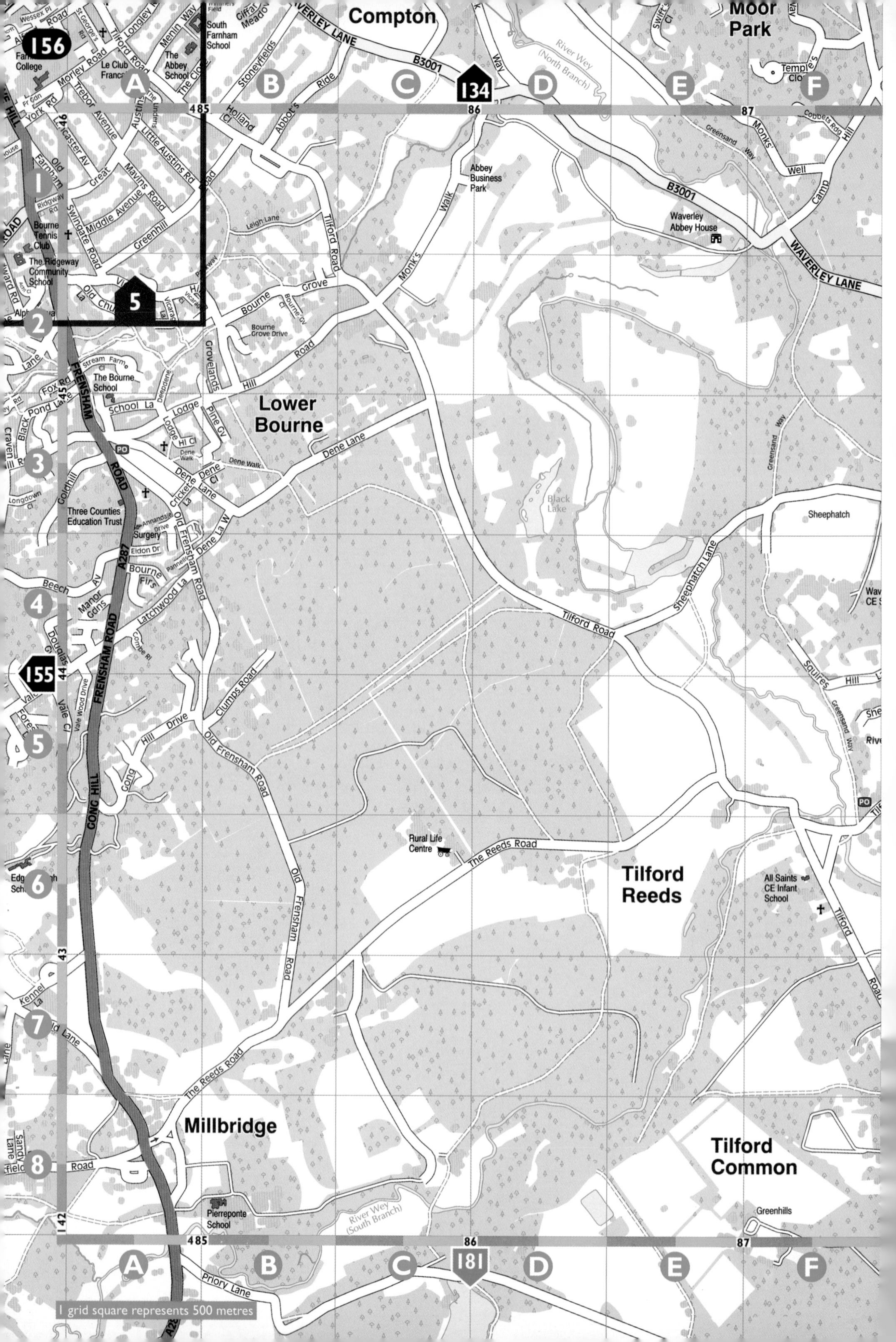

156
134
5
155
181
Compton
Moor Park
Lower Bourne
Tilford Reeds
Millbridge
Tilford Common
WAVERLEY LANE
B3001
FRENSHAM ROAD
GONG HILL
A287
Tilford Road
The Reeds Road
Old Frensham Road
Dene Lane
Bourne Grove
Hill Road
Monk's Walk
Sheephatch Lane
Clumps Road
Gong Hill Drive
Tilford Road
Greensand Way
River Wey (North Branch)
River Wey (South Branch)
Black Lake
Waverley Abbey House
Abbey Business Park
South Farnham School
The Abbey School
Farnham College
Le Club Francais
Bourne Tennis Club
The Ridgeway Community School
The Bourne School
Three Counties Education Trust
Surgery
Rural Life Centre
All Saints CE Infant School
Pierrepont School
Sheephatch
Greenhills
Priory Lane
485
86
87
46
45
44
43
142
1 grid square represents 500 metres

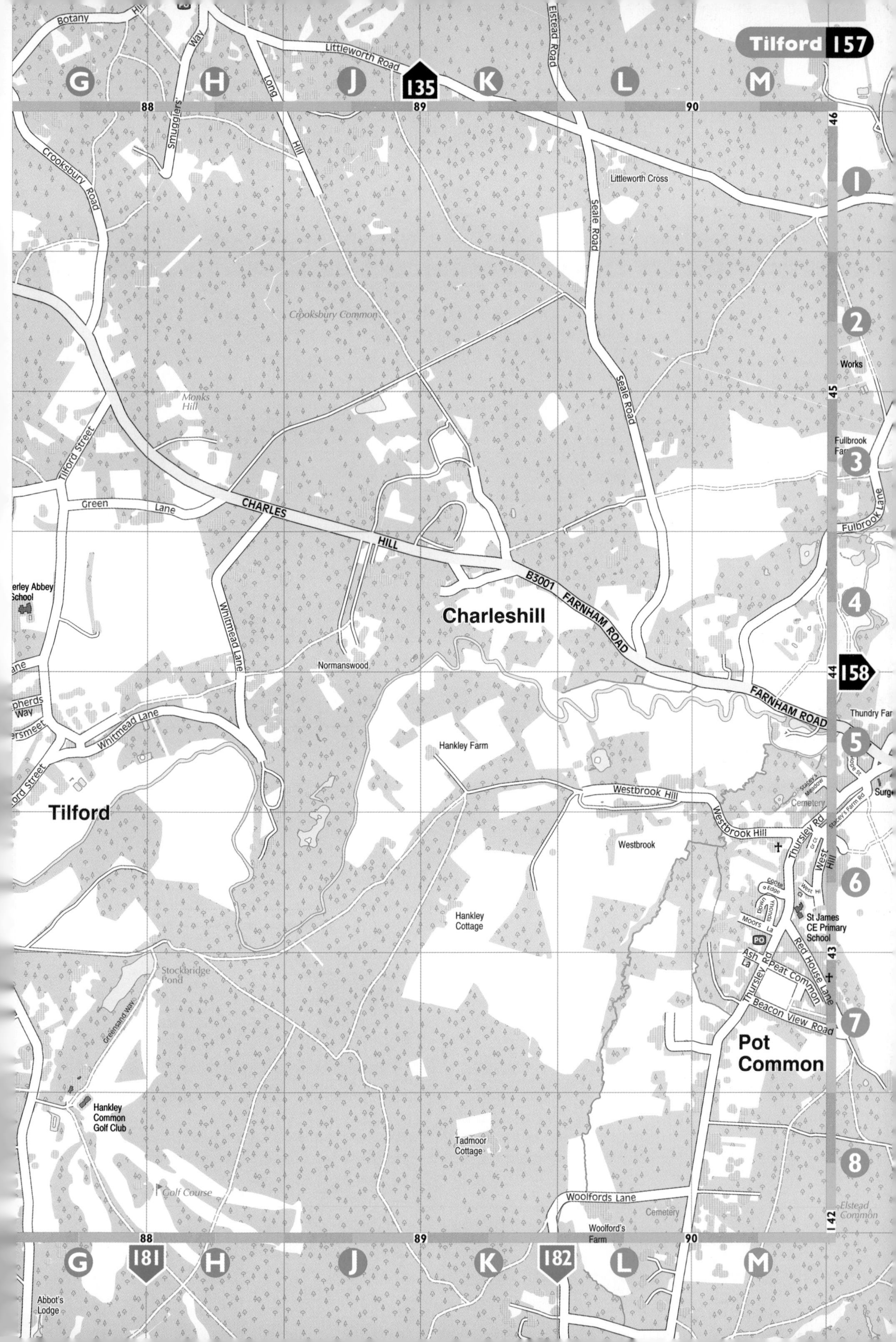

G H J **135** K L M

88 89 90

46

1

Littleworth Road

Botany

Littleworth Cross

Smugglers' Way

Long Hill

Elstead Road

Crooksbury Road

Crooksbury Common

Seale Road

45

Works

2

Monks Hill

Fullbrook Farm

3

Tilford Street

Green Lane

CHARLES

Fulbrook Lane

Whitmead Lane

HILL

B3001 FARNHAM ROAD

Charleshill

rerley Abbey School

4

Normanswood

44 **158**

FARNHAM ROAD

Thundry Far

Hankley Farm

5

pherds Way

Whitmead Lane

ord Street

Westbrook Hill

Hankley Cottage

Westbrook Hill

Cemetery

Stanley's Farm Rd

Surge

Tilford

Westbrook

Thursley Rd

West Hill

6

Codge Edge

West Hill

Victoria

Moors La

St James CE Primary School

Stockbridge Pond

PO

Greensand Way

43

Ash La

Thursley Rd

Peat common La

7

Hankley Common Golf Club

Beacon View Road

Thursley Rd

Pot Common

Golf Course

Tadmoor Cottage

42

Elstead Common

8

Woolfords Lane

Cemetery

Woolford's Farm

88 89 90

G **181** H J K **182** L M

Abbot's Lodge

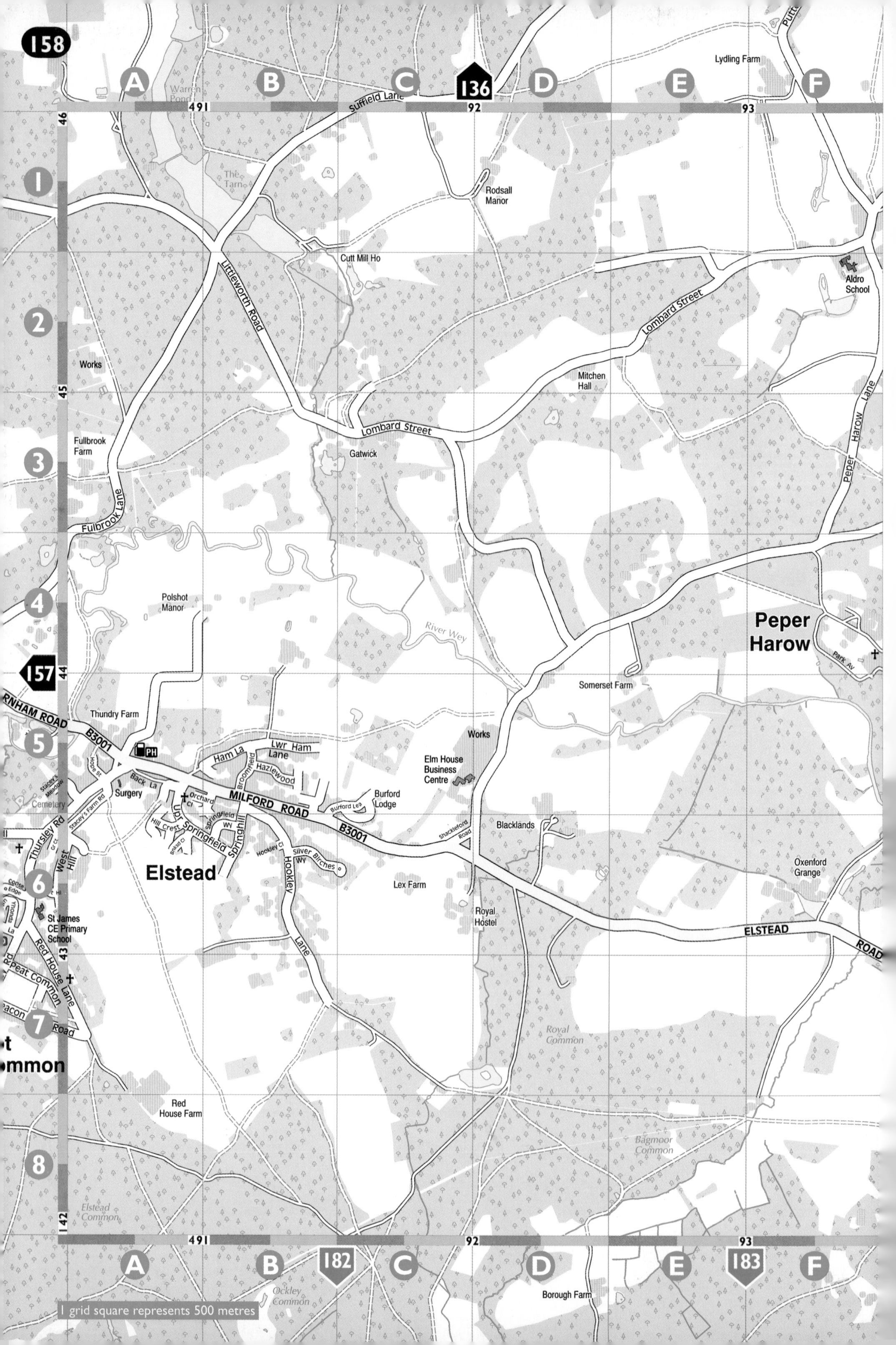

136
Suffield Lane
Warren Pond
Lydling Farm
491
92
93
46
The Tarn
Rodsall Manor
Cutt Mill Ho
Littleworth Road
Aldro School
Lombard Street
Works
Mitchen Hall
45
Fullbrook Farm
Gatwick
Peper Harow Lane
Fulbrook Lane
Polshot Manor
River Wey
Peper Harow
Park Av
157
44
Somerset Farm
Thundry Farm
B3001
PH
Works
Ham La
Lwr Ham Lane
Hazlewood
Broomfield
Elm House Business Centre
Back La
Surgery
Orchard Cl
MILFORD ROAD
Burford Lodge
Burford Lea
Cemetery
Stacey's Farm Rd
Upr Springfield
Springfield Wy
Springhill
Hill Crest
Shackleford Road
Blacklands
Thursley Rd
West Hill
Hookley Cl
Silver Birches Wy
Hookley Lane
B3001
Elstead
Lex Farm
Oxenford Grange
St James CE Primary School
Royal Hostel
ELSTEAD ROAD
43
Red House Lane
Peat Common
Royal Common
Red House Farm
Bagmoor Common
42
Elstead Common
491
92
93
182
183
Ockley Common
Borough Farm
A
B
C
D
E
F
1
2
3
4
5
6
7
8

1 grid square represents 500 metres

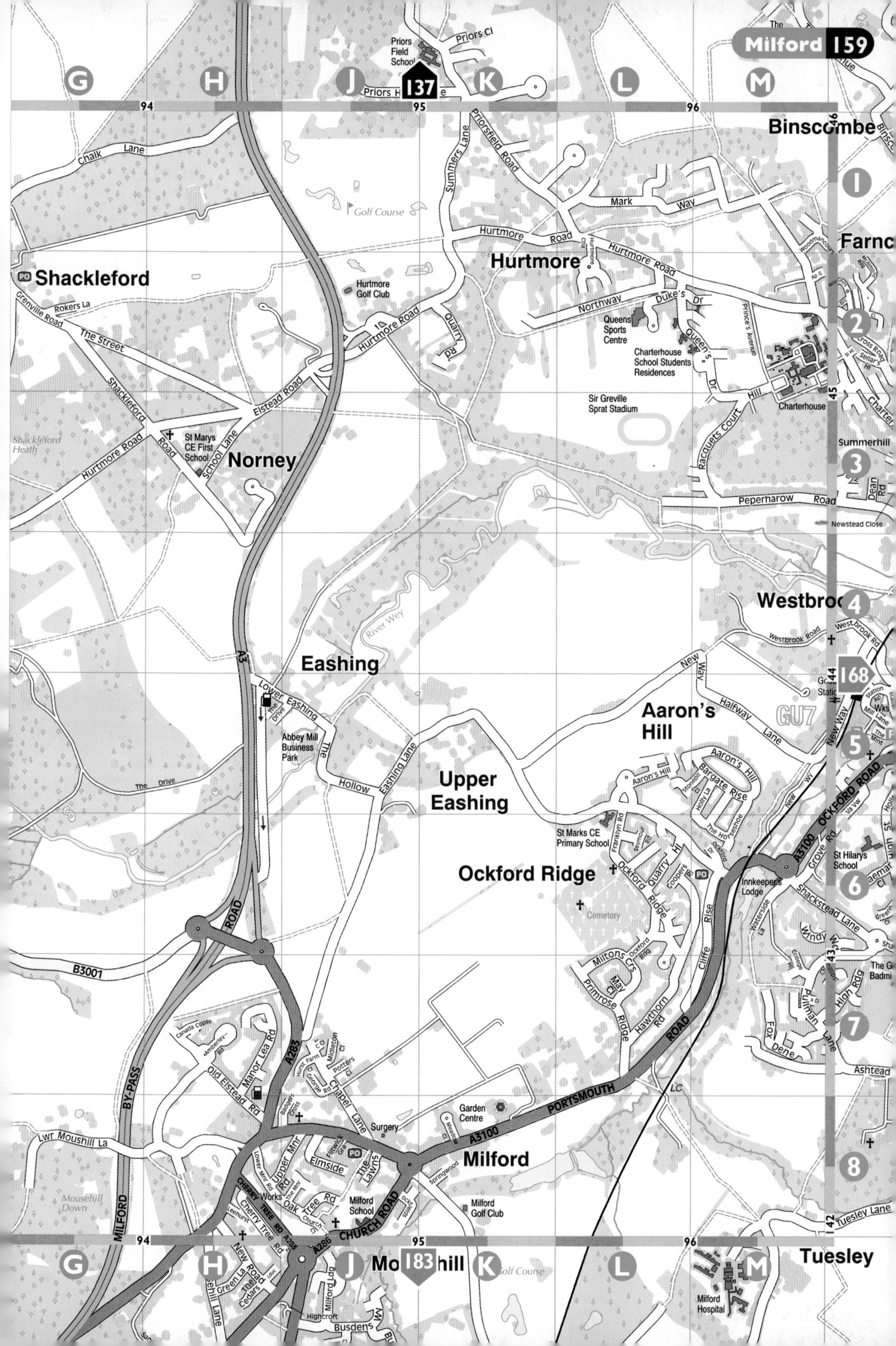
137
Priors Field School
Priors Cl
Binscombe
Chalk Lane
Golf Course
Summers Lane
Priorsfield Road
Mark Way
Hurtmore Road
Farnc
Hurtmore
Shackleford
Hurtmore Golf Club
Northway
Duke's Dr
Rokers La
Grenville Road
The Street
Hurtmore Road
Quarry Rd
Queens Sports Centre
Charterhouse School Students Residences
Queen's Dr
Prince's Avenue
Elstead Road
Shackleford Road
Sir Greville Sprat Stadium
Charterhouse
Shackleford Heath
St Marys CE First School
School Lane
Norney
Racquets Court
Summerhill
Peperharow Road
Dean Rd
Newstead Close
Westbrook Road
Westbroo
River Wey
A3
Eashing
New Way
Lower Eashing
The Drive
Abbey Mill Business Park
The Hollow
Eashing Lane
Halfway Lane
Aaron's Hill
GU7
168
The Drive
Upper Eashing
Aaron's Hill
Bargate Rise
Holly La
The Horseshoe
A3100 OCKFORD ROAD
St Marks CE Primary School
Franklyn Rd
Seymour Rd
Quarry Hl
Coopers Ri
Ockford Ridge
Ockford Ridge
Cemetery
Innkeeper's Lodge
St Hilarys School
Shackstead Lane
Waterside La
Grove Rd
Windy
ROAD
B3001
Miltons Crs
Ockford Rdg
Primrose Ridge
May Cl
Hawthorn Rd
Cliffe Rise
College Hl
High Rdg
Pullman Lane
Fox Dene
Ashtead
Canada Copse
Amberley Rd
Manor Lea Rd
A283
Old Elstead Rd
Hurst Farm Cl
Midleton Cl
Potters Cl
George Rd
Chapel Lane
Badgers Cross
PORTSMOUTH ROAD
LC
Garden Centre
BY-PASS
Lwr Moushill La
Surgery
A3100
Upper Mnr Rd
Elmside
The Lawns
Milford
Springwood
Lower Mnr Rd
Works
Oak Tree Rd
Milford School
CHURCH ROAD
Milford Golf Club
Mousehill Down
CHERRY TREE RD
Cherry Tree Rd
A286
A283
MILFORD
Tuesley Lane
New Road
Green La
The Cedars
Mo 183 hill
Golf Course
Milford Hospital
Tuesley
Busdens Wy
Highcroft
Milford Ldg
94
95
96
G H J K L M
1 2 3 4 5 6 7 8
42 43 44 45 46

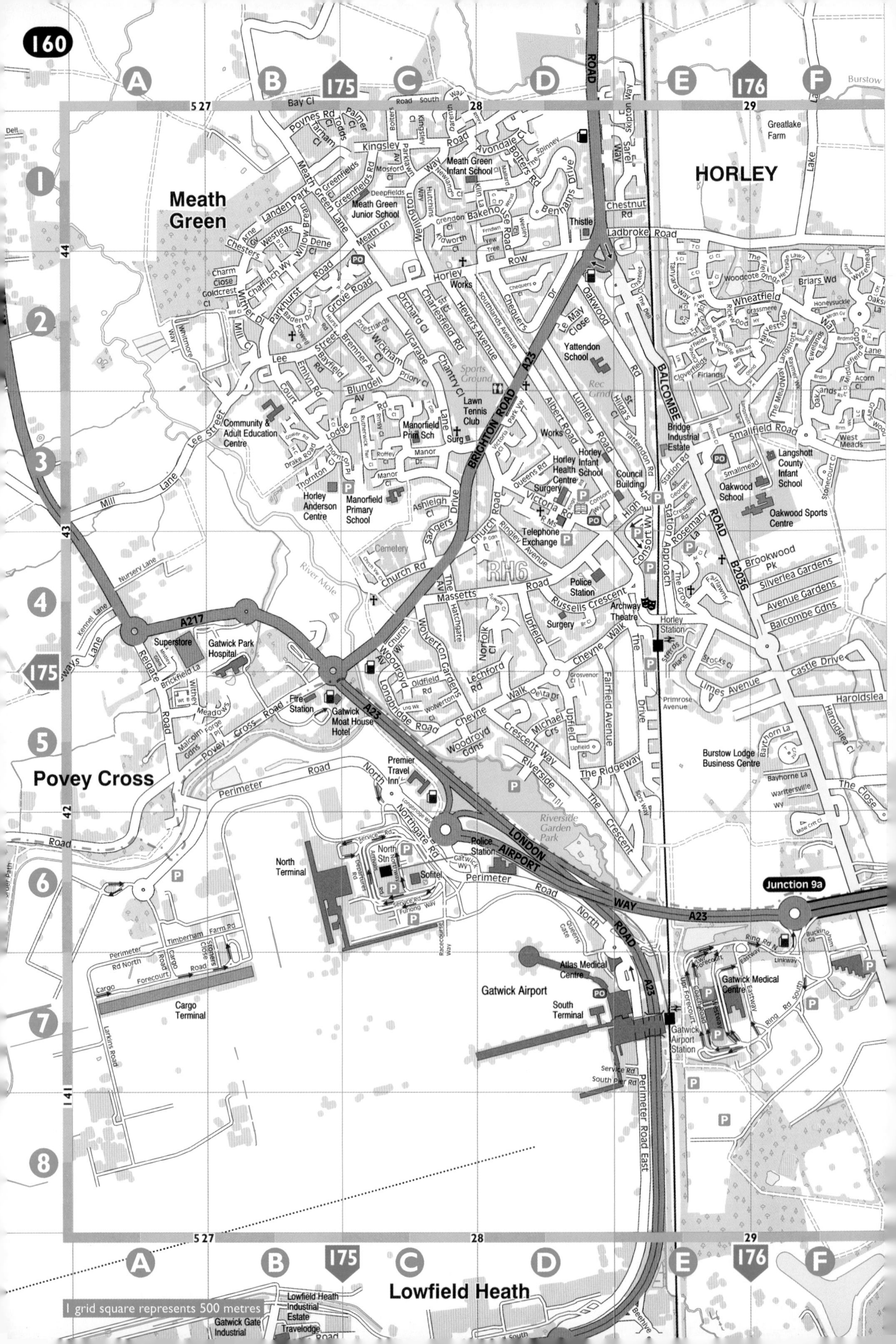

HORLEY

Meath Green

Povey Cross

Lowfield Heath

RH6

Junction 9a

1 grid square represents 500 metres

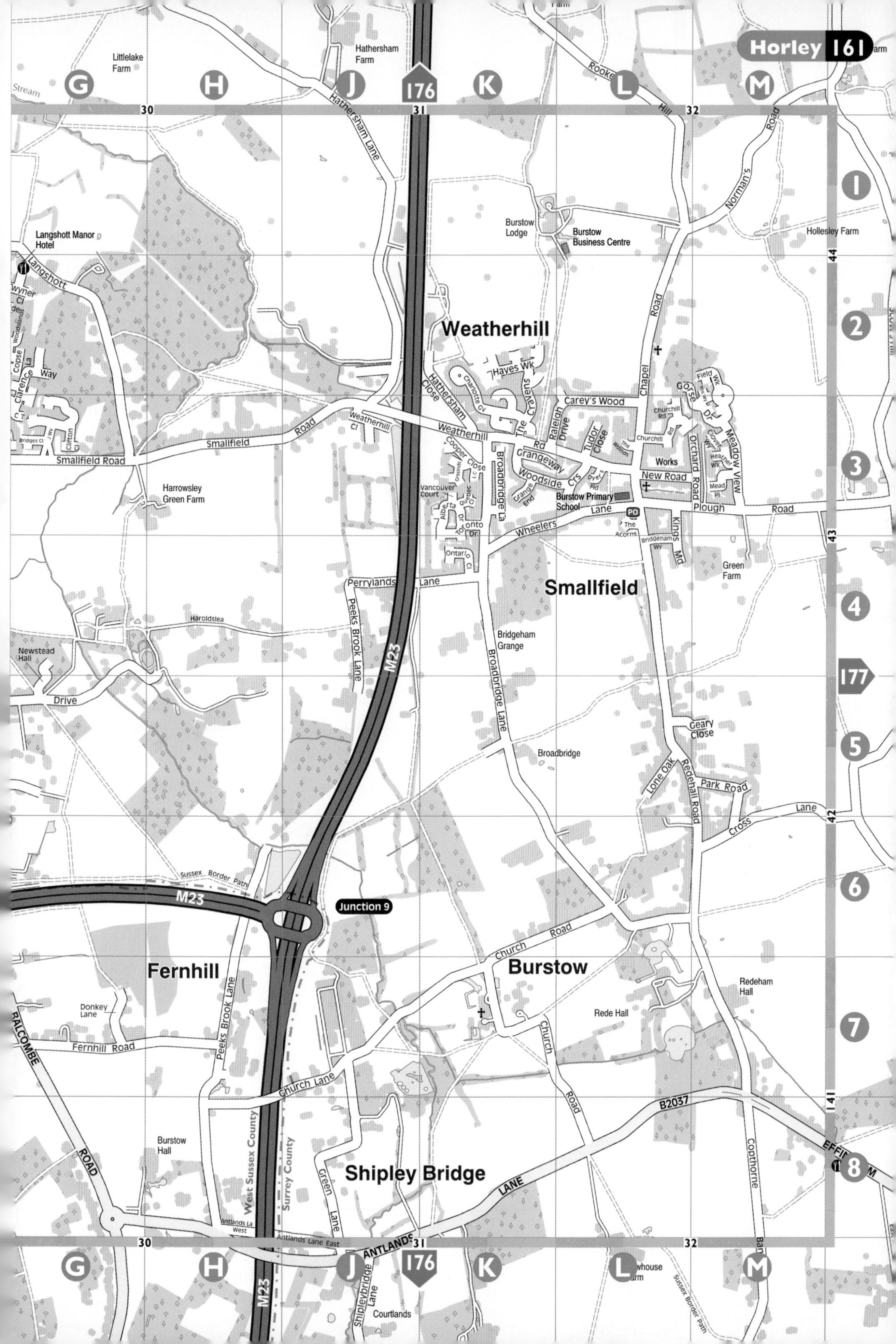

Littlelake Farm
Hathersham Farm
Stream
G
H
J
176
K
L
M
30
31
32
Hathersham Lane
Rookery Hill
Norman's Road
Langshott Manor Hotel
Langshott
Burstow Lodge
Burstow Business Centre
Hollesley Farm
44
Weatherhill
Chapel Road
Hayes Wk
Field Wk
Gorse Dr
Carey's Wood
Hathersham Close
Weatherhill Cl
Weatherhill Rd
The Cravens
Raleigh Drive
Tudor Close
Churchill Rd
Churchill
Works
Orchard Road
Meadow View
Clarence Way
Copse La
Clifton Cl
Bridges Cl
Smallfield Road
Cooper Close
Broadbridge La
Grangeway
Woodside Crs
New Road
Heather Wk
Mead Pl
Harrowsley Green Farm
Vancouver Court
Quebec Cl
Alberta Dr
Toronto Dr
Grange End
Burstow Primary School
Wheelers Lane
Plough Road
The Acorns
Kings Md
Bridgeham Wy
43
Ontario Cl
Green Farm
Perrylands Lane
Smallfield
Haroldslea
Peeks Brook Lane
M23
Bridgeham Grange
Newstead Hall
Drive
177
Broadbridge Lane
Geary Close
Broadbridge
Lone Oak
Redehall Road
Park Road
Cross Lane
42
Sussex Border Path
M23
Junction 9
Church Road
Fernhill
Burstow
Redeham Hall
Peeks Brook Lane
Donkey Lane
Rede Hall
Fernhill Road
Church Road
Ralcombe Road
Church Lane
B2037
41
Burstow Hall
West Sussex County
Surrey County
Green Lane
Shipley Bridge
Copthorne Bank
Lane
Antlands La West
Antlands Lane East
Antlands
Shipleybridge Lane
Courtlands
Sussex Border Path

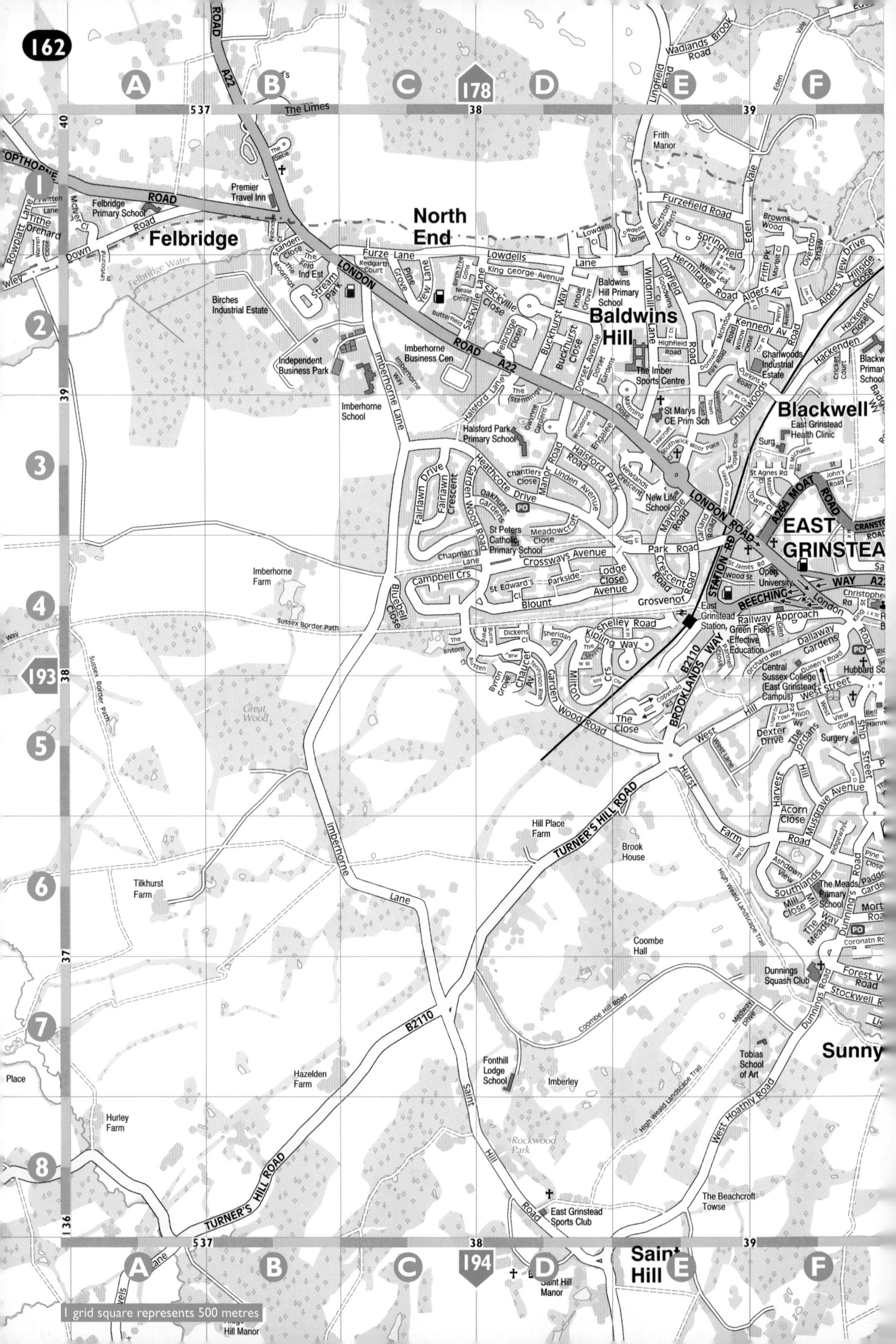
Felbridge
North End
Baldwins Hill
Blackwell
EAST GRINSTEAD
Sunny
Saint Hill
LONDON ROAD A22
COPTHORNE ROAD
TURNER'S HILL ROAD
B2110
Imberhorne Lane
Saint Hill Road
West Hoathly Road
Felbridge Primary School
Premier Travel Inn
Birches Industrial Estate
Independent Business Park
Imberhorne Business Cen
Imberhorne School
Halsford Park Primary School
Baldwins Hill Primary School
The Imber Sports Centre
St Marys CE Prim Sch
St Peters Catholic Primary School
New Life School
East Grinstead Health Clinic
Charlwoods Industrial Estate
Open University
East Grinstead Station
Green Field Effective Education
Central Sussex College (East Grinstead Campus)
The Meads Primary School
Dunnings Squash Club
Tobias School of Art
East Grinstead Sports Club
Saint Hill Manor
Imberhorne Farm
Tilkhurst Farm
Hazelden Farm
Hurley Farm
Hill Place Farm
Brook House
Coombe Hall
Fonthill Lodge School
Imberley
Rockwood Park
Great Wood
The Beachcroft Towse
Frith Manor
Sussex Border Path
High Weald Landscape Trail
Felbridge Water
1 grid square represents 500 metres

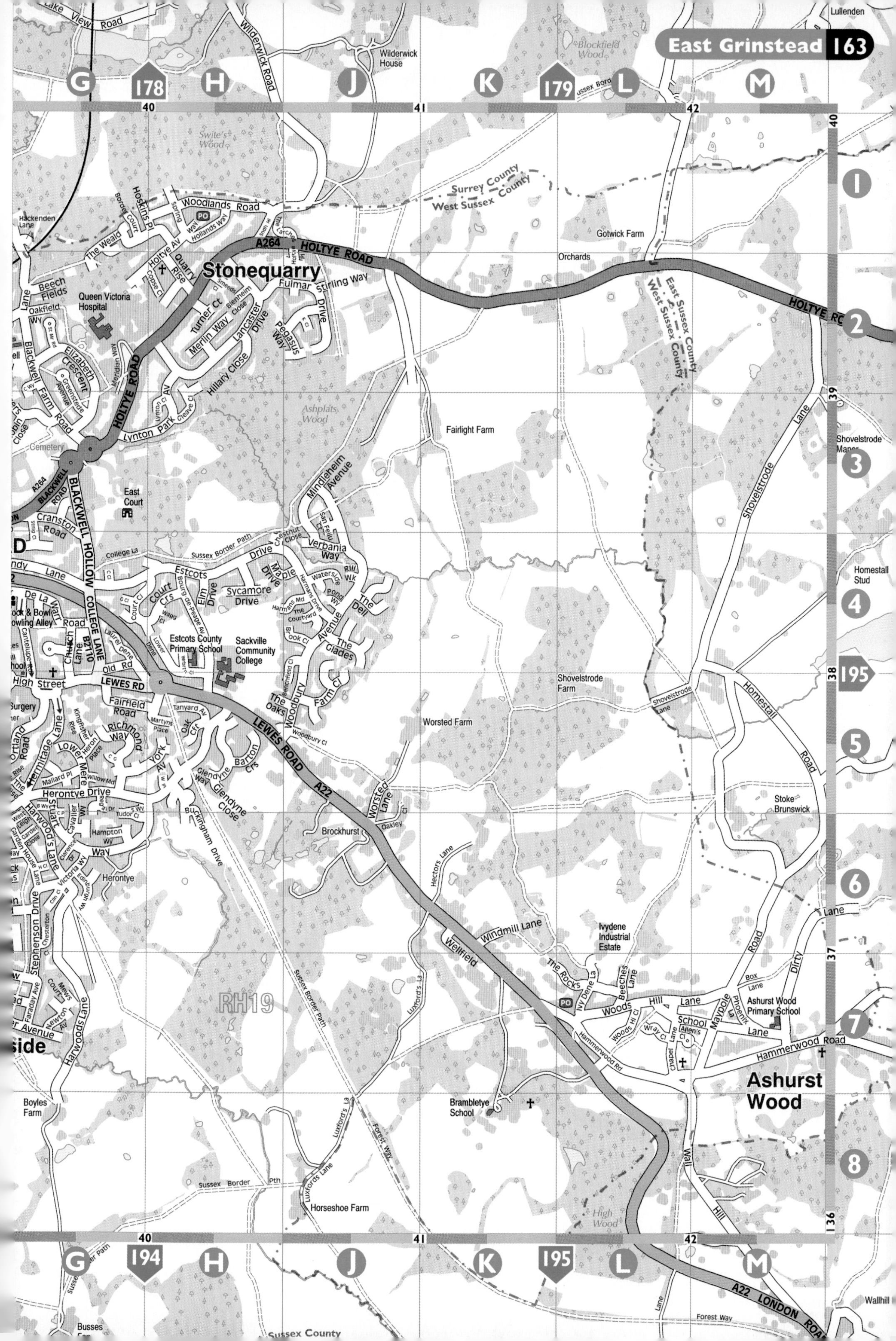

Stonequarry
Ashurst Wood
HOLTYE ROAD
A264
LEWES ROAD
A22
A22 LONDON ROAD
BLACKWELL HOLLOW
COLLEGE LANE
B2110
Surrey County
West Sussex County
East Sussex County
Queen Victoria Hospital
Estcots County Primary School
Sackville Community College
Gotwick Farm
Orchards
Fairlight Farm
Shovelstrode Farm
Worsted Farm
Brockhurst
Stoke Brunswick
Ivydene Industrial Estate
Ashurst Wood Primary School
Brambletye School
Horseshoe Farm
Boyles Farm
Homestall Stud
Shovelstrode Manor
Wilderwick House
Lullenden
Wallhill
Herontye
Cemetery
East Court
Swite's Wood
Ashplats Wood
Blockfield Wood
High Wood
RH19
Woodlands Road
Mindleheim Avenue
Verbania Way
Estcots Drive
Sycamore Drive
Windmill Lane
Woods Hill Lane
Hammerwood Road
School Lane
Maypole Rd
Dirty Lane
Homestall Road
Shovelstrode Lane
Hectors Lane
Luxford's Lane
Forest Way
Sussex Border Path
Wellfield
Worsted Lane
Buckingham Drive
Glendyne Close
Barton Crs
Herontye Drive
Harwoods Lane
Stephenson Drive
Lynton Park
Hillary Close
Lancaster Drive
Merlin Way
Turner Ct
Pegasus Way
Fulmar Drive
Stirling Way
Elizabeth Crescent
Blackwell Farm Road
Beech Fields
Cranston Road
De La Warr Road
High Street
Fairfield Road
Richmond Way
Hermitage Lane
Old Rd
178
179
194
195
163

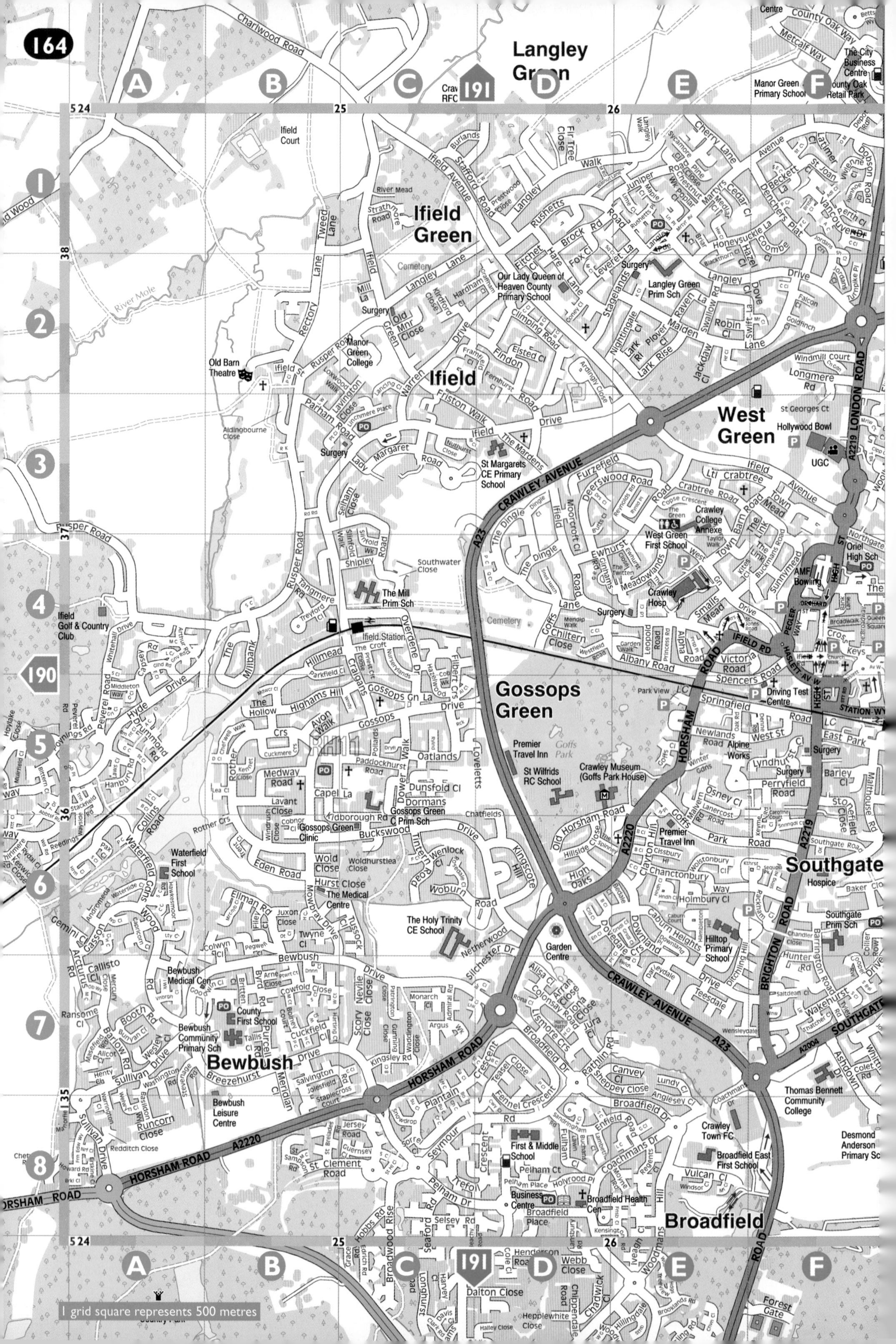

164
Langley Green
191
Ifield Green
Ifield
West Green
Gossops Green
Southgate
Bewbush
Broadfield
190
Crawley Avenue
A23
Horsham Road
A2220
London Road
A2219
Brighton Road
Ifield Avenue
Charlwood Road
Rusper Road
Ifield Court
Old Barn Theatre
Manor Green College
St Margarets CE Primary School
Our Lady Queen of Heaven County Primary School
Langley Green Prim Sch
The Mill Prim Sch
Ifield Station
Ifield Golf & Country Club
West Green First School
Crawley College Annexe
Crawley Hosp
Hollywood Bowl
UGC
Oriel High Sch
Premier Travel Inn
St Wilfrids RC School
Crawley Museum (Goffs Park House)
Gossops Green C Prim Sch
Gossops Green Clinic
The Medical Centre
The Holy Trinity CE School
Waterfield First School
Bewbush Medical Cen
County First School
Bewbush Community Primary Sch
Bewbush Leisure Centre
Garden Centre
Hilltop Primary School
Southgate Prim Sch
Hospice
Thomas Bennett Community College
Crawley Town FC
Broadfield East First School
First & Middle School
Broadfield Health Cen
Business Centre
Driving Test Centre
Manor Green Primary School
The City Business Centre
County Oak Retail Park
Desmond Anderson Primary Sc
Forest Gate
1 grid square represents 500 metres

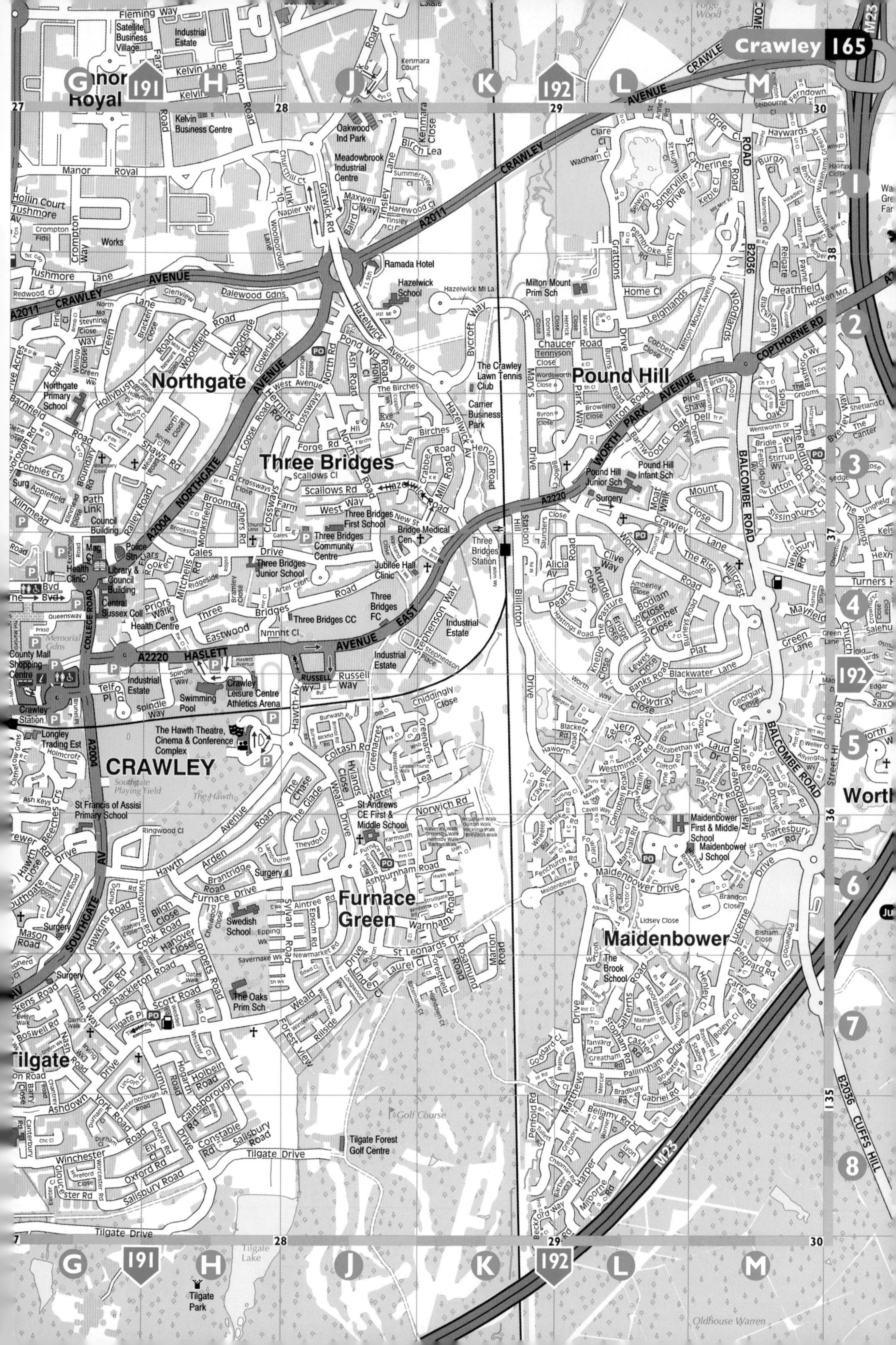
G
191
H
J
K
192
L
M
Manor Royal
Fleming Way
Satellite Business Village
Industrial Estate
Kelvin Business Centre
Newton Road
Oakwood Ind Park
Meadowbrook Industrial Centre
Kenmara Court
Crompton Way
Works
Tushmore Lane
CRAWLEY AVENUE
A2011
Ramada Hotel
Hazelwick School
Milton Mount Prim Sch
Northgate
Northgate Primary School
Three Bridges
Pound Hill
The Crawley Lawn Tennis Club
Carrier Business Park
Three Bridges First School
Three Bridges Community Centre
Three Bridges Junior School
Bridge Medical Cen
Jubilee Hall Clinic
Three Bridges Station
Three Bridges FC
Three Bridges CC
Industrial Estate
Pound Hill Junior Sch
Pound Hill Infant Sch
Surgery
WORTH PARK AVENUE
A2220
BALCOMBE ROAD
B2036
COPTHORNE RD
Council Building
Police Stn
Library & Council Building
Health Clinic
Central Sussex Coll
Health Centre
County Mall Shopping Centre
Crawley Station
Longley Trading Est
HASLETT AVENUE EAST
A2220
COLLEGE ROAD
A2004
NORTHGATE AVENUE
Crawley Leisure Centre Athletics Arena
Swimming Pool
The Hawth Theatre, Cinema & Conference Complex
CRAWLEY
Southgate Playing Field
The Hawth
St Francis of Assisi Primary School
Hawth Avenue
St Andrews CE First & Middle School
Furnace Green
Swedish School
The Oaks Prim Sch
Maidenbower
Maidenbower First & Middle School
Maidenbower J School
The Brook School
SOUTHGATE AV
Tilgate
Tilgate Drive
Tilgate Forest Golf Centre
Golf Course
M23
B2036 CUFFS HILL
Worth
Tilgate Lake
Tilgate Park
Oldhouse Warren
27
28
29
30
35
36
37
38
2
3
4
5
6
7
8

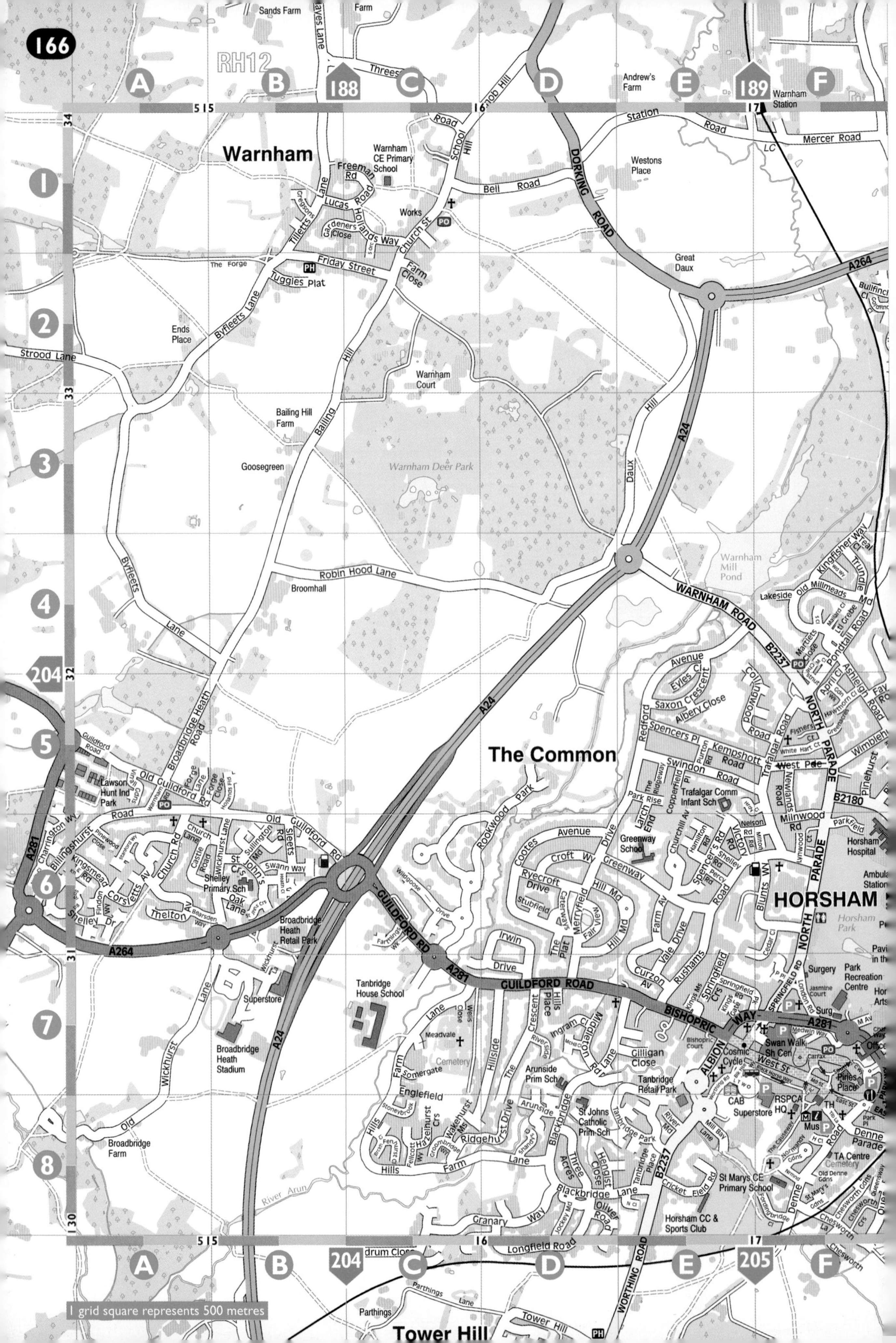

Warnham
The Common
HORSHAM
Tower Hill
Warnham Deer Park
Warnham Mill Pond
Broadbridge Heath Stadium
Tanbridge House School
Horsham Hospital
Broadbridge Heath Retail Park
Tanbridge Retail Park
Swan Walk Sh Cen
Horsham CC & Sports Club
St Marys CE Primary School
Warnham CE Primary School
Shelley Primary Sch
Trafalgar Comm Infant Sch
Greenway School
Arunside Prim Sch
St Johns Catholic Prim Sch
Warnham Station
DORKING ROAD
WARNHAM ROAD
GUILDFORD ROAD
BISHOPRIC
ALBION WAY
NORTH PARADE
WORTHING ROAD
A24
A264
A281
B2237
Robin Hood Lane
Byfleets Lane
Broadbridge Heath Road
Friday Street
Bell Road
Station Road
Mercer Road
Strood Lane
Ends Place
Goosegreen
Broomhall
Bailing Hill Farm
Warnham Court
Great Daux
Weston's Place
Andrew's Farm
Broadbridge Farm
Parthings
Cemetery
River Arun
1 grid square represents 500 metres

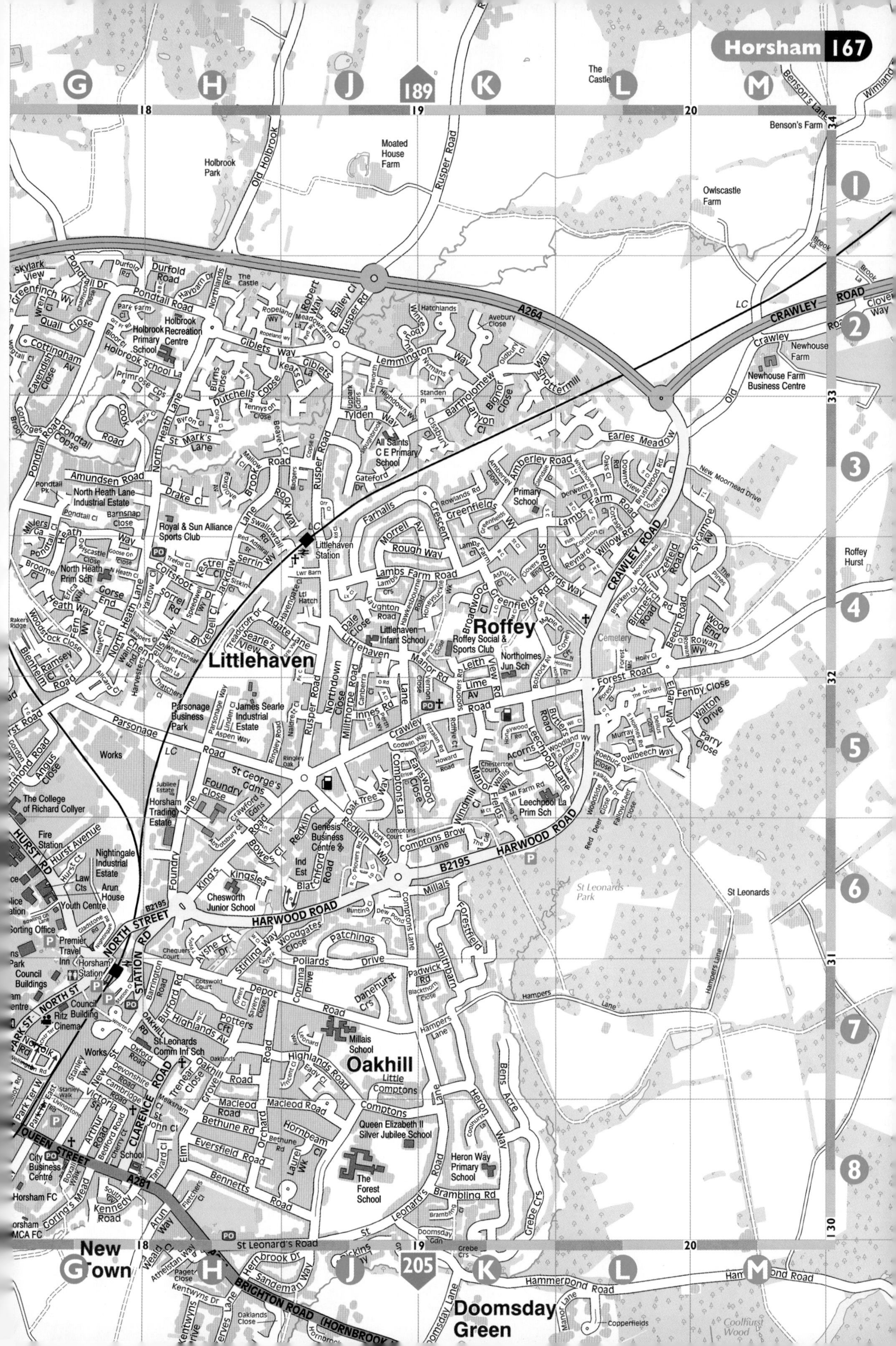

G H J 189 K L M

Benson's Lane
Wimland
Benson's Farm

The Castle
Owlscastle Farm

I

Holbrook Park

Moated House Farm

Old Holbrook
Rusper Road

Brook La
LC
CRAWLEY ROAD
Clover Way

2

Crawley
Newhouse Farm
Newhouse Farm Business Centre

A264

Skylark View
Greenfinch Wy
Wren Cl
Quail Close
Cottingham Av
Cavendish Close

Pondtail Dr
Durfold Road
Durfold Road
Haybarn Dr
Northlands

The Castle
Robert Way
Bailey Cl
Rusper Rd

Ropeland Meadow Wy
Ropeland Wy

Hatchlands
Avebury Close

Lemmington Way
Nymans
Standen Pl
Bartholomew Way
Bignor Close
Lynton Cl
Shottermill Way

Earles Meadow
New Moorhead Drive

Roffey Hurst

3

Park Farm
Holbrook Primary Centre
Holbrook Recreation
Holbrook School La

Giblets Way
Giblets La
Keats La
Burns Close

Dutchells Copse
Tennys Close

Tylden Way
All Saints C E Primary School
Gateford Dr

Peworth
Highdown Wy

Primary School

Amberley Road
Amberley Road
Greenfields
Willow Rd
Lambs Farm Road
Crawley Road
Downsview
Brushwood Rd
Oaks Rd
Cotman
Reynard
Lambs Farm Rd

Primrose Cps
St Mark's Lane
Byron Cl

Beaver Cl
Rusper Road
Rook Way

Rowlands Rd
Greenfields
Lambs Farm Road

Sycamore Av
The Pines
Wood End
Rowan Wy

4

North Heath Prim Sch
Gorse End
Heath Way
Fern Way
Ramsey Road
Blenheim Road
Woodstock Close

Drake Cl
Amundsen Road
North Heath Lane Industrial Estate
Pondtail Cl
Barnsnap Close
Pondtail Pk
Heath Way
Broome
Pondtail
North Heath Lane
Gorse End
Chennells

Royal & Sun Alliance Sports Club
PO
Trefoil Cl
Coltsfoot Rd
Kestrel Cl
Serrin Wy
Lwr Barn

Littlehaven Station

Farnalls
Morrell Av
Rough Way
Lambs Cl
Ltl Hatch

Laughton Road
Littlehaven Infant School

Crescent
Shepherds Way
Broadwood
Greenfields

Church Rd
Birches
Beech Road

Cemetery

Roffey
Northolmes Jun Sch
Roffey Social & Sports Club

Forest Road
The Orchard

Fenby Close
Walton Drive
Parry Close
Owlbeech Way
Roebuck Close
Fallow Deer Close

5

The College of Richard Collyer
Fire Station
Hurst Rd
Hurst Avenue
Nightingale Industrial Estate

Parsonage Business Park
James Searle Industrial Estate
Parsonage Road
Searle's View
Agate Lane
Dale Close
Innes Rd
Canberra
Vernon Rd
PO
Crawley Road
Godwin Way

Leith View
Lime Av
Manor Road

Chesterton Court
Wallis
Leechpool La Prim Sch

Leechpool Lane
Woodland Wy
Windmill

St Leonards Park
St Leonards

6

Law Cts
Arun House
Youth Centre
Sorting Office
Premier Travel Inn
Horsham Station

Foundry Close
Horsham Trading Estate
St George's Cns
Foundry Lane
Crawford Gdns
King's
Kingslea
Chesworth Junior School

Genesis Business Centre
Ind Est
Redkiln Close
Bower
Redkiln Way
Comptons Brow Lane
HARWOOD ROAD
B2195

Comptons Court

7

Council Buildings
North St
Ritz Cinema
Station Rd
North Street
B2195

HARWOOD ROAD
Ayshe Ct Dr
Stirling Way
Woodgates Close
Pollards
Patchings Drive

Depot
Coruna Drive
Danehurst Crs
Padwick Rd
Blackthorn Close

Hampers Lane
Hampers

8

Park
City Business Centre
Horsham FC
Horsham MCA FC

Highlands Av
St Leonards Comm Inf Sch
Oxford Road
Potters Crt
Highlands Road
Macleod Road
Bethune Rd
Eversfield Road
Bennetts Road

Oakhill
Little Comptons
Comptons
Queen Elizabeth II Silver Jubilee School
The Forest School

Millais School
Smitham Lane
Bens Acre
Heron Way
Heron Way Primary School
Brambling Rd
Grebe Crs

QUEEN STREET
A281
Arun Way
St Leonard's Road
PO
Brighton Road (Hornbrook)
Athelstan Way
Paget Cl
Kentwyns Rise
Oaklands Close

Weald
Hornbrook Dr
Sandeman Way
Perkins
Doomsday La
Grebe Crs

Doomsday Green
Manor Lane
Copperfields
Hammerpond Road
Coolhurst Wood

New Town
G H 18 J 205 K 19 L 20 M

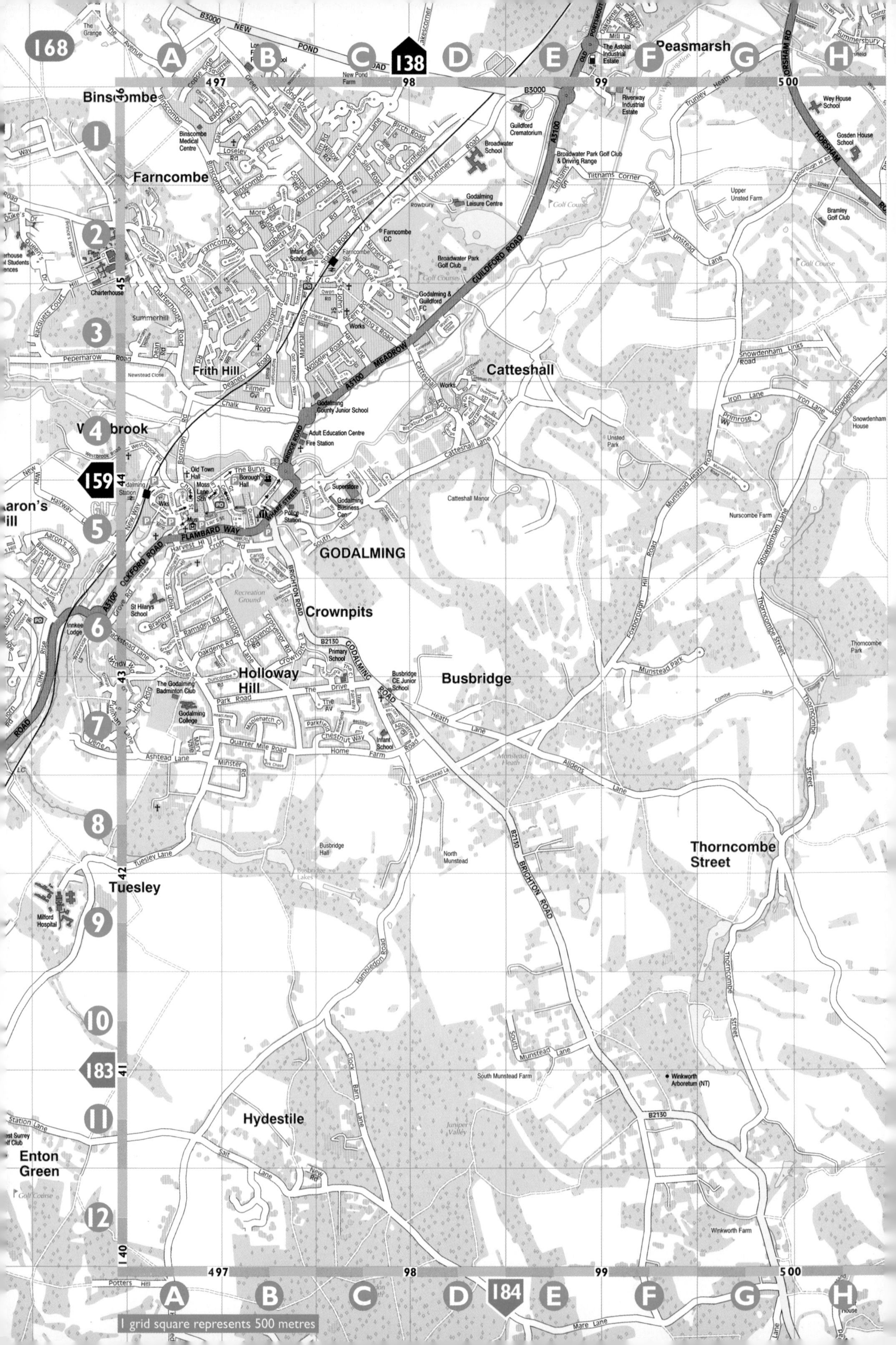

168
138
159
183
184
A
B
C
D
E
F
G
H
1
2
3
4
5
6
7
8
9
10
11
12
497
98
99
500
46
45
44
43
42
41
40
Binscombe
Farncombe
Peasmarsh
Frith Hill
Catteshall
GODALMING
Crownpits
Holloway Hill
Busbridge
Tuesley
Thorncombe Street
Hydestile
Enton Green
Summerhill
Charterhouse
Milford Hospital
Winkworth Arboretum (NT)
Busbridge Hall
North Munstead
South Munstead Farm
Catteshall Manor
Nurscombe Farm
Thorncombe Park
Snowdenham House
Upper Unsted Farm
Winkworth Farm
Godalming Leisure Centre
Broadwater School
Guildford Crematorium
Broadwater Park Golf Club & Driving Range
Broadwater Park Golf Club
Godalming & Guildford FC
Godalming County Junior School
Adult Education Centre
Fire Station
Superstore
Police Station
Godalming College
The Godalming Badminton Club
St Hilarys School
Wey House School
Gosden House School
Bramley Golf Club
Riverway Industrial Estate
The Astolat Industrial Estate
Binscombe Medical Centre
Farncombe CC
Busbridge CE Junior School
B3000
A3100
B2130
NEW POND ROAD
GUILDFORD ROAD
MEADROW
BRIDGE ROAD
FLAMBARD WAY
OCKFORD ROAD
BRIGHTON ROAD
GODALMING ROAD
HORSHAM RD
Peperharow Road
Chalk Road
Catteshall Lane
Munstead Heath Road
Snowdenham Links Road
Iron Lane
Alldens Lane
Heath Lane
Quarter Mile Road
Home Farm Road
Park Road
Hambledon Road
Clock Barn Lane
Salt Lane
Station Lane
Tuesley Lane
Ashtead Lane
Munstead Park
South Munstead Lane
Mare Lane
Potters Hill
1 grid square represents 500 metres

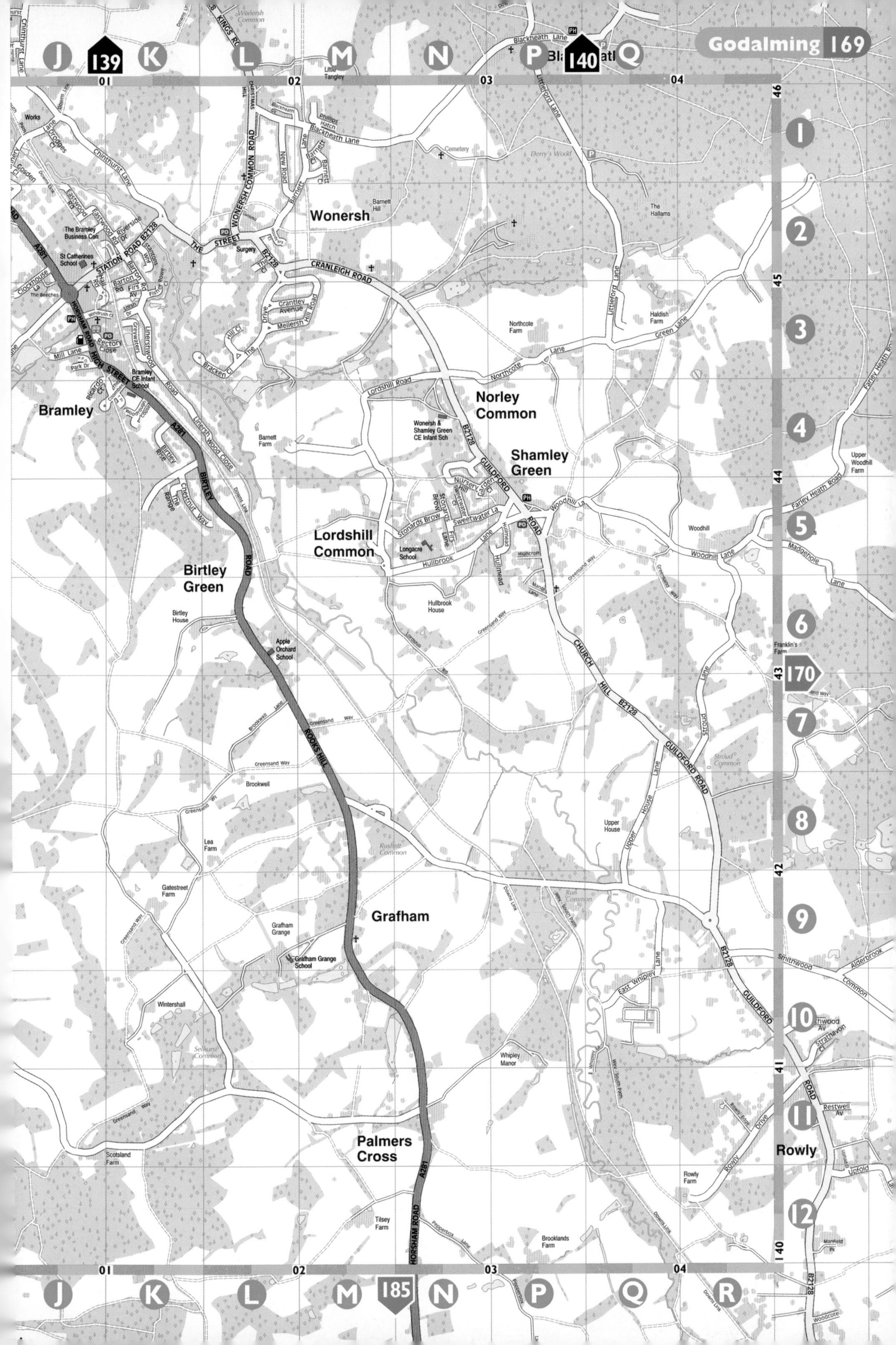

J **139** K L M N P **140** Q

01 02 03 04

I
2
3
4
5
6 **170**
7
8
9
10
11
12

46
45
44
43
42
41
140

Wonersh

Bramley

Norley Common

Shamley Green

Lordshill Common

Birtley Green

Grafham

Palmers Cross

Rowly

St Catherines School
The Bramley Business Cen
STATION ROAD B2128
Barton Rd
Rectory Close
HIGH STREET
Mill Lane
Park Dr
Bramley CE Infant School
The Beeches
Clockhouse
A281
Linersh Wood Close
Chestnut Way
BIRTLEY ROAD
Birtley Rise
Birtley House
Apple Orchard School
Lea Farm
Gatestreet Farm
Wintershall
Scotsland Farm
Greensand Way
Greensand Wy
Brookwell
Greensand Way
ROOKS HILL
Greensand Way
Gratham Grange
Gratham Grange School
Tilsey Farm
HORSHAM ROAD
A281

THE STREET
WONERSH COMMON ROAD
New Road
Blackheath Lane
Barnett
Little Tangley
Blackheath Lane
Blackheath
PH
Littleford Lane
Derry's Wood
P
Cemetery
The Hallams
Barnett Hill
Surgery
Grantley Avenue
Mellersh Cl
Mill Ct
The Drive
CRANLEIGH ROAD
Barnett Farm
Lordshill Road
Wonersh & Shamley Green CE Infant Sch
GUILDFORD
Stortords Brow
Sweetwater La
Nursery
Longacre School
Hullbrook
Hullmead
Hullbrook House
PO
PH
Highcroft
ROAD
Woodhill
Woodhill
Woodhill Lane
Maddehole Lane
CHURCH HILL B2128
GUILDFORD ROAD
Stroud
Stroud Common
Upper House
Rushett Common
Run Common
East Whipley
Whipley Manor
Smithwood Common
Strathavon
Alderbrook Common
B2128
Rowly Farm
Restwell Av
Roxby Drive
Upfold
Manfield Pk
B2128
Northcote Farm
Northcote Lane
Haldish Farm
Green Lane
Farley Heath Road
Upper Woodhill Farm
Franklin's Farm
2nd Way

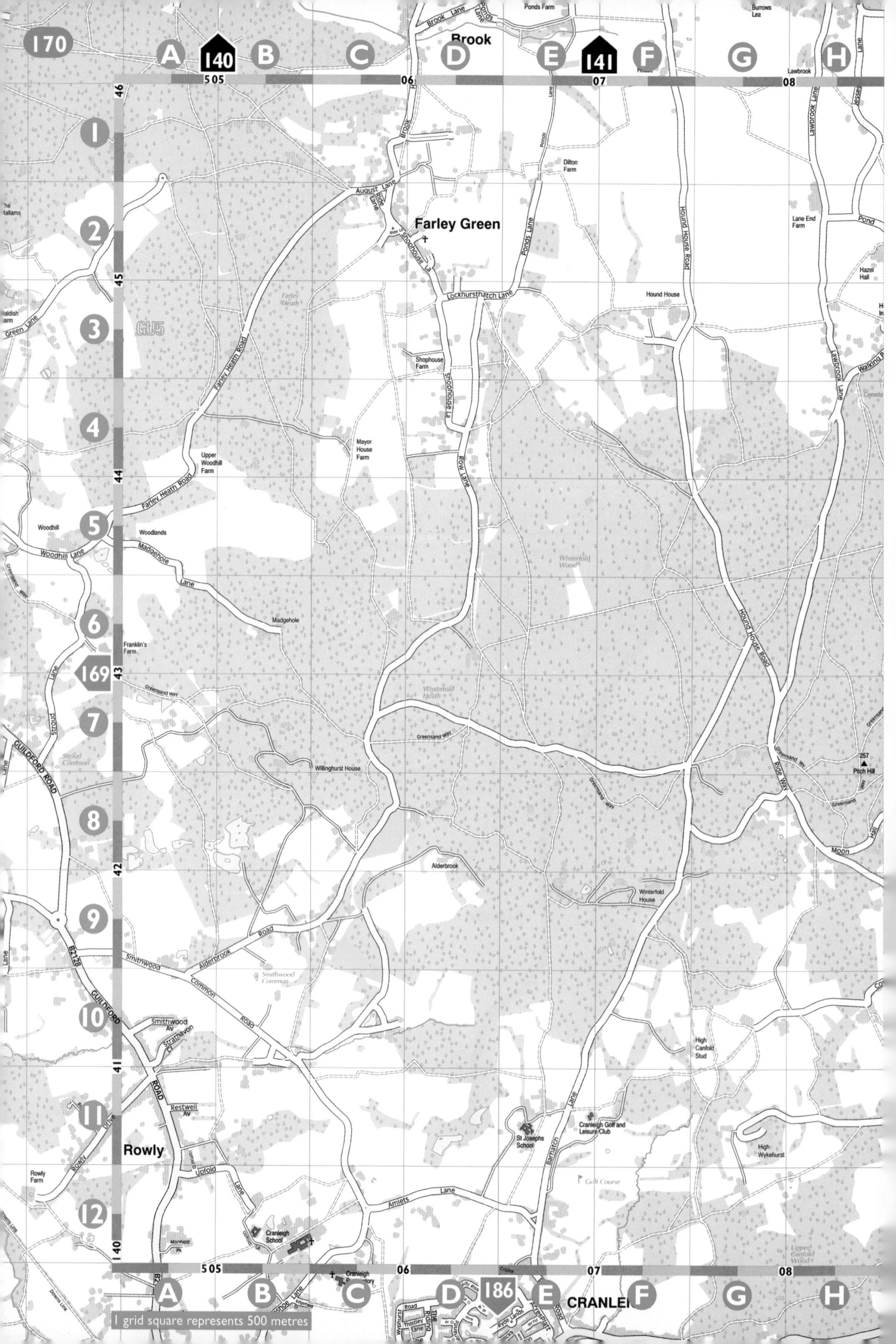

170
140
141
169
186
Brook
Farley Green
Rowly
CRANLEIGH
Ponds Farm
Burrows Lea
Lawbrook
Dilton Farm
Lane End Farm
Hazel Hall
Hound House
Shophouse Farm
Mayor House Farm
Upper Woodhill Farm
Woodhill
Woodlands
Madgehole
Franklin's Farm
Winterfold Wood
Winterfold Heath
Willinghurst House
Alderbrook
Winterfold House
Pitch Hill
Smithwood Common
Stroud Common
High Canfold Stud
High Wykehurst
St Josephs School
Cranleigh Golf and Leisure Club
Golf Course
Cranleigh School
Rowly Farm
Upper Canfold Wood
GU5
Brook Lane
August Lane
Farley Heath Road
Lockhursthatch Lane
Shophouse La
Row Lane
Ponds Lane
Hound House Road
Lawbrook Lane
Ride Way
Madgehole Lane
Woodhill Lane
Greensand Way
GUILDFORD ROAD
B2128
Smithwood Common Road
Alderbrook Road
Smithwood Av
Strathavon Cl
Restwell Av
Upfold Lane
Amlets Lane
Barnhatch Lane
Rowly Drive
Stroud Lane
1 grid square represents 500 metres

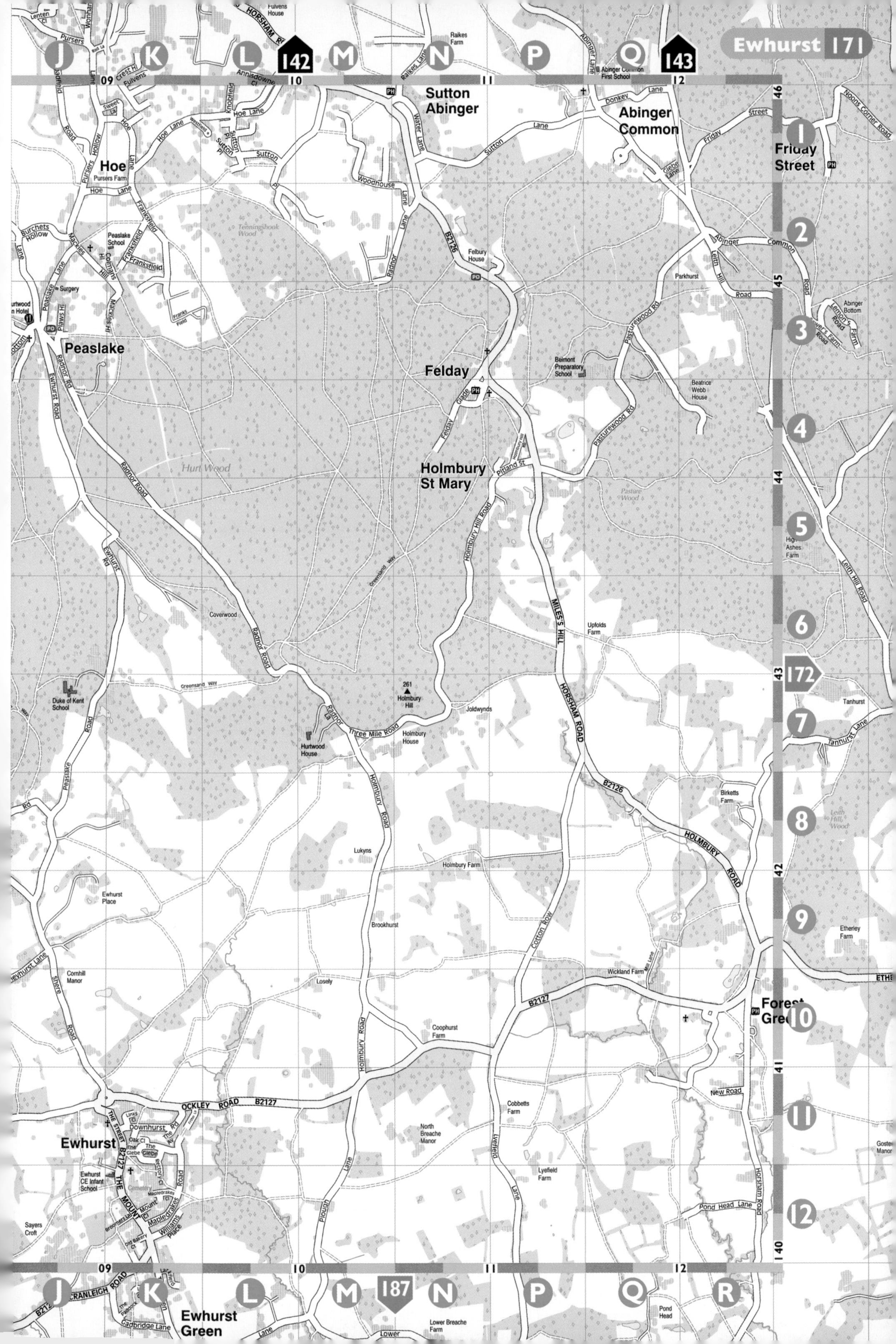
J
K
L
142
M
N
P
Q
143
09
10
11
12
Sutton Abinger
Abinger Common
Friday Street
Hoe
Peaslake
Felday
Holmbury St Mary
Hurt Wood
Tenningshook Wood
Pasture Wood
Leith Hill Wood
Coverwood
Upfolds Farm
Duke of Kent School
Holmbury Hill
Hurtwood House
Holmbury House
Joldwynds
Lukyns
Holmbury Farm
Birketts Farm
Brookhurst
Ewhurst Place
Cornhill Manor
Losely
Wickland Farm
Coophurst Farm
Cobbetts Farm
North Breache Manor
Lyefield Farm
Ewhurst
Ewhurst CE Infant School
Sayers Croft
Etherley Farm
Tanhurst
High Ashes Farm
Beatrice Webb House
Belmont Preparatory School
Parkhurst
Felbury House
Pursers Farm
Peaslake School
Surgery
Abinger Common First School
Raikes Farm
Fulvens House
Abinger Bottom
HORSHAM ROAD
MILES'S HILL
B2126
B2127
HOLMBURY ROAD
OCKLEY ROAD
THE MOUNT
THE STREET
Radnor Road
Ewhurst Road
Peaslake Road
Shere Road
Holmbury Road
Three Mile Road
Holmbury Hill Road
Cotton Row
Lyefield Lane
Plough Lane
Horsham Road
Pond Head Lane
New Road
Leith Hill Road
Abinger Common Road
Pasturewood Rd
Sutton Lane
Hoe Lane
Franksfield
Woodhouse Lane
Water Lane
Radnor Lane
Friday Street
Donkey Lane
Tanhurst Lane
Greensand Way
Forest Green
172
1
2
3
4
5
6
7
8
9
10
11
12
46
45
44
43
42
41
140
R
187
Ewhurst Green
CRANLEIGH ROAD
Cadbridge Lane
Pond Head
Lower Breache Farm
Gosterwood Manor

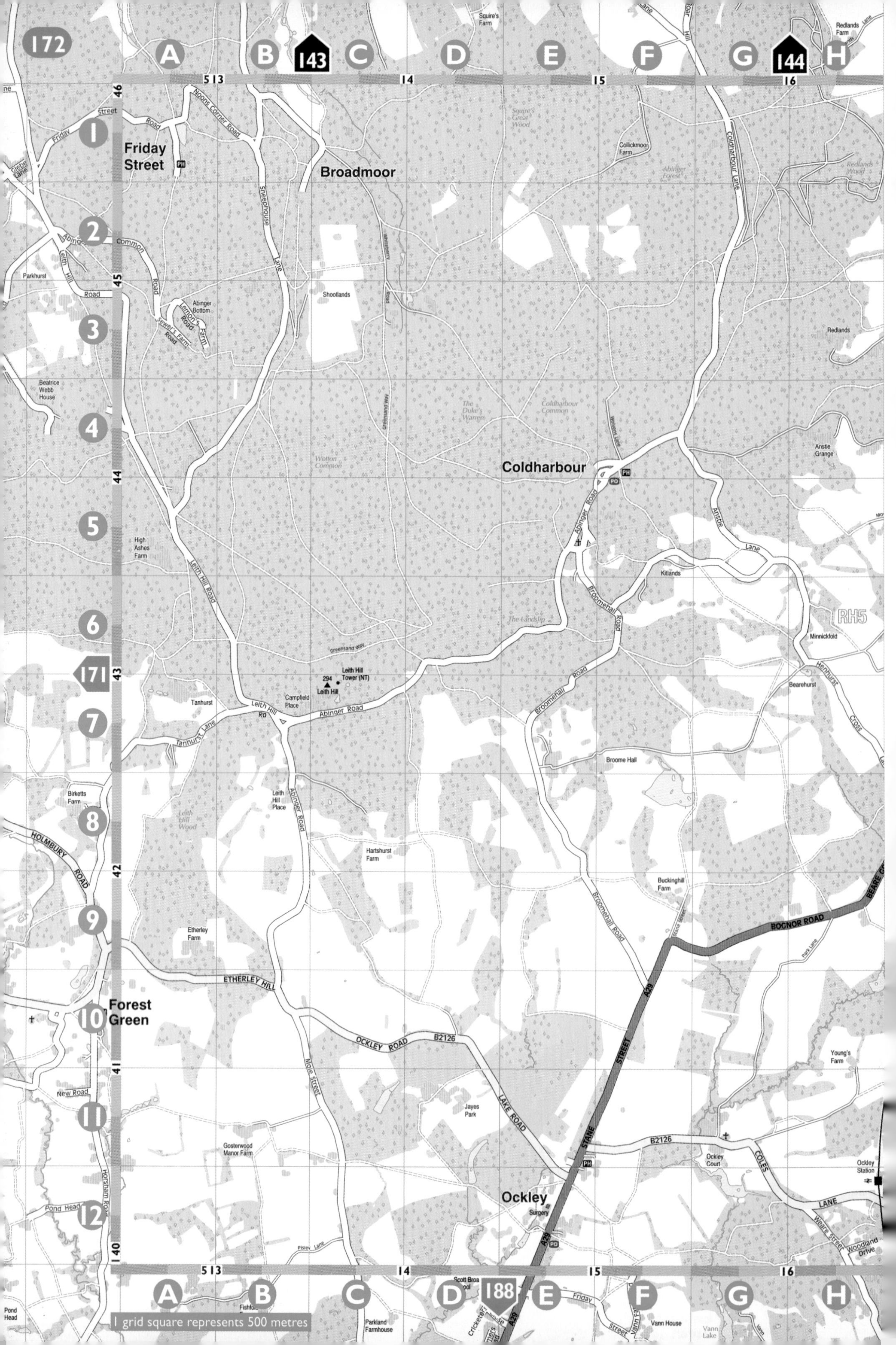
172
143
144
171
188
Friday Street
Broadmoor
Coldharbour
Forest Green
Ockley
Leith Hill
Leith Hill Tower (NT)
294
Campfield Place
Leith Hill Place
Leith Hill Wood
Abinger Bottom
Parkhurst
Beatrice Webb House
High Ashes Farm
Tanhurst
Birketts Farm
Etherley Farm
Gosterwood Manor Farm
Hartshurst Farm
Jayes Park
Shootlands
Squire's Farm
Squire's Great Wood
Collickmoor Farm
Abinger Forest
Redlands Farm
Redlands Wood
Redlands
Anstie Grange
Kitlands
Minnickfold
Bearehurst
Broome Hall
Buckinghill Farm
Young's Farm
Ockley Court
Ockley Station
Surgery
Vann House
Vann Lake
Parkland Farmhouse
Pond Head
The Duke's Warren
Coldharbour Common
Wotton Common
The Landslip
Greensand Way
RH5
Noons Corner Road
Sheephouse Lane
Leith Hill Road
Abinger Road
Broomehall Road
Coldharbour Lane
Anstie Lane
Henhurst Cross
Tanhurst Lane
Holmbury Road
Etherley Hill
Ockley Road B2126
Lake Road
Mole Street
Stane Street
A29
Bognor Road
Beare Green
Coles Lane
Weare Street
Woodland Drive
Horsham Road
New Road
Pond Head
Pisley Lane
Friday Street
Abinger Common Road
Sewers Farm Road
Lemon's Farm Road
Friday Road
Glebe Lane
Park Lane
1 grid square represents 500 metres

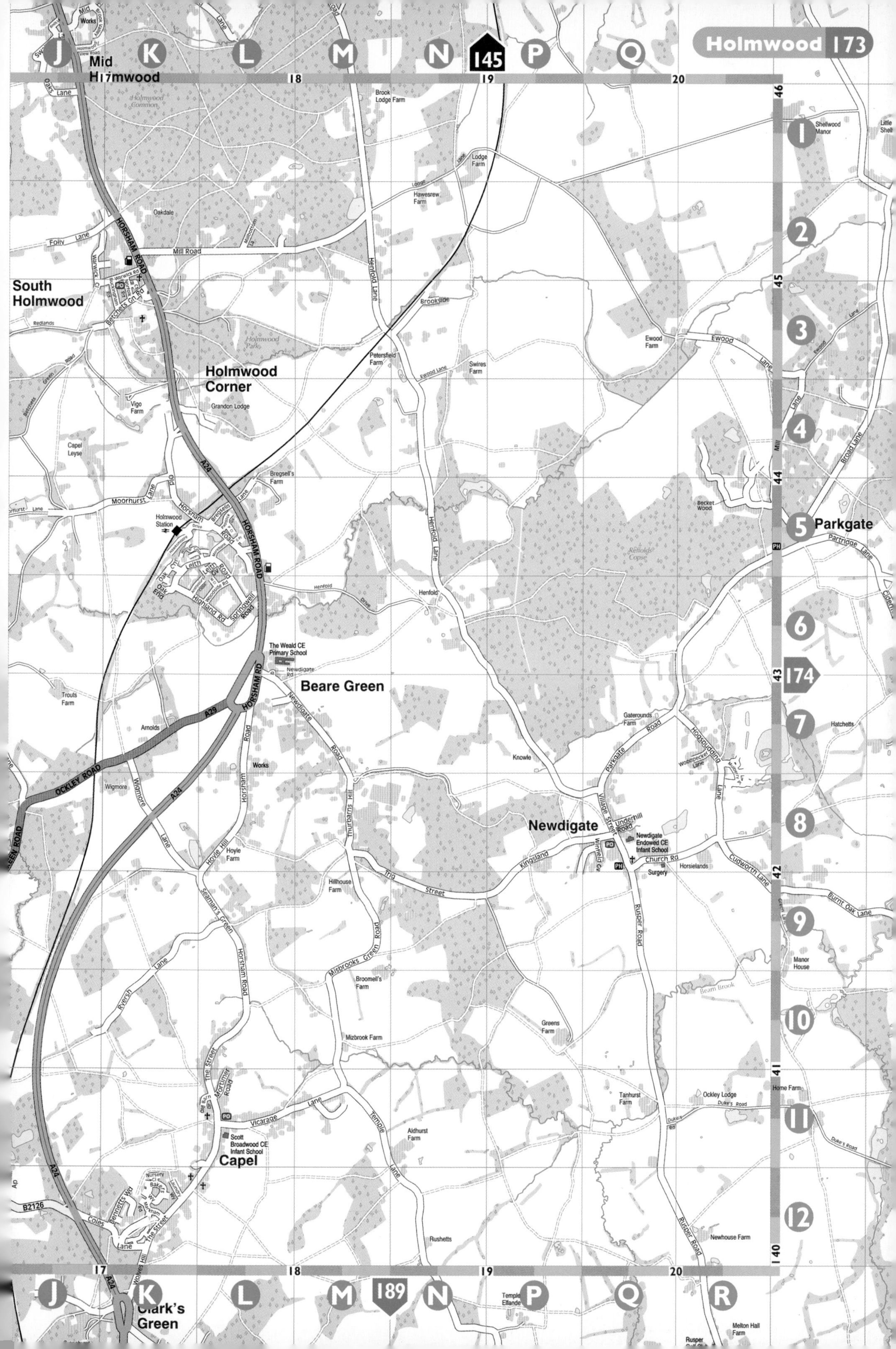

J K L M N **145** P Q

18 **19** **20**

46

1 Shellwood Manor · Little Shell

2

45

3 Ewood Farm · Ewood

4

44

5 Parkgate · Partridge Lane

6

43 **174**

7 Hatchetts

8

42

9 Manor House

10

41

11 Home Farm · Ockley Lodge · Duke's Road

12 Newhouse Farm

40

Mid Holmwood

South Holmwood

Holmwood Common

Oakdale

Folly Lane

Mill Road

Holmwood Corner

Grandon Lodge

Vigo Farm

Capel Leyse

Moorhurst Lane

Holmwood Station

Bregsell's Farm

The Weald CE Primary School

Newdigate Rd

Beare Green

Trouts Farm

Arnolds

Wigmore

Works

OCKLEY ROAD

HORSHAM RD

A29

A24

B2126

Brook Lodge Farm

Hawesrew Farm

Brookside

Petersfield Farm

Swires Farm

Henfold Lane

Henfold

Becket Wood

Renolds Copse

Gaterounds Farm

Knowle

Newdigate

Newdigate Endowed CE Infant School

Surgery

Horsielands

Woodspeck Lane

Hogspudding Lane

Cudworth Lane

Burnt Oak Lane

Thunderhill

Trig Street

Hillhouse Farm

Mizbrooks Green Road

Broomell's Farm

Mizbrook Farm

Greens Farm

Beam Brook

Kingsland

Winfield Gn

Rusper Road

Village Street

Underhill Road

Church Rd

Parkgate

Ockley Lodge

Duke's Road

Tanhurst Farm

Seaman's Green

Hoyle Hill

Hoyle Farm

Kerch Lane

The Street

Horsham Road

Mortimer Road

Vicarage Lane

Scott Broadwood CE Infant School

Capel

Temple Lane

Aldhurst Farm

Rushetts

Rusper Road

Newhouse Farm

Temple Ellande

Melton Hall Farm

Rusper

Clark's Green

Wolves Hill

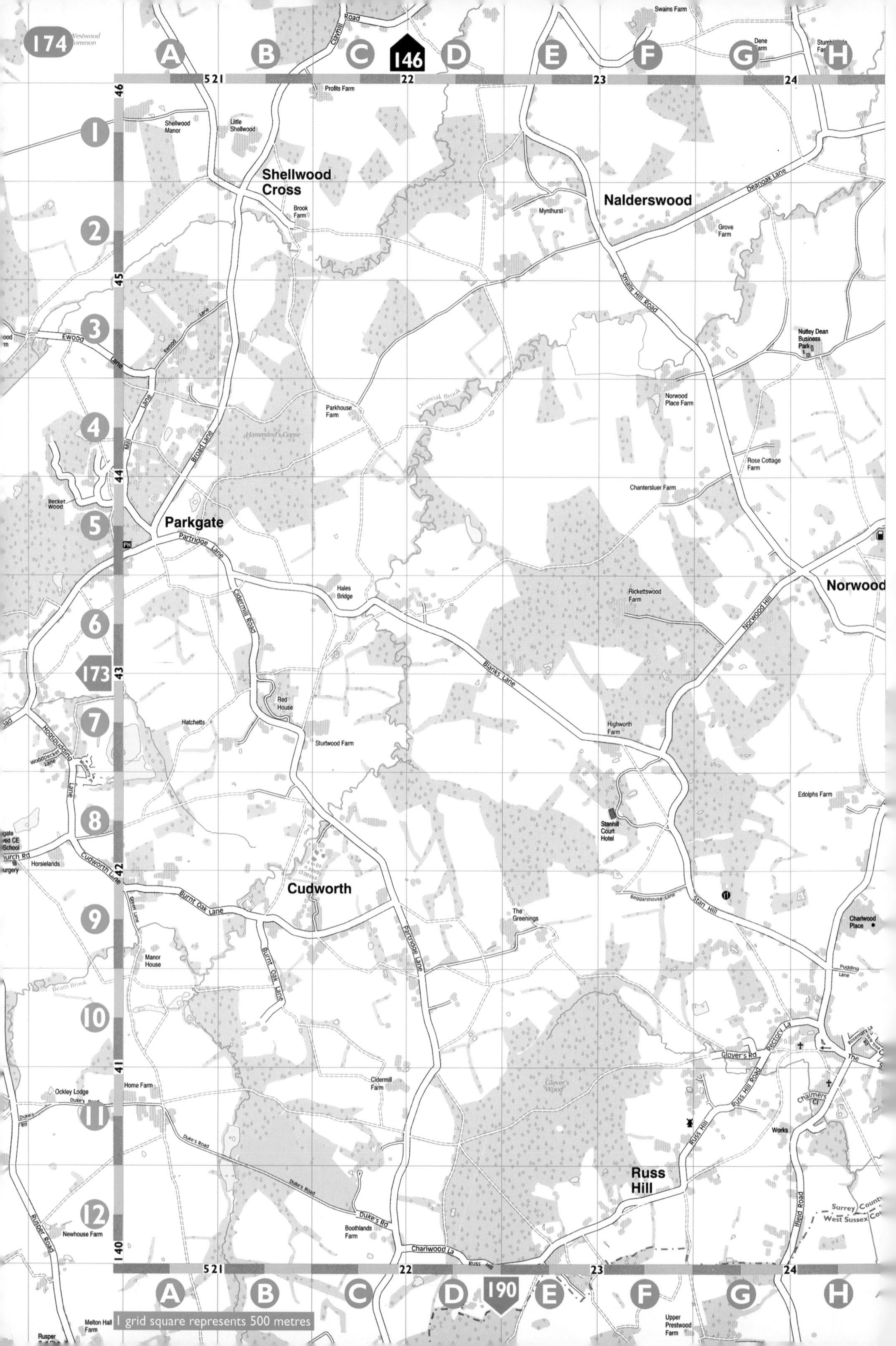

174
Westwood Common
146
173
190
Shellwood Cross
Nalderswood
Parkgate
Norwood
Cudworth
Russ Hill
Swains Farm
Dene Farm
Profits Farm
Shellwood Manor
Little Shellwood
Brook Farm
Mynthurst
Grove Farm
Deanoak Lane
Smalls Hill Road
Nutley Dean Business Park
Norwood Place Farm
Parkhouse Farm
Deanoak Brook
Hammond's Copse
Rose Cottage Farm
Chantersluer Farm
Becket Wood
Ewood Lane
Mill Lane
Broad Lane
Partridge Lane
Hales Bridge
Rickettswood Farm
Norwood Hill
Cidermill Road
Blanks Lane
Red House
Hatchetts
Sturtwood Farm
Highworth Farm
Hogspudding Lane
Woodpecker Lane
Edolphs Farm
Stanhill Court Hotel
Horsielands
Cudworth Lane
Burnt Oak Lane
Beggarshouse Lane
Stan Hill
The Greenings
Charlwood Place
Green Lane
Manor House
Partridge Lane
Pudding Lane
Beam Brook
Rectory La
Glover's Rd
Glover's Wood
Russ Hill Road
Home Farm
Ockley Lodge
Duke's Road
Cidermill Farm
Chalmers Cl
Works
Russ Hill
Duke's Rd
Ifield Road
Surrey County
West Sussex County
Rusper Road
Newhouse Farm
Boothlands Farm
Charlwood La
Upper Prestwood Farm
Melton Hall Farm
Rusper
1 grid square represents 500 metres
A B C D E F G H
1 2 3 4 5 6 7 8 9 10 11 12
521 22 23 24
46 45 44 43 42 41 140

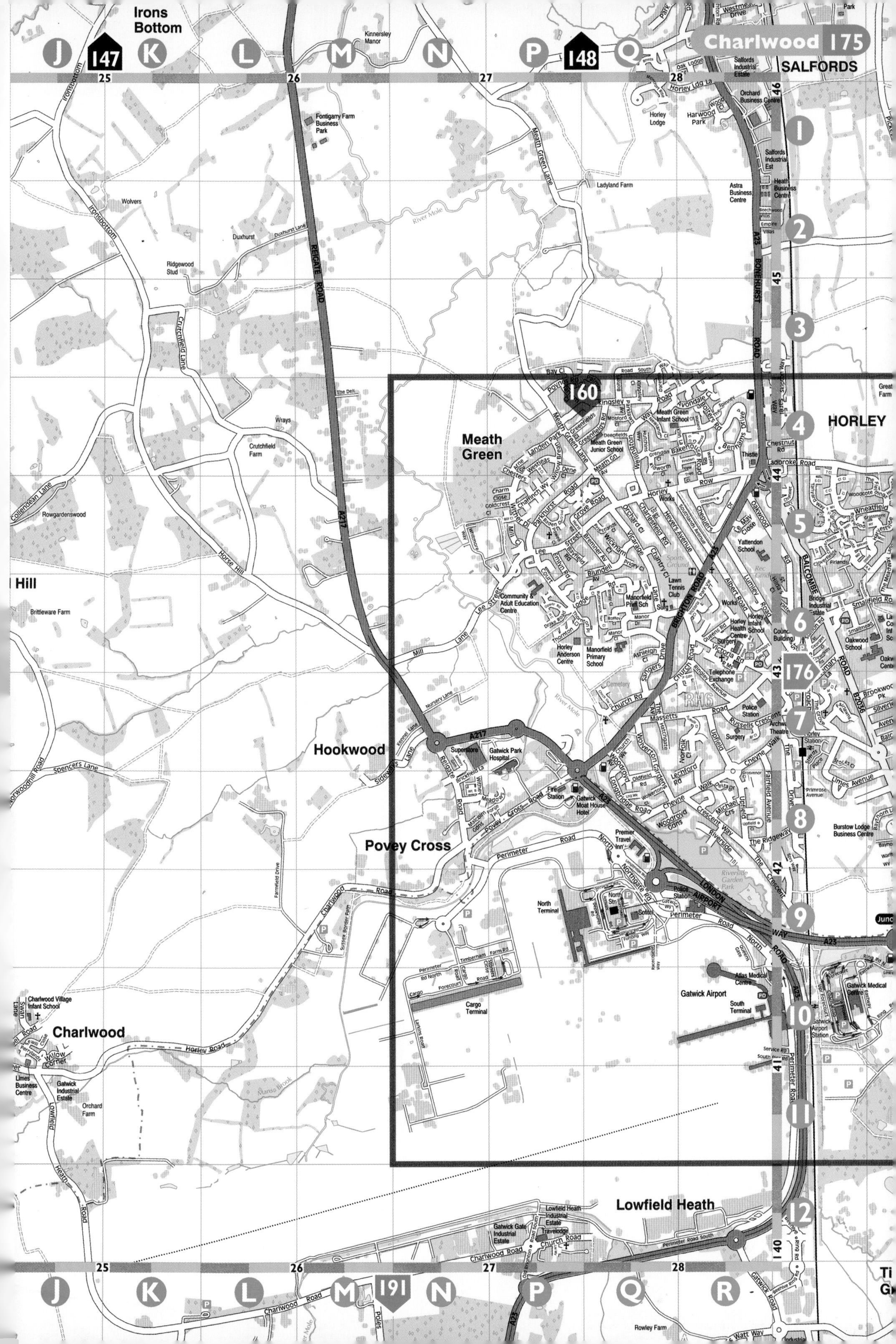
Irons Bottom
147
148
160
176
191
SALFORDS
HORLEY
Meath Green
Hookwood
Povey Cross
Charlwood
Lowfield Heath
Gatwick Airport
North Terminal
South Terminal
Cargo Terminal
REIGATE ROAD
BONEHURST ROAD
BRIGHTON ROAD
LONDON ROAD
AIRPORT WAY
BALCOMBE ROAD
Horley Road
Charlwood Road
Perimeter Road
Ironsbottom
Horse Hill
Crutchfield Lane
Lee Street
Mill Lane
Meath Green Lane
Victoria Road
Church Road
Massetts Road
Upfield
Lowfield Heath Road
Charlwood Road
Perimeter Road South
River Mole
Wolvers
Duxhurst
Ridgewood Stud
Crutchfield Farm
Wrays
Rowgardenswood
Brittleware Farm
Ladyland Farm
Fontigarry Farm Business Park
Kinnersley Manor
Gatwick Park Hospital
Superstore
Fire Station
Gatwick Moat House Hotel
Premier Travel Inn
Sofitel
Police Station
Horley Station
Gatwick Airport Station
Atlas Medical Centre
Gatwick Medical Centre
Charlwood Village Infant School
Gatwick Industrial Estate
Limes Business Centre
Orchard Farm
Lowfield Heath Industrial Estate
Gatwick Gate Industrial Estate
Travelodge
Rowley Farm
Burstow Lodge Business Centre
Salfords Industrial Estate
Orchard Business Centre
Harwood Park
Horley Lodge
Astra Business Centre
Heath Business Centre
Yattendon School
Manorfield Primary School
Horley Anderson Centre
Community & Adult Education Centre
Meath Green Infant School
Meath Green Junior School
Horley Infant School
Horley Health Centre
Telephone Exchange
Riverside Garden Park
RH6
J K L M N P Q R
25 26 27 28
1 2 3 4 5 6 7 8 9 10 11 12
40 41 42 43 44 45 46

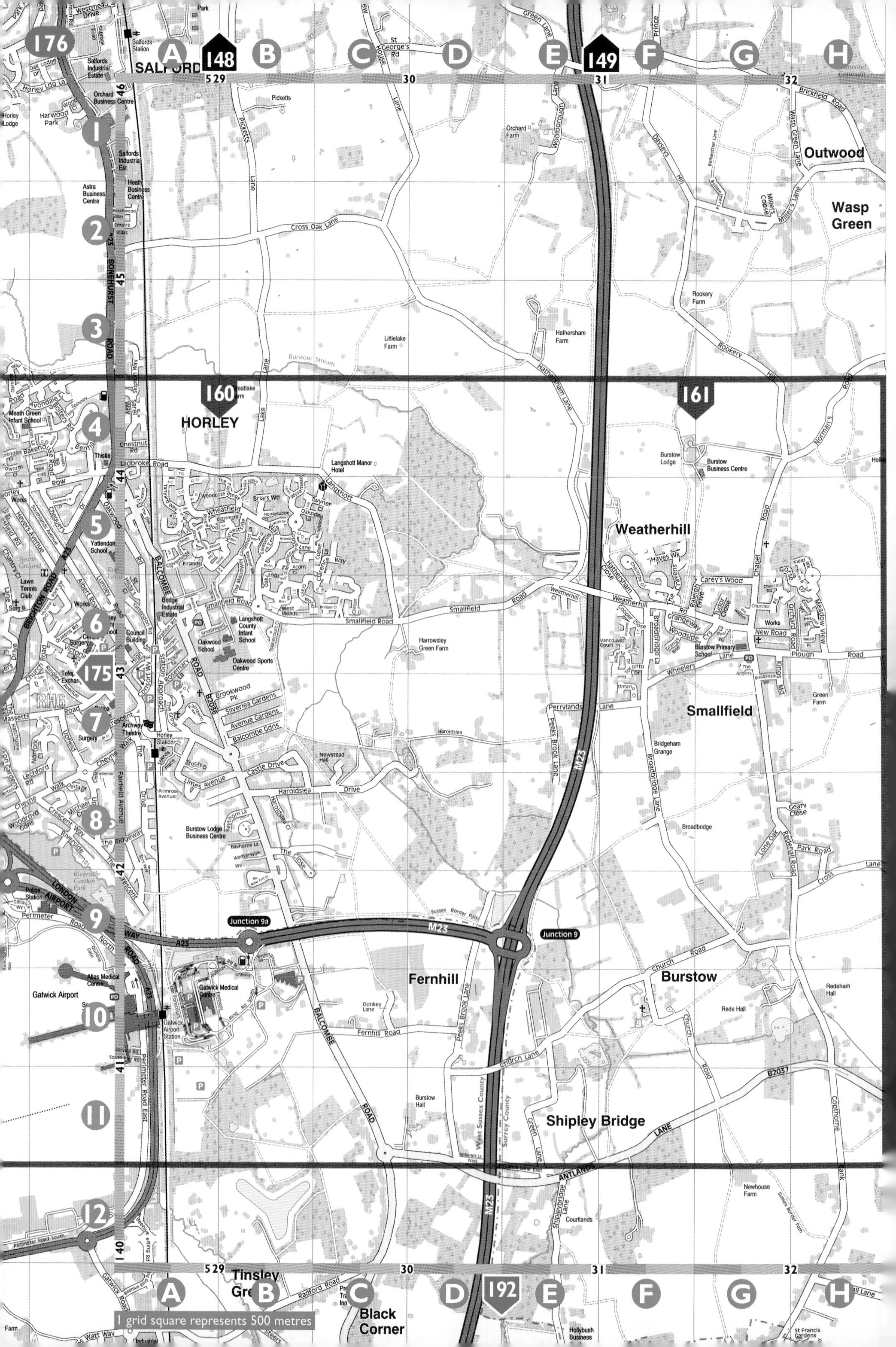

176
148
149
160
161
175
192
SALFORD
HORLEY
Outwood
Wasp Green
Weatherhill
Smallfield
Fernhill
Burstow
Shipley Bridge
Gatwick Airport
Tinsley Green
Black Corner
Junction 9a
Junction 9
M23
A23
B2036
B2037
Salfords Station
Horley Station
Gatwick Airport Station
Cross Oak Lane
Smallfield Road
Balcombe Road
Brighton Road
Bonehurst Road
Picketts Lane
Lake Lane
Hathersham Lane
Rookery Hill
Chapel Road
Broadbridge Lane
Church Road
Antlands Lane
Fernhill Road
Peeks Brook Lane
Copthorne Bank
Haroldslea Drive
Castle Drive
Limes Avenue
Langshott
Weatherhill Road
Plough Lane
Wheelers Lane
Perryland Lane
Redehall Road
Burstow Stream
Langshott Manor Hotel
Langshott County Infant School
Oakwood School
Oakwood Sports Centre
Burstow Lodge Business Centre
Burstow Business Centre
Burstow Primary School
Gatwick Medical Centre
Atlas Medical Centre
Yattendon School
Meath Green Infant School
Littlelake Farm
Hathersham Farm
Orchard Farm
Rookery Farm
Harrowsley Green Farm
Newstead Hall
Burstow Hall
Donkey Lane
Redeham Hall
Rede Hall
Broadbridge
Bridgeham Grange
Newhouse Farm
Courtlands
Green Farm
Riverside Garden Park
RH6
1 grid square represents 500 metres

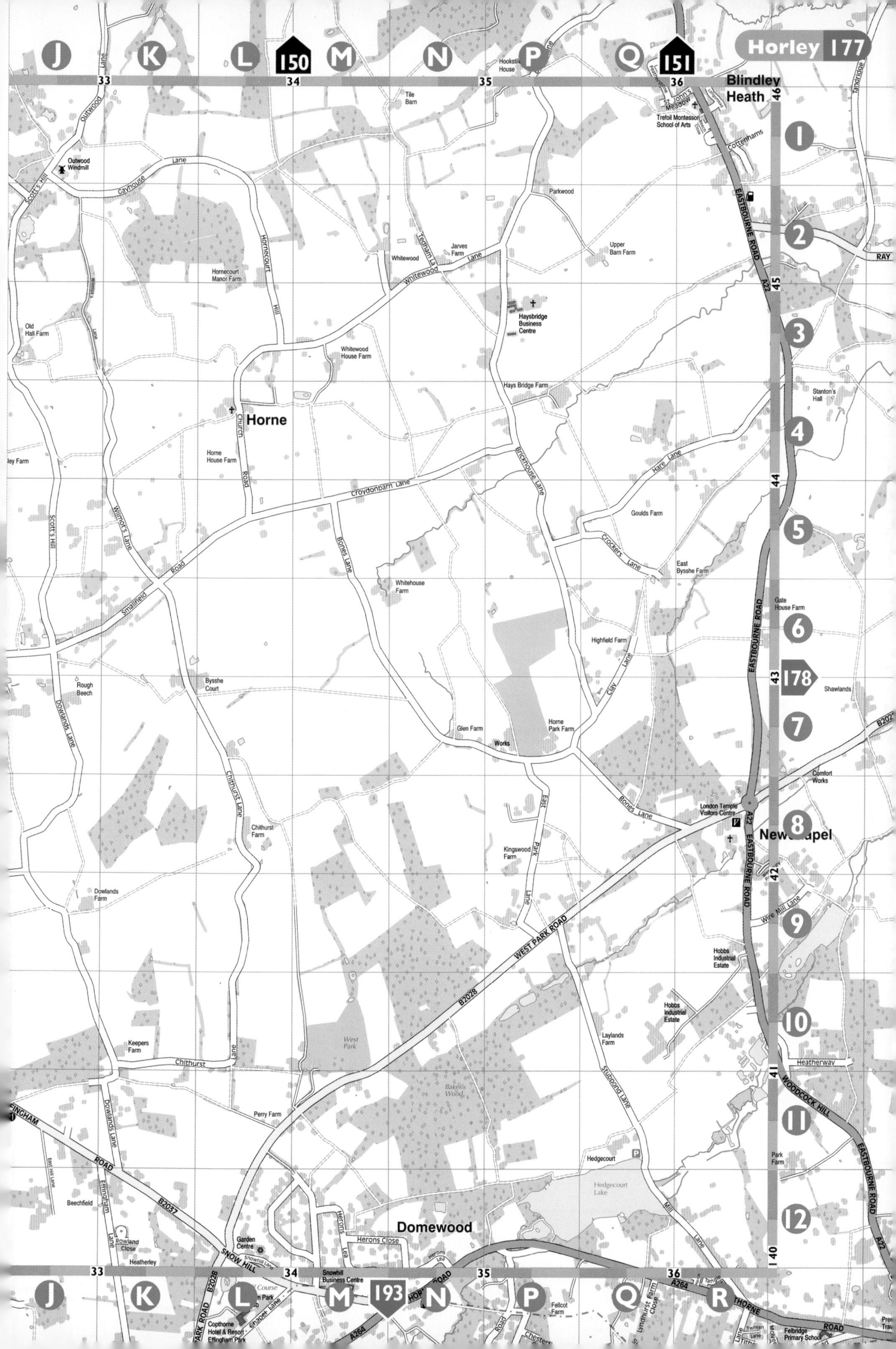
Blindley Heath
Horne
Newchapel
Domewood
Outwood Windmill
Old Hall Farm
Hornecourt Manor Farm
Whitewood
Jarves Farm
Upper Barn Farm
Parkwood
Haysbridge Business Centre
Whitewood House Farm
Hays Bridge Farm
Horne House Farm
Goulds Farm
East Bysshe Farm
Whitehouse Farm
Highfield Farm
Gate House Farm
Rough Beech
Bysshe Court
Glen Farm
Works
Horne Park Farm
Shawlands
Comfort Works
London Temple Visitors Centre
Chithurst Farm
Kingswood Farm
Dowlands Farm
Hobbs Industrial Estate
Keepers Farm
West Park
Laylands Farm
Bakers Wood
Perry Farm
Hedgecourt
Hedgecourt Lake
Park Farm
Beechfield
Garden Centre
Snowhill Business Centre
Fellcot Farm
Felbridge Primary School
Trefoil Montessori School of Arts
Tile Barn
Hookstile House
Stanton's Hall
Cottenhams
EASTBOURNE ROAD
A22
WEST PARK ROAD
B2028
B2037
A264
WOODCOCK HILL
SNOW HILL
Croydonbarn Lane
Smallfield Road
Whitewood Lane
Cayhouse Lane
Hornecourt Hill
Church Road
Bones Lane
Brickhouse Lane
Crockers Lane
Hare Lane
Clay Lane
East Park Lane
Chithurst Lane
Wilmot's Lane
Dowlands Lane
Scott's Hill
Outwood Lane
Stubpond Lane
Mill Lane
Wire Mill Lane
Heatherway
Herons Close
Herons Lea
Effingham Lane
Rowland Close
Heatherley
Snowhill Lane
Chapel Lane
St John's Meadow
Lynchmere Farm Close
Tandridge
RAY
Copthorne Hotel & Resort Effingham Park
J K L M N P Q R
150 151 178 193
33 34 35 36
40 41 42 43 44 45 46
1 2 3 4 5 6 7 8 9 10 11 12

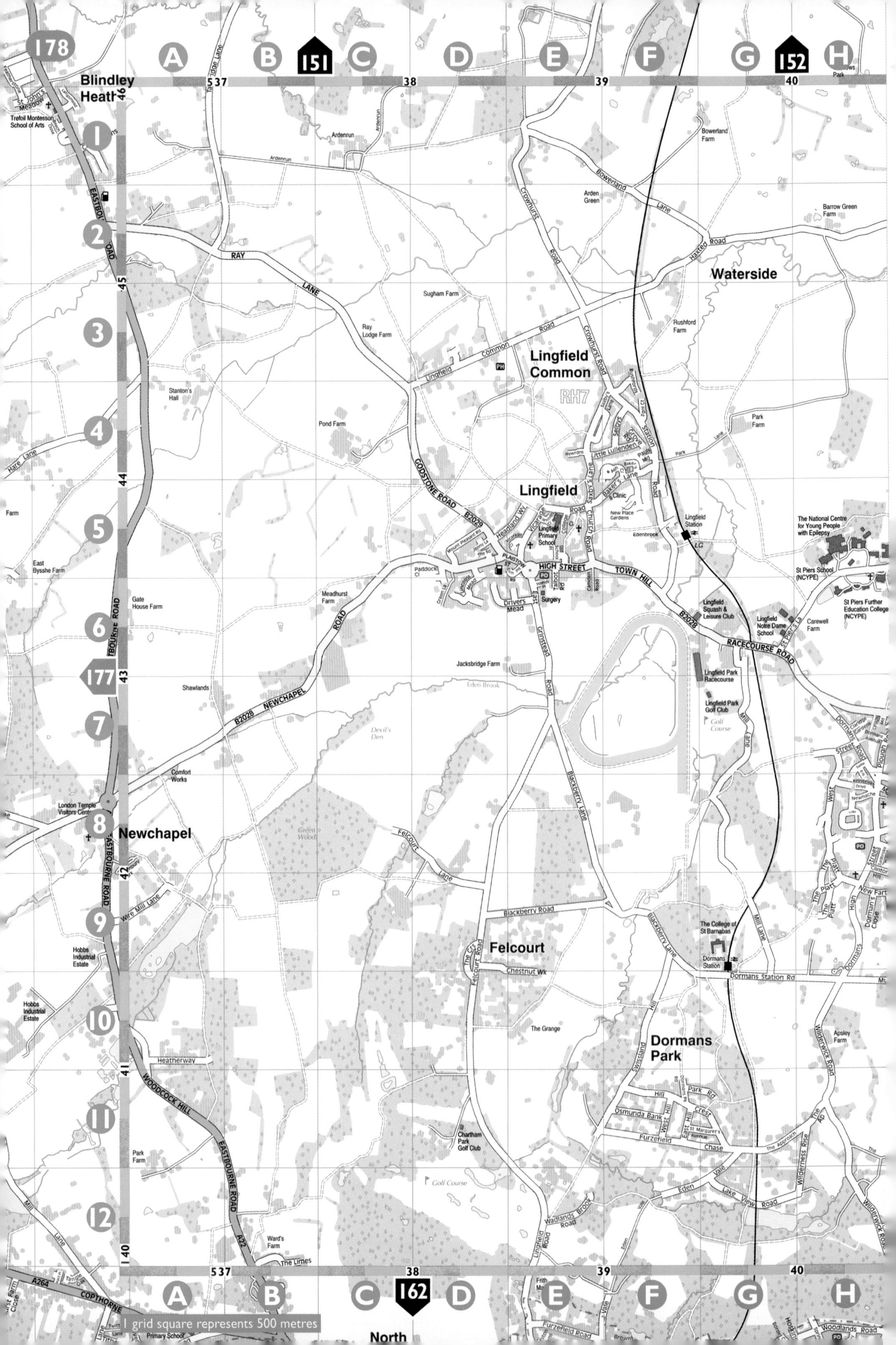

A   B   151   C   D   E   F   G   152   H

Blindley
Heath   5 37   46   38   39   40

1
Trefoil Montessori
School of Arts
St John's
Meadow

Ardenrun   Ardenrun   Bowerland
Farm

2   RAY   Ardenrun   Arden
Green   Bowerland
Lane   Haxted
Road   Waterside

45   LANE   Sugham Farm   Rushford
Farm   Barrow Green
Farm

3   Ray
Lodge Farm   Lingfield
Common   Lingfield
Common

Stanton's
Hall   GODSTONE ROAD   B2029   Crowhurst   RH7   Park
Farm

4   Pond Farm   Lingfield

44   Little Lullenden's
Mount Pleasant Rd   Lingfield
Primary School   Clinic   New Place
Gardens   Lingfield
Station   LC   The National Centre
for Young People
with Epilepsy

5   East
Bysshe Farm   Meadhurst
Farm   Paddock
Cl   HIGH STREET   Surgery   TOWN HILL   Edenbrook   St Piers School
(NCYPE)

Gate
House Farm   B2028   NEWCHAPEL   Lingfield
Squash &
Leisure Club   Lingfield
Notre Dame
School   Carewell
Farm   St Piers Further
Education College
(NCYPE)

6   ROAD   B2029   Drivers
Mead   B2028   RACECOURSE ROAD

177   43   Jacksbridge Farm   Shawlands   Eden Brook   Lingfield Park
Racecourse

7   Devil's
Den   Comfort
Works   Lingfield Park
Golf Club   Golf
Course

London Temple
Visitors Centr   Green
Wood   Felcourt
Lane   Dormans
Lane

8   Newchapel   Blackberry Road   The College of
St Barnabas   Dormans
Station

42   Wire Mill Lane   Blackberry Road   Dormans Station Rd

9   Hobbs
Industrial Estate   Felcourt   Chestnut Wk   Dormans
Park

10   The Grange   Apsley
Farm

Hobbs
Industrial
Estate   Heatherway   Chartham
Park
Golf Club   Dormans
Park   Osmunda Bank   Furzefield

41   WOODCOCK HILL   EASTBOURNE ROAD   West
Hill   Park Rd   Crest   St Margaret's
Avenue   Chase

11   Park
Farm   A22   Golf Course   Eden   Lake View Road   Wilderness Rise

12   40   Ward's
Farm   The Limes   Wadlands Brook   Frith   Furzefield Road   Woodlands Road

A264   COPTHORNE   5 37   38   162   39   40

A   B   C   D   E   F   G   H

1 grid square represents 500 metres

North

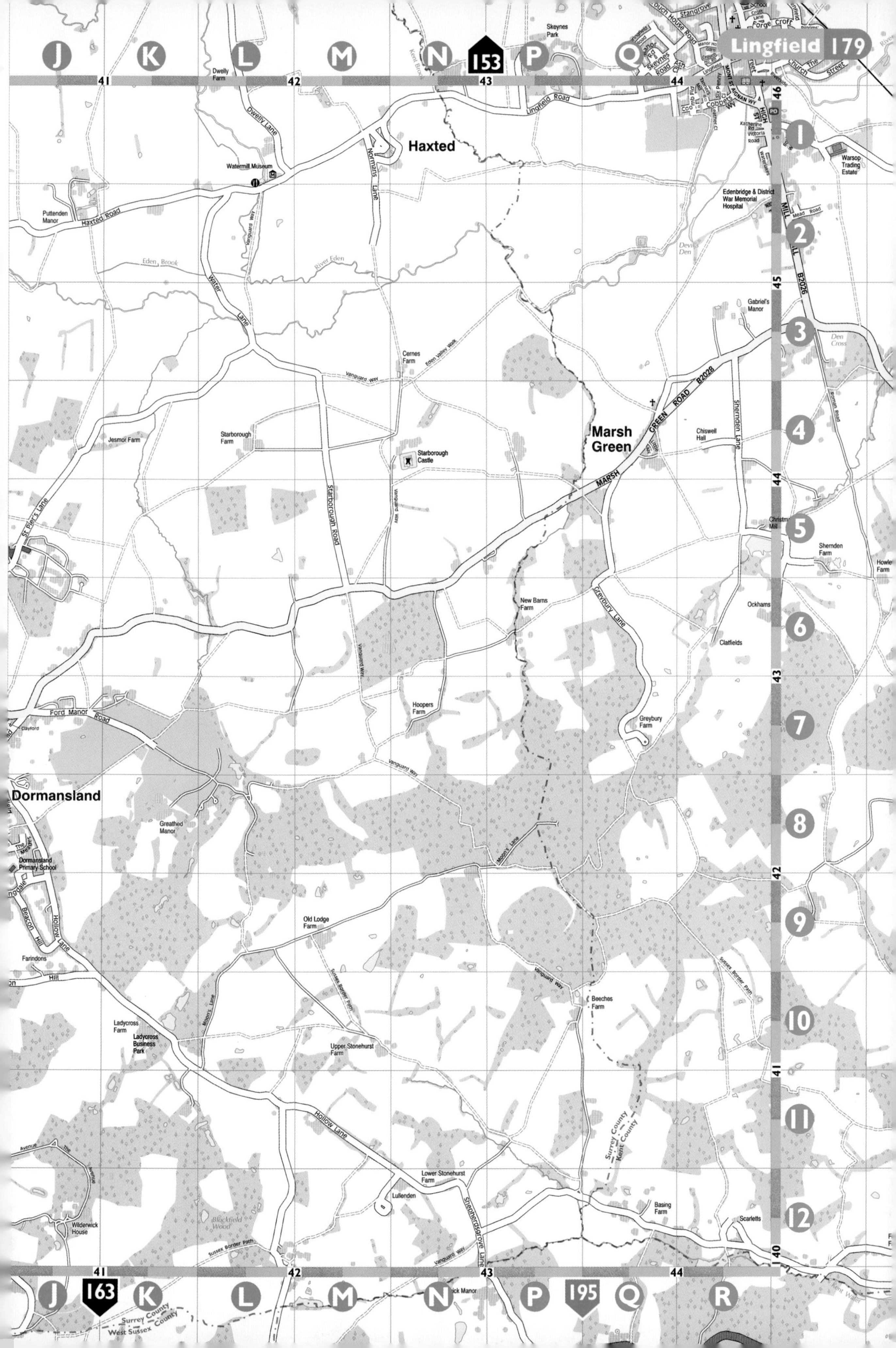

J K L M N **153** P Q

41 42 43 44

Skeynes
Park

Dwelly
Farm

Haxted

Dwelly Lane

Lingfield Road

Edenbridge & District
War Memorial
Hospital

Watermill Museum

Norman's Lane

Puttenden
Manor

Haxted Road

Gabriel's
Manor

Eden Brook

River Eden

Cernes
Farm

Eden Valley Walk

Vanguard Way

Marsh
Green

GREEN ROAD B2028

Chiswell
Hall

Shernden Lane

Jesmor Farm

Starborough
Farm

Starborough Castle

MARSH

Christmas
Mill

Shernden
Farm

St Piers Lane

Starborough Road

New Barns
Farm

Gradoury Lane

Ockhams

Clatfields

Greybury
Farm

Ford Manor Road

Vanguard Way

Hoopers
Farm

Clayford

Dormansland

Greathed
Manor

The
Dormansland
Primary School

Beacon Hill Lane

Hollow Lane

Old Lodge
Farm

Vanguard Way

Moore's Lane

Moore's Lane

Sussex Border Path

Beeches
Farm

Farindons

Hill

Ladycross
Farm

Ladycross
Business
Park

Moore's Lane

Upper Stonehurst
Farm

Sussex Border Path

Surrey County
Kent County

Hollow Lane

Avenue

Lower Stonehurst
Farm

Lullenden

Stonehedgeprove Lane

Basing
Farm

Scarletts

Wilderwick
House

Blockfield
Wood

Sussex Border Path

Vanguard Way

Surrey County
West Sussex County

I

2

3

4

5

6

7

8

9

10

11

12

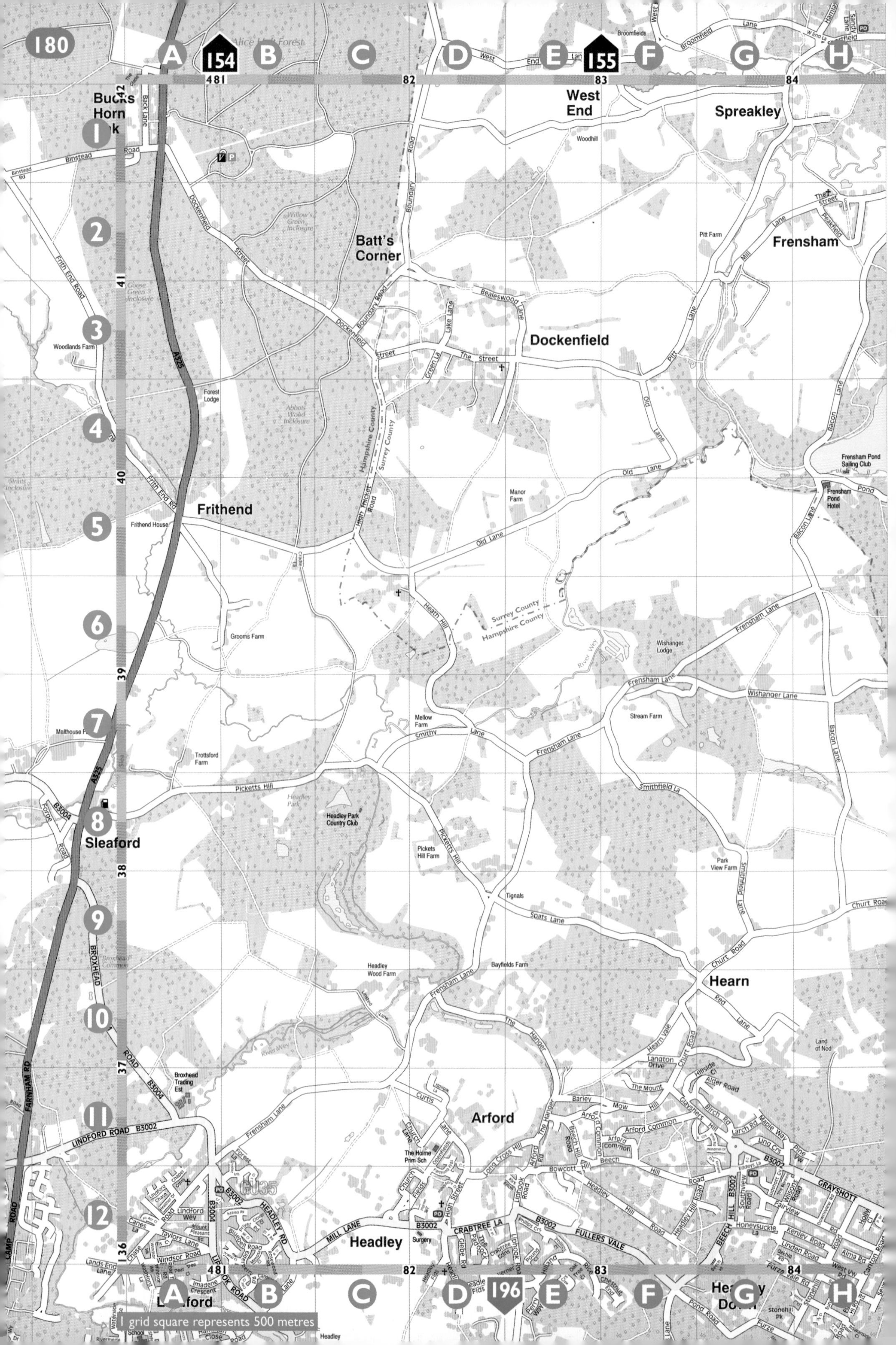
154
155
196
A
B
C
D
E
F
G
H
Bucks Horn Oak
West End
Spreakley
Batt's Corner
Frensham
Dockenfield
Frithend
Sleaford
Hearn
Arford
Headley
Lindford
Headley Down
Alice Holt Forest
Binstead Road
Dockenfield Street
Boundary Road
Bealeswood Lane
The Street
Old Lane
Pitt Lane
Bacon Lane
Frensham Lane
Wishanger Lane
Smithfield Lane
Churt Road
Picketts Hill
Smithy Lane
Spats Lane
Heath Hill
High Thicket Road
Hampshire County
Surrey County
River Wey
Frith End Road
Broxhead Road
Farnham Rd
Lindford Road B3002
Frensham Pond Sailing Club
Frensham Pond Hotel
Headley Park Country Club
Broxhead Trading Est
Mill Lane
Crabtree La
Fullers Vale
Grayshott
Beech Hill
1 grid square represents 500 metres

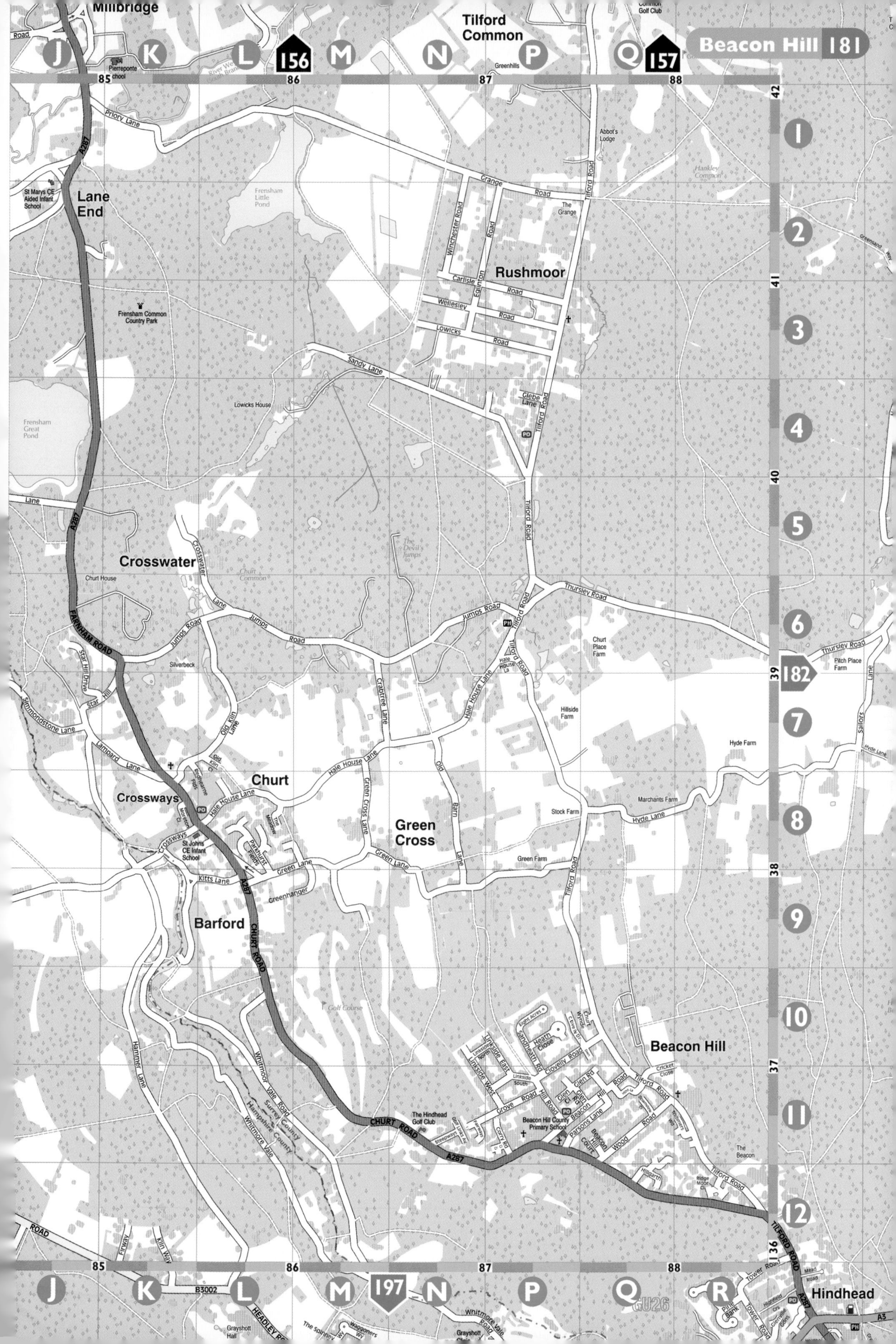

Millbridge
Tilford Common
156
157
182
197
Lane End
Rushmoor
Crosswater
Churt
Crossways
Green Cross
Barford
Beacon Hill
Hindhead
Frensham Little Pond
Frensham Great Pond
Frensham Common Country Park
St Marys CE Aided Infant School
Priory Lane
Grange Road
The Grange
Abbot's Lodge
Hankley Common
Tilford Road
Winchester Road
Eggleton Road
Carlisle Road
Wellesley Road
Lowicks Road
Sandy Lane
Glebe Lane
Lowicks House
The Devil's Jumps
Churt Common
Churt House
Jumps Road
Thursley Road
Farnham Road
Star Hill Drive
Star Hill
Simmondstone Lane
Lampard Lane
Old Kiln Lane
Silverbeck
Crabtree Lane
Hale House Lane
Green Cross Lane
Old Barn Lane
Church Place Farm
Pitch Place Farm
Hillside Farm
Hyde Farm
Hyde Lane
Sailors Lane
Marchants Farm
Stock Farm
Green Farm
Green Lane
Kitts Lane
Greenhanger
St Johns CE Infant School
Parkhurst Fields
Churt Road
Golf Course
Whitmoor Vale Road
Whitmore Vale
Surrey County
Hampshire County
Hammer Lane
The Hindhead Golf Club
Beacon Hill County Primary School
Linkside East
Linkside West
Linkside North
Linkside South
Heath Close
Sandheath Road
Clovelly Road
Glen Road
Grove Road
Hill Road
Beacon Hill Road
Parsons Lane
Beacon Court
Wood Road
Cricket Close
Tilford Road
The Beacon
Ridge Moor Cl.
Hillgarth
Churt Wynde
A287
B3002
A3
Headley Road
Tower Road
Pine Bank
Whitmore Vale Road
Grayshott Hall
Grayshott
The Spinney
Waggoners Way
Firway
Kiln Way
GU26

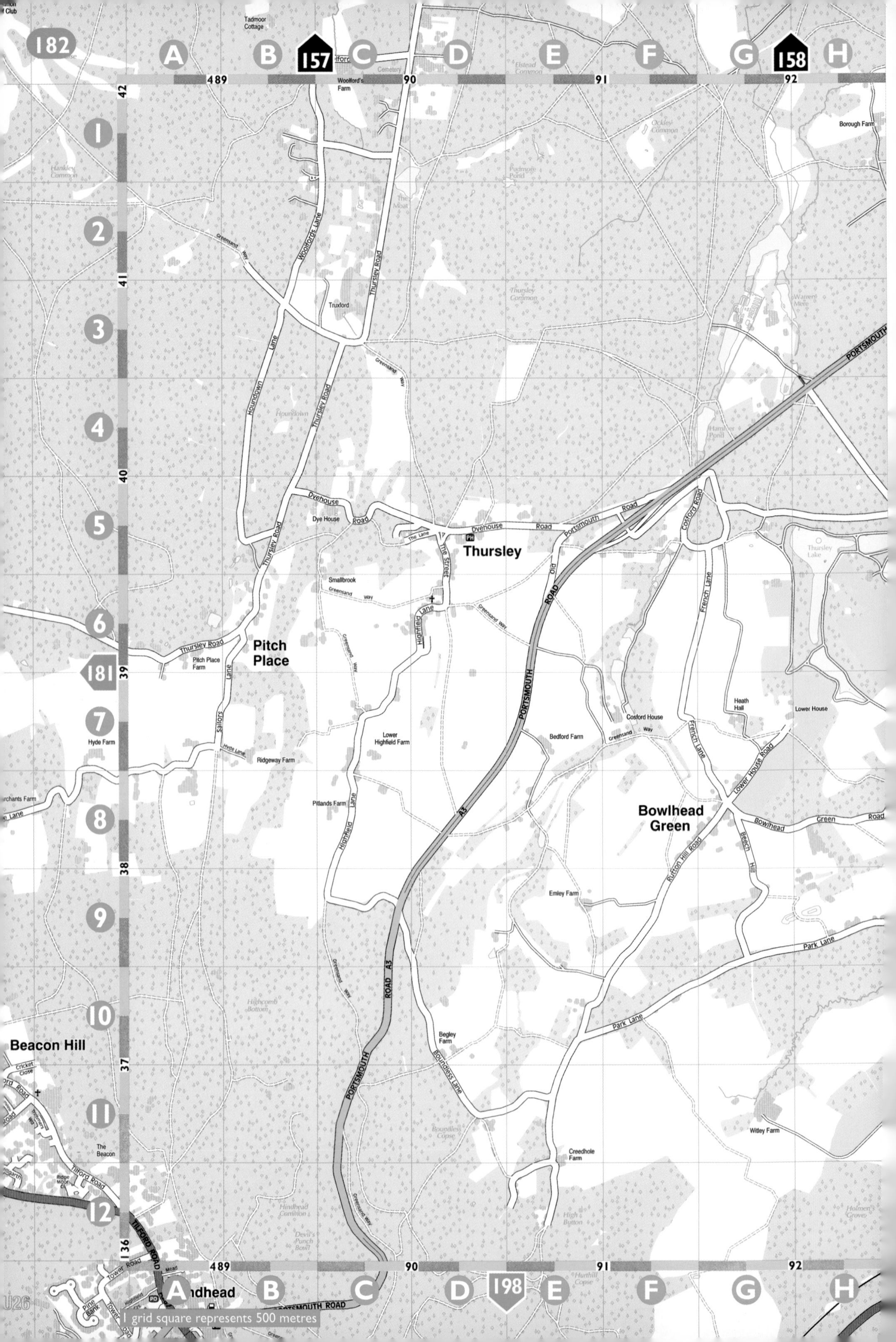
Thursley
Pitch Place
Bowlhead Green
Beacon Hill
Thursley Road
Dyehouse Road
Dye House
Smallbrook
Greensand Way
Highfield Lane
Lower Highfield Farm
Pitlands Farm
Ridgeway Farm
Hyde Lane
Sailors Lane
Pitch Place Farm
Hyde Farm
Houndown Lane
Houndown
Woolfords Lane
Woolford's Farm
Truxford
Tadmoor Cottage
Hankley Common
Cemetery
Elstead Common
Ockley Common
Pudmore Pond
The Moat
Thursley Common
Warren Mere
Hammer Pond
Borough Farm
Portsmouth Road
Old Portsmouth Road
The Street
The Lane
Cosford Road
French Lane
Thursley Lake
Heath Hall
Lower House
Lower House Road
Cosford House
Bedford Farm
Bowlhead Green Road
Beech Hill
Rutton Hill Road
Emley Farm
Park Lane
Begley Farm
Boundless Lane
Boundless Copse
Creedhole Farm
High Button
Holmen's Grove
Witley Farm
Highcomb Bottom
Hindhead Common
Devil's Punch Bowl
Hurthill Copse
The Beacon
Cricket Close
Tilford Road
Ridge Moor Cl
Tower Road
Pine Bank
Hindhead
A3
1 grid square represents 500 metres
182
157
158
181
198
A B C D E F G H
1 2 3 4 5 6 7 8 9 10 11 12
489 90 91 92
42 41 40 39 38 37 136

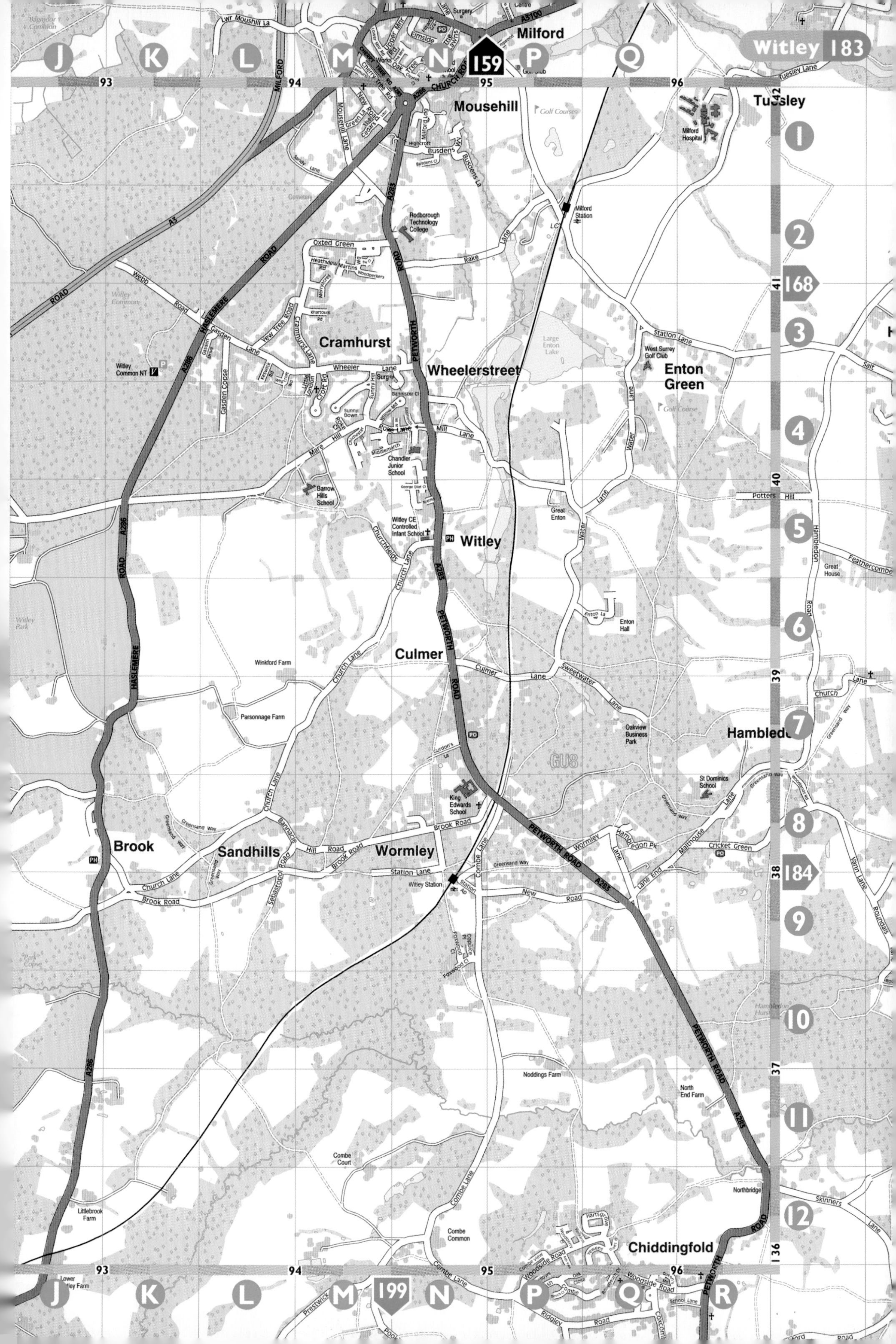
Milford
159
Mousehill
Tuesley
Milford Hospital
Milford Station
Rodborough Technology College
Oxted Green
Cramhurst
Wheelerstreet
Large Enton Lake
West Surrey Golf Club
Enton Green
Witley Common NT
Chandler Junior School
Barrow Hills School
Witley CE Controlled Infant School
Witley
Great Enton
Enton Hall
Witley Park
Winkford Farm
Culmer
Parsonnage Farm
Oakview Business Park
Hambledon
GU8
St Dominics School
King Edwards School
Brook
Sandhills
Wormley
Witley Station
Noddings Farm
North End Farm
Combe Court
Northbridge
Littlebrook Farm
Combe Common
Chiddingfold
199
168
184
HASLEMERE ROAD
PETWORTH ROAD
A286
A283
A3
A3100
Golf Course
Station Lane
Church Lane
Brook Road
Combe Lane
Water Lane
Culmer Lane
Sweetwater Lane
Hambledon Road
Potters Hill
Woodside Road
Skinners Lane

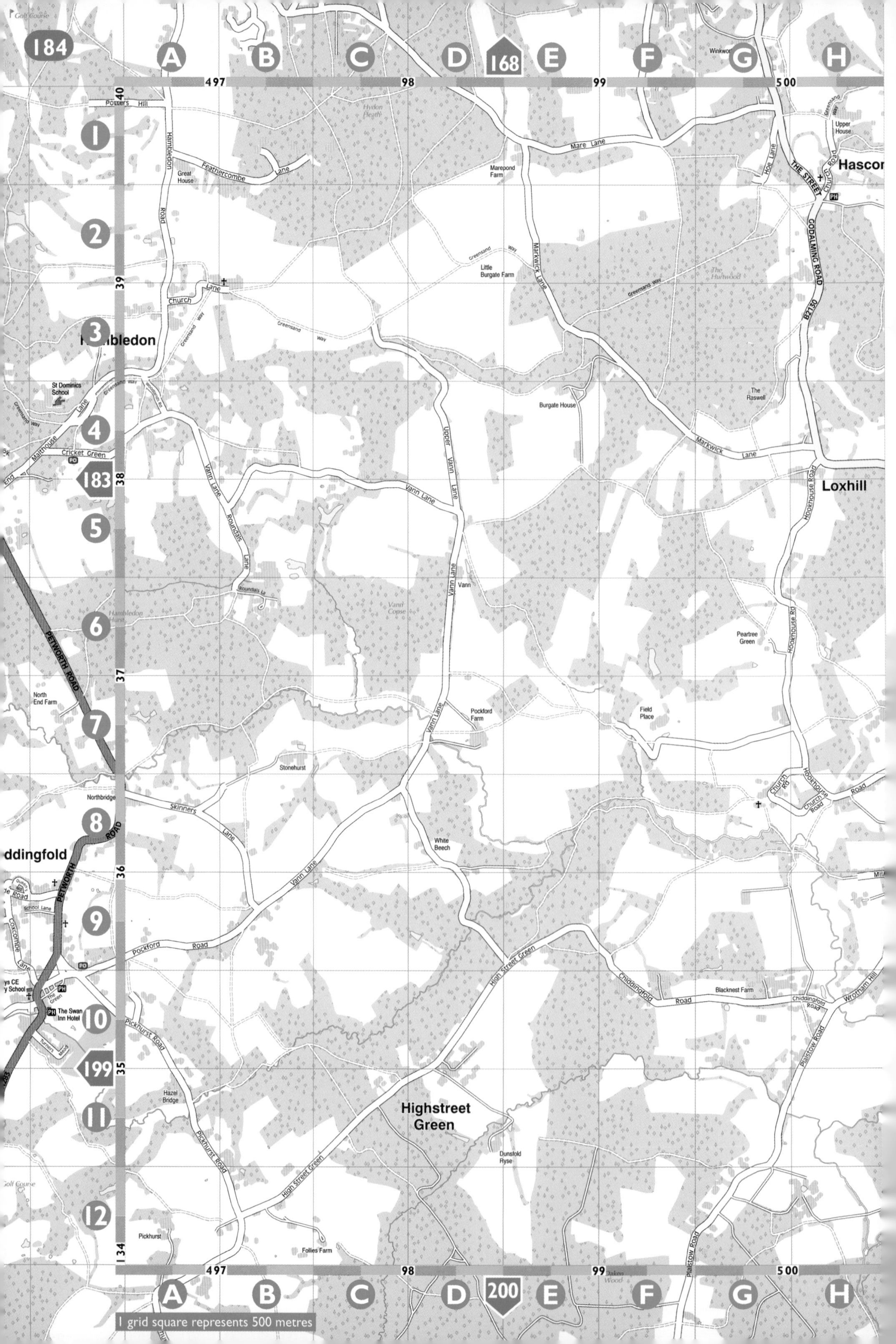

184
168
183
199
200
A B C D E F G H
1 2 3 4 5 6 7 8 9 10 11 12
497
98
99
500
40
39
38
37
36
35
134
Potters Hill
Hambledon Road
Feathercombe Lane
Great House
Hydon Heath
Mare Lane
Marepond Farm
Winkworth
Upper House
Hascombe
Hoe Lane
THE STREET
Church Road
GODALMING ROAD
B2130
Greensand Way
Little Burgate Farm
Markwick Lane
The Hurtwood
Church Lane
Hambledon
St Dominics School
Maithouse Lane
Cricket Green
PO
Burgate House
The Raswell
Markwick Lane
Loxhill
Hookhouse Road
Upper Vann Lane
Vann Lane
Roundals Lane
Roundals La
Vann
Vann Copse
Hambledon Hurst
Peartree Green
PETWORTH ROAD
North End Farm
Pockford Farm
Field Place
Stonehurst
Northbridge
Skinners Lane
Church Rd
Hookhouse Road
Church Road
ddingfold
PETWORTH ROAD
White Beech
School Lane
Coxcombe Lane
Pockford Road
High Street Green
Chiddingfold Road
Blacknest Farm
Chiddingfold Road
Wrotham Hill
The Green
PH
The Swan Inn Hotel
Pickhurst Road
Plaistow Road
Hazel Bridge
Highstreet Green
Dunsfold Ryse
Golf Course
Pickhurst
Follies Farm
Plaistow Road
Jaken Wood
1 grid square represents 500 metres

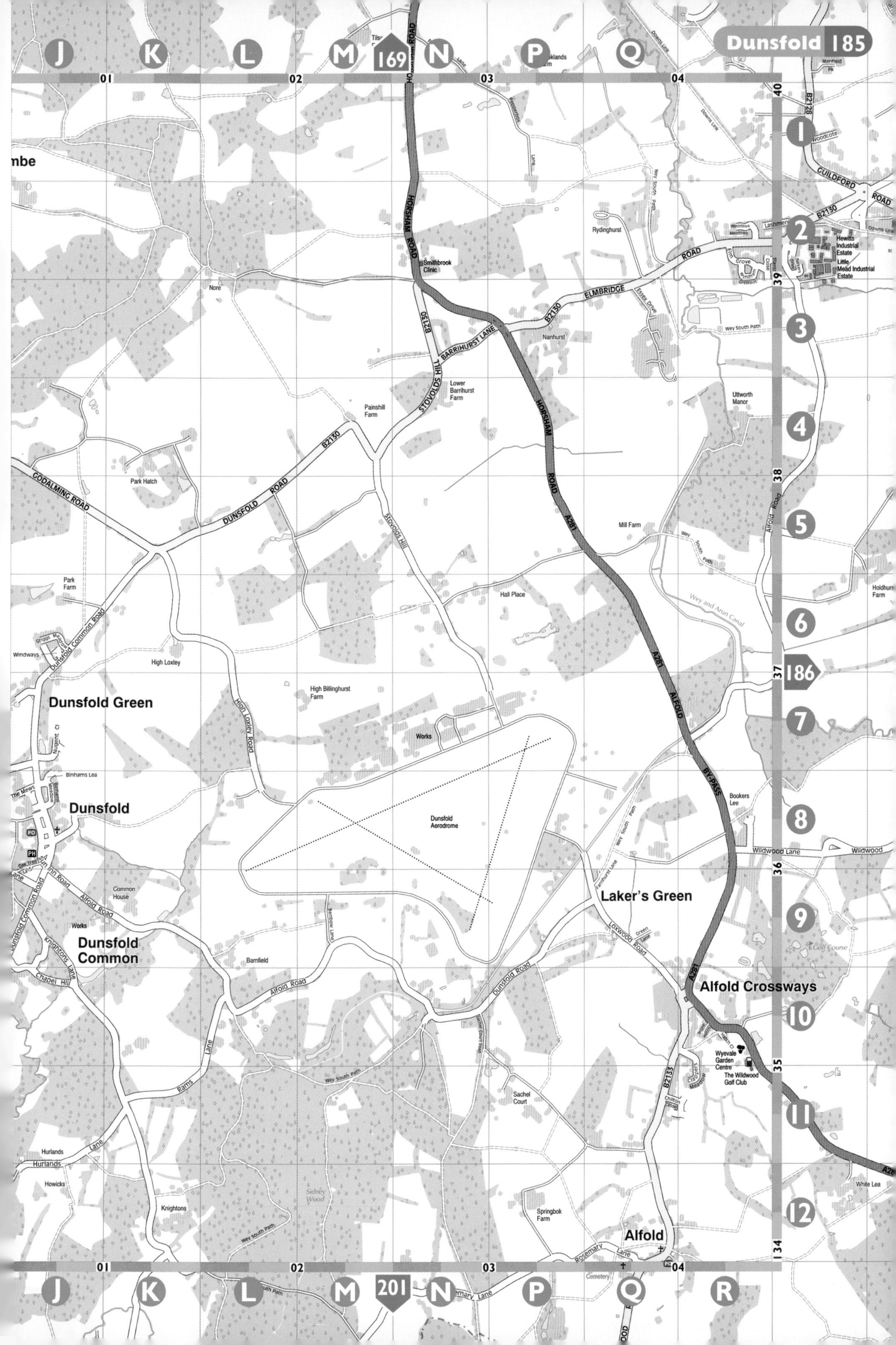
Dunsfold Green
Dunsfold
Dunsfold Common
Laker's Green
Alfold Crossways
Alfold
Dunsfold Aerodrome
HORSHAM ROAD
ALFOLD BY-PASS
A281
B2130
ELMBRIDGE ROAD
BARRIHURST LANE
STOVOLDS HILL
DUNSFOLD ROAD
GODALMING ROAD
GUILDFORD ROAD
B2128
B2133
Dunsfold Common Road
High Loxley Road
Alfold Road
Loxwood Road
Wildwood Lane
Rams Lane
Hurlands Lane
Chapel Hill
Knightons Lane
Rosemary Lane
Wey South Path
Wey and Arun Canal
Downs Link
Smithbrook Clinic
Nore
Rydinghurst
Nanhurst
Lower Barrihurst Farm
Painshill Farm
Park Hatch
Park Farm
Windways
High Loxley
High Billinghurst Farm
Works
Hall Place
Mill Farm
Uttworth Manor
Bookers Lee
Common House
Barnfield
Sachel Court
Springbok Farm
Sidney Wood
Hurlands
Howicks
Knightons
Cemetery
Wyevale Garden Centre
The Wildwood Golf Club
Golf Course
White Lea
Holdhurst Farm
Hewitts Industrial Estate
Little Mead Industrial Estate
Binhams Lea
The Mews
Nugent Cl
Chilton Close
Woodcote
Lashmere
Elm Grove
Essex Drive
169
186
201
J K L M N P Q R
01 02 03 04
34 35 36 37 38 39 40
1 2 3 4 5 6 7 8 9 10 11 12

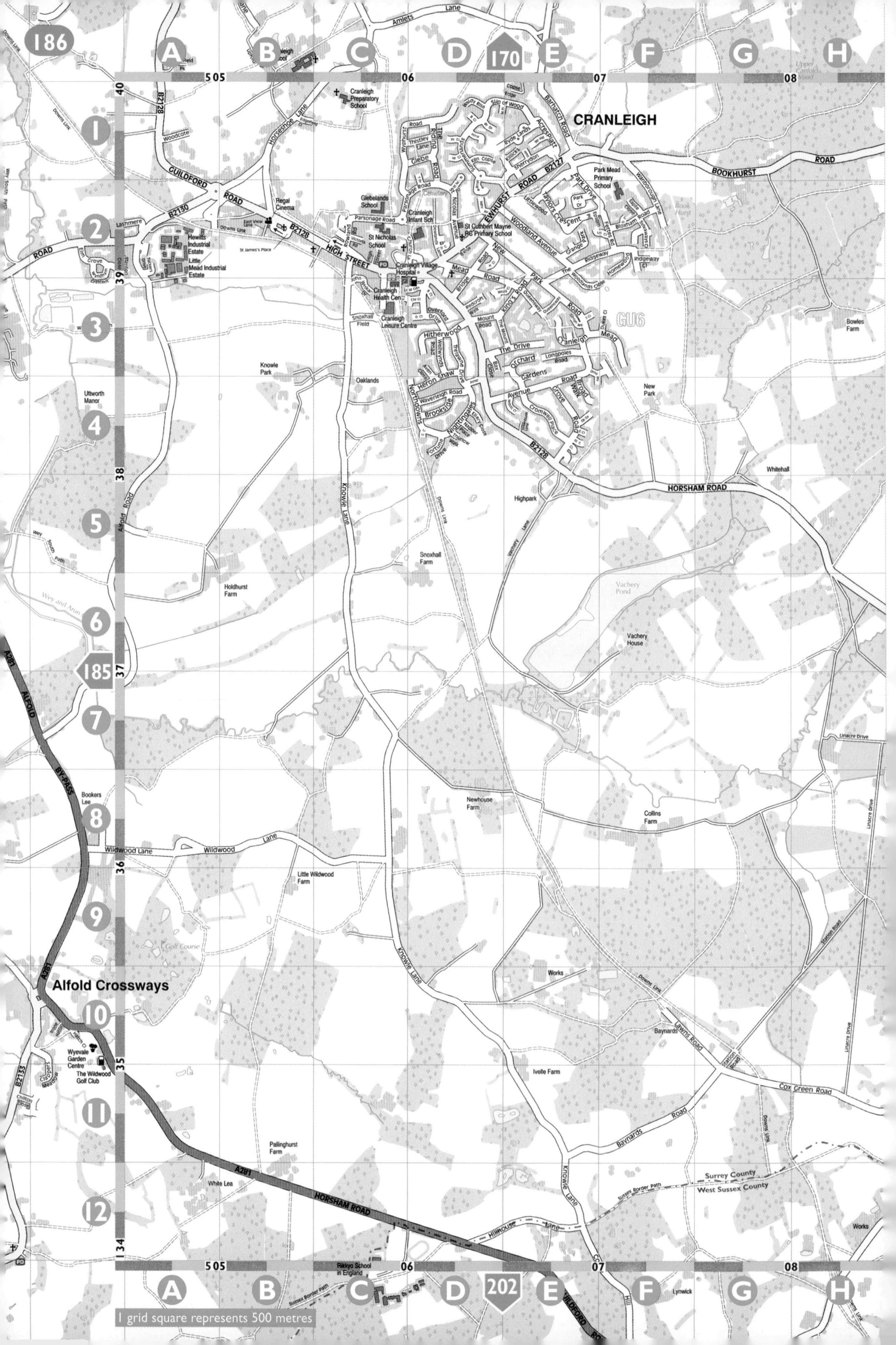
186
170
185
202
CRANLEIGH
Alfold Crossways
GU6
Guildford Road
High Street
Ewhurst Road
Bookhurst Road
Horsham Road
Knowle Lane
Alfold Road
Wildwood Lane
Alfold By-pass
Cox Green Road
Baynards Road
Lawns Road
Station Road
Hillhouse Lane
Amlets Lane
Downs Link
Wey South Path
Sussex Border Path
Surrey County
West Sussex County
Cranleigh Preparatory School
Park Mead Primary School
Glebelands School
Cranleigh Infant Sch
St Nicholas School
St Cuthbert Mayne RC Primary School
Cranleigh Village Hospital
Cranleigh Health Cen
Cranleigh Leisure Centre
Regal Cinema
Hewitts Industrial Estate
Little Mead Industrial Estate
Knowle Park
Oaklands
Uttworth Manor
Holdhurst Farm
Snoxhall Farm
Highpark
Vachery Pond
Vachery House
New Park
Whitehall
Bowles Farm
Newhouse Farm
Collins Farm
Little Wildwood Farm
Bookers Lee
Wyevale Garden Centre
The Wildwood Golf Club
Golf Course
Works
Baynards
Ivelle Farm
Pallinghurst Farm
White Lea
Rikkyo School in England
Lynwick
Linacre Drive
1 grid square represents 500 metres

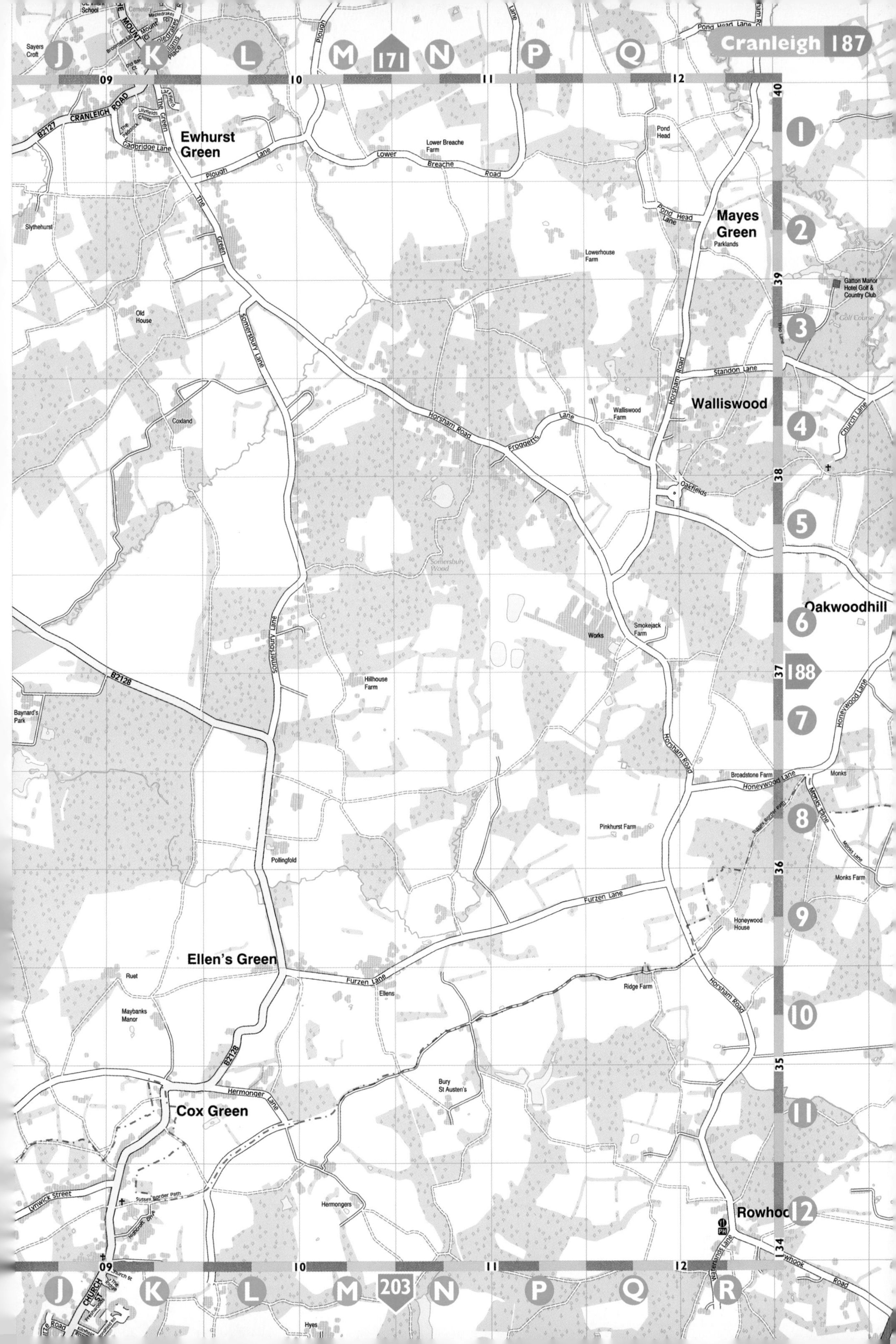
Ewhurst Green
Mayes Green
Walliswood
Oakwoodhill
Ellen's Green
Cox Green
Rowhook
Sayers Croft
Slythehurst
Old House
Coxland
Baynard's Park
Ruet
Maybanks Manor
Lower Breache Farm
Lower Breache Road
Plough Lane
Cadbridge Lane
CRANLEIGH ROAD
B2127
B2128
The Green
Somersbury Lane
Somersbury Wood
Horsham Road
Froggetts Lane
Pond Head
Pond Head Lane
Parklands
Lowerhouse Farm
Gatton Manor Hotel Golf & Country Club
Golf Course
Standon Lane
Walliswood Farm
Church Lane
Oakfields
Works
Smokejack Farm
Hillhouse Farm
Honeywood Lane
Broadstone Farm
Monks
Monks Lane
Monks Farm
Sussex Border Path
Pinkhurst Farm
Pollingfold
Furzen Lane
Honeywood House
Ellens
Ridge Farm
Bury St Austen's
Hermonger Lane
Hermongers
Lynwick Street
Church St
Waterlands Lane
Rowhook Road
Hyes
171
188
203
J K L M N P Q R
09 10 11 12
40 39 38 37 36 35 34
1 2 3 4 5 6 7 8 9 10 11 12

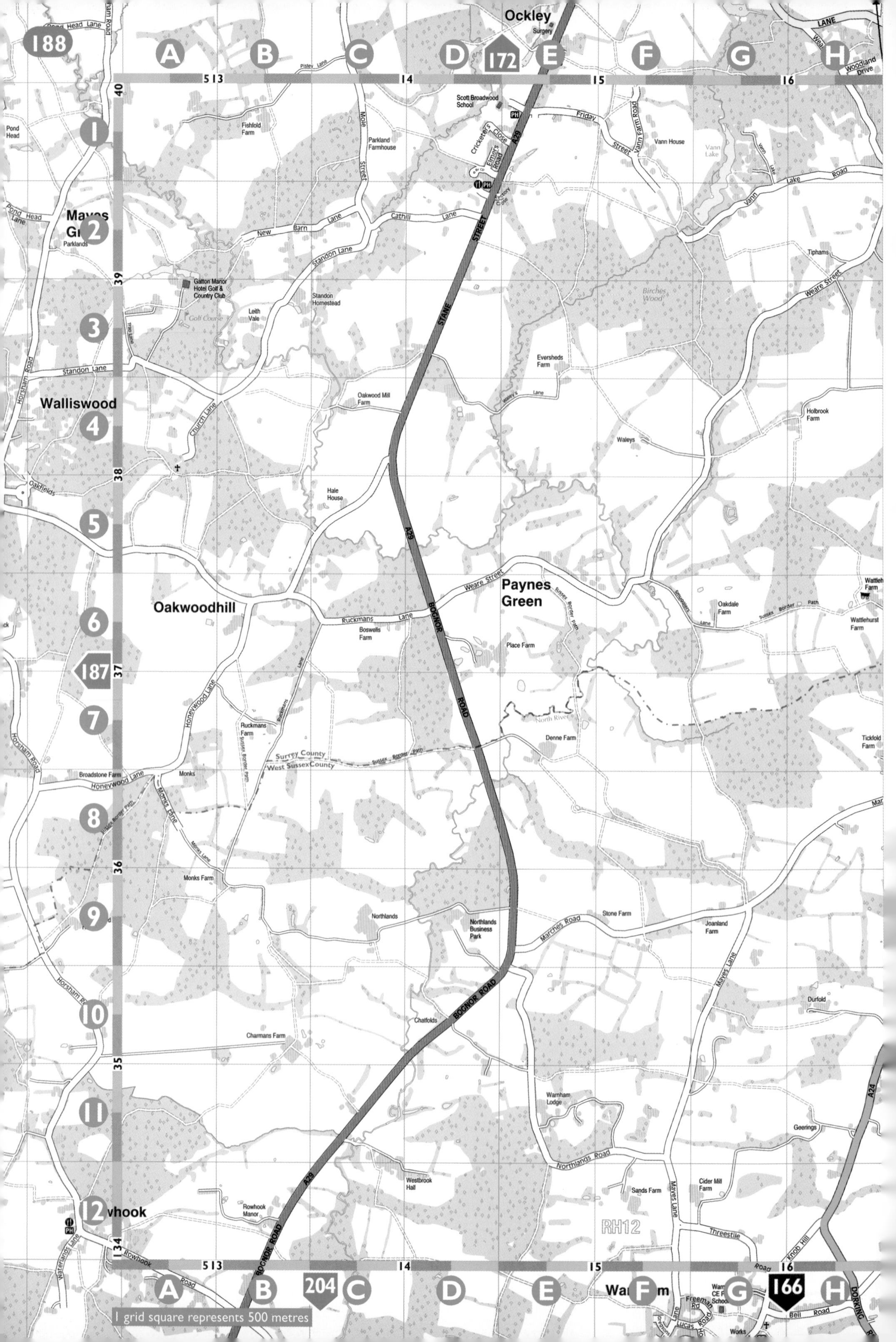

188 (top left corner)

172 (top center, with house icon)

187 (left side)

204 (bottom center, with marker)

166 (bottom right, with marker)

Grid references — top: **A** 513 **B** 14 **C** **D** 172 **E** 15 **F** **G** 16 **H**

Grid references — bottom: **A** 513 **B** 204 **C** **D** **E** **F** War m **G** 166 **H**

Row numbers (left side): 1, 2, 3, 4, 5, 6, 7, 8, 9, 10, 11, 12

Grid line numbers: 40, 39, 38, 37, 36, 35, 34

Place names and features:
- Ockley
- Surgery
- Scott Broadwood School
- PH
- Friday Street
- Vann House
- Vann Lake
- Pistley Lane
- Fishfold Farm
- Mole Street
- Parkland Farmhouse
- Crickets Hill
- Emms Road
- Rectory Close
- Mayes Green
- Parklands
- New Barn Lane
- Cathill Lane
- Standon Lane
- Vann Lake Road
- Tiphams
- Weare Street
- Birches Wood
- Gatton Manor Hotel Golf & Country Club
- Standon Homestead
- Leith Vale
- Golf Course
- STANE STREET
- Eversheds Farm
- Holbrook Farm
- Walliswood
- Standon Lane
- Church Lane
- Oakwood Mill Farm
- Waleys Lane
- Waleys
- Hale House
- Oakfields
- Hookham Road
- Weare Street
- Paynes Green
- Surrey Border Path
- Wattlehurst
- Oakdale Farm
- Wattlehurst Farm
- Oakwoodhill
- Ruckmans Lane
- Boswells Farm
- Place Farm
- Sussex Border Path
- Honeywood Lane
- Ruckmans Farm
- Sussex Border Path
- BOGNOR ROAD
- North River
- Denne Farm
- Tickfold Farm
- Surrey County
- West Sussex County
- Broadstone Farm
- Monks
- Honeywood Lane
- Monks Lane
- Sussex Border Path
- Sussex - Bognor path
- Monks Farm
- Northlands
- Northlands Business Park
- Stone Farm
- Marches Road
- Joanland Farm
- Mayes Lane
- Charmans Farm
- Durfold
- Chatfolds
- BOGNOR ROAD
- Warnham Lodge
- Geerings
- A24
- Rowhook
- PH
- Waterbroker Lane
- Rowhook Manor
- Westbrook Hall
- RH12
- Northlands Road
- Sands Farm
- Cider Mill Farm
- Mayes Lane
- Threestile
- Warnham
- Bell Road
- DORKING RD
- Freemans Rd
- Lucas Road
- Works
- A29
- Bognor Road
- Hook Road
- Lane
- Woodland Drive
- LANE
- West Lane

1 grid square represents 500 metres

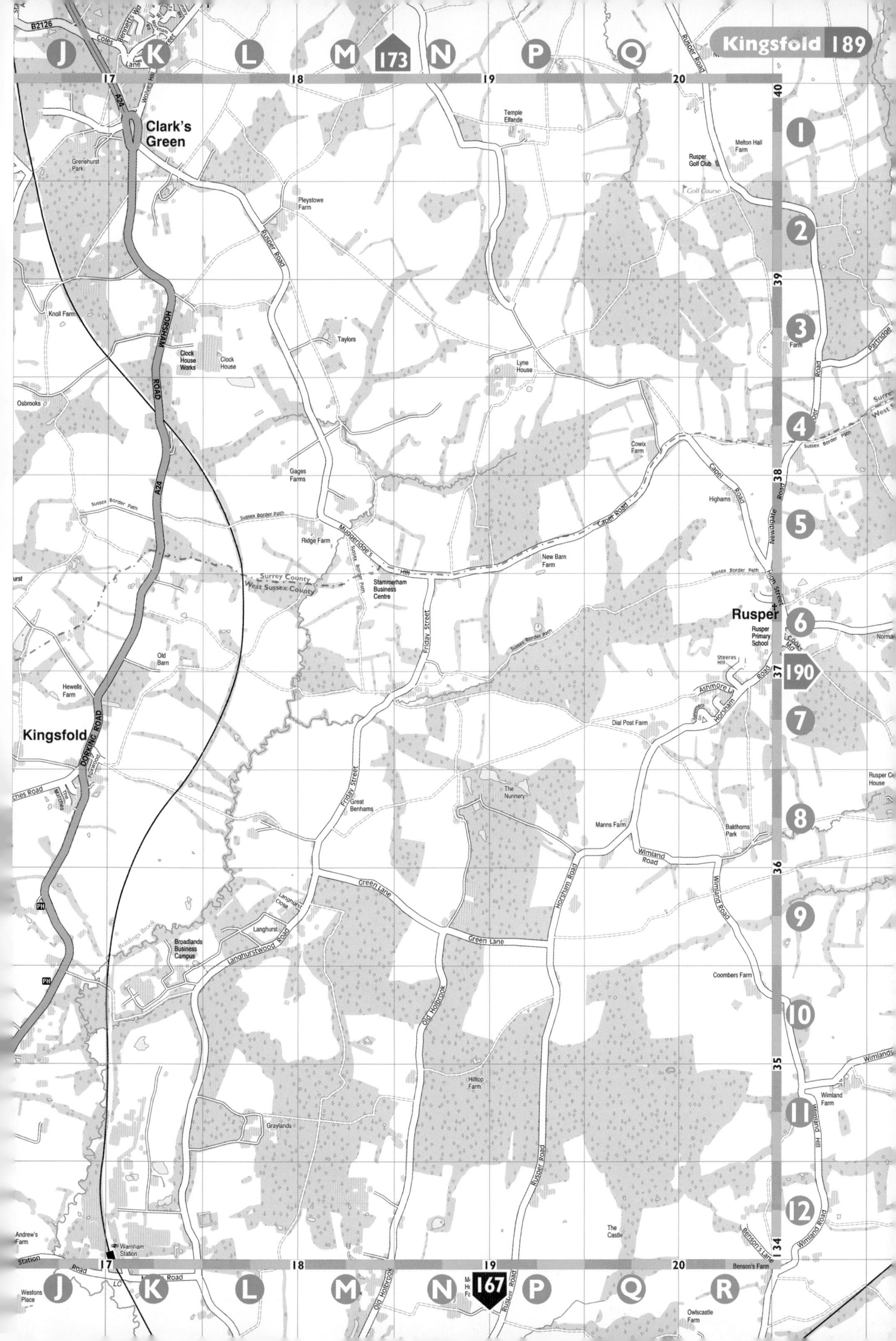
Clark's Green
Kingsfold
Rusper
Greenhurst Park
Knoll Farm
Osbrooks
Clock House Works
Clock House
Pleystowe Farm
Taylors
Gages Farms
Ridge Farm
Temple Elfande
Lyne House
Cowix Farm
New Barn Farm
Stammerham Business Centre
Melton Hall Farm
Rusper Golf Club
Golf Course
Highams
Rusper Primary School
Steeres Hill
Dial Post Farm
The Nunnery
Great Benhams
Manns Farm
Baldhorns Park
Old Barn
Hewells Farm
Langhurst
Broadlands Business Campus
Coombers Farm
Hilltop Farm
Graylands
The Castle
Wimland Farm
Warnham Station
Benson's Farm
Owlscastle Farm
Westons Place
HORSHAM ROAD
DORKING ROAD
A24
Rusper Road
Capel Road
Friday Street
Green Lane
Horsham Road
Wimland Road
Old Holbrook
Langhurstwood Road
Newdigate Road
High Street
Ashmore La
Benson's Lane
Wimland Hill
Sussex Border Path
Surrey County
West Sussex County
Muggeridge's Hill
Boldings Brook
B2126
173
167
190
J K L M N P Q R
17 18 19 20
1 2 3 4 5 6 7 8 9 10 11 12
40 39 38 37 36 35 34

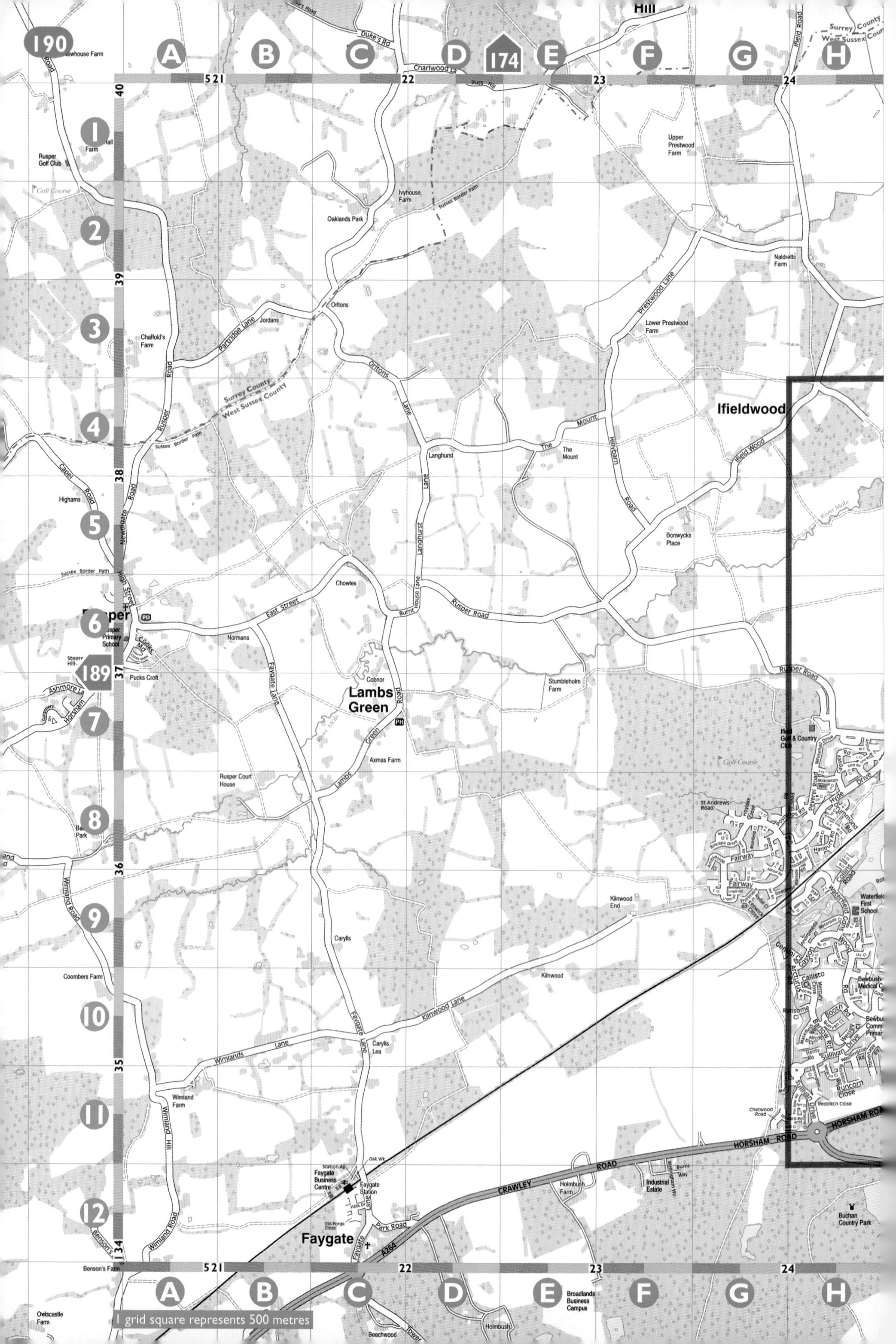
190
174
189
A
B
C
D
E
F
G
H
521
22
23
24
Lambs Green
Ifieldwood
Faygate
Rusper
Surrey County
West Sussex County
Rusper Road
East Street
Faygate Lane
Langhurst Lane
Orltons Lane
Prestwood Lane
Hillybarn Road
Ifield Wood
The Mount
Kilnwood Lane
Wimlands Lane
Wimland Road
Wimland Hill
Newdigate Road
Capel Road
Partridge Lane
Burnt House Lane
Lambs Green Road
CRAWLEY ROAD
HORSHAM ROAD
Park Road
Charlwood La
Duke's Rd
Russ Hill
Chowles
Normans
Cobnor
Axmas Farm
Langhurst
Orltons
Jordans
Chaffold's Farm
Oaklands Park
Ivyhouse Farm
Upper Prestwood Farm
Lower Prestwood Farm
Naldretts Farm
Bonwycks Place
Stumbleholm Farm
Kilnwood End
Kilnwood
Carylls
Carylls Lea
Wimland Farm
Coombers Farm
Rusper Court House
Pucks Croft
Highams
Rusper Golf Club
Ifield Golf & Country Club
Faygate Business Centre
Faygate Station
Holmbush Farm
Industrial Estate
Buchan Country Park
Broadlands Business Campus
Owlscastle Farm
Benson's Farm
Beechwood
Holmbush
Fairway
Peverel Road
Hyde Drive
Runcorn Close
Sullivan Drive
1 grid square represents 500 metres

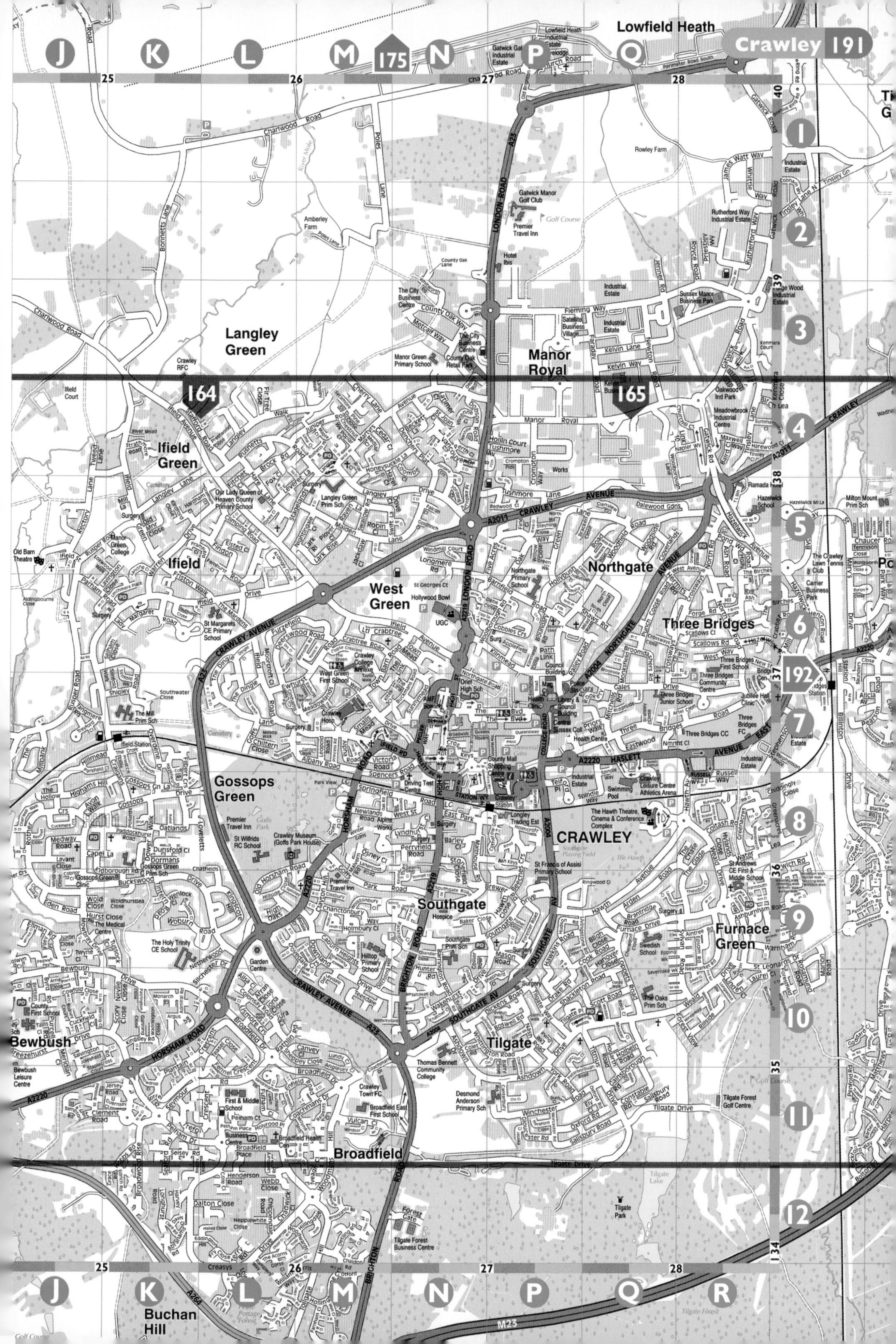

Lowfield Heath
Langley Green
Manor Royal
Ifield Green
Ifield
West Green
Northgate
Three Bridges
Gossops Green
CRAWLEY
Southgate
Furnace Green
Bewbush
Tilgate
Broadfield
Buchan Hill
164
165
175
192
CRAWLEY AVENUE
LONDON ROAD
BRIGHTON ROAD
HORSHAM ROAD
SOUTHGATE AV
HASLETT AVENUE
NORTHGATE
M23
A23
A2011
A2220
A2004
A2219
A264
Charlwood Road
Gatwick Road
Tilgate Park
Tilgate Forest Golf Centre
The Hawth Theatre, Cinema & Conference Complex
Crawley Station
Three Bridges Station
Ifield Station
County Mall Shopping Centre
Crawley Leisure Centre Athletics Arena
Thomas Bennett Community College
Tilgate Forest Business Centre
J
K
L
M
N
P
Q
R
25
26
27
28
1
2
3
4
5
6
7
8
9
10
11
12

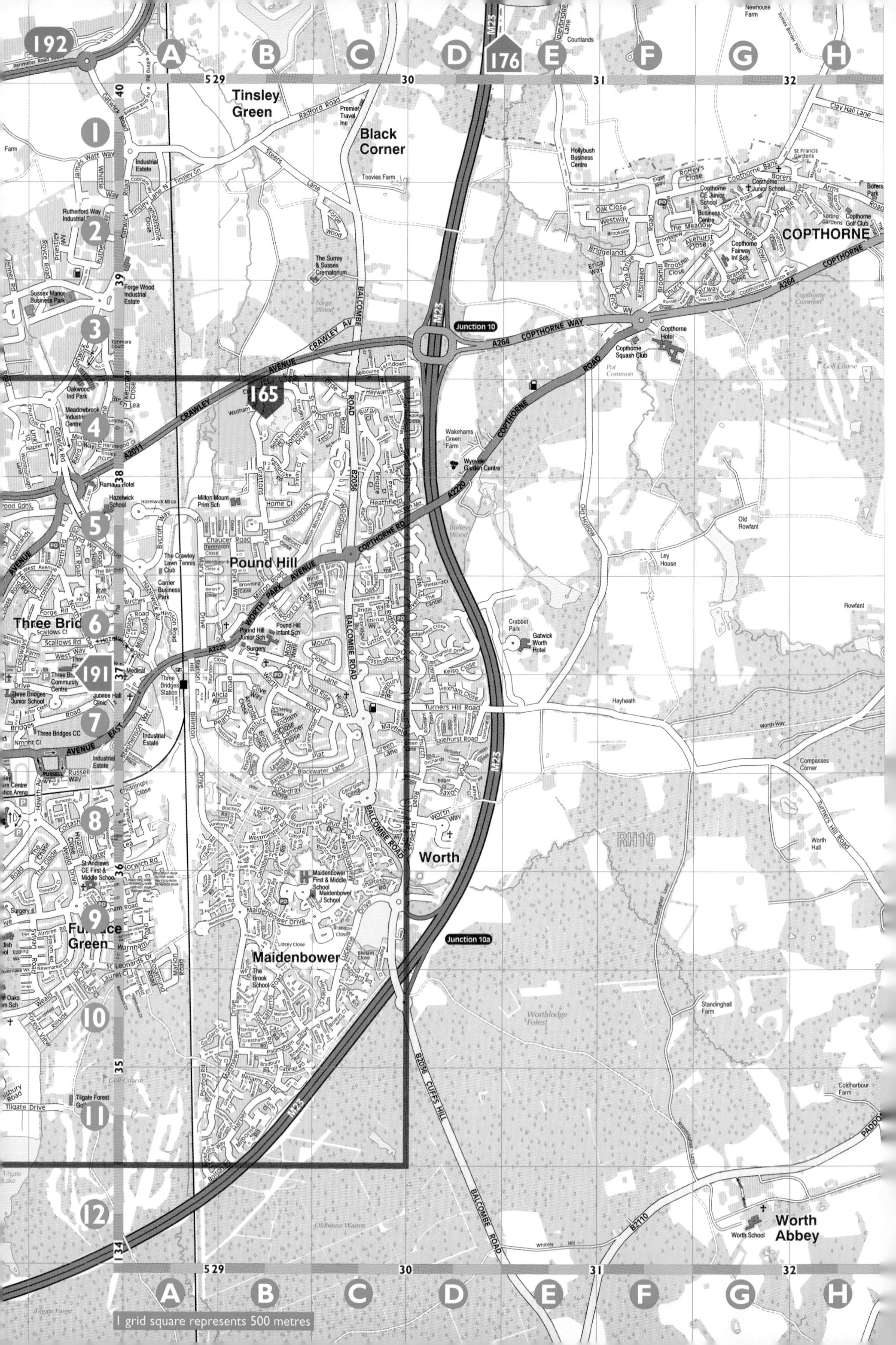

192
176
165
191
A
B
C
D
E
F
G
H
1
2
3
4
5
6
7
8
9
10
11
12
529
30
31
32
40
39
38
37
36
35
134
Tinsley Green
Black Corner
COPTHORNE
Pound Hill
Three Bridges
Furnace Green
Maidenbower
Worth
Worth Abbey
Junction 10
Junction 10a
M23
A264 COPTHORNE WAY
A2011
A2220
B2036
B2110
BALCOMBE ROAD
CRAWLEY AVENUE
COPTHORNE ROAD
WORTH PARK AVENUE
CUFFS HILL
Radford Road
Premier Travel Inn
Toovies Farm
The Surrey & Sussex Crematorium
Forge Wood
Forge Wood Industrial Estate
Sussex Manor Business Park
Rutherford Way Industrial Estate
Industrial Estate
Oakwood Ind Park
Meadowbrook Industrial Centre
Ramada Hotel
Hazelwick School
Milton Mount Prim Sch
The Crawley Lawn Tennis Club
Three Bridges Station
Pound Hill Junior Sch
Pound Hill Infant Sch
Three Bridges Community Centre
Three Bridges Junior School
Three Bridges CC
Jubilee Hall Clinic
St Andrews CE First & Middle School
Maidenbower First & Middle School
Maidenbower J School
The Brook School
Tilgate Forest Golf
Tilgate Drive
Tilgate Lake
Tilgate Forest
Golf Course
Hollybush Business Centre
Courtlands
Newhouse Farm
Clay Hall Lane
St Francis Gardens
Copthorne Bank
Copthorne CE Junior School
Copthorne Junior School
Copthorne Fairway Inf Sch
Copthorne Golf Club
Copthorne Hotel
Copthorne Squash Club
Copthorne Common
Pot Common
Wakehams Green Farm
Wyevale Garden Centre
Burleys Wood
Old Hollow
Old Rowfant
Ley House
Rowfant
Crabbet Park
Gatwick Worth Hotel
Hayheath
Turners Hill Road
Worth Way
Compasses Corner
Worth Hall
RH10
Worthlodge Forest
Standinghall Farm
Standinghall Lane
Coldharbour Farm
Worth School
Whitely Hill
Oldhouse Warren
1 grid square represents 500 metres

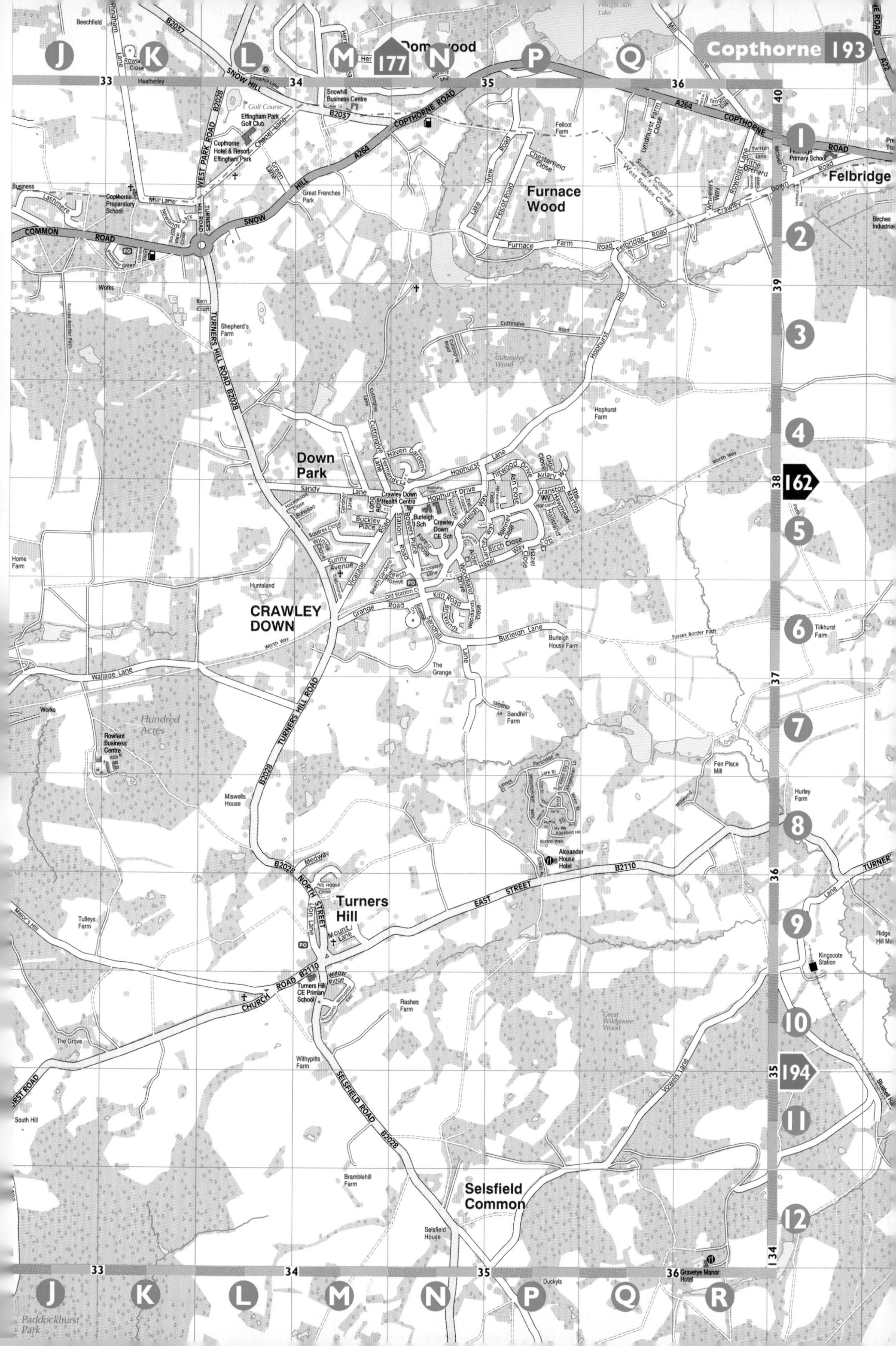

J
K
L
M
N
P
Q
R
177
162
194
33
34
35
36
37
38
39
40
1
2
3
4
5
6
7
8
9
10
11
12
Beechfield
Heatherley
Snow Hill
B2037
Snowhill Business Centre
Golf Course
Effingham Park Golf Club
Copthorne Hotel & Resort Effingham Park
Chapel Lane
West Park Road
B2028
A264
Copthorne Road
Fellcot Farm
Lyndhurst Farm Close
Copthorne
Felbridge Primary School
Felbridge
Felbridge Water
Birches Industrial
Surrey County
West Sussex County
Crawley Down Road
Rowplatt Lane
Wheelers Way
Tithe Orchard
Twitten Lane
Furnace Wood
Chesterfield Close
Felcot Road
Lake View Road
Furnace Farm Road
Felbridge Road
Business
Lashmere
Copthorne Preparatory School
Mill Lane
Newlands
Turners Hill Road
Common Road
Snow Hill
Green Lane
Great Frenches Park
Works
Sussex Border Path
Shepherd's Farm
Cuttinglye Road
Cuttinglye Wood
Cuttinglye Lane
Hophurst Hill
Hophurst Farm
Hophurst Lane
Turners Hill Road B2028
Down Park
Sandy Lane
Haven Gardens
Fermandy La
Crawley Down Health Centre
Hophurst Drive
Tiltwood Drive
Ash Close
Aviary Wy
Granston Wy
The Martins
Hawthorns
Hallsland
Burleigh Sch
Crawley Down CE Sch
Burleigh Way
Hillside
Spinney Close
Birch Close
Hazel Way
Hazel Close
Copse Cl
Larches Way
Alder Cl
Buckley Place
Long Acre
Gardner Lane
Station Road
Bowers Place
Forest Close
Squires Close
Hazelwood Close
Burlwood
Wyntie Close
Sunny Avenue
Vicarage
Beech Gardens
Beech Holme
Brickyard Lane
Woodland Drive
Old Station Cl
Grange Road
Kiln Road
Sandhill Lane
Bricklands
Home Farm
Huntsland
CRAWLEY DOWN
Worth Way
Burleigh Lane
Burleigh House Farm
The Grange
Sussex Border Path
Tilkhurst Farm
Wallage Lane
Works
Hundred Acres
Rowfant Business Centre
Sandhill Farm
Fen Place Mill
Hurley Farm
Partridge Pl
Lark Ri
Linnet
Woodpecker Way
Wren St
Blackbird Hill
Kestrel Walk
Jay Wk
Miswells House
Alexander House Hotel
B2110
East Street
Turners Hill Road
Medway
Hill House Close
North Street
Turners Hill
Lion Lane
Mount Lane
Major's Hill
Tulleys Farm
Church Road
Willow Ridge
Turners Hill CE Primary School
Withypitts East
Rashes Farm
Great Wildgoose Wood
Kingscote Station
Ridge Hill
Lane
The Grove
Withypitts Farm
Selsfield Road
Vowels Lane
South Hill
Bluebell
Bramblehill Farm
Selsfield Common
Selsfield House
Duckyls
Gravetye Manor Hotel
Paddockhurst Park

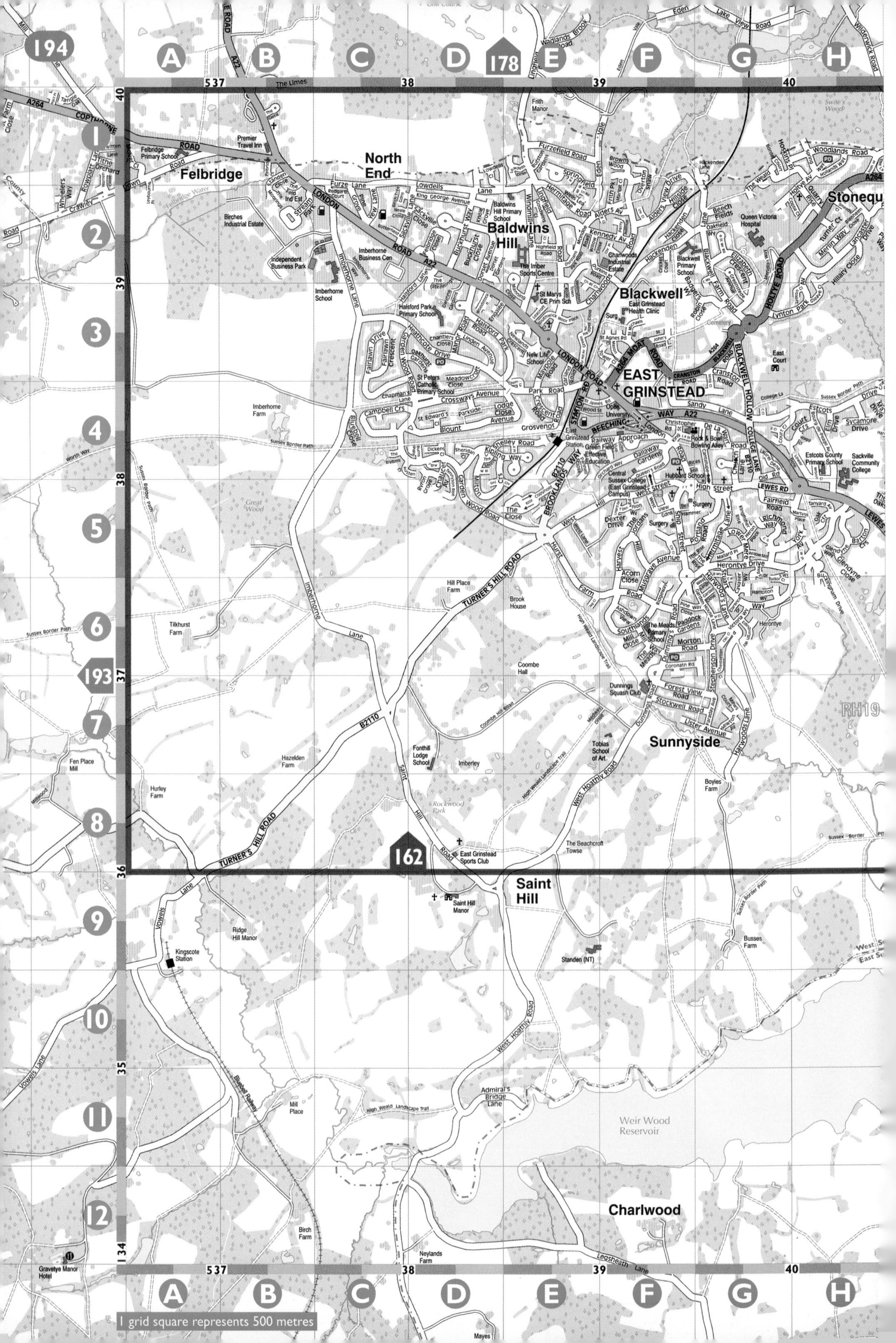

194
178
193
162
A
B
C
D
E
F
G
H
537
38
39
40
36
37
35
1 34
1
2
3
4
5
6
7
8
9
10
11
12
Felbridge
North End
Baldwins Hill
Blackwell
EAST GRINSTEAD
Stonequ
Sunnyside
Saint Hill
Charlwood
A264
A22
B2110
COPTHORNE ROAD
LONDON ROAD
TURNER'S HILL ROAD
HOLTYE ROAD
LEWES RD
BEECHING WAY
BROOKLANDS WAY
CRANSTON ROAD
MOAT ROAD
BLACKWELL HOLLOW
COLLEGE LANE
Imberhorne Lane
Saint Hill Road
West Hoathly Road
Legsheath Lane
Vowels Lane
Coombe Hill Road
Furze Lane
Lowdells Lane
King George Avenue
Crossways Avenue
Park Road
Sandy Lane
High Street
West Street
Felbridge Primary School
Premier Travel Inn
Birches Industrial Estate
Independent Business Park
Imberhorne Business Cen
Imberhorne School
Halsford Park Primary School
St Peters Catholic Primary School
Baldwins Hill Primary School
The Imber Sports Centre
St Marys CE Prim Sch
New Life School
Charlwoods Industrial Estate
East Grinstead Health Clinic
Blackwell Primary School
Queen Victoria Hospital
East Grinstead Station
Open University
Central Sussex College (East Grinstead Campus)
Hubbard School
Rock & Bowl Bowling Alley
Estcots County Primary School
Sackville Community College
The Meads Primary School
Dunnings Squash Club
Tobias School of Art
Fonthill Lodge School
East Grinstead Sports Club
Saint Hill Manor
Standen (NT)
Kingscote Station
Gravetye Manor Hotel
Weir Wood Reservoir
Imberhorne Farm
Tilkhurst Farm
Hill Place Farm
Brook House
Coombe Hall
Hazelden Farm
Hurley Farm
Fen Place Mill
Imberley
Rockwood Park
Boyles Farm
Busses Farm
Ridge Hill Manor
Mill Place
Birch Farm
Neylands Farm
Admiral's Bridge Lane
The Beachcroft Towse
Great Wood
Frith Manor
Swite's Wood
Bluebell Railway
Sussex Border Path
High Weald Landscape Trail
Worth Way
RH19
Mayes
1 grid square represents 500 metres

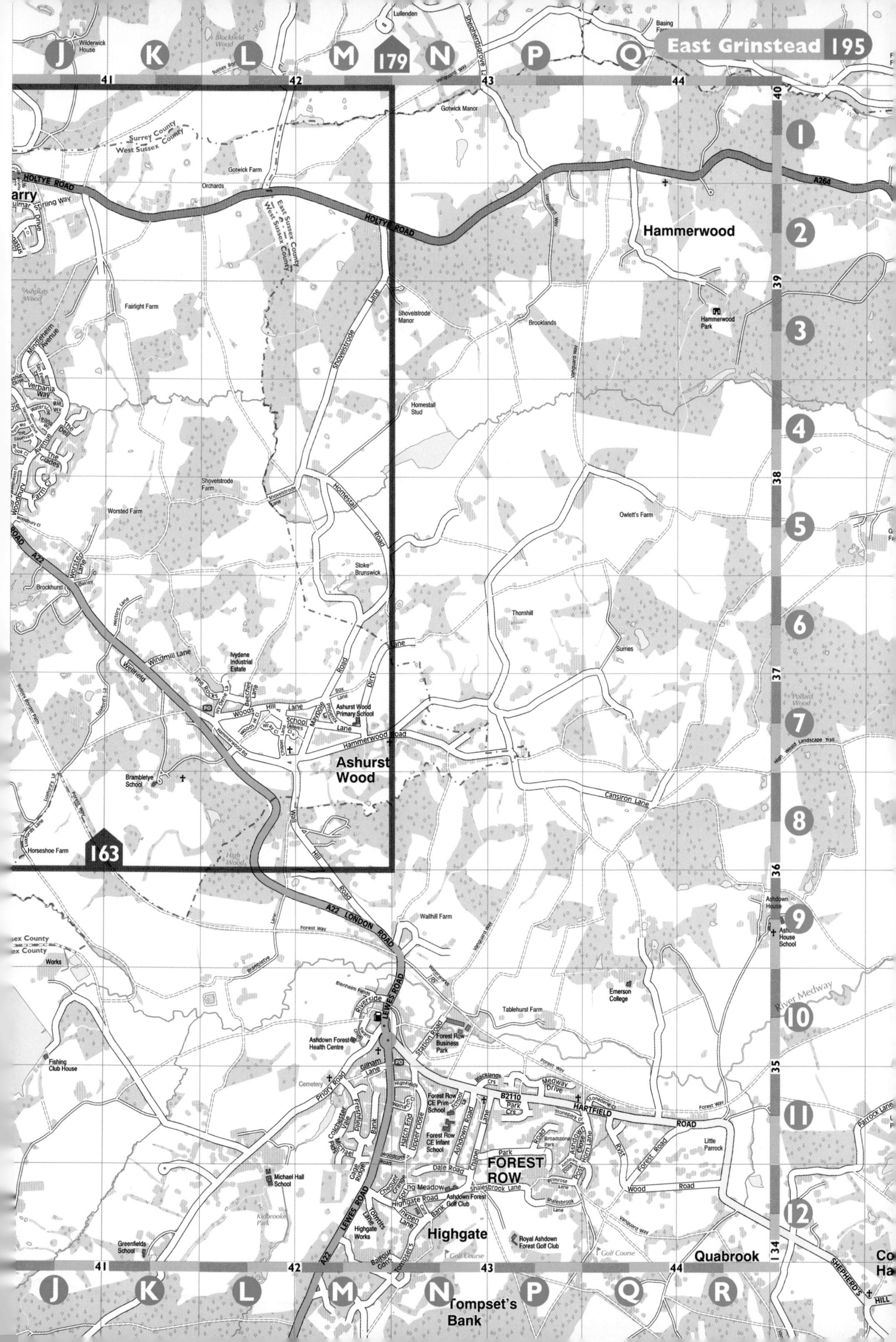

J K L M 179 N P Q

41 42 43 44 40

1

A264

HOLTYE ROAD

Hammerwood 2

39

Hammerwood Park 3

38 4

Owlett's Farm 5

Thornhill 6

Surries

37

Pollard Wood 7

Ashurst Wood 8

Cansiron Lane

36

Ashdown House 9

River Medway 10

35

HARTFIELD 11

FOREST ROW 12

Highgate 34

Quabrook

41 42 43 44

J K L M N P Q R

Tompset's Bank

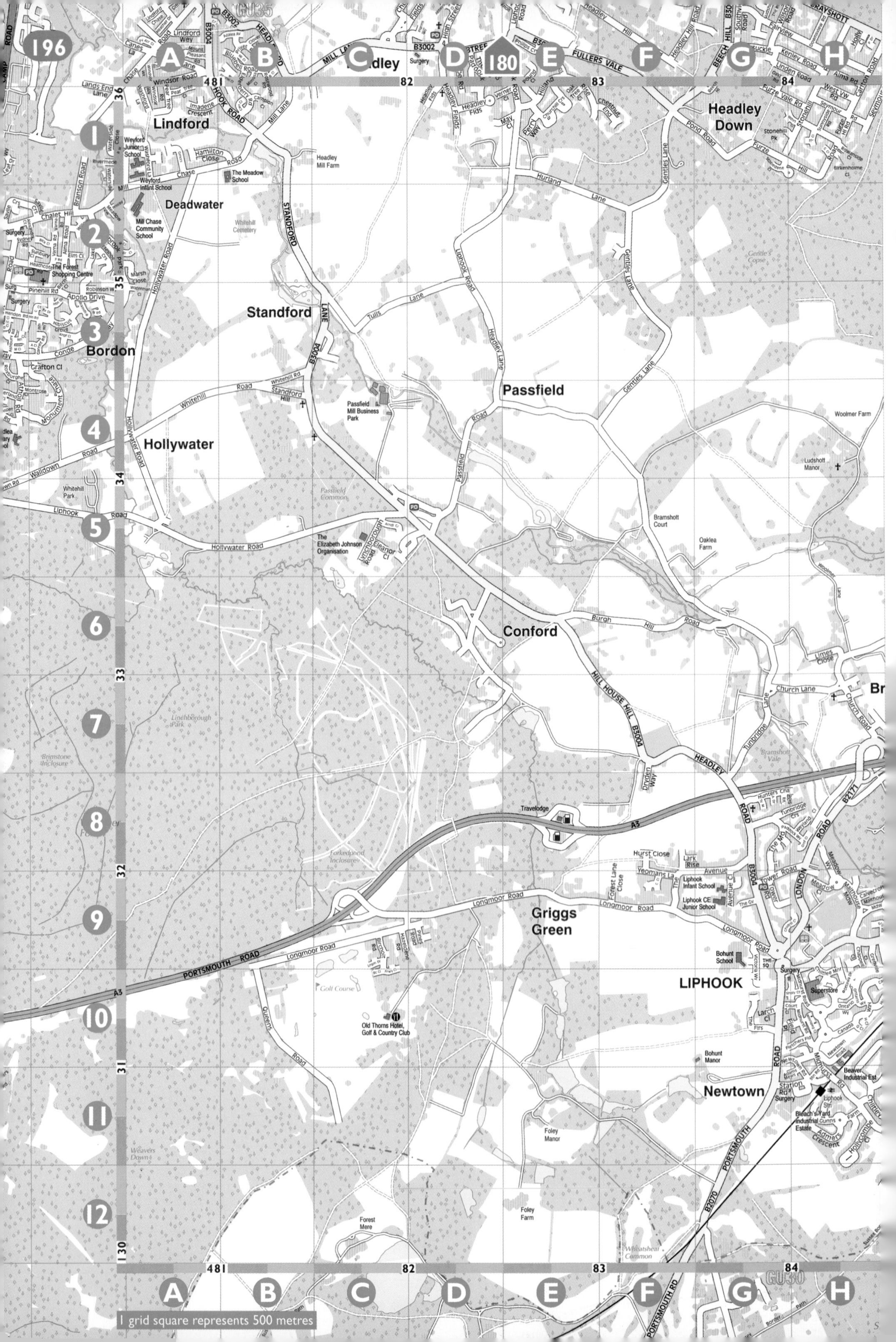

196
180
Lindford
Deadwater
Bordon
Standford
Hollywater
Passfield
Headley Down
Conford
Griggs Green
LIPHOOK
Newtown
Headley Mill Farm
The Meadow School
Weyford Junior School
Weyford Infant School
Mill Chase Community School
Whitehill Cemetery
The Forest Shopping Centre
Passfield Mill Business Park
The Elizabeth Johnson Organisation
Passfield Common
Whitehill Park
Woolmer Farm
Ludshott Manor
Bramshott Court
Oaklea Farm
Linchborough Park
Brimstone Inclosure
Forkedpond Inclosure
Travelodge
Liphook Infant School
Liphook CE Junior School
Bohunt School
Superstore
Golf Course
Old Thorns Hotel, Golf & Country Club
Bohunt Manor
Beaver Industrial Est
Bleach's Yard Industrial Estate
Foley Manor
Foley Farm
Forest Mere
Wheatsheaf Common
Weavers Down
STANDFORD LANE
HOOK ROAD
MILL LANE
FULLERS VALE
BEECH HILL
Hollywater Road
Whitehill Road
Liphook Road
Headley Lane
Gentles Lane
Hurland Lane
Tulls Lane
Passfield Road
Burgh Hill Road
HILL HOUSE HILL
HEADLEY ROAD
LONDON ROAD
PORTSMOUTH ROAD
Longmoor Road
Church Lane
Tunbridge Lane
A3
B3004
B3002
B2070
B2131
GU35
GU30
481
82
83
84
130
31
32
33
34
35
36
1 grid square represents 500 metres

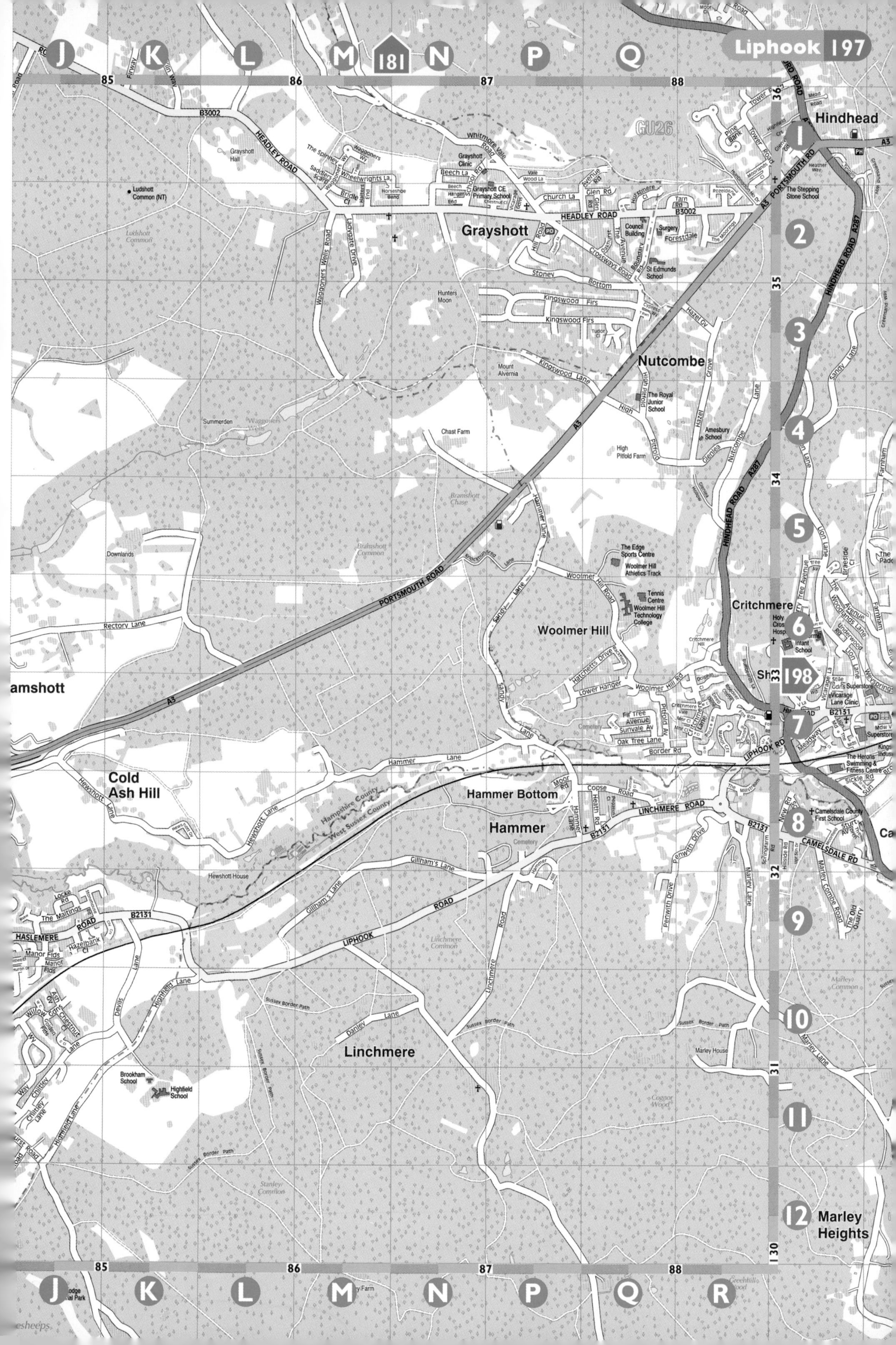
Hindhead
Grayshott
Nutcombe
Woolmer Hill
Critchmere
Cold Ash Hill
Hammer Bottom
Hammer
Linchmere
Marley Heights
HEADLEY ROAD
PORTSMOUTH ROAD
HINDHEAD ROAD
LINCHMERE ROAD
LIPHOOK ROAD
HASLEMERE ROAD
CAMELSDALE RD
Hammer Lane
Marley Lane
Sandy Lane
Rectory Lane

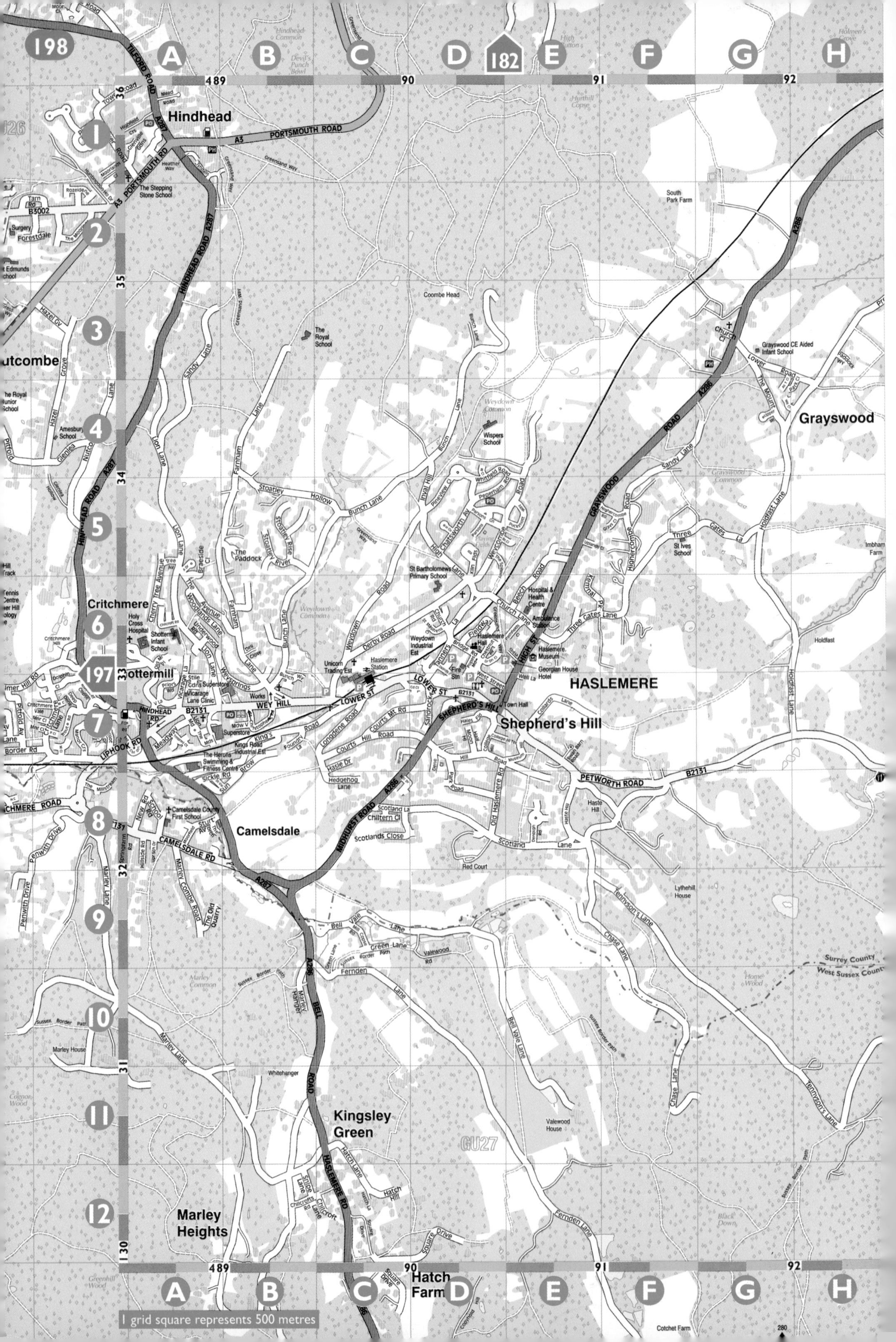
198
182
197
A
B
C
D
E
F
G
H
489
90
91
92
Hindhead
PORTSMOUTH ROAD
HINDHEAD ROAD
TILFORD ROAD
The Stepping Stone School
Forestdale
Critchmere
Holy Cross Hospital
Shottermill Infant School
Shottermill
HINDHEAD RD
WEY HILL
LOWER ST
LIPHOOK RD
The Herons Swimming & Fitness Centre
Camelsdale County First School
Camelsdale
CAMELSDALE RD
Marley Lane
The Royal School
Coombe Head
Weydown Common
Wispers School
St Bartholomews Primary School
Haslemere Station
Unicorn Trading Est
Weydown Industrial Est
Hospital & Health Centre
Ambulance Station
Haslemere Museum
Georgian House Hotel
HASLEMERE
Town Hall
Shepherd's Hill
PETWORTH ROAD
MIDHURST ROAD
GRAYSWOOD ROAD
HIGH ST
Grayswood
Grayswood CE Aided Infant School
South Park Farm
St Ives School
Holdfast
Haste Hill
Red Court
Lythehill House
Surrey County
West Sussex County
Valewood House
Kingsley Green
Marley Heights
Marley House
Whitehanger
BELL ROAD
HASLEMERE RD
Hatch Farm
GU27
Cotchet Farm
1 grid square represents 500 metres

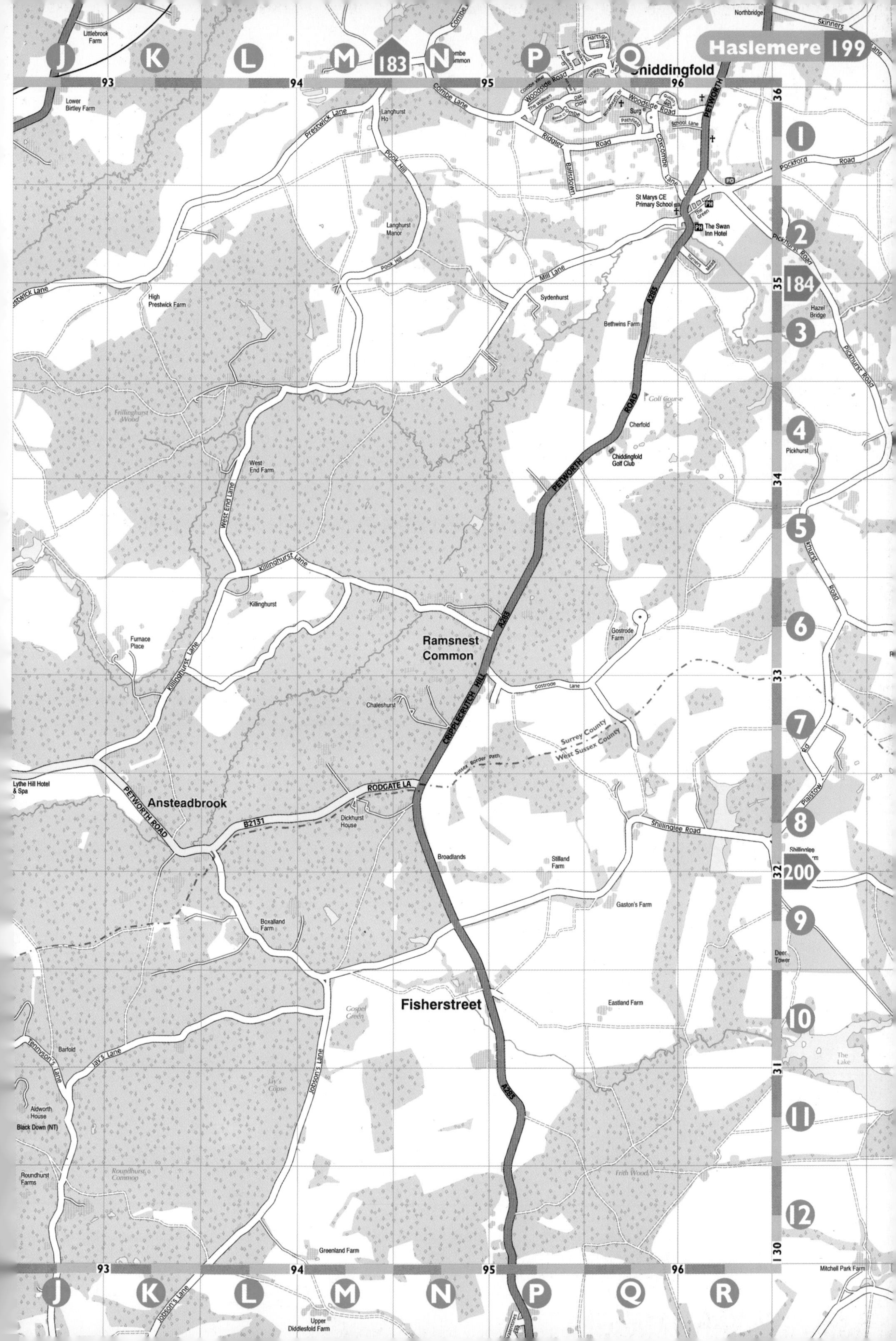
Chiddingfold
Ramsnest
Common
Ansteadbrook
Fisherstreet
Littlebrook Farm
Lower Birtley Farm
Northbridge
Skinners
Prestwick Lane
Combe Lane
Woodside Road
Ridgley Road
Coxcombe Lane
School Lane
Pockford Road
St Marys CE Primary School
The Green
The Swan Inn Hotel
Langhurst Ho
Langhurst Manor
Pook Hill
Mill Lane
High Prestwick Farm
Sydenhurst
Bethwins Farm
Pickhurst Road
Hazel Bridge
Golf Course
Cherfold
Chiddingfold Golf Club
Pickhurst
Frillinghurst Wood
West End Farm
West End Lane
Killinghurst Lane
Killinghurst
Furnace Place
PETWORTH ROAD
A283
Gostrode Farm
Gostrode Lane
CRIPPLECRUTCH HILL
Chaleshurst
Surrey County
West Sussex County
Sussex Border Path
RODGATE LA
B2131
Dickhurst House
Lythe Hill Hotel & Spa
Shillinglee Road
Broadlands
Stilland Farm
Gaston's Farm
Boxalland Farm
Deer Tower
Eastland Farm
Gospel Green
Tennyson's Lane
Jay's Lane
Jobson's Lane
Barfold
Jay's Copse
Aldworth House
Black Down (NT)
The Lake
Roundhurst Farms
Roundhurst Common
Frith Wood
Greenland Farm
Mitchell Park Farm
Upper Diddlesfold Farm
183
184
200
93
94
95
96
36
35
34
33
32
31
130
J
K
L
M
N
P
Q
R
1
2
3
4
5
6
7
8
9
10
11
12

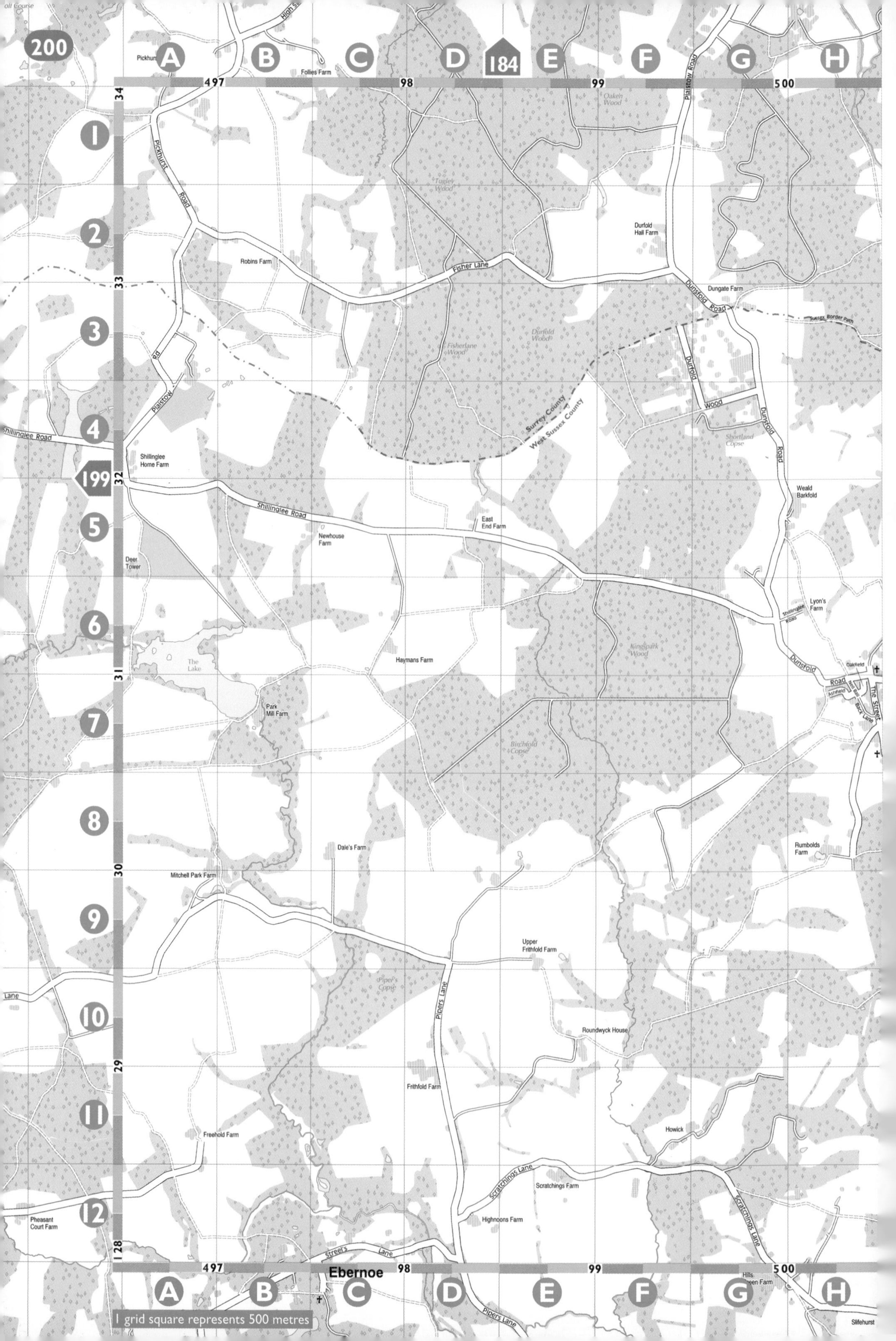

200
184
199
A
B
C
D
E
F
G
H
497
98
99
500
34
33
32
31
30
29
128
1
2
3
4
5
6
7
8
9
10
11
12
Pickhurst Road
Follies Farm
Oaken Wood
Plaistow Road
Tugley Wood
Durfold Hall Farm
Robins Farm
Fisher Lane
Dungate Farm
Dunsfold Road
Sussex Border Path
Durfold Wood
Fisherlane Wood
Plaistow Rd
Surrey County
West Sussex County
Wood
Shortland Copse
Shillinglee Road
Shillinglee Home Farm
Weald Barkfold
East End Farm
Newhouse Farm
Deer Tower
Lyon's Farm
Kingspark Wood
The Lake
Haymans Farm
Oakfield
Ashfield
The Street
Back Lane
Park Mill Farm
Birchfold Copse
Rumbolds Farm
Dale's Farm
Mitchell Park Farm
Upper Frithfold Farm
Piper's Copse
Lane
Pipers Lane
Roundwyck House
Frithfold Farm
Howick
Freehold Farm
Scratchings Lane
Scratchings Farm
Highnoons Farm
Pheasant Court Farm
Streel's Lane
Ebernoe
Pipers Lane
Slifehurst
1 grid square represents 500 metres

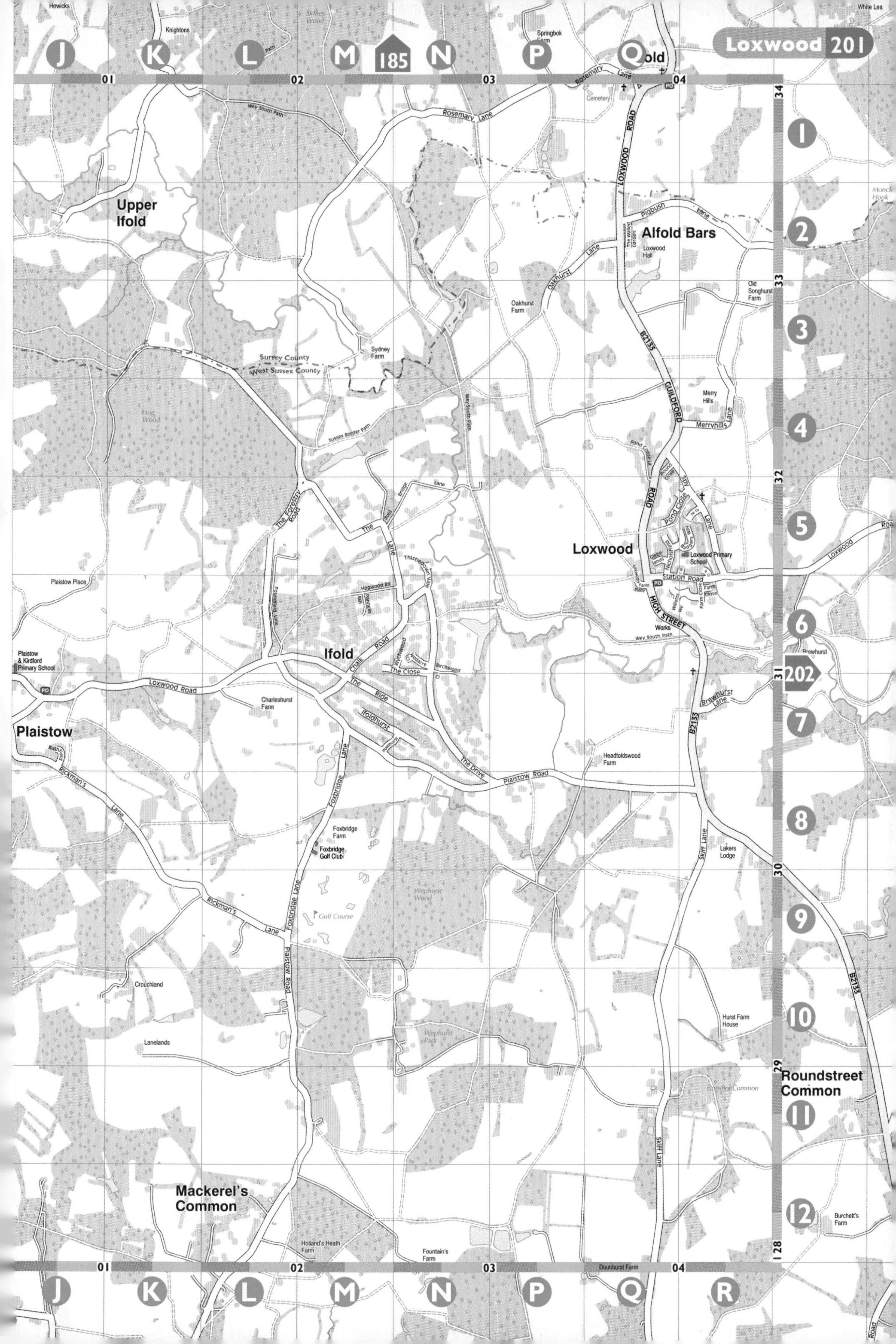

Upper Ifold
Alfold Bars
Loxwood
Ifold
Plaistow
Roundstreet Common
Mackerel's Common
Loxwood Road
Rosemary Lane
Plaistow Road
Rickman's Lane
Foxbridge Lane
Station Road
High Street
Guildford Road
Skiff Lane
Brewhurst Lane
Merryhills Lane
Chalk Road
The Ride
The Drive
The Close
The Lane
The Forestry Road
Surrey County
West Sussex County
Sussex Border Path
Wey South Path
Loxwood Primary School
Plaistow & Kirdford Primary School
Foxbridge Golf Club
Golf Course
Wephurst Wood
Hog Wood
Oakhurst Farm
Sydney Farm
Charleshurst Farm
Headfoldswood Farm
Foxbridge Farm
Lakers Lodge
Hurst Farm House
Crouchland
Lanelands
Holland's Heath Farm
Fountain's Farm
Dounhurst Farm
Burchett's Farm
Old Songhurst Farm
Merry Hills
Loxwood Hall
Plaistow Place
Gunshot Common
Brewhurst
B2133
185
202

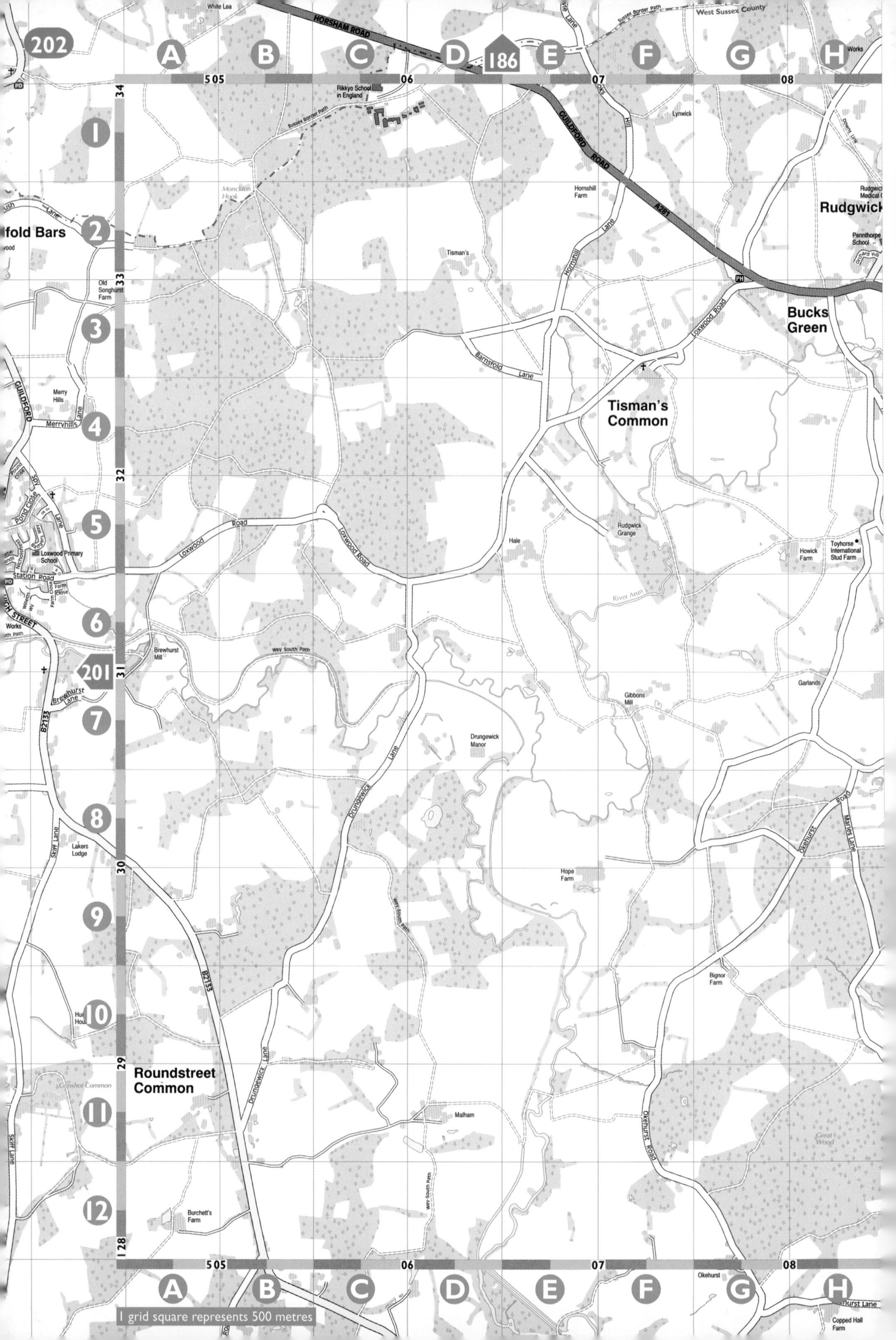

202

186

201

A B C D E F G H

34
5 05 06 07 08

White Lea
HORSHAM ROAD
West Sussex County

Rikkyo School
in England

Sussex Border Path

Monckton Hook

Rudgwick
Medical C

Rudgwick

fold Bars

Old Songhurst
Farm

Merry
Hills

Merryhills Lane

GUILDFORD

Pennthorpe
School

Hornshill
Farm

Bucks
Green

Tisman's

Hornshill Lane

GUILDFORD ROAD A281

Lynwick

Lynwick

PH

Barnsfold Lane

Tisman's
Common

Rudgwick
Grange

Loxwood Road

Hale

Howick
Farm

Toyhorse
International
Stud Farm

Loxwood Primary
School

Loxwood Road

Loxwood Road

Station Road

Pond Close

HIGH STREET

Works

River Arun

Brewhurst
Mill

Wey South Path

Garlands

Gibbons
Mill

Brewhurst Lane

B2133

Drungewick
Manor

Drungewick Lane

Lakers
Lodge

Skiff Lane

Hope
Farm

Okehurst Road

Marles Lane

Bignor
Farm

B2133

Hu
Hou

Roundstreet
Common

Cramhot Common

Drungewick Lane

Malham

Wey South Path

Okehurst Road

Great
Wood

Skiff Lane

Burchett's
Farm

Okehurst

Copped Hall
Farm

1 28
5 05 06 07 08

A B C D E F G H

I grid square represents 500 metres

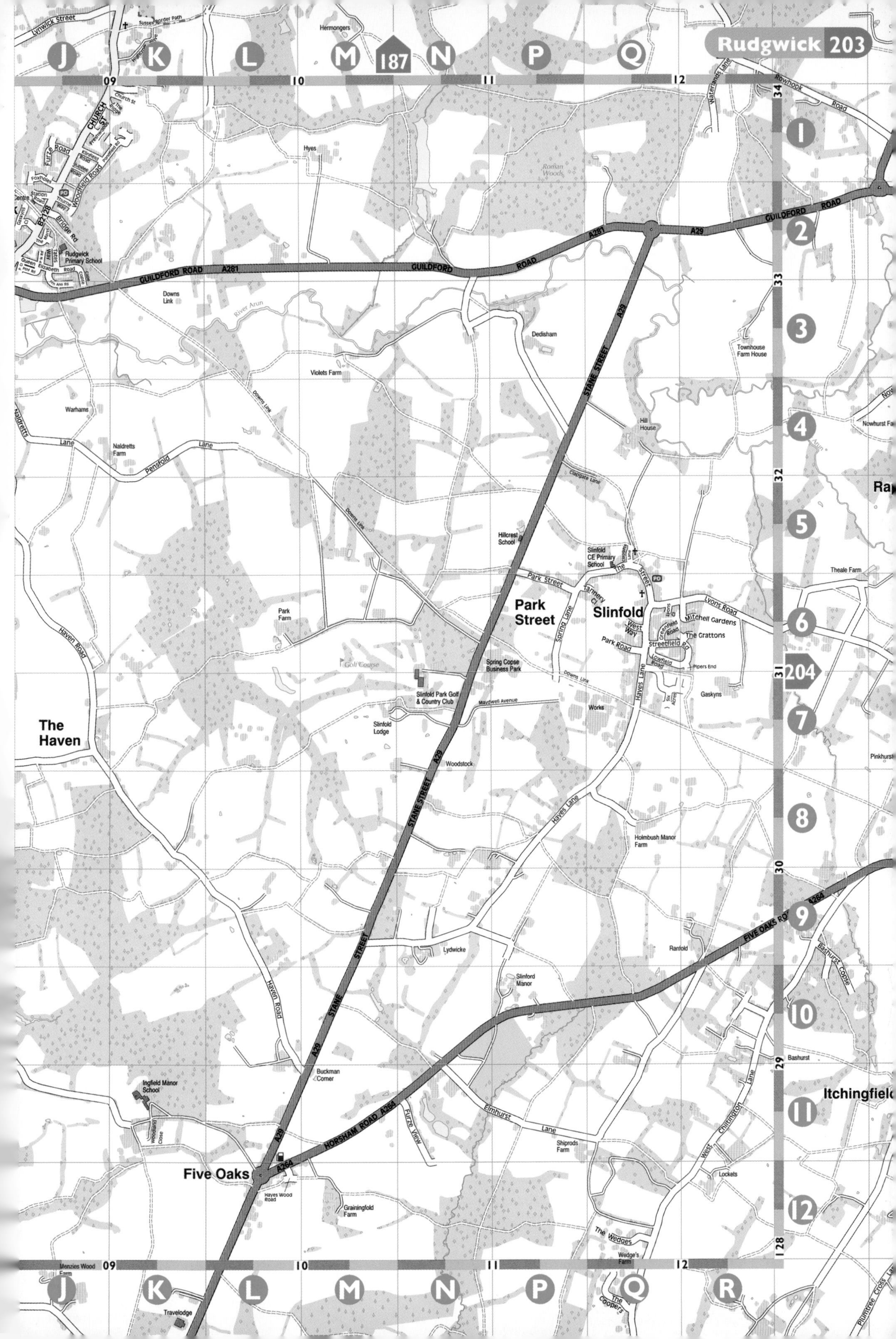
J
K
L
M
187
N
P
Q
09
10
11
12
34
1
2
3
4
32
5
6
31
204
7
8
30
9
10
29
11
12
128
R
Lynwick Street
Sussex Border Path
Hermongers
CHURCH ST
Church St
Furze Road
Woodfield Road
Foxholes
Station
Centre
B2128
Bridge Rd
Rudgwick Primary School
Queen Elizabeth Road
GUILDFORD ROAD
A281
GUILDFORD
ROAD
A29
Hyes
Roman Woods
Waterlands Lane
Rowhook
Road
Downs Link
River Arun
Dedisham
Townhouse Farm House
STANE STREET
Violets Farm
Nowhurst Farm
Hill House
Naldretts
Lane
Warnhams
Naldretts Farm
Pensfold
Lane
Downs Link
Clapgate Lane
Ra
Hillcrest School
Slinfold CE Primary School
The Street
Park Street
Tannery Cl
Theale Farm
Park Farm
Park Street
Slinfold
Spring Lane
West Way
Lyons Road
Mitchell Gardens
Greenfield Road
The Grattons
Park Road
Streetfield Rd
Lowfield Road
Pipers End
Haven Road
Golf Course
Spring Copse Business Park
Downs Link
Slinfold Park Golf & Country Club
Maydwell Avenue
Six Acres
Gaskyns
Works
Hayes Lane
Slinfold Lodge
The Haven
Woodstock
Pinkhurst
Hayes Lane
Holmbush Manor Farm
STANE STREET
A29
FIVE OAKS RD
A264
Bashurst Copse
Lydwicke
Ranfold
Slinford Manor
Haven Road
STANE
STREET
A29
Bashurst
Buckman Corner
Itchingfield
Ingfield Manor School
Furze View
Elmhurst
Lane
Chiltington Lane
West
Woodland Close
HORSHAM ROAD
A264
A29
Shiprods Farm
Five Oaks
Hayes Wood Road
Lockets
Grainingfold Farm
The Wedges
Wedge's Farm
Menzies Wood Farm
The Coopers
Travelodge
Plumtree Cross La

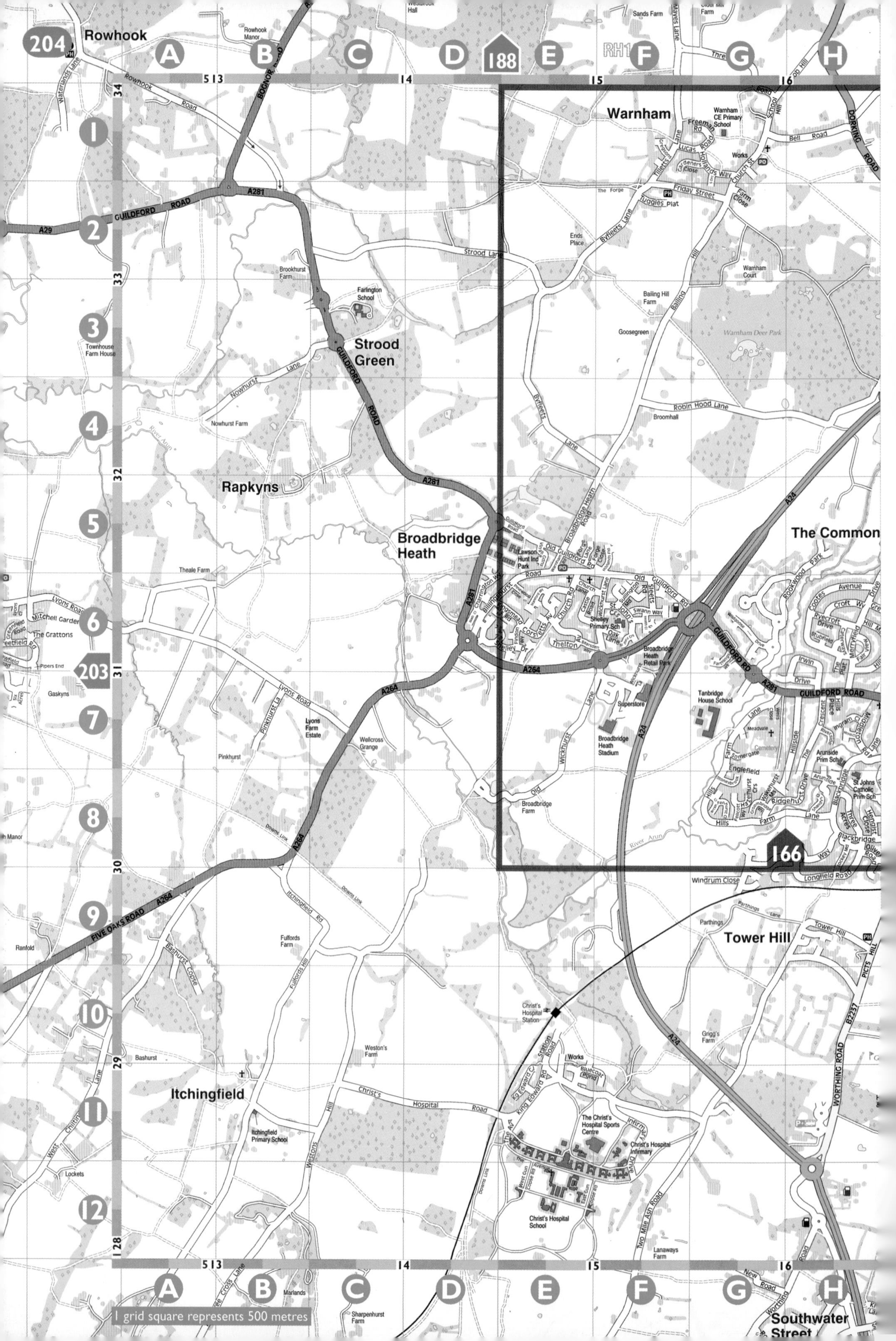

204
Rowhook
188
203
166
Warnham
Strood Green
Rapkyns
Broadbridge Heath
The Common
Tower Hill
Itchingfield
Southwater Street
Warnham Deer Park
Christ's Hospital School
Christ's Hospital Station
Broadbridge Heath Stadium
Tanbridge House School
Shelley Primary Sch
Itchingfield Primary School
Farlington School
GUILDFORD ROAD
FIVE OAKS ROAD
WORTHING ROAD
DORKING ROAD
BOGNOR ROAD
A281
A264
A24
A29
B2237
River Arun
1 grid square represents 500 metres

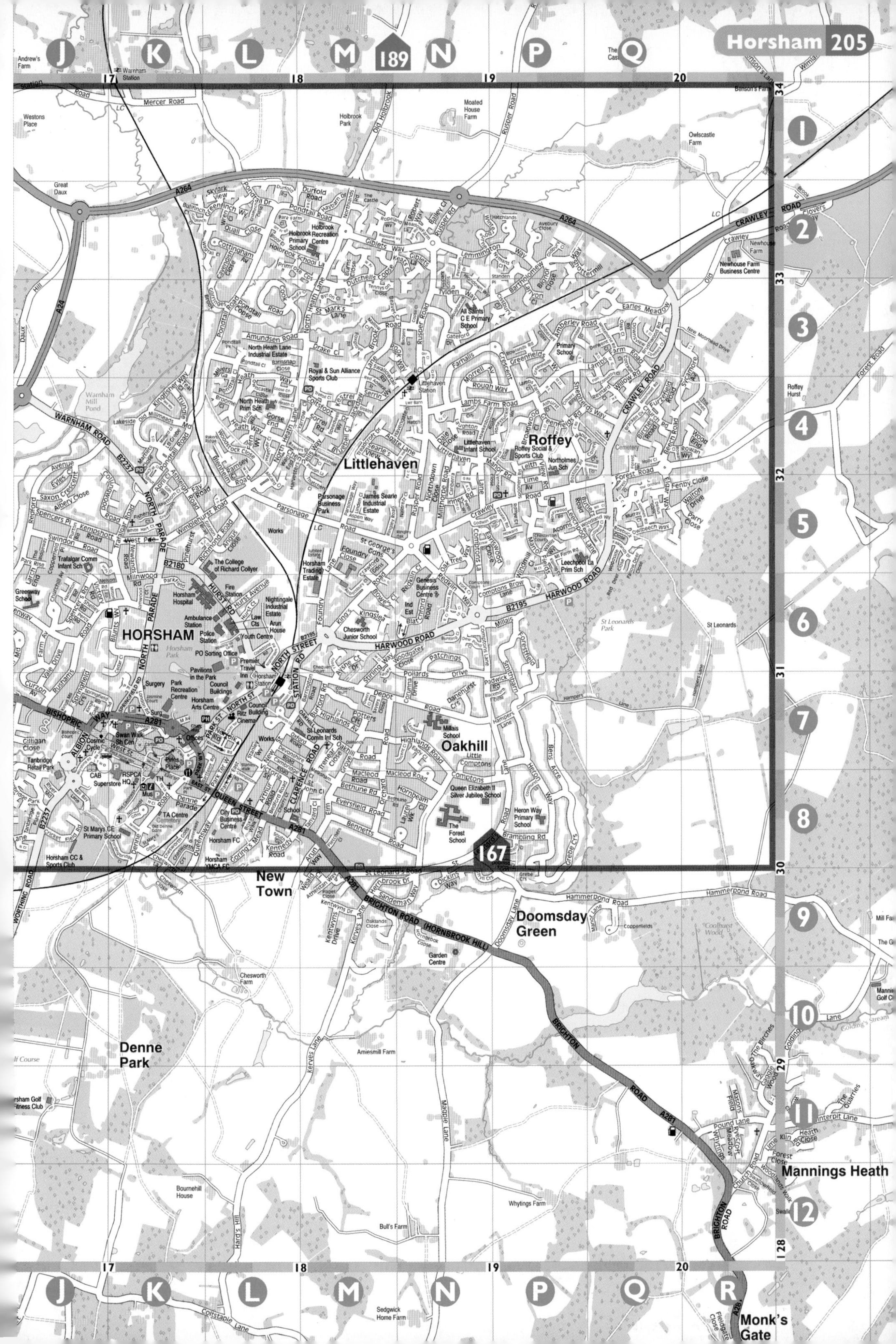
J
K
L
M
189
N
P
Q
17
18
19
20
34
33
32
31
30
29
28
1
2
3
4
5
6
7
8
9
10
11
12
Warnham Station
Mercer Road
Westons Place
Holbrook Park
Old Holbrook
Moated House Farm
Rusper Road
Owlscastle Farm
Great Daux
A264
A24
Daux Hill
Crawley Road
Newhouse Farm
Newhouse Farm Business Centre
Pondtail Road
Holbrook Primary School
Holbrook Recreation Centre
North Heath Lane
St Mark's Lane
Amundsen Road
North Heath Lane Industrial Estate
Royal & Sun Alliance Sports Club
Littlehaven Station
Littlehaven
All Saints C E Primary School
Earles Meadow
Primary School
Roffey
Roffey Hurst
Forest Road
Littlehaven Infant School
Roffey Social & Sports Club
Northolmes Jun Sch
Warnham Mill Pond
Warnham Road
North Parade
Parsonage Business Park
James Searle Industrial Estate
Parsonage Road
Works
Horsham Trading Estate
Foundry Lane
Genesis Business Centre
Leechpool La Prim Sch
Harwood Road
B2195
St Leonards Park
St Leonards
The College of Richard Collyer
Horsham Hospital
Fire Station
Nightingale Industrial Estate
Ambulance Station
Police Station
Law Cts
Arun House
Youth Centre
Chesworth Junior School
HORSHAM
Horsham Park
PO Sorting Office
Pavilions in the Park
Premier Travel Inn
Horsham Station
North Street
Station Rd
Surgery
Park Recreation Centre
Council Buildings
Horsham Arts Centre
Ritz Cinema
Millais School
Oakhill
Trafalgar Comm Infant Sch
Greenway School
Bishopric
Albion Way
A281
Swan Walk Sh Cen
Cosmic Cycle
Tanbridge Retail Park
CAB
RSPCA HQ
Superstore
Mus
Denne Parade
TA Centre
St Leonards Comm Inf Sch
Clarence Road
Queen Street
St Marys CE Primary School
City Business Centre
Horsham FC
Horsham CC & Sports Club
Horsham YMCA FC
Queen Elizabeth II Silver Jubilee School
The Forest School
Heron Way Primary School
167
Brampling Rd
Worthing Road
New Town
St Leonard's Road
Hammerpond Road
Doomsday Green
Doomsday Lane
Brighton Road (Hornbrook Hill)
Garden Centre
Copperfields
Coolhurst Wood
Chesworth Farm
Denne Park
Amiesmill Farm
Kerves Lane
Magpie Lane
Brighton Road
Golding Lane
Interpit Lane
Mannings Heath
Pound Lane
Church Road
Bournehill House
Whytings Farm
Bull's Farm
Hard's Hill
Sedgwick Home Farm
Coltstaple Lane
R
Monk's Gate
A281
A281

Aaron's Hill 159 L5
Abbey Mead 40 E6
Abbotswood 117 J6
Abinger Common 171 Q1
Abinger Hammer 142 B6
Addington 69 K5
Addiscombe 3 L3
Addlestone 58 F4
Addlestonemoor 58 F1
Albury 140 F5
Albury Heath 141 H7
Aldershot 112 F6
Alfold 185 Q12
Alfold Bars 201 Q2
Alfold Crossways 185 R10
Anerley 50 D2
Ansteadbrook 199 K8
Anthonys 77 K2
Aperfield 91 J7
Arford 180 D11
Artington 138 E5
Ascot 36 F2
Ash 113 K6
Ashford 23 K5
Ashford Common 24 A7
Ash Green 136 A1
Ashley Park 60 D2
Ashtead 83 H8
Ashurst Wood 163 M7
Ash Vale 113 K3
Badshot Lea 134 E3
Bagshot 54 A6
Bagshot Heath 54 B8
Baldwins Hill 162 D2
Balham 30 C1
Bandonhill 67 G4
Banstead 85 K6
Barford 181 K9
Barnes 19 L3
Barwell 62 F6
Batt's Corner 180 C2
Beacon Hill 181 Q10
Beare Green 173 M7
Beaumont 20 E2
Beckenham 51 K2
Beddington 67 H1
Beddington Corner 48 D7
Bellfields 116 F5
Bell Green 33 J4
Bellingham 33 K5
Belmont 65 K7
Benhilton 65 L2
Berrylands 45 J6
Berry's Green 91 K6
Betchworth 123 M7
Bewbush 164 B7
Biggin Hill 91 G6
Binscombe 159 M1
Birch Hill 34 F7
Birtley Green 169 K5
Bishopsgate 20 C5
Bisley 75 L6
Blackbrook 145 H7
Black Corner 192 C1
Blackheath 140 B8
Blacknest 37 M3
Blackwater 72 A5
Blackwell 162 F3
Bletchingley 128 A8
Blindley Heath 151 H8
Boundstone 155 L5
The Bourne 155 M3
Bowlhead Green 182 F8
Bowling Alley 132 B1
Box Hill 123 K6
Bracknell 35 G3
Bramley 169 J4
Bramshott 196 H7
Brands Hill 12 E2
Brentford 18 A1
Brentford End 17 L1
Brewer Street 127 M5
Brick Hill 55 M3
Bridge End 99 L2
Broadbridge Heath 204 C5
Broadfield 164 E8
Broadford 138 F7
Broad Green 23 B1
Broadham Green 129 M6
Broadmoor 172 C1
Brockham 145 K1
Brockham Park 145 M5
Brook 141 H8
Brook 183 K8
Brooklands 59 J7
Brookwood 95 K2
Broomhall 37 J7
Buckland 124 D7
Bucks Green 202 G3
Bullbrook 35 J2
Bunce Common 146 A7
Burgh Heath 105 G1
Burntcommon 98 C7
Burpham 117 K4
Burrowhill 56 C7
Burrows Cross 141 L7
Burstow 161 K7
Burwood Park 60 D4
Busbridge 168 D7
Bushbury 145 K5
Bushey Mead 47 G3
Bushy Hill 117 L6
Byfleet 79 G3
Camberley 73 H2
Camelsdale 198 B8
Cannon Hill 47 G4
Capel 173 L11
Carshalton 66 B3
Carshalton Beeches 66 B7
Carshalton on the Hill 66 C6
Cartbridge 97 L4
Castle Green 76 A3
Caterham 108 B5
Catford 33 M2
Catteshall 168 D3
Chaldon 107 L6
Charleshill 157 K4
Charlton 41 M2
Charlwood 175 J10
Charlwood 194 F12
Chattern Hill 23 L5
Chavey Down 35 L2
Cheam 65 H4
Cheapside 37 H2
Chelsham 89 K7
Chertsey 40 D7
Chertsey Meads 41 H8
Chessington 63 H5
Chiddingfold 183 Q12
Chilworth 139 M6
Chipstead 106 D1
Chobham 56 A8
Christmaspie 136 E1
Church End 99 J3
Church Town 128 F5
Churt 181 L8
Claremont Park 61 K6
Clark's Green 189 K1
Claygate 62 C5
Clock House 86 F4
Cobham 80 D4
Cold Ash Hill 197 K8
Coldharbour 172 E4
Cole Park 17 K8
Coles Meads 126 C5
College Town 52 B8
Collier's Wood 30 A8
Colnbrook 12 F3
The Common 166 D5
Compton 134 C8
Compton 137 K6
Coney Hall 70 B3
Conford 196 E6
Coombe 28 B8
Cooper's Hill 21 G4
Copse Hill 28 D8
Copthorne 192 G2
Cottenham Park 46 E1
Coulsdon 87 H6
Cove 92 B3
Cox Green 187 K11
Cramhurst 183 M3
Cranford 15 K2
Cranleigh 186 E1
Crawley 165 G5
Crawley Down 193 L6
Crawley Hill 73 H4
Critchmere 197 R6
Crockham Hill 131 M7
Crondall 132 B2
Crooked Billet 28 E7
Crosswater 181 K5
Crossways 181 K8
Crowhurst 152 A6
Crowhurst Lane End 151 K4
Crownpits 168 B6
Crown Wood 35 G6
Croydon 2 E7
Crystal Palace 32 D7
Cudworth 174 B9
Culmer 183 N6
Dawesgreen 146 B6
Deadwater 196 A2
Deepcut 93 M3
Deepdene 145 G2
Denbies 122 A8
Denne Park 205 K10
Dippenhall 133 G7
Dockenfield 180 E3
Domewood 177 N12
Donkey Town 75 G3
Doomsday Green 205 P9
Dora's Green 132 F4
Dorking 144 E3
Dormansland 179 J8
Dormans Park 178 F10
Doversgreen 147 L4
Downe 91 J1
Down Park 193 M4
Downside 100 E1
Dulwich 32 C3
Dulwich Village 32 B1
Dunsfold 185 J8
Dunsfold Common 185 J9
Dunsfold Green 185 J7
Earlsfield 29 M2
Earlswood 148 C2
Eashing 159 J4
East Bedfont 23 L1
East Clandon 119 H5
East Ewell 65 G8
East Green 154 B3
East Grinstead 162 F3
Easthampstead 34 E4
East Horsley 120 A1
East Molesey 43 M5
East Sheen 19 G7
Edenbridge 153 K7
Eden Park 51 J4
Effingham 121 G1
Egham 21 K7
Egham Hythe 22 A7
Egham Wick 20 C8
Ellen's Green 187 K9
Elm Corner 99 K1
Elmers End 51 G3
Elstead 158 A6
Englefield Green 20 E8
Enton Green 183 Q3
Epsom 83 M4
Esher 61 M3
Ewell 64 D7
Ewhurst 171 J11
Ewhurst Green 187 K1
Ewshot 132 F1
Fairlands 116 A5
Fairmile 81 J2
Farleigh 89 J4
Farleigh Court 89 K4
Farley Green 170 D2
Farnborough 71 L4
Farnborough 92 D5
Farnborough Green 92 F4
Farnborough Park 93 G6
Farnborough Street 92 F4
Farncombe 168 A1
Farnham 5 H4
Faygate 190 B12
Felbridge 162 A1
Felcourt 178 D9
Felday 171 N3
Feltham 24 E3
Felthamhill 24 B7
Fernhill 161 H7
Fetcham 102 A5
Fickleshole 90 B4
Field Common 43 J7
Fisherstreet 199 N10
Five Oaks 203 K12
Flexford 115 G8
Folly Hill 133 K4
Forestdale 69 H7
Forest Green 171 R10
Forest Hill 33 G2
Forest Row 195 N12
Fox Corner 95 M7
Fox Lane 72 C8
Fredley 122 E3
Frensham 180 G2
Friday Street 172 A1
Frimley 72 F8
Frimley Green 93 J2
Frimley Ridge 73 K6
Frithend 180 A5
Frith Hill 168 A3
Furnace Green 165 J6
Furnace Wood 193 P2
Furzedown 30 E5
Gadbrook 146 A4
Gatton 126 C2
Giggshill 44 D7
Givons Grove 103 G7
Godalming 168 C5
Godstone 128 E5
Goldworth Park 76 D6
Gomshall 141 M6
Goodley Stock 131 L4
Gossops Green 164 D5
Grafham 169 M9
Grayshott 197 N2
Grayswood 198 H4
Great Bookham 101 L8
Great Burgh 84 F7
Great Hollands 34 B6
Green Cross 181 N8
Griggs Green 196 E9
Grove Park 19 G3
Guildford 7 C8
Guildford Park 6 C5
Hackbridge 66 E1
Hale 134 A4
Ham 27 G4
Hambledon 183 R7
Hammer 197 P8
Hammer Bottom 197 N8
Hammerwood 195 Q2
Hamm Moor 59 G3
Hampton 43 L1
Hampton Hill 25 M5
Hampton Wick 8 A5
Hamsey Green 88 F5
Hanworth 25 G4
Hanworth 34 D7
Harlington 14 F1
Harmans Water 35 G4
Harmondsworth 13 M1
Hascombe 184 H1
Haslemere 198 E7
Hatton 15 H6
Hatton Hill 55 G3
The Haven 203 J7
Hawk's Hill 102 C6
Hawley 72 B6
Hawley Lane 92 E2
Haxted 179 N1
Hazelwood 91 M1
Headley 103 M8
Headley 180 C12
Headley Down 196 G1
Hearn 180 G10
Heath End 134 A2
Heatherside 73 L5
Hersham 60 F4
Heston 16 C2
High Curley 74 B1
Highgate 195 N12
Highstreet Green 184 C11
Hill Park 111 L5
Hinchley Wood 62 C2
Hindhead 198 A1
Hoe 171 J1
Hog Hatch 133 J3
Holland 130 D7
Holloway Hill 168 B7
Hollywater 196 A4
Holmbury St Mary 171 N4
Holmethorpe 126 E6
Holmwood Corner 173 L3
Holt Pound 155 G5
Hook 63 H4
Hook Heath 96 E2
Hookwood 175 M7
Hooley 106 D4
Horley 160 E1
Horne 177 L4
Horsell 10 B3
Horsham 166 F6
Horton 12 D5
Hounslow 16 D4
Hounslow West 16 A5
Hurst Green 130 B6
Hurst Park 43 M2
Hurtmore 159 K2
Hydestile 168 B11
Hythe End 21 L4
Ifield 164 C2
Ifield Green 164 C1
Ifieldwood 190 G4
Ifold 201 M6
Irons Bottom 147 K8
Isleworth 17 L5
Itchingfield 204 A11
Jacobs Well 116 F3
Kenley 88 A6
Keston 71 G3
Keston Mark 71 G2
Kew 18 C2
Kingfield 97 H2
Kingsfold 189 J7
Kingsley Green 198 C11
Kingston upon Thames 8 E4
Kingston Vale 28 A6
Kingswood 105 J5
Knaphill 75 M8
Knight's Hill 31 M2
Knowle Green 22 E6
Knowle Hill 38 E7
Laker's Green 185 Q9
Laleham 40 F3
Laleham Burway 40 E5
Lambs Green 190 C7
Lampton 16 E3
Lane End 181 J2
Langley Green 191 L3
Langley Vale 104 A2
Leatherhead 102 B3
Leaves Green 91 G1
Leigh 146 D7
Lightwater 74 F1
Limpsfield 130 C1
Limpsfield Chart 131 J5
Limpsfield Common 130 E4
Linchmere 197 M10
Lindford 196 A1
Lingfield 178 E5
Lingfield Common 178 E3
Liphook 196 F10
Little Bookham 101 H7
Littlefield Common 115 L3
Littlehaven 167 H4
Little Heath 81 J4
Littleton 41 L3
Littleton 138 D6
Littleton Common 23 L8
Littlewick 76 C6
Little Woodcote 86 D1
Locksbottom 71 L2
Logmore Green 143 L7
Longcross 56 E2
Long Ditton 44 E8
Longford 13 L3
Lordshill Common 169 M5
Lower Ashtead 102 F1
Lower Bourne 156 B3
Lower Feltham 24 B4
Lower Green 61 L1
Lower Halliford 42 A7
Lower Kingswood 105 K8
Lower Sunbury 42 D3
Lower Sydenham 33 G5
Lowfield Heath 175 Q12
Loxhill 184 H5
Loxwood 201 P5
Lucas Green 75 G5
Luxted 91 K4
Mackerel's Common 201 K12
Maidenbower 165 L6
Malden Rushett 82 E2
Manor Royal 191 P3
Margery 125 K3
Marley Heights 198 A12
Marlpit Hill 153 L5
Marsh Green 179 Q4
Martin's Heron 35 K3
Martyr's Green 100 B2
Maybury 11 J5
Mayes Green 187 R2
Mayford 96 F4
May's Green 100 C2
Mead Vale 147 M3
Meath Green 160 A1
Merle Common 152 D2
Merrow 117 M7
Merstham 126 E2
Merton 47 K1
Merton Park 47 J2
Mickleham 122 F2
Middle Bourne 155 M2
Mid Holmwood 144 E8
Milford 159 K8
Millbridge 156 A8
Mimbridge 76 E3
Mitcham 48 D3
Mogador 125 G3
Monks Orchard 50 F7
Montgomery Lines 112 F5
Moorhouse Bank 131 K2
Moor Park 134 E8
Morden 47 K4
Morden Park 47 H6
Mortlake 18 F4
Motspur Park 46 D6
Mount Hermon 10 C9
Mousehill 183 N1
Mugswell 105 L7
Mytchett 93 H6
Mytchett Place 93 L7
Nalderswood 174 F2
Nash 70 E5
Netherne on The Hill 107 G4
New Addington 70 A6
New Beckenham 33 H7
Newchapel 177 R8
Newdigate 173 P8
New Haw 58 F6
Newlands Corner 140 E2
New Malden 46 C3
Newtown 196 G11
New Town 205 L9
Norbiton 9 J6
Norbury 49 L2
Nork 85 G6
Norley Common 169 N4
Normandy 114 E5
Norney 159 H3
North Ascot 35 M2
North Camp 112 E3
North Cheam 65 G2
North End 162 C1
North Feltham 15 L7
Northgate 165 H2
North Holmwood 144 E7
North Looe 84 F3
North Sheen 18 E4
North Town 113 H7
Norwood Hill 174 H6
Norwood New Town 32 A7
Nutcombe 197 Q3
Nutfield 127 J8
Oakhill 167 J7
Oakwoodhill 188 A6
Oatlands Park 60 B3
Ockford Ridge 159 K6
Ockham 99 K4
Ockley 172 E12
Old Coulsdon 107 L2
Old Malden 46 A7
Old Woking 97 L2
Onslow Village 138 B2
Osterley 16 F2
Ottershaw 57 M4
Outwood 176 H1
Owlsmoor 52 A7
Oxshott 81 M3
Oxted 130 A3
Pachesham Park 82 D6
Pains Hill 130 F5
Palmers Cross 169 M11
Park Barn 116 B7
Parkgate 174 A5
Park Langley 51 M6
Park Street 203 P6
Passfield 196 E4
Paynes Green 188 E6
Peaslake 171 J3
Peasmarsh 138 F8
Penge 32 F8
Peper Harow 158 F4
Petersham 27 H2
Pirbright 95 J5
Pitch Place 116 C3
Pitch Place 182 B6
Pixham 122 F7
Plaistow 201 J7
Pot Common 157 M7
Pound Hill 165 L2
Povey Cross 175 M8
Poyle 13 H3
Prey Heath 96 E5
Priestwood 34 B2
Purley 87 K2
Putney Heath 28 F1
Putney Vale 28 D4
Puttenham 136 E4
Pyle Hill 97 G7
Pyrford 78 C5
Pyrford Green 78 E7
Pyrford Village 78 B8
Quabrook 195 R12
Rafborough 92 B6
Ramsnest Common 199 N6
Ranmore Common 121 M7
Rapkyns 204 B5
Raynes Park 46 F3
Redhill 126 D6
Reigate 125 J8
Reigate Hill 125 J6
Richmond 18 B7
Richmond Hill 18 B8
Ridge Green 149 H3
Ripley 98 E3
The Rise 37 H6
Roehampton 19 J7
Roffey 167 K4
Rosehill 47 L8
Rose Hill 144 D2
Roundshaw 67 J5
Roundstreet Common 202 A11
Rowhook 187 R12
Rowledge 155 J6
Rowly 170 A11
Row Town 58 C5
Rudgwick 202 H2
Runfold 134 F6
Rushmoor 181 P2
Rusper 189 R6
Russell Hill 67 J8
Russ Hill 174 F12
Rydens 60 F1
Rydeshill 116 A6
Saint Hill 194 E9
Salfords 148 E8
Sanderstead 88 D1
Sandhills 183 L8
The Sands 135 H7
Sandy Cross 135 J5
Scotswood 37 G8
Seale 135 L5
Seething Wells 44 E6
Selhurst 50 A5
Selsdon 68 F8
Selsfield Common 193 N12
Send 97 M6
Send Grove 97 L8
Send Marsh 98 C5
Shackleford 159 G2
Shalford 139 J7
Shamley Green 169 P4
Sheerwater 77 M3
Sheets Heath 95 J1
Shellwood Cross 174 B1
Shepherd's Hill 198 D7
Shepperton 41 K6
Shepperton Green 41 K4
Shere 141 K4
Shipley Bridge 161 J8
Shirley 68 F1
Shortfield Common 155 L7
Shortheath 155 L3
Shottermill 197 R7
Shrubs Hill 37 M6
Sidlow 147 L7
Slinfold 203 Q6
Slyfield 117 G5
Smallfield 161 K4
South Ascot 36 D6
South Beddington 67 G5
South Croydon 67 L5
South Earlswood 148 B5
Southend 33 M5
South Farnborough 93 G8
Southfields 29 K2
Southgate 164 F6
South Godstone 151 J4
South Holmwood 173 J3
South Merstham 127 G4
South Norwood 50 A3
South Nutfield 149 H2
South Park 147 H3
South Street 111 J1
South Wimbledon 29 M6
Spitals Cross 153 M6
Spreakley 180 G1
Spring Grove 17 G3
Spring Park 69 K1

Staines	22 C5	Sutton Green	97 J7	Tulse Hill	31 L2	West Barnes	46 F5	Windlesham	54 E5
Standford	196 B3	Sydenham	33 G6	Turners Hill	193 M9	West Bedfont	23 J1	Wisley	79 H5
Stanwell	14 A8	Tadworth	104 F4	Twickenham	26 B2	Westbrook	159 M5	Witley	183 N5
Stanwell Moor	13 K8	Tandridge	129 K7	Tyler's Green	128 E4	West Byfleet	78 E3	Woking	10 F6
St George's Hill	59 M7	Tatsfield	111 G2	Tyrrell's Wood	103 K5	West Clandon	118 E3	Woldingham	109 K5
St Helier	47 M8	Teddington	26 A7	Upper Eashing	159 K5	Westcott	143 L3	Woldingham Garden Village	109 J3
St Johns	96 D1	Thames Ditton	44 D7	Upper Elmers End	51 J5	West Dulwich	32 A3	Wonersh	169 M2
St Margarets	17 M8	Thorncombe Street	168 F8	Upper Hale	133 L3	West End	61 J4	Woodbridge Hill	6 A1
Stoke D'Abernon	81 H5	Thornton Heath	49 L3	Upper Halliford	42 A4	West End	75 J4	Woodcote	84 A6
Stonebridge	145 G5	Thorpe	39 M3	Upper Ifold	201 K2	West End	180 E1	Woodcote	87 H1
Stonehill	57 H5	Thorpe Green	39 K4	Upper Norwood	50 A1	West Ewell	64 A5	Woodcote Green	66 E8
Stoneleigh	64 C4	Thorpe Lea	21 M8	Upper Shirley	68 F3	Westfield	97 J4	Woodham	58 D8
Stonequarry	163 H2	Three Bridges	165 H3	Upper Sydenham	32 D5	West Green	164 E3	Woodhatch	147 K3
Stoughton	116 E5	Thursley	182 D5	Upper Tooting	30 B4	West Heath	92 B4	Woodlands	17 G5
Strawberry Hill	26 A4	Tilford	157 G6	Valley End	55 K4	West Hill	29 H1	Woodmansterne	86 A5
Streatham	31 H6	Tilford Common	156 E8	Virginia Water	38 F3	West Horsley	119 L2	Woodside	50 D6
Streatham Hill	31 H2	Tilford Reeds	156 E6	Waddon	67 H1	Westhumble	122 D5	Wood Street Village	115 K6
Streatham Park	30 F5	Tilgate	164 F7	Wallington	66 D4	West Molesey	43 J4	Woolmer Hill	197 N6
Streatham Vale	30 E8	Tinsley Green	192 B1	Walliswood	187 R4	West Norwood	31 M5	Worcester Park	64 E1
Strood Green	204 C3	Tisman's Common	202 F4	Walton-on-Thames	42 D8	Weston Green	44 B8	Wormley	183 M8
Stroude	39 J2	Titsey	110 F7	Walton on the Hill	104 C6	Weybourne	134 C3	Worplesdon	116 A1
Summerstown	30 A3	Tittenhurst	37 K4	Wanborough	136 E3	Weybridge	59 K3	Worth	192 D8
Sunbury	42 B1	Tolworth	45 K8	Wandle Park	2 A6	Wheelerstreet	183 N3	Worth Abbey	192 G12
Sunbury Common	24 C8	Tongham	135 J3	Warlingham	89 G8	Whitebushes	148 E5	Wotton	143 H5
Sunningdale	37 K5	Tooting	30 C6	Warnham	166 B1	Whiteley Village	60 C7	Wray Common	126 A6
Sunninghill	37 G5	Tooting Graveney	30 B4	Warren Corner	132 F2	Whitton	16 F8	Wraysbury	12 C8
Sunnymeads	12 B6	Tower Hill	144 E4	Warwick Wold	127 K3	Whyteleafe	88 C8	Wrecclesham	155 J3
Sunnyside	162 F7	Tower Hill	204 C9	Wasp Green	176 H2	Wildridings	34 C4	The Wrythe	66 B1
Surbiton	45 G8	Troy Town	153 J4	Waterside	178 G2	Willey Green	115 G5	Wyke	114 C6
Sutton	65 K4	Trumpsgreen	38 F6	Weatherhill	161 K2	Wimbledon	29 H6	York Town	72 D5
Sutton Abinger	171 N1	Tuesley	183 R1	The Wells	83 J4	Wimble Hill	132 D7		

USING THE STREET INDEX

Street names are listed alphabetically. Each street name is followed by its postal town or area locality, the Postcode District, the page number, and the reference to the square in which the name is found.

Standard index entries are shown as follows:

Aaron's Hl *GODL* GU7 .... **159** M5

Street names and selected addresses not shown on the map due to scale restrictions are shown in the index with an asterisk:

Abbey Cha *CHERT* KT16 * **40** E6

GENERAL ABBREVIATIONS

ACC	ACCESS	CTYD	COURTYARD	HLS	HILLS	MWY	MOTORWAY
ALY	ALLEY	CUTT	CUTTINGS	HO	HOUSE	N	NORTH
AP	APPROACH	CV	COVE	HOL	HOLLOW	NE	NORTH EAST
AR	ARCADE	CYN	CANYON	HOSP	HOSPITAL	NW	NORTH WEST
ASS	ASSOCIATION	DEPT	DEPARTMENT	HRB	HARBOUR	O/P	OVERPASS
AV	AVENUE	DL	DALE	HTH	HEATH	OFF	OFFICE
BCH	BEACH	DM	DAM	HTS	HEIGHTS	ORCH	ORCHARD
BLDS	BUILDINGS	DR	DRIVE	HVN	HAVEN	OV	OVAL
BND	BEND	DRO	DROVE	HWY	HIGHWAY	PAL	PALACE
BNK	BANK	DRY	DRIVEWAY	IMP	IMPERIAL	PAS	PASSAGE
BR	BRIDGE	DWGS	DWELLINGS	IN	INLET	PAV	PAVILION
BRK	BROOK	E	EAST	IND EST	INDUSTRIAL ESTATE	PDE	PARADE
BTM	BOTTOM	EMB	EMBANKMENT	INF	INFIRMARY	PH	PUBLIC HOUSE
BUS	BUSINESS	EMBY	EMBASSY	INFO	INFORMATION	PK	PARK
BVD	BOULEVARD	ESP	ESPLANADE	INT	INTERCHANGE	PKWY	PARKWAY
BY	BYPASS	EST	ESTATE	IS	ISLAND	PL	PLACE
CATH	CATHEDRAL	EX	EXCHANGE	JCT	JUNCTION	PLN	PLAIN
CEM	CEMETERY	EXPY	EXPRESSWAY	JTY	JETTY	PLNS	PLAINS
CEN	CENTRE	EXT	EXTENSION	KG	KING	PLZ	PLAZA
CFT	CROFT	F/O	FLYOVER	KNL	KNOLL	POL	POLICE STATION
CH	CHURCH	FC	FOOTBALL CLUB	L	LAKE	PR	PRINCE
CHA	CHASE	FK	FORK	LA	LANE	PREC	PRECINCT
CHYD	CHURCHYARD	FLD	FIELD	LDG	LODGE	PREP	PREPARATORY
CIR	CIRCLE	FLDS	FIELDS	LGT	LIGHT	PRIM	PRIMARY
CIRC	CIRCUS	FLS	FALLS	LK	LOCK	PROM	PROMENADE
CL	CLOSE	FM	FARM	LKS	LAKES	PRS	PRINCESS
CLFS	CLIFFS	FT	FORT	LNDG	LANDING	PRT	PORT
CMP	CAMP	FTS	FLATS	LTL	LITTLE	PT	POINT
CNR	CORNER	FWY	FREEWAY	LWR	LOWER	PTH	PATH
CO	COUNTY	FY	FERRY	MAG	MAGISTRATE	PZ	PIAZZA
COLL	COLLEGE	GA	GATE	MAN	MANSIONS	QD	QUADRANT
COM	COMMON	GAL	GALLERY	MD	MEAD	QU	QUEEN
COMM	COMMISSION	GDN	GARDEN	MDW	MEADOWS	QY	QUAY
CON	CONVENT	GDNS	GARDENS	MEM	MEMORIAL	R	RIVER
COT	COTTAGE	GLD	GLADE	MI	MILL	RBT	ROUNDABOUT
COTS	COTTAGES	GLN	GLEN	MKT	MARKET	RD	ROAD
CP	CAPE	GN	GREEN	MKTS	MARKETS	RDG	RIDGE
CPS	COPSE	GND	GROUND	ML	MALL	REP	REPUBLIC
CR	CREEK	GRA	GRANGE	MNR	MANOR	RES	RESERVOIR
CREM	CREMATORIUM	GRG	GARAGE	MS	MEWS	RFC	RUGBY FOOTBALL CLUB
CRS	CRESCENT	GT	GREAT	MSN	MISSION	RI	RISE
CSWY	CAUSEWAY	GTWY	GATEWAY	MT	MOUNT	RP	RAMP
CT	COURT	GV	GROVE	MTN	MOUNTAIN	RW	ROW
CTRL	CENTRAL	HGR	HIGHER	MTS	MOUNTAINS	S	SOUTH
CTS	COURTS	HL	HILL	MUS	MUSEUM	SCH	SCHOOL

SE	SOUTH EAST
SER	SERVICE AREA
SH	SHORE
SHOP	SHOPPING
SKWY	SKYWAY
SMT	SUMMIT
SOC	SOCIETY
SP	SPUR
SPR	SPRING
SQ	SQUARE
ST	STREET
STN	STATION
STR	STREAM
STRD	STRAND
SW	SOUTH WEST
TDG	TRADING
TER	TERRACE
THWY	THROUGHWAY
TNL	TUNNEL
TOLL	TOLLWAY
TPK	TURNPIKE
TR	TRACK
TRL	TRAIL
TWR	TOWER
U/P	UNDERPASS
UNI	UNIVERSITY
UPR	UPPER
V	VALE
VA	VALLEY
VIAD	VIADUCT
VIL	VILLA
VIS	VISTA
VLG	VILLAGE
VLS	VILLAS
VW	VIEW
W	WEST
WD	WOOD
WHF	WHARF
WK	WALK
WKS	WALKS
WLS	WELLS
WY	WAY
YD	YARD
YHA	YOUTH HOSTEL

POSTCODE TOWNS AND AREA ABBREVIATIONS

ADL/WDHM	Addlestone/Woodham	CHERT	Chertsey	FROW	Forest Row	LIPH	Liphook
ALDT	Aldershot	CHOB/PIR	Chobham/Pirbright	FSTH	Forest Hill	LISS	Liss
ALTN	Alton	CHSGTN	Chessington	FUL/PGN	Fulham/Parsons Green	LTWR	Lightwater
ASC	Ascot	CHSWK	Chiswick	GDST	Godstone	MFD/CHID	Milford/Chiddingfold
ASHF	Ashford (Surrey)	CLAP	Clapham	GODL	Godalming	MORT/ESHN	Mortlake/East Sheen
ASHTD	Ashtead	COB	Cobham	GSHT	Grayshott	MRDN	Morden
ASHV	Ash Vale	COUL/CHIP	Coulsdon/Chipstead	GT/LBKH	Great Bookham/	MTCM	Mitcham
BAGS	Bagshot	CRAN	Cranleigh		Little Bookham	NRWD	Norwood
BAL	Balham	CRAWE	Crawley east	GU	Guildford	NWDGN	Norwood Green
BARN	Barnes	CRAWW	Crawley west	GUW	Guildford west	NWMAL	New Malden
BECK	Beckenham	CROY/NA	Croydon/New Addington	HASM	Haslemere	ORP	Orpington
BELMT	Belmont	CTHM	Caterham	HAYES	Hayes	OXTED	Oxted
BF/WBF	Byfleet/West Byfleet	CWTH	Crowthorne	HEST	Heston	PETW	Petworth
BFOR	Bracknell Forest/Windlesham	DORK	Dorking	HMSMTH	Hammersmith	PGE/AN	Penge/Anerley
BH/WHM	Biggin Hill/Westerham	DTCH/LGLY	Datchet/Langley	HNHL	Herne Hill	PUR/KEN	Purley/Kenley
BIL	Billingshurst	DUL	Dulwich	HOR/WEW	Horton/West Ewell	PUT/ROE	Putney/Roehampton
BLKW	Blackwater	E/WMO/HCT	East & West Molesey/	HORL	Horley	RCH/KEW	Richmond/Kew
BMLY	Bromley		Hampton Court	HORS	Horsham	RCHPK/HAM	Richmond Park/Ham
BNFD	Binfield	EBED/NFELT	East Bedfont/	HPTN	Hampton	RDKG	Rural Dorking
BNSTD	Banstead		North Feltham	HRTF	Hartfield	REDH	Redhill
BOR	Bordon	EDEN	Edenbridge	HSLW	Hounslow	REIG	Reigate
BRAK	Bracknell	EDUL	East Dulwich	HSLWW	Hounslow west	RFNM	Rural Farnham
BRKHM/BTCW	Brockham/Betchworth	EGH	Egham	HTHAIR	Heathrow Airport	RGUE	Rural Guildford east
BROCKY	Brockley	EGRIN	East Grinstead	HYS/HAR	Hayes/Harlington	RGUW	Rural Guildford west
BRXS/STRHM	Brixton south/	EHSLY	East Horsley	ISLW	Isleworth	RHWH	Rural Haywards Heath
	Streatham Hill	EPSOM	Epsom	KUT/HW	Kingston upon Thames/	RPLY/SEND	Ripley/Send
BRYLDS	Berrylands	ESH/CLAY	Esher/Claygate		Hampton Wick	RSEV	Rural Sevenoaks
BTFD	Brentford	EW	Ewell	KUTN/CMB	Kingston upon Thames	RYNPK	Raynes Park
BTSEA	Battersea	EWKG	Wokingham east		north/Coombe	SAND/SEL	Sanderstead/Selsdon
CAR	Carshalton	FARN	Farnborough	KWD/TDW/WH	Kingswood/Tadworth/	SHGR	Shamley Green
CAT	Catford	FELT	Feltham		Walton on the Hill	SHPTN	Shepperton
CBLY	Camberley	FNM	Farnham	LHD/OX	Leatherhead/Oxshott	SHST	Sandhurst
CHEAM	Cheam	FRIM	Frimley	LING	Lingfield	SNWD	South Norwood

STA	Staines
STMC/STPC	St Mary Cray/
	St Paul's Cray
STRHM/NOR	Streatham/Norbury
STWL/WRAY	Stanwell/Wraysbury
SUN	Sunbury
SURB	Surbiton
SUT	Sutton
SWTR	Southwater
SYD	Sydenham
TEDD	Teddington
THDIT	Thames Ditton
THHTH	Thornton Heath
TOOT	Tooting
TWK	Twickenham
VW	Virginia Water
WAND/EARL	Wandsworth/Earlsfield
WARL	Warlingham
WDR/YW	West Drayton/Yiewsley
WDSR	Windsor
WEY	Weybridge
WHTN	Whitton
WIM/MER	Wimbledon/Merton
WLGTN	Wallington
WNWD	West Norwood
WOKN/KNAP	Woking north/Knaphill
WOKS/MYFD	Woking south/Mayford
WOT/HER	Walton-on-Thames/
	Hersham
WPK	Worcester Park
WWKM	West Wickham

1

1st Av KWD/TDW/WH KT20 105 H7
2nd Av KWD/TDW/WH KT20 105 H7
3rd Av KWD/TDW/WH KT20 105 H7
4th Av KWD/TDW/WH KT20 105 H7
6th Av KWD/TDW/WH KT20 105 H7
7th Av KWD/TDW/WH KT20 105 H7
8th Av KWD/TDW/WH KT20 105 H8
9th Av KWD/TDW/WH KT20 105 H7
10th Av KWD/TDW/WH KT20 105 H8
11th Av KWD/TDW/WH KT20 105 H7
12th Av KWD/TDW/WH KT20 105 H8
13th Av KWD/TDW/WH KT20 105 H8
14th Av KWD/TDW/WH KT20 105 H8
15th Av KWD/TDW/WH KT20 105 J8
16th Av KWD/TDW/WH KT20 105 H8

A

Aaron's Hl GODL GU7 159 M5
Abbess Cl BRXS/STRHM SW2 31 L2
Abbetts La CBLY GU15 72 E6
Abbey Cha CHERT KT16 * 40 E6
Abbey Cl BRAK RG12 35 G5
WOKS/MYFD GU22 78 B6
Abbey Ct CHERT KT16 * 40 E7
Abbeydore Cl BOR GU35 180 D12
Abbey Dr STA TW18 40 F4
TOOT SW17 30 D6
Abbeyfield Cl MTCM CR4 48 B2
Abbey Gdns CHERT KT16 40 D6
Abbey Gn CHERT KT16 40 D6
Abbey La BECK BR3 33 K8
Abbey Ms ISLW TW7 17 L3
STA TW18 * 40 F3
Abbey Pk BECK BR3 33 K8
Abbey Pl CHERT KT16 * 40 D3
Abbey Rd CHERT KT16 40 E7
CROY/NA CR0 2 B7
SAND/SEL CR2 69 G8
SHPTN TW17 41 K8
VW GU25 39 G5
WIM/MER SW19 29 M8
WOKN/KNAP GU21 76 F7
Abbey St FNM GU9 5 J4
Abbey Wk E/WMO/HCT KT8 43 L3
Abbey Wy FARN GU14 92 F5
Abbey Wd ASC SL5 37 K7
Abbeywood ASHV GU12 * 113 L5
Abbot Cl BF/WBF KT14 59 G8
STA TW18 23 G8
Abbot Rd GU GU1 7 H8
Abbots Av HOR/WEW KT19 83 K1
Abbotsbury BRAK RG12 34 C5
Abbotsbury Ct SWTR RH13 167 H6
Abbotsbury Rd MRDN SM4 47 L4
WWKM BR4 70 C1
Abbot's Cl GUW GU2 138 B3
Abbots Dr VW GU25 38 F4
Abbotsfield Rd CRAWW RH11 190 G8
Abbotsford Cl
WOKS/MYFD GU22 11 H5
Abbots Gn CROY/NA CR0 69 G5
Abbots La PUR/KEN CR8 87 M6
Abbotsleigh Cl BELMT SM2 65 L6
Abbotsleigh Rd
STRHM/NOR SW16 30 F5
Abbotsmede Cl TWK TW1 26 C3
Abbots Pk BRXS/STRHM SW2 31 K2
Abbot's Ride FNM GU9 156 B1
Abbots Rd CHEAM SM3 65 H3
Abbotstone Rd PUT/ROE SW15 19 M5
Abbots Wk CTHM CR3 108 E4
Abbots Wy BECK BR3 51 H5
CHERT KT16 40 C7
GU GU1 118 A7
Abbotswood GU GU1 117 J6
Abbotswood Cl GU GU1 117 J5
Abbotswood Dr WEY KT13 60 A8
Abbotswood Rd
STRHM/NOR SW16 31 G4
Abbott Av RYNPK SW20 47 G2
Abbott Cl HPTN TW12 25 H7
Abbotts Md
RCHPK/HAM TW10 * 26 F5
Abbotts Ri REDH RH1 126 D6
Abbotts Rd MTCM CR4 48 F4
Abbotts Tilt WOT/HER KT12 61 H2
Abelia Cl CHOB/PIR GU24 75 H3
Abercairn Rd
STRHM/NOR SW16 30 F8
Aberconway Rd MRDN SM4 47 L3
Abercorn Cl SAND/SEL CR2 89 G2
Abercorn Wy
WOKN/KNAP GU21 76 D8
Aberdare Cl WWKM BR4 69 M1
Aberdeen Rd CROY/NA CR0 67 M3
Aberdeen Ter GSHT GU26 * 197 Q2
Aberfoyle Rd
STRHM/NOR SW16 31 G8
Abingdon Cl BRAK RG12 35 H5
WIM/MER SW19 29 M7
WOKN/KNAP GU21 76 E8
Abingdon Rd
STRHM/NOR SW16 49 H1
Abinger Av BELMT SM2 64 F7
Abinger Cl CROY/NA CR0 69 M5
RDKG RH5 144 F6
WLGTN SM6 67 H4
Abinger Common Rd
RDKG RH5 171 R2
Abinger Dr NRWD SE19 31 M8
REDH RH1 148 B2
Abinger Gdns ISLW TW7 17 H5
Abinger La RDKG RH5 142 F8
Abinger Rd RDKG RH5 172 B8
REDH RH1 148 B3
Abinger Wy RGUE GU4 117 L3
Aboyne Dr RYNPK SW20 46 D2
Aboyne Rd TOOT SW17 30 A4
Abrahams Rd CRAWW RH11 191 K12
Acacia Av BTFD TW8 17 L2
SHPTN TW17 41 K5
SHST GU47 52 A8
STWL/WRAY TW19 12 B6
WOKS/MYFD GU22 97 G2
Acacia Cl ADL/WDHM KT15 58 C8
Acacia Ct BRAK RG12 34 E3
Acacia Dr ADL/WDHM KT15 78 C1
BNSTD SM7 85 G4
CHEAM SM3 47 J8
Acacia Gdns WWKM BR4 69 M1
Acacia Gv DUL SE21 32 A3
NWMAL KT3 46 B3
Acacia Ms WDR/YW UB7 14 A1
Acacia Rd BECK BR3 51 J3
GU GU1 7 G3
HPTN TW12 25 K7
MTCM CR4 48 D2
STA TW18 22 E6
STRHM/NOR SW16 49 H1
Academy Cl CBLY GU15 73 H1
Academy Gdns CROY/NA CR0 3 K4
Academy Pl SHST GU47 72 B2
Accommodation La
WDR/YW UB7 13 M1
Accommodation Rd
CHERT KT16 57 H3
Ace Pde CHSGTN KT9 63 H2
Acer Dr CHOB/PIR GU24 75 J3
Acer Rd BH/WHM TN16 91 G6
Acheulian Cl FNM GU9 5 K9
Achilles Pl WOKN/KNAP GU21 76 F7
Ackroyd Rd FSTH SE23 33 G1
Acorn Cl EGRIN RH19 162 F5
HORL RH6 160 F2
HPTN TW12 25 L7
Acorn Gdns NRWD SE19 50 C1
Acorn Gv HYS/HAR UB3 15 J2
KWD/TDW/WH KT20 105 J6
WOKS/MYFD GU22 * 97 H3
Acorn Keep FNM GU9 134 A1
Acorns SWTR RH13 167 K5
The Acorns CRAWW RH11 191 L12
HORL RH6 161 L3
Acorns Wy ESH/CLAY KT10 61 M4
Acorn Wy FSTH SE23 33 G4
ORP BR6 71 L3
Acre La CAR SM5 66 D3
Acre Rd KUTN/CMB KT2 9 G3
WIM/MER SW19 30 A7
Acres Gdns
KWD/TDW/WH KT20 104 F1
Acres Platt CRAN GU6 186 E1
Acuba Rd WAND/EARL SW18 29 L3
Adair Cl SNWD SE25 50 E3
Adair Gdns CTHM CR3 107 M3
Adam Cl CAT SE6 33 K4
FSTH SE23 32 F3
Adams Cl BRYLDS KT5 45 J6
Adams Cft CHOB/PIR GU24 94 F2
Adams Ms LIPH GU30 196 G11
TOOT SW17 30 C3
Adamson Wy BECK BR3 51 M5
Adams Park Rd FNM GU9 134 A5
Adamsrill Rd SYD SE26 33 G5
Adams Rd BECK BR3 51 H5
Adams Wk KUT/HW KT1 8 E6
Adams Wy CROY/NA CR0 50 C6
Adam Wk FUL/PGN SW6 * 19 M2
Adare Wk STRHM/NOR SW16 31 J4
Addington Gv SYD SE26 33 H5
Addington Rd CROY/NA CR0 49 K8
SAND/SEL CR2 88 D1
WWKM BR4 69 M3
Addington Village Rd
CROY/NA CR0 69 J5
Addiscombe Av CROY/NA CR0 3 L2
Addiscombe Court Rd
CROY/NA CR0 3 H4
Addiscombe Gv CROY/NA CR0 2 F6
Addiscombe Rd CROY/NA CR0 3 G6
Addison Av HSLW TW3 16 F3
Addison Cl CTHM CR3 108 A4
Addison Gdns BRYLDS KT5 45 J4
Addison Rd CTHM CR3 108 A3
FRIM GU16 93 H1
GU GU1 7 L7
SNWD SE25 50 D4
TEDD TW11 26 E7
Addison's Cl CROY/NA CR0 69 J1
Addlestone Moor
ADL/WDHM KT15 58 F1
Addlestone Pk
ADL/WDHM KT15 58 E4
Addlestone Rd
ADL/WDHM KT15 59 J3
Adecroft Wy E/WMO/HCT KT8 43 M3
Adela Av NWMAL KT3 46 E5
Adelaide Cl CRAWW RH11 164 F1
HORS RH12 167 J5
Adelaide Pl WEY KT13 60 A3
Adelaide Rd ASHF TW15 23 G6
HEST TW5 16 B3
RCH/KEW TW9 18 C6
SURB KT6 45 H5
TEDD TW11 26 C7
WOT/HER KT12 60 D2
Adelina Ms BAL SW12 31 G2
Adelphi Cl CRAWE RH10 165 M6
Adelphi Rd EW KT17 84 A3
Adenmore Rd CAT SE6 33 K1
Adlers La RDKG RH5 122 D5
Adlington Pl FARN GU14 93 H7
Admers Crs LIPH GU30 196 H11
Admiral Rd CRAWW RH11 164 C7
Admiral's Bridge La
EGRIN RH19 194 D11
Admirals Ct GU GU1 117 L7
Admiralty Rd TEDD TW11 26 C8
Admiralty Wy CBLY GU15 72 C5
Adolf St CAT SE6 33 K5
Advance Rd WNWD SE27 31 M5
Aerodrome Wy HEST TW5 15 M1
Aerospace Bvd FARN GU14 112 D2
Agar Cl SURB KT6 63 J1
Agate La HORS RH12 167 H4
Agates La ASHTD KT21 83 G8
Agincourt Pl ASC SL5 36 F3
Agnes Riley Gdns CLAP SW4 * 30 F1
Agnes Scott Ct WEY KT13 59 L2
Agnew Rd FSTH SE23 33 H1
Agraria Rd GUW GU2 6 C6
Ailsa Av TWK TW1 17 K7
Ailsa Cl CRAWW RH11 164 D7
Ailsa Rd TWK TW1 17 L7
Ainger Cl ASHV GU12 113 G7
Ainsdale Wy WOKN/KNAP GU21 76 D7
Ainsworth Rd CROY/NA CR0 2 B5
Aintree Cl DTCH/LGLY SL3 13 H3
Aintree Rd CRAWE RH10 165 J6
Aircraft Esp FARN GU14 92 F8
Airedale Rd BAL SW12 30 C1
Airport Wy HORL RH6 160 D6
STWL/WRAY TW19 13 K6
Aisne Rd FRIM GU16 74 B8
Aitken Cl MTCM CR4 48 C7
Aitken Rd CAT SE6 33 L3
Akabusi Cl CROY/NA CR0 50 D6
Akehurst Cl CRAWE RH10 192 F2
Akehurst St PUT/ROE SW15 19 K8
Akerman Rd SURB KT6 44 F6
Alamein Rd ALDT GU11 112 E6
Alanbrooke Cl
WOKN/KNAP GU21 75 M8
Alanbrooke Rd ALDT GU11 113 G3
Alan Hilton Ct CHERT KT16 * 58 A5
Alan Rd WIM/MER SW19 29 H6
Alan Turing Rd GUW GU2 116 A8
Albain Crs ASHF TW15 23 H3
Albany Cl ESH/CLAY KT10 61 K7
MORT/ESHN SW14 18 E6
Albany Crs ESH/CLAY KT10 62 B5
Albany Ms KUTN/CMB KT2 8 D1
SUT SM1 65 L4
Albany Pde BTFD TW8 * 18 B1
Albany Pk DTCH/LGLY SL3 13 G2
FRIM GU16 72 F8
Albany Park Rd KUTN/CMB KT2 8 D1
LHD/OX KT22 102 D1
Albany Pl BTFD TW8 18 A1
EGH TW20 21 K5
Albany Rd BTFD TW8 18 A1
CRAWW RH11 164 E4
NWMAL KT3 46 A4
RCHPK/HAM TW10 * 18 C7
WIM/MER SW19 29 L6
WOT/HER KT12 61 G3
The Albanys REIG RH2 125 K5
Albany Ter RCHPK/HAM TW10 * 18 C7
The Albany KUTN/CMB KT2 8 D1
Albatross Gdns SAND/SEL CR2 89 G1
Albemarle Av WHTN TW2 25 J2
Albemarle Gdns NWMAL KT3 46 A4
Albemarle Pk BECK BR3 * 51 L1
Albemarle Rd BECK BR3 51 L1
Alberta Av SUT SM1 65 H3
Alberta Dr HORL RH6 161 K3
Albert Av CHERT KT16 40 D3
Albert Carr Gdns
STRHM/NOR SW16 31 H6
Albert Dr STA TW18 22 C6
WIM/MER SW19 29 H3
WOKN/KNAP GU21 77 M4
Albert Gv RYNPK SW20 47 G1
Albertine Cl EW KT17 84 E6
Albert Rd ADL/WDHM KT15 59 G2
ALDT GU11 112 E7
ASHF TW15 23 J6
ASHTD KT21 83 J8
BAGS GU19 54 B8
BNFD RG42 34 E1
CBLY GU15 * 72 F3
EGH TW20 21 G7
EW KT17 84 C3
FARN GU14 92 F7
HORL RH6 160 D3
HPTN TW12 25 M6
HSLW TW3 16 D6
KUT/HW KT1 9 G6
MTCM CR4 48 C3
NWMAL KT3 46 C4
PGE/AN SE20 33 G8
RCHPK/HAM TW10 18 B7
REDH RH1 126 F3
SNWD SE25 50 E4
SUT SM1 66 A4
TEDD TW11 26 C7
TWK TW1 26 C2
WARL CR6 89 H7
Albert Rd North REIG RH2 125 J7
Albery Cl HORS RH12 166 E5
Albion Cl CRAWE RH10 165 M5
Albion Ms REIG RH2 * 147 M2
Albion Pde WOKN/KNAP GU21 * 75 M7
Albion Pl SNWD SE25 * 50 D3
Albion Rd BELMT SM2 66 A5
HSLW TW3 16 D6
KUTN/CMB KT2 45 M1
REIG RH2 147 M1
WHTN TW2 26 B2
Albion St CROY/NA CR0 2 A4
Albion Villas Rd SYD SE26 32 F4
Albion Wy EDEN TN8 153 M5
HORS RH12 166 E7
Albury Av BELMT SM2 64 F7
ISLW TW7 17 J2
Albury Cl CHERT KT16 56 D2
HOR/WEW KT19 63 L7
HPTN TW12 25 K7
Albury Keep HORL RH6 160 E2
Albury Rd CHSGTN KT9 63 H4
GU GU1 7 M5
REDH RH1 126 F3
WOT/HER KT12 60 B5
Albury St SHGR GU5 140 F5
Alcester Rd WLGTN SM6 66 E3
Alcock Cl WLGTN SM6 67 G6
Alcock Rd HEST TW5 16 A2
Alcocks Cl KWD/TDW/WH KT20 105 H2
Alcocks La
KWD/TDW/WH KT20 105 H2
Alcorn Cl CHEAM SM3 65 K1
Aldenham Ter BRAK RG12 34 F6
Aldenholme WEY KT13 60 B5
Alderbrook Rd CRAN GU6 170 A10
Alderbury Rd BARN SW13 19 K1
Alder Cl ASHV GU12 113 K2
CRAWE RH10 193 N5
EGH TW20 21 H6
Aldercombe La CTHM CR3 128 B1
Alder Cft COUL/CHIP CR5 87 H7
Alderman Judge Ml KUT/HW KT1 8 E7
Aldermoor Rd CAT SE6 33 J4
Alderney Av HEST TW5 16 E2
Alder Rd BOR GU35 180 G11
MORT/ESHN SW14 19 G5
Alders Av EGRIN RH19 162 E2
Aldersbrook Dr KUTN/CMB KT2 27 J7
Aldersey Rd GU GU1 7 M4
Aldersgrove E/WMO/HCT KT8 44 A5
Aldershot Rd ASHV GU12 113 J8
CHOB/PIR GU24 95 H8
RGUW GU3 115 H4
Alderside Wk EGH TW20 21 H6
Aldersmead Av CROY/NA CR0 51 G6
Aldersmead Rd BECK BR3 33 H8
Alders Rd REIG RH2 125 L6
Alderstead La REDH RH1 107 G7
The Alders BF/WBF KT14 78 F2
FELT TW13 25 H6
FNM GU9 134 D3
HEST TW5 16 C1
STRHM/NOR SW16 * 30 F5
WWKM BR4 51 L8
Alders View Dr EGRIN RH19 162 F2
Alderton Rd CROY/NA CR0 3 K1
Alderwick Dr HSLW TW3 17 G5
Alderwood Cl CTHM CR3 108 B7
Aldingbourne Cl CRAWW RH11 164 B3
Aldis Ms TOOT SW17 30 B6
Aldis St TOOT SW17 30 B6
Aldren Rd TOOT SW17 29 M4
Aldrich Crs CROY/NA CR0 69 M7
Aldrich Gdns CHEAM SM3 65 J2
Aldrich Ter WAND/EARL SW18 29 M3
Aldridge Ri NWMAL KT3 46 B7
Aldrington Rd
STRHM/NOR SW16 30 F6
Aldrin Pl FARN GU14 92 A5
Aldwick Cl FARN GU14 92 D3
Aldwick Rd CROY/NA CR0 67 J2
Aldworth Cl BRAK RG12 34 D4
Alexander Cl WHTN TW2 26 B3
Alexander Crs CTHM CR3 107 M4
Alexander Evans Ms FSTH SE23 33 G3
Alexander Godley Cl
ASHTD KT21 103 J1
Alexander Pl OXTED RH8 130 B2
Alexander Rd COUL/CHIP CR5 86 E5
EGH TW20 21 L6
REIG RH2 147 K3
Alexanders Wk CTHM CR3 108 C8
Alexander Wk BRAK RG12 34 E5
Alexandra Av CBLY GU15 72 D4
SUT SM1 65 K2
WARL CR6 89 J7
Alexandra Cl ASHF TW15 24 A8
STA TW18 23 G7
WOT/HER KT12 60 D1
Alexandra Ct CRAWE RH10 * 164 F5
FARN GU14 92 F8
Alexandra Dr BRYLDS KT5 45 K7
NRWD SE19 32 B6
Alexandra Gdns CAR SM5 66 D7
HSLW TW3 16 E4
WOKN/KNAP GU21 75 M8
Alexandra Pl CROY/NA CR0 3 G3
GU GU1 7 L7
SNWD SE25 50 A5
Alexandra Rd ADL/WDHM KT15 59 G3
ALDT GU11 112 C7
ASHF TW15 24 A8
ASHV GU12 113 J8
BH/WHM TN16 110 E1
BTFD TW8 * 18 A1
CROY/NA CR0 3 G3
EGH TW20 20 F7
EW KT17 84 C3
FARN GU14 92 F7
HSLW TW3 16 E4
KUTN/CMB KT2 9 J3
MORT/ESHN SW14 19 G5
MTCM CR4 30 B8
PGE/AN SE20 33 G7
RCH/KEW TW9 18 C4
THDIT KT7 44 C5
TWK TW1 17 M8
WARL CR6 89 H7
WIM/MER SW19 29 K6
Alexandra Sq MRDN SM4 47 K5
Alexandra Ter ALDT GU11 * 112 D7
GU GU1 7 J5
Alexandra Wy HOR/WEW KT19 83 K5
Alfold By-Pass CRAN GU6 185 Q7
Alfold Rd MFD/CHID GU8 185 J9
Alfonso Cl ASHV GU12 134 F1
Alford Cl RGUE GU4 117 J5
Alford Gn CROY/NA CR0 70 A5
Alfred Cl CRAWE RH10 192 D8
Alfred Rd FELT TW13 24 F3
FNM GU9 5 K5
KUT/HW KT1 8 F9
SNWD SE25 50 D5
SUT SM1 65 M4
Alfreton Cl WIM/MER SW19 29 G4
Alfriston BRYLDS KT5 45 J6
Alfriston Av CROY/NA CR0 49 H7
Alfriston Cl BRYLDS KT5 45 J6
Alfriston Rd FRIM GU16 93 M2
Algar Rd ISLW TW7 17 K5
Algarve Rd WAND/EARL SW18 29 L2
Alice Rd ALDT GU11 112 E7
Alice Ruston Pl
WOKS/MYFD GU22 96 F1
Alice Wy HSLW TW3 16 E6
Alicia Av CRAWE RH10 165 K4
Alington Gv WLGTN SM6 67 G7
Alison Cl CROY/NA CR0 51 G8
FARN GU14 92 C6
WOKN/KNAP GU21 10 D1
Alison Dr CBLY GU15 73 J4
Alison's Rd ALDT GU11 112 D4
Alison Wy ALDT GU11 112 C7
Allan Cl NWMAL KT3 46 A5
Allbrook Cl TEDD TW11 26 B6
Allcard Cl HORS RH12 167 G4
Allcot Cl CRAWW RH11 164 A7
EBED/NFELT TW14 24 C2
Allden Av ASHV GU12 135 G2
Allden Gdns ASHV GU12 135 G2
Alldens La MFD/CHID GU8 168 E7
Allder Wy SAND/SEL CR2 67 L6
Allee Dr LIPH GU30 196 G8
Allenby Av SAND/SEL CR2 67 M7
Allenby Rd BH/WHM TN16 91 H7
CBLY GU15 72 D3
FSTH SE23 33 H4
Allen Cl MTCM CR4 48 E1
SUN TW16 42 E1
Allendale Cl SYD SE26 33 G6
Allen House Pk
WOKS/MYFD GU22 96 F2
Allen Rd BECK BR3 51 G2
CROY/NA CR0 49 J7
GT/LBKH KT23 101 L8
SUN TW16 42 E1
Allen's Cl EGRIN RH19 163 L7
Allerford Rd CAT SE6 33 L5
Alleyn Crs DUL SE21 32 A3
Alleyn Pk DUL SE21 32 A3
Alleyn Rd DUL SE21 32 A4
Allgood Cl MRDN SM4 47 G6
All Hallows Av
WOKS/MYFD GU22 95 L4
Alliance Cl HSLWW TW4 16 C7
Allingham Rd REIG RH2 147 K3
Allington Av SHPTN TW17 42 B3
Allington Cl WIM/MER SW19 29 G6
Allison Gv DUL SE21 32 B2
Alloway Cl WOKN/KNAP GU21 76 E8
All Saints Crs FARN GU14 72 B8
All Saints Dr SAND/SEL CR2 88 C2
All Saints Rd LTWR GU18 54 F8
SUT SM1 65 L2
WIM/MER SW19 29 M8
Allsmoor La BRAK RG12 35 J3
All Souls Av CHOB/PIR GU24 95 L3
All Souls' Rd ASC SL5 36 D5
Allum Gv KWD/TDW/WH KT20 104 E3
Allwood Cl SYD SE26 33 G5
Allyington Wy CRAWE RH10 165 M5
Allyn Cl STA TW18 22 C7
Alma Cl ASHV GU12 113 G6
WOKN/KNAP GU21 76 B7
Alma Crs SUT SM1 65 H4
Alma Gdns FRIM GU16 94 A1
Alma La FNM GU9 133 M2
Alma Pl NRWD SE19 32 C8
THHTH CR7 49 K5
Alma Rd BOR GU35 180 H12
CAR SM5 66 B4
ESH/CLAY KT10 44 B8
REIG RH2 125 L7
Alma Ter WAND/EARL SW18 30 A1
Alma Wy FNM GU9 134 A2
Almer Rd RYNPK SW20 28 D8
Almners Rd CHERT KT16 39 M7
Almond Av CAR SM5 66 C1
WOKS/MYFD GU22 97 G3
Almond Cl CRAWW RH11 164 C5
EGH TW20 20 E7
FARN GU14 92 D2
FELT TW13 24 D2
GU GU1 117 G4
SHPTN TW17 41 M2
Almond Gv BTFD TW8 17 L2
Almond Rd HOR/WEW KT19 84 A1
Almond Wy MTCM CR4 49 G5
Almorah Rd HEST TW5 16 A3
Almsgate RGUW GU3 137 M7
Alms Heath RPLY/SEND GU23 99 L3
Almshouse La CHSGTN KT9 62 F7
Alnwick Gv MRDN SM4 47 L4
Alphabet Gdns CAR SM5 48 A6
Alpha Pl MRDN SM4 * 47 G7
Alpha Rd ASHV GU12 113 G8
BRYLDS KT5 45 J6
CHOB/PIR GU24 56 C8
CRAWW RH11 164 E4
CROY/NA CR0 3 G3
TEDD TW11 26 A6
WOKS/MYFD GU22 11 K3
Alpha Wy EGH TW20 39 M1
Alphea Cl WIM/MER SW19 30 B8
Alphington Av FRIM GU16 73 J8
Alphington Gn FRIM GU16 73 H8
Alpine Av BRYLDS KT5 63 M1
Alpine Cl ASC SL5 * 36 C5
CROY/NA CR0 3 G8
FARN GU14 92 A6
Alpine Rd REDH RH1 126 D5
WOT/HER KT12 42 D7
Alpine Vw CAR SM5 66 B4
Alresford Rd GUW GU2 6 A5
Alric Av NWMAL KT3 46 B3
Alsford Cl LTWR GU18 74 C2
Alsom Av WPK KT4 64 C3
Alston Cl SURB KT6 44 E7
Alston Rd TOOT SW17 30 A5
Alterton Cl WOKN/KNAP GU21 76 D7
Alt Gv WIM/MER SW19 29 J8
Althorne Rd REDH RH1 148 D2
Althorp Rd TOOT SW17 30 C2
Alton Cl ISLW TW7 17 J4
Alton Ct STA TW18 40 B1
Alton Gdns BECK BR3 33 K8
WHTN TW2 17 G8
Alton Rd CROY/NA CR0 67 K3
PUT/ROE SW15 28 D2
RCH/KEW TW9 18 B6
RFNM GU10 4 B8
Altyre Cl BECK BR3 51 J5
Altyre Rd CROY/NA CR0 2 F6
Altyre Wy BECK BR3 51 J5
Alvernia Cl GODL GU7 159 M7
Alverstoke Gdns ALDT GU11 112 B8
Alverstone Av
WAND/EARL SW18 29 K3
Alverstone Rd NWMAL KT3 46 C4
Alverston Gdns SNWD SE25 50 B5
Alvia Gdns SUT SM1 65 M3
Alway Av HOR/WEW KT19 63 M4
Alwin Pl FNM GU9 133 M2
Alwyn Cl CROY/NA CR0 69 L6
Alwyne Ct WOKN/KNAP GU21 10 D4
Alwyne Rd WIM/MER SW19 29 J7
Alwyns Cl CHERT KT16 40 D6
Alwyns La CHERT KT16 40 C6
Amalgamated Dr BTFD TW8 17 K1
Ambassador BRAK RG12 34 C5
Ambassador Cl HSLW TW3 16 B4
Ambercroft Wy
COUL/CHIP CR5 107 L1
Amber Hl CBLY GU15 73 M5
Amberley Cl CRAWE RH10 165 L4
HORS RH12 167 K3
RPLY/SEND GU23 98 C7
Amberley Ct CRAWW RH11 * 191 N2
Amberley Dr ADL/WDHM KT15 58 C8

Amberley Gdns HOR/WEW KT19 64 C3
Amberley Gra ALDT GU11 134 C1
Amberley Gv CROY/NA CR0 3 J2
SYD SE26 32 E5
Amberley Rd HORS RH12 167 K3
MFD/CHID GU8 159 H7
Amberley Wy HSLWW TW4 15 M7
MRDN SM4 47 J7
Amberside Cl ISLW TW7 17 G8
Amberwood Cl WLGTN SM6 67 H4
Amberwood Dr CBLY GU15 73 J2
Amberwood Ri NWMAL KT3 46 B6
Amblecote COB KT11 81 G1
Ambleside Av BECK BR3 51 H5
STRHM/NOR SW16 31 G5
WOT/HER KT12 42 F8
Ambleside Cl CRAWW RH11 190 G8
FARN GU14 92 B5
FRIM GU16 93 K7
REDH RH1 148 E5
Ambleside Crs FNM GU9 133 K3
Ambleside Dr
EBED/NFELT TW14 24 C2
Ambleside Gdns BELMT SM2 65 M5
SAND/SEL CR2 69 G8
Ambleside Rd LTWR GU18 74 D1
Ambleside Wy EGH TW20 21 L8
Ambrey Wy WLGTN SM6 67 G7
Amen Cnr TOOT SW17 30 D7
Amersham Rd CROY/NA CR0 49 M6
Amesbury Av
BRXS/STRHM SW2 31 H3
Amesbury Cl WPK KT4 46 F8
Amesbury Rd FELT TW13 25 G3
Amey Dr GT/LBKH KT23 101 M6
Amhurst Gdns ISLW TW7 17 J3
Amis Av ADL/WDHM KT15 78 D1
HOR/WEW KT19 63 K5
Amis Rd WOKN/KNAP GU21 96 B1
Amity Gv RYNPK SW20 46 F1
Amlets La CRAN GU6 170 C12
Ampere Wy CROY/NA CR0 49 J8
Amroth Cl FSTH SE23 32 E2
Amstel Wy WOKN/KNAP GU21 76 C8
Amundsen Rd HORS RH12 167 G3
Amyand Cottages TWK TW1 17 L8
Amyand Park Gdns TWK TW1 26 E1
Amyand Park Rd TWK TW1 26 D1
Amy Cl WLGTN SM6 67 H6
Amy Rd OXTED RH8 130 B3
Ancaster Crs NWMAL KT3 46 D6
Ancaster Dr ASC SL5 36 B1
Ancaster Rd BECK BR3 51 G3
Anchorage Cl WIM/MER SW19 29 K6
Anchor Cl RGUW GU3 114 F5
Anchor Ct HORS RH12 * 166 F8
Anchor Hl WOKN/KNAP GU21 76 A7
Anchor Meadow FARN GU14 92 C5
Anders Cnr BNFD RG42 34 C1
Anderson Cl CHEAM SM3 47 K8
HOR/WEW KT19 83 L2
Anderson Dr ASHF TW15 23 M5
Anderson Pl BAGS GU19 54 B5
Anderson Rd WEY KT13 * 60 A2
Anderson's Pl HSLW TW3 16 E6
Andover Cl EBED/NFELT TW14 24 C2
HOR/WEW KT19 84 A1
Andover Rd WHTN TW2 26 A2
Andover Wy ALDT GU11 134 E2
Andrewartha Rd FARN GU14 93 H8
Andrew's Cl EW KT17 84 C4
WPK KT4 65 G1
Andrews Rd FARN GU14 92 B4
Andromeda Cl CRAWW RH11 164 A6
Anerley Gv NRWD SE19 32 C8
Anerley Hl NRWD SE19 32 C7
Anerley Pk PGE/AN SE20 32 E8
Anerley Park Rd PGE/AN SE20 32 E8
Anerley Rd PGE/AN SE20 50 E1
Anerley Station Rd
PGE/AN SE20 50 E1
Anerley V NRWD SE19 32 C8
Anfield Cl BAL SW12 30 F1
Angelfield HSLW TW3 16 E7
Angel Ga GU GU1 7 G6
Angel Hl SUT SM1 65 L2
Angel Hill Dr SUT SM1 65 L2
Angelica Gdns CROY/NA CR0 51 G8
Angelica Rd CHOB/PIR GU24 75 K5
GUW GU2 116 D4
Angel Pl REIG RH2 * 147 L2
Angel Rd THDIT KT7 44 D8
Anglers Reach SURB KT6 * 45 G5
Anglesea Rd KUT/HW KT1 45 G4
Anglesey Av FARN GU14 92 C2
Anglesey Cl ASHF TW15 23 K5
CRAWW RH11 164 E7
Anglesey Court Rd CAR SM5 66 D5
Anglesey Gdns CAR SM5 66 D5
Anglesey Rd ASHV GU12 113 G8
Angles Rd STRHM/NOR SW16 31 H5
Angus Cl CHSGTN KT9 63 K4
HORS RH12 167 G5
Anlaby Rd TEDD TW11 26 B6
Annandale Dr RFNM GU10 156 A3
Annandale Rd CROY/NA CR0 3 M5
GUW GU2 6 D7
Anne Armstrong Cl ALDT GU11 113 G4
Anne Boleyn's Wk CHEAM SM3 65 G6
KUTN/CMB KT2 27 H6
Anne Case Ms NWMAL KT3 * 46 A3
Anners Cl EGH TW20 39 M3
Annesley Dr CROY/NA CR0 69 J2
Anne's Wk CTHM CR3 108 B2
Annett Cl SHPTN TW17 42 B4
Annett Rd WOT/HER KT12 42 D7
Annie Brookes Cl STA TW18 22 A4
Anningsley Pk CHERT KT16 57 L8
Annisdowne Cl RDKG RH5 142 C8
Annsworthy Av THHTH CR7 50 A3
Ansell Gv CAR SM5 48 C8
Ansell Rd DORK RH4 144 E1
FRIM GU16 93 H1
TOOT SW17 30 B4
Anselm Cl CROY/NA CR0 3 J7
Ansford Rd BMLY BR1 33 M6
Ansley Cl SAND/SEL CR2 88 E4
Anson Cl ALDT GU11 112 C6
PUR/KEN CR8 108 A2
Anstead MFD/CHID GU8 * 199 R2
Anstice Cl CHSWK W4 19 H2
Anstiebury Cl RDKG RH5 173 K6
Anstie La RDKG RH5 172 G5
Anthony Pl GSHT GU26 * 198 A4
Anthony Rd SNWD SE25 50 D6
Anthony Wall BNFD RG42 35 J1
Antlands La HORL RH6 176 E12
Antlands La East HORL RH6 161 H8
Antlands La West HORL RH6 161 H8
Anton Crs SUT SM1 65 K2
Antrobus Cl SUT SM1 65 J4
Anvil Cl STRHM/NOR SW16 30 F8
Anvil La COB KT11 80 D5
Anvil Rd SUN TW16 42 D3
Anyards Rd COB KT11 80 E4
Anzio Cl ALDT GU11 112 D7
Anzio Gdns CTHM CR3 107 M3
Apeldoorn Dr WLGTN SM6 67 H7
Aperdele Rd LHD/OX KT22 82 D8
Aperfield Rd BH/WHM TN16 91 H7
Apers Av WOKS/MYFD GU22 97 J3
Apex Cl BECK BR3 51 L1
Apex Dr FRIM GU16 73 G8
Apley Rd REIG RH2 147 K3
Aplin Wy ISLW TW7 17 H3
LTWR GU18 54 D8
Apollo Pl WOKN/KNAP GU21 * 96 D1
Apollo Ri FARN GU14 92 A5
Apostle Wy THHTH CR7 49 L2
Apperlie Dr BRKHM/BTCW RH3 145 M1
Appleby Cl WHTN TW2 26 A3
Appleby Gdns
EBED/NFELT TW14 * 24 C2
Appledore BRAK RG12 34 C6
Appledore Cl TOOT SW17 30 C3
Appledore Ms FARN GU14 92 D2
Appledown Ri COUL/CHIP CR5 86 F5
Applefield CRAWE RH10 165 G3
Applegarth CROY/NA CR0 69 L6
ESH/CLAY KT10 62 C4
Apple Garth GODL GU7 159 M2
Applegarth Av GUW GU2 116 A8
Apple Gv CHSGTN KT9 63 H3
Applelands Cl RFNM GU10 155 K5
Apple Market KUT/HW KT1 8 D7
Appleton Gdns NWMAL KT3 46 D6
Apple Tree Cl LHD/OX KT22 101 M6
Appletree Cl GODL GU7 168 C7
PGE/AN SE20 50 E1
Appletree Ct RGUE GU4 118 A6
Appletree Pl BNFD RG42 34 D1
Apple Trees Pl
WOKS/MYFD GU22 * 96 F1
Apple Tree Wy SHST GU47 52 A8
Appley Dr CBLY GU15 72 E4
Approach Rd ASHF TW15 23 M7
BH/WHM TN16 110 E4
E/WMO/HCT KT8 43 K5
FNM GU9 5 J5
PUR/KEN CR8 87 K2
RYNPK SW20 46 F2
The Approach EGRIN RH19 178 H11
April Cl ASHTD KT21 83 J8
CBLY GU15 72 F7
FELT TW13 24 D4
HORS RH12 166 F5
April Gln FSTH SE23 33 G4
Aprilwood Cl ADL/WDHM KT15 78 C1
Apsley Rd NWMAL KT3 45 M3
SNWD SE25 50 E4
Aquila Cl LHD/OX KT22 103 H3
Arabella Dr PUT/ROE SW15 19 H6
Aragon Av EW KT17 64 E7
THDIT KT7 44 C5
Aragon Cl CROY/NA CR0 70 B8
SUN TW16 24 C8
Aragon Ct BRAK RG12 34 F4
Aragon Pl MRDN SM4 47 G7
Aragon Rd KUTN/CMB KT2 27 H6
MRDN SM4 47 G7
Aram Ct WOKS/MYFD GU22 * 11 K2
Arbor Cl BECK BR3 51 L2
Arborfield Cl BRXS/STRHM SW2 31 J2
Arbour Cl LHD/OX KT22 102 C5
Arbrook La ESH/CLAY KT10 62 A5
Arbutus Cl REDH RH1 147 M2
Arbutus Rd REDH RH1 147 M2
Arcade Pde CHSGTN KT9 * 63 H3
Arcadia Cl CAR SM5 66 D3
Arcadian Pl WAND/EARL SW18 29 J1
Archdale Pl NWMAL KT3 9 M8
Archer Cl KUTN/CMB KT2 8 E2
Archer Rd SNWD SE25 50 E4
Arch Rd WOT/HER KT12 61 G2
Archway Cl WIM/MER SW19 29 L5
WLGTN SM6 * 67 H2
Archway Ms DORK RH4 144 D1
Archway St BARN SW13 19 H5
Arcturus Rd CRAWW RH11 164 A6
Arden Cl BRAK RG12 35 K2
REIG RH2 147 L4
Arden Gv ORP BR6 71 L3
Arden Rd CRAWE RH10 165 H6
Ardenrun LING RH7 178 B1
Ardent Cl SNWD SE25 50 B3
Ardesley Wd WEY KT13 60 B3
Ardfern Av STRHM/NOR SW16 49 K3
Ardingly BRAK RG12 34 D6
Ardingly Cl CRAWW RH11 164 D2
CROY/NA CR0 69 G2
Ardleigh Gdns CHEAM SM3 47 K8
Ardley Cl CAT SE6 33 H4
Ardlui Rd WNWD SE27 31 M3
Ardmay Gdns SURB KT6 45 H5
Ardmore Av GUW GU2 116 E6
Ardmore Wy GUW GU2 116 E6
Ardrossan Av CBLY GU15 73 K5
Ardrossan Gdns WPK KT4 64 D2
Ardshiel Dr REDH RH1 148 B2
Ardwell Rd BRXS/STRHM SW2 31 H3
Arena La ALDT GU11 112 B5
Arethusa Wy CHOB/PIR GU24 75 J6
Arford Common BOR GU35 180 F11
Arford Rd BOR GU35 180 E11
Argent Cl EGH TW20 21 M7
Argent Ct SURB KT6 * 63 K1
Argent Ter SHST GU47 * 72 B1
Argosy Gdns STA TW18 22 C7
Argosy La STWL/WRAY TW19 23 G1
Argus Wk CRAWW RH11 164 C7
Argyle Av HSLW TW3 16 D8
Argyle Rd HSLW TW3 16 E7
Argyle St CHOB/PIR GU24 94 D3
Ariel Wy HSLWW TW4 15 L5
Arkell Gv NRWD SE19 31 L8
Arkindale Rd CAT SE6 33 M4
Arkwright Dr BNFD RG42 34 A2
Arkwright Rd DTCH/LGLY SL3 13 H4
SAND/SEL CR2 68 C8
Arlington Cl BNFD RG42 34 D1
SUT SM1 65 K1
TWK TW1 * 17 M8
Arlington Dr CAR SM5 66 C1
Arlington Ldg WEY KT13 59 L3
Arlington Rd ASHF TW15 23 J6
RCHPK/HAM TW10 27 G3
SURB KT6 45 G6
TEDD TW11 26 C5
TWK TW1 17 M8
Arlington Sq BRAK RG12 34 D2
Arlington Ter ALDT GU11 112 C7
Armadale Rd
EBED/NFELT TW14 15 K7
WOKN/KNAP GU21 76 D7
Armfield Cl E/WMO/HCT KT8 43 J5
Armfield Crs MTCM CR4 48 C2
Armitage Ct ASC SL5 36 F6
Armitage Dr FRIM GU16 73 J8
Armstrong Cl WOT/HER KT12 42 D6
Armstrong Ml FARN GU14 92 A5
Armstrong Rd EGH TW20 20 F7
FELT TW13 25 H6
Armytage Rd HEST TW5 16 A2
Arnal Crs WAND/EARL SW18 29 H1
Arncliffe BRAK RG12 34 D5
Arndale Wy EGH TW20 21 K6
Arne Cl CRAWW RH11 164 B7
Arne Gv HORL RH6 160 B1
Arnewood Cl LHD/OX KT22 81 L4
PUT/ROE SW15 28 D2
Arney's La MTCM CR4 48 D6
Arnfield Cl CRAWW RH11 164 A5
Arnhem Dr CROY/NA CR0 90 A1
Arnison Rd E/WMO/HCT KT8 44 A4
Arnold Crs ISLW TW7 17 G7
Arnold Dr CHSGTN KT9 63 G5
Arnold Rd STA TW18 22 F8
TOOT SW17 30 C8
WOKN/KNAP GU21 11 J3
Arnulf St CAT SE6 33 L5
Arnull's Rd STRHM/NOR SW16 31 L7
Arosa Rd TWK TW1 18 A8
Arragon Gdns
STRHM/NOR SW16 31 H8
WWKM BR4 69 L2
Arragon Rd TWK TW1 26 D2
WAND/EARL SW18 29 K2
Arragon Wk BF/WBF KT14 79 J3
Arran Cl CRAWW RH11 164 D7
WLGTN SM6 66 F3
Arran Rd CAT SE6 33 L3
Arran Wy ESH/CLAY KT10 61 L1
Arras Av MRDN SM4 47 M5
Arreton Md WOKN/KNAP GU21 77 H4
Arrivals Rd HORL RH6 160 C6
Arrol Rd BECK BR3 50 F3
Arrow Rd FARN GU14 92 C7
Artel Cft CRAWE RH10 165 H4
Arterberry Rd RYNPK SW20 28 F8
Arthur Cl BAGS GU19 54 B8
FNM GU9 5 H6
Arthur Rd BH/WHM TN16 90 F5
CRAWW RH11 164 A4
FNM GU9 5 H7
KUTN/CMB KT2 9 J3
NWMAL KT3 46 E5
SWTR RH13 167 G8
WIM/MER SW19 29 K5
Arthur's Bridge Rd
WOKN/KNAP GU21 10 A6
Arthur St ALDT GU11 112 E8
Artillery Rd ALDT GU11 112 E7
ALDT GU11 113 G2
GU GU1 7 G5
Artillery Ter GU GU1 7 G4
Artington Cl ORP BR6 71 M3
Artington Wk GUW GU2 6 F9
Arundel Av EW KT17 64 E8
MRDN SM4 47 J4
SAND/SEL CR2 68 D8
Arundel Cl CRAWE RH10 165 L4
CROY/NA CR0 2 A8
HPTN TW12 25 L6
LIPH GU30 196 C5
Arundel Pl FNM GU9 5 G3
Arundel Rd BELMT SM2 65 J6
CBLY GU15 73 M5
CROY/NA CR0 50 A6
DORK RH4 144 D2
HSLWW TW4 15 M5
KUT/HW KT1 9 M6
Arundel Ter BARN SW13 19 L1
Arunside HORS RH12 166 D8
Arun Wy SWTR RH13 167 H8
Aschurch Rd CROY/NA CR0 3 K1
Ascot Ct ALDT GU11 112 D8
Ascot Ms WLGTN SM6 66 F7
Ascot Pk ASC SL5 * 36 B3
Ascot Rd EBED/NFELT TW14 23 K2
TOOT SW17 30 D7
Ashbourne BRAK RG12 34 C6
Ashbourne Cl ASHV GU12 113 M6
COUL/CHIP CR5 86 F8
Ashbourne Rd MTCM CR4 30 D7
Ashbourne Ter WIM/MER SW19 29 K8
Ashbrook Rd WDSR SL4 20 E1
Ashburnham Pk
ESH/CLAY KT10 61 M3
Ashburnham Rd CRAWE RH10 165 J6
RCHPK/HAM TW10 26 E4
Ashburton Av CROY/NA CR0 50 E8
Ashburton Cl CROY/NA CR0 3 L4
Ashburton Gdns CROY/NA CR0 3 L5
Ashburton Rd CROY/NA CR0 3 L5
Ashbury Crs RGUE GU4 117 M6
Ashbury Dr BLKW GU17 72 D8
Ashbury Pl WIM/MER SW19 29 M7
Ashby Av CHSGTN KT9 63 K5
Ashby Wk CROY/NA CR0 49 M6
Ashby Wy WDR/YW UB7 14 D2
Ash Church Rd ASHV GU12 113 L7
Ash Cl ASHV GU12 113 L6
CAR SM5 66 C1
CRAWE RH10 193 P4
EDEN TN8 153 L8
KWD/TDW/WH KT20 123 M5
LING RH7 178 F4
NWMAL KT3 46 A2
PGE/AN SE20 50 F2
REDH RH1 126 F4
WOKS/MYFD GU22 78 D5
WOKS/MYFD GU22 97 H2
Ash Combe MFD/CHID GU8 199 P1
Ashcombe Av SURB KT6 45 G7
Ashcombe Dr EDEN TN8 153 L5
Ashcombe Pde
WOKS/MYFD GU22 * 97 K2
Ashcombe Rd CAR SM5 66 D5
DORK RH4 122 D8
REDH RH1 126 F1
WIM/MER SW19 29 K6
Ashcombe Sq NWMAL KT3 45 M3
Ashcombe Ter
KWD/TDW/WH KT20 104 E2
Ash Ct HOR/WEW KT19 63 M3
Ashcroft RGUE GU4 139 H7
Ashcroft Pk COB KT11 81 H2
Ashcroft Ri COUL/CHIP CR5 87 H6
Ashcroft Rd CHSGTN KT9 63 J2
Ashdale GT/LBKH KT23 101 M8
Ashdale Cl STWL/WRAY TW19 23 H3
WHTN TW2 25 L1
Ashdene Cl ASHF TW15 * 23 M8
Ashdene Crs ASHV GU12 113 K6
Ashdene Rd ASHV GU12 113 K6
Ashdown Av FARN GU14 93 H7
Ashdown Cl BECK BR3 51 L2
BRAK RG12 35 J2
FROW RH18 195 P11
REIG RH2 147 L4
WOKS/MYFD GU22 10 C9
Ashdown Ct CRAWE RH10 * 165 H7
Ashdown Dr CRAWE RH10 165 G8
Ashdown Gdns SAND/SEL CR2 88 E5
Ashdown Pl THDIT KT7 44 D6
Ashdown Rd EW KT17 84 C3
FROW RH18 195 N11
KUT/HW KT1 8 E7
REIG RH2 147 L4
Ashdown Vw EGRIN RH19 162 F6
Ashdown Wy TOOT SW17 30 D3
Ash Dr REDH RH1 148 D2
Ashenden Rd GUW GU2 116 C8
Ashen Gv WIM/MER SW19 29 K4
Ashen V SAND/SEL CR2 69 G7
Asher Dr ASC SL5 35 M1
Ashfield BIL RH14 200 H7
Ashfield Av FELT TW13 24 E2
Ashfield Cl BECK BR3 33 K8
RCHPK/HAM TW10 27 H2
Ashford Av ASHF TW15 23 L7
Ashford Cl ASHF TW15 23 H5
Ashford Crs ASHF TW15 23 H4
Ashford Gdns COB KT11 81 G6
Ashford Rd ASHF TW15 23 M8
FELT TW13 24 A5
STA TW18 23 G8
Ash Green La East ASHV GU12 135 M1
Ash Green La West
RFNM GU10 135 J1
Ash Green Rd ASHV GU12 113 M8
Ash Gv EBED/NFELT TW14 24 B2
GUW GU2 6 A3
HEST TW5 16 A3
LIPH GU30 197 J10
PGE/AN SE20 50 F2
STA TW18 22 F7
WWKM BR4 69 M1
Ashgrove Rd ASHF TW15 23 M6
Ash Hill Rd ASHV GU12 113 M6
Ash Keys CRAWE RH10 165 G5
Ashlake Rd STRHM/NOR SW16 31 H5
Ash La MFD/CHID GU8 157 M7
Ashleigh Av EGH TW20 21 M8
Ashleigh Cl HORL RH6 160 C3
Ashleigh Gdns SUT SM1 65 L1
Ashleigh Rd HORS RH12 166 F4
MORT/ESHN SW14 19 H5
PGE/AN SE20 50 E3
Ashley Av EPSOM KT18 84 A3
MRDN SM4 47 K5
Ashley Cl FRIM GU16 93 K3
GT/LBKH KT23 101 J7
RFNM GU10 132 C2
WOT/HER KT12 42 B8
Ashley Ct EPSOM KT18 84 A3
WOKN/KNAP GU21 * 76 C8
Ashley Dr BNSTD SM7 85 K4
ISLW TW7 17 H1
WHTN TW2 25 L2
WOT/HER KT12 60 D2
Ashley Gdns RCHPK/HAM TW10 27 G4
Ashley La CROY/NA CR0 67 L3
Ashley Park Av WOT/HER KT12 42 C8
Ashley Park Crs WOT/HER KT12 42 D8
Ashley Park Rd WOT/HER KT12 60 D1
Ashley Ri WOT/HER KT12 60 D2
Ashley Rd DORK RH4 143 M3
EPSOM KT18 84 C7
FARN GU14 93 G5
HOR/WEW KT19 84 A3
HPTN TW12 43 K1
RCH/KEW TW9 18 B5
THDIT KT7 44 C6
THHTH CR7 49 J4
WIM/MER SW19 29 L7
WOKN/KNAP GU21 76 C8
WOT/HER KT12 60 C3
Ashley Wy CHOB/PIR GU24 75 G3
Ashling Rd CROY/NA CR0 3 M3
Ash Lodge Cl ASHV GU12 113 K8
Ash Lodge Dr ASHV GU12 113 K8
Ashlone Rd PUT/ROE SW15 19 M5
Ashlyn's Pk COB KT11 81 H3
Ashlyns Wy CHSGTN KT9 63 G5
Ashmead Rd EBED/NFELT TW14 24 D2
Ashmere Cl CHEAM SM3 65 G4
Ash Ms EPSOM KT18 84 B4
Ashmore La HAYES BR2 90 F1
HORS RH12 189 R7
Ashridge FARN GU14 92 C2
Ashridge Gn BNFD RG42 34 E1
Ashridge Wy MRDN SM4 47 J4
SUN TW16 24 D7
Ash Rd ASHV GU12 134 F1
CHEAM SM3 47 H8
CHOB/PIR GU24 95 K8
CRAWE RH10 165 J2
CROY/NA CR0 69 K1
SHPTN TW17 41 K4
WOKS/MYFD GU22 97 H2
Ash St ASHV GU12 113 K8
Ashtead La GODL GU7 168 A7
Ashtead Woods Rd ASHTD KT21 82 F6
Ashton Cl SUT SM1 65 K3
WOT/HER KT12 60 E5
Ashton Gdns HSLWW TW4 16 C6
Ashton Rd WOKN/KNAP GU21 76 C7
Ashtree Av MTCM CR4 48 A2
Ash Tree Cl CROY/NA CR0 51 H6
HASM GU27 198 G4
Ashtree Cl ORP BR6 71 L3
Ash Tree Cl SURB KT6 45 H8
Ashtrees CRAN GU6 186 D4
Ash Tree Wy CROY/NA CR0 51 H5
Ashurst Cl HORS RH12 167 K4
LHD/OX KT22 102 D3
PGE/AN SE20 50 E1
PUR/KEN CR8 88 A5
Ashurst Dr CRAWE RH10 165 M4
KWD/TDW/WH KT20 123 L4
SHPTN TW17 41 H5
Ashurst Gdns
BRXS/STRHM SW2 * 31 K2
Ashurst Pk ASC SL5 * 37 G3
Ashurst Pl DORK RH4 144 F1
Ashurst Rd ASHV GU12 113 J5
KWD/TDW/WH KT20 104 E3
Ashurst Wk CROY/NA CR0 68 E1
Ash V MFD/CHID GU8 183 P12
Ashvale Rd TOOT SW17 30 C6
Ashview Cl ASHF TW15 23 H7
Ashview Gdns ASHF TW15 23 H6
Ashwell Av CBLY GU15 73 J3
Ashwick Cl CTHM CR3 108 D7
Ashwood WARL CR6 108 F2
Ashwood Gdns CROY/NA CR0 69 L5
Ashwood Pk LHD/OX KT22 101 M5
WOKS/MYFD GU22 11 G8
Ashwood Rd EGH TW20 20 E7
WOKS/MYFD GU22 10 F8
Ashworth Pl GUW GU2 * 116 C8
Aslett St WAND/EARL SW18 29 L1
Asmar Cl COUL/CHIP CR5 87 H5
Aspen Cl COB KT11 81 H6
RGUE GU4 118 A5
STA TW18 22 C4
Aspen Gdns ASHF TW15 23 M6
MTCM CR4 48 D5
Aspen Gv ASHV GU12 135 H1
Aspen V CTHM CR3 88 C8
Aspen Wy BNSTD SM7 85 G4
FELT TW13 24 E4
HORS RH12 167 H5
Asprey Gv CTHM CR3 108 D6
Assembly Wk CAR SM5 48 B7
Assher Rd WOT/HER KT12 61 H2
Astleham Wy SHPTN TW17 41 H3
Aston Cl ASHTD KT21 82 F8
Aston Gn HSLWW TW4 15 M4
Aston Rd ESH/CLAY KT10 62 B4
RYNPK SW20 46 F2
Astonville St WAND/EARL SW18 29 K2
Aston Wy EPSOM KT18 84 C6
Astor Cl ADL/WDHM KT15 59 G3
KUTN/CMB KT2 27 L7
Astoria Pde ASHF TW15 * 23 K5
STRHM/NOR SW16 * 31 H4
Asylum Arch Rd REDH RH1 148 C3
Atalanta Cl PUR/KEN CR8 67 K8
Atbara Rd TEDD TW11 26 E7
Atcham Rd HSLW TW3 16 F6
Atfield Gv BFOR GU20 55 G5
Atheldene Rd
WAND/EARL SW18 29 L2
Athelney St CAT SE6 33 K4
Athelstan Cl CRAWE RH10 192 D7
Athelstan Rd KUT/HW KT1 45 J4
Athelstan Wy SWTR RH13 205 M9
Athena Cl KUT/HW KT1 9 G8
Atherfield Rd REIG RH2 147 M3
Atherley Wy HSLWW TW4 25 J1
Atherton Cl RGUE GU4 139 H6
STWL/WRAY TW19 14 A8
Atherton Dr WIM/MER SW19 29 G5
Atherton Rd BARN SW13 19 K2
Athlone ESH/CLAY KT10 62 B5
Athlone Rd BRXS/STRHM SW2 31 J1
Atkins Cl WOKN/KNAP GU21 76 D8
Atkins Dr WWKM BR4 70 A2
Atkinson Ct HORL RH6 * 160 E4
Atkinson Rd CRAWE RH10 165 L6
Atkins Rd BAL SW12 30 F1
Attebrouche Ct BRAK RG12 35 G7
Attfield Cl ASHV GU12 113 J8
Attlee Cl THHTH CR7 49 M6
Attwood Cl SAND/SEL CR2 88 E4
Atwood GT/LBKH KT23 101 H6
Atwood Av RCH/KEW TW9 18 D4
Aubyn Hl WNWD SE27 31 M5
Aubyn Sq PUT/ROE SW15 19 K6
Auchinleck Ct CRAWE RH10 * 193 N6
Auchinleck Wy ALDT GU11 112 B7
Auckland Cl CRAWW RH11 164 F1
NRWD SE19 50 C1
Auckland Hl WNWD SE27 31 M5
Auckland Ri NRWD SE19 50 B1
Auckland Rd CTHM CR3 108 B4
KUT/HW KT1 45 J4
NRWD SE19 50 C1
Aucklands Gdns NRWD SE19 50 B1
Auden Pl CHEAM SM3 * 64 F3
Audley Cl ADL/WDHM KT15 58 E4
Audley Dr WARL CR6 88 F5
Audley Firs WOT/HER KT12 60 E3
Audley Pl BELMT SM2 65 L6
Audley Rd RCHPK/HAM TW10 18 C7
Audley Wy ASC SL5 36 A3
Audrey Cl BECK BR3 51 L6
Audric Cl KUTN/CMB KT2 9 J4
Augur Cl STA TW18 22 C6
Augusta Cl E/WMO/HCT KT8 43 J3
Augusta Rd WHTN TW2 25 M3
Augustine Cl DTCH/LGLY SL3 13 H5
August La SHGR GU5 170 C2

Augustus Cl BTFD TW8 18 A2
Augustus Gdns CBLY GU15 73 M4
Augustus Rd WIM/MER SW19 29 H2
Aultone Wy CAR SM5 66 C2
SUT SM1 65 L1
Aurelia Gdns CROY/NA CR0 49 J5
Aurelia Rd CROY/NA CR0 49 H6
Auriol Cl WPK KT4 64 B2
Auriol Park Rd WPK KT4 64 B2
Aurum Cl HORL RH6 160 E4
Austen Cl EGRIN RH19 162 C4
Austen Rd FARN GU14 92 D3
GU GU1 7 M6
Austin Cl COUL/CHIP CR5 87 L8
FSTH SE23 33 H1
Austyn Gdns BRYLDS KT5 * 45 L8
Autumn Cl WIM/MER SW19 29 M7
Autumn Dr BELMT SM2 65 L7
Avalon Cl RYNPK SW20 47 H2
Avard Gdns ORP BR6 71 M3
Avarn Rd TOOT SW17 30 C7
Avebury BRAK RG12 34 D6
Avebury Cl HORS RH12 167 K2
Avebury Pk SURB KT6 * 45 G6
Avebury Rd WIM/MER SW19 47 J1
Aveley La FNM GU9 155 L2
Aveling Cl CRAWE RH10 165 L6
PUR/KEN CR8 87 J3
Aven Cl CRAN GU6 186 D3
Avening Rd WAND/EARL SW18 29 K1
Avenue C ADL/WDHM KT15 59 H2
Avenue Cl HEST TW5 15 L3
KWD/TDW/WH KT20 104 E4
LIPH GU30 196 G9
Avenue Crs HEST TW5 15 L3
Avenue De Cagny
CHOB/PIR GU24 95 J4
Avenue Elmers SURB KT6 45 H5
Avenue Gdns HEST TW5 * 15 K2
HORL RH6 160 F4
MORT/ESHN SW14 19 H5
TEDD TW11 26 C8
Avenue One ADL/WDHM KT15 59 H3
Avenue Pde SUN TW16 * 42 E3
Avenue Park Rd WNWD SE27 31 L3
Avenue Rd BELMT SM2 65 K8
BH/WHM TN16 111 H2
BNSTD SM7 85 L5
COB KT11 81 G6
CRAN GU6 186 E4
CTHM CR3 108 A4
EPSOM KT18 84 A4
FARN GU14 93 G5
FELT TW13 24 C4
GSHT GU26 197 Q2
HPTN TW12 43 L1
ISLW TW7 17 H3
KUT/HW KT1 8 F8
NWMAL KT3 46 B3
PGE/AN SE20 50 F1
RYNPK SW20 46 E2
SNWD SE25 50 D2
STA TW18 22 A6
STRHM/NOR SW16 49 G2
TEDD TW11 26 D8
WLGTN SM6 66 F6
Avenue South BRYLDS KT5 45 J7
Avenue Sucy CBLY GU15 72 D5
Avenue Ter NWMAL KT3 45 M3
The Avenue ADL/WDHM KT15 58 D8
ASHV GU12 134 F2
BECK BR3 51 L1
BELMT SM2 65 J7
BH/WHM TN16 111 K5
BRKHM/BTCW RH3 123 K8
BRYLDS KT5 45 J6
CAR SM5 66 D6
CBLY GU15 72 E5
CHOB/PIR GU24 56 C7
COUL/CHIP CR5 87 G5
CRAN GU6 171 K11
CROY/NA CR0 3 G7
CTHM CR3 108 D1
EGH TW20 21 L5
EGRIN RH19 178 H11
ESH/CLAY KT10 62 B5
EW KT17 64 F6
GODL GU7 168 C7
GSHT GU26 197 Q2
HASM GU27 198 A6
HEST TW5 15 K3
HORL RH6 160 C4
HPTN TW12 25 J7
HSLW TW3 16 F7
KWD/TDW/WH KT20 104 E4
LHD/OX KT22 82 C2
LIPH GU30 196 F9
LTWR GU18 54 D8
RCH/KEW TW9 18 C4
REDH RH1 149 H3
RFNM GU10 155 H5
RGUW GU3 116 B1
RGUW GU3 137 M8
STA TW18 40 E1
STWL/WRAY TW19 12 B6
SUN TW16 42 E2
SWTR RH13 204 E11
TWK TW1 17 M7
WPK KT4 64 C1
Avenue Three ADL/WDHM KT15 59 H2
Avenue Two ADL/WDHM KT15 59 H3
Averil Gv STRHM/NOR SW16 31 L7
Avern Gdns E/WMO/HCT KT8 43 L4
Avern Rd E/WMO/HCT KT8 43 L4
Aviary Rd WOKS/MYFD GU22 78 D6
Aviary Wy CRAWE RH10 193 P4
Aviemore Cl BECK BR3 51 J5
Aviemore Wy BECK BR3 51 H5
Avington Cl GU GU1 7 K3
Avington Gv PGE/AN SE20 32 F8
Avoca Rd TOOT SW17 30 D5
Avocet Crs SHST GU47 72 A1
Avon Cl ADL/WDHM KT15 58 D5
ASHV GU12 113 J8
FARN GU14 92 B2
SUT SM1 65 M3
WPK KT4 64 D1
Avondale ASHV GU12 113 J2
Avondale Av ESH/CLAY KT10 62 D2
STA TW18 22 C8
WPK KT4 46 C8
Avondale Cl HORL RH6 160 C1
WOT/HER KT12 60 F4
Avondale Gdns HSLWW TW4 16 C7
Avondale Rd ALDT GU11 134 E1
ASHF TW15 23 G4
MORT/ESHN SW14 19 G5
SAND/SEL CR2 67 M5
WIM/MER SW19 29 L6
Avonmead WOKN/KNAP GU21 76 F8
Avonmore Av GU GU1 7 M2
Avon Rd FNM GU9 5 J6
SUN TW16 24 C8
Avonstowe Cl ORP BR6 71 M2
Avon Wk CRAWW RH11 164 B5
Avonwick Rd HSLW TW3 16 E4
Avro Wy BF/WBF KT14 59 H8
WEY KT13 79 H1
WLGTN SM6 67 H6
Axbridge BRAK RG12 35 H5
Axes La REDH RH1 148 F7
Axwood EPSOM KT18 83 M5
Ayebridges Av EGH TW20 21 M8
Ayjay Cl ALDT GU11 134 E2
Aylesford Av BECK BR3 51 H5
Aylesworth Sp WDSR SL4 20 E1
Aylett Rd ISLW TW7 17 H4
SNWD SE25 50 E4
Ayliffe Cl KUT/HW KT1 9 J6
Ayling Ct FNM GU9 134 C2
Ayling Hl ALDT GU11 112 C8
Ayling La ALDT GU11 134 C1
Aylward Rd FSTH SE23 33 G3
RYNPK SW20 47 J2
Aymer Cl STA TW18 40 B1
Aymer Dr STA TW18 40 B1
Aysgarth BRAK RG12 34 C6
Ayshe Court Dr SWTR RH13 167 H7
Azalea Av BOR GU35 180 B12
Azalea Ct WOKS/MYFD GU22 10 A9
Azalea Dr HASM GU27 198 A5
Azalea Wy CBLY GU15 73 L3

B

Babbacombe Cl CHSGTN KT9 63 G4
Babbs Md FNM GU9 4 F5
Baber Bridge Pde
EBED/NFELT TW14 * 15 M8
Baber Dr EBED/NFELT TW14 15 M8
Babington Rd
STRHM/NOR SW16 31 G6
Babylon La
KWD/TDW/WH KT20 125 L1
Bachelor's La RPLY/SEND GU23 99 K6
Back Gn WOT/HER KT12 60 F5
Back La BIL RH14 200 H7
BTFD TW8 18 A2
CRAWE RH10 192 H11
MFD/CHID GU8 158 A5
RCHPK/HAM TW10 26 F4
RFNM GU10 180 A1
RGUE GU4 119 G5
Backley Gdns CROY/NA CR0 50 D6
Back Rd TEDD TW11 26 B8
Bacon Cl SHST GU47 72 A3
Bacon La RFNM GU10 180 H5
Badajos Rd ALDT GU11 112 C6
Baden Cl STA TW18 22 D8
Baden Dr HORL RH6 160 B2
Baden Powell Cl SURB KT6 63 J1
Baden Rd GUW GU2 116 D6
Bader Cl PUR/KEN CR8 88 A5
Badger Cl FELT TW13 24 E4
GUW GU2 116 E5
HSLWW TW4 15 M5
Badger Dr LTWR GU18 54 D8
Badgers Cl ASHF TW15 * 23 J6
GODL GU7 168 A1
HORS RH12 167 J3
WOKN/KNAP GU21 76 F8
Badgers Copse CBLY GU15 73 H6
WPK KT4 64 C1
Badgers Ct WPK KT4 * 64 C1
Badgers Cross MFD/CHID GU8 159 J8
Badgers Hl VW GU25 38 F5
Badgers Hollow GODL GU7 168 A3
Badgers La WARL CR6 108 F1
Badgers Wk CTHM CR3 88 C8
NWMAL KT3 46 B2
PUR/KEN CR8 86 F1
Badgers Wy BIL RH14 201 R5
BRAK RG12 35 J1
EGRIN RH19 162 F2
Badgers Wd CTHM CR3 107 M7
Badger Wy ASHV GU12 113 G6
RFNM GU10 133 G1
Badgerwood Dr FRIM GU16 73 G7
Badingham Dr LHD/OX KT22 102 B6
Badshot Lea Rd FNM GU9 134 E3
Badshot Pk FNM GU9 134 D3
Bagot Cl ASHTD KT21 83 J6
Bagshot Gn BAGS GU19 54 B7
Bagshot Rd ASC SL5 36 E8
BRAK RG12 34 E3
CHOB/PIR GU24 75 L1
EGH TW20 20 F8
WOKN/KNAP GU21 95 L1
Bahram Rd HOR/WEW KT19 64 A8
Baigents La BFOR GU20 55 G5
Bailes La RGUW GU3 115 G7
Bailey Cl FRIM GU16 93 G1
HORS RH12 167 J2
Bailey Crs CHSGTN KT9 63 G6
Bailey Pl SYD SE26 32 F7
Bailey Rd DORK RH4 143 M3
Bailing Hl HORS RH12 166 B3
Baillie Rd GU GU1 7 L6
Bain Av CBLY GU15 72 E8
Bainbridge Cl
RCHPK/HAM TW10 27 H6
Baines Cl SAND/SEL CR2 68 A4
Bainton Md WOKN/KNAP GU21 76 D7
Baird Cl CRAWE RH10 165 J1
Baird Dr RGUW GU3 115 L7
Baird Gdns NRWD SE19 32 B5
Baird Rd FARN GU14 92 F3
Bakeham La EGH TW20 20 F8
Bakehouse Barn Cl
HORS RH12 167 H2
Bakehouse Ms ALDT GU11 * 112 D7
Bakehouse Rd HORL RH6 160 C1
Baker Cl CRAWE RH10 164 F6
Baker La MTCM CR4 48 D2
Baker's Cl LING RH7 178 F4
PUR/KEN CR8 87 M4
Bakers End RYNPK SW20 47 H2
Bakers Gdns CAR SM5 66 B1
Baker's La LING RH7 178 F5
Bakers Md GDST RH9 128 F4
Baker St WEY KT13 59 K3
Bakers Wy RDKG RH5 173 K12
Bakewell Wy NWMAL KT3 46 B2
Balaclava Rd SURB KT6 44 F7
Balchins La DORK RH4 143 K3
Balcombe Gdns HORL RH6 160 F4
Balcombe Rd CRAWE RH10 165 M3
CRAWE RH10 192 D12
HORL RH6 160 E2
Baldreys FNM GU9 4 F8
Baldry Gdns STRHM/NOR SW16 31 H7
Baldwin Cl CRAWE RH10 * 165 L7
Baldwin Crs RGUE GU4 117 M6
Baldwin Gdns HSLW TW3 16 F3
Baldwins Fld EGRIN RH19 * 162 D1
Balfont Cl SAND/SEL CR2 88 D3
Balfour Av WOKS/MYFD GU22 97 H4
Balfour Crs BRAK RG12 34 E5
Balfour Rd CAR SM5 66 C6
HSLW TW3 16 E5
SNWD SE25 50 D4
WEY KT13 59 J3
WIM/MER SW19 29 L8
Balgowan Cl NWMAL KT3 46 B4
Balgowan Rd BECK BR3 51 H3
Balham Gv BAL SW12 30 D1
Balham High Rd BAL SW12 30 E2
Balham Hl BAL SW12 30 E1
Balham New Rd BAL SW12 30 E1
Balham Park Rd BAL SW12 30 C2
Balham Station Rd BAL SW12 30 D2
Balintore Ct SHST GU47 72 A2
The Ballands North
LHD/OX KT22 102 B4
The Ballands South
LHD/OX KT22 102 B5
Ballantyne Dr
KWD/TDW/WH KT20 105 J3
Ballantyne Rd FARN GU14 92 D3
Ballard Cl KUTN/CMB KT2 28 A8
Ballard Rd CBLY GU15 73 K1
Ballards Farm Rd
SAND/SEL CR2 68 D5
Ballards Gn
KWD/TDW/WH KT20 105 H1
Ballards La OXTED RH8 130 F3
Ballards Ri SAND/SEL CR2 68 D5
Ballards Wy SAND/SEL CR2 68 D5
Ballater Rd SAND/SEL CR2 68 C4
Ballencrieff Rd ASC SL5 37 J7
Ballfield Rd GODL GU7 168 A3
Ballina St FSTH SE23 33 G1
Balliol Cl CRAWE RH10 165 L1
Balliol Wy SHST GU47 52 B8
Balloon Rd FARN GU14 92 E7
Ballsdown MFD/CHID GU8 199 P1
Ball & Wicket La FNM GU9 133 M2
Balmoral Av BECK BR3 51 H4
Balmoral Crs E/WMO/HCT KT8 43 K3
FNM GU9 133 L3
Balmoral Dr FRIM GU16 93 H1
WOKS/MYFD GU22 11 M3
Balmoral Gdns SAND/SEL CR2 68 A8
Balmoral Rd ASHV GU12 113 K5
KUT/HW KT1 45 J4
WPK KT4 64 E2
Balmoral Wy BELMT SM2 65 K8
Balmuir Gdns PUT/ROE SW15 19 M6
Balquhain Cl ASHTD KT21 83 G7
Baltic Cl WIM/MER SW19 30 A8
Balvernie Gv WAND/EARL SW18 29 J1
Bampfylde Cl WLGTN SM6 66 F2
Bampton Rd FSTH SE23 33 G4
Bampton Wy
WOKN/KNAP GU21 76 D8
Banavie Gdns BECK BR3 51 L1
Banbury BRAK RG12 35 H7
Banbury Cl FRIM GU16 93 J2
Banbury Ct BELMT SM2 * 65 K6
Bancroft Cl ASHF TW15 * 23 K6
Bancroft Ct REIG RH2 125 L8
Bancroft Rd CRAWE RH10 165 M5
REIG RH2 125 K8
Banders Ri GU GU1 117 M7
Band La EGH TW20 21 J6
Bandon Ri WLGTN SM6 67 G5
Bangalore St PUT/ROE SW15 19 M5
Bank Av MTCM CR4 48 A2
Bankhurst Rd CAT SE6 33 J1
Bank La CRAWE RH10 164 F4
KUTN/CMB KT2 8 E2
PUT/ROE SW15 19 H7
Bank Rd ALDT GU11 113 G4
Bankside FNM GU9 134 C2
SAND/SEL CR2 68 C5
WOKN/KNAP GU21 76 E8
Bankside Cl BH/WHM TN16 90 F8
CAR SM5 66 B4
ISLW TW7 17 J6
MFD/CHID GU8 158 A6
Bankside Dr THDIT KT7 62 E1
Bank's La EHSLY KT24 100 E4
Banks Rd CRAWE RH10 165 L5
Banks Wy RGUE GU4 117 J5
Bank Ter CRAWE RH10 * 164 F5
The Bank CRAWE RH10 * 193 M9
Bank Willow RCHPK/HAM TW10 26 E4
Bannacie Hill Rd
MFD/CHID GU8 183 L8
Bannister Cl BRXS/STRHM SW2 31 K2
MFD/CHID GU8 183 N4
Bannister's Rd GUW GU2 138 C2
Bannow Cl HOR/WEW KT19 64 B3
Banstead Rd BNSTD SM7 85 H3
CAR SM5 66 B5
CTHM CR3 108 A4
EW KT17 64 E8
PUR/KEN CR8 87 K1
Banstead Rd South BELMT SM2 65 M8
Banstead Wy WLGTN SM6 67 H4
Barbara Cl SHPTN TW17 41 L5
Barber Cl CRAWE RH10 165 L8
Barber Dr CRAN GU6 186 D1
Barberry Wy BLKW GU17 72 C6
Barbon Cl CBLY GU15 74 A6
Barclay Cl LHD/OX KT22 101 L5
Barclay Rd CROY/NA CR0 2 E7
Barcombe Av
BRXS/STRHM SW2 31 H3
Bardney Rd MRDN SM4 47 L4
Bardolph Av CROY/NA CR0 69 J7
Bardolph Rd RCH/KEW TW9 18 C6
Bardon Wk WOKN/KNAP GU21 * 76 E7
Bardsley Cl CROY/NA CR0 3 J7
Bardsley Dr FNM GU9 4 E9
Barfields REDH RH1 127 L7
Barfreston Wy PGE/AN SE20 50 E1
Bargate Cl NWMAL KT3 46 D7
Bargate Ri GODL GU7 159 M5
Barge Cl ALDT GU11 113 H4
Bargery Rd CAT SE6 33 L2
Barge Wk KUT/HW KT1 8 C8
Bargrove Cl PGE/AN SE20 32 D8
Bargrove Crs CAT SE6 33 J3
Barham Cl WEY KT13 59 M3
Barham Rd RYNPK SW20 28 D8
SAND/SEL CR2 67 M3
Barhatch La CRAN GU6 170 E11
Barhatch Rd CRAN GU6 186 E1
Baring Rd CROY/NA CR0 3 M3
Barker Cl CHERT KT16 40 B7
NWMAL KT3 45 L4
Barker Rd CHERT KT16 40 B7
Barkers Meadow ASC SL5 36 A1
Barker Wk STRHM/NOR SW16 31 G4
Barkis Md SHST GU47 52 B7
Barkway Dr ORP BR6 71 K3
Barley Cl CRAWE RH10 164 F5
Barley Mow Cl
WOKN/KNAP GU21 76 A7
Barley Mow Ct
BRKHM/BTCW RH3 123 M8
Barley Mow Hl BOR GU35 180 E11
Barley Mow La
WOKN/KNAP GU21 75 M6
Barley Mow Rd EGH TW20 20 F6
Barley Mow Wy SHPTN TW17 41 K4
Barlow Cl WLGTN SM6 67 H5
Barlow Rd CRAWW RH11 164 A7
HPTN TW12 25 K8
Barmeston Rd CAT SE6 33 L3
Barmouth Rd CROY/NA CR0 69 G1
Barnard Cl FRIM GU16 93 J1
SUN TW16 24 E8
WLGTN SM6 67 G6
Barnard Gdns NWMAL KT3 46 D4
Barnard Pl EW KT17 64 F8
Barnard Rd MTCM CR4 48 D3
WARL CR6 109 L1
Barnards Pl SAND/SEL CR2 67 L7
Barnard Wy ALDT GU11 112 C6
Barnato Cl BF/WBF KT14 79 H2
Barnby Rd WOKN/KNAP GU21 76 A7
Barn Cl BNSTD SM7 86 A5
BRAK RG12 35 G2
CBLY GU15 73 H3
KWD/TDW/WH KT20 * 123 J6
Barn Ct CRAWE RH10 193 K3
Barn Crs PUR/KEN CR8 88 A3
Barncroft FNM GU9 5 J5
Barneby Cl WHTN TW2 26 B2
Barnes Av BARN SW13 19 K2
Barnes Br CHSWK W4 19 H4
Barnes Cl FARN GU14 93 G5
Barnes End NWMAL KT3 46 D5
Barnes High St BARN SW13 19 J4
Barnes Rd FRIM GU16 93 H1
GODL GU7 168 B1
Barnes Wallis Cl EHSLY KT24 121 G1
Barnes Wallis Dr BF/WBF KT14 79 H1
Barnet Dr HAYES BR2 71 H1
Barnett Cl LHD/OX KT22 102 E1
SHGR GU5 169 M1
Barnett Ct BRAK RG12 * 34 F2
Barnett Gn BRAK RG12 34 E6
Barnett La LTWR GU18 74 C2
SHGR GU5 169 L2
Barnett Rw RGUE GU4 117 G3
Barnett's Shaw OXTED RH8 130 A1
Barnetts Wy OXTED RH8 130 A1
Barnett Wood La ASHTD KT21 82 F8
LHD/OX KT22 102 E1
Barnet Wood Rd HAYES BR2 70 F1
Barn Fld BNSTD SM7 85 L4
Barnfield CRAN GU6 186 D2
NWMAL KT3 46 B6
Barnfield Av CROY/NA CR0 50 F8
KUTN/CMB KT2 27 G5
MTCM CR4 48 E4
Barnfield Cl COUL/CHIP CR5 107 M1
TOOT SW17 29 M4
Barnfield Gdns KUTN/CMB KT2 27 H6
Barnfield Rd BH/WHM TN16 111 G2
CRAWE RH10 164 F3
SAND/SEL CR2 68 B7
Barnfield Wy OXTED RH8 130 D7
Barnlea Cl FELT TW13 25 H3
Barnmead CHOB/PIR GU24 56 C8
Barn Meadow La
GT/LBKH KT23 101 J6
Barnmead Rd BECK BR3 51 G1
Barn Rd ADL/WDHM KT15 58 E7
Barnsbury Cl NWMAL KT3 45 M4
Barnsbury Crs BRYLDS KT5 45 M8
Barnsbury La BRYLDS KT5 63 L1
Barnscroft RYNPK SW20 46 E3
Barnsfold La HORS RH12 202 D3
Barnsford Crs CHOB/PIR GU24 75 K2
Barnsley Cl ASHV GU12 93 L8
Barnsnap Cl HORS RH12 167 G3
Barnway EGH TW20 20 F6
Barnwood Cl CRAWE RH10 165 L3
GUW GU2 116 B6
Barnwood Ct GUW GU2 116 B6
Barnwood Rd GUW GU2 116 B7
The Barnyard
KWD/TDW/WH KT20 104 D6
Baron Cl BELMT SM2 65 L8
Baron Gv MTCM CR4 48 B4
Baronsfield Rd TWK TW1 * 17 L8
Baron's Hurst EPSOM KT18 83 M6
Baronsmead Rd BARN SW13 19 K3
The Barons TWK TW1 17 L8
Baron's Wk CROY/NA CR0 51 H6
Barons Wy EGH TW20 22 A7
REIG RH2 147 K4
Barossa Rd CBLY GU15 73 G2
Barrack Pth WOKN/KNAP GU21 76 C8
Barrack Rd ALDT GU11 * 112 D7
GUW GU2 116 D6
HSLWW TW4 16 A6
Barrens Brae
WOKS/MYFD GU22 11 H8
Barrens Cl WOKS/MYFD GU22 * 11 H9
Barrens Pk WOKS/MYFD GU22 11 H8
Barrett Rd LHD/OX KT22 101 M7
Barrhill Rd BRXS/STRHM SW2 31 H3
Barricane WOKN/KNAP GU21 96 E1
Barrie Cl COUL/CHIP CR5 86 F6
Barrie Rd FNM GU9 133 K2
Barrihurst La CRAN GU6 185 N3
Barringer Sq TOOT SW17 30 D5
Barrington Ct DORK RH4 144 D3
Barrington Ldg WEY KT13 59 M4
Barrington Rd CHEAM SM3 47 K8
CRAWE RH10 164 F6
DORK RH4 * 144 D3
PUR/KEN CR8 86 F2
SWTR RH13 167 H7
Barrington Wk NRWD SE19 * 32 B7
Barrow Av CAR SM5 66 C6
Barrow Green Rd OXTED RH8 129 K5
Barrow Hedges Cl CAR SM5 66 B6
Barrow Hedges Wy CAR SM5 66 B6
Barrow Hl WPK KT4 64 B1
Barrow Hill Cl WPK KT4 64 B1
Barrow Rd CROY/NA CR0 67 K4
STRHM/NOR SW16 31 G7
Barr's La WOKN/KNAP GU21 76 B6
Barry Cl CRAWE RH10 165 G7
Barry Sq BRAK RG12 35 G7
Barry Ter ASHF TW15 * 23 J3
Barsons Cl PGE/AN SE20 32 F8
The Bars GU GU1 7 G6
Barston Rd WNWD SE27 31 M3
Barstow Crs BRXS/STRHM SW2 31 J2
Bartholemew Ct DORK RH4 * 144 D3
Bartholomew Cl HASM GU27 198 D5
Bartholomew Wy HORS RH12 167 K3
Bartlett Pl FRIM GU16 93 J4
Bartlett Rd BH/WHM TN16 111 M8
Bartlett St SAND/SEL CR2 68 A4
Barton Cl ADL/WDHM KT15 58 D5
ALDT GU11 112 B8
SHPTN TW17 41 L6
Barton Crs EGRIN RH19 163 H5
Barton Gn NWMAL KT3 46 A2
Barton Pl RGUE GU4 * 117 L5
Barton Rd SHGR GU5 169 K3
The Barton COB KT11 81 G2
Barton Wk CRAWE RH10 165 K6
Barts Cl BECK BR3 51 K5
Barttelot Rd HORS RH12 166 F8
Barwell Cl CHSGTN KT9 * 62 F6
Barwell La CHSGTN KT9 62 F6
Barwood Av WWKM BR4 51 L8
Basden Gv FELT TW13 25 K3
Basemoors BRAK RG12 35 H2
Bashford Wy CRAWE RH10 165 M2
Bashurst Copse SWTR RH13 204 A9
Basildene Rd HSLWW TW4 16 A5
Basildon Cl BELMT SM2 65 L7
Basildon Wy CRAWW RH11 164 A7
Basil Gdns CROY/NA CR0 51 G8
WNWD SE27 31 M6
Basing Cl THDIT KT7 44 C7
Basing Dr ALDT GU11 134 E2
Basingfield Rd THDIT KT7 44 C7
Basinghall Gdns BELMT SM2 65 L7
Basing Rd BNSTD SM7 85 J5
Basing Wy THDIT KT7 44 C7
Baskerville Rd
WAND/EARL SW18 30 B1
Basset Cl ADL/WDHM KT15 58 E8
Basset Dr REIG RH2 125 K7
Bassett Cl BELMT SM2 65 L7
FRIM GU16 93 H1
Bassett Gdns ISLW TW7 16 F2
Bassett Rd CRAWE RH10 165 M7
WOKS/MYFD GU22 11 L4
Bassetts Cl ORP BR6 71 L3
Bassetts Hl LING RH7 178 H7
Bassetts Wy ORP BR6 71 L3
Bassingham Rd
WAND/EARL SW18 29 M1
Baston Manor Rd WWKM BR4 70 E2
Baston Rd HAYES BR2 70 E1
Bat And Ball La FNM GU9 155 K3
Batavia Cl SUN TW16 42 F1
Batavia Rd SUN TW16 42 E1
Batcombe Md BRAK RG12 35 H7
Bateman Ct CRAWE RH10 * 165 J7
Batemans Ct CRAWE RH10 165 J7
Bates Crs CROY/NA CR0 67 K5
STRHM/NOR SW16 30 F8
Bateson Wy WOKN/KNAP GU21 77 M4
Bates Wk ADL/WDHM KT15 58 F5
Bathgate Rd WIM/MER SW19 29 G4
Bath House Rd CROY/NA CR0 49 H8
Bath Pas KUT/HW KT1 8 D7
Bath Rd CBLY GU15 72 F3
DTCH/LGLY SL3 13 J3
HSLWW TW4 15 M3
Bathurst Av WIM/MER SW19 47 L1
Batley Cl MTCM CR4 48 C7
Batsworth Rd MTCM CR4 48 A3
Batten Av WOKN/KNAP GU21 96 B1
Battlebridge La REDH RH1 126 E4
Battle Cl WIM/MER SW19 29 M7
Batts Hl REIG RH2 126 B7
The Baulk WAND/EARL SW18 29 K1
Bavant Rd STRHM/NOR SW16 49 H2
Bawtree Cl BELMT SM2 65 M8
Bax Cl CRAN GU6 186 D3
Baxter Av REDH RH1 126 B8
Baxter Cl CRAWE RH10 165 K6
Bayards WARL CR6 88 F8
Bay Cl HORL RH6 175 P3
Bayeux KWD/TDW/WH KT20 105 G4
Bayfield Av FRIM GU16 73 H7
Bayfield Rd HORL RH6 160 B2
Bayford Cl BLKW GU17 72 D8
Bayham Rd MRDN SM4 47 L4

Bayhorne La HORL RH6 160 F5
Bayleaf Cl HPTN TW12 26 A6
Bayliss Ct GU GU1 6 F5
Baylis Wk CRAWW RH11 * 191 L12
Baynards Rd HORS RH12 186 F11
Bay Rd BRAK RG12 35 H2
Bays Cl SYD SE26 32 F6
Baysfarm Ct WDR/YW UB7 13 M3
Baythorn La HORL RH6 160 F5
Bay Tree Av LHD/OX KT22 102 D2
Bazalgette Cl NWMAL KT3 45 M5
Bazalgette Gdns NWMAL KT3 46 A5
Beachborough Rd BMLY BR1 33 M5
Beach Gv FELT TW13 25 K4
Beachy Rd CRAWW RH11 191 L12
Beacon Cl BNSTD SM7 85 G6
RFNM GU10 155 K4
Beacon Ct DTCH/LGLY SL3 12 F2
SWTR RH13 * 167 K5
Beacon Hl LING RH7 179 J9
WOKN/KNAP GU21 96 F1
Beacon Hill Ct GSHT GU26 181 Q11
Beacon Hill Pk GSHT GU26 * 181 N12
Beacon Hill Rd GSHT GU26 181 P11
Beacon Pl CROY/NA CR0 67 H2
Beacon Rd FARN GU14 112 E1
HTHAIR TW6 14 D8
Beaconsfield Gdns
ESH/CLAY KT10 62 B6
Beaconsfield Pl EW KT17 84 B2
Beaconsfield Rd CROY/NA CR0 50 A6
EPSOM KT18 104 A1
ESH/CLAY KT10 62 B6
NWMAL KT3 46 A2
SURB KT6 45 J7
TWK TW1 26 E1
WOKS/MYFD GU22 97 J2
Beacon View Rd
MFD/CHID GU8 157 M7
Beacon Wy BNSTD SM7 85 G6
Beadles La OXTED RH8 130 A4
Beadlow Cl CAR SM5 48 A6
Beadman Pl WNWD SE27 * 31 L5
Beadman St WNWD SE27 31 L5
Beadnell Rd FSTH SE23 33 G2
Beaford Gv RYNPK SW20 47 H3
Beagle Cl FELT TW13 24 E5
Beales La RFNM GU10 155 J2
WEY KT13 59 L2
Beales Rd GT/LBKH KT23 121 L1
Bealeswood La RFNM GU10 180 D3
Beam Hollow FNM GU9 133 M2
Beardell St NRWD SE19 32 C7
Beard Rd KUTN/CMB KT2 27 J6
Beard's Hl HPTN TW12 43 K1
Beard's Hill Cl HPTN TW12 43 K1
Beards Rd ASHF TW15 24 B7
Beare Green Rd RDKG RH5 172 H9
Bearfield Rd KUTN/CMB KT2 8 E3
Bear La FNM GU9 5 H2
Bear Rd FELT TW13 25 G5
Bears Den
KWD/TDW/WH KT20 105 J4
Bearsden Wy HORS RH12 166 A6
Bearstead Ter BECK BR3 * 51 K1
Bearwood Cl ADL/WDHM KT15 58 D5
Beasley's Ait SUN TW16 42 D6
Beasley's Ait La SUN TW16 42 C6
Beatrice Av STRHM/NOR SW16 49 J3
Beatrice Rd OXTED RH8 130 B2
RCHPK/HAM TW10 18 C7
Beattie Cl EBED/NFELT TW14 24 C2
GT/LBKH KT23 101 J6
Beatty Av GU GU1 117 K7
Beauchamp Rd
E/WMO/HCT KT8 43 L5
NRWD SE19 50 A1
SUT SM1 65 K4
TWK TW1 26 D1
Beauchamp Ter BARN SW13 19 L5
Beauclare Cl LHD/OX KT22 103 G3
Beauclerk Cl FELT TW13 24 E2
Beaufighter Rd FARN GU14 112 D1
Beaufort Cl PUT/ROE SW15 28 F2
REIG RH2 125 J7
WOKS/MYFD GU22 11 L3
Beaufort Gdns ASC SL5 36 B1
HEST TW5 16 B3
STRHM/NOR SW16 31 J8
Beaufort Rd ASHV GU12 113 J3
FNM GU9 5 J2
KUT/HW KT1 45 H4
RCHPK/HAM TW10 26 F5
REIG RH2 125 J7
TWK TW1 26 F1
WOKS/MYFD GU22 11 L4
Beauforts EGH TW20 20 F6
Beaufort Wy EW KT17 64 D6
Beaufront Cl CBLY GU15 73 K2
Beaufront Rd CBLY GU15 73 K2
Beaulieu Av SYD SE26 32 E5
Beaulieu Cl BRAK RG12 35 J3
HSLWW TW4 16 C7
MTCM CR4 48 D1
TWK TW1 18 A8
Beaumaris Pde FRIM GU16 93 J1
Beaumont Av RCH/KEW TW9 18 C5
Beaumont Cl CRAWW RH11 164 A5
KUTN/CMB KT2 9 K3
Beaumont Dr ASHF TW15 24 A6
Beaumont Gdns BRAK RG12 35 H5
Beaumont Gv ALDT GU11 112 B7
Beaumont Pl ISLW TW7 17 J7
Beaumont Rd NRWD SE19 31 M7
PUR/KEN CR8 87 K3
WIM/MER SW19 29 H1
Beaumonts REDH RH1 148 C8
Beaver Cl HORS RH12 167 H3
HPTN TW12 43 L1
MRDN SM4 46 F7
PGE/AN SE20 * 32 D8
Beavers Cl FNM GU9 4 E4
RGUW GU3 116 B7
Beavers Crs HSLWW TW4 16 A6
Beavers Hl FNM GU9 4 D3
Beavers La HSLWW TW4 15 M5
Beavers Rd FNM GU9 4 F4
Beck Ct BECK BR3 51 G3
Beckenham Hill Rd BECK BR3 33 L7
Beckenham Place Pk BECK BR3 33 L8
Beckenham Rd WWKM BR4 51 L7
Beckenshaw Gdns BNSTD SM7 86 B5
Becket Cl SNWD SE25 50 D6
WIM/MER SW19 * 47 L1
Beckett Av PUR/KEN CR8 87 L5
Beckett Cl STRHM/NOR SW16 31 G3
Beckett La CRAWW RH11 164 F1
Becketts Cl EBED/NFELT TW14 15 L8
Becketts Pl KUT/HW KT1 8 C5
Beckett Wk BECK BR3 33 H7
Beckett Wy EGRIN RH19 163 G5
Becket Wd RDKG RH5 173 R5
Beckford Av BRAK RG12 34 E6
Beckford Rd CROY/NA CR0 50 C6
Beckford Wy CRAWE RH10 192 A12
Beck Gdns FNM GU9 133 K3
Beckingham Rd GUW GU2 6 A1
Beck La BECK BR3 51 G3
Beck River Pk BECK BR3 51 J1
Beck Wy BECK BR3 51 J3
Beckway Rd STRHM/NOR SW16 49 G2
Beclands Rd TOOT SW17 30 D7
Becmead Av STRHM/NOR SW16 31 G5
Becondale Rd NRWD SE19 32 B6
Bedale Cl CRAWW RH11 164 E6
Beddington Farm Rd
CROY/NA CR0 49 H8
Beddington Gdns CAR SM5 66 D5
Beddington Gv WLGTN SM6 67 G4
Beddington La CROY/NA CR0 49 G7
Beddington Ter CROY/NA CR0 * 49 J7
Beddlestead La
BH/WHM TN16 110 D3
WARL CR6 90 C8
Bedfont Cl EBED/NFELT TW14 14 F8
MTCM CR4 48 D2
Bedfont Ct STWL/WRAY TW19 13 K5
Bedfont Court Est
STWL/WRAY TW19 * 13 L6
Bedfont Green Cl
EBED/NFELT TW14 23 M2
Bedfont La EBED/NFELT TW14 24 B1
Bedfont Rd EBED/NFELT TW14 23 M2
FELT TW13 24 C4
STWL/WRAY TW19 14 C8
Bedford Av FRIM GU16 93 J4
Bedford Cl CHSWK W4 19 H1
WOKN/KNAP GU21 76 F5
Bedford Crs FRIM GU16 93 H3
Bedford Hl BAL SW12 30 E3
Bedford La ASC SL5 37 L5
FRIM GU16 93 J3
Bedford Pk CROY/NA CR0 2 D4
Bedford Pl CROY/NA CR0 2 E4
Bedford Rd GU GU1 6 F6
SWTR RH13 167 G8
WHTN TW2 26 A4
WPK KT4 64 F1
Bedgebury Gdns
WIM/MER SW19 29 H3
Bedlow Wy CROY/NA CR0 67 J3
Bedser Cl THHTH CR7 49 M3
WOKN/KNAP GU21 11 G4
Bedster Gdns E/WMO/HCT KT8 43 L2
Bedwardine Rd NRWD SE19 32 B8
Beech Av BH/WHM TN16 111 G1
BTFD TW8 17 J1
CBLY GU15 73 G5
EHSLY KT24 121 G4
RFNM GU10 155 M4
SAND/SEL CR2 88 A1
Beech Cl ASHF TW15 24 A6
ASHV GU12 135 H1
BF/WBF KT14 79 H2
CAR SM5 66 C1
COB KT11 81 K2
DORK RH4 144 C1
EGRIN RH19 * 162 E3
EHSLY KT24 121 G2
LING RH7 177 R1
MFD/CHID GU8 199 P1
PUT/ROE SW15 28 D1
STWL/WRAY TW19 23 G1
SUN TW16 43 G2
WIM/MER SW19 28 F7
WOT/HER KT12 60 F3
Beech Close Ct COB KT11 81 J1
Beech Copse SAND/SEL CR2 68 B4
Beech Crs KWD/TDW/WH KT20 123 M4
Beechcroft ASHTD KT21 103 J1
Beechcroft Av NWMAL KT3 45 M1
PUR/KEN CR8 88 A5
Beechcroft Cl ASC SL5 37 G4
HEST TW5 16 B2
LIPH GU30 196 C10
STRHM/NOR SW16 31 J6
Beechcroft Dr GUW GU2 138 A3
Beechcroft Mnr WEY KT13 60 A2
Beechcroft Rd CHSGTN KT9 63 J3
MORT/ESHN SW14 * 18 F5
TOOT SW17 30 C4
Beech Dell HAYES BR2 71 J3
Beechdene
KWD/TDW/WH KT20 104 E4
Beech Dr BLKW GU17 72 A5
KWD/TDW/WH KT20 105 J4
REIG RH2 126 A8
RPLY/SEND GU23 98 C6
Beechen Cliff Wy ISLW TW7 17 J4
Beechen La
KWD/TDW/WH KT20 105 J7
Beechen Pl FSTH SE23 32 F3
The Beeches Av CAR SM5 66 B6
Beeches Cl
KWD/TDW/WH KT20 105 K5
PGE/AN SE20 50 F1
Beeches Crs CRAWE RH10 165 G6
Beeches La EGRIN RH19 163 L7
Beeches Rd CHEAM SM3 47 H8
TOOT SW17 30 B4
The Beeches ASHV GU12 93 J8
BNSTD SM7 85 L6
LHD/OX KT22 102 B6
SHGR GU5 169 J3
STA TW18 * 22 D6
Beeches Wk BELMT SM2 66 A7
Beeches Wd
KWD/TDW/WH KT20 105 K4
Beechey Cl CRAWE RH10 192 G2
Beechey Wy CRAWE RH10 192 G2
Beech Farm Rd WARL CR6 110 A2
Beechfield BNSTD SM7 85 L3
Beechfield Rd CAT SE6 33 J2
Beech Flds EGRIN RH19 163 G2
Beech Gdns CRAWE RH10 193 M6
WOKN/KNAP GU21 10 C2
Beech Gln BRAK RG12 34 E4
Beech Gv ADL/WDHM KT15 58 E3
CHOB/PIR GU24 94 F2
CTHM CR3 108 B8
EPSOM KT18 84 E7
GT/LBKH KT23 121 K1
GUW GU2 116 C8
MTCM CR4 49 G5
NWMAL KT3 46 A3
WOKS/MYFD GU22 97 G5
Beech Hall CHERT KT16 * 57 M6
Beech Hanger End GSHT GU26 197 N2
Beech Hl BOR GU35 180 G12
MFD/CHID GU8 182 G8
WOKS/MYFD GU22 97 G5
Beech Hill Rd ASC SL5 37 H6
BOR GU35 180 E11
Beech Holme CRAWE RH10 193 M5
Beech Holt LHD/OX KT22 102 F4
Beech House Rd CROY/NA CR0 2 E8
Beeching Cl ASHV GU12 113 L6
Beeching Wy EGRIN RH19 162 E4
Beech La GSHT GU26 197 N1
GUW GU2 6 E9
RGUW GU3 114 D8
Beechlawn GU GU1 7 L5
Beechmeads COB KT11 * 81 G3
Beechmont Av VW GU25 39 G6
Beechmore Gdns CHEAM SM3 65 G1
Beechnut Rd ASHV GU12 112 E8
Beecholme BNSTD SM7 * 85 H4
Beecholme Av MTCM CR4 48 E1
Beech Rd BH/WHM TN16 90 F7
EBED/NFELT TW14 24 B1
EW KT17 84 C5
FARN GU14 92 E2
FRIM GU16 93 J3
HASM GU27 198 E6
HORS RH12 167 L4
REDH RH1 106 F8
REIG RH2 125 K6
STRHM/NOR SW16 49 H2
WEY KT13 60 A3
Beechrow KUTN/CMB KT2 27 H5
Beechside CRAWE RH10 165 G5
Beechtree Av EGH TW20 20 E7
Beech Tree Cl CRAWE RH10 * 164 F3
Beech Tree Dr FNM GU9 134 D4
Beech Tree La STA TW18 * 40 E2
Beech Tree Pl SUT SM1 65 L4
Beech V WOKS/MYFD GU22 10 E8
Beech Wk EW KT17 84 D1
Beech Wy EW KT17 84 C5
GODL GU7 168 A6
SAND/SEL CR2 89 G3
WHTN TW2 25 K4
Beechway GU GU1 117 L7
Beechwood
KWD/TDW/WH KT20 * 123 L5
Beechwood Av COUL/CHIP CR5 86 E5
KWD/TDW/WH KT20 105 K3
RCH/KEW TW9 18 D3
STA TW18 22 E7
SUN TW16 24 D7
THHTH CR7 49 L4
WEY KT13 60 B3
Beechwood Cl SURB KT6 44 F7
WEY KT13 60 B3
WOKN/KNAP GU21 76 B7
Beechwood Dr COB KT11 81 K1
HAYES BR2 71 G3
Beechwood Gdns CTHM CR3 108 D4
Beechwood La WARL CR6 109 G1
Beechwood Mnr WEY KT13 60 B3
Beechwood Pk LHD/OX KT22 102 F4
Beechwood Rd CTHM CR3 108 D4
SAND/SEL CR2 68 B7
VW GU25 38 E7
WOKN/KNAP GU21 76 B8
Beechwood Vls REDH RH1 175 R2
Beecot La WOT/HER KT12 60 F1
Beeding Cl HORS RH12 167 K4
Beedon Dr BRAK RG12 34 A6
Beehive Ring Rd HORL RH6 176 A12
Beehive Rd BRAK RG12 34 A2
STA TW18 22 C6
Beehive Wy REIG RH2 147 L4
Beeken Dene ORP BR6 71 M3
Beeleigh Rd MRDN SM4 47 L4
Beeston Wy EBED/NFELT TW14 15 M8
Beeton's Av ASHV GU12 113 K5
Beggarshouse La HORL RH6 174 F9
Beggars La CHOB/PIR GU24 75 M1
RDKG RH5 142 B5
Beggar's Roost La SUT SM1 65 K5
Begonia Pl HPTN TW12 25 K7
Behenna Cl CRAWW RH11 164 A5
Beira St BAL SW12 30 E1
Beldam Bridge Rd
CHOB/PIR GU24 75 K3
Beldham Gdns
E/WMO/HCT KT8 43 L3
Beldham Rd FNM GU9 4 D9
Belfast Rd SNWD SE25 50 E4
Belfield Rd HOR/WEW KT19 64 A7
The Belfry REDH RH1 126 C7
Belgrade Rd HPTN TW12 43 L1
Belgrave Cl WOT/HER KT12 60 E3
Belgrave Ct BLKW GU17 72 A6
Belgrave Crs SUN TW16 42 E1
Belgrave Mnr
WOKS/MYFD GU22 10 C9
Belgrave Rd BARN SW13 19 J2
HSLWW TW4 16 C5
MTCM CR4 48 A3
SNWD SE25 50 C4
SUN TW16 42 E1
Belgrave Wk MTCM CR4 48 A3
Belgravia Ms KUT/HW KT1 45 G4
Bellamy Rd CRAWE RH10 165 L8
Bellamy St BAL SW12 30 E1
Belland Dr ALDT GU11 112 B8
Bel La FELT TW13 25 H4
Bellasis Av BRXS/STRHM SW2 31 H2
Bell Bridge Rd CHERT KT16 40 C8
Bell Cl FARN GU14 92 F3
Bell Crs COUL/CHIP CR5 106 E3
Bell Dr WAND/EARL SW18 29 H1
Bellever Hl CBLY GU15 73 H4
Belle Vue Cl ASHV GU12 113 G7
STA TW18 40 D1
Bellevue Pk THHTH CR7 49 M3
Belle Vue Rd ASHV GU12 113 G8
ORP BR6 71 K8
Bellevue Rd BARN SW13 19 K4
KUT/HW KT1 8 F9
TOOT SW17 30 C1
Bellew Rd FRIM GU16 93 M2
Bellew St TOOT SW17 29 M4
Bellfield CROY/NA CR0 69 J7
Bellfields Rd GU GU1 117 G6
Bell Gn SYD SE26 33 H5
Bell Green La SYD SE26 33 J6
Bell Hammer EGRIN RH19 162 F5
Bellingham Cl CBLY GU15 73 M5
Bellingham Dr REIG RH2 125 J8
Bellingham Gn CAT SE6 33 K4
Bellingham Rd CAT SE6 33 M4
Bell La LHD/OX KT22 102 A5
RFNM GU10 155 H6
TWK TW1 26 D2
Bell Lane Cl LHD/OX KT22 102 A5
Bellmarsh Rd ADL/WDHM KT15 58 E3
Bell Meadow GDST RH9 128 F6
NRWD SE19 32 B5
Belloc Cl CRAWE RH10 165 K3
Belloc Ct SWTR RH13 * 167 K6
Bello Cl HNHL SE24 31 L2
Bell Pde HSLW TW3 * 16 E6
WWKM BR4 * 69 M1
Bell Pl BAGS GU19 54 C6
Bell Rd E/WMO/HCT KT8 44 A5
HASM GU27 198 B10
HORS RH12 166 D1
HSLW TW3 16 E6
Bells La DTCH/LGLY SL3 12 E5
Bell St REIG RH2 125 K8
Belltrees Gv STRHM/NOR SW16 31 J6
Bell Vale La HASM GU27 198 C9
Bellweir Cl STWL/WRAY TW19 21 L3
Bellwether La REDH RH1 176 G1
Belmont Av GUW GU2 116 C5
NWMAL KT3 46 D5
Belmont Cl FARN GU14 92 C2
Belmont Ms CBLY GU15 72 F6
Belmont Ri BELMT SM2 65 J6
Belmont Rd BECK BR3 51 H2
BELMT SM2 65 K8
CBLY GU15 72 F5
LHD/OX KT22 102 D4
REIG RH2 147 M1
SNWD SE25 50 E5
WHTN TW2 26 A3
WLGTN SM6 66 F4
Belmore Av WOKS/MYFD GU22 78 A6
Beloe Cl PUT/ROE SW15 19 K6
Belsize Gdns SUT SM1 65 L3
Belsize Rd FARN GU14 92 F8
Belstone Ms FARN GU14 92 D2
Beltane Dr WIM/MER SW19 29 G4
Belthorn Crs BAL SW12 30 F1
Belton Rd CBLY GU15 73 H6
Belvedere Av WIM/MER SW19 29 H6
Belvedere Cl ESH/CLAY KT10 61 L4
GUW GU2 116 E6
TEDD TW11 26 B6
WEY KT13 59 K4
Belvedere Ct BLKW GU17 72 A6
Belvedere Dr WIM/MER SW19 29 H6
Belvedere Gdns
E/WMO/HCT KT8 43 J5
Belvedere Gv WIM/MER SW19 29 H6
Belvedere Rd BH/WHM TN16 91 J8
FARN GU14 92 F7
NRWD SE19 32 C8
Belvedere Sq WIM/MER SW19 29 H6
Belvoir Cl FRIM GU16 73 J8
Belvoir Rd EDUL SE22 32 D1
Benbow La MFD/CHID GU8 185 M9
Benbrick Rd GUW GU2 6 A5
Benbury Cl BMLY BR1 33 M6
The Bence EGH TW20 39 L3
Bench Fld SAND/SEL CR2 68 C5
Benchfield Cl EGRIN RH19 163 H5
The Bench RCHPK/HAM TW10 * 26 F4
Bencombe Rd PUR/KEN CR8 87 K4
Bencroft Rd STRHM/NOR SW16 30 F8
Bencurtis Pk WWKM BR4 70 A2
Bendon Va WAND/EARL SW18 29 L1
Benedict Dr EBED/NFELT TW14 24 A1
Benedict Rd MTCM CR4 48 A3
Benedict Whf MTCM CR4 48 B3
Benen-stock Rd
STWL/WRAY TW19 13 K8
Benett Gdns STRHM/NOR SW16 49 H2
Benfleet Cl COB KT11 81 H2
SUT SM1 65 M2
Benham Cl CHSGTN KT9 62 F5
COUL/CHIP CR5 87 L8
Benham Gdns HSLWW TW4 16 C7
Benhams Dr HORL RH6 160 D1
Benhill Av SUT SM1 65 M3
Benhill Rd SUT SM1 66 A2
Benhill Wood Rd SUT SM1 65 M3
Benhilton Gdns SUT SM1 65 L2
Benhurst Cl SAND/SEL CR2 69 G8
Benhurst Gdns SAND/SEL CR2 68 F8
Benhurst La STRHM/NOR SW16 31 K6
Benjamin Ms BAL SW12 30 F1
Benjamin Rd CRAWE RH10 165 M6
Benn Cl OXTED RH8 130 D8
Benner La CHOB/PIR GU24 75 J2
Bennet Cl KUT/HW KT1 8 B5
Bennett Cl COB KT11 80 D3
CRAWE RH10 165 K8
HSLWW TW4 16 B7
Bennett Ct CBLY GU15 72 F4
Bennetts Av CROY/NA CR0 69 H1
Bennetts Cl MTCM CR4 48 E1
Bennetts Farm Pl
GT/LBKH KT23 101 J7
Bennetts Ri ALDT GU11 134 F1
Bennetts Rd SWTR RH13 167 H8
Bennett St CHSWK W4 19 H1
Bennetts Wy CROY/NA CR0 69 H1
Bennetts Wd RDKG RH5 173 K12
Bennett Wy RGUE GU4 118 D3
Bens Acre SWTR RH13 167 K7
Bensbury Cl PUT/ROE SW15 28 E1
Bensham Cl THHTH CR7 49 M4
Bensham Gv THHTH CR7 49 M2
Bensham La CROY/NA CR0 2 B1
THHTH CR7 49 L4
Bensham Manor Rd
THHTH CR7 49 M4
Benson Cl HSLW TW3 16 D6
Benson Rd CROY/NA CR0 67 K2
FSTH SE23 32 F2
Benson's La HORS RH12 189 R12
Benthall Gdns PUR/KEN CR8 87 M6
Bentham Av WOKN/KNAP GU21 11 L1
Bentley Copse CBLY GU15 73 L5
Bentley Dr WEY KT13 59 K7
Benton's La WNWD SE27 31 M5
Benton's Ri WNWD SE27 32 A6
Bentsbrook Cl RDKG RH5 144 E6
Bentsbrook Pk RDKG RH5 144 E6
Bentsbrook Rd RDKG RH5 144 E6
Benwell Ct SUN TW16 * 42 D1
Ben Well Rd CHOB/PIR GU24 95 K1
Benwood Ct SUT SM1 65 M2
Beomonds Rw CHERT KT16 * 40 D7
Berberis Cl GU GU1 116 F6
Bere Rd BRAK RG12 35 H6
Beresford Av BRYLDS KT5 45 L8
TWK TW1 17 M8
Beresford Cl FRIM GU16 93 J3
Beresford Gdns HSLWW TW4 16 C7
Beresford Rd BELMT SM2 65 J6
DORK RH4 144 E2
KUTN/CMB KT2 9 G4
NWMAL KT3 45 M4
Bergenia Ct CHOB/PIR GU24 75 H3
Berkeley Av HSLWW TW4 15 K3
Berkeley Cl CRAWW RH11 190 G11
KUTN/CMB KT2 8 E2
STWL/WRAY TW19 22 A3
Berkeley Ct WEY KT13 60 A1
WLGTN SM6 66 F2
Berkeley Crs FRIM GU16 93 K1
Berkeley Dr E/WMO/HCT KT8 43 J3
Berkeley Gdns BF/WBF KT14 78 C4
ESH/CLAY KT10 62 D6
WOT/HER KT12 42 C7
Berkeley Ms SUN TW16 42 F3
Berkeley Pl EPSOM KT18 84 A5
WIM/MER SW19 29 G7
Berkeley Rd BARN SW13 19 K3
The Berkeleys LHD/OX KT22 102 B6
SNWD SE25 * 50 D4
Berkeley Waye HEST TW5 16 B2
Berkley Cl WHTN TW2 * 26 B4
Berkley Ct GU GU1 7 K3
Berkshire Cl CTHM CR3 108 A4
Berkshire Corpse Rd
ALDT GU11 112 B2
Berkshire Rd CBLY GU15 73 J1
Berkshire Wy MTCM CR4 49 H4
Bernard Gdns WIM/MER SW19 29 J6
Bernard Rd WLGTN SM6 66 E4
Bernel Dr CROY/NA CR0 69 J2
Berne Rd THHTH CR7 49 L5
Berney Rd CROY/NA CR0 2 E2
Berridge Rd NRWD SE19 32 A6
Berrington Dr EHSLY KT24 100 C6
Berrybank SHST GU47 72 B3
Berrycroft BRAK RG12 35 G1
Berrylands BRYLDS KT5 45 K5
RYNPK SW20 46 F3
Berrylands Rd BRYLDS KT5 45 J6
Berry La DUL SE21 32 A5
RGUW GU3 96 A6
Berryman's La SYD SE26 33 G5
Berry Meade ASHTD KT21 83 J7
Berry Meade Cl ASHTD KT21 83 J7
Berryscroft Rd STA TW18 22 F8
Berry's Green Rd
BH/WHM TN16 91 L6
Berry's Hl BH/WHM TN16 91 L5
Berry's La BF/WBF KT14 79 G1
Berry Wk ASHTD KT21 103 J1
Bertal Rd TOOT SW17 30 A5
Bertie Rd SYD SE26 33 G7
Bertram Rd KUTN/CMB KT2 9 J2
Bert Rd THHTH CR7 49 M5
Berwick Cl WHTN TW2 25 K2
Berwick Gdns SUT SM1 65 M2
Berwyn Av HSLW TW3 16 E3
Berwyn Rd HNHL SE24 31 L2
RCHPK/HAM TW10 18 E6
Berystede KUTN/CMB KT2 9 L3
Besley St STRHM/NOR SW16 30 F7
Bessant Dr RCH/KEW TW9 18 E3
Bessborough Rd
PUT/ROE SW15 28 D2
Beswick Gdns BRAK RG12 35 J1
Beta Rd CHOB/PIR GU24 56 C8
FARN GU14 92 C4
WOKS/MYFD GU22 11 K3
Beta Wy EGH TW20 39 M1
Betchets Green Rd RDKG RH5 173 K3
Betchley Cl EGRIN RH19 162 F2
Betchworth Cl SUT SM1 66 A4
Betchworth Wy CROY/NA CR0 69 M7
Bethany Pl WOKN/KNAP GU21 * 10 A7
Bethany Waye
EBED/NFELT TW14 24 B1
Bethel Cl FNM GU9 134 A3
Bethel La FNM GU9 134 A3
Bethersden Cl BECK BR3 33 J8
Bethune Cl CRAWE RH10 165 M5
Bethune Rd SWTR RH13 167 H8
Betjeman Cl COUL/CHIP CR5 87 J7
Betley Ct WOT/HER KT12 60 E2
Betony Cl CROY/NA CR0 51 G8
Betts Cl BECK BR3 51 H2
Betts Wy CRAWE RH10 191 N3
PGE/AN SE20 50 E2
SURB KT6 44 E8
Betula Cl PUR/KEN CR8 88 A5
Between Streets COB KT11 80 E4
Beulah Av THHTH CR7 * 49 M2
Beulah Crs THHTH CR7 49 M2
Beulah Gv CROY/NA CR0 49 M6
Beulah Hl NRWD SE19 31 M7
Beulah Rd SUT SM1 65 K3
THHTH CR7 49 M3
WIM/MER SW19 29 J8
Beulah Wk CTHM CR3 109 H2

Bevan Ct CROY/NA CR0 67 K4
Bevan Ga BNFD RG42 34 D1
Bevan Pk EW KT17 84 C1
Beverley Av HSLWW TW4 16 C6
RYNPK SW20 46 C1
Beverley Cl ADL/WDHM KT15 59 G4
ASHV GU12 113 J8
BARN SW13 19 K4
CBLY GU15 73 M3
CHSGTN KT9 62 F3
EW KT17 84 F1
WEY KT13 60 B1
Beverley Crs FARN GU14 92 C6
Beverley Gdns BARN SW13 19 J5
WPK KT4 46 D8
Beverley Hts REIG RH2 125 L6
Beverley La KUTN/CMB KT2 28 B8
Beverley Ms CRAWE RH10 165 J5
Beverley Rd BARN SW13 19 J5
CTHM CR3 88 B7
HAYES BR2 71 H1
KUT/HW KT1 8 B4
MTCM CR4 49 G4
NWMAL KT3 46 D4
PGE/AN SE20 50 E2
SUN TW16 42 C1
WPK KT4 64 F1
Beverley Wy KUTN/CMB KT2 46 C1
Beverstone Rd THHTH CR7 49 K4
Bevill Cl SNWD SE25 50 D3
Bevington Rd BECK BR3 51 L2
Bevin Sq TOOT SW17 30 C4
Bewbush Dr CRAWW RH11 164 B7
Bewley St WIM/MER SW19 29 M7
Bewlys Rd WNWD SE27 31 L6
Bexhill Cl FELT TW13 25 H3
Bexhill Rd MORT/ESHN SW14 18 F5
Beynon Rd CAR SM5 66 C4
Bicester Rd RCH/KEW TW9 18 D5
Bickersteth Rd TOOT SW17 30 C7
Bickley St TOOT SW17 30 B6
Bicknell Rd FRIM GU16 73 H7
Bickney Wy LHD/OX KT22 101 M4
Bicknoller Cl BELMT SM2 65 L8
Biddulph Rd SAND/SEL CR2 67 M7
Bideford Cl FARN GU14 92 D2
FELT TW13 25 J4
Bidhams Crs
KWD/TDW/WH KT20 104 F3
The Bield REIG RH2 147 K2
Big Common La REDH RH1 127 L7
Biggin Av MTCM CR4 48 C1
Biggin Cl CRAWW RH11 164 E6
Biggin Hl NRWD SE19 31 L8
Biggin Wy NRWD SE19 31 L8
Bigginwood Rd
STRHM/NOR SW16 31 L8
Bignor Cl HORS RH12 167 K3
Bilberry Cl CRAWW RH11 164 D7
Billesden Rd CHOB/PIR GU24 94 F3
Billingshurst Rd HORS RH12 204 D6
Billinton Dr CRAWE RH10 165 K4
Billockby Cl CHSGTN KT9 63 J5
Binfield Rd BF/WBF KT14 79 H2
BNFD RG42 34 D1
SAND/SEL CR2 68 C4
Bingham Dr STA TW18 23 G8
WOKN/KNAP GU21 76 C8
Bingham Rd CROY/NA CR0 3 L4
Bingley Rd SUN TW16 24 D8
Binhams Lea MFD/CHID GU8 185 J8
Binhams Meadow
MFD/CHID GU8 185 J8
Binney Ct CRAWE RH10 165 M1
CRAWE RH10 192 D4
Binscombe GODL GU7 168 A1
Binscombe Crs GODL GU7 168 B2
Binscombe La GODL GU7 168 A1
Binstead Cl CRAWW RH11 164 D2
Binsted Dr BLKW GU17 72 A4
Binton La RFNM GU10 135 H7
Birchanger GODL GU7 168 B5
Birchanger Rd SNWD SE25 50 D5
Birch Av CTHM CR3 108 A6
Birch Cir GODL GU7 168 C1
Birch Cl ADL/WDHM KT15 59 G7
BTFD TW8 17 L2
CBLY GU15 73 H1
CRAWE RH10 193 P5
HSLW TW3 17 G5
RFNM GU10 155 K5
RPLY/SEND GU23 98 C7
TEDD TW11 26 D6
WOKN/KNAP GU21 96 F1
Birch Ct WLGTN SM6 66 E3
Birchcroft Cl CTHM CR3 107 M7
Birchdale Cl BF/WBF KT14 78 F1
Birch Dr BLKW GU17 72 A6
Birchend Cl SAND/SEL CR2 68 A5
Birches Cl EPSOM KT18 84 B5
MTCM CR4 48 C3
Birches Rd HORS RH12 167 L4
The Birches CRAWE RH10 165 J3
EHSLY KT24 100 B8
FARN GU14 92 A5
HSLWW TW4 * 25 J1
ORP BR6 71 K3
SWTR RH13 205 R10
WOKS/MYFD GU22 10 E7
Birchett Rd ALDT GU11 112 D7
FARN GU14 92 B4
Birchetts Cl BNFD RG42 34 E1
Birchfield Cl ADL/WDHM KT15 58 E3
COUL/CHIP CR5 87 J6
Birchfield Est HORL RH6 * 190 G1
Birchfield Gv EW KT17 64 F8
Birchfields CBLY GU15 72 F5
Birchgate Ms
KWD/TDW/WH KT20 * 104 F3
Birch Gn STA TW18 22 C5
Birch Gv BRAK RG12 34 F4
GU GU1 * 116 F5
KWD/TDW/WH KT20 105 J6
SHPTN TW17 42 B2
WOKS/MYFD GU22 78 A5
Birchgrove COB KT11 80 F4
Birch Hl CROY/NA CR0 69 G4
Birch Hill Rd BRAK RG12 34 E7
Birchington Rd BRYLDS KT5 45 J7
Birchlands Av BAL SW12 30 C1
Birch La ASC SL5 35 K1
CHOB/PIR GU24 75 G2
PUR/KEN CR8 87 H1
Birch Lea CRAWE RH10 165 J1
Birch Md ORP BR6 71 K1
Bircholt Rd LIPH GU30 196 C9
Birch Platt CHOB/PIR GU24 75 G3
Birch Rd BFOR GU20 55 H5
BOR GU35 180 G11
FELT TW13 25 G6
GODL GU7 168 C1
Birch Tree Av WWKM BR4 70 C4
Birch Tree Gdns EGRIN RH19 162 C2
Birch Tree Vw LTWR GU18 54 D8
Birch Tree Wy CROY/NA CR0 68 E1
Birch V COB KT11 81 K3
Birch Wk MTCM CR4 48 E1
Birch Wy ASHV GU12 113 K2
WARL CR6 89 H8
Birchway REDH RH1 148 E2
Birchwood Av BECK BR3 51 J4
WLGTN SM6 66 D2
Birchwood Cl BIL RH14 201 N6
CRAWE RH10 165 L7
HORL RH6 160 E2
MRDN SM4 47 L4
Birchwood Dr BF/WBF KT14 78 D2
LTWR GU18 54 F8
Birchwood Gv HPTN TW12 25 K7
Birchwood La CTHM CR3 107 L7
Birchwood Rd BF/WBF KT14 78 D2
TOOT SW17 30 E6
Birdham Cl CRAWW RH11 164 D2
Birdhaven RFNM GU10 155 K4
Bird House La ORP BR6 91 K4
Birdhurst Av SAND/SEL CR2 68 A3
Birdhurst Gdns SAND/SEL CR2 68 A3
Birdhurst Ri SAND/SEL CR2 68 B4
Birdhurst Rd SAND/SEL CR2 68 B4
WIM/MER SW19 30 B7
Bird-in-Hand Ms FSTH SE23 32 F3
Bird-in-Hand Pas FSTH SE23 32 F3
Birds Gv WOKN/KNAP GU21 75 L8
Birds Hill Dr LHD/OX KT22 82 A3
Birds Hill Ri LHD/OX KT22 82 A3
Birds Hill Rd LHD/OX KT22 82 A2
Birdswood Dr
WOKN/KNAP GU21 96 B1
Bird Wk WHTN TW2 25 J2
Birdwood Cl SAND/SEL CR2 88 F1
TEDD TW11 26 B5
Birdwood Rd CBLY GU15 72 C3
Birkbeck Hl DUL SE21 31 L3
Birkbeck Pl DUL SE21 31 L2
SHST GU47 52 B8
Birkbeck Rd BECK BR3 51 G2
WIM/MER SW19 29 L6
Birkdale BRAK RG12 34 B6
Birkdale Dr CRAWW RH11 190 G8
Birkdale Gdns CROY/NA CR0 69 G3
Birkenhead Av KUTN/CMB KT2 9 G6
Birkenholme Cl BOR GU35 196 H1
Birkheads Rd REIG RH2 125 K7
Birkwood Cl BAL SW12 31 G1
Birnham Cl RPLY/SEND GU23 98 G4
Birtley Ri SHGR GU5 169 K4
Birtley Rd SHGR GU5 169 K4
Biscoe Cl HEST TW5 16 D1
Bisenden Rd CROY/NA CR0 3 G5
Bisham Cl CAR SM5 48 C7
CRAWE RH10 165 M6
Bishop Cl RCHPK/HAM TW10 27 G4
Bishopdale BRAK RG12 34 D4
Bishop Duppas Pk
SHPTN TW17 42 A7
Bishop Fox Wy
E/WMO/HCT KT8 43 J4
Bishopric HORS RH12 166 E7
Bishopric Ct HORS RH12 166 E7
Bishop's Cl COUL/CHIP CR5 87 K8
SUT SM1 65 K2
Bishops Dr EBED/NFELT TW14 15 G8
Bishopsford Rd MRDN SM4 47 M7
Bishopsgate Rd EGH TW20 20 D4
Bishops Gv BFOR GU20 54 F5
HPTN TW12 25 J5
Bishop's Hall KUT/HW KT1 8 D6
Bishops Hl WOT/HER KT12 42 D7
Bishop's Md FNM GU9 5 G4
Bishopsmead Cl EHSLY KT24 120 C2
HOR/WEW KT19 64 A8
Bishopsmead Dr EHSLY KT24 120 C3
Bishops Park Rd
STRHM/NOR SW16 49 H1
Bishop's Pl SUT SM1 65 M4
Bishop's Rd CROY/NA CR0 2 A2
FNM GU9 133 L5
Bishopsthorpe Rd SYD SE26 32 F5
Bishop Sumner Dr FNM GU9 133 M3
Bishops Wk CROY/NA CR0 69 G4
Bishops Wy EGH TW20 22 A7
Bishops Wd WOKN/KNAP GU21 76 C7
Bisley Cl WPK KT4 46 F8
Bitmead Cl CRAWW RH11 * 164 A5
Bittams La CHERT KT16 58 A3
Bittern Cl ALDT GU11 134 D2
CRAWW RH11 190 G8
SHST GU47 72 A1
Bitterne Dr WOKN/KNAP GU21 76 C7
Bittoms Ct KUT/HW KT1 * 8 D8
The Bittoms KUT/HW KT1 8 D9
Blackberry Cl GU GU1 116 E5
SHPTN TW17 42 B4
Blackberry Farm Cl HEST TW5 16 B2
Blackberry La LING RH7 178 E7
Blackberry Rd EGRIN RH19 178 D9
Blackbird Cl SHST GU47 72 A1
Blackbird Hl CRAWE RH10 193 P8
Blackborough Cl REIG RH2 125 M8
Blackborough Rd REIG RH2 126 A8
Blackbridge La HORS RH12 166 D8
Blackbridge Rd
WOKS/MYFD GU22 97 G2
Blackbrook Rd RDKG RH5 145 H7
The Blackburn GT/LBKH KT23 101 J6
Blackburn Wy GODL GU7 168 C4
Blackbush Cl BELMT SM2 65 L6
Blackcap Cl CRAWW RH11 164 E6
Blackcap Pl SHST GU47 72 B1
Black Dog Wk CRAWE RH10 165 G2
Blackdown Av
WOKS/MYFD GU22 78 B5
Blackdown Cl
WOKS/MYFD GU22 11 M3
Blackdown Rd FRIM GU16 93 M2
Black Eagle Cl BH/WHM TN16 131 M1
Blackenham Rd TOOT SW17 30 C5
Blackett Cl STA TW18 40 B2
Blackett Rd CRAWE RH10 165 L5
Blackfold Rd CRAWE RH10 165 J5
Blackford Cl SAND/SEL CR2 67 L7
Blackheath CRAWE RH10 165 M2
Blackheath Gv SHGR GU5 169 L1
Blackheath La SHGR GU5 169 M1
Blackhills ESH/CLAY KT10 61 J7
Blackhorse Cl CROY/NA CR0 3 M1
KWD/TDW/WH KT20 125 L3
Blackhorse Rd
WOKS/MYFD GU22 96 A2
Black Horse Wy HORS RH12 166 F7
Blacklands Crs FROW RH18 195 N11
Blacklands Meadow
REDH RH1 127 H7
Blacklands Rd CAT SE6 33 M5
Blackman Gdns ALDT GU11 134 E1
Blackman's La WARL CR6 90 B4
Blackmeadows BRAK RG12 34 F6
Blackmoor Cl ASC SL5 36 A2
Blackmoor Wd ASC SL5 36 A2
Blackmore Crs
WOKN/KNAP GU21 77 M4
Blackmore's Gv TEDD TW11 26 D7
Blackness La HAYES BR2 71 G7
WOKS/MYFD GU22 10 D9
Blacknest Rd ALTN GU34 154 B7
ASC SL5 38 A3
Black Pond La RFNM GU10 155 M3
Black Potts Copse
WOKS/MYFD GU22 96 E1
Black Prince Cl BF/WBF KT14 79 J4
Blackshaw Rd TOOT SW17 30 A6
Blacksmith Cl ASHTD KT21 103 J1
Blacksmith La RGUE GU4 139 M5
Blacksmiths Hl SAND/SEL CR2 88 E3
Blacksmiths La CHERT KT16 40 D7
STA TW18 40 E3
Blackstone Cl FARN GU14 92 A3
REDH RH1 148 B1
Blackstone Hl REDH RH1 126 B8
Blackstroud La East
LTWR GU18 75 G1
Blackstroud La West
LTWR GU18 75 G1
Blackthorn Cl CRAWW RH11 164 E2
REIG RH2 147 M2
SWTR RH13 167 J7
Blackthorn Ct HEST TW5 16 B2
Blackthorn Crs FARN GU14 92 C1
Blackthorn Dr LTWR GU18 74 E2
Blackthorne Av CROY/NA CR0 50 F8
Blackthorne Crs DTCH/LGLY SL3 13 H4
Blackthorne Rd DTCH/LGLY SL3 13 H5
GT/LBKH KT23 101 M8
Blackthorn Pl GU GU1 * 116 F5
Blackthorn Rd BH/WHM TN16 91 H6
REIG RH2 147 M2
Blackwater Cl ASHV GU12 113 K8
Blackwater La CRAWE RH10 165 L5
Blackwater Pk ASHV GU12 113 H8
Blackwater Wy ASHV GU12 135 H1
Blackwell Av GUW GU2 116 A8
Blackwell Hollow EGRIN RH19 163 G3
Blackwell Rd EGRIN RH19 163 G3
Blackwood Cl BF/WBF KT14 78 F2
Bladen Cl WEY KT13 60 A5
Blades Cl LHD/OX KT22 103 G2
Bladon Cl GU GU1 117 K7
Blagdon Rd NWMAL KT3 46 C4
Blagdon Wk TEDD TW11 8 A1
Blair Av ESH/CLAY KT10 61 M1
Blairderry Rd
BRXS/STRHM SW2 31 H3
Blaise Cl FARN GU14 93 G6
Blake Cl CAR SM5 48 B8
CRAWE RH10 165 H8
Blakeden Dr ESH/CLAY KT10 62 C6
Blakehall Rd CAR SM5 66 C5
Blakemore Gdns BARN SW13 19 L1
Blakemore Rd
STRHM/NOR SW16 31 H4
THHTH CR7 49 J5
Blakeney Av BECK BR3 51 J1
Blakeney Cl HOR/WEW KT19 84 A1
Blakeney Rd BECK BR3 51 J1
Blake Rd CROY/NA CR0 3 G5
MTCM CR4 48 B3
Blakes Av NWMAL KT3 46 C5
Blake's Gn WWKM BR4 51 M7
Blake's La EHSLY KT24 119 J5
NWMAL KT3 46 C5
Blakes Ter NWMAL KT3 46 D5
Blakewood Cl FELT TW13 24 F5
Blanchards Hl RGUE GU4 117 H1
Blanchland Rd MRDN SM4 47 L5
Blanchman's Rd WARL CR6 89 H8
Blandford Av BECK BR3 51 H2
WHTN TW2 25 L2
Blandford Cl CROY/NA CR0 67 H2
WOKS/MYFD GU22 11 J6
Blandford Rd BECK BR3 51 G2
TEDD TW11 26 A6
Blane's La ASC SL5 35 M6
Blanford Ms REIG RH2 126 A8
Blanford Rd REIG RH2 147 M1
Blanks La HORL RH6 174 D6
Blatchford Rd SWTR RH13 167 J6
Blays Cl EGH TW20 20 F7
Blay's La EGH TW20 20 E7
Blean Gv PGE/AN SE20 32 F8
Blegborough Rd
STRHM/NOR SW16 30 F7
Blencarn Cl WOKN/KNAP GU21 76 D6
Blenheim Cl BF/WBF KT14 78 C3
CRAWE RH10 192 C3
EGRIN RH19 163 H2
RFNM GU10 135 H2
RYNPK SW20 46 F3
WLGTN SM6 66 F6
Blenheim Ct FARN GU14 93 G7
Blenheim Crs FNM GU9 133 K3
SAND/SEL CR2 67 M6
Blenheim Flds FROW RH18 195 M10
Blenheim Gdns KUTN/CMB KT2 9 L3
SAND/SEL CR2 88 D2
WLGTN SM6 66 F5
WOKS/MYFD GU22 96 E1
Blenheim Pk ALDT GU11 112 F2
Blenheim Park Rd
SAND/SEL CR2 67 M7
Blenheim Pl TEDD TW11 26 C6
Blenheim Rd FARN GU14 112 F2
HOR/WEW KT19 84 A1
HORS RH12 167 G4
PGE/AN SE20 32 F8
RYNPK SW20 46 F3
SUT SM1 65 K2
Blenheim Wy ISLW TW7 17 K3
Bleriot Rd HEST TW5 15 M2
Bletchingley Cl REDH RH1 126 F3
Bletchingley Rd GDST RH9 128 D5
REDH RH1 126 F3
REDH RH1 127 K7
Bletchingly Cl THHTH CR7 49 L4
Blewburton Wk BRAK RG12 35 H4
Blewfield GODL GU7 168 C7
Bligh Cl CRAWE RH10 165 H6
Blighton La RFNM GU10 135 G7
Blincoe Cl WIM/MER SW19 29 G3
Blindley Ct LING RH7 * 177 R1
Blindley Rd CRAWE RH10 165 M1
Blomfield Dl BNFD RG42 34 A2
Blondell Cl WDR/YW UB7 14 A1
Bloomfield Cl
WOKN/KNAP GU21 76 B8
Bloomfield Rd KUT/HW KT1 45 H4
Bloom Gv WNWD SE27 31 L4
Bloomhall Rd NRWD SE19 32 A6
Bloomsbury Cl HOR/WEW KT19 64 A8
Bloor Cl HORS RH12 167 G2
Blossom Cl SAND/SEL CR2 68 C4
Blossom Waye HEST TW5 16 B1
Blount Av EGRIN RH19 162 D4
Bloxham Crs HPTN TW12 43 J1
Bloxham Rd CRAN GU6 186 F2
Bloxworth Cl BRAK RG12 35 J4
WLGTN SM6 66 F2
Blue Ball La EGH TW20 21 J6
Blue Barn Wy WEY KT13 79 K1
Bluebell Cl CRAWW RH11 * 164 D7
EGRIN RH19 162 C4
HORS RH12 167 H4
ORP BR6 71 M1
SYD SE26 32 C5
WLGTN SM6 48 E8
Bluebell Ct WOKS/MYFD GU22 * 10 A9
Bluebell Hl BRAK RG12 35 H1
Bluebell La EHSLY KT24 120 B3
Bluebell Ri LTWR GU18 74 E1
Bluebell Rd BOR GU35 180 B12
Blueberry Gdns COUL/CHIP CR5 87 J6
Blue Cedars BNSTD SM7 85 G4
Blue Cedars Pl COB KT11 81 G2
Bluecoat Pond SWTR RH13 204 E11
Blue Coat Wk BRAK RG12 35 G5
Bluefield Cl HPTN TW12 25 K6
Bluegates EW KT17 64 D6
Bluehouse Gdns OXTED RH8 130 D2
Bluehouse La OXTED RH8 130 B2
Blue Leaves Av
COUL/CHIP CR5 107 G4
Blue Riband Est CROY/NA CR0 * 2 A5
Bluethroat Cl SHST GU47 72 B1
Bluff Cove ALDT GU11 112 F6
Blundel La COB KT11 81 J6
Blundell Av HORL RH6 160 C2
Blunden Rd FARN GU14 92 C4
Blunt Rd SAND/SEL CR2 68 A4
Blunts Av WDR/YW UB7 14 D2
Blunts Wy HORS RH12 166 F6
Blyth Cl TWK TW1 17 J8
Blythe Cl CAT SE6 33 J1
Blythe Hl CAT SE6 33 J1
Blythe Hill La CAT SE6 33 J1
Blythe Hill Pl FSTH SE23 * 33 H1
Blytheswood Pl
STRHM/NOR SW16 31 J5
Blythe V CAT SE6 33 J2
Blythewood La ASC SL5 36 A3
Blythwood Dr FRIM GU16 73 G7
The Blytons EGRIN RH19 162 C4
Board School Rd
WOKN/KNAP GU21 10 F4
Boar Hl DORK RH4 144 B8
Bockhampton Rd
KUTN/CMB KT2 9 H2
Boddicott Cl WIM/MER SW19 29 H3
Bodens Ride ASC SL5 36 C8
Bodiam Cl CRAWE RH10 165 L4
Bodiam Rd STRHM/NOR SW16 49 G1
Bodley Cl NWMAL KT3 46 B5
Bodley Rd NWMAL KT3 46 B6
Bodmin Gv MRDN SM4 47 L4
Bodmin St WAND/EARL SW18 29 K2
Bodnant Gdns RYNPK SW20 46 D3
Bofors Rd FARN GU14 112 D1
Bog La BRAK RG12 35 J5
Bognor Rd HORS RH12 204 B1
RDKG RH5 172 G9
RDKG RH5 188 D6
Boileau Rd BARN SW13 19 K2
Bois Hall Rd ADL/WDHM KT15 59 G4
Bolderwood Wy WWKM BR4 69 L1
Bolding House La
CHOB/PIR GU24 75 J3
Boleyn Av EW KT17 64 D8
Boleyn Cl CRAWE RH10 165 M7
STA TW18 22 B6
Boleyn Dr E/WMO/HCT KT8 43 J3
Boleyn Gdns WWKM BR4 69 L1
Boleyn Wk LHD/OX KT22 102 C2
Bolney Ct CRAWW RH11 164 B7
Bolsover Gv REDH RH1 127 H3
Bolstead Rd MTCM CR4 48 E1
Bolters La BNSTD SM7 85 J5
Bolters Rd HORL RH6 160 D1
Bolters Rd South HORL RH6 160 C1
Bolton Cl CHSGTN KT9 63 G5
Bolton Dr MRDN SM4 47 M7
Bolton Gdns TEDD TW11 26 D7
Bolton Rd CHSGTN KT9 63 G5
CHSWK W4 18 F2
CRAWE RH10 192 A12
Boltons Cl WOKS/MYFD GU22 78 D5
Bolton's La HYS/HAR UB3 14 F2
WOKS/MYFD GU22 78 D6
Bomer Cl WDR/YW UB7 14 D2
Bonchurch Cl BELMT SM2 65 L6
Bond Gdns WLGTN SM6 66 F3
Bond Rd MTCM CR4 48 C2
SURB KT6 63 J1
WARL CR6 89 G8
Bond's La RDKG RH5 144 E8
Bond St EGH TW20 20 E7
Bond Wy BRAK RG12 34 E2
Bonehurst Rd HORL RH6 175 R2
Bone Mill La GDST RH9 129 H8
Bones La HORL RH6 177 M5
Bonner Hill Rd KUT/HW KT1 9 H8
Bonners Cl WOKS/MYFD GU22 97 J4
Bonnetts La CRAWW RH11 191 K2
Bonnys Rd REIG RH2 125 G8
Bonser Rd TWK TW1 26 C3
Bonsey Cl WOKS/MYFD GU22 97 H3
Bonsey La WOKS/MYFD GU22 97 H3
Bonsey's La CHOB/PIR GU24 57 H7
Bonsor Dr KWD/TDW/WH KT20 105 H4
Bookham Ct GT/LBKH KT23 101 J5
Bookham Gv GT/LBKH KT23 101 L8
Bookham Rd COB KT11 101 G2
Bookhurst Hl CRAN GU6 * 186 G1
Bookhurst Rd CRAN GU6 186 G1
Boole Hts BRAK RG12 34 D6
Booth Dr STA TW18 23 G7
Booth Rd CRAWW RH11 164 A7
CROY/NA CR0 2 B6
Booth Wy SWTR RH13 * 167 H6
Borage Cl CRAWW RH11 164 C7
Border Cha CRAWE RH10 192 F3
Border Ct EGRIN RH19 163 G1
Border Crs SYD SE26 32 E6
Border End HASM GU27 * 197 Q7
Border Gdns CROY/NA CR0 69 L3
Border Ga MTCM CR4 48 B1
Border Rd HASM GU27 197 Q7
SYD SE26 32 E6
Bordesley Rd MRDN SM4 47 L4
Bordon Wk PUT/ROE SW15 28 D1
The Boreen BOR GU35 180 G12
Borelli Ms FNM GU9 5 J3
Borers Arms Rd CRAWE RH10 192 G1
Borers Cl CRAWE RH10 * 192 H2
Borland Rd TEDD TW11 26 E7
Borneo St PUT/ROE SW15 19 M5
Borough Hl CROY/NA CR0 2 A8
Borough Rd BH/WHM TN16 111 G3
GODL GU7 168 A4
ISLW TW7 17 H3
KUTN/CMB KT2 9 J4
MTCM CR4 48 B2
The Borough
BRKHM/BTCW RH3 145 K1
FNM GU9 5 H3
RFNM GU10 132 B3
Borrowdale Cl CRAWW RH11 164 D6
EGH TW20 21 L8
SAND/SEL CR2 88 C3
Borrowdale Dr SAND/SEL CR2 88 C2
Bosbury Rd CAT SE6 33 M4
Boscombe Cl EGH TW20 * 21 M8
Boscombe Rd TOOT SW17 30 D7
WIM/MER SW19 47 K1
WPK KT4 46 F8
Bosham Rd CRAWE RH10 165 L7
Boshers Gdns EGH TW20 21 J7
Bosman Dr BFOR GU20 54 E2
Bostock Av HORS RH12 167 K5
Boston Gdns CHSWK W4 19 H1
Boston Park Rd BTFD TW8 * 17 M1
Boston Rd CROY/NA CR0 49 J6
Boswell Rd CRAWE RH10 165 G7
THHTH CR7 49 M4
Botany Hl RFNM GU10 135 G8
Boterys Cross REDH RH1 * 127 L7
Bothwell Rd CROY/NA CR0 69 M8
Botleys Pk CHERT KT16 * 57 M4
Botsford Rd RYNPK SW20 47 H2
Bottom Harrow Rd VW GU25 39 J6
Boucher Cl TEDD TW11 26 C6
Boughton Hall Av
RPLY/SEND GU23 98 C6
Bouldish Farm Rd ASC SL5 36 C5
Boulevards ALDT GU11 * 112 D7
The Boulevard CRAWE RH10 164 F4
Boulogne Rd CROY/NA CR0 49 M6
Boulters Rd ALDT GU11 112 E8
Boulthurst Wy OXTED RH8 130 D6
Boundaries Rd BAL SW12 30 C3
FELT TW13 24 F2
Boundary Cl CRAWE RH10 165 G3
KUT/HW KT1 9 L8
Boundary Rd ASHF TW15 22 F6
CAR SM5 66 D7
CRAWE RH10 165 G3
FARN GU14 92 F7
GSHT GU26 197 Q2
RFNM GU10 180 D2
WIM/MER SW19 30 A7
WOKN/KNAP GU21 11 G3
Boundary Rd East
ADL/WDHM KT15 58 E7
Boundary Rd North
ADL/WDHM KT15 58 E7
Boundary Rd West
ADL/WDHM KT15 58 E7
Boundary Wy CROY/NA CR0 69 K4
WOKN/KNAP GU21 11 J2
Boundless La MFD/CHID GU8 182 D10
Boundstone Cl RFNM GU10 155 L4
Boundstone Rd RFNM GU10 155 J5
Bourdon Rd PGE/AN SE20 50 F2
Bourg-de-peage Av
EGRIN RH19 163 H4
Bourke Hl COUL/CHIP CR5 86 C8
Bourne Av CHERT KT16 40 D3
Bourne Cl BF/WBF KT14 78 E3
ISLW TW7 17 H5
RGUE GU4 139 L6
THDIT KT7 62 C1
Bourne Ct ALDT GU11 134 D1
BF/WBF KT14 * 79 H3
Bourne Dene RFNM GU10 155 K4
Bourne Dr MTCM CR4 48 A2
Bournefield Rd CTHM CR3 88 C8
Bourne Firs RFNM GU10 156 A4

Bourne Gv ASHTD KT21 103 G1
RFNM GU10 156 B2
Bourne Grove Cl RFNM GU10 156 B2
Bourne Grove Dr RFNM GU10 156 B2
Bourne Hts FNM GU9 * 5 K8
Bourne La CTHM CR3 108 A3
Bourne Meadow EGH TW20 39 L4
Bournemouth Rd
WIM/MER SW19 47 K1
Bourne Park Cl PUR/KEN CR8 88 B6
Bourne Rd ADL/WDHM KT15 58 E7
GODL GU7 168 C1
REDH RH1 126 F4
VW GU25 39 G5
Bourneside VW GU25 38 D7
Bourneside Gdns CAT SE6 33 M6
Bourneside Rd
ADL/WDHM KT15 59 G4
Bourne St CROY/NA CR0 2 B6
Bournevale Rd
STRHM/NOR SW16 31 H5
Bourne Vw PUR/KEN CR8 88 A5
Bourne Wy ADL/WDHM KT15 58 F4
HAYES BR2 70 D1
HOR/WEW KT19 63 M3
SUT SM1 65 J4
WOKS/MYFD GU22 97 G4
Bournville Rd CAT SE6 33 K1
Bousley Ri CHERT KT16 58 A6
Bouverie Gdns PUR/KEN CR8 87 H4
Bouverie Rd COUL/CHIP CR5 86 D8
Boveney Rd FSTH SE23 33 G1
Bovill Rd FSTH SE23 33 G1
Bowater Rdg WEY KT13 60 A8
Bowater Rd CRAWE RH10 165 L7
Bowcott Hl BOR GU35 180 E12
Bowden Cl EBED/NFELT TW14 24 B2
Bowden Rd ASC SL5 36 F5
Bowen Dr DUL SE21 32 B4
Bowens Wd CROY/NA CR0 * 69 J7
Bowenswood CROY/NA CR0 69 J7
Bowen Wy COUL/CHIP CR5 107 G4
Bower Ct WOKS/MYFD GU22 11 K3
Bower Hill Cl REDH RH1 149 H2
Bower Hill La REDH RH1 149 G1
Bowerland La LING RH7 178 E1
Bower Rd RFNM GU10 155 K4
Bowers Cl RGUE GU4 117 K4
Bowers Farm Dr RGUE GU4 117 K4
Bowers La RGUE GU4 117 K3
Bowers Pl CRAWE RH10 193 N5
Bowes Cl SWTR RH13 167 H6
Bowes Rd STA TW18 22 B7
WOT/HER KT12 60 E1
Bowfell Rd HMSMTH W6 19 M1
Bowie Cl CLAP SW4 31 G1
Bowland Dr BRAK RG12 35 H7
Bowley Cl NRWD SE19 * 32 C7
Bowley La NRWD SE19 32 C6
Bowlhead Green Rd
MFD/CHID GU8 182 G8
Bowling Court Gn FRIM GU16 93 H2
Bowling Green Cl
PUT/ROE SW15 28 E1
Bowling Green La HORS RH12 167 G6
Bowling Green Rd
CHOB/PIR GU24 56 B7
Bowman Ct CRAWE RH10 * 164 F3
Bowman Ms WAND/EARL SW18 29 J2
Bowmans Lea FSTH SE23 32 F1
Bowman's Meadow
WLGTN SM6 66 E2
Bowness Crs PUT/ROE SW15 28 B6
Bowness Dr HSLWW TW4 16 B6
Bowness Rd CAT SE6 33 L1
Bowry Dr STWL/WRAY TW19 12 C8
Bowsley Ct FELT TW13 24 D3
The Bowsprit COB KT11 80 F5
Bowyers Cl ASHTD KT21 83 J8
Bowyers Ct TWK TW1 17 L6
Bowyer Wk ASC SL5 36 B1
Boxall's Gv ALDT GU11 134 D2
Boxall's La ALDT GU11 134 D2
Boxall Wk SWTR RH13 167 G8
Box Cl CRAWW RH11 191 M12
Boxford Cl SAND/SEL CR2 89 G2
Boxford Rdg BRAK RG12 34 E3
Boxgrove Av GU GU1 117 K6
Boxgrove La GU GU1 117 K7
Boxgrove Rd GU GU1 117 K7
Boxhill Rd DORK RH4 123 H8
KWD/TDW/WH KT20 124 A4
Boxhill Wy BRKHM/BTCW RH3 145 L4
Box La EGRIN RH19 163 M7
Boxley Rd MRDN SM4 47 M4
Box Ridge Av PUR/KEN CR8 87 J2
Box Tree Wk REDH RH1 147 M3
Boxwood Wy WARL CR6 89 G7
Boyd Cl KUTN/CMB KT2 9 K2
Boyd Ct BNFD RG42 34 D1
Boyd Rd WIM/MER SW19 30 A7
Boyle Farm Rd THDIT KT7 44 D6
Brabazon Av WLGTN SM6 67 H6
Brabazon Rd HEST TW5 15 M2
Brabon Rd FARN GU14 92 C4
Brabourne Cl NRWD SE19 32 B6
Bracebridge CBLY GU15 72 D4
Bracewood Gdns CROY/NA CR0 3 J7
Bracken Av CROY/NA CR0 69 K2
Bracken Bank ASC SL5 35 M1
Bracken Cl CRAWE RH10 165 G2
CRAWE RH10 192 G3
GT/LBKH KT23 101 J6
SHGR GU5 169 L3
SUN TW16 * 24 C7
WHTN TW2 25 K1
WOKS/MYFD GU22 10 F7
Brackendale Cl CBLY GU15 73 H6
HSLW TW3 16 E3
Brackendale Rd CBLY GU15 73 G5
Brackendene ASHV GU12 113 M6
Brackendene Cl
WOKN/KNAP GU21 11 G1
Bracken End ISLW TW7 17 G7
Bracken Gdns BARN SW13 19 K4
Bracken Gv HORS RH12 167 L4
Brackenhill COB KT11 81 K2
Brackenlea GODL GU7 168 A2
Bracken Pth EPSOM KT18 83 L3
Brackenside HORL RH6 160 E2
The Brackens ASC SL5 * 35 L3
Bracken Wy CHOB/PIR GU24 56 C8
RGUW GU3 116 B6
Brackenwood CBLY GU15 74 A4
SUN TW16 42 D1
Brackenwood Rd
WOKN/KNAP GU21 96 A1
Bracklesham Cl FARN GU14 92 D2
Brackley WEY KT13 60 A4
Brackley Cl WLGTN SM6 67 H6
Brackley Rd BECK BR3 33 J8
Bracklyn Av EGRIN RH19 * 178 H11
Bracknell Beeches BRAK RG12 * 34 E3
Bracknell Cl CBLY GU15 53 J8
Bracknell Rd BAGS GU19 54 A3
CBLY GU15 53 K7
Bracondale ESH/CLAY KT10 61 M4
Bradbury Rd CRAWE RH10 165 L7
Braddock Cl ISLW TW7 17 J5
Braddon Rd RCH/KEW TW9 18 C5
Bradenhurst Cl CTHM CR3 108 C8
Bradfield Cl RGUE GU4 117 K5
WOKS/MYFD GU22 10 D7
Bradfields BRAK RG12 35 G6
Bradford Cl SYD SE26 32 E5
Bradford Dr HOR/WEW KT19 64 D5
Brading Rd BRXS/STRHM SW2 31 J1
CROY/NA CR0 49 J6
Bradley Cl BELMT SM2 65 L8
Bradley La RDKG RH5 122 E6
Bradley Rd NRWD SE19 31 M7
Bradmore Wy COUL/CHIP CR5 87 H8
Bradshaw Cl WIM/MER SW19 29 K7
Bradshaws Cl SNWD SE25 50 D2
Bradstock Rd EW KT17 64 E4
Braemar Av SAND/SEL CR2 67 M8
THHTH CR7 49 L3
WIM/MER SW19 29 K3
Braemar Cl FRIM GU16 93 J1
GODL GU7 168 A6
Braemar Gdns WWKM BR4 51 M8
Braemar Rd BTFD TW8 18 A1
WPK KT4 64 E2
Braeside ADL/WDHM KT15 78 E1
BECK BR3 33 K6
Braeside Av RYNPK SW20 47 H1
Braeside Cl HASM GU27 198 A5
Braeside Rd STRHM/NOR SW16 30 F8
Braes Md REDH RH1 149 H1
Brafferton Rd CROY/NA CR0 2 C9
Bragg Rd TEDD TW11 26 B8
Braid Cl FELT TW13 25 J3
Brailsford Cl WIM/MER SW19 30 B8
Brainton Av EBED/NFELT TW14 24 E1
Brake Rd FARN GU14 92 B8
Brakey Hl REDH RH1 128 B8
Bramber Cl CRAWE RH10 165 G2
Bramber Wy WARL CR6 89 J6
Bramble Acres Cl BELMT SM2 65 K6
Bramble Bank FRIM GU16 93 K3
Bramble Banks CAR SM5 66 D7
Bramble Cl BECK BR3 51 M5
CRAWE RH10 192 G2
CROY/NA CR0 69 K3
REDH RH1 148 D2
RGUW GU3 116 B6
SHPTN TW17 42 A4
Brambledene Cl
WOKN/KNAP GU21 76 F8
Brambledown STA TW18 40 E1
Brambledown Rd CAR SM5 66 D6
SAND/SEL CR2 68 B6
Bramble Hall La
KWD/TDW/WH KT20 * 123 J6
Bramble La HPTN TW12 25 J6
Bramble Ri COB KT11 80 F5
Brambles Cl ASHV GU12 113 L8
CTHM CR3 108 B4
ISLW TW7 17 L2
Brambles Pk SHGR GU5 169 J3
The Brambles GODL GU7 168 A2
RFNM GU10 * 132 B3
SUT SM1 66 A1
WIM/MER SW19 * 29 J6
Brambleton Av FNM GU9 5 G8
Brambletye La FROW RH18 195 L10
Brambletye Park Rd
REDH RH1 148 C2
Brambletye Rd CRAWE RH10 165 J5
Bramble Wk EPSOM KT18 83 L4
REDH RH1 * 148 D2
Bramble Wy RPLY/SEND GU23 98 C6
Bramblewood REDH RH1 126 E3
Bramblewood Cl CAR SM5 48 B8
Brambling Cl SWTR RH13 167 K8
Brambling Rd SWTR RH13 167 K8
Bramcote CBLY GU15 73 M4
Bramcote Av MTCM CR4 48 C4
Bramcote Rd PUT/ROE SW15 19 L6
Bramerton Rd BECK BR3 51 J3
Bramham Gdns CHSGTN KT9 * 63 G4
Bramley Av COUL/CHIP CR5 86 F5
SHPTN TW17 42 B3
Bramley Cl CHERT KT16 40 E8
CRAWE RH10 165 H4
REDH RH1 148 B2
SAND/SEL CR2 67 L4
STA TW18 22 F7
WHTN TW2 16 F8
Bramley Gv ASHTD KT21 103 H1
Bramley Hl SAND/SEL CR2 67 M3
Bramley Hyrst SAND/SEL CR2 * 67 M4
Bramley Rd BELMT SM2 65 G7
CBLY GU15 72 E7
SUT SM1 66 A4
Bramley Wk HORL RH6 160 F3
Bramley Wy ASHTD KT21 83 J7
HSLWW TW4 16 C7
WWKM BR4 69 L1
Brampton Gdns WOT/HER KT12 60 F4
Brampton Rd CROY/NA CR0 3 J1
Bramshaw Ri NWMAL KT3 46 B6
Bramshott Ct LIPH GU30 * 196 F5
Bramston Rd MTCM CR4 30 C8
Bramswell Rd GODL GU7 168 C3
Bramwell Cl SUN TW16 43 G2
Brancaster La PUR/KEN CR8 87 M1
Brancaster Rd
STRHM/NOR SW16 31 H4
Brandon Cl CBLY GU15 74 A5
CRAWE RH10 165 M6
Brandon Rd SUT SM1 65 L3
Brandreth Rd TOOT SW17 30 E3
The Brandries WLGTN SM6 67 G2
Brandsland REIG RH2 147 L4
Brands Rd DTCH/LGLY SL3 12 E1
Brandy Wy BELMT SM2 65 K6
Brangbourne Rd BMLY BR1 33 M6
Brangwyn Crs WIM/MER SW19 48 A2
Branksome Cl CBLY GU15 73 H3
WOT/HER KT12 61 G1
Branksome Hill Rd SHST GU47 72 B2
Branksome Park Rd CBLY GU15 73 H3
Branksome Rd WIM/MER SW19 47 L2
Branksome Wy NWMAL KT3 45 M2
Bransby Rd CHSGTN KT9 63 H6
Branstone Rd RCH/KEW TW9 18 C3
Brantridge Rd CRAWE RH10 165 H6
Brants Br BRAK RG12 35 H2
Brantwood Av ISLW TW7 17 K6
Brantwood Dr BF/WBF KT14 78 C3
Brantwood Gdns BF/WBF KT14 78 C3
Brantwood Rd SAND/SEL CR2 67 M7
Brasenose Dr BARN SW13 19 M1
Brassey Cl EBED/NFELT TW14 * 24 D2
OXTED RH8 130 D3
Brassey Hl OXTED RH8 130 D4
Brassey Rd OXTED RH8 130 D3
Brasted Cl BELMT SM2 65 K8
SYD SE26 32 F5
Brathway Rd
WAND/EARL SW18 29 K1
Brattain Ct BRAK RG12 35 G3
Bravington Cl SHPTN TW17 41 J5
Braxted Pk STRHM/NOR SW16 31 J7
Braybourne Dr ISLW TW7 17 J2
Braybrooke Gdns NRWD SE19 32 B8
Bray Cl CRAWE RH10 165 M6
Braycourt Av WOT/HER KT12 42 F7
Bray Gdns WOKS/MYFD GU22 78 B6
Bray Rd COB KT11 81 H6
GUW GU2 6 C6
Braywood Av EGH TW20 21 J7
Breakfield COUL/CHIP CR5 87 H6
Breamore Cl PUT/ROE SW15 28 D2
Breamwater Gdns
RCHPK/HAM TW10 26 E4
Breasley Cl PUT/ROE SW15 19 L6
Brecon Cl FARN GU14 92 A2
MTCM CR4 49 H4
WPK KT4 64 F1
Bredhurst Cl PGE/AN SE20 32 F7
Bredon Rd CROY/NA CR0 3 J2
Bredune PUR/KEN CR8 88 A5
Breech La KWD/TDW/WH KT20 104 D7
The Breech SHST GU47 72 B2
Breezehurst Dr CRAWW RH11 164 B7
Bregsells La RDKG RH5 173 L5
Bremer Rd STA TW18 22 D4
Bremner Av HORL RH6 160 C2
Brenda Rd TOOT SW17 30 C3
Brende Gdns E/WMO/HCT KT8 43 L4
Brendon Cl ESH/CLAY KT10 61 M5
HYS/HAR UB3 14 F2
Brendon Dr ESH/CLAY KT10 61 M5
Brendon Rd FARN GU14 92 A2
Brenley Cl MTCM CR4 48 D3
Brent Lea BTFD TW8 17 M2
Brentmoor Rd CHOB/PIR GU24 74 F3
Brent Rd BTFD TW8 17 M1
SAND/SEL CR2 68 E7
Brentside BTFD TW8 17 M1
Brent Wy BTFD TW8 18 A2
Bret Harte Rd FRIM GU16 73 H8
Bretlands Rd CHERT KT16 58 B1
Brettgrave HOR/WEW KT19 63 M8
Brettingham Cl
CRAWW RH11 * 164 A7
Brewer Rd CRAWE RH10 164 F6
Brewers Cl FARN GU14 92 D4
Brewer St REDH RH1 127 M5
Brewery La BF/WBF KT14 79 H3
Brewery Rd WOKN/KNAP GU21 10 B5
Brew House Rd
BRKHM/BTCW RH3 145 L4
Brewhurst La BIL RH14 201 R7
Breydon Wk CRAWE RH10 165 K6
Brian Av SAND/SEL CR2 88 B2
Briane Rd HOR/WEW KT19 63 M8
Briar Av LTWR GU18 74 D1
STRHM/NOR SW16 31 J8
Briar Bank CAR SM5 66 D7
Briar Cl BF/WBF KT14 78 E1
CRAWW RH11 164 E1
HPTN TW12 25 J6
ISLW TW7 17 J7
WARL CR6 89 K6
Briar Gv SAND/SEL CR2 88 D3
Briar Hl PUR/KEN CR8 87 H1
Briar La CAR SM5 66 D7
CROY/NA CR0 69 L3
Briar Patch GODL GU7 168 A3
Briar Rd RPLY/SEND GU23 97 L6
SHPTN TW17 41 J5
STRHM/NOR SW16 49 H3
WHTN TW2 26 B2
Briars Cl FARN GU14 92 A6
Briars Ct LHD/OX KT22 82 A4
The Briars ASHV GU12 113 L8
Briars Wd HORL RH6 160 F2
Briarswood Cl CRAWE RH10 165 M2
Briar Wk BF/WBF KT14 78 D2
PUT/ROE SW15 19 L6
Briar Wy RGUE GU4 117 L4
Briarwood Cl FELT TW13 24 B4
Briarwood Ct WPK KT4 * 46 D8
Briarwood Rd EW KT17 64 D5
WOKN/KNAP GU21 96 A1
Brick Farm Cl RCH/KEW TW9 18 E3
Brickfield Cl BTFD TW8 17 M2
Brickfield Farm Gdns ORP BR6 71 M3
Brickfield La HORL RH6 160 A5
HYS/HAR UB3 15 G1
Brickfield Rd REDH RH1 176 H1
THHTH CR7 49 L1
WIM/MER SW19 29 L5
Brickhouse La GDST RH9 177 P4
Brick Kiln La OXTED RH8 130 F4
Bricklands CRAWE RH10 193 N6
Bricksbury Hl FNM GU9 133 M2
Brickwood Cl SYD SE26 32 E4
Brickwood Rd CROY/NA CR0 3 G5
Brickyard Copse RDKG RH5 188 D1
Brickyard La CRAWE RH10 193 N5
RDKG RH5 143 G7
Brideake Cl CRAWW RH11 164 C7
Bridge Barn La
WOKN/KNAP GU21 76 F7
Bridge Cl BF/WBF KT14 79 J2
STA TW18 22 B5
WOKN/KNAP GU21 76 F7
WOT/HER KT12 42 C7
Bridge Ct WOKN/KNAP GU21 10 A6
Bridge End CBLY GU15 72 E5
Bridgefield FNM GU9 5 L3
Bridgefield Cl BNSTD SM7 84 F5
Bridgefield Rd SUT SM1 65 K5
Bridge Gdns ASHF TW15 23 M8
E/WMO/HCT KT8 44 A4
Bridgeham Cl WEY KT13 59 K4
Bridgeham Wy HORL RH6 161 L4
Bridgehill Cl GUW GU2 116 D6
Bridgelands CRAWE RH10 192 E2
Bridgelands Cl BECK BR3 33 J8
Bridge La VW GU25 39 H6
Bridgeman Rd TEDD TW11 26 D7
Bridgemead FRIM GU16 93 G1
Bridge Ms WOKN/KNAP GU21 10 A6
Bridge Pde STRHM/NOR SW16 * 31 H6
Bridge Pk RGUE GU4 * 117 M5
Bridge Pl CROY/NA CR0 2 F3
Bridge Rd ALDT GU11 134 D1
ASC SL5 37 G5
BAGS GU19 54 B5
BECK BR3 33 J8
CBLY GU15 72 E6
CHERT KT16 40 E7
CHSGTN KT9 63 H4
COB KT11 80 E5
CRAN GU6 186 D3
E/WMO/HCT KT8 44 B4
EW KT17 84 C2
FARN GU14 92 C5
GODL GU7 168 B4
HASM GU27 198 D6
HORS RH12 203 J2
HSLW TW3 17 G5
SUT SM1 65 L5
TWK TW1 17 L8
WEY KT13 59 J3
WLGTN SM6 66 E4
Bridge Rw CROY/NA CR0 * 2 F3
Bridges Cl HORL RH6 161 G3
Bridges La CROY/NA CR0 67 H3
Bridge Sq FNM GU9 5 J4
Bridge St DTCH/LGLY SL3 13 G2
GODL GU7 168 B5
GU GU1 6 F6
LHD/OX KT22 102 D4
TWK TW1 18 A8
WOT/HER KT12 42 C8
Bridgetown Cl NRWD SE19 32 B6
Bridge Vw ASC SL5 37 L7
Bridgewater Rd WEY KT13 60 A5
Bridge Wy COUL/CHIP CR5 106 B1
WHTN TW2 25 M1
Bridgewood Cl PGE/AN SE20 32 E8
Bridgewood Rd
STRHM/NOR SW16 31 G8
WPK KT4 64 D3
Bridgford St WAND/EARL SW18 29 M4
Bridle Cl GSHT GU26 197 M2
HOR/WEW KT19 63 M3
KUT/HW KT1 45 G4
SUN TW16 42 D3
Bridle La COB KT11 81 L5
TWK TW1 17 L8
Bridle Pth CROY/NA CR0 67 H2
The Bridle Pth EW KT17 64 F8
Bridlepath Wy
EBED/NFELT TW14 24 B1
Bridle Rd CROY/NA CR0 69 K1
ESH/CLAY KT10 62 E5
EW KT17 84 C3
The Bridle Rd PUR/KEN CR8 67 H8
Bridle Wy CRAWE RH10 165 M3
CROY/NA CR0 69 K4
ORP BR6 71 M3
Bridleway Cl EW KT17 64 F8
The Bridle Wy WLGTN SM6 66 F3
Bridlington Cl BH/WHM TN16 110 E1
Bridport Rd THHTH CR7 49 K3
Brier Lea KWD/TDW/WH KT20 105 J8
Brierley CROY/NA CR0 69 L5
Brierley Cl SNWD SE25 50 D4
Brierley Rd BAL SW12 30 F3
Brierly Cl GUW GU2 116 D6
Brier Rd KWD/TDW/WH KT20 104 E1
Brigade Pl CTHM CR3 107 M4
Briggs Cl MTCM CR4 48 E1
Bright Hl GU GU1 7 J7
Brightlands Rd REIG RH2 125 M6
Brightman Rd
WAND/EARL SW18 30 A2
Brighton Cl ADL/WDHM KT15 58 F4
Brighton Rd ADL/WDHM KT15 58 F3
ALDT GU11 134 F1
BELMT SM2 65 L8
BNSTD SM7 85 J4
COUL/CHIP CR5 106 E3
CRAWE RH10 164 F7
HORL RH6 160 C3
KWD/TDW/WH KT20 105 J8
MFD/CHID GU8 168 E8
PUR/KEN CR8 87 H4
REDH RH1 148 D8
SURB KT6 44 F6
SWTR RH13 205 P10
Brighton Rd (Hornbrook Hill)
SWTR RH13 205 N9
Brighton Ter REDH RH1 * 148 C1
Brightside Av STA TW18 22 F8
Brightwell Cl CROY/NA CR0 49 K8
Brightwell Crs TOOT SW17 30 C6
Brightwells Rd FNM GU9 5 J3
Brigstock Rd COUL/CHIP CR5 86 E5
THHTH CR7 49 L5
Brimshot La CHOB/PIR GU24 56 B7
Brindle Cl ALDT GU11 134 E2
The Brindles BNSTD SM7 85 J7
Brinkley Rd WPK KT4 64 E1
Brinsworth Cl WHTN TW2 26 A2
Brisbane Av WIM/MER SW19 47 L1
Brisbane Cl CRAWW RH11 164 F1
Briscoe Rd WIM/MER SW19 30 A7
Brisson Cl ESH/CLAY KT10 61 J5
Bristol Cl CRAWE RH10 165 M1
STWL/WRAY TW19 14 B8
WLGTN SM6 67 H7
Bristol Rd MRDN SM4 47 M5
Bristow Rd CBLY GU15 72 E6
CROY/NA CR0 67 H3
HSLW TW3 16 E5
NRWD SE19 32 B6
Britannia La WHTN TW2 25 M1
Britannia Rd BRYLDS KT5 45 J7
Britannia Wy STWL/WRAY TW19 23 G1
Briton Cl SAND/SEL CR2 88 B1
Briton Crs SAND/SEL CR2 88 B1
Briton Hill Rd SAND/SEL CR2 68 B8
Brittain Rd WOT/HER KT12 61 G4
Britten Cl ASHV GU12 113 L7
CRAWW RH11 164 B7
Brittens Cl GUW GU2 116 D3
Brixton Hill Pl
BRXS/STRHM SW2 31 H1
Broadacre STA TW18 22 D6
Broad Acres GODL GU7 168 B1
Broadacres RGUW GU3 116 B6
Broadbridge Heath Rd
HORS RH12 166 A5
Broadbridge La HORL RH6 161 K4
Broad Cl WOT/HER KT12 61 G2
Broadcoombe SAND/SEL CR2 69 G6
Broadeaves Cl SAND/SEL CR2 68 B4
Broadfield Cl
KWD/TDW/WH KT20 104 F2
Broadfield Dr CRAWW RH11 164 E8
Broadfield Pk CRAWW RH11 * 164 F8
Broadfield Pl CRAWW RH11 164 D8
Broadfield Rd SHGR GU5 142 A8
Broadfields E/WMO/HCT KT8 44 A6
Broadford La CHOB/PIR GU24 76 B2
Broadford Pk RGUE GU4 139 G7
Broadford Rd RGUE GU4 139 G7
Broadgates Rd
WAND/EARL SW18 30 A2
Broad Green Av CROY/NA CR0 2 A1
Broadham Green Rd
OXTED RH8 130 A7
Broadham Pl OXTED RH8 130 A6
Broad Ha'Penny RFNM GU10 155 K4
Broad Hwy COB KT11 81 G4
Broadhurst ASHTD KT21 83 H6
Broadhurst Gdns REIG RH2 147 L3
Broadlands FARN GU14 93 H7
FELT TW13 25 J4
FRIM GU16 93 J1
HORL RH6 160 F2
Broadlands Av SHPTN TW17 41 M6
STRHM/NOR SW16 31 H3
Broadlands Cl
STRHM/NOR SW16 31 H3
Broadlands Dr ASC SL5 36 F7
WARL CR6 108 F1
Broadlands Wy NWMAL KT3 46 C6
Broad La BRAK RG12 34 F3
HPTN TW12 25 J8
RDKG RH5 174 A4
Broadley Gn BFOR GU20 55 G6
Broadmead ASHTD KT21 83 H8
CAT SE6 33 K4
FARN GU14 92 A6
HORL RH6 160 F2
REDH RH1 * 126 F2
Broadmead Av WPK KT4 46 D7
Broadmead Cl HPTN TW12 25 K7
Broadmeads RPLY/SEND GU23 97 L4
Broad Oak SUN TW16 24 C7
Broad Oaks SURB KT6 45 L8
Broadoaks Crs BF/WBF KT14 78 E4
Broadstone Pk FROW RH18 195 P11
Broad St CHOB/PIR GU24 75 G2
RGUW GU3 116 A6
TEDD TW11 26 C7
Broadview Rd
STRHM/NOR SW16 31 G8
Broad Wk COUL/CHIP CR5 106 D4
CRAN GU6 186 E4
CTHM CR3 108 C4
EPSOM KT18 104 F1
FRIM GU16 73 H7
HEST TW5 16 A3
RCH/KEW TW9 18 C2
Broadwalk CRAWE RH10 164 F4
Broadwater Cl
STWL/WRAY TW19 21 H1
WOKN/KNAP GU21 78 A2
WOT/HER KT12 60 D4
Broadwater Gdns ORP BR6 71 L3
Broadwater Ri GU GU1 139 K1
Broadwater Rd TOOT SW17 30 B5
Broadwater Rd North
WOT/HER KT12 60 C4
Broadwater Rd South
WOT/HER KT12 60 D4
Broad Wy FARN GU14 112 D1
Broadway BRAK RG12 34 E2
STA TW18 * 22 E6
SUT SM1 65 M3
WOKN/KNAP GU21 95 L1
Broadway Av CROY/NA CR0 50 A5
TWK TW1 17 L8
Broadway Cl SAND/SEL CR2 88 E4
Broadway Ct
WIM/MER SW19 * 29 K7
Broadway Gdns MTCM CR4 48 B4
Broadway Rd LTWR GU18 54 F8
The Broadway
ADL/WDHM KT15 58 D8
CHEAM SM3 65 H5
CRAWE RH10 164 F4
STA TW18 40 F3
THDIT KT7 44 B8
WIM/MER SW19 29 J7
WOKN/KNAP GU21 10 E5
Broadwell Rd RFNM GU10 155 J3
Broadwood Cl HORS RH12 167 K4
Broadwood Ri CRAWW RH11 191 K12
Broadwood Rd
COUL/CHIP CR5 107 G3
Brock Cl FRIM GU16 94 A1
Brockdene Dr HAYES BR2 71 G1
Brockenhurst E/WMO/HCT KT8 43 J5
Brockenhurst Av WPK KT4 46 B8

Brockenhurst Cl WOKN/KNAP GU21 77 J4
Brockenhurst Rd ALDT GU11 134 E1
ASC SL5 36 E5
BRAK RG12 35 J3
CROY/NA CR0 50 E7
Brockenhurst Wy STRHM/NOR SW16 49 G2
Brockham Cl WIM/MER SW19 29 J6
Brockham Crs CROY/NA CR0 70 A6
Brockham Dr BRXS/STRHM SW2 31 J1
Brockham Hill Pk KWD/TDW/WH KT20 123 M5
Brockhamhurst Rd BRKHM/BTCW RH3 145 L7
Brockham La BRKHM/BTCW RH3 123 K8
Brockhill WOKN/KNAP GU21 * 76 D7
Brockhurst Cl HORS RH12 166 C8
Brockhurst Ldg FNM GU9 155 L2
Brocklebank Rd WAND/EARL SW18 29 M1
Brocklesby Rd SNWD SE25 50 E4
Brockley Combe WEY KT13 60 A4
Brockley Pk FSTH SE23 33 H1
Brockley Ri FSTH SE23 33 H1
Brockley Vw FSTH SE23 33 H1
Brock Rd CRAWW RH11 164 D1
Brock's Cl GODL GU7 168 D4
Brocks Dr CHEAM SM3 65 H2
RGUW GU3 115 M4
Brockshot Cl BTFD TW8 18 A1
Brock Wy VW GU25 38 F5
Brockway Cl GU GU1 117 L7
Brockwell Av BECK BR3 51 M5
Brockwell Park Gdns HNHL SE24 31 L1
Brodie Rd GU GU1 7 J6
Brodrick Gv GT/LBKH KT23 101 K8
Brodrick Rd TOOT SW17 30 C2
Brograve Gdns BECK BR3 51 L2
Broke Ct RGUE GU4 117 M5
Brokes Crs REIG RH2 125 K6
Brokes Rd REIG RH2 125 K6
Bromford Cl OXTED RH8 130 D7
Bromley Rd BECK BR3 51 K1
CAT SE6 33 L3
Brompton Cl HSLWW TW4 16 C7
Bronson Rd RYNPK SW20 47 G2
The Brontes EGRIN RH19 * 162 E4
Brook Av FNM GU9 134 C2
Brook Cl DORK RH4 122 F8
EGRIN RH19 163 H4
HOR/WEW KT19 64 B7
RYNPK SW20 46 E3
SHST GU47 52 B8
STWL/WRAY TW19 23 J1
TOOT SW17 30 D3
Brook Ct BECK BR3 * 51 J1
Brookdale Rd CAT SE6 33 L1
Brook Dr BRAK RG12 * 35 H4
Brooke End OXTED RH8 * 130 D7
Brooke Forest RGUW GU3 115 M4
Brookehowse Rd CAT SE6 33 L4
Brookers Cl ASHTD KT21 82 F7
Brook Farm Rd COB KT11 81 G5
Brookfield GODL GU7 168 D1
WOKN/KNAP GU21 76 E6
Brookfield Av SUT SM1 66 B2
Brookfield Cl ASHTD KT21 103 H2
CHERT KT16 58 A5
REDH RH1 148 D6
Brookfield Gdns ESH/CLAY KT10 62 C5
Brookfield Pl COB KT11 81 H5
Brookfield Rd ASHV GU12 113 H7
Brookfields Av MTCM CR4 48 B5
Brook Gdns BARN SW13 19 J5
FARN GU14 92 C7
KUTN/CMB KT2 45 M1
Brook Gn BNFD RG42 34 C1
Brook Hl OXTED RH8 129 M4
SHGR GU5 170 C1
Brookhill Cl CRAWE RH10 192 F2
Brookhill Rd CRAWE RH10 192 F3
Brookhouse Rd FARN GU14 92 C6
Brookhurst Fld HORS RH12 * 203 J1
Brookhurst Rd ADL/WDHM KT15 58 E5
Brooklands GDST RH9 * 150 F7
Brooklands Av WIM/MER SW19 29 L3
Brooklands Cl COB KT11 81 H5
FNM GU9 134 A2
RFNM GU10 154 A4
SUN TW16 42 B1
Brooklands La WEY KT13 59 J5
Brooklands Pl HPTN TW12 25 L6
Brooklands Rd CRAWW RH11 191 M12
FNM GU9 134 B2
THDIT KT7 44 C8
WEY KT13 79 K1
Brooklands Ter SUN TW16 * 42 D4
The Brooklands ISLW TW7 * 17 G3
Brooklands Wy EGRIN RH19 162 E5
FNM GU9 134 B2
REDH RH1 126 B6
Brook La CHOB/PIR GU24 76 A1
RPLY/SEND GU23 98 B4
SHGR GU5 141 H8
Brookley Cl RFNM GU10 134 E6
Brookleys CHOB/PIR GU24 56 C8
Brooklyn Av SNWD SE25 50 E4
Brooklyn Cl CAR SM5 66 B1
WOKS/MYFD GU22 10 C9
Brooklyn Ct WOKS/MYFD GU22 10 C9
Brooklyn Gv SNWD SE25 50 E4
Brooklyn Rd SNWD SE25 50 E4
WOKS/MYFD GU22 10 C8
Brookmead CROY/NA CR0 48 F6
Brook Md HOR/WEW KT19 64 B5
Brookmead Ct CRAN GU6 186 D3
FNM GU9 4 F5
Brookmead Rd CROY/NA CR0 48 F6
Brook Rd BAGS GU19 54 B7
CBLY GU15 72 E5
HORS RH12 167 H3
MFD/CHID GU8 183 K9
REDH RH1 126 F2
REDH RH1 148 C1
RGUE GU4 139 M6
SURB KT6 63 H1
THHTH CR7 49 M4
TWK TW1 17 K8
Brook Rd South BTFD TW8 18 A1
Brooks Cl WEY KT13 59 K8
Brookscroft CROY/NA CR0 69 J8
Brookside CAR SM5 66 D4
CHERT KT16 40 B7
CRAN GU6 186 D2
CRAWE RH10 165 H3
CRAWE RH10 192 F2
DTCH/LGLY SL3 12 F2
FNM GU9 133 M3
GDST RH9 151 G4
RDKG RH5 173 N3
RGUE GU4 117 G3
Brookside Av ASHF TW15 22 F6
STWL/WRAY TW19 12 A5
Brookside Cl FELT TW13 24 D4
Brookside Crs WPK KT4 46 D8
Brookside Pk FARN GU14 * 72 D8
Brookside Wy CROY/NA CR0 51 G6
Brooks La CHSWK W4 18 D1
Brook St KUT/HW KT1 8 E7
Brookswood RGUE GU4 139 M7
The Brook CRAWE RH10 164 F3
Brook Va RDKG RH5 144 E8
Brookview CRAWE RH10 192 F2
Brookview Rd STRHM/NOR SW16 30 F6
Brook Wy LHD/OX KT22 82 D8
Brookwell La SHGR GU5 169 L7
Brookwood HORL RH6 160 E2
Brookwood Av BARN SW13 19 J5
Brookwood Br CHOB/PIR GU24 95 L2
Brookwood Lye Rd CHOB/PIR GU24 95 M2
Brookwood Pk HORL RH6 160 E4
Brookwood Rd FARN GU14 93 G5
HSLW TW3 16 E4
WAND/EARL SW18 29 J2
Broom Bank WARL CR6 109 M1
Broom Cl ESH/CLAY KT10 61 L4
TEDD TW11 8 C2
Broomcroft Dr WOKS/MYFD GU22 78 A5
Broomdashers Rd CRAWE RH10 165 H3
Broome Cl EPSOM KT18 104 A8
HORS RH12 167 G4
Broome Ct BRAK RG12 34 E3
Broomehall Rd RDKG RH5 172 E7
Broome Rd HPTN TW12 43 J1
Broomers La CRAN GU6 171 K12
Broomfield GUW GU2 116 B7
Broom Fld LTWR GU18 74 D2
Broomfield MFD/CHID GU8 158 B5
SUN TW16 42 D1
Broomfield Cl RGUW GU3 116 B6
WOKS/MYFD GU22 78 A6
Broomfield Ct WEY KT13 59 K5
Broomfield La RFNM GU10 155 K8
Broomfield Pk ASC SL5 37 L7
DORK RH4 143 M3
Broomfield Ride LHD/OX KT22 82 A2
Broomfield Rd ADL/WDHM KT15 78 E1
BECK BR3 51 H4
RCH/KEW TW9 18 C3
SURB KT6 45 J8
TEDD TW11 26 F7
Broomfields ESH/CLAY KT10 61 M4
Broom Gdns CROY/NA CR0 69 K2
Broom Hall LHD/OX KT22 81 M4
Broomhall End WOKN/KNAP GU21 10 D3
Broomhall La ASC SL5 37 J6
WOKN/KNAP GU21 10 D4
Broomhall Rd SAND/SEL CR2 68 A7
WOKN/KNAP GU21 10 D4
Broomhill RFNM GU10 133 G1
Broomhill Rd FARN GU14 92 A4
Broomhurst Ct DORK RH4 144 E4
Broomlands La OXTED RH8 131 H1
Broom La CHOB/PIR GU24 56 B7
Broomleaf Cnr FNM GU9 5 M4
Broomleaf Rd FNM GU9 5 M3
Broomloan La SUT SM1 65 K1
Broom Lock TEDD TW11 * 26 F6
Broom Pk TEDD TW11 8 C3
Broom Rd CROY/NA CR0 69 K2
TEDD TW11 26 F7
Broomsquires Rd BAGS GU19 54 B7
Broom Water TEDD TW11 26 F7
Broom Water West TEDD TW11 26 F6
Broom Wy BLKW GU17 72 A5
WEY KT13 60 A3
Broomwood Cl CROY/NA CR0 51 G5
Broomwood Wy RFNM GU10 155 M3
Broseley Gv SYD SE26 33 H6
Broster Gdns SNWD SE25 50 C3
Brougham Pl FNM GU9 133 L2
Brough Cl KUTN/CMB KT2 * 27 G6
Broughton Av RCHPK/HAM TW10 26 F5
Broughton Ms FRIM GU16 73 J8
Broughton Rd THHTH CR7 49 K6
Browells La FELT TW13 24 F3
Brown Cl WLGTN SM6 67 H6
Browngraves Rd HYS/HAR UB3 14 F2
Brownhill Rd CAT SE6 33 M1
Browning Av SUT SM1 66 B3
WPK KT4 46 E8
Browning Cl CBLY GU15 73 M5
CRAWE RH10 165 L3
HPTN TW12 25 J5
Browning Rd LHD/OX KT22 102 A7
Brownings EDEN TN8 153 M5
The Brownings EGRIN RH19 162 D4
Browning Wy HEST TW5 16 A3
Brownlow Rd CROY/NA CR0 3 H9
REDH RH1 126 B8
Brownrigg Crs BRAK RG12 35 H1
Brownrigg Rd ASHF TW15 23 K5
Brown's Hl REDH RH1 150 A7
Browns La EHSLY KT24 121 G1
Brown's Rd BRYLDS KT5 45 J7
Browns Wk RFNM GU10 155 J4
Browns Wd EGRIN RH19 162 F1
The Brow REDH RH1 148 D5
Broxholm Rd WNWD SE27 31 K4
Brox La CHERT KT16 58 A7
Brox Rd CHERT KT16 57 M7
Broxted Rd FSTH SE23 33 J3
Bruce Av SHPTN TW17 41 M6
Bruce Cl BF/WBF KT14 79 G3
Bruce Dr SAND/SEL CR2 69 G7
Bruce Rd MTCM CR4 30 D8
SNWD SE25 50 A4
Brudenell Rd TOOT SW17 30 C4
Brumana Cl WEY KT13 59 L5
Brumfield Rd HOR/WEW KT19 63 M4
Brunel Cl HEST TW5 15 L2
NRWD SE19 32 C7
Brunel Pl CRAWE RH10 165 G5
Brunel Wk WHTN TW2 25 K1
Brunner Ct CHERT KT16 57 M4
Brunswick BRAK RG12 34 D7
Brunswick Cl CRAWE RH10 165 J6
THDIT KT7 44 C8
WHTN TW2 26 A4
WOT/HER KT12 60 F1
Brunswick Dr CHOB/PIR GU24 95 G2
Brunswick Gv COB KT11 80 F3
Brunswick Ms STRHM/NOR SW16 31 G7
Brunswick Pl NRWD SE19 32 D8
Brunswick Rd CHOB/PIR GU24 95 G3
FRIM GU16 93 M3
KUTN/CMB KT2 9 J4
SUT SM1 65 L3
Bruntile Cl FARN GU14 93 G8
Brushfield Wy WOKN/KNAP GU21 75 M8
Brushwood Rd HORS RH12 167 L3
Bruton Rd MRDN SM4 47 M4
Bruton Wy BRAK RG12 35 H7
Bryan Cl SUN TW16 24 D8
Bryanston Av WHTN TW2 25 L2
Bryanstone Av GUW GU2 116 C4
Bryanstone Cl GUW GU2 116 C5
Bryanstone Gv GUW GU2 116 C4
Bryce Cl HORS RH12 167 K4
Bryce Gdns ALDT GU11 134 F2
Bryden Cl SYD SE26 33 H6
Brympton Cl DORK RH4 144 D4
Brynford Cl WOKN/KNAP GU21 10 D1
Bryn Rd RFNM GU10 155 J2
Bryony Rd GU GU1 117 L5
Bryony Wy SUN TW16 24 D7
Buchans Lawn CRAWW RH11 164 D8
The Buchan CBLY GU15 73 K1
Bucharest Rd WAND/EARL SW18 29 M1
Buckfast Rd MRDN SM4 47 L4
Buckham Thorns Rd BH/WHM TN16 111 M8
Buckhurst Av CAR SM5 48 B8
Buckhurst Cl EGRIN RH19 162 D2
REDH RH1 126 B6
Buckhurst Hl BRAK RG12 35 J4
Buckhurst La ASC SL5 37 J3
Buckhurst Rd ASC SL5 37 J2
BH/WHM TN16 111 L3
FRIM GU16 93 J3
Buckhurst Wy EGRIN RH19 162 D2
Buckingham Av E/WMO/HCT KT8 43 L2
EBED/NFELT TW14 15 L8
THHTH CR7 49 K1
Buckingham Cl GU GU1 7 M2
HPTN TW12 25 J6
Buckingham Ct BELMT SM2 * 65 K7
Buckingham Dr EGRIN RH19 163 H6
Buckingham Gdns E/WMO/HCT KT8 43 L2
THHTH CR7 49 K2
Buckingham Ga HORL RH6 160 F6
Buckingham La FSTH SE23 33 H1
Buckingham Rd HPTN TW12 25 J5
KUT/HW KT1 45 J4
MTCM CR4 49 H5
RCHPK/HAM TW10 27 G3
RDKG RH5 173 K2
Buckingham Wy FRIM GU16 93 J1
WLGTN SM6 66 F7
Buckland Cl FARN GU14 92 F2
Buckland La BRKHM/BTCW RH3 124 E5
Buckland Rd BELMT SM2 64 F8
CHSGTN KT9 63 J4
KWD/TDW/WH KT20 125 J3
REIG RH2 125 G7
Bucklands Rd TEDD TW11 26 F7
Bucklands Whf KUT/HW KT1 * 8 D6
Buckland Wk MRDN SM4 47 M4
Buckland Wy WPK KT4 46 F8
Bucklebury BRAK RG12 34 D7
Buckleigh Av RYNPK SW20 47 J3
Buckleigh Rd STRHM/NOR SW16 31 G7
Buckleigh Wy NRWD SE19 * 32 C8
Bucklers' Wy CAR SM5 66 C2
Buckles Wy BNSTD SM7 85 H6
Buckley Pl CRAWE RH10 193 M5
Buckmans Rd CRAWW RH11 164 F4
Bucknall Wy BECK BR3 51 M4
Bucknills Cl EPSOM KT18 83 M4
Bucks Cl BF/WBF KT14 78 E4
Buckswood Dr CRAWW RH11 164 C6
Budebury Rd STA TW18 22 C6
Budge La MTCM CR4 48 C7
Budgen Cl CRAWE RH10 165 M1
Budgen Dr REDH RH1 126 D5
Budham Wy BRAK RG12 34 E6
Buff Av BNSTD SM7 85 L5
Buffbeards La HASM GU27 197 R6
Buffers La LHD/OX KT22 102 D1
Bug Hl WARL CR6 109 G2
Bugkingham Wy FRIM GU16 73 J8
Bulganak Rd THHTH CR7 49 M4
Bulkeley Cl EGH TW20 20 F6
Bullard Rd TEDD TW11 * 26 C7
Bullbeggars La GDST RH9 128 F6
WOKN/KNAP GU21 76 E6
Bullbrook Dr BRAK RG12 35 H1
Bullbrook Rw BRAK RG12 35 H2
Buller Ct FARN GU14 92 F8
Buller Rd ALDT GU11 112 E5
THHTH CR7 50 A3
Bullers Rd FNM GU9 134 B3
Bullfinch Cl HORL RH6 160 B2
HORS RH12 166 F2
SHST GU47 72 B1
Bullfinch Rd SAND/SEL CR2 69 G8
Bull Hl LHD/OX KT22 102 D3
Bull La BNFD RG42 34 E1
RGUE GU4 97 J8
Bullrush Cl CAR SM5 66 B1
CROY/NA CR0 50 B6
Bulls Aly MORT/ESHN SW14 * 19 G5
Bullswater Common Rd CHOB/PIR GU24 95 K7
Bulstrode Av HSLW TW3 16 C5
Bulstrode Gdns HSLW TW3 16 D5
Bulstrode Rd HSLW TW3 16 D5
Bunbury Wy EW KT17 84 E6
Bunce Common Rd REIG RH2 146 A7
Bunce Dr CTHM CR3 108 A5
Bunch La HASM GU27 198 B6
Bunch Wy HASM GU27 198 B7
Bundys Wy STA TW18 22 C7
Bungalow Rd FARN GU14 92 E7
SNWD SE25 50 B4
The Bungalows STRHM/NOR SW16 30 E8
Bunting Cl MTCM CR4 48 C5
SWTR RH13 167 J6
The Buntings FNM GU9 4 D9
Bunyan Cl CRAWW RH11 164 A7
Bunyard Dr WOKN/KNAP GU21 77 M4
Burbage Gn BRAK RG12 35 J5
Burbeach Cl CRAWW RH11 164 D7
Burberry Cl NWMAL KT3 46 B2
Burbidge Rd SHPTN TW17 41 K4
Burbury Woods CBLY GU15 73 H3
Burchets Hollow SHGR GU5 171 J2
Burchetts Wy SHPTN TW17 41 L6
Burcote WEY KT13 60 A5
Burcote Rd WAND/EARL SW18 30 A2
Burcott Gdns ADL/WDHM KT15 59 G5
Burcott Rd PUR/KEN CR8 87 K4
Burdenshot Hl RGUW GU3 96 D7
Burdenshott Av RCHPK/HAM TW10 18 E6
Burdenshott Rd RGUW GU3 96 D6
Burden Wy GUW GU2 116 E3
Burdett Av RYNPK SW20 46 D1
Burdett Cl CRAWE RH10 165 M5
Burdett Rd CROY/NA CR0 50 A6
RCH/KEW TW9 18 C4
Burdock Cl CRAWW RH11 164 C8
CROY/NA CR0 51 G8
LTWR GU18 74 E1
Burdon La BELMT SM2 65 J7
Burdon Pk BELMT SM2 65 J7
Burfield Cl TOOT SW17 29 M5
Burfield Dr WARL CR6 108 F1
Burfield Rd WDSR SL4 20 D1
Burford La EW KT17 84 F1
Burford Lea MFD/CHID GU8 158 B5
Burford Rd CAT SE6 33 J3
CBLY GU15 72 E5
SUT SM1 65 K1
SWTR RH13 167 H7
WPK KT4 46 D7
Burford Wy CROY/NA CR0 69 M6
Burges Gv BARN SW13 19 L2
Burges Rd STA TW18 22 D7
Burgess Cl FELT TW13 25 H5
Burgess Rd SUT SM1 65 L3
Burges Wy STA TW18 22 D6
Burgh Cl CRAWE RH10 165 M1
Burghead Cl SHST GU47 72 A2
Burghfield EW KT17 84 C5
Burgh Heath Rd EW KT17 84 C5
Burgh Hill Rd LIPH GU30 196 E6
Burghill Rd SYD SE26 33 G5
Burghley Av NWMAL KT3 46 A1
Burghley Hall Cl WIM/MER SW19 * 29 H2
Burghley Pl MTCM CR4 48 C4
Burghley Rd WIM/MER SW19 29 H5
Burgh Mt BNSTD SM7 85 J5
Burgh Wd BNSTD SM7 85 H5
Burgos Cl CROY/NA CR0 67 K5
Burgoyne Rd CBLY GU15 73 K3
SNWD SE25 50 C4
SUN TW16 24 C7
Burham Cl PGE/AN SE20 32 F8
Burhill Rd WOT/HER KT12 60 F7
Burke Cl PUT/ROE SW15 19 H6
Burlands CRAWW RH11 164 C1
Burlea Cl WOT/HER KT12 60 E4
Burleigh Av WLGTN SM6 66 D2
Burleigh Cl ADL/WDHM KT15 58 E4
CRAWE RH10 193 N5
Burleigh Gdns ASHF TW15 23 M6
WOKN/KNAP GU21 * 10 F4
Burleigh La ASC SL5 36 B1
CRAWE RH10 193 P6
Burleigh Pk COB KT11 81 H2
Burleigh Rd ADL/WDHM KT15 58 E3
ASC SL5 36 C1
CHEAM SM3 47 H8
FRIM GU16 93 G1
Burleigh Wk CAT SE6 33 M2
Burleigh Wy CRAWE RH10 193 N5
Burley Cl BIL RH14 201 R5
STRHM/NOR SW16 49 G2
Burleys Rd CRAWE RH10 165 M4
Burlingham Cl RGUE GU4 118 A6
The Burlings ASC SL5 36 B2
Burlington Av RCH/KEW TW9 18 D3
Burlington Cl EBED/NFELT TW14 24 A1
ORP BR6 71 L1
Burlington Ct ALDT GU11 112 C8
Burlington La CHSWK W4 18 F2
Burlington Pl REIG RH2 125 K7
Burlington Rd ISLW TW7 17 G3
NWMAL KT3 46 C4
THHTH CR7 49 M2
Burlsdon Wy BRAK RG12 35 H1
Burma Rd CHERT KT16 56 C1
Burma Ter NRWD SE19 * 32 B6
Burmester Rd TOOT SW17 29 M4
Burnaby Crs CHSWK W4 18 E1
Burnaby Gdns CHSWK W4 18 E1
Burnbury Rd BAL SW12 30 F2
Burn Cl ADL/WDHM KT15 59 G3
LHD/OX KT22 81 M5
Burne-Jones Dr SHST GU47 72 A3
Burnell Av RCHPK/HAM TW10 26 F6
Burnell Rd SUT SM1 65 L3
Burnet Av GU GU1 117 L5
Burnet Cl CHOB/PIR GU24 75 H3
Burnet Gv HOR/WEW KT19 83 M3
Burney Av BRYLDS KT5 45 J5
Burney Cl LHD/OX KT22 101 M7
Burney Rd RDKG RH5 122 D5
Burnham Cl WOKN/KNAP GU21 76 A8
Burnham Dr REIG RH2 125 K7
WPK KT4 65 G1
Burnham Gdns CROY/NA CR0 3 K2
HSLWW TW4 15 L3
Burnham Pl SWTR RH13 * 167 G8
Burnham Rd MRDN SM4 47 L5
WOKN/KNAP GU21 76 A8
Burnhams Rd GT/LBKH KT23 101 H6
Burnham St KUTN/CMB KT2 9 J5
Burnham Wy SYD SE26 33 J6
Burnhill Rd BECK BR3 51 K2
Burn Moor Cha BRAK RG12 35 H7
Burnsall Cl FARN GU14 92 E3
Burns Av EBED/NFELT TW14 15 K8
Burns Cl CAR SM5 66 D7
FARN GU14 92 C3
HORS RH12 167 H2
WIM/MER SW19 30 A7
Burns Dr BNSTD SM7 85 H4
Burnside ASHTD KT21 83 J8
Burnside Cl TWK TW1 17 K8
Burns Rd CRAWE RH10 165 L2
Burns Wy EGRIN RH19 162 D4
HEST TW5 16 A3
HORS RH12 190 F12
Burnt Common Cl RPLY/SEND GU23 98 C7
Burntcommon La RPLY/SEND GU23 98 D7
Burnt Hill Rd RFNM GU10 155 K3
Burnt Hill Wy RFNM GU10 155 L4
Burnt House La HORS RH12 190 C6
Burnt Oak La RDKG RH5 174 B9
Burnt Pollard La LTWR GU18 55 H8
Burntwood Cl CTHM CR3 108 D3
WAND/EARL SW18 * 30 A2
Burntwood Grange Rd WAND/EARL SW18 30 A2
Burntwood La CTHM CR3 108 D3
TOOT SW17 30 A3
Burntwood Vw NRWD SE19 * 32 C6
Burnwood Park Rd WOT/HER KT12 60 E3
Burpham La RGUE GU4 117 K4
Burrell Cl CROY/NA CR0 51 H6
Burrell Rd FRIM GU16 92 F1
Burrell Rw BECK BR3 51 K2
The Burrell DORK RH4 143 M3
Burr Hill La CHOB/PIR GU24 56 B7
Burritt Rd KUT/HW KT1 9 J7
Burrow Hill Gn CHOB/PIR GU24 56 A7
Burrows Cl GT/LBKH KT23 101 J6
GUW GU2 116 C7
Burrows Hill Cl STWL/WRAY TW19 13 L6
Burrows La SHGR GU5 141 M6
Burr Rd WAND/EARL SW18 29 K2
Burrwood Gdns ASHV GU12 113 K5
Burstead Cl COB KT11 81 G3
Burston Gdns EGRIN RH19 162 E1
Burstow Rd RYNPK SW20 47 H1
Burtenshaw Rd THDIT KT7 44 D7
Burton Cl CHSGTN KT9 63 G6
HORL RH6 160 D4
THHTH CR7 50 A3
Burton Gdns HEST TW5 16 C3
Burton Rd KUTN/CMB KT2 8 F3
Burtons Ct HORS RH12 * 166 F7
Burton's Rd HPTN TW12 25 L5
Burtwell La WNWD SE27 32 A5
Burwash Rd CRAWE RH10 165 J5
Burway Crs CHERT KT16 40 D4
Burwood Av HAYES BR2 70 E1
PUR/KEN CR8 87 L4
Burwood Cl GU GU1 117 M7
REIG RH2 126 A8
SURB KT6 45 K8
WOT/HER KT12 60 F5
Burwood Rd WEY KT13 60 A6
Bury Cl WOKN/KNAP GU21 10 A4
Bury Flds GUW GU2 6 F8
Bury Gv MRDN SM4 47 L5
Bury La WOKN/KNAP GU21 76 F6
Bury Ms GUW GU2 * 6 F8
The Burys GODL GU7 168 B4
Bury St GUW GU2 6 F8
Busbridge La GODL GU7 168 B6
Busch Cl ISLW TW7 17 L3
Busdens Cl MFD/CHID GU8 183 N1
Busdens La MFD/CHID GU8 183 N1
Busdens Wy MFD/CHID GU8 183 N1
Bushbury La BRKHM/BTCW RH3 145 K5
Bush Cl ADL/WDHM KT15 58 F4
Bushell Cl BRXS/STRHM SW2 31 J3
Bushetts Gv REDH RH1 126 E3
Bushey Cl PUR/KEN CR8 88 C6
Bushey Cft OXTED RH8 129 M4
Bushey La SUT SM1 65 K2
Bushey Rd CROY/NA CR0 69 K1
RYNPK SW20 46 F2
SUT SM1 65 L3
Bushfield BIL RH14 201 J7
Bushfield Dr REDH RH1 148 D5
Bush La RPLY/SEND GU23 98 A6
Bushnell Rd TOOT SW17 30 E3
Bush Rd RCH/KEW TW9 18 C1
SHPTN TW17 41 J5
Bushwood Rd RCH/KEW TW9 18 D1
Bushy Hill Dr GU GU1 117 M7
Bushy Park Gdns HPTN TW12 26 A6
Bushy Park Rd TEDD TW11 26 E8
Bushy Rd LHD/OX KT22 101 L4
TEDD TW11 26 B7
Bushy Shaw ASHTD KT21 82 F7
Busk Crs FARN GU14 92 C6
Butchers Yd ORP BR6 91 K1
Bute Av RCHPK/HAM TW10 27 H3
Bute Gdns RCHPK/HAM TW10 * 27 H2
WLGTN SM6 66 F4
Bute Gdns West WLGTN SM6 66 F4
Bute Rd CROY/NA CR0 49 K8

WLGTN SM6 66 F3
Butler Rd *BAGS* GU19 54 C7
Butlers Cl *HSLWW* TW4 16 C6
Butlers Dene Rd *CTHM* CR3 109 J2
Butlers Hl *EHSLY* KT24 119 L4
Butlers Rd *SWTR* RH13 167 K5
Butt Cl *CRAN* GU6 186 D1
Buttercup Cl *BOR* GU35 180 B12
Buttercup Sq
STWL/WRAY TW19 * 23 G2
Butterfield *CBLY* GU15 72 E5
EGRIN RH19 162 C2
Butterfield Cl *TWK* TW1 17 J8
Butterfly Wk *WARL* CR6 108 F2
Butter Hl *CAR* SM5 66 D2
DORK RH4 144 D2
Buttermer Cl *RFNM* GU10 155 H2
Buttermere Cl
EBED/NFELT TW14 24 C2
FARN GU14 92 B5
HORS RH12 167 L3
MRDN SM4 47 G6
Buttermere Ct *ASHV* GU12 * 113 J5
Buttermere Dr *CBLY* GU15 74 A5
Buttermere Gdns *BRAK* RG12 34 F3
PUR/KEN CR8 88 A3
Buttermere Wy *EGH* TW20 21 L8
Buttersteep Ri *ASC* SL5 35 M8
Butts Cl *CRAWW* RH11 164 D3
Butts Crs *FELT* TW13 25 K4
Butts Rd *WOKN/KNAP* GU21 10 C7
The Butts *BTFD* TW8 18 A1
Buxton Av *CTHM* CR3 108 B3
Buxton Crs *CHEAM* SM3 65 H3
Buxton Dr *NWMAL* KT3 46 A2
Buxton La *CTHM* CR3 108 B3
Buxton Rd *ASHF* TW15 23 G6
MORT/ESHN SW14 19 H5
THHTH CR7 49 L5
Byards Cft *STRHM/NOR* SW16 49 G1
Bychurch End *TEDD* TW11 * 26 C6
Bycroft St *PGE/AN* SE20 33 G8
Bycroft Wy *CRAWE* RH10 165 K2
Byerley Wy *CRAWE* RH10 192 D6
Byers La *GDST* RH9 150 F8
Bye Ways *WHTN* TW2 25 L4
The Byeways *BRYLDS* KT5 45 K5
The Byeway *MORT/ESHN* SW14 18 F5
Byfeld Gdns *BARN* SW13 19 K3
Byfield Rd *ISLW* TW7 17 K5
Byfleet Rd *ADL/WDHM* KT15 59 G7
COB KT11 79 L2
Byfleets La *HORS* RH12 166 A4
Bygrove *CROY/NA* CR0 69 L5
Bygrove Rd *WIM/MER* SW19 30 A7
Byland Cl *CAR* SM5 47 M7
Bylands *WOKS/MYFD* GU22 11 G9
Byne Rd *CAR* SM5 66 B1
SYD SE26 32 F7
Bynes Rd *SAND/SEL* CR2 68 A6
By Pass Rd *LHD/OX* KT22 102 E2
Byrd Rd *CRAWW* RH11 164 B7
Byrefield Rd *GUW* GU2 116 C5
Byrne Rd *BAL* SW12 30 E2
Byron Av *CBLY* GU15 73 L6
COUL/CHIP CR5 87 H5
HSLWW TW4 15 L4
NWMAL KT3 46 D5
SUT SM1 66 A3
Byron Av East *SUT* SM1 66 A3
Byron Cl *CRAWE* RH10 165 K3
HORS RH12 167 H3
HPTN TW12 25 J5
PGE/AN SE20 * 50 E3
SYD SE26 * 33 H5
WOKN/KNAP GU21 76 B7
WOT/HER KT12 43 H8
Byron Gdns *SUT* SM1 66 A3
Byron Gv *EGRIN* RH19 162 D5
Byron Pl *LHD/OX* KT22 102 E4
Byron Rd *ADL/WDHM* KT15 59 G3
SAND/SEL CR2 68 E8
Byton Rd *TOOT* SW17 30 C7
Byttom Hl *RDKG* RH5 122 F1
Byward Av *EBED/NFELT* TW14 15 M8
The Byways *HOR/WEW* KT19 64 C3
The Byway *BELMT* SM2 66 A7
Bywood *BRAK* RG12 34 D7
Bywood Av *CROY/NA* CR0 50 F6
Bywood Cl *PUR/KEN* CR8 87 L5
Byworth Cl *FNM* GU9 4 D3
Byworth Rd *FNM* GU9 4 D4

C

Cabbell Pl *ADL/WDHM* KT15 58 F3
Cabell Rd *GUW* GU2 116 B7
Caberfeigh Cl *REDH* RH1 126 B8
Caberfeigh Pl *REDH* RH1 * 126 A8
Cabin Moss *BRAK* RG12 35 H7
Cabrera Av *VW* GU25 39 G5
Cabrera Cl *VW* GU25 38 F6
Cabrol Rd *FARN* GU14 92 D4
Caburn Ct *CRAWW* RH11 164 E6
Caburn Hts *CRAWW* RH11 164 E6
The Cackstones
CRAWE RH10 * 165 M3
Cadbury Cl *ISLW* TW7 17 K3
SUN TW16 24 B8
Cadbury Rd *SUN* TW16 24 B8
Caddy Cl *EGH* TW20 21 K6
Cadmer Cl *NWMAL* KT3 46 B4
Cadnam Cl *ALDT* GU11 134 F3
Cadogan Cl *TEDD* TW11 26 B6
Cadogan Ct *BELMT* SM2 65 L5
Cadogan Pl *PUR/KEN* CR8 87 M7
Cadogan Rd *ALDT* GU11 113 G2
SURB KT6 45 G5
Caenshill Ga *WEY* KT13 59 K6
Caenshill Rd *WEY* KT13 59 K6
Caenswood Hl *WEY* KT13 59 K8
Caenwood Cl *WEY* KT13 59 K5
Caen Wood Rd *ASHTD* KT21 82 F8
Caerleon Cl *ESH/CLAY* KT10 62 E6
GSHT GU26 181 P11
Caernarvon *FRIM* GU16 93 J1
Caernarvon Cl *MTCM* CR4 49 H3
Caesar's Camp Rd *CBLY* GU15 73 K1
Caesar's Cl *CBLY* GU15 73 K1
Caesars Wk *MTCM* CR4 48 C5
Caesar's Wy *SHPTN* TW17 42 A6
Caffins Cl *CRAWE* RH10 165 G2
Cage Yd *REIG* RH2 * 125 K8
Caillard Rd *BF/WBF* KT14 79 G1
Cain Rd *BNFD* RG42 34 B2
Cain's La *EBED/NFELT* TW14 15 G7
Cairn Cl *CBLY* GU15 73 L6
Cairngorm Pl *FARN* GU14 92 B2
Cairo New Rd *CROY/NA* CR0 2 B6
Caistor Rd *BAL* SW12 30 E1
Caithness Dr *EPSOM* KT18 84 A4
Caithness Rd *MTCM* CR4 30 E8
Calbourne Rd *BAL* SW12 30 C1
Caldbeck Av *WPK* KT4 64 E1
Calderdale Cl *CRAWW* RH11 164 D6
Calder Rd *MRDN* SM4 47 M5
Calder Wy *DTCH/LGLY* SL3 13 H5
Caldwell Rd *BFOR* GU20 55 G4
Caledonian Wy *HORL* RH6 * 160 E6
Caledonia Rd
STWL/WRAY TW19 23 H2
Caledon Pl *RGUE* GU4 117 K5
Caledon Rd *WLGTN* SM6 66 D3
Calfridus Wy *BRAK* RG12 35 H3
California Cl *BELMT* SM2 65 K8
California Rd *NWMAL* KT3 45 M4
Callander Rd *CAT* SE6 33 L3
Calley Down Crs *CROY/NA* CR0 70 A8
Callis Farm Cl
STWL/WRAY TW19 14 B8
Callisto Cl *CRAWW* RH11 164 A7
Callow Fld *PUR/KEN* CR8 87 K3
Callow Hl *VW* GU25 38 F2
Calluna Ct *WOKS/MYFD* GU22 10 E7
Calluna Dr *CRAWE* RH10 192 F3
Calonne Rd *WIM/MER* SW19 29 G5
Calshot Rd *HTHAIR* TW6 14 E4
Calshot Wy *FRIM* GU16 93 K2
HTHAIR TW6 14 D4
Calthorpe Gdns *SUT* SM1 65 M2
Calton Gdns *ALDT* GU11 134 F2
Calvecroft *LIPH* GU30 196 H9
Calverley Cl *BECK* BR3 33 L7
Calverley Rd *EW* KT17 64 D5
Calvert Cl *ASHV* GU12 113 G8
Calvert Crs *DORK* RH4 122 E8
Calvert Rd *DORK* RH4 122 E8
EHSLY KT24 120 E2
Calvin Cl *CBLY* GU15 73 L5
Camac Rd *WHTN* TW2 26 A2
Camber Cl *CRAWE* RH10 165 L4
Camberley Av *RYNPK* SW20 46 E2
Camberley Cl *CHEAM* SM3 65 G2
Camberley Rd *HTHAIR* TW6 14 D5
Camborne Cl *HTHAIR* TW6 14 D5
Camborne Crs *HTHAIR* TW6 14 D5
Camborne Ms
WAND/EARL SW18 29 K1
Camborne Rd *BELMT* SM2 65 K6
CROY/NA CR0 3 L2
MRDN SM4 47 G6
WAND/EARL SW18 29 K1
Camborne Wy *HEST* TW5 16 D3
Cambray Rd *BAL* SW12 30 F2
Cambria Cl *HSLW* TW3 16 D6
Cambria Ct *EBED/NFELT* TW14 24 E1
Cambria Gdns
STWL/WRAY TW19 23 H1
Cambrian Cl *CBLY* GU15 72 E4
WNWD SE27 31 L4
Cambrian Rd *FARN* GU14 92 A2
RCHPK/HAM TW10 18 C8
Cambridge Av *NWMAL* KT3 46 C2
Cambridge Cl *HSLWW* TW4 16 B6
RYNPK SW20 46 E1
WDR/YW UB7 14 A1
WOKN/KNAP GU21 76 C8
Cambridge Crs *TEDD* TW11 * 26 D6
Cambridge Gdns *KUT/HW* KT1 9 J7
Cambridge Gv *PGE/AN* SE20 * 50 E1
Cambridge Grove Rd
KUT/HW KT1 9 J7
Cambridge Lodge Pk
HORL RH6 * 175 R3
Cambridge Pk *TWK* TW1 27 G1
Cambridge Rd *ALDT* GU11 112 C7
ASHF TW15 23 M8
BARN SW13 19 J4
CAR SM5 66 B5
E/WMO/HCT KT8 43 J4
HPTN TW12 25 J8
HSLWW TW4 16 B6
KUT/HW KT1 9 J7
MTCM CR4 48 F3
NWMAL KT3 46 A4
PGE/AN SE20 50 D3
RCH/KEW TW9 18 D2
RYNPK SW20 46 E1
SHST GU47 52 B8
SWTR RH13 167 G7
TEDD TW11 26 D5
TWK TW1 18 A8
WOT/HER KT12 42 E6
Cambridge Rd East *FARN* GU14 92 F8
Cambridge Rd West *FARN* GU14 92 F8
Cambridge Sq *REDH* RH1 148 D3
Camden Av *FELT* TW13 24 F3
Camden Gdns *SUT* SM1 65 L4
THHTH CR7 49 L3
Camden Hill Rd *NRWD* SE19 32 B7
Camden Rd *CAR* SM5 66 C3
LING RH7 178 E6
SUT SM1 65 L4
Camden Wy *THHTH* CR7 49 L3
Camel Gv *KUT/CMB* KT2 27 G6
Camellia Ct *CHOB/PIR* GU24 75 J3
Camellia Pl *WHTN* TW2 25 L1
Camelot Cl *BH/WHM* TN16 90 F6
WIM/MER SW19 29 J5
Camelsdale Rd *HASM* GU27 198 A8
Camel Wy *FARN* GU14 112 D1
Cameron Cl *CRAN* GU6 186 D4
Cameron Pl *STRHM/NOR* SW16 31 K4
Cameron Rd *ALDT* GU11 113 G2
CAT SE6 * 33 J3
CROY/NA CR0 49 L6
Camilla Cl *GT/LBKH* KT23 101 L7
SUN TW16 * 24 B7
Camilla Dr *RDKG* RH5 122 D4
Camille Cl *SNWD* SE25 50 D3
Camm Gdns *KUT/HW* KT1 9 H6
THDIT KT7 44 B7
Camomile Av *MTCM* CR4 48 C1
Campbell Av *WOKS/MYFD* GU22 97 J3
Campbell Cl *ALDT* GU11 134 E2
BF/WBF KT14 79 G1
STRHM/NOR SW16 * 31 G6
WHTN TW2 26 A2
Campbell Crs *EGRIN* RH19 162 C4
Campbell Pl *FRIM* GU16 73 J6
Campbell Rd *ALDT* GU11 112 D6
CRAWE RH10 165 L6
CROY/NA CR0 2 A1
CTHM CR3 108 A3
WEY KT13 59 K6
WHTN TW2 26 A3
Campden Rd *SAND/SEL* CR2 68 B4
Campen Cl *WIM/MER* SW19 29 H3
Camp End Rd *WEY* KT13 79 M1
Camp Farm Rd *ALDT* GU11 113 G4
Camp Hl *RFNM* GU10 156 F1
Camphill Ct *BF/WBF* KT14 78 D2
Camphill Rd *BF/WBF* KT14 78 D2
Campion Cl *BLKW* GU17 72 C6
BOR GU35 196 B1
CROY/NA CR0 68 B3
Campion Dr
KWD/TDW/WH KT20 104 E2
Campion Rd *ISLW* TW7 17 J3
PUT/ROE SW15 19 M6
Camp Rd *CTHM* CR3 109 H3
FARN GU14 112 F1
WIM/MER SW19 28 F6
Camp Vw *WIM/MER* SW19 28 E6
Camrose Av *FELT* TW13 24 E5
Camrose Cl *CROY/NA* CR0 51 H7
MRDN SM4 47 K4
Canada Av *REDH* RH1 148 D4
Canada Copse *MFD/CHID* GU8 159 H7
Canada Dr *REDH* RH1 148 D4
Canada Rd *BF/WBF* KT14 79 G1
COB KT11 80 F3
FRIM GU16 94 A1
Canada Wy *LIPH* GU30 196 H10
Canadian Av *CAT* SE6 33 L2
Canal Cl *ALDT* GU11 113 G4
Canal Wk *CROY/NA* CR0 50 B6
Canberra Cl *CRAWW* RH11 164 F1
HORS RH12 167 J5
Canberra Pl *HORS* RH12 * 167 J4
Canberra Rd *HTHAIR* TW6 14 D5
Canberra Wy *FARN* GU14 112 C1
Canbury Av *KUTN/CMB* KT2 9 G5
Canbury Ms *SYD* SE26 32 D4
Canbury Park Rd *KUTN/CMB* KT2 9 G5
Candleford Ga *LIPH* GU30 * 196 G9
Candler Ms *TWK* TW1 26 D1
Candlerush Cl
WOKS/MYFD GU22 11 K5
Candover Cl *WDR/YW* UB7 14 A2
Candy Cft *GT/LBKH* KT23 101 L8
Canes La *BOR* GU35 180 A12
Canewden Cl
WOKS/MYFD GU22 10 D9
Canford Dr *ADL/WDHM* KT15 58 E1
Canford Gdns *NWMAL* KT3 46 B6
Canford Pl *TEDD* TW11 8 A1
Canham Rd *SNWD* SE25 50 B3
Can Hatch *KWD/TDW/WH* KT20 85 H8
Canmore Gdns
STRHM/NOR SW16 30 F8
Canning Rd *ASHV* GU12 113 G7
CROY/NA CR0 3 J5
Cannizaro Rd *WIM/MER* SW19 28 F7
Cannon Cl *HPTN* TW12 25 L7
RYNPK SW20 46 F3
SHST GU47 72 C1
Cannon Crs *CHOB/PIR* GU24 76 B1
Cannon Gv *LHD/OX* KT22 102 B4
Cannon Hl *BRAK* RG12 34 F6
Cannon Hill La *RYNPK* SW20 47 G5
Cannon Side *LHD/OX* KT22 102 B4
Cannon Wy *E/WMO/HCT* KT8 43 K4
LHD/OX KT22 102 B3
Canonbie Rd *FSTH* SE23 32 F1
Canons Cl *REIG* RH2 125 J7
Canon's Hl *COUL/CHIP* CR5 87 K8
Canons La
KWD/TDW/WH KT20 105 H1
Canon's Wk *CROY/NA* CR0 69 G2
Canopus Wy *STWL/WRAY* TW19 23 H1
Cansiron La *EGRIN* RH19 195 Q8
Cantelupe Ms *EGRIN* RH19 * 162 F4
Canterbury Cl *BECK* BR3 51 L1
WPK KT4 65 G1
Canterbury Ct *DORK* RH4 * 144 D1
Canterbury Gv *WNWD* SE27 31 L4
Canterbury Rd *ASHV* GU12 113 K6
CRAWE RH10 165 G8
CROY/NA CR0 49 J7
FARN GU14 93 G7
FELT TW13 25 H3
GUW GU2 116 C6
MRDN SM4 47 M6
The Canter *CRAWE* RH10 192 D6
Cantley Gdns *NRWD* SE19 50 C1
Canvey Cl *CRAWW* RH11 164 E7
Cape Copse *HORS* RH12 203 J2
Capel Av *WLGTN* SM6 67 J4
Capel La *CRAWW* RH11 164 B5
Capel Rd *HORS* RH12 189 R4
Capern Rd *WAND/EARL* SW18 29 M2
Capper Rd *CBLY* GU15 72 D2
Capricorn Cl *CRAWW* RH11 164 A6
Capri Rd *CROY/NA* CR0 3 K2
Capsey Rd *CRAWW* RH11 164 A5
Capstans Whf
WOKN/KNAP GU21 76 C8
Caradon Cl *WOKN/KNAP* GU21 76 E8
Caraway Cl *CRAWW* RH11 164 D8
Caraway Pl *GUW* GU2 116 D3
WLGTN SM6 * 66 E2
Carberry Rd *NRWD* SE19 32 B7
Carbery La *ASC* SL5 36 E3
Cardamom Cl *GUW* GU2 116 D4
Card Hl *FROW* RH18 195 N12
Cardigan Cl *WOKN/KNAP* GU21 76 B8
Cardigan Rd *BARN* SW13 19 K4
RCHPK/HAM TW10 18 B8
WIM/MER SW19 29 M7
Cardinal Av *KUTN/CMB* KT2 27 H6
MRDN SM4 47 H6
Cardinal Cl *MRDN* SM4 47 H6
SAND/SEL CR2 88 D3
WPK KT4 64 D3
Cardinal Crs *NWMAL* KT3 45 M2
Cardinal Dr *WOT/HER* KT12 43 G8
Cardinal Rd *FELT* TW13 24 E2
The Cardinals *BRAK* RG12 * 34 E4
RFNM GU10 135 J2
Cardinal's Wk *HPTN* TW12 25 M8
SUN TW16 24 B7
Cardingham *WOKN/KNAP* GU21 76 D7
Cardington Sq *HSLWW* TW4 16 A6
Cardwell Crs *ASC* SL5 36 F5
Cardwells Keep *GUW* GU2 116 D5
Carew Cl *COUL/CHIP* CR5 107 L1
Carew Rd *ASHF* TW15 23 M7
MTCM CR4 48 D2
THHTH CR7 49 L3
WLGTN SM6 66 F5
Careys Copse *HORL* RH6 * 161 L2
Carey's Wd *HORL* RH6 161 L3
Carfax *HORS* RH12 166 F7
Carfax Av *RFNM* GU10 135 J1
Cargate Av *ALDT* GU11 112 D8
Cargate Gv *ALDT* GU11 112 C8
Cargate Hl *ALDT* GU11 112 C8
Cargate Ter *ALDT* GU11 112 C8
Cargill Rd *WAND/EARL* SW18 29 M2
Cargo Forecourt Rd
HORL RH6 160 A7
Cargo Rd *HORL* RH6 160 A6
Cargreen Rd *SNWD* SE25 50 C4
Carholme Rd *FSTH* SE23 33 J2
Carisbrooke *FRIM* GU16 93 J1
Carisbrooke Cl *HSLWW* TW4 25 H2
Carisbrooke Rd *MTCM* CR4 49 H4
Carleton Av *WLGTN* SM6 67 G7
Carleton Cl *ESH/CLAY* KT10 44 A8
Carlingford Rd *MRDN* SM4 47 G6
Carlin Pl *CBLY* GU15 72 F5
Carlinwark Dr *CBLY* GU15 73 J2
Carlisle Cl *KUTN/CMB* KT2 9 K4
Carlisle Rd *HPTN* TW12 25 L8
RFNM GU10 181 N2
SUT SM1 65 J5
Carlisle Wy *TOOT* SW17 30 D6
Carlos St *GODL* GU7 168 B5
Carlton Av *EBED/NFELT* TW14 15 M8
SAND/SEL CR2 68 A6
Carlton Cl *CBLY* GU15 73 L6
CHSGTN KT9 63 G5
WOKN/KNAP GU21 77 J4
Carlton Ct *HORL* RH6 * 160 E1
Carlton Crs *CHEAM* SM3 65 H3
Carlton Dene *EW* KT17 * 64 E4
Carlton Gn *REDH* RH1 126 B5
Carlton Park Av *RYNPK* SW20 46 F2
Carlton Pl *WEY* KT13 * 59 L3
Carlton Rd *BOR* GU35 196 H1
GDST RH9 150 F7
MORT/ESHN SW14 18 F5
NWMAL KT3 46 B2
REIG RH2 126 A6
SAND/SEL CR2 68 A6
SUN TW16 24 C8
WOKN/KNAP GU21 77 K4
WOT/HER KT12 42 E7
Carlton Ter *SYD* SE26 32 F4
Carlton Tye *HORL* RH6 161 G3
Carlwell St *TOOT* SW17 30 B6
Carlyle Cl *E/WMO/HCT* KT8 43 L2
Carlyle Rd *CROY/NA* CR0 3 M5
STA TW18 22 C8
Carlyon Cl *FARN* GU14 92 F5
FRIM GU16 93 J5
Carlys Cl *BECK* BR3 51 G2
Carmalt Gdns *PUT/ROE* SW15 19 M6
WOT/HER KT12 60 F4
Carmarthen Cl *FARN* GU14 92 C2
Carmel Cl *WOKS/MYFD* GU22 * 10 D8
Carmel Wy *RCH/KEW* TW9 18 D4
Carmichael Rd *SNWD* SE25 50 D5
Carminia Rd *TOOT* SW17 30 E3
Carmino Ter *LIPH* GU30 * 196 G9
Carnac St *WNWD* SE27 32 A5
Carnegie Cl *SURB* KT6 63 J1
Carnegie Pl *WIM/MER* SW19 29 G4
Carnforth Cl *HOR/WEW* KT19 63 L5
Carnforth Rd
STRHM/NOR SW16 31 G8
Carnoustie *BRAK* RG12 34 B7
Carolina Rd *THHTH* CR7 49 L2
Caroline Cl *CROY/NA* CR0 3 H9
STRHM/NOR SW16 31 J4
Caroline Ct *ASHF* TW15 23 L7
CRAWW RH11 164 F5
Caroline Pl *HYS/HAR* UB3 15 H2
Caroline Rd *WIM/MER* SW19 29 J8
Caroline Wy *FRIM* GU16 73 J8
Carolyn Cl *WOKN/KNAP* GU21 96 C1
Carrick Cl *ISLW* TW7 17 K5
Carrick Ga *ESH/CLAY* KT10 61 M2
Carrington Av *HSLW* TW3 16 E7
Carrington Cl *CROY/NA* CR0 51 H7
REDH RH1 126 C7
Carrington La *ASHV* GU12 113 J1
Carrington Pl *ESH/CLAY* KT10 * 61 L3
Carrington Rd
RCHPK/HAM TW10 18 D6
Carroll Av *GU* GU1 117 L8
Carroll Crs *ASC* SL5 36 C4
Carrow Rd *WOT/HER* KT12 61 G2
Carshalton Gv *SUT* SM1 66 A3
Carshalton Park Rd *CAR* SM5 66 C5
Carshalton Pl *CAR* SM5 66 D3
Carshalton Rd *BNSTD* SM7 86 C3
CBLY GU15 53 K8
MTCM CR4 48 D5
SUT SM1 65 M4
Carslake Rd *PUT/ROE* SW15 19 M8
Carson Rd *DUL* SE21 31 M3
Carstairs Rd *CAT* SE6 33 M4
Carswell Rd *CAT* SE6 33 M1
Cartbridge Cl *RPLY/SEND* GU23 97 L5
Carter Cl *WLGTN* SM6 67 G6
Carter Rd *CRAWE* RH10 165 M7
WIM/MER SW19 30 A7
Carters Cl *GU* GU1 117 H4
WPK KT4 65 G1
Carters La *WOKS/MYFD* GU22 97 M2
Cartersmead Cl *HORL* RH6 160 E2
Carter's Rd *EW* KT17 84 C5
Carters Wk *FNM* GU9 134 A1
Carthouse La
WOKN/KNAP GU21 76 B4
Cartmel Cl *REIG* RH2 126 B7
Cartmel Gdns *MRDN* SM4 47 M5
Cartwright Wy *BARN* SW13 19 L2
Cascades *CROY/NA* CR0 69 J8
Caselden Cl *ADL/WDHM* KT15 58 F4
Casewick Rd *WNWD* SE27 31 L6
Casher Rd *CRAWE* RH10 165 L7
Cassilis Rd *TWK* TW1 17 L8
Cassino Cl *ALDT* GU11 112 E7
Cassiobury Av
EBED/NFELT TW14 24 C1
Cassland Rd *THHTH* CR7 50 A4
Casslee Rd *CAT* SE6 33 J1
Castello Av *PUT/ROE* SW15 19 M7
Castelnau *BARN* SW13 19 L2
Castlands Rd *CAT* SE6 33 J3
Castle Av *EW* KT17 64 D7
Castle Cl *CBLY* GU15 73 J5
REDH RH1 127 M7
REIG RH2 147 L4
WIM/MER SW19 29 G4
Castlecombe Dr
WIM/MER SW19 29 G1
Castle Ct *SYD* SE26 33 H5
Castlecraig Ct *SHST* GU47 * 72 A2
Castledine Rd *PGE/AN* SE20 32 E8
Castle Dr *HORL* RH6 160 F5
REIG RH2 147 K4
Castle Fld *FNM* GU9 5 G2
Castlefield Rd *REIG* RH2 125 K7
Castle Gdns *DORK* RH4 123 J8
Castlegate *RCH/KEW* TW9 18 C5
Castle Gn *WEY* KT13 60 B2
Castle Grove Rd
CHOB/PIR GU24 76 B2
Castle Hl *FNM* GU9 5 G2
GU GU1 7 H8
Castle Hill Av *CROY/NA* CR0 69 L7
Castle Hill Rd *EGH* TW20 20 E5
Castlemaine Av *EW* KT17 64 E7
SAND/SEL CR2 68 C4
Castle Ms *TOOT* SW17 30 B5
Castle Pde *EW* KT17 * 64 D6
Castle Rd *ALDT* GU11 112 B5
CBLY GU15 73 J4
COUL/CHIP CR5 106 B2
EPSOM KT18 83 L5
HORS RH12 166 A6
ISLW TW7 17 J4
WEY KT13 60 B2
WOKN/KNAP GU21 77 J4
Castle Sq *REDH* RH1 127 M7
Castle St *FNM* GU9 5 H2
GU GU1 7 G7
KUT/HW KT1 8 E6
REDH RH1 127 L7
The Castle *HORS* RH12 167 H2
Castleton Cl *BNSTD* SM7 85 K5
CROY/NA CR0 51 H6
Castleton Dr *BNSTD* SM7 85 K5
Castleton Rd *MTCM* CR4 49 G4
Castle View Rd *WEY* KT13 59 L3
Castle Wk *SUN* TW16 * 42 F3
Castle Wy *EW* KT17 64 D8
FELT TW13 24 F5
WIM/MER SW19 29 G4
Castle Yd *RCH/KEW* TW9 18 A7
Caswell Cl *FARN* GU14 92 C3
Catalina Rd *HTHAIR* TW6 14 E5
Catalpa Cl *GU* GU1 * 116 F6
Catena Ri *LTWR* GU18 54 D8
Caterfield La *LING* RH7 152 C7
Cater Gdns *RGUW* GU3 116 B6
Caterham-By-Pass *CTHM* CR3 108 E4
Caterham Cl *CHOB/PIR* GU24 95 H3
Caterham Dr *COUL/CHIP* CR5 107 M1
Caterways *HORS* RH12 166 D6
Catford Broadway *CAT* SE6 33 L1
Catford Hl *CAT* SE6 33 J2
Catford Island *CAT* SE6 * 33 L1
Catford Rd *CAT* SE6 33 K2
Cathedral Cl *GUW* GU2 6 C5
Cathedral Hl *GUW* GU2 6 B2
Cathedral Vw *GUW* GU2 116 C8
Catherine Cl *BF/WBF* KT14 79 H4
Catherine Dr *RCH/KEW* TW9 18 B6
SUN TW16 24 C8
Catherine Gdns *HSLW* TW3 17 G6
Catherine Howard Ct
WEY KT13 * 59 L2
Catherine Rd *SURB* KT6 45 G5
Catherine Wheel Rd *BTFD* TW8 18 A2
Cathill La *RDKG* RH5 188 C2
Catlin Crs *SHPTN* TW17 42 A5
Catlin Gdns *GDST* RH9 128 E4
Catling Cl *FSTH* SE23 32 F4
Cator Cl *CROY/NA* CR0 90 B1
Cator Crs *CROY/NA* CR0 90 B1
Cator La *BECK* BR3 51 J2
Cator Rd *CAR* SM5 66 C4
SYD SE26 33 G7
Catteshall Hatch *GODL* GU7 168 D3
Catteshall La *GODL* GU7 168 D4
Catteshall Rd *GODL* GU7 168 D3
Causeway *EBED/NFELT* TW14 15 L6
The Causeway *BELMT* SM2 65 M7
CAR SM5 66 D2
CHSGTN KT9 63 H3
ESH/CLAY KT10 62 C6
HORS RH12 166 F8
STA TW18 21 M5
TEDD TW11 26 C7
WIM/MER SW19 28 F6
Cavalier Wy *EGRIN* RH19 163 G6
Cavalry Ct *ALDT* GU11 112 B7
Cavalry Crs *HSLWW* TW4 16 A6
Cavan's Rd *ALDT* GU11 112 F3
Cavell Wy *CRAWE* RH10 165 L5
HOR/WEW KT19 83 K1
WOKN/KNAP GU21 75 M8
Cavendish Av *NWMAL* KT3 46 E5
Cavendish Cl *HORS* RH12 167 G2
SUN TW16 24 C7
Cavendish Ct *BLKW* GU17 72 A6
SUN TW16 24 C7
Cavendish Dr *ESH/CLAY* KT10 62 B4

Cavendish Gdns REDH RH1 126 D7
Cavendish Meads ASC SL5 37 G6
Cavendish Ms ALDT GU11 112 D8
Cavendish Pde HSLWW TW4 * 16 B4
Cavendish Rd ALDT GU11 112 D8
BAL SW12 30 F1
BELMT SM2 65 M6
CHSWK W4 18 F3
CROY/NA CR0 2 A3
NWMAL KT3 46 C5
REDH RH1 126 D8
SUN TW16 24 C7
WEY KT13 59 L7
WIM/MER SW19 30 B8
WOKS/MYFD GU22 10 A9
Cavendish Ter FELT TW13 * 24 D3
Cavendish Wk HOR/WEW KT19 83 L1
Cavendish Wy WWKM BR4 51 L8
Cavenham Cl
WOKS/MYFD GU22 10 C9
Caverleigh Wy WPK KT4 46 D8
Cave Rd RCHPK/HAM TW10 26 F5
Caversham Av CHEAM SM3 65 H1
Caversham Rd KUT/HW KT1 9 G6
Cawnpore St NRWD SE19 32 B6
Cawsey Wy WOKN/KNAP GU21 10 D6
Caxton Av ADL/WDHM KT15 58 D5
Caxton Cl CRAWE RH10 164 F7
Caxton Gdns GUW GU2 6 C1
Caxton La OXTED RH8 131 H5
Caxton Ms BTFD TW8 * 18 A2
Caxton Ri REDH RH1 126 D7
Caxton Rd WIM/MER SW19 29 M6
Cayton Rd COUL/CHIP CR5 106 F4
Cearn Wy COUL/CHIP CR5 87 J6
Cecil Cl ASHF TW15 23 M7
CHSGTN KT9 63 G3
Cecil Pl MTCM CR4 48 C5
Cecil Rd ASHF TW15 23 M8
CROY/NA CR0 49 H6
HSLW TW3 16 F5
SUT SM1 65 J5
WIM/MER SW19 29 L8
Cedar Av BLKW GU17 72 A4
COB KT11 80 E4
WHTN TW2 16 E8
Cedar Cl ASHV GU12 135 H1
BAGS GU19 54 B6
CAR SM5 66 C5
CRAWW RH11 164 E1
DORK RH4 144 E2
DUL SE21 31 M2
ESH/CLAY KT10 61 J6
EW KT17 84 C4
HAYES BR2 71 H2
HORS RH12 166 F7
KUTN/CMB KT2 28 A5
REIG RH2 147 M2
STA TW18 40 F2
WARL CR6 89 H8
Cedar Ct ADL/WDHM KT15 58 F3
EGH TW20 21 K5
HASM GU27 198 D7
WIM/MER SW19 29 G4
Cedar Crs HAYES BR2 71 H2
Cedarcroft Rd CHSGTN KT9 63 J3
Cedar Dr ASC SL5 37 K7
EDEN TN8 153 L7
LHD/OX KT22 102 B5
Cedar Gdns BELMT SM2 65 M5
WOKN/KNAP GU21 76 E8
Cedar Gv CHOB/PIR GU24 75 K5
WEY KT13 59 M3
Cedar Hts RCHPK/HAM TW10 27 H2
Cedar Hl EPSOM KT18 83 M5
Cedar Pk CTHM CR3 108 B3
Cedar Rd BELMT SM2 65 M5
COB KT11 80 E4
CROY/NA CR0 3 G5
E/WMO/HCT KT8 44 B4
EBED/NFELT TW14 24 A2
FARN GU14 92 F6
HSLWW TW4 15 M4
TEDD TW11 26 D6
WEY KT13 59 K2
WOKS/MYFD GU22 96 E2
Cedars BNSTD SM7 86 C4
Cedars Av MTCM CR4 48 D4
Cedars Ct GU GU1 * 117 K5
Cedars Rd BARN SW13 19 J4
BECK BR3 51 H2
CROY/NA CR0 67 H2
KUT/HW KT1 8 A4
MRDN SM4 47 K4
The Cedars BF/WBF KT14 79 J2
GU GU1 117 K5
LHD/OX KT22 103 G3
MFD/CHID GU8 183 M1
REIG RH2 126 A8
TEDD TW11 26 C7
Cedar Ter RCH/KEW TW9 18 B6
Cedar Tree Gv WNWD SE27 31 L6
Cedarville Gdns
STRHM/NOR SW16 31 J7
Cedar Wk ESH/CLAY KT10 62 C5
KWD/TDW/WH KT20 105 J3
PUR/KEN CR8 87 M6
Cedar Wy GU GU1 116 F5
SUN TW16 24 B8
Cedarways FNM GU9 155 L2
Celandine Cl CRAWW RH11 * 164 C8
Celandine Rd WOT/HER KT12 61 H3
Celia Crs ASHF TW15 23 G7
Celtic Rd BF/WBF KT14 79 H4
Cemetery La SHPTN TW17 41 L7
Cemetery Pales
CHOB/PIR GU24 95 K4
Centennial Ct BRAK RG12 * 34 D2
Central Ar ASHF TW15 * 23 J5
Central Av E/WMO/HCT KT8 43 J5
HSLW TW3 16 F6
WLGTN SM6 67 H4
Central Hl NRWD SE19 31 M6
Central Pde CROY/NA CR0 69 M8
E/WMO/HCT KT8 * 43 J4
HORL RH6 * 160 D3
PGE/AN SE20 * 33 G8
STRHM/NOR SW16 * 31 H5
SURB KT6 * 45 H6
Central Park Est HSLWW TW4 * 16 A6
Central Pl SNWD SE25 * 50 D4
Central Rd MRDN SM4 47 L5
WPK KT4 64 D1
Central Sq E/WMO/HCT KT8 43 J4
Central Ter BECK BR3 * 51 G3
Central Wy CAR SM5 66 B6
EBED/NFELT TW14 15 L7
OXTED RH8 130 A1
Centre Terrace Rd FARN GU14 112 D1
The Centre FELT TW13 24 D3
Centurion Cl SHST GU47 72 A1
Centurion Ct WLGTN SM6 * 66 E1
Century Ct WOKN/KNAP GU21 10 E4
Century Rd EGH TW20 21 M6
Cerne Rd MRDN SM4 47 M6
Cerotus Pl CHERT KT16 40 C7
Chadacre Rd EW KT17 64 E4
Chadhurst Cl RDKG RH5 145 G5
Chadwick Av WIM/MER SW19 29 K7
Chadwick Cl CRAWW RH11 191 L12
PUT/ROE SW15 28 C1
TEDD TW11 26 D7
Chadwick Pl SURB KT6 44 F6
Chadworth Wy ESH/CLAY KT10 62 A4
Chaffers Md ASHTD KT21 83 J6
Chaffinch Av CROY/NA CR0 51 G6
Chaffinch Cl CRAWW RH11 164 F2
CROY/NA CR0 51 G5
HORS RH12 167 G2
SHST GU47 72 B1
SURB KT6 63 K2
Chaffinch Rd BECK BR3 51 H1
Chaffinch Wy HORL RH6 160 B2
Chailey Cl CRAWW RH11 164 C7
HEST TW5 16 A3
Chailey Pl WOT/HER KT12 61 H3
Chalcot Cl BELMT SM2 65 K6
Chalcot Ms STRHM/NOR SW16 31 H4
Chalcott Gdns SURB KT6 * 44 F8
Chalcraft Cl LIPH GU30 196 F9
Chaldon Cl REDH RH1 148 B2
Chaldon Common Rd
CTHM CR3 107 M6
Chaldon Rd CRAWW RH11 191 M12
CTHM CR3 108 A5
Chaldon Wy COUL/CHIP CR5 87 H7
Chalfont Dr FARN GU14 92 F7
Chalfont Ms WAND/EARL SW18 29 J2
Chalfont Rd SNWD SE25 50 C3
Chalford Cl E/WMO/HCT KT8 43 K4
Chalford Rd DUL SE21 32 A5
Chalgrove Av MRDN SM4 47 K5
Chalgrove Rd BELMT SM2 66 A6
Chalice Cl WLGTN SM6 67 G5
Chalkenden Cl PGE/AN SE20 32 E8
Chalk La ASHTD KT21 103 K1
EHSLY KT24 120 C5
EPSOM KT18 84 B6
MFD/CHID GU8 159 G1
Chalkley Cl MTCM CR4 48 C2
Chalk Paddock EPSOM KT18 84 A5
Chalkpit La BRKHM/BTCW RH3 123 L7
DORK RH4 122 D8
Chalk Pit La GT/LBKH KT23 121 J1
Chalkpit La OXTED RH8 129 M1
Chalk Pit Rd BNSTD SM7 85 K5
EPSOM KT18 103 M1
SUT SM1 65 M4
Chalkpit Ter DORK RH4 122 D8
Chalkpit Wd OXTED RH8 130 A1
Chalk Rd BIL RH14 201 M6
GODL GU7 168 B4
Chalky La CHSGTN KT9 63 G7
Challenge Ct LHD/OX KT22 102 E1
Challenge Rd ASHF TW15 23 M4
Challice Wy BRXS/STRHM SW2 31 J2
Challin St PGE/AN SE20 50 F1
Challis Pl BNFD RG42 34 B1
Challock Cl BH/WHM TN16 90 F6
Challoners Cl E/WMO/HCT KT8 44 A4
Chalmers Cl HORL RH6 174 H11
Chalmers Rd ASHF TW15 23 L5
BNSTD SM7 85 M5
Chalmers Rd East ASHF TW15 23 L5
Chalmers Wy
EBED/NFELT TW14 15 L7
TWK TW1 17 L6
Chamberlain Crs WWKM BR4 51 L8
Chamberlain Gdns HSLW TW3 16 F3
Chamberlain Wy SURB KT6 45 H7
Chamber La RFNM GU10 154 F1
Chambers Rd ASHV GU12 113 L3
Champion Crs SYD SE26 33 H5
Champion Down EHSLY KT24 121 H2
Champion Rd SYD SE26 33 H5
Champness Cl WNWD SE27 32 A5
Champney Cl DTCH/LGLY SL3 12 D5
Champneys Cl BELMT SM2 65 J6
Chancellor Gdns SAND/SEL CR2 67 L7
Chancellor Gv DUL SE21 31 M3
Chancellors Whf HMSMTH W6 19 M1
Chancery La BECK BR3 51 L2
Chancery Ms TOOT SW17 30 B3
Chanctonbury Cha REDH RH1 148 E1
Chanctonbury Dr ASC SL5 37 H7
Chanctonbury Gdns
BELMT SM2 65 L6
Chanctonbury Wy
CRAWW RH11 164 E6
Chandler Cl CRAWE RH10 164 F6
HPTN TW12 43 J1
Chandlers Cl EBED/NFELT TW14 24 C1
Chandlers Rd ASHV GU12 113 L5
Chandos Rd STA TW18 22 A6
Channel Cl HEST TW5 16 D3
Channings WOKN/KNAP GU21 10 D1
Chantilly Wk HOR/WEW KT19 63 M8
Chantlers Cl EGRIN RH19 162 D3
Chanton Dr BELMT SM2 64 F8
Chantrey Cl ASHTD KT21 102 F1
Chantrey Rd CRAWE RH10 165 G7
Chantry Cl FNM GU9 4 D4
HORL RH6 160 C2
SUN TW16 24 D8
Chantry Hurst EPSOM KT18 84 A5
Chantry La SHGR GU5 141 J5
Chantry Rd BAGS GU19 54 A7
CHERT KT16 40 E8
CHSGTN KT9 63 J4
RGUE GU4 139 L6
The Chantrys FNM GU9 4 D5
Chantry View Rd GU GU1 139 H3
Chantry Wy MTCM CR4 48 A3
Chapel Av ADL/WDHM KT15 58 E3
CHOB/PIR GU24 95 L3
Chapel Cl MFD/CHID GU8 159 J7
Chapel Ct DORK RH4 * 144 D2
Chapel Gdns BOR GU35 180 A12
Chapel Gn PUR/KEN CR8 87 K3
Chapel Gv ADL/WDHM KT15 58 E3
EPSOM KT18 104 F1
Chapel Hl EHSLY KT24 121 G1
MFD/CHID GU8 185 J10
Chapelhouse Cl GUW GU2 116 B8
Chapel La BAGS GU19 54 A7
CHOB/PIR GU24 95 K5
CRAWE RH10 193 L1
DORK RH4 143 M3
EGRIN RH19 163 L7
FARN GU14 92 C1
FROW RH18 195 N12
GT/LBKH KT23 121 M2
MFD/CHID GU8 159 J7
Chapel Mill Rd KUT/HW KT1 9 H9
Chapel Park Rd
ADL/WDHM KT15 58 E3
Chapel Rd CBLY GU15 72 E4
HORL RH6 161 L2
HORL RH6 174 H10
HSLW TW3 16 E5
KWD/TDW/WH KT20 104 F5
OXTED RH8 130 F4
REDH RH1 126 C8
RFNM GU10 155 H6
TWK TW1 26 E1
WARL CR6 89 G8
WNWD SE27 31 L5
Chapel Sq CBLY GU15 72 C3
VW GU25 39 H3
Chapel St FARN GU14 93 G3
GU GU1 7 G7
WOKN/KNAP GU21 10 E6
Chapel Vw SAND/SEL CR2 68 F6
Chapel Wk COUL/CHIP CR5 107 G4
Chapel Wy EPSOM KT18 104 F1
Chaplain's Hl CWTH RG45 52 A5
Chaplin Crs SUN TW16 24 B7
Chapman Rd CRAWE RH10 165 K8
CROY/NA CR0 49 K8
Chapman's La EGRIN RH19 162 C4
Chapman Sq WIM/MER SW19 29 G3
Chappell Cl LIPH GU30 196 H9
Chapter Wy HPTN TW12 25 K5
Chara Pl CHSWK W4 19 G1
Chargate Cl WOT/HER KT12 60 D5
Charlbury Cl BRAK RG12 35 J4
Charlecote Cl FARN GU14 93 G6
Charlecote Gv SYD SE26 32 E4
Charles Babbage Cl
CHSGTN KT9 62 F6
Charles Cobb Gdns
CROY/NA CR0 67 K4
Charles Dickens Ter
PGE/AN SE20 * 32 F8
Charlesfield Rd HORL RH6 160 C2
Charles Haller St
BRXS/STRHM SW2 31 K1
Charles Hl RFNM GU10 157 H3
Charles Rd STA TW18 23 G7
WIM/MER SW19 47 K1
Charles Sq BRAK RG12 34 F2
Charles St BARN SW13 19 H5
CBLY GU15 72 F4
CHERT KT16 40 C8
CROY/NA CR0 2 C7
HSLW TW3 16 C4
Charleston Cl FELT TW13 24 D4
Charleston Ct CRAWE RH10 165 K7
Charleville Circ SYD SE26 32 D6
Charlmont Rd TOOT SW17 30 B7
Charlock Cl CRAWW RH11 164 C8
Charlock Wy GU GU1 117 L6
Charlotte Cl FNM GU9 134 A1
Charlotte Ct ESH/CLAY KT10 61 M4
Charlotte Gv HORL RH6 161 K2
Charlotte Ms ESH/CLAY KT10 * 61 L3
Charlotte Pde FSTH SE23 * 33 H3
Charlotte Rd BARN SW13 19 J3
WLGTN SM6 66 F5
Charlton Av WOT/HER KT12 60 E3
Charlton Ct SHST GU47 52 A8
Charlton Dr BH/WHM TN16 91 G7
Charlton Gdns COUL/CHIP CR5 86 F8
Charlton Kings WEY KT13 60 B3
Charlton La SHPTN TW17 41 M3
Charlton Rd SHPTN TW17 41 M2
Charlwood CROY/NA CR0 69 J7
Charlwood Cl GT/LBKH KT23 101 L6
Charlwood Dr LHD/OX KT22 82 A5
Charlwood La RDKG RH5 174 D12
Charlwood Pl REIG RH2 125 J8
Charlwood Rd CRAWW RH11 191 J3
HORL RH6 175 M9
Charlwoods Pl EGRIN RH19 162 F2
Charlwoods Rd EGRIN RH19 162 E3
Charlwood Wk CRAWW RH11 164 D1
Charman Rd REDH RH1 126 B8
Charmans Cl HORS RH12 * 167 L4
Charm Cl HORL RH6 160 B2
Charminster Av
WIM/MER SW19 47 K2
Charminster Rd WPK KT4 47 G8
Charnwood ASC SL5 37 J6
Charnwood Av WIM/MER SW19 47 K2
Charnwood Cl NWMAL KT3 46 B4
Charnwood Rd SNWD SE25 50 A5
Charrington Rd CROY/NA CR0 2 B6
Charrington Wy HORS RH12 204 D6
Charsley Rd CAT SE6 33 L3
Charta Rd EGH TW20 21 M6
Chart Cl CROY/NA CR0 50 F6
MTCM CR4 48 C4
RDKG RH5 144 F4
Chart Downs RDKG RH5 144 F4
Charter Crs HSLWW TW4 16 B6
Charterhouse Cl BRAK RG12 35 H5
Charterhouse Rd GODL GU7 168 A3
Charter Pl STA TW18 22 D7
Charter Rd KUT/HW KT1 9 L8
Charters Cl NRWD SE19 32 B6
Charters La ASC SL5 37 G5
Charter Sq KUT/HW KT1 9 M7
Charters Rd ASC SL5 37 J7
Charters Wy ASC SL5 37 J7
Charter Wk HASM GU27 * 198 D7
Chartfield Av PUT/ROE SW15 19 L7
Chartfield Rd REIG RH2 147 M1
Chart Gdns RDKG RH5 144 F5
Chartham Gv WNWD SE27 31 K4
Chartham Rd SNWD SE25 50 E3
Chart House Rd ASHV GU12 113 K2
Chart La DORK RH4 144 E2
REIG RH2 125 L8
Chart La South RDKG RH5 145 G4
Charts Cl CRAN GU6 186 D3
Chart Wy HORS RH12 166 F7
Chartway REIG RH2 125 L8
Chartwell FNM GU9 155 J3
FRIM GU16 93 H4
Chartwell Cl CROY/NA CR0 2 E3
Chartwell Gdns ALDT GU11 112 F2
Chartwell Pl CHEAM SM3 65 H3
EPSOM KT18 84 B4
Chartwell Wy PGE/AN SE20 50 E1
Charwood STRHM/NOR SW16 * 31 K5
Chase Ct RYNPK SW20 47 H2
Chase End HOR/WEW KT19 84 A2
Chasefield Cl RGUE GU4 117 K5
Chasefield Rd TOOT SW17 30 C5
Chase Gdns WHTN TW2 17 G8
Chase La HASM GU27 198 F9
Chaseley Dr SAND/SEL CR2 68 A8
Chasemore Cl MTCM CR4 48 C7
Chasemore Gdns CROY/NA CR0 67 K4
Chase Pln GSHT GU26 * 197 P4
Chase Rd BOR GU35 180 A12
HOR/WEW KT19 84 A2
Chaseside Av RYNPK SW20 47 H1
Chaseside Gdns CHERT KT16 40 E7
The Chase ASHTD KT21 82 F8
COUL/CHIP CR5 86 F4
CRAWE RH10 165 J5
EHSLY KT24 100 C8
FARN GU14 93 G3
GUW GU2 6 A5
KWD/TDW/WH KT20 105 M3
LHD/OX KT22 81 M5
REIG RH2 126 A8
STRHM/NOR SW16 31 J8
SUN TW16 42 E1
WLGTN SM6 67 H4
Chatelet Cl HORL RH6 160 E2
Chatfield Cl FARN GU14 92 F7
Chatfield Ct CTHM CR3 108 A4
Chatfield Dr RGUE GU4 117 M6
Chatfield Rd CROY/NA CR0 2 B3
Chatfields CRAWW RH11 164 C6
Chatham Cl CHEAM SM3 47 J7
Chatham Rd KUT/HW KT1 9 J6
Chatsfield EW KT17 64 D8
Chatsworth Av HASM GU27 198 D5
RYNPK SW20 47 H1
Chatsworth Cl CHSWK W4 * 18 F1
WWKM BR4 70 C1
Chatsworth Crs HSLW TW3 17 G6
Chatsworth Gdns NWMAL KT3 * 46 C5
Chatsworth Gv FNM GU9 133 L3
Chatsworth Hts CBLY GU15 73 K2
Chatsworth Pl LHD/OX KT22 82 A2
MTCM CR4 48 C3
TEDD TW11 26 D5
Chatsworth Rd CHEAM SM3 65 G3
CHSWK W4 18 F1
CROY/NA CR0 2 F9
FARN GU14 93 H6
Chatsworth Wy WNWD SE27 31 M3
Chattern Hl ASHF TW15 23 L5
Chattern Rd ASHF TW15 23 M5
Chatton Rw CHOB/PIR GU24 75 K7
Chaucer Av EGRIN RH19 162 D5
HSLWW TW4 15 L4
RCH/KEW TW9 18 D4
WEY KT13 59 K6
Chaucer Cl BNSTD SM7 85 H4
Chaucer Ct GUW GU2 6 F8
Chaucer Gdns SUT SM1 65 K3
Chaucer Gn CROY/NA CR0 50 E7
Chaucer Gv CBLY GU15 73 G4
Chaucer Rd ASHF TW15 23 H5
CRAWE RH10 165 K2
FARN GU14 92 C3
SUT SM1 65 K3
Chaucer Wy ADL/WDHM KT15 58 D5
Chaundlers Cft RFNM GU10 132 C4
Chavasse Wy FARN GU14 92 A4
Chave Cft EPSOM KT18 * 104 F1
Chavecroft Ter EPSOM KT18 * 104 F1
Chaworth Cl CHERT KT16 57 M5
Chaworth Rd CHERT KT16 57 M5
Cheam Cl BRAK RG12 35 G5
KWD/TDW/WH KT20 104 E3
Cheam Common Rd WPK KT4 64 E1
Cheam Park Wy CHEAM SM3 65 G5
Cheam Rd BELMT SM2 65 G7
EW KT17 64 E8
Cheapside WOKN/KNAP GU21 10 A1
Cheapside Rd ASC SL5 36 F3
Cheeseman Cl HPTN TW12 25 H7
Cheetah Rd FARN GU14 92 E7
Chellows La LING RH7 152 C7
Chelmsford Cl BELMT SM2 65 K7
Chelsea Cl HPTN TW12 25 M7
WPK KT4 46 D7
Chelsea Gdns CHEAM SM3 65 H3
Chelsea Sq CAR SM5 66 C7
Chelsfield Gdns SYD SE26 32 F4
Chelsham Court Rd WARL CR6 90 A8
Chelsham Rd SAND/SEL CR2 68 A6
Cheltenham Av TWK TW1 26 D1
Cheltenham Cl NWMAL KT3 45 M3
Chelwood Cl COUL/CHIP CR5 106 F1
CRAWE RH10 165 H6
EW KT17 84 C2
Chelwood Gdns RCH/KEW TW9 18 D4
Cheniston Cl BF/WBF KT14 78 D3
Chennells Wy HORS RH12 167 G4
Chepstow Cl CRAWE RH10 192 D7
Chepstow Ri CROY/NA CR0 3 H7
Chepstow Rd CROY/NA CR0 3 H7
Chequer Gra FROW RH18 195 M12
Chequer Rd EGRIN RH19 * 163 G4
Chequers Cl HORL RH6 160 D2
KWD/TDW/WH KT20 104 D7
Chequers Ct SWTR RH13 167 H6
Chequers Dr HORL RH6 160 D2
Chequers La
KWD/TDW/WH KT20 104 D7
Chequers Pl DORK RH4 144 E2
Chequer Tree Cl
WOKN/KNAP GU21 76 B6
Cherbury Cl BRAK RG12 35 H3
Cherimoya Gdns
E/WMO/HCT KT8 43 L3
Cherington Wy ASC SL5 * 36 B2
Cheriton Ct WOT/HER KT12 42 F8
Cheriton Sq TOOT SW17 30 D3
Cheriton Wy BLKW GU17 72 A4
Cherkley LHD/OX KT22 * 103 G8
Cherkley Hl LHD/OX KT22 102 F8
Cherrimans Orch HASM GU27 198 A7
Cherry Cl BNSTD SM7 85 G4
BRXS/STRHM SW2 * 31 K1
CAR SM5 66 C1
MRDN SM4 47 H4
Cherrycot Ri ORP BR6 71 M3
Cherry Ct SWTR RH13 167 G8
Cherry Crs BTFD TW8 17 L2
Cherrydale Rd CBLY GU15 74 A4
Cherry Green Cl REDH RH1 148 E2
Cherry Hill Gdns CROY/NA CR0 67 J3
Cherryhurst MFD/CHID GU8 * 183 Q8
Cherry La CRAWW RH11 164 E1
Cherry Orch ASHTD KT21 83 L8
STA TW18 22 D6
Cherry Orchard Gdns
CROY/NA CR0 2 F4
E/WMO/HCT KT8 43 J3
Cherry Orchard Rd
CROY/NA CR0 2 F4
E/WMO/HCT KT8 43 K3
HAYES BR2 71 H1
Cherry St WOKN/KNAP GU21 10 C7
Cherry Tree Av GUW GU2 116 C8
HASM GU27 198 A6
STA TW18 22 E7
Cherry Tree Cl CRAWE RH10 165 M2
SHST GU47 52 A8
Cherry Tree Ct COUL/CHIP CR5 87 J8
Cherry Tree Dr BRAK RG12 35 G3
STRHM/NOR SW16 * 31 H4
Cherry Tree Gn SAND/SEL CR2 88 E4
Cherry Tree La GODL GU7 168 A1
Cherry Tree Rd MFD/CHID GU8 159 H8
RFNM GU10 155 H6
Cherrytrees COUL/CHIP CR5 107 G3
Cherry Tree Wk BECK BR3 51 J4
WWKM BR4 70 C3
Cherry Wy DTCH/LGLY SL3 12 F5
HOR/WEW KT19 64 A5
SHPTN TW17 42 A4
Cherrywood Av EGH TW20 20 E7
Cherrywood Cl KUTN/CMB KT2 9 J3
Cherrywood La RYNPK SW20 47 H4
Cherrywood Rd FARN GU14 92 D2
Chertsey Bridge Rd
CHERT KT16 41 G7
Chertsey Cl PUR/KEN CR8 87 L5
Chertsey Crs CROY/NA CR0 69 M8
Chertsey Dr CHEAM SM3 65 H1
Chertsey La HOR/WEW KT19 83 K2
STA TW18 40 B1
Chertsey Rd ADL/WDHM KT15 58 F2
BF/WBF KT14 79 G1
BFOR GU20 55 H5
CHOB/PIR GU24 56 D8
SHPTN TW17 41 H7
SUN TW16 24 B7
TWK TW1 17 K8
WHTN TW2 25 M2
WOKN/KNAP GU21 10 F4
Chertsey St GU GU1 7 H5
TOOT SW17 30 D6
Chertsey Wk CHERT KT16 * 40 D7
Chervil Cl FELT TW13 24 D4
Cherwell Cl DTCH/LGLY SL3 12 E1
Cherwell Ct HOR/WEW KT19 63 M3
Cherwell Wk CRAWW RH11 164 B5
Cheselden Rd GU GU1 7 J6
Cheseman St SYD SE26 32 E4
Chesfield Rd KUTN/CMB KT2 8 F2
Chesham Cl BELMT SM2 65 H8
Chesham Crs PGE/AN SE20 50 F1
Chesham Ms GU GU1 7 K6
Chesham Rd GU GU1 7 K6
KUT/HW KT1 9 J5
KWD/TDW/WH KT20 105 J8
PGE/AN SE20 50 F2
WARL CR6 89 K6
Cheshire Cl CHERT KT16 58 A5
MTCM CR4 49 H3
Cheshire Gdns CHSGTN KT9 63 G5
Chesney Crs CROY/NA CR0 69 M6
Chessholme Rd ASHF TW15 23 M7
Chessington Cl HOR/WEW KT19 63 M5
Chessington Hall Gdns
CHSGTN KT9 63 G6
Chessington Hill Pk
CHSGTN KT9 63 K5
Chessington Pde CHSGTN KT9 * 63 G4
Chessington Rd CHSGTN KT9 63 K5
Chessington Wy WWKM BR4 69 L1
Chester Av RCHPK/HAM TW10 18 C8
WHTN TW2 25 J2
Chesterblade La BRAK RG12 35 G7
Chester Cl ASHF TW15 24 A6
ASHV GU12 113 L7
BARN SW13 * 19 L5
DORK RH4 122 F8
GUW GU2 116 C6
SUT SM1 65 K1
Chesterfield Cl EGRIN RH19 193 P1
Chesterfield Dr ESH/CLAY KT10 62 D1
Chesterfield Rd ASHF TW15 23 H6
CHSWK W4 18 F1
HOR/WEW KT19 64 A6
Chester Gdns MRDN SM4 47 M5
Chester Rd ASHV GU12 113 L6
EHSLY KT24 120 E2
HSLWW TW4 15 L5
HTHAIR TW6 14 D5
WIM/MER SW19 28 F7
Chesters HORL RH6 160 B1
Chesters Rd CBLY GU15 73 L4
The Chesters NWMAL KT3 46 B1
Chesterton Cl EGRIN RH19 163 G6

Chesterton Ct SWTR RH13 167 K5
Chesterton Dr REDH RH1 127 H2
STWL/WRAY TW19 23 J2
Chesterton Ter KUT/HW KT1 9 J7
Chester Wy RFNM GU10 135 J3
Chestnut Av ASHV GU12 135 H2
BH/WHM TN16 111 G4
CBLY GU15 73 K3
ESH/CLAY KT10 44 A7
FNM GU9 4 E8
GUW GU2 138 F4
HASM GU27 198 D6
HOR/WEW KT19 64 B3
HPTN TW12 25 K8
MORT/ESHN SW14 * 19 G5
TEDD TW11 26 C8
VW GU25 38 C4
WEY KT13 59 M6
WOT/HER KT12 60 B7
WWKM BR4 70 B4
Chestnut Cl ADL/WDHM KT15 59 G4
ASHF TW15 23 L5
BLKW GU17 * 72 B4
CAR SM5 48 C8
CAT SE6 33 M5
EDEN TN8 153 L7
EGH TW20 20 E7
EGRIN RH19 163 H4
GSHT GU26 197 N2
HYS/HAR UB3 14 E2
KWD/TDW/WH KT20 105 K5
LIPH GU30 197 J10
REDH RH1 148 E2
RPLY/SEND GU23 98 D7
STRHM/NOR SW16 31 K5
SUN TW16 24 C7
Chestnut Copse OXTED RH8 130 E7
Chestnut Ct ASHV GU12 113 G7
Chestnut Dr EGH TW20 21 G7
Chestnut End BOR GU35 196 E1
Chestnut Gdns HORS RH12 166 F4
Chestnut Gv BAL SW12 30 D1
ISLW TW7 17 K6
MTCM CR4 49 G5
NWMAL KT3 46 A3
SAND/SEL CR2 68 E6
STA TW18 22 F7
WOKS/MYFD GU22 97 H2
Chestnut La CHOB/PIR GU24 55 M5
WEY KT13 59 L4
Chestnut Mnr WLGTN SM6 66 E3
Chestnut Manor Cl STA TW18 22 E6
Chestnut Md REDH RH1 126 B7
Chestnut Pl ASHTD KT21 103 H1
SYD SE26 32 C5
WEY KT13 * 59 L4
Chestnut Rd ASHF TW15 23 K5
FARN GU14 92 D4
GU GU1 7 G3
HORL RH6 160 D1
KUTN/CMB KT2 8 E3
RYNPK SW20 47 G2
WHTN TW2 26 B3
WNWD SE27 31 L4
The Chestnuts BECK BR3 * 51 G3
WOT/HER KT12 60 D1
Chestnut Ter SUT SM1 * 65 L3
Chestnut Wk CRAWW RH11 164 E1
EGRIN RH19 178 D10
SHPTN TW17 42 B5
Chestnut Wy FELT TW13 24 E4
GODL GU7 168 C7
SHGR GU5 169 K5
Cheston Av CROY/NA CR0 51 H8
Chesworth Cl SWTR RH13 205 K9
Chesworth Crs SWTR RH13 166 F8
Chesworth Gdns SWTR RH13 166 F8
Chesworth La SWTR RH13 166 F8
Chetwode Dr EPSOM KT18 85 G8
Chetwode Pl ASHV GU12 134 F2
Chetwode Rd EPSOM KT18 104 F1
KWD/TDW/WH KT20 105 G1
TOOT SW17 30 C4
Chetwode Ter ALDT GU11 112 B8
Chetwood Rd CRAWW RH11 190 G11
Chevening Cl CRAWW RH11 191 M12
Chevening Rd NRWD SE19 32 A8
Cheviot Cl BELMT SM2 66 A7
BNSTD SM7 85 L5
CBLY GU15 73 M5
FARN GU14 92 B2
HYS/HAR UB3 15 G2
Cheviot Rd WNWD SE27 31 L6
Cheviot Wk CRAWW RH11 * 164 D4
Chewter La BFOR GU20 54 E3
Cheyham Gdns BELMT SM2 65 G8
Cheyham Wy BELMT SM2 65 H8
Cheylesmore Dr FRIM GU16 74 A6
Cheyne Av WHTN TW2 25 J2
Cheyne Cl HAYES BR2 71 H2
Cheyne Ct BNSTD SM7 85 L5
Cheyne Hl BRYLDS KT5 45 J4
Cheyne Park Dr WWKM BR4 69 M2
Cheyne Rd ASHF TW15 24 A7
Cheyne Wk CROY/NA CR0 3 M6
HORL RH6 160 D4
Cheyne Wy FARN GU14 92 C2
Chichele Gdns CROY/NA CR0 3 H9
Chichele Rd OXTED RH8 130 B2
Chichester Cl CRAWE RH10 165 G8
DORK RH4 122 E8
HPTN TW12 25 J7
MFD/CHID GU8 183 M4
Chichester Ct EW KT17 * 64 C7
Chichester Dr PUR/KEN CR8 87 J2
Chichester Rd ASHV GU12 113 K6
CROY/NA CR0 3 H8
DORK RH4 122 E7
Chichester Ter HORS RH12 167 G7
Chichester Wy
EBED/NFELT TW14 24 F1
Chiddingfold Rd
MFD/CHID GU8 184 F10
Chiddingly Cl CRAWE RH10 165 J5
Chiddingstone Cl BELMT SM2 65 K8
Chilberton Dr REDH RH1 126 F4
Chilbrook Rd COB KT11 80 D8
Chilcroft La HASM GU27 198 C12
Chilcroft Rd HASM GU27 198 A6
Chilcrofts Rd HASM GU27 198 B12
Childebert Rd TOOT SW17 30 E3
Childerstone Cl LIPH GU30 196 G9
Childs Hall Dr GT/LBKH KT23 101 J7
Childs Hall Rd GT/LBKH KT23 101 J7
Childs La NRWD SE19 * 32 B7
Chilham Cl FRIM GU16 93 J1
Chillerton Rd TOOT SW17 30 D6
Chillingham Wy CBLY GU15 72 F5
Chillingworth Gdns TWK TW1 * 26 C3
Chilmans Dr GT/LBKH KT23 101 L7
Chilmark Gdns NWMAL KT3 46 C6
REDH RH1 127 H3
Chilmark Rd STRHM/NOR SW16 49 G2
Chilmead REDH RH1 * 126 C7
Chilmead La REDH RH1 127 G6
Chilsey Green Rd CHERT KT16 40 B6
Chiltenhurst EDEN TN8 153 K7
Chiltern Av FARN GU14 92 A5
WHTN TW2 25 K2
Chiltern Cl CRAWW RH11 164 D4
CROY/NA CR0 3 H8
HASM GU27 198 C8
STA TW18 22 D6
WPK KT4 64 F1
Chiltern Dr BRYLDS KT5 45 L6
Chiltern Rd BELMT SM2 65 M8
The Chilterns BELMT SM2 * 65 L7
Chilthorne Cl CAT SE6 33 J1
Chiltlee Cl LIPH GU30 196 H9
Chiltlee Mnr LIPH GU30 196 H9
Chiltley La LIPH GU30 197 J11
Chiltley Wy LIPH GU30 196 H11
Chilton Cl CRAN GU6 185 Q11
Chilton Rd RCH/KEW TW9 18 D5
Chiltons Cl BNSTD SM7 85 L5
Chilvers Cl WHTN TW2 26 B3
Chilworth Gdns SUT SM1 65 M2
Chilworth Rd SHGR GU5 140 D5
Chinchilla Dr HSLWW TW4 15 M4
The Chine DORK RH4 * 144 E1
RFNM GU10 155 J4
Chingford Av FARN GU14 92 F4
Chinthurst La RGUE GU4 139 H7
Chinthurst Ms COUL/CHIP CR5 86 F5
Chinthurst Pk RGUE GU4 139 H8
Chippendale Rd CRAWW RH11 191 L12
Chipstead Av THHTH CR7 49 L4
Chipstead Cl BELMT SM2 65 L7
COUL/CHIP CR5 86 D7
NRWD SE19 32 C8
REDH RH1 148 C1
Chipstead Ct
WOKN/KNAP GU21 76 B7
Chipstead La COUL/CHIP CR5 105 L6
Chipstead Rd BNSTD SM7 85 J7
Chipstead Station Pde
COUL/CHIP CR5 86 C8
Chipstead Valley Rd
COUL/CHIP CR5 86 E6
Chipstead Wy BNSTD SM7 86 C7
Chirton Wk WOKN/KNAP GU21 76 D8
Chisbury Cl BRAK RG12 35 H6
Chisholm Rd CROY/NA CR0 3 H5
RCHPK/HAM TW10 18 C8
Chislehurst Rd
RCHPK/HAM TW10 18 B8
Chislet Cl BECK BR3 33 K8
Chiswick Br CHSWK W4 18 F4
Chiswick Cl CROY/NA CR0 67 J2
Chiswick House Grounds
CHSWK W4 * 19 G1
Chiswick La South CHSWK W4 19 J1
Chiswick Ml CHSWK W4 19 J1
Chiswick Quay CHSWK W4 18 F3
Chiswick Sq CHSWK W4 19 H1
Chiswick Staithe CHSWK W4 18 E3
Chiswick Village CHSWK W4 18 D1
Chithurst La CRAWE RH10 177 K10
Chitterfield Ga WDR/YW UB7 14 D2
Chitty's Wk RGUW GU3 116 C4
Chivenor Gv KUTN/CMB KT2 27 G6
Chobham Cl CHERT KT16 57 L5
Chobham Gdns
WIM/MER SW19 29 G3
Chobham La CHERT KT16 56 D1
Chobham Park La
CHOB/PIR GU24 56 D8
Chobham Rd ASC SL5 55 M1
CHERT KT16 57 K6
FRIM GU16 73 H7
WOKN/KNAP GU21 10 D3
WOKN/KNAP GU21 75 L8
Choir Gn WOKN/KNAP GU21 76 B7
Cholmley Rd THDIT KT7 44 E6
Cholmley Ter THDIT KT7 * 44 E7
Chrislaine Cl STWL/WRAY TW19 14 A8
Chrismas Av ASHV GU12 112 F8
Chrismas Pl ASHV GU12 112 F8
Christabel Cl ISLW TW7 17 H5
Christchurch Av TEDD TW11 26 D6
Christchurch Cl
WIM/MER SW19 30 A8
Christ Church Mt
HOR/WEW KT19 83 L2
Christchurch Pk BELMT SM2 65 M6
Christ Church Rd BECK BR3 * 51 K2
BRYLDS KT5 45 J7
EPSOM KT18 83 H2
Christchurch Rd
BRXS/STRHM SW2 31 J2
MORT/ESHN SW14 18 E7
PUR/KEN CR8 67 K8
VW GU25 38 E3
WIM/MER SW19 48 A1
Christchurch Wy
WOKN/KNAP GU21 10 E5
Christian Flds
STRHM/NOR SW16 31 K8
Christie Cl GT/LBKH KT23 101 J7
LTWR GU18 54 E8
Christie Dr CROY/NA CR0 50 D5
Christies EGRIN RH19 162 E5
Christie Wk COUL/CHIP CR5 107 L1
Christine Cl ASHV GU12 113 J8
Christmas Hl SHGR GU5 139 L8
Christmaspie Av RGUW GU3 114 E8
Christopher Rd EGRIN RH19 162 F4
Christ's Hospital Rd
SWTR RH13 204 C11
Christy Est ASHV GU12 * 113 H7
Christy Rd BH/WHM TN16 90 F5
Chrystie La GT/LBKH KT23 101 L8
Chuck's La
KWD/TDW/WH KT20 104 E6
Chudleigh Gdns SUT SM1 65 M2
Chudleigh Rd WHTN TW2 17 H8
Chulsa Rd SYD SE26 32 E6
Chumleigh Wk BRYLDS KT5 45 J4
Church Ap DUL SE21 32 A4
EGH TW20 39 M3
Church Av BECK BR3 51 K1
FARN GU14 92 F7
MORT/ESHN SW14 19 G6
Church Cir FARN GU14 92 F8
Church Cl ADL/WDHM KT15 58 E3
CHOB/PIR GU24 95 J2
EW KT17 * 84 B3
HASM GU27 198 G3
HSLW TW3 16 C4
KWD/TDW/WH KT20 125 J1
LHD/OX KT22 102 A6
MFD/CHID GU8 159 J8
STA TW18 40 F3
WOKN/KNAP GU21 10 B3
Church Ct REIG RH2 125 L8
Churchcroft Cl BAL SW12 * 30 D1
Church Dr WWKM BR4 70 B2
Church Farm La CHEAM SM3 65 H5
Churchfield Rd REIG RH2 125 J7
WEY KT13 59 K3
WOT/HER KT12 42 D8
Church Flds BOR GU35 180 D12
Churchfields E/WMO/HCT KT8 43 K3
MFD/CHID GU8 183 M5
RGUE GU4 117 K3
WOKN/KNAP GU21 10 C3
Churchfields Av FELT TW13 25 J4
WEY KT13 59 L3
Churchfields Rd BECK BR3 51 G2
Church Gdns LHD/OX KT22 * 102 E2
Church Gn
KWD/TDW/WH KT20 * 104 D6
WOT/HER KT12 60 F5
Church Gv KUT/HW KT1 8 B5
Church Hl ASHV GU12 134 E1
BH/WHM TN16 91 M5
BH/WHM TN16 111 G4
CAR SM5 66 C4
CBLY GU15 73 H4
CTHM CR3 108 C6
PUR/KEN CR8 67 H8
REDH RH1 106 E8
REDH RH1 127 J7
SHGR GU5 141 K5
SHGR GU5 169 P6
WIM/MER SW19 29 J6
WOKN/KNAP GU21 10 A4
WOKS/MYFD GU22 78 C7
Church Hill Rd CHEAM SM3 65 G3
SURB KT6 45 H5
Church Hill Ter RFNM GU10 * 132 C3
Churchill Av ASHV GU12 134 F1
HORS RH12 166 E6
Churchill Cl EBED/NFELT TW14 24 C2
LHD/OX KT22 102 B5
WARL CR6 88 F7
Churchill Ct CRAWE RH10 165 H1
Churchill Crs BOR GU35 196 E1
FARN GU14 92 E2
Churchill Dr WEY KT13 59 M2
Churchill Rd ASC SL5 36 C2
GU GU1 7 K5
HOR/WEW KT19 83 K1
HORL RH6 161 L3
SAND/SEL CR2 67 M7
Churchill Wy BH/WHM TN16 91 G5
SUN TW16 24 D6
Churchlands ALDT GU11 134 E1
Church La ASC SL5 37 G4
ASC SL5 37 K3
ASHV GU12 113 L7
BOR GU35 180 C11
CHOB/PIR GU24 75 K5
CHOB/PIR GU24 95 G4
CHSGTN KT9 63 J5
COUL/CHIP CR5 106 D4
CRAN GU6 186 C2
CRAWE RH10 165 H3
CRAWE RH10 192 F3
CTHM CR3 107 K5
EGRIN RH19 163 G4
EPSOM KT18 103 M7
FARN GU14 92 B5
GDST RH9 129 G6
GSHT GU26 197 P2
HASM GU27 198 D6
HORL RH6 161 H7
HORS RH12 166 A6
LIPH GU30 196 G7
MFD/CHID GU8 183 K9
MFD/CHID GU8 184 A3
OXTED RH8 130 B3
RDKG RH5 188 A4
REDH RH1 128 A7
RFNM GU10 133 G2
RFNM GU10 155 H6
RFNM GU10 155 J2
RGUW GU3 116 B1
RPLY/SEND GU23 97 L8
SHGR GU5 140 E5
SHGR GU5 141 K5
TEDD TW11 26 C6
THDIT KT7 44 C6
TOOT SW17 30 C6
TOOT SW17 30 E5
TWK TW1 26 D2
WARL CR6 89 G7
WARL CR6 89 M6
WEY KT13 59 K3
WIM/MER SW19 47 K2
WLGTN SM6 67 G2
Church Lane Av
COUL/CHIP CR5 106 E4
Church Lane Dr
COUL/CHIP CR5 106 E4
Church La East ALDT GU11 134 E1
Church La West ALDT GU11 112 C8
Churchley Rd SYD SE26 32 E5
Church Meadow SURB KT6 62 F1
Church Ms ADL/WDHM KT15 58 F3
Churchmore Rd
STRHM/NOR SW16 48 F1
Church Paddock Ct
WLGTN SM6 67 G2
Church Pde ASHF TW15 * 23 J5
Church Pk CRAWW RH11 * 164 C3
Church Pth ASHV GU12 113 K6
MTCM CR4 48 B3
RYNPK SW20 47 J2
WOKN/KNAP GU21 10 E5
Church Pl MTCM CR4 48 B3
Church Ri CHSGTN KT9 63 J5
FSTH SE23 33 G2
Church Rd ADL/WDHM KT15 58 D4
ALDT GU11 134 F1
ASC SL5 35 L1
ASC SL5 36 D4
ASC SL5 37 K6
ASHF TW15 23 K6
ASHTD KT21 83 G8
BAGS GU19 54 A6
BARN SW13 19 K4
BF/WBF KT14 79 H3
BFOR GU20 54 E5
BH/WHM TN16 91 G7
BRAK RG12 34 F2
CBLY GU15 72 C2
CHEAM SM3 65 H5
CHOB/PIR GU24 75 J2
CRAWE RH10 192 D7
CRAWE RH10 192 G2
CRAWE RH10 193 L10
CROY/NA CR0 2 C8
CTHM CR3 88 C8
CTHM CR3 108 C5
CTHM CR3 109 G3
E/WMO/HCT KT8 44 A4
EGH TW20 21 K6
ESH/CLAY KT10 62 C5
EW KT17 84 B3
FELT TW13 24 F6
FRIM GU16 93 G1
GT/LBKH KT23 101 J5
GU GU1 7 G5
HASM GU27 198 D6
HAYES BR2 71 G6
HEST TW5 16 D2
HOR/WEW KT19 64 A6
HORL RH6 160 C4
HORL RH6 161 K7
HORL RH6 175 P12
HORL RH6 177 L4
HORS RH12 166 A6
HORS RH12 167 L4
ISLW TW7 17 G3
KUT/HW KT1 9 G6
LHD/OX KT22 102 E4
LING RH7 178 E5
LIPH GU30 196 H7
MFD/CHID GU8 183 N1
MFD/CHID GU8 184 G8
MFD/CHID GU8 184 H2
NRWD SE19 32 B8
ORP BR6 71 M4
PUR/KEN CR8 67 H8
PUR/KEN CR8 88 A5
RCHPK/HAM TW10 18 B7
RCHPK/HAM TW10 27 H5
RDKG RH5 173 Q8
REDH RH1 148 B2
REIG RH2 147 K2
SHPTN TW17 41 L7
SHST GU47 52 A8
SURB KT6 44 F8
SWTR RH13 205 R12
TEDD TW11 26 B5
WARL CR6 89 G7
WIM/MER SW19 29 H6
WIM/MER SW19 48 A2
WLGTN SM6 66 F2
WOKN/KNAP GU21 10 C3
WOKN/KNAP GU21 96 D1
WPK KT4 46 B8
Church Rd East FARN GU14 93 G8
Church Rd West FARN GU14 92 F8
Church Rw RPLY/SEND GU23 * 98 F3
Church Side EPSOM KT18 83 L3
Churchside Cl BH/WHM TN16 90 F8
Church Sq SHPTN TW17 41 L7
Church St ALDT GU11 112 C8
BRKHM/BTCW RH3 146 B1
CHSWK W4 19 H1
COB KT11 80 E5
CRAWW RH11 164 E4
CROY/NA CR0 2 B7
DORK RH4 144 D2
EHSLY KT24 121 G1
ESH/CLAY KT10 61 L3
EW KT17 64 D7
EW KT17 84 B3
GODL GU7 168 A5
HORS RH12 166 C2
HORS RH12 203 K1
HPTN TW12 43 M1
HSLW TW3 16 F7
ISLW TW7 17 L5
KUT/HW KT1 8 D7
LHD/OX KT22 102 E4
REIG RH2 125 L8
RFNM GU10 132 B3
STA TW18 22 B5
SUN TW16 42 D2
TWK TW1 26 D2
WEY KT13 59 K3
WOKS/MYFD GU22 97 M3
WOT/HER KT12 42 D8
Church St East
WOKN/KNAP GU21 10 E5
Church St West
WOKN/KNAP GU21 10 C6
Church Ter RCHPK/HAM TW10 18 A7
RDKG RH5 * 173 K3
Church V FSTH SE23 32 F3
Church Vw ASHV GU12 113 K7
FSTH SE23 33 G3
Church View Cl HORL RH6 160 C4
Churchview Rd WHTN TW2 26 A2
Church Wk BTFD TW8 17 M1
CRAWE RH10 164 F4
CTHM CR3 108 D6
HORL RH6 160 C4
LHD/OX KT22 102 E4
REIG RH2 125 L8
RYNPK SW20 46 F3
STRHM/NOR SW16 48 F2
THDIT KT7 44 C6
WEY KT13 59 K2
WOT/HER KT12 42 D8
Church Wy OXTED RH8 130 C6
SAND/SEL CR2 68 C8
Churston Cl
BRXS/STRHM SW2 * 31 L2
Churston Dr MRDN SM4 47 G5
Churton Pl CHSWK W4 * 18 E1
Churt Rd BOR GU35 180 F10
RFNM GU10 181 L9
Churt Wynde GSHT GU26 181 Q10
Chuters Cl BF/WBF KT14 79 J2
Chuters Gv EW KT17 84 C2
Cibber Rd FSTH SE23 33 G3
Cidermill Rd RDKG RH5 174 B6
Cinder Pth WOKS/MYFD GU22 96 F1
Cinnamon Cl CROY/NA CR0 * 49 H7
Cinnamon Gdns GUW GU2 116 D3
Cintra Pk NRWD SE19 32 C8
Circle Gdns BF/WBF KT14 79 J3
WIM/MER SW19 47 K3
Circle Rd WOT/HER KT12 60 B8
The Circle GODL GU7 168 C3
The Circus LHD/OX KT22 * 102 E2
Cissbury Cl HORS RH12 167 K3
Cissbury Hl CRAWW RH11 164 E6
Clacket La BH/WHM TN16 111 H6
Clairvale Rd HEST TW5 16 A3
Clairview Rd STRHM/NOR SW16 30 E6
Clairville MFD/CHID GU8 * 199 P1
Clandon Av EGH TW20 21 M8
Clandon Cl EW KT17 64 C5
Clandon Ct FARN GU14 93 G6
Clandon Rd GU GU1 7 K5
RGUE GU4 98 D8
Clandon Ter RYNPK SW20 * 47 G2
Clanfield Ride BLKW GU17 72 A4
Clapgate La SWTR RH13 203 Q5
Clapham Park Est CLAP SW4 * 31 G1
Clappers Ga CRAWE RH10 164 F3
Clappers La CHOB/PIR GU24 75 M1
Clappers Meadow CRAN GU6 185 R11
Clappers Orch CRAN GU6 * 185 Q10
Clare Cl BF/WBF KT14 78 D3
CRAWE RH10 165 L1
Clare Ct CTHM CR3 109 K5
Clare Crs LHD/OX KT22 82 D8
Claredale WOKS/MYFD GU22 97 H1
Clare Gdns EGH TW20 21 K6
Clare Hl ESH/CLAY KT10 61 L4
Clare Hill (No 2) ESH/CLAY KT10 61 L4
Clare Lawn Av
MORT/ESHN SW14 19 G7
Clare Md RFNM GU10 155 J6
Claremont Av CBLY GU15 73 J4
ESH/CLAY KT10 61 J5
NWMAL KT3 46 E5
SUN TW16 42 E1
WOT/HER KT12 61 G3
Claremont Cl BRXS/STRHM SW2 31 J2
ORP BR6 71 K3
SAND/SEL CR2 88 E5
WOT/HER KT12 60 F4
Claremont Ct DORK RH4 144 E3
Claremont Dr ESH/CLAY KT10 61 L6
SHPTN TW17 41 L6
WOKS/MYFD GU22 97 H1
Claremont End ESH/CLAY KT10 61 L5
Claremont Gdns SURB KT6 45 H4
Claremont Gv CHSWK W4 19 H2
Claremont La ESH/CLAY KT10 61 L4
Claremont Park Rd
ESH/CLAY KT10 61 L5
Claremont Rd BF/WBF KT14 78 D2
CROY/NA CR0 3 M3
ESH/CLAY KT10 62 B6
REDH RH1 126 D5
STA TW18 22 A6
SURB KT6 45 H5
TEDD TW11 26 C6
TWK TW1 26 E1
Claremont Ter THDIT KT7 * 44 E7
Claremount Cl EPSOM KT18 84 F7
Claremount Gdns EPSOM KT18 84 F7
Clarence Av CLAP SW4 31 G1
NWMAL KT3 45 M2
Clarence Cl ASHV GU12 112 F7
WOT/HER KT12 60 E3
Clarence Ct HORL RH6 * 161 G2
Clarence Dr CBLY GU15 73 L2
EGH TW20 20 F5
EGRIN RH19 163 G6
Clarence La PUT/ROE SW15 19 J8
Clarence Ms TOOT SW17 29 M4
Clarence Rd BH/WHM TN16 91 J8
CROY/NA CR0 2 E1
RCH/KEW TW9 18 C3
REDH RH1 148 A3
SUT SM1 65 L3
SWTR RH13 167 G8
TEDD TW11 26 C7
WIM/MER SW19 29 L7
WLGTN SM6 66 E4
WOT/HER KT12 60 E3
Clarence St EGH TW20 21 J7
KUT/HW KT1 8 D6
RCH/KEW TW9 18 B6
STA TW18 22 B5
Clarence Ter HSLW TW3 16 E6
Clarence Wk REDH RH1 148 A3
Clarence Wy HORL RH6 161 G3
Clarendon Ct BLKW GU17 72 A6
Clarendon Crs WHTN TW2 26 A4
Clarendon Dr PUT/ROE SW15 19 M6
Clarendon Ga CHERT KT16 58 A5
Clarendon Gv MTCM CR4 48 C3
Clarendon Ms ASHTD KT21 * 103 H1
Clarendon Rd ASHF TW15 23 J5
CROY/NA CR0 2 B5
REDH RH1 126 C7
WIM/MER SW19 30 B8
WLGTN SM6 66 F4
Clarens St CAT SE6 33 J3
Clare Rd HSLWW TW4 16 C5
STWL/WRAY TW19 23 G2
The Clares CTHM CR3 108 D6
Claret Gdns SNWD SE25 50 B4
Clareville Rd CTHM CR3 108 D6

STMC/STPC BR5 71 M1
Clare Wd LHD/OX KT22 82 D8
Clarewood Dr CBLY GU15 73 H3
Clarice Wy WLGTN SM6 67 H7
Claridge Gdns LING RH7 178 H7
Claridges Md LING RH7 178 H7
Clarke Crs SHST GU47 72 B2
Clarke's Av WPK KT4 47 G8
Clark Rd CRAWW RH11 191 K12
Clarks Hl RFNM GU10 132 F7
Clarks La OXTED RH8 110 E5
Clark Wy HEST TW5 16 A2
Claudia Pl WIM/MER SW19 29 H2
Claverdale Rd
BRXS/STRHM SW2 31 J1
Claverdon BRAK RG12 34 D7
Clavering Av BARN SW13 19 L1
Clavering Cl TEDD TW11 26 D5
Clay Av MTCM CR4 48 E2
Claycart Rd ALDT GU11 112 A6
Claydon Dr CROY/NA CR0 67 H3
Claydon Gdns BLKW GU17 72 D8
Claydon Rd WOKN/KNAP GU21 76 D6
Clayford LING RH7 179 J7
Claygate Crs CROY/NA CR0 69 M5
Claygate La ESH/CLAY KT10 62 D2
THDIT KT7 44 D8
Claygate Lodge Cl
ESH/CLAY KT10 62 B6
Claygate Rd DORK RH4 144 E4
Clay Hall La CRAWE RH10 192 H1
Clayhall La REIG RH2 147 H3
Clayhanger RGUE GU4 117 M6
Clayhill Cl BRAK RG12 35 J3
REIG RH2 146 D7
Clayhill Rd REIG RH2 146 C8
Clay La EPSOM KT18 103 L6
LING RH7 177 Q7
REDH RH1 148 F1
RGUE GU4 117 G2
STWL/WRAY TW19 23 J1
Claymore Cl MRDN SM4 47 K7
Claypole Dr HEST TW5 16 B3
Clays Cl EGRIN RH19 162 F5
Clayton Barracks ALDT GU11 113 G5
Clayton Ct FNM GU9 * 5 H4
Clayton Dr GUW GU2 116 C5
Clayton Gv BRAK RG12 35 H1
Clayton Hl CRAWW RH11 164 E6
Clayton Md GDST RH9 128 E4
Clayton Rd CHSGTN KT9 62 F3
EW KT17 84 B2
FARN GU14 72 C8
ISLW TW7 17 H5
Cleardene DORK RH4 144 E2
Cleardown WOKS/MYFD GU22 11 J8
Clearsprings LTWR GU18 74 C1
The Clears REIG RH2 125 H6
Clearwater Pl SURB KT6 44 F6
Cleaveland Rd SURB KT6 45 G5
Cleave Prior COUL/CHIP CR5 106 B1
Cleaverholme Cl SNWD SE25 50 E6
Cleeve Hl FSTH SE23 32 E2
Cleeve Rd LHD/OX KT22 102 D2
The Cleeve GU GU1 117 K8
Cleeve Wy PUT/ROE SW15 19 J8
SUT SM1 47 L8
Clement Cl PUR/KEN CR8 87 L6
Clement Rd BECK BR3 51 G2
WIM/MER SW19 29 H6
Clements Rd WOT/HER KT12 60 E1
Clensham La SUT SM1 65 K1
Clerks Cft REDH RH1 128 A7
Clevedon WEY KT13 60 A4
Clevedon Ct FARN GU14 93 G6
FRIM GU16 93 K1
Clevedon Gdns HEST TW5 15 L4
Clevedon Rd KUT/HW KT1 9 J6
PGE/AN SE20 51 G1
TWK TW1 18 A8
Cleveland Av HPTN TW12 25 J8
Cleveland Cl WOT/HER KT12 60 E2
Cleveland Dr STA TW18 40 E2
Cleveland Gdns BARN SW13 19 J4
WPK KT4 64 B1
Cleveland Ri MRDN SM4 47 G7
Cleveland Rd BARN SW13 19 J4
ISLW TW7 17 K6
NWMAL KT3 46 B4
WPK KT4 64 B1
Cleves Av EW KT17 64 E7
Cleves Cl COB KT11 80 E4
Cleves Crs CROY/NA CR0 89 M1
Cleves Rd RCHPK/HAM TW10 26 F4
Cleves Wy HPTN TW12 25 J8
SUN TW16 24 C7
Cleves Wd WEY KT13 60 B2
Clewborough Dr CBLY GU15 73 L3
Clews La CHOB/PIR GU24 75 K6
Clifden Rd BTFD TW8 18 A1
TWK TW1 26 C2
Cliff End PUR/KEN CR8 87 L2
Cliffe Ri GODL GU7 159 M7
Cliffe Rd SAND/SEL CR2 68 A4
Clifford Av MORT/ESHN SW14 18 F4
WLGTN SM6 66 F3
Clifford Gv ASHF TW15 23 K5
Clifford Manor Rd RGUE GU4 139 H4
Clifford Rd HSLWW TW4 16 A5
RCHPK/HAM TW10 27 G3
SNWD SE25 50 D4
Clifton Av BELMT SM2 85 L1
FELT TW13 24 F4
Clifton Cl ADL/WDHM KT15 58 E1
CTHM CR3 108 A5
HORL RH6 161 G3
ORP BR6 71 M4
RFNM GU10 155 K5
Clifton Ct BECK BR3 * 51 L1
Clifton Gdns FRIM GU16 93 J3
Clifton Ms SNWD SE25 50 B4
Clifton Pde FELT TW13 * 24 F5
Clifton Park Av RYNPK SW20 46 F2
Clifton Pl BNSTD SM7 85 K5
KUTN/CMB KT2 * 9 J5
Clifton Rd COUL/CHIP CR5 86 E5
CRAWE RH10 165 L5
HTHAIR TW6 * 14 E6
ISLW TW7 17 H4
KUTN/CMB KT2 9 J5
SNWD SE25 50 B4
TEDD TW11 26 B5
WIM/MER SW19 29 G7
WLGTN SM6 66 E4
Clifton's La REIG RH2 125 G7
Clifton Ter DORK RH4 * 144 E3
Cliftonville DORK RH4 144 E3
Clifton Wy WOKN/KNAP GU21 76 C7
Climping Rd CRAWW RH11 164 D2
Cline Rd GU GU1 7 L7
Clinton Av E/WMO/HCT KT8 43 M4
Clinton Cl WEY KT13 59 L2
WOKN/KNAP GU21 76 A8
Clinton Hl LING RH7 178 H8
Clinton Rd LHD/OX KT22 102 F5
Clintons Gn BNFD RG42 34 D1
Clinton Ter SUT SM1 * 65 M3
Clippesby Cl CHSGTN KT9 * 63 J5
Clipstone Rd HSLW TW3 16 D5
Clitherow Gdns CRAWE RH10 165 G5
Cliveden Pl SHPTN TW17 41 L6
Cliveden Rd WIM/MER SW19 47 J1
Clive Gn BRAK RG12 34 E5
Clive Rd ASHV GU12 113 G8
DUL SE21 32 A4
EBED/NFELT TW14 15 K8
ESH/CLAY KT10 61 L3
TWK TW1 26 C5
WIM/MER SW19 30 B7
Clive Wy CRAWE RH10 165 L4
Clock Barn La MFD/CHID GU8 168 C10
Clock House Cl BF/WBF KT14 79 J3
Clockhouse Cl WIM/MER SW19 28 F3
Clock House Ct HASM GU27 * 198 D7
Clockhouse La ASHF TW15 23 K5
SHGR GU5 169 J3
Clockhouse La East EGH TW20 21 L8
Clockhouse La West EGH TW20 21 K8
Clock House Md LHD/OX KT22 81 L4
Clockhouse Rd BECK BR3 51 H3
Clockhouse Rd FARN GU14 92 E5
Clock Tower Rd ISLW TW7 17 J5
Clodhouse Hl
WOKS/MYFD GU22 96 A4
Cloister Cl TEDD TW11 26 E6
Cloister Gdns SNWD SE25 50 E6
The Cloisters FRIM GU16 73 G8
WOKS/MYFD GU22 97 L3
Clonmel Rd TEDD TW11 26 A5
Clonmore St WAND/EARL SW18 29 J2
The Close ASC SL5 36 A2
BECK BR3 51 H4
BF/WBF KT14 78 D3
BH/WHM TN16 * 91 L6
BIL RH14 201 M6
BRAK RG12 34 F4
BRKHM/BTCW RH3 145 L4
CAR SM5 66 B7
CHEAM SM3 47 J7
EGRIN RH19 162 E5
FNM GU9 5 M6
FRIM GU16 92 F1
GODL GU7 168 C6
HORL RH6 160 F5
ISLW TW7 17 G4
LTWR GU18 54 D8
MTCM CR4 48 C4
NWMAL KT3 45 M2
PUR/KEN CR8 67 J8
RCH/KEW TW9 18 E5
REIG RH2 147 L1
SHGR GU5 169 L2
SHST GU47 72 B1
SNWD SE25 * 50 D6
SURB KT6 45 H7
VW GU25 39 G5
WOKS/MYFD GU22 11 J5
Closeworth Rd FARN GU14 113 H1
Cloudesdale Rd TOOT SW17 30 E3
Clouston Cl WLGTN SM6 67 H4
Clouston Rd FARN GU14 92 C4
Clovelly Av WARL CR6 88 E8
Clovelly Dr GSHT GU26 181 P10
Clovelly Rd GSHT GU26 181 P11
HSLW TW3 16 D4
Clover Cl BOR GU35 180 B12
Clover Ct WOKS/MYFD GU22 10 A8
Cloverfields HORL RH6 160 E2
Clover Hl COUL/CHIP CR5 106 E3
Cloverlands CRAWE RH10 165 H2
Clover Lea GODL GU7 168 B1
Clover Rd GUW GU2 116 B7
Clovers End HORS RH12 167 K4
Clover Wy HORL RH6 161 M3
WLGTN SM6 48 D8
Cloves Farm Wd BNFD RG42 * 34 A2
Clowders Rd CAT SE6 33 J4
Clowser Cl SUT SM1 65 M4
Clubhouse Rd ALDT GU11 112 C4
Club La CWTH RG45 52 A4
Clump Av KWD/TDW/WH KT20 123 M5
Clumps Rd RFNM GU10 156 B5
The Clumps ASHF TW15 24 A5
Clyde Av SAND/SEL CR2 88 E5
Clyde Cl REDH RH1 126 D7
Clyde Rd CROY/NA CR0 3 J5
STWL/WRAY TW19 23 G2
SUT SM1 65 K4
WLGTN SM6 66 F4
Clydesdale Cl ISLW TW7 17 J5
Clydesdale Gdns
RCHPK/HAM TW10 18 E6
Clyde Ter FSTH SE23 32 F3
Clyde V FSTH SE23 32 F3
Clymping Dene
EBED/NFELT TW14 24 E1
Clyve Wy STA TW18 40 B1
Coach House Cl FRIM GU16 73 H6
Coach House La
WIM/MER SW19 29 G5
Coach House Ms REDH RH1 * 148 C1
Coachlads Av GUW GU2 116 C8
Coachmans Dr CRAWW RH11 164 D8
Coach Rd BRKHM/BTCW RH3 145 K2
CHERT KT16 57 M5
DORK RH4 123 H8
HORL RH6 160 E7
Coalecroft Rd PUT/ROE SW15 19 M6
Coast Hl DORK RH4 143 J4
Coast Hill La DORK RH4 143 K4
Coates Cl THHTH CR7 49 M3
Cobalt Cl BECK BR3 51 G4
Cobb Cl DTCH/LGLY SL3 12 A3
Cobbets Rdg RFNM GU10 134 F8
Cobbets Wy EDEN TN8 179 R1
Cobbett Cl CRAWE RH10 165 L2
Cobbett Hill Rd RGUW GU3 115 H2
Cobbett Rd GUW GU2 116 B7
WHTN TW2 25 K2
Cobbetts Cl WOKN/KNAP GU21 76 E6
Cobbetts Farm CHOB/PIR GU24 75 K5
Cobbetts Hl WEY KT13 59 L6
Cobbetts Ms FNM GU9 * 5 G3
Cobbetts Wk CHOB/PIR GU24 75 K6
Cobbetts Wy FNM GU9 155 J3
Cobbler's Wk TEDD TW11 26 B8
Cobbles Crs CRAWE RH10 165 G3
Cobblestone Pl CROY/NA CR0 2 C4
Cobb's Rd HSLWW TW4 16 C6
Cob Cl CRAWE RH10 193 P5
Cobden La HASM GU27 198 E6
Cobden Ms SYD SE26 32 E6
Cobden Rd SNWD SE25 50 D5
Cobham Av NWMAL KT3 46 D5
Cobham Cl WLGTN SM6 67 H5
Cobham Park Rd COB KT11 80 E7
Cobham Rd COB KT11 81 K8
HEST TW5 15 M2
KUT/HW KT1 9 K6
Cobham Wy CRAWE RH10 192 A1
EHSLY KT24 100 B7
Cobnor Cl CRAWW RH11 164 B6
Cobs Wy ADL/WDHM KT15 58 F8
Coburg Crs BRXS/STRHM SW2 31 J2
Cob Wk CRAWW RH11 164 C5
Cochrane Pl BFOR GU20 55 G4
Cochrane Rd WIM/MER SW19 29 H8
Cockcrow Hl SURB KT6 * 45 G8
Cock La LHD/OX KT22 101 M4
Cocks Crs NWMAL KT3 46 C4
Cockshot Hl REIG RH2 147 L2
Cockshot Rd REIG RH2 147 L2
Codrington Ct
WOKN/KNAP GU21 76 C8
Codrington Hl FSTH SE23 33 H1
Cody Cl ASHV GU12 113 J4
WLGTN SM6 67 G6
Cody Rd FARN GU14 92 C6
Coe Av SNWD SE25 50 D6
Coe Cl ALDT GU11 112 D8
Cokenor Wd RFNM GU10 155 J3
Cokers La DUL SE21 31 M2
Colborne Wy WPK KT4 64 F2
Colburn Av CTHM CR3 108 C6
Colburn Crs RGUE GU4 117 K5
Colburn Wy SUT SM1 66 A2
Colby Rd NRWD SE19 32 B6
WOT/HER KT12 42 D8
Colchester V FROW RH18 195 M11
Colcokes Rd BNSTD SM7 85 K6
Coldharbour Cl EGH TW20 39 M3
Cold Harbour La FARN GU14 92 C1
Coldharbour La
CHOB/PIR GU24 75 J1
DORK RH4 144 D4
DORK RH4 172 G1
EGH TW20 39 M3
PUR/KEN CR8 67 K8
REDH RH1 128 C8
WOKS/MYFD GU22 78 C5
Coldharbour Rd BF/WBF KT14 78 C4
CROY/NA CR0 67 K4
Coldharbour Wy CROY/NA CR0 67 K4
Coldshott OXTED RH8 130 D7
Coldstream Rd CTHM CR3 107 M4
Cole Av ALDT GU11 112 C6
Colebrook CHERT KT16 58 A5
Colebrook Pl CHERT KT16 * 57 M6
Colebrooke Rd REDH RH1 126 B6
Colebrook Rd
STRHM/NOR SW16 49 H1
Cole Cl CRAWW RH11 191 L12
Coleford Bridge Rd FARN GU14 93 G5
Coleford Cl FRIM GU16 93 J6
Coleford Paddocks FRIM GU16 93 J5
Cole Gdns HEST TW5 15 K2
Colekitchen La SHGR GU5 141 M4
Coleman Cl SNWD SE25 50 D2
Coleman Rd ASHV GU12 113 G8
Cole Park Gdns TWK TW1 17 K8
Cole Park Rd TWK TW1 26 D1
Coleridge Av SUT SM1 66 B3
Coleridge Cl HORS RH12 167 H3
Coleridge Crs DTCH/LGLY SL3 13 H3
Coleridge Rd ASHF TW15 23 H5
CROY/NA CR0 50 F7
Cole Rd TWK TW1 17 K8
Colesburg Rd BECK BR3 51 J3
Colescroft Hl PUR/KEN CR8 87 K5
Coleshill Rd TEDD TW11 26 B7
Coles La RDKG RH5 172 G11
Colesmead Rd REDH RH1 126 C5
Coleson Hill Rd RFNM GU10 155 J4
Colet Rd CRAWE RH10 164 F7
Coleville Rd FARN GU14 92 C4
Coley Av WOKS/MYFD GU22 11 G7
Colfe Rd FSTH SE23 33 H2
Colgate Cl CRAWW RH11 164 D2
Colin Cl CROY/NA CR0 69 J2
WWKM BR4 70 C2
Colinette Rd PUT/ROE SW15 19 M6
Colin Rd CTHM CR3 108 D5
Coliston Rd WAND/EARL SW18 29 K1
Collamore Av
WAND/EARL SW18 30 B2
Collard Cl PUR/KEN CR8 108 A2
Collards Ga HASM GU27 * 198 E7
Collards La HASM GU27 198 E7
College Av EGH TW20 21 L7
EW KT17 84 C4
College Cl ADL/WDHM KT15 59 G2
CBLY GU15 73 G1
EGRIN RH19 163 G4
LING RH7 178 E5
WHTN TW2 26 A2
College Crs REDH RH1 126 D5
SHST GU47 72 B1
College Dr THDIT KT7 44 B7
College Gdns FNM GU9 5 G3
NWMAL KT3 46 C5
TOOT SW17 30 B3
College Gn NRWD SE19 32 B8
College Hl GODL GU7 159 M6
HASM GU27 198 D7
College Hill Ter HASM GU27 198 D7
College La EGRIN RH19 163 G4
WOKS/MYFD GU22 96 F1
College Ride BAGS GU19 53 M7
CBLY GU15 73 G2
College Rd ASHV GU12 113 K6
BRAK RG12 34 F4
CRAWE RH10 165 G4
CROY/NA CR0 2 E6
DUL SE21 32 B1
EW KT17 84 D4
GU GU1 7 G5
ISLW TW7 17 J3
SHST GU47 72 B2
WIM/MER SW19 30 A7
WOKS/MYFD GU22 11 K4
The College EW KT17 * 84 D5
College Wy ASHF TW15 23 J5
Collendean La HORL RH6 175 J5
Collens Fld CHOB/PIR GU24 95 H6
Colley La REIG RH2 125 H5
Colley Manor Dr REIG RH2 125 G7
Colley Wy REIG RH2 125 H5
Collier Cl FARN GU14 92 A4
HOR/WEW KT19 63 K5
Collier Rw CRAWE RH10 164 F7
Colliers CTHM CR3 108 D7
Colliers Cl WOKN/KNAP GU21 76 E7
Colliers Water La THHTH CR7 49 K5
Colliers Wd HAYES BR2 71 G4
Collier Wy RGUE GU4 118 A6
Collingdon CRAN GU6 186 E4
Collingdon Ct CRAN GU6 * 186 E4
Collingsbourne
ADL/WDHM KT15 * 58 E3
Collingtree Rd SYD SE26 32 F5
Collingwood FARN GU14 93 H7
Collingwood Av BRYLDS KT5 45 M8
Colling Wood Cl PGE/AN SE20 50 E1
Collingwood Cl EGRIN RH19 163 G6
HORL RH6 160 E2
WHTN TW2 25 K1
Collingwood Crs GU GU1 117 K7
Collingwood Grange Cl
CBLY GU15 73 L1
Collingwood Ri CBLY GU15 73 K2
Collingwood Rd CRAWE RH10 165 M5
HORS RH12 166 E4
MTCM CR4 48 B2
SUT SM1 65 K3
Collins Gdns ASHV GU12 113 L7
Collins Rd CRAWW RH11 164 A6
Collyer Av CROY/NA CR0 67 H3
Collyer Rd CROY/NA CR0 67 H3
Collyers Crs LIPH GU30 197 K9
Colman Cl EPSOM KT18 84 F7
Colmans Hl SHGR GU5 171 J2
Colman Wy REDH RH1 126 B6
Colmer Rd STRHM/NOR SW16 31 H8
Colnbrook By-Pass
DTCH/LGLY SL3 12 F1
WDR/YW UB7 13 L2
Colndale Rd DTCH/LGLY SL3 13 H4
Colne Bank DTCH/LGLY SL3 12 F5
Colne Ct HOR/WEW KT19 63 M3
Colne Dr WOT/HER KT12 61 G2
Colne Rd WHTN TW2 26 B2
Colne Valley Wy
STWL/WRAY TW19 22 B2
Colne Wy ASHV GU12 113 K8
STWL/WRAY TW19 21 M4
Colonel's La CHERT KT16 40 D6
Colonial Av WHTN TW2 16 F8
Colonial Rd EBED/NFELT TW14 24 B1
Colonsay Rd CRAWW RH11 164 D7
Colson Rd CROY/NA CR0 3 G5
Colson Wy STRHM/NOR SW16 30 F5
Colston Av CAR SM5 66 B3
Colston Rd MORT/ESHN SW14 18 F6
Coltash Rd CRAWE RH10 165 J5
Coltsfoot Dr GU GU1 117 L5
HORS RH12 167 H4
Coltsfoot La OXTED RH8 130 C7
Colts Foot Rd BOR GU35 180 B12
Columbia Av WPK KT4 46 C7
Columbine Av SAND/SEL CR2 67 L6
Colville Gdns LTWR GU18 74 F1
Colvin Cl SYD SE26 32 F6
Colvin Rd THHTH CR7 49 K5
Colwith Rd HMSMTH W6 19 M1
Colwood Gdns WIM/MER SW19 30 A8
Colworth Rd CROY/NA CR0 3 L3
Colwyn Cl CRAWW RH11 164 A6
STRHM/NOR SW16 30 F6
Colwyn Crs HSLW TW3 16 F3
Colyton Cl WOKN/KNAP GU21 76 F8
Colyton La STRHM/NOR SW16 31 K8
Combe La FARN GU14 92 D3
MFD/CHID GU8 183 N12
SHGR GU5 141 K2
SHGR GU5 168 H7
WOT/HER KT12 60 C7
Combemartin Rd
WAND/EARL SW18 29 H1
Combe Ri RFNM GU10 156 A4
Combermere Rd MRDN SM4 47 L6
Combe Rd GODL GU7 168 B1
Combe Vw MFD/CHID GU8 199 P1
Comeragh Cl
WOKS/MYFD GU22 96 D1
Comet Cl ASHV GU12 113 J4
Comet Rd STWL/WRAY TW19 23 G1
Comforts Farm Av OXTED RH8 130 C7
Commerce Rd BTFD TW8 17 M1
Commerce Wy CROY/NA CR0 67 J2
EDEN TN8 153 M6
Commercial Rd ASHV GU12 134 F1
GU GU1 7 G6
STA TW18 22 D7
Commercial Wy
WOKN/KNAP GU21 10 E5
Commodore Pde
STRHM/NOR SW16 * 31 J8
Common Cl WOKN/KNAP GU21 77 G4
Commondale PUT/ROE SW15 19 M4
Commonfield Rd BNSTD SM7 85 K4
Commonfields CHOB/PIR GU24 75 J3
Common La ADL/WDHM KT15 58 F7
ESH/CLAY KT10 62 D6
Common Rd BARN SW13 19 K5
ESH/CLAY KT10 62 D5
REDH RH1 148 C2
Common Side EPSOM KT18 83 K5
Commonside GT/LBKH KT23 101 K5
HAYES BR2 70 F3
Commonside Cl BELMT SM2 85 L1
COUL/CHIP CR5 107 L2
Commonside East MTCM CR4 48 D3
Commonside West MTCM CR4 48 D3
Commonwealth Rd CTHM CR3 108 D5
Community Cl HEST TW5 15 L3
Como Rd FSTH SE23 33 H3
Compass Cl ASHF TW15 23 M8
Compass Hl RCHPK/HAM TW10 18 A8
Compassion Cl CRAWW RH11 164 A5
Comper Cl CRAWW RH11 164 A6
Comport Gn CROY/NA CR0 90 B2
Compound Rd FARN GU14 92 D7
Compton Cl BRAK RG12 34 B6
ESH/CLAY KT10 62 A5
Compton Crs CHSGTN KT9 63 H5
CHSWK W4 18 F1
Compton Rd CROY/NA CR0 50 E8
WIM/MER SW19 29 J7
Comptons Brow La
SWTR RH13 167 J6
Comptons Ct SWTR RH13 167 J6
Comptons La SWTR RH13 167 J6
Compton Wy RFNM GU10 134 D7
Comsaye Wk BRAK RG12 34 F5
Conaways Cl EW KT17 64 D8
Concorde Cl HSLW TW3 16 E4
Condor Ct GUW GU2 6 F8
Condor Rd FARN GU14 92 E7
STA TW18 40 F3
Conduit La SAND/SEL CR2 68 D4
The Conduit REDH RH1 128 A3
Coneyberry REIG RH2 147 M4
Coneybury REDH RH1 128 B8
Coneybury Cl WARL CR6 108 E1
Coney Cl CRAWW RH11 164 D2
Coney Cft HORS RH12 167 L4
Coney Hall Pde WWKM BR4 * 70 B2
Coney Hill Rd WWKM BR4 70 B1
Coneyhurst La CRAN GU6 170 H10
Conford Dr RGUE GU4 139 H7
Coniers Wy RGUE GU4 117 L5
Conifer Cl REIG RH2 125 K6
Conifer Dr CBLY GU15 73 K3
Conifer Gdns
STRHM/NOR SW16 31 J4
SUT SM1 65 L1
Conifer La EGH TW20 21 M6
Conifer Pk EW KT17 84 B1
Conifers WEY KT13 60 B3
Conifers Cl HORS RH12 167 L3
TEDD TW11 26 E8
Coningsby BRAK RG12 34 F4
Coningsby Rd SAND/SEL CR2 67 M7
Conisborough Crs CAT SE6 33 M4
Conista Ct WOKN/KNAP GU21 76 C6
Coniston Cl BARN SW13 19 J2
CBLY GU15 73 M6
CHSWK W4 18 F3
CRAWW RH11 190 G9
FARN GU14 92 B6
HORS RH12 167 L4
MRDN SM4 47 G6
Coniston Ct ASHV GU12 * 113 J5
LTWR GU18 54 E8
Coniston Dr FNM GU9 133 K3
Coniston Gdns BELMT SM2 * 66 A5
Coniston Rd COUL/CHIP CR5 86 F6
CROY/NA CR0 3 L2
WHTN TW2 16 E8
WOKS/MYFD GU22 97 L2
Coniston Wy CHSGTN KT9 63 H2
EGH TW20 21 L8
REIG RH2 126 B7
Connaught Av ASHF TW15 23 H5
HSLWW TW4 16 B7
MORT/ESHN SW14 18 F5
Connaught Barracks
ALDT GU11 113 G3
Connaught Cl SUT SM1 66 A1
Connaught Crs CHOB/PIR GU24 95 J2
Connaught Dr WEY KT13 79 J1
Connaught Gdns CRAWE RH10 164 F2
MRDN SM4 47 M5
Connaught Rd ASHV GU12 112 F8
BAGS GU19 53 M6
CBLY GU15 73 J4
CHOB/PIR GU24 95 J2
NWMAL KT3 46 B4
RCHPK/HAM TW10 * 18 C7
SUT SM1 66 A1
TEDD TW11 26 A6
Connop Wy FRIM GU16 73 J6
Conquest Rd ADL/WDHM KT15 58 D4
Conrad Dr WPK KT4 46 F8
Consfield Av NWMAL KT3 46 D4
Consort Dr CBLY GU15 73 M2
Consort Ms ISLW TW7 17 G8
Consort Wy HORL RH6 160 D3
Consort Wy East HORL RH6 160 E4
Constable Gdns ISLW TW7 17 G7
Constable Rd CRAWE RH10 165 H8
Constable Wk DUL SE21 32 C4
Constable Wy SHST GU47 72 B3
Constance Rd CROY/NA CR0 2 B1
SUT SM1 65 M3
WHTN TW2 25 L1
Constitution Hl
WOKS/MYFD GU22 10 D8
Control Tower Rd HTHAIR TW6 14 D5
Convent Cl BECK BR3 33 M8
Convent Hl NRWD SE19 31 M7
Convent La COB KT11 80 C2
Convent Rd ASHF TW15 23 L6
Conway Dr ASHF TW15 23 M7
BELMT SM2 65 L5
FARN GU14 92 A4
Conway Gdns MTCM CR4 49 G4
Conway Rd FELT TW13 25 G6
HSLWW TW4 25 J1
RYNPK SW20 46 F1
Conyers Cl WOT/HER KT12 61 G4
Conyers Rd STRHM/NOR SW16 31 G6
Cookes La CHEAM SM3 65 H5
Cookham Rd BRAK RG12 34 B2
Cook Rd CRAWE RH10 165 G6

HORS RH12 167 G3
Cooks Hl HORS RH12 186 E12
Cooks Md HORS RH12 190 A6
Cooks Meadow HORS RH12 190 A6
Cook Wy GUW GU2 116 A7
Coolarne Ri CBLY GU15 73 K3
Coolgardie Rd ASHF TW15 23 M6
Coolhurst La SWTR RH13 167 K8
Coombe Av CROY/NA CR0 68 B3
Coombe Bank NWMAL KT3 46 B1
Coombe Cl CRAWW RH11 164 F1
FRIM GU16 93 G1
HSLW TW3 16 D6
Coombe Crs HPTN TW12 25 H8
Coombe Dr ADL/WDHM KT15 58 C5
Coombe End KUTN/CMB KT2 28 A8
Coombefield Cl NWMAL KT3 46 B5
Coombe Gdns NWMAL KT3 46 C4
Coombe Hill Gld KUTN/CMB KT2 28 B8
Coombe Hill Rd EGRIN RH19 162 D7
KUTN/CMB KT2 28 B8
Coombe House Cha
NWMAL KT3 46 A1
Coombelands La
ADL/WDHM KT15 58 D5
Coombe La CROY/NA CR0 68 E4
RGUW GU3 115 M2
RYNPK SW20 46 C1
Coombe La West KUTN/CMB KT2 9 M5
Coombe Mnr CHOB/PIR GU24 75 L5
Coombe Neville KUTN/CMB KT2 27 M8
Coombe Pk KUTN/CMB KT2 27 M6
Coombe Pine BRAK RG12 35 G6
Coombe Ridings
KUTN/CMB KT2 27 M6
Coombe Ri KUTN/CMB KT2 45 M1
Coombe Rd CROY/NA CR0 2 E9
HPTN TW12 25 J7
KUT/HW KT1 9 K5
NWMAL KT3 46 B3
SAND/SEL CR2 68 C3
SYD SE26 32 E5
Coomber Wy CROY/NA CR0 49 H7
The Coombes SHGR GU5 169 K4
The Coombe
BRKHM/BTCW RH3 124 A5
Coombe Vls
WAND/EARL SW18 * 29 K1
Coombe Wy BF/WBF KT14 79 J2
Coombe Wood Hl
PUR/KEN CR8 87 M2
Coombe Wood Rd
KUTN/CMB KT2 27 M6
Coomb Fld EDEN TN8 179 R1
Cooper Cl HORL RH6 161 K3
Cooper Crs CAR SM5 66 C2
Cooper Rd BFOR GU20 55 G5
CROY/NA CR0 67 K4
GU GU1 7 K7
Cooper Rw CRAWE RH10 164 F7
Coopers Cl STA TW18 22 B6
Coopers Hill Dr CHOB/PIR GU24 94 F2
Cooper's Hill La EGH TW20 20 F4
Cooper's Hill Rd REDH RH1 127 J7
Coopers Ms BECK BR3 51 K2
Coopers Ri GODL GU7 159 L6
Coopers Yd NRWD SE19 32 B7
Cootes Av HORS RH12 166 D6
Copelands Cl CBLY GU15 74 A5
Copeman Cl SYD SE26 32 F6
Copenhagen Wy
WOT/HER KT12 60 E2
Copers Cope Rd BECK BR3 33 J8
Copgate Pth STRHM/NOR SW16 31 J7
Copleigh Dr
KWD/TDW/WH KT20 105 H2
Copley Cl REDH RH1 126 B6
WOKN/KNAP GU21 96 B1
Copley Pk STRHM/NOR SW16 31 J7
Copley Wy
KWD/TDW/WH KT20 105 G2
Copnall Wy HORS RH12 166 F7
Coppard Gdns CHSGTN KT9 62 F5
Copped Hall Dr CBLY GU15 73 M3
Copped Hall Wy CBLY GU15 73 M3
Copper Beech Cl
WOKS/MYFD GU22 96 E3
Copper Cl NRWD SE19 32 C8
Copperfield Av SHST GU47 52 B7
Copperfield Cl SAND/SEL CR2 87 M1
Copperfield Pl HORS RH12 166 E6
Copperfield Ri
ADL/WDHM KT15 58 C4
Copperfields LHD/OX KT22 101 M4
SUN TW16 * 24 C7
SWTR RH13 205 Q9
Copper Mill Dr ISLW TW7 17 J4
Copper Mill La TOOT SW17 29 M5
Coppermill Rd
STWL/WRAY TW19 12 E8
Coppice Cl BECK BR3 51 L4
FNM GU9 134 B3
GUW GU2 116 A7
RYNPK SW20 46 F3
Coppice Dr PUT/ROE SW15 19 K8
STWL/WRAY TW19 21 G1
Coppice La REIG RH2 125 J6
Coppice Pl MFD/CHID GU8 183 N9
Coppice Rd HORS RH12 167 K4
The Coppice ASHF TW15 23 L7
CRAWE RH10 193 N5
Coppice Wk CRAWE RH10 165 J3
Copping Cl CROY/NA CR0 3 H9
The Coppins CROY/NA CR0 69 L5
Coppsfield E/WMO/HCT KT8 43 K3
Copse Av FNM GU9 134 B2
WWKM BR4 69 L2
Copse Cl CBLY GU15 73 K4
CRAWE RH10 193 N5
EGRIN RH19 163 G2
HORS RH12 167 J3
RGUE GU4 139 M6
Copse Crs CRAWW RH11 164 E3
Copse Edge CRAN GU6 186 E1
MFD/CHID GU8 157 M6
RGUE GU4 * 117 M5
Copse Edge Av EW KT17 84 C3
Copse End CBLY GU15 73 J3
Copse Gld SURB KT6 45 G8
Copse Hl BELMT SM2 65 L6
PUR/KEN CR8 87 H3
RYNPK SW20 46 D1
Copse La HORL RH6 160 F2
Copsem Dr ESH/CLAY KT10 61 L5
Copsem La ESH/CLAY KT10 61 L5
Copsem Wy ESH/CLAY KT10 61 M5
Copsen Wd LHD/OX KT22 81 M1
Copse Rd COB KT11 80 E3
HASM GU27 197 Q8
REDH RH1 147 M2
WOKN/KNAP GU21 76 C8
Copse Side GODL GU7 168 A1
The Copse BRAK RG12 * 35 G3
CTHM CR3 108 D8
FARN GU14 92 A6
LHD/OX KT22 101 L5
REDH RH1 149 H2
RFNM GU10 155 J5
Copse Vw SAND/SEL CR2 69 H7
Copse Wy RFNM GU10 155 J3
Copsleigh Av REDH RH1 148 D7
Copsleigh Cl REDH RH1 148 D6
Copsleigh Wy REDH RH1 148 D6
Copthall Gdns TWK TW1 26 D2
Copthall Wy ADL/WDHM KT15 58 C8
Copt Hill La
KWD/TDW/WH KT20 105 H2
Copthorne Av BAL SW12 31 G1
HAYES BR2 71 J1
Copthorne Bank CRAWE RH10 192 G1
HORL RH6 161 M8
Copthorne Cl SHPTN TW17 41 M6
Copthorne Common Rd
CRAWE RH10 192 H2
Copthorne Ct LHD/OX KT22 * 102 D3
Copthorne Dr LTWR GU18 54 E8
Copthorne Ri SAND/SEL CR2 88 A3
Copthorne Rd CRAWE RH10 165 M2
CRAWE RH10 192 D4
CRAWE RH10 193 N1
EGRIN RH19 193 R1
LHD/OX KT22 102 E2
Copthorne Wy CRAWE RH10 192 E3
Copyhold Rd EGRIN RH19 162 E5
Corban Rd HSLW TW3 16 D5
Corbet Cl WLGTN SM6 48 D8
Corbet Rd EW KT17 64 B8
Corbett Cl CROY/NA CR0 90 A2
Corbett Dr LTWR GU18 74 C2
Corby Cl EGH TW20 20 F7
Corby Dr EGH TW20 20 F7
Cordelia Cft BNFD RG42 35 H1
Cordelia Gdns ASHV GU12 113 J1
STWL/WRAY TW19 23 H1
Cordelia Rd STWL/WRAY TW19 23 H1
Corderoy Pl CHERT KT16 40 B6
Cordrey Gdns COUL/CHIP CR5 87 H5
Cordwalles Rd CBLY GU15 73 J1
Coresbrook Wy
WOKN/KNAP GU21 75 L8
Corfe Cl ASHTD KT21 82 F8
HSLWW TW4 25 H2
Corfe Gdns FRIM GU16 73 J8
Corfe Wy FARN GU14 93 H8
Coriander Crs GUW GU2 116 D3
Corkran Rd SURB KT6 45 G7
Corkscrew Hl WWKM BR4 69 M1
Cormongers La REDH RH1 127 G7
Cormorant Pl SHST GU47 72 B1
Cornbunting Cl SHST GU47 72 A2
Cornelia Cl FARN GU14 * 92 A6
Corner Farm Cl
KWD/TDW/WH KT20 104 F4
Corner Fielde
BRXS/STRHM SW2 * 31 J2
Cornerside ASHF TW15 23 M8
Corney Reach Wy CHSWK W4 19 H2
Corney Rd CHSWK W4 19 H1
Cornfield Rd REIG RH2 147 M1
Cornfields GODL GU7 168 C1
Cornflower La CROY/NA CR0 51 G8
Cornford Gv BAL SW12 30 E3
Cornhill Cl ADL/WDHM KT15 58 E1
Cornish Gv PGE/AN SE20 50 E1
Cornwall Av BF/WBF KT14 79 J4
ESH/CLAY KT10 62 C6
Cornwall Cl CBLY GU15 73 J2
Cornwall Gdns EGRIN RH19 163 G5
SNWD SE25 * 50 C4
Cornwallis Cl CTHM CR3 107 M4
Cornwall Rd BELMT SM2 65 J6
CROY/NA CR0 2 A5
TWK TW1 26 D1
Cornwall Wy STA TW18 22 B7
Coronation Rd ALDT GU11 134 E2
ASC SL5 36 D6
EGRIN RH19 162 F6
The Coronet HORL RH6 160 F5
Corporation Av HSLWW TW4 16 B6
Corrib Dr SUT SM1 66 B4
Corrie Gdns VW GU25 38 F7
Corrie Rd ADL/WDHM KT15 59 G3
WOKS/MYFD GU22 97 L2
Corrigan Av COUL/CHIP CR5 86 D5
Corry Rd GSHT GU26 181 P11
Corsair Cl STWL/WRAY TW19 23 G1
Corsair Rd STWL/WRAY TW19 23 H1
Corscombe Cl KUTN/CMB KT2 27 M6
Corsehill St STRHM/NOR SW16 30 F7
Corsellis Sq TWK TW1 17 L6
Corsletts Av HORS RH12 166 A6
Cortis Rd PUT/ROE SW15 19 L8
Cortis Ter PUT/ROE SW15 19 L7
Corunna Dr SWTR RH13 167 J7
Cosdach Av WLGTN SM6 67 G6
Cosedge Crs CROY/NA CR0 67 K4
Cosford Rd MFD/CHID GU8 182 F5
Coteford St TOOT SW17 30 C5
Cotelands CROY/NA CR0 3 G7
Cotford Rd THHTH CR7 49 M4
Cotherstone HOR/WEW KT19 64 A7
Cotherstone Rd
BRXS/STRHM SW2 31 J2
Cotland Acres REDH RH1 148 A2
Cotsford Av NWMAL KT3 45 M5
Cotswold Cl CRAWW RH11 164 D4
ESH/CLAY KT10 62 C1
FARN GU14 92 B2
KUTN/CMB KT2 9 M1
STA TW18 22 D6
Cotswold Ct SWTR RH13 167 H7
Cotswold Rd BELMT SM2 65 L8
HPTN TW12 25 K7
Cotswold St WNWD SE27 31 L5
Cotswold Wy WPK KT4 64 F1
Cottage Cl CHERT KT16 57 M5
HORS RH12 167 L3
Cottage Farm Wy EGH TW20 * 39 M3
Cottage Gdns FARN GU14 92 C5
Cottage Gv SURB KT6 45 G6
Cottage Pl CRAWE RH10 193 K2
Cottage Rd HOR/WEW KT19 64 A6
Cottenham Dr RYNPK SW20 28 E8
Cottenham Park Rd
RYNPK SW20 46 D1
Cottenham Pl RYNPK SW20 28 E8
Cottenhams LING RH7 177 R1
Cotterill Rd SURB KT6 63 J1
Cottesbrooke Cl DTCH/LGLY SL3 13 G3
Cottesloe Cl CHOB/PIR GU24 75 J6
Cottesmore BRAK RG12 34 D7
Cottimore Av WOT/HER KT12 42 E8
Cottimore Crs WOT/HER KT12 42 E7
Cottimore La WOT/HER KT12 42 F8
Cottimore Ter WOT/HER KT12 42 E7
Cottingham Av HORS RH12 167 G2
Cottingham Rd PGE/AN SE20 33 G8
Cottington Rd FELT TW13 25 G5
Cotton Cl ALDT GU11 112 C6
Cottongrass Cl CROY/NA CR0 51 G8
Cotton Rw RDKG RH5 171 P9
Cotts Wood Dr RGUE GU4 117 K3
Couchmore Av ESH/CLAY KT10 62 B1
Coulsdon Court Rd
COUL/CHIP CR5 87 J6
Coulsdon La COUL/CHIP CR5 106 D1
Coulsdon Pl CTHM CR3 108 A4
Coulsdon Ri COUL/CHIP CR5 87 H7
Coulsdon Rd COUL/CHIP CR5 87 J6
COUL/CHIP CR5 107 K2
Countisbury Gdns
ADL/WDHM KT15 58 E4
Country Wy FELT TW13 24 F6
County Oak La CRAWE RH10 191 N2
County Oak Wy CRAWW RH11 191 N3
County Pde BTFD TW8 * 18 A2
County Rd THHTH CR7 49 L2
Courland Rd ADL/WDHM KT15 58 E2
Course Rd ASC SL5 36 D3
Court Av COUL/CHIP CR5 87 K8
Court Bushes Rd CTHM CR3 108 D1
Court Cl EGRIN RH19 163 G4
LIPH GU30 196 G10
WHTN TW2 25 L4
Court Close Av WHTN TW2 25 L4
Court Crs CHSGTN KT9 63 G5
EGRIN RH19 163 G4
Court Downs Rd BECK BR3 51 L2
Court Dr CROY/NA CR0 67 J3
SUT SM1 66 B3
Courtenay Av BELMT SM2 65 K7
Courtenay Ms
WOKN/KNAP GU21 11 G3
Courtenay Rd FNM GU9 134 B3
PGE/AN SE20 33 G8
WOKN/KNAP GU21 11 G3
WPK KT4 64 F2
Court Farm Av HOR/WEW KT19 64 A4
Court Farm Gdns
HOR/WEW KT19 * 84 A1
Court Farm Pk WARL CR6 * 88 D6
Court Farm Rd WARL CR6 88 D8
Courtfield Ri WWKM BR4 70 A2
Courtfield Rd ASHF TW15 23 L7
Court Gdns CBLY GU15 73 G4
Court Haw BNSTD SM7 86 B5
Court Hl SAND/SEL CR2 88 B5
Courthope Rd WIM/MER SW19 29 H6
Courthope Vls WIM/MER SW19 29 H8
Courtland Av
STRHM/NOR SW16 31 J8
Courtlands RCHPK/HAM TW10 18 D7
Courtlands Av ESH/CLAY KT10 61 J5
HPTN TW12 25 J7
RCH/KEW TW9 18 E4
Courtlands Cl SAND/SEL CR2 68 C8
Courtlands Crs BNSTD SM7 85 K6
Courtlands Dr HOR/WEW KT19 64 B5
Courtlands Rd BRYLDS KT5 45 K7
Court La DUL SE21 32 C1
HOR/WEW KT19 83 M3
Court Lane Gdns DUL SE21 32 B1
Courtleas COB KT11 81 K3
Court Lodge Rd HORL RH6 160 B2
Courtney Cl NRWD SE19 * 32 B7
Courtney Crs CAR SM5 66 C6
Courtney Pl COB KT11 81 J2
Courtney Rd CROY/NA CR0 67 K2
HTHAIR TW6 14 D5
WIM/MER SW19 30 B8
Courtney Wy HTHAIR TW6 14 D5
Court Rd ALDT GU11 112 D7
BNSTD SM7 85 K5
CTHM CR3 108 A5
GDST RH9 128 F5
SNWD SE25 50 C2
Courts Hill Rd HASM GU27 198 C7
Courtside SYD SE26 * 32 F4
Courts Mount Rd HASM GU27 198 C7
The Court GUW GU2 * 6 F8
WARL CR6 89 H8
Court Wy WHTN TW2 26 C1
Court Wood La CROY/NA CR0 69 J8
The Courtyard BF/WBF KT14 78 D2
CRAWE RH10 * 164 F5
EGRIN RH19 163 H4
HORS RH12 * 166 F7
Coutts Av CHSGTN KT9 63 H4
Coval Gdns MORT/ESHN SW14 18 E6
Coval La MORT/ESHN SW14 18 E6
Coval Rd MORT/ESHN SW14 18 F6
Coveham Crs COB KT11 80 D3
Coventry Rd SNWD SE25 50 D4
Coverack Cl CROY/NA CR0 51 H7
Coverdale Gdns CROY/NA CR0 3 J7
Cove Rd FARN GU14 92 D5
Covert Cl CRAWE RH10 165 G3
Covert La BRAK RG12 34 F4
Coverton Rd TOOT SW17 30 B5
Coverts Cl FNM GU9 134 B5
Coverts Rd ESH/CLAY KT10 62 C6
The Covert ASC SL5 36 E7
FARN GU14 92 B1
NRWD SE19 * 32 C8
Covey Cl FARN GU14 92 D1
WIM/MER SW19 47 L2
The Covey CRAWE RH10 165 M2
CRAWE RH10 * 192 D5
Covington Gdns
STRHM/NOR SW16 31 L8
Covington Wy
STRHM/NOR SW16 31 L8
Cowbridge Meadow
CHOB/PIR GU24 95 J5
Cowden St CAT SE6 33 K5
Cowdray Cl CRAWE RH10 165 L5
Cowdrey Rd WIM/MER SW19 29 L7
Cowfold Cl CRAWW RH11 164 B7
Cowick Rd TOOT SW17 30 C5
Cow La GODL GU7 168 A5
Cowleaze Rd KUTN/CMB KT2 8 F5
Cowley Av CHERT KT16 40 C7
Cowley Cl SAND/SEL CR2 68 F7
Cowley Crs WOT/HER KT12 60 F3
Cowley La CHERT KT16 40 C7
Cowley Rd MORT/ESHN SW14 19 H5
Coworth Cl ASC SL5 37 L5
Coworth Pk ASC SL5 * 37 M3
Coworth Rd ASC SL5 37 K5
Cowper Av SUT SM1 66 A3
Cowper Cl CHERT KT16 40 C6
Cowper Gdns WLGTN SM6 66 F5
Cowper Rd KUTN/CMB KT2 27 J6
WIM/MER SW19 29 M7
Cowshot Crs CHOB/PIR GU24 95 G2
Cowslip Cl BOR GU35 196 B1
Cowslip La RDKG RH5 122 D2
Coxbridge Mdw FNM GU9 4 D5
Coxcombe La MFD/CHID GU8 199 Q1
Coxdean EPSOM KT18 104 F1
Coxes Av SHPTN TW17 * 42 B3
Coxgreen SHST GU47 72 A3
Cox Green Rd HORS RH12 186 G11
Cox La CHSGTN KT9 63 J3
HOR/WEW KT19 63 M4
Coxley Ri PUR/KEN CR8 87 M3
Coxs Av SHPTN TW17 42 B3
Coxwell Rd NRWD SE19 32 B8
Crabbet Rd CRAWE RH10 165 K3
Crabbs Croft Cl ORP BR6 * 71 M4
Crab Hill La REDH RH1 149 J4
Crabtree Cl GT/LBKH KT23 101 M8
Crabtree Dr LHD/OX KT22 102 F7
Crabtree Gdns BOR GU35 180 D12
Crabtree La BOR GU35 180 D12
EPSOM KT18 103 M8
GT/LBKH KT23 101 M8
RDKG RH5 122 C4
RFNM GU10 181 M7
Crabtree Rd CBLY GU15 72 E7
CRAWW RH11 164 E3
EGH TW20 39 M2
Craddocks Av ASHTD KT21 83 J6
Cradhurst Cl DORK RH4 143 M3
Cradle La BOR GU35 180 B5
Craigans CRAWW RH11 164 C4
Craigen Av CROY/NA CR0 50 E8
Craignair Rd BRXS/STRHM SW2 31 J1
Craignish Av STRHM/NOR SW16 49 J2
Craig Rd RCHPK/HAM TW10 26 F5
Craigwell Av FELT TW13 24 D4
Craigwell Cl STA TW18 40 B1
Crakell Rd REIG RH2 147 M1
Crake Pl SHST GU47 72 A1
Cramhurst La MFD/CHID GU8 183 M3
Crampshaw La ASHTD KT21 103 J2
Crampton Rd PGE/AN SE20 32 F7
Cranborne Av SURB KT6 63 K2
Cranborne Wk CRAWE RH10 165 H6
Cranbourne Cl HORL RH6 * 160 E1
STRHM/NOR SW16 49 H3
Cranbrook Dr ESH/CLAY KT10 43 M8
WHTN TW2 25 L2
Cranbrook Rd HSLWW TW4 16 C6
THHTH CR7 49 M2
WIM/MER SW19 29 H8
Crane Av ISLW TW7 17 K7
Cranebank Ms TWK TW1 * 17 L7
Cranebrook WHTN TW2 25 M3
Crane Ct MORT/ESHN SW14 * 18 F6
SHST GU47 72 A1
Craneford Cl WHTN TW2 26 C1
Craneford Wy WHTN TW2 26 B1
Crane Lodge Rd HEST TW5 15 L1
Crane Park Rd WHTN TW2 25 L3
Crane Rd STWL/WRAY TW19 14 D8
WHTN TW2 26 B2
Cranes Dr BRYLDS KT5 45 H4
Cranes Pk BRYLDS KT5 45 H4
Cranes Park Av BRYLDS KT5 45 H4
Cranes Park Crs BRYLDS KT5 45 J4
Craneswater HYS/HAR UB3 15 J2
Crane Wy WHTN TW2 25 M1
Cranfield Rd East CAR SM5 66 D7
Cranfield Rd West CAR SM5 * 66 C7
Cranford Av STWL/WRAY TW19 23 H1
Cranford Cl PUR/KEN CR8 87 M3
RYNPK SW20 * 46 E1
STWL/WRAY TW19 23 H1
Cranford La HEST TW5 15 M2
HYS/HAR UB3 15 G1
Cranford Ri ESH/CLAY KT10 61 M4
Cranleigh Cl PGE/AN SE20 50 E2
SAND/SEL CR2 88 D2
Cranleigh Ct FARN GU14 92 C5
Cranleigh Gdns KUTN/CMB KT2 27 J7
SAND/SEL CR2 88 D2
SNWD SE25 50 B3
SUT SM1 65 L1
Cranleigh Md CRAN GU6 186 E3
Cranleigh Rd CRAN GU6 187 J1
ESH/CLAY KT10 43 M8
FELT TW13 24 C5
SHGR GU5 169 M2
WIM/MER SW19 47 K3
Cranley Cl GU GU1 117 K8
Cranley Dene GU GU1 117 K8
Cranley Gdns WLGTN SM6 66 F6
Cranley Pl WOKN/KNAP GU21 * 76 A8
Cranley Rd GU GU1 7 M4
WOT/HER KT12 60 C5
Cranmer Cl MRDN SM4 47 G6
WARL CR6 89 H7
WEY KT13 59 K6
Cranmer Ct HPTN TW12 25 L6
Cranmer Farm Cl MTCM CR4 48 C4
Cranmer Gdns WARL CR6 89 H7
Cranmer Rd CROY/NA CR0 2 B7
HPTN TW12 25 L6
KUTN/CMB KT2 27 H6
MTCM CR4 48 C4
Cranmer Ter TOOT SW17 30 A6
Cranmore Av ISLW TW7 16 F2
Cranmore Cl ALDT GU11 112 B8
Cranmore Gdns ALDT GU11 112 B8
Cranmore La ALDT GU11 112 B8
EHSLY KT24 119 L3
Cranmore Rd FRIM GU16 93 J5
Cranston Cl HSLW TW3 16 B4
REIG RH2 147 L1
Cranston Rd EGRIN RH19 162 F3
FSTH SE23 33 H2
Cranstoun Cl RGUW GU3 116 C4
Crantock Rd CAT SE6 33 M3
Cranwell Gv LTWR GU18 74 C1
SHPTN TW17 41 J4
Craster Rd BRXS/STRHM SW2 31 J1
Cravan Av FELT TW13 24 D3
Craven Cl RFNM GU10 155 M3
Craven Gdns WIM/MER SW19 29 L6
Craven Rd CRAWE RH10 165 K5
CROY/NA CR0 50 E8
KUTN/CMB KT2 9 G4
The Cravens HORL RH6 161 K3
Crawford Cl ISLW TW7 17 H4
Crawford Gdns CBLY GU15 72 E4
SWTR RH13 167 H6
Crawley Av CRAWE RH10 165 G2
CRAWE RH10 192 B3
CRAWW RH11 164 D3
CRAWW RH11 164 D7
Crawley Down Rd EGRIN RH19 193 R2
Crawley Dr CBLY GU15 73 J3
Crawley Goods Yd
CRAWE RH10 * 192 A3
Crawley Hl CBLY GU15 73 J4
Crawley La CRAWE RH10 165 L3
Crawley Market
CRAWE RH10 * 164 F4
Crawley Rdg CBLY GU15 73 J3
Crawley Rd HORS RH12 167 J5
Crawley Wood Cl CBLY GU15 73 J4
Crawshaw Rd CHERT KT16 58 A5
Crawters Cl CRAWE RH10 165 H3
Cray Av ASHTD KT21 83 H6
Crayke Hl CHSGTN KT9 63 H6
Crayonne Cl SUN TW16 42 B1
Credenhill St STRHM/NOR SW16 30 F7
Crediton Wy ESH/CLAY KT10 62 D4
Credon Cl FARN GU14 92 B4
Creek Rd E/WMO/HCT KT8 44 B4
The Creek SUN TW16 42 D5
Creeland Gv CAT SE6 33 J2
Cree's Meadow BFOR GU20 * 55 G6
Cremorne Gdns
HOR/WEW KT19 64 A7
Crerar Cl FARN GU14 92 A6
Crescent Ct HORL RH6 * 160 D5
Crescent Gdns WIM/MER SW19 29 K4
Crescent Gv MTCM CR4 48 B4
Crescent La ASHV GU12 113 L4
Crescent Rd BECK BR3 51 L2
CTHM CR3 108 D6
EGRIN RH19 162 E4
KUTN/CMB KT2 9 K2
REDH RH1 127 M7
REIG RH2 147 K2
RYNPK SW20 47 G1
SHPTN TW17 41 M5
The Crescent ASHF TW15 23 J6
BARN SW13 19 J4
BECK BR3 51 K1
BELMT SM2 85 K1
BRAK RG12 34 F4
CHERT KT16 40 D3
CROY/NA CR0 50 A6
CTHM CR3 109 K5
E/WMO/HCT KT8 43 J4
EGH TW20 21 J7
EGRIN RH19 178 D9
EPSOM KT18 83 K5
FARN GU14 92 F6
FNM GU9 134 A1
GUW GU2 6 A1
HORL RH6 160 D5
HORS RH12 166 D7
HYS/HAR UB3 14 F2
LHD/OX KT22 102 E4
NWMAL KT3 45 M2
REDH RH1 * 148 A3
REIG RH2 125 L8
SHPTN TW17 42 C7
SURB KT6 45 H5
SUT SM1 66 A4
WEY KT13 59 K2
WIM/MER SW19 29 K4
Crescent Wy HORL RH6 160 D5
STRHM/NOR SW16 31 J8
Crescent Wood Rd SYD SE26 32 D4
Cressall Cl LHD/OX KT22 102 E2
Cressall Md LHD/OX KT22 102 E2
Cressida Cha BNFD RG42 * 35 H1
Cressingham Gv SUT SM1 65 M3
Cresswell Rd FELT TW13 25 H4
SNWD SE25 50 D4
TWK TW1 18 A8
Cressys Cnr HSLW TW3 * 16 E5
Cresta Dr ADL/WDHM KT15 58 C8
Crest Hl SHGR GU5 142 B8
Creston Av WOKN/KNAP GU21 76 B7
Creston Wy WPK KT4 47 G8
Crest Rd SAND/SEL CR2 68 E6
The Crest BRYLDS KT5 45 K5
Crestway PUT/ROE SW15 19 K8
Crestwood Wy HSLWW TW4 16 C7
Creswell WOKN/KNAP GU21 * 76 A7
Creswell Cnr
WOKN/KNAP GU21 * 76 A7
Creswell Dr BECK BR3 51 L5
Crewdson Rd HORL RH6 160 E3
Crewe's Av WARL CR6 88 F6
Crewe's Cl WARL CR6 88 F6
Crewe's La WARL CR6 89 G6
Crichton Av WLGTN SM6 67 G4
Crichton Rd CAR SM5 66 C6

Cricket Ct EGRIN RH19 162 F2
Cricketers Cl CHSGTN KT9 63 G4
RDKG RH5 188 D1
Cricketers La BFOR GU20 55 G4
Cricketers Ms BAL SW12 30 E1
Cricketers Wk SYD SE26 32 F6
Cricket Field Gv CWTH RG45 52 A5
Cricket Field Rd HORS RH12 166 E8
Cricket Gn MFD/CHID GU8 183 R8
MTCM CR4 48 C4
Cricket Hl REDH RH1 149 J2
Cricket La BECK BR3 33 H7
RFNM GU10 156 A3
Cricket Lea BOR GU35 180 A12
Cricketts Hl SHGR GU5 141 K5
Cricket Vw WEY KT13 59 L4
Cricket Wy WEY KT13 60 B1
Cricklade Av BRXS/STRHM SW2 31 K5
Criffel Av BRXS/STRHM SW2 31 G3
Crimea Rd ALDT GU11 112 E7
Crimp Hl WDSR SL4 20 C1
Cripley Rd FARN GU14 92 B4
Cripplecrutch Hl
MFD/CHID GU8 199 N7
Crispen Rd FELT TW13 25 H5
Crispin Crs CROY/NA CR0 67 G2
Critchmere Hl HASM GU27 197 R6
Critchmere La HASM GU27 197 R7
Critchmere V HASM GU27 197 Q7
Critten La RDKG RH5 121 G6
Cricket Cl GSHT GU26 181 Q11
Crocker Cl ASC SL5 36 C1
Crockers La LING RH7 177 Q5
Crockerton Rd TOOT SW17 30 C3
Crockford Cl ADL/WDHM KT15 58 F3
Crockford Park Rd
ADL/WDHM KT15 58 F4
Crockham Cl CRAWW RH11 164 E6
Crocknorth Rd EHSLY KT24 120 C5
Crocus Cl CROY/NA CR0 51 G8
Croffets KWD/TDW/WH KT20 105 G3
Croft Av DORK RH4 122 E8
WWKM BR4 51 M8
Croft Cl HYS/HAR UB3 14 F2
Croft Ct EDEN TN8 153 M8
SUT SM1 * 66 A1
Crofters Cl FRIM GU16 74 A8
ISLW TW7 17 G7
REDH RH1 148 E2
Crofters Md CROY/NA CR0 69 J7
Croft La EDEN TN8 153 M8
RFNM GU10 132 B4
Croftleigh Av PUR/KEN CR8 87 K6
Crofton ASHTD KT21 83 H8
Crofton Av CHSWK W4 18 F2
ORP BR6 71 M1
WOT/HER KT12 60 F2
Crofton Cl BRAK RG12 35 H5
CHERT KT16 57 M6
Crofton Rd ORP BR6 71 K3
Crofton Ter RCH/KEW TW9 18 C6
Croft Rd ALDT GU11 134 E1
BH/WHM TN16 111 L8
CTHM CR3 109 J4
GODL GU7 168 A5
MFD/CHID GU8 183 M4
STRHM/NOR SW16 31 K8
SUT SM1 66 A4
WIM/MER SW19 29 M8
Crofts Cl MFD/CHID GU8 183 Q12
The Crofts SHPTN TW17 42 B4
The Croft CRAWW RH11 164 C4
HEST TW5 16 B2
Croft Wy FRIM GU16 73 J8
HORS RH12 166 D6
RCHPK/HAM TW10 26 E4
Croham Cl SAND/SEL CR2 68 B5
Croham Manor Rd
SAND/SEL CR2 68 B6
Croham Mt SAND/SEL CR2 68 B6
Croham Park Av SAND/SEL CR2 68 C4
Croham Rd SAND/SEL CR2 68 B4
Croham Valley Rd
SAND/SEL CR2 68 D5
Croindene Rd
STRHM/NOR SW16 49 H1
Cromer Hyde MRDN SM4 * 47 L5
Cromer Rd HTHAIR TW6 14 D5
SNWD SE25 50 E3
TOOT SW17 30 D7
Cromer Rd West HTHAIR TW6 14 D5
Cromford Wy NWMAL KT3 46 A1
Crompton Flds CRAWE RH10 165 G1
Crompton Wy CRAWE RH10 165 G2
Cromwell Av NWMAL KT3 46 C5
Cromwell Cl WOT/HER KT12 42 E8
Cromwell Gv CTHM CR3 107 M3
Cromwell Pl CRAN GU6 186 E4
EGRIN RH19 163 G6
MORT/ESHN SW14 18 F5
Cromwell Rd ASC SL5 36 E4
BECK BR3 51 H2
CBLY GU15 73 G2
CROY/NA CR0 2 D1
CTHM CR3 107 M3
FELT TW13 24 E2
HSLW TW3 16 D6
KUTN/CMB KT2 8 F5
REDH RH1 126 C8
TEDD TW11 26 D7
WIM/MER SW19 29 K6
WOT/HER KT12 60 E1
WPK KT4 64 A2
Cromwell St HSLW TW3 16 D6
Cromwell Ter HSLW TW3 * 16 D6
Cromwell Wy FARN GU14 92 E2
Crondall Ct CBLY GU15 72 E5
Crondall La RFNM GU10 132 F7
Crondall Rd RFNM GU10 154 D2
Cronks Hl REIG RH2 147 M1
Cronks Hill Cl REDH RH1 148 A2
Cronks Hill Rd REDH RH1 148 A2
Crooksbury Rd RFNM GU10 134 E6
Crosby Cl FELT TW13 25 H5
Crosby Hill Dr CBLY GU15 73 J2
Crosby Wy FNM GU9 4 F5
Crossacres WOKS/MYFD GU22 78 B6
Cross Deep TWK TW1 26 C4
Cross Deep Gdns TWK TW1 26 C3
Cross Fell BRAK RG12 34 D4
Crossfield Pl WEY KT13 59 L6
Cross Gdns FRIM GU16 93 J3
Cross Gates Cl BRAK RG12 35 J3
Cross Keys CRAWE RH10 164 F4
Cross Lances Rd HSLW TW3 16 E6
Crossland Rd REDH RH1 126 D8
THHTH CR7 49 L6
Crosslands CHERT KT16 58 B2
Crosslands Rd HOR/WEW KT19 64 A5
Cross La CHERT KT16 57 L5
FRIM GU16 93 J3
HORL RH6 161 M6
Cross Lanes GU GU1 7 L4
Crossley Cl BH/WHM TN16 91 G5
Cross Oak La REDH RH1 176 B2
Crosspath CRAWE RH10 * 165 G3
Cross Rd ASC SL5 37 J8
ASHV GU12 113 L6
BELMT SM2 65 K8
CROY/NA CR0 2 F3
FARN GU14 92 B8
FELT TW13 25 H5
HAYES BR2 71 H1
KUTN/CMB KT2 9 H3
KWD/TDW/WH KT20 104 F4
PUR/KEN CR8 87 L3
SUT SM1 66 A4
WEY KT13 * 60 A2
WIM/MER SW19 29 K8
The Crossroads EHSLY KT24 121 G2
Cross St BARN SW13 19 H4
FARN GU14 112 F1
HPTN TW12 25 M6
Crosswater La RFNM GU10 181 K5
Crossway BRAK RG12 34 F2
NWMAL KT3 46 F4
WOT/HER KT12 60 E1
Crossways ASHV GU12 112 F8
BELMT SM2 66 A7
BH/WHM TN16 110 F2
CRAWE RH10 165 J3
EGH TW20 22 A7
EHSLY KT24 121 G1
RFNM GU10 181 K8
SAND/SEL CR2 69 J6
SUN TW16 42 C1
Crossways Av EGRIN RH19 162 D4
Crossways Cl CRAWE RH10 165 H3
Crossways La REIG RH2 125 M2
Crossways Rd BECK BR3 51 K4
GSHT GU26 197 Q2
MTCM CR4 48 E3
The Crossways BRYLDS KT5 * 45 L8
COUL/CHIP CR5 107 J1
GUW GU2 138 C2
HEST TW5 16 C2
REDH RH1 126 E3
Crosswell Cl SHPTN TW17 41 M2
Crossweys GU GU1 * 7 G7
Crouch Cl BECK BR3 33 K7
Crouch House Rd EDEN TN8 153 K6
Crouchmans Cl SYD SE26 32 C4
Crouch Oak La
ADL/WDHM KT15 58 F3
Crowberry Cl CRAWW RH11 164 C8
Crowborough Cl WARL CR6 89 H8
Crowborough Dr WARL CR6 89 H8
Crowborough Rd TOOT SW17 30 D6
Crowcroft Cl GUW GU2 116 E4
Crow Hl ORP BR6 71 J8
Crowhurst Cl CRAWE RH10 192 D7
Crowhurst La OXTED RH8 152 A4
Crowhurst Md GDST RH9 128 F4
Crowhurst Rd LING RH7 178 E3
Crowhurst Village Rd
LING RH7 152 B7
Crowland Rd THHTH CR7 * 50 A4
Crowland Wk MRDN SM4 47 L6
Crowley Crs CROY/NA CR0 67 K4
Crown Ar KUT/HW KT1 8 D7
Crownbourne Ct SUT SM1 * 65 L3
Crown Cl DTCH/LGLY SL3 12 F2
WOT/HER KT12 42 F7
Crown Dl NRWD SE19 31 M7
Crown Dr FNM GU9 134 D4
Crown Hts GU GU1 139 H3
Crown Hl CROY/NA CR0 2 D6
Crown Hill Ct ASC SL5 36 E5
Crown La FNM GU9 134 D4
MRDN SM4 47 K3
STRHM/NOR SW16 31 K6
VW GU25 39 G6
Crown Lane Gdns
STRHM/NOR SW16 * 31 K6
Crown Meadow DTCH/LGLY SL3 12 E2
Crown Pde MRDN SM4 * 47 L4
Crownpits La GODL GU7 168 B6
Crown Pl SHST GU47 52 B8
Crown Ri CHERT KT16 40 C8
Crown Rd KUTN/CMB KT2 45 M1
MRDN SM4 47 K4
SUT SM1 65 L3
TWK TW1 17 L8
VW GU25 38 F6
Crown Rw BRAK RG12 35 G6
Crown Sq WOKN/KNAP GU21 10 E5
Crown St EGH TW20 21 K6
Crown Ter RCH/KEW TW9 18 C6
Crowntree Cl ISLW TW7 17 J1
Crown Yd HSLW TW3 16 F5
Crowther Rd SNWD SE25 50 D4
Crowthorne Cl
WAND/EARL SW18 29 J1
Crowthorne Rd BRAK RG12 34 C8
Crowthorne Rd North
BRAK RG12 34 E3
Croxden Wk MRDN SM4 47 M6
Croxted Cl DUL SE21 31 M1
Croxted Rd DUL SE21 31 M1
Croyde Cl FARN GU14 92 D3
Croydonbarn La GDST RH9 177 M5
The Croydon F/O CROY/NA CR0 2 C9
Croydon Gv CROY/NA CR0 2 A3
Croydon La BNSTD SM7 86 A3
Croydon La South BNSTD SM7 85 L4
Croydon Rd BECK BR3 51 G5
BH/WHM TN16 111 M8
CTHM CR3 108 D4
MTCM CR4 48 E5
PGE/AN SE20 50 E2
REIG RH2 125 M7
WARL CR6 110 A4
WLGTN SM6 66 E3
WWKM BR4 70 B2
Croylands Dr SURB KT6 45 H7
Croysdale Av SUN TW16 42 D3
Crozier Dr SAND/SEL CR2 68 E8
Cruikshank Lea SHST GU47 72 B3
Crunden Rd SAND/SEL CR2 68 A6
Crusader Gdns CROY/NA CR0 3 H8
Crusoe Rd MTCM CR4 30 C8
Crutchfield La HORL RH6 175 K3
WOT/HER KT12 60 E1
Crystal Palace NRWD SE19 * 32 D8
Crystal Palace Pde NRWD SE19 32 C7
Crystal Palace Park Rd
SYD SE26 32 D6
Crystal Ter NRWD SE19 32 A7
Cubitt St CROY/NA CR0 67 J4
Cubitt Wy WOKN/KNAP GU21 76 A8
Cuckfield Cl CRAWW RH11 164 B7
Cuckmere Crs CRAWW RH11 164 B5
Cuckoo La CHOB/PIR GU24 75 G3
Cuckoo V CHOB/PIR GU24 75 G3
Cuda's Cl HOR/WEW KT19 64 C3
Cuddington Av WPK KT4 64 C2
Cuddington Cl
KWD/TDW/WH KT20 104 F2
Cuddington Gld
HOR/WEW KT19 83 K2
Cuddington Park Cl BNSTD SM7 85 J3
Cuddington Wy BELMT SM2 85 G2
Cudham Cl BELMT SM2 65 K8
Cudham Dr CROY/NA CR0 69 L8
Cudham La North RSEV TN14 91 M4
Cudham La South RSEV TN14 91 M5
Cudham Rd BH/WHM TN16 111 H1
ORP BR6 91 K1
Cudham St CAT SE6 33 M1
Cudworth La RDKG RH5 173 R8
Cudworth Pk RDKG RH5 * 174 B9
Cuffs Hl CRAWE RH10 192 D11
Cullens Ms ALDT GU11 * 112 D8
Cullerne Cl EW KT17 64 C8
Cullesden Rd PUR/KEN CR8 87 L5
Cull's Rd RGUW GU3 114 E8
Culmer La MFD/CHID GU8 183 N6
Culmington Rd SAND/SEL CR2 67 M6
Culsac Rd SURB KT6 63 H1
Culverden Rd BAL SW12 30 F4
Culverden Ter WEY KT13 * 60 A2
Culver Dr OXTED RH8 130 B4
Culverhay ASHTD KT21 83 H6
Culverhouse Gdns
STRHM/NOR SW16 31 J5
Culverlands Crs ASHV GU12 113 J6
Culverley Rd CAT SE6 33 L2
Culver Rd SHST GU47 52 A8
Culvers Av CAR SM5 66 C1
Culvers Retreat CAR SM5 48 C8
Culvers Wy CAR SM5 66 C2
Cumberland Av GUW GU2 116 D3
Cumberland Cl HOR/WEW KT19 64 B8
RYNPK SW20 29 G8
TWK TW1 17 L8
Cumberland Dr BRAK RG12 35 G1
CHSGTN KT9 63 H2
ESH/CLAY KT10 62 D1
Cumberland Pl SUN TW16 42 D4
Cumberland Rd ASHF TW15 23 G4
BARN SW13 19 J3
CBLY GU15 73 M5
RCH/KEW TW9 18 D3
SNWD SE25 50 E6
Cumberlands PUR/KEN CR8 88 A5
Cumberland St STA TW18 22 A6
Cumberland Ter PGE/AN SE20 * 32 E8
Cumberlow Av SNWD SE25 50 D3
Cumbernauld Gdns SUN TW16 24 C6
Cumbrae Gdns SURB KT6 63 G1
Cumbria Ct FARN GU14 93 H8
Cumnor Gdns EW KT17 64 D5
Cumnor Ri PUR/KEN CR8 87 M7
Cumnor Rd BELMT SM2 65 M5
Cumnor Wy BRAK RG12 35 H4
Cunliffe Cl EPSOM KT18 103 L6
Cunliffe Rd HOR/WEW KT19 64 C3
Cunliffe St STRHM/NOR SW16 30 F7
Cunningham Av GU GU1 117 K7
Cunningham Cl WWKM BR4 69 L1
Cunningham Rd BNSTD SM7 86 A5
Cunnington Rd FARN GU14 93 H8
Cunworth Ct BRAK RG12 34 B6
Curfew Bell Rd CHERT KT16 40 C7
Curlew Cl SAND/SEL CR2 89 G1
Curlew Gdns RGUE GU4 118 A6
Curley Hill Rd LTWR GU18 74 B2
Curling Cl COUL/CHIP CR5 107 J2
Curling V GUW GU2 6 A8
Curly Bridge Cl FARN GU14 92 C1
Curnick's La WNWD SE27 31 M5
Curran Av WLGTN SM6 66 D2
Currie Hill Cl WIM/MER SW19 29 J5
Curtis Cl BOR GU35 180 D11
CBLY GU15 73 M2
Curtis Field Rd
STRHM/NOR SW16 31 J5
Curtis La BOR GU35 180 D11
Curtis Rd DORK RH4 144 C1
HOR/WEW KT19 63 M3
HSLWW TW4 25 J1
Curvan Cl EW KT17 64 C8
Curzon Av HORS RH12 166 E7
Curzon Br CHOB/PIR GU24 94 D4
Curzon Cl WEY KT13 59 K3
Curzon Rd THHTH CR7 49 K6
WEY KT13 59 K3
Cusack Cl TWK TW1 * 26 C5
Cuthbert Gdns SNWD SE25 50 B3
Cuthbert Rd ASHV GU12 113 K3
CROY/NA CR0 2 B6
Cuttinglye La CRAWE RH10 193 M4
Cuttinglye Rd CRAWE RH10 193 N3
Cutts Rd ALDT GU11 113 G2
Cyclamen Cl HPTN TW12 25 K7
Cyclamen Wy HOR/WEW KT19 63 M4
Cygnet Av EBED/NFELT TW14 24 F1
The Cygnets FELT TW13 25 H5
STA TW18 22 C6
Cypress FARN GU14 72 C8
Cypress Av WHTN TW2 25 M1
Cypress Ct VW GU25 39 J4
Cypress Gv ASHV GU12 113 J2
Cypress Rd GU GU1 116 F6
SNWD SE25 50 B2
Cypress Wk EGH TW20 20 E7
Cypress Wy BNSTD SM7 85 G4
GSHT GU26 197 Q3
Cyprians Av CHOB/PIR GU24 95 L3
Cyprus Rd FRIM GU16 94 A1

D

D'Abernon Cl ESH/CLAY KT10 61 K3
D'Abernon Dr COB KT11 81 H6
Dacre Rd CROY/NA CR0 49 H7
Dacres Est FSTH SE23 * 33 G4
Dacres Rd FSTH SE23 33 G4
Daffodil Cl CROY/NA CR0 51 G8
HPTN TW12 25 K7
Daffodil Dr CHOB/PIR GU24 75 K6
Dafforne Rd TOOT SW17 30 C4
Dagden Rd RGUE GU4 139 H6
Dagley La RGUE GU4 139 G7
Dagmar Rd KUTN/CMB KT2 9 H4
SNWD SE25 50 B4
Dagnall Pk SNWD SE25 50 B5
Dagnall Rd SNWD SE25 50 B5
Dagnan Rd BAL SW12 30 E1
Dahlia Gdns MTCM CR4 49 G4
Dahomey Rd
STRHM/NOR SW16 30 F7
Daimler Wy WLGTN SM6 67 H6
Dairy Cl THHTH CR7 49 M2
Dairyfields CRAWW RH11 164 C5
Dairy Gate Rd FARN GU14 112 E1
Dairy La EDEN TN8 131 L8
Dairymans Wk RGUE GU4 117 L3
Daisy Cl CROY/NA CR0 51 G8
Daisy Meadow EGH TW20 21 K6
Dakin Cl CRAWE RH10 165 L8
The Dakins EGRIN RH19 162 F5
Dakota Cl WLGTN SM6 67 J6
Dalcross BRAK RG12 35 H6
Dalcross Rd HSLWW TW4 16 B4
Dale Av HSLWW TW4 16 B5
Dalebury Rd TOOT SW17 30 C3
Dale Cl ADL/WDHM KT15 58 E4
ASC SL5 37 K5
HORS RH12 167 J4
RFNM GU10 155 J2
Dalegarth Gdns PUR/KEN CR8 88 A3
Daleham Av EGH TW20 21 K7
Dale Lodge Rd ASC SL5 37 K5
Dale Park Av CAR SM5 66 C1
Dale Park Rd NRWD SE19 49 M1
Dale Rd FROW RH18 195 N12
PUR/KEN CR8 87 K2
SUN TW16 * 24 C8
SUT SM1 65 J3
WOT/HER KT12 42 C7
Daleside Rd HOR/WEW KT19 64 A5
STRHM/NOR SW16 30 E6
The Dale HAYES BR2 71 G3
Dale Vw EPSOM KT18 103 L5
HASM GU27 198 A8
WOKN/KNAP GU21 76 D8
Dalewood Gdns CRAWE RH10 165 H2
WPK KT4 64 E1
Dalkeith Rd DUL SE21 31 M2
Dallas Rd CHEAM SM3 65 H5
SYD SE26 32 E5
Dallaway Gdns EGRIN RH19 162 F4
Dalley Ct SHST GU47 72 A2
Dallington Cl WOT/HER KT12 60 F5
Dalmain Rd FSTH SE23 33 G2
Dalmally Rd CROY/NA CR0 3 K2
Dalmeny Av STRHM/NOR SW16 49 K2
Dalmeny Crs HSLW TW3 17 G6
Dalmeny Rd CAR SM5 66 D6
WPK KT4 64 E2
Dalmore Av ESH/CLAY KT10 62 C5
Dalmore Rd DUL SE21 31 M3
Dalston Cl CBLY GU15 74 A6
Dalton Av MTCM CR4 48 B2
Dalton Cl CRAWW RH11 191 K12
Dalton St WNWD SE27 31 L3
Damask Cl CHOB/PIR GU24 75 H3
Dampier Wk CRAWW RH11 * 191 L12
Danbrook Rd
STRHM/NOR SW16 49 H1
Danbury Ms WLGTN SM6 66 E3
Dancer Rd RCH/KEW TW9 18 D5
Danebury CROY/NA CR0 69 L5
Danebury Av PUT/ROE SW15 28 C1
Daneby Rd CAT SE6 33 M4
Dane Ct WOKS/MYFD GU22 78 C5
Danecourt Gdns CROY/NA CR0 3 K7
Danehurst Cl EGH TW20 21 H7
Danehurst Crs SWTR RH13 167 J7
Danemere St PUT/ROE SW15 19 M5
Danemore La GDST RH9 151 H7
Dane Rd ASHF TW15 23 M7
WARL CR6 89 G7
WIM/MER SW19 47 M1
Danesbury Rd FELT TW13 24 E2
Danes Cl LHD/OX KT22 81 M4
Danescourt Crs SUT SM1 65 M1
Danesfield RPLY/SEND GU23 98 C5
Danesfield Cl WOT/HER KT12 60 E2
Danes Hl WOKS/MYFD GU22 11 H7
Daneshill REDH RH1 126 B7
Daneshill La REDH RH1 126 B7
Danes Hill School Dr
LHD/OX KT22 * 82 A4
Danesmead COB KT11 81 K1
Danesrood GU GU1 7 L5
Danes Wy LHD/OX KT22 82 A4
Daneswood Av CAT SE6 33 M4
Daneswood Cl WEY KT13 59 L4
Danetree Cl HOR/WEW KT19 63 M6
Danetree Rd HOR/WEW KT19 63 M6
Daniel Cl HSLWW TW4 25 J1
TOOT SW17 30 B7
Daniell Wy CROY/NA CR0 49 H8
Daniels La WARL CR6 89 J6
Daniel Wy BNSTD SM7 85 L4
Danley La HASM GU27 197 M10
Dan Manson Dr CHSWK W4 19 G4
Danses Cl RGUE GU4 118 A6
Danvers Wy CTHM CR3 107 M5
Dapdune Rd GU GU1 7 G4
Darby Cl CTHM CR3 107 M4
Darby Crs SUN TW16 42 F2
Darby Gdns SUN TW16 42 F2
Darcy Av WLGTN SM6 66 F3
Darcy Cl COUL/CHIP CR5 107 L1
Darcy Pl ASHTD KT21 83 J7
Darcy Rd ASHTD KT21 83 J7
D'Arcy Rd CHEAM SM3 65 G3
Darcy Rd ISLW TW7 17 K3
STRHM/NOR SW16 49 H2
Darell Rd RCH/KEW TW9 18 D5
Darenth Wy HORL RH6 160 C1
Darfield Rd RGUE GU4 117 K5
Dargate Cl NRWD SE19 32 C8
Dark La RGUW GU3 136 E5
Darlaston Rd WIM/MER SW19 29 G8
Darley Cl ADL/WDHM KT15 58 F4
CROY/NA CR0 51 G6
Darleydale CRAWW RH11 164 E7
Darleydale Cl SHST GU47 52 A7
Darley Dene Ct
ADL/WDHM KT15 * 58 F3
Darley Dr NWMAL KT3 46 A2
Darley Gdns MRDN SM4 47 L6
Darlington Rd WNWD SE27 31 L6
Darmaine Cl SAND/SEL CR2 67 M6
Darnley Pk WEY KT13 59 L2
Darracott Cl CBLY GU15 73 M1
Dart Cl DTCH/LGLY SL3 12 E1
Dartmouth Av
WOKN/KNAP GU21 77 M4
Dartmouth Cl BRAK RG12 35 H3
Dartmouth Pl CHSWK W4 19 H1
FSTH SE23 32 F3
Dartmouth Rd SYD SE26 32 E4
Dartnell Av BF/WBF KT14 78 F2
Dartnell Cl BF/WBF KT14 78 E2
Dartnell Ct BF/WBF KT14 78 F2
Dartnell Crs BF/WBF KT14 78 E2
Dartnell Park Rd BF/WBF KT14 78 E2
Dartnell Pl BF/WBF KT14 78 E2
Dartnell Rd CROY/NA CR0 3 J1
Dart Rd FARN GU14 92 A3
Darvel Cl WOKN/KNAP GU21 76 D6
Darvill Hts FNM GU9 * 5 K4
Darvills La FNM GU9 5 K3
Darwall Dr ASC SL5 36 A2
Darwin Cl HORS RH12 167 J5
Darwin Gv ALDT GU11 112 F6
Daryngton Dr GU GU1 117 L8
Dashwood Cl BF/WBF KT14 78 F2
BRAK RG12 35 G1
Dashwood Lang Rd
ADL/WDHM KT15 59 H3
Dassett Rd WNWD SE27 31 L6
Datchet Rd CAT SE6 33 J4
DTCH/LGLY SL3 12 C5
Daux Hl HORS RH12 166 E3
Davenport Cl TEDD TW11 * 26 D7
Davenport Rd BRAK RG12 35 H1
Daventry Cl DTCH/LGLY SL3 13 J3
Daventry Ct BNFD RG42 34 E1
David Cl HYS/HAR UB3 15 G2
David Rd DTCH/LGLY SL3 13 J4
Davidson Rd CROY/NA CR0 3 G3
David's Rd FSTH SE23 32 F2
David Twigg Cl KUTN/CMB KT2 8 F4
Davies Cl CROY/NA CR0 50 C6
GODL GU7 168 A2
Davies Wk ISLW TW7 17 G3
Davis Cl CRAWW RH11 191 K12
Davis Gdns SHST GU47 72 B2
Davis Rd CHSGTN KT9 63 K3
WEY KT13 59 J8
Davos Cl WOKS/MYFD GU22 97 H1
Dawell Dr BH/WHM TN16 90 F7
Dawes Av ISLW TW7 17 K7
Dawes Ct ESH/CLAY KT10 61 L3
Dawley Ride DTCH/LGLY SL3 13 H3
Dawlish Av WAND/EARL SW18 29 L3
Dawnay Cl ASC SL5 36 C1
Dawnay Gdns
WAND/EARL SW18 30 A3
Dawnay Rd CBLY GU15 72 E1
GT/LBKH KT23 101 L8
WAND/EARL SW18 29 M3
Dawn Cl HSLWW TW4 16 B5
Dawney Hl CHOB/PIR GU24 95 H3
Dawneys Rd CHOB/PIR GU24 95 H4
Dawn Redwood Cl
DTCH/LGLY SL3 12 D5
Dawsmere Cl CBLY GU15 73 M4
Dawson Rd BF/WBF KT14 79 G1
KUT/HW KT1 9 H8
Daybrook Rd WIM/MER SW19 47 L2
Daylesford Av PUT/ROE SW15 19 K6
Daymerslea Rdg LHD/OX KT22 102 F3
Day's Acre SAND/SEL CR2 68 C8
Daysbrook Rd
BRXS/STRHM SW2 31 J2
Dayseys Hl REDH RH1 176 F1
Dayspring GUW GU2 116 E4
Deacon Cl COB KT11 100 E1
CTHM CR3 107 M5
PUR/KEN CR8 67 H7
Deacon Ct LING RH7 * 178 D5
Deacon Fld GUW GU2 6 B2
Deacon Rd KUTN/CMB KT2 9 G5
Deacons Wk HPTN TW12 25 K5
Deadbrook La ASHV GU12 113 H6
Deal Rd TOOT SW17 30 D7
Dealtry Rd PUT/ROE SW15 19 M6
Dean Cl WOKS/MYFD GU22 78 B6
Deanery Rd EDEN TN8 131 M8
GODL GU7 168 B4
Deanhill Ct MORT/ESHN SW14 * 18 E6
Deanhill Rd MORT/ESHN SW14 18 E6
Dean La REDH RH1 106 F6
Deanoak La REIG RH2 174 G2
Dean Pde CBLY GU15 * 73 J1
Dean Rd CROY/NA CR0 68 A3
GODL GU7 168 A3
HPTN TW12 25 K6
HSLW TW3 16 E7
Deans Cl CHSWK W4 18 E1
CROY/NA CR0 3 J7
KWD/TDW/WH KT20 104 E6
Deans Ct BFOR GU20 55 G6
Deansfield CTHM CR3 108 C7
Deansgate BRAK RG12 34 D7
Deans Gate Cl FSTH SE23 33 G4

Deans La KWD/TDW/WH KT20 104 E7
REDH RH1 127 K7
Deans Rd REDH RH1 126 F4
SUT SM1 65 L2
Deans Wk COUL/CHIP CR5 87 K8
Dean Wk GT/LBKH KT23 101 L8
De'Arn Gdns MTCM CR4 48 B3
Debden Cl KUTN/CMB KT2 27 G6
Deborah Cl ISLW TW7 17 H3
De Broome Rd FELT TW13 24 F2
De Burgh Gdns
KWD/TDW/WH KT20 105 G1
De Burgh Pk BNSTD SM7 85 L5
Deburgh Rd WIM/MER SW19 29 M8
Decimus Cl THHTH CR7 * 50 A4
Dedisham Cl CRAWE RH10 165 J5
Dedswell Dr RGUE GU4 118 D3
Deedman Cl ASHV GU12 113 K7
Deepcut Bridge Rd FRIM GU16 74 A8
Deepdale BRAK RG12 34 D4
WIM/MER SW19 29 G5
Deep Dene HASM GU27 197 R7
Deepdene RFNM GU10 156 A3
Deepdene Av CROY/NA CR0 3 K8
RDKG RH5 144 F2
Deepdene Avenue Rd
DORK RH4 122 F8
Deepdene Dr RDKG RH5 144 F1
Deepdene Gdns
BRXS/STRHM SW2 31 J1
DORK RH4 144 E1
Deepdene Park Rd RDKG RH5 144 F1
Deepdene V DORK RH4 122 F8
Deepdene Wd RDKG RH5 145 G2
Deepfield Rd BRAK RG12 35 G2
Deepfields HORL RH6 160 C1
Deepfield Wy COUL/CHIP CR5 87 H6
Deep Pool La CHOB/PIR GU24 76 D3
Deeprose Cl GUW GU2 116 E4
Deepwell Cl ISLW TW7 17 K3
Deep Well Dr CBLY GU15 73 H4
Deerbarn Rd GUW GU2 6 C1
Deerbrook Rd HNHL SE24 31 L2
Deerhurst Cl FELT TW13 24 D5
Deerhurst Crs HPTN TW12 25 M6
Deerhurst Rd
STRHM/NOR SW16 31 J6
Deerings Rd REIG RH2 125 L8
Deerleap BOR GU35 * 196 H1
Deer Leap LTWR GU18 74 D1
Deerleap Rd DORK RH4 143 L3
Dee Rd RCH/KEW TW9 18 C6
Deer Park Cl KUTN/CMB KT2 9 L2
Deer Park Gdns MTCM CR4 * 48 A4
Deer Park Rd WIM/MER SW19 47 L2
Deer Park Wy WWKM BR4 70 C1
Deer Rock Hl BRAK RG12 34 F6
Deer Rock Rd CBLY GU15 73 J2
Deers Farm Cl RPLY/SEND GU23 79 H6
Deerswood Cl CRAWW RH11 164 D3
CTHM CR3 108 D6
Deerswood Rd CRAWW RH11 164 D3
Deeside Rd TOOT SW17 30 A4
Dee Wy HOR/WEW KT19 64 B8
Defiant Wy WLGTN SM6 67 H6
Defoe Av RCH/KEW TW9 18 D2
Defoe Cl TOOT SW17 30 B7
Defoe Pl TOOT SW17 30 B3
De Frene Rd SYD SE26 33 G5
De Havilland Dr WEY KT13 79 H1
De Havilland Rd HEST TW5 15 M2
De Havilland Wy
STWL/WRAY TW19 14 A8
Delabole Rd REDH RH1 127 H3
Delagarde Rd BH/WHM TN16 111 M8
Delamare Crs CROY/NA CR0 50 F6
Delamere Rd REIG RH2 147 L4
RYNPK SW20 47 G1
Delaporte Cl EW KT17 84 B2
De Lara Wy WOKN/KNAP GU21 10 A8
Delcombe Av WPK KT4 46 F8
Delderfield ASHTD KT21 103 G2
Delfont Cl CRAWE RH10 165 M6
Delia St WAND/EARL SW18 29 L1
Delius Gdns SWTR RH13 167 L5
Dellbow Rd EBED/NFELT TW14 15 L5
Dell Campus BRAK RG12 * 34 B2
Dell Cl HASM GU27 198 B6
LHD/OX KT22 102 A5
RDKG RH5 122 F1
WLGTN SM6 66 F3
Dellfield Cl BECK BR3 51 M1
Dell Gv FRIM GU16 73 J7
Dell La EW KT17 64 D4
Dell Rd EW KT17 64 D5
The Dell BECK BR3 * 33 K8
BTFD TW8 17 M1
EBED/NFELT TW14 24 E1
EGRIN RH19 163 J4
FNM GU9 133 M2
HORL RH6 160 E2
HORL RH6 175 M4
KWD/TDW/WH KT20 104 F3
NRWD SE19 50 C1
REIG RH2 * 125 K7
WOKN/KNAP GU21 96 F1
Dell Wk NWMAL KT3 46 B2
Delmey Cl CROY/NA CR0 3 K7
Delta Cl CHOB/PIR GU24 56 C8
WPK KT4 64 B2
Delta Dr HORL RH6 160 D5
Delta Rd CHOB/PIR GU24 56 C8
WOKN/KNAP GU21 11 G3
WPK KT4 64 B2
Delta Wy EGH TW20 39 M1
Delves KWD/TDW/WH KT20 105 G3
Delville Cl FARN GU14 92 A6
Demesne Rd WLGTN SM6 67 G3
De Montfort Pde
STRHM/NOR SW16 * 31 H4
De Montfort Rd
STRHM/NOR SW16 31 H4
Denbigh Cl SUT SM1 65 J4
Denbigh Gdns
RCHPK/HAM TW10 18 C7
Denbigh Rd HASM GU27 198 E8
HSLW TW3 16 E4
Denby Rd COB KT11 80 F2
Denchers Plat CRAWW RH11 164 F1
Dencliffe STA TW15 * 23 K6
Dendy St BAL SW12 30 D2
Dene Av HSLW TW3 16 C5
Dene Cl ASHV GU12 113 M7
BRAK RG12 34 F1
CBLY GU15 73 K1
COUL/CHIP CR5 106 B1
HASM GU27 198 D7
HORL RH6 160 B1
RFNM GU10 156 A3
WPK KT4 64 C1
Denefield Dr PUR/KEN CR8 88 A5
Dene Gdns THDIT KT7 62 D1
Denehurst Gdns
RCHPK/HAM TW10 18 D6
WHTN TW2 26 A1
Dene La RFNM GU10 156 A3
Dene La West RFNM GU10 156 A4
Dene Pl WOKN/KNAP GU21 76 E8
Dene Rd ASHTD KT21 103 J1
FARN GU14 92 C6
GU GU1 7 J5
Dene St DORK RH4 144 E2
Dene Street Gdns DORK RH4 144 E2
The Dene BELMT SM2 85 J1
CROY/NA CR0 69 G3
E/WMO/HCT KT8 43 J5
Dene Tye CRAWE RH10 165 L3
Dene Wk RFNM GU10 156 B3
Denewood EW KT17 * 84 B3
Denfield DORK RH4 144 E4
Denham Crs MTCM CR4 48 C4
Denham Gv BRAK RG12 * 34 F6
Denham Pl RDKG RH5 * 173 L5
Denham Rd EBED/NFELT TW14 24 F1
EGH TW20 21 K5
EW KT17 84 C2
Denholm Gdns RGUE GU4 117 K5
Denison Rd FELT TW13 24 C5
WIM/MER SW19 30 A7
Denleigh Gdns THDIT KT7 * 44 B6
Denly Wy LTWR GU18 54 F8
Denman Dr ASHF TW15 23 L7
ESH/CLAY KT10 62 D4
Denmans CRAWE RH10 165 M3
Denmark Av WIM/MER SW19 29 H8
Denmark Ct MRDN SM4 47 K5
Denmark Gdns CAR SM5 66 C2
Denmark Rd CAR SM5 66 C2
KUT/HW KT1 8 F9
SNWD SE25 50 E5
WHTN TW2 26 A4
WIM/MER SW19 29 G7
Denmark Sq ASHV GU12 113 H7
Denmark St ASHV GU12 113 G7
Denmead Ct BRAK RG12 35 H6
Denmead Rd CROY/NA CR0 2 B3
Dennan Rd SURB KT6 45 J8
Denne Pde HORS RH12 166 F8
Denne Rd CRAWW RH11 164 F5
HORS RH12 166 F8
Dennett Rd CROY/NA CR0 2 A1
Dennettsland Rd EDEN TN8 131 M8
Denning Av CROY/NA CR0 67 K4
Denning Cl HPTN TW12 25 J7
The Denningtons WPK KT4 64 B1
Dennis Cl REDH RH1 126 B6
Dennis Park Crs RYNPK SW20 47 H1
Dennis Reeve Cl MTCM CR4 48 C1
Dennis Rd E/WMO/HCT KT8 43 M4
Dennistoun Cl CBLY GU15 73 G4
Dennis Wy GU GU1 117 H3
Densham Dr PUR/KEN CR8 87 K4
Densole Cl BECK BR3 * 51 H1
Denton Cl REDH RH1 148 D5
Denton Gv WOT/HER KT12 61 H1
Denton Rd TWK TW1 18 A8
Denton Wy FRIM GU16 73 G7
WOKN/KNAP GU21 76 D7
Dents Gv KWD/TDW/WH KT20 125 J2
Denvale Trade Pk MTCM CR4 48 A4
Denvale Wk WOKN/KNAP GU21 76 D8
Denzil Rd GUW GU2 6 D6
Departures Rd HORL RH6 160 C6
Depot Rd CRAWW RH11 164 F1
EW KT17 84 B3
HSLW TW3 17 G5
SWTR RH13 167 H7
Derby Arms Rd EPSOM KT18 84 C7
Derby Cl EPSOM KT18 104 E1
Derby Hl FSTH SE23 32 F3
Derby Hill Crs FSTH SE23 32 F3
Derby Rd BRYLDS KT5 45 K8
CROY/NA CR0 2 B4
GUW GU2 116 C8
HASM GU27 198 C6
HSLW TW3 16 E6
MORT/ESHN SW14 18 E6
SUT SM1 65 J5
WIM/MER SW19 29 K8
Derby Stables Rd EPSOM KT18 84 B7
Derek Av HOR/WEW KT19 63 K5
WLGTN SM6 66 E2
Derek Cl HOR/WEW KT19 63 L4
Deri Dene Cl
STWL/WRAY TW19 * 14 B8
Dering Pl CROY/NA CR0 67 M3
Dering Rd CROY/NA CR0 67 M3
Derinton Rd TOOT SW17 30 D5
Deronda Rd HNHL SE24 31 L2
De Ros Pl EGH TW20 21 K7
Deroy Cl CAR SM5 66 C5
Derrick Av SAND/SEL CR2 67 M8
Derrick Rd BECK BR3 51 J3
Derry Cl ASHV GU12 113 J4
Derrydown WOKS/MYFD GU22 96 E3
Derry Rd CROY/NA CR0 67 H2
FARN GU14 72 C8
Derwent Av ASHV GU12 113 J5
PUT/ROE SW15 28 B5
Derwent Cl ADL/WDHM KT15 59 G4
CRAWW RH11 164 B5
EBED/NFELT TW14 24 C2
ESH/CLAY KT10 62 B5
FARN GU14 92 A5
FNM GU9 133 K3
HORS RH12 167 L3
Derwent Dr PUR/KEN CR8 88 A4
Derwent Rd EGH TW20 21 L7
LTWR GU18 74 E1
PGE/AN SE20 50 D2
RYNPK SW20 47 G6
WHTN TW2 16 E8
Desborough Cl SHPTN TW17 41 K7
Desford Wy ASHF TW15 23 J3
Desmond Tutu Dr FSTH SE23 33 H2
Detillens La OXTED RH8 130 D3
Detling Rd CRAWW RH11 191 M12
Dettingen Crs FRIM GU16 94 A1
Dettingen Rd FRIM GU16 94 B1
Devana End CAR SM5 66 C2
Devas Rd RYNPK SW20 46 F1
Devenish La ASC SL5 37 G8
Devenish Rd ASC SL5 37 G6
Deveraux Cl BECK BR3 51 M5
De Vere Cl WLGTN SM6 67 H6
Devereux La BARN SW13 19 L2
Devey Cl KUTN/CMB KT2 28 C8
Devil's La EGH TW20 21 M7
LIPH GU30 197 K10
Devitt Cl ASHTD KT21 83 K6
Devoil Cl RGUE GU4 117 L4
Devoke Wy WOT/HER KT12 61 G1
Devon Av WHTN TW2 25 M2
Devon Bank GUW GU2 6 F9
Devon Cl HOR/WEW KT19 83 K2
PUR/KEN CR8 88 B6
SHST GU47 72 A2
Devon Crs REDH RH1 126 A8
Devoncroft Gdns TWK TW1 26 D1
Devon Rd ALDT GU11 112 B2
BELMT SM2 65 H7
REDH RH1 126 F4
WOT/HER KT12 60 F3
Devonshire Av BELMT SM2 65 M6
KWD/TDW/WH KT20 123 M5
WOKN/KNAP GU21 77 M4
Devonshire Ct FELT TW13 * 24 E3
Devonshire Dr CBLY GU15 73 J2
SURB KT6 45 G8
Devonshire Gdns CHSWK W4 18 F2
Devonshire Pl ALDT GU11 112 C8
Devonshire Rd BELMT SM2 65 M6
CAR SM5 66 D3
CROY/NA CR0 2 E1
FELT TW13 25 H4
FSTH SE23 33 G1
SWTR RH13 167 G7
WEY KT13 * 59 K3
WIM/MER SW19 30 B8
Devonshire Wy CROY/NA CR0 69 J1
Devon Wy CHSGTN KT9 62 F3
HOR/WEW KT19 63 L4
Devon Waye HEST TW5 16 D2
Dewar Cl CRAWW RH11 * 164 A5
Dewey St TOOT SW17 30 C6
Dewlands GDST RH9 128 F5
Dewlands Cl CRAN GU6 186 D2
Dewlands La CRAN GU6 186 D2
Dew Pond Cl SWTR RH13 167 J6
Dewsbury Gdns WPK KT4 64 D2
Dexter Dr EGRIN RH19 162 F5
Diamedes Av STWL/WRAY TW19 23 J1
Diamond Hl CBLY GU15 73 H2
Diamond Rdg CBLY GU15 73 G2
Diamond Wy FARN GU14 112 B1
Diana Gdns SURB KT6 63 J1
Dianthus Cl CHERT KT16 40 B7
Dianthus Ct WOKS/MYFD GU22 10 B8
Dibdin Cl SUT SM1 65 K2
Dibdin Rd SUT SM1 65 K2
Diceland Rd BNSTD SM7 85 J6
Dickens Cl EGRIN RH19 162 D4
RCHPK/HAM TW10 27 H3
Dickens Dr ADL/WDHM KT15 58 C5
Dickenson Rd FELT TW13 24 F6
Dickenson's La SNWD SE25 50 D6
Dickenson's Pl SNWD SE25 50 D6
Dickens Pl DTCH/LGLY SL3 13 H3
Dickens Rd CRAWE RH10 164 F7
Dickens Wood Cl NRWD SE19 31 L8
Dickerage Hl NWMAL KT3 45 M2
Dickerage La NWMAL KT3 45 M3
Dickerage Rd KUT/HW KT1 45 M1
Dickins Wy SWTR RH13 205 N9
Dick Turpin Wy
EBED/NFELT TW14 15 J6
Digby Pl CROY/NA CR0 3 K7
Digby Wy BF/WBF KT14 79 J2
Digdens Ri EPSOM KT18 83 M5
Dillwyn Cl SYD SE26 33 H5
Dilston Rd LHD/OX KT22 102 D1
Dilton Gdns PUT/ROE SW15 28 D2
Dingle Cl CRAWW RH11 164 B4
Dingle Rd ASHF TW15 23 L6
The Dingle CRAWW RH11 164 D4
Dingley La STRHM/NOR SW16 31 G3
Dingley Wy FARN GU14 112 D1
Dingwall Av CROY/NA CR0 2 D6
Dingwall Rd CAR SM5 66 C7
CROY/NA CR0 2 E5
WAND/EARL SW18 29 M1
Dinsdale Cl WOKS/MYFD GU22 10 F7
Dinsdale Gdns SNWD SE25 50 B4
Dinsmore Rd BAL SW12 30 E1
Dinton Rd KUTN/CMB KT2 9 H2
WIM/MER SW19 30 A7
Dippenhall Rd RFNM GU10 132 E7
Dippenhall St RFNM GU10 132 D4
Dirdene Cl EW KT17 84 C2
Dirdene Gdns EW KT17 84 C2
Dirdene Gv EW KT17 84 B2
Dirtham La EHSLY KT24 120 E3
Dirty La EGRIN RH19 163 M7
Discovery Pk BRAK RG12 * 35 G8
Disraeli Ct DTCH/LGLY SL3 12 E1
Ditches La COUL/CHIP CR5 87 G7
Ditchling BRAK RG12 34 D7
Ditchling Hl CRAWW RH11 164 E7
Ditton Cl THDIT KT7 44 D7
Dittoncroft Cl CROY/NA CR0 68 B3
Ditton Grange Cl SURB KT6 45 G8
Ditton Grange Dr SURB KT6 45 G8
Ditton Hl SURB KT6 44 F8
Ditton Hill Rd SURB KT6 44 F8
Ditton Lawn THDIT KT7 44 D8
Ditton Park Rd DTCH/LGLY SL3 12 B1
Ditton Pl PGE/AN SE20 * 50 E1
Ditton Reach THDIT KT7 44 E6
Ditton Rd DTCH/LGLY SL3 12 A3
SURB KT6 45 H8
Dixon Dr WEY KT13 59 J8
Dixon Pl WWKM BR4 51 L8
Dixon Rd SNWD SE25 50 B3
Dobbins Pl CRAWW RH11 190 G8
Dobson Rd CRAWW RH11 164 F1
Dockenfield St RFNM GU10 180 A2
Dockett Eddy La SHPTN TW17 41 J7
Dockett Moorings
CHERT KT16 * 41 J8
Dock Rd BTFD TW8 * 18 A2
Dockwell Cl EBED/NFELT TW14 15 K6
Doctors Cl SYD SE26 32 F6
Doctors La CTHM CR3 107 K6
Dodbrooke Rd WNWD SE27 31 K4
Dodds Crs BF/WBF KT14 78 E4
Dodd's La WOKS/MYFD GU22 78 D4
Dodds Pk BRKHM/BTCW RH3 145 L2
Doel Cl WIM/MER SW19 29 M8
Dogflud Wy FNM GU9 5 K2
Doggett Rd CAT SE6 33 K1
Doggetts Cl EDEN TN8 179 R1
Doghurst Av WDR/YW UB7 14 E2
Doghurst Dr WDR/YW UB7 14 E2
Doghurst La COUL/CHIP CR5 106 C2
Dolby Ter HORL RH6 * 174 H11
Dollary Pde KUT/HW KT1 * 9 L8
Dollis Cl CRAWE RH10 165 L5
Dollis Dr FNM GU9 5 L1
Dolphin Cl HASM GU27 197 R7
SURB KT6 45 G6
Dolphin Ct BRAK RG12 34 F4
STA TW18 22 D4
Dolphin Ct North STA TW18 * 22 D4
Dolphin Est SUN TW16 * 42 B1
Dolphin Rd SUN TW16 42 B1
Dolphin Rd North SUN TW16 42 A1
Dolphin Rd South SUN TW16 42 A1
Dolphin Rd West SUN TW16 42 B1
Dolphin Sq CHSWK W4 * 19 H2
Dolphin St KUT/HW KT1 8 E6
Doman Rd CBLY GU15 72 D5
Dome Hl CTHM CR3 128 B1
Dome Hill Pk SYD SE26 32 C5
Dome Hill Peak CTHM CR3 108 B8
Dome Wy REDH RH1 126 C7
Dominion Cl HSLW TW3 17 G4
Dominion Rd CROY/NA CR0 3 J1
Donald Rd CROY/NA CR0 49 J6
Donald Woods Gdns
BRYLDS KT5 63 L1
Doncaster Wk CRAWE RH10 * 165 J6
Doncastle Rd BRAK RG12 34 C3
Donkey Aly EDUL SE22 32 D1
Donkey La HORL RH6 161 G7
RDKG RH5 171 Q1
Donnafields CHOB/PIR GU24 75 K6
Donne Cl CRAWE RH10 165 K2
Donne Gdns WOKS/MYFD GU22 78 B5
Donne Pl MTCM CR4 48 E4
Donnington Cl CBLY GU15 72 E5
Donnington Ct CRAWW RH11 164 B7
Donnington Rd WPK KT4 64 D1
Donnybrook BRAK RG12 34 D7
Donnybrook Rd
STRHM/NOR SW16 30 F8
Donovan Cl HOR/WEW KT19 64 A8
Doods Park Rd REIG RH2 125 M8
Doods Pl REIG RH2 * 125 M7
Doods Rd REIG RH2 125 M7
Doods Wy REIG RH2 126 A7
Doomsday Gdn SWTR RH13 167 J8
Doomsday La SWTR RH13 205 P9
Doone Cl TEDD TW11 26 D7
Doral Wy CAR SM5 66 C4
Doran Dr REDH RH1 126 A8
Doran Gdns REDH RH1 * 126 A8
Dora Rd WIM/MER SW19 29 K6
Dora's Green La RFNM GU10 132 E7
Dorcas Ct CBLY GU15 72 E6
Dorchester Ct
WOKS/MYFD GU22 11 H4
Dorchester Dr
EBED/NFELT TW14 15 H8
Dorchester Gv CHSWK W4 19 H1
Dorchester Ms TWK TW1 17 M8
Dorchester Pde
STRHM/NOR SW16 * 31 H3
Dorchester Rd MRDN SM4 47 L7
WEY KT13 59 L2
WPK KT4 46 F8
Doreen Cl FARN GU14 92 A1
Dore Gdns MRDN SM4 47 L7
Dorian Ct WARL CR6 * 108 E1
Dorian Dr ASC SL5 37 H1
Doric Dr KWD/TDW/WH KT20 105 J2
Dorien Rd RYNPK SW20 47 G2
Dorin Ct WARL CR6 * 108 E2
WOKS/MYFD GU22 78 B5
Doris Rd ASHF TW15 24 A7
Dorking Cl WPK KT4 65 G1
Dorking Rd ASHTD KT21 83 L5
GT/LBKH KT23 121 L1
HORS RH12 166 D1
KWD/TDW/WH KT20 124 C2
LHD/OX KT22 102 E5
RGUE GU4 140 A6
SHGR GU5 142 A5
Dorlcote Rd WAND/EARL SW18 30 A1
Dorling Dr EW KT17 84 C2
Dorly Cl SHPTN TW17 42 B4
Dormans CRAWW RH11 164 C5
Dormans Av LING RH7 178 H7
Dorman's Cl LING RH7 178 H9
Dormans High St LING RH7 178 H10
Dormans Park Rd EGRIN RH19 162 E2
EGRIN RH19 178 F11
Dormans Rd LING RH7 178 H7
Dormans Station Rd LING RH7 178 G10
Dormers Cl GODL GU7 168 A2
Dorney Gv WEY KT13 59 L1
Dorney Wy HSLWW TW4 16 B7
Dornford Gdns
COUL/CHIP CR5 107 M1
Dornton Rd BAL SW12 30 E3
SAND/SEL CR2 68 B4
Dorrington Wy BECK BR3 51 M5
Dorrit Crs RGUW GU3 116 B6
Dorset Av EGRIN RH19 162 D2
Dorset Dr WOKS/MYFD GU22 11 K6
Dorset Gdns EGRIN RH19 162 D2
MTCM CR4 49 J4
Dorset Rd ASHF TW15 23 G4
ASHV GU12 113 K4
BECK BR3 51 G3
BELMT SM2 65 K8
MTCM CR4 48 B2
WIM/MER SW19 47 K1
Dorset Wy BF/WBF KT14 79 G1
WHTN TW2 25 M2
Dorset Waye HEST TW5 16 C2
Dorton Wy RPLY/SEND GU23 98 E3
Douai Cl FARN GU14 92 F5
Douai Gv HPTN TW12 43 M1
Douglas Av NWMAL KT3 46 E4
Douglas Cl RGUE GU4 117 G2
WLGTN SM6 67 H5
Douglas Ct CTHM CR3 * 107 M4
Douglas Dr CROY/NA CR0 69 K2
GODL GU7 168 C4
Douglas Gv RFNM GU10 155 M4
Douglas La STWL/WRAY TW19 12 C7
Douglas Ms BNSTD SM7 85 J6
Douglas Rd ADL/WDHM KT15 58 E2
ESH/CLAY KT10 61 L1
HSLW TW3 16 E5
KUT/HW KT1 9 L7
REIG RH2 125 K7
STWL/WRAY TW19 14 A8
SURB KT6 63 J1
The Doultons STA TW18 22 D7
Dounesforth Gdns
WAND/EARL SW18 29 L2
Dove Cl CRAWW RH11 164 F2
SAND/SEL CR2 89 G1
WLGTN SM6 67 J6
Dovecote Cl WEY KT13 59 L2
Dovedale Cl RGUE GU4 117 K5
SHST GU47 52 A7
Dovedale Crs CRAWW RH11 164 D6
Dovedale Ri MTCM CR4 30 C8
Dovehouse Gn WEY KT13 60 A3
Dover Ct CRAN GU6 186 F2
Dovercourt Av THHTH CR7 49 K4
Dovercourt La SUT SM1 65 M2
Doverfield Rd RGUE GU4 117 K5
Dover Gdns CAR SM5 66 C2
Dover House Rd
PUT/ROE SW15 19 K6
Dover Park Dr PUT/ROE SW15 19 L8
Dover Rd NRWD SE19 32 A7
Dovers Green Rd REIG RH2 147 L5
Doversmead WOKN/KNAP GU21 76 B6
Dover Ter RCH/KEW TW9 * 18 D4
Doves Cl HAYES BR2 71 H1
Doveton Rd SAND/SEL CR2 68 A4
Dowdeswell Cl PUT/ROE SW15 19 H6
Dowding Rd BH/WHM TN16 91 G5
Dower Av WLGTN SM6 66 E7
Dower Wk CRAWW RH11 164 C5
Dowlands La HORL RH6 177 J7
Dowlans Cl GT/LBKH KT23 121 K1
Dowlans Rd GT/LBKH KT23 121 L1
Dowman Cl WIM/MER SW19 29 L8
Downe Av RSEV TN14 91 M2
Downe Cl HORL RH6 160 B1
Downer Meadow GODL GU7 168 B1
Downe Rd HAYES BR2 71 H7
MTCM CR4 48 C2
ORP BR6 91 M4
Downes Cl TWK TW1 17 L8
Downfield WPK KT4 46 C8
Down Hall Rd KUT/HW KT1 8 D5
Downham Ct WOT/HER KT12 * 60 F2
Downhurst Rd CRAN GU6 171 K11
Downing Av GUW GU2 138 C1
Downing St FNM GU9 5 H3
Downland Cl COUL/CHIP CR5 86 E4
EPSOM KT18 84 E8
Downland Dr CRAWW RH11 164 E6
Downland Gdns EPSOM KT18 84 E8
Downland Pl CRAWW RH11 164 E6
Downlands Rd PUR/KEN CR8 87 H3
Downland Wy EPSOM KT18 84 E8
Down La RGUW GU3 137 L4
Downmill Rd BRAK RG12 34 C2
Down Rd GU GU1 117 L8
TEDD TW11 26 E7
Downs Av EPSOM KT18 84 C5
Downs Cl FARN GU14 92 B2
Downs Court Rd PUR/KEN CR8 87 M3
Downs Hill Rd EPSOM KT18 * 84 B5
Downshire Wy BRAK RG12 34 D3
Downside BECK BR3 * 51 K1
CHERT KT16 * 40 C8
EPSOM KT18 84 B4
GSHT GU26 181 Q10
SUN TW16 42 D1
TWK TW1 26 C4
Downside Bridge Rd COB KT11 80 E5
Downside Cl WIM/MER SW19 29 M7
Downside Common COB KT11 80 E8
Downside Common Rd
COB KT11 80 F8
Downside Orch
WOKS/MYFD GU22 11 G6
Downside Rd BELMT SM2 66 A5
COB KT11 80 E8
RGUE GU4 139 L1
Downs La LHD/OX KT22 102 E5
Downs Link CRAN GU6 185 R1
HORS RH12 202 H1
RGUE GU4 140 B5
SHGR GU5 169 J1
SWTR RH13 203 M5
Downs Lodge Ct EW KT17 * 84 B4
Downs Rd BECK BR3 51 L2
BELMT SM2 85 L1
COUL/CHIP CR5 87 G8
EPSOM KT18 103 M2
PUR/KEN CR8 87 L1
RDKG RH5 122 F2
THHTH CR7 49 M1
Downs Side BELMT SM2 85 J1
The Downs LHD/OX KT22 102 F7
RYNPK SW20 29 G8
Down St E/WMO/HCT KT8 43 K5
Downs Vw DORK RH4 122 F8
ISLW TW7 17 J3
KWD/TDW/WH KT20 104 E3
Downsview Av
WOKS/MYFD GU22 97 J3
Downsview Cl COB KT11 100 E1
Downsview Gdns DORK RH4 144 E3
NRWD SE19 31 M8
Downs View Rd GT/LBKH KT23 121 M1

Downsview Rd BOR GU35 180 H12
HORS RH12 167 L3
NRWD SE19 31 M8
Downs Wy EPSOM KT18 84 C6
GT/LBKH KT23 101 M8
KWD/TDW/WH KT20 104 E3
OXTED RH8 130 B1
Downsway CTHM CR3 88 C6
GU GU1 118 A8
SAND/SEL CR2 88 B1
Downsway Cl
KWD/TDW/WH KT20 104 D3
The Downsway BELMT SM2 65 M7
Downs Wd EPSOM KT18 84 E7
Downswood REIG RH2 126 A6
Downton Av BRXS/STRHM SW2 31 J3
Downview Cl GSHT GU26 181 Q11
Down Yhonda MFD/CHID GU8 157 M6
Doyle Rd SNWD SE25 50 D4
Draco Ga PUT/ROE SW15 * 19 M5
Dragon La WEY KT13 59 K8
Drake Av CTHM CR3 107 M4
FRIM GU16 93 K8
STA TW18 22 C6
Drake Cl BRAK RG12 34 E5
HORS RH12 167 H3
Drakefield Rd TOOT SW17 30 D4
Drake Rd CHSGTN KT9 63 K4
CRAWE RH10 165 G7
CROY/NA CR0 49 J7
HORL RH6 160 B3
MTCM CR4 48 D6
Drake's Cl ESH/CLAY KT10 61 K4
Drakes Wy WOKS/MYFD GU22 97 G4
Drakewood Rd
STRHM/NOR SW16 31 G8
Drax Av RYNPK SW20 28 D8
Draxmont WIM/MER SW19 29 H7
Draycot Rd SURB KT6 45 K8
Draycott BRAK RG12 35 H5
Dray Ct GUW GU2 6 C6
Drayhorse Dr BAGS GU19 54 B7
Draymans Wy ISLW TW7 17 J5
Drayton Cl BRAK RG12 35 G2
HSLWW TW4 16 C7
LHD/OX KT22 102 A5
Drayton Rd CROY/NA CR0 2 B5
Dresden Wy WEY KT13 59 M4
Drew Pl CTHM CR3 108 A5
Drewstead Rd
STRHM/NOR SW16 31 G3
Drifters Dr FRIM GU16 74 A8
The Drift EHSLY KT24 100 B6
HAYES BR2 71 G2
Drift Wy DTCH/LGLY SL3 12 F3
The Driftway BNSTD SM7 84 F5
LHD/OX KT22 102 F5
MTCM CR4 48 D1
Driftwood Dr PUR/KEN CR8 87 M7
Drill Hall Rd CHERT KT16 40 D7
Drive Rd COUL/CHIP CR5 107 J2
Drivers Md LING RH7 178 D6
The Drive ASHF TW15 24 A8
BECK BR3 51 K2
BELMT SM2 85 J2
BIL RH14 201 N7
BNSTD SM7 85 H7
COB KT11 81 H4
COUL/CHIP CR5 87 H4
CRAN GU6 186 D3
CRAWE RH10 192 H2
EBED/NFELT TW14 24 E1
ESH/CLAY KT10 43 M8
FNM GU9 5 H9
GODL GU7 159 H5
GODL GU7 168 B7
GUW GU2 116 C8
GUW GU2 138 C2
HOR/WEW KT19 64 C5
HORL RH6 160 E4
HSLW TW3 17 G4
KUTN/CMB KT2 27 M8
KWD/TDW/WH KT20 * 105 K6
LHD/OX KT22 102 B4
LHD/OX KT22 103 H5
LHD/OX KT22 103 K6
MRDN SM4 47 M5
RGUW GU3 138 E4
RYNPK SW20 28 F8
SHGR GU5 169 L3
STWL/WRAY TW19 12 A7
SURB KT6 * 45 H7
THHTH CR7 50 A4
WLGTN SM6 66 F8
WOKS/MYFD GU22 96 E2
Dr Johnson Av TOOT SW17 30 E4
Drodges Cl SHGR GU5 169 J1
Droitwich Cl BRAK RG12 35 G3
SYD SE26 32 D4
Drove Rd RGUE GU4 140 D2
Drovers Rd SAND/SEL CR2 68 A4
Drovers Wy ASHV GU12 113 M8
BRAK RG12 35 J3
FNM GU9 133 K3
Druid's Cl ASHTD KT21 103 J2
Drumaline Rdg WPK KT4 64 B1
Drummond Cl BRAK RG12 35 J1
Drummond Rd CRAWW RH11 164 A5
CROY/NA CR0 2 C6
GU GU1 7 G4
Drummonds Pl RCH/KEW TW9 18 B6
Drungewick La BIL RH14 202 B11
Drury Cl CRAWE RH10 165 M6
Drury Crs CROY/NA CR0 67 K1
Dry Arch Rd ASC SL5 37 J7
Dryburgh Rd PUT/ROE SW15 19 M6
Dryden BRAK RG12 34 D7
Dryden Rd FARN GU14 92 C3
WIM/MER SW19 29 M7
Dryden Wy LIPH GU30 196 F8
Drynham Pk WEY KT13 60 B2
Duchess Cl SUT SM1 65 M3
Duchess Ct WEY KT13 60 A2
Duchess of Kent Barracks
ALDT GU11 112 E6
Duchess of Kent Cl GUW GU2 116 D4
Dudley Cl ADL/WDHM KT15 58 E2
Dudley Dr MRDN SM4 47 H8
Dudley Gv EPSOM KT18 83 M4
Dudley Rd ASHF TW15 23 J6
EBED/NFELT TW14 24 A2
KUT/HW KT1 9 G7
RCH/KEW TW9 18 C4
WIM/MER SW19 29 K7
WOT/HER KT12 42 D6
Dudset La HEST TW5 15 K3
Duffield Rd
KWD/TDW/WH KT20 104 E6
Duffins Orch CHERT KT16 57 M6
Duke Cl CRAWE RH10 165 L8
Duke of Cambridge Cl
WHTN TW2 17 G8
Duke of Cornwall Av
CBLY GU15 53 G8
Duke of Edinburgh Rd
SUT SM1 66 A2
Dukes Av HSLWW TW4 16 B6
NWMAL KT3 46 B3
RCHPK/HAM TW10 26 F5
Dukes Cl ASHF TW15 23 M5
CRAN GU6 186 F3
FNM GU9 * 133 K3
HPTN TW12 25 J6
Dukes Covert BAGS GU19 54 B3
Duke's Dr GODL GU7 159 L2
Dukes Hl BAGS GU19 54 B4
CTHM CR3 109 H2
Dukeshill Rd BNFD RG42 34 E1
Dukes Pk ALDT GU11 113 G3
Dukes Ride RDKG RH5 145 G5
Duke's Rd RDKG RH5 173 R11
WOT/HER KT12 61 G4
Dukesthorpe Rd SYD SE26 33 G5
Duke St RCH/KEW TW9 18 A6
SUT SM1 66 A3
WOKN/KNAP GU21 10 F5
Dukes Wy WWKM BR4 70 B2
Dulverton Rd SAND/SEL CR2 68 F8
Dulwich Common DUL SE21 32 A2
The Dulwich Oaks DUL SE21 * 32 C4
Dulwich Wood Av NRWD SE19 32 B6
Dulwich Wood Pk NRWD SE19 32 B5
Dumbleton Cl KUT/HW KT1 9 L5
Dump Rd FARN GU14 92 B8
Dumville Dr GDST RH9 128 E5
Dunally Pk SHPTN TW17 42 A7
Dunbar Av BECK BR3 51 H4
STRHM/NOR SW16 49 K2
Dunbar Ct WOT/HER KT12 60 F1
Dunbar Rd FRIM GU16 93 J2
NWMAL KT3 45 M4
Dunbar St WNWD SE27 31 M4
Dunboe Pl SHPTN TW17 41 M7
Duncan Dr GU GU1 117 K7
Duncan Gdns STA TW18 22 D7
Duncan Rd
KWD/TDW/WH KT20 105 H1
RCH/KEW TW9 18 B6
Duncombe Hl FSTH SE23 33 H1
Duncombe Rd GODL GU7 168 A7
Duncroft Cl REIG RH2 125 J8
Dundaff Cl CBLY GU15 73 K4
Dundas Cl BRAK RG12 34 E4
Dundas Gdns E/WMO/HCT KT8 43 L3
Dundee Rd SNWD SE25 50 E5
Dundela Gdns WPK KT4 64 E3
Dundonald Rd WIM/MER SW19 29 J8
Dundrey Crs REDH RH1 127 H3
Dunedin Dr CTHM CR3 108 B7
Dunelm Gv WNWD SE27 31 M5
Dunfee Wy BF/WBF KT14 79 H2
Dunfield Rd CAT SE6 33 L6
Dunford Br CHERT KT16 77 L1
Dungarvan Av PUT/ROE SW15 19 K6
Dungates La
BRKHM/BTCW RH3 124 D7
Dunheved Cl THHTH CR7 49 K6
Dunheved Rd North
THHTH CR7 49 K6
Dunheved Rd South
THHTH CR7 49 K6
Dunheved Rd West THHTH CR7 49 K6
Dunkeld Rd SNWD SE25 50 A4
Dunkirk St WNWD SE27 * 31 M5
Dunleary Cl HSLWW TW4 25 J1
Dunley Dr CROY/NA CR0 69 M5
Dunlin Cl REDH RH1 148 B5
Dunlin Ri RGUE GU4 118 A6
Dunmail Dr PUR/KEN CR8 88 B4
Dunmore GUW GU2 116 A7
Dunmore Rd RYNPK SW20 46 F1
Dunmow Cl FELT TW13 * 25 H5
Dunnets WOKN/KNAP GU21 76 B7
Dunnings Rd EGRIN RH19 162 F7
Dunnymans Rd BNSTD SM7 85 J5
Dunoon Gdns FSTH SE23 * 33 G1
Dunoon Rd FSTH SE23 32 F1
Dunottar Cl REDH RH1 148 A2
Dunraven Av REDH RH1 148 E8
Dunsbury Cl BELMT SM2 65 L7
Dunsdon Av GUW GU2 6 D6
Dunsfold Cl CRAWW RH11 164 C5
Dunsfold Common Rd
MFD/CHID GU8 185 J6
Dunsfold Ri COUL/CHIP CR5 87 G3
Dunsfold Rd BIL RH14 200 H6
CRAN GU6 185 P10
MFD/CHID GU8 185 L5
MFD/CHID GU8 200 F2
Dunsfold Wy CROY/NA CR0 69 M6
Dunsmore Rd WOT/HER KT12 42 E5
Dunstable Rd E/WMO/HCT KT8 43 J4
RCH/KEW TW9 18 B6
Dunstall Pk FARN GU14 92 D2
Dunstall Rd RYNPK SW20 28 E7
Dunstall Wy E/WMO/HCT KT8 43 L3
Dunstan Rd COUL/CHIP CR5 87 G7
Dunstan's Rd EDUL SE22 32 D1
Dunster Av MRDN SM4 47 G8
Dunton Cl SURB KT6 45 H8
Duntshill Rd WAND/EARL SW18 29 L2
Dunvegan Cl E/WMO/HCT KT8 43 L4
Dupont Rd RYNPK SW20 47 G2
Duppas Av CROY/NA CR0 2 B9
Duppas Cl SHPTN TW17 42 A5
Duppas Hill Rd CROY/NA CR0 67 K3
Duppas Hill Ter CROY/NA CR0 2 B8
Duppas Rd CROY/NA CR0 67 K2
Dura Den Cl BECK BR3 33 L8
Durban Rd BECK BR3 51 J2
WNWD SE27 31 M5
Durbin Rd CHSGTN KT9 63 H3
Durfold Dr REIG RH2 125 M8
Durfold Rd HORS RH12 167 H2
Durfold Wd BIL RH14 200 F3
Durford Crs PUT/ROE SW15 28 D2
Durham Av HEST TW5 16 C1
Durham Cl CRAWE RH10 165 G8
GUW GU2 116 C6
Durham Dr FRIM GU16 74 A8
Durham Rd EBED/NFELT TW14 24 F1
RYNPK SW20 46 E1
SHST GU47 52 B7
Durham Ter PGE/AN SE20 * 32 E8
Durkins Rd EGRIN RH19 162 E2
Durleston Park Dr
GT/LBKH KT23 101 M7
Durley Md BRAK RG12 35 J5
Durlston Rd KUTN/CMB KT2 8 E1
Durning Rd NRWD SE19 32 A6
Durnsford Av WIM/MER SW19 29 K3
Durnsford Rd WIM/MER SW19 29 K3
Durnsford Wy CRAN GU6 186 E3
Durrell Wy SHPTN TW17 42 A6
Durrington Av RYNPK SW20 28 F8
Durrington Park Rd
RYNPK SW20 46 F1
Dutch Barn Cl
STWL/WRAY TW19 14 A8
Dutchells Copse HORS RH12 167 H3
Dutch Gdns KUTN/CMB KT2 9 L1
Duval Pl BAGS GU19 54 B6
Duxhurst La REIG RH2 175 L2
Dwelly La EDEN TN8 152 F5
Dyehouse Rd MFD/CHID GU8 182 B5
Dyers Fld HORL RH6 161 L3
Dyer's La PUT/ROE SW15 19 L5
Dykes Pth WOKN/KNAP GU21 11 L1
Dynevor Pl RGUW GU3 115 M4
Dynevor Rd RCHPK/HAM TW10 18 B7
Dysart Av KUTN/CMB KT2 26 F6
Dyson Ct DORK RH4 * 144 D2
Dyson Wk CRAWW RH11 * 191 L12

E

Eady Cl SWTR RH13 167 J7
Eagle Cl WLGTN SM6 67 H5
Eagle Hl NRWD SE19 32 A7
Eagle Rd GU GU1 7 H4
HTHAIR TW6 15 J5
Eagles Dr BH/WHM TN16 91 G8
Eardley Rd STRHM/NOR SW16 30 F7
Earldom Rd PUT/ROE SW15 19 M6
Earle Gdns KUTN/CMB KT2 8 F1
Earles Meadow HORS RH12 167 L3
Earleswood COB KT11 81 G2
Earleydene ASC SL5 36 E8
Earl of Chester Dr FRIM GU16 94 A1
Earl Rd MORT/ESHN SW14 18 F6
Earlsbrook Rd REDH RH1 148 C2
Earlsfield Rd WAND/EARL SW18 29 M2
Earls Gv CBLY GU15 73 H3
Earls Ms WAND/EARL SW18 29 M1
Earlsthorpe Rd SYD SE26 33 G5
Earlswood BRAK RG12 34 E7
Earlswood Av THHTH CR7 49 K5
Earlswood Cl SWTR RH13 167 J5
Earlswood Rd REDH RH1 148 C2
Early Commons CRAWE RH10 165 H3
Easby Crs MRDN SM4 47 L6
Eashing La GODL GU7 159 J5
Easington Pl GU GU1 7 M5
East Av FNM GU9 134 A3
WLGTN SM6 67 J4
Eastbank Rd HPTN TW12 25 M6
Eastbourne Gdns
MORT/ESHN SW14 18 F5
Eastbourne Rd CHSWK W4 18 F1
EGRIN RH19 178 A11
FELT TW13 25 G3
GDST RH9 128 F6
TOOT SW17 30 D7
Eastbrook Cl WOKN/KNAP GU21 11 H3
Eastbury La RGUW GU3 137 K6
Eastbury Rd KUTN/CMB KT2 8 E3
Eastchurch Rd HTHAIR TW6 15 H5
Eastcote Av E/WMO/HCT KT8 43 J5
East Ct EGRIN RH19 * 163 G3
Eastcroft Rd HOR/WEW KT19 64 B6
Eastdean Av EPSOM KT18 83 L3
East Dr CAR SM5 66 B7
VW GU25 38 E6
Eastern Av CHERT KT16 40 D3
CHOB/PIR GU24 95 L3
Eastern La CWTH RG45 52 C5
Eastern Perimeter Rd
HTHAIR TW6 15 H4
Eastern Rd ASHV GU12 113 H7
BRAK RG12 35 G2
Eastern Vw BH/WHM TN16 90 F7
Easter Wy GDST RH9 151 J4
Eastfield Rd REDH RH1 148 F2
Eastfields MFD/CHID GU8 183 N4
Eastfields Rd MTCM CR4 48 D2
East Flexford La RGUW GU3 137 J3
East Gdns TOOT SW17 30 B7
WOKS/MYFD GU22 11 L5
Eastgate BNSTD SM7 85 J4
Eastgate Ct GU GU1 * 7 J6
Eastgate Gdns GU GU1 7 J5
East Grinstead Rd LING RH7 178 E6
East Gun Copse Rd
SWTR RH13 204 E12
Easthampstead Rd BNFD RG42 34 D2
East Hl BH/WHM TN16 90 E8
EGRIN RH19 178 F11
OXTED RH8 130 C3
SAND/SEL CR2 68 B8
WOKS/MYFD GU22 11 L4
East Hill La CRAWE RH10 177 J11
East Hill Rd OXTED RH8 130 B3
East India Wy CROY/NA CR0 3 J3
Eastlands Cl OXTED RH8 130 A1
Eastlands Wy OXTED RH8 130 A1
East La EHSLY KT24 99 M8
KUT/HW KT1 8 D8
Eastleigh Cl BELMT SM2 65 L6
Eastleigh Wy
EBED/NFELT TW14 24 D2
Eastmead FARN GU14 92 E6
WOKN/KNAP GU21 76 E7
East Meads GUW GU2 138 C1
Eastmearn Rd WNWD SE27 31 M3
East Ms HORS RH12 * 166 F7
Eastmont Rd ESH/CLAY KT10 62 C1
Eastney Rd CROY/NA CR0 2 A3
Eastnor Pl REIG RH2 * 147 K2
Eastnor Rd REIG RH2 147 J2
East Pk CRAWE RH10 164 F5
East Park La LING RH7 177 P8
East Parkside WARL CR6 89 K6
East Pl WNWD SE27 31 M5
East Rp HTHAIR TW6 14 E3
East Ring RFNM GU10 135 K2
East Rd EBED/NFELT TW14 24 A1
KUTN/CMB KT2 8 F4
REIG RH2 125 J7
WEY KT13 60 A6
WIM/MER SW19 29 M7
East Shalford La RGUE GU4 139 K5
East Sheen Av
MORT/ESHN SW14 19 G7
East Station Rd ASHV GU12 112 E8
East Stratton Cl BRAK RG12 35 J5
East St BTFD TW8 17 M2
CRAWE RH10 193 N9
EW KT17 84 B2
FNM GU9 5 J2
GT/LBKH KT23 101 L7
HORS RH12 166 F8
HORS RH12 190 B6
East View La CRAN GU6 186 B2
East Wk REIG RH2 125 L8
East Wy CROY/NA CR0 69 H1
Eastway GUW GU2 116 C8
HOR/WEW KT19 83 M2
HORL RH6 160 E7
MRDN SM4 47 G5
WLGTN SM6 66 F3
Eastwell Cl BECK BR3 51 H1
East Whipley La SHGR GU5 169 Q11
Eastwick Dr GT/LBKH KT23 101 L6
Eastwick Park Av
GT/LBKH KT23 101 L6
Eastwick Rd GT/LBKH KT23 101 L7
WOT/HER KT12 60 E5
Eastwood CRAWE RH10 165 H4
Eastwood Rd SHGR GU5 169 J2
Eastwood St STRHM/NOR SW16 30 F7
Eastworth Rd CHERT KT16 40 C8
Eaton Dr KUTN/CMB KT2 9 K3
Eaton Pk COB KT11 81 H4
Eaton Park Rd COB KT11 81 H4
Eaton Rd BELMT SM2 66 A5
CBLY GU15 72 E5
HSLW TW3 17 G6
Eatonville Rd TOOT SW17 30 C3
Eatonville Vls TOOT SW17 30 C3
Eaves Cl ADL/WDHM KT15 58 F5
Ebba's Wy EPSOM KT18 83 L5
Ebbisham La
KWD/TDW/WH KT20 104 C3
Ebbisham Rd EPSOM KT18 83 L5
WPK KT4 64 F1
Ebenezer Wk
STRHM/NOR SW16 48 F1
Ebsworth St FSTH SE23 33 G1
Ebury Cl HAYES BR2 71 H2
Ecclesbourne Rd THHTH CR7 49 M5
Eccleshill RDKG RH5 144 F6
Echelforde Dr ASHF TW15 23 K5
Echo Barn La RFNM GU10 155 H4
Echo Pit Rd GU GU1 139 H4
Ecob Cl RGUW GU3 116 C4
Ecton Rd ADL/WDHM KT15 58 E3
Eddeys Cl BOR GU35 180 G11
Eddeys La BOR GU35 180 G12
Eddington Hl CRAWW RH11 191 K12
Eddington Rd BRAK RG12 34 B6
Eddy Rd ASHV GU12 112 F8
Ede Cl HSLW TW3 16 C5
Edenbrook LING RH7 178 F5
Eden Cl ADL/WDHM KT15 58 E8
Edencourt Rd
STRHM/NOR SW16 30 E7
Edencroft SHGR GU5 169 K2
Edenfield Gdns WPK KT4 64 C2
Eden Grove Rd BF/WBF KT14 79 H3
Eden Pde BECK BR3 * 51 H4
Eden Park Av BECK BR3 51 K5
Eden Rd BECK BR3 51 H4
CRAWW RH11 164 B6
CROY/NA CR0 2 E9
WNWD SE27 31 L6
Edenside Rd GT/LBKH KT23 101 J6
Edensor Rd CHSWK W4 19 H2
Eden St KUT/HW KT1 8 E7
Eden V EGRIN RH19 162 F1
Edenvale Rd MTCM CR4 30 D8
Eden Valley Wk EDEN TN8 179 N3
Eden Wy BECK BR3 51 K5
WARL CR6 89 H8
Ederline Av STRHM/NOR SW16 49 J3
Edgar Cl CRAWE RH10 192 D8
Edgar Rd BH/WHM TN16 111 G3
HSLWW TW4 25 J1
SAND/SEL CR2 68 A8
Edgeborough Ct GU GU1 * 7 M6
Edge Cl WEY KT13 59 K6
Edgecombe Cl KUTN/CMB KT2 28 A8
Edgecoombe SAND/SEL CR2 69 G7
Edgefield Cl CRAN GU6 186 B1
REDH RH1 148 D5
Edge Hl WIM/MER SW19 29 G8
Edgehill Ct WOT/HER KT12 * 42 F8
Edgehill Rd MTCM CR4 48 E1
PUR/KEN CR8 67 K8
Edgeley GT/LBKH KT23 101 H6
Edgell Cl VW GU25 39 J3
Edgell Rd STA TW18 22 C7
Edgemoor Rd FRIM GU16 73 M6
Edge Point Cl WNWD SE27 31 L6
Edgewood Gn CROY/NA CR0 51 G8
Edgeworth Cl CTHM CR3 88 D8
Edgington Rd
STRHM/NOR SW16 31 G7
Edinburgh Ct KUT/HW KT1 * 8 E8
Edinburgh Dr STA TW18 23 G7
Edinburgh Rd SUT SM1 65 M1
Edinburgh Wy EGRIN RH19 163 G6
Edith Gdns BRYLDS KT5 45 L7
Edith Rd SNWD SE25 50 A5
WIM/MER SW19 29 L7
Edmonds Ct BRAK RG12 * 34 F1
Edmund Gv FELT TW13 25 J3
Edmund Rd MTCM CR4 48 B3
Edna Rd RYNPK SW20 47 G2
Edrich Rd CRAWW RH11 191 K12
Edridge Rd CROY/NA CR0 2 D8
Edward Av CBLY GU15 72 D4
MRDN SM4 48 A5
Edward Cl HPTN TW12 25 M6
Edward Ct STA TW18 22 F7
Edward Ii Av BF/WBF KT14 79 J4
Edward Rd BFOR GU20 55 G5
BH/WHM TN16 91 H8
COUL/CHIP CR5 87 G5
CROY/NA CR0 3 H1
EBED/NFELT TW14 15 G7
FNM GU9 5 J9
HPTN TW12 25 M6
PGE/AN SE20 33 G8
Edwards Cl WPK KT4 65 G1
Edward St ALDT GU11 112 C7
Edward Wy ASHF TW15 23 J3
Edwin Cl EHSLY KT24 100 A7
Edwin Rd EHSLY KT24 99 M7
WHTN TW2 26 B2
Eelmoor Plain Rd ALDT GU11 112 A5
Eelmoor Rd ALDT GU11 112 A4
FARN GU14 92 C7
Effingham Cl BELMT SM2 65 L6
Effingham Common Rd
EHSLY KT24 100 F7
Effingham Ct
WOKS/MYFD GU22 * 10 D9
Effingham La CRAWE RH10 177 K12
Effingham Pl EHSLY KT24 121 G1
Effingham Rd CROY/NA CR0 49 J7
HORL RH6 161 M8
REIG RH2 147 L1
SURB KT6 44 E7
Effort St TOOT SW17 30 B6
Effra Rd WIM/MER SW19 29 L7
Egerton Pl WEY KT13 59 M5
Egerton Rd GUW GU2 138 B1
NWMAL KT3 46 C4
SHST GU47 72 B3
SNWD SE25 50 B3
WEY KT13 59 M5
WHTN TW2 26 B1
Egerton Wy HYS/HAR UB3 14 E2
Eggars Fld RFNM GU10 154 A4
Eggar's Hl ALDT GU11 134 D1
Egham By-pass EGH TW20 21 J5
Egham Cl CHEAM SM3 65 H1
Egham Crs CHEAM SM3 65 G2
Egham Hl EGH TW20 21 G7
Egleston Rd MRDN SM4 47 L6
Egley Dr WOKS/MYFD GU22 97 G4
Egley Rd WOKS/MYFD GU22 97 G4
Eglinton Rd RFNM GU10 181 N3
Eglise Rd WARL CR6 89 H7
Egliston Ms PUT/ROE SW15 19 M5
Egliston Rd PUT/ROE SW15 19 M5
Egmont Av SURB KT6 45 K8
Egmont Park Rd
KWD/TDW/WH KT20 104 D7
Egmont Rd BELMT SM2 65 M6
NWMAL KT3 46 C4
SURB KT6 45 J8
WOT/HER KT12 42 E7
Egmont Wy
KWD/TDW/WH KT20 105 H1
Egremont Rd WNWD SE27 31 K4
Egret Gdns ALDT GU11 134 D2
Eight Acres GSHT GU26 181 P10
Eighteenth Rd MTCM CR4 49 H4
Eighth Av
KWD/TDW/WH KT20 * 105 J8
Eileen Rd SNWD SE25 50 A5
Eindhoven Cl CAR SM5 48 D8
WIM/MER SW19 48 A1
Eland Rd ASHV GU12 113 G8
CROY/NA CR0 2 A7
Elberon Av CROY/NA CR0 48 F6
Elborough Rd SNWD SE25 50 D5
Elborough St
WAND/EARL SW18 29 K2
Elbow Meadow
DTCH/LGLY SL3 * 13 J3
Elcho Rd CHOB/PIR GU24 94 F1
Elderberry Rd BOR GU35 180 B12
Elder Cl RGUE GU4 117 K5
Eldergrove FARN GU14 93 H7
Elder Oak Cl PGE/AN SE20 50 E1
Elder Rd CHOB/PIR GU24 75 K5
WNWD SE27 31 M6
Eldersley Cl REDH RH1 126 C6
Eldersley Gdns REDH RH1 126 C6
Elderslie Cl BECK BR3 51 K6
Elderton Rd SYD SE26 33 H5
Eldertree Wy MTCM CR4 48 E1
Elder Wy RDKG RH5 144 F6
Eldon Av CROY/NA CR0 68 F1
HEST TW5 16 D2
Eldon Dr RFNM GU10 156 A4
Eldon Pk SNWD SE25 50 E4
Eldon Rd CTHM CR3 108 A3
Eldridge Cl EBED/NFELT TW14 24 D2
Eleanora Ter SUT SM1 * 65 M4
Eleanor Av HOR/WEW KT19 64 A8
Eleanor Cl LIPH GU30 196 C5
Eleanor Gv BARN SW13 19 H5
Electra Av HTHAIR TW6 15 J5
Electric Pde SURB KT6 45 G6
Eleventh Av
KWD/TDW/WH KT20 * 105 J8
Elfin Gv TEDD TW11 26 C6
Elfrida Crs CAT SE6 33 K5
Elgal Cl ORP BR6 71 L4
Elgar Av BRYLDS KT5 45 L8
STRHM/NOR SW16 49 H3
Elgar Wy SWTR RH13 167 L5
Elger Wy CRAWE RH10 192 F1
Elgin Av ASHF TW15 23 M7
Elgin Crs CTHM CR3 108 D4
HTHAIR TW6 15 H4
Elgin Gdns GU GU1 117 K7
Elgin Pl WEY KT13 * 59 M5
Elgin Rd CROY/NA CR0 3 K5
SUT SM1 65 M2

WEY KT13 59 K5
WLGTN SM6 66 F5
Elgin Wy FRIM GU16 93 J2
Eliot Bank FSTH SE23 32 E3
Eliot Cl CBLY GU15 73 L2
Eliot Dr HASM GU27 197 R7
Eliot Gdns PUT/ROE SW15 19 K6
Elizabethan Wy CRAWE RH10 165 L5
STWL/WRAY TW19 23 G1
Elizabeth Av BAGS GU19 54 C7
STA TW18 22 F7
Elizabeth Cl BRAK RG12 34 F4
SUT SM1 65 J3
Elizabeth Cottages
RCH/KEW TW9 18 C3
Elizabeth Ct GODL GU7 168 B2
HORL RH6 * 160 D3
Elizabeth Crs EGRIN RH19 163 G2
Elizabeth Gdns ASC SL5 36 E5
ISLW TW7 17 K6
SUN TW16 42 F3
Elizabeth Rd GODL GU7 168 B2
Elizabeth Wy FELT TW13 24 F5
NRWD SE19 32 A8
Elkins Gdns RGUE GU4 117 K5
Elkins Gv FNM GU9 * 4 C4
Elland Rd WOT/HER KT12 61 G1
Ellenborough Cl BRAK RG12 35 G1
Ellenborough Pl
PUT/ROE SW15 19 K6
Ellenbridge Wy SAND/SEL CR2 68 B7
Elleray Ct ASHV GU12 113 K4
Elleray Rd TEDD TW11 26 C7
Ellerdine Rd HSLW TW3 16 F6
Ellerker Gdns
RCHPK/HAM TW10 18 B8
Ellerman Av WHTN TW2 25 J2
Ellerton Rd BARN SW13 * 19 K3
RYNPK SW20 28 D8
SURB KT6 63 J1
WAND/EARL SW18 30 A2
Ellery Cl CRAN GU6 186 D4
Ellery Rd NRWD SE19 32 A8
Elles Av GU GU1 117 L8
Elles Cl FARN GU14 92 E6
Ellesfield Av BRAK RG12 34 B4
Ellesmere Av BECK BR3 51 L2
Ellesmere Dr SAND/SEL CR2 88 E4
Ellesmere Pl WOT/HER KT12 60 B4
Ellesmere Rd TWK TW1 17 M8
WEY KT13 60 B5
Elles Rd FARN GU14 92 D7
Ellice Rd OXTED RH8 130 C3
Ellies Ms ASHF TW15 23 H3
Ellingham Rd CHSGTN KT9 63 G5
Ellington Rd FELT TW13 24 C5
HSLW TW3 16 E4
Ellington Wy EPSOM KT18 84 E7
Elliot Cl CRAWE RH10 165 L5
Elliott Ct WOKN/KNAP GU21 * 11 H4
Elliott Gdns SHPTN TW17 41 K4
Elliott Ri ASC SL5 36 A2
Elliott Rd THHTH CR7 49 L4
Ellis Av GUW GU2 138 C2
Ellis Cl COUL/CHIP CR5 107 J2
Ellis Farm Cl WOKS/MYFD GU22 97 G4
Ellisfield Dr PUT/ROE SW15 28 C1
Ellison Rd BARN SW13 19 J4
STRHM/NOR SW16 31 G8
Ellison Wy RFNM GU10 135 J2
Ellis Rd COUL/CHIP CR5 107 J2
MTCM CR4 48 C6
Ellman Rd CRAWW RH11 164 B6
Ellora Rd STRHM/NOR SW16 31 G6
Ellson Cl CRAWE RH10 165 L6
Ellwood Pl CRAWW RH11 * 164 B4
Elm Bank CHOB/PIR GU24 * 76 B1
Elmbank Av EGH TW20 20 E8
GUW GU2 6 B6
Elm Bank Gdns BARN SW13 19 H4
Elmbourne Rd TOOT SW17 30 E4
Elmbridge Av BRYLDS KT5 45 M6
Elmbridge La
WOKS/MYFD GU22 97 J1
Elmbridge Rd CRAN GU6 185 Q3
Elmbrook Cl SUN TW16 42 E1
Elmbrook Rd SUT SM1 65 J3
Elm Cl BRYLDS KT5 45 M7
CAR SM5 48 C8
KWD/TDW/WH KT20 123 M4
LHD/OX KT22 102 E4
RPLY/SEND GU23 98 D6
RYNPK SW20 46 F4
SAND/SEL CR2 68 A5
STWL/WRAY TW19 23 G2
WARL CR6 89 G7
WHTN TW2 25 L3
WOKN/KNAP GU21 10 A2
Elm Ct WOKN/KNAP GU21 76 A7
Elmcourt Rd WNWD SE27 31 L3
Elm Crs FNM GU9 134 A2
KUTN/CMB KT2 8 F5
Elmcroft GT/LBKH KT23 * 101 K6
Elmcroft Cl CHSGTN KT9 * 63 H2
EBED/NFELT TW14 15 J8
FRIM GU16 93 J2
Elmcroft Dr ASHF TW15 * 23 K6
CHSGTN KT9 63 H2
Elmdene BRYLDS KT5 45 M8
Elmdene Cl BECK BR3 51 J5
Elmdene Ct WOKS/MYFD GU22 10 D9
Elmdon Rd HSLWW TW4 16 A4
HTHAIR TW6 15 J5
Elm Dr CHOB/PIR GU24 56 C8
EGRIN RH19 163 H4
LHD/OX KT22 102 E4
SUN TW16 42 F2
Elmer Gdns ISLW TW7 17 G5
Elmer Ms LHD/OX KT22 102 D5
Elmer Rd CAT SE6 33 M1
Elmer's Dr TEDD TW11 26 E7
Elmers End Rd BECK BR3 50 F3
Elmerside Rd BECK BR3 51 H4
Elmers Rd RDKG RH5 188 D1
SNWD SE25 3 M1
Elmfield GT/LBKH KT23 101 K5
Elmfield Av MTCM CR4 48 D1
TEDD TW11 26 C6
Elmfield Rd TOOT SW17 30 E3
Elmfield Wy SAND/SEL CR2 68 C7
Elm Gdns EPSOM KT18 104 F1
ESH/CLAY KT10 62 C5
MTCM CR4 49 G4
Elmgate Av FELT TW13 24 E4
Elm Gv CHOB/PIR GU24 75 K6
CRAN GU6 185 R2
CTHM CR3 108 B4
EPSOM KT18 83 M4
FNM GU9 133 M2
KUTN/CMB KT2 8 F5
SUT SM1 65 L3
SWTR RH13 167 H8
WIM/MER SW19 29 H8
Elmgrove Cl WOKN/KNAP GU21 96 A1
Elm Grove Pde CAR SM5 66 D2
Elm Grove Rd BARN SW13 19 K4
COB KT11 81 G6
Elmgrove Rd CROY/NA CR0 50 E7
Elm Grove Rd FARN GU14 92 E5
Elmgrove Rd WEY KT13 59 K3
Elmhurst Av MTCM CR4 30 D8
Elmhurst Ct GU GU1 7 M5
Elmhurst Dr DORK RH4 144 E4
Elmhurst La SWTR RH13 203 N11
Elm La CAT SE6 33 J3
RFNM GU10 135 J1
RPLY/SEND GU23 99 J1
Elmore Rd COUL/CHIP CR5 106 C3
Elm Pk ASC SL5 37 H8
Elmpark Gdns SAND/SEL CR2 68 F8
Elm Park Rd SNWD SE25 50 C3
Elm Pl ALDT GU11 134 F1
Elm Rd BECK BR3 51 J2
CHSGTN KT9 63 H3
EBED/NFELT TW14 24 A2
ESH/CLAY KT10 62 C5
EW KT17 64 C5
FNM GU9 134 A2
GODL GU7 168 C1
KUTN/CMB KT2 9 H3
LHD/OX KT22 102 E4
MORT/ESHN SW14 18 F5
NWMAL KT3 46 A3
PUR/KEN CR8 87 L3
REDH RH1 126 B8
THHTH CR7 49 M4
WARL CR6 89 G7
WLGTN SM6 48 D8
WOKN/KNAP GU21 10 A8
WOKN/KNAP GU21 10 F1
Elm Rd West CHEAM SM3 47 J7
Elmshaw Rd PUT/ROE SW15 19 K7
Elmshorn EW KT17 84 F6
Elmside CROY/NA CR0 69 L5
GUW GU2 6 A6
MFD/CHID GU8 159 J8
Elmsleigh Rd FARN GU14 92 D5
STA TW18 22 C6
WHTN TW2 26 A3
Elmslie Cl EPSOM KT18 83 M4
Elms Rd ALDT GU11 112 D8
Elmstead Cl HOR/WEW KT19 64 B4
Elmstead Gdns WPK KT4 64 D2
Elmstead Rd BF/WBF KT14 78 D3
The Elms BARN SW13 19 J5
BLKW GU17 * 72 A5
ESH/CLAY KT10 * 62 C6
RFNM GU10 135 J2
TOOT SW17 * 30 D4
WARL CR6 88 F5
WLGTN SM6 * 66 F3
Elmsway ASHF TW15 23 J6
Elmswood GT/LBKH KT23 101 J6
Elmsworth Av HSLW TW3 16 E4
Elm Tree Av ESH/CLAY KT10 44 A7
Elm Tree Cl ASHF TW15 23 L6
CHERT KT16 58 B1
HORL RH6 * 160 D2
Elmtree Cl BF/WBF KT14 79 H3
Elmtree Rd TEDD TW11 26 B6
Elm Vw ASHV GU12 113 L6
Elm Wk ORP BR6 71 J2
RYNPK SW20 46 F4
Elm Wy HOR/WEW KT19 64 A4
WPK KT4 64 F2
Elmwood Av FELT TW13 24 E4
Elmwood Cl EW KT17 64 D6
WLGTN SM6 66 E1
Elmwood Ct ASHTD KT21 83 G7
Elmwood Dr EW KT17 64 D6
Elmwood Rd CHSWK W4 18 F1
CROY/NA CR0 2 B1
MTCM CR4 48 C3
REDH RH1 126 D4
WOKN/KNAP GU21 96 A1
Elmworth Gv DUL SE21 32 A3
Elsdon Rd WOKN/KNAP GU21 76 D8
Elsenham St WAND/EARL SW18 29 J2
Elsenwood Crs CBLY GU15 73 K3
Elsenwood Dr CBLY GU15 73 K2
Elsinore Av STWL/WRAY TW19 * 23 H1
Elsinore Rd FSTH SE23 33 H1
Elsinore Wy RCH/KEW TW9 18 E5
Elsley Cl FRIM GU16 93 J3
Elsrick Av MRDN SM4 47 K5
Elstan Wy CROY/NA CR0 51 H7
Elstead Rd MFD/CHID GU8 158 E6
RFNM GU10 135 K4
Elsted Cl CRAWW RH11 164 D2
Elston Pl ASHV GU12 134 F1
Elston Rd ASHV GU12 134 F1
Elsworth Cl EBED/NFELT TW14 24 B2
Elsworthy THDIT KT7 44 B6
Elthorne Ct FELT TW13 24 F2
Elton Cl KUT/HW KT1 8 B3
Elton Rd KUTN/CMB KT2 9 J4
PUR/KEN CR8 86 F2
Elveden Cl WOKS/MYFD GU22 78 E7
Elveden Pl WOKS/MYFD GU22 * 78 E7
Elveden Rd COB KT11 80 E1
Elvino Rd SYD SE26 33 G6
Elwell Cl EGH TW20 21 K7
Elwill Wy BECK BR3 51 M4
Ely Cl CRAWE RH10 165 H8
FRIM GU16 93 K2
NWMAL KT3 46 C2
Ely Pl GUW GU2 * 116 C6
Ely Rd CROY/NA CR0 50 A5
HTHAIR TW6 15 J4
Elystan Cl WLGTN SM6 66 F7
The Embankment
STWL/WRAY TW19 20 F1
TWK TW1 26 D2
Embassy Ct WLGTN SM6 * 66 E5
Ember Cl ADL/WDHM KT15 59 G4
Embercourt Rd THDIT KT7 44 B6
Ember Farm Av
E/WMO/HCT KT8 44 A6
Ember Farm Wy
E/WMO/HCT KT8 44 A5
Ember Gdns THDIT KT7 44 B7
Ember La ESH/CLAY KT10 44 A8
Emberwood CRAWW RH11 * 164 F2
Embleton Rd BOR GU35 180 G11
Emerton Rd LHD/OX KT22 101 M2
Emery Down Cl BRAK RG12 35 K3
Emily Davison Dr EPSOM KT18 84 E8
Emley Rd ADL/WDHM KT15 58 D2
Emlyn La LHD/OX KT22 102 D4
Emlyn Rd HORL RH6 160 B2
REDH RH1 148 D2
Emmanuel Cl GUW GU2 116 D5
Emmanuel Rd BAL SW12 30 F2
Emma Ter RYNPK SW20 * 28 F8
Emmetts Cl WOKN/KNAP GU21 10 A5
Empire Vls REDH RH1 175 R2
Empress Av FARN GU14 92 E4
Emsworth Cl CRAWE RH10 * 165 L7
Emsworth St BRXS/STRHM SW2 31 J3
Ena Rd STRHM/NOR SW16 49 H3
Endale Cl CAR SM5 66 C1
Endeavour Wy CROY/NA CR0 49 H7
WIM/MER SW19 29 L5
Endlesham Rd BAL SW12 30 D1
Endsleigh Cl SAND/SEL CR2 68 F8
Endsleigh Gdns SURB KT6 44 F6
WOT/HER KT12 60 F4
Endsleigh Rd REDH RH1 126 F3
Ends Pl HORS RH12 * 204 D2
Endway BRYLDS KT5 45 K7
Endymion Rd
BRXS/STRHM SW2 31 J1
Enfield Rd ASHV GU12 113 L4
CRAWW RH11 164 D8
HTHAIR TW6 15 H4
Engadine Cl CROY/NA CR0 3 J8
Engadine St WAND/EARL SW18 29 J2
Engalee EGRIN RH19 162 D3
England Wy NWMAL KT3 45 L4
Englefield HORS RH12 166 C7
Englefield Cl CROY/NA CR0 49 M6
EGH TW20 20 F7
Englefield Rd
WOKN/KNAP GU21 * 75 M7
Engleheart Dr
EBED/NFELT TW14 15 J8
Engleheart Rd CAT SE6 33 L1
Englehurst EGH TW20 20 F7
Englemere Pk ASC SL5 36 A4
COB KT11 81 L4
Englesfield CBLY GU15 73 M4
Engliff La WOKS/MYFD GU22 98 C5
English Gdns STWL/WRAY TW19 12 A6
Enmore Av SNWD SE25 50 D5
Enmore Gdns
MORT/ESHN SW14 19 H7
Enmore Rd PUT/ROE SW15 19 M6
SNWD SE25 50 D5
Ennerdale BRAK RG12 34 D4
Ennerdale Cl CRAWW RH11 164 D6
EBED/NFELT TW14 24 C2
SUT SM1 65 J3
Ennerdale Gv FNM GU9 133 K3
Ennerdale Rd RCH/KEW TW9 18 C4
Ennismore Av GU GU1 7 L4
Ennismore Gdns THDIT KT7 44 B6
Ensign Cl PUR/KEN CR8 67 K8
STWL/WRAY TW19 23 G2
Ensign Wy STWL/WRAY TW19 23 G2
WLGTN SM6 67 H6
Enterdent Rd GDST RH9 128 F8
Enterprise Cl CROY/NA CR0 49 K8
Enterprise Est GU GU1 * 117 H4
Enterprise Wy EDEN TN8 153 L6
TEDD TW11 26 C6
Enton La MFD/CHID GU8 183 Q6
Envis Wy RGUW GU3 115 M4
Envoy Av HTHAIR TW6 15 J5
Eothen Cl CTHM CR3 108 D6
Epping Wk CRAWE RH10 165 H6
Epping Wy BRAK RG12 35 J4
Epsom Cl CBLY GU15 72 F1
Epsom College EW KT17 * 84 B4
Epsom La North EPSOM KT18 104 E1
Epsom La South
KWD/TDW/WH KT20 104 F3
Epsom Pl CRAN GU6 186 E2
Epsom Rd ASHTD KT21 83 J8
CRAWE RH10 165 J6
CROY/NA CR0 67 K3
EHSLY KT24 120 A3
EW KT17 64 C8
GU GU1 7 L6
LHD/OX KT22 102 E3
MRDN SM4 47 J6
RGUE GU4 118 B7
RGUE GU4 119 G5
Epsom Sq HTHAIR TW6 * 15 J4
Epts Rd FARN GU14 112 E1
Epworth Rd ISLW TW7 17 L2
Eresby Dr BECK BR3 51 K8
Erica Cl CHOB/PIR GU24 75 H3
Erica Ct WOKS/MYFD GU22 10 A8
Erica Gdns CROY/NA CR0 69 L3
Erica Wy CRAWE RH10 192 F3
HORS RH12 167 G4
Eridge Cl CRAWE RH10 165 L4
Eriswell Crs WOT/HER KT12 60 C5
Eriswell Rd WOT/HER KT12 60 C4
Erkenwald Cl CHERT KT16 40 B6
Erles Rd LIPH GU30 196 H9
Ermine Cl HSLWW TW4 15 M4
Ermyn Cl LHD/OX KT22 103 G3
Ermyn Wy LHD/OX KT22 103 G3
Erncroft Wy TWK TW1 17 J8
Ernest Av WNWD SE27 31 L5
Ernest Cl BECK BR3 51 K5
RFNM GU10 155 L3
Ernest Gdns CHSWK W4 18 E1
Ernest Gv BECK BR3 51 J5
Ernest Rd KUT/HW KT1 9 L7
Ernest Sq KUT/HW KT1 9 L7
Ernle Rd RYNPK SW20 28 E8
Erpingham Rd PUT/ROE SW15 19 M5
Erridge Rd WIM/MER SW19 47 K2
Errol Gdns NWMAL KT3 46 D4
Erskine Cl CRAWW RH11 164 A8
SUT SM1 66 B2
Erskine Rd SUT SM1 66 A3
Esam Wy STRHM/NOR SW16 31 K6
Escombe Dr GUW GU2 116 E3
Escot Rd SUN TW16 24 B8
Escott Pl CHERT KT16 57 M5
Esher Av CHEAM SM3 65 G2
WOT/HER KT12 42 E8
Esher Cl ESH/CLAY KT10 61 L4
Esher Crs HTHAIR TW6 15 J4
Esher Gn ESH/CLAY KT10 61 L3
Esher Green Dr ESH/CLAY KT10 61 K2
Esher Ms MTCM CR4 48 D3
Esher Park Av ESH/CLAY KT10 61 M4
Esher Place Av ESH/CLAY KT10 61 L3
Esher Rd CBLY GU15 53 K8
E/WMO/HCT KT8 44 A5
WOT/HER KT12 61 H3
Eskdale Ct ASHV GU12 * 113 J5
Eskdale Gdns PUR/KEN CR8 88 A4
Eskdale Wy CBLY GU15 73 M5
Eskmont Rdg NRWD SE19 32 B8
Esparto St WAND/EARL SW18 29 L1
Essendene Cl CTHM CR3 108 B5
Essendene Rd CTHM CR3 108 B5
Essenden Rd SAND/SEL CR2 68 B6
Essex Av ISLW TW7 17 H5
Essex Cl ADL/WDHM KT15 58 F3
FRIM GU16 93 K2
MRDN SM4 47 G7
Essex Ct BARN SW13 19 J4
Essex Dr CRAN GU6 185 Q3
Essex Gv NRWD SE19 32 A7
Estcots Dr EGRIN RH19 163 H4
Estcourt Rd SNWD SE25 50 E6
Estella Av NWMAL KT3 46 E4
Estoria Cl BRXS/STRHM SW2 31 K1
Estreham Rd
STRHM/NOR SW16 31 G7
Estridge Cl HSLW TW3 16 D6
Eswyn Rd TOOT SW17 30 C5
Ethelbert Rd RYNPK SW20 47 G1
Ethelbert St BAL SW12 30 E2
Ethel Rd ASHF TW15 23 H6
Etherley Hl RDKG RH5 172 B10
Etherstone Rd
STRHM/NOR SW16 31 J5
Eton Av HEST TW5 16 C1
NWMAL KT3 46 A5
Eton Cl WAND/EARL SW18 29 L1
Eton Ct STA TW18 22 C6
Eton Pl FNM GU9 133 L2
Eton Rd HYS/HAR UB3 15 J2
Eton St RCH/KEW TW9 18 A7
Etton Rd HSLW TW3 16 F7
Etwell Pl BRYLDS KT5 45 J6
Eureka Rd KUT/HW KT1 9 J7
Europa Park Rd GU GU1 6 F1
Eustace Rd RGUE GU4 118 A6
Euston Rd CROY/NA CR0 49 K8
Evans Cl CRAWE RH10 165 M5
Evans Gv FELT TW13 25 K3
Evedon BRAK RG12 34 E7
Evelina Rd PGE/AN SE20 32 F8
Eveline Rd MTCM CR4 48 C1
Evelyn Av ALDT GU11 134 E1
Evelyn Cl WHTN TW2 25 L1
WOKS/MYFD GU22 97 G2
Evelyn Crs SUN TW16 42 C1
Evelyn Gdns GDST RH9 128 F4
RCH/KEW TW9 18 B6
Evelyn Rd RCH/KEW TW9 18 B5
RCHPK/HAM TW10 26 F4
WIM/MER SW19 29 L6
Evelyn Ter RCH/KEW TW9 18 B5
Evelyn Wk CRAWE RH10 165 G7
Evelyn Wy COB KT11 81 J6
HOR/WEW KT19 83 K1
SUN TW16 42 C1
WLGTN SM6 67 G3
Evelyn Woods Rd ALDT GU11 112 F2
Everdon Rd BARN SW13 19 K1
Everest Ct WOKN/KNAP GU21 * 76 B6
Everest Rd CBLY GU15 73 G1
STWL/WRAY TW19 23 G1
Everglade BH/WHM TN16 91 G8
The Everglades HSLW TW3 * 16 F5
Evergreen Cl PGE/AN SE20 32 F8
Evergreen Ct
STWL/WRAY TW19 * 23 G1
Evergreen Rd FRIM GU16 73 J7
Evergreen Wy
STWL/WRAY TW19 23 G1
Everlands Cl
WOKS/MYFD GU22 10 C8
Eve Rd ISLW TW7 17 K6
WOKN/KNAP GU21 11 J2
Eversfield Rd RCH/KEW TW9 18 C4
REIG RH2 125 L8
SWTR RH13 167 H8
Eversley Crs ISLW TW7 17 G3
Eversley Pk WIM/MER SW19 28 E6
Eversley Rd BRYLDS KT5 45 J4
NRWD SE19 32 A8
Eversley Wy CROY/NA CR0 69 K2
EGH TW20 39 M2
Everton Rd CROY/NA CR0 3 L3
Evesham Cl BELMT SM2 65 K6
REIG RH2 125 J7
Evesham Gn MRDN SM4 47 L6
Evesham Rd MRDN SM4 47 L6
REIG RH2 125 J7
Evesham Rd North REIG RH2 125 J7
Evesham Ter SURB KT6 * 45 G6
Ewart Rd FSTH SE23 33 G1
Ewelands HORL RH6 160 F2
Ewell By-pass EW KT17 64 D6
Ewell Court Av HOR/WEW KT19 64 B4
Ewell Downs Rd EW KT17 84 D1
Ewell House Gv EW KT17 64 C8
Ewell House Pde EW KT17 * 64 C8
Ewell Park Gdns EW KT17 64 D6
Ewell Park Wy EW KT17 64 D5
Ewell Rd CHEAM SM3 65 G5
SURB KT6 44 E7
SURB KT6 45 G6
Ewelme Rd FSTH SE23 32 F2
Ewen Crs BRXS/STRHM SW2 31 K1
Ewhurst Av SAND/SEL CR2 68 C8
Ewhurst Cl BELMT SM2 64 F7
CRAWW RH11 164 E4
Ewhurst Rd CRAN GU6 186 D2
CRAWW RH11 164 D4
SHGR GU5 171 J3
Ewins Cl ASHV GU12 113 K7
Ewood La RDKG RH5 173 N3
Exbury Rd CAT SE6 33 K3
Excalibur Cl CRAWW RH11 164 A4
Excelsior Cl KUT/HW KT1 9 J7
Exchange Rd ASC SL5 36 F5
CRAWE RH10 165 G4
Exeforde Av ASHF TW15 23 K5
Exeter Cl CRAWE RH10 165 G8
Exeter Pl GUW GU2 * 116 C6
Exeter Rd ASHV GU12 113 K6
CROY/NA CR0 3 H2
FELT TW13 25 J4
HTHAIR TW6 15 H5
Exeter Wy HTHAIR TW6 15 H4
Exhibition Rd FARN GU14 112 D1
Explorer Av STWL/WRAY TW19 23 H2
Eyhurst Cl
KWD/TDW/WH KT20 105 J6
Eyhurst Pk
KWD/TDW/WH KT20 * 105 M5
Eyhurst Sp
KWD/TDW/WH KT20 105 J6
Eyles Cl HORS RH12 166 E5
Eylewood Rd WNWD SE27 31 M6
Eynella Rd DUL SE21 32 C1
Eyston Dr WEY KT13 59 K8

F

The Facade FSTH SE23 * 32 F3
REIG RH2 125 K7
Factory La CROY/NA CR0 2 A5
Fagg's Rd EBED/NFELT TW14 15 K7
Fairacre ISLW TW7 * 17 G3
NWMAL KT3 46 B3
Fairacres COB KT11 81 G2
CROY/NA CR0 69 J7
KWD/TDW/WH KT20 104 F3
RFNM GU10 * 155 J5
Fairbairn Cl PUR/KEN CR8 87 K3
Fairbank Av ORP BR6 71 L1
Fairborne Wy GUW GU2 116 D5
Fairbourne COB KT11 81 G3
Fairbourne Cl
WOKN/KNAP GU21 76 D7
Fairbourne La CTHM CR3 107 M4
Fairchildes Av CROY/NA CR0 90 A2
Fairchildes Rd WARL CR6 90 A5
Faircross BRAK RG12 34 E3
Fairdale Gdns PUT/ROE SW15 19 L6
Fairdene Rd COUL/CHIP CR5 87 G8
Fairfax BNFD RG42 34 D1
Fairfax Av EW KT17 64 E7
REDH RH1 126 C7
Fairfax Cl OXTED RH8 130 A4
WOT/HER KT12 42 E8
Fairfax Ms FARN GU14 93 G7
PUT/ROE SW15 19 M6
Fairfax Rd FARN GU14 92 E2
TEDD TW11 26 D8
WOKS/MYFD GU22 97 L2
Fairfield Ap STWL/WRAY TW19 12 A8
Fairfield Av HORL RH6 160 D4
STA TW18 22 C5
WHTN TW2 25 L2
Fairfield Cl GT/LBKH KT23 101 L7
GUW GU2 6 A2
HOR/WEW KT19 64 B4
MTCM CR4 30 B8
Fairfield Cnr KUT/HW KT1 * 9 G7
Fairfield Dr DORK RH4 122 E8
FRIM GU16 73 H6
Fairfield East KUT/HW KT1 8 F6
Fairfield La CHOB/PIR GU24 75 J2
Fairfield North KUTN/CMB KT2 8 F6
Fairfield Pk COB KT11 81 G4
Fairfield Pth CROY/NA CR0 2 F7
Fairfield Pl KUT/HW KT1 8 F8
Fairfield Ri GUW GU2 116 C7
Fairfield Rd BECK BR3 51 K2
CROY/NA CR0 2 F7
EGRIN RH19 163 G5
KUT/HW KT1 8 F7
LHD/OX KT22 102 E3
STWL/WRAY TW19 12 A8
Fairfields CAT SE6 33 L1
CHERT KT16 * 40 E8
Fairfield South KUT/HW KT1 8 F8
The Fairfield FNM GU9 5 K4
Fairfield Wy COUL/CHIP CR5 87 G4
HOR/WEW KT19 64 B4
Fairfield West KUT/HW KT1 8 F7
Fairford Av CROY/NA CR0 51 G5
Fairford Cl BF/WBF KT14 78 C4
CROY/NA CR0 51 G5
REIG RH2 125 M6
Fairford Ct BELMT SM2 * 65 L6
Fairford Gdns WPK KT4 64 C2
Fairgreen Rd THHTH CR7 49 L5
Fairhaven EGH TW20 21 J6
Fairhaven Av CROY/NA CR0 51 G6
Fairhaven Rd REDH RH1 126 D4
Fairholme EBED/NFELT TW14 24 A1
Fairholme Crs ASHTD KT21 82 F7
Fairholme Gdns FNM GU9 5 K6
Fairholme Rd ASHF TW15 23 H6
CROY/NA CR0 49 K7
SUT SM1 65 J5
Fairlands Av RGUW GU3 115 M4
SUT SM1 65 K1
THHTH CR7 49 J4
Fairlands Rd RGUW GU3 115 M3
Fair La COUL/CHIP CR5 105 M7
Fairlawn GT/LBKH KT23 101 J6
WEY KT13 * 60 B4
Fairlawn Cl ESH/CLAY KT10 62 C5
FELT TW13 25 J5
KUTN/CMB KT2 27 M7
Fairlawn Crs EGRIN RH19 162 C3
Fairlawn Dr EGRIN RH19 162 C3
REDH RH1 148 B2

Fairlawn Gv BNSTD SM7 86 A3
Fairlawn Pk SYD SE26 33 H6
WOKN/KNAP GU21 77 H4
Fairlawn Rd CAR SM5 85 M1
WIM/MER SW19 29 J8
Fairlawns ADL/WDHM KT15 78 C1
HORL RH6 160 E4
SUN TW16 42 D3
TWK TW1 17 M8
Fairlawns Cl STA TW18 22 E7
Fairlie Gdns FSTH SE23 32 F1
Fairlight Cl WPK KT4 64 F3
Fairlight Rd TOOT SW17 30 A5
Fairmead BRYLDS KT5 45 L8
WOKN/KNAP GU21 76 F8
Fairmead Cl HEST TW5 16 A2
NWMAL KT3 46 A3
SHST GU47 72 B2
Fairmead Ct CBLY GU15 72 F5
Fairmead Rd CROY/NA CR0 49 K7
EDEN TN8 153 L4
Fairmeads COB KT11 81 H3
Fairmile Av COB KT11 81 H4
STRHM/NOR SW16 31 G6
Fairmile Ct COB KT11 81 H2
Fairmile Hts COB KT11 81 K3
Fairmile La COB KT11 81 G2
Fairmile Pk Copse COB KT11 81 J2
Fairmile Park Rd COB KT11 81 J3
Fair Oak Cl LHD/OX KT22 82 A1
Fairoak Cl PUR/KEN CR8 87 L5
Fairoak La LHD/OX KT22 82 B1
Fairoaks RGUW GU3 * 115 K3
Fairs Rd LHD/OX KT22 102 D1
Fairstone Ct HORL RH6 160 E2
Fair St HSLW TW3 16 F5
Fairview EW KT17 84 F1
Fair Vw HORS RH12 166 D6
Fairview Av WOKS/MYFD GU22 10 D8
Fairview Ct SYD SE26 * 33 H5
WOKS/MYFD GU22 10 E8
Fairview Dr SHPTN TW17 41 J5
Fairview Gdns FNM GU9 134 A3
Fairview Pl BRXS/STRHM SW2 31 J1
Fairview Rd ASHV GU12 113 L6
BOR GU35 180 G12
EW KT17 84 C1
STRHM/NOR SW16 49 J1
SUT SM1 66 A4
Fairview Ter BOR GU35 * 180 F11
Fairwater Dr ADL/WDHM KT15 59 G7
Fairway CAR SM5 85 M1
CHERT KT16 40 E8
CRAWE RH10 192 G3
CRAWW RH11 190 G8
GU GU1 118 A8
RYNPK SW20 46 F3
Fairway Cl CRAWE RH10 192 F3
CROY/NA CR0 51 H5
HOR/WEW KT19 63 M3
LIPH GU30 196 C10
WOKS/MYFD GU22 96 E1
Fairway Hts CBLY GU15 73 L3
Fairways ASHF TW15 23 K7
GSHT GU26 181 N11
ISLW TW7 * 17 H3
PUR/KEN CR8 87 M7
TEDD TW11 8 C2
The Fairways REDH RH1 148 A3
The Fairway CBLY GU15 73 K6
E/WMO/HCT KT8 43 L3
FNM GU9 134 A2
GODL GU7 168 C7
LHD/OX KT22 82 D8
NWMAL KT3 46 A1
RGUW GU3 95 M6
WEY KT13 79 K1
Fairwell La EHSLY KT24 119 L2
Fairwyn Rd SYD SE26 33 H4
Fakenham Wy SHST GU47 52 A8
Falaise EGH TW20 21 H6
Falaise Cl ALDT GU11 112 E6
Falcon Cl CHSWK W4 18 E1
CRAWW RH11 164 F2
LTWR GU18 74 C1
Falcon Dr STWL/WRAY TW19 14 A8
Falconhurst LHD/OX KT22 82 A5
Falcon Rd GU GU1 7 H4
HPTN TW12 25 J8
Falcons Cl BH/WHM TN16 91 G7
Falcon Wy SUN TW16 42 B2
Falconwood EGH TW20 21 H6
EHSLY KT24 100 C6
Falcon Wd LHD/OX KT22 102 C2
Falconwood Rd CROY/NA CR0 69 K6
Falcourt Cl SUT SM1 65 L4
Falkland Gv DORK RH4 144 D3
Falkland Park Av SNWD SE25 50 B3
Falkland Rd DORK RH4 144 D3
Falklands Dr SWTR RH13 167 L5
Falkner Rd FNM GU9 4 F3
Fallow Deer Cl SWTR RH13 167 L6
Fallowfield Wy HORL RH6 160 E2
Fallsbrook Rd
STRHM/NOR SW16 30 E7
Falmer Cl CRAWW RH11 164 F6
Falmouth Cl CBLY GU15 73 K5
Falmouth Rd WOT/HER KT12 60 F3
Falstone WOKN/KNAP GU21 76 E8
Fambridge Cl SYD SE26 33 J5
Famet Av PUR/KEN CR8 87 M3
Famet Cl PUR/KEN CR8 87 M3
Famet Wk PUR/KEN CR8 87 M3
Fanes Cl BNFD RG42 34 C1
Fanshawe Rd
RCHPK/HAM TW10 26 F5
Fanthorpe St PUT/ROE SW15 19 M5
Faraday Av EGRIN RH19 163 G7
Faraday Pl E/WMO/HCT KT8 43 K4
Faraday Rd CRAWE RH10 191 Q3
E/WMO/HCT KT8 43 K4
FARN GU14 92 F3
GU GU1 6 F3
WIM/MER SW19 29 L7
Farebrothers HORS RH12 * 166 C1
Fareham Rd EBED/NFELT TW14 24 F1
Farewell Pl MTCM CR4 48 A1
Farhalls Crs HORS RH12 167 J3
Faringdon Dr BRAK RG12 35 G5
Faris Barn Dr ADL/WDHM KT15 78 C2
Faris La ADL/WDHM KT15 78 C1
Farleigh Court Rd
CROY/NA CR0 67 J1
WARL CR6 89 J4
Farleigh Dean Crs
CROY/NA CR0 89 L1
Farleigh Rd ADL/WDHM KT15 78 D1
WARL CR6 89 H7
Farleton Cl WEY KT13 60 A5
Farley Copse BNFD RG42 34 B1
Farley Ct FARN GU14 * 93 G7
Farleycroft BH/WHM TN16 111 L8
Farley Heath Rd SHGR GU5 170 A5
Farley La BH/WHM TN16 131 L1
Farley Nursery BH/WHM TN16 131 M1
Farley Pk OXTED RH8 130 A4
Farley Pl SNWD SE25 50 D4
Farley Rd CAT SE6 33 M1
SAND/SEL CR2 68 E6
Farleys Cl EHSLY KT24 99 M8
Farlington Pl PUT/ROE SW15 28 E1
Farlton Rd WAND/EARL SW18 29 L1
Farm Av HORS RH12 166 E6
STRHM/NOR SW16 31 H5
Farm Cl ASC SL5 36 F5
BELMT SM2 66 A6
BF/WBF KT14 79 J2
BIL RH14 201 R6
BNFD RG42 34 C1
CHERT KT16 39 K6
CRAWE RH10 165 H3
EGRIN RH19 163 J5
EHSLY KT24 120 C2
GU GU1 117 G5
HORS RH12 166 C2
LHD/OX KT22 102 A6
RGUW GU3 115 M3
SHPTN TW17 41 K7
STA TW18 22 B6
WLGTN SM6 66 F8
WWKM BR4 70 C2
Farm Ct FRIM GU16 * 73 J7
Farmdale Rd CAR SM5 66 B6
Farm Dr CROY/NA CR0 69 J1
PUR/KEN CR8 87 G2
Farmer's Rd STA TW18 22 B6
Farmfield Dr HORL RH6 175 L9
Farm Flds SAND/SEL CR2 88 C1
Farmhouse Cl
WOKS/MYFD GU22 78 A5
Farmhouse Rd
STRHM/NOR SW16 30 F8
Farmington Av SUT SM1 66 A2
Farm La ADL/WDHM KT15 58 D5
ASHTD KT21 83 L8
CROY/NA CR0 69 J1
EHSLY KT24 120 C2
PUR/KEN CR8 66 F8
RFNM GU10 132 B4
RPLY/SEND GU23 97 M5
Farmleigh Cl CRAWE RH10 165 L2
Farmleigh Gv WOT/HER KT12 60 C4
Farm Rd ASHV GU12 113 H6
BELMT SM2 66 A6
ESH/CLAY KT10 43 K8
FRIM GU16 73 H7
HSLWW TW4 25 H2
MRDN SM4 47 L5
STA TW18 22 E7
WARL CR6 109 H1
WOKS/MYFD GU22 97 L2
Farmstead Dr EDEN TN8 153 M6
Farmstead Rd CAT SE6 33 L5
The Farm WIM/MER SW19 * 29 G1
Farmview COB KT11 81 G6
Farm Wk ASHV GU12 135 M1
GUW GU2 138 C2
Farm Wy STWL/WRAY TW19 13 J8
WPK KT4 64 F2
Farnan Rd STRHM/NOR SW16 31 H6
Farnborough Av SAND/SEL CR2 69 H6
Farnborough Common
ORP BR6 71 K3
Farnborough Crs
SAND/SEL CR2 69 H7
Farnborough Ga FARN GU14 * 92 F2
Farnborough Rd ALDT GU11 112 A8
FARN GU14 112 E1
FNM GU9 134 A1
Farnborough St FARN GU14 93 G4
Farnborough Wy ORP BR6 71 L4
Farncombe Hl GODL GU7 168 A2
Farncombe St GODL GU7 168 B2
Farnell Rd ISLW TW7 17 G5
STA TW18 22 D4
Farnham By-Pass FNM GU9 4 D7
Farnham Cl BRAK RG12 35 G2
Farnham Gdns RYNPK SW20 46 E2
Farnham La HASM GU27 198 B4
Farnham Park Cl FNM GU9 133 L3
Farnham Rd GUW GU2 6 E7
MFD/CHID GU8 157 M5
RFNM GU10 181 J6
Farnhurst La CRAN GU6 185 Q9
Farningham BRAK RG12 35 H6
Farningham Crs CTHM CR3 108 D5
Farningham Rd CTHM CR3 108 D5
Farnley WOKN/KNAP GU21 76 C7
Farnley Rd SNWD SE25 50 A4
Farquhar Rd NRWD SE19 32 C6
WIM/MER SW19 29 K4
Farquharson Rd CROY/NA CR0 2 C2
Farrell Cl CBLY GU15 72 E6
Farren Rd FSTH SE23 33 H3
Farriers Cl EW KT17 84 B2
The Farriers SHGR GU5 169 K4
Farrington Acres WEY KT13 * 60 A2
Farriers Rd EW KT17 84 B1
Farthing Flds BOR GU35 180 D12
Farthingham La CRAN GU6 171 K11
Farthings WOKN/KNAP GU21 76 B6
Farthings Hl HORS RH12 * 166 E8
The Farthings KUTN/CMB KT2 9 K4
Farthing St HAYES BR2 71 J6
Farthings Wk HORS RH12 166 C6
Fassett Rd KUT/HW KT1 45 H4
Fauconberg Rd CHSWK W4 18 F1
Faulkner Pl BAGS GU19 54 B5
Faulkner's Rd WOT/HER KT12 60 F4
Faversham Rd BECK BR3 51 J2
CAT SE6 33 J1
MRDN SM4 47 L6
SHST GU47 52 A8
Fawcett Cl STRHM/NOR SW16 31 K5
Fawcett Rd CROY/NA CR0 2 C8
Fawcus Cl ESH/CLAY KT10 62 B5
Fawler Md BRAK RG12 35 J4
Fawns Manor Rd
EBED/NFELT TW14 24 A2
Fawsley Cl DTCH/LGLY SL3 13 H2
Faygate La GDST RH9 151 H6
HORS RH12 190 B6
Faygate Rd BRXS/STRHM SW2 31 J3
Fayland Av STRHM/NOR SW16 30 F6
Fay Rd HORS RH12 166 F5
Fearn Cl EHSLY KT24 120 B3
Fearnley Crs HPTN TW12 25 J7
Featherbed La SAND/SEL CR2 69 J6
Feathercombe La
MFD/CHID GU8 184 A1
Feathers La STWL/WRAY TW19 21 K3
Featherstone LING RH7 151 G8
Featherstone Av FSTH SE23 32 E3
Fee Farm Rd ESH/CLAY KT10 62 C6
Felbridge Av CRAWE RH10 165 M3
Felbridge Cl BELMT SM2 65 L7
EGRIN RH19 162 D2
FRIM GU16 73 J7
STRHM/NOR SW16 31 K5
Felbridge Ct EGRIN RH19 162 B1
Felbridge Pl EGRIN RH19 * 162 B1
Felbridge Rd EGRIN RH19 193 Q2
Felcot Rd EGRIN RH19 193 P2
Felcott Cl WOT/HER KT12 60 F2
Felcott Rd WOT/HER KT12 60 F2
Felcourt La EGRIN RH19 178 C8
Felcourt Rd EGRIN RH19 178 D10
Felday Gld RDKG RH5 171 N4
Felday Rd RDKG RH5 142 C6
The Feld EGRIN RH19 162 B2
Felix Dr RGUE GU4 118 D2
Felix La SHPTN TW17 42 C6
Felix Rd WOT/HER KT12 42 D6
Felland Wy REIG RH2 148 A4
Fellbrook RCHPK/HAM TW10 26 E4
Fellcott Wy HORS RH12 166 C8
Fellmongers Yd CROY/NA CR0 2 C7
Fellowes Rd CAR SM5 66 B2
Fellow Gn CHOB/PIR GU24 75 J3
Fellow Green Rd
CHOB/PIR GU24 75 J3
Fellows Rd FARN GU14 93 G8
Fell Rd CROY/NA CR0 2 D7
Felmingham Rd PGE/AN SE20 50 F2
Felsham Rd PUT/ROE SW15 19 M5
Felstead Rd HOR/WEW KT19 84 A1
Feltham Av E/WMO/HCT KT8 44 B4
Felthambrook Wy FELT TW13 24 E5
Feltham Hill Rd ASHF TW15 23 K6
Feltham Rd ASHF TW15 23 L5
MTCM CR4 48 C2
REDH RH1 148 C5
Fenby Cl SWTR RH13 167 L5
Fenchurch Rd CRAWE RH10 165 K6
Fencote BRAK RG12 35 G7
Fendall Rd HOR/WEW KT19 63 M4
Fengates Rd REDH RH1 126 B8
Fenhurst Cl HORS RH12 166 C8
Fennel Cl ASC SL5 36 D4
CROY/NA CR0 51 G8
GU GU1 117 L5
Fennel Crs CRAWW RH11 164 D7
Fennells Md HOR/WEW KT19 64 C7
Fennscombe Ct
CHOB/PIR GU24 75 H3
Fenns La CHOB/PIR GU24 75 H3
Fenn's Wy WOKN/KNAP GU21 10 D2
Fenton Av STA TW18 22 F7
Fenton Cl REDH RH1 126 D8
Fenton Rd REDH RH1 126 D8
Fentum Rd GUW GU2 116 D6
Fenwick Cl WOKN/KNAP GU21 76 E8
Fenwick Pl SAND/SEL CR2 67 L6
Ferguson Av BRYLDS KT5 45 J5
Ferguson Cl BECK BR3 51 M3
Fermandy La CRAWE RH10 193 M4
Fermor Dr ALDT GU11 112 C6
Fermor Rd FSTH SE23 33 H2
Fern Av MTCM CR4 49 G4
Fernbank Av WOT/HER KT12 43 H7
Fernbank Crs ASC SL5 36 A1
Fernbank Pl ASC SL5 35 M1
Fernbank Rd ADL/WDHM KT15 58 D4
ASC SL5 36 A2
Fernbrae Cl RFNM GU10 155 L7
Fern Cl FRIM GU16 73 M6
WARL CR6 89 H8
Ferndale RGUW GU3 116 B6
Ferndale Av CHERT KT16 58 B2
HSLWW TW4 16 B5
Ferndale Rd ASHF TW15 23 G6
BNSTD SM7 85 J6
SNWD SE25 50 E5
WOKN/KNAP GU21 10 E4
Fernden La HASM GU27 198 D10
Fernden Ri GODL GU7 168 B2
Ferndown CRAWE RH10 192 C3
HORL RH6 160 D1
Ferndown Cl BELMT SM2 66 A5
GU GU1 139 K1
Ferndown Gdns COB KT11 80 F4
FARN GU14 92 B5
The Fernery STA TW18 22 B6
Ferney Ct BF/WBF KT14 79 G2
Ferney Meade Wy ISLW TW7 17 K4
Fern Gv EBED/NFELT TW14 24 E1
Fernham Rd THHTH CR7 49 M4
Fernhill LHD/OX KT22 82 A4
Fernhill Cl BLKW GU17 72 B8
CRAWE RH10 193 N4
FNM GU9 133 L3
WOKS/MYFD GU22 96 F2
Fernhill Dr FNM GU9 133 L3
Fernhill Gdns KUTN/CMB KT2 27 G6
Fernhill La BLKW GU17 72 C8
FNM GU9 133 L2
WOKS/MYFD GU22 96 F2
Fernhill Pk WOKS/MYFD GU22 96 F2
Fernhill Rd BLKW GU17 72 B7
FARN GU14 92 B2
HORL RH6 161 G7
Fernhill Wk BLKW GU17 72 C8
Fernhurst Cl CRAWW RH11 164 D2
Fernhurst Rd ASHF TW15 23 M5
CROY/NA CR0 3 M2
Ferniehurst CBLY GU15 73 J5
Fernihough Cl WEY KT13 79 K1
Fernlands Cl CHERT KT16 58 B2
Fernlea GT/LBKH KT23 101 L6
Fernlea Rd BAL SW12 30 E2
MTCM CR4 48 D2
Fernleigh Cl CROY/NA CR0 67 K3
WOT/HER KT12 60 E2
Fernleigh Ri FRIM GU16 93 M2
Fern Rd GODL GU7 168 C3
Ferns Cl SAND/SEL CR2 68 E8
Fernside Av FELT TW13 24 E5
Fernside Rd BAL SW12 30 C2
Ferns Md FNM GU9 4 F5
The Ferns FNM GU9 * 133 M2
Fernthorpe Rd
STRHM/NOR SW16 30 F7
Fern Towers CTHM CR3 108 D7
Fern Wk ASHF TW15 23 G6
Fern Wy HORS RH12 167 G4
Fernwood Av
STRHM/NOR SW16 31 G5
Feroners Cl CRAWE RH10 165 J6
Ferrard Cl ASC SL5 36 A1
Ferraro Cl HEST TW5 16 D1
Ferrers Av WLGTN SM6 67 G3
Ferrers Rd STRHM/NOR SW16 31 G6
Ferriers Wy EPSOM KT18 104 F1
Ferrings DUL SE21 32 B3
Ferris Av CROY/NA CR0 69 J2
Ferry Av STA TW18 22 B8
Ferry La BARN SW13 19 J1
BTFD TW8 18 B1
CHERT KT16 40 D6
GUW GU2 138 F4
SHPTN TW17 41 K8
STA TW18 40 F3
STWL/WRAY TW19 21 L3
Ferrymoor RCHPK/HAM TW10 26 E4
Ferry Rd BARN SW13 19 K2
E/WMO/HCT KT8 43 K3
TEDD TW11 26 E6
THDIT KT7 44 E6
Ferry Sq BTFD TW8 18 B1
Fetcham Common La
LHD/OX KT22 101 L3
Fetcham Park Dr
LHD/OX KT22 102 B5
Fettes Rd CRAN GU6 186 F2
Fiddicroft Av BNSTD SM7 85 L5
Field Cl CHSGTN KT9 62 F4
E/WMO/HCT KT8 43 L5
HSLWW TW4 15 L3
HYS/HAR UB3 14 F2
RGUE GU4 118 A6
SAND/SEL CR2 88 E4
Fieldcommon La
WOT/HER KT12 43 H8
Field Ct OXTED RH8 130 B2
Field End CHOB/PIR GU24 75 J3
COUL/CHIP CR5 87 G4
FNM GU9 134 C5
Fieldend HORS RH12 167 L4
TEDD TW11 26 C5
Fieldend Rd STRHM/NOR SW16 48 F1
Fielden Pl BRAK RG12 35 G2
Fielders Gn GU GU1 117 K8
Field House Cl ASC SL5 36 D8
Fieldhouse Rd BAL SW12 30 F2
Fieldhurst Cl ADL/WDHM KT15 58 E4
Fielding Av WHTN TW2 25 M4
Fielding Rd SHST GU47 72 B3
The Fieldings BNSTD SM7 85 J7
FSTH SE23 32 F2
HORL RH6 160 E2
WOKN/KNAP GU21 76 C6
Field La BTFD TW8 17 M2
FRIM GU16 73 H8
GODL GU7 168 C2
TEDD TW11 26 D6
Field Pk BRAK RG12 35 G1
Fieldpark Gdns CROY/NA CR0 51 H8
Field Pl LIPH GU30 196 G10
NWMAL KT3 46 C6
Field Rd EBED/NFELT TW14 15 L8
FARN GU14 72 C8
Fieldsend Rd CHEAM SM3 65 H4
Fieldside Cl ORP BR6 71 M3
Field Stores Ap ALDT GU11 112 F6
Field Vw EGH TW20 21 M6
FELT TW13 24 A5
Fieldview HORL RH6 160 E2
WAND/EARL SW18 30 A2
Field Wk HORL RH6 161 M2
Field Wy ASHV GU12 113 H7
CROY/NA CR0 69 L6
RFNM GU10 135 J2
RPLY/SEND GU23 98 C7
Fieldway HASM GU27 198 D6
Fifehead Cl ASHF TW15 23 H7
Fife Rd KUT/HW KT1 8 E6
MORT/ESHN SW14 18 F7
Fife Wy GT/LBKH KT23 101 K7
Fifield La RFNM GU10 155 M7
Fifield Pth FSTH SE23 33 G4
Fifteenth Av
KWD/TDW/WH KT20 * 105 J8
Fifth Av KWD/TDW/WH KT20 * 105 J8
Fifth Cross Rd WHTN TW2 26 A3
Figge's Rd MTCM CR4 30 D8
Figgswood COUL/CHIP CR5 106 F4
Filbert Crs CRAWW RH11 164 C4
Filby Rd CHSGTN KT9 63 J5
Filey Cl BELMT SM2 65 M6
BH/WHM TN16 110 E1
CRAWW RH11 164 B6
Filmer Gv GODL GU7 168 B4
Finborough Rd TOOT SW17 30 C8
Finch Av WNWD SE27 32 A5
Finch Cl WOKN/KNAP GU21 75 M7
Finch Crs CRAWE RH10 193 P8
Finch Dr EBED/NFELT TW14 25 G1
Finches Ri GU GU1 117 L6
Finch Rd GU GU1 7 H4
Findhorn Cl SHST GU47 72 A2
The Findings FARN GU14 92 B1
Findlay Dr RGUW GU3 116 C4
Findon Rd CRAWW RH11 164 D2
Findon Wy HORS RH12 166 A6
Finlay Gdns ADL/WDHM KT15 58 F3
Finlays Cl CHSGTN KT9 63 K4
Finmere BRAK RG12 34 F6
Finnart Cl WEY KT13 59 M3
Finney Dr BFOR GU20 55 G5
Finsbury Cl CRAWW RH11 164 E8
Finstock Gn BRAK RG12 35 J4
Fintry Pl FARN GU14 92 B2
Fiona Cl GT/LBKH KT23 101 K6
Fir Acre Rd ASHV GU12 113 K3
Firbank Dr WOKN/KNAP GU21 96 E1
Firbank La WOKN/KNAP GU21 96 E1
Firbank Pl EGH TW20 20 E7
Fir Cl WOT/HER KT12 42 D7
Fircroft Cl WOKS/MYFD GU22 10 E8
Fircroft Ct WOKS/MYFD GU22 10 E8
Fircroft Rd CHSGTN KT9 63 J3
TOOT SW17 30 C4
Fircroft Wy EDEN TN8 153 M6
Firdene BRYLDS KT5 45 M8
Fir Dene ORP BR6 71 J2
Fir Dr BLKW GU17 72 A6
Fireball Hl ASC SL5 37 G7
Fire Bell Aly SURB KT6 45 H6
Firebell Ms SURB KT6 45 H6
Firefly Cl WLGTN SM6 * 67 H6
Fire Station Rd ALDT GU11 112 E6
Firfield Rd ADL/WDHM KT15 58 D3
FNM GU9 155 K2
Firfields WEY KT13 59 L6
Fir Grange Av WEY KT13 59 L4
Fir Gv NWMAL KT3 46 C6
Firgrove WOKN/KNAP GU21 96 D1
Firgrove Ct FNM GU9 5 J5
Firgrove Hl FNM GU9 5 J6
Firgrove Pde FARN GU14 * 92 E5
Firgrove Rd FARN GU14 92 E5
Firhill Rd CAT SE6 33 K4
Firlands BRAK RG12 34 F5
HORL RH6 160 E2
WEY KT13 60 B5
Firlands Av CBLY GU15 73 G4
Firle Cl CRAWE RH10 165 G2
Firle Ct EW KT17 * 84 C2
Firle Pl WAND/EARL SW18 29 M1
Fir Rd CHEAM SM3 47 J8
FELT TW13 25 G6
Firs Av MORT/ESHN SW14 18 F6
SHGR GU5 169 K3
Firsby Av CROY/NA CR0 51 G8
Firs Cl DORK RH4 144 D4
ESH/CLAY KT10 62 B5
FARN GU14 92 F7
FSTH SE23 33 G1
MTCM CR4 48 E2
Firsdene Cl CHERT KT16 58 A5
Firs Dr HEST TW5 15 L2
Firs La SHGR GU5 169 N5
Firs Rd PUR/KEN CR8 87 L5
First Av ADL/WDHM KT15 58 E7
E/WMO/HCT KT8 43 J4
HOR/WEW KT19 64 B7
KWD/TDW/WH KT20 * 105 J8
MORT/ESHN SW14 19 H4
WOT/HER KT12 42 E6
First Cl E/WMO/HCT KT8 43 M4
First Cross Rd WHTN TW2 26 B3
The Firs BF/WBF KT14 * 79 G2
EBED/NFELT TW14 * 15 H8
GT/LBKH KT23 * 101 L7
LIPH GU30 196 G10
RGUW GU3 138 E4
First Quarter HOR/WEW KT19 * 84 B1
Firstway RYNPK SW20 46 F2
Firsway GUW GU2 116 C7
Firswood Av HOR/WEW KT19 64 B4
Fir Tree Av HASM GU27 197 Q7
Firtree Av MTCM CR4 48 D2
Fir Tree Cl ASC SL5 36 D7
CRAWW RH11 164 D1
ESH/CLAY KT10 61 M4
EW KT17 84 F5
HOR/WEW KT19 64 C3
LHD/OX KT22 102 F5
STRHM/NOR SW16 30 F6
Fir Tree Gdns CROY/NA CR0 69 K3
Fir Tree Gv CAR SM5 66 C6
Fir Tree Pl ASHF TW15 * 23 K5
Fir Tree Rd EW KT17 84 E6
GU GU1 116 F5
HSLWW TW4 16 B6
LHD/OX KT22 102 F5
Fir Tree Wk REIG RH2 126 A8
Fir Wk CHEAM SM3 65 G5
Firway GSHT GU26 181 K12
Firwood Cl WOKN/KNAP GU21 96 B2
Firwood Dr CBLY GU15 72 F4
Firwood Rd VW GU25 38 B6
Fisher Cl CRAWE RH10 165 G6
CROY/NA CR0 3 J4
WOT/HER KT12 60 E3
Fisherdene ESH/CLAY KT10 62 D6
Fisher La MFD/CHID GU8 200 D2
Fisherman Cl
RCHPK/HAM TW10 26 F5
Fishermen's Cl ALDT GU11 113 H4
Fisher Rowe Cl SHGR GU5 169 K3
Fishers Ct HORS RH12 166 F5
Fishers Wd ASC SL5 37 M8
Fishponds Rd HAYES BR2 71 G4
TOOT SW17 30 B5
Fitchet Cl CRAWW RH11 164 D2
Fitzalan Rd ESH/CLAY KT10 62 B6
SWTR RH13 167 K5
Fitzgeorge Av NWMAL KT3 46 A1
Fitzgerald Av
MORT/ESHN SW14 19 H5
Fitzgerald Rd
MORT/ESHN SW14 19 G5
THDIT KT7 44 D6
Fitzjames Av CROY/NA CR0 3 M6
Fitzjohn Cl RGUE GU4 117 M5
Fitzrobert Pl EGH TW20 21 K7
Fitzroy Cl BRAK RG12 34 D6
Fitzroy Crs CHSWK W4 * 19 G2
Fitzroy Gdns NRWD SE19 32 B8
Fitzwilliam Av RCH/KEW TW9 18 C4
Fitz Wygram Cl HPTN TW12 25 M6
Fiveacre Cl CROY/NA CR0 49 K6
Five Acres CRAWE RH10 165 G2
Five Acres Cl BOR GU35 180 A12

Five Elms Rd HAYES BR2 70 F2
Five Oaks Cl WOKN/KNAP GU21 96 A1
Five Oaks Rd SWTR RH13 203 R9
Flag Cl CROY/NA CR0 51 G8
Flambard Wy GODL GU7 168 A5
Flamborough Cl
BH/WHM TN16 110 E1
Flamsteed Hts CRAWW RH11 * 191 L12
Flanchford Rd REIG RH2 146 F5
Flanders Crs TOOT SW17 30 C8
Flather Cl STRHM/NOR SW16 30 F7
Flaxley Rd MRDN SM4 47 L6
Fleece Rd SURB KT6 44 F8
Fleet Cl E/WMO/HCT KT8 43 J5
Fleetside E/WMO/HCT KT8 43 K5
Fleet Ter CAT SE6 * 33 M1
Fleetway EGH TW20 39 M3
Fleetwood Cl CHSGTN KT9 63 G6
CROY/NA CR0 3 J7
KWD/TDW/WH KT20 105 G3
Fleetwood Ct BF/WBF KT14 78 D3
Fleetwood Rd KUT/HW KT1 9 M8
Fleetwood Sq KUT/HW KT1 9 M8
Fleming Cl FARN GU14 93 G3
Fleming Ct CROY/NA CR0 67 K6
Fleming Md MTCM CR4 30 B8
Fleming Wy CRAWE RH10 191 P3
ISLW TW7 17 J5
Flemish Flds CHERT KT16 40 D7
Fletcher Cl CHERT KT16 58 A5
CRAWE RH10 165 G6
Fletcher Gdns BNFD RG42 34 A1
Fletcher Rd CHERT KT16 58 A5
Fletchers Cl SWTR RH13 167 H8
Fletchers Fld LIPH GU30 196 G10
Flexford Gn BRAK RG12 34 B6
Flexford Rd RGUW GU3 136 E1
Flint Cl BNSTD SM7 85 L4
CRAWE RH10 165 K7
GT/LBKH KT23 101 M8
REDH RH1 126 C7
Flintgrove BRAK RG12 35 G1
Flint Hl DORK RH4 144 E4
Flint Hill Cl DORK RH4 144 E5
Flintlock Cl STWL/WRAY TW19 13 K6
Flitwick Gra MFD/CHID GU8 159 J8
Flock Mill Pl WAND/EARL SW18 29 L2
Flood La TWK TW1 * 26 D2
Flora Gdns CROY/NA CR0 89 M1
Florence Av ADL/WDHM KT15 78 D1
MRDN SM4 47 M5
Florence Cl WOT/HER KT12 42 E7
Florence Gdns CHSWK W4 18 F1
STA TW18 22 E8
Florence Rd BECK BR3 51 G2
FELT TW13 24 E2
KUTN/CMB KT2 9 H3
SAND/SEL CR2 68 A7
SHST GU47 72 B2
WIM/MER SW19 29 L7
WOT/HER KT12 42 E7
Florence Wy BAL SW12 30 C2
WOKN/KNAP GU21 75 M8
Florian Av SUT SM1 66 A3
Florida Rd RGUE GU4 139 H6
THHTH CR7 49 L1
Floss St PUT/ROE SW15 19 M4
Flower Crs CHERT KT16 57 L5
Flower La GDST RH9 129 G3
Flower Wk GUW GU2 6 F9
Floyds La WOKS/MYFD GU22 78 D6
Floyer Cl RCHPK/HAM TW10 18 C7
Foden Rd ALDT GU11 112 D8
Foley Ms ESH/CLAY KT10 62 B5
Foley Rd BH/WHM TN16 91 G8
ESH/CLAY KT10 62 B6
Follyfield Rd BNSTD SM7 85 K4
Folly Hl FNM GU9 133 K4
Folly La RDKG RH5 173 J2
Folly La North FNM GU9 133 L2
Folly La South FNM GU9 133 K3
The Folly LTWR GU18 * 74 E2
Fontaine Rd STRHM/NOR SW16 31 J7
Fontana Cl CRAWE RH10 165 M5
Fontenoy Rd BAL SW12 30 E3
Fontley Wy PUT/ROE SW15 28 D1
Fontmell Cl ASHF TW15 23 K6
Fontmell Pk ASHF TW15 23 J6
Fontwell Cl ASHV GU12 113 G7
Fontwell Rd CRAWE RH10 165 J7
The Footpath PUT/ROE SW15 * 19 K7
Forbes Cha SHST GU47 72 A2
Forbes Cl CRAWE RH10 165 K8
Fordbridge Rd ASHF TW15 23 H7
SUN TW16 42 B6
Ford Cl ASHF TW15 23 H7
SHPTN TW17 41 K5
THHTH CR7 49 L6
Fordingbridge Cl CHERT KT16 * 40 E8
HORS RH12 166 F8
Ford La RFNM GU10 155 L3
Ford Manor Rd LING RH7 179 J7
Fordmill Rd CAT SE6 33 K3
Ford Rd ASHF TW15 23 J5
CHERT KT16 40 E8
CHOB/PIR GU24 55 M8
CHOB/PIR GU24 75 J5
WOKS/MYFD GU22 97 L2
Fordwater Rd CHERT KT16 40 E8
Fordwells Dr BRAK RG12 35 J4
Foreman Pk ASHV GU12 113 L7
Foreman Rd ASHV GU12 113 L8
Forest Cl ASC SL5 35 M3
CRAWE RH10 193 N5
EHSLY KT24 100 C7
SWTR RH13 167 L5
SWTR RH13 205 R11
WOKS/MYFD GU22 78 A5
Forest Crs ASHTD KT21 83 K6
Forestdale GSHT GU26 197 Q2
Forest Dr HAYES BR2 71 H3
KWD/TDW/WH KT20 105 K3
RFNM GU10 155 M5
SUN TW16 24 C8
Forester Rd CRAWE RH10 165 G6
GUW GU2 116 D4
Foresters Cl WLGTN SM6 67 G6
WOKN/KNAP GU21 76 C8
Foresters Dr WLGTN SM6 67 G6
Foresters Sq BRAK RG12 35 H3
Foresters Wy CWTH RG45 52 C2
Forestfield CRAWE RH10 165 K6
SWTR RH13 167 K6
Forest Ga CRAWW RH11 191 N12
Forest Gld RFNM GU10 155 G6
Forest Gn BRAK RG12 35 G2
Forest Hills CBLY GU15 72 E5
Forestholme Cl FSTH SE23 32 F3
SYD SE26 32 F6
Forest La BOR GU35 180 B11
EHSLY KT24 100 C6
Forest Lane Cl LIPH GU30 196 F9
Forest Ms HORS RH12 167 L4
Forest Oaks SWTR RH13 167 L5
Forest Rdg BECK BR3 51 K3
HAYES BR2 71 H3
Forest Rd CHEAM SM3 47 K8
EHSLY KT24 100 C7
FELT TW13 24 F4
FROW RH18 195 Q12
HORS RH12 167 L5
RCH/KEW TW9 18 D2
WOKS/MYFD GU22 78 A5
The Forestry Rd BIL RH14 201 L5
Forest Side WPK KT4 46 C8
Forest Vw CRAWE RH10 165 H7
Forest View Rd EGRIN RH19 162 F7
Forest Wy ASHTD KT21 83 K7
EGRIN RH19 163 J8
Forge Av COUL/CHIP CR5 107 K2
Forge Bridge La
COUL/CHIP CR5 106 E4
Forge Cl FNM GU9 5 M1
HORS RH12 166 B5
Forge Cft EDEN TN8 153 M8
Forge Dr ESH/CLAY KT10 62 D6
Forge End WOKN/KNAP GU21 10 C6
Forgefield BH/WHM TN16 91 G6
Forge La ALDT GU11 112 C3
CHEAM SM3 65 H6
CRAWE RH10 * 165 J3
FELT TW13 25 H6
HORS RH12 166 B5
RCHPK/HAM TW10 27 H2
SUN TW16 42 D3
Forge Ms CROY/NA CR0 69 K4
SUN TW16 * 42 D3
Forge Pl HORL RH6 160 B5
Forge Rd CRAWE RH10 165 J3
The Forge HORL RH6 * 174 H10
HORS RH12 166 B2
Forge Wd CRAWE RH10 192 C2
Forrester Pth SYD SE26 32 F5
Forrest Gdns
STRHM/NOR SW16 49 J3
Forster Rd BECK BR3 51 H3
BRXS/STRHM SW2 31 H1
Forsyte Crs NRWD SE19 50 B1
Forsythia Pl GU GU1 * 116 F6
Forsyth Rd WOKN/KNAP GU21 11 M1
Fortescue Av WHTN TW2 25 M4
Fortescue Rd WEY KT13 59 J3
WIM/MER SW19 30 A8
Forth Cl FARN GU14 92 A3
Fort La REIG RH2 125 L4
Fort Rd GU GU1 7 J9
KWD/TDW/WH KT20 123 L5
Fortrose Cl SHST GU47 72 A2
Fortrose Gdns
BRXS/STRHM SW2 31 H2
Fortune Dr CRAN GU6 186 D4
Fortyfoot Rd LHD/OX KT22 102 F3
The Forum E/WMO/HCT KT8 43 L4
Forval Cl MTCM CR4 48 C5
Foss Av CROY/NA CR0 67 K4
Fosse Wy BF/WBF KT14 78 C3
Fossewood Dr CBLY GU15 73 G1
Foss Rd TOOT SW17 30 A5
Fosterdown GDST RH9 128 E3
Fosters Gv BFOR GU20 54 E3
Fosters La WOKN/KNAP GU21 75 M7
Foulser Rd TOOT SW17 30 C4
Foulsham Rd THHTH CR7 49 M3
Founders Gdns NRWD SE19 31 M8
Foundry Cl SWTR RH13 167 H5
Foundry Ct CHERT KT16 40 D7
Foundry La DTCH/LGLY SL3 12 E5
HASM GU27 198 B7
SWTR RH13 167 H6
Foundry Ms HSLW TW3 16 E6
Foundry Pl WAND/EARL SW18 * 29 L1
Fountain Dr CAR SM5 66 C7
NRWD SE19 32 C5
WLGTN SM6 86 E1
Fountain Rd REDH RH1 148 B2
THHTH CR7 49 M2
TOOT SW17 30 A6
Fountains Av FELT TW13 25 J4
Fountains Cl CRAWW RH11 164 C6
FELT TW13 25 J3
Fountains Garth BRAK RG12 34 D3
Four Acres COB KT11 81 H3
GU GU1 117 M6
Four Elms Rd EDEN TN8 153 M7
Four Seasons Crs CHEAM SM3 65 J1
Fourteenth Av
KWD/TDW/WH KT20 * 105 J8
Fourth Av
KWD/TDW/WH KT20 * 105 J8
Fourth Cross Rd WHTN TW2 26 A3
Fourth Dr COUL/CHIP CR5 87 G6
Four Wents COB KT11 80 E3
Fowler Av FARN GU14 92 E7
Fowler Cl CRAWE RH10 165 L6
Fowler Rd FARN GU14 92 C7
Fowlers La BNFD RG42 34 E1
Fowlers Md CHOB/PIR GU24 56 B7
Fowler's Rd ALDT GU11 112 F4
Foxacre CTHM CR3 108 B4
Foxborough Hill Rd
MFD/CHID GU8 168 F6
Foxbourne Rd TOOT SW17 30 D3
Foxbridge La BIL RH14 201 M8
Foxburrows Av GUW GU2 116 C8
Fox Cl CRAWW RH11 164 D2
WEY KT13 60 A4
WOKS/MYFD GU22 78 A5
Foxcombe CROY/NA CR0 69 L5
Fox Ct ASHV GU12 113 H6
Fox Covert LHD/OX KT22 102 A6
LTWR GU18 74 D1
Fox Covert Cl ASC SL5 36 F5
Fox Dene GODL GU7 159 M7
Foxdown Cl CBLY GU15 72 F4
Foxearth Cl BH/WHM TN16 91 H8
Foxearth Rd SAND/SEL CR2 68 F8
Foxearth Sp SAND/SEL CR2 68 F7
Foxenden Rd GU GU1 7 J5
Foxes Pth RGUE GU4 97 J8
Foxglove Av HORS RH12 167 H3
Foxglove Cl STWL/WRAY TW19 23 G2
Foxglove Gdns PUR/KEN CR8 87 H1
RGUE GU4 117 M6
Foxglove La CHSGTN KT9 63 K3
Foxglove Wy WLGTN SM6 48 D8
Fox Gv WOT/HER KT12 42 E7
Foxgrove Av BECK BR3 33 L8
Foxgrove Dr WOKN/KNAP GU21 11 G1
Foxgrove Rd BECK BR3 33 M8
Foxhanger Gdns
WOKS/MYFD GU22 11 H4
Fox Hl NRWD SE19 32 C8
Foxhill Crs CBLY GU15 73 L1
Fox Hill Gdns NRWD SE19 32 C8
Foxhills WOKN/KNAP GU21 76 F8
Foxhills Cl CHERT KT16 57 L5
Fox Hills La ASHV GU12 113 M6
Fox Hills Rd CHERT KT16 57 K4
Foxholes HORS RH12 203 J1
WEY KT13 60 A4
Foxhurst Rd ASHV GU12 113 K4
Foxlake Rd BF/WBF KT14 79 J2
Fox La GT/LBKH KT23 101 J6
HAYES BR2 70 E4
REIG RH2 125 L5
Fox La North CHERT KT16 40 C8
Fox La South CHERT KT16 * 40 C8
Foxleigh Cha HORS RH12 167 J5
Foxley Cl REDH RH1 148 D5
Foxley Gdns PUR/KEN CR8 87 L3
Foxley Hill Rd PUR/KEN CR8 87 K2
Foxley La PUR/KEN CR8 67 H8
Foxley Rd PUR/KEN CR8 87 L4
THHTH CR7 49 L4
Foxoak Hl WOT/HER KT12 60 B8
Foxon Cl CTHM CR3 108 B3
Foxon La CTHM CR3 108 A3
Foxon Lane Gdns CTHM CR3 108 B3
Fox Rd BRAK RG12 34 F4
HASM GU27 197 R7
RFNM GU10 155 M3
Foxton Gv MTCM CR4 48 A2
Foxwarren ESH/CLAY KT10 62 C7
Fox Wy RFNM GU10 133 G1
Foxwood HORS RH12 189 J8
Foxwood Cl FELT TW13 24 E4
MFD/CHID GU8 183 N10
Fox Yd FNM GU9 5 G3
Frailey Cl WOKS/MYFD GU22 11 K4
Frailey Hl WOKS/MYFD GU22 11 K3
Framfield Cl CRAWW RH11 164 C2
Framfield Rd MTCM CR4 30 D8
Frampton Cl BELMT SM2 65 K6
Frampton Rd HSLWW TW4 16 B7
France Hill Dr CBLY GU15 72 F4
Franche Court Rd TOOT SW17 29 M4
Francis Av FELT TW13 24 D4
Francis Barber Cl
STRHM/NOR SW16 * 31 J5
Franciscan Rd TOOT SW17 30 D5
Francis Chichester Cl ASC SL5 36 E5
Francis Cl HOR/WEW KT19 64 A3
SHPTN TW17 41 K4
Francis Ct GUW GU2 * 116 E6
Francis Edwards Wy
CRAWW RH11 164 A8
Francis Gv WIM/MER SW19 29 J8
Francis Rd CROY/NA CR0 2 B1
CTHM CR3 108 A4
HSLWW TW4 16 A4
WLGTN SM6 66 F5
Frank Dixon Cl DUL SE21 32 B1
Frank Dixon Wy DUL SE21 32 B2
Franklands Dr ADL/WDHM KT15 58 C6
Franklin Cl KUT/HW KT1 9 J8
WNWD SE27 31 L4
Franklin Ct GUW GU2 116 C8
Franklin Crs MTCM CR4 48 F4
Franklin Rd CRAWE RH10 165 L5
PGE/AN SE20 32 F8
Franklin Wy CROY/NA CR0 49 H8
Franklyn Rd GODL GU7 159 L6
WOT/HER KT12 42 E6
Franks Av NWMAL KT3 45 M4
Franksfield SHGR GU5 171 K2
Franks Fld SHGR GU5 171 K3
Franks Rd GUW GU2 116 D5
Fransfield Gv SYD SE26 32 E4
Frant Cl PGE/AN SE20 32 F8
Frant Fld EDEN TN8 153 M8
Frant Rd THHTH CR7 49 L5
Fraser Md SHST GU47 72 B3
Fraser Rd BNFD RG42 34 E1
Frederick Cl SUT SM1 65 J3
Frederick Gdns CROY/NA CR0 49 L6
SUT SM1 65 J4
Frederick Rd SUT SM1 65 J4
Frederick Sanger Rd
GUW GU2 138 A1
Frederick St ALDT GU11 112 D7
Freeborn Wy BRAK RG12 35 H1
Freedown La BNSTD SM7 85 L8
Freelands Av SAND/SEL CR2 69 G7
Freelands Rd COB KT11 80 E4
Freeman Cl SHPTN TW17 42 B4
Freeman Dr E/WMO/HCT KT8 43 J4
Freeman Rd HORS RH12 166 B1
MRDN SM4 48 A5
Freemantle Rd BAGS GU19 54 C6
Freemason's Rd CROY/NA CR0 3 G3
Free Prae Rd CHERT KT16 40 D8
Freesia Dr CHOB/PIR GU24 75 K6
Freestone Yd DTCH/LGLY SL3 * 13 G3
Freethorpe Cl NRWD SE19 50 B1
Frenchaye ADL/WDHM KT15 58 F4
Frenches Rd REDH RH1 126 E5
The Frenches REDH RH1 126 D6
French Gdns BLKW GU17 72 A5
COB KT11 80 F4
Frenchlands Hatch
EHSLY KT24 120 B1
French La MFD/CHID GU8 182 F7
French St SUN TW16 42 F2
French's Wls WOKN/KNAP GU21 76 E7
Frensham BRAK RG12 35 G6
Frensham Ct RFNM GU10 155 L5
Frensham Dr CROY/NA CR0 69 M6
PUT/ROE SW15 28 D4
Frensham Heights Rd
RFNM GU10 155 K7
Frensham La BOR GU35 180 B11
RFNM GU10 180 F7
Frensham Rd FNM GU9 5 K9
PUR/KEN CR8 87 L4
RFNM GU10 156 A2
Frensham V RFNM GU10 155 M5
Frensham Wy EW KT17 84 F6
Freshborough Ct GU GU1 7 L5
Freshfield Bank FROW RH18 195 M11
Freshfield Cl CRAWE RH10 165 J5
Freshfields CROY/NA CR0 51 J7
Freshford St TOOT SW17 29 M4
Freshmount Gdns
HOR/WEW KT19 83 L1
Freshwater Cl TOOT SW17 30 D7
Freshwater Pde HORS RH12 * 166 E7
Freshwater Rd TOOT SW17 30 D7
Freshwood Cl BECK BR3 51 L1
Freshwoods HORS RH12 203 J1
Freshwood Wy WLGTN SM6 66 F7
Frewin Rd WAND/EARL SW18 30 A2
Friar Ms WNWD SE27 31 L4
Friars Av PUT/ROE SW15 28 C4
Friars Cft RGUE GU4 117 M5
Friars Fld FNM GU9 5 G2
Friar's Ga GUW GU2 6 A8
Friars Keep BRAK RG12 34 E4
Friars La RCH/KEW TW9 18 A7
Friars Orch LHD/OX KT22 102 A3
Friars Ri WOKS/MYFD GU22 11 H8
Friars Rd VW GU25 39 G4
Friars Rookery CRAWE RH10 165 G4
Friars Stile Rd
RCHPK/HAM TW10 18 B8
Friars Wy CHERT KT16 40 D6
Friars Wd CROY/NA CR0 * 69 H7
Friarswood CROY/NA CR0 69 H7
Friary Br GU GU1 6 F7
Friary Ct WOKN/KNAP GU21 76 C8
Friary Pas GU GU1 6 F7
Friary Rd ASC SL5 36 E6
Friary St GU GU1 6 F7
The Friary GU GU1 * 6 F6
Friary Wy CRAWE RH10 164 F5
Friday Rd MTCM CR4 30 C8
Friday St HORS RH12 166 B2
HORS RH12 189 M8
RDKG RH5 188 E1
Friday Street Rd RDKG RH5 171 R1
Friend Av ASHV GU12 113 G8
Friends Cl CRAWW RH11 164 F1
Friendship Wy BRAK RG12 34 E3
Friends' Rd CROY/NA CR0 2 E7
PUR/KEN CR8 87 L2
Frimley Av WLGTN SM6 67 H4
Frimley Cl CROY/NA CR0 69 M6
WIM/MER SW19 29 H3
Frimley Crs CROY/NA CR0 69 M6
Frimley Gdns MTCM CR4 48 B3
Frimley Green Rd FRIM GU16 93 H2
Frimley Grove Gdns FRIM GU16 73 G8
Frimley Hall Dr CBLY GU15 73 J3
Frimley High St FRIM GU16 92 F1
Frimley Rd ASHV GU12 93 K8
CBLY GU15 72 E5
CHSGTN KT9 63 G4
Frinton Rd TOOT SW17 30 D7
Friston Wk CRAWW RH11 164 C3
Fritham Cl NWMAL KT3 46 B6
Frith End Rd BOR GU35 180 A5
Frith Hill Rd FRIM GU16 73 K8
GODL GU7 168 A3
Frith Knowle WOT/HER KT12 60 E4
Frith Pk EGRIN RH19 162 F2
Frith Rd CROY/NA CR0 2 C6
Friths Dr REIG RH2 125 L5
Frithwald Rd CHERT KT16 40 C7
Frobisher BRAK RG12 34 F7
Frobisher Cl PUR/KEN CR8 87 M7
Frobisher Crs
STWL/WRAY TW19 23 H1
Frobisher Gdns GU GU1 117 K7
Frodsham Wy SHST GU47 52 B7
Froggetts La RDKG RH5 187 P4
Frog Grove La RGUW GU3 115 J5
Frog La BRAK RG12 34 D3
RGUE GU4 97 H7
Frogmore Cl CHEAM SM3 65 G2
Frogmore Gdns CHEAM SM3 65 H3
Frogmore Park Dr BLKW GU17 72 A5
Frome Cl FARN GU14 92 A3
Fromondes Rd CHEAM SM3 65 H4
Fromow Gdns BFOR GU20 55 G5
Froxfield Down BRAK RG12 35 J5
Fruen Rd EBED/NFELT TW14 24 C1
Fry Cl CRAWW RH11 191 L12
Fryday Grove Ms BAL SW12 30 F1
Fryern Wd CTHM CR3 107 M6
Fryston Av COUL/CHIP CR5 86 E4
CROY/NA CR0 3 M6
Fuchsia Wy CHOB/PIR GU24 75 H3
Fulbourne Cl REDH RH1 126 B6
Fulbrook La MFD/CHID GU8 158 A3
Fulford Rd CTHM CR3 108 A3
HOR/WEW KT19 64 A6
Fulfords Hl SWTR RH13 204 B10
Fulham Cl CRAWW RH11 164 D8
Fullbrook Av ADL/WDHM KT15 78 D1
Fullbrooks Av WPK KT4 46 C8
Fullers Av SURB KT6 63 J1
Fullers Farm Rd EHSLY KT24 119 L7
Fullers Rd RFNM GU10 155 G5
Fullers V BOR GU35 180 E12
Fullers Wy North SURB KT6 63 J2
Fullers Wy South CHSGTN KT9 63 H5
Fuller's Wd CROY/NA CR0 69 K4
Fullers Wood La REDH RH1 126 F8
Fullerton Cl BF/WBF KT14 79 J4
Fullerton Dr BF/WBF KT14 79 H4
Fullerton Rd BF/WBF KT14 79 H4
CAR SM5 66 B7
CROY/NA CR0 3 J2
Fullerton Wy BF/WBF KT14 79 H4
Fullmer Wy ADL/WDHM KT15 58 C8
Fulmar Cl CRAWW RH11 * 190 G8
Fulmar Ct BRYLDS KT5 45 J6
Fulmar Dr EGRIN RH19 163 H2
Fulmer Cl HPTN TW12 25 H6
Fulstone Cl HSLWW TW4 16 C6
Fulvens SHGR GU5 171 K1
Fulwell Park Av WHTN TW2 25 M3
Fulwell Rd TEDD TW11 26 A5
Fulwood Gdns TWK TW1 17 J8
Fulwood Wk WIM/MER SW19 29 H2
Furlong Cl WLGTN SM6 48 E8
Furlong Rd DORK RH4 143 M3
Furlong Wy HORL RH6 160 C6
The Furlough
WOKS/MYFD GU22 11 H4
Furmage St WAND/EARL SW18 29 L1
Furnace Dr CRAWE RH10 165 H6
Furnace Farm Rd
CRAWE RH10 * 165 J6
EGRIN RH19 193 P2
Furnace Pde CRAWE RH10 165 J6
Furnace Pl CRAWE RH10 165 J6
Furneaux Av WNWD SE27 31 L6
Furness Rd MRDN SM4 47 L6
Furnival Cl VW GU25 39 G6
Furrows Pl CTHM CR3 108 C5
The Furrows WOT/HER KT12 60 F1
Furse Cl CBLY GU15 73 L5
Furtherfield Cl CROY/NA CR0 49 K6
Furzebank ASC SL5 37 G4
Furze Cl ASHV GU12 113 K2
REDH RH1 126 C7
Furzedown Cl EGH TW20 21 H7
Furzedown Dr TOOT SW17 30 E6
Furzedown Rd BELMT SM2 85 M1
TOOT SW17 30 E6
Furzefield CRAWW RH11 164 D3
Furze Fld LHD/OX KT22 82 A3
Furzefield Cha EGRIN RH19 178 F11
Furzefield Crs REIG RH2 147 M2
Furzefield Rd EGRIN RH19 162 E1
HORS RH12 167 L4
REIG RH2 147 M2
Furze Gv KWD/TDW/WH KT20 105 J3
Furze Hl KWD/TDW/WH KT20 105 J3
PUR/KEN CR8 87 H1
Furzehill REDH RH1 126 B7
Furze Hill Rd BOR GU35 196 H1
Furze La EGRIN RH19 162 C2
GODL GU7 168 C1
PUR/KEN CR8 87 H1
Furzemoors BRAK RG12 34 E5
Furzen La HORS RH12 187 M10
Furze Pl REDH RH1 * 126 C7
Furze Rd ADL/WDHM KT15 58 C5
HORS RH12 203 J1
THHTH CR7 49 M3
Furze Vale Rd BOR GU35 196 G1
Furze Vw SWTR RH13 203 N11
Furzewood SUN TW16 42 D1
Fyfield Cl BLKW GU17 72 A4

G

Gable Ct SYD SE26 32 E5
Gable End FARN GU14 * 92 E5
Gable Ms HAYES BR2 71 H1
Gables Av ASHF TW15 23 J6
Gables Cl ASHV GU12 113 K4
FARN GU14 92 D5
WOKS/MYFD GU22 97 J2
The Gables BNSTD SM7 85 J7
HORS RH12 167 G5
LHD/OX KT22 81 M2
NRWD SE19 * 50 B1
WEY KT13 59 M4
WOKS/MYFD GU22 * 10 B9
Gables Wy BNSTD SM7 85 J6
Gabriel Cl FELT TW13 25 H5
Gabriel Dr CBLY GU15 73 L5
Gabriel Rd CRAWE RH10 165 L8
Gabriel St FSTH SE23 33 G1
Gadbridge La CRAN GU6 187 K1
Gadbrook Rd
BRKHM/BTCW RH3 145 M6
Gadesden Rd HOR/WEW KT19 63 M5
Gaffney Cl ALDT GU11 113 G2
Gage Cl CRAWE RH10 193 P4
Gage Rdg FROW RH18 195 M12
Gaggle Wd SWTR RH13 205 R11
Gainsborough BRAK RG12 34 F6
Gainsborough Cl BECK BR3 33 K8
CBLY GU15 73 J2
ESH/CLAY KT10 * 44 A8
FARN GU14 93 G7
Gainsborough Ct
WOT/HER KT12 60 D3
Gainsborough Dr ASC SL5 36 A3
SAND/SEL CR2 88 D3
Gainsborough Gdns HSLW TW3 17 G7
Gainsborough Ms DUL SE21 31 M2
SYD SE26 * 32 E4
Gainsborough Rd
CRAWE RH10 165 H8
HOR/WEW KT19 63 M8
NWMAL KT3 46 A6
RCH/KEW TW9 18 C4
Gainsborough Ter BELMT SM2 * 65 J6
Gaist Av CTHM CR3 108 E4
Galahad Rd CRAWW RH11 164 A4
Galata Rd BARN SW13 19 K2
Gale Barracks ALDT GU11 * 112 E5
Gale Cl HPTN TW12 25 H7
MTCM CR4 48 A3
Gale Crs BNSTD SM7 85 K7
Gale Dr LTWR GU18 54 D8
Galen Cl HOR/WEW KT19 83 K1
Gales Cl RGUE GU4 * 118 A5
Gales Dr CRAWE RH10 165 H4
Gales Pl CRAWE RH10 165 H4
Galgate Cl WIM/MER SW19 29 H2
The Galleries ALDT GU11 * 112 D7
Gallery Rd DUL SE21 32 A2
Galleymead Rd DTCH/LGLY SL3 13 J3
The Gallop BELMT SM2 66 A7
SAND/SEL CR2 68 E6
Galloway Pth CROY/NA CR0 68 A3
Gallwey Rd ALDT GU11 112 F6
Galpin's Rd THHTH CR7 49 H4

Galsworthy Rd CHERT KT16 * 40 D7
KUTN/CMB KT2 9 L4
Galton Rd ASC SL5 37 J6
Galvins Cl GUW GU2 116 D5
Gambles La RPLY/SEND GU23 98 F7
Gambole Rd TOOT SW17 30 B5
Gander Green Crs HPTN TW12 43 K1
Gander Green La CHEAM SM3 65 H1
Gangers Hl GDST RH9 129 J1
Ganghill GU GU1 117 K6
Gapemouth Rd CHOB/PIR GU24 94 B4
Gap Rd WIM/MER SW19 29 K6
Garbetts Wy RFNM GU10 135 H3
Garbrand Wk EW KT17 64 C7
Garden Av MTCM CR4 30 E8
Garden Cl ADL/WDHM KT15 59 G3
ASHF TW15 23 M7
BNSTD SM7 85 K5
FARN GU14 92 B7
HPTN TW12 25 J6
LHD/OX KT22 102 F6
PUT/ROE SW15 28 E1
SHGR GU5 169 N5
WLGTN SM6 67 H4
Gardeners Cl HORS RH12 166 B1
Gardeners Gn HORS RH12 189 R7
Gardener's Hill Rd RFNM GU10 155 L5
Gardeners Rd CROY/NA CR0 2 B4
Gardener's Wk GT/LBKH KT23 101 L8
Gardenia Ct CHOB/PIR GU24 75 J2
Garden La BRXS/STRHM SW2 31 J2
Garden Pl HORS RH12 * 166 F5
Garden Rd PGE/AN SE20 50 F1
RCH/KEW TW9 18 D5
WOT/HER KT12 42 E6
The Gardens BECK BR3 51 M2
CHOB/PIR GU24 95 J4
COB KT11 * 99 M1
EBED/NFELT TW14 15 G8
ESH/CLAY KT10 61 K3
RFNM GU10 135 J2
Garden Wk BECK BR3 51 J1
COUL/CHIP CR5 106 E5
CRAWW RH11 164 E4
HORS RH12 166 F5
Garden Wood Rd EGRIN RH19 162 D4
Gardner La CRAWE RH10 193 M5
Gardner Pl EBED/NFELT TW14 15 L8
Gardner Rd GU GU1 7 G3
Garendon Gdns MRDN SM4 47 L7
Garendon Rd MRDN SM4 47 L7
Gareth Cl WPK KT4 65 G1
Garfield Rd ADL/WDHM KT15 58 F4
CBLY GU15 72 F4
TWK TW1 26 D2
WIM/MER SW19 29 M7
Garibaldi Rd REDH RH1 148 C1
Garland Ct EGRIN RH19 * 162 E4
Garland Rd EGRIN RH19 162 E4
Garlands Rd LHD/OX KT22 102 E3
REDH RH1 126 C8
Garland Wy CTHM CR3 108 A4
Garlichill Rd EPSOM KT18 84 E7
Garlies Rd FSTH SE23 33 H4
Garnet Rd THTH CR7 49 M4
Garrad's Rd STRHM/NOR SW16 31 G4
Garrard Rd BNSTD SM7 85 K6
Garratt Cl CROY/NA CR0 67 H3
Garratt La WAND/EARL SW18 29 L1
Garratts La BNSTD SM7 85 J6
Garratt Ter TOOT SW17 30 B5
Garrett Cl CRAWE RH10 165 L6
Garrick Cl RCH/KEW TW9 17 M7
STA TW18 22 D8
WOT/HER KT12 60 E3
Garrick Crs CROY/NA CR0 3 G6
Garrick Gdns E/WMO/HCT KT8 43 K3
Garrick Rd RCH/KEW TW9 18 D2
Garrick Wk CRAWE RH10 165 G7
Garrick Wy FRIM GU16 93 H3
Garrison Cl HSLWW TW4 16 C7
Garrison La CHSGTN KT9 63 H6
The Garrones CRAWE RH10 * 192 D6
Garside Cl HPTN TW12 25 L8
Garson La STWL/WRAY TW19 21 G1
Garson Rd ESH/CLAY KT10 61 J4
Garston La PUR/KEN CR8 88 A5
The Garstons GT/LBKH KT23 101 J7
Garswood BRAK RG12 35 G6
Garth Cl FNM GU9 4 F9
KUTN/CMB KT2 27 J6
MRDN SM4 47 G7
Garthorne Rd FSTH SE23 33 G1
Garth Rd KUTN/CMB KT2 27 J6
MRDN SM4 47 G8
Garthside KUTN/CMB KT2 27 H6
The Garth ASHV GU12 113 J8
COB KT11 81 H3
FARN GU14 93 G5
HPTN TW12 25 L7
Gartmoor Gdns
WIM/MER SW19 29 J2
Garton Cl CRAWW RH11 164 A5
Gascoigne Rd CROY/NA CR0 69 M8
WEY KT13 59 L2
Gasden Copse MFD/CHID GU8 183 L4
Gasden Dr MFD/CHID GU8 183 L3
Gasden La MFD/CHID GU8 183 L3
Gaskyns Cl HORS RH12 203 J2
Gassiot Rd TOOT SW17 30 C5
Gassiot Wy SUT SM1 66 A2
Gasson Wood Rd
CRAWW RH11 164 A6
Gaston Bell Cl RCH/KEW TW9 18 C5
Gaston Bridge Rd SHPTN TW17 42 B5
Gaston Rd MTCM CR4 48 D3
Gaston Wy SHPTN TW17 42 A5
Gatcombe Crs ASC SL5 36 C1
Gateford Dr HORS RH12 167 J3
Gatehouse Cl KUTN/CMB KT2 27 M8
Gates Cl CRAWE RH10 165 L8
Gatesden Cl LHD/OX KT22 101 M5
Gatesden Rd LHD/OX KT22 101 M5
Gates Green Rd WWKM BR4 70 D3
Gateside Rd TOOT SW17 30 C4
Gatestone Rd NRWD SE19 32 B7
Gateways GU GU1 139 L1
The Gateways RCH/KEW TW9 * 18 A6
The Gateway
WOKN/KNAP GU21 77 L4
Gatfield Gv FELT TW13 25 K3
Gatley Av HOR/WEW KT19 63 L4
Gatley Dr RGUE GU4 117 J5
Gatton Bottom REIG RH2 126 C2
Gatton Cl BELMT SM2 * 65 L7
REIG RH2 125 M5
Gatton Park Rd REIG RH2 126 A5
Gatton Rd REIG RH2 125 M5
TOOT SW17 30 B5
Gatwick Rd HORL RH6 191 R1
WAND/EARL SW18 29 J1
Gatwick Wy HORL RH6 160 C6
Gauntlet Crs PUR/KEN CR8 108 A1
Gauntlett Rd SUT SM1 66 A4
Gavell Rd COB KT11 80 D3
Gaveston Cl BF/WBF KT14 79 J3
Gaveston Rd LHD/OX KT22 102 D2
Gavina Cl MRDN SM4 48 B5
Gawton Crs COUL/CHIP CR5 106 F3
Gayfere Rd EW KT17 64 D4
Gayhouse La REDH RH1 177 K2
Gayler Cl REDH RH1 128 C8
Gaynesford Rd CAR SM5 66 C6
FSTH SE23 33 G3
Gayton Cl ASHTD KT21 83 H8
Gaywood Cl BRXS/STRHM SW2 31 J2
Gaywood Rd ASHTD KT21 83 J8
Gearing Cl TOOT SW17 30 E5
Geary Cl HORL RH6 161 L5
Geffers Ride ASC SL5 36 B3
Gemini Cl CRAWW RH11 190 G9
Gemmell Cl PUR/KEN CR8 87 J4
Genesis Cl STWL/WRAY TW19 23 J2
Geneva Cl SHPTN TW17 42 B2
Geneva Rd KUT/HW KT1 45 H4
THTH CR7 49 M5
Genoa Av PUT/ROE SW15 19 M7
Genoa Rd PGE/AN SE20 50 F1
Gentles La LIPH GU30 196 F4
Genyn Rd GUW GU2 6 D7
George Denyer Cl HASM GU27 198 D6
George Eliot Cl MFD/CHID GU8 183 N5
George Gdns ALDT GU11 134 F2
George Groves Rd
PGE/AN SE20 50 D1
Georgeham Rd SHST GU47 52 A7
George Horley Pl RDKG RH5 * 173 Q8
Georgelands RPLY/SEND GU23 98 E3
George Rd GODL GU7 168 B2
GU GU1 7 G4
KUTN/CMB KT2 9 M2
MFD/CHID GU8 159 J7
NWMAL KT3 46 C4
George's Rd BH/WHM TN16 111 G2
Georges Ter CTHM CR3 108 A4
George St CHOB/PIR GU24 94 D3
CROY/NA CR0 2 E6
HSLW TW3 16 C4
RCH/KEW TW9 18 A7
STA TW18 22 C5
Georgetown Cl NRWD SE19 32 A6
George Wyver Cl
WIM/MER SW19 29 H1
Georgian Cl CBLY GU15 73 H2
CRAWE RH10 165 M5
STA TW18 22 E5
Georgia Rd NWMAL KT3 45 M4
THTH CR7 49 L1
Geraldine Rd CHSWK W4 18 D1
Gerald's Gv BNSTD SM7 85 G4
Gerard Av HSLWW TW4 25 K1
Gerard Rd BARN SW13 19 J3
Germander Dr CHOB/PIR GU24 75 K6
Gerrards Md BNSTD SM7 85 J6
Ghent St CAT SE6 33 K3
Ghyll Crs SWTR RH13 205 N9
Giant Arches Rd HNHL SE24 31 M1
Gibbet La CBLY GU15 73 K2
Gibbon Rd KUTN/CMB KT2 8 F4
Gibbons Cl CRAWE RH10 * 165 L7
Gibbon Wk PUT/ROE SW15 * 19 K6
Gibb's Acre CHOB/PIR GU24 95 J5
Gibbs Av NRWD SE19 32 A7
Gibbs Brook La OXTED RH8 130 A8
Gibbs Cl NRWD SE19 * 32 A6
Gibbs Sq NRWD SE19 * 32 A6
Giblets La HORS RH12 167 J2
Giblets Wy HORS RH12 167 H2
Gibraltar Crs HOR/WEW KT19 64 B8
Gibson Cl CHSGTN KT9 * 62 F4
ISLW TW7 17 G5
Gibson Pl STWL/WRAY TW19 13 M8
Gibson Rd SUT SM1 65 L4
Gibson's Hl STRHM/NOR SW16 31 K8
Gidd Hl COUL/CHIP CR5 86 D6
Giffard Dr FARN GU14 92 C3
Giffards Cl EGRIN RH19 163 G4
Giffards Meadow FNM GU9 134 B8
Giffard Wy GUW GU2 116 D5
Giggs Hill Gdns THDIT KT7 44 D8
Giggs Hill Rd THDIT KT7 44 D7
Gilbert Cl WIM/MER SW19 * 47 L1
Gilbert Rd FRIM GU16 72 F8
WIM/MER SW19 29 M8
Gilbert St HSLW TW3 16 F5
Gilbey Rd TOOT SW17 30 B5
Gilders Rd CHSGTN KT9 63 J6
Giles Coppice NRWD SE19 32 C5
Giles Md EPSOM KT18 * 84 B4
Giles Travers Cl EGH TW20 39 M3
Gilham La FROW RH18 195 M11
Gilham's Av BNSTD SM7 85 G2
Gill Av GUW GU2 138 B1
Gillet Ct SWTR RH13 * 167 L5
Gillett Ct SWTR RH13 167 L5
Gillett Rd THTH CR7 50 A4
Gillham's La HASM GU27 197 M9
Gilliam Gv PUR/KEN CR8 67 K8
Gillian Av ASHV GU12 134 F1
Gillian Cl ASHV GU12 135 G1
Gillian Park Rd CHEAM SM3 47 J8
Gillian Ter BRYLDS KT5 * 45 J6
Gilliat Dr RGUE GU4 118 A6
Gilligan Cl HORS RH12 166 E7
Gilmais GT/LBKH KT23 101 M7
Gilmore Crs ASHF TW15 23 K6
Gilpin Av MORT/ESHN SW14 19 G6
Gilpin Cl MTCM CR4 48 B2
Gilpin Crs WHTN TW2 25 L1
Gilpin Wy HYS/HAR UB3 15 G2
Gilsland Rd THTH CR7 50 A4
Gilson Ct WDSR SL4 20 F1
Gimcrack Hl LHD/OX KT22 102 E4
Ginhams Rd CRAWW RH11 164 D4
Gipsy Hl NRWD SE19 32 B6
Gipsy La BRAK RG12 35 G3
PUT/ROE SW15 19 K5
Gipsy Rd WNWD SE27 32 A5
Gipsy Road Gdns WNWD SE27 31 M5
Girdwood Rd
WAND/EARL SW18 29 H1
Girling Wy EBED/NFELT TW14 15 K5
Girton Cl SHST GU47 52 B8
Girton Gdns CROY/NA CR0 69 K2
Girton Rd SYD SE26 33 G6
Gisbourne Cl WLGTN SM6 67 G2
Glade Cl SURB KT6 * 63 G1
Glade Gdns CROY/NA CR0 51 H7
Gladeside CROY/NA CR0 51 G7
Glade Sp KWD/TDW/WH KT20 105 L3
The Glades EGRIN RH19 163 J4
The Glade ASC SL5 36 F5
BELMT SM2 65 H7
BF/WBF KT14 78 B3
COUL/CHIP CR5 107 K1
CRAWE RH10 165 J6
CROY/NA CR0 51 G5
EW KT17 64 D5
FNM GU9 134 A2
FRIM GU16 93 J7
KWD/TDW/WH KT20 105 L3
LHD/OX KT22 101 L4
RFNM GU10 154 E8
STA TW18 22 E8
SWTR RH13 167 K6
WWKM BR4 69 L2
Gladiator Wy FARN GU14 112 D1
Gladioli Cl HPTN TW12 25 K7
Gladsmuir Cl WOT/HER KT12 60 F1
Gladstone Av
EBED/NFELT TW14 15 K8
WHTN TW2 26 A1
Gladstone Gdns HSLW TW3 16 F3
Gladstone Ms PGE/AN SE20 33 G8
Gladstone Pl E/WMO/HCT KT8 * 44 B5
Gladstone Rd ASHTD KT21 83 G8
CROY/NA CR0 2 F2
HORS RH12 167 G6
KUT/HW KT1 9 K8
ORP BR6 71 M4
SURB KT6 63 G1
WIM/MER SW19 29 K8
Gladstone Ter WNWD SE27 * 31 M5
Glamis Cl FRIM GU16 93 J2
Glamorgan Cl MTCM CR4 49 H3
Glamorgan Rd KUT/HW KT1 8 B3
Glanfield Rd BECK BR3 51 J4
The Glanty EGH TW20 21 M5
Glasbrook Av WHTN TW2 25 J2
Glasford St TOOT SW17 30 C7
Glastonbury Rd MRDN SM4 47 K7
Glayshers Hl BOR GU35 180 F11
Glazebrook Cl DUL SE21 32 A3
Glazebrook Rd TEDD TW11 26 C8
Glaziers La RGUW GU3 114 F7
Gleave Cl EGRIN RH19 163 H3
Glebe Av MTCM CR4 48 B2
Glebe Cl ALDT GU11 134 D2
CRAWE RH10 164 F3
GT/LBKH KT23 101 K8
LTWR GU18 54 F8
SAND/SEL CR2 88 C2
Glebe Cottages RGUE GU4 118 E6
Glebe Gdns BF/WBF KT14 79 G4
NWMAL KT3 46 B7
Glebe Hyrst SAND/SEL CR2 88 C2
Glebeland Gdns SHPTN TW17 41 M6
Glebeland Rd CBLY GU15 72 C5
Glebelands BIL RH14 201 Q5
CRAWE RH10 193 M5
E/WMO/HCT KT8 43 L5
ESH/CLAY KT10 62 C7
Glebelands Meadow
CRAN GU6 * 185 Q12
Glebelands Rd
EBED/NFELT TW14 24 D1
Glebe La RDKG RH5 171 Q1
RFNM GU10 181 P4
Glebe Pth MTCM CR4 48 C3
Glebe Rd ASHTD KT21 83 G8
BARN SW13 19 K4
BELMT SM2 65 H7
BOR GU35 180 D12
CAR SM5 66 C5
CRAN GU6 186 D1
DORK RH4 144 C2
EGH TW20 21 M7
FARN GU14 92 C4
REDH RH1 106 D6
RFNM GU10 132 C3
STA TW18 22 E6
WARL CR6 89 G7
Glebe Side TWK TW1 17 J8
Glebe Sq MTCM CR4 * 48 C3
The Glebe BLKW GU17 72 B5
CRAN GU6 171 K11
CRAWE RH10 192 G2
EGRIN RH19 162 B1
HORL RH6 160 C3
REIG RH2 146 D7
STRHM/NOR SW16 * 31 G5
WPK KT4 46 C8
Glebe Wy FELT TW13 25 K4
SAND/SEL CR2 88 C2
WWKM BR4 69 M1
Glebewood BRAK RG12 34 F5
Gledhow Wd
KWD/TDW/WH KT20 105 L4
Glen Albyn Rd WIM/MER SW19 29 G3
Glena Mt SUT SM1 65 M3
Glen Av ASHF TW15 23 K5
Glenavon Cl ESH/CLAY KT10 62 D5
Glenbuck Rd SURB KT6 45 G6
Glenburnie Rd TOOT SW17 30 C4
Glencairn Rd STRHM/NOR SW16 31 H8
Glen Cl GSHT GU26 181 P11
KWD/TDW/WH KT20 105 H5
SHPTN TW17 41 K4
Glencoe Cl FRIM GU16 93 J1
Glencoe Rd WEY KT13 59 K2
Glen Ct ADL/WDHM KT15 * 58 C4
Glendale Cl HORS RH12 167 K3
WOKN/KNAP GU21 76 F8
Glendale Dr RGUE GU4 117 M4
WIM/MER SW19 29 J6
Glen Dale Ms BECK BR3 51 L1
Glendale Ri PUR/KEN CR8 87 L5
Glendene Av EHSLY KT24 100 B8
Glendower Gdns
MORT/ESHN SW14 19 G5
Glendower Rd
MORT/ESHN SW14 19 G5
Glendyne Cl EGRIN RH19 163 H5
Glendyne Wy EGRIN RH19 163 H5
Gleneagle Ms
STRHM/NOR SW16 31 G6
Gleneagle Rd
STRHM/NOR SW16 31 G6
Gleneagles Cl
STWL/WRAY TW19 13 M8
Gleneagles Ct CRAWE RH10 * 164 F5
Gleneldon Ms
STRHM/NOR SW16 31 H6
Gleneldon Rd
STRHM/NOR SW16 31 H5
Glenfield Cl BRKHM/BTCW RH3 145 L3
Glenfield Rd ASHF TW15 23 L7
BAL SW12 30 F2
BNSTD SM7 85 L5
BRKHM/BTCW RH3 145 L4
Glen Gdns CROY/NA CR0 67 K2
Glenheadon Cl LHD/OX KT22 103 G5
Glenheadon Ri LHD/OX KT22 103 G5
Glenhurst BFOR GU20 54 D3
Glenhurst Cl BLKW GU17 72 B5
Glenhurst Ri NRWD SE19 31 M8
Glenhurst Rd BTFD TW8 17 M1
Glen Innes SHST GU47 52 C8
Glenister Park Rd
STRHM/NOR SW16 31 G8
Glenlea GSHT GU26 197 R4
Glenlea Hollow GSHT GU26 197 R5
Glenmore Cl ADL/WDHM KT15 58 E2
Glenmount Rd FRIM GU16 93 K7
Glenn Av PUR/KEN CR8 87 L1
Glennie Rd WNWD SE27 31 K4
Glen Rd CHSGTN KT9 63 H2
GSHT GU26 197 Q2
Glen Road End WLGTN SM6 66 E7
Glenside Cl PUR/KEN CR8 88 A5
Glentanner Wy TOOT SW17 30 A4
Glentham Rd BARN SW13 19 K1
The Glen ADL/WDHM KT15 58 C4
ASC SL5 * 37 G4
BELMT SM2 * 65 M5
CROY/NA CR0 69 G2
FNM GU9 133 M3
ORP BR6 71 J2
Glenthorne Av CROY/NA CR0 50 F8
Glenthorne Cl CHEAM SM3 47 K8
Glenthorne Gdns CHEAM SM3 47 K8
Glenthorne Rd KUT/HW KT1 45 J4
Glenthorpe Rd MRDN SM4 47 G5
Glenview Cl CRAWE RH10 165 H2
Glenville Gdns GSHT GU26 198 A1
Glenville Rd KUTN/CMB KT2 9 J4
Glen Vue EGRIN RH19 162 F4
Glenwood BRAK RG12 35 G4
RDKG RH5 144 F4
Glenwood Rd CAT SE6 33 J2
EW KT17 64 D5
HSLW TW3 17 G5
Glenwood Rw NRWD SE19 * 50 C1
Glenwood Wy CROY/NA CR0 51 G6
Glorney Md FNM GU9 134 D3
Glory Md DORK RH4 144 F5
Glossop Rd SAND/SEL CR2 68 A7
Gloster Rd NWMAL KT3 46 B4
WOKS/MYFD GU22 97 K2
Gloucester Cl FRIM GU16 93 H3
THDIT KT7 * 44 D8
Gloucester Ct MTCM CR4 * 49 H5
RCH/KEW TW9 * 18 D2
Gloucester Crs STA TW18 23 G7
Gloucester Dr STA TW18 21 M4
Gloucester Gdns SUT SM1 65 L1
Gloucester Rd ALDT GU11 134 F2
BAGS GU19 54 B6
CRAWE RH10 165 G8
CROY/NA CR0 2 F3
FELT TW13 24 F2
GUW GU2 116 C6
HPTN TW12 25 L8
HSLWW TW4 16 B6
KUT/HW KT1 9 K7
RCH/KEW TW9 18 D2
REDH RH1 126 C7
TEDD TW11 26 B6
WHTN TW2 25 M2
Glovers Cl BH/WHM TN16 90 E6
Glover's Rd HORL RH6 174 G10
REIG RH2 147 L1
Glyn Cl EW KT17 64 D7
SNWD SE25 50 B2
Glyndebourne Pk ORP BR6 71 L2
Glynde Pl HORS RH12 166 F8
Glyn Rd WPK KT4 65 G1
Glynswood CBLY GU15 73 J6
RFNM GU10 155 K5
Goaters Rd ASC SL5 35 M2
Goat Rd MTCM CR4 48 D7
Goatsfield Rd BH/WHM TN16 110 F2
Goat Whf BTFD TW8 18 B1
Godalming Av WLGTN SM6 67 H4
Godalming Rd GODL GU7 168 C6
MFD/CHID GU8 184 H2
Goddard Cl CRAWE RH10 165 K7
GUW GU2 116 D4
SHPTN TW17 41 J3
Goddard Rd BECK BR3 51 G4
Goddards La CBLY GU15 72 E6
Godfrey Av WHTN TW2 26 A1
Godfrey Cl SHST GU47 72 A2
Godfrey Wy HSLWW TW4 25 H1
Godley Rd BF/WBF KT14 79 J3
WAND/EARL SW18 30 A2
Godolphin Cl BELMT SM2 85 J1
Godolphin Ct CRAWE RH10 * 164 F5
Godolphin Rd WEY KT13 60 A5
Godric Crs CROY/NA CR0 70 A8
Godson Rd CROY/NA CR0 67 K2
Godstone Green Rd GDST RH9 128 E5
Godstone Hl GDST RH9 128 E2
Godstone Mt PUR/KEN CR8 * 87 L2
Godstone Rd CTHM CR3 108 D6
LING RH7 178 D4
OXTED RH8 129 M4
PUR/KEN CR8 87 L3
REDH RH1 128 B7
SUT SM1 65 M3
TWK TW1 17 K8
Godwin Cl HOR/WEW KT19 63 M5
Godwin Wy SWTR RH13 167 J5
Goffs Cl CRAWW RH11 164 E5
Goffs La CRAWW RH11 164 D4
Goffs Park Rd CRAWW RH11 164 E5
Goffs Rd ASHF TW15 24 A7
Gogmore Farm Cl CHERT KT16 40 B7
Gogmore La CHERT KT16 40 D7
Goidel Cl WLGTN SM6 67 G3
Goldcliff Cl MRDN SM4 47 K7
Goldcrest Cl HORL RH6 160 A2
Goldcrest Wy CROY/NA CR0 70 A7
PUR/KEN CR8 67 G8
Gold Cup La ASC SL5 36 A1
Golden Ct HSLW TW3 17 G4
Goldenfield Cl LIPH GU30 197 J10
Golden Flds LIPH GU30 197 J10
Golden Orb Wd BNFD RG42 34 A1
Goldfinch Cl ALDT GU11 134 C1
CRAWW RH11 164 F2
HORS RH12 166 F2
Goldfinch Gdns RGUE GU4 118 A7
Goldfinch Rd SAND/SEL CR2 69 H8
Goldhill RFNM GU10 155 M3
Golding Cl CRAWE RH10 165 L5
The Goldings
WOKN/KNAP GU21 76 C6
Gold La ALDT GU11 113 H5
Goldney Rd CBLY GU15 73 L5
Goldrings Rd LHD/OX KT22 81 M3
Goldsmiths Cl
WOKN/KNAP GU21 76 F8
Goldstone Farm Vw
GT/LBKH KT23 * 121 K1
Goldsworth Orch
WOKN/KNAP GU21 76 D8
Goldsworth Rd
WOKN/KNAP GU21 10 A7
Goldwell Rd THTH CR7 49 J4
Gole Rd CHOB/PIR GU24 95 G3
Golf Cl THTH CR7 49 K1
WOKS/MYFD GU22 78 B4
Golf Club Dr KUTN/CMB KT2 28 A8
Golf Club Rd WEY KT13 59 L8
WOKS/MYFD GU22 96 E2
Golf Dr CBLY GU15 73 J5
Golf Links Av GSHT GU26 181 N11
Golf Rd PUR/KEN CR8 88 A8
Golf Side BELMT SM2 85 H1
WHTN TW2 26 A4
Golf Side Cl NWMAL KT3 46 B2
Gomer Gdns TEDD TW11 26 D7
Gomer Pl TEDD TW11 26 D7
Gomshall Av WLGTN SM6 67 H4
Gomshall Gdns PUR/KEN CR8 88 B5
Gomshall La SHGR GU5 141 K5
Gomshall Rd BELMT SM2 64 F8
Gong Hl RFNM GU10 156 A6
Gong Hill Dr RFNM GU10 156 A5
Gonston Cl WIM/MER SW19 29 H3
Gonville Rd THTH CR7 49 J5
Goodden Crs FARN GU14 92 C7
Goodenough Cl
COUL/CHIP CR5 107 K2
Goodenough Rd
WIM/MER SW19 29 J8
Goodenough Wy
COUL/CHIP CR5 107 J2
Goodhew Rd CROY/NA CR0 50 D6
Gooding Cl NWMAL KT3 45 M4
Goodley Stock Rd EDEN TN8 131 L3
Goodman Crs
BRXS/STRHM SW2 31 H3
Goodways Dr BRAK RG12 34 F2
Goodwin Cl CRAWW RH11 164 A7
EDEN TN8 153 L7
MTCM CR4 48 A3
Goodwin Gdns CROY/NA CR0 67 L5
Goodwin Rd CROY/NA CR0 67 L4
Goodwins Cl EGRIN RH19 162 E2
Goodwood Cl CBLY GU15 72 F1
CRAWE RH10 165 J7
MRDN SM4 47 K4
Goodwood Pde BECK BR3 * 51 H4
Goodwood Pl FARN GU14 93 H6
Goodwood Rd REDH RH1 126 C6
Goodwyns Rd DORK RH4 144 E5
Goose Gn SHGR GU5 141 M5
Goose Green Cl HORS RH12 167 G4
Goose La WOKS/MYFD GU22 96 E4
Goose Rye Rd RGUW GU3 96 A8
Goossens Cl SUT SM1 65 M4
Gordon Av CBLY GU15 72 E5
MORT/ESHN SW14 19 H6
SAND/SEL CR2 67 M8
TWK TW1 17 K7
Gordon Cl CHERT KT16 58 B2
STA TW18 22 E7
Gordon Ct REDH RH1 * 148 C2
Gordon Crs CBLY GU15 72 F5
CROY/NA CR0 3 H3
Gordondale Rd WIM/MER SW19 29 K3
Gordon Dr CHERT KT16 58 B2
SHPTN TW17 42 A6
Gordon Rd ALDT GU11 112 D8
ASHF TW15 23 H4
BECK BR3 51 J3
BRYLDS KT5 45 J7
CAR SM5 66 C5
CBLY GU15 72 F5
CTHM CR3 108 A3
CWTH RG45 52 A6
ESH/CLAY KT10 62 B6
FARN GU14 113 G1
HORS RH12 167 G5
HSLW TW3 16 F6
KUTN/CMB KT2 9 G5
RCH/KEW TW9 18 C4
REDH RH1 126 D5
SHPTN TW17 42 A6
Gordons Wy OXTED RH8 130 A2
Gore Rd RYNPK SW20 46 F2
Goring Rd STA TW18 22 A6
Goring's Md SWTR RH13 167 G8

Gorling Cl CRAWW RH11 164 A5
Gorringe Park Av MTCM CR4 30 C8
Gorringes Brook HORS RH12 167 G3
Gorse Bank LTWR GU18 * 74 D1
Gorse Cl CRAWE RH10 192 G3
KWD/TDW/WH KT20 104 E2
RFNM GU10 155 K3
Gorse Ct RGUE GU4 117 M6
Gorse Dr HORL RH6 161 L2
Gorse End HORS RH12 167 G4
Gorse Hill La VW GU25 39 G4
Gorse Hill Rd VW GU25 39 G4
Gorselands Cl ASHV GU12 113 K4
BF/WBF KT14 78 F1
BOR GU35 196 H1
Gorse La CHOB/PIR GU24 56 B6
RFNM GU10 155 K3
Gorse Ri TOOT SW17 30 D6
Gorse Rd CROY/NA CR0 69 K2
FRIM GU16 73 H7
Gorsewood Rd
WOKN/KNAP GU21 96 A1
Gort Cl ALDT GU11 113 H2
Gosberton Rd BAL SW12 30 C2
Gosbury Hl CHSGTN KT9 63 H3
Gosden Cl CRAWE RH10 165 J5
SHGR GU5 169 J1
Gosden Hill Rd RGUE GU4 117 M4
Gosden Rd CHOB/PIR GU24 75 J3
Gosfield Rd HOR/WEW KT19 84 A2
Gosnell Cl FRIM GU16 74 A6
Gossops Dr CRAWW RH11 164 C5
Gossops Green La
CRAWW RH11 164 C5
Gostling Rd WHTN TW2 25 K2
Goston Gdns THHTH CR7 49 K3
Gostrode La MFD/CHID GU8 199 P7
Gothic Ct HYS/HAR UB3 15 G1
Gothic Rd WHTN TW2 26 A3
Goudhurst Cl CRAWE RH10 192 D7
Gough's La BRAK RG12 34 F1
Gould Ct RGUE GU4 118 A6
Goulding Gdns THHTH CR7 49 M2
Gould Rd EBED/NFELT TW14 24 B1
WHTN TW2 26 B2
Government House Rd
FARN GU14 112 D2
Government Rd ALDT GU11 113 H5
Governor's Rd CBLY GU15 72 C3
Govett Av SHPTN TW17 * 41 M5
Govett Gv BFOR GU20 55 G4
Gower Pk SHST GU47 72 A2
Gower Rd HORL RH6 160 B3
ISLW TW7 17 J1
WEY KT13 60 A5
The Gower EGH TW20 39 L3
Gowland Pl BECK BR3 51 J2
Gowlland Cl CROY/NA CR0 3 L1
Gowrie Pl CTHM CR3 107 M4
Graburn Wy E/WMO/HCT KT8 44 A3
Grace Bennett Cl FARN GU14 * 92 D2
Gracedale Rd
STRHM/NOR SW16 30 E6
Gracefield Gdns
STRHM/NOR SW16 31 H4
Grace Rd CRAWW RH11 191 K12
CROY/NA CR0 49 M6
Gracious Pond Rd
CHOB/PIR GU24 56 C6
The Gradient SYD SE26 32 D5
Graemesdyke Av
MORT/ESHN SW14 18 E5
Graffham Cl CRAWW RH11 164 D2
Grafton Cl BF/WBF KT14 78 C3
HSLWW TW4 25 H2
WPK KT4 64 B2
Grafton Park Rd WPK KT4 64 B1
Grafton Rd CROY/NA CR0 49 K8
NWMAL KT3 46 B4
WPK KT4 64 A2
Grafton Wy E/WMO/HCT KT8 43 J4
Graham Av MTCM CR4 48 D1
Graham Cl CROY/NA CR0 69 K1
Graham Gdns SURB KT6 45 H8
Graham Rd BFOR GU20 54 F5
HPTN TW12 25 K5
MTCM CR4 48 D1
PUR/KEN CR8 87 K3
WIM/MER SW19 29 J8
Grainger Rd ISLW TW7 17 J4
Grampian Cl BELMT SM2 65 M6
HYS/HAR UB3 15 G2
Gramsci Wy CAT SE6 33 L4
Granada St TOOT SW17 30 C6
Granard Av PUT/ROE SW15 19 L7
Granard Rd BTSEA SW11 30 C1
Granary Cl HORL RH6 160 D1
Granary Wy HORS RH12 166 C8
Grand Av BRYLDS KT5 45 L6
CBLY GU15 72 F3
Grand Dr RYNPK SW20 46 F4
Granden Rd
STRHM/NOR SW16 * 49 H2
Grandison Rd WPK KT4 64 F1
Grand Pde CRAWE RH10 * 164 F4
MORT/ESHN SW14 * 18 F6
SURB KT6 * 45 K8
Grand Stand Rd EPSOM KT18 84 C7
Grand View Av BH/WHM TN16 90 F7
Grange Av SNWD SE25 50 B2
WHTN TW2 26 B3
Grangecliffe Gdns SNWD SE25 50 B2
Grange Cl BH/WHM TN16 * 111 M8
CRAWE RH10 165 J2
E/WMO/HCT KT8 43 L4
EDEN TN8 153 M8
GODL GU7 168 D4
GUW GU2 116 E4
LHD/OX KT22 103 G2
REDH RH1 126 E2
REDH RH1 128 A7
STWL/WRAY TW19 12 B8
Grange Ct BELMT SM2 * 65 L6
EGH TW20 * 21 J6
GDST RH9 151 H4
GUW GU2 * 116 E4
RFNM GU10 * 135 H3
WLGTN SM6 * 66 E2
WOT/HER KT12 60 D1
Grange Crs CRAWE RH10 193 N6
Grange Dr REDH RH1 126 E2
WOKN/KNAP GU21 10 D1
Grange End HORL RH6 161 K3
Grange Farm Rd ASHV GU12 113 K6
Grangefields Rd RGUE GU4 117 G2
Grange Gdns BNSTD SM7 85 L3
SNWD SE25 50 B2
Grange Hl SNWD SE25 50 B2
Grange La DUL SE21 32 C3
Grange Meadow BNSTD SM7 85 L3
Grange Ms FELT TW13 * 24 A4
Grangemill Rd CAT SE6 33 K4
Grangemill Wy CAT SE6 33 K3
Grangemount LHD/OX KT22 103 G2
Grange Pk CRAN GU6 186 E2
WOKN/KNAP GU21 10 D1
Grange Park Pl RYNPK SW20 28 E8
Grange Park Rd THHTH CR7 50 A3
Grange Pl STA TW18 40 F2
WOT/HER KT12 60 D1
Grange Rd ADL/WDHM KT15 58 D8
ASHV GU12 113 L8
BARN SW13 19 K3
BELMT SM2 65 K6
BRAK RG12 34 F1
CBLY GU15 73 H4
CHOB/PIR GU24 95 G4
CHSGTN KT9 63 H3
CRAWE RH10 193 M6
CTHM CR3 108 D7
E/WMO/HCT KT8 43 L4
EGH TW20 21 J6
FARN GU14 92 E2
GUW GU2 116 E3
KUT/HW KT1 8 E8
LHD/OX KT22 103 G2
ORP BR6 71 M1
RFNM GU10 135 H3
RFNM GU10 181 N1
SAND/SEL CR2 67 M8
SNWD SE25 50 A3
WOT/HER KT12 61 H3
The Grange CHOB/PIR GU24 56 B8
CROY/NA CR0 69 J1
NWMAL KT3 * 46 D5
WIM/MER SW19 29 G7
WOT/HER KT12 60 E1
WPK KT4 64 A3
Grange V BELMT SM2 65 L6
Grangeway HORL RH6 161 K3
Grangewood La BECK BR3 33 J7
Granston Wy CRAWE RH10 193 P5
Grantchester KUT/HW KT1 * 9 J7
Grant Cl SHPTN TW17 41 L6
Grantham Cl SHST GU47 52 B8
Grantham Rd CHSWK W4 19 H2
Grantley Av SHGR GU5 169 L3
Grantley Cl RGUE GU4 139 H7
Grantley Ct FNM GU9 155 J3
Grantley Gdns GUW GU2 6 B1
Grantley Pl ESH/CLAY KT10 61 L4
Grantley Rd GUW GU2 6 A1
HSLWW TW4 15 M4
Granton Rd STRHM/NOR SW16 48 F1
Grant Rd CROY/NA CR0 3 J3
Grants La EDEN TN8 153 G3
OXTED RH8 130 F7
Grant Wk ASC SL5 37 H8
Grant Wy ISLW TW7 17 K1
Grantwood Cl REDH RH1 148 D5
Granville Av FELT TW13 24 D3
HSLW TW3 16 D7
Granville Cl BF/WBF KT14 79 J3
CROY/NA CR0 3 G7
WEY KT13 59 M5
Granville Gdns
STRHM/NOR SW16 49 J1
Granville Rd BH/WHM TN16 111 M8
OXTED RH8 130 C3
WAND/EARL SW18 29 K1
WEY KT13 59 M6
WIM/MER SW19 29 K8
WOKS/MYFD GU22 97 J2
Grapsome Cl CHSGTN KT9 62 F6
Grasmere Av HSLW TW3 16 E8
ORP BR6 71 L2
PUT/ROE SW15 28 A5
WIM/MER SW19 47 K3
Grasmere Cl EBED/NFELT TW14 24 C2
EGH TW20 21 L8
GU GU1 117 L7
Grasmere Gdns HORS RH12 167 L3
ORP BR6 71 L2
Grasmere Rd FARN GU14 92 B6
FNM GU9 133 K3
LTWR GU18 54 E8
ORP BR6 71 L2
PUR/KEN CR8 87 L1
SNWD SE25 50 E6
STRHM/NOR SW16 31 J6
Grasmere Wy BF/WBF KT14 79 J2
Grasslands HORL RH6 161 K3
Grassmere HORL RH6 160 E2
Grassmount FSTH SE23 32 E3
WLGTN SM6 66 F8
Grassway WLGTN SM6 66 F3
Grattons Dr CRAWE RH10 165 L1
The Grattons SWTR RH13 203 R6
Gravel Hl CROY/NA CR0 69 H5
LHD/OX KT22 102 D3
Gravel Hill Rd RFNM GU10 154 D4
Gravelly Hl CTHM CR3 128 C2
Gravel Pits La SHGR GU5 141 M5
Gravel Rd FARN GU14 113 G1
FNM GU9 133 L2
HAYES BR2 71 H1
WHTN TW2 26 B2
Gravenel Gdns TOOT SW17 * 30 B6
Graveney Gv PGE/AN SE20 32 F8
Graveney Rd CRAWE RH10 165 L5
TOOT SW17 30 B5
Gravetts La RGUW GU3 116 B5
Gravetye Cl CRAWE RH10 165 J6
Grayham Crs NWMAL KT3 46 A4
Grayham Rd NWMAL KT3 46 A4
Graylands WOKN/KNAP GU21 10 C3
Graylands Cl WOKN/KNAP GU21 10 C4
Gray Pl CHERT KT16 58 A5
Grays Cl HASM GU27 198 F5
Grayscroft Rd
STRHM/NOR SW16 31 G8
Grayshott Laurels BOR GU35 180 B11
Grayshott Rd BOR GU35 180 H12
Grays La ASHF TW15 23 L5
ASHTD KT21 103 J1
Grays Rd BH/WHM TN16 111 L3
GODL GU7 168 C2
Grays Wd HORL RH6 160 F3
Grayswood Dr FRIM GU16 93 K8
Grayswood Gdns RYNPK SW20 46 E2
Grayswood Ms HASM GU27 * 198 G3
Grayswood Rd HASM GU27 198 E5
Great Austins FNM GU9 5 L8
Great Brownings DUL SE21 32 C5
Great Chertsey Rd CHSWK W4 19 G3
FELT TW13 25 J4
Great Ellshams BNSTD SM7 85 K6
Great Elms EW KT17 * 84 C1
Greatfield Cl FARN GU14 92 E1
Greatfield Rd FARN GU14 92 D1
Greatford Dr GU GU1 118 A8
Great Gatton Cl CROY/NA CR0 51 H7
Great George St GODL GU7 168 B5
Great Goodwin Dr GU GU1 117 L6
Greatham Rd CRAWE RH10 165 L7
Great Hollands Rd BRAK RG12 34 C6
Great Hollands Sq BRAK RG12 34 C6
Great House Ct EGRIN RH19 * 163 G5
Greatlake Ct HORL RH6 160 E2
Great Oaks Pk RGUE GU4 117 L4
Great Quarry GU GU1 7 H9
Great South-west Rd
EBED/NFELT TW14 23 M1
Great Tattenhams EPSOM KT18 84 F8
Great West Rd HEST TW5 16 B4
ISLW TW7 17 H2
Great West Rd Chiswick
CHSWK W4 19 J1
Great West Rd Ellesmere Rd
CHSWK W4 18 F1
Great West Rd Hogarth La
CHSWK W4 19 G1
Greatwood Cl CHERT KT16 57 M7
Great Woodcote Dr
PUR/KEN CR8 67 G8
Great Woodcote Pk
PUR/KEN CR8 67 H8
Greaves Pl TOOT SW17 30 B5
Grebe Ct SUT SM1 65 J4
Grebe Crs SWTR RH13 167 K8
SWTR RH13 205 P9
Grebe Ter KUT/HW KT1 * 8 E8
Grecian Crs NRWD SE19 31 L7
Green Acre ALDT GU11 112 C8
Greenacre Ct EGH TW20 * 20 F7
Greenacre Pl WLGTN SM6 66 E1
Green Acres CROY/NA CR0 3 J7
Greenacres BOR GU35 196 A1
CRAWE RH10 165 K5
GT/LBKH KT23 101 K6
HORS RH12 166 F5
KWD/TDW/WH KT20 125 J2
OXTED RH8 130 B1
RFNM GU10 134 F7
Greenacres Cl ORP BR6 71 M3
Greenbush La CRAN GU6 186 E4
Green Chain Wk SYD SE26 33 G7
Green Cl CAR SM5 66 C1
FELT TW13 25 H6
Green Court Av CROY/NA CR0 68 E1
Green Court Gdns
CROY/NA CR0 68 E1
Greencroft FARN GU14 92 E5
GU GU1 117 L8
Greencroft Rd HEST TW5 16 C3
Green Cross La RFNM GU10 181 M8
Green Curve BNSTD SM7 85 J5
Green Dene EHSLY KT24 141 M1
Green Dr RPLY/SEND GU23 98 C5
Greene Fielde End STA TW18 23 G8
Green End CHSGTN KT9 63 G3
Green Farm Rd BAGS GU19 54 C6
Greenfield Av BRYLDS KT5 45 L7
Greenfield Cl LIPH GU30 196 H8
Greenfield Link COUL/CHIP CR5 87 H5
Greenfield Rd FNM GU9 155 J2
SWTR RH13 203 Q6
Greenfields Cl HORL RH6 160 B1
HORS RH12 167 K3
Greenfields Pl RDKG RH5 173 L5
Greenfields Rd HORL RH6 160 B1
HORS RH12 167 K4
Greenfields Wy HORS RH12 167 K3
Greenfinch Wy HORS RH12 167 G2
Greenford Rd SUT SM1 65 L3
Green Gdns ORP BR6 71 M4
Greenham Wk
WOKN/KNAP GU21 76 F8
Greenham Wd BRAK RG12 34 F7
Greenhanger RFNM GU10 181 L9
Greenhayes Av BNSTD SM7 85 K5
Greenhayes Cl REIG RH2 125 M8
Greenhayes Gdns BNSTD SM7 85 K5
Green Hedges Av EGRIN RH19 162 E3
Green Hedges Cl EGRIN RH19 162 E3
Green Heights Ct
WOKS/MYFD GU22 96 F2
Greenheys Pl
WOKS/MYFD GU22 10 F6
Green Hl ORP BR6 91 H2
Greenhill SUT SM1 65 M1
Greenhill Av CTHM CR3 108 E3
Green Hill Cl CBLY GU15 73 M3
Greenhill Cl FNM GU9 155 K2
GODL GU7 168 A6
Greenhill Gdns RGUE GU4 117 M5
Greenhill La WARL CR6 89 H7
Green Hill Rd CBLY GU15 73 M3
Greenhill Rd FNM GU9 5 M8
Greenhill Wy FNM GU9 155 K3
Greenholme CBLY GU15 74 A4
Greenhow BRAK RG12 34 D3
Greenhurst La OXTED RH8 130 D6
Greenhurst Rd WNWD SE27 31 K6
Greening Wd GSHT GU26 * 182 A12
Greenlake Ter STA TW18 * 22 D8
Greenlands CHERT KT16 57 M2
HOR/WEW KT19 63 L4
Greenlands Rd CBLY GU15 72 E8
STA TW18 22 D5
WEY KT13 59 L2
Greenland Wy CROY/NA CR0 49 G7
Green La ASC SL5 37 H1
ASHTD KT21 82 F7
BAGS GU19 54 C7
BF/WBF KT14 79 J2
BLKW GU17 72 B5
CHERT KT16 58 B1
CHOB/PIR GU24 56 C8
CHSGTN KT9 63 H7
COB KT11 81 H2
CRAN GU6 185 Q9
CRAWE RH10 165 G2
CRAWE RH10 165 M4
CRAWE RH10 193 L1
CTHM CR3 107 M5
E/WMO/HCT KT8 43 L5
EGH TW20 21 L6
EGH TW20 39 M2
FELT TW13 25 H6
FNM GU9 4 F8
FNM GU9 134 C3
GODL GU7 138 B8
GU GU1 117 L8
HASM GU27 198 C10
HORL RH6 161 J8
HORS RH12 189 M9
HSLWW TW4 15 M6
KWD/TDW/WH KT20 105 J8
LHD/OX KT22 103 G3
LING RH7 178 D6
MFD/CHID GU8 183 M1
MRDN SM4 47 L7
NWMAL KT3 45 M5
PGE/AN SE20 33 G8
PUR/KEN CR8 86 F1
RDKG RH5 174 A9
REDH RH1 126 B6
REDH RH1 148 D5
REDH RH1 149 J8
REIG RH2 125 J8
RFNM GU10 157 G3
RFNM GU10 180 D3
RFNM GU10 181 L9
RGUE GU4 118 D1
RGUW GU3 115 K6
RPLY/SEND GU23 99 L6
SHGR GU5 169 Q3
SHPTN TW17 41 M6
STA TW18 40 B1
SUN TW16 24 C8
THHTH CR7 49 L1
WOT/HER KT12 60 E4
WPK KT4 46 E7
Green Lane Av WOT/HER KT12 60 E4
Green Lane Cl BF/WBF KT14 79 J2
CBLY GU15 72 F2
CHERT KT16 58 B1
Green La East RGUW GU3 136 D1
Green Lane Gdns THHTH CR7 49 M2
Green Lanes HOR/WEW KT19 64 B7
Green La West ASHV GU12 136 B1
EHSLY KT24 99 K7
Greenlaw Gdns NWMAL KT3 46 C7
Green Leaf Av WLGTN SM6 67 G3
Greenleaf Cl
BRXS/STRHM SW2 * 31 K1
Greenlea Pk WIM/MER SW19 * 48 B1
Greenleas FRIM GU16 73 H7
Green Leas SUN TW16 24 C8
Green Leas Cl SUN TW16 24 C7
Greenleaves Ct ASHF TW15 * 23 L7
Greenlink Wk RCH/KEW TW9 18 E3
Green Man La
EBED/NFELT TW14 15 K6
Green Md ESH/CLAY KT10 61 J5
Greenmead Cl SNWD SE25 50 D5
Greenmeads WOKS/MYFD GU22 97 H4
Greenoak Ri BH/WHM TN16 90 F8
Greenoak Wy WIM/MER SW19 29 G5
Greenock Rd
STRHM/NOR SW16 49 G1
Greeno Crs SHPTN TW17 41 K5
Green Pde HSLW TW3 * 16 E8
Green Pk STA TW18 22 B4
Green Rd EGH TW20 39 L4
Greensand Cl REDH RH1 127 G2
Greensand Rd REDH RH1 126 D7
Greensand Wy
BRKHM/BTCW RH3 145 M1
DORK RH4 144 B3
EDEN TN8 131 M5
FNM GU9 5 K4
GDST RH9 129 G8
GSHT GU26 198 B3
MFD/CHID GU8 182 D6
MFD/CHID GU8 184 H1
OXTED RH8 110 B8
RDKG RH5 122 A8
REDH RH1 127 L8
REDH RH1 148 B3
REDH RH1 150 E1
REIG RH2 125 H6
RFNM GU10 157 G7
SHGR GU5 169 K11
Greenside RPLY/SEND GU23 * 98 F3
Greenside Cl RGUE GU4 117 M6
Greenside Dr ASHTD KT21 82 E8
Greenside Rd CROY/NA CR0 49 K7
Green Springs RFNM GU10 132 C2
Greenstead Gdns
PUT/ROE SW15 19 K7
Greenstede Av EGRIN RH19 163 G2
Green St SUN TW16 42 D1
The Green ASHF TW15 * 23 G6
BRAK RG12 34 E4
CAR SM5 * 66 D3
CRAN GU6 187 K2
CRAWE RH10 192 G2
CRAWW RH11 164 E3
CROY/NA CR0 69 J7
CTHM CR3 109 K5
EGH TW20 20 F5
EW KT17 84 D2
FELT TW13 24 E3
FNM GU9 133 M3
FNM GU9 134 E3
FRIM GU16 93 J3
GDST RH9 128 E6
HEST TW5 16 D1
KWD/TDW/WH KT20 105 G5
KWD/TDW/WH KT20 105 H1
LHD/OX KT22 102 A6
MFD/CHID GU8 199 R2
MRDN SM4 47 H4
NWMAL KT3 45 M3
RCH/KEW TW9 18 A7
RFNM GU10 135 H8
STWL/WRAY TW19 12 B8
SUT SM1 65 L2
WHTN TW2 26 B2
Greenvale Rd
WOKN/KNAP GU21 96 A1
Green Vw CHSGTN KT9 63 J6
Greenview Av BECK BR3 51 H6
Green Wk CRAWE RH10 165 G2
Green Wy ASHV GU12 113 H6
REDH RH1 126 B6
SUN TW16 42 D4
Greenway BH/WHM TN16 110 F2
GT/LBKH KT23 101 L5
HORS RH12 166 D6
RYNPK SW20 46 F4
WLGTN SM6 66 F3
Greenway Cl BF/WBF KT14 78 D3
Greenway Dr STA TW18 40 F1
Greenway Gdns CROY/NA CR0 69 J2
Greenways BECK BR3 51 K2
EGH TW20 21 H7
ESH/CLAY KT10 62 B3
KWD/TDW/WH KT20 104 D7
Greenways Dr ASC SL5 37 H8
The Greenways TWK TW1 * 17 K8
The Greenway EPSOM KT18 83 K5
HSLWW TW4 * 16 C6
OXTED RH8 130 D7
Greenwell Cl GDST RH9 128 E4
Greenwich Cl CRAWW RH11 164 E8
Green Wd ASC SL5 35 M1
Greenwood Cl ADL/WDHM KT15 78 C1
MRDN SM4 47 H4
THDIT KT7 44 D8
Greenwood Cottages ASC SL5 37 M6
Greenwood Ct CRAWW RH11 * 191 L12
Greenwood Dr REDH RH1 148 D5
Greenwood Gdns CTHM CR3 108 D7
OXTED RH8 130 D8
Greenwood La HPTN TW12 25 L6
Greenwood Pk KUTN/CMB KT2 28 B8
Greenwood Rd CHOB/PIR GU24 94 E3
CROY/NA CR0 2 B1
ISLW TW7 17 H5
MTCM CR4 49 G3
THDIT KT7 44 D8
WOKN/KNAP GU21 96 B2
The Greenwood GU GU1 117 K8
Green Wrythe Crs CAR SM5 48 B8
Green Wrythe La CAR SM5 48 A6
Gregory Cl CRAWE RH10 165 L8
WOKN/KNAP GU21 76 F7
Gregsons HORS RH12 166 B1
Grenaby Av CROY/NA CR0 2 E2
Grenaby Rd CROY/NA CR0 2 E2
Grenadier Pl CTHM CR3 107 M4
Grenadier Rd ASHV GU12 113 L5
Grena Gdns RCH/KEW TW9 18 C6
Grena Rd RCH/KEW TW9 18 C6
Grendon Cl HORL RH6 160 C1
Grenfell Rd TOOT SW17 30 C7
Grennell Cl SUT SM1 66 A1
Grennell Rd SUT SM1 65 M1
Grenside Rd WEY KT13 59 L2
Grenville Cl BRYLDS KT5 45 M8
COB KT11 81 G3
LIPH GU30 196 H9
Grenville Gdns FRIM GU16 93 H3
Grenville Ms HPTN TW12 25 L6
Grenville Rd CROY/NA CR0 69 M8
MFD/CHID GU8 159 G2
Grenville Sq BRAK RG12 34 F2
Gresham Av WARL CR6 89 H8
Gresham Cl OXTED RH8 130 C3
Gresham Rd BECK BR3 51 H2
HPTN TW12 25 K7
HSLW TW3 16 F3
OXTED RH8 130 C3
SNWD SE25 * 50 D4
STA TW18 22 C6
Greshams Wy EDEN TN8 153 K7
Gresham Wk CRAWE RH10 165 G7
Gresham Wy FRIM GU16 93 H3
WIM/MER SW19 29 K4
Greta Bank EHSLY KT24 99 M8
Greville Av SAND/SEL CR2 69 G8
Greville Cl ALDT GU11 112 D7
ASHTD KT21 103 H1
GUW GU2 116 B8
TWK TW1 26 E1
Greville Ct GT/LBKH KT23 101 M7
Greville Park Av ASHTD KT21 83 H8
Greville Park Rd ASHTD KT21 83 H8
Greville Rd RCHPK/HAM TW10 18 C8
Grey Alders BNSTD SM7 84 F4
Greybury La EDEN TN8 179 Q6
Greycot Rd BECK BR3 33 K6
Greyfields Cl PUR/KEN CR8 87 L3
Greyfriars Dr ASC SL5 36 E6
CHOB/PIR GU24 75 K5
Greyfriars Rd RPLY/SEND GU23 98 D6
Greyhound Cl ASHV GU12 113 J8
Greyhound La
STRHM/NOR SW16 31 H7
Greyhound Rd SUT SM1 65 M4
Greyhound Slip CRAWE RH10 165 M3
Greyhound Ter
STRHM/NOR SW16 48 F1
Greys Ct ALDT GU11 112 B7
Greys Park Cl HAYES BR2 70 F4
Greystead Pk RFNM GU10 155 H3
Greystead Rd FSTH SE23 32 F1
Greystone Cl SAND/SEL CR2 88 F1
Greystones Cl REDH RH1 148 A2
Greystones Dr REIG RH2 125 M6
Greyswood St
STRHM/NOR SW16 30 E7
Greythorne Rd
WOKN/KNAP GU21 76 D8
Greywaters SHGR GU5 169 K3
Grice Av BH/WHM TN16 90 E3
Grier Cl CRAWW RH11 164 A5
Grieve Cl RFNM GU10 135 H2
Griffin Ct ASHTD KT21 * 103 H1
Griffin Wy GT/LBKH KT23 101 K8
SUN TW16 42 D2
Griffiths Rd WIM/MER SW19 29 K8

Griffon Cl FARN GU14 92 A6
Griggs Meadow
MFD/CHID GU8 185 J6
Grimwade Av CROY/NA CR0 3 M8
Grimwood Rd TWK TW1 26 C1
Grindall Cl CROY/NA CR0 67 L3
Grindley Gdns CROY/NA CR0 * 50 C6
Grindstone Crs
WOKN/KNAP GU21 75 L8
Grisedale Cl CRAWW RH11 164 E6
PUR/KEN CR8 88 B4
Grisedale Gdns PUR/KEN CR8 88 B4
Grobars Av WOKN/KNAP GU21 76 F5
Groombridge Cl WOT/HER KT12 60 E4
Groombridge Wy HORS RH12 166 C8
Groom Crs WAND/EARL SW18 30 A1
Groomfield Cl TOOT SW17 30 D5
The Grooms CRAWE RH10 165 M6
Grosse Wy PUT/ROE SW15 19 L8
Grosvenor Av CAR SM5 66 C5
MORT/ESHN SW14 19 H5
Grosvenor Cl HORL RH6 160 D5
Grosvenor Ct BLKW GU17 72 A6
Grosvenor Gdns
KUTN/CMB KT2 27 G7
MORT/ESHN SW14 19 H5
WLGTN SM6 66 F6
Grosvenor Hl WIM/MER SW19 29 H7
Grosvenor Ms REIG RH2 147 L3
Grosvenor Pl WEY KT13 60 A2
Grosvenor Rd ALDT GU11 112 D7
BTFD TW8 18 A1
CHOB/PIR GU24 76 A3
EGRIN RH19 162 E4
EPSOM KT18 104 B1
GODL GU7 168 B6
HSLWW TW4 16 C5
RCHPK/HAM TW10 18 B7
SNWD SE25 50 D4
STA TW18 22 D8
TWK TW1 26 D1
WLGTN SM6 66 E5
WWKM BR4 69 L1
Groton Rd WAND/EARL SW18 29 L3
Grotto Rd TWK TW1 26 C3
WEY KT13 59 M3
Grove Av EW KT17 84 B3
SUT SM1 65 K5
TWK TW1 26 C2
Grove Cl CRAN GU6 186 E4
FSTH SE23 33 G2
HAYES BR2 70 D1
HOR/WEW KT19 63 K8
KUT/HW KT1 45 J4
WDSR SL4 20 E1
Grove Ct E/WMO/HCT KT8 44 A5
EGH TW20 21 K6
Grove Crs FELT TW13 25 H5
KUT/HW KT1 8 E9
WOT/HER KT12 42 E7
Grove Cross Rd FRIM GU16 73 G8
Grove End BAGS GU19 54 C5
Grove End La ESH/CLAY KT10 44 A8
Grove End Rd FNM GU9 5 G9
Grove Farm Pk FRIM GU16 * 93 J8
Grovefields Av FRIM GU16 73 G8
Grove Footpath BRYLDS KT5 45 H4
Grove Gdns TEDD TW11 26 D5
Grove Heath La
RPLY/SEND GU23 98 F6
Grove Heath North
RPLY/SEND GU23 98 E4
Grove Heath Rd
RPLY/SEND GU23 98 E5
Grovehill Rd REDH RH1 126 B8
Groveland Av
STRHM/NOR SW16 31 J8
Groveland Rd BECK BR3 51 J3
Grovelands E/WMO/HCT KT8 43 K4
RFNM GU10 156 B2
Grovelands Rd PUR/KEN CR8 87 J2
Groveland Wy NWMAL KT3 45 M5
Grove La COUL/CHIP CR5 86 E5
KUT/HW KT1 45 H4
Groveley Rd SUN TW16 24 C6
Grove Park Br CHSWK W4 18 F2
Grove Park Gdns CHSWK W4 18 E2
Grove Park Rd CHSWK W4 18 E2
Grove Park Ter CHSWK W4 18 F2
Grove Pl WEY KT13 59 M4
Grove Rd ASHTD KT21 83 J8
ASHV GU12 113 K5
BARN SW13 19 J4
BH/WHM TN16 110 F2
CBLY GU15 73 H4
CHERT KT16 40 C6
CRAN GU6 186 E4
E/WMO/HCT KT8 44 A4
EW KT17 84 B3
GODL GU7 159 M6
GSHT GU26 181 P11
GU GU1 117 M8
HORL RH6 160 B2
HSLW TW3 16 E6
ISLW TW7 17 H3
LING RH7 178 F4
MTCM CR4 48 E2
RCHPK/HAM TW10 18 C8
SHPTN TW17 41 M6
SURB KT6 45 G5
SUT SM1 65 L5
THHTH CR7 49 K4
WHTN TW2 26 A4
WIM/MER SW19 29 M8
WOKN/KNAP GU21 10 F4
Groveside GT/LBKH KT23 121 K1
Groveside Cl CAR SM5 66 B1
GT/LBKH KT23 121 K1
Grovestile Waye
EBED/NFELT TW14 24 A1
Grove Ter TEDD TW11 26 D5
The Grove ADL/WDHM KT15 58 E4
ALDT GU11 112 D8
ASC SL5 35 M1
BH/WHM TN16 91 G8
COUL/CHIP CR5 87 C5
CRAWW RH11 164 E4
CTHM CR3 107 L3
EGH TW20 21 K6
EW KT17 84 B3
FARN GU14 93 G8
FRIM GU16 73 G8
GU GU1 * 7 L7
HORL RH6 160 E4
ISLW TW7 17 H3
LIPH GU30 196 G9
TEDD TW11 26 D5
WOKN/KNAP GU21 10 E4
WOT/HER KT12 42 E7
WWKM BR4 69 M2
Grove Wy ESH/CLAY KT10 43 M8
Grove Wood Hl COUL/CHIP CR5 87 G4
Grub St OXTED RH8 130 F3
Guardian Ct MFD/CHID GU8 157 M6
Guards Av CTHM CR3 107 M4
Guards Ct ASC SL5 37 L7
Guerdon Pl BRAK RG12 35 G7
Guernsey Cl CRAWW RH11 164 C8
HEST TW5 16 D3
RGUE GU4 117 K3
Guernsey Farm Dr
WOKN/KNAP GU21 10 B1
Guernsey Gv HNHL SE24 31 M1
Guildables La EDEN TN8 131 H8
Guildcroft GU GU1 117 K8
Guildersfield Rd
STRHM/NOR SW16 31 H8
Guildford Av FELT TW13 24 D3
Guildford Business Park Rd
GUW GU2 6 C2
Guildford La SHGR GU5 140 D4
Guildford Park Av GUW GU2 6 D5
Guildford Park Rd GUW GU2 6 D6
Guildford Rd ASHV GU12 135 G2
BAGS GU19 54 C7
BIL RH14 201 Q4
CHERT KT16 57 L8
CHERT KT16 58 A2
CHOB/PIR GU24 75 H2
CHOB/PIR GU24 95 J5
CRAN GU6 186 A1
CROY/NA CR0 50 A6
DORK RH4 143 L4
FNM GU9 5 M1
FRIM GU16 93 K4
GODL GU7 168 D3
GT/LBKH KT23 121 J2
HORS RH12 202 E1
HORS RH12 204 C3
LHD/OX KT22 102 B6
RDKG RH5 142 D6
RFNM GU10 134 D5
RGUE GU4 96 F7
SHGR GU5 169 N4
SWTR RH13 203 N2
WOKS/MYFD GU22 10 D6
Guildford Rd East FARN GU14 92 F8
Guildford Rd West FARN GU14 92 F8
Guildford St CHERT KT16 40 D7
STA TW18 22 D7
Guildford Wy WLGTN SM6 67 H4
Guildown Av GUW GU2 138 E3
Guildown Rd GUW GU2 138 E3
Guileshill La RPLY/SEND GU23 99 H4
Guilford Av BRYLDS KT5 45 J5
Guillemont Flds FARN GU14 92 A4
Guinevere Rd CRAWW RH11 164 A4
Guinness Ct CROY/NA CR0 * 3 J6
Gulley Rd FARN GU14 112 D1
Gumbrells Cl RGUW GU3 115 M4
Gumley Gdns ISLW TW7 17 K5
Gumping Rd STMC/STPC BR5 71 M1
Gun Hl ALDT GU11 112 E6
Gunnell Cl CROY/NA CR0 50 C6
SYD SE26 * 32 D5
Gunners Rd WAND/EARL SW18 30 A3
Gunning Cl CRAWW RH11 164 C7
Gunns Farm LIPH GU30 196 H11
Gun Pit Rd LING RH7 178 D5
Gunters Md LHD/OX KT22 * 81 M1
Gunton Rd TOOT SW17 30 D7
Gurdon's La MFD/CHID GU8 183 N7
Gurney Crs CROY/NA CR0 49 J8
Gurney Rd CAR SM5 66 D3
Gurney's Cl REDH RH1 148 C1
Guyatt Gdns MTCM CR4 48 D2
Guy Rd WLGTN SM6 67 H2
Gwydor Rd BECK BR3 51 G4
Gwynne Av CROY/NA CR0 51 G7
Gwynne Gdns EGRIN RH19 162 D3
Gwynne Rd CTHM CR3 108 A5
Gwynne Whf CHSWK W4 19 J1

H

Habershon Dr FRIM GU16 74 A7
Haccombe Rd WIM/MER SW19 29 M7
Hackbridge Park Gdns
CAR SM5 66 C1
Hackbridge Rd CAR SM5 66 D1
Hackenden Cl EGRIN RH19 162 F2
Hackenden La EGRIN RH19 162 F2
Hacketts La WOKS/MYFD GU22 78 C5
Hackhurst La RDKG RH5 142 C5
Hackington Crs BECK BR3 33 K7
Haddon Cl NWMAL KT3 46 C5
Haddon Rd SUT SM1 65 L3
Hadfield Rd STWL/WRAY TW19 14 A8
Hadleigh Cl RYNPK SW20 47 J2
Hadleigh Dr BELMT SM2 65 K7
Hadley Pl WEY KT13 59 K6
Hadley Rd MTCM CR4 49 G4
Hadleys RFNM GU10 155 H6
Hadley Wood Ri PUR/KEN CR8 87 L5
Hadmans Cl HORS RH12 166 F8
Hadrian Cl STWL/WRAY TW19 23 H1
Hadrian Wy STWL/WRAY TW19 23 H1
Haggard Rd TWK TW1 26 E1
Haigh Crs REDH RH1 148 E2
Haig Rd ASHV GU12 112 F8
BH/WHM TN16 91 H7
CBLY GU15 72 C3
Hailes Cl WIM/MER SW19 29 M7
Hailsham Av BRXS/STRHM SW2 31 J3
Hailsham Cl SHST GU47 52 A8
SURB KT6 45 G7
Hailsham Rd TOOT SW17 30 D7
Haines Ct WEY KT13 60 A4
Haines Wk MRDN SM4 47 L7
Haining Gdns FRIM GU16 93 K6
Hainthorpe Rd WNWD SE27 31 L4
Haldane Pl WAND/EARL SW18 29 L2
Halebourne La CHOB/PIR GU24 55 K8
Hale Cl ORP BR6 71 M3
Hale End BRAK RG12 35 J4
Hale Ends WOKS/MYFD GU22 96 E3
Hale House La RFNM GU10 181 M8
Hale Pit Rd GT/LBKH KT23 101 M8
Hale Pl FNM GU9 134 B4
Hale Reeds FNM GU9 134 A3
Hale Rd FNM GU9 5 M1
Hales Fld HASM GU27 198 D7
Hales Oak GT/LBKH KT23 101 M8
Halesowen Rd MRDN SM4 47 L7
Hale St STA TW18 22 B5
Haleswood COB KT11 80 E4
Hale Wy FRIM GU16 73 G8
Halewood BRAK RG12 34 C6
Half Acre BTFD TW8 18 A1
Half Acre Ms BTFD TW8 18 A2
Half Moon Hl HASM GU27 198 D7
Halford Rd RCHPK/HAM TW10 18 B7
Halfpenny Cl RGUE GU4 140 A6
Halfpenny La ASC SL5 37 K7
RGUE GU4 139 M3
Halfway Gn WOT/HER KT12 60 E2
Halfway La GODL GU7 159 M5
Haliburton Rd TWK TW1 17 K7
Halifax Cl CRAWE RH10 192 D4
FARN GU14 92 C6
TEDD TW11 26 B7
Halifax St SYD SE26 32 E4
Halifax Wy FARN GU14 112 C2
Halimote Rd ALDT GU11 112 D8
Haling Gv SAND/SEL CR2 67 M6
Haling Park Gdns
SAND/SEL CR2 67 L5
Haling Park Rd SAND/SEL CR2 67 L5
Haling Rd SAND/SEL CR2 68 A5
Hallam Rd GODL GU7 168 C3
Halland Cl CRAWE RH10 165 J3
Hall Cl CBLY GU15 73 H3
GODL GU7 168 B2
Hall Ct TEDD TW11 26 C6
Hall Dene Cl GU GU1 117 M7
Hall Dr SYD SE26 32 F6
Halley Cl CRAWW RH11 191 L12
Halley Dr ASC SL5 36 A2
Halley's Ap WOKN/KNAP GU21 76 D8
Halley's Ct WOKN/KNAP GU21 * 76 D8
Halley's Wk ADL/WDHM KT15 58 F6
Hall Farm Dr WHTN TW2 26 A1
Hallgrove Bottom BAGS GU19 54 C4
Hall Hl OXTED RH8 130 A6
The Halliards WOT/HER KT12 42 D6
Halliford Cl SHPTN TW17 42 B3
Halliford Rd SHPTN TW17 42 B5
Hallington Cl WOKN/KNAP GU21 76 E7
Hall La HYS/HAR UB3 15 G2
Hallmark Cl SHST GU47 72 B1
Hallmead Rd SUT SM1 65 L2
Hallowell Av CROY/NA CR0 67 H3
Hallowell Cl MTCM CR4 48 D3
Hallowes Cl GUW GU2 116 E3
Hallowfield Wy MTCM CR4 48 A3
Hallows Gv SUN TW16 24 C6
Hall Pl WOKN/KNAP GU21 11 G4
Hall Place Dr WEY KT13 60 B4
Hall Rd FARN GU14 92 E8
ISLW TW7 17 G7
SHGR GU5 169 J2
WLGTN SM6 66 E7
Halls Dr HORS RH12 190 C12
Halls Farm Cl
WOKN/KNAP GU21 76 A7
Hallsland CRAWE RH10 193 P5
Hallsland Wy OXTED RH8 130 C7
Halnaker Wk CRAWW RH11 * 164 B7
Halsford La EGRIN RH19 162 C3
Halsford Park Rd EGRIN RH19 162 D3
Halstead Cl CROY/NA CR0 2 C7
Halters End GSHT GU26 197 M2
Hamble Av BLKW GU17 72 A4
Hamble Cl WOKN/KNAP GU21 76 D7
Hambledon Gdns SNWD SE25 50 C3
Hambledon Hl EPSOM KT18 83 M6
Hambledon Pk MFD/CHID GU8 183 Q8
Hambledon Pl DUL SE21 32 C2
GT/LBKH KT23 101 K5
Hambledon Rd CTHM CR3 108 A5
MFD/CHID GU8 184 A1
WAND/EARL SW18 29 J1
Hambledon V EPSOM KT18 83 M6
Hambleton WDSR SL4 * 20 F2
Hambleton Cl FRIM GU16 73 L6
WPK KT4 64 F1
Hambleton Hl CRAWW RH11 164 E6
Hambrook Rd SNWD SE25 50 E3
Hambro Rd STRHM/NOR SW16 31 G7
Ham Common
RCHPK/HAM TW10 27 G4
Ham Croft Cl FELT TW13 24 D4
Hamesmoor Rd FRIM GU16 93 H5
Hamesmoor Wy FRIM GU16 93 J5
Ham Farm Rd
RCHPK/HAM TW10 27 G5
Hamfield Cl OXTED RH8 129 M1
Ham Gate Av
RCHPK/HAM TW10 27 J5
Hamilton Av CHEAM SM3 65 H1
COB KT11 80 D3
SURB KT6 63 K1
WOKS/MYFD GU22 78 B6
Hamilton Cl BOR GU35 196 A1
CHERT KT16 40 C8
FELT TW13 24 C6
GUW GU2 * 116 D3
HOR/WEW KT19 83 M2
PUR/KEN CR8 87 L2
TEDD TW11 26 E7
Hamilton Crs HSLW TW3 16 E7
Hamilton Dr ASC SL5 37 H7
GUW GU2 116 D3
Hamilton Gordon Ct GU GU1 6 F2
Hamilton Ms WEY KT13 * 59 K3
Hamilton Pde FELT TW13 * 24 D5
Hamilton Pl ALDT GU11 112 C8
GUW GU2 116 D3
KWD/TDW/WH KT20 105 J5
SUN TW16 24 E8
Hamilton Rd BTFD TW8 18 A1
FELT TW13 24 B6
HORS RH12 166 E6
THHTH CR7 50 A3
WHTN TW2 26 B2
WIM/MER SW19 29 L8
WNWD SE27 32 A5
Hamilton Road Ms
WIM/MER SW19 29 L8
Hamilton Wy WLGTN SM6 67 G7
Ham La EGH TW20 20 E5
MFD/CHID GU8 158 B5
Hamlash La RFNM GU10 155 M8
Hamlet Rd NRWD SE19 32 C8
Hamlet St BNFD RG42 35 H1
Hamlyn Gdns NRWD SE19 32 B8
Hamm Ct WEY KT13 59 J2
Hamm Court Est WEY KT13 59 J1
Hammerfield Dr RDKG RH5 142 C7
Hammer Hl HASM GU27 197 P9
Hammer La GSHT GU26 181 K10
GSHT GU26 197 P5
HASM GU27 197 M7
HASM GU27 197 P8
Hammerpond Rd SWTR RH13 205 P9
Hammersley Rd ALDT GU11 112 E2
Hammersmith Bridge Rd
BARN SW13 19 L1
Hammersmith Emb
HMSMTH W6 * 19 M1
Hammerwood Copse
HASM GU27 197 Q8
Hammerwood Rd EGRIN RH19 163 M7
Hammer Yd CRAWE RH10 * 164 F5
Hamm Moor La
ADL/WDHM KT15 59 H4
Hammond Av MTCM CR4 48 E2
Hammond Cl HPTN TW12 43 K1
WOKN/KNAP GU21 76 F5
Hammond Rd
WOKN/KNAP GU21 76 F5
Hammond Wy LTWR GU18 54 E8
Hamond Cl SAND/SEL CR2 67 L7
Hampden Av BECK BR3 51 H2
Hampden Cl CRAWE RH10 * 165 M1
CRAWE RH10 192 D4
Hampden Rd BECK BR3 51 H2
KUT/HW KT1 9 K8
Hampers La SWTR RH13 167 K7
Hampshire Cl ASHV GU12 135 G2
Hampshire Rd CBLY GU15 73 J1
Hampstead La DORK RH4 144 C3
Hampstead Rd DORK RH4 144 D3
Hampstead Wk CRAWW
RH11 * 164 E8
Hampton Cl RYNPK SW20 * 28 F8
WOKN/KNAP GU21 95 L1
Hampton Court Av
E/WMO/HCT KT8 44 A6
Hampton Court Crs
E/WMO/HCT KT8 * 44 A3
Hampton Court Est THDIT KT7 * 44 B5
Hampton Court Rd HPTN TW12 44 A2
Hampton Court Wy
E/WMO/HCT KT8 44 B4
ESH/CLAY KT10 62 B1
Hampton Gv EW KT17 84 C1
Hampton La FELT TW13 25 H5
Hampton Rd CROY/NA CR0 49 M6
FNM GU9 133 K3
REDH RH1 148 C5
WHTN TW2 26 A4
WPK KT4 64 D1
Hampton Rd East FELT TW13 25 J5
Hampton Rd West FELT TW13 25 H3
Hampton Wy EGRIN RH19 163 G6
Ham Ridings RCHPK/HAM TW10 27 J6
Hamsey Green Gdns WARL CR6 88 F6
Hamsey Wy SAND/SEL CR2 88 E4
Ham St RCHPK/HAM TW10 26 F3
The Ham BTFD TW8 17 M2
Ham Vw CROY/NA CR0 51 H6
Hanbury Dr BH/WHM TN16 90 E3
Hanbury Rd CRAWW RH11 164 A5
Hanbury Wy CBLY GU15 72 F6
Hancock Rd NRWD SE19 32 A7
Hancocks Mt ASC SL5 37 G6
Handcroft Cl RFNM GU10 132 C1
Handcroft Rd CROY/NA CR0 2 A2
Handley Page Rd WLGTN SM6 67 J6
Handside Cl WPK KT4 47 G8
Hanford Cl WAND/EARL SW18 29 K2
Hanger Hl WEY KT13 59 L4
The Hanger BOR GU35 180 D10
Hang Grove Hl ORP BR6 91 L3
Hanley Pl BECK BR3 33 K8
Hannah Cl BECK BR3 51 L3
Hannam's Farm RFNM GU10 132 B3
Hannen Rd WNWD SE27 * 31 L4
Hannibal Rd STWL/WRAY TW19 23 H1
Hannibal Wy CROY/NA CR0 67 J4
Hanover Av FELT TW13 24 D2
Hanover Cl CHEAM SM3 65 H3
CRAWE RH10 165 H6
EGH TW20 20 E7
FRIM GU16 73 H8
RCH/KEW TW9 18 D2
REDH RH1 126 F2
Hanover Ct DORK RH4 144 C2
WOKS/MYFD GU22 10 B9
Hanover Gdns BRAK RG12 34 C7
FARN GU14 92 B3
Hanover Rd WIM/MER SW19 29 M8
Hanover St CROY/NA CR0 2 B7
Hanover Wk WEY KT13 60 A2
Hansler Gv E/WMO/HCT KT8 44 A5
Hanson Cl BAL SW12 30 E1
BECK BR3 * 33 L7
CBLY GU15 73 L2
MORT/ESHN SW14 18 F5
RGUE GU4 117 J5
Hanworth Cl BRAK RG12 34 F6
Hanworth La CHERT KT16 40 C8
Hanworth Rd BRAK RG12 34 D7
FELT TW13 24 E2
HSLW TW3 16 D6
HSLWW TW4 25 J1
REDH RH1 148 C5
SUN TW16 24 D8
Hanworth Ter HSLW TW3 16 E6
Harberson Rd BAL SW12 30 E2
Harbledown Rd SAND/SEL CR2 88 D1
Harborough Rd
STRHM/NOR SW16 31 J5
Harbour Cl FARN GU14 92 D1
Harbourfield Rd BNSTD SM7 85 L5
Harbridge Av PUT/ROE SW15 28 C1
Harbury Rd CAR SM5 66 B7
Harcourt STWL/WRAY TW19 12 B8
Harcourt Av WLGTN SM6 66 E3
Harcourt Cl EGH TW20 21 M7
ISLW TW7 17 K5
Harcourt Fld WLGTN SM6 66 E3
Harcourt Rd BRAK RG12 34 E6
CBLY GU15 72 E4
THHTH CR7 49 J6
WIM/MER SW19 29 K8
WLGTN SM6 66 E3
Harcourt Wy GDST RH9 151 H3
Hardcastle Cl CROY/NA CR0 50 D6
Hardcourts Cl WWKM BR4 69 L3
Hardell Cl EGH TW20 21 K6
Hardel Wk BRXS/STRHM SW2 31 K1
Harden Farm Cl
COUL/CHIP CR5 106 F3
Hardham Cl CRAWW RH11 164 C2
Harding Cl CROY/NA CR0 3 K7
KUTN/CMB KT2 9 G4
Harding Rd EPSOM KT18 104 B1
Hardings La PGE/AN SE20 33 G7
Hardman Rd KUTN/CMB KT2 8 F6
Hard's Hl SWTR RH13 205 L12
Hardwell Wy BRAK RG12 35 H4
Hardwick Cl LHD/OX KT22 81 M5
Hardwicke Av HEST TW5 * 16 D3
Hardwicke Rd
RCHPK/HAM TW10 26 F5
REIG RH2 125 K7
Hardwick La CHERT KT16 39 M7
Hardwick Pl STRHM/NOR SW16 30 F8
Hardwick Rd REDH RH1 148 A2
Hardy Cl CRAWE RH10 165 L3
HORL RH6 160 B3
HORS RH12 166 E5
RDKG RH5 144 E6
Hardy Rd WIM/MER SW19 29 L8
Harebell Hl COB KT11 81 G4
Harecroft DORK RH4 144 F5
LHD/OX KT22 101 L5
Haredon Cl FSTH SE23 32 F1
Harefield ESH/CLAY KT10 62 B2
Harefield Av BELMT SM2 65 H7
Harefield Rd STRHM/NOR SW16 31 J8
Hare Hl ADL/WDHM KT15 58 C5
Hare Hill Cl WOKS/MYFD GU22 78 D5
Harelands Cl WOKN/KNAP GU21 76 F7
Hare La CRAWW RH11 164 D1
ESH/CLAY KT10 62 B5
GODL GU7 168 C3
LING RH7 177 Q4
Harendon KWD/TDW/WH KT20 104 F3
Hares Bank CROY/NA CR0 70 A8
Harestone Dr CTHM CR3 108 C7
Harestone Hl CTHM CR3 108 D7
Harestone La CTHM CR3 108 B7
Harestone Valley Rd
CTHM CR3 108 C7
Harewood Cl CRAWE RH10 165 J1
REIG RH2 125 M6
Harewood Gdns SAND/SEL CR2 88 E5
Harewood Rd ISLW TW7 17 J2
RGUE GU4 117 M5
SAND/SEL CR2 68 B5
WIM/MER SW19 30 B7
Harfield Rd SUN TW16 43 G2
Harkness Cl EW KT17 84 F6
Harland Av CROY/NA CR0 3 K7
Harland Cl WIM/MER SW19 47 L3
Harlands Gv ORP BR6 71 L3
Harlech Gdns HEST TW5 15 M1
Harlech Rd BLKW GU17 72 A5
Harlequin Av BTFD TW8 17 K1
Harlequin Cl ISLW TW7 17 H7
Harlequin Rd TEDD TW11 * 26 E8
Harlington Cl HYS/HAR UB3 14 F2
Harlington Rd East
EBED/NFELT TW14 24 E1
Harlington Rd West
EBED/NFELT TW14 15 L8
Harman Pl PUR/KEN CR8 87 L1
Harmans Dr EGRIN RH19 163 J4
Harmans Md EGRIN RH19 163 H4
Harmans Water Rd BRAK RG12 35 G5
Harmondsworth La
WDR/YW UB7 14 B1
Harmony Cl CRAWW RH11 164 A6
WLGTN SM6 67 H7
Harms Gv RGUE GU4 117 M5
Harold Rd CRAWE RH10 192 D8
NRWD SE19 32 A8
SUT SM1 66 A3
Haroldslea HORL RH6 161 H4
Haroldslea Cl HORL RH6 160 F5
Haroldslea Dr HORL RH6 160 F5
Harpenden Rd WNWD SE27 31 L3
Harper Dr CRAWE RH10 165 L8
Harper's Rd ASHV GU12 113 M7
Harpers Yd ISLW TW7 * 17 J4
Harpesford Av VW GU25 38 F5
Harps Oak La REDH RH1 106 C7
Harpswood Cl COUL/CHIP CR5 106 F4
Harpurs KWD/TDW/WH KT20 105 G3
Harrier Cl CRAN GU6 186 D1
Harriet Cl BRXS/STRHM SW2 31 K1
Harriet Gdns CROY/NA CR0 3 M5
Harrington Cl CROY/NA CR0 67 H1
REIG RH2 146 D7
Harrington Rd SNWD SE25 50 D4
Harriotts Cl ASHTD KT21 103 G2
Harriotts La ASHTD KT21 102 F1
Harris Cl CRAWW RH11 164 D7
HSLW TW3 16 D3
Harrison Cl REIG RH2 147 L1
Harrison Ct SHPTN TW17 * 41 L5
Harrison's Ri CROY/NA CR0 2 A7
Harrison Wy SHPTN TW17 41 L5
Harris Pth CRAWW RH11 164 D7
Harris Wy SUN TW16 42 B1
Harrow Cl ADL/WDHM KT15 58 E1
CHSGTN KT9 63 G6
DORK RH4 144 D3
Harrowdene CRAN GU6 186 D1
Harrowdene Gdns TEDD TW11 26 D8

Harrow Gdns WARL CR6 89 J6
Harrowlands Pk DORK RH4 144 E3
Harrow La GODL GU7 168 B2
Harrow Rd CAR SM5 66 B5
EBED/NFELT TW14 23 K2
WARL CR6 89 J5
Harrow Rd East DORK RH4 144 E4
Harrow Rd West DORK RH4 144 D4
Harrowsley Ct HORL RH6 160 E2
Harrow Wy SHPTN TW17 41 M2
Hart Cl FARN GU14 92 B1
REDH RH1 128 C7
Hart Dene Ct BAGS GU19 54 B6
Harte Rd HSLW TW3 16 C4
Hartfield Crs WIM/MER SW19 29 J8
WWKM BR4 70 D2
Hartfield Gv PGE/AN SE20 50 E1
Hartfield Rd CHSGTN KT9 63 G4
FROW RH18 195 P11
WIM/MER SW19 29 J8
WWKM BR4 70 D3
Hartford Ri CBLY GU15 73 G3
Hartford Rd HOR/WEW KT19 63 K5
Hart Gdns DORK RH4 144 E1
Hartham Cl ISLW TW7 17 K3
Hartham Rd ISLW TW7 17 J3
Harting Ct CRAWW RH11 164 B7
Hartington Cl ORP BR6 71 M4
REIG RH2 125 K6
Hartington Pl REIG RH2 * 125 K6
Hartington Rd CHSWK W4 18 F3
TWK TW1 26 E1
Hartland Cl ADL/WDHM KT15 58 F8
Hartland Pl FARN GU14 92 D2
Hartland Rd ADL/WDHM KT15 58 D6
HPTN TW12 25 L5
ISLW TW7 17 K5
MRDN SM4 47 K7
The Hartlands HEST TW5 15 L1
Hartland Wy CROY/NA CR0 69 H1
MRDN SM4 47 J7
Hartley Down PUR/KEN CR8 87 J5
Hartley Farm PUR/KEN CR8 87 J5
Hartley Hl PUR/KEN CR8 87 J5
Hartley Old Rd PUR/KEN CR8 87 J4
Hartley Rd CROY/NA CR0 2 C1
Hartley Wy PUR/KEN CR8 87 J5
Hart Rd BF/WBF KT14 79 H3
DORK RH4 144 E1
Hartscroft CROY/NA CR0 69 H7
Harts Gdns GUW GU2 116 E5
Hartsgrove MFD/CHID GU8 183 Q12
Hartshill GUW GU2 116 A7
Hart's La GDST RH9 151 G2
Hartspiece Rd REDH RH1 148 E2
Hart Sq MRDN SM4 * 47 L5
Hartswood RDKG RH5 145 G5
Hartswood Av REIG RH2 147 K4
The Hart FNM GU9 5 G3
Harvard Rd ISLW TW7 17 H3
SHST GU47 52 C8
Harvest Bank Rd WWKM BR4 70 D2
Harvester Rd HOR/WEW KT19 64 A8
Harvesters HORS RH12 167 G5
Harvesters Cl ISLW TW7 17 G7
Harvest Hl EGRIN RH19 162 F5
GODL GU7 168 A5
Harvest La THDIT KT7 44 D6
Harvest Ride BNFD RG42 35 J1
Harvest Rd CRAWE RH10 165 L6
EGH TW20 21 G6
FELT TW13 24 D5
Harvestside HORL RH6 160 F2
Harvey Cl CRAWW RH11 191 K12
Harvey Dr HPTN TW12 43 L1
Harvey Gdns GU GU1 * 7 K6
Harvey Rd GU GU1 7 J7
HSLWW TW4 25 J1
WOT/HER KT12 42 D7
Harwarden Cl CRAWE RH10 193 P5
Harwood Av MTCM CR4 48 B3
Harwood Gdns WDSR SL4 20 E1
Harwood Pk REDH RH1 175 R1
Harwood Rd SWTR RH13 167 H6
Harwoods Cl EGRIN RH19 163 G6
Harwood's La EGRIN RH19 163 G5
Haseley End FSTH SE23 * 32 F1
Haseltine Rd SYD SE26 33 J5
Haslam Av CHEAM SM3 47 H8
Hasle Dr HASM GU27 198 C8
Haslemere Av HEST TW5 15 M4
MTCM CR4 48 A2
WAND/EARL SW18 29 L3
Haslemere Cl FRIM GU16 73 M6
HPTN TW12 25 J6
WLGTN SM6 67 H4
Haslemere Rd HASM GU27 198 C11
LIPH GU30 197 J9
MFD/CHID GU8 183 K7
THHTH CR7 49 L5
Haslett Av CRAWE RH10 165 H4
Haslett Av East CRAWE RH10 165 J4
Haslett Av West CRAWE RH10 164 F5
Haslett Rd SHPTN TW17 42 B2
Hassocks Cl SYD SE26 32 E4
Hassocks Ct CRAWW RH11 164 B7
Hassocks Rd STRHM/NOR SW16 49 G1
Hassock Wd HAYES BR2 71 G3
Haste Hl HASM GU27 198 E8
Haste Hill Top HASM GU27 * 198 E8
Hastings Cl FRIM GU16 93 K2
Hastings Dr SURB KT6 44 F6
Hastings Rd CRAWE RH10 165 K4
CROY/NA CR0 3 J3
Hatch Cl ADL/WDHM KT15 58 E2
CRAN GU6 185 R10
Hatch End BFOR GU20 54 F5
FROW RH18 195 N11
The Hatches FNM GU9 4 D8
FRIM GU16 93 J3
Hatchett Rd EBED/NFELT TW14 23 M2
Hatchetts Dr HASM GU27 197 P7
Hatch Gdns
KWD/TDW/WH KT20 105 G2
Hatchgate HORL RH6 160 C4
Hatchgate Copse BRAK RG12 34 B6
Hatch Hl HASM GU27 198 C12
Hatchlands HORS RH12 167 K2
Hatchlands Rd REDH RH1 126 B8
Hatch La COB KT11 99 L1
HASM GU27 198 C12
REDH RH1 149 J6
WDR/YW UB7 14 A2
Hatch Pl KUTN/CMB KT2 27 J6
Hatch Rd STRHM/NOR SW16 49 H2
Hatfield Cl BELMT SM2 65 K7
BF/WBF KT14 * 79 J5
MTCM CR4 * 48 A4
Hatfield Ct CBLY GU15 72 E4
Hatfield Gdns FARN GU14 93 H6
Hatfield Rd ASHTD KT21 103 J1
Hathaway Rd CROY/NA CR0 2 B2
Hatherleigh Cl CHSGTN KT9 63 G4
MRDN SM4 47 K4
Hatherley Rd RCH/KEW TW9 18 C3
Hatherop Rd HPTN TW12 25 J8
Hathersham Cl HORL RH6 161 K2
Hathersham La HORL RH6 176 E3
Hatherwood LHD/OX KT22 103 G3
Hatton Cross Est HTHAIR TW6 * 15 J6
Hatton Gdns MTCM CR4 48 C5
Hatton Gn EBED/NFELT TW14 15 K6
Hatton Hl BFOR GU20 54 F4
Hatton Rd CROY/NA CR0 49 K8
EBED/NFELT TW14 23 M1
HTHAIR TW6 15 J6
Hatton Rd North HTHAIR TW6 15 G3
Havana Rd WIM/MER SW19 29 K3
Havelock Rd CROY/NA CR0 3 K5
WIM/MER SW19 29 M6
Havelock Wk FSTH SE23 32 F2
Haven Cl WIM/MER SW19 29 G4
Haven Ct BRYLDS KT5 * 45 J6
Haven Gdns CRAWE RH10 193 M4
Havengate HORS RH12 167 J4
Haven Rd ASHF TW15 23 L5
BIL RH14 203 J6
The Haven MFD/CHID GU8 * 183 Q8
RCH/KEW TW9 18 D5
SUN TW16 24 D8
Haven Wy FNM GU9 134 A5
Haverfield Est BTFD TW8 18 B1
Haverfield Gdns RCH/KEW TW9 18 D2
Haverhill Rd BAL SW12 30 F2
Havers Av WOT/HER KT12 61 G4
Haversham Cl CRAWE RH10 165 H4
TWK TW1 27 G1
Haversham Dr BRAK RG12 34 E6
Havisham Pl NRWD SE19 31 L7
Hawarden Gv HNHL SE24 31 M1
Hawarden Rd CTHM CR3 107 M3
Hawes La WWKM BR4 51 M8
Hawes Rd KWD/TDW/WH KT20 105 G2
Haweswater Ct ASHV GU12 * 113 J5
Hawke Rd NRWD SE19 32 A7
Hawker Rd ASHV GU12 113 J4
CROY/NA CR0 67 K5
Hawkesbourne Rd HORS RH12 167 J4
Hawkesbury Rd PUT/ROE SW15 19 L7
Hawkesfield Rd FSTH SE23 33 H3
Hawkes Leap BFOR GU20 54 E3
Hawkesley Cl TWK TW1 26 D5
Hawkesmoore Dr RDKG RH5 173 K5
Hawkesmoor Rd
CRAWW RH11 164 A6
Hawkes Rd EBED/NFELT TW14 24 D1
MTCM CR4 48 B1
Hawkesworth Dr BAGS GU19 54 A8
Hawkewood Rd SUN TW16 42 D3
Hawkhirst Rd PUR/KEN CR8 88 A6
Hawkhurst COB KT11 81 K4
Hawkhurst Rd
STRHM/NOR SW16 31 G8
Hawkhurst Wk CRAWE RH10 165 K6
Hawkhurst Wy NWMAL KT3 46 A5
WWKM BR4 69 L1
Hawkins Cl BRAK RG12 35 K2
Hawkins Rd CRAWE RH10 165 G6
TEDD TW11 26 E7
Hawkins Wy CAT SE6 33 K6
Hawk La BRAK RG12 35 G4
Hawkley Gdns WNWD SE27 31 L3
Hawksbrook La BECK BR3 51 M6
Hawkshaw Cl LIPH GU30 197 J9
Hawk's Hl LHD/OX KT22 102 C5
Hawkshill Cl ESH/CLAY KT10 61 K5
Hawks Hill Cl LHD/OX KT22 102 C5
Hawks Hill Ct LHD/OX KT22 102 C5
Hawkshill Pl ESH/CLAY KT10 * 61 K5
Hawkshill Wy ESH/CLAY KT10 61 J5
Hawks Rd KUT/HW KT1 9 H7
Hawksview COB KT11 81 J3
Hawksway STA TW18 22 C4
Hawkswell Cl
WOKN/KNAP GU21 76 C7
Hawkswood Av FRIM GU16 73 J7
Hawkwood Dell GT/LBKH KT23 101 K8
Hawkwood Ri GT/LBKH KT23 101 K8
Hawley Cl HPTN TW12 25 J7
Hawley Gn BLKW GU17 72 B6
Hawley Gv BLKW GU17 72 B7
Hawley La FARN GU14 92 E1
Hawley Rd BLKW GU17 72 C6
Hawley Wy ASHF TW15 23 K6
Hawmead CRAWE RH10 193 P5
Haworth Rd CRAWE RH10 165 K5
Hawth Av CRAWE RH10 165 J5
Hawth Cl CRAWE RH10 165 G6
Hawthorn Av THHTH CR7 49 L1
Hawthorn Cl ASHV GU12 135 H1
BNFD RG42 34 D1
BNSTD SM7 85 H4
CRAWW RH11 164 E1
EDEN TN8 153 L7
HEST TW5 15 L2
HORS RH12 166 F5
HPTN TW12 25 K6
REDH RH1 148 D5
WOKS/MYFD GU22 97 H2
Hawthorn Ct FARN GU14 112 F1
Hawthorn Crs SAND/SEL CR2 88 F1
Hawthorndene Cl HAYES BR2 * 70 C1
Hawthorndene Rd HAYES BR2 70 D1
Hawthorn Dr WWKM BR4 70 B3
Hawthorne Av BH/WHM TN16 91 G5
CAR SM5 66 D6
MTCM CR4 48 A2
Hawthorne Ct
STWL/WRAY TW19 * 23 G1
Hawthorne Crs BLKW GU17 72 B5
Hawthorne Pl EW KT17 84 B2
Hawthorne Rd STA TW18 21 M6
Hawthorne Wy RGUE GU4 117 L4
Hawthorn Gv PGE/AN SE20 50 E1
Hawthorn Hatch BTFD TW8 17 L2
Hawthorn La RFNM GU10 155 J6
Hawthorn Pl RGUE GU4 * 117 G3
RGUE GU4 118 A6
Hawthorn Rd BTFD TW8 17 L2
FELT TW13 24 D2
FRIM GU16 73 J7
GODL GU7 159 L7
RPLY/SEND GU23 98 C6
SUT SM1 66 A4
WLGTN SM6 66 E6
WOKS/MYFD GU22 97 H2
The Hawthorns DTCH/LGLY SL3 13 J3
EW KT17 64 C5
OXTED RH8 130 D7
Hawthorn Ter WEY KT13 * 79 K1
Hawthorn Wy ADL/WDHM KT15 58 E8
CHOB/PIR GU24 75 K6
REDH RH1 148 E2
SHPTN TW17 42 A4
Haxted Rd LING RH7 178 F2
Haybarn Dr HORS RH12 167 H2
Haycroft Cl COUL/CHIP CR5 107 L1
Haycroft Rd SURB KT6 63 G1
Hayden Ct ADL/WDHM KT15 58 E8
Haydn Av PUR/KEN CR8 87 K5
Haydon Park Rd
WIM/MER SW19 29 K6
Haydon Pl GU GU1 7 G5
Haydon's Rd WIM/MER SW19 29 L6
Hayes Barton
WOKS/MYFD GU22 78 A6
Hayes Cl HAYES BR2 70 D1
Hayes Crs CHEAM SM3 65 G3
Hayes Gdn HAYES BR2 70 D1
Hayes La PUR/KEN CR8 87 L6
SWTR RH13 203 P8
The Hayes EPSOM KT18 104 A1
Hayes Wk HORL RH6 161 K2
Hayes Wy BECK BR3 51 M4
Hayes Wood Rd BIL RH14 203 L12
Hayfields HORL RH6 160 F2
Haygarth Pl WIM/MER SW19 29 G6
Haygreen Cl KUTN/CMB KT2 9 L1
Haylett Gdns KUT/HW KT1 * 45 G4
Hayling Av FELT TW13 24 D4
Haymeads Dr ESH/CLAY KT10 61 M5
Haymer Gdns WPK KT4 64 D2
Hayne Rd BECK BR3 51 J2
Haynes Cl RPLY/SEND GU23 98 E4
Haynes La NRWD SE19 32 B7
Haynt Wk RYNPK SW20 47 H3
Haysleigh Gdns PGE/AN SE20 50 D2
Hays Wk BELMT SM2 65 G8
Haywain CTHM CR3 107 M4
Hayward Cl WIM/MER SW19 29 L8
Haywardens LING RH7 178 E4
Hayward Gdns PUT/ROE SW15 19 M8
Hayward Rd THDIT KT7 44 C8
Haywards CRAWE RH10 165 M1
Haywood BRAK RG12 34 F7
Hazel Av FARN GU14 92 C7
GU GU1 116 F4
Hazel Bank BRYLDS KT5 45 M8
Hazelbank Cl LIPH GU30 197 J9
Hazelbank Rd CHERT KT16 40 F7
Hazelbury Cl WIM/MER SW19 47 K1
Hazel Cl BTFD TW8 * 17 L2
CRAWE RH10 193 P5
CRAWW RH11 164 E1
CROY/NA CR0 51 G7
EGH TW20 20 E7
MTCM CR4 49 G4
REIG RH2 147 M2
WHTN TW2 25 M1
Hazel Ct COB KT11 80 D3
Hazeldene ADL/WDHM KT15 58 F4
Hazeldene Ct PUR/KEN CR8 88 A5
Hazeldene Rd LIPH GU30 196 C9
Hazel Dr RPLY/SEND GU23 98 C7
Hazel Gv GSHT GU26 197 R4
ORP BR6 71 L1
STA TW18 22 E7
SYD SE26 33 G5
Hazelhurst HORL RH6 160 F2
Hazelhurst Cl RGUE GU4 117 L3
Hazelhurst Crs HORS RH12 166 C8
Hazelhurst Dr CRAWE RH10 192 D7
Hazelhurst Rd TOOT SW17 29 M5
Hazell Hl BRAK RG12 34 F3
Hazell Rd FNM GU9 4 C4
Hazel Md EW KT17 64 D8
Hazelmere Cl
EBED/NFELT TW14 15 G8
LHD/OX KT22 102 E1
Hazel Pde LHD/OX KT22 * 101 M4
Hazel Rd ASHV GU12 135 M2
BF/WBF KT14 78 D4
FRIM GU16 93 K7
REIG RH2 147 M3
Hazel Wy COUL/CHIP CR5 106 C1
CRAWE RH10 193 N5
LHD/OX KT22 101 M4
Hazelway Cl LHD/OX KT22 101 M5
Hazelwick Av CRAWE RH10 165 K3
Hazelwick Mill La
CRAWE RH10 165 K2
Hazelwick Rd CRAWE RH10 165 J3
Hazelwood CRAWW RH11 164 C4
DORK RH4 * 144 E3
Hazelwood Av MRDN SM4 47 L4
Hazelwood Cl CRAWE RH10 193 L5
Hazelwood Ct SURB KT6 45 H6
Hazelwood Gv SAND/SEL CR2 88 E4
Hazelwood Hts OXTED RH8 130 D5
Hazelwood La COUL/CHIP CR5 106 C1
Hazelwood Rd OXTED RH8 130 E6
WOKN/KNAP GU21 76 B8
Hazledean Rd CROY/NA CR0 2 F6
Hazledene Rd CHSWK W4 18 F1
Hazlemere Gdns WPK KT4 46 D8
Hazlewell Rd PUT/ROE SW15 19 M7
Hazlewood MFD/CHID GU8 158 B5
Hazlitt Cl FELT TW13 25 H5
Hazon Wy HOR/WEW KT19 84 A2
Headcorn Rd THHTH CR7 49 J4
Headington Rd
WAND/EARL SW18 29 M2
Headlam Rd CLAP SW4 31 G1
Headland Wy LING RH7 178 D5
Headley Av WLGTN SM6 67 J4
Headley Cl CHSGTN KT9 63 K5
CRAWE RH10 165 M1
Headley Common Rd
EPSOM KT18 124 A1
Headley Dr CROY/NA CR0 69 M6
EPSOM KT18 104 E1
Headley Flds BOR GU35 180 D12
Headley Gv EPSOM KT18 124 A2
KWD/TDW/WH KT20 104 E2
Headley Heath Ap
KWD/TDW/WH KT20 123 L4
Headley Hill Rd BOR GU35 180 F12
Headley La LIPH GU30 196 D3
Headley Pde EPSOM KT18 * 104 A1
Headley Rd BOR GU35 180 B12
EPSOM KT18 83 M8
GSHT GU26 197 L1
LHD/OX KT22 102 F4
LIPH GU30 196 F7
RDKG RH5 122 F3
Headway Cl RCHPK/HAM TW10 26 F5
The Headway EW KT17 64 C7
Hearn V BOR GU35 180 F10
Hearnville Rd BAL SW12 30 D2
Hearn Wk BRAK RG12 35 H1
Heatham Pk WHTN TW2 26 C1
Heathbridge WEY KT13 * 59 K5
Heath Cl BNSTD SM7 85 L4
FNM GU9 133 M2
GSHT GU26 181 P10
HORS RH12 166 B6
HYS/HAR UB3 15 G2
SAND/SEL CR2 67 L5
STWL/WRAY TW19 13 M8
VW GU25 39 G4
Heathcote
KWD/TDW/WH KT20 105 G4
Heathcote Cl ASHV GU12 * 113 K6
Heathcote Dr EGRIN RH19 162 C3
Heathcote Rd ASHV GU12 113 L6
CBLY GU15 73 G4
EPSOM KT18 84 A4
TWK TW1 17 L8
Heathcroft Av SUN TW16 24 C8
Heathdale Av HSLWW TW4 16 B5
Heathdene
KWD/TDW/WH KT20 105 H1
Heathdene Rd
STRHM/NOR SW16 31 J8
WLGTN SM6 66 E6
Heathdown Rd
WOKS/MYFD GU22 78 A5
Heath Dr BELMT SM2 65 M7
CHOB/PIR GU24 95 K2
KWD/TDW/WH KT20 104 E8
RPLY/SEND GU23 97 L5
RYNPK SW20 46 F4
Heathedge SYD SE26 * 32 E3
Heatherbank Cl COB KT11 81 G1
Heather Cl ADL/WDHM KT15 58 E8
ALDT GU11 112 B8
ASHV GU12 113 L4
CRAWE RH10 192 G3
FNM GU9 155 J3
GUW GU2 116 E6
HORS RH12 167 G4
HPTN TW12 43 J1
ISLW TW7 17 G7
KWD/TDW/WH KT20 105 H4
REDH RH1 126 E5
WOKN/KNAP GU21 76 E5
Heatherdale Cl KUTN/CMB KT2 9 K1
Heatherdale Rd CBLY GU15 72 F5
Heatherdeane EHSLY KT24 100 A7
Heatherdene Cl MTCM CR4 48 A4
Heather Dr ASC SL5 37 L7
BOR GU35 180 A12
Heather Gdns BELMT SM2 65 K5
Heatherlands HORL RH6 * 160 F2
SUN TW16 24 D7
Heatherley Cl CBLY GU15 72 E4
Heatherley Rd CBLY GU15 72 E4
Heather Md FRIM GU16 73 J7
Heathermount BRAK RG12 35 H4
Heather Pl ESH/CLAY KT10 61 L3
Heatherset Cl ESH/CLAY KT10 61 M4
Heatherset Gdns
STRHM/NOR SW16 31 J8
Heatherside Cl
GT/LBKH KT23 * 101 J7
Heatherside Dr VW GU25 38 D6
Heatherside Rd
HOR/WEW KT19 64 A6
Heathers Land DORK RH4 144 F5
The Heathers
STWL/WRAY TW19 23 J1
Heathervale Rd
ADL/WDHM KT15 58 E8
Heathervale Wy
ADL/WDHM KT15 58 F8
Heather Wk CHOB/PIR GU24 95 G3
HORL RH6 161 M3
Heather Wy CHOB/PIR GU24 56 B6
Heatherway EGRIN RH19 178 A10
Heather Wy GSHT GU26 198 A1
SAND/SEL CR2 69 G7
Heathfield COB KT11 81 K4
CRAWE RH10 165 M2
Heathfield Av ASC SL5 37 H5
WAND/EARL SW18 30 A1
Heathfield Cl ASHTD KT21 102 F1
GODL GU7 168 A7
HAYES BR2 70 F4
WOKS/MYFD GU22 11 H7
Heathfield Dr MTCM CR4 30 B8
REDH RH1 148 B5
Heathfield Gdns CROY/NA CR0 2 D9
Heathfield North WHTN TW2 26 B1
Heathfield Rd HAYES BR2 70 F4
SAND/SEL CR2 68 A4
WOKS/MYFD GU22 11 H8
WOT/HER KT12 61 H3
Heathfield South WHTN TW2 26 C1
Heathfield Sq
WAND/EARL SW18 30 A1
Heathfield V SAND/SEL CR2 69 G7
Heath Gdns TWK TW1 26 C2
Heath Gv PGE/AN SE20 32 F8
SUN TW16 24 C8
Heath Hl DORK RH4 144 E2
RFNM GU10 180 D6
Heath House Rd
WOKS/MYFD GU22 96 A4
Heathhurst Rd SAND/SEL CR2 68 B7
Heathlands
KWD/TDW/WH KT20 105 G4
Heathlands Cl SUN TW16 42 D2
TWK TW1 26 C3
WOKN/KNAP GU21 77 H4
Heathlands Ct HSLWW TW4 16 B7
Heathland St ALDT GU11 112 D7
Heathlands Wy HSLWW TW4 16 B7
Heath La FNM GU9 133 M2
GODL GU7 168 D7
RFNM GU10 132 D3
SHGR GU5 141 H7
Heath Md WIM/MER SW19 29 G4
Heath Mill La RGUW GU3 95 M7
Heathmoors BRAK RG12 34 F5
Heathpark Dr BFOR GU20 55 H5
Heath Pl BAGS GU19 * 54 B6
Heath Ridge Gn COB KT11 81 K3
Heath Ri CBLY GU15 73 G4
DORK RH4 143 M4
VW GU25 39 G4
Heathrise RPLY/SEND GU23 98 E5
Heath Rd BAGS GU19 54 B6
CTHM CR3 108 A5
HASM GU27 197 Q8
HSLW TW3 16 F6
LHD/OX KT22 81 M2
THHTH CR7 49 M3
TWK TW1 26 C2
WEY KT13 59 K4
WOKN/KNAP GU21 10 E1
Heathrow SHGR GU5 141 M5
Heathrow Cl WDR/YW UB7 13 L3
Heathside ESH/CLAY KT10 62 B2
HSLWW TW4 25 J1
WEY KT13 59 L4
Heathside Cl ESH/CLAY KT10 62 B2
Heathside Ct
KWD/TDW/WH KT20 104 E5
Heathside Crs
WOKS/MYFD GU22 10 E6
Heathside Gdns
WOKS/MYFD GU22 11 G6
Heathside La GSHT GU26 181 Q11
Heathside Pk CBLY GU15 73 M2
Heathside Park Rd
WOKS/MYFD GU22 10 F7
Heathside Pl EPSOM KT18 85 G8
Heathside Rd
WOKS/MYFD GU22 10 E7
The Heath CTHM CR3 107 M6
Heathvale Bridge Rd
ASHV GU12 113 K3
Heath Vw EHSLY KT24 100 D7
Heathview Gdns
PUT/ROE SW15 28 F1
Heathview Rd MFD/CHID GU8 183 M2
THHTH CR7 49 K4
Heathway ASC SL5 36 B1
CBLY GU15 73 G4
CROY/NA CR0 69 J2
CTHM CR3 107 M7
EHSLY KT24 100 C6
Heath Wy HORS RH12 167 G4
Heathway Cl CBLY GU15 73 G4
Heathyfields Rd FNM GU9 133 J3
Heaton Rd MTCM CR4 30 D8
Hebdon Rd TOOT SW17 30 B4
Hectors La EGRIN RH19 163 K6
Heddon Cl ISLW TW7 17 K6
Heddon Wk FARN GU14 92 D2
Hedgecourt Pl EGRIN RH19 193 R1
Hedgehog La HASM GU27 198 C8
Hedgerley Ct
WOKN/KNAP GU21 76 F7
Hedgeside CRAWW RH11 191 M12
Hedgeway GUW GU2 6 A7
Hedingham Cl HORL RH6 160 F2
Hedley Rd WHTN TW2 25 K1
Heenan Cl FRIM GU16 93 H2
Heidegger Crs BARN SW13 19 L2
Heighton Gdns CROY/NA CR0 67 L4
Heights Cl BNSTD SM7 85 H6
RYNPK SW20 28 E8
The Heights BECK BR3 * 33 M8
WEY KT13 * 59 K8
Helder St SAND/SEL CR2 68 A5
Heldmann Cl HSLW TW3 17 G6
Helen Av EBED/NFELT TW14 24 E1
Helen Cl E/WMO/HCT KT8 43 L4
Helen Ct FARN GU14 92 E5
Helford Wk WOKN/KNAP GU21 76 D8
Helgiford Gdns SUN TW16 24 B8
Helios Rd WLGTN SM6 48 D8
Helksham Cl SHST GU47 52 A8
Helm Cl HOR/WEW KT19 83 K2
Helme Cl WIM/MER SW19 29 J6
Helmsdale BRAK RG12 35 H5
WOKN/KNAP GU21 76 E8
Helmsdale Rd
STRHM/NOR SW16 48 F1
Helvellyn Cl EGH TW20 21 L8
Helvetia St CAT SE6 33 J3
Hemingford Rd CHEAM SM3 64 F3
Hemlock Cl
KWD/TDW/WH KT20 105 H5
Hemming Cl HPTN TW12 43 K1
Hempshaw Av BNSTD SM7 86 C6
Hemsby Rd CHSGTN KT9 63 J5
Hemsby Wk CRAWE RH10 165 K6
Henbit Cl KWD/TDW/WH KT20 104 E1
Henchley Dene RGUE GU4 118 A5
Henderson Av GUW GU2 116 E4
Henderson Rd BH/WHM TN16 90 F2
CRAWW RH11 191 L12
CROY/NA CR0 50 A6
WAND/EARL SW18 30 B1
Hendham Rd TOOT SW17 30 B3
Hendon Gv HOR/WEW KT19 63 K7
Hendon Ter ASHF TW15 * 24 A7
Hendon Wy STWL/WRAY TW19 14 A7
Heneage Crs CROY/NA CR0 69 M8
Henfield Rd WIM/MER SW19 47 J1
Henfold Dr RDKG RH5 173 M6
Henfold La RDKG RH5 173 M2
Hengelo Gdns MTCM CR4 48 A4

Hengist Cl HORS RH12 .... 166 D8
Hengrave Rd FSTH SE23 .... 32 F1
Hengrove Crs ASHF TW15 ...... 23 G4
Henhurst Cross La RDKG RH5 .172 H6
Henley Av CHEAM SM3 .... 65 H2
Henley Bank GUW GU2 .... 6 A8
Henley Cl CRAWE RH10 .... 165 M7
    FARN GU14 .... 92 H1
    ISLW TW7 .... 17 J3
Henley Ct WOKS/MYFD GU22 ...97 K2
Henley Dr FRIM GU16 .... 93 J7
    KUTN/CMB KT2 .... 28 C8
Henley Ga CHOB/PIR GU24 ... 114 F1
Henley Pk RGUW GU3 * 115 G3
Henley Wy FELT TW13 .... 25 G6
Hennel Cl FSTH SE23 .... 32 F4
Hennessy Ct WOKN/KNAP GU21 ..77 M3
Henry Doulton Dr TOOT SW17 . 30 D1
Henry Macaulay Av
    KUTN/CMB KT2 .... 8 C7
Henry Peters Dr TEDD TW11 ... 26 A6
Hensford Gdns SYD SE26 .... 32 E5
Henshaw Cl CRAWW RH11 ..... 164 B6
Henslow Wy WOKN/KNAP GU21 ..78 A4
Henson Cl ORP BR6 .... 71 L1
Henson Rd CRAWE RH10 .... 165 K3
Henty Cl CRAWW RH11 .... 164 A1
Henty Wk PUT/ROE SW15 ...... 19 L7
Hepple Cl ISLW TW7 .... 17 L4
Hepplewhite Cl CRAWW RH11 . 191 L12
Hepworth Cft SHST GU47 .... 72 B3
Hepworth Rd
    STRHM/NOR SW16 .... 31 H8
Hepworth Wy WOT/HER KT12 . 42 C8
Herald Gdns WLGTN SM6 .... 66 E2
Herbert Cl BRAK RG12 .... 34 E5
Herbert Crs WOKN/KNAP GU21 .76 B8
Herbert Gdns CHSWK W4 .... 18 L1
Herbert Rd KUT/HW KT1 * 9
    WIM/MER SW19 .... 29 J8
Hereford Cl CRAWE RH10 ...... 165 K3
    EPSOM KT18 .... 84 A1
    GUW GU2 .... 116 C3
    STA TW18 .... 40 E1
Hereford Copse
    WOKS/MYFD GU22 .... 96 E1
Hereford Gdns WHTN TW2 * ... 25 M2
Hereford La FNM GU9 .... 133 L3
Hereford Rd FELT TW13 .... 24 F2
Hereford Wy CHSGTN KT9 ...... 62 F4
Hereward Av PUR/KEN CR8 .... 67 K8
Hereward Rd TOOT SW17 .... 30 D5
Heriot Rd CHERT KT16 .... 40 D7
Heritage Ct EGH TW20 .... 21 J6
Heritage HI HAYES BR2 .... 70 F4
Heritage Lawn HORL RH6 ...... 160 F2
Herlwyn Gdns TOOT SW17 ...... 30 C5
Herm Cl CRAWW RH11 * 164 C4
    ISLW TW7 .... 16 F7
Hermes Wy WLGTN SM6 .... 67 G6
Hermitage Cl ESH/CLAY KT10 .. 62 D5
    FARN GU14 .... 93 C8
    FRIM GU16 .... 73 J8
    RCHPK/HAM TW10 * 18 A7
    SHPTN TW17 .... 41 M7
Hermitage Dr ASC SL5 .... 36 B2
Hermitage Gdns NRWD SE19 ... 31 M8
Hermitage La CROY/NA CR0 ..... 3 K1
    EGRIN RH19 .... 163 G5
    STRHM/NOR SW16 .... 31 J8
Hermitage Pde ASC SL5 * 36 D3
Hermitage Rd EGRIN RH19 ..... 162 E2
    NRWD SE19 .... 31 M8
    PUR/KEN CR8 .... 87 M6
    WOKN/KNAP GU21 .... 96 A2
The Hermitage BARN SW13 * ... 19 J3
    FELT TW13 * 24 C4
    FSTH SE23 .... 32 F2
    KUT/HW KT1 * 45 G4
    RCHPK/HAM TW10 .... 18 B7
Hermitage Woods Crs
    WOKN/KNAP GU21 .... 96 A2
Hermits Rd CRAWE RH10 ...... 165 H2
Hermonger La HORS RH12 .... 187 L11
Hernbrook Dr SWTR RH13 ..... 205 M9
Herndon Cl EGH TW20 .... 21 K5
Herne Rd SURB KT6 .... 63 G1
Heron Cl ASC SL5 .... 36 A1
    CRAWW RH11 .... 164 C2
    FRIM GU16 .... 93 J5
    GUW GU2 .... 116 E5
Heron Ct DORK RH4 * 144 D1
    KUT/HW KT1 * 8 E9
Heron Dl ADL/WDHM KT15 ...... 59 G4
Herondale BRAK RG12 .... 34 F7
    HASM GU27 .... 197 M5
    SAND/SEL CR2 .... 69 G7
Herondale Av
    WAND/EARL SW18 .... 30 A1
Heronfield EGH TW20 .... 20 F7
Heron Pl EGRIN RH19 .... 163 G5
Heron Rd CROY/NA CR0 .... 3 H5
    TWK TW1 .... 17 K6
The Heronry WOT/HER KT12 ... 60 D5
Herons Cl CRAWE RH10 .... 177 M12
Heronscourt LTWR GU18 .... 74 F1
Heronscroft LTWR GU18 .... 74 F1
Herons Cft WEY KT13 .... 59 M5
Heron Shaw CRAN GU6 .... 186 D4
Herons Lea CRAWE RH10 ..... 177 N12
Herons Pl ISLW TW7 .... 17 L5
Herons Wy CHOB/PIR GU24 .... 95 G3
Heronswood Rd HORL RH6 .... 160 E2
Herons Wood Ct HORL RH6 * .. 160 E2
Herontye Dr EGRIN RH19 .... 163 G5
Heron Wy EBED/NFELT TW14 .. 15 K6
    SWTR RH13 .... 167 K7
Heron Wood Rd ASHV GU12 ... 135 G3
Herretts Gdns ASHV GU12 .... 113 G8
Herrett St ASHV GU12 .... 135 G1
Herrick Cl CRAWE RH10 .... 165 L2
    FRIM GU16 .... 73 M6
Herrings La BFOR GU20 .... 55 G4
Herschell Rd FSTH SE23 .... 33 G1
Herschel Wk CRAWW RH11 * . 191 L12
Hersham Centre
    WOT/HER KT12 * 61 G4
Hersham Cl PUT/ROE SW15 .... 28 D1
Hersham Gdns WOT/HER KT12 . 60 E3
Hersham Pl WOT/HER KT12 * ... 61 G4

Hersham Rd WOT/HER KT12 .... 60 E1
Hershell Ct MORT/ESHN SW14 * ..18 E6
Hertford Av MORT/ESHN SW14 ..19 H4
Hertford Wy MTCM CR4 .... 49 H4
Hesiers Hl WARL CR6 .... 90 B7
Hesiers Rd WARL CR6 .... 90 B6
Hesketh Cl CRAN GU6 .... 186 D2
Heslop Rd BAL SW12 .... 30 C2
Hessle Gv EW KT17 .... 84 C1
Hesterman Wy CROY/NA CR0 ... 49 H8
Hester Ter RCH/KEW TW9 ...... 18 D5
Heston Av HEST TW5 .... 16 B2
Heston Grange La HEST TW5 ... 16 C1
Heston Rd HEST TW5 .... 16 D2
    REDH RH1 .... 148 C5
Hetherington Rd SHPTN TW17 . 41 M2
Hethersett Cl REIG RH2 .... 125 M5
Hevers Av HORL RH6 .... 160 C2
Hewers Wy
    KWD/TDW/WH KT20 .... 104 C2
Hewitt Cl CROY/NA CR0 .... 69 K2
Hewlett Pl BAGS GU19 .... 54 B6
Hewshott Gv LIPH GU30 .... 197 K8
Hewshott La LIPH GU30 .... 197 J8
Hexham Cl CRAWE RH10 ...... 192 D7
    SHST GU47 .... 52 A7
Hexham Gdns ISLW TW7 .... 17 K2
Hexham Rd MRDN SM4 .... 47 L8
    WNWD SE27 .... 31 M3
Hextalls La REDH RH1 .... 128 A2
Heybridge Av
    STRHM/NOR SW16 .... 31 J7
Heyford Av RYNPK SW20 .... 47 J3
Heyford Rd MTCM CR4 .... 48 B2
Heymede LHD/OX KT22 .... 102 F5
Heythorpe Cl
    WOKN/KNAP GU21 .... 76 C7
Heythorp St WAND/EARL SW18 . 29 J3
Heywood Dr BAGS GU19 .... 53 M7
Hibernia Gdns HSLW TW3 .... 16 D7
Hibernia Rd HSLW TW3 .... 16 D6
Hickling Wk CRAWE RH10 ..... 165 K6
Hickmans Cl GDST RH9 .... 128 F6
Hidcote Cl WOKS/MYFD GU22 . 11 K4
Hidcote Gdns RYNPK SW20 .... 46 E3
Higgs La BAGS GU19 .... 54 A6
Highacre DORK RH4 .... 144 E5
Highams Hl CRAWW RH11 ..... 164 B5
Highams La CHOB/PIR GU24 ... 55 K5
Highbank Pl
    WAND/EARL SW18 * 29 L2
High Barn Rd EHSLY KT24 ..... 121 G3
Highbarrow Rd CROY/NA CR0 .... 3 K1
High Beech BRAK RG12 .... 35 J4
    SAND/SEL CR2 .... 68 B6
High Beeches BNSTD SM7 .... 85 G4
    FRIM GU16 .... 93 K8
High Beeches Cl PUR/KEN CR8 .. 67 G8
High Broom Crs WWKM BR4 .... 51 L7
Highbury Av THHTH CR7 .... 49 M2
Highbury Cl NWMAL KT3 .... 45 M4
    WWKM BR4 .... 69 L1
Highbury Crs CBLY GU15 .... 73 J2
Highbury Gv HASM GU27 ...... 198 D5
Highbury Rd WIM/MER SW19 ... 29 H6
High Cedar Dr RYNPK SW20 .... 28 E8
Highclere ASC SL5 .... 37 G5
    GU GU1 .... 117 K6
Highclere Cl BRAK RG12 .... 35 H2
    PUR/KEN CR8 .... 87 M5
Highclere Ct WOKN/KNAP GU21 . 75 G2
    DCR CBLY GU15 .... 73 K2
Highclere Gdns
    WOKN/KNAP GU21 .... 75 M7
Highclere Rd ASHV GU12 ...... 135 G1
    NWMAL KT3 .... 46 A3
    WOKN/KNAP GU21 .... 75 M7
Highclere St SYD SE26 .... 33 H5
Highcliffe Dr PUT/ROE SW15 ... 19 J8
High Coombe Pl
    KUTN/CMB KT2 .... 28 A7
Highcotts La RGUE GU4 .... 98 D3
Highcroft MFD/CHID GU8 ..... 183 N1
    SHGR GU5 .... 169 P5
Highcroft Ct GT/LBKH KT23 ... 101 K5
Highcroft Rd CRAWE RH10 .... 187 P1
Highdaun Dr STRHM/NOR SW16 . 49 J4
Highdown WPK KT4 .... 64 B3
Highdown Cl CRAWE RH10 .... 165 K7
    CROY/NA CR0 .... 2 D7
    CTHM CR3 .... 108 B5
    DORK RH4 .... 144 E2
    DTCH/LGLY SL3 * 12 F2
    EDEN TN8 .... 153 M8
    ESH/CLAY KT10 .... 61 L4
    ESH/CLAY KT10 .... 62 C5
    EW KT17 .... 64 C8
    FARN GU14 .... 112 F1
    FELT TW13 .... 24 D3
    GDST RH9 .... 128 F5
    GODL GU7 .... 168 A6
    GT/LBKH KT23 .... 101 L7
    GU GU1 .... 7 H6
    GUW GU2 .... 6 F7
    HASM GU27 .... 198 D6
    HEST TW5 .... 15 L2
    HOR/WEW KT19 .... 84 A3
    HORL RH6 .... 160 E3
    HORS RH12 .... 189 R5
    HPTN TW12 .... 43 L1
    HSLW TW3 .... 16 F4
    HYS/HAR UB3 .... 15 G1
    KUT/HW KT1 * 8 D5
    KWD/TDW/WH KT20 .... 104 F5
    LHD/OX KT22 .... 82 A3
    LHD/OX KT22 .... 102 A4
    LING RH7 .... 178 E5
    NWMAL KT3 .... 46 B4
    ORP BR6 .... 71 M4
    ORP BR6 .... 91 K1
    OXTED RH8 .... 130 A4
    OXTED RH8 .... 130 E2
    PGE/AN SE20 .... 32 F8
    PUR/KEN CR8 .... 87 K1
    REDH RH1 .... 126 D5
    REDH RH1 .... 127 J8
    REDH RH1 .... 128 A7
    REIG RH2 .... 125 A7
    RFNM GU10 .... 155 H6
    RPLY/SEND GU23 .... 98 F3

High Flds ASC SL5 .... 37 J5
Highfields ASHTD KT21 .... 103 C3
    EHSLY KT24 .... 120 C2
    FROW RH18 .... 195 N11
    LHD/OX KT22 .... 102 A3
High Foleys ESH/CLAY KT10 ... 62 E6
High Garth ESH/CLAY KT10 .... 61 M5
Highgate La FARN GU14 .... 92 H4
Highgate Rd FROW RH18 ..... 195 N12
Highgrove FARN GU14 .... 92 D5
Highgrove Av ASC SL5 .... 36 C1
Highgrove Ms CAR SM5 .... 66 B2
Highland Cft BECK BR3 .... 33 L6
Highland Pk FELT TW13 .... 24 C5
Highland Rd ASHV GU12 .... 113 C7
    CBLY GU15 .... 73 H1
    NRWD SE19 .... 32 B7
    PUR/KEN CR8 .... 87 K4
    RDKG RH5 .... 173 K6
Highlands Av LHD/OX KT22 ... 102 F4
    SWTR RH13 .... 167 H7
Highlands Cl FNM GU9 .... 155 L2
    HSLW TW3 .... 16 E3
    LHD/OX KT22 .... 102 A4
Highlands Crs SWTR RH13 .... 167 H7
Highlands La
    WOKS/MYFD GU22 .... 97 H3
Highlands Pk LHD/OX KT22 ... 103 G5
Highlands Rd FNM GU9 .... 133 M2
    LHD/OX KT22 .... 102 F4
    REIG RH2 .... 126 A7
    SWTR RH13 .... 167 J7
The Highlands EHSLY KT24 .... 100 C8
High La CTHM CR3 .... 109 J1
    HASM GU27 .... 198 D5
    WARL CR6 .... 89 J8
High Level Dr SYD SE26 .... 32 D5
High Limes NRWD SE19 .... 32 B7
High Loxley Rd
    MFD/CHID GU8 .... 185 L12
High Md WWKM BR4 .... 70 A1
High Meadow Cl DORK RH4 ... 144 E4
High Meadow Pl CHERT KT16 .. 40 C6
High Oaks CRAWW RH11 ...... 164 D6
The High Pde
    STRHM/NOR SW16 * 31 H4
High Park Av EHSLY KT24 ..... 100 C8
High Park Rd FNM GU9 .... 5 H2
    RCH/KEW TW9 .... 18 D3
High Pth WIM/MER SW19 .... 47 L1
High Path Rd GU GU1 .... 117 M8
High Pewley GU GU1 * 7 J8
High Pine Cl WEY KT13 .... 59 M4
High Pines WARL CR6 .... 108 F1
High Pitfold GSHT GU26 .... 197 Q4
Highpoint WEY KT13 .... 59 K4
High Rdg GODL GU7 .... 168 A7
Highridge Cl EPSOM KT18 ...... 84 B5
High Rd BF/WBF KT14 .... 79 J3
    COUL/CHIP CR5 .... 106 B6
High Standing CTHM CR3 ...... 107 M7
High St ADL/WDHM KT15 .... 58 E3
    ALDT GU11 .... 112 F7
    ASC SL5 .... 36 C3
    ASC SL5 .... 37 G3
    ASC SL5 .... 37 K5
    BAGS GU19 .... 54 B6
    BECK BR3 .... 51 K2
    BH/WHM TN16 .... 131 M1
    BIL RH14 .... 201 Q6
    BNSTD SM7 .... 85 K5
    BOR GU35 .... 180 D12
    BRAK RG12 .... 34 E2
    BTFD TW8 .... 18 A1
    CAR SM5 .... 66 C4
    CBLY GU15 .... 73 G3
    CHEAM SM3 .... 65 H5
    CHOB/PIR GU24 .... 75 H2
    CHOB/PIR GU24 .... 76 B1
    COB KT11 .... 80 E4
    CRAN GU6 .... 186 C2
    CRAWE RH10 .... 164 F5
    CROY/NA CR0 .... 2 D7
    CTHM CR3 .... 108 B5
    DORK RH4 .... 144 E2
    DTCH/LGLY SL3 * 12 F2
    EDEN TN8 .... 153 M8
    E/WMO/HCT KT8 .... 43 K4
    EGH TW20 .... 21 K6
    ESH/CLAY KT10 .... 61 L4
    ESH/CLAY KT10 .... 62 C5
    EW KT17 .... 64 C8
    FARN GU14 .... 112 F1
    FELT TW13 .... 24 D3
    GDST RH9 .... 128 F5
    GODL GU7 .... 168 A6
    GT/LBKH KT23 .... 101 L7
    GU GU1 .... 7 H6
    GUW GU2 .... 6 F7
    HASM GU27 .... 198 D6
    HEST TW5 .... 15 L2
    HOR/WEW KT19 .... 84 A3
    HORL RH6 .... 160 E3
    HORS RH12 .... 189 R5
    HPTN TW12 .... 43 L1
    HSLW TW3 .... 16 F4
    HYS/HAR UB3 .... 15 G1
    KUT/HW KT1 * 8 D5
    KWD/TDW/WH KT20 .... 104 F5
    LHD/OX KT22 .... 82 A3
    LHD/OX KT22 .... 102 A4
    LING RH7 .... 178 E5
    NWMAL KT3 .... 46 B4
    ORP BR6 .... 71 M4
    ORP BR6 .... 91 K1
    OXTED RH8 .... 130 A4
    OXTED RH8 .... 130 E2
    PGE/AN SE20 .... 32 F8
    PUR/KEN CR8 .... 87 K1
    REDH RH1 .... 126 D5
    REDH RH1 .... 127 J8
    REDH RH1 .... 128 A7
    REIG RH2 .... 125 A7
    RFNM GU10 .... 155 H6
    RPLY/SEND GU23 .... 98 F3

SHGR GU5 .... 169 J3
SHPTN TW17 .... 41 M6
SNWD SE25 .... 50 C4
STA TW18 .... 22 C5
STWL/WRAY TW19 .... 12 B8
STWL/WRAY TW19 .... 14 A8
SUT SM1 .... 65 L3
TEDD TW11 .... 26 D6
THDIT KT7 .... 44 D7
THHTH CR7 .... 49 M4
WDR/YW UB7 .... 14 A1
WEY KT13 .... 59 K3
WHTN TW2 .... 25 M1
WIM/MER SW19 .... 29 G6
WOKN/KNAP GU21 .... 10 E6
WOKN/KNAP GU21 .... 75 M8
WOKN/KNAP GU21 .... 76 F6
WOKS/MYFD GU22 .... 97 K3
WOT/HER KT12 .... 42 B5
WWKM BR4 .... 51 L8
High Street Collier's Wd
    WIM/MER SW19 .... 30 A8
High Street Gn MFD/CHID GU8 . 184 B12
High Street Harlington
    HYS/HAR UB3 .... 15 G2
High Street Ms WIM/MER SW19 . 29 H6
High Thicket Rd RFNM GU10 .. 180 C5
High Tree Cl ADL/WDHM KT15 . 58 D4
High Trees BRXS/STRHM SW2 . 31 K2
    CROY/NA CR0 .... 51 H8
High Trees Cl CTHM CR3 ...... 108 C4
High Trees Rd REIG RH2 .... 148 A1
High Vw BELMT SM2 .... 85 J1
    SHGR GU5 .... 141 M5
Highview COUL/CHIP CR5 .... 86 D6
Highwood Cl FSTH SE23 .... 32 D2
    ORP BR6 .... 71 M1
    PUR/KEN CR8 .... 87 M7
Highwood Dr ORP BR6 .... 71 M1
Highwoods CTHM CR3 .... 108 B7
    LHD/OX KT22 .... 102 F3
Highworth SWTR RH13 * 167 J8
Hilary Av MTCM CR4 .... 48 D3
Hilbert Rd CHEAM SM3 .... 65 G3
Hilborough Cl WIM/MER SW19 . 29 M8
Hilda Vale Rd ORP BR6 .... 71 K3
Hidenley Cl REDH RH1 .... 127 G2
The Hildens DORK RH4 .... 143 M4
Hilder Gdns FARN GU14 .... 93 G6
Hilders Cl EDEN TN8 .... 153 L5
Hilders La EDEN TN8 .... 153 J5
The Hilders ASHTD KT21 .... 83 L7
Hildreth St BAL SW12 .... 30 E2
Hilgay GU GU1 .... 7 L4
Hilgay Cl GU GU1 .... 7 L4
Hilland Ri BOR GU35 .... 196 E1
Hillars Heath Rd
    COUL/CHIP CR5 .... 87 H5
Hillary Cl EGRIN RH19 .... 163 H3
    FNM GU9 .... 5 H9
Hillary Crs WOT/HER KT12 ..... 42 F8
Hillary Dr ISLW TW7 .... 17 J6
Hillary Rd FNM GU9 .... 5 G9
Hillbarn SAND/SEL CR2 .... 88 B3
Hillberry BRAK RG12 .... 34 F7
Hillborough Cl
    WIM/MER SW19 * 29 M8
Hillbrook Gdns WEY KT13 ...... 59 K6
Hillbrook Ri FNM GU9 .... 133 K3
Hillbrook Rd TOOT SW17 .... 30 C4
Hillbrow NWMAL KT3 .... 46 C3
Hillbrow Cl RGUW GU3 .... 115 L4
Hillbrow Ct OXTED RH8 .... 130 F3
Hillbrow Rd ESH/CLAY KT10 ... 61 M3
Hillbury Cl WARL CR6 .... 88 F4
Hillbury Gdns WARL CR6 .... 88 F8
Hillbury Rd TOOT SW17 .... 30 E4
    WARL CR6 .... 88 D7
Hill Cl COB KT11 .... 81 H1
    PUR/KEN CR8 .... 87 M2
    SHGR GU5 .... 169 J5
    WOKN/KNAP GU21 .... 10 A2
Hill Copse Vw BRAK RG12 ...... 35 H1
Hillcote Av STRHM/NOR SW16 . 31 K8
Hill Ct FARN GU14 .... 72 C8
Hill Crs BRYLDS KT5 .... 45 J5
    WPK KT4 .... 64 F1
Hill Crest EGRIN RH19 .... 178 F11
    MFD/CHID GU8 .... 183 A6
    SURB KT6 * 45 H7
Hillcrest FNM GU9 * 134 V1
    KWD/TDW/WH KT20 .... 123 L5
    WEY KT13 .... 59 L3
Hillcrest Av CRAWE RH10 ..... 165 M4
    EPSOM KT18 .... 84 D5
    SYD SE26 .... 32 D5
Hillcrest Cl BECK BR3 .... 51 J8
    CRAWE RH10 .... 165 M4
    EPSOM KT18 .... 84 C4
    SYD SE26 .... 32 D5
Hillcrest Dr RFNM GU10 .... 155 L6
Hillcrest Gdns ESH/CLAY KT10 . 62 C3
Hillcrest Rd BH/WHM TN16 .... 91 G6
    CBLY GU15 .... 73 L2
    CTHM CR3 .... 88 C7
    EDEN TN8 .... 153 L6
    GUW GU2 .... 116 C7
    PUR/KEN CR8 .... 87 J2
    SUT SM1 .... 65 L4
Hillcroft Av PUR/KEN CR8 ...... 87 K3
Hillcroft Rd BELMT SM2 .... 66 D8
Hillcross Av MRDN SM4 .... 47 H6
Hilldale Rd SUT SM1 .... 65 J3
Hilldeane Rd PUR/KEN CR8 .... 67 K8
Hilldown Rd STRHM/NOR SW16 . 31 H8
Hillersdon BARN SW13 .... 19 K4
Hilley Field La LHD/OX KT22 .. 101 M4

Hill Farm Cl HASM GU27 * 198 A8
Hillfield Av MRDN SM4 .... 48 B6
Hillfield Cl GU GU1 .... 117 M6
Hill Field Rd HPTN TW12 .... 25 J8
Hillfield Pde MRDN SM4 * 48 A6
Hillfield Rd REDH RH1 .... 126 D8
Hillford Pl REDH RH1 .... 148 D6
Hillgarth GSHT GU26 .... 181 Q12
Hill Hse Cl WEY KT13 .... 25 J3
Hill House Cl CRAWE RH10 ... 193 N6
Hill House Dr HPTN TW12 .... 43 K1
    REIG RH2 .... 147 L2
    WEY KT13 .... 79 K1
Hillhouse La HORS RH12 ...... 186 D12
Hill House Rd
    STRHM/NOR SW16 .... 31 J6
Hillhurst Gdns CTHM CR3 .... 108 B2
Hillier Gdns CROY/NA CR0 ..... 67 K4
Hillier Pl CHSGTN KT9 .... 63 G5
Hillier Rd GU GU1 .... 117 K8
Hillier's La CROY/NA CR0 .... 67 H2
Hillingdale BH/WHM TN16 ...... 90 E8
    CRAWW RH11 .... 191 M12
Hillingdon Av
    STWL/WRAY TW19 .... 23 H2
Hill La KWD/TDW/WH KT20 ... 105 H3
Hillmead CRAWW RH11 .... 164 B4
Hill Md HORS RH12 .... 166 D6
Hillmont Rd ESH/CLAY KT10 ... 62 B2
Hillmore Gv SYD SE26 .... 33 G6
Hillmount WOKS/MYFD GU22 .. 10 E8
Hill Pk LHD/OX KT22 .... 102 C1
Hill Park Ct LHD/OX KT22 * ... 102 C1
Hill Pl CRAWW RH11 .... 164 E5
Hill Ri DORK RH4 .... 122 D8
    ESH/CLAY KT10 .... 62 E1
    RCHPK/HAM TW10 .... 18 A7
Hillrise DTCH/LGLY SL3 .... 12 D1
Hill Rd CAR SM5 .... 66 B5
    GSHT GU26 .... 197 R7
    HASM GU27 .... 198 D2
    LHD/OX KT22 .... 101 L4
    MTCM CR4 .... 48 E1
    PUR/KEN CR8 .... 87 J2
    SUT SM1 .... 65 L4
Hillsborough Ct FARN GU14 ... 92 B1
Hillsborough Pk CBLY GU15 .... 73 M4
Hill School Rd RFNM GU10 ... 155 J2
Hills Farm La HORS RH12 .... 166 D8
Hillside ASC SL5 .... 36 F5
    BNSTD SM7 .... 85 H5
    CBLY GU15 .... 72 C2
    CRAWE RH10 .... 193 N5
    ESH/CLAY KT10 .... 61 L4
    HORS RH12 .... 166 D7
    VW GU25 .... 38 F6
    WIM/MER SW19 .... 29 G7
    WOKS/MYFD GU22 .... 97 G2
Hillside Av PUR/KEN CR8 .... 87 L3
Hillside Cl BNSTD SM7 .... 85 H6
    BOR GU35 .... 180 F11
    BRKHM/BTCW RH3 .... 145 K1
    CRAWW RH11 .... 164 D6
    EGRIN RH19 .... 162 F2
    MRDN SM4 .... 47 H4
    WOKN/KNAP GU21 .... 76 A7
Hillside Crs FRIM GU16 .... 93 J2
Hillside Gdns ADL/WDHM KT15 . 58 C4
    BRKHM/BTCW RH3 .... 123 K8
    BRXS/STRHM SW2 * 31 K3
    WLGTN SM6 .... 66 F6
Hillside La FNM GU9 .... 134 A2
    HAYES BR2 .... 70 D1
Hillside Pk ASC SL5 .... 37 J8
Hillside Rd ASHTD KT21 .... 113 L6
    ASHV GU12 .... 113 J6
    BELMT SM2 .... 65 J6
    BH/WHM TN16 .... 111 H1
    BRXS/STRHM SW2 * 31 J3
    COUL/CHIP CR5 .... 87 H8
    CROY/NA CR0 .... 88 D8
    CTHM CR3 .... 88 F8
    EW KT17 .... 64 F8
    FNM GU9 .... 134 B2
    HASM GU27 .... 198 A8
    RFNM GU10 .... 155 L6
Hillside Wy GODL GU7 .... 168 A2
Hillsmead Wy SAND/SEL CR2 .. 88 D4
Hills Pl HORS RH12 .... 166 D7
Hillspur Cl GUW GU2 .... 116 C7
Hillspur Rd GUW GU2 .... 116 C7
Hill St RCH/KEW TW9 .... 18 A7
Hillswood Dr CHERT KT16 ...... 57 M3
The Hill CTHM CR3 .... 108 C6
Hill Top CHEAM SM3 .... 47 J7
Hilltop Cl ASC SL5 .... 37 H2
    LHD/OX KT22 .... 102 F5
    RGUW GU3 .... 116 C4
Hilltop Rd FNM GU9 .... 107 K8
Hilltop Ri GT/LBKH KT23 ...... 101 M8
Hilltop Rd CTHM CR3 .... 88 B7
    REIG RH2 .... 147 L2
Hilltop Wk CTHM CR3 .... 109 H2
Hill Vw CHOB/PIR GU24 * 55 M3
Hillview CTHM CR3 .... 88 C7
    RYNPK SW20 .... 28 E8
    RYNPK SW20 * 46 E1
Hill View Cl
    KWD/TDW/WH KT20 .... 104 F5
    PUR/KEN CR8 .... 87 L1
Hillview Ct WOKS/MYFD GU22 . 10 C6
Hill View Crs GUW GU2 .... 116 C6
Hillview Dr REDH RH1 .... 148 D1
Hill View Rd ESH/CLAY KT10 ... 62 D6
    FNM GU9 .... 4 D3
    STWL/WRAY TW19 .... 12 F8
Hillview Rd SUT SM1 .... 65 M2
    TWK TW1 .... 17 H8
    WOKS/MYFD GU22 .... 10 E8
Hillworth BECK BR3 * 51 L2
Hillworth Rd BRXS/STRHM SW2 . 31 K1
Hillybarn Rd CRAWW RH11 .... 190 F6
Hilton Wy SAND/SEL CR2 .... 88 E5
Himley Rd TOOT SW17 .... 30 B6
Hinaidi Wy FARN GU14 .... 112 C1
Hinchley Cl ESH/CLAY KT10 .... 62 C2
Hinchley Dr ESH/CLAY KT10 ... 62 C2

Hinchley Wy ESH/CLAY KT10 62 D2
Hindell Cl FARN GU14 92 D1
Hindhead Cl CRAWW RH11 164 E6
Hindhead Rd HASM GU27 197 R5
Hindhead Wy WLGTN SM6 67 H4
Hindsley's Pl FSTH SE23 32 F3
Hine Cl COUL/CHIP CR5 106 F4
Hinstock Cl FARN GU14 92 D6
Hinton Av HSLWW TW4 16 A6
Hinton Rd WLGTN SM6 66 F5
Hipley St WOKS/MYFD GU22 97 L2
Hitchcock Cl SHPTN TW17 41 J3
Hitchings Wy REIG RH2 147 K4
Hitherbury Cl GUW GU2 138 F3
Hitherfield Rd
STRHM/NOR SW16 31 J3
Hitherhooks Hl BNFD RG42 34 B1
Hithermoor Rd
STWL/WRAY TW19 13 K8
Hitherwood CRAN GU6 186 D3
Hitherwood Cl REIG RH2 126 A6
Hitherwood Dr NRWD SE19 32 C5
H Jones Crs ALDT GU11 112 F6
Hoadly Rd STRHM/NOR SW16 31 G4
Hobart Gdns THHTH CR7 50 A3
Hobart Pl RCHPK/HAM TW10 27 J1
Hobart Rd WPK KT4 64 E2
Hobbes Wk PUT/ROE SW15 19 L7
Hobbs Cl BF/WBF KT14 78 E3
Hobbs Rd CRAWW RH11 191 K12
WNWD SE27 31 M5
Hocken Md CRAWE RH10 165 M2
Hockering Gdns
WOKS/MYFD GU22 11 J7
Hockering Rd
WOKS/MYFD GU22 11 H7
Hockford Cl CHOB/PIR GU24 95 L8
Hodges Cl BAGS GU19 54 A8
Hodgkin Cl CRAWE RH10 165 K5
Hodgson Gdns RGUE GU4 117 K5
Hoebrook Cl WOKS/MYFD GU22 97 H3
Hoe La MFD/CHID GU8 184 G1
SHGR GU5 171 K2
Hoffmann Gdns SAND/SEL CR2 68 D5
Hogarth Av ASHF TW15 23 M7
Hogarth Cl SHST GU47 72 B3
Hogarth Crs CROY/NA CR0 2 D2
WIM/MER SW19 48 A1
Hogarth Gdns HEST TW5 16 D2
Hogarth Rd CRAWE RH10 165 H7
Hogarth Ter CHSWK W4 * 19 H1
Hogarth Wy HPTN TW12 43 M1
Hogden La EHSLY KT24 121 H5
Hogden Rd RDKG RH5 121 H8
Hoghatch La FNM GU9 133 K3
Hogscross La COUL/CHIP CR5 106 C4
Hogshill La COB KT11 80 F4
Hogsmill Wy HOR/WEW KT19 63 M4
Hogspudding La RDKG RH5 173 R7
Hogtrough La OXTED RH8 129 L2
REDH RH1 149 G1
Hogwood Rd BIL RH14 201 M6
Holbeach Rd CAT SE6 33 K1
Holbeck BRAK RG12 34 C6
Holbein Rd CRAWE RH10 165 H7
Holborn Wy MTCM CR4 48 C2
Holbreck Pl WOKS/MYFD GU22 10 E7
Holbrook Cl FNM GU9 134 C1
Holbrook Meadow EGH TW20 21 M7
Holbrook School La
HORS RH12 167 G2
Holbrook Wy ALDT GU11 134 E2
Holcon Ct REDH RH1 126 D5
Holderness Rd ISLW TW7 17 K3
TOOT SW17 30 C4
Holderness Wy WNWD SE27 31 L6
Holder Rd ASHV GU12 113 H8
CRAWE RH10 165 K7
Holdfast La HASM GU27 198 G5
Hole Hl DORK RH4 143 L2
Hole La EDEN TN8 153 K3
Holford Rd GU GU1 117 M8
Holland Av BELMT SM2 65 K6
RYNPK SW20 46 C1
Holland Cl FNM GU9 134 B8
HAYES BR2 70 C1
REDH RH1 126 C8
Holland Crs OXTED RH8 130 D7
Holland Dr FSTH SE23 33 H4
Holland Gdns EGH TW20 40 C2
Holland La OXTED RH8 130 D7
Holland Pines BRAK RG12 34 C7
Holland Rd OXTED RH8 130 D7
SNWD SE25 50 D5
Hollands Fld HORS RH12 166 B5
The Hollands
WOKS/MYFD GU22 10 D8
WPK KT4 46 C8
Hollands Wy EGRIN RH19 163 H1
HORS RH12 166 C1
Holland Wy HAYES BR2 70 C1
Holles Cl HPTN TW12 25 K7
Hollies Av BF/WBF KT14 78 C3
Hollies Cl STRHM/NOR SW16 31 K7
TWK TW1 26 C3
Hollies Ct ADL/WDHM KT15 58 F4
The Hollies ADL/WDHM KT15 * 58 F4
BLKW GU17 * 72 C8
OXTED RH8 130 E7
WOKN/KNAP GU21 * 76 A7
Hollies Wy BAL SW12 * 30 D1
Hollin Ct CRAWE RH10 165 G1
Hollingsworth Rd
CROY/NA CR0 68 E5
Hollington Crs NWMAL KT3 46 C6
Hollingworth Cl
E/WMO/HCT KT8 43 J4
Hollis Rw REDH RH1 * 148 C2
Hollis Wood Dr RFNM GU10 155 H4
Hollman Gdns
STRHM/NOR SW16 31 L7
Holloway Dr VW GU25 39 H4
Holloway Hl CHERT KT16 57 M2
GODL GU7 168 A5
Holloway St HSLW TW3 16 E5
Hollow Cl GUW GU2 6 C5
Hollow La BOR GU35 180 D11
LING RH7 179 J9
RDKG RH5 143 G7
VW GU25 38 F3
The Hollow CRAWW RH11 164 B5
GODL GU7 159 J5
Holly Av ADL/WDHM KT15 58 D8
FRIM GU16 73 L6
WOT/HER KT12 43 G8
Hollybank CHOB/PIR GU24 75 J3
Hollybank Cl HPTN TW12 25 K6
Hollybank Rd BF/WBF KT14 78 D4
Holly Bank Rd
WOKS/MYFD GU22 96 E2
Hollybush Cl CRAWE RH10 165 G3
Hollybush La ALDT GU11 113 H3
Holly Bush La HPTN TW12 25 J8
Hollybush Rd CRAWE RH10 165 G3
KUTN/CMB KT2 27 H6
Hollybush Ter NRWD SE19 * 32 B7
Hollybush Tr BFOR GU20 54 C3
Holly Cl ASHV GU12 112 F7
BECK BR3 51 M4
BOR GU35 180 H12
CHERT KT16 56 D2
CRAWE RH10 165 J2
ECH TW20 20 E7
FARN GU14 92 D5
FELT TW13 25 H6
HORS RH12 167 L4
WOKN/KNAP GU21 96 E1
Hollycombe EGH TW20 20 F5
Hollycombe Cl LIPH GU30 196 H11
Holly Crs BECK BR3 51 J5
Hollycroft Cl SAND/SEL CR2 68 B4
WDR/YW UB7 14 D1
Hollycroft Gdns WDR/YW UB7 14 D1
Hollydale Dr HAYES BR2 71 J2
Hollyfield Rd BRYLDS KT5 45 J7
Hollyfields Cl CBLY GU15 72 E4
Holly Gn WEY KT13 60 A3
Hollygrove Cl HSLW TW3 16 C6
Holly Hedge Cl FRIM GU16 73 H7
Holly Hedge Rd COB KT11 80 E4
FRIM GU16 73 H7
Holly Hill Dr BNSTD SM7 85 K7
Holly Hock CHOB/PIR GU24 75 K5
Holly Hough
KWD/TDW/WH KT20 123 L4
Holly La BNSTD SM7 86 A8
GODL GU7 159 M5
RGUW GU3 116 A3
Holly La East BNSTD SM7 85 L6
Holly La West BNSTD SM7 85 L7
Holly Lea RGUE GU4 117 G2
Hollymead CAR SM5 66 C2
Hollymead Rd COUL/CHIP CR5 86 D8
Hollymoor La HOR/WEW KT19 64 A8
Holly Pde COB KT11 80 E5
Hollyridge HASM GU27 198 D7
Holly Rd ASHV GU12 112 F8
FARN GU14 92 C5
HPTN TW12 25 M7
HSLW TW3 16 E6
REIG RH2 147 L2
TWK TW1 26 D2
Holly Spring La BRAK RG12 35 G1
Hollytree Cl WIM/MER SW19 29 G2
Hollytree Gdns FRIM GU16 93 G1
Holly Tree Rd CTHM CR3 108 B4
Hollywater Rd LIPH GU30 196 A5
Holly Wy BLKW GU17 72 A5
MTCM CR4 49 G4
Hollywoods CROY/NA CR0 69 J8
Holman Ct EW KT17 * 64 D7
Holman Rd HOR/WEW KT19 63 M4
Holmbank Dr SHPTN TW17 42 B4
Holmbury Cl CRAWW RH11 164 E6
Holmbury Ct WIM/MER SW19 30 B8
Holmbury Dr RDKG RH5 144 F5
Holmbury Gv CROY/NA CR0 69 J6
Holmbury Hill Rd RDKG RH5 171 N5
Holmbury Rd CRAN GU6 171 M11
RDKG RH5 171 R8
Holmbush Ct HORS RH12 * 190 E12
Holm Cl ADL/WDHM KT15 78 B2
Holmcroft CRAWE RH10 165 G5
KWD/TDW/WH KT20 104 E7
Holmdene Cl BECK BR3 51 M2
Holmes Cl ASC SL5 36 F6
PUR/KEN CR8 87 J3
WOKS/MYFD GU22 97 J3
Holmesdale Av
MORT/ESHN SW14 18 E5
Holmesdale Cl GU GU1 117 L7
SNWD SE25 50 C3
Holmesdale Pk REDH RH1 * 127 J8
Holmesdale Rd CROY/NA CR0 50 A5
RCH/KEW TW9 18 C3
RDKG RH5 144 E6
REDH RH1 149 J2
REIG RH2 125 L7
TEDD TW11 8 A2
Holmesdale Ter RDKG RH5 * 144 E6
Holmes Rd TWK TW1 26 C3
WIM/MER SW19 29 M8
Holmethorpe Av REDH RH1 126 E5
Holmewood Gdns
BRXS/STRHM SW2 31 J1
Holmewood Rd
BRXS/STRHM SW2 31 H1
SNWD SE25 50 B3
Holming End HORS RH12 167 L4
Holmlea Rd DTCH/LGLY SL3 12 A3
Holmshaw Cl SYD SE26 33 H5
Holmsley Cl NWMAL KT3 46 C6
Holmwood Av SAND/SEL CR2 88 C3
Holmwood Cl ADL/WDHM KT15 58 D4
BELMT SM2 65 G7
EHSLY KT24 120 B2
Holmwood Gdns WLGTN SM6 66 E5
Holmwood Rd BELMT SM2 64 F7
CHSGTN KT9 63 H4
Holmwood View Rd
RDKG RH5 144 E8
Holne Cha MRDN SM4 47 K6
Holroyd Rd ESH/CLAY KT10 62 D7
PUT/ROE SW15 19 M6
Holsart Cl KWD/TDW/WH KT20 104 E4
Holstein Av WEY KT13 59 K3
Holsworthy Wy CHSGTN KT9 62 F4
Holt Cl FARN GU14 92 F2
Holton Heath BRAK RG12 35 J4
Holt Pound La RFNM GU10 154 F4
The Holt MRDN SM4 * 47 K4
WLGTN SM6 66 F3
Holtwood Rd LHD/OX KT22 81 M3
Holtye Av EGRIN RH19 163 G2
Holtye Pl EGRIN RH19 163 H2
Holtye Rd EGRIN RH19 163 G3
EGRIN RH19 163 M2
Holtye Wk CRAWE RH10 * 165 J6
Holwood Cl WOT/HER KT12 60 F1
Holwood Park Av ORP BR6 71 J3
Holybourne Av PUT/ROE SW15 28 D1
Holyoake Av WOKN/KNAP GU21 76 F7
Holyoake Crs
WOKN/KNAP GU21 76 F7
Holyport Rd FUL/PGN SW6 19 M2
Holyrood Pl CRAWW RH11 164 D8
Holywell Cl FARN GU14 92 D2
STWL/WRAY TW19 23 H2
Holywell Wy STWL/WRAY TW19 23 H2
Hombrook Dr BNFD RG42 34 B1
Home Cl CAR SM5 66 C1
CRAWE RH10 165 L2
LHD/OX KT22 102 A3
VW GU25 39 G6
Home Ct FELT TW13 * 24 D2
SURB KT6 * 45 G5
Homecroft Rd SYD SE26 32 F6
Home Farm Cl
BRKHM/BTCW RH3 146 B1
CHERT KT16 57 K6
EPSOM KT18 85 G7
ESH/CLAY KT10 61 L5
FARN GU14 93 G3
SHPTN TW17 42 B4
THDIT KT7 44 C7
Home Farm Gdns
WOT/HER KT12 60 F1
Home Farm Rd GODL GU7 168 C7
Homefield MFD/CHID GU8 * 182 D6
Homefield Cl ADL/WDHM KT15 78 B2
HORL RH6 160 E2
LHD/OX KT22 102 F3
Homefield Gdns
KWD/TDW/WH KT20 104 F2
WIM/MER SW19 47 M2
Homefield Ms BECK BR3 * 51 K1
Homefield Pk SUT SM1 65 L5
Homefield Rd COUL/CHIP CR5 107 L2
WARL CR6 108 F1
WIM/MER SW19 29 H7
WOT/HER KT12 43 J7
The Homefield MRDN SM4 * 47 K4
Homeland Dr BELMT SM2 65 L7
Homelands LHD/OX KT22 102 F3
Homelands Dr NRWD SE19 32 B8
Homelea Cl FARN GU14 92 E1
Homeleigh Crs ASHV GU12 113 K1
Home Meadow BNSTD SM7 85 K6
Homemead Rd CROY/NA CR0 48 F6
Home Pk OXTED RH8 130 D5
Home Park Cl SHGR GU5 169 J3
Home Park Ct KUT/HW KT1 * 45 G4
Home Park Rd WIM/MER SW19 29 J5
Home Park Ter KUT/HW KT1 8 C6
Home Park Wk KUT/HW KT1 45 G4
Homer Rd CROY/NA CR0 51 G6
Homersham Rd KUT/HW KT1 9 K6
Homesdale Rd CTHM CR3 108 A5
Homestall GUW GU2 116 A8
Homestall Rd EGRIN RH19 163 M5
Homestead CRAN GU6 186 E1
Homestead Gdns
ESH/CLAY KT10 62 B4
Homestead Rd CTHM CR3 108 A5
EDEN TN8 153 L4
STA TW18 22 E7
Homestead Wy CROY/NA CR0 89 M1
Homewaters Av SUN TW16 42 D1
Homewood CRAN GU6 186 F2
Homewood Cl HPTN TW12 25 J7
Homewood Gdns SNWD SE25 * 50 B5
Honeybrook Rd BAL SW12 30 F1
Honeycrock La REDH RH1 148 D7
Honeyhill Rd BNFD RG42 34 D1
Honeypot La EDEN TN8 153 G5
Honeypots Rd
WOKS/MYFD GU22 97 G4
Honeysuckle Bottom
EHSLY KT24 120 B8
Honeysuckle Cl HORL RH6 160 F2
Honeysuckle Gdns
CROY/NA CR0 51 G7
Honeysuckle La BOR GU35 180 G12
CRAWW RH11 164 E1
Honeysuckle Wk HORS RH12 167 K4
Honeywood La RDKG RH5 187 R8
Honeywood Rd ISLW TW7 * 17 K6
SWTR RH13 167 K5
Honeywood Wk CAR SM5 66 C3
Honister Hts PUR/KEN CR8 88 A4
Honley Rd CAT SE6 33 L1
Honnor Gdns ISLW TW7 17 G4
Honnor Rd STA TW18 23 G8
Honor Oak Pk FSTH SE23 32 F1
Honor Oak Rd FSTH SE23 32 F2
Hood Av MORT/ESHN SW14 18 F7
Hood Cl CROY/NA CR0 2 B4
Hood Rd RYNPK SW20 28 C8
Hooke Rd EHSLY KT24 100 C7
Hookfield HOR/WEW KT19 83 M3
Hook Heath Av
WOKS/MYFD GU22 96 E1
Hook Heath Gdns
WOKS/MYFD GU22 96 C3
Hook Heath Rd
WOKS/MYFD GU22 96 C3
Hook Hl SAND/SEL CR2 68 B8
Hook Hill La WOKS/MYFD GU22 96 E3
Hook Hill Pk WOKS/MYFD GU22 96 E3
Hookhouse Rd
MFD/CHID GU8 184 H7
Hook La CHOB/PIR GU24 74 F3
RGUW GU3 137 G7
SHGR GU5 141 L7
Hookley Cl MFD/CHID GU8 158 B6
Hookley La MFD/CHID GU8 158 B6
Hook Mill La LTWR GU18 55 G7
Hook Ri North SURB KT6 63 K2
Hook Ri South CHSGTN KT9 63 J2
Hook Rd CHSGTN KT9 63 G4
HOR/WEW KT19 63 M6
Hookstile La FNM GU9 5 J6
Hookstone La CHOB/PIR GU24 75 J1
Hook Underpass (Kingston By-Pass)
CHSGTN KT9 63 G2
Hookwood Cnr OXTED RH8 130 E2
Hooley La REDH RH1 148 C1
Hope Av BRAK RG12 35 H7
Hope Cl SUT SM1 65 M4
Hope Ct CRAWW RH11 * 191 L12
Hope Fountain CBLY GU15 73 J5
Hope Grant's Rd ALDT GU11 112 D5
Hope La FNM GU9 133 L3
Hopeman Cl SHST GU47 72 A2
Hopes Cl HEST TW5 16 D1
Hope St MFD/CHID GU8 158 A5
Hope Wy ALDT GU11 112 C7
Hopfield WOKN/KNAP GU21 10 C3
Hopfield Av BF/WBF KT14 79 H2
Hophurst Cl CRAWE RH10 193 N5
Hophurst Dr CRAWE RH10 193 N5
Hophurst Hl CRAWE RH10 193 Q3
Hophurst La CRAWE RH10 193 N4
Hopkin Cl GUW GU2 116 E4
Hopkins Ct CRAWW RH11 * 191 L12
Hopper V BRAK RG12 34 D6
The Hoppety
KWD/TDW/WH KT20 105 G4
Hoppingwood Av NWMAL KT3 46 B3
Hopton Gdns NWMAL KT3 46 D6
Hopton Pde
STRHM/NOR SW16 * 31 H6
Hopton Rd STRHM/NOR SW16 31 H6
Hopwood Cl TOOT SW17 29 M4
Horace Rd KUT/HW KT1 9 G9
Horatio Av BNFD RG42 35 H1
Horatius Wy CROY/NA CR0 67 J5
Horewood Rd BRAK RG12 34 E6
Horley Lodge La REDH RH1 175 Q1
Horley Rd HORL RH6 175 K10
REDH RH1 148 C3
Horley Rw HORL RH6 160 C2
Hormer Cl SHST GU47 52 A8
Hornbeam Cl SHST GU47 52 A8
SWTR RH13 167 J8
Hornbeam Crs BTFD TW8 17 L2
Hornbeam Gdns NWMAL KT3 46 D6
Hornbeam Rd GU GU1 116 F5
REIG RH2 147 M3
Hornbrook Copse SWTR RH13 205 N9
Hornby Av BRAK RG12 35 G7
Hornchurch Cl KUTN/CMB KT2 27 G6
Hornchurch Hl CTHM CR3 88 C7
Horndean Cl CRAWE RH10 192 C3
PUT/ROE SW15 28 D2
Horndean Rd BRAK RG12 35 J6
Hornecourt Hl HORL RH6 177 L2
Horner La MTCM CR4 48 A2
Horne Rd SHPTN TW17 41 J4
Horne Wy PUT/ROE SW15 19 M4
Hornhatch RGUE GU4 139 L7
Hornhatch Cl RGUE GU4 139 L6
Hornhatch La RGUE GU4 139 K6
Horniman Dr FSTH SE23 32 E2
Horniman Gdns FSTH SE23 * 32 E2
Horn Rd FARN GU14 92 B4
Hornshill La HORS RH12 202 E2
Horsebrass Dr BAGS GU19 54 B7
Horsecroft BNSTD SM7 85 J7
Horsecroft Mdw BNSTD SM7 * 85 K6
Horse Fair KUT/HW KT1 8 C6
Horse Gate Ride ASC SL5 36 D6
Horse Hl HORL RH6 175 L5
Horsell Birch WOKN/KNAP GU21 76 E5
Horsell Common Rd
WOKN/KNAP GU21 76 F4
Horsell Ct CHERT KT16 40 E7
Horsell Moor WOKN/KNAP GU21 10 A6
Horsell Pk WOKN/KNAP GU21 10 C5
Horsell Park Cl
WOKN/KNAP GU21 10 B5
Horsell Ri WOKN/KNAP GU21 10 B1
Horsell Rise Cl
WOKN/KNAP GU21 10 B1
Horsell V WOKN/KNAP GU21 10 C3
Horsell Wy WOKN/KNAP GU21 76 F6
Horseshoe Bend GSHT GU26 197 M2
Horseshoe Cl CBLY GU15 73 J1
CRAWE RH10 165 M3
CRAWE RH10 * 192 D6
Horseshoe Crs CBLY GU15 73 J1
Horseshoe La ASHV GU12 113 K3
CRAN GU6 186 B1
Horseshoe La West GU GU1 117 L7
Horseshoe Rdg WEY KT13 79 M1
The Horseshoe BNSTD SM7 85 J5
COUL/CHIP CR5 87 G3
GODL GU7 159 M6
Horsham Gates SWTR RH13 * 167 H6
Horsham Rd BIL RH14 203 M11
CRAN GU6 185 N2
CRAN GU6 186 F5
CRAN GU6 187 M4
CRAWW RH11 164 A8
DORK RH4 144 D3
EBED/NFELT TW14 14 F8
HORS RH12 186 C12
HORS RH12 189 P9
RDKG RH5 142 C8
RDKG RH5 171 P7
RDKG RH5 171 R12
RDKG RH5 173 L8
RDKG RH5 187 Q4
RDKG RH5 187 Q7
RDKG RH5 189 K3
SHGR GU5 168 H1
SHGR GU5 185 N1
SHST GU47 52 A8
Horshoe La East GU GU1 117 L7
Horsley Cl HOR/WEW KT19 84 A3
Horsley Dr CROY/NA CR0 69 M6
KUTN/CMB KT2 27 G6
Horsley Rd COB KT11 100 E1
Horsneile La BNFD RG42 34 E1
Horton Crs HOR/WEW KT19 83 L1
Horton Gdns DTCH/LGLY SL3 * 12 C5
HOR/WEW KT19 83 M1
Horton Hl HOR/WEW KT19 83 M1
Horton La HOR/WEW KT19 83 K2
Horton Rd DTCH/LGLY SL3 12 B4
DTCH/LGLY SL3 13 H5
Horton Wy CROY/NA CR0 51 G5
Horvath Cl WEY KT13 60 A3
Hosack Rd TOOT SW17 30 C3
Hoskins Pl EGRIN RH19 163 G1
Hoskins Rd OXTED RH8 130 B3
Hoskins Wk OXTED RH8 130 B3
Hospital Bridge Rd WHTN TW2 25 L3
Hospital Hl ALDT GU11 112 D6
Hospital Rd ALDT GU11 112 D6
HSLW TW3 16 D5
Hostel Rd FARN GU14 112 E1
Hotham Cl E/WMO/HCT KT8 43 K3
Hotham Rd PUT/ROE SW15 19 M5
WIM/MER SW19 29 M8
Houblon Rd RCHPK/HAM TW10 18 B7
Houghton Cl HPTN TW12 25 H7
Houghton Rd CRAWE RH10 * 165 L7
Houlder Crs CROY/NA CR0 67 L5
Houlton Ct BAGS GU19 54 B7
Hound House Rd SHGR GU5 141 K7
Houndown La MFD/CHID GU8 182 B4
Hounslow Av HSLW TW3 16 E7
Hounslow Gdns HSLW TW3 16 E7
Hounslow Rd
EBED/NFELT TW14 24 E1
FELT TW13 25 G4
WHTN TW2 16 F8
Houseman Rd FARN GU14 92 C3
Houston Rd FSTH SE23 33 H3
SURB KT6 44 E6
Hove Gdns SUT SM1 47 L8
Howard Av EW KT17 64 D8
Howard Cl ASHTD KT21 83 J8
EHSLY KT24 100 A7
HPTN TW12 25 M8
KWD/TDW/WH KT20 104 C7
LHD/OX KT22 102 F5
SUN TW16 24 C7
Howard Cole Wy ALDT GU11 112 B7
Howard Gdns GU GU1 117 K7
Howard Pl REIG RH2 125 K6
Howard Rdg RGUE GU4 117 K4
Howard Rd COUL/CHIP CR5 86 F5
CRAWW RH11 190 G11
DORK RH4 144 D2
EHSLY KT24 100 D4
GT/LBKH KT23 121 L1
ISLW TW7 17 J5
NWMAL KT3 46 B3
PGE/AN SE20 50 F1
RDKG RH5 * 144 F6
REIG RH2 147 L1
SNWD SE25 50 D5
SURB KT6 45 J6
SWTR RH13 167 K5
Howards Cl WOKS/MYFD GU22 97 K2
Howards Crest Cl BECK BR3 51 M2
Howards La ADL/WDHM KT15 58 B5
PUT/ROE SW15 19 M6
Howards Rd WOKS/MYFD GU22 97 J2
Howard St THDIT KT7 44 E7
Howards Yd WAND/EARL SW18 29 L1
Howberry Rd THHTH CR7 50 A1
Howden Rd SNWD SE25 50 C2
Howe Dr CTHM CR3 108 A4
Howell Hl BELMT SM2 * 64 F8
Howell Hill Cl EW KT17 84 F1
Howell Hill Gv EW KT17 84 F1
Howgate Rd MORT/ESHN SW14 19 G5
Howitts Cl ESH/CLAY KT10 61 K5
How La COUL/CHIP CR5 86 D8
Howley Rd CROY/NA CR0 2 B7
Howsman Rd BARN SW13 19 K1
Howson Ter
RCHPK/HAM TW10 * 18 B8
Hoylake Cl CRAWW RH11 190 G8
Hoylake Gdns MTCM CR4 48 F3
Hoyle Hl RDKG RH5 173 L8
Hoyle Rd TOOT SW17 30 B6
Hubbard Dr CHSGTN KT9 62 F5
Hubbard Rd WNWD SE27 31 M5
Hubberholme BRAK RG12 34 D3
Hubert Cl WIM/MER SW19 * 47 M1
Huddleston Crs REDH RH1 127 G2
Hudson Cl LIPH GU30 196 H10
Hudson Ct GUW GU2 116 C8
Hudson Rd CRAWE RH10 165 G6
HYS/HAR UB3 15 G1
Hudsons KWD/TDW/WH KT20 105 G3
Huggins Pl BRXS/STRHM SW2 31 J2
Hughenden Rd WPK KT4 46 D7
Hughes Rd ASHF TW15 23 M8
Hughes Wk CROY/NA CR0 2 C1
Hullbrook La SHGR GU5 169 N5
Hullmead SHGR GU5 169 P5
Hulton Cl LHD/OX KT22 102 F5
Hulverston Cl BELMT SM2 65 L8
Humber Wy SHST GU47 72 A1
Humbolt Cl GUW GU2 116 B8
Hummer Rd EGH TW20 21 K5
Humphrey Cl LHD/OX KT22 101 M4
Hungry Hill La
RPLY/SEND GU23 98 F8
Hunstanton Cl CRAWW RH11 190 G8
DTCH/LGLY SL3 12 F2
Hunston Rd MRDN SM4 47 L8
Hunter Cl BAL SW12 30 D2
WLGTN SM6 67 H6
Hunter Rd CRAWE RH10 164 F7
FARN GU14 92 C6
GU GU1 7 K6
RYNPK SW20 46 F1
THHTH CR7 50 A3
Hunters Cha GDST RH9 151 J3
LIPH GU30 196 G8
Hunters Cl HOR/WEW KT19 83 M3
Hunters Ct RCH/KEW TW9 18 A7
Huntersfield Cl REIG RH2 125 L5
Hunters Ga REDH RH1 127 J7
Hunter's Gv ORP BR6 71 M3
Hunters Meadow NRWD SE19 32 B5
Hunters Rd CHSGTN KT9 63 H2
Hunters Wy CROY/NA CR0 3 H9
Hunting Cl ESH/CLAY KT10 61 K3
Huntingdon Cl MTCM CR4 49 H4
Huntingdon Gdns CHSWK W4 * 18 F2
WPK KT4 64 F2
Huntingdon House Dr
GSHT GU26 197 R1
Huntingdon Rd REDH RH1 126 C8
WOKN/KNAP GU21 76 B7
Huntingfield CROY/NA CR0 69 J6
Huntingfield Rd PUT/ROE SW15 19 K6
Huntingfield Wy EGH TW20 22 A8

Huntingford Cl GSHT GU26 * 181 P10
Hunting Gate Dr CHSGTN KT9 63 H6
Hunting Gate Ms WHTN TW2 * 26 B2
Huntley Cl STWL/WRAY TW19 23 H1
Huntley Wy RYNPK SW20 * 46 D2
Huntly Rd SNWD SE25 50 B4
Hunts Cl GUW GU2 116 A7
Huntsgreen Ct BRAK RG12 34 F3
Hunts Hill Rd RGUW GU3 114 D4
Huntsman Cl FELT TW13 24 E5
Huntsmans Cl WARL CR6 108 F1
Huntsmans Meadow ASC SL5 36 C1
Huntsman's Ms FRIM GU16 93 J5
Huntsmoor Rd HOR/WEW KT19 64 A4
Huntspill St TOOT SW17 29 M4
Hunts Slip Rd DUL SE21 32 B4
Hurland La BOR GU35 196 E1
Hurlands Cl FNM GU9 134 C5
Hurlands La MFD/CHID GU8 185 J12
Hurlands Pl FNM GU9 134 C5
Hurley Cl WOT/HER KT12 60 E1
Hurley Gdns RGUE GU4 117 K5
Hurlford WOKN/KNAP GU21 76 D7
Hurlstone Rd SNWD SE25 50 A5
Hurn Court Rd HSLWW TW4 16 A4
Hurnford Cl SAND/SEL CR2 68 B8
Huron Dr LIPH GU30 196 H10
Huron Rd TOOT SW17 30 D3
Hurricane Rd WLGTN SM6 67 H6
Hurricane Wy FARN GU14 112 C2
Hurst Av HORS RH12 167 G6
Hurstbourne Rd FSTH SE23 33 H2
Hurst Cl BRAK RG12 * 34 D5
CHSGTN KT9 63 K4
CRAWW RH11 164 B6
EPSOM KT18 103 M6
LIPH GU30 196 F8
WOKS/MYFD GU22 96 F2
Hurst Ct HORS RH12 167 G6
Hurstcourt Rd SUT SM1 47 L8
Hurst Cft GU GU1 7 K9
Hurstdene Av STA TW18 22 E7
Hurst Dr KWD/TDW/WH KT20 104 D8
Hurst Farm Cl MFD/CHID GU8 159 J7
Hurst Farm Rd EGRIN RH19 162 E5
Hurstfield Rd E/WMO/HCT KT8 43 K3
Hurst Green Cl OXTED RH8 130 D6
Hurst Green Rd OXTED RH8 130 D6
Hurst Gv WOT/HER KT12 42 C8
Hurst Hl Cottages SHGR GU5 * 169 K4
Hurstlands OXTED RH8 130 D6
Hurst La E/WMO/HCT KT8 43 M4
EGH TW20 39 J3
EPSOM KT18 104 A4
Hurstleigh Cl REDH RH1 126 C6
Hurstleigh Dr REDH RH1 126 C6
Hurstmere Cl GSHT GU26 197 Q2
Hurst Rd ALDT GU11 112 F6
CROY/NA CR0 68 A4
E/WMO/HCT KT8 43 M3
EPSOM KT18 104 B5
FARN GU14 92 E1
HOR/WEW KT19 84 A1
HORL RH6 160 B2
HORS RH12 167 G6
WOT/HER KT12 43 G4
Hurst View Rd SAND/SEL CR2 68 B6
Hurst Wy SAND/SEL CR2 68 B5
WOKS/MYFD GU22 78 B4
Hurstwood ASC SL5 36 D6
Hurtmore Cha GODL GU7 159 L1
Hurtmore Rd MFD/CHID GU8 159 G3
Hurtwood Rd WOT/HER KT12 43 J7
Hussar Ct ALDT GU11 112 B7
Hussars Cl HSLWW TW4 16 B5
Hutchingson's Rd
CROY/NA CR0 89 M1
Hutchins Wy HORL RH6 160 C1
Hutton Cl BFOR GU20 55 G6
Hutton Rd ASHV GU12 113 K3
Huxley Cl GODL GU7 168 A2
Huxley Rd GUW GU2 138 A1
Hyacinth Cl HPTN TW12 25 K7
Hyacinth Rd PUT/ROE SW15 28 D2
Hyde Dr CRAWW RH11 164 A5
Hyde Farm Ms BAL SW12 31 G2
Hyde La MFD/CHID GU8 182 B7
RFNM GU10 132 A2
RFNM GU10 181 Q8
Hyde Rd RCHPK/HAM TW10 18 C7
SAND/SEL CR2 88 B3
Hyde Ter ASHF TW15 24 B7
Hydethorpe Rd BAL SW12 30 F2
Hyde Wk MRDN SM4 47 K7
Hylands Cl CRAWE RH10 165 J5
Hylands Ms EPSOM KT18 83 M5
Hylands Rd EPSOM KT18 83 M5
Hyndewood FSTH SE23 33 G4
Hyperion Ct CRAWW RH11 164 A6
Hyperion Pl HOR/WEW KT19 64 A7
Hythe Cl BRAK RG12 35 H5
Hythe End Rd
STWL/WRAY TW19 21 K3
Hythe Field Av EGH TW20 22 A7
Hythe Park Rd EGH TW20 21 M6
Hythe Rd STA TW18 22 A6
THHTH CR7 50 A2
The Hythe STA TW18 22 B6

I

Iberian Av WLGTN SM6 67 G3
Iberian Wy CBLY GU15 73 K3
Ibis La CHSWK W4 18 F3
Ibsley Gdns PUT/ROE SW15 28 D2
Icehouse Wd OXTED RH8 130 C5
Icklingham Rd COB KT11 80 F2
Idlecombe Rd TOOT SW17 30 D7
Idmiston Rd WNWD SE27 31 M4
WPK KT4 46 C7
Idmiston Sq WPK KT4 46 C7
Ifield Av CRAWW RH11 164 C1
CRAWW RH11 164 E3
Ifield Cl REDH RH1 148 B3
Ifield Dr CRAWW RH11 164 C3
Ifield Gn CRAWW RH11 164 C1
Ifield Pk CRAWW RH11 * 164 B4
Ifield Rd CRAWW RH11 164 D3
HORL RH6 174 H12
Ifield St CRAWW RH11 164 B2
Ifield Wd CRAWW RH11 190 G4
Ifold Bridge La BIL RH14 201 M5
Ifoldhurst BIL RH14 201 M7
Ifold Rd REDH RH1 148 D2
Ikona Ct WEY KT13 * 59 M4
Ildersly Gv DUL SE21 32 A3
Ilex Cl EGH TW20 20 E8
SUN TW16 42 F2
Ilex Wy STRHM/NOR SW16 31 K6
Ilkley Cl NRWD SE19 * 32 A7
Illingworth Cl MTCM CR4 48 A3
Illingworth Gv BRAK RG12 35 J1
Imadene Crs BOR GU35 196 A1
Imber Cross THDIT KT7 * 44 C7
Imber Gv ESH/CLAY KT10 44 A7
Imberhorne La EGRIN RH19 162 B6
Imberhorne Wy EGRIN RH19 162 C2
Imber Park Rd ESH/CLAY KT10 44 A8
Imjin Cl ALDT GU11 112 E6
Imperial Gdns MTCM CR4 48 E3
Imperial Pk LHD/OX KT22 * 102 D2
Imperial Rd EBED/NFELT TW14 24 B1
Imperial Wy CROY/NA CR0 67 K5
Imran Ct ASHV GU12 134 F1
Ince Rd WOT/HER KT12 60 B4
Inchmery Rd CAT SE6 33 L3
Inchwood BRAK RG12 34 F8
CROY/NA CR0 69 L3
Infirmary Dr SWTR RH13 204 F11
Ingatestone Rd SNWD SE25 50 E5
Ingham Cl SAND/SEL CR2 69 G7
Ingham Rd SAND/SEL CR2 68 F7
Ingleboro Dr PUR/KEN CR8 88 A3
Ingleby Wy WLGTN SM6 67 G7
Ingle Dell CBLY GU15 73 G5
Inglehurst ADL/WDHM KT15 58 E8
Inglemere Rd FSTH SE23 33 G4
TOOT SW17 30 C8
Ingleside DTCH/LGLY SL3 13 H3
Ingleside Cl BECK BR3 33 K8
Ingleton BRAK RG12 34 D3
Ingleton Rd CAR SM5 66 B7
Inglewood CHERT KT16 58 C2
CROY/NA CR0 69 H7
WOKN/KNAP GU21 76 E8
Inglewood Av CBLY GU15 73 M5
Inglis Rd CROY/NA CR0 3 K3
Ingram Cl HORS RH12 166 D7
Ingram Rd THHTH CR7 49 M1
Ingrams Cl WOT/HER KT12 60 F4
Ingress V BNFD RG42 * 34 C1
Inholms La RDKG RH5 144 F6
Inkerman Pde
WOKN/KNAP GU21 * 76 B8
Inkerman Rd
WOKN/KNAP GU21 76 B8
Inkerman Wy
WOKN/KNAP GU21 76 B8
Inkpen La FROW RH18 195 N12
Inman Rd WAND/EARL SW18 29 M1
Inner Park Rd WIM/MER SW19 29 G3
Inner Ring East HTHAIR TW6 14 E5
Innes Cl RYNPK SW20 47 H2
Innes Gdns PUT/ROE SW15 19 L8
Innes Rd HORS RH12 167 J5
Innes Yd CROY/NA CR0 2 D8
Innings La BNFD RG42 35 G1
Institute Rd ASHV GU12 113 G8
DORK RH4 143 M3
Instow Gdns FARN GU14 92 D2
International Wy SUN TW16 42 B1
Inval Hl HASM GU27 198 D5
Inveresk Gdns WPK KT4 64 C2
Inverness Rd HSLW TW3 16 C6
WPK KT4 47 G8
Inverness Wy SHST GU47 72 A2
Invicta Cl EBED/NFELT TW14 24 C2
Invincible Rd FARN GU14 92 D6
Inwood Av COUL/CHIP CR5 107 K2
HSLW TW3 16 F5
Inwood Cl CROY/NA CR0 69 H1
Inwood Rd HSLW TW3 16 F6
Iona Cl CAT SE6 33 K1
CRAWW RH11 164 D7
MRDN SM4 47 L7
Ipswich Rd TOOT SW17 30 D7
Irene Rd COB KT11 81 L4
Ireton Av WOT/HER KT12 60 C1
Iris Cl CROY/NA CR0 51 G8
SURB KT6 * 45 J7
Iris Rd CHOB/PIR GU24 75 K5
HOR/WEW KT19 63 L4
Iron La SHGR GU5 168 H4
Ironsbottom REIG RH2 175 J2
Irvine Dr FARN GU14 92 B1
Irvine Pl VW GU25 39 H5
Irving Wk CRAWE RH10 165 G7
Irwin Dr HORS RH12 166 D7
Irwin Rd GUW GU2 6 B7
Isabella Ct RCHPK/HAM TW10 18 C8
Isabella Dr ORP BR6 71 M3
Isabella Pl KUTN/CMB KT2 27 J6
Isbells Dr REIG RH2 147 L2
Isham Rd STRHM/NOR SW16 49 H2
Isis St WAND/EARL SW18 29 M3
Isis Wy SHST GU47 72 A1
Island Cl STA TW18 22 B5
Island Farm Av
E/WMO/HCT KT8 43 J5
Island Farm Rd
E/WMO/HCT KT8 43 J5
Island Rd MTCM CR4 30 C8
Islay Gdns HSLWW TW4 16 A7
Itchel La RFNM GU10 132 A2
Itchingfield Rd SWTR RH13 204 B9
Itchingwood Common Rd
OXTED RH8 130 F7
Ivanhoe Cl CRAWW RH11 164 F1
Ivanhoe Rd HSLWW TW4 16 A5
Iveagh Cl CRAWW RH11 191 M12
Iveagh Rd GUW GU2 6 C6
Ively Rd FARN GU14 92 A8
Iverna Gdns EBED/NFELT TW14 15 G7
Ivers Wy CROY/NA CR0 69 L6
Ivor Cl GU GU1 7 M5
Ivory Ct FELT TW13 24 D2
Ivory Wk CRAWW RH11 164 A7
Ivybank GODL GU7 168 B3
Ivybridge Cl TWK TW1 17 K8
Ivychurch Cl PGE/AN SE20 32 E8
Ivy Cl SUN TW16 42 F2
Ivydale Rd CAR SM5 66 C1
Ivyday Gv STRHM/NOR SW16 31 J4
Ivydene E/WMO/HCT KT8 43 J5
WOKN/KNAP GU21 75 L8
Ivydene Cl REDH RH1 148 E5
SUT SM1 65 M3
Ivy Dene La EGRIN RH19 163 L7
Ivy Dr LTWR GU18 74 D2
Ivy Gdns MTCM CR4 49 G3
Ivy La FNM GU9 5 H3
HSLWW TW4 16 C6
WOKS/MYFD GU22 11 J7
Ivy Mill Cl GDST RH9 128 E6
Ivy Mill La GDST RH9 128 D6
Ivymount Rd WNWD SE27 31 K4
Ivy Rd ASHV GU12 113 H7
HSLW TW3 16 E6
SURB KT6 * 63 K1
TOOT SW17 30 B6

J

Jacaranda Cl NWMAL KT3 46 B3
Jackass La GDST RH9 129 J5
HAYES BR2 70 E5
Jackdaw Cl CRAWW RH11 164 E2
Jackdaw La HORS RH12 167 H4
Jack Good Child Wy
KUT/HW KT1 9 L8
Jackman's La
WOKN/KNAP GU21 96 E1
Jackson Cl BRAK RG12 34 E5
EPSOM KT18 84 A4
Jackson Rd HAYES BR2 71 H1
Jackson's Pl CROY/NA CR0 2 F4
Jackson's Wy CROY/NA CR0 69 K2
Jacob Cl BNFD RG42 34 A2
Jacobean Cl CRAWE RH10 165 L5
Jacob Rd CBLY GU15 72 D2
Jacobs Well Rd RGUE GU4 117 G3
Jaggard Wy BAL SW12 30 C1
Jaguar Rd FARN GU14 92 E7
Jail La BH/WHM TN16 91 G5
Jamaica Rd THHTH CR7 49 L6
James Rd ALDT GU11 113 G2
CBLY GU15 72 E7
RGUW GU3 138 F8
James St HSLW TW3 17 G5
Jameston BRAK RG12 34 F8
James Watt Wy CRAWE RH10 191 R1
James Wy CBLY GU15 72 E7
Jamnagar Cl STA TW18 22 C7
Janoway Hill La
WOKN/KNAP GU21 96 F1
Japonica Cl WOKN/KNAP GU21 76 F8
Jarrett Cl BRXS/STRHM SW2 31 L2
Jarrow Cl MRDN SM4 47 L5
Jarvis Rd SAND/SEL CR2 68 A5
Jasmine Cl ORP BR6 71 L1
REDH RH1 148 D5
WOKN/KNAP GU21 76 C6
Jasmine Ct HORS RH12 166 F7
Jasmine Gdns CROY/NA CR0 69 L2
Jasmine Gv PGE/AN SE20 50 E1
Jasmine Rd HOR/WEW KT19 63 L5
Jasmin Rd HOR/WEW KT19 63 L5
Jason Cl REDH RH1 148 B5
WEY KT13 59 M4
Jasons Dr RGUE GU4 117 M5
Jasper Rd NRWD SE19 32 C7
Jay Av ADL/WDHM KT15 * 59 H2
Jay's La HASM GU27 199 J10
Jays Nest Cl BLKW GU17 72 A5
Jay Wk CRAWE RH10 193 P8
Jean Batten Cl WLGTN SM6 67 J6
Jefferies Rd EHSLY KT24 119 L5
Jeffries Pas GU GU1 7 H6
Jeffs Cl HPTN TW12 * 25 L7
Jeffs Rd SUT SM1 65 J3
Jemmett Cl KUTN/CMB KT2 9 L5
Jengar Cl SUT SM1 65 L3
Jenkins' Hill London Rd
BAGS GU19 53 M8
Jenner Dr CHOB/PIR GU24 75 K3
Jenner Rd CRAWE RH10 191 Q2
GU GU1 7 J6
Jenners Cl LING RH7 178 E5
Jenner Wy HOR/WEW KT19 63 K7
Jennett Rd CROY/NA CR0 67 K2
Jennings Cl ADL/WDHM KT15 58 F7
SURB KT6 44 F7
Jennings Wy HORL RH6 161 G3
Jenny La LING RH7 178 D5
Jennys Wy COUL/CHIP CR5 106 F4
Jenson Wy NRWD SE19 32 C8
Jeppo's La MTCM CR4 48 C4
Jersey Brow Rd FARN GU14 92 D7
Jersey Cl CHERT KT16 58 C2
RGUE GU4 117 L3
Jersey Rd CRAWW RH11 164 C8
HEST TW5 16 E3
TOOT SW17 30 E8
Jerviston Gdns
STRHM/NOR SW16 31 K7
Jesmond Cl MTCM CR4 48 E3
Jesmond Rd CROY/NA CR0 3 K1
Jessamy Rd WEY KT13 59 K1
Jesses La SHGR GU5 170 H1
Jessiman Ter SHPTN TW17 41 K5
Jessops Wy CROY/NA CR0 48 F6
Jevington BRAK RG12 34 F7
Jewels Hl WARL CR6 90 D2
Jews Wk SYD SE26 32 E5
Jeypore Rd WAND/EARL SW18 29 M1
Jig's La South BNFD RG42 35 H1
Jillian Cl HPTN TW12 25 K8
Jobson's La HASM GU27 199 M11
Jocelyn Rd RCH/KEW TW9 18 B5
Jockey Md HORS RH12 166 D8
Jock's La BNFD RG42 34 B1
Jodrell Cl ISLW TW7 17 K3
John Austin Cl KUTN/CMB KT2 9 G5
John Cl ALDT GU11 134 B1
John Cobb Rd WEY KT13 59 K6
John Russell Cl GUW GU2 116 D5
John's Cl ASHF TW15 23 M5
Johnsdale OXTED RH8 130 C3
Johns La MRDN SM4 47 M5
Johnson Rd CROY/NA CR0 2 E1
HEST TW5 15 M2
Johnson's Cl CAR SM5 66 C2
Johnsons Dr HPTN TW12 43 M1
Johnson Wk CRAWE RH10 164 F7
John's Rd BH/WHM TN16 111 G2
John's Ter CROY/NA CR0 3 G4
Johnston Wk GUW GU2 116 D4
John St HSLW TW3 16 B4
SNWD SE25 50 D4
Johns Wk CTHM CR3 108 D1
John Wiskar Dr CRAN GU6 186 C3
Joinville Pl ADL/WDHM KT15 59 G3
Jolesfield CRAWW RH11 164 B7
Jolive Ct GU GU1 * 139 K1
Jolliffe Rd REDH RH1 106 F8
Jones Cnr ASC SL5 36 B1
Jonson Cl MTCM CR4 48 E4
Jordan Cl SAND/SEL CR2 88 C1
Jordans Cl CRAWW RH11 164 F2
GU GU1 117 K7
REDH RH1 148 D5
STWL/WRAY TW19 22 F1
Jordans Crs CRAWW RH11 164 F1
Jordans Ms WHTN TW2 26 B3
The Jordans EGRIN RH19 162 F5
Josephine Av
KWD/TDW/WH KT20 125 J1
Josephine Cl
KWD/TDW/WH KT20 125 J1
Joseph Locke Wy
ESH/CLAY KT10 61 K1
Joseph's Rd GU GU1 6 F1
Joshua Cl SAND/SEL CR2 67 L6
Jubilee Av ASC SL5 36 B1
WHTN TW2 25 M2
Jubilee Cl ASC SL5 36 B1
KUT/HW KT1 8 B5
STWL/WRAY TW19 22 F1
Jubilee Crs ADL/WDHM KT15 59 G4
Jubilee Dr ASHV GU12 113 K3
Jubilee Est SWTR RH13 167 H5
Jubilee Hall Rd FARN GU14 92 F5
Jubilee La GSHT GU26 197 P2
RFNM GU10 155 K4
Jubilee Rd ALDT GU11 134 E2
CHEAM SM3 65 G6
FRIM GU16 93 K7
HORS RH12 203 J1
Jubilee Ter BRKHM/BTCW RH3 145 M4
DORK RH4 144 E1
Jubilee Wk CRAWE RH10 165 J4
Jubilee Wy CHSGTN KT9 63 L2
EBED/NFELT TW14 24 D2
WIM/MER SW19 47 L1
Judges Ter EGRIN RH19 162 F5
Judge Wk ESH/CLAY KT10 62 B5
Julian Cl WOKN/KNAP GU21 76 F8
Julian Hl WEY KT13 59 K6
Julian Tayler Pth FSTH SE23 * 32 E3
Julien Rd COUL/CHIP CR5 86 F5
Julius Hl BNFD RG42 35 J1
Jumps Rd RFNM GU10 181 L6
Junction Rd ASHF TW15 23 M6
DORK RH4 144 D2
LTWR GU18 54 E8
SAND/SEL CR2 68 A5
June Cl COUL/CHIP CR5 86 E4
June La REDH RH1 148 E7
Junewood Cl ADL/WDHM KT15 78 C1
Juniper BRAK RG12 34 F8
Juniper Cl BH/WHM TN16 91 H7
CHSGTN KT9 63 J4
GU GU1 116 E3
OXTED RH8 130 E7
REIG RH2 147 M2
Juniper Dr CHOB/PIR GU24 75 K5
Juniper Gdns MTCM CR4 48 F1
SUN TW16 24 C7
Juniper Rd CRAWW RH11 164 E1
REIG RH2 147 M2
Jura Cl CRAWW RH11 164 D7
Justin Cl BTFD TW8 18 A2
Jutland Pl EGH TW20 21 M6
Jutland Rd CAT SE6 33 M1
Juxon Cl CRAWW RH11 164 B6

K

Kangley Bridge Rd SYD SE26 33 J6
Kashmir Cl ADL/WDHM KT15 59 G7
Katharine St CROY/NA CR0 2 D7
Katherine Cl ADL/WDHM KT15 58 D5
Katherine Rd EDEN TN8 179 R1
Kay Av ADL/WDHM KT15 59 H2
Kay Crs BOR GU35 180 G11
Kaye Don Wy WEY KT13 59 K8
Kayemoor Rd BELMT SM2 66 B6
Kaynes Pk ASC SL5 36 B1
Keable Rd RFNM GU10 155 J2
Kearton Cl PUR/KEN CR8 87 M7
Keates Gn BNFD RG42 34 E1
Keats Av REDH RH1 126 D6
Keats Cl HORS RH12 167 H2
WIM/MER SW19 30 A7
Keats Pl EGRIN RH19 162 E4
Keats Wy CROY/NA CR0 50 F6
Keble Cl CRAWE RH10 165 M1
WPK KT4 46 C8
Keble Pl BARN SW13 19 L1
Keble St TOOT SW17 29 M5
Keble Wy SHST GU47 52 B7
Keeley Rd CROY/NA CR0 2 C6
Keens Cl STRHM/NOR SW16 31 G6
Keens La RGUW GU3 116 C4
Keens Park Rd RGUW GU3 116 C4
Keen's Rd CROY/NA CR0 2 D9
Keepers Cl RGUE GU4 118 A5
Keepers Combe BRAK RG12 35 G6
Keepers Ms TEDD TW11 26 F7
Keepers Wk VW GU25 39 G5
The Keep KUTN/CMB KT2 9 G2
Keevil Dr WIM/MER SW19 29 G1
Keith Lucas Rd FARN GU14 92 C7
Keith Park Crs BH/WHM TN16 90 F2
Keldholme BRAK RG12 34 D3
Kelling Gdns CROY/NA CR0 2 A1
Kellino St TOOT SW17 30 C5
Kelly Cl SHPTN TW17 42 B2
Kelsall Ms RCH/KEW TW9 18 E3
Kelsey Cl HORL RH6 160 C3
Kelsey La BECK BR3 51 K3
Kelsey Park Av BECK BR3 51 L3
Kelsey Park Rd BECK BR3 51 K2
Kelsey Sq BECK BR3 51 K2
Kelsey Wy BECK BR3 51 K3
Kelso Cl CRAWE RH10 192 D6
Kelso Rd CAR SM5 47 M7
Kelvedon Av WOT/HER KT12 60 B6
Kelvedon Cl KUTN/CMB KT2 27 K7
Kelvin Av LHD/OX KT22 102 C2
Kelvinbrook E/WMO/HCT KT8 43 L3
Kelvin Cl HOR/WEW KT19 63 K5
Kelvin Dr TWK TW1 17 L8
Kelvin Gdns CROY/NA CR0 49 H7
Kelvin Gv CHSGTN KT9 63 G2
SYD SE26 32 E4
Kelvington Cl CROY/NA CR0 51 H7
Kelvin La CRAWE RH10 191 Q3
Kelvin Wy CRAWE RH10 191 Q3
Kemble Cl WEY KT13 60 A3
Kemble Dr HAYES BR2 71 H2
Kemble Rd CROY/NA CR0 2 A7
FSTH SE23 33 G2
Kembleside Rd BH/WHM TN16 90 F8
Kemerton Rd BECK BR3 51 L2
CROY/NA CR0 3 J2
Kemishford WOKS/MYFD GU22 96 D5
Kemnal Pk HASM GU27 198 E5
Kemp Ct BAGS GU19 54 C7
Kemp Gdns CROY/NA CR0 49 M6
Kempshott Rd HORS RH12 166 E5
STRHM/NOR SW16 31 H8
Kempton Av SUN TW16 42 E1
Kempton Ct FARN GU14 92 C7
SUN TW16 42 E1
Kempton Pk SUN TW16 * 42 F1
Kempton Rd HPTN TW12 43 J2
Kempton Wk CROY/NA CR0 51 H6
Kemsing Cl THHTH CR7 * 49 M4
Kemsley Rd BH/WHM TN16 111 G1
Kendal Cl EBED/NFELT TW14 24 C2
FARN GU14 * 92 B5
REIG RH2 126 A7
Kendale Cl CRAWE RH10 165 L8
Kendal Gdns SUT SM1 65 M1
Kendal Gv CBLY GU15 74 A5
Kendall Av BECK BR3 51 H2
SAND/SEL CR2 68 A7
Kendall Av South
SAND/SEL CR2 67 M8
Kendall Rd BECK BR3 51 H2
ISLW TW7 17 K4
Kendor Av HOR/WEW KT19 83 M1
Kendra Hall Rd SAND/SEL CR2 67 L6
Kendrey Gdns WHTN TW2 17 H8
Kenilford Rd BAL SW12 30 E1
Kenilworth Av BRAK RG12 34 F1
COB KT11 81 L4
WIM/MER SW19 29 K6
Kenilworth Cl BNSTD SM7 85 L6
CRAWW RH11 164 D8
Kenilworth Dr WOT/HER KT12 61 G2
Kenilworth Gdns STA TW18 22 F6
Kenilworth Rd ASHF TW15 23 G4
EW KT17 64 D5
PGE/AN SE20 51 G1
Kenilworth Ter BELMT SM2 65 K6
Kenley Aerodrome
PUR/KEN CR8 88 A4
Kenley Gdns THHTH CR7 49 L4
Kenley La PUR/KEN CR8 87 M5
Kenley Rd BOR GU35 180 G12
KUT/HW KT1 9 M6
TWK TW1 17 K8
WIM/MER SW19 47 K3
Kenley Wk CHEAM SM3 65 G3
Kenlor Rd TOOT SW17 30 A6
Kenmara Cl CRAWE RH10 165 K1
Kenmara Ct CRAWE RH10 191 R3
Kenmare Dr MTCM CR4 30 C8
Kenmare Rd THHTH CR7 49 K6
Kenmore Cl FRIM GU16 93 G1
Kenmore Rd PUR/KEN CR8 87 L4
Kennard Ct FROW RH18 * 195 M10
Kennedy Av EGRIN RH19 162 E2
Kennedy Cl MTCM CR4 48 D2
Kennedy Rd SWTR RH13 167 G8
Kennel Av ASC SL5 36 C1
Kennel Cl LHD/OX KT22 101 M6
Kennel Gn ASC SL5 36 B1
Kennel La BFOR GU20 54 F4
HORL RH6 160 A4
LHD/OX KT22 101 M5
RFNM GU10 155 M7
Kennel Wd ASC SL5 36 C1
Kennelwood Crs CROY/NA CR0 90 A1
Kennet Cl ASHV GU12 113 K8
CRAWW RH11 164 B5
FARN GU14 92 A3
Kenneth Rd BNSTD SM7 86 A5
Kennet Rd ISLW TW7 17 J5
Kenny Dr CAR SM5 66 D7
Kenrick Sq REDH RH1 128 B8
Kensington Av THHTH CR7 49 K1
Kensington Gdns KUT/HW KT1 8 D9
Kensington Rd CRAWW RH11 164 D8
Kensington Ter SAND/SEL CR2 68 A6
Kent Cl MTCM CR4 49 H4
STA TW18 23 G7
Kent Dr TEDD TW11 26 B6
Kent Gate Wy CROY/NA CR0 69 J5
Kent Hatch Rd OXTED RH8 130 F4
Kent House La BECK BR3 33 H7
Kent House Rd BECK BR3 33 G8
Kentigern Dr CWTH RG45 52 B4
Kenton Av SUN TW16 43 G2
Kenton Cl BRAK RG12 35 G2
FRIM GU16 73 J7
Kenton Wy WOKN/KNAP GU21 76 C7
Kent Rd BFOR GU20 55 G4
E/WMO/HCT KT8 43 M4
KUT/HW KT1 8 D8
RCH/KEW TW9 18 D2
WOKS/MYFD GU22 11 K3
WWKM BR4 51 L8
Kent Wy SURB KT6 63 H2
Kentwode Gn BARN SW13 19 K2
Kentwyns Dr SWTR RH13 205 M9
Kentwyns Ri REDH RH1 149 J1

Kenwood Cl WDR/YW UB7 14 D1
Kenwood Dr BECK BR3 51 M3
WOT/HER KT12 60 E5
Kenwood Pk WEY KT13 60 A5
Kenwood Rdg PUR/KEN CR8 87 L7
Kenworth Gv LTWR GU18 54 C8
Kenwyn Rd RYNPK SW20 46 F1
Kenya Ct HORL RH6 * 160 C2
Kenyngton Dr SUN TW16 24 D6
Kenyons EHSLY KT24 119 L2
Keogh Barracks ASHV GU12 113 K1
Keogh Cl ASHV GU12 93 L8
Keppel Rd DORK RH4 122 E8
Keppel Sp WDSR SL4 20 E1
Kepple Pl BAGS GU19 54 B6
Kernel Ct GU GU1 * 6 E3
Kerria Wy CHOB/PIR GU24 75 J3
Kerrill Av COUL/CHIP CR5 107 K1
Kerry Ter WOKN/KNAP GU21 11 J3
Kersey Dr SAND/SEL CR2 88 F2
Kerves La SWTR RH13 205 M11
Keston Av ADL/WDHM KT15 78 D1
COUL/CHIP CR5 107 K1
HAYES BR2 70 F4
Keston Gdns HAYES BR2 70 F5
Keston Park Cl HAYES BR2 71 J3
Keston Rd THHTH CR7 49 J6
Kestrel Av STA TW18 22 C4
Kestrel Cl CRAWW RH11 164 E2
HOR/WEW KT19 83 K1
HORS RH12 167 H4
KUTN/CMB KT2 27 G5
RFNM GU10 133 G2
RGUE GU4 118 A6
Kestrel Rd FARN GU14 92 E7
Kestrel Wk CRAWE RH10 193 P8
Kestrel Wy CROY/NA CR0 70 A7
WOKN/KNAP GU21 76 E5
Keswick Av PUT/ROE SW15 28 B6
SHPTN TW17 42 B3
WIM/MER SW19 47 K2
Keswick Cl CBLY GU15 73 M5
CRAWW RH11 190 G9
SUT SM1 65 M3
Keswick Dr LTWR GU18 74 E1
Keswick Rd EGH TW20 21 L8
GT/LBKH KT23 101 M7
MFD/CHID GU8 183 L3
WHTN TW2 16 F8
WWKM BR4 70 B1
Kettering St STRHM/NOR SW16 30 E7
Kettlewell Cl WOKN/KNAP GU21 10 C1
Kettlewell Hl WOKN/KNAP GU21 10 C1
Kevan Dr RPLY/SEND GU23 98 B7
Kevin Cl HSLWW TW4 16 A4
Kew Br RCH/KEW TW9 18 D1
Kew Bridge Arches
CHSWK W4 * 18 D1
Kew Bridge Rd BTFD TW8 18 C1
Kew Crs CHEAM SM3 65 J2
Kew Foot Rd RCH/KEW TW9 18 B6
Kew Gardens Rd RCH/KEW TW9 18 C2
Kew Gn RCH/KEW TW9 18 C1
Kew Meadow Pth
RCH/KEW TW9 18 D3
Kew Riverside Pk
RCH/KEW TW9 18 E2
Kew Rd RCH/KEW TW9 18 B6
RCH/KEW TW9 18 C1
Keymer Cl BH/WHM TN16 90 F6
Keymer Rd BRXS/STRHM SW2 31 J3
CRAWW RH11 164 F6
Keynsham Rd MRDN SM4 47 L8
Keynsham Wy SHST GU47 52 A7
Keysham Av HEST TW5 15 K3
Keywood Dr SUN TW16 24 D7
Khama Rd TOOT SW17 30 B5
Khartoum Rd MFD/CHID GU8 183 M3
TOOT SW17 30 A5
Kibble Gn BRAK RG12 34 F6
Kidborough Down
GT/LBKH KT23 121 K1
Kidborough Rd CRAWW RH11 164 B6
Kidderminster Pl CROY/NA CR0 2 B3
Kidderminster Rd CROY/NA CR0 2 B3
Kidmans Cl HORS RH12 167 J4
Kidworth Cl HORL RH6 160 C1
Kier Pk ASC SL5 36 F3
Kilberry Cl ISLW TW7 17 G3
Kilcorral Cl EW KT17 84 D4
Kilburns Mill Cl WLGTN SM6 66 E1
Killester Gdns WPK KT4 64 E3
Killicks CRAN GU6 186 E1
Killieser Av BRXS/STRHM SW2 31 H3
Killinghurst La HASM GU27 199 K7
Kilmarnock Pk REIG RH2 125 L7
Kilmartin Av STRHM/NOR SW16 49 K3
Kilmartin Gdns FRIM GU16 73 J8
Kilmington Cl BRAK RG12 35 H7
Kilmington Rd BARN SW13 19 K1
Kilmiston Av SHPTN TW17 41 M6
Kilmore Dr CBLY GU15 73 L5
Kilmorey Gdns TWK TW1 17 L7
Kilmorey Rd TWK TW1 17 L6
Kilmorie Rd FSTH SE23 33 H2
Kilmuir Cl SHST GU47 72 A2
Kiln Cl HYS/HAR UB3 15 G1
Kiln Copse CRAN GU6 186 D1
Kilnfield Rd HORS RH12 203 J1
Kiln Flds HASM GU27 198 D5
Kiln La ASC SL5 37 K5
BRAK RG12 34 D2
BRKHM/BTCW RH3 145 L1
EW KT17 84 B2
HORL RH6 160 C1
RFNM GU10 155 M3
RPLY/SEND GU23 98 E6
Kilnmead CRAWE RH10 165 G3
Kilnmead Cl CRAWE RH10 165 G3
Kiln Mdw RGUW GU3 115 M4
Kiln Ms TOOT SW17 30 A6
Kiln Rd CRAWE RH10 193 N6
Kilnside BRAK RG12 * 34 F1
ESH/CLAY KT10 62 D6
The Kilns FNM GU9 * 134 A4
Kiln Wy ALDT GU11 134 E2
GSHT GU26 181 K12
Kilnwood La HORS RH12 190 D10
Kilross Rd EBED/NFELT TW14 24 A2
Kilrue La WOT/HER KT12 60 C3
Kilrush Ter WOKN/KNAP GU21 11 H3
Kilsha Rd WOT/HER KT12 42 E6
Kimber Ct RGUE GU4 * 118 A6
Kimberley BRAK RG12 34 F8
Kimberley Cl HORL RH6 160 B3
Kimberley Pl PUR/KEN CR8 87 K1
Kimberley Ride COB KT11 81 L3
Kimberley Rd BECK BR3 51 G2
CRAWE RH10 165 K3
CROY/NA CR0 49 L6
Kimber Rd WAND/EARL SW18 29 L1
Kimbers La FNM GU9 5 M1
Kimble Rd WIM/MER SW19 30 A7
Kimmeridge BRAK RG12 35 H6
Kimpton Rd CHEAM SM3 65 J2
Kinburn Dr EGH TW20 21 H6
Kindersley Cl EGRIN RH19 163 J2
Kinfauns Rd BRXS/STRHM SW2 31 K3
King Alfred Av CAT SE6 33 K5
King Charles Crs BRYLDS KT5 45 J7
King Charles' Rd BRYLDS KT5 45 J6
King Charles Wk
WIM/MER SW19 * 29 H2
Kingcup Cl CROY/NA CR0 51 G8
Kingcup Dr CHOB/PIR GU24 75 K5
King Edward Cl SWTR RH13 204 E11
King Edward Dr CHSGTN KT9 63 H2
King Edward Rd SWTR RH13 204 E11
King Edwards Cl ASC SL5 * 36 B1
King Edward's Gv TEDD TW11 26 E7
King Edwards Ri ASC SL5 36 B1
King Edwards Rd ASC SL5 36 B1
Kingfield Cl WOKS/MYFD GU22 97 J2
Kingfield Dr WOKS/MYFD GU22 97 J2
Kingfield Gdns
WOKS/MYFD GU22 97 J2
Kingfield Rd WOKS/MYFD GU22 97 J2
Kingfisher Cl CRAWE RH10 165 J1
WOT/HER KT12 61 H4
Kingfisher Ct DORK RH4 * 144 D1
Kingfisher Dr
RCHPK/HAM TW10 26 F5
REDH RH1 126 D5
RGUE GU4 117 M6
STA TW18 22 C5
Kingfisher Gdns SAND/SEL CR2 69 G8
Kingfisher La CRAWE RH10 193 P8
Kingfisher Ri EGRIN RH19 163 G5
Kingfisher Wk ASHV GU12 113 J6
Kingfisher Wy BECK BR3 51 G5
HORS RH12 166 F4
King Gdns CROY/NA CR0 67 L4
King Garth Ms FSTH SE23 32 F3
King George Av EGRIN RH19 162 D2
WOT/HER KT12 43 G8
King George Cl FARN GU14 93 G7
SUN TW16 * 24 B6
King George's Dr
ADL/WDHM KT15 58 D8
King George Sq
RCHPK/HAM TW10 18 C8
King George VI Av MTCM CR4 48 C4
Kingham Cl WAND/EARL SW18 29 M1
King Henry's Dr CROY/NA CR0 69 M7
King Henry's Reach
HMSMTH W6 19 M1
King Henry's Rd KUT/HW KT1 9 M8
Kingpost Pde RGUE GU4 * 117 L4
Kings Apartments CBLY GU15 72 F5
Kings Av BAL SW12 31 G2
BF/WBF KT14 79 G2
CAR SM5 66 B6
CHOB/PIR GU24 95 G1
HSLW TW3 16 E3
NWMAL KT3 46 C4
REDH RH1 148 B2
RFNM GU10 135 H1
SUN TW16 24 C6
Kingsbridge Rd MRDN SM4 47 G7
WOT/HER KT12 42 E7
Kingsbrook LHD/OX KT22 82 D8
Kingsbury Crs STA TW18 22 A5
Kingsbury Dr WDSR SL4 20 D1
Kings Cha E/WMO/HCT KT8 43 M3
Kingsclear Pk CBLY GU15 73 G5
Kingsclere Cl PUT/ROE SW15 28 D1
Kingscliffe Gdns
WIM/MER SW19 29 J2
King's Cl STA TW18 23 G8
THDIT KT7 44 D6
WOT/HER KT12 * 42 E8
Kings Copse EGRIN RH19 * 163 G5
Kingscote Hl CRAWW RH11 164 D6
Kingscote Rd CROY/NA CR0 50 E7
NWMAL KT3 46 A3
Kings Ct KWD/TDW/WH KT20 104 F4
RFNM GU10 135 H1
SWTR RH13 * 167 H6
Kingscourt Rd
STRHM/NOR SW16 31 G4
King's Crs CBLY GU15 72 F1
Kingscroft Rd BNSTD SM7 86 A5
LHD/OX KT22 102 E2
Kings Cross La REDH RH1 149 J3
Kingsdale Rd PGE/AN SE20 51 G1
Kingsdene
KWD/TDW/WH KT20 104 E3
Kingsdown Av SAND/SEL CR2 67 M7
Kingsdowne Rd SURB KT6 45 H7
Kingsdown Rd CHEAM SM3 65 H4
EW KT17 84 D3
Kings Dr BRYLDS KT5 45 K7
THDIT KT7 44 E6
The Kings Dr WOT/HER KT12 60 C7
Kings Farm Av
RCHPK/HAM TW10 18 D6
Kingsfold Ct HORS RH12 * 189 J8
Kingsgate CRAWE RH10 * 165 G4
Kings Ga HORS RH12 166 E7
Kingsgate Rd KUT/HW KT1 8 E5
Kings Hall Rd BECK BR3 33 G8
King's Head La BF/WBF KT14 79 G1
Kingshill Av WPK KT4 46 D7
Kings Keep KUT/HW KT1 * 45 H4
Kingsland RDKG RH5 173 P8
Kingsland Ct CRAWE RH10 * 165 J4
Kings La BFOR GU20 55 H4
EGH TW20 20 D6
RFNM GU10 155 J3
SUT SM1 66 A4
Kingslawn Cl PUT/ROE SW15 19 L7
Kingslea LHD/OX KT22 102 D2
SWTR RH13 167 H6
Kingsleigh Cl BTFD TW8 18 A1
Kingsleigh Pl MTCM CR4 48 C3
Kingsley Av BNSTD SM7 85 K5
CBLY GU15 72 F5
EGH TW20 20 E7
HSLW TW3 16 F4
SUT SM1 66 A3
Kingsley Cl HORL RH6 175 N4
HORL RH6 175 Q4
Kingsley Dr WPK KT4 64 C1
Kingsley Gv REIG RH2 147 K3
Kingsley Rd CRAWW RH11 164 C7
CROY/NA CR0 49 K8
FARN GU14 92 C3
HORL RH6 160 C1
HSLW TW3 16 F4
WIM/MER SW19 29 L6
Kingslyn Crs NRWD SE19 50 B1
Kingsmead BH/WHM TN16 91 G6
CRAN GU6 186 D2
FARN GU14 92 E5
FRIM GU16 93 H2
Kings Md HORL RH6 161 L3
Kingsmead RCHPK/HAM TW10 18 C8
Kings Md REDH RH1 149 H2
Kingsmead WOKN/KNAP GU21 11 H3
Kingsmead Av MTCM CR4 48 F3
SUN TW16 42 F3
SURB KT6 63 K1
WPK KT4 64 E2
Kingsmead Cl HOR/WEW KT19 64 A6
TEDD TW11 26 E7
Kings Mead Pk ESH/CLAY KT10 62 B6
Kingsmead Pl HORS RH12 204 D6
Kingsmead Rd
BRXS/STRHM SW2 31 K3
HORS RH12 204 D6
Kingsmere Rd BNFD RG42 34 C1
WIM/MER SW19 29 G3
Kings Ms FRIM GU16 93 J3
HORS RH12 166 E7
Kings Mill La REDH RH1 149 G4
Kingsnympton Pk KUTN/CMB KT2 9 M1
King's Paddock HPTN TW12 43 M1
Kings Pde CAR SM5 * 66 B2
King's Pas KUTN/CMB KT2 8 D4
The Kings Peace GSHT GU26 * 197 P2
King's Ride ASC SL5 35 M4
CBLY GU15 53 G8
Kings Rd ADL/WDHM KT15 58 E8
ALDT GU11 112 B8
ASC SL5 37 H5
BELMT SM2 65 K8
BH/WHM TN16 90 F7
CHOB/PIR GU24 75 K4
CRAN GU6 186 E3
EGH TW20 21 K5
FELT TW13 24 F2
GODL GU7 168 C3
HASM GU27 198 B7
HORL RH6 160 D4
KUTN/CMB KT2 8 F3
MORT/ESHN SW14 19 G5
MTCM CR4 48 D3
RCHPK/HAM TW10 18 C7
RGUE GU4 139 H7
SHGR GU5 139 L8
SNWD SE25 50 D3
SURB KT6 44 F8
SWTR RH13 167 H6
TEDD TW11 26 A6
TWK TW1 17 L8
WIM/MER SW19 29 K7
WOKN/KNAP GU21 11 H3
WOT/HER KT12 60 E1
Kings Shade Wk
HOR/WEW KT19 * 84 A3
King's Rd GU GU1 7 H4
Kingsthorpe Rd SYD SE26 33 G5
Kingston Av CHEAM SM3 65 H2
EBED/NFELT TW14 15 H8
EHSLY KT24 100 B8
LHD/OX KT22 102 E3
Kingston Br KUT/HW KT1 8 C6
Kingston By-Pass BRYLDS KT5 45 M8
ESH/CLAY KT10 62 A5
RYNPK SW20 28 C7
SURB KT6 63 J2
Kingston Cl TEDD TW11 26 E7
Kingston Crs ASHF TW15 22 F6
BECK BR3 51 J1
Kingston Gdns CROY/NA CR0 67 H2
Kingston Hall Rd KUT/HW KT1 8 D8
Kingston Hl KUTN/CMB KT2 9 K4
Kingston Hill Pl KUTN/CMB KT2 27 M5
Kingston House Gdns
LHD/OX KT22 * 102 E3
Kingston La EHSLY KT24 119 K1
TEDD TW11 26 E7
Kingston Ldg NWMAL KT3 46 B4
Kingston Ri ADL/WDHM KT15 58 D8
Kingston Rd ASHF TW15 23 J7
BRYLDS KT5 63 L1
CBLY GU15 53 K8
HOR/WEW KT19 64 B4
LHD/OX KT22 102 D1
NWMAL KT3 46 A4
PUT/ROE SW15 28 E2
RYNPK SW20 47 H2
STA TW18 22 D5
TEDD TW11 26 E7
WIM/MER SW19 29 K8
Kingston Sq NRWD SE19 32 A6
Kingston V PUT/ROE SW15 28 A5
King St CHERT KT16 40 D8
EGRIN RH19 162 F4
RCH/KEW TW9 18 A7
TWK TW1 26 D2
King Street Pde TWK TW1 * 26 D2
King's Wk CBLY GU15 72 C3
SAND/SEL CR2 88 E4
Kings Warren LHD/OX KT22 81 M1
Kingsway ALDT GU11 112 C8
BLKW GU17 72 B5
Kings Wy CROY/NA CR0 67 J4
Kingsway MORT/ESHN SW14 18 E5
NWMAL KT3 46 F4
STWL/WRAY TW19 23 G2
WOKN/KNAP GU21 10 A8
WWKM BR4 70 C2
Kingsway Av SAND/SEL CR2 68 F7
WOKN/KNAP GU21 10 B7
Kingsway Rd CHEAM SM3 65 H6
Kingsway Ter WEY KT13 59 K7
The Kingsway EW KT17 64 C8
Kingswick Cl ASC SL5 37 H4
Kingswick Dr ASC SL5 37 G4
Kingswood Av HPTN TW12 25 L7
HSLW TW3 16 C4
SAND/SEL CR2 88 E5
THHTH CR7 49 K5
Kingswood Cl ASHF TW15 23 M5
EGH TW20 21 G5
GU GU1 117 M7
NWMAL KT3 46 C6
SURB KT6 45 H7
WEY KT13 59 L6
Kingswood Creek
STWL/WRAY TW19 12 A7
Kingswood Dr BELMT SM2 65 L7
CAR SM5 48 C8
DUL SE21 32 B5
Kingswood Firs GSHT GU26 197 P3
Kingswood La GSHT GU26 197 P3
WARL CR6 88 F5
Kingswood Ri EGH TW20 21 G6
Kingswood Rd
KWD/TDW/WH KT20 104 E3
PGE/AN SE20 32 F7
WIM/MER SW19 47 J1
Kingswood Wy SAND/SEL CR2 89 G2
WLGTN SM6 67 H4
Kingsworth Cl BECK BR3 51 H5
Kingsworthy Cl KUT/HW KT1 9 H8
Kings Yd ASC SL5 * 36 B4
Kinloss Rd CAR SM5 47 M7
Kinnaird Av CHSWK W4 18 F2
Kinnersley Mnr REIG RH2 * 147 M8
Kinnersley Wk REIG RH2 147 K5
Kinnibrugh Dr LING RH7 178 H8
Kinross Av ASC SL5 36 C5
WPK KT4 64 D1
Kinross Cl SUN TW16 24 C6
Kinross Ct ASC SL5 36 C5
Kinross Dr SUN TW16 24 C6
Kintyre Cl STRHM/NOR SW16 49 J2
Kinver Rd SYD SE26 32 F5
Kipings KWD/TDW/WH KT20 105 G4
Kipling Cl CRAWE RH10 165 L2
Kipling Ct SWTR RH13 167 K5
Kipling Dr WIM/MER SW19 30 A7
Kipling Wy EGRIN RH19 162 D4
Kirby Cl HOR/WEW KT19 64 C4
Kirby Rd WOKN/KNAP GU21 10 A5
Kirdford Cl CRAWW RH11 164 C2
Kirkdale SYD SE26 32 E3
Kirkdale Cnr SYD SE26 * 32 F5
Kirkefields GUW GU2 116 D5
Kirkham Cl SHST GU47 52 A7
Kirk Knoll BOR GU35 180 E12
Kirkland Av WOKN/KNAP GU21 76 B6
Kirkland Ter BECK BR3 33 K7
Kirkleas Rd SURB KT6 45 H8
Kirklees Rd THHTH CR7 49 K5
Kirkley Rd WIM/MER SW19 47 K1
Kirkly Cl SAND/SEL CR2 68 B7
Kirkstall Gdns
BRXS/STRHM SW2 31 G2
Kirkstall Rd BRXS/STRHM SW2 31 H2
Kirksted Rd MRDN SM4 47 L8
Kirkstone Cl CBLY GU15 74 A5
Kirrane Cl NWMAL KT3 46 C5
Kirriemuir Gdns ASHV GU12 114 A6
Kirtley Rd SYD SE26 33 H5
Kitchener Rd ALDT GU11 113 G3
THHTH CR7 50 A3
Kites Cl CRAWW RH11 164 E4
Kithurst Cl CRAWW RH11 164 E6
Kitley Gdns NRWD SE19 50 C1
Kitsmead CRAWE RH10 192 F3
Kitsmead La CHERT KT16 57 G1
VW GU25 38 F8
Kitson Rd BARN SW13 19 K3
Kittiwake Cl CRAWW RH11 190 G9
SAND/SEL CR2 69 H8
Kitts La RFNM GU10 181 L9
Knapdale Cl FSTH SE23 32 E3
Knapmill Rd CAT SE6 33 K3
Knapmill Wy CAT SE6 33 K3
Knapp Rd ASHF TW15 23 J5
Knapton Ms TOOT SW17 30 D7
Knaresborough Dr
WAND/EARL SW18 29 L2
Kneller Gdns ISLW TW7 17 G8
Kneller Rd NWMAL KT3 46 B7
WHTN TW2 16 F8
Knepp Cl CRAWE RH10 165 L4
Knevett Ter HSLW TW3 16 D6
Knighton Cl CRAWE RH10 192 C3
SAND/SEL CR2 67 L7
Knighton Park Rd SYD SE26 33 G6
Knighton Rd REDH RH1 148 D2
Knightons La MFD/CHID GU8 185 J9
Knightsbridge Crs STA TW18 22 E7
Knightsbridge Rd CBLY GU15 73 H2
Knights Cl E/WMO/HCT KT8 43 J5
EGH TW20 * 22 A7
Knight's Hl WNWD SE27 31 L6
Knight's Hill Sq WNWD SE27 31 L5
Knight's Pk KUT/HW KT1 8 F8
Knights Pl REDH RH1 126 D7
Knights Rd FNM GU9 134 B2
Knights Wy CBLY GU15 73 M5
Knightswood BRAK RG12 34 E8
WOKN/KNAP GU21 76 C8
Knightwood Cl REIG RH2 147 K2
Knightwood Crs NWMAL KT3 46 B6
Knipp Hl COB KT11 81 J3
Knobfield RDKG RH5 171 L1
Knob Hl HORS RH12 188 H12
Knockhundred La GSHT GU26 197 N5
Knole Cl CRAWE RH10 165 M3
CROY/NA CR0 * 50 F6
Knole Gv EGRIN RH19 162 D2
Knole Wd ASC SL5 * 37 H8
Knollmead BRYLDS KT5 45 M8
Knoll Park Rd CHERT KT16 40 C8
Knoll Quarry GODL GU7 168 B3
Knoll Rd CBLY GU15 73 G3
DORK RH4 144 D4
GODL GU7 168 A3
Knolls Cl WPK KT4 64 E2
The Knolls EW KT17 84 F6
The Knoll BECK BR3 51 L1
CHERT KT16 40 C8
COB KT11 81 K3
HAYES BR2 70 D1
LHD/OX KT22 102 F3
Knoll Wd GODL GU7 168 B3
Knollys Cl STRHM/NOR SW16 31 L4
Knollys Rd ALDT GU11 112 C6
STRHM/NOR SW16 31 K4
The Knook SHST GU47 * 72 A2
Knowle Cl CRAWE RH10 192 H2
Knowle Dr CRAWE RH10 192 G2
Knowle Gdns BF/WBF KT14 78 C3
Knowle Gn STA TW18 22 D6
Knowle Gv VW GU25 38 F7
Knowle Grove Cl VW GU25 38 F7
Knowle Hl VW GU25 38 E7
Knowle La CRAN GU6 186 C5
HORS RH12 186 E12
Knowle Pk COB KT11 81 H5
Knowle Park Av STA TW18 22 E7
Knowle Rd HAYES BR2 71 H1
WHTN TW2 26 B2
The Knowle BOR GU35 180 G11
KWD/TDW/WH KT20 * 104 E3
Knowl Hl WOKS/MYFD GU22 11 K8
Knowsley Ter
MFD/CHID GU8 * 199 P1
Knox Rd GUW GU2 116 D3
Kohat Ct ALDT GU11 * 112 C7
Kohat Rd WIM/MER SW19 29 L6
Kohima Cl ALDT GU11 112 E7
Koonowla Cl BH/WHM TN16 91 G5
Kooringa WARL CR6 108 E1
Korda Cl SHPTN TW17 41 J3
Krooner Rd CBLY GU15 72 E6
Kuala Gdns STRHM/NOR SW16 49 J1
Kyle Cl BRAK RG12 34 E3
Kynaston Av THHTH CR7 49 M5
Kynaston Ct CTHM CR3 108 B7
Kynaston Crs THHTH CR7 49 M5
Kynaston Rd THHTH CR7 49 M5
Kynersley Cl CAR SM5 66 C2

L

Laburnum Av SUT SM1 66 B2
Laburnum Cl GU GU1 116 F5
Laburnum Crs SUN TW16 42 E1
Laburnum Gdns CROY/NA CR0 51 G7
Laburnum Gv DTCH/LGLY SL3 12 D1
HSLW TW3 16 C6
NWMAL KT3 46 A2
Laburnum Pl EGH TW20 20 E7
Laburnum Rd ALDT GU11 112 D8
CHERT KT16 40 D8
EPSOM KT18 84 B3
FNM GU9 134 B2
MTCM CR4 48 D2
WIM/MER SW19 29 M8
WOKS/MYFD GU22 97 G2
Laburnum Wy
STWL/WRAY TW19 23 J2
Lacey Av COUL/CHIP CR5 107 K2
Lacey Cl EGH TW20 22 A8
Lacey Dr COUL/CHIP CR5 107 K2
HPTN TW12 43 J1
Lackford Rd COUL/CHIP CR5 86 C8
Lacock Cl WIM/MER SW19 29 M7
Lacrosse Wy STRHM/NOR SW16 49 G1
Lacy Gn COUL/CHIP CR5 107 K2
Ladas Rd WNWD SE27 31 M6
Ladbroke Gv REDH RH1 126 D7
Ladbroke Hurst LING RH7 178 H8
Ladbroke Rd EPSOM KT18 84 A4
HORL RH6 160 D1
REDH RH1 126 D6
Ladbrook Rd SNWD SE25 50 A3
Ladderstile Ride
KUTN/CMB KT2 27 L6
Ladybank BRAK RG12 34 E8
Lady Booth Rd KUT/HW KT1 8 E7
Ladycroft Gdns ORP BR6 71 M4
Ladycroft Wy ORP BR6 71 M4
Ladycross MFD/CHID GU8 183 M1
Ladyegate Cl RDKG RH5 145 G1
Ladyegate Rd RDKG RH5 144 F2
Lady Forsdyke Wy
HOR/WEW KT19 63 K7
Ladygate Dr GSHT GU26 197 M2
Ladygrove CROY/NA CR0 69 H7
Ladygrove Dr RGUE GU4 117 L3
Lady Harewood Wy
HOR/WEW KT19 63 K7
Lady Hay WPK KT4 64 C1
Lady Margaret Rd ASC SL5 37 J8
CRAWW RH11 164 C3
Ladymead GU GU1 6 F1
Ladymead Cl CRAWE RH10 165 L7
Ladymount WLGTN SM6 67 G3
Ladyship Ter EDUL SE22 * 32 E1
Ladythorpe Cl ADL/WDHM KT15 58 E3
Ladywood Rd SURB KT6 63 K1
Laffan's Rd ALDT GU11 112 C4
Lafone Av FELT TW13 24 F2
Lagham Ct GDST RH9 * 151 H4
Lagham Pk GDST RH9 151 H3
Lagham Rd GDST RH9 151 H4
Laglands Cl REIG RH2 125 M6
Laings Av MTCM CR4 48 C2
Lainlock Pl HSLW TW3 16 E3
Lainson St WAND/EARL SW18 29 K1
Lairdale Cl DUL SE21 31 M2
Laird Ct BAGS GU19 54 B8
Laitwood Rd BAL SW12 30 E2
Lake Cl BF/WBF KT14 79 G2
Lake Gdns RCHPK/HAM TW10 26 E4
WLGTN SM6 66 E2
Lakehall Gdns THHTH CR7 49 L5
Lakehall Rd THHTH CR7 49 L5
Lakehurst Rd HOR/WEW KT19 64 B4
Lakeland Dr FRIM GU16 73 H8
Lake La HORL RH6 160 F1
RFNM GU10 180 D3
Lake Rd CROY/NA CR0 69 J1
FRIM GU16 93 K3
RDKG RH5 172 D11

VW GU25 38 E5
WIM/MER SW19 29 J6
Lakers Ri BNSTD SM7 86 B6
Lakes Cl RGUE GU4 139 L6
Lakeside BECK BR3 51 L3
HOR/WEW KT19 64 B5
HORS RH12 166 F4
REDH RH1 126 D6
WEY KT13 60 B1
WLGTN SM6 66 E3
WOKN/KNAP GU21 96 B1
Lakeside Cl ASHV GU12 113 J5
SNWD SE25 50 D2
WOKN/KNAP GU21 96 B1
Lakeside Dr ESH/CLAY KT10 61 M5
HAYES BR2 71 H2
Lakeside Gdns FARN GU14 92 A2
Lakeside Gra WEY KT13 59 M2
Lakeside Rd ASHV GU12 113 J5
DTCH/LGLY SL3 13 J2
FARN GU14 112 D2
The Lake Side BLKW GU17 72 A5
Lakes Rd HAYES BR2 70 F4
Lake Vw RDKG RH5 144 F5
Lake View Rd EGRIN RH19 178 G12
EGRIN RH19 193 N2
Lakeview Rd WNWD SE27 31 K6
Laleham Abbey STA TW18 * 40 F4
Laleham Cl STA TW18 40 E1
Laleham Ct SUT SM1 * 65 M4
WOKN/KNAP GU21 * 10 D3
Laleham Reach CHERT KT16 40 E2
Laleham Rd CAT SE6 33 M1
SHPTN TW17 41 J4
STA TW18 22 C7
Lamberhurst Rd WNWD SE27 31 K5
Lamberhurst Wk CRAWE RH10 165 J5
Lambert Av RCH/KEW TW9 18 D5
Lambert Cl BH/WHM TN16 91 G6
Lambert Rd BNSTD SM7 85 K4
Lambert's Pl CROY/NA CR0 2 F3
Lambert's Rd BRYLDS KT5 45 H5
Lambeth Cl CRAWW RH11 164 D8
Lambeth Rd CROY/NA CR0 49 K8
Lambeth Wk CRAWW RH11 * 164 D8
Lambly Hl VW GU25 39 H3
Lambourn Cl EGRIN RH19 162 F2
Lambourne Av
WIM/MER SW19 29 J5
Lambourne Cl CRAWE RH10 165 H6
Lambourne Crs
WOKN/KNAP GU21 78 A3
Lambourne Dr BAGS GU19 54 A7
COB KT11 80 F5
Lambourne Gv BRAK RG12 35 H2
KUT/HW KT1 9 L6
Lambourne Wy RFNM GU10 135 H2
Lambs Crs HORS RH12 167 J4
Lambs Farm Cl HORS RH12 167 K4
Lambs Farm Rd HORS RH12 167 J4
Lambs Green Rd HORS RH12 190 C8
Lambton Rd RYNPK SW20 46 F2
Lambyn Cft HORL RH6 160 F2
Lammas Av MTCM CR4 48 D2
Lammas Cl GODL GU7 168 D3
STA TW18 22 B4
Lammas Dr STA TW18 22 A5
Lammas La ESH/CLAY KT10 61 K3
Lammas Rd GODL GU7 168 D4
RCHPK/HAM TW10 26 F5
Lammermoor Rd BAL SW12 * 30 E1
Lamorna WOKS/MYFD GU22 * 10 D8
Lampard La RFNM GU10 181 J7
Lampeter Cl WOKS/MYFD GU22 10 C8
Lampton Av HSLW TW3 16 D3
Lampton House Cl
WIM/MER SW19 29 G5
Lampton Park Rd HSLW TW3 16 E4
Lampton Rd HSLW TW3 16 E4
Lanark Cl FRIM GU16 73 H7
SWTR RH13 167 H7
Lancaster Av FNM GU9 5 K7
GU GU1 7 M7
MTCM CR4 49 H4
WIM/MER SW19 29 G6
WNWD SE27 31 L3
Lancaster Cl ASHF TW15 23 H5
ASHV GU12 113 J4
CRAWE RH10 165 M1
EGH TW20 21 G6
STWL/WRAY TW19 14 B8
WOKN/KNAP GU21 11 G4
WPK KT4 46 E7
Lancaster Ct WOT/HER KT12 42 D7
Lancaster Dr CBLY GU15 73 G3
EGRIN RH19 163 H2
Lancaster Gdn KUTN/CMB KT2 27 G6
Lancaster Gdns KUTN/CMB KT2 27 H6
WIM/MER SW19 29 H6
Lancaster Ms
RCHPK/HAM TW10 18 B8
Lancaster Pk
RCHPK/HAM TW10 18 B7
Lancaster Pl TWK TW1 26 D1
WIM/MER SW19 29 G6
Lancaster Rd FARN GU14 92 E8
SNWD SE25 50 D3
WIM/MER SW19 29 G6
Lancaster Wy FARN GU14 92 F2
WPK KT4 46 F7
Lancastrian Rd WLGTN SM6 67 H6
Lancelot Cl CRAWW RH11 164 A4
Lancer Ct ALDT GU11 * 112 B7
Lancing Cl CRAWW RH11 164 C3
Lancing Rd CROY/NA CR0 49 J6
FELT TW13 24 C3
Landau Ter HAYES BR2 71 H3
Landen Pk HORL RH6 160 B1
Landford Rd PUT/ROE SW15 19 M5
Landgrove Rd WIM/MER SW19 29 K5
Landon Wy ASHF TW15 * 23 L7
Landscape Rd WARL CR6 108 E1
Landseer Cl SHST GU47 72 B3
WIM/MER SW19 47 M1
Landseer Rd NWMAL KT3 46 A7
SUT SM1 65 K5
Lane Cl ADL/WDHM KT15 58 D4
Lane End EPSOM KT18 83 L4
MFD/CHID GU8 183 Q9
Lane End Dr WOKN/KNAP GU21 75 M7
Lane Gdns ESH/CLAY KT10 62 C6
Lanercost Rd
BRXS/STRHM SW2 31 K3
CRAWW RH11 164 E5
The Lane BIL RH14 201 M5
CHERT KT16 40 D3
MFD/CHID GU8 182 C5
VW GU25 39 H3
Laneway PUT/ROE SW15 19 L7
Langaller La LHD/OX KT22 101 L3
Langbourne Wy ESH/CLAY KT10 62 C5
Lang Cl LHD/OX KT22 101 L5
Langcroft Cl CAR SM5 66 C2
Langdale Av MTCM CR4 48 C3
Langdale Cl FARN GU14 92 B5
MORT/ESHN SW14 18 E6
ORP BR6 71 L2
WOKN/KNAP GU21 76 F6
Langdale Ct ASHV GU12 * 113 J4
Langdale Dr ASC SL5 36 B2
Langdale Pde MTCM CR4 * 48 C2
Langdale Rd CRAWW RH11 190 G9
THHTH CR7 49 K4
Langdon Cl CBLY GU15 73 M5
Langdon Pl MORT/ESHN SW14 18 F5
Langdon Rd MRDN SM4 47 M5
Langdon Wk MRDN SM4 47 M5
Langham Cl GODL GU7 168 C4
Langham Dene PUR/KEN CR8 87 L5
Langham Gdns
RCHPK/HAM TW10 26 F5
Langham House Cl
RCHPK/HAM TW10 27 G5
Langham Pk GODL GU7 168 C4
Langham Pl CHSWK W4 19 H1
EGH TW20 21 J6
Langham Rd RYNPK SW20 46 F1
TEDD TW11 26 E6
Langholm Cl BAL SW12 31 G1
Langhorn Dr WHTN TW2 26 B1
Langhurst Cl HORS RH12 189 L9
Langhurst La CRAWW RH11 190 D5
Langhurstwood Rd
HORS RH12 189 L9
Langland Gdns CROY/NA CR0 69 J1
Langlands Ri HOR/WEW KT19 83 M3
Langley Av SURB KT6 45 G8
WPK KT4 65 G1
Langley Cl EPSOM KT18 104 A1
GU GU1 6 F1
Langley Ct BECK BR3 * 51 L4
Langley Crs HYS/HAR UB3 15 J2
Langley Dr ALDT GU11 134 D1
CBLY GU15 73 G3
CRAWW RH11 164 E2
Langley Gv NWMAL KT3 46 A2
Langley La CRAWW RH11 164 C2
Langley Oaks Av SAND/SEL CR2 68 D8
Langley Pde CRAWW RH11 164 E1
Langley Park Rd BELMT SM2 65 M5
Langley Pl CRAWW RH11 164 E1
Langley Rd BECK BR3 51 G4
ISLW TW7 17 J4
SAND/SEL CR2 69 G7
STA TW18 22 C7
SURB KT6 45 H7
WIM/MER SW19 47 J1
Langley Vale Rd EPSOM KT18 84 A8
Langley Wk CRAWW RH11 164 E1
WOKS/MYFD GU22 10 C9
Langmans Wy
WOKN/KNAP GU21 76 B6
Langmead St WNWD SE27 31 L5
Langport Ct WOT/HER KT12 42 F8
Langridge Dr EGRIN RH19 162 F5
Langridge Ms HPTN TW12 25 J7
Langroyd Rd TOOT SW17 30 C3
Langshott HORL RH6 161 G2
Langshott Cl ADL/WDHM KT15 58 B8
Langshott La HORL RH6 160 F2
Langside Av PUT/ROE SW15 19 K6
Langsmead LING RH7 177 R1
Langstone Cl CRAWE RH10 165 L7
Langton Av EW KT17 84 C1
Langton Cl ADL/WDHM KT15 58 E2
WOKN/KNAP GU21 76 C7
Langton Dr BOR GU35 180 F10
Langton Ri EDUL SE22 32 E1
Langton Rd E/WMO/HCT KT8 43 M5
Langton Wy CROY/NA CR0 3 H9
EGH TW20 21 M7
Langwood Cha TEDD TW11 8 B1
Langwood Cl ASHTD KT21 83 K7
Lanigan Dr HSLW TW3 16 E7
Lankton Cl BECK BR3 51 M1
Lansbury Av EBED/NFELT TW14 15 L8
Lansbury Rd CRAWW RH11 191 L12
Lansdell Rd MTCM CR4 48 D2
Lansdown GU GU1 117 K8
Lansdown Cl HORS RH12 167 L3
WOKN/KNAP GU21 96 C1
WOT/HER KT12 42 F8
Lansdowne Cl BRYLDS KT5 63 L1
RYNPK SW20 29 G8
TWK TW1 26 C2
Lansdowne Copse WPK KT4 * 64 D1
Lansdowne Ct WPK KT4 64 D1
Lansdowne Hl WNWD SE27 31 L4
Lansdowne Pl NRWD SE19 32 C8
Lansdowne Rd ALDT GU11 112 D8
CROY/NA CR0 2 D5
FRIM GU16 93 K1
HOR/WEW KT19 63 M6
HSLW TW3 16 E5
PUR/KEN CR8 87 K2
RYNPK SW20 28 F8
STA TW18 22 E8
Lansdowne Wood Cl
WNWD SE27 31 L4
Lantern Cl ORP BR6 71 L3
PUT/ROE SW15 19 K6
Lanyon Cl HORS RH12 167 K3
Lanyon Ms HORS RH12 * 167 K3
Lapse Wood Wk FSTH SE23 32 E2
Lapwing Cl SAND/SEL CR2 69 H8
SWTR RH13 167 J6
Lapwing Gv RGUE GU4 118 A6
Lara Cl CHSGTN KT9 63 H6
Larbert Rd STRHM/NOR SW16 48 F1
Larby Pl EW KT17 64 B8
Larch Av ASC SL5 37 H5
GU GU1 116 F5
Larch Cl BAL SW12 30 E3
CBLY GU15 53 H8
KWD/TDW/WH KT20 105 M3
LIPH GU30 196 G10
REDH RH1 147 M2
WARL CR6 109 H1
Larch Crs HOR/WEW KT19 63 L5
Larch Dene ORP BR6 71 K1
Larch End HORS RH12 166 E6
Larches Av MORT/ESHN SW14 19 G6
The Larches EGRIN RH19 163 H1
HORS RH12 167 M3
WOKN/KNAP GU21 10 D3
Larches Wy CRAWE RH10 193 P5
Larch Rd BOR GU35 180 G11
Larch Tree Wy CROY/NA CR0 69 K2
Larchwood Cl BNSTD SM7 85 H6
Larchwood Dr EGH TW20 20 E7
Larchwood Gld CBLY GU15 73 K2
Larchwood Rd
WOKN/KNAP GU21 96 A2
Larcombe Cl CROY/NA CR0 68 C3
Larges Bridge Dr BRAK RG12 34 F3
Larges La BRAK RG12 34 F2
Largewood Av SURB KT6 63 K1
Lark Av STA TW18 22 C4
Larkbere Rd SYD SE26 33 H5
Larkfield COB KT11 80 D3
CRAN GU6 187 K1
Larkfield Cl FNM GU9 4 C2
Larkfield Ct HORL RH6 161 K3
Larkfield Rd FNM GU9 4 C3
RCH/KEW TW9 18 B6
Larkhall Cl WOT/HER KT12 60 F5
Larkham Cl FELT TW13 24 B4
Larkin Cl COUL/CHIP CR5 87 J7
Larkins Rd HORL RH6 160 A7
Lark Ri CRAWE RH10 193 P7
CRAWW RH11 164 E2
EHSLY KT24 120 B5
LIPH GU30 196 F8
Larksfield EGH TW20 20 E8
HORL RH6 160 E2
Larkspur Cl ALDT GU11 134 D2
Larkspur Wy HOR/WEW KT19 63 M4
RDKG RH5 145 G5
Larks Wy WOKN/KNAP GU21 75 M6
Lark Wy CAR SM5 48 B7
Larpent Av PUT/ROE SW15 19 M7
Lascombe La RGUW GU3 136 D5
Lashmere CRAN GU6 185 R2
CRAWE RH10 193 J2
Lasswade Rd CHERT KT16 40 C7
Latchmere Cl
RCHPK/HAM TW10 27 H6
Latchmere La KUTN/CMB KT2 27 J7
Latchmere Rd KUTN/CMB KT2 8 F2
Latchwood La RFNM GU10 156 A4
Lateward Rd BTFD TW8 18 A1
Latham Av FRIM GU16 73 H7
Latham Cl BH/WHM TN16 90 F6
Latham Rd TWK TW1 26 C1
Latham's Wy CROY/NA CR0 49 J8
Latimer BRAK RG12 34 E8
Latimer Cl CRAWW RH11 164 F1
WOKS/MYFD GU22 11 K3
WPK KT4 64 E3
Latimer Ct REDH RH1 148 C2
Latimer Rd CROY/NA CR0 2 B7
GODL GU7 168 B5
TEDD TW11 26 C6
WIM/MER SW19 29 L7
La Tourne Gdns ORP BR6 71 M2
Lattimer Pl CHSWK W4 19 H2
Latton Cl ESH/CLAY KT10 61 L3
WOT/HER KT12 43 J7
Latymer Cl WEY KT13 59 M3
Laud Dr CRAWE RH10 165 M5
Lauder Cl FRIM GU16 73 H7
Lauderdale FARN GU14 92 A7
Lauderdale Dr
RCHPK/HAM TW10 27 G4
Laud St CROY/NA CR0 2 C8
Laughton Rd HORS RH12 167 J4
Laundry La SHST GU47 72 B4
Laundry Rd GU GU1 6 F5
Laundry Wy RDKG RH5 173 K12
Lauradale BRAK RG12 34 D4
Laurel Av EGH TW20 20 E6
TWK TW1 26 C2
Laurel Bank CHOB/PIR GU24 * 76 B1
Laurel Cl CBLY GU15 73 G5
CRAWE RH10 165 J7
DTCH/LGLY SL3 13 H2
TOOT SW17 30 B6
Laurel Crs CROY/NA CR0 69 K2
WOKN/KNAP GU21 77 M3
Laurel Dene EGRIN RH19 163 G4
Laureldene RGUW GU3 114 E8
Laurel Dr OXTED RH8 130 C5
Laurel Gdns ALDT GU11 134 D2
HSLWW TW4 16 B6
Laurel Gv PGE/AN SE20 32 E8
RFNM GU10 155 J4
SYD SE26 33 G6
Laurel Rd BARN SW13 19 K4
HPTN TW12 26 A6
RYNPK SW20 46 E1
The Laurels BNSTD SM7 85 J7
COB KT11 81 H5
CRAWE RH10 * 165 J1
FNM GU9 134 C2
Laurel Wk SWTR RH13 167 J8
Laurier Rd CROY/NA CR0 3 J1
Lauriston Cl WOKN/KNAP GU21 76 A7
Lauriston Rd WIM/MER SW19 29 G7
Lauser Rd STWL/WRAY TW19 22 F1
Laustan Cl GU GU1 117 M8
Lavant Cl CRAWW RH11 164 B5
Lavender Av MTCM CR4 48 B1
WPK KT4 64 F2
Lavender Cl CAR SM5 66 D3
COUL/CHIP CR5 * 106 F1
CTHM CR3 107 M7
REDH RH1 148 E5
Lavender Ct E/WMO/HCT KT8 43 L3
Lavender Ga LHD/OX KT22 81 L3
Lavender Gv MTCM CR4 48 B1
Lavender La RFNM GU10 155 J5
Lavender Park Rd
BF/WBF KT14 * 78 D3
Lavender Rd CROY/NA CR0 49 J6
HOR/WEW KT19 63 L4
SUT SM1 66 A3
WLGTN SM6 66 D4
WOKS/MYFD GU22 11 K4
Lavender V WLGTN SM6 67 G5
Lavender Wy CROY/NA CR0 51 G6
Lavengro Rd WNWD SE27 31 M3
Lavenham Rd
WAND/EARL SW18 29 J3
Laverstoke Gdns
PUT/ROE SW15 28 C1
Lavington Cl CRAWW RH11 164 B3
Lavington Rd CROY/NA CR0 67 J2
Lawbrook La SHGR GU5 170 H1
Lawday Link FNM GU9 133 K2
Lawday Pl FNM GU9 133 K2
Lawday Place La FNM GU9 133 K2
Lawdon Gdns CROY/NA CR0 67 L3
Lawford Gdns PUR/KEN CR8 87 M6
Lawford Rd CHSWK W4 18 F2
Lawford's Hill Rd RGUW GU3 95 M6
Lawn Cl NWMAL KT3 46 B2
Lawn Crs RCH/KEW TW9 18 D4
Lawn Rd BECK BR3 33 K8
GUW GU2 6 F9
Lawnsmead SHGR GU5 169 L2
Lawns Rd HORS RH12 186 F10
The Lawns BELMT SM2 65 H6
DTCH/LGLY SL3 * 13 H3
FARN GU14 92 B6
MFD/CHID GU8 159 J8
NRWD SE19 50 A1
Lawrence Av NWMAL KT3 46 B7
Lawrence Cl RGUE GU4 117 L3
Lawrence Crs BFOR GU20 55 G5
Lawrence Gv BNFD RG42 34 A1
Lawrence La
BRKHM/BTCW RH3 124 E6
Lawrence Pde ISLW TW7 * 17 L5
Lawrence Rd HPTN TW12 25 J8
HSLWW TW4 15 M6
RCHPK/HAM TW10 26 F5
SNWD SE25 50 C4
WWKM BR4 70 D3
Lawrence Wy CBLY GU15 72 C5
Lawrie Park Av SYD SE26 32 E6
Lawrie Park Crs SYD SE26 32 E6
Lawrie Park Gdns SYD SE26 32 E6
Lawrie Park Rd SYD SE26 32 F7
Laws Cl CRAWW RH11 164 A5
SNWD SE25 50 A4
Lawson Cl WIM/MER SW19 29 G4
Lawson Ter SHGR GU5 * 169 L2
Lawson Wk CAR SM5 66 C8
Lawson Wy ASC SL5 37 L6
Laws Ter ALDT GU11 112 F6
Laxton Gdns REDH RH1 127 G2
Layard Rd THHTH CR7 50 A2
Layburn Crs DTCH/LGLY SL3 12 E1
Layhams Rd HAYES BR2 70 C8
WWKM BR4 70 B3
Layton Ct WEY KT13 59 L3
Layton Crs CROY/NA CR0 67 K4
Layton Pl RCH/KEW TW9 18 D3
Layton Rd HSLW TW3 16 E6
Layton's La SUN TW16 42 C2
Lazell Gdns BRKHM/BTCW RH3 145 M6
Leach Gv LHD/OX KT22 102 F4
Lea Cl ASHV GU12 113 K8
CRAWW RH11 164 B5
FNM GU9 134 D3
WHTN TW2 25 J1
Lea Ct FNM GU9 134 C2
Leacroft ASC SL5 37 K5
EGRIN RH19 162 E3
STA TW18 22 E6
Leacroft Av BAL SW12 30 C1
Leacroft Cl PUR/KEN CR8 87 M6
STA TW18 22 E5
Leaf Cl THDIT KT7 44 B5
Leaf Gv WNWD SE27 31 K6
Leafield Cl STRHM/NOR SW16 31 L7
WOKN/KNAP GU21 76 E8
Leafield Copse BRAK RG12 35 J4
Leafield Rd RYNPK SW20 47 J3
SUT SM1 65 K1
Leafy Gv HAYES BR2 70 F4
Leafy Wy CROY/NA CR0 3 J6
Leamington Av MRDN SM4 47 J4
Leamington Cl HSLW TW3 16 F7
Leander Rd THHTH CR7 49 J4
Leapale La GU GU1 7 G6
Leapale Rd GU GU1 7 G6
Lea Rd BECK BR3 51 K2
CBLY GU15 72 E7
Leas Cl CHSGTN KT9 63 J6
Leaside GT/LBKH KT23 101 K5
Leas La WARL CR6 89 G8
Leas Rd GU GU1 6 F5
WARL CR6 89 G8
The Leas STA TW18 * 22 D5
The Lea EGH TW20 21 L8
Leather Cl EDEN TN8 179 R1
MTCM CR4 48 D2
Leatherhead By-Pass Rd
LHD/OX KT22 103 G4
Leatherhead Rd
GT/LBKH KT23 101 L8
LHD/OX KT22 82 A5
LHD/OX KT22 103 G3
Leather La SHGR GU5 141 M5
Leaveland Cl BECK BR3 51 K4
Leavesden Rd WEY KT13 59 L4
Leaves Gn BRAK RG12 35 G6
Leaves Green Crs HAYES BR2 90 F1
Leaves Green Rd HAYES BR2 91 G1
Lea Wy ASHV GU12 113 J6
Leaway FNM GU9 * 134 D4
Leazes Av CTHM CR3 107 K5
Lebanon Av FELT TW13 25 G6
Lebanon Dr COB KT11 81 K3
Lebanon Gdns BH/WHM TN16 91 G7
Lebanon Pk TWK TW1 26 E1
Lebanon Rd CROY/NA CR0 3 H4
Lechford Rd HORL RH6 160 C5
Leckford Rd WAND/EARL SW18 29 M3
Leconfield Av BARN SW13 19 J5
Ledbury Rd CROY/NA CR0 67 M3
REIG RH2 125 K8
Ledger Cl GU GU1 117 L6
Ledger Dr ADL/WDHM KT15 58 C5
Ledgers Rd WARL CR6 89 K6
Ledrington Rd NRWD SE19 32 C7
Lee Acre DORK RH4 * 144 F5
Leechcroft Rd WLGTN SM6 66 D2
Leech La EPSOM KT18 103 M8
Leechpool La SWTR RH13 167 K5
Lee Ct ALDT GU11 134 E1
Leehurst MFD/CHID GU8 159 H8
Lee Rd ALDT GU11 112 B7
WIM/MER SW19 47 L1
Leeside HORS RH12 * 189 R7
The Lees CROY/NA CR0 69 J1
Lee St HORL RH6 160 B2
Leeward Gdns WIM/MER SW19 29 H7
The Leeways CHEAM SM3 * 65 H5
Leewood Wy EHSLY KT24 120 F1
Lefroy's Fld RFNM GU10 132 C1
Legge Crs ALDT GU11 112 B8
Legrace Av HSLWW TW4 16 A4
Legsheath La EGRIN RH19 194 E12
Leicester BRAK RG12 35 G7
Leicester Av MTCM CR4 49 H4
Leicester Cl WPK KT4 64 F3
Leicester Rd CROY/NA CR0 3 H2
Leigham Av STRHM/NOR SW16 31 H4
Leigham Cl STRHM/NOR SW16 31 J4
Leigham Court Rd
STRHM/NOR SW16 31 J4
Leigham Dr ISLW TW7 17 H2
Leigham Hall Pde
STRHM/NOR SW16 * 31 H4
Leigham V STRHM/NOR SW16 31 K4
Leigh Cl ADL/WDHM KT15 58 C6
NWMAL KT3 46 A4
Leigh Court Cl COB KT11 80 F4
Leigh Crs CROY/NA CR0 69 L6
Leigh Hill Rd COB KT11 80 F5
Leighlands CRAWE RH10 165 L2
Leigh La FNM GU9 156 B1
Leigh Orchard Cl
STRHM/NOR SW16 31 J4
Leigh Pl COB KT11 80 F5
FELT TW13 24 F2
Leigh Place La GDST RH9 129 G6
Leigh Place Rd REIG RH2 146 D6
Leigh Rd BRKHM/BTCW RH3 145 M6
COB KT11 80 E3
HSLW TW3 17 G6
The Leigh KUTN/CMB KT2 28 B7
Leighton Gdns SAND/SEL CR2 88 E3
Leighton St CROY/NA CR0 2 A4
Leighton Wy EPSOM KT18 84 A4
Leinster Av MORT/ESHN SW14 18 F5
Leisure La BF/WBF KT14 * 78 E2
Leithcote Gdns
STRHM/NOR SW16 31 J5
Leithcote Pth
STRHM/NOR SW16 31 J4
Leith Dr ALDT GU11 112 C7
Leith Gv RDKG RH5 173 L5
Leith Hill Rd RDKG RH5 171 R2
Leith Lea RDKG RH5 * 173 L5
Leith Rd EW KT17 84 B2
RDKG RH5 173 K5
Leith Vw RDKG RH5 144 F6
Leith View Rd HORS RH12 167 K4
Lela Av HSLWW TW4 15 M4
Le Marchant Rd FRIM GU16 73 J6
Le May Cl HORL RH6 160 D2
Lemington Gv BRAK RG12 34 E6
Lemmington Wy HORS RH12 167 J2
Lemon's Farm Rd RDKG RH5 172 A3
Lendore Rd FRIM GU16 93 G1
Lenelby Rd SURB KT6 45 K8
Lenham Rd SUT SM1 65 L3
THHTH CR7 50 A2
Lennard Av WWKM BR4 70 B1
Lennard Cl WWKM BR4 70 B1
Lennard Rd CROY/NA CR0 2 C3
PGE/AN SE20 33 G7
SYD SE26 32 F7
Lennard Ter PGE/AN SE20 * 33 G7
Lennox Gdns CROY/NA CR0 67 L3
Lenten Cl SHGR GU5 142 A8
Lenton Ri RCH/KEW TW9 18 B5
Leof Crs CAT SE6 33 L6
Leominster Rd MRDN SM4 47 M6
Leominster Wk MRDN SM4 47 M6
Leonard Av MRDN SM4 47 M5
Leonard Cl FRIM GU16 93 G1
Leonard Pl HAYES BR2 * 71 H2
Leonard Rd STRHM/NOR SW16 48 F1
Leonardslee Ct CRAWE RH10 * 165 K7
Leonard Wy SWTR RH13 167 J7
Leopold Av FARN GU14 92 E4
WIM/MER SW19 29 J6
Leopold Rd CRAWW RH11 164 E4
WIM/MER SW19 29 K6
Le Personne Rd CTHM CR3 108 A4
Leppington BRAK RG12 34 E8
Leret Wy LHD/OX KT22 102 D3
Lesbourne Rd REIG RH2 147 L1
Lescombe Cl FSTH SE23 33 H4
Lescombe Rd FSTH SE23 33 H4
Leslie Gdns BELMT SM2 65 K6
Leslie Gv CROY/NA CR0 2 F3
Leslie Grove Pl CROY/NA CR0 3 G4
Leslie Park Rd CROY/NA CR0 3 G4
Leslie Rd CHOB/PIR GU24 56 A8
DORK RH4 123 G8
Lessingham Av TOOT SW17 30 C5
Lessing St FSTH SE23 33 H1
Lessness Rd MRDN SM4 47 M6
Lestock Cl SNWD SE25 50 D3
Letchworth Av
EBED/NFELT TW14 24 C1
Letchworth St TOOT SW17 30 C5
Letcombe Sq BRAK RG12 35 J4
Levana Cl WIM/MER SW19 29 H2
Levendale Rd FSTH SE23 33 H3
Leveret Cl CROY/NA CR0 90 A1
Leveret La CRAWW RH11 164 D2
Leverette Cl ASHV GU12 113 G6
Leverkusen Rd BRAK RG12 34 E3
Levern Dr FNM GU9 133 M3
Leverson St STRHM/NOR SW16 30 F7
Levett Rd LHD/OX KT22 102 E2
Levylsdene GU GU1 118 A8
Lewes Cl CRAWE RH10 165 L4
Lewesdon Cl WIM/MER SW19 29 G2

Lewes Rd EGRIN RH19 163 H5
FROW RH18 195 M10
Lewin Rd MORT/ESHN SW14 19 G5
STRHM/NOR SW16 31 G7
Lewins Rd EPSOM KT18 83 L4
Lewis Cl ADL/WDHM KT15 58 F3
Lewisham Cl CRAWW RH11 164 E8
Lewisham Wy SHST GU47 52 A8
Lewis Rd MTCM CR4 48 B2
RCH/KEW TW9 * 18 A7
SUT SM1 65 L3
Lewiston Cl WPK KT4 46 E7
Lexden Rd MTCM CR4 49 G4
Lexington Ct PUR/KEN CR8 67 M8
Lexton Gdns BAL SW12 31 G2
Leyborne Pk RCH/KEW TW9 18 D3
Leybourne Av BF/WBF KT14 79 J3
Leybourne Cl BF/WBF KT14 79 J3
CRAWW RH11 191 M12
Leybourne Pl EGRIN RH19 162 A2
Leyburn Gdns CROY/NA CR0 3 H6
Leycester Cl BFOR GU20 54 E3
Leyfield WPK KT4 64 B1
Leylands La STWL/WRAY TW19 13 J7
Ley Rd FARN GU14 92 D1
Leys Rd LHD/OX KT22 82 A2
The Leys WOT/HER KT12 * 61 H3
Leyton Rd WIM/MER SW19 29 M8
Liberty Av WIM/MER SW19 48 A1
Liberty Hall Rd
ADL/WDHM KT15 58 D4
Liberty La ADL/WDHM KT15 58 E4
Liberty Ri ADL/WDHM KT15 58 D5
Library Rd FARN GU14 92 E7
Lichfield Gdns RCH/KEW TW9 * 18 B7
Lichfield Rd HSLWW TW4 15 M5
RCH/KEW TW9 18 C3
Lichfields BRAK RG12 35 H2
Lichfield Ter RCH/KEW TW9 * 18 B7
Lichfield Wy SAND/SEL CR2 69 G8
Lickfolds Rd RFNM GU10 155 H7
Liddell Wy ASC SL5 36 D5
Liddington Hall Dr RGUW GU3 116 B5
Liddington New Rd
RGUW GU3 116 B5
Lidiard Rd WAND/EARL SW18 29 M3
Lido Rd GU GU1 7 H2
Lidsey Cl CRAWE RH10 165 L6
Lidstone Cl WOKN/KNAP GU21 76 E7
Lightwater Meadow
LTWR GU18 74 E1
Lightwater Rd LTWR GU18 74 E1
Lightwood BRAK RG12 35 G6
Lilac Av WOKS/MYFD GU22 97 G2
Lilac Cl GU GU1 116 F4
Lilac Gdns CROY/NA CR0 69 K2
Lilian Rd STRHM/NOR SW16 48 F1
Lille Barracks ALDT GU11 113 G1
Lilleshall Rd MRDN SM4 48 A6
Lilley Dr KWD/TDW/WH KT20 105 L4
Lillian Rd BARN SW13 19 K1
Lillie Rd BH/WHM TN16 91 G8
Lilliott's La LHD/OX KT22 102 D1
Lilyfields Cha CRAN GU6 187 K1
Lily Hill Dr BRAK RG12 35 H2
Lily Hill Rd BRAK RG12 35 J2
Lime Av CBLY GU15 73 K3
HORS RH12 167 K5
Limebush Cl ADL/WDHM KT15 58 F7
Lime Cl CRAWE RH10 192 G2
CRAWW RH11 164 E1
REIG RH2 147 L3
RGUE GU4 118 E2
Lime Crs SUN TW16 42 F2
Limecroft Cl HOR/WEW KT19 64 A6
Limecroft Rd
WOKN/KNAP GU21 75 L7
Lime Gv ADL/WDHM KT15 58 D3
GU GU1 116 F4
NWMAL KT3 46 A3
ORP BR6 71 L1
RGUE GU4 118 E2
TWK TW1 17 J8
WARL CR6 109 H1
WOKS/MYFD GU22 97 H3
Lime Kiln Rd SWTR RH13 205 R11
Lime Meadow Av
SAND/SEL CR2 88 D3
Limerick Cl BAL SW12 31 F1
BNFD RG42 34 D1
Limes Av BARN SW13 19 J4
CAR SM5 48 C8
CROY/NA CR0 67 J2
HORL RH6 160 E5
PGE/AN SE20 32 E8
Limes Cl ASHF TW15 23 K6
CAR SM5 66 C1
LIPH GU30 196 H6
Limes Field Rd
MORT/ESHN SW14 19 H5
Limes Rd BECK BR3 51 L2
CROY/NA CR0 50 A6
EGH TW20 21 J6
WEY KT13 59 K3
Limes Rw ORP BR6 71 L4
The Limes EDEN TN8 153 M8
EGRIN RH19 178 B12
LHD/OX KT22 102 E5
WOKN/KNAP GU21 10 A2
WOKN/KNAP GU21 * 11 G4
Lime St ALDT GU11 112 C7
Lime Tree Av THDIT KT7 44 B8
Limetree Cl BRXS/STRHM SW2 31 J2
Lime Tree Cl GT/LBKH KT23 101 K6
Lime Tree Gv CROY/NA CR0 69 J2
Limetree Pl MTCM CR4 48 E1
Lime Tree Rd HEST TW5 16 E3
Lime Tree Ter CAT SE6 * 33 J2
Lime Tree Wk VW GU25 39 H4
WWKM BR4 70 C3
Lime Wk BRAK RG12 34 F4
Limeway Ter DORK RH4 122 D8
Limewood Cl BECK BR3 51 M5
WOKN/KNAP GU21 96 A2
Limpsfield Av THTH CR7 49 J5
WIM/MER SW19 29 G3
Limpsfield Rd SAND/SEL CR2 88 D2
WARL CR6 109 K1
Linacre Dr CRAN GU6 186 H7
HORS RH12 186 H10
Lince La DORK RH4 144 A2
Linchmere Pl CRAWW RH11 164 C3
Linchmere Rd HASM GU27 197 P10
Lincoln Av WHTN TW2 25 M3
WIM/MER SW19 29 G4
Lincoln Cl ASHV GU12 113 K4
CBLY GU15 73 L5
CRAWE RH10 165 G7
Lincoln Dr WOKS/MYFD GU22 78 B5
Lincoln Rd DORK RH4 122 F8
FARN GU14 92 D8
FELT TW13 25 J4
GUW GU2 116 C6
MTCM CR4 49 H5
NWMAL KT3 45 M3
SNWD SE25 50 E3
WPK KT4 46 E8
Lincolns Md LING RH7 178 D6
Lincoln Ter BELMT SM2 * 65 K6
Lincoln Wy SUN TW16 42 B1
Lindale Cl VW GU25 38 C4
Linden Av COUL/CHIP CR5 86 E6
EGRIN RH19 162 D3
HSLW TW3 16 E7
THHTH CR7 49 L4
Linden Cl ADL/WDHM KT15 78 D1
CRAWE RH10 165 J7
HORS RH12 167 H5
KWD/TDW/WH KT20 105 G2
THDIT KT7 44 D7
Linden Ct CBLY GU15 73 J2
EGH TW20 20 E7
LHD/OX KT22 102 E3
Linden Crs KUT/HW KT1 9 H7
Linden Dr CTHM CR3 107 M6
Linden Gdns LHD/OX KT22 102 F3
Linden Gv NWMAL KT3 46 B3
SYD SE26 32 F7
TEDD TW11 26 C6
WARL CR6 89 H8
WOT/HER KT12 60 C1
Lindenhill Rd BNFD RG42 34 C1
Linden Lea DORK RH4 * 144 F4
Linden Leas WWKM BR4 70 A1
Linden Pit Pth LHD/OX KT22 102 E3
Linden Pl EHSLY KT24 * 100 B8
EW KT17 84 B2
MTCM CR4 48 B4
Linden Rd BOR GU35 180 G12
GU GU1 7 G3
HPTN TW12 43 K1
LHD/OX KT22 102 E3
WEY KT13 59 M7
Lindens Cl EHSLY KT24 121 H2
The Lindens CHSWK W4 18 F3
CRAWE RH10 192 G2
CROY/NA CR0 69 M5
FNM GU9 5 M6
Linden Wy PUR/KEN CR8 66 F8
RPLY/SEND GU23 98 C7
SHPTN TW17 41 M5
WOKS/MYFD GU22 97 J3
Lindfield Gdns GU GU1 7 M2
Lindfield Rd CROY/NA CR0 50 C6
Lindfield Ter
WOKN/KNAP GU21 * 76 F6
Lindford Cha BOR GU35 180 A12
Lindford Wey BOR GU35 180 A12
Lindgren Wk CRAWW RH11 * 191 L12
Lindisfarne Rd RYNPK SW20 28 D8
Lindley Pl RCH/KEW TW9 18 D5
Lindley Rd GDST RH9 128 F4
WOT/HER KT12 61 H2
Lindores Rd CAR SM5 47 M7
Lind Rd SUT SM1 65 M3
Lindsay Cl CHSGTN KT9 63 H6
HOR/WEW KT19 83 M3
STWL/WRAY TW19 14 A8
Lindsay Dr SHPTN TW17 42 A6
Lindsay Rd ADL/WDHM KT15 78 D1
HPTN TW12 25 L5
WPK KT4 64 E1
Lindsey Cl MTCM CR4 49 H4
Lindsey Gdns
EBED/NFELT TW14 * 24 A1
Lindum Dene ALDT GU11 112 D8
Lindum Rd TEDD TW11 8 A3
Lindway WNWD SE27 31 L6
Linersh Dr SHGR GU5 169 K3
Linersh Wood Cl SHGR GU5 169 K4
Linershwood Rd SHGR GU5 169 K3
Linfield Cl WOT/HER KT12 * 60 E4
Ling Crs BOR GU35 180 G11
Ling Dr LTWR GU18 74 C2
Lingfield Av KUT/HW KT1 45 H4
Lingfield Common Rd
LING RH7 178 D4
Lingfield Dr CRAWE RH10 192 D6
Lingfield Gdns COUL/CHIP CR5 107 L1
Lingfield Rd EDEN TN8 179 P1
EGRIN RH19 178 E12
WIM/MER SW19 29 G7
WPK KT4 64 F2
Lingwell Rd TOOT SW17 30 B4
Lingwood BRAK RG12 34 F6
Lingwood Gdns ISLW TW7 17 H2
Link 10 CRAWE RH10 165 J1
Linkfield E/WMO/HCT KT8 43 K3
Linkfield Gdns REDH RH1 126 B8
Linkfield La REDH RH1 126 C7
Linkfield Rd ISLW TW7 17 J4
Linkfield St REDH RH1 126 B8
Link La WLGTN SM6 67 G5
Link Rd ADL/WDHM KT15 59 H3
EBED/NFELT TW14 24 C1
FARN GU14 112 A1
WLGTN SM6 48 D8
Links Av MRDN SM4 47 K4
Links Brow LHD/OX KT22 102 B5
Links Cl ASHTD KT21 82 F7
CRAN GU6 171 K11
Linkscroft Av ASHF TW15 23 L7
Links Gdns STRHM/NOR SW16 31 K8
Links Green Wy COB KT11 81 K4
Linkside NWMAL KT3 46 B2
Linkside East GSHT GU26 181 N10
Linkside North GSHT GU26 181 N10
Linkside South GSHT GU26 181 P11
Linkside West GSHT GU26 181 N10
Links Pl ASHTD KT21 83 G7
Links Rd ASHF TW15 23 H6
ASHTD KT21 82 F7
EW KT17 84 D3
SHGR GU5 168 H2
TOOT SW17 30 D7
WWKM BR4 51 M8
The Links ASC SL5 36 B2
WOT/HER KT12 60 D1
Links View Av
BRKHM/BTCW RH3 123 K8
Linksview Ct HPTN TW12 * 26 A5
Links View Rd CROY/NA CR0 69 K2
HPTN TW12 25 M6
Links Wy BECK BR3 51 K6
GT/LBKH KT23 121 H2
The Link CRAWW RH11 164 F4
TEDD TW11 26 C7
Link Wy RCHPK/HAM TW10 26 E3
STA TW18 22 E7
Linkway CBLY GU15 72 F5
GUW GU2 116 C8
HORL RH6 160 F7
NWMAL KT3 46 E4
RYNPK SW20 46 E3
WOKS/MYFD GU22 11 M5
The Linkway BELMT SM2 65 M7
Linnell Rd REDH RH1 148 D1
Linnet Cl CRAWE RH10 193 P8
SAND/SEL CR2 69 G8
Linnet Gv RGUE GU4 118 A6
Linnet Ms BAL SW12 30 D1
Linnett Cl CRAWE RH10 * 193 P7
Linsford La FRIM GU16 93 J6
Linslade Cl HSLWW TW4 16 B7
Linstead Rd FARN GU14 92 B1
Linstead Wy WAND/EARL SW18 29 H1
Linsted La BOR GU35 180 C10
Linton Cl CAR SM5 48 C7
Linton Gld CROY/NA CR0 69 H8
Linton Gv WNWD SE27 31 L6
Linton's La EW KT17 84 B2
Lintott Ct STWL/WRAY TW19 14 A8
Lintott Gdns SWTR RH13 167 H6
Lion Av TWK TW1 26 C2
Lion Cl SHPTN TW17 41 H3
Lion Gate Gdns RCH/KEW TW9 18 C5
Lion Green Rd COUL/CHIP CR5 87 G5
Lion & Lamb Wy FNM GU9 5 G3
Lion & Lamb Yd FNM GU9 * 5 H3
Lion La CRAWE RH10 193 M9
GSHT GU26 198 A4
Lion Md HASM GU27 198 A7
Lion Park Av CHSGTN KT9 63 K3
Lion Rd CROY/NA CR0 49 M5
FARN GU14 92 E7
TWK TW1 26 C2
Lion Wy BTFD TW8 18 A2
Lion Wharf Rd ISLW TW7 17 L5
Liphook Crs FSTH SE23 32 F1
Liphook Rd BOR GU35 180 A12
HASM GU27 197 M9
Lipsham Cl BNSTD SM7 86 A3
Lisbon Av WHTN TW2 25 M3
Liscombe BRAK RG12 34 E7
Liskeard Dr FARN GU14 92 D3
Lisle Cl TOOT SW17 30 E5
Lismore WIM/MER SW19 * 29 J6
Lismore Cl ISLW TW7 17 K4
Lismore Crs CRAWW RH11 164 D7
Lismore Rd SAND/SEL CR2 68 B5
Lissant Cl SURB KT6 44 F7
Lissoms Rd COUL/CHIP CR5 86 D8
Lister Av EGRIN RH19 162 F7
Lister Cl MTCM CR4 30 B8
Litchfield Av MRDN SM4 47 J7
Litchfield Rd SUT SM1 65 M3
Litchfield Wy GUW GU2 138 C2
Lithgow's Rd HTHAIR TW6 15 H6
Little Acre BECK BR3 51 K3
Little Aly EDEN TN8 179 Q4
Little Austins Rd FNM GU9 5 M7
Little Birch Cl ADL/WDHM KT15 59 G7
Little Bookham St
GT/LBKH KT23 101 J6
Little Bornes DUL SE21 32 B5
Little Borough
BRKHM/BTCW RH3 145 K1
Littlebrook Cl CROY/NA CR0 51 G6
Little Brownings FSTH SE23 32 E3
Little Browns La EDEN TN8 153 H5
Little Chesters
KWD/TDW/WH KT20 104 D7
Little Collins REDH RH1 * 176 G2
Little Common La REDH RH1 127 L6
Little Comptons SWTR RH13 167 J7
Littlecote Cl WIM/MER SW19 29 G1
Little Ct WWKM BR4 70 B1
Little Crabtree CRAWW RH11 164 E3
Little Cranmore La
EHSLY KT24 119 L2
Littlecroft Rd EGH TW20 21 J6
Littledale Cl BRAK RG12 35 H3
Little Dimocks BAL SW12 30 E3
Little East Fld COUL/CHIP CR5 107 G3
Little Elms HYS/HAR UB3 15 G2
Little Ferry Rd TWK TW1 * 26 E2
Littlefield Cl ASHV GU12 113 K8
KUT/HW KT1 8 F7
RGUW GU3 116 A4
Littlefield Gdns ASHV GU12 113 K8
Littlefield Wy RGUW GU3 115 M4
Littleford La RGUE GU4 140 B8
SHGR GU5 169 Q3
Little Grebe HORS RH12 166 F4
Little Green La CHERT KT16 58 B2
FNM GU9 155 K2
Little Gv DORK RH4 * 144 F4
Little Halliards WOT/HER KT12 42 D6
Little Hatch HORS RH12 167 J4
Little Haven La HORS RH12 167 J4
Littlehaven La HORS RH12 167 J5
Littleheath La COB KT11 81 K4
Little Heath Rd CHOB/PIR GU24 56 B7
Littleheath Rd SAND/SEL CR2 68 E7
Little Hide GU GU1 117 L6
Little Kiln GODL GU7 168 B1
Little King St EGRIN RH19 162 F4
Little London MFD/CHID GU8 183 M4
SHGR GU5 141 H7
Little Lullenden LING RH7 178 E4
Little Manor Gdns CRAN GU6 186 C3
Littlemead ESH/CLAY KT10 62 A3
Little Md WOKN/KNAP GU21 76 C6
Little Moreton Cl
BF/WBF KT14 * 78 E2
Little Oak Cl SHPTN TW17 41 J4
Little Orch ADL/WDHM KT15 78 D1
WOKN/KNAP GU21 77 K4
Little Orchards EPSOM KT18 84 B4
Little Orchard Wy RGUE GU4 139 H7
Little Paddock CBLY GU15 73 K1
Little Park Dr FELT TW13 25 G3
Little Platt GUW GU2 116 A7
Little Queens Rd TEDD TW11 26 C7
Little Riding WOKS/MYFD GU22 11 J4
Little Ringdale BRAK RG12 35 H4
Little Roke Av PUR/KEN CR8 87 L4
Little Roke Rd PUR/KEN CR8 87 M4
Littlers Cl WIM/MER SW19 48 A1
Little St Leonards
MORT/ESHN SW14 18 F5
Littlestone Cl BECK BR3 33 K7
Little St GUW GU2 116 E4
Little Sutton La DTCH/LGLY SL3 12 E1
Little Thatch GODL GU7 168 C3
Little Thurbans Cl FNM GU9 155 K3
Littleton La REIG RH2 147 H2
RGUW GU3 138 D6
SHPTN TW17 41 H5
Littleton Rd ASHF TW15 23 M8
Littleton St WAND/EARL SW18 29 M3
Little Tumners Ct GODL GU7 168 B2
Little Warren Cl RGUE GU4 139 L2
Little Wellington St
ALDT GU11 112 D7
Littlewick Rd
WOKN/KNAP GU21 76 A6
Littlewood CRAN GU6 186 E2
Little Woodcote Est
WLGTN SM6 * 66 E8
Little Woodcote La CAR SM5 86 E2
Littleworth Av ESH/CLAY KT10 62 A4
Littleworth Common Rd
ESH/CLAY KT10 62 A2
Littleworth La ESH/CLAY KT10 62 A3
Littleworth Pl ESH/CLAY KT10 62 A3
Littleworth Rd ESH/CLAY KT10 62 A4
RFNM GU10 135 J8
RGUW GU3 158 B2
Littlt Halliards WOT/HER KT12 * 42 D6
Liverpool Rd KUTN/CMB KT2 9 K2
THHTH CR7 49 M3
Livesey Cl KUT/HW KT1 9 G8
Livingstone Rd CRAWE RH10 165 G6
CTHM CR3 108 A4
HSLW TW3 16 F6
SWTR RH13 167 G8
THHTH CR7 50 A2
Llanaway Cl GODL GU7 168 C3
Llanaway Rd GODL GU7 168 C3
Llanthony Rd MRDN SM4 48 A6
Llanvair Cl ASC SL5 36 D6
Llanvair Dr ASC SL5 36 C7
Lloyd Av COUL/CHIP CR5 86 D4
STRHM/NOR SW16 49 H1
Lloyd Park Av CROY/NA CR0 68 C3
Lloyd Rd WPK KT4 64 F2
Lloyds Ct CRAWE RH10 * 165 G1
Lloyds Wy BECK BR3 51 H5
Lobelia Rd CHOB/PIR GU24 75 K5
Lochaline St HMSMTH W6 19 M1
Lochinvar St BAL SW12 30 E1
Lochinver BRAK RG12 34 E7
Lock Cl ADL/WDHM KT15 78 B2
Locke-king Cl WEY KT13 59 K6
Locke King Rd WEY KT13 59 K6
Locke Rd LIPH GU30 197 J9
Lockesley Sq SURB KT6 * 45 G6
Lockestone Cl WEY KT13 59 J5
Locke Wy WOKN/KNAP GU21 10 F5
Lockfield Dr WOKN/KNAP GU21 10 A6
Lockhart Rd COB KT11 80 F3
Lockhursthatch La SHGR GU5 170 D3
Lock La WOKS/MYFD GU22 78 E6
Lock Rd ALDT GU11 113 G4
GU GU1 117 G4
RCHPK/HAM TW10 26 F5
Lock's La MTCM CR4 48 D1
Locksley Dr WOKN/KNAP GU21 76 C7
Locksmeade Rd
RCHPK/HAM TW10 26 E5
Locks Meadow LING RH7 178 H8
Lockstone WEY KT13 59 J5
Lockswood CHOB/PIR GU24 95 J2
Lockton Cha ASC SL5 36 A3
Lockwood Cl FARN GU14 92 B1
HORS RH12 167 K4
SYD SE26 33 G5
Lockwood Ct CRAWE RH10 * 165 H2
Lockwood Pth
WOKN/KNAP GU21 78 A3
Lockwood Wy CHSGTN KT9 63 K4
Locomotive Dr
EBED/NFELT TW14 24 D2
Loddon Cl CBLY GU15 73 K3
Loddon Rd FARN GU14 92 A3
Loddon Wy ASHV GU12 113 K8
Loder Cl WOKN/KNAP GU21 78 A3
Lodge Av CROY/NA CR0 67 J2
Lodgebottom Rd RDKG RH5 123 K1
Lodge Cl COB KT11 81 J6
CRAWW RH11 164 E4
EGH TW20 21 G6
EGRIN RH19 162 D4
EW KT17 64 F8
ISLW TW7 17 L3
LHD/OX KT22 102 A4
RDKG RH5 144 F6
WLGTN SM6 48 D8
Lodge Gdns BECK BR3 51 J5
Lodge Hl PUR/KEN CR8 87 K5
Lodge Hill Cl RFNM GU10 156 A3
Lodge Hill Rd RFNM GU10 156 A3
Lodge La BH/WHM TN16 131 M1
CROY/NA CR0 69 L6
RDKG RH5 173 N2
REDH RH1 148 B8
Lodge Pl SUT SM1 65 L4
Lodge Rd CROY/NA CR0 49 L6
LHD/OX KT22 101 M4
SUT SM1 65 L4
WLGTN SM6 66 E4
Lodge Wk WARL CR6 89 K6
Lodge Wy ASHF TW15 23 H3
SHPTN TW17 41 M2
Lodsworth FARN GU14 92 A6
Lofthouse Pl CHSGTN KT9 62 F5
Logan Cl HSLWW TW4 16 C5
Logmore La DORK RH4 144 B7
Lois Dr SHPTN TW17 41 L5
Lollesworth La EHSLY KT24 99 M8
Loman Rd FRIM GU16 93 K6
Lomas Cl CROY/NA CR0 69 M6
Lombard Rd WIM/MER SW19 47 L2
Lombard St MFD/CHID GU8 158 C3
Lombardy Cl WOKN/KNAP GU21 76 C7
Lomond Gdns SAND/SEL CR2 69 H6
Loncin Mead Av
ADL/WDHM KT15 58 F7
London La SHGR GU5 141 K5
London Loop BNSTD SM7 85 J3
COUL/CHIP CR5 107 H1
CROY/NA CR0 69 G2
PUR/KEN CR8 88 B5
WWKM BR4 70 A2
London Rd ASC SL5 35 M3
ASHF TW15 22 F4
BFOR GU20 54 F2
BH/WHM TN16 111 M5
BLKW GU17 72 B5
BRAK RG12 35 G2
CBLY GU15 72 F3
CHEAM SM3 65 H1
CRAWE RH10 164 F3
CRAWE RH10 191 P2
CROY/NA CR0 2 B3
CTHM CR3 108 A5
DORK RH4 122 E8
DTCH/LGLY SL3 12 D1
EGH TW20 20 F8
EGRIN RH19 162 F4
EW KT17 64 C7
FROW RH18 195 M9
FSTH SE23 32 F2
GU GU1 7 K4
HORL RH6 160 D6
HORS RH12 166 F7
ISLW TW7 17 H4
KUTN/CMB KT2 9 G6
LIPH GU30 196 H9
MRDN SM4 47 K5
MTCM CR4 48 B4
MTCM CR4 48 D7
REDH RH1 126 D5
REIG RH2 125 K7
RPLY/SEND GU23 98 B8
STA TW18 22 C5
STRHM/NOR SW16 49 J2
TWK TW1 26 D1
WLGTN SM6 66 E3
London Rd North REDH RH1 106 E6
London Rd South REDH RH1 126 E4
London Sq GU GU1 * 7 K4
London St CHERT KT16 40 D7
The London Temple
LING RH7 * 177 R8
Loneacre BFOR GU20 * 55 H5
Lone Oak HORL RH6 161 L5
Lonesome La REIG RH2 147 M4
Lonesome Wy MTCM CR4 48 E1
Longacre ASHV GU12 113 K7
Long Acre CRAWE RH10 193 M5
Longacre Pl CAR SM5 * 66 D5
Long Av CHOB/PIR GU24 95 K3
Longbourne Wy CHERT KT16 40 C6
Longboyds COB KT11 80 E5
Long Br FNM GU9 5 J4
Longbridge Rd HORL RH6 160 C5
Longbridge Wk HORL RH6 160 C5
Longbridge Wy HORL RH6 160 C5
Longchamp Cl HORL RH6 160 F3
Long Copse Cl GT/LBKH KT23 101 L5
Longcroft Av BNSTD SM7 85 M4
Long Cross Hl BOR GU35 180 D12
Longcross Rd CHERT KT16 56 E2
Longdene Rd HASM GU27 198 C7
Longdon Wd HAYES BR2 71 H3
Longdown Cl RFNM GU10 155 M3
Longdown La North EW KT17 84 D3
Longdown La South EW KT17 84 D5
Longdown Rd CAT SE6 33 K5
EW KT17 84 D4
RFNM GU10 155 L4
RGUE GU4 139 L3
Long Dyke GU GU1 117 L6
Longfellow Rd WPK KT4 46 D8
Longfield Av WLGTN SM6 48 D8
Longfield Cl FARN GU14 92 D1
Longfield Crs
KWD/TDW/WH KT20 104 F2
SYD SE26 32 F4
Longfield Dr MORT/ESHN SW14 18 E7
MTCM CR4 48 B1
Longfield Rd ASHV GU12 113 K7
DORK RH4 144 C3
HORS RH12 204 H9
Longfield St WAND/EARL SW18 29 K1
Longford Av EBED/NFELT TW14 15 H8
STWL/WRAY TW19 23 H2
Longford Cl CBLY GU15 73 G5
FELT TW13 25 H4
HPTN TW12 25 K5
Longford Ct HOR/WEW KT19 63 M3
HPTN TW12 25 L7
Longford Gdns SUT SM1 65 M2
Longford Rd WHTN TW2 25 K2
Longford Wy STWL/WRAY TW19 23 H2
Long Garden Pl FNM GU9 5 H2
Long Garden Wk FNM GU9 5 H3
Long Garden Wk East FNM GU9 5 H3
Long Garden Wk West FNM GU9 5 H2
Long Garden Wy FNM GU9 5 G3
Long Gore GODL GU7 168 B1
Long Grove Rd HOR/WEW KT19 63 M8
PUR/KEN CR8 87 H1
Longheath Dr GT/LBKH KT23 101 H6
Longheath Gdns CROY/NA CR0 50 F5
Long Hl CTHM CR3 109 H3
RFNM GU10 135 H8
Long Hill Rd ASC SL5 35 L1
Longhope Dr RFNM GU10 155 K3
Longhurst Rd CRAWW RH11 191 K12
CROY/NA CR0 50 E6
EHSLY KT24 120 B3
Longlands Av COUL/CHIP CR5 86 E4

Long La CROY/NA CR0......50 F6
STWL/WRAY TW19......23 J4
Longleat Sq FARN GU14......93 H6
Longleat Wy FARN TW14......23 H7
Longley Rd CROY/NA CR0......2 A2
FNM GU9......5 L5
TOOT SW17......30 B7
Long Lodge Dr WOT/HER KT12......60 F7
Longmead GU GU1......117 M8
Longmead CI FRTH CR3......108 B3
Longmeadow FRIM GU16......73 J6
GT/LBKH KT23......101 J7
Long Meadow CI WWKM BR4......51 M7
Longmead Rd HOR/WEW KT19......64 B8
THDIT KT7......44 C7
TOOT SW17......30 C6
Longmere Gdns
KWD/TDW/WH KT20......104 F1
Longmere Rd CRAWE RH10......164 F1
Longmoor Dr LIPH GU30......196 C9
Longmoor Rd LIPH GU30......196 B9
Longmoors BNFD RG42......34 B1
Longmore Rd WOT/HER KT12......61 H3
Longpoles Rd CRAN GU6......186 E3
Long Reach RPLY/SEND GU23......99 L6
Longridge Gv
WOKS/MYFD GU22......78 B4
The Long Rd RFNM GU10......155 J6
Longs CI WOKS/MYFD GU22......78 D6
Longsdon Wy CTHM CR3......108 D6
Long Shaw LHD/OX KT22......102 D1
Longshot La BRAK RG12......34 B2
Longside CI EGH TW20......39 M1
Longstone Rd TOOT SW17......30 E6
Longthornton Rd
STRHM/NOR SW16......48 F2
Longton Av SYD SE26......32 D5
Longton Gv SYD SE26......32 E5
Long Wk EPSOM KT18......104 F1
NWMAL KT3......45 M3
The Long Wk WDSR SL4......20 A2
Longwater Rd BRAK RG12......34 F6
Longwood Ct WPK KT4......64 D1
Longwood Dr PUT/ROE SW15......19 K8
Longwood Rd PUR/KEN CR8......88 A6
Longwood Vw CRAWE RH10......165 J7
Lonsdale Gdns THHTH CR7......49 J4
Lonsdale Ms RCH/KEW TW9 *......18 D3
Lonsdale Rd BARN SW13......19 J2
DORK RH4......144 E1
SNWD SE25......50 E4
WEY KT13......59 K6
Loop Rd EPSOM KT18......83 M6
WOKS/MYFD GU22......97 J2
Loppets Rd CRAWE RH10......165 H6
Loraine Gdns ASHTD KT21......83 H7
Loraine Rd CHSWK W4......18 E1
Lord Chancellor Wk
KUTN/CMB KT2......45 M1
Lord Knyvett CI
STWL/WRAY TW19......14 A8
Lord Knyvetts Ct
STWL/WRAY TW19 *......14 B8
Lordsbury Fld WLGTN SM6......66 F8
Lords CI DUL SE21......31 M3
FELT TW13......25 H3
Lordsgrove CI
KWD/TDW/WH KT20......104 E2
Lordshill Rd SHGR GU5......169 M4
Lordship La EDUL SE22......32 D2
Loretto CI CRAN GU6......186 E2
Lorian Dr REIG RH2......125 M7
Loriners CRAWE RH10......164 F7
Loriners CI COB KT11......80 D4
Loring Rd ISLW TW7......17 J4
Lorne Av CROY/NA CR0......51 G2
WOKN/KNAP GU21......96 A1
Lorne Gdns CROY/NA CR0......51 H7
WOKN/KNAP GU21......96 A1
Lorne Rd RCHPK/HAM TW10......18 C7
The Lorne GT/LBKH KT23......101 K8
Lorraine Rd CBLY GU15......73 J1
Lory Rd BAGS GU19......54 B5
Loseberry Rd ESH/CLAY KT10......62 A4
Loseley Rd GODL GU7......168 B1
Lothian Rd CHOB/PIR GU24......94 D3
Lothian Wd
KWD/TDW/WH KT20......104 E4
Lotus Rd BH/WHM TN16......91 J4
Loubet St TOOT SW17......30 C7
Loudwater CI SUN TW16......42 D4
Loughborough BRAK RG12......35 H6
Louise Margaret Rd
ALDT GU11......112 F7
Louis Flds RGUW GU3......115 H4
Louisville Rd TOOT SW17......30 D4
Lovedean Ct BRAK RG12......35 H6
Lovekyn CI KUTN/CMB KT2......8 F6
Lovelace CI EHSLY KT24......100 C5
Lovelace Dr WOKS/MYFD GU22......78 C5
Lovelace Gdns SURB KT6......45 G7
WOT/HER KT12......60 F4
Lovelace Rd BRAK RG12......34 B4
DUL SE21......31 M3
SURB KT6......44 F7
Lovelands La CHOB/PIR GU24......75 M3
KWD/TDW/WH KT20......125 L1
Love La CHEAM SM3......65 H5
GDST RH9......128 F6
KWD/TDW/WH KT20......104 D8
MRDN SM4......47 K7
MTCM CR4......48 B3
SNWD SE25......50 E3
SURB KT6......63 G1
Loveletts CRAWW RH11......164 C5
Lovell Rd RCHPK/HAM TW10......26 H1
Lovells CI LTWR GU18......54 E8
Lovelock CI PUR/KEN CR8......87 M7
Lovers La RFNM GU10......180 H1
Lovett Dr CAR SM5......47 M7
Lovett Rd STA TW18......21 L5
Lovibonds Av ORP BR6......71 L4
Lowbury BRAK RG12......35 H4
Lowburys DORK RH4......144 D5
Lowdells CI EGRIN RH19......162 E1
Lowdells Dr EGRIN RH19......162 E1
Lowdells La EGRIN RH19......162 D2
Lowe CI ALDT GU11......112 C6
Lower Addiscombe Rd
CROY/NA CR0......2 F3
Lower Barn CI HORS RH12......167 J4
Lower Barn Rd PUR/KEN CR8......87 M2

Lower Breache Rd CRAN GU6......187 M1
Lower Bridge Rd REDH RH11......126 C8
Lower Broadmoor Rd
CWTH RG45......52 A5
Lower Church La FNM GU9......5 H4
Lower Church St CROY/NA CR0......2 B6
Lower Common South
PUT/ROE SW15......19 L5
Lower Coombe St CROY/NA CR0......2 C9
Lower Ct BH/WHM TN16......91 G6
Lower Ct Rd HOR/WEW KT19......84 A1
Lower Court Rd
HOR/WEW KT19......83 M1
Lower Dene EGRIN RH19......163 G4
Lower Downs Rd RYNPK SW20......47 G1
Lower Dunnymans BNSTD SM7......85 J4
Lower Eashing GODL GU7......159 H5
Lower Edgeborough Rd GU GU1......7 L5
Lower Farm Rd EHSLY KT24......100 E6
Lower Farnham Rd
ALDT GU11......134 F2
Lower Forecourt HORL RH6......160 E7
Lower Green Gdns WPK KT4......46 D8
Lower Green Rd ESH/CLAY KT10......61 L1
Lower Gn West MTCM CR4......48 B3
Lower Grove Rd
RCHPK/HAM TW10......18 C8
Lower Guildford Rd
WOKN/KNAP GU21......76 A7
Lower Ham La MFD/CHID GU8......158 B5
Lower Hampton Rd SUN TW16......43 G4
Lower Ham Rd KUTN/CMB KT2......27 C7
Lower Hanger HASM GU27......197 P7
Lower Hill Rd HOR/WEW KT19......83 L1
Lower House Rd
MFD/CHID GU8......182 G8
Lower Kings Rd KUTN/CMB KT2......8 E4
Lower Manor Rd GODL GU7......168 B3
MFD/CHID GU8......159 H8
Lower Marsh La BRYLDS KT5......45 J4
Lower Mere EGRIN RH19......163 G5
Lower Mill Fld BAGS GU19......54 A5
Lower Morden La MRDN SM4......46 F6
Lower Mortlake Rd
RCH/KEW TW9......18 D5
Lower Moushill La
MFD/CHID GU8......159 G8
Lower Newport Rd
ASHV GU12......113 G8
Lower Northfield BNSTD SM7......85 J4
Lower Park Rd COUL/CHIP CR5......86 B8
Lower Peryers EHSLY KT24......120 B2
Lower Pillory Down CAR SM5......86 D3
Lower Richmond Rd
PUT/ROE SW15......19 M5
RCH/KEW TW9......18 D5
Lower Sandfields
RPLY/SEND GU23......98 A5
Lower Sand Hills SURB KT6......44 F7
Lower Sawleywood
BNSTD SM7......85 J4
Lower Shott GT/LBKH KT23......101 L8
Lower South St GODL GU7......168 A5
Lower South Vw FNM GU9......5 J3
Lower St HASM GU27......198 D7
SHGR GU5......141 K5
Lower Sunbury Rd
E/WMO/HCT KT8......43 J2
Lower Tanbridge Wy
HORS RH12......166 E7
Lower Teddington Rd
KUT/HW KT1......8 C5
Lower Terrace Rd FARN GU14......112 D1
Lower Village Rd ASC SL5......36 F5
Lower Weybourne La
FNM GU9......134 C3
Lower Wood Rd ESH/CLAY KT10......62 E5
Lowfield CI LTWR GU18......74 D1
Lowfield Heath Rd HORL RH6......175 J11
Lowfield Rd SWTR RH13......203 G6
Lowfield Wy HORL RH6......175 P12
Lowicks Rd RFNM GU10......181 N3
Lowlands Rd STWL/WRAY TW19......14 A7
Low La FNM GU9......134 E3
Lowndes Buildings FNM GU9......5 H2
Lowry CI SHST GU47......72 A3
Lowry Crs MTCM CR4......48 B3
Lowther HI FSTH SE23......33 H1
Lowther Rd BARN SW13......19 J3
KUTN/CMB KT2......9 H4
Loxford Rd CTHM CR3......108 C7
Loxford Wy CTHM CR3......108 C7
Loxley CI SYD SE26......33 G1
Loxley Rd HPTN TW12......25 J5
WAND/EARL SW18......30 A2
Loxton Rd FSTH SE23......33 G2
Loxwood Farm PI BIL RH14......201 Q5
Loxwood Rd BIL RH14......201 K7
BIL RH14......201 Q2
CRAN GU6......185 Q9
Loxwood Wk CRAWW RH11......164 B3
Lucan Dr STA TW18......23 G8
Lucas CI EGRIN RH19 *......163 G4
Lucas Fld HASM GU27......197 R7
Lucas Green Rd
CHOB/PIR GU24......75 G5
Lucas Rd HORS RH12......166 B1
PGE/AN SE20......32 F7
Lucerne CI WOKS/MYFD GU22......97 H1
Lucerne Dr CRAWE RH10......165 M6
Lucerne Rd THHTH CR7......49 L5
Lucie Av ASHF TW15......23 L7
Lucien Rd TOOT SW17......30 D5
WIM/MER SW19......29 K3
Luciline Dr EDEN TN8......179 R1
Luddington Av VW GU25......39 J2
Ludford CI CROY/NA CR0......2 A9
Ludlow BRAK RG12......34 E7
Ludlow CI FRIM GU16......93 K2
Ludlow Rd FELT TW13......24 D4
GUW GU2......6 D6
Ludovick Wk PUT/ROE SW15......19 H6
Ludshott Gv BOR GU35......180 G12
Luke Rd ALDT GU11......134 B1
Luke Rd East ALDT GU11......134 B1

Lullarook CI BH/WHM TN16......90 F6
Lullington Rd PGE/AN SE20......32 D8
Lulworth Av HEST TW5......16 C1
Lulworth Crs MTCM CR4......48 B2
FARN GU14......92 D2
Lulworth CI CRAWW RH11......164 C6
Lumley Gdns CHEAM SM3......65 H4
Lumley Rd CHEAM SM3......65 H5
HORL RH6......160 D2
Luna Rd THHTH CR7......49 M3
Lundy CI CRAWW RH11......164 C7
Lunghurst Rd CTHM CR3......109 K3
Lunham Rd NRWD SE19......32 B7
Lupin CI BAGS GU19......53 M8
BRXS/STRHM SW2......31 K3
CROY/NA CR0......51 G8
Lushington Dr COB KT11......80 E4
Lushington Rd CAT SE6......33 L5
Lusted Hall La BH/WHM TN16......110 F2
Lusteds CI DORK RH4......144 F5
Luther Ms TEDD TW11......26 C6
Luther Rd TEDD TW11......26 C6
Luttrell Av PUT/ROE SW15......19 L7
Lutwyche Rd FSTH SE23......33 J3
Lutyens CI CRAWW RH11......164 A6
Luxford CI HORS RH12......167 J4
Luxfords La EGRIN RH19......163 J8
Lyall Av DUL SE21......32 B5
Lyall PI FNM GU9......133 L2
Lych Wy WOKN/KNAP GU21......10 B4
Lyconby Gdns CROY/NA CR0......51 H6
Lydbury BRAK RG12......35 J3
Lydden Gv WAND/EARL SW18......29 L1
Lydden Rd WAND/EARL SW18......29 L1
Lydford CI FARN GU14 *......92 D2
Lydhurst Av BRXS/STRHM SW2......31 J3
Lydney BRAK RG12......34 E7
Lydney CI WIM/MER SW19......29 H3
Lye Copse Av FARN GU14......92 E1
Lyefield La RDKG RH5......171 P11
The Lye KWD/TDW/WH KT20......104 F4
Lyfield LHD/OX KT22......81 L4
Lyford Rd WAND/EARL SW18......30 A1
Lyle CI MTCM CR4......48 D7
Lymbourne CI BELMT SM2......65 K8
Lymden Gdns REIG RH2......147 L2
Lymer Av NRWD SE19......32 C6
Lyme Regis Rd BNSTD SM7......85 J7
Lymescote Gdns SUT SM1......65 K1
Lyminge Gdns
WAND/EARL SW18......30 B2
Lymington CI
STRHM/NOR SW16......49 G2
Lymington Gdns
HOR/WEW KT19......64 C4
Lynchborough Rd LIPH GU30......196 C5
Lynchen CI HEST TW5......15 K3
Lynchford La FARN GU14......93 H8
Lynchford Rd FARN GU14......112 F1
FARN GU14......113 H1
Lynch Rd FNM GU9......5 M4
Lyncroft Gdns EW KT17......64 C7
HSLW TW3......16 F7
Lyndale THDIT KT7 *......44 B7
Lyndale Hampton Court Wy
THDIT KT7......44 B7
Lyndale Rd REDH RH1......126 C5
Lyndhurst Av ALDT GU11......134 F3
BRYLDS KT5......45 L8
STRHM/NOR SW16......49 G2
SUN TW16......42 D3
WHTN TW2......25 J2
Lyndhurst CI BRAK RG12......35 K3
CRAWW RH11......164 F5
CROY/NA CR0......3 J8
ORP BR6......71 L3
WOKN/KNAP GU21......10 B2
Lyndhurst Ct BELMT SM2 *......65 K6
Lyndhurst Dr NWMAL KT3......46 B6
Lyndhurst Farm CI
EGRIN RH19......193 Q1
Lyndhurst Prior SNWD SE25 *......50 B3
Lyndhurst Rd ASC SL5......36 D4
COUL/CHIP CR5......86 D6
REIG RH2......147 K3
THHTH CR7......49 K4
Lyndhurst Wy BELMT SM2......65 K7
CHERT KT16......58 B7
Lyndon Av WLGTN SM6......66 D2
Lyndon Yd TOOT SW17......29 L5
Lyndum PI BOR GU35 *......180 A12
Lyne CI VW GU25......39 J6
Lyne Crossing Rd CHERT KT16......39 K6
Lynegrove Av ASHF TW15......23 M6
Lyne La EGH TW20......39 K5
Lyne Rd VW GU25......39 H6
Lynmead CI EDEN TN8......153 L5
Lynmouth Av MRDN SM4......47 G6
Lynmouth Gdns HEST TW5......16 A3
Lynn CI ASHF TW15......24 A6
Lynn CI SAND/SEL CR2......88 F1
Lynne Wk ESH/CLAY KT10......61 M4
Lynn Rd BAL SW12......30 E1
Lynn Wk REIG RH2......147 L4
Lynn Wy FARN GU14......92 C2
Lynscott Wy SAND/SEL CR2......67 L7
Lynsted Ct BECK BR3......51 H2
Lynton CI CHSGTN KT9......63 H3
EGRIN RH19......163 G3
ISLW TW7......17 J6
Lynton Park Av EGRIN RH19......163 G3
Lynton Rd CROY/NA CR0......49 K6
NWMAL KT3......46 A5
Lynwick St HORS RH12......187 J12
Lynwood GUW GU2......6 C7
Lynwood Av COUL/CHIP CR5......86 D5
EPSOM KT18......84 C3
EW KT17......84 C4
Lynwood CI BOR GU35......180 B12
WOKN/KNAP GU21......78 A3
Lynwood Crs ASC SL5......37 H6
Lynwood Dr FRIM GU16......93 K6
WPK KT4......64 D1
Lynwood Gdns CROY/NA CR0......67 G3
Lynwood Rd EW KT17......84 C4

REDH RH1......126 D6
THDIT KT7......62 C7
TOOT SW17......30 D7
Lynwood Ter WIM/MER SW19 *......47 J1
Lynx HI EHSLY KT24......120 C2
Lyon CI CRAWE RH10......165 L8
Lyon Rd WIM/MER SW19......47 M1
WOT/HER KT12......61 H1
Lyons CI SWTR RH13......203 Q6
Lyons Ct DORK RH4......144 E2
Lyonsdene
KWD/TDW/WH KT20......125 J1
Lyons Dr GUW GU2......116 D3
Lyons Rd SWTR RH13......203 R6
Lyon Wy FRIM GU16......72 F8
Lyoth End STMC/STPC BR5......71 M1
Lyric CI CRAWE RH10......165 M6
Lyric Ms SYD SE26......32 F5
Lyric Rd BARN SW13......19 J3
Lysander Gdns SURB KT6......45 J6
Lysander Rd CROY/NA CR0......67 J5
Lysander Wy FARN GU14......92 E3
ORP BR6......71 M2
Lysons Av ASHV GU12......113 J1
Lysons Rd ALDT GU11......112 D8
Lysons Wk PUT/ROE SW15 *......19 K7
Lyster Ms COB KT11......80 F3
Lytchet Minster CI BRAK RG12......35 J5
Lytchgate CI SAND/SEL CR2......68 B6
Lytcott Dr E/WMO/HCT KT8......43 J3
Lytham BRAK RG12......34 C4
Lytham Rd FSTH SE23......33 C2
Lytton Dr CRAWE RH10......165 M3
Lytton Gdns WLGTN SM6......67 G3
Lytton Pk COB KT11......81 J2
Lytton Rd WOKS/MYFD GU22......11 J5
Lyveden Rd TOOT SW17......30 B7
Lywood CI
KWD/TDW/WH KT20......104 F4

M

Mabbotts KWD/TDW/WH KT20......105 G3
Mabel St WOKN/KNAP GU21......10 A7
Maberley Crs NRWD SE19......32 D8
Maberley Rd BECK BR3......51 G3
NRWD SE19......50 C1
Macadam Av CWTH RG45 *......52 A3
Macaulay Av ESH/CLAY KT10......62 B1
Macaulay Rd CTHM CR3......108 B3
Macbeth Ct BNFD RG42......35 H1
Macclesfield Rd SNWD SE25......50 E5
Macdonald Rd FNM GU9......133 C2
LTWR GU18......74 C1
Macdowall Rd GUW GU2......116 D3
Macfarlane La ISLW TW7......17 J1
Mackenzie Rd BECK BR3......51 H1
Mackie Rd BRXS/STRHM SW2......31 K1
Mackies HI SHGR GU5......171 K3
Macleod Rd SWTR RH13......167 H8
Macmillan Wy TOOT SW17......30 E5
Macnaghten Woods CBLY GU15......73 H3
Mada Rd ORP BR6......71 L2
Maddison Ct TEDD TW11......26 C7
Maddox Dr CRAWE RH10......165 M5
Maddox La GT/LBKH KT23......101 H5
Maddox Pk GT/LBKH KT23......101 H5
Madehurst Ct CRAWW RH11......164 B7
Madeira Av HORS RH12......166 F7
Madeira Crs BF/WBF KT14......78 C5
Madeira Rd BF/WBF KT14......78 C5
MTCM CR4......48 C4
STRHM/NOR SW16......31 H6
Madeira Wk EPSOM KT18......84 A4
REIG RH2......126 A7
Madeline Rd PGE/AN SE20......32 D8
Madgehole La SHGR GU5......170 A5
Madingley BRAK RG12......34 E8
Madox Brown End SHST GU47......72 B3
Madrid Rd BARN SW13......19 K3
GUW GU2......6 C7
Maesmaur Rd BH/WHM TN16......111 J3
Mafeking Av BTFD TW8......18 B1
Mafeking Rd STWL/WRAY TW19......21 J3
Magazine PI LHD/OX KT22......102 C4
Magazine Rd CTHM CR3......107 L4
FARN GU14......112 A1
Magdala Rd ISLW TW7......17 K5
SAND/SEL CR2......68 A6
Magdalen CI BF/WBF KT14......79 H4
Magdalen Crs BF/WBF KT14......79 H4
Magdale CI CRAWE RH10......165 L1
Magdalene Rd SHPTN TW17......41 J4
SHST GU47......52 C7
Magdalen Rd
WAND/EARL SW18......30 M2
Magellan Ter CRAWE RH10 *......191 R3
Magna Carta La
STWL/WRAY TW19......21 H7
Magna Rd EGH TW20......20 E7
SHST GU47......52 A8
Magnolia CI KUTN/CMB KT2......9 M1
Magnolia Ct HORL RH6 *......160 D3
Magnolia CI BH/WHM TN16......91 G6
Magnolia PI GU GU1......116 F2
Magnolia Wy CHSWK W4......18 E1
HOR/WEW KT19......63 M4
RDKG RH5......145 G5
Magnolia Whf CHSWK W4 *......18 E1
Magpie CI COUL/CHIP CR5......86 F6
RFNM GU10......133 G1
Magpie La SWTR RH13......205 N11
Maguire Dr FRIM GU16......73 M6
RCHPK/HAM TW10......26 H1
Mahonia CI CHOB/PIR GU24 *......75 G3
Maida Rd ALDT GU11......112 C6
Maidenbower Dr CRAWE RH10......165 M6
Maidenbower La CRAWE RH10......165 M5
Maidenbower PI CRAWE RH10......165 L6
Maiden La CRAWW RH11......164 E2
Maidenshaw Rd
HOR/WEW KT19......84 A2
Main Gate Rd FARN GU14......92 C8
Mainprize Rd BRAK RG12......35 H1
Main Rd BH/WHM TN16......91 G3
EDEN TN8......153 L2
Mainstone CI FRIM GU16......93 M2
Mainstone Crs CHOB/PIR GU24......95 G3
Mainstone Rd CHOB/PIR GU24......75 J6
Main St ADL/WDHM KT15......59 H2

FELT TW13......25 G6
Maise Webster CI
STWL/WRAY TW19......23 G1
Maitland CI BF/WBF KT14......78 D3
HSLWW TW4......16 C5
WOT/HER KT12......61 H1
Maitland Rd FARN GU14......112 E1
PGE/AN SE20......33 G7
Maitlands CI RFNM GU10......135 H3
Maizecroft HORL RH6......160 F2
Major's Farm Rd
DTCH/LGLY SL3......12 B2
Major's HI CRAWE RH10......193 J9
Malacca Farm RGUE GU4......118 E2
Malan CI BH/WHM TN16......91 H7
Malbrook Rd PUT/ROE SW15......19 L6
Malcolm CI PGE/AN SE20 *......32 F8
Malcolm Dr SURB KT6......45 G8
Malcolm Gdns HORL RH6......160 A5
Malcolm Rd COUL/CHIP CR5......87 G5
PGE/AN SE20......32 F8
SNWD SE25......50 D6
WIM/MER SW19......29 H7
Malden Av SNWD SE25......50 E4
Malden Green Av WPK KT4......46 C8
Malden HI NWMAL KT3......46 C3
Malden Hill Gdns NWMAL KT3......46 C3
Malden Pk NWMAL KT3......46 C5
Malden Rd CHEAM SM3......65 G3
NWMAL KT3......46 C7
Malden Wy NWMAL KT3......46 E4
Maldon CI WLGTN SM6......66 E4
Malet CI EGH TW20 *......22 A7
Maley Av WNWD SE27......31 L3
Malham CI CRAWE RH10......165 L7
Malham Fell BRAK RG12......34 D4
Malham Rd FSTH SE23......33 C2
Mallard CI ASHV GU12......113 J7
HASM GU27......197 R7
HORL RH6......160 D3
HORS RH12......166 F4
REDH RH1......126 D5
WHTN TW2......25 K1
Mallard Ct DORK RH4 *......144 C1
Mallard PI EGRIN RH19......163 G5
TWK TW1......26 D4
Mallard Rd SAND/SEL CR2......69 G8
Mallard's Reach WEY KT13......60 A1
The Mallards FRIM GU16......73 J7
STA TW18......40 E2
Mallards Wy LTWR GU18......74 D1
Mallard Wk BECK BR3......51 G5
Mallard Wy WLGTN SM6......66 F7
Malling CI CROY/NA CR0......50 F6
Malling Gdns MRDN SM4......47 M6
Mallinson Rd CROY/NA CR0......67 G2
Mallow CI BOR GU35......180 B12
CROY/NA CR0......51 G8
HORS RH12......167 H3
REDH RH1......126 E3
Mallow Crs RGUE GU4......117 L5
Mallowdale Rd BRAK RG12......35 H7
The Mall MORT/ESHN SW14......18 F4
SURB KT6......45 G5
Malmains Wy BECK BR3......51 M4
Malmesbury Rd MRDN SM4......47 M7
Malmstone Av REDH RH1......126 F3
Malory CI BECK BR3......51 H2
Malta Rd FRIM GU16......94 A1
Maltby Rd CHSGTN KT9......63 K5
Malt HI EGH TW20......21 H6
Malt House CI WDSR SL4......20 E1
Malthouse Ct CHOB/PIR GU24 *......75 J2
RGUE GU4 *......139 H5
Malthouse Dr FELT TW13......25 G6
CHSWK W4......18 E1
Malthouse La CHOB/PIR GU24......75 J2
MFD/CHID GU8......183 R8
RGUW GU3......95 M6
Malthouse Md MFD/CHID GU8......183 N4
Malthouse Mdw LIPH GU30......196 G4
Malthouse Rd CRAWW RH11......164 F5
The Maltings BF/WBF KT14......79 H3
LIPH GU30......197 J9
OXTED RH8......130 C7
SHGR GU5 *......141 M5
SNWD SE25 *......50 B3
STA TW18......22 B5
Malting Wy ISLW TW7......17 J5
Malus CI ADL/WDHM KT15......58 C6
Malus Dr ADL/WDHM KT15......58 C6
Malvern CI CHERT KT16......57 M5
MTCM CR4......48 C3
SURB KT6......45 H8
Malvern Dr FELT TW13......25 G6
Malvern Rd CRAWW RH11......164 E6
FARN GU14......92 A2
HPTN TW12......25 K1
HYS/HAR UB3......15 H1
SURB KT6......63 H1
THHTH CR7......49 K4
The Malyons SHPTN TW17 *......42 A6
Manbre Rd HMSMTH W6......19 M1
Manchester CI THHTH CR7......49 M3
Mandeville CI GUW GU2......116 D5
WIM/MER SW19......29 H8
Mandeville Dr SURB KT6......45 G8
Mandeville Rd ISLW TW7......17 K4
SHPTN TW17......41 K5
Mandora Rd ALDT GU11......112 C4
Mandrake Rd TOOT SW17......30 C4
Manfield Pk CRAN GU6......170 A12
Manfield Rd ASHV GU12......113 K7
Mangles Rd GU GU1......117 L6
Manley Bridge Rd RFNM GU10......155 H5
Mannamead EPSOM KT18......104 B1
Mannamead CI EPSOM KT18......104 B1
Mann CI CROY/NA CR0......2 C7
Manning CI EGRIN RH19......162 E3
Manning PI RCHPK/HAM TW10......18 C8
Manning Rd CRAWE RH10......165 J1
Manningtree CI
WIM/MER SW19......29 H2
Mann's CI ISLW TW7......17 J7
Manoel Rd WHTN TW2......25 M3
Manor Av CTHM CR3......108 B6
HSLWW TW4......16 A5
Manor Cha WEY KT13......59 L4
Manor CI EHSLY KT24......120 D3
GDST RH9......151 J4
HASM GU27......197 R7
HORL RH6......160 C2

RFNM GU10 135 J2
WARL CR6 89 H7
WOKS/MYFD GU22 78 C6
WPK KT4 46 B8
Manor Ct E/WMO/HCT KT8 * 43 K4
HORS RH12 * 167 K5
KUTN/CMB KT2 * 9 K5
WEY KT13 59 L3
Manor Crs BF/WBF KT14 79 J3
BRYLDS KT5 45 K6
CHOB/PIR GU24 95 G2
GUW GU2 116 E6
HASM GU27 197 R7
HOR/WEW KT19 83 K2
Manorcrofts Rd EGH TW20 21 K7
Manordene Cl THDIT KT7 44 D8
Manor Dr ADL/WDHM KT15 58 D8
BRYLDS KT5 45 K6
ESH/CLAY KT10 62 C2
FELT TW13 25 G6
HOR/WEW KT19 64 B5
HORL RH6 160 C3
SUN TW16 42 D2
Manor Dr North NWMAL KT3 46 A7
The Manor Dr WPK KT4 46 B8
Manor Farm RGUW GU3 136 F3
Manor Farm Av SHPTN TW17 41 L6
Manor Farm Cl ASHV GU12 * 113 J8
RGUW GU3 114 E6
Manor Farm Ct EGH TW20 * 21 K6
Manor Farm La EGH TW20 21 K6
Manor Farm Rd
STRHM/NOR SW16 49 K2
Manorfields CRAWW RH11 190 G11
Manor Flds LIPH GU30 197 J9
SWTR RH13 167 K5
Manor Gdns EHSLY KT24 121 G2
GODL GU7 168 B2
GUW GU2 116 E6
HPTN TW12 25 L8
RCH/KEW TW9 18 C6
RFNM GU10 156 A4
RYNPK SW20 47 J2
SAND/SEL CR2 68 C5
SUN TW16 42 D1
Manorgate Rd KUTN/CMB KT2 9 J5
Manor Green Rd
HOR/WEW KT19 83 M2
Manor Gv BECK BR3 51 L2
RCH/KEW TW9 18 D6
Manor Hl BNSTD SM7 86 C5
Manor House Ct EPSOM KT18 * 83 M3
SHPTN TW17 * 41 L7
Manor House Dr
WOT/HER KT12 60 C4
Manor House Gdns EDEN TN8 153 M8
Manorhouse La GT/LBKH KT23 101 H8
Manor House Wy ISLW TW7 17 L5
Manor La FELT TW13 24 D3
HYS/HAR UB3 15 G1
KWD/TDW/WH KT20 125 K3
SHGR GU5 169 P6
SUN TW16 42 E2
SUT SM1 65 M4
SWTR RH13 205 Q9
Manor Lea Rd MFD/CHID GU8 159 H7
Manor Leaze EGH TW20 21 L6
Manor Mt FSTH SE23 32 F2
Manor Pk RCH/KEW TW9 18 C6
STA TW18 22 A4
Manor Park Cl WWKM BR4 51 L8
Manor Park Est ASHV GU12 * 112 F8
Manor Park Rd SUT SM1 65 M4
WWKM BR4 51 L8
Manor Pl EBED/NFELT TW14 24 D2
GT/LBKH KT23 101 K8
MTCM CR4 48 F3
STA TW18 22 E6
SUT SM1 65 L4
Manor Rd ALDT GU11 134 D1
ASHF TW15 23 J6
ASHV GU12 113 J8
BECK BR3 51 K2
BELMT SM2 65 J6
BH/WHM TN16 111 H2
E/WMO/HCT KT8 44 A4
EDEN TN8 153 L8
EGRIN RH19 162 D3
FARN GU14 93 G6
FNM GU9 134 B5
GUW GU2 116 E6
HORS RH12 167 J4
MTCM CR4 48 F3
RCH/KEW TW9 18 C5
REDH RH1 126 F3
REIG RH2 125 J6
RFNM GU10 135 J1
RPLY/SEND GU23 98 C5
RYNPK SW20 47 J2
SNWD SE25 50 D4
TEDD TW11 26 D6
WHTN TW2 25 M3
WLGTN SM6 66 E3
WOKN/KNAP GU21 76 F6
WOT/HER KT12 42 D7
WWKM BR4 69 L1
Manor Rd North
ESH/CLAY KT10 62 C2
WLGTN SM6 66 E3
Manor Rd South
ESH/CLAY KT10 62 B3
Manor Royal CRAWE RH10 165 G1
Manorside Cl RFNM GU10 135 J1
The Manor MFD/CHID GU8 159 J8
Manor Wk ASHV GU12 112 E8
WEY KT13 59 L4
Manor Wy BAGS GU19 54 B7
BECK BR3 51 K3
BNSTD SM7 86 C6
EGH TW20 21 J7
GUW GU2 138 B3
LHD/OX KT22 81 M6
MTCM CR4 48 F3
PUR/KEN CR8 87 H2
SAND/SEL CR2 68 B5
WOKS/MYFD GU22 97 L2
WPK KT4 46 B8
The Manor Wy WLGTN SM6 66 E3
Manor Wood Rd PUR/KEN CR8 87 H3
Mansard Beeches TOOT SW17 30 D6
Manse Cl HYS/HAR UB3 15 G1
Mansel Cl GUW GU2 116 E3
Mansell Wy CTHM CR3 107 M4
Mansel Rd WIM/MER SW19 29 H7
Mansfield Cl ASC SL5 36 A2
Mansfield Crs BRAK RG12 34 E6
Mansfield Dr REDH RH1 127 G2
Mansfield Pl ASC SL5 36 A2
Mansfield Rd CHSGTN KT9 62 F4
SAND/SEL CR2 68 A5
Manship Rd MTCM CR4 48 D1
Manston Cl PGE/AN SE20 50 F1
Manston Dr BRAK RG12 34 E6
Manston Gv KUTN/CMB KT2 27 G6
Manston Rd RGUE GU4 117 K4
Mantilla Rd TOOT SW17 30 D5
Mantlet Cl STRHM/NOR SW16 30 F8
Manton Ter ADL/WDHM KT15 * 58 F3
Manville Gdns TOOT SW17 30 E4
Manville Rd TOOT SW17 30 D3
Manygate La SHPTN TW17 41 M6
Many Gates BAL SW12 30 E3
Maori Rd GU GU1 7 M4
Maple Cl ASHV GU12 113 J2
CRAWW RH11 164 E1
CTHM CR3 88 C7
HORS RH12 167 K4
HPTN TW12 25 J7
MTCM CR4 48 E1
Maple Ct ASHF TW15 24 A8
EGH TW20 20 E7
NWMAL KT3 46 A3
Mapledale Av CROY/NA CR0 3 M7
Mapledrakes Cl CRAN GU6 171 K12
Mapledrakes Rd CRAN GU6 171 K12
Maple Dr EGRIN RH19 163 H4
LTWR GU18 74 C1
Maple Gdns STWL/WRAY TW19 23 H3
Maple Gv BTFD TW8 17 L2
GU GU1 117 G6
WOKS/MYFD GU22 97 H3
Maplehatch Cl GODL GU7 168 B7
Maplehurst LHD/OX KT22 102 A5
Maplehurst Cl KUT/HW KT1 45 H4
Maple Leaf Cl FARN GU14 92 C6
Maple Ms STRHM/NOR SW16 31 J6
Maple Pl BNSTD SM7 85 G4
Maple Rd ASHTD KT21 103 G1
CTHM CR3 88 C7
PGE/AN SE20 50 E1
REDH RH1 148 C4
RPLY/SEND GU23 98 D6
SURB KT6 45 H5
Maplestead Rd
BRXS/STRHM SW2 31 J1
The Maples BNSTD SM7 85 L3
CHERT KT16 57 L5
ESH/CLAY KT10 * 62 D6
KUT/HW KT1 * 8 A3
Maplethorpe Rd THHTH CR7 49 K4
Maple Wk ASHV GU12 135 G1
Maple Wy BOR GU35 180 G11
COUL/CHIP CR5 106 E3
FELT TW13 24 D4
Marble Hill Cl TWK TW1 26 E1
Marble Hill Gdns TWK TW1 26 E1
Marbles Wy
KWD/TDW/WH KT20 105 G1
Marcheria Cl BRAK RG12 * 34 E6
Marches Rd HORS RH12 188 E9
The Marches HORS RH12 189 J8
Marchmont Rd
RCHPK/HAM TW10 18 C7
WLGTN SM6 66 F7
March Rd TWK TW1 26 C1
WEY KT13 59 K4
Marchside Cl HEST TW5 16 A3
Marcus Ct WOKS/MYFD GU22 * 10 E7
Marcuse Rd CTHM CR3 107 M5
Mardale CBLY GU15 73 M5
Mardell Rd CROY/NA CR0 51 G5
Marden Crs CROY/NA CR0 49 J6
Marden Rd CROY/NA CR0 49 J6
The Mardens CRAWW RH11 164 D3
Mare Hl MFD/CHID GU8 183 M4
Mare La MFD/CHID GU8 184 E1
Mareschal Rd GUW GU2 6 E8
Maresfield CROY/NA CR0 3 H7
Mareth Cl ALDT GU11 112 E7
Marfield Cl WPK KT4 46 D8
Marfleet Cl CAR SM5 66 B1
Margaret Cl STA TW18 23 G8
Margaret Lockwood Cl
KUT/HW KT1 * 45 J4
Margaret Rd GU GU1 6 F5
Margaret Wy COUL/CHIP CR5 107 L1
Margery Gv
KWD/TDW/WH KT20 125 H3
Margery La
KWD/TDW/WH KT20 125 J3
Margin Dr WIM/MER SW19 29 G6
Marham Gdns MRDN SM4 47 M6
WAND/EARL SW18 30 B2
Marian Rd STRHM/NOR SW16 48 F1
Maria Theresa Cl NWMAL KT3 46 A5
Mariette Wy WLGTN SM6 67 H7
Marigold Ct GU GU1 117 H5
Marigold Dr CHOB/PIR GU24 75 K5
Marigold Wy CROY/NA CR0 51 G8
Marina Av NWMAL KT3 46 E6
Marina Cl CHERT KT16 40 E8
Marina Pde STA TW18 * 40 E1
Marina Wy TEDD TW11 8 C2
Mariner Gdns
RCHPK/HAM TW10 26 E4
Mariners Dr RGUW GU3 114 E6
Marion Av SHPTN TW17 41 L5
Marion Ms DUL SE21 32 A4
Marion Rd CRAWE RH10 165 K7
THHTH CR7 49 M5
Marius Rd TOOT SW17 30 D3
Marjoram Cl GUW GU2 116 D4
Mark Cl HAYES BR2 71 H3
Markedge La COUL/CHIP CR5 106 C6
REDH RH1 126 C1
Markenfield Rd GU GU1 7 G4
Markenhorn GODL GU7 168 A2
Market Field Rd REDH RH1 126 C7
Marketfield Wy REDH RH1 126 C8
Market Pde EW KT17 * 64 C7
FELT TW13 * 25 H3
SNWD SE25 * 50 D4
Market Pl BRAK RG12 34 E2
BTFD TW8 17 M2
DTCH/LGLY SL3 * 12 F2
KUT/HW KT1 8 D7
Market Rd RCH/KEW TW9 18 D5
Market Sq BH/WHM TN16 131 M1
HORS RH12 * 166 F8
Market St BRAK RG12 34 E2
GU GU1 7 G6
Market Ter BTFD TW8 * 18 B1
Markfield CROY/NA CR0 * 69 J8
Markfield Rd CTHM CR3 108 E8
Markham Ct CBLY GU15 73 G3
Markham Rd RDKG RH5 173 K12
Markhole Cl HPTN TW12 25 J8
Mark Oak La LHD/OX KT22 101 K3
Marksbury Av RCH/KEW TW9 18 D5
Marks Rd WARL CR6 89 H8
Mark St REIG RH2 125 L7
Mark Ter RYNPK SW20 * 28 F8
Markville Gdns CTHM CR3 108 D7
Mark Wy GODL GU7 159 L1
The Markway SUN TW16 42 F2
Markwell Cl SYD SE26 32 E5
Markwick La MFD/CHID GU8 184 E2
Marlborough Rd ISLW TW7 17 L2
Marlborough Cl CRAWW RH11 164 E8
HORS RH12 167 G4
WIM/MER SW19 30 B7
WOT/HER KT12 61 G2
Marlborough Crs HYS/HAR UB3 15 G2
Marlborough Dr WEY KT13 59 M2
Marlborough Ms BNSTD SM7 85 K5
Marlborough Ri CBLY GU15 73 H3
Marlborough Rd ASHF TW15 23 H6
DORK RH4 144 E2
FELT TW13 25 G3
HPTN TW12 25 K7
HYS/HAR UB3 15 G2
RCHPK/HAM TW10 18 B8
SAND/SEL CR2 67 M6
SUT SM1 65 K2
WIM/MER SW19 30 B7
WOKN/KNAP GU21 11 G4
The Marld ASHTD KT21 83 J8
Marler Rd FSTH SE23 33 J2
Marles La BIL RH14 202 H8
Marley Cl ADL/WDHM KT15 58 C5
Marley Combe Rd HASM GU27 198 A8
Marley Hanger HASM GU27 198 B10
Marley La HASM GU27 197 R8
Marley Ri DORK RH4 144 D5
Marlhurst EDEN TN8 153 L5
Marlin Cl SUN TW16 24 B7
Marlingdene Cl HPTN TW12 25 K7
Marlings Cl CTHM CR3 88 B7
Marlins Cl SUT SM1 * 65 M4
Marlow Cl PGE/AN SE20 50 E3
Marlow Ct CRAWE RH10 164 F3
Marlow Crs TWK TW1 17 J8
Marlow Dr CHEAM SM3 65 G2
Marlowe Wy CROY/NA CR0 67 H1
Marlow Rd PGE/AN SE20 50 E3
Marlpit Av COUL/CHIP CR5 87 H7
Marlpit Cl EDEN TN8 153 M5
EGRIN RH19 162 F2
Marlpit La COUL/CHIP CR5 87 H7
Marlyns Cl RGUE GU4 117 K4
Marlyns Dr RGUE GU4 117 K5
Marmot Rd HSLWW TW4 16 A5
Marnell Wy HSLWW TW4 16 A5
Marneys Cl EPSOM KT18 83 K5
Marnfield Crs
BRXS/STRHM SW2 31 J2
Marnham Pl ADL/WDHM KT15 58 F3
Maroons Wy CAT SE6 33 K6
Marrick Cl PUT/ROE SW15 19 K6
Marriott Cl EBED/NFELT TW14 15 G8
Marriott Lodge Cl
ADL/WDHM KT15 58 F2
Marrowbrook Cl FARN GU14 92 D6
Marrowbrook La FARN GU14 92 D6
Marrowells WEY KT13 60 B2
Marryat Cl HSLWW TW4 16 C6
Marryat Pl WIM/MER SW19 29 H5
Marryat Rd WIM/MER SW19 29 G6
Marshall Cl FARN GU14 92 C2
FRIM GU16 74 A7
HSLWW TW4 16 C7
SAND/SEL CR2 88 D3
Marshall Pde
WOKS/MYFD GU22 * 78 C5
Marshall Pl ADL/WDHM KT15 58 F7
Marshall Rd CRAWE RH10 165 L6
GODL GU7 168 B3
SHST GU47 72 A2
Marshalls Cl HOR/WEW KT19 83 M3
Marshall's Rd SUT SM1 65 L3
Marsh Av HOR/WEW KT19 64 B8
MTCM CR4 48 C2
Marsh Cl BOR GU35 196 A2
Marsh Farm Rd WHTN TW2 26 C2
Marsh Green Rd EDEN TN8 179 Q5
Marsh La ADL/WDHM KT15 58 E3
Marshwood Rd LTWR GU18 75 G1
Marston HOR/WEW KT19 83 M1
Marston Av CHSGTN KT9 63 H5
Marston Ct WOT/HER KT12 * 42 F8
Marston Dr FARN GU14 92 E2
WARL CR6 89 H8
Marston Rd FNM GU9 4 D5
TEDD TW11 26 E6
WOKN/KNAP GU21 76 E7
Marston Wy ASC SL5 36 B2
NRWD SE19 31 L8
Martel Cl CBLY GU15 73 M2
Martell Rd DUL SE21 32 A4
Martens Pl GODL GU7 168 B3
Martin Cl CRAWW RH11 164 F2
SAND/SEL CR2 89 G1
WARL CR6 88 E6
Martin Crs CROY/NA CR0 49 J8
Martindale MORT/ESHN SW14 18 F7
Martindale Av CBLY GU15 73 M6
Martindale Cl RGUE GU4 118 A6
Martindale Pl MFD/CHID GU8 * 199 P1
Martindale Rd BAL SW12 30 E1
HSLWW TW4 16 B6
WOKN/KNAP GU21 76 C8
Martineau Cl ESH/CLAY KT10 62 A3
Martineau Dr DORK RH4 144 E4
TWK TW1 17 L6
Martingale Cl SUN TW16 42 D4
Martingale Ct ALDT GU11 112 B7
Martingales Cl
RCHPK/HAM TW10 27 G4
Martin Gv MRDN SM4 47 K3
Martin Rd GUW GU2 116 D6
Martins Cl BLKW GU17 72 A5
GU GU1 117 M7
WWKM BR4 70 A1
Martins La BRAK RG12 35 H3
Martins Pk FARN GU14 * 92 A2
The Martins CRAWE RH10 193 P5
SYD SE26 32 E6
Martins Wd MFD/CHID GU8 183 M2
Martinsyde WOKS/MYFD GU22 11 M5
Martin Wy FRIM GU16 73 H8
MRDN SM4 47 H3
WOKN/KNAP GU21 76 D8
Martlets Cl HORS RH12 166 F4
The Martlets CRAWE RH10 165 G4
Martletts Cnr HORS RH12 * 203 J2
Marton Cl CAT SE6 33 K4
The Marts HORS RH12 203 J2
Martyns Pl EGRIN RH19 163 G5
Martyr Rd GU GU1 7 G6
Martyrs Av CRAWW RH11 164 E1
Martyrs La WOKN/KNAP GU21 77 L2
Marvell Cl CRAWE RH10 165 L2
Marwell BH/WHM TN16 111 L8
Marwell Cl WWKM BR4 70 C1
Mary Adelaide Cl
PUT/ROE SW15 28 B4
Maryhill Cl PUR/KEN CR8 87 M7
Maryland Rd THHTH CR7 49 L1
Maryland Wy SUN TW16 42 D2
Mary Rd GU GU1 6 F5
Mary Rose Cl HPTN TW12 43 K1
Mary's Ter TWK TW1 26 D1
Mary V GODL GU7 168 A7
Masefield Rd CRAWW RH11 164 A7
HPTN TW12 25 J5
Masefield Vw ORP BR6 71 M2
Masefield Wy
STWL/WRAY TW19 23 J2
Maskall Cl BRXS/STRHM SW2 * 31 K2
Maskell Rd TOOT SW17 29 M4
Mason Cl EGRIN RH19 162 F3
HPTN TW12 43 J1
RYNPK SW20 47 G1
Masonic Hall Rd CHERT KT16 40 C6
Mason Rd CRAWE RH10 165 G6
FARN GU14 92 B3
Mason's Av CROY/NA CR0 2 D8
Mason's Bridge Rd REDH RH1 148 E5
Masons Ct EW KT17 * 64 D7
Masons Fld SWTR RH13 205 R11
Masons Paddock DORK RH4 122 D8
Mason's Pl MTCM CR4 48 C1
Mason Wy ALDT GU11 134 E2
Massetts Rd HORL RH6 160 C4
Massingberd Wy TOOT SW17 30 E5
Master Cl OXTED RH8 130 B3
Masters Cl STRHM/NOR SW16 30 F7
Maswell Park Crs HSLW TW3 16 F7
Maswell Park Rd HSLW TW3 16 E7
Matham Rd E/WMO/HCT KT8 44 A5
Mathews Ter ALDT GU11 * 112 F7
Mathias Cl EPSOM KT18 83 M3
Mathisen Wy DTCH/LGLY SL3 13 H3
Matilda Cl NRWD SE19 32 A8
Matlock Crs CHEAM SM3 65 H3
Matlock Gdns CHEAM SM3 65 H3
Matlock Pl CHEAM SM3 65 H3
Matlock Rd CTHM CR3 108 B4
Matlock Wy NWMAL KT3 46 A1
Matthew Arnold Cl COB KT11 80 D4
STA TW18 22 F7
Matthew Ct MTCM CR4 49 G5
Matthew Rd ALDT GU11 134 B1
Matthews Dr CRAWE RH10 165 L8
Matthew's Gdns CROY/NA CR0 90 A1
Matthews La STA TW18 22 C5
Matthews Rd CBLY GU15 72 F1
Matthew's St REIG RH2 147 K4
Matthey Pl CRAWE RH10 165 M1
Maultway Cl CBLY GU15 73 L1
Maultway Crs CBLY GU15 73 L1
Maultway North CBLY GU15 53 L8
The Maultway CBLY GU15 73 L1
Maunsell Pk CRAWE RH10 165 K4
Maurice Av CTHM CR3 108 A4
Mavins Rd FNM GU9 5 L7
Mavis Av HOR/WEW KT19 64 B4
Mavis Cl HOR/WEW KT19 64 B4
Mawbey Rd CHERT KT16 58 A5
Mawson Cl RYNPK SW20 47 H2
Mawson La CHSWK W4 19 J1
Maxton Wk CRAWW RH11 * 164 D8
Maxwell Cl CROY/NA CR0 49 H8
Maxwell Dr BF/WBF KT14 78 F1
Maxwell Rd ASHF TW15 23 M7
Maxwell Wy CRAWE RH10 165 J1
May Bate Av KUTN/CMB KT2 8 D4
Maybelle Cl RDKG RH5 173 L6
Mayberry Pl BRYLDS KT5 45 J7
Maybourne Cl SYD SE26 * 32 E7
Maybourne Ri
WOKS/MYFD GU22 97 G6
Maybury Cl FRIM GU16 93 G1
KWD/TDW/WH KT20 105 H1
Maybury Hl WOKN/KNAP GU21 11 J3
Maybury Rd WOKN/KNAP GU21 11 G5
Maybury St TOOT SW17 30 B6
May Cl BOR GU35 196 D1
CHSGTN KT9 63 J5
GODL GU7 159 L7
SHST GU47 72 A1
May Crs ASHV GU12 113 H8
Maycross Av MRDN SM4 47 J4
Mayday Rd THHTH CR7 49 L6
Maydwell Av SWTR RH13 203 N7
Mayell Cl LHD/OX KT22 102 F5
Mayes Cl CRAWE RH10 165 L5
WARL CR6 89 G8
Mayes La HORS RH12 188 F12
Mayfair Av WHTN TW2 25 M1
WPK KT4 46 D8
Mayfair Cl BECK BR3 51 L1
SURB KT6 45 H8
Mayfield CRAWE RH10 165 M4
LHD/OX KT22 102 F3
LING RH7 178 H8
RFNM GU10 155 J6
Mayfield Av ADL/WDHM KT15 58 E8
Mayfield Cl ADL/WDHM KT15 58 F8
ASHF TW15 23 L7
FNM GU9 134 E3
PGE/AN SE20 * 50 E1
REDH RH1 148 D6
THDIT KT7 44 E8
WOT/HER KT12 60 D3
Mayfield Crs THHTH CR7 49 J4
Mayfield Gdns
ADL/WDHM KT15 58 E8
STA TW18 22 C8
WOT/HER KT12 60 D3
Mayfield Gn GT/LBKH KT23 121 K1
Mayfield Rd BELMT SM2 66 A5
CBLY GU15 * 72 E8
FARN GU14 92 C2
SAND/SEL CR2 68 A7
THHTH CR7 49 J4
WEY KT13 59 J4
WIM/MER SW19 47 J1
WOT/HER KT12 60 D3
Mayflower Cl CRAWE RH10 165 M5
Mayford Cl BAL SW12 30 C1
BECK BR3 51 G3
WOKS/MYFD GU22 97 G4
Mayford Rd BAL SW12 30 C1
Mayhurst Av WOKS/MYFD GU22 11 L4
Mayhurst Cl WOKS/MYFD GU22 11 L4
Mayhurst Crs
WOKS/MYFD GU22 11 L4
Maynard Cl CRAWE RH10 192 H1
Maynooth Gdns CAR SM5 48 C7
Mayo Rd CROY/NA CR0 50 A5
WOT/HER KT12 42 D7
Mayow Rd SYD SE26 33 G5
Maypole Rd EGRIN RH19 162 E3
EGRIN RH19 163 M7
May Rd WHTN TW2 26 B2
Mayroyd Av SURB KT6 63 K1
Mays Cl WEY KT13 59 J8
Mays Cft BRAK RG12 * 34 D4
Maysfield Rd RPLY/SEND GU23 98 A5
Mays Gn COB KT11 * 100 C2
Mays Gv RPLY/SEND GU23 98 A5
Mays Rd TEDD TW11 26 A6
Maytree Cl GU GU1 116 E5
Maytree Ct MTCM CR4 48 D3
Maytrees WOKN/KNAP GU21 75 M7
Maytree Wk
BRXS/STRHM SW2 * 31 K3
Maywater Cl SAND/SEL CR2 88 A1
Maywood Cl BECK BR3 * 33 L8
Maywood Dr CBLY GU15 73 L2
Maze Rd RCH/KEW TW9 18 D2
McAlmont Rdg GODL GU7 168 A2
McCarthy Rd FELT TW13 25 G6
McDonough Cl CHSGTN KT9 63 H3
McDougall Ct RCH/KEW TW9 18 D4
McGrigor Barracks ALDT GU11 112 E6
McIndoe Rd EGRIN RH19 162 E2
McIntosh Cl WLGTN SM6 67 H6
McIver Cl EGRIN RH19 162 A1
McKay Cl ALDT GU11 112 F6
McKay Rd RYNPK SW20 28 E8
McKenzie Wy HOR/WEW KT19 63 K8
McRae La MTCM CR4 48 C7
Mead Av REDH RH1 148 D8
Mead Cl CRAN GU6 186 D3
EGH TW20 21 L7
REDH RH1 126 D5
Mead Ct EGH TW20 21 M7
WOKN/KNAP GU21 76 B7
Mead Crs GT/LBKH KT23 101 K7
SUT SM1 66 B3
Mead Dr COUL/CHIP CR5 87 H4
Meade Cl CHSWK W4 18 D1
Mead End ASHTD KT21 83 J6
Meades Cl LING RH7 178 H8
The Meades LING RH7 179 J8
WEY KT13 * 60 A5
Meadfoot Rd
STRHM/NOR SW16 48 F1
Meadhurst Pk SUN TW16 24 B7
Meadhurst Rd CHERT KT16 * 40 E8
Meadlands Dr
RCHPK/HAM TW10 27 G3
Mead La CHERT KT16 40 F8
FNM GU9 5 G4
Meadow Ap CRAWE RH10 192 F2
Meadow Av CROY/NA CR0 51 G6
Meadowbank BRYLDS KT5 45 J6
Meadow Bank EHSLY KT24 120 C1
FNM GU9 5 G5
Meadowbank Cl FUL/PGN SW6 19 M2
Meadowbank Gdns HEST TW5 15 K3
Meadowbank Rd LTWR GU18 54 F8
Meadowbrook OXTED RH8 129 M4
Meadowbrook Cl
DTCH/LGLY SL3 13 H4
Meadowbrook Rd DORK RH4 144 D1
Meadow Cl ASHV GU12 93 J8
BLKW GU17 72 A5
CAT SE6 33 K6
CRAWE RH10 192 F2
ESH/CLAY KT10 62 C2
GODL GU7 168 B2
HORS RH12 167 K4
HSLWW TW4 16 D8
LIPH GU30 196 H9
MFD/CHID GU8 159 K8
PUR/KEN CR8 87 G3
RCHPK/HAM TW10 27 H2
RYNPK SW20 46 F4
WOT/HER KT12 61 J3
Meadow Ct EPSOM KT18 83 M3
STA TW18 22 B4
Meadowcroft Cl CRAWW RH11 164 B5
EGRIN RH19 162 D3
Meadow Croft Cl HORL RH6 160 F6
Meadow Dr RPLY/SEND GU23 98 C5
Meadow Farm La HORS RH12 167 J2
Meadow Gdns STA TW18 22 A6
Meadow Gate Av FARN GU14 92 C7
Meadow Hl COUL/CHIP CR5 86 F3
NWMAL KT3 46 B6
Meadowlands COB KT11 80 D3
CRAWW RH11 164 E4

OXTED RH8 130 D8
RGUE GU4 118 E4
Meadow La EDEN TN8 153 L5
LHD/OX KT22 101 M4
Meadowlea Cl WDR/YW UB7 14 A1
Meadow Pl CHSWK W4 * 19 H2
Meadow Ri COUL/CHIP CR5 87 G3
WOKN/KNAP GU21 75 M7
Meadow Rd ASHF TW15 24 A6
ASHTD KT21 83 H7
ESH/CLAY KT10 62 B4
FARN GU14 92 E2
FELT TW13 25 H3
RGUE GU4 117 K4
SUT SM1 66 B3
VW GU25 38 B5
WIM/MER SW19 29 M8
Meadows End SUN TW16 42 D1
Meadowside GT/LBKH KT23 101 K5
HORL RH6 160 E2
TWK TW1 27 G1
WOT/HER KT12 60 F1
Meadowside Rd BELMT SM2 65 H7
Meadows Leigh Cl WEY KT13 59 M2
The Meadows GUW GU2 138 F3
RFNM GU10 181 L8
WARL CR6 89 G7
Meadow Stile CROY/NA CR0 2 D8
Meadowsweet Cl NWMAL KT3 46 F5
The Meadow CRAWE RH10 192 B7
Meadow V HASM GU27 198 B7
Meadow Vw CHERT KT16 40 F4
HORL RH6 161 M3
STWL/WRAY TW19 13 J7
Meadowview Rd CAT SE6 33 K5
HOR/WEW KT19 64 B7
Meadow View Rd THHTH CR7 49 L4
Meadow Wk EW KT17 64 C6
KWD/TDW/WH KT20 104 E6
WLGTN SM6 66 E2
Meadow Wy ADL/WDHM KT15 58 E3
ASHV GU12 113 J6
CHOB/PIR GU24 75 J3
CHSGTN KT9 63 H4
EHSLY KT24 100 A7
GT/LBKH KT23 101 L5
KWD/TDW/WH KT20 85 H7
LIPH GU30 196 H8
ORP BR6 71 K2
REIG RH2 147 L4
RFNM GU10 155 J6
Meadow Waye HEST TW5 16 B2
Mead Pth WIM/MER SW19 30 A7
Mead Pl CROY/NA CR0 2 B4
HORL RH6 161 M3
Mead Rd CRAN GU6 186 D2
CRAWE RH10 165 H3
CTHM CR3 108 C5
GSHT GU26 198 A1
RCHPK/HAM TW10 26 F4
WOT/HER KT12 61 H3
Meadrow GODL GU7 168 C3
Meadside Cl BECK BR3 51 H1
Meads Rd GU GU1 117 L8
The Meads CHEAM SM3 65 G2
EGRIN RH19 162 F6
HASM GU27 198 A7
MRDN SM4 * 48 B5
WEY KT13 59 M5
The Mead ASHTD KT21 103 H1
BECK BR3 51 M2
DORK RH4 * 144 F5
FARN GU14 * 92 E6
LIPH GU30 196 G8
WLGTN SM6 67 G5
Meadvale HORS RH12 166 C7
Meadvale Rd CROY/NA CR0 3 K1
Mead Wy COUL/CHIP CR5 87 H8
CROY/NA CR0 69 H1
RGUE GU4 117 M3
Meadway ASHF TW15 23 K5
BECK BR3 51 M1
BRYLDS KT5 45 M8
EHSLY KT24 121 H2
ESH/CLAY KT10 61 L7
FRIM GU16 73 J7
HASM GU27 198 A7
HOR/WEW KT19 83 M3
LHD/OX KT22 82 A4
RYNPK SW20 46 F4
STA TW18 22 D8
WARL CR6 88 F6
WHTN TW2 26 A2
Meadway Cl STA TW18 22 C8
Meadway Dr ADL/WDHM KT15 58 F6
WOKN/KNAP GU21 76 F6
The Meadway HORL RH6 160 F3
Meaford Wy PGE/AN SE20 32 E8
Meare Cl KWD/TDW/WH KT20 104 F5
Meath Green Av HORL RH6 160 C1
Meath Green La HORL RH6 175 P1
Medawar Rd GUW GU2 138 A1
Medcroft Gdns
MORT/ESHN SW14 18 F6
Mede Cl STWL/WRAY TW19 21 G2
Mede Fld LHD/OX KT22 102 A6
Medfield St PUT/ROE SW15 28 D1
Medhurst Cl CHOB/PIR GU24 56 C7
Medina Av ESH/CLAY KT10 62 B2
Medlake Rd EGH TW20 21 M7
Medland Cl WLGTN SM6 48 D8
Medlar Cl CRAWW RH11 164 E1
GU GU1 116 F6
Medlar Dr BLKW GU17 72 C6
Medway CRAWE RH10 193 M8
Medway Cl CROY/NA CR0 50 F6
Medway Dr EGRIN RH19 162 E7
FARN GU14 92 B2
FROW RH18 195 P11
Medway Rd CRAWW RH11 164 B5
Medwin Wy HORS RH12 166 F7
Melbourne Cl WLGTN SM6 66 F4
Melbourne Ms CAT SE6 33 M1
Melbourne Rd TEDD TW11 26 F7
WIM/MER SW19 47 K1
WLGTN SM6 66 E4
Melbourne Wy HORS RH12 * 167 J4
Melbury Cl BF/WBF KT14 78 D4
CHERT KT16 40 D7
ESH/CLAY KT10 62 E5
Melbury Gdns RYNPK SW20 46 E1
Meldone Cl BRYLDS KT5 45 L6
Meldrum Cl OXTED RH8 130 C6
Melfield Gdns CAT SE6 33 L5
Melfont Av THHTH CR7 49 L3
Melford Cl CHSGTN KT9 63 J4
Melford Rd EDUL SE22 32 D2
Melfort Rd THHTH CR7 49 L3
Melksham Cl SWTR RH13 167 H7
Meller Cl CROY/NA CR0 67 H2
Mellersh Hill Rd SHGR GU5 169 L3
Mellison Rd TOOT SW17 30 B6
Melliss Av RCH/KEW TW9 18 E3
Mellor Cl WOT/HER KT12 43 J7
Mellow Cl BNSTD SM7 85 L4
Mellows Rd WLGTN SM6 67 G4
Melody Rd BH/WHM TN16 90 F8
Melrose BRAK RG12 34 E8
Melrose Av MTCM CR4 30 E8
STRHM/NOR SW16 49 J3
WHTN TW2 25 L1
WIM/MER SW19 29 J3
Melrose Gdns NWMAL KT3 46 A3
WOT/HER KT12 60 F4
Melrose Rd BARN SW13 19 J4
BH/WHM TN16 90 F6
COUL/CHIP CR5 86 E5
WEY KT13 59 K4
WIM/MER SW19 47 K2
Melrose Vls BECK BR3 * 51 K2
Melsa Rd MRDN SM4 47 M6
Melton Flds HOR/WEW KT19 64 A7
Melton Pl HOR/WEW KT19 64 A7
Melton Rd REDH RH1 126 F4
Melville Av FRIM GU16 73 J8
RYNPK SW20 28 D8
SAND/SEL CR2 68 C4
Melville Rd BARN SW13 19 K3
Melville Ter FNM GU9 * 5 G4
Melvin Rd PGE/AN SE20 50 F1
Melvinshaw LHD/OX KT22 102 F3
Membury Cl FRIM GU16 93 K2
Membury Wk BRAK RG12 35 H4
Memorial Cl HEST TW5 16 C1
OXTED RH8 130 A1
Memorial Sq KUT/HW KT1 8 D6
Mendip Cl HYS/HAR UB3 15 G2
SYD SE26 32 F5
WPK KT4 64 F1
Mendip Rd BRAK RG12 35 H5
FARN GU14 92 B2
Mendip Wk CRAWW RH11 164 D4
Menin Wy FNM GU9 5 M6
Menlo Gdns NRWD SE19 32 A8
Meon Cl FARN GU14 92 A3
KWD/TDW/WH KT20 104 E4
Meopham Rd MTCM CR4 48 F1
Merantum Wy
WIM/MER SW19 47 M1
Mercer Cl CRAWE RH10 165 L7
THDIT KT7 44 C7
Mercer Rd HORS RH12 166 F1
Merchants Cl SNWD SE25 50 D4
WOKN/KNAP GU21 75 M7
Mercury Centre
EBED/NFELT TW14 * 15 K7
Mercury Cl CRAWW RH11 164 A7
Merebank RDKG RH5 173 L5
Merebank La WLGTN SM6 67 J4
Mere Cl ORP BR6 71 L1
WIM/MER SW19 29 G1
Meredyth Rd BARN SW13 19 K4
Mere End CROY/NA CR0 51 G7
Merefield Gdns
KWD/TDW/WH KT20 105 G1
Mere Rd KWD/TDW/WH KT20 104 E6
SHPTN TW17 * 41 L6
WEY KT13 60 A2
Mereside ORP BR6 71 K1
Mereside Pk ASHF TW15 * 23 M5
Merevale Crs MRDN SM4 47 M6
Mereway Rd WHTN TW2 26 A2
Merewood Gdns CROY/NA CR0 51 G7
Mereworth Dr CRAWE RH10 165 M2
Meridian Cl CRAWW RH11 164 B7
Meridian Gv HORL RH6 160 F2
Meridian Wy EGRIN RH19 163 G2
Merland Cl
KWD/TDW/WH KT20 104 F2
Merland Gn
KWD/TDW/WH KT20 104 F2
Merland Ri EPSOM KT18 104 F1
Merle Common Rd
OXTED RH8 152 D2
Merlewood BRAK RG12 35 G5
Merlewood Cl CTHM CR3 108 A2
Merlin Cl CRAWW RH11 164 A4
CROY/NA CR0 3 G9
DTCH/LGLY SL3 * 12 E1
MTCM CR4 48 B3
WLGTN SM6 67 J5
Merlin Gv BECK BR3 51 J4
Merlin Rd FARN GU14 92 E7
Merlins Cl FNM GU9 5 J6
Merlin Wy EGRIN RH19 163 H2
FARN GU14 92 A6
Merrilands Rd WPK KT4 46 F8
Merrilyn Cl ESH/CLAY KT10 62 D5
Merrin Hl SAND/SEL CR2 88 B2
Merritt Gdns CHSGTN KT9 62 F5
Merrivale Gdns
WOKN/KNAP GU21 76 F7
Merrow Cha GU GU1 117 M8
Merrow Common Rd
RGUE GU4 118 A5
Merrow Copse GU GU1 117 L7
Merrow Ct GU GU1 * 118 A8
Merrow Cft GU GU1 117 M7
Merrow La RGUE GU4 117 M3
Merrow Pl RGUE GU4 118 A6
Merrow Rd BELMT SM2 65 G7
Merrow St RGUE GU4 118 A6
Merrow Wy CROY/NA CR0 69 M5
GU GU1 * 118 A7
Merrow Woods GU GU1 117 L6
Merryacres MFD/CHID GU8 183 M3
Merryfield Dr HORS RH12 166 D6
Merryfield Wy CAT SE6 33 L1
Merryhill Rd BNFD RG42 34 D1
Merryhills Cl BH/WHM TN16 91 G6
Merryhills La BIL RH14 201 R4
Merrylands CHERT KT16 58 B2
Merrylands Farm
GT/LBKH KT23 101 J6
Merrylands Rd GT/LBKH KT23 101 J5
Merrymeet BNSTD SM7 86 C4
Merryweather Ct NWMAL KT3 46 B5
Merrywood Gv
KWD/TDW/WH KT20 125 G4
Merrywood Pk CBLY GU15 73 J5
REIG RH2 125 L6
Mersham Pl PGE/AN SE20 50 E1
THHTH CR7 50 A2
Mersham Rd THHTH CR7 50 A3
Merstham Rd REDH RH1 127 K4
Merthyr Ter BARN SW13 19 L1
Merton Cl SHST GU47 52 C7
Merton Gdns
KWD/TDW/WH KT20 105 G1
Merton Hall Gdns RYNPK SW20 47 H1
Merton Hall Rd WIM/MER SW19 47 H1
Merton High St
WIM/MER SW19 29 M8
Merton Pl WIM/MER SW19 * 47 M1
Merton Rd SNWD SE25 50 C5
WAND/EARL SW18 29 K2
WIM/MER SW19 29 L8
Merton Wy E/WMO/HCT KT8 43 M4
LHD/OX KT22 102 D1
Mervyn Rd SHPTN TW17 41 M7
Metcalf Rd ASHF TW15 23 L6
Metcalf Wy CRAWW RH11 191 N3
Meteor Wy FARN GU14 92 D8
WLGTN SM6 67 H6
Meudon Av FARN GU14 92 E6
Mews Ct EGRIN RH19 163 G7
Mewsend BH/WHM TN16 91 G8
The Mews BECK BR3 * 51 K1
GU GU1 * 118 A8
HORS RH12 * 166 A5
MFD/CHID GU8 185 J8
REIG RH2 * 125 L7
STRHM/NOR SW16 * 49 J1
TWK TW1 * 17 L8
Meyrick Cl WOKN/KNAP GU21 76 B6
Michael Crs HORL RH6 160 D5
Michael Flds FROW RH18 195 M11
Michael La GUW GU2 116 E3
Michaelmas Cl RYNPK SW20 46 F3
Michael Rd SNWD SE25 50 B3
Micheldever Wy BRAK RG12 35 J5
Michelet Cl LTWR GU18 54 E8
Michelham Gdns
KWD/TDW/WH KT20 * 104 F2
TWK TW1 26 C4
Michell Cl HORS RH12 166 D7
Mickleham Dr LHD/OX KT22 102 F8
Mickleham Gdns CHEAM SM3 65 H5
Mickleham Wy CROY/NA CR0 70 A6
Middle Av FNM GU9 5 L8
Middle Bourne La RFNM GU10 155 L3
Middle Church La FNM GU9 5 H4
Middle Cl CBLY GU15 73 M3
COUL/CHIP CR5 107 K2
EW KT17 84 B2
Middle Farm Pl EHSLY KT24 121 G1
Middlefield FNM GU9 4 F9
HORL RH6 160 F2
Middlefields CROY/NA CR0 69 H7
Middle Gordon Rd CBLY GU15 72 F4
Middle Green Cl BRYLDS KT5 45 J6
Middle Hl ALDT GU11 112 D7
EGH TW20 20 F6
Middle La EW KT17 84 B2
TEDD TW11 26 C7
Middlemarch MFD/CHID GU8 183 M4
Middlemead Cl GT/LBKH KT23 101 L6
Middlemead Rd GT/LBKH KT23 101 L7
Middlemoor Rd FRIM GU16 93 H1
Middle Old Pk FNM GU9 133 J5
Middle Rd LHD/OX KT22 102 E3
STRHM/NOR SW16 48 F2
Middlesex Rd MTCM CR4 49 H5
Middle St BRKHM/BTCW RH3 145 L2
CROY/NA CR0 2 D6
HORS RH12 166 F7
SHGR GU5 141 K5
Middleton Gdns FARN GU14 92 B3
Middleton Rd CAR SM5 48 B7
CBLY GU15 73 H3
COB KT11 100 E1
HOR/WEW KT19 * 64 A8
HORS RH12 166 D7
MRDN SM4 47 M6
NWMAL KT3 45 M3
Middleton Wy CRAWW RH11 164 A5
Middle Wk WOKN/KNAP GU21 10 E5
Middle Wy STRHM/NOR SW16 49 G2
Midgley Rd CRAWE RH10 165 H2
Midholm Rd CROY/NA CR0 69 H2
Mid Holmwood La RDKG RH5 144 F7
Midhope Cl WOKS/MYFD GU22 97 H1
Midhope Gdns
WOKS/MYFD GU22 10 C9
Midhope Rd WOKS/MYFD GU22 10 C9
Midhurst Av CROY/NA CR0 49 K7
Midhurst Cl CRAWW RH11 164 C3
Midhurst Rd HASM GU27 198 C8
LIPH GU30 196 H10
Midleton Cl MFD/CHID GU8 159 J7
Midleton Industrial Estate Rd
GUW GU2 6 D1
Midleton Rd GUW GU2 6 A4
GUW GU2 116 C8
Midmoor Rd BAL SW12 30 F2
WIM/MER SW19 47 G1
Mid St REDH RH1 127 J8
Midsummer Av HSLWW TW4 16 C6
Midsummer Wk
WOKN/KNAP GU21 10 A3
Midway CHEAM SM3 47 J7
WOT/HER KT12 60 E1
Midway Av CHERT KT16 40 E3
EGH TW20 39 L3
Midway Cl STA TW18 22 E4
Miena Wy ASHTD KT21 83 G7
Mike Hawthorn Dr FNM GU9 5 K2
Milbanke Ct BRAK RG12 34 C2
Milbanke Wy BRAK RG12 34 C2
Milborne Rd CRAWE RH10 165 L8
Milbourne La ESH/CLAY KT10 61 M5
Milbrook ESH/CLAY KT10 61 M5
Milburn Wk EPSOM KT18 84 B5
Milden Cl FRIM GU16 93 K3
Milden Gdns FRIM GU16 93 K3
Mile Pth WOKS/MYFD GU22 96 F1
Mile Rd WLGTN SM6 48 D8
Miles La COB KT11 81 H3
OXTED RH8 151 K2
Miles Pl BRYLDS KT5 * 45 J4
LTWR GU18 74 C2
Miles Rd ASHV GU12 113 L6
HOR/WEW KT19 84 A2
MTCM CR4 48 B3
Miles's Hl RDKG RH5 171 P6
Milestone Cl BELMT SM2 66 A5
RPLY/SEND GU23 98 D4
Milestone Rd NRWD SE19 32 C7
Milford By-Pass Rd
MFD/CHID GU8 183 L1
Milford Ct RDKG RH5 173 K3
Milford Gv SUT SM1 65 M3
Milford Ldg MFD/CHID GU8 183 N1
Milford Ms STRHM/NOR SW16 31 J4
Milford Rd MFD/CHID GU8 158 B5
Milkhouse Ga GU GU1 7 H7
Milking La ORP BR6 91 H2
Milkwood Rd RGUE GU4 * 139 J7
Millais SWTR RH13 167 K6
Millais Cl CRAWW RH11 164 B8
Millais Ct SWTR RH13 167 K5
Millais Crs HOR/WEW KT19 64 B4
Millais Rd NWMAL KT3 46 B7
Millais Wy HOR/WEW KT19 63 M3
Millan Cl ADL/WDHM KT15 58 E8
The Millbank CRAWW RH11 164 B5
Mill Bay La HORS RH12 166 E8
Millbottom La RDKG RH5 173 L2
Millbourne Rd FELT TW13 25 H5
Millbrook GU GU1 7 G7
WEY KT13 60 B3
Millbrook Wy DTCH/LGLY SL3 13 H4
Mill Cl BAGS GU19 54 A6
CAR SM5 * 66 D1
EGRIN RH19 162 F6
GT/LBKH KT23 101 K6
HASM GU27 197 R7
HORL RH6 160 B2
Millcombe Cl WOKN/KNAP GU21 76 E8
Mill Copse Rd HASM GU27 198 C9
Millennium Wy BNFD RG42 34 E1
Miller Cl MTCM CR4 48 C7
Miller Rd CROY/NA CR0 49 J8
RGUE GU4 117 M5
WIM/MER SW19 30 A7
Millers Cl STA TW18 22 E6
Millers Copse EPSOM KT18 104 A1
REDH RH1 176 G2
Millers Ga HORS RH12 167 G3
Miller's La REDH RH1 176 G2
Mill Farm Av SUN TW16 24 B8
Mill Farm Crs HSLWW TW4 25 H2
Mill Farm Rd SWTR RH13 167 K5
Mill Fld BAGS GU19 54 A6
Millfield SUN TW16 42 A1
Millfield La
KWD/TDW/WH KT20 105 K7
Millfield Rd HSLWW TW4 25 H2
Millford WOKN/KNAP GU21 76 E7
Mill Gdns SYD SE26 32 E5
Mill Gn MTCM CR4 * 48 D7
Mill Green Rd MTCM CR4 48 D7
Millhedge Cl COB KT11 81 H6
Mill Hl BARN SW13 19 K5
BRKHM/BTCW RH3 145 L1
Mill Hill La BRKHM/BTCW RH3 123 L8
Mill Hill Rd BARN SW13 19 L5
Mill House La EGH TW20 39 L4
Millhouse Pl WNWD SE27 31 L5
Millins Cl SHST GU47 52 A8
Mill La ASC SL5 37 L2
BF/WBF KT14 79 K3
BOR GU35 196 B1
BRAK RG12 34 D5
CAR SM5 66 D3
CHOB/PIR GU24 95 G6
CRAWE RH10 193 K2
CRAWW RH11 164 C2
CROY/NA CR0 67 K2
DORK RH4 144 E1
DTCH/LGLY SL3 12 E5
EGH TW20 39 M4
EGRIN RH19 177 Q12
EW KT17 64 C7
GODL GU7 168 A5
GU GU1 7 G7
HORL RH6 160 A3
LHD/OX KT22 102 D4
LING RH7 178 G7
MFD/CHID GU8 183 N4
MFD/CHID GU8 184 H9
MFD/CHID GU8 199 P2
ORP BR6 71 K8
OXTED RH8 130 C6
OXTED RH8 131 J5
RDKG RH5 171 Q10
RDKG RH5 174 A4
REDH RH1 126 F5
RFNM GU10 180 G2
RGUW GU3 138 F8
RPLY/SEND GU23 99 G1
SHGR GU5 140 C5
SHGR GU5 169 J3
Millmead BF/WBF KT14 79 J2
GUW GU2 6 F7
Mill Md STA TW18 22 C5
Millmead Ct GUW GU2 * 6 F8
Millmead Ter GUW GU2 6 F8
Mill Pl DTCH/LGLY SL3 12 A4
KUT/HW KT1 9 G8
Mill Plat ISLW TW7 17 K5
Mill Plat Av ISLW TW7 17 K4
Millpond Ct ADL/WDHM KT15 59 H4
Mill Pond Rd BFOR GU20 54 E3
Mill Reach SHGR GU5 140 C5
Mill Ride ASC SL5 36 A1
Mill Rd COB KT11 80 F5
CRAWE RH10 165 K3
ESH/CLAY KT10 61 K1
EW KT17 84 C2
KWD/TDW/WH KT20 105 G5
RDKG RH5 173 K2
WHTN TW2 25 M3
WIM/MER SW19 29 M8
Mill Shaw OXTED RH8 130 C6
Millshot Cl FUL/PGN SW6 19 M3
Millside CAR SM5 66 C1
Millside Ct GT/LBKH KT23 * 101 K7
Millside Pl ISLW TW7 17 L4
Mills Rd WOT/HER KT12 60 F4
Mills Sp WDSR SL4 20 E1
Millstead Cl
KWD/TDW/WH KT20 104 E5
Mill Stream FNM GU9 134 B3
The Millstream HASM GU27 197 R8
Mill St DTCH/LGLY SL3 13 G2
KUT/HW KT1 8 F8
REDH RH1 148 B1
Millthorpe Rd HORS RH12 167 J5
Mill Vw CRAN GU6 * 186 A2
Mill View Cl EW KT17 64 C6
Millview Cl REIG RH2 126 A6
Mill View Gdns CROY/NA CR0 69 G2
Mill Wy EBED/NFELT TW14 15 L7
EGRIN RH19 162 F6
LHD/OX KT22 103 J7
Millway REIG RH2 126 A8
Millwood CRAWE RH10 193 R8
Millwood Rd HSLW TW3 16 F7
Milman Cl BRAK RG12 35 J2
Milne Cl CRAWW RH11 164 A7
Milne Pk East CROY/NA CR0 90 A1
Milne Pk West CROY/NA CR0 90 A1
Milner Ap CTHM CR3 108 D3
Milner Cl CTHM CR3 108 D4
Milner Dr COB KT11 81 J2
WHTN TW2 26 A1
Milner Rd CTHM CR3 108 D4
KUT/HW KT1 8 D9
MRDN SM4 48 A5
THHTH CR7 49 M3
WIM/MER SW19 47 L1
Milnthorpe Rd CHSWK W4 19 G1
Milnwood Rd HORS RH12 166 F6
Milton Av CROY/NA CR0 2 F2
DORK RH4 144 A3
SUT SM1 66 A2
Milton Cl BRAK RG12 34 D6
DTCH/LGLY SL3 12 D5
SUT SM1 66 A2
Miltoncourt La DORK RH4 144 B2
Milton Crs EGRIN RH19 162 D4
Milton Dr SHPTN TW17 41 H4
Milton Gdns EPSOM KT18 84 B4
STWL/WRAY TW19 23 J2
Milton Mount Av CRAWE RH10 165 M1
Milton Pk EGH TW20 * 21 K8
Milton Rd ADL/WDHM KT15 58 D5
CRAWE RH10 165 L3
CROY/NA CR0 2 F2
CTHM CR3 108 A3
EGH TW20 21 J6
HORS RH12 166 F6
HPTN TW12 25 K8
MORT/ESHN SW14 19 G5
MTCM CR4 30 D8
SUT SM1 65 K2
WIM/MER SW19 29 M7
WLGTN SM6 66 F5
WOT/HER KT12 61 G2
Miltons Crs GODL GU7 159 L7
Milton St DORK RH4 144 A3
Miltons Yd MFD/CHID GU8 * 183 N5
Milton Wy LHD/OX KT22 101 M7
Mimosa Cl BOR GU35 180 B12
Mina Rd WIM/MER SW19 47 K1
Minchin Cl LHD/OX KT22 102 D4
Mincing La CHOB/PIR GU24 56 C7
Minden Rd CHEAM SM3 65 H1
PGE/AN SE20 50 E1
Mindleheim Av EGRIN RH19 163 J3
Minehead Rd
STRHM/NOR SW16 31 J6
Minehurst Rd FRIM GU16 93 J5
Minerva Cl STWL/WRAY TW19 * 13 K7
Minerva Rd FARN GU14 92 E8
KUT/HW KT1 9 G7
Minimax Cl EBED/NFELT TW14 15 K8
Mink Ct HSLWW TW4 15 M4
Minley Cl FARN GU14 92 B5
Minniedale BRYLDS KT5 45 J5
Minorca Av FRIM GU16 74 B7
Minorca Rd FRIM GU16 74 B8
WEY KT13 59 K3
Minshull Pl BECK BR3 * 33 K8
Minstead Cl BRAK RG12 35 J3
Minstead Gdns PUT/ROE SW15 28 C1
Minstead Wy NWMAL KT3 46 B6
Minster Av SUT SM1 65 K1
Minster Ct CBLY GU15 * 72 C5
Minster Dr CROY/NA CR0 3 G9
Minster Gdns E/WMO/HCT KT8 43 J4
Minsterley Av SHPTN TW17 42 B4
Minster Rd GODL GU7 168 A7
Minstrel Gdns BRYLDS KT5 45 J4
Mint Gdns DORK RH4 144 D1
Mint La KWD/TDW/WH KT20 125 K3
Mint Rd BNSTD SM7 85 M6
WLGTN SM6 66 E4
Mint St GODL GU7 168 A5
The Mint GODL GU7 168 A5
Mint Wk CROY/NA CR0 2 D7
WARL CR6 89 G7
WOKN/KNAP GU21 76 B7
Misbrooks Green Rd
RDKG RH5 173 M10
Missenden Cl
EBED/NFELT TW14 24 C2
Missenden Gdns MRDN SM4 47 M6
Mistletoe Cl CROY/NA CR0 51 G8
Mistley Gdns HORL RH6 160 A4
Misty's Fld WOT/HER KT12 42 F8
Mitcham Ct CBLY GU15 53 K8
Mitcham La STRHM/NOR SW16 30 F6
Mitcham Pk MTCM CR4 48 C4
Mitcham Rd CBLY GU15 53 K8
CROY/NA CR0 49 H6
TOOT SW17 30 C6
Mitchell Gdns SWTR RH13 203 R6
Mitchells Cl RGUE GU4 139 H6
Mitchells Rd CRAWE RH10 165 H4
Mitchley Av PUR/KEN CR8 88 A3
Mitchley Gv SAND/SEL CR2 88 D3
Mitchley Hl SAND/SEL CR2 88 C3
Mitchley Vw SAND/SEL CR2 88 D3

Mitre Cl *BELMT* SM2 65 M6
SHPTN TW17 42 A6
Mixbury Gv *WEY* KT13 60 A5
Mixnams La *CHERT* KT16 40 D3
Mizen Cl *COB* KT11 81 G4
Mizen Wy *COB* KT11 80 F5
Moat Ct *ASHTD* KT21 83 H7
Moated Farm Dr
ADL/WDHM KT15 58 F6
Moat Rd *EGRIN* RH19 162 F3
Moat Side *FELT* TW13 24 F5
Moats La *REDH* RH1 149 J6
The Moat *NWMAL* KT3 46 B1
Moat Wk *CRAWE* RH10 165 L3
Moberly Rd *CLAP* SW4 31 G1
Moffat Rd *THHTH* CR7 49 M2
TOOT SW17 30 B5
Mogador Rd
KWD/TDW/WH KT20 125 H2
Mogden La *ISLW* TW7 17 J7
Moir Cl *SAND/SEL* CR2 68 D7
Mole Abbey Gdns
E/WMO/HCT KT8 43 K3
Mole Cl *CRAWW* RH11 164 D2
FARN GU14 92 A3
Mole Ct *HOR/WEW* KT19 63 M3
Molember Rd *E/WMO/HCT* KT8 44 B5
Mole Rd *LHD/OX* KT22 102 A3
WOT/HER KT12 61 G4
Molesey Av *E/WMO/HCT* KT8 43 J5
Molesey Cl *WOT/HER* KT12 61 H3
Molesey Dr *CHEAM* SM3 65 H1
Molesey Park Av
E/WMO/HCT KT8 43 L5
Molesey Park Cl
E/WMO/HCT KT8 43 M5
Molesey Park Rd
E/WMO/HCT KT8 43 L5
Molesey Rd *E/WMO/HCT* KT8 43 H5
WOT/HER KT12 61 G4
Molesham Cl *E/WMO/HCT* KT8 43 L3
Molesham Wy *E/WMO/HCT* KT8 43 L4
Moles Hl *LHD/OX* KT22 82 A1
Moles Md *EDEN* TN8 153 M7
Mole St *RDKG* RH5 172 B10
Mole Valley Pl *ASHTD* KT21 103 G1
Mollison Dr *WLGTN* SM6 67 H6
Molly Huggins Cl *BAL* SW12 30 F1
Molyneux Dr *TOOT* SW17 30 E5
Molyneux Rd *BFOR* GU20 54 F5
GODL GU7 168 C2
WEY KT13 59 K3
Monahan Av *PUR/KEN* CR8 87 J2
Monarch Cl *CRAWW* RH11 164 C7
EBED/NFELT TW14 24 B1
WWKM BR4 70 C3
Monarch Ms *STRHM/NOR* SW16 31 K6
Monarch Pde *MTCM* CR4 * 48 C2
Monaveen Gdns
E/WMO/HCT KT8 43 L3
Mondial Wy *HYS/HAR* UB3 14 F2
Money Av *CTHM* CR3 108 A4
Money Rd *CTHM* CR3 108 A4
Mongers La *EW* KT17 64 D8
Monivea Rd *BECK* BR3 33 J8
Monkleigh Rd *MRDN* SM4 47 H3
Monks Av *E/WMO/HCT* KT8 43 J5
Monks Cl *ASC* SL5 36 E6
FARN GU14 92 F5
Monks Crs *ADL/WDHM* KT15 58 E4
WOT/HER KT12 42 E8
Monksdene Gdns *SUT* SM1 65 L2
Monks Dr *ASC* SL5 36 E6
Monksfield *CRAWE* RH10 165 H4
Monks Gn *LHD/OX* KT22 101 M3
Monkshanger *FNM* GU9 134 B7
Monks La *EDEN* TN8 153 G3
RDKG RH5 188 A8
Monks Orchard Rd *BECK* BR3 51 K8
Monks Rd *BNSTD* SM7 85 K7
VW GU25 39 G4
Monks Wk *ASC* SL5 36 E6
FNM GU9 156 C2
REIG RH2 125 L8
Monks Wy *BECK* BR3 51 K6
STA TW18 23 G8
Monks' Well *RFNM* GU10 156 F1
Monkswell La *COUL/CHIP* CR5 105 L6
Monk Ter *FSTH* SE23 33 J3
Monkton La *FNM* GU9 134 B4
Monmouth Av *KUT/HW* KT1 8 B3
Monmouth Cl *MTCM* CR4 49 H4
Monro Dr *GUW* GU2 116 E5
Monroe Dr *MORT/ESHN* SW14 18 E7
Monro Pl *HOR/WEW* KT19 63 K7
Mons Barracks *ALDT* GU11 112 F4
Mons Cl *ALDT* GU11 113 H2
Monson Rd *REDH* RH1 126 C5
Mons Wk *EGH* TW20 21 M6
Montacute Cl *FARN* GU14 93 G5
Montacute Rd *CAT* SE6 33 J1
CROY/NA CR0 69 M7
MRDN SM4 48 A6
Montague Av *SAND/SEL* CR2 88 B2
Montague Cl *CBLY* GU15 72 E4
LTWR GU18 54 D8
WOT/HER KT12 42 D7
Montague Dr *CTHM* CR3 107 M4
Montague Rd *CROY/NA* CR0 2 B3
HSLW TW3 16 E5
RCHPK/HAM TW10 18 B8
WIM/MER SW19 29 L8
Montagu Gdns *WLGTN* SM6 66 F3
Montana Cl *SAND/SEL* CR2 68 A8
Montana Gdns *SUT* SM1 65 M4
SYD SE26 33 J6
Montana Rd *RYNPK* SW20 46 F1
TOOT SW17 30 D4
Montem Rd *FSTH* SE23 33 J1
NWMAL KT3 46 B4
Montford Rd *SUN* TW16 42 D4
Montfort Pl *WIM/MER* SW19 29 G2
Montfort Ri *REDH* RH1 148 C8
Montgomerie Dr *GUW* GU2 116 D3
Montgomerie Ms *FSTH* SE23 32 F1
Montgomery Av
ESH/CLAY KT10 62 B1
Montgomery Cl *MTCM* CR4 * 49 H4
Montgomery Gdns *BELMT* SM2 66 A6
Montgomery Rd *FARN* GU14 92 C6
WOKS/MYFD GU22 10 D8
Montolieu Gdns *PUT/ROE* SW15 19 L7
Montpelier Rd *PUR/KEN* CR8 67 L8
SUT SM1 65 M3
Montpelier Rw *TWK* TW1 26 E1
Montrave Rd *PGE/AN* SE20 32 F7
Montrell Rd *BRXS/STRHM* SW2 31 H2
Montrose Av *WHTN* TW2 25 L1
Montrose Cl *ASHF* TW15 23 M7
FRIM GU16 73 H7
Montrose Gdns *LHD/OX* KT22 82 A2
MTCM CR4 48 C3
SUT SM1 65 L1
Montrose Rd
EBED/NFELT TW14 15 G8
Montrose Wk *WEY* KT13 59 L2
Montrose Wy *DTCH/LGLY* SL3 12 A3
FSTH SE23 33 G2
Montrouge Crs *EW* KT17 84 F6
Mont St Aignan Wy *EDEN* TN8 153 M8
Montserrat Cl *NRWD* SE19 32 A6
Monument Hl *WEY* KT13 59 L3
Monument Rd *WEY* KT13 59 L3
Monument Wy East
WOKN/KNAP GU21 11 J2
Monument Wy West
WOKN/KNAP GU21 11 H2
Moon Hall Rd *CRAN* GU6 170 H8
Moons Hl *RFNM* GU10 155 L7
Moon's La *LING* RH7 179 L10
SWTR RH13 167 G8
Moor Cl *SHST* GU47 52 B8
Moorcroft Cl *CRAWW* RH11 164 D3
Moorcroft Rd
STRHM/NOR SW16 31 H4
Moordale Av *BNFD* RG42 34 B1
Moore Cl *ADL/WDHM* KT15 58 E4
MORT/ESHN SW14 18 F5
MTCM CR4 * 48 E2
RFNM GU10 135 J1
Moore Grove Crs *EGH* TW20 21 H8
Moore Rd *CHOB/PIR* GU24 94 E3
NRWD SE19 31 M7
Moore's Rd *DORK* RH4 144 E1
Moore Wy *BELMT* SM2 65 K7
Moorfield *HASM* GU27 198 A8
RDKG RH5 * 173 L2
Moorfield Point *GU* GU1 117 H4
Moorfield Rd *CHSGTN* KT9 63 H4
GU GU1 117 H4
Moorfields Cl *STA* TW18 40 B1
Moorhayes Dr *STA* TW18 40 F3
Moorhead Rd *HORS* RH12 167 L4
Moorholme *WOKS/MYFD* GU22 10 D9
Moorhouse Rd *OXTED* RH8 131 J4
Moorhurst La *RDKG* RH5 172 H5
The Moorings *BF/WBF* KT14 78 F2
CHSWK W4 * 18 D1
EGRIN RH19 162 B2
GSHT GU26 197 R2
GT/LBKH KT23 101 K7
WDSR SL4 20 F1
Moorland Cl *WHTN* TW2 25 K1
Moorland Rd *CRAWE* RH10 165 L7
WDR/YW UB7 13 M2
Moorlands Cl *GSHT* GU26 197 R1
Moorlands Rd *CBLY* GU15 72 D5
The Moorlands
WOKS/MYFD GU22 97 J3
Moor La *CHSGTN* KT9 63 J4
STA TW18 22 B4
STWL/WRAY TW19 21 M2
WDR/YW UB7 13 M1
WOKS/MYFD GU22 97 H4
Moormead Dr *HOR/WEW* KT19 64 B4
Moor Mead Rd *TWK* TW1 17 K8
Moormede Crs *STA* TW18 22 C5
Moor Pk *HORL* RH6 * 160 E4
Moor Park Crs *CRAWW* RH11 190 G8
Moor Park Gdns
KUTN/CMB KT2 28 B8
Moor Park La *FNM* GU9 134 C6
Moor Park Wy *FNM* GU9 134 C7
Moor Pl *BFOR* GU20 54 E4
EGRIN RH19 162 E3
Moor Rd *FARN* GU14 92 D1
FRIM GU16 93 J1
HASM GU27 197 P8
Moorside Cl *FARN* GU14 72 D8
Moors La *MFD/CHID* GU8 157 M6
Moorsom Wy *COUL/CHIP* CR5 87 G7
The Moors *RFNM* GU10 135 J2
Moray Av *SHST* GU47 72 A2
Morden Cl *BRAK* RG12 35 J4
KWD/TDW/WH KT20 105 G2
Morden Ct *MRDN* SM4 47 L4
Morden Court Pde
MRDN SM4 * 47 L3
Morden Gdns *MTCM* CR4 48 A4
Morden Hall Rd *MRDN* SM4 47 L3
Morden Rd *MTCM* CR4 48 A4
WIM/MER SW19 47 L2
Morden Wy *CHEAM* SM3 47 K7
Morecambe Cl *CRAWW* RH11 164 B6
More Cir *GODL* GU7 168 B2
More Cl *PUR/KEN* CR8 87 J1
Morecoombe Cl *KUTN/CMB* KT2 9 M2
Morecote Cl *RGUE* GU4 139 H7
Moreland Cl *DTCH/LGLY* SL3 12 F2
More La *ESH/CLAY* KT10 61 L2
Morella Cl *VW* GU25 38 F4
Morella Rd *BTSEA* SW11 30 C1
Moremead Rd *CAT* SE6 33 J5
Morena St *CAT* SE6 33 L1
More Rd *GODL* GU7 168 B2
Moresby Av *BRYLDS* KT5 45 L7
Moretaine Rd *ASHF* TW15 23 G4
Moreton Av *ISLW* TW7 17 G3
Moreton Cl *RFNM* GU10 181 K8
Moreton Rd *SAND/SEL* CR2 68 A4
WPK KT4 64 D1
Moring Rd *TOOT* SW17 30 D5
Morkyns Wk *DUL* SE21 * 32 B4
Morland Av *CROY/NA* CR0 3 H3
Morland Cl *HPTN* TW12 25 J6
MTCM CR4 48 B3
Morland Rd *ALDT* GU11 134 F2
CROY/NA CR0 3 J2
PGE/AN SE20 33 G8
SUT SM1 65 M4
Morland's Rd *ALDT* GU11 113 G4
Morley Cl *ORP* BR6 71 L1
Morley Rd *CHEAM* SM3 47 J8
FNM GU9 5 K6
SAND/SEL CR2 68 C8
TWK TW1 18 A8
Morningside Rd *WPK* KT4 64 E1
Mornington Crs *HEST* TW5 15 L3
Mornington Rd *ASHF* TW15 23 M6
Mornington Wk
RCHPK/HAM TW10 26 F5
Morrell Av *HORS* RH12 167 J4
Morris Cl *CROY/NA* CR0 51 H6
Morris Gdns *WAND/EARL* SW18 29 K1
Morrish Rd *BRXS/STRHM* SW2 31 H1
Morris Rd *FARN* GU14 113 G1
ISLW TW7 17 J5
REDH RH1 149 H2
Morston Cl
KWD/TDW/WH KT20 104 E2
Mortimer Cl *STRHM/NOR* SW16 31 G3
Mortimer Crs *WPK* KT4 64 A2
Mortimer Rd *BH/WHM* TN16 90 F2
MTCM CR4 48 C1
RDKG RH5 173 L11
Mortlake Cl *CROY/NA* CR0 67 J2
Mortlake Dr *MTCM* CR4 48 B1
Mortlake High St
MORT/ESHN SW14 19 G5
Mortlake Rd *RCH/KEW* TW9 18 D2
Morton *KWD/TDW/WH* KT20 105 G3
Morton Cl *FRIM* GU16 93 J2
WLGTN SM6 67 J6
WOKN/KNAP GU21 76 F5
Morton Gdns *WLGTN* SM6 66 F4
Morton Rd *EGRIN* RH19 162 F6
MRDN SM4 48 A5
WOKN/KNAP GU21 76 F5
Morval Cl *FARN* GU14 92 B5
Morven Rd *TOOT* SW17 30 C4
Moselle Cl *FARN* GU14 92 A4
Moselle Rd *BH/WHM* TN16 91 H8
Mosford Cl *HORL* RH6 160 C1
Mospey Crs *EW* KT17 84 C5
Mossfield *COB* KT11 80 D3
Moss Gdns *FELT* TW13 24 D3
SAND/SEL CR2 69 G6
Moss La *GODL* GU7 168 A5
Mosslea Rd *CTHM* CR3 88 C6
ORP BR6 71 M2
PGE/AN SE20 32 F8
Mossville Gdns *MRDN* SM4 47 J3
Mostyn Rd *WIM/MER* SW19 47 J2
Mostyn Ter *REDH* RH1 148 D1
Moth Cl *WLGTN* SM6 67 H6
Motspur Pk *NWMAL* KT3 46 C6
Motts Hill La
KWD/TDW/WH KT20 104 D5
Mouchotte Cl *BH/WHM* TN16 90 E2
Moulton Av *HSLW* TW3 16 B4
Mountacre Cl *SYD* SE26 32 C5
Mount Adon Pk *EDUL* SE22 32 D1
Mount Angelus Rd
PUT/ROE SW15 28 C1
Mount Ararat Rd
RCHPK/HAM TW10 18 B7
Mount Ash Rd *SYD* SE26 32 E4
Mount Av *CTHM* CR3 107 M6
Mountbatten Cl
CRAWW RH11 * 164 E8
NRWD SE19 32 B6
Mount Cl *CAR* SM5 66 D7
CRAN GU6 171 K12
CRAWE RH10 165 L3
LHD/OX KT22 102 C5
PUR/KEN CR8 87 M6
WOKS/MYFD GU22 96 E3
The Mount Cl *VW* GU25 39 G6
Mountcombe Cl *SURB* KT6 45 H7
Mount Ct *GUW* GU2 * 6 F7
WWKM BR4 70 B1
The Mount Dr *REIG* RH2 125 M6
Mountearl Gdns
STRHM/NOR SW16 31 J4
Mount Ephraim La
STRHM/NOR SW16 31 G4
Mount Ephraim Rd
STRHM/NOR SW16 31 G4
Mount Felix *WOT/HER* KT12 42 C8
Mount Gdns *SYD* SE26 32 E4
Mount Hermon Cl
WOKS/MYFD GU22 10 C8
Mount Hermon Rd
WOKS/MYFD GU22 10 B9
Mount La *BRAK* RG12 34 F3
CRAWE RH10 193 M9
Mount Lee *EGH* TW20 21 H6
Mount Nod Rd
STRHM/NOR SW16 31 J4
Mount Pk *CAR* SM5 66 D7
Mount Park Av *SAND/SEL* CR2 67 L7
Mount Pl *GUW* GU2 * 6 F7
Mount Pleasant *BH/WHM* TN16 91 G7
BRAK RG12 34 F3
EHSLY KT24 119 L3
EHSLY KT24 121 H2
EW KT17 64 C8
FNM GU9 4 E4
GUW GU2 6 E8
RDKG RH5 * 142 C6
WEY KT13 59 K2
WNWD SE27 31 M5
Mount Pleasant Cl *LTWR* GU18 54 D8
Mount Pleasant Rd
ASHV GU12 112 F7
BOR GU35 180 A12
CTHM CR3 108 D5
LING RH7 178 D5
NWMAL KT3 45 M3
Mount Ri *FSTH* SE23 32 F3
REDH RH1 148 A2
Mount Rd *CHOB/PIR* GU24 76 E2
CHSGTN KT9 63 J4
CRAN GU6 186 D3
FELT TW13 25 H4
MTCM CR4 48 A2
NRWD SE19 * 32 A7
NWMAL KT3 46 A3
WIM/MER SW19 29 K3
WOKS/MYFD GU22 96 E3
Mountsfield Cl
STWL/WRAY TW19 13 K7
Mountside *GUW* GU2 6 D8
Mount St *DORK* RH4 144 D2
The Mount *BOR* GU35 180 F11
COUL/CHIP CR5 86 D5
CRAN GU6 171 K12
CRAN GU6 186 D3
CRAWW RH11 190 E4
ESH/CLAY KT10 61 K5
EW KT17 64 C8
EW KT17 64 E3
GUW GU2 6 D9
HASM GU27 198 G3
KWD/TDW/WH KT20 105 J8
LHD/OX KT22 102 B5
NWMAL KT3 46 C3
VW GU25 39 G6
WARL CR6 108 D1
WEY KT13 60 B1
WOKN/KNAP GU21 10 A8
Mount Vw *ALDT* GU11 112 D8
Mountview Cl *REDH* RH1 148 B2
Mountview Dr *REDH* RH1 148 B2
Mount View Rd *ESH/CLAY* KT10 62 E6
Mount Vls *WNWD* SE27 31 L4
Mount Wy *CAR* SM5 66 D7
Mountwood *E/WMO/HCT* KT8 43 L3
Mountwood Cl *SAND/SEL* CR2 68 E8
Mousehill La *MFD/CHID* GU8 183 M1
Mowbray Av *BF/WBF* KT14 79 H3
Mowbray Crs *EGH* TW20 21 K6
Mowbray Dr *CRAWW* RH11 164 B6
Mowbray Gdns *DORK* RH4 122 E8
Mowbray Rd *NRWD* SE19 50 C1
RCHPK/HAM TW10 26 F4
Mower Pl *CRAN* GU6 186 D1
Moyne Rd *CRAWW* RH11 164 E8
Moys Cl *CROY/NA* CR0 49 H6
Moyser Rd *STRHM/NOR* SW16 30 E6
Muchelney Rd *MRDN* SM4 47 M6
Muckhatch La *EGH* TW20 39 L3
Muggeridge Cl *SAND/SEL* CR2 68 A4
Muggeridge's Hl *RDKG* RH5 189 M5
Muirdown Av
MORT/ESHN SW14 18 F6
Muirfield Cl *CRAWW* RH11 190 G8
Muirfield Rd *WOKN/KNAP* GU21 76 D8
Muirkirk Rd *CAT* SE6 33 M2
Mulberry Av *STWL/WRAY* TW19 23 H2
Mulberry Cl *ASHV* GU12 113 K5
HORS RH12 166 F4
SHST GU47 72 A1
STRHM/NOR SW16 30 F5
WEY KT13 59 L2
WOKN/KNAP GU21 77 H4
Mulberry Crs *BTFD* TW8 17 L2
Mulberry La *CROY/NA* CR0 3 K4
Mulberry Pl *RDKG* RH5 173 R7
Mulberry Rd *CRAWW* RH11 164 D1
Mulberry Trees *SHPTN* TW17 42 A7
Mulgrave Rd *BELMT* SM2 65 J6
CROY/NA CR0 2 E8
FRIM GU16 73 J7
Mulgrave Wy
WOKN/KNAP GU21 76 B8
Mulholland Cl *MTCM* CR4 48 E2
Mullards Cl *MTCM* CR4 48 C8
Mullens Rd *EGH* TW20 21 M6
Mullins Pth *MORT/ESHN* SW14 19 G5
Mulroy Dr *CBLY* GU15 73 K3
Multon Rd *WAND/EARL* SW18 30 A1
Muncaster Cl *ASHF* TW15 23 K5
Muncaster Rd *ASHF* TW15 23 L6
Muncies Ms *CAT* SE6 33 M3
Munday's Boro *RGUW* GU3 136 D5
Munday's Boro Rd *RGUW* GU3 136 E5
Munnery Wy *ORP* BR6 71 K2
Munnings Dr *SHST* GU47 72 A3
Munnings Gdns *ISLW* TW7 17 G7
Munslow Gdns *SUT* SM1 65 M3
Munstead Heath Rd
MFD/CHID GU8 168 F5
Munstead Pk *MFD/CHID* GU8 168 F6
Munstead Vw *RGUW* GU3 138 E4
Munstead View Rd *SHGR* GU5 168 G4
Munster Av *HSLWW* TW4 16 B6
Munster Rd *TEDD* TW11 8 A1
Murdoch Cl *STA* TW18 22 D6
Murfett Cl *WIM/MER* SW19 29 H3
Murray Av *HSLW* TW3 16 E7
Murray Ct *ASC* SL5 36 F6
SWTR RH13 167 L5
Murray Rd *CHERT* KT16 58 A5
FARN GU14 92 C6
RCHPK/HAM TW10 26 E3
WIM/MER SW19 29 G7
Murray's La *BF/WBF* KT14 79 G4
Murray's Rd *ALDT* GU11 113 G4
Murrell Rd *ASHV* GU12 113 K6
Murrells La *CBLY* GU15 72 E6
Murrells Wk *GT/LBKH* KT23 101 K5
Murrey Ct *SWTR* RH13 * 167 L5
The Murreys *ASHTD* KT21 83 G8
Muschamp Rd *CAR* SM5 66 B1
Museum Hl *HASM* GU27 198 E7
Musgrave Av *EGRIN* RH19 162 F6
Musgrave Rd *ISLW* TW7 17 J3
Musquash Wy *HSLWW* TW4 15 M4
Mustard Mill Rd *STA* TW18 22 C5
Mutton Hl *LING* RH7 178 H10
Mutton Oaks *BRAK* RG12 34 A1
Muybridge Rd *NWMAL* KT3 45 M2
Myers Wy *FRIM* GU16 74 A7
Mylis Cl *SYD* SE26 32 E5
Mylor Cl *WOKN/KNAP* GU21 77 H4
Mynn's Cl *EPSOM* KT18 83 L4
Myrna Cl *WIM/MER* SW19 30 B8
Myrtle Av *EBED/NFELT* TW14 15 H6
Myrtle Cl *DTCH/LGLY* SL3 13 H3
LTWR GU18 74 E1
Myrtle Dr *BLKW* GU17 72 A5
Myrtle Gv *NWMAL* KT3 45 M2
Myrtle Rd *CROY/NA* CR0 69 K2
DORK RH4 144 D1
HPTN TW12 25 M7
HSLW TW3 16 F4
SUT SM1 65 M4
Mytchett Farm Pk
FRIM GU16 * 93 J7
Mytchett Heath *FRIM* GU16 93 K6
Mytchett Lake Rd *FRIM* GU16 93 K8
Mytchett Place Rd *FRIM* GU16 93 K8
Mytchett Rd *FRIM* GU16 93 J5
Myton Rd *DUL* SE21 32 A4

N

Nailsworth Crs *REDH* RH1 127 G3
Nairn Cl *FRIM* GU16 73 H7
Naldrett Cl *HORS* RH12 167 J5
Naldretts La *HORS* RH12 202 H4
Nallhead Rd *FELT* TW13 24 F6
Namba Roy Cl
STRHM/NOR SW16 31 J5
Namton Dr *THHTH* CR7 49 J4
Napier Cl *ALDT* GU11 113 H2
Napier Ct *CTHM* CR3 108 B4
Napier Dr *CBLY* GU15 73 K2
Napier Gdns *GU* GU1 117 L7
Napier Rd *ASHF* TW15 24 A8
ISLW TW7 17 K6
SAND/SEL CR2 68 A6
SNWD SE25 50 E4
WDR/YW UB7 14 A3
Napier Wk *ASHF* TW15 24 A8
Napier Wy *CRAWE* RH10 165 H1
Napoleon Av *FARN* GU14 92 E3
Napoleon Rd *TWK* TW1 * 26 E1
Napper Cl *ASC* SL5 35 M2
Napper Pl *CRAN* GU6 186 D4
Narrow La *WARL* CR6 108 E1
Naseby *BRAK* RG12 34 E8
Naseby Cl *ISLW* TW7 17 H3
Naseby Ct *WOT/HER* KT12 * 60 F1
Naseby Rd *NRWD* SE19 32 A7
Nash Cl *FARN* GU14 92 C5
SUT SM1 66 A2
Nash Gdns *ASC* SL5 36 A2
REDH RH1 126 C6
Nash La *HAYES* BR2 70 D5
Nash Rd *CRAWE* RH10 165 G7
Nassau Rd *BARN* SW13 19 J3
Nasturtium Dr *CHOB/PIR* GU24 75 K5
Natalie Cl *EBED/NFELT* TW14 24 A1
Natal Rd *STRHM/NOR* SW16 31 G7
THHTH CR7 50 A3
Neale Cl *EGRIN* RH19 162 C2
Neal Ter *FSTH* SE23 * 33 G2
Neath Gdns *MRDN* SM4 47 M6
Neb La *OXTED* RH8 129 M5
Needles Bank *GDST* RH9 128 E5
Needles Cl *HORS* RH12 166 E8
Neil Cl *ASHF* TW15 23 M6
Nelgarde Rd *CAT* SE6 33 K1
Nell Ball *BIL* RH14 200 H7
Nell Gwynn Av *SHPTN* TW17 42 A6
Nell Gwynne Av *ASC* SL5 37 G4
Nell Gwynne Cl *HOR/WEW* KT19 83 K1
Nello James Gdns *WNWD* SE27 32 A5
Nelson Cl *ASHV* GU12 112 F8
BH/WHM TN16 91 H7
BRAK RG12 35 H2
CRAWE RH10 165 L5
CROY/NA CR0 2 B4
EBED/NFELT TW14 * 24 C2
FNM GU9 134 A1
WOT/HER KT12 42 E8
Nelson Gdns *GU* GU1 117 K7
HSLW TW3 16 D8
Nelson Grove Rd
WIM/MER SW19 47 L1
Nelson Rd *ASHF* TW15 23 H6
CTHM CR3 108 A5
FNM GU9 134 A1
HORS RH12 166 E6
HTHAIR TW6 14 C3
NWMAL KT3 46 A5
WHTN TW2 25 M1
WIM/MER SW19 29 L8
Nelson St *ALDT* GU11 112 D7
Nelson Wk *HOR/WEW* KT19 63 K7
Nelson Wy *CBLY* GU15 72 C5
Nene Gdns *FELT* TW13 25 J3
Nene Rd *HTHAIR* TW6 14 E3
Nepean St *PUT/ROE* SW15 19 K8
Neptune Cl *CRAWW* RH11 164 A6
Neptune Rd *HTHAIR* TW6 * 14 F3
Nesbitt Sq *NRWD* SE19 * 32 B8
Netheravon Rd South
CHSWK W4 19 J1
Netherby Pk *WEY* KT13 60 B4
Netherby Rd *FSTH* SE23 32 F1
Nethercote Av
WOKN/KNAP GU21 76 C7
Netherfield Rd *TOOT* SW17 30 D4
The Netherlands
COUL/CHIP CR5 106 F1
Netherleigh Pk *REDH* RH1 149 H3
Nether Mt *GUW* GU2 6 D8
Nethern Court Rd *CTHM* CR3 109 K5
Netherne Dr *COUL/CHIP* CR5 106 F4
Netherne La *COUL/CHIP* CR5 106 F4
Netherton *BRAK* RG12 34 D4
Netherton Rd *TWK* TW1 17 K7
Netherwood *CRAWW* RH11 164 C7
Netley Cl *CHEAM* SM3 65 G4
CROY/NA CR0 69 M6
SHGR GU5 141 M4
Netley Dr *WOT/HER* KT12 43 J7
Netley Gdns *MRDN* SM4 47 M7
Netley Rd *BTFD* TW8 18 B1
MRDN SM4 47 M7
Netley St *FARN* GU14 112 F1
Nettlecombe *BRAK* RG12 35 G5
Nettlecombe Cl *BELMT* SM2 65 L7
Nettlefold Pl *WNWD* SE27 31 L4
Nettlestead Cl *BECK* BR3 33 J8
Nettles Ter *GU* GU1 7 G3
Nettleton Rd *HTHAIR* TW6 14 E3
Nettlewood Rd
STRHM/NOR SW16 31 G8
Neuchatel Rd *CAT* SE6 33 J3
Neuman Crs *BRAK* RG12 34 D6
Nevada Cl *FARN* GU14 92 A6
NWMAL KT3 45 M4
Nevelle Cl *BNFD* RG42 34 A1
Nevile Cl *CRAWW* RH11 164 C7
Neville Av *NWMAL* KT3 46 A1
Neville Cl *BNSTD* SM7 85 L4
ESH/CLAY KT10 61 J5
HSLW TW3 16 D4
Neville Duke Rd *FARN* GU14 92 C1

Neville Rd CROY/NA CR0 2 F1
KUT/HW KT1 9 K6
RCHPK/HAM TW10 26 F4
Neville Wk CAR SM5 48 B7
Nevil Wk CAR SM5 * 48 B7
Nevis Rd TOOT SW17 30 D3
Newall Rd HTHAIR TW6 14 F3
Newark Cl RGUE GU4 117 L3
RPLY/SEND GU23 98 C3
Newark Ct WOT/HER KT12 42 F8
Newark La RPLY/SEND GU23 98 C2
Newark Rd BFOR GU20 54 E3
CRAWE RH10 165 H2
SAND/SEL CR2 68 A5
New Barn Cl WLGTN SM6 67 J5
New Barn La CTHM CR3 88 B7
RDKG RH5 188 B2
New Barns Av MTCM CR4 49 G4
New Battlebridge La
REDH RH1 126 E4
New Berry La WOT/HER KT12 61 G4
Newbolt Av CHEAM SM3 64 F4
Newborough Gn NWMAL KT3 46 A4
Newbridge Cl HORS RH12 204 D6
Newbury Gdns HOR/WEW KT19 64 F4
Newbury Rd CRAWE RH10 165 M4
HTHAIR TW6 14 C3
New Cswy REIG RH2 147 L3
Newchapel Rd LING RH7 178 B7
New Cl FELT TW13 25 H6
WIM/MER SW19 47 M3
Newcombe Gdns HSLWW TW4 16 C6
Newcome Gdns
STRHM/NOR SW16 31 H5
Newcome Pl ASHV GU12 135 G2
Newcome Rd FNM GU9 134 B2
New Coppice
WOKN/KNAP GU21 96 B1
New Cross Rd GUW GU2 116 D6
New Dawn Cl FARN GU14 92 A6
Newdigate STRHM/NOR SW16 * 31 K5
Newdigate Rd HORS RH12 190 A5
RDKG RH5 173 L7
Newenham Rd GT/LBKH KT23 101 K8
Newent Cl CAR SM5 48 C8
New Farthingdale LING RH7 178 H9
Newfield Av FARN GU14 92 B3
Newfield Cl HPTN TW12 43 K1
Newfield Rd ASHV GU12 113 K3
New Forest Ride BRAK RG12 35 H7
Newfoundland Rd FRIM GU16 94 A1
Newgate CROY/NA CR0 2 D3
Newgate Cl FELT TW13 25 H3
New Green Pl
BRXS/STRHM SW2 31 K1
NRWD SE19 32 B7
Newhache LING RH7 178 H8
Newhall Gdns WOT/HER KT12 60 F1
Newhaven Crs ASHF TW15 24 A6
Newhaven Rd SNWD SE25 50 A5
New Haw Rd ADL/WDHM KT15 58 F5
New Heston Rd HEST TW5 16 C2
Newhouse Cl NWMAL KT3 46 B7
New House Farm La
RGUW GU3 115 L6
New House La REDH RH1 149 G8
New House Ter EDEN TN8 * 153 M7
Newhouse Wk MRDN SM4 47 M7
New Inn La GU GU1 117 L5
New Kelvin Av TEDD TW11 26 B7
Newlands GU GU1 7 M7
Newlands Av THDIT KT7 44 B8
WOKS/MYFD GU22 97 J3
Newlands Cl HORL RH6 160 C1
WOT/HER KT12 61 H3
Newlands Crs EGRIN RH19 162 E3
GU GU1 7 M7
Newlands Dr ASHV GU12 113 L5
DTCH/LGLY SL3 13 H5
Newlands Pk CRAWE RH10 193 K2
SYD SE26 32 F7
Newlands Pl FROW RH18 * 195 N10
Newlands Rd CBLY GU15 72 E8
CRAWW RH11 164 E5
HORS RH12 166 F5
STRHM/NOR SW16 49 H2
The Newlands WLGTN SM6 66 F6
Newlands Wy CHSGTN KT9 62 F4
Newlands Wd CROY/NA CR0 69 J7
Newlands Woods
CROY/NA CR0 * 69 J7
New La RGUE GU4 97 J6
New Lodge Dr OXTED RH8 130 C2
Newman Cl CRAWE RH10 165 L5
Newman Rd CROY/NA CR0 49 J7
Newmans Ct FNM GU9 133 K3
Newmans Pl ASC SL5 37 L7
Newmarket Rd CRAWE RH10 165 J7
New Meadow ASC SL5 36 A1
New Mile Rd ASC SL5 36 E2
Newminster Rd MRDN SM4 47 M6
New Moorhead Dr HORS RH12 167 M3
Newnham Cl THHTH CR7 49 M2
New North Rd REIG RH2 147 J3
New Pde ASHF TW15 * 23 J5
DORK RH4 * 144 E1
GT/LBKH KT23 * 101 M8
New Park Rd ASHF TW15 23 M6
BRXS/STRHM SW2 31 H2
CRAN GU6 186 D2
New Pl ASC SL5 * 55 H1
New Place Gdns LING RH7 178 F5
REDH RH1 126 C7
New Pond Rd GODL GU7 138 B8
Newport Rd ASHV GU12 112 F8
BARN SW13 19 K3
HTHAIR TW6 14 D3
Newquay Rd CAT SE6 33 L3
New Rd BAGS GU19 54 D5
BLKW GU17 72 B5
BRAK RG12 35 G2
BTFD TW8 * 18 A1
DTCH/LGLY SL3 12 A3
E/WMO/HCT KT8 43 K3
EBED/NFELT TW14 15 G8
ESH/CLAY KT10 61 M3
FELT TW13 25 H6
HASM GU27 198 A8
HORL RH6 161 L3
HSLW TW3 16 E6
HYS/HAR UB3 14 F2
KUTN/CMB KT2 9 J2
KWD/TDW/WH KT20 104 F5
MFD/CHID GU8 168 B12
MFD/CHID GU8 183 M1
MFD/CHID GU8 183 P9
MTCM CR4 48 D8
OXTED RH8 130 E4
OXTED RH8 151 K2
RCHPK/HAM TW10 26 F5
RDKG RH5 171 R11
RFNM GU10 135 J3
RGUE GU4 119 H5
RGUE GU4 139 L7
SHGR GU5 141 G5
SHGR GU5 141 M5
SHGR GU5 169 L1
SHPTN TW17 41 K3
STA TW18 21 M6
WEY KT13 59 M4
New Road Hl HAYES BR2 71 H7
Newry Rd TWK TW1 17 K6
Newsham Rd
WOKN/KNAP GU21 76 C7
New Site ADL/WDHM KT15 * 59 H3
Newstead Cl GODL GU7 168 A3
Newstead Hall HORL RH6 161 G4
Newstead Ri CTHM CR3 108 E8
Newstead Wk CAR SM5 47 M7
Newstead Wy WIM/MER SW19 29 G5
New St BH/WHM TN16 131 M1
CRAWE RH10 165 J3
STA TW18 22 D5
SWTR RH13 167 G7
Newton Av EGRIN RH19 163 G7
Newton Rd CRAWE RH10 191 Q3
FARN GU14 93 G3
HTHAIR TW6 14 B3
ISLW TW7 17 J4
PUR/KEN CR8 86 F2
WIM/MER SW19 29 H8
Newton Wy RFNM GU10 135 H2
Newton Wood Rd ASHTD KT21 83 J6
New Town CRAWE RH10 192 G2
Newtown Rd LIPH GU30 196 H10
New Wy GODL GU7 159 M5
New Wickham La EGH TW20 21 K8
New Zealand Av
WOT/HER KT12 42 D8
Nexus Pk ASHV GU12 113 J1
Nicholas Gdns
WOKS/MYFD GU22 78 B6
Nicholas Rd CROY/NA CR0 67 H3
Nicholes Rd HSLW TW3 16 D6
Nicholsfield BIL RH14 201 Q5
Nicholson Ms EGH TW20 * 21 K6
KUT/HW KT1 45 H4
Nicholson Rd CROY/NA CR0 3 K3
Nicholson Wk EGH TW20 21 K6
Nicola Cl SAND/SEL CR2 67 M5
Nicosia Rd WAND/EARL SW18 30 B1
Niederwald Rd SYD SE26 33 H5
Nigel Fisher Wy CHSGTN KT9 62 F6
Nightingale Av EHSLY KT24 100 A7
Nightingale Cl BH/WHM TN16 90 F5
CAR SM5 66 D1
CHSWK W4 18 F1
COB KT11 81 G1
CRAWW RH11 164 E2
EGRIN RH19 162 E6
HOR/WEW KT19 83 K2
Nightingale Crs BRAK RG12 34 F5
EHSLY KT24 100 A7
Nightingale Dr FRIM GU16 93 K6
HOR/WEW KT19 63 L5
Nightingale La CRAWE RH10 193 P8
RCHPK/HAM TW10 27 H1
Nightingale Ms KUT/HW KT1 * 8 D8
Nightingale Rd ASHV GU12 113 M6
CAR SM5 66 C2
E/WMO/HCT KT8 43 L5
EHSLY KT24 100 C7
ESH/CLAY KT10 61 J4
GODL GU7 168 B3
GU GU1 7 H3
HORS RH12 167 G6
HPTN TW12 25 K7
SAND/SEL CR2 89 G1
WOT/HER KT12 * 42 F7
Nightingales CRAN GU6 186 D4
Nightingale Shott EGH TW20 21 J7
Nightingale Sq BAL SW12 30 D1
The Nightingales
STWL/WRAY TW19 23 J2
Nightingale Wy REDH RH1 128 B8
Nightjar Cl RFNM GU10 133 G1
Nimbus Rd HOR/WEW KT19 64 A8
Nimrod Rd STRHM/NOR SW16 30 E7
Nineacres Wy COUL/CHIP CR5 87 H6
Nine Elms Cl EBED/NFELT TW14 24 C2
Ninehams Cl CTHM CR3 108 A2
Ninehams Gdns CTHM CR3 108 A2
Ninehams Rd BH/WHM TN16 111 G3
CTHM CR3 108 A3
Nine Mile Ride BRAK RG12 34 D8
Nineteenth Rd MTCM CR4 49 H4
Ninhams Wd ORP BR6 71 K3
Ninth Av KWD/TDW/WH KT20 * 105 J8
Niton Rd RCH/KEW TW9 * 18 D5
Niven Cl CRAWE RH10 165 M5
Noahs Ct CRAWE RH10 * 193 M9
Nobel Dr HYS/HAR UB3 15 H2
Noble Cnr HEST TW5 * 16 D3
Nobles Wy EGH TW20 21 H8
Noke Dr REDH RH1 126 D7
Nonsuch Court Av EW KT17 64 E8
Nonsuch Pl CHEAM SM3 * 65 G6
Nonsuch Wk BELMT SM2 65 G8
Noons Corner Rd RDKG RH5 172 A1
Norbiton Av KUT/HW KT1 9 K6
Norbiton Common Rd
KUT/HW KT1 9 M8
Norbury Av HSLW TW3 17 G7
STRHM/NOR SW16 49 J1
Norbury Cl STRHM/NOR SW16 49 K1
Norbury Court Rd
STRHM/NOR SW16 49 H2
Norbury Crs STRHM/NOR SW16 49 K2
Norbury Cross
STRHM/NOR SW16 49 H3
Norbury Hl STRHM/NOR SW16 31 K8
Norbury Ri STRHM/NOR SW16 49 H3
Norbury Rd FELT TW13 24 C4
REIG RH2 125 J8
THHTH CR7 49 M2
Norbury Wy GT/LBKH KT23 101 M7
Norcroft Gdns EDUL SE22 32 D1
Norcutt Rd WHTN TW2 26 B2
Norfolk Av SAND/SEL CR2 68 D8
Norfolk Cl CRAWW RH11 164 A8
HORL RH6 160 D4
TWK TW1 * 17 L8
Norfolk Farm Cl
WOKS/MYFD GU22 11 M3
Norfolk Farm Rd
WOKS/MYFD GU22 78 A5
Norfolk Gdns
WOKN/KNAP GU21 * 96 C1
Norfolk House Rd
STRHM/NOR SW16 31 G4
Norfolk La RDKG RH5 144 E8
Norfolk Rd DORK RH4 144 D2
ESH/CLAY KT10 62 B4
FELT TW13 24 F2
HORS RH12 167 G7
RDKG RH5 173 K3
THHTH CR7 49 M3
WIM/MER SW19 30 B8
Norgrove St BAL SW12 30 D2
Norheads La BH/WHM TN16 90 D8
Norhyrst Av SNWD SE25 50 C3
Nork Gdns BNSTD SM7 85 H4
Nork Ri BNSTD SM7 85 G6
Nork Wy BNSTD SM7 85 G5
Norlands La EGH TW20 40 B2
Norley V PUT/ROE SW15 28 D2
Norman Av EW KT17 84 C2
FELT TW13 25 H3
SAND/SEL CR2 67 M8
TWK TW1 26 E1
Norman Cl EPSOM KT18 104 E1
ORP BR6 71 M2
Norman Colyer Ct
HOR/WEW KT19 * 64 A8
Norman Crs HEST TW5 16 A2
Normandy HORS RH12 166 F8
Normandy Cl CRAWE RH10 165 K6
EGRIN RH19 * 163 G5
FRIM GU16 94 B1
SYD SE26 33 H4
Normandy Common La
RGUW GU3 114 E5
Normandy Gdns HORS RH12 166 F8
Normandy Wk EGH TW20 * 21 M6
Normanhurst Cl CRAWE RH10 165 H4
Normanhurst Dr TWK TW1 17 L7
Normanhurst Rd
BRXS/STRHM SW2 31 J3
WOT/HER KT12 61 G1
Norman Keep BNFD RG42 35 J1
Norman Rd ASHF TW15 24 A7
SUT SM1 65 K4
THHTH CR7 49 L5
WIM/MER SW19 29 M8
Normansfield Av KUT/HW KT1 8 B3
Normans La EDEN TN8 179 M1
Norman's Rd HORL RH6 161 M1
Normanton Av
WAND/EARL SW18 29 K3
Normanton Rd SAND/SEL CR2 68 B5
Normanton St FSTH SE23 33 G3
Normington Cl
STRHM/NOR SW16 31 K6
Norrels Dr EHSLY KT24 100 C8
Norrels Ride EHSLY KT24 100 C8
Norstead Pl PUT/ROE SW15 28 D3
North Acre BNSTD SM7 85 J6
Northampton Cl BRAK RG12 35 G3
Northampton Rd CROY/NA CR0 3 L5
Northanger Rd
STRHM/NOR SW16 31 H7
North Av CAR SM5 66 D6
FNM GU9 134 A2
RCH/KEW TW9 18 D3
WOT/HER KT12 60 C7
Northborough Rd
STRHM/NOR SW16 49 H2
Northbourne GODL GU7 168 C1
Northbrook Copse BRAK RG12 35 J6
Northbrook Rd ALDT GU11 134 E1
CROY/NA CR0 50 A5
Northcliffe Cl WPK KT4 64 B2
North Cl ASHV GU12 113 H8
CRAWE RH10 165 H3
EBED/NFELT TW14 15 G8
FARN GU14 92 D1
MRDN SM4 47 H4
RDKG RH5 144 F6
North Common WEY KT13 * 59 M3
Northcote ADL/WDHM KT15 59 G3
Northcote Av BRYLDS KT5 45 K7
ISLW TW7 17 K7
Northcote Crs EHSLY KT24 99 M7
Northcote La SHGR GU5 169 P4
Northcote Rd ASHV GU12 113 K2
CROY/NA CR0 50 A6
EHSLY KT24 99 M7
FARN GU14 92 B3
NWMAL KT3 45 M3
TWK TW1 17 K7
Northcott BRAK RG12 34 D8
Northcott Gdns FARN GU14 92 A4
Northcroft Cl EGH TW20 20 E6
Northcroft Gdns EGH TW20 20 E6
Northcroft Rd EGH TW20 20 E6
HOR/WEW KT19 64 B6
Northcroft Vls EGH TW20 20 E6
North Dene HSLW TW3 16 E3
North Down SAND/SEL CR2 88 B1
Northdown Cl HORS RH12 167 J5
Northdown La GU GU1 7 K9
Northdown Rd BELMT SM2 65 K8
CTHM CR3 109 K7
Northdowns CRAN GU6 186 D4
North Downs Crs CROY/NA CR0 69 L8
North Downs Rd CROY/NA CR0 69 L8
North Downs Wy
BRKHM/BTCW RH3 124 A6
CTHM CR3 128 A1
GDST RH9 129 J2
KWD/TDW/WH KT20 123 J6
RDKG RH5 143 H1
REDH RH1 107 H8
RFNM GU10 134 D7
RGUE GU4 139 K4
RGUW GU3 136 C6
WARL CR6 110 D5
Northdown Ter EGRIN RH19 * 162 E2
North Dr BECK BR3 51 L4
CHOB/PIR GU24 94 F3
HSLW TW3 16 F4
STRHM/NOR SW16 30 F5
VW GU25 38 B5
North End CROY/NA CR0 2 C5
EGRIN RH19 * 162 C2
North End La ASC SL5 37 K7
ORP BR6 71 L7
Northernhay Wk MRDN SM4 47 H4
Northern Perimeter Rd
HTHAIR TW6 14 F3
Northern Perimeter Rd (West)
WDR/YW UB7 13 M3
Northey Av BELMT SM2 65 G8
North Farm Rd FARN GU14 92 B1
Northfield LTWR GU18 74 E1
MFD/CHID GU8 183 N5
RGUE GU4 139 H8
Northfield Cl ASHV GU12 113 G8
Northfield Ct STA TW18 40 E1
Northfield Crs CHEAM SM3 65 H3
Northfield Pl WEY KT13 59 L6
Northfield Rd COB KT11 80 D3
North Field Rd HEST TW5 16 A1
Northfield Rd STA TW18 40 E1
Northfields ASHTD KT21 103 H1
EW KT17 84 B1
North Gdns WIM/MER SW19 30 A8
Northgate Av CRAWE RH10 165 H3
Northgate Dr CBLY GU15 73 K2
Northgate Pl CRAWE RH10 165 G3
Northgate Rd CRAWE RH10 164 F4
North Gate Rd FARN GU14 92 E7
Northgate Rd HORL RH6 160 C5
North Gn BRAK RG12 35 G1
North Gv CHERT KT16 40 C6
North Heath Cl HORS RH12 167 G4
North Heath La HORS RH12 167 G4
North Holmes Cl HORS RH12 167 L4
Northington Cl BRAK RG12 35 J6
Northlands RDKG RH5 * 173 Q8
Northlands Rd HORS RH12 167 H2
HORS RH12 188 E12
North La ASHV GU12 113 G6
TEDD TW11 26 C7
North Lodge Dr ASC SL5 35 M2
North Looe EW KT17 * 84 F3
North Md CRAWE RH10 165 G2
REDH RH1 126 C5
Northmead FARN GU14 92 E5
North Moors GU GU1 117 H4
North Munstead La
MFD/CHID GU8 168 D8
Northolt Rd WDR/YW UB7 14 A3
North Pde CHSGTN KT9 63 J4
HORS RH12 166 F6
North Park La GDST RH9 128 D3
North Pl MTCM CR4 30 C8
TEDD TW11 26 C7
Northpoint Cl SUT SM1 65 M2
North Pole La HAYES BR2 70 D5
North Rd ALDT GU11 113 G2
ASC SL5 35 L1
ASHV GU12 113 J5
BTFD TW8 18 B1
CRAWE RH10 165 J3
EBED/NFELT TW14 15 G8
FARN GU14 113 G2
GUW GU2 116 E5
HEST TW5 15 M1
RCH/KEW TW9 18 D4
REIG RH2 147 J3
SURB KT6 45 G6
WIM/MER SW19 29 M7
WOKN/KNAP GU21 11 G3
WOT/HER KT12 60 F4
WWKM BR4 51 L8
Northrop Rd HTHAIR TW6 15 H3
North Side RFNM GU10 135 K2
Northspur Rd SUT SM1 65 K2
North Station Ap REDH RH1 * 149 J2
Northstead Rd
BRXS/STRHM SW2 31 K3
North St CAR SM5 66 C3
CRAWE RH10 193 M9
DORK RH4 144 D2
EGH TW20 21 J6
GODL GU7 168 B2
GU GU1 7 G6
HORS RH12 167 G7
ISLW TW7 17 K5
LHD/OX KT22 102 D3
REDH RH1 126 C7
Northumberland Av ISLW TW7 17 J3
Northumberland Cl
STWL/WRAY TW19 14 B8
Northumberland Crs
EBED/NFELT TW14 15 H8
Northumberland Gdns
MTCM CR4 49 H5
North Vw WIM/MER SW19 28 E6
North View Crs EPSOM KT18 84 F7
North Wk CROY/NA CR0 69 L4
Northway GODL GU7 159 L2
GUW GU2 116 D6
HORL RH6 160 C6
MRDN SM4 47 H3
WLGTN SM6 66 F3
Northway Rd CROY/NA CR0 50 C6
North Weald La KUTN/CMB KT2 26 F6
Northwood Av PUR/KEN CR8 87 K3
WOKN/KNAP GU21 76 A8
Northwood Pk CRAWE RH10 * 191 R3
Northwood Rd CAR SM5 66 D5
FSTH SE23 33 J2
HTHAIR TW6 14 A3
THHTH CR7 49 M2
North Worple Wy
MORT/ESHN SW14 19 G5
Norton Av BRYLDS KT5 45 L7
Norton Cl RGUW GU3 116 A1
Norton Gdns STRHM/NOR SW16 49 H2
Norton Pk ASC SL5 36 F5
Norton Rd CBLY GU15 73 M5
Norwich Av CBLY GU15 73 H6
Norwich Rd CRAWE RH10 165 J6
THHTH CR7 49 M3
Norwood Cl EHSLY KT24 121 H2
WHTN TW2 26 A3
Norwood Crs HTHAIR TW6 14 F3
Norwood Farm La COB KT11 80 D1
Norwood High St WNWD SE27 31 M5
Norwood Hl HORL RH6 174 G6
Norwoodhill Rd HORL RH6 175 J8
Norwood Park Rd WNWD SE27 31 M6
Norwood Rd EHSLY KT24 121 H2
HNHL SE24 31 L2
Notley End EGH TW20 * 20 F8
Notson Rd SNWD SE25 50 E4
Nottingham Cl
WOKN/KNAP GU21 76 C8
Nottingham Rd ISLW TW7 17 J4
SAND/SEL CR2 67 M4
TOOT SW17 30 C2
Nova Ms CHEAM SM3 47 H7
Nova Rd CROY/NA CR0 2 B3
Nowell Rd BARN SW13 19 K1
Nower Rd DORK RH4 144 D2
Nowhurst La HORS RH12 204 B4
Noyna Rd TOOT SW17 30 C4
Nuffield Dr SHST GU47 52 C8
Nugent Cl MFD/CHID GU8 185 J7
Nugent Rd GUW GU2 138 A1
SNWD SE25 50 C3
Nunappleton Wy OXTED RH8 130 D6
Nuneaton BRAK RG12 35 H6
Nunns Fld RDKG RH5 * 173 K11
Nuns Wk VW GU25 39 G5
Nursery Av CROY/NA CR0 69 G1
Nursery Cl ADL/WDHM KT15 58 C8
CROY/NA CR0 69 G1
EBED/NFELT TW14 24 E1
EW KT17 64 B8
FRIM GU16 93 J2
KWD/TDW/WH KT20 104 E7
RDKG RH5 173 K12
WOKN/KNAP GU21 76 F6
Nursery Gdns HSLWW TW4 16 C7
RGUE GU4 139 L6
STA TW18 22 E8
SUN TW16 42 C2
Nursery Hl SHGR GU5 169 N5
Nurserylands CRAWW RH11 164 C4
Nursery La ASC SL5 36 B1
HORL RH6 160 A4
Nursery Rd GODL GU7 168 C2
KWD/TDW/WH KT20 104 E7
MTCM CR4 48 B3
SUN TW16 42 B2
SUT SM1 65 M3
THHTH CR7 50 A4
WIM/MER SW19 29 H8
WIM/MER SW19 47 L2
WOKN/KNAP GU21 76 A7
Nursery Wy OXTED RH8 * 130 B3
STWL/WRAY TW19 12 A8
Nutbourne FNM GU9 134 B2
Nutcombe La DORK RH4 144 C2
GSHT GU26 197 R4
Nutcroft Gv LHD/OX KT22 102 B4
Nutfield Cl CAR SM5 66 B2
Nutfield Marsh Rd REDH RH1 127 H5
Nutfield Rd COUL/CHIP CR5 86 D6
REDH RH1 126 E8
THHTH CR7 49 L4
Nutfield Wy ORP BR6 71 K1
Nuthatch Cl RFNM GU10 133 G2
Nuthatch Gdns REIG RH2 147 M4
Nuthatch Wy CRAWE RH10 193 P8
Nuthurst BRAK RG12 35 H5
Nuthurst Av BRXS/STRHM SW2 31 J3
CRAN GU6 186 D2
Nuthurst Cl CRAWW RH11 164 C3
Nutley BRAK RG12 34 D8
Nutley La REIG RH2 125 J7
Nutshell La FNM GU9 133 M3
Nutty La SHPTN TW17 41 M4
Nutwell St TOOT SW17 30 B6
Nutwood Av
BRKHM/BTCW RH3 145 M1
Nutwood Cl
BRKHM/BTCW RH3 145 M1
Nyefield Pk
KWD/TDW/WH KT20 104 D8
Nylands Av RCH/KEW TW9 18 D4
Nymans Cl HORS RH12 167 K2
Nymans Ct CRAWE RH10 * 165 K7
Nymans Gdns RYNPK SW20 46 E3
Nyon Gv CAT SE6 33 J3

O

Oakapple Cl CRAWW RH11 191 L12
SAND/SEL CR2 88 E4
Oak Av CHOB/PIR GU24 95 K3
CROY/NA CR0 69 K1
EGH TW20 21 M8
HEST TW5 16 A2
HPTN TW12 25 H6
SHST GU47 52 A8
Oakbank CROY/NA CR0 69 M5
LHD/OX KT22 101 M5
WOKS/MYFD GU22 10 D9
Oakbank Av WOT/HER KT12 43 J7
Oak Cl CRAN GU6 171 K11
CRAWE RH10 192 E2
GODL GU7 168 B1
KWD/TDW/WH KT20 123 L4
MFD/CHID GU8 199 P1
Oakcombe Cl NWMAL KT3 46 B1
Oak Cnr RDKG RH5 173 K6
Oak Cottage Cl RGUW GU3 115 M7
Oak Ct CRAWE RH10 * 191 N3
FNM GU9 5 H6
Oak Cft EGRIN RH19 163 H5
Oakcroft Cl BF/WBF KT14 78 C4
Oakcroft Rd BF/WBF KT14 78 C4
CHSGTN KT9 63 J3
Oakcroft Vls CHSGTN KT9 63 J3
Oakdale BRAK RG12 35 G6
Oakdale La EDEN TN8 131 M7
Oakdale Rd HOR/WEW KT19 64 A7
STRHM/NOR SW16 31 H6
WEY KT13 59 K2

Oakdale Wy MTCM CR4 48 D7
Oak Dell CRAWE RH10 165 L3
Oakdene ASC SL5 37 J6
CHOB/PIR GU24 56 C8
KWD/TDW/WH KT20 105 H2
Oakdene Av THDIT KT7 44 D8
Oakdene Cl BRKHM/BTCW RH3 145 M2
GT/LBKH KT23 121 M1
Oakdene Dr BRYLDS KT5 45 M8
Oakdene Ms CHEAM SM3 47 J8
Oakdene Pl RGUW GU3 138 F8
Oakdene Rd
BRKHM/BTCW RH3 145 M3
COB KT11 80 E4
GODL GU7 168 A6
GT/LBKH KT23 101 J6
REDH RH1 126 C8
RGUW GU3 138 F8
Oak Dr KWD/TDW/WH KT20 123 L4
Oaken Coppice ASHTD KT21 103 K1
Oaken Copse CBLY GU15 73 M2
Oaken Copse Crs FARN GU14 92 E2
Oak End RDKG RH5 173 K6
Oaken Dr ESH/CLAY KT10 62 C5
Oak End Wy ADL/WDHM KT15 78 B2
Oakengates BRAK RG12 34 D8
Oaken La ESH/CLAY KT10 62 B3
Oakenshaw Cl SURB KT6 45 H7
Oakfield BIL RH14 200 H6
WOKN/KNAP GU21 76 B6
Oakfield Cl NWMAL KT3 46 C5
WEY KT13 59 M3
Oakfield Dr REIG RH2 125 K6
Oakfield Gdns BECK BR3 51 K5
CAR SM5 48 B8
Oakfield Gld WEY KT13 59 M3
Oakfield La HAYES BR2 70 F3
Oakfield Rd ASHF TW15 23 L5
ASHTD KT21 83 H8
BLKW GU17 72 B5
COB KT11 80 E3
CROY/NA CR0 2 C3
EDEN TN8 153 L5
PGE/AN SE20 32 E8
WIM/MER SW19 29 G4
Oakfields BF/WBF KT14 78 E4
CBLY GU15 * 72 E4
CRAWE RH10 165 M3
RDKG RH5 187 R5
RGUW GU3 116 B6
WOT/HER KT12 42 D8
Oakfield Wy EGRIN RH19 163 G2
Oak Gdns CROY/NA CR0 69 K1
Oak Grange Rd RGUE GU4 118 E3
Oak Gv BIL RH14 201 R5
CRAN GU6 186 E4
SUN TW16 24 E8
WWKM BR4 69 M1
Oak Grove Crs CBLY GU15 72 C3
Oak Grove Rd PGE/AN SE20 50 F1
Oakhall Dr SUN TW16 24 C6
Oakham Cl CAT SE6 * 33 J3
Oakhaven CRAWE RH10 164 F6
Oak Hl EPSOM KT18 84 A6
Oakhill ESH/CLAY KT10 62 D5
Oak Hl RGUE GU4 117 M4
RGUW GU3 115 K6
SURB KT6 45 H7
Oakhill Cl ASHTD KT21 82 F8
Oak Hill Crs SURB KT6 45 H7
Oakhill Gdns WEY KT13 60 B1
Oak Hill Gv SURB KT6 45 H6
Oak Hill Rd SURB KT6 * 45 H6
Oakhill Rd ADL/WDHM KT15 58 C5
ASHTD KT21 82 F8
BECK BR3 51 M2
BOR GU35 180 G12
REIG RH2 147 L1
STRHM/NOR SW16 49 H1
SUT SM1 65 L2
SWTR RH13 167 H7
Oakhurst CHOB/PIR GU24 56 B7
GSHT GU26 197 Q2
Oakhurst Cl TEDD TW11 26 B6
Oakhurst Gdns EGRIN RH19 162 D3
Oakhurst La BIL RH14 201 P3
Oakhurst Ms SWTR RH13 * 167 K5
Oakhurst Ri CAR SM5 66 B8
Oakhurst Rd HOR/WEW KT19 63 M5
Oakington Cl SUN TW16 42 F2
Oakington Dr SUN TW16 42 F2
Oakland Av FNM GU9 134 B2
Oaklands GDST RH9 151 H4
HASM GU27 198 D6
HORL RH6 160 F3
LHD/OX KT22 102 A6
PUR/KEN CR8 87 M4
SWTR RH13 167 H7
Oaklands Av ESH/CLAY KT10 44 A8
ISLW TW7 17 J1
THHTH CR7 49 K4
WWKM BR4 69 L2
Oaklands Cl CHSGTN KT9 62 F3
RGUE GU4 139 H8
SWTR RH13 205 M9
Oaklands Ct ADL/WDHM KT15 58 E2
Oaklands Dr REDH RH1 148 E2
Oaklands Gdns PUR/KEN CR8 87 M4
Oaklands La BH/WHM TN16 90 F5
Oaklands Rd MORT/ESHN SW14 19 G5
Oaklands Wy
KWD/TDW/WH KT20 104 F4
WLGTN SM6 66 F6
Oakland Wy HOR/WEW KT19 64 A5
Oak La EGH TW20 20 F4
HORS RH12 166 B6
ISLW TW7 17 H6
TWK TW1 26 D1
WOKS/MYFD GU22 11 K4
Oaklawn Rd LHD/OX KT22 82 B8
Oaklea ASHV GU12 113 K4
Oak Leaf Cl HOR/WEW KT19 * 83 M2
Oakleigh Av SURB KT6 45 K8
Oakleigh Ct OXTED RH8 * 130 B3
Oakleigh Rd HORS RH12 167 J5
Oakleigh Wy MTCM CR4 48 E1
SURB KT6 45 K8
Oakley Av CROY/NA CR0 67 H3
Oakley Cl ADL/WDHM KT15 59 G3
EGRIN RH19 163 J6
ISLW TW7 17 G3
Oakley Ct MTCM CR4 48 D7
Oakley Dell RGUE GU4 117 M6
Oakley Dr HAYES BR2 71 H2
Oakley Gdns BNSTD SM7 85 L5
BRKHM/BTCW RH3 145 M6
Oakley Rd CBLY GU15 72 E5
HAYES BR2 71 H2
SNWD SE25 50 E5
WARL CR6 88 D8
Oak Lodge Cl WOT/HER KT12 60 F4
Oak Lodge Dr REDH RH1 148 D8
WWKM BR4 51 L7
Oak Md GODL GU7 168 A1
Oakmead Gn EPSOM KT18 83 M5
Oakmead Pl MTCM CR4 48 B1
Oakmead Rd BAL SW12 30 E2
CROY/NA CR0 49 G6
Oak Pk BF/WBF KT14 78 B3
Oak Park Gdns WIM/MER SW19 29 G2
Oakridge CHOB/PIR GU24 75 J3
Oak Rdg DORK RH4 144 E5
Oak Rd COB KT11 81 G5
CRAWW RH11 164 E5
CTHM CR3 108 B4
FARN GU14 92 F6
LHD/OX KT22 102 D1
NWMAL KT3 46 A2
REIG RH2 125 L7
Oak Rw MTCM CR4 48 F2
Oaks Av FELT TW13 25 H3
NRWD SE19 32 B6
WPK KT4 64 E3
Oaks Cl HORS RH12 167 L3
LHD/OX KT22 102 D3
Oaksford Av SYD SE26 32 E4
Oakshade Rd LHD/OX KT22 81 M4
Oakshaw OXTED RH8 130 A1
Oakshaw Rd WAND/EARL SW18 29 L1
Oakside Ct HORL RH6 160 F2
Oakside La HORL RH6 160 F2
Oaks La CROY/NA CR0 68 F2
RDKG RH5 144 E8
Oaks Pk BNSTD SM7 * 86 C2
The Oaks Pk RDKG RH5 * 173 L8
Oaks Rd CROY/NA CR0 68 E4
PUR/KEN CR8 87 L4
REIG RH2 126 A7
STWL/WRAY TW19 14 A7
WOKN/KNAP GU21 10 C6
The Oaks BF/WBF KT14 78 D4
BRAK RG12 35 G2
CHSGTN KT9 62 F2
DORK RH4 * 144 E5
EGRIN RH19 163 H5
EPSOM KT18 84 B4
FELT TW13 * 25 H3
MFD/CHID GU8 * 199 Q1
MRDN SM4 * 47 H4
STA TW18 * 22 C5
WOKN/KNAP GU21 * 10 C6
Oaks Tr CAR SM5 66 D8
Oaks Wy CAR SM5 66 C6
EPSOM KT18 104 E1
PUR/KEN CR8 87 M4
RPLY/SEND GU23 98 D6
SURB KT6 63 G1
Oak Tree Cl ASHV GU12 93 J8
ASHV GU12 135 G1
BOR GU35 196 E1
EGRIN RH19 * 162 D2
RGUE GU4 116 F2
RGUE GU4 117 M3
VW GU25 39 G6
WOKN/KNAP GU21 75 L8
Oak Tree Dr EGH TW20 20 F6
GU GU1 116 F4
Oak Tree La HASM GU27 197 Q7
MFD/CHID GU8 185 J8
Oak Tree Rd MFD/CHID GU8 159 J8
WOKN/KNAP GU21 75 L8
Oaktrees ASHV GU12 113 J8
FNM GU9 133 L3
Oak Tree Vw FNM GU9 134 A3
Oaktree Wk CTHM CR3 108 B4
Oak Tree Wy SWTR RH13 167 J5
Oak Vw EDEN TN8 153 L7
Oakview Gv CROY/NA CR0 51 H8
Oakview Rd CAT SE6 33 L6
Oak Wk HORS RH12 190 C11
Oak Wy CRAWE RH10 165 G2
CROY/NA CR0 51 G6
EBED/NFELT TW14 24 B2
REIG RH2 148 A1
ASHTD KT21 83 K6
Oakway ASHV GU12 135 G1
RYNPK SW20 46 F4
SWTR RH13 205 R10
WOKN/KNAP GU21 96 B1
Oakway Dr FRIM GU16 73 H8
Oakwood GUW GU2 116 D3
WLGTN SM6 66 E7
Oakwood Av BECK BR3 51 M2
HOR/WEW KT19 63 K7
MTCM CR4 48 A2
PUR/KEN CR8 87 L2
Oakwood Cl EHSLY KT24 120 B1
REDH RH1 126 D8
REDH RH1 * 149 J2
Oakwood Ct CHOB/PIR GU24 75 K6
Oakwood Dr EHSLY KT24 120 B1
NRWD SE19 32 A7
Oakwood Gdns ORP BR6 71 M1
SUT SM1 65 K1
WOKN/KNAP GU21 75 K8
Oakwood Pl CROY/NA CR0 49 K6
Oakwood Ri CTHM CR3 108 B7
Oakwood Rd BFOR GU20 55 H5
BRAK RG12 35 H2
CROY/NA CR0 49 K6
HORL RH6 160 D2
ORP BR6 71 M1
REDH RH1 127 K3
RYNPK SW20 46 D1
VW GU25 38 F5
WOKN/KNAP GU21 96 B1
Oareborough BRAK RG12 35 H4
Oarsman Pl E/WMO/HCT KT8 44 B4
Oast House Cl
STWL/WRAY TW19 21 H1
Oast House La FNM GU9 134 A4
Oast La ALDT GU11 134 E2
Oast Rd OXTED RH8 130 C5
Oates Wk CRAWE RH10 165 H7
Oatfield Rd
KWD/TDW/WH KT20 104 E3
Oatlands CRAWW RH11 164 C5
HORL RH6 160 E2
Oatlands Av WEY KT13 60 A4
Oatlands Cha WEY KT13 60 B2
Oatlands Cl WEY KT13 59 M3
Oatlands Dr WEY KT13 59 L3
Oatlands Gn WEY KT13 60 A2
Oatlands Mere WEY KT13 60 A2
Oatlands Rd
KWD/TDW/WH KT20 105 H1
Oban Rd THHTH CR7 50 A4
Obelisk Wy CBLY GU15 72 F3
Oberon Wy CRAWW RH11 164 A7
SHPTN TW17 41 H3
Observatory Rd
MORT/ESHN SW14 18 F6
Occam Rd GUW GU2 116 A8
Ockenden Cl
WOKS/MYFD GU22 * 10 F8
Ockenden Gdns
WOKS/MYFD GU22 10 E8
Ockenden Rd
WOKS/MYFD GU22 10 E8
Ockfields MFD/CHID GU8 159 J8
Ockford Dr GODL GU7 159 M6
Ockford Rdg GODL GU7 159 L7
Ockford Rd GODL GU7 159 M6
Ockham Dr EHSLY KT24 100 A6
Ockham La COB KT11 80 D8
RPLY/SEND GU23 99 M2
Ockham Rd North
RPLY/SEND GU23 99 L4
Ockham Rd South EHSLY KT24 120 B1
Ockley Ct RGUE GU4 117 L3
Ockley Rd CRAN GU6 171 K11
CROY/NA CR0 49 J7
RDKG RH5 172 C10
RDKG RH5 173 J8
STRHM/NOR SW16 31 H5
Ockleys Md GDST RH9 128 F3
O'Connor Rd ALDT GU11 113 G2
Octagon Rd WOT/HER KT12 60 C8
Octavia BRAK RG12 34 D8
Octavia Cl MTCM CR4 48 B5
Octavia Rd ISLW TW7 17 J5
Octavia Wy STA TW18 22 D7
Odard Rd E/WMO/HCT KT8 43 K4
Odeon Pde ISLW TW7 * 17 H4
Odiham Rd RFNM GU10 132 E1
Ogden Pk BRAK RG12 35 H3
O'Gorman Av FARN GU14 92 E7
Okeburn Rd TOOT SW17 30 D6
Okehurst Rd BIL RH14 202 F11
Okingham Cl SHST GU47 52 A8
Old Acre BF/WBF KT14 78 D4
Oldacre CHOB/PIR GU24 75 J2
Old Av BF/WBF KT14 78 B4
WEY KT13 59 M6
Old Avenue Cl
WOKN/KNAP GU21 78 B3
Old Bakery Ct CRAN GU6 171 K12
Old Barn Cl BELMT SM2 65 H6
Old Barn Dr RDKG RH5 173 L11
Old Barn La CTHM CR3 88 C6
RFNM GU10 181 N7
Old Barn Rd EPSOM KT18 83 M7
Old Barn Vw GODL GU7 * 159 M7
Old Bisley Rd FRIM GU16 73 K7
Old Bracknell Cl BRAK RG12 34 E3
Old Bracknell La East
BRAK RG12 34 E3
Old Bracknell La West
BRAK RG12 34 D3
Old Brickfield Rd ALDT GU11 134 E2
Old Bridge Rd RFNM GU10 134 E5
Old Bridge St KUT/HW KT1 8 C6
Old Brighton Rd South
HORL RH6 191 P1
Oldbury BRAK RG12 34 C3
Oldbury Cl FRIM GU16 93 J1
HORS RH12 167 K2
Oldbury Rd CHERT KT16 40 B7
Old Chapel La ASHV GU12 113 K7
Old Charlton Rd SHPTN TW17 41 M5
Old Char Whf DORK RH4 144 C1
Old Chertsey Rd
CHOB/PIR GU24 56 E8
Old Chestnut Av
ESH/CLAY KT10 61 K5
Old Church La FNM GU9 5 L9
Old Church Pth ESH/CLAY KT10 61 L3
Old Claygate La ESH/CLAY KT10 62 D5
Old Common COB KT11 * 80 E2
Old Common Rd COB KT11 80 E2
Old Compton La FNM GU9 134 B8
Old Convent EGRIN RH19 * 162 F3
Old Cote Dr HEST TW5 16 D1
Old Ct ASHTD KT21 103 H1
Old Court Rd GUW GU2 6 B5
Old Crawley Rd HORS RH12 167 M3
Old Cross Tree Wy ASHV GU12 135 M1
Old Dairy Ms BAL SW12 30 D2
Old Dean Rd CBLY GU15 73 G2
Old Deer Pk RCH/KEW TW9 * 18 C5
Old Deer Park Gdns
RCH/KEW TW9 18 B5
Old Denne Gdns HORS RH12 166 F8
Old Devonshire Rd BAL SW12 30 E1
Old Dock Cl RCH/KEW TW9 18 D1
Old Dr SHGR GU5 * 141 M4
Old Elstead Rd MFD/CHID GU8 159 H7
Olden La PUR/KEN CR8 87 K2
Old Esher Cl WOT/HER KT12 * 61 G4
Old Esher Rd WOT/HER KT12 61 G4
Old Farleigh Rd SAND/SEL CR2 68 F8
WARL CR6 89 J5
Old Farm Cl HSLWW TW4 16 C6
Old Farmhouse Dr
LHD/OX KT22 82 A5
Old Farm Pl ASHV GU12 113 J5
Old Farm Rd GU GU1 117 G5
HPTN TW12 25 J7
Old Farnham La FNM GU9 5 K7
RFNM GU10 132 D8
Oldfield Gdns ASHTD KT21 103 G1
Oldfield Rd HORL RH6 160 C5
HPTN TW12 43 K1
WIM/MER SW19 29 H7
Oldfields Rd SUT SM1 65 K1
Oldfieldwood
WOKS/MYFD GU22 11 K5
Old Forge Cl HORS RH12 190 C12
Old Forge Crs SHPTN TW17 41 L6
Old Fox Cl CTHM CR3 107 L3
Old Frensham Rd RFNM GU10 156 A3
Old Green La CBLY GU15 72 F2
Old Guildford Rd FRIM GU16 93 M4
HORS RH12 166 B6
Old Haslemere Rd HASM GU27 198 D8
Old Heath Wy FNM GU9 * 133 M2
Old Hl WOKS/MYFD GU22 97 G2
Old Holbrook HORS RH12 167 H1
Old Hollow CRAWE RH10 192 E5
Old Horsham Rd CRAWW RH11 164 D6
RDKG RH5 173 K4
Old Hospital Cl BAL SW12 * 30 C2
Old House Cl EW KT17 64 C8
WIM/MER SW19 29 H6
Old House Gdns TWK TW1 * 17 M8
Oldhouse La BFOR GU20 54 F7
CHOB/PIR GU24 75 K4
Old House Ms HORS RH12 * 166 F7
Old Kiln Cl RFNM GU10 181 L7
Old Kiln La BRKHM/BTCW RH3 123 M8
RFNM GU10 181 L7
Old Kingston Rd WPK KT4 63 M2
Old Lands Hl BRAK RG12 35 G1
Old La ALDT GU11 134 D2
ASHV GU12 113 H6
BH/WHM TN16 111 G3
COB KT11 100 B2
OXTED RH8 130 C4
RFNM GU10 180 D5
Old Lane Gdns EHSLY KT24 100 C4
Old Lodge Cl GODL GU7 * 159 L6
Old Lodge La PUR/KEN CR8 87 J3
Old London Rd EPSOM KT18 84 D8
KUTN/CMB KT2 8 F6
RDKG RH5 122 F2
Old Malden La WPK KT4 64 B1
Old Malt Wy WOKN/KNAP GU21 10 B5
Old Manor Cl CRAWW RH11 164 C2
Old Manor Dr ISLW TW7 16 F8
Old Manor Gdns RGUE GU4 139 M6
Old Martyrs CRAWW RH11 164 F1
Old Merrow St RGUE GU4 117 M5
Old Mill La REDH RH1 126 E2
Old Millmeads HORS RH12 166 F4
Old Mill Pl HASM GU27 198 A6
STWL/WRAY TW19 12 E8
Old Nursery Pl ASHF TW15 23 L6
Old Oak Av COUL/CHIP CR5 106 B1
Old Oak Cl COB KT11 80 E3
Old Orch BF/WBF KT14 79 J2
SUN TW16 42 F2
Old Orchards CRAWE RH10 192 D7
The Old Orch FNM GU9 4 D9
Old Palace Rd CROY/NA CR0 2 B7
GUW GU2 6 B6
WEY KT13 59 L2
Old Palace Yd RCH/KEW TW9 17 M7
Old Park Cl FNM GU9 133 K3
Old Park La RFNM GU10 133 J2
Old Park Ms HEST TW5 16 C2
Old Parvis Rd BF/WBF KT14 78 F2
Old Pasture Rd FRIM GU16 73 J6
Old Pond Cl CBLY GU15 72 E8
Old Portsmouth Rd CBLY GU15 73 K5
MFD/CHID GU8 182 E5
RGUW GU3 138 E8
Old Pottery Cl REIG RH2 147 L2
Old Pound Cl ISLW TW7 17 K3
The Old Quarry HASM GU27 198 A9
Old Rectory Cl
KWD/TDW/WH KT20 104 D6
Old Rectory Dr ASHV GU12 113 L7
Old Rectory Gdns FARN GU14 93 G5
GODL GU7 168 C7
Old Rectory La EHSLY KT24 100 B8
Old Redstone Dr REDH RH1 148 D1
Old Reigate Rd DORK RH4 123 H8
Oldridge Rd BAL SW12 30 D1
Old Rd ADL/WDHM KT15 58 C6
BRKHM/BTCW RH3 124 C7
EGRIN RH19 163 G5
Old School Cl ASHV GU12 113 K6
BECK BR3 51 G2
GU GU1 7 G4
Old School Ct
STWL/WRAY TW19 21 J1
Old School La
BRKHM/BTCW RH3 145 K3
Old School Ms WEY KT13 60 A3
Old School Pl CROY/NA CR0 67 K3
LING RH7 178 E5
WOKS/MYFD GU22 97 H3
Old Schools La EW KT17 64 C7
Old School Sq THDIT KT7 44 C6
Old School Ter CHEAM SM3 * 65 G6
Old Station Ap LHD/OX KT22 102 D3
Old Station Cl CRAWE RH10 193 M6
Old Station Gdns TEDD TW11 * 26 D7
Old Station La
STWL/WRAY TW19 12 C8
Old Station Wy GODL GU7 168 B3
Oldstead BRAK RG12 35 G5
The Old Surrey Ms GDST RH9 * 128 F4
Old Swan Yd CAR SM5 66 C3
Old Town CROY/NA CR0 2 B7
Old Town Ms FNM GU9 * 4 F4
Old Tye Av BH/WHM TN16 91 H6
Old Westhall Cl WARL CR6 108 F1
Old Wickhurst La HORS RH12 166 A8
Old Woking Rd BF/WBF KT14 78 D3
WOKS/MYFD GU22 97 M2
Oliver Av SNWD SE25 50 C3
Oliver Cl ADL/WDHM KT15 58 E3
CHSWK W4 18 E1
Oliver Gv SNWD SE25 50 C4
Olive Rd WIM/MER SW19 * 29 M8
Oliver Rd ASC SL5 36 E4
HORS RH12 166 D8
NWMAL KT3 45 M2
SUT SM1 66 A3
Olivier Rd CRAWE RH10 165 M5
Ollerton BRAK RG12 34 D8
Olley Cl WLGTN SM6 67 H6
Olveston Wk CAR SM5 48 A6
Olyffe Dr BECK BR3 51 M1
Omega Rd WOKN/KNAP GU21 11 H2
Omega Wy EGH TW20 39 M1
One Tree Hill Rd RGUE GU4 139 L2
Ongar Cl ADL/WDHM KT15 58 C5
Ongar Hl ADL/WDHM KT15 58 D5
Ongar Pl ADL/WDHM KT15 58 D5
Ongar Rd ADL/WDHM KT15 58 D4
Onslow Av BELMT SM2 65 J8
RCHPK/HAM TW10 18 B7
Onslow Cl WOKS/MYFD GU22 11 H5
Onslow Crs WOKS/MYFD GU22 11 H5
Onslow Gdns SAND/SEL CR2 88 D2
THDIT KT7 44 B8
WLGTN SM6 66 F6
Onslow Ms CHERT KT16 40 C6
Onslow Rd ASC SL5 37 L7
CROY/NA CR0 49 K7
GU GU1 7 H4
NWMAL KT3 46 D4
RCHPK/HAM TW10 18 B8
WOT/HER KT12 60 D3
Onslow St GU GU1 6 F7
Onslow Wy THDIT KT7 44 B8
WOKS/MYFD GU22 78 C5
Ontario Cl HORL RH6 161 K4
Ontario Wy LIPH GU30 196 H10
Openfields BOR GU35 180 D11
Openview WAND/EARL SW18 29 M2
Opladen Wy BRAK RG12 34 F5
Opossum Wy HSLWW TW4 15 M5
Opus Pk GU GU1 * 117 G4
Orange Court La ORP BR6 71 K7
The Orangery
RCHPK/HAM TW10 26 F3
Orchard Av ADL/WDHM KT15 78 C1
ASHF TW15 23 M7
CROY/NA CR0 69 H1
EBED/NFELT TW14 15 G7
HEST TW5 16 B2
MTCM CR4 48 D8
NWMAL KT3 46 B2
THDIT KT7 44 D8
Orchard Cl ASHF TW15 23 M7
ASHV GU12 113 K4
BLKW GU17 72 C8
BNSTD SM7 85 L4
CHOB/PIR GU24 75 G3
EDEN TN8 153 L7
EHSLY KT24 100 C6
FNM GU9 134 D3
GU GU1 117 L8
HOR/WEW KT19 * 63 L5
HORL RH6 160 C2
LHD/OX KT22 102 A4
MFD/CHID GU8 158 A5
RGUW GU3 114 E8
RYNPK SW20 46 F4
WOKS/MYFD GU22 11 K4
WOT/HER KT12 42 E7
Orchard Ct BRAK RG12 * 34 F2
WLGTN SM6 * 66 E4
WPK KT4 * 46 D8
Orchard Dr ASHTD KT21 103 G2
EDEN TN8 153 L7
SHPTN TW17 42 B3
WOKN/KNAP GU21 10 E2
Orchard End CTHM CR3 108 B4
LHD/OX KT22 101 M6
RFNM GU10 155 J6
WEY KT13 60 B1
Orchardfield Rd GODL GU7 168 C2
Orchard Gdns ASHV GU12 134 F1
CHSGTN KT9 63 H3
CRAN GU6 186 E3
EHSLY KT24 121 H2
EPSOM KT18 83 M5
Orchard Ga ESH/CLAY KT10 44 A8
Orchard Gv CROY/NA CR0 51 H7
PGE/AN SE20 32 D8
Orchard Hl BFOR GU20 55 G6
HORS RH12 202 H2
Orchard La E/WMO/HCT KT8 44 A6
RYNPK SW20 46 E1
Orchard Lea Cl
WOKS/MYFD GU22 78 B5
Orchardleigh LHD/OX KT22 102 E4
Orchard Mains
WOKS/MYFD GU22 96 F2
Orchard Mew
WOKN/KNAP GU21 75 L8
Orchard Ms TOOT SW17 29 M4
Orchard Ri CROY/NA CR0 51 H8
KUTN/CMB KT2 45 M1
RCHPK/HAM TW10 18 E6
Orchard Rd BTFD TW8 17 M1
CHSGTN KT9 63 H3
DORK RH4 144 E3
FARN GU14 92 D5
FELT TW13 24 D2
FNM GU9 134 D3
GUW GU2 138 C2
HORL RH6 161 L3
HPTN TW12 25 J8
HSLWW TW4 16 C7
KUT/HW KT1 8 E7
ORP BR6 71 L4
RCH/KEW TW9 18 D5
REIG RH2 125 L8
RGUE GU4 117 L4
RGUE GU4 139 H6
SAND/SEL CR2 88 E4
SHGR GU5 141 K5
SUN TW16 24 E8
SUT SM1 65 K4
SWTR RH13 167 H8
TWK TW1 17 K7
WDSR SL4 20 E1
Orchards Cl BF/WBF KT14 78 D4
The Orchards CRAWW RH11 190 G8
Orchard St CRAWW RH11 164 F4
THDIT KT7 44 E8
The Orchard EW KT17 64 C6
HASM GU27 198 A8
HORL RH6 * 160 D3
LTWR GU18 74 E1
RDKG RH5 144 F6
SWTR RH13 167 L5
VW GU25 39 H5
WEY KT13 59 L3
WOKN/KNAP GU21 76 E6

WOKS/MYFD GU22 97 H4
Orchard Wy ADL/WDHM KT15 58 E4
ASHF TW15 23 J3
ASHV GU12 134 F1
CBLY GU15 72 E7
CROY/NA CR0 51 H7
DORK RH4 144 E3
EGRIN RH19 162 F4
ESH/CLAY KT10 61 M5
KWD/TDW/WH KT20 105 H8
OXTED RH8 130 D7
REIG RH2 147 L3
RGUW GU3 * 96 A6
RGUW GU3 114 E8
RPLY/SEND GU23 97 M7
SUT SM1 66 A3
Orchid Cl CHSGTN KT9 62 F6
Orchid Ct EGH TW20 21 L5
Orchid Dr CHOB/PIR GU24 75 K5
Orchid Gdns HSLWW TW4 16 C6
Orde Cl CRAWE RH10 165 M1
Ordnance Cl FELT TW13 24 D3
Ordnance Rd ASHV GU12 113 G6
Oregano Wy GUW GU2 116 D3
Oregon Cl NWMAL KT3 45 M4
Orestan La EHSLY KT24 120 F1
Orford Gdns TWK TW1 26 C3
Orford Rd CAT SE6 33 L4
Oriel Cl CRAWE RH10 165 L1
MTCM CR4 49 G4
Oriel Dr BARN SW13 19 M1
Oriel Hl CBLY GU15 73 G5
Oriental Cl WOKS/MYFD GU22 10 F5
Oriental Rd ASC SL5 37 G4
WOKS/MYFD GU22 10 F6
Orion BRAK RG12 34 D8
Orlando Gdns HOR/WEW KT19 64 A8
Orleans Rd NRWD SE19 32 A7
TWK TW1 26 E1
Orltons La HORS RH12 190 C3
Ormanton Rd SYD SE26 32 D5
Ormeley Rd BAL SW12 30 E1
Orme Rd KUT/HW KT1 9 M6
SUT SM1 65 L5
Ormerod Gdns MTCM CR4 48 D2
Ormesby Wk CRAWE RH10 165 K6
Ormond Av HPTN TW12 43 L1
ORP BR6 71 M1
Ormond Crs HPTN TW12 25 L8
Ormond Dr HPTN TW12 25 L8
Ormonde Av HOR/WEW KT19 64 A7
Ormonde Pl WEY KT13 * 60 A5
Ormonde Rd GODL GU7 168 B3
MORT/ESHN SW14 18 E5
WOKN/KNAP GU21 76 F6
Ormond Rd RCHPK/HAM TW10 18 A7
Ormsby BELMT SM2 * 65 L6
Ormside Wy REDH RH1 126 E4
Orpin Rd REDH RH1 126 F4
Orpwood Cl HPTN TW12 25 J7
Orwell Cl FARN GU14 92 B2
Orwell Gdns REIG RH2 147 L2
Osborne Av STWL/WRAY TW19 23 H2
Osborne Cl BECK BR3 51 H4
FELT TW13 25 G6
Osborne Dr LTWR GU18 74 D1
Osborne Gdns THHTH CR7 49 M2
Osborne Rd EGH TW20 21 J7
FARN GU14 112 F1
HSLW TW3 16 C5
KUTN/CMB KT2 8 E2
REDH RH1 126 D5
THHTH CR7 49 M2
WOT/HER KT12 42 D8
Osborne Ter TOOT SW17 * 30 D6
Osborne Wy CHSGTN KT9 63 J4
Osborn La FSTH SE23 33 H1
Osborn Rd FNM GU9 134 A5
Osier Pl EGH TW20 21 M7
Osier Wy BNSTD SM7 85 H4
MTCM CR4 48 B5
Oslac Rd CAT SE6 33 L6
Osmond Gdns WLGTN SM6 66 F4
Osmunda Bank EGRIN RH19 178 F11
Osmund Cl CRAWE RH10 192 D7
Osnaburgh Hl CBLY GU15 72 E4
Osney Cl CRAWW RH11 164 E5
Osney Wk MRDN SM4 48 A6
Osprey Gdns ALDT GU11 134 D2
SAND/SEL CR2 69 G8
Ospringe Cl PGE/AN SE20 32 F8
Ostade Rd BRXS/STRHM SW2 31 J1
Osterley Av ISLW TW7 17 G2
Osterley Crs ISLW TW7 17 H3
Osterley Gdns THHTH CR7 49 M2
Osterley Rd ISLW TW7 17 H2
Ostlers Dr ASHF TW15 23 M6
Oswald Cl LHD/OX KT22 101 M4
Oswald Rd LHD/OX KT22 101 M4
Osward CROY/NA CR0 69 J8
Osward Rd BAL SW12 30 C3
Otford Cl PGE/AN SE20 50 F1
Othello Gv BNFD RG42 * 35 H1
Ottawa Dr LIPH GU30 196 H10
Otterbourne Pl EGRIN RH19 * 162 C4
Otterbourne Rd CROY/NA CR0 2 C5
Otterburn Gdns ISLW TW7 17 K2
Otterburn St TOOT SW17 30 C7
Otter Cl CHERT KT16 57 L5
Ottersden St CAT SE6 33 K5
Ottermead La CHERT KT16 57 M5
Otto Cl CAT SE6 33 J4
SYD SE26 32 E4
Ottways Av ASHTD KT21 103 G1
Ottways La ASHTD KT21 103 H1
Otway Cl CRAWW RH11 164 B6
Oulton Wk CRAWE RH10 165 K6
Ouseley Rd BAL SW12 30 C2
STWL/WRAY TW19 20 F1
Outdowns EHSLY KT24 120 E4
Outram Pl WEY KT13 59 M4
Outram Rd CROY/NA CR0 3 K5
Outwood La
KWD/TDW/WH KT20 105 L4
REDH RH1 128 A8
Oval Rd CROY/NA CR0 2 F5
The Oval BNSTD SM7 85 K4
GODL GU7 168 C2
GUW GU2 6 B5
RGUW GU3 115 L7
Overbrae BECK BR3 33 K7
Overbrook EHSLY KT24 119 L3
GODL GU7 168 D4
Overbury Av BECK BR3 51 L3
Overbury Crs CROY/NA CR0 69 M8
Overdale ASHTD KT21 83 H6
RDKG RH5 144 F1
REDH RH1 127 M7
Overdale Av NWMAL KT3 45 M2
Overdale Ri FRIM GU16 73 H6
Overdene Dr CRAWW RH11 164 C4
Overdown Rd CAT SE6 33 K5
Overford Cl CRAN GU6 186 D3
Overford Dr CRAN GU6 186 D3
Overhill WARL CR6 108 F1
Overhill Rd EDUL SE22 32 D1
PUR/KEN CR8 67 K7
Overlord Cl CBLY GU15 72 F1
Overlord Ct LHD/OX KT22 102 A3
Overstand Cl BECK BR3 51 K5
Overstone Gdns CROY/NA CR0 51 J7
Overthorpe Cl
WOKN/KNAP GU21 76 B7
Overton Cl ALDT GU11 134 F3
ISLW TW7 17 J3
Overton Rd BELMT SM2 65 K6
Overton Shaw EGRIN RH19 162 F2
Overton's Yd CROY/NA CR0 2 C7
Oveton Wy GT/LBKH KT23 101 K8
Ovett Cl NRWD SE19 32 B7
Ovington Ct WOKN/KNAP GU21 76 C6
Owen Cl CROY/NA CR0 50 A6
Owen Pl LHD/OX KT22 * 102 E4
Owen Rd BFOR GU20 55 G4
GODL GU7 168 C3
Owens Wy FSTH SE23 33 H1
Owen Wk PGE/AN SE20 32 D8
Owers Cl SWTR RH13 167 H7
Owlbeech Wy SWTR RH13 167 L5
Owl Cl SAND/SEL CR2 69 G8
Owletts CRAWE RH10 165 M3
Owlscastle Cl HORS RH12 167 G4
Owlsmoor Rd SHST GU47 72 A1
Ownstead Gdns SAND/SEL CR2 88 C1
Ownsted Hl CROY/NA CR0 69 M8
Oxdowne Cl COB KT11 81 L4
Oxenden Ct RFNM GU10 135 H1
Oxenden Rd RFNM GU10 135 H1
Oxenhope BRAK RG12 34 D4
Oxford Av HYS/HAR UB3 15 J2
RYNPK SW20 47 H2
Oxford Cl ASHF TW15 23 M8
MTCM CR4 48 F3
Oxford Crs NWMAL KT3 46 A6
Oxford Rd CAR SM5 66 B5
CRAWE RH10 165 H8
FARN GU14 92 F8
GU GU1 7 H7
NRWD SE19 32 A7
REDH RH1 126 B7
SHST GU47 52 B7
SWTR RH13 167 G7
TEDD TW11 26 A6
WLGTN SM6 * 66 F4
Oxford Rw SUN TW16 * 42 F3
Oxford Ter GU GU1 7 H7
Oxford Wy FELT TW13 25 G5
Oxleigh Cl NWMAL KT3 46 B5
Oxshott Ri COB KT11 81 H4
Oxshott Rd LHD/OX KT22 82 C6
Oxshott Wy COB KT11 81 H5
Oxted Cl MTCM CR4 48 A3
Oxted Gn MFD/CHID GU8 183 M2
Oxted Rd GDST RH9 129 J5
Oxtoby Wy STRHM/NOR SW16 49 G1
Oyster La BF/WBF KT14 79 H2

P

Pacific Cl EBED/NFELT TW14 24 C2
Packway FNM GU9 5 M9
Padbrook OXTED RH8 130 D3
Padbury Cl EBED/NFELT TW14 24 A2
Paddock Cl CBLY GU15 73 K3
LING RH7 178 D5
MFD/CHID GU8 * 183 R8
ORP BR6 71 L3
OXTED RH8 130 C5
RDKG RH5 173 L5
SYD SE26 33 G5
WPK KT4 46 B8
Paddock Gdns EGRIN RH19 162 F6
NRWD SE19 32 B7
Paddock Gv RDKG RH5 173 L5
Paddockhurst Rd
CRAWE RH10 192 H11
CRAWW RH11 164 C5
Paddocks Cl COB KT11 80 F4
Paddocks Md
WOKN/KNAP GU21 76 B6
Paddocks Rd RGUE GU4 117 K4
The Paddocks GT/LBKH KT23 101 L8
RGUW GU3 114 F8
WEY KT13 60 B2
WEY KT13 * 79 H1
Paddocks Wy ASHTD KT21 83 H8
CHERT KT16 40 E8
The Paddock BH/WHM TN16 111 M8
BOR GU35 180 D12
BRAK RG12 34 F3
CRAN GU6 187 K1
CRAWE RH10 165 M3
DORK RH4 143 L3
GODL GU7 168 C6
GSHT GU26 197 M1
GU GU1 118 A7
HASM GU27 198 B5
RFNM GU10 * 155 J5
VW GU25 * 39 H6
Paddock Wk WARL CR6 108 E1
Paddock Wy HASM GU27 198 H3
LIPH GU30 196 G8
OXTED RH8 130 C5
WOKN/KNAP GU21 77 L4
Padley Cl CHSGTN KT9 63 J4
Padstow Wk EBED/NFELT TW14 24 C2
Padua Rd PGE/AN SE20 50 F1
Padwick Rd SWTR RH13 167 J7
Pageant Wk CROY/NA CR0 3 G7
Page Cl HPTN TW12 25 H7
Page Crs CROY/NA CR0 67 L4
Pagehurst Rd CROY/NA CR0 3 M1
Page Rd EBED/NFELT TW14 15 G8
Pages Yd CHSWK W4 * 19 H1
Paget Av SUT SM1 66 A2
Paget Cl CBLY GU15 73 L2
HPTN TW12 26 A5
SWTR RH13 205 M9
Paget La ISLW TW7 17 G5
Paget Pl KUTN/CMB KT2 * 27 M7
THDIT KT7 44 C8
Pagewood Cl CRAWE RH10 165 M6
Pagoda Av RCH/KEW TW9 18 C5
Pagoda Gv WNWD SE27 31 L3
Pain's Cl MTCM CR4 48 E2
Pains Hl COB KT11 * 80 C4
OXTED RH8 130 F6
Pains Hill Pk COB KT11 * 80 C3
Paisley Rd CAR SM5 48 A8
Paisley Ter CAR SM5 48 A8
Pakenham Cl BAL SW12 30 D2
Pakenham Dr ALDT GU11 112 C6
Pakenham Rd BRAK RG12 35 G7
Palace Dr WEY KT13 59 L2
Palace Gdns West WEY KT13 59 L2
Palace Gn CROY/NA CR0 69 J6
Palace Gv NRWD SE19 32 C8
Palace Rd ADL/WDHM KT15 58 E7
BH/WHM TN16 111 K3
BRXS/STRHM SW2 31 J2
E/WMO/HCT KT8 43 M3
KUT/HW KT1 45 G4
NRWD SE19 32 C8
Palace Sq NRWD SE19 32 C8
Palace Vw CROY/NA CR0 69 J3
Palestine Gv WIM/MER SW19 48 A1
Palewell Common Dr
MORT/ESHN SW14 19 G7
Palewell Pk MORT/ESHN SW14 19 G7
Pallant Wy ORP BR6 71 K2
Pallingham Dr CRAWE RH10 165 L7
Palmer Av CHEAM SM3 64 F3
Palmer Cl HEST TW5 16 D3
HORL RH6 175 N4
REDH RH1 148 D1
WWKM BR4 70 A1
Palmer Crs CHERT KT16 58 A5
KUT/HW KT1 8 E8
Palmer Rd CRAWE RH10 165 L7
Palmersfield Rd BNSTD SM7 85 K4
Palmers Gv E/WMO/HCT KT8 43 K4
Palmer's Ldg GUW GU2 6 B6
Palmers Rd MORT/ESHN SW14 18 F5
STRHM/NOR SW16 49 J2
Palmerston Cl FARN GU14 92 A6
REDH RH1 148 B3
WOKN/KNAP GU21 77 K4
Palmerston Gv WIM/MER SW19 29 K8
Palmerston Rd CAR SM5 66 C3
CROY/NA CR0 50 A5
HSLW TW3 16 F3
MORT/ESHN SW14 18 F6
ORP BR6 71 M3
SUT SM1 65 M4
WHTN TW2 17 J8
WIM/MER SW19 29 K8
Palmers Whf KUT/HW KT1 * 8 C7
Palm Gv GU GU1 116 F3
Pampisford Rd PUR/KEN CR8 87 K1
Pams Wy HOR/WEW KT19 64 A4
Pankhurst Cl ISLW TW7 17 J5
Pankhurst Dr BRAK RG12 35 G5
Pankhurst Rd WOT/HER KT12 42 F7
Pankridge St RFNM GU10 132 C2
Panmuir Rd RYNPK SW20 46 E1
Panmure Rd SYD SE26 32 E4
Pannell Cl EGRIN RH19 162 E4
Pannells RFNM GU10 156 A4
Pannells Ash BIL RH14 201 M6
Pannells Cl CHERT KT16 40 C8
Pannells Ct GU GU1 7 H6
Pan's Gdns CBLY GU15 73 J5
Pantile Rd WEY KT13 60 A3
Pantiles BOR GU35 * 180 G12
Pantiles Cl WOKN/KNAP GU21 76 E8
Panton Cl CROY/NA CR0 2 B3
Papercourt La
RPLY/SEND GU23 98 C4
Paper Ms DORK RH4 144 E1
Papermill Cl CAR SM5 66 D3
Papworth Wy
BRXS/STRHM SW2 31 K1
Parade Cl RPLY/SEND GU23 97 M5
Parade Ct EHSLY KT24 * 100 B8
Parade Ms BRXS/STRHM SW2 31 L3
The Parade ASHV GU12 * 113 K5
BH/WHM TN16 * 110 F3
CAR SM5 66 C4
CRAWE RH10 165 G3
CROY/NA CR0 * 49 H6
EGRIN RH19 * 162 C2
EPSOM KT18 84 A3
ESH/CLAY KT10 62 B5
FRIM GU16 * 93 G1
GUW GU2 * 116 E3
HORS RH12 * 166 D6
KUT/HW KT1 * 8 F6
KWD/TDW/WH KT20 * 105 H1
LHD/OX KT22 * 102 E2
PGE/AN SE20 * 50 F1
RCH/KEW TW9 * 18 D5
STA TW18 * 22 A6
SUN TW16 24 C8
SUT SM1 * 65 J2
SYD SE26 * 32 E5
VW GU25 * 39 G6
WLGTN SM6 * 67 J4
WOKN/KNAP GU21 * 10 C6
Paradise Rd RCH/KEW TW9 18 B7
Paragon Gv BRYLDS KT5 45 J6
Parbury Ri CHSGTN KT9 63 H5
Parchmore Rd THHTH CR7 49 L2
Parchmore Wy THHTH CR7 49 L2
Pares Cl WOKN/KNAP GU21 10 A3
Parfitts Cl FNM GU9 4 E4
Parfour Dr PUR/KEN CR8 87 M6
Parfrey St HMSMTH W6 19 M1
Parham Rd CRAWW RH11 164 B3
Parish Cl ASHV GU12 113 L8
FNM GU9 133 K3
Parish La PGE/AN SE20 33 G8
Parish Rd FARN GU14 112 E1
Park Av CAR SM5 66 D5
CBLY GU15 72 F5
CTHM CR3 108 B6
EDEN TN8 153 L7
EGH TW20 21 M8
HSLW TW3 16 E8
MFD/CHID GU8 158 F4
MORT/ESHN SW14 19 G6
MTCM CR4 30 E8
ORP BR6 71 J1
REDH RH1 148 C8
SHPTN TW17 42 B3
STA TW18 22 C7
STWL/WRAY TW19 12 A7
WWKM BR4 69 M1
Park Av East EW KT17 64 D5
Park Av West EW KT17 64 D5
Park Barn Dr GUW GU2 116 B7
Park Barn East GUW GU2 116 C7
Park Barn Pde GUW GU2 * 116 B8
Park Cha GODL GU7 168 B7
GU GU1 7 J4
Park Cl ADL/WDHM KT15 58 E8
BRKHM/BTCW RH3 145 L5
CAR SM5 66 C5
EGH TW20 * 20 C6
ESH/CLAY KT10 61 J5
HASM GU27 198 G4
HPTN TW12 43 M1
HSLW TW3 16 F7
KUTN/CMB KT2 9 J3
LHD/OX KT22 102 A6
OXTED RH8 130 C2
RFNM GU10 154 D7
WOT/HER KT12 60 C1
Park Copse RDKG RH5 145 G2
Park Corner Dr EHSLY KT24 120 B2
Park Ct BF/WBF KT14 * 78 D3
DUL SE21 * 32 A4
NWMAL KT3 46 A4
SYD SE26 * 32 E7
WOKS/MYFD GU22 10 E8
Park Crs ASC SL5 37 J5
FROW RH18 195 P11
WHTN TW2 26 A2
Parkdale Crs WPK KT4 64 A2
Park Dr ASC SL5 37 J6
CRAN GU6 186 E2
MORT/ESHN SW14 19 G7
SHGR GU5 169 J3
WEY KT13 59 L4
WOKS/MYFD GU22 10 E8
Parker Cl CAR SM5 66 C5
CRAWE RH10 165 M5
Parke Rd BARN SW13 19 K3
SUN TW16 42 D4
Parker Rd CROY/NA CR0 2 D9
Parker's Cl ASHTD KT21 103 H1
Parker's Hl ASHTD KT21 103 H1
Parker's La ASHTD KT21 103 J1
Parker Ter FSTH SE23 33 J3
Park Farm Cl HORS RH12 167 G2
Park Farm Rd KUTN/CMB KT2 8 F2
Parkfield GODL GU7 168 B7
HORS RH12 166 F6
Parkfield Av FELT TW13 24 D4
MORT/ESHN SW14 19 H6
Parkfield Cl CRAWW RH11 164 B4
Parkfield Crs FELT TW13 24 D4
Parkfield Pde FELT TW13 * 24 D4
Parkfield Rd FELT TW13 24 D4
Parkfields CROY/NA CR0 51 J8
LHD/OX KT22 82 A1
PUT/ROE SW15 19 M6
Parkfields Av RYNPK SW20 46 E1
Parkfields Cl CAR SM5 66 D3
Parkfields Rd KUTN/CMB KT2 27 J6
Park Gdns KUTN/CMB KT2 27 J6
Parkgate Cl KUTN/CMB KT2 27 L7
Park Gate Ct HPTN TW12 * 25 M6
WOKS/MYFD GU22 * 10 D8
Parkgate Gdns
MORT/ESHN SW14 19 G7
Parkgate Rd RDKG RH5 173 Q7
REIG RH2 147 L1
WLGTN SM6 66 D4
Park Gn GT/LBKH KT23 101 K6
Park Hall Rd DUL SE21 32 A4
REIG RH2 125 K6
Park Hl CAR SM5 66 C5
FSTH SE23 32 E3
RCHPK/HAM TW10 18 C8
Parkhill Cl BLKW GU17 72 A5
Park Hill Cl CAR SM5 66 B4
Park Hill Ri CROY/NA CR0 3 J7
Parkhill Rd BLKW GU17 72 A5
Park Hill Rd CROY/NA CR0 3 H9
EW KT17 84 C1
WLGTN SM6 66 E6
Park Horsley EHSLY KT24 120 D3
Park House Dr REIG RH2 147 J2
Park House Gdns TWK TW1 17 M7
Parkhurst HOR/WEW KT19 63 M8
Parkhurst Flds RFNM GU10 181 L8
Parkhurst Gv HORL RH6 160 B2
Parkhurst Rd GUW GU2 6 B1
HORL RH6 160 B2
SUT SM1 66 A3
Parkland Dr BRAK RG12 35 H1
Parkland Gv ASHF TW15 23 K5
FNM GU9 134 C1
Parkland Rd ASHF TW15 23 K5
Parklands ADL/WDHM KT15 58 F4
BRYLDS KT5 45 J5
GT/LBKH KT23 101 K5
OXTED RH8 130 B5
RDKG RH5 144 E6
Parklands Cl MORT/ESHN SW14 18 F7
Parklands Pde HEST TW5 * 16 A4
Parklands Pl GU GU1 117 L8
Parklands Rd
STRHM/NOR SW16 30 E6
Parklands Wy WPK KT4 64 B1
Park La ASHTD KT21 83 J8
CAR SM5 66 D4
CBLY GU15 * 72 F4
CHEAM SM3 65 H5
COUL/CHIP CR5 107 G3
CROY/NA CR0 2 E8
DTCH/LGLY SL3 12 D5
HEST TW5 15 K2
LING RH7 178 F4
MFD/CHID GU8 182 F10
RCH/KEW TW9 18 A6
RDKG RH5 172 H9
REIG RH2 125 J8
RGUE GU4 118 A5
TEDD TW11 26 C7
Park La East REIG RH2 147 J3
Parklawn Av EPSOM KT18 83 L3
HORL RH6 160 C1
Park Lawn Rd WEY KT13 59 M3
Parkleigh Rd WIM/MER SW19 47 L2
Park Ley Rd CTHM CR3 109 G2
Parkleys RCHPK/HAM TW10 27 G5
Parkleys Pde
RCHPK/HAM TW10 * 27 G5
Parkmead PUT/ROE SW15 19 L8
Park Ms STWL/WRAY TW19 23 J1
Parkpale La
BRKHM/BTCW RH3 145 K5
Park Pde CRAN GU6 * 186 E1
Park Pl HORS RH12 166 F8
HPTN TW12 25 M7
WOKS/MYFD GU22 10 E8
Park Ri HORS RH12 166 E5
LHD/OX KT22 102 D3
Park Rise Cl LHD/OX KT22 102 E3
Park Rise Rd FSTH SE23 33 H2
Park Rd ALDT GU11 134 E2
ASHF TW15 23 L6
ASHTD KT21 83 H8
BECK BR3 33 J8
BNSTD SM7 85 M6
BRAK RG12 35 G2
BRYLDS KT5 45 J6
CBLY GU15 72 F4
CHEAM SM3 65 H5
CHSWK W4 19 G1
CTHM CR3 108 B5
E/WMO/HCT KT8 43 M4
EGH TW20 21 K5
EGRIN RH19 162 E4
EGRIN RH19 178 F11
ESH/CLAY KT10 61 L3
FARN GU14 93 H8
FELT TW13 25 G5
FNM GU9 134 A5
FROW RH18 195 P11
GODL GU7 168 A7
GU GU1 7 G4
HASM GU27 198 D7
HORL RH6 161 M5
HORS RH12 190 C12
HPTN TW12 25 M6
HSLW TW3 16 F7
ISLW TW7 17 L3
KUT/HW KT1 8 B5
KUTN/CMB KT2 27 J6
LING RH7 152 B6
NWMAL KT3 46 A4
OXTED RH8 130 C2
PUR/KEN CR8 87 M5
RCHPK/HAM TW10 18 C8
REDH RH1 126 C6
SHGR GU5 141 J7
SHPTN TW17 41 K8
SNWD SE25 50 B4
STWL/WRAY TW19 13 M8
SUN TW16 24 E8
SWTR RH13 203 Q6
TEDD TW11 26 C8
TWK TW1 17 M8
WARL CR6 90 B4
WIM/MER SW19 30 A7
WLGTN SM6 66 E1
WOKS/MYFD GU22 11 G6
Park Rd North CHSWK W4 19 G1
Park Rw FNM GU9 5 H2
Parkshot RCH/KEW TW9 18 A6
Park Side ADL/WDHM KT15 58 E8
Parkside BECK BR3 * 51 L2
CHEAM SM3 65 H5
CRAWE RH10 165 G4
EGRIN RH19 162 D4
FNM GU9 133 M3
HPTN TW12 26 A6
WIM/MER SW19 29 G6
Parkside Av WIM/MER SW19 29 G6
Parkside Cl EHSLY KT24 100 C7
PGE/AN SE20 32 F8
Parkside Crs BRYLDS KT5 45 M6
Parkside Gdns COUL/CHIP CR5 86 E7
WIM/MER SW19 29 G5
Parkside Ms HORS RH12 * 167 G7
WARL CR6 89 K6
Parkside Pl EHSLY KT24 100 B7
STA TW18 22 D7
Parkside Rd ASC SL5 37 K6
HSLW TW3 16 E7
Parkstead Rd PUT/ROE SW15 19 K7
Parkstone Dr CBLY GU15 72 F5
Park St BAGS GU19 54 B6
CBLY GU15 72 F3
CROY/NA CR0 2 D6
DTCH/LGLY SL3 13 G3
GU GU1 6 F7
HORS RH12 167 G7
SWTR RH13 203 P6
TEDD TW11 26 B7
Park Ter CAR SM5 * 66 B2
WPK KT4 46 D8
Park Ter East SWTR RH13 167 G8
Park Ter West HORS RH12 167 G8
The Park CAR SM5 66 C4
GT/LBKH KT23 101 K7
Parkthorne Rd BAL SW12 31 G1
Park Vw ADL/WDHM KT15 * 58 F4
BAGS GU19 54 A6
CRAWW RH11 164 E5
CTHM CR3 108 D7
EW KT17 * 84 C3
GT/LBKH KT23 101 K7
HORL RH6 160 D3
NWMAL KT3 46 C3
Park View Cl EDEN TN8 153 L7
Park View Ct
WOKS/MYFD GU22 10 E9
Park View Dr MTCM CR4 48 A2
Park View Gdns EGRIN RH19 * 162 E2
Parkview Rd CROY/NA CR0 3 M3

Park View Rd CTHM CR3 109 J4
REDH RH1 148 D7
Parkview V RGUE GU4 117 M5
Park Vls TOOT SW17 * 30 B6
Park Wy CRAWE RH10 165 L2
E/WMO/HCT KT8 43 M3
EBED/NFELT TW14 24 E1
GT/LBKH KT23 101 K5
HORS RH12 166 F8
Parkway CBLY GU15 72 F6
CROY/NA CR0 69 M7
DORK RH4 144 D1
GU GU1 7 H1
RYNPK SW20 47 G4
WEY KT13 60 A3
The Parkway HEST TW5 15 K1
Parkwood BECK BR3 33 K8
Parkwood Av ESH/CLAY KT10 43 M8
Park Wood Cl BNSTD SM7 85 G5
Parkwood Gv SUN TW16 42 D3
Parkwood Rd BH/WHM TN16 111 H3
Park Wood Rd BNSTD SM7 85 G5
Parkwood Rd ISLW TW7 17 J3
REDH RH1 127 H7
WIM/MER SW19 29 J6
Park Wood Vw BNSTD SM7 84 F6
Park Works Rd REDH RH1 127 J7
Parley Dr WOKN/KNAP GU21 76 F8
Parliamentary Rd
CHOB/PIR GU24 94 D3
Parnell Cl CRAWE RH10 165 M6
Parnell Gdns WEY KT13 79 J1
Parnham Av LTWR GU18 75 G1
Parr Av EW KT17 64 E7
Parr Cl LHD/OX KT22 102 C2
Parris Cft DORK RH4 144 F5
Parrs Cl SAND/SEL CR2 68 A7
Parr's Pl HPTN TW12 25 K8
Parry Cl EW KT17 64 D6
SWTR RH13 167 M5
Parry Dr WEY KT13 59 K8
Parry Rd SNWD SE25 50 B3
Parsonage Cl WARL CR6 89 H6
Parsonage La DORK RH4 143 M3
Parsonage Rd CRAN GU6 186 C2
EGH TW20 21 G6
HORS RH12 167 G5
Parsonage Sq DORK RH4 144 D1
Parsonage Wy FRIM GU16 73 H8
HORS RH12 167 H5
Parsons Cl HASM GU27 198 D5
HORL RH6 160 B2
Parsonsfield Cl BNSTD SM7 85 G5
Parsonsfield Rd BNSTD SM7 85 G6
Parsons Gn GU GU1 117 G6
HASM GU27 198 D5
Parsons La GSHT GU26 181 P11
Parson's Md CROY/NA CR0 2 B4
E/WMO/HCT KT8 43 M3
Parsons Rd DTCH/LGLY SL3 12 C1
Parthia Cl KWD/TDW/WH KT20 104 E1
Parthings La HORS RH12 204 G9
Partridge Cl FRIM GU16 73 H8
RFNM GU10 133 G1
Partridge Dr ORP BR6 71 M2
Partridge Knoll PUR/KEN CR8 87 L2
Partridge La HORS RH12 190 B3
RDKG RH5 174 A5
RDKG RH5 174 C9
Partridge Md BNSTD SM7 84 F5
Partridge Pl CRAWE RH10 193 P7
Partridge Rd HPTN TW12 25 J7
Partridge Wy RGUE GU4 118 A6
Parvis Rd BF/WBF KT14 78 F2
BF/WBF KT14 79 J2
Paschal Rd CBLY GU15 73 J1
Passfield Rd LIPH GU30 196 D5
Pastens Rd OXTED RH8 130 F5
Paston Cl WLGTN SM6 66 F2
The Pasture CRAWE RH10 165 L4
Pasturewood Rd RDKG RH5 171 Q4
Patching Cl CRAWW RH11 164 B3
Patchings SWTR RH13 167 J6
Paterson Cl FRIM GU16 73 M6
Pates Manor Dr
EBED/NFELT TW14 24 A1
Pathfield MFD/CHID GU8 199 Q1
Pathfield Cl HORS RH12 203 J2
Pathfield Rd HORS RH12 203 J2
STRHM/NOR SW16 31 G7
Pathfields SHGR GU5 141 K6
Pathfields Cl HASM GU27 198 E6
Path Link CRAWE RH10 165 G3
The Path WIM/MER SW19 47 L1
The Pathway RPLY/SEND GU23 98 C7
Patmore La WOT/HER KT12 60 C5
Patrington Cl CRAWW RH11 164 C7
Pattenden Rd CAT SE6 33 J2
Patten Rd WAND/EARL SW18 30 B1
Patterdale Cl CRAWW RH11 164 E7
Patterson Rd NRWD SE19 32 C7
Paul Cl ALDT GU11 134 B1
Paul Gdns CROY/NA CR0 3 J6
Pauline Crs WHTN TW2 25 M2
Pauls Md LING RH7 178 F4
Paul's Pl ASHTD KT21 103 L1
The Pavement REDH RH1 * 126 C8
TEDD TW11 * 26 E8
WIM/MER SW19 * 29 J7
WNWD SE27 * 31 M5
Pavilion Gdns STA TW18 22 E8
Pavilion Rd ALDT GU11 112 B8
The Pavilions End CBLY GU15 73 G6
Pavilion Wy EGRIN RH19 162 F5
Pavilion Sq TOOT SW17 30 B4
Pawley Cl RFNM GU10 135 J2
Pawleyne Cl PGE/AN SE20 32 F8
Pawson's Rd THHTH CR7 49 M6
Pax Cl CRAWW RH11 164 A6
Paxton Cl RCH/KEW TW9 18 C4
WOT/HER KT12 * 42 F7
Paxton Gdns WOKN/KNAP GU21 78 B3
Paxton Pl WNWD SE27 32 B5
Paxton Rd CHSWK W4 19 H1
FSTH SE23 33 H4
Payne Cl CRAWE RH10 165 M2
Paynesfield Av
MORT/ESHN SW14 19 G5
Paynesfield Rd BH/WHM TN16 110 F2
Peabody Cl CROY/NA CR0 50 F8
Peabody Est HNHL SE24 31 L1
Peabody Hl DUL SE21 31 L2
Peabody Rd FARN GU14 93 G8
Peace Cl SNWD SE25 50 B4
Peacemaker Cl CRAWW RH11 164 A6
Peaches Cl BELMT SM2 65 H6
Peach Rd FELT TW13 24 D2
Peach Tree Cl FARN GU14 92 D2
Peacock Av EBED/NFELT TW14 24 A2
Peacock Gdns SAND/SEL CR2 69 H8
Peacock La BRAK RG12 34 A4
Peakfield RFNM GU10 180 H2
Peak Hl SYD SE26 32 F5
Peak Hill Av SYD SE26 32 F5
Peak Hill Gdns SYD SE26 32 F5
Peak Rd GUW GU2 116 D5
Peaks Hl PUR/KEN CR8 67 H8
Peaks Hill Ri PUR/KEN CR8 67 H8
The Peak SYD SE26 32 F4
Peall Rd CROY/NA CR0 49 J6
Pear Av SHPTN TW17 42 B3
Pearce Cl MTCM CR4 48 D2
Pearcefield Av FSTH SE23 32 F2
Pearfield Rd FSTH SE23 33 H4
Pearl Ct WOKN/KNAP GU21 76 B6
Pearmain Cl SHPTN TW17 41 L5
Pears Av SHPTN TW17 * 42 B3
Pearson Rd CRAWE RH10 165 K4
Pearson Wy MTCM CR4 48 D1
Pears Rd HSLW TW3 16 F5
Peartree Av TOOT SW17 30 C7
Pear Tree Cl ADL/WDHM KT15 58 D4
BOR GU35 196 A1
MTCM CR4 48 B2
Peartree Cl SAND/SEL CR2 88 E4
Pear Tree Hl REDH RH1 * 175 R1
Pear Tree La RFNM GU10 155 J6
Pear Tree Rd ADL/WDHM KT15 58 D4
ASHF TW15 23 M6
BOR GU35 180 A12
Peary Cl HORS RH12 167 G3
Peaslake La SHGR GU5 171 J3
Peaslake Rd CRAN GU6 171 J8
Peat Common MFD/CHID GU8 157 M7
Peatmore Av
WOKS/MYFD GU22 78 D6
Peatmore Cl WOKS/MYFD GU22 78 D6
Peatmore Dr CHOB/PIR GU24 94 F3
Pebble Cl EPSOM KT18 124 B2
Pebble Hl EHSLY KT24 119 M7
Pebblehill Rd
BRKHM/BTCW RH3 124 B4
Pebble La LHD/OX KT22 103 K4
Peckarmans Wd SYD SE26 32 D4
Pedleaf Cl LHD/OX KT22 102 A6
Peek Crs WIM/MER SW19 29 G6
Peeks Brook La HORL RH6 161 H7
Peel Av FRIM GU16 93 K2
Peel Rd ORP BR6 71 M3
Pegasus Av ASHV GU12 113 H6
Pegasus Cl HASM GU27 197 Q8
Pegasus Rd CROY/NA CR0 67 K5
FARN GU14 92 E7
Pegasus Wy EGRIN RH19 163 H2
Peggotty Pl SHST GU47 52 B7
Pegg Rd HEST TW5 16 A2
Pegler Wy CRAWW RH11 164 F4
Pegwell Cl CRAWW RH11 164 B6
Peket Cl STA TW18 40 B1
Pelham Ct CRAWW RH11 164 D8
HORS RH12 * 166 E7
Pelham Dr CRAWW RH11 164 C8
Pelham Pl CRAWW RH11 164 D8
RFNM GU10 155 K5
Pelham Rd PGE/AN SE20 50 F2
WIM/MER SW19 29 K8
Pelhams Cl ESH/CLAY KT10 61 K3
Pelhams Wk ESH/CLAY KT10 61 K3
Pelham Wy GT/LBKH KT23 101 L8
Pelling Hl WDSR SL4 20 E1
Pelton Av BELMT SM2 65 L8
Pemberley Cha HOR/WEW KT19 63 L4
Pemberley Cl HOR/WEW KT19 63 L4
Pemberton Pl ESH/CLAY KT10 61 M2
Pemberton Rd
E/WMO/HCT KT8 43 M4
Pembley Gn CRAWE RH10 193 K2
Pembridge Av WHTN TW2 25 J2
Pembroke BRAK RG12 34 C7
Pembroke Av BRYLDS KT5 45 L5
WOT/HER KT12 61 G3
Pembroke Broadway
CBLY GU15 72 F4
Pembroke Cl ASC SL5 37 G5
BNSTD SM7 85 L7
Pembroke Gdns
WOKS/MYFD GU22 11 H7
Pembroke Pl ISLW TW7 17 H4
Pembroke Rd CRAWE RH10 165 L1
MTCM CR4 48 D2
SNWD SE25 50 B4
WOKS/MYFD GU22 11 H6
Pembury Av WPK KT4 46 D8
Pembury Cl COUL/CHIP CR5 86 D4
Pembury Ct HYS/HAR UB3 15 G1
Pembury Pl ASHV GU12 112 F8
Pembury Rd SNWD SE25 50 D4
Pemdevon Rd CROY/NA CR0 49 K7
Penates ESH/CLAY KT10 62 A3
Penberth Rd CAT SE6 33 M3
Pendarves Rd RYNPK SW20 46 F1
Pendell Av HYS/HAR UB3 15 J2
Pendell Ms REDH RH1 * 148 C1
Pendell Rd REDH RH1 127 L5
Pendennis Cl BF/WBF KT14 78 D4
Pendennis Rd
STRHM/NOR SW16 31 H5
Penderel Rd HSLW TW3 16 D7
Pendine Pl BRAK RG12 34 E5
Pendlebury BRAK RG12 34 D7
Pendle Rd STRHM/NOR SW16 30 E7
Pendleton Cl REDH RH1 148 C2
Pendleton Rd REDH RH1 148 A3
Pendragon Wy CBLY GU15 74 A5
Penerley Rd CAT SE6 33 L2
Penfold Cl CROY/NA CR0 67 K2
Penfold Cft FNM GU9 134 C5
Penfold Rd CRAWE RH10 165 K8
Penge La PGE/AN SE20 32 F8
Penge Rd SNWD SE25 50 D3
Pengilly Rd FNM GU9 5 G4
Penhurst WOKN/KNAP GU21 77 J4
Peninsular Cl CBLY GU15 73 L2
EBED/NFELT TW14 15 G8
Penistone Rd
STRHM/NOR SW16 31 H8
Penlee Cl EDEN TN8 153 M7
The Pennards SUN TW16 42 F3
Penn Cl CRAWW RH11 164 F1
Penn Ct CRAWW RH11 * 164 B4
Pennefather's Rd ALDT GU11 112 C6
Penner Cl WIM/MER SW19 29 H3
Penners Gdns SURB KT6 45 H7
Pennine Cl CRAWW RH11 164 D4
Pennine Wy FARN GU14 92 B2
HYS/HAR UB3 15 G2
Pennings Av GUW GU2 116 C5
Pennington Dr WEY KT13 60 B2
Penn Rd DTCH/LGLY SL3 12 A3
Penns Wd FARN GU14 93 G8
Penns Yd FNM GU9 5 G3
Pennycroft CROY/NA CR0 69 H7
Penny Dr RGUW GU3 115 L7
Pennyfield COB KT11 80 D3
Penny La SHPTN TW17 42 B7
Pennymead Dr EHSLY KT24 120 C1
Pennypot La CHOB/PIR GU24 75 L3
Penrhyn Cl ASHV GU12 * 112 E8
CTHM CR3 108 A2
Penrhyn Crs MORT/ESHN SW14 18 F6
Penrhyn Gdns KUT/HW KT1 45 H4
Penrhyn Rd KUT/HW KT1 8 E9
Penrith Cl BECK BR3 51 L1
REIG RH2 126 B7
Penrith Pl WNWD SE27 31 L3
Penrith Rd NWMAL KT3 46 A4
THHTH CR7 49 M2
Penrith St STRHM/NOR SW16 30 F7
Penrose Ct EGH TW20 20 F7
Penrose Rd LHD/OX KT22 101 M4
Penryn Dr BOR GU35 180 H12
Pensfold La HORS RH12 203 K4
Pensford Av RCH/KEW TW9 18 D2
Penshurst Cl CRAWE RH10 165 M3
Penshurst Ri FRIM GU16 93 J1
Penshurst Rd THHTH CR7 49 L5
Penshurst Wy BELMT SM2 65 K6
Pentelow Gdns
EBED/NFELT TW14 15 K8
Pentire Cl WOKN/KNAP GU21 77 H4
Pentland Av SHPTN TW17 41 K5
Pentlands Cl MTCM CR4 48 E3
Pentlow St PUT/ROE SW15 19 M4
Pentney Rd BAL SW12 30 F2
RYNPK SW20 47 H1
Penton Av STA TW18 22 C8
Penton Hall Dr STA TW18 40 D1
Penton Hook Rd STA TW18 22 D8
Penton Rd STA TW18 22 C8
Pentreath Av GUW GU2 138 C1
Penwerris Av ISLW TW7 16 F2
Penwith Dr HASM GU27 197 R8
Penwith Rd WAND/EARL SW18 29 L3
Penwith Wk WOKS/MYFD GU22 10 A9
Penwood End
WOKS/MYFD GU22 96 E3
Penwood Gdns BRAK RG12 34 A6
Penwortham Rd SAND/SEL CR2 68 A8
STRHM/NOR SW16 30 E7
Peperham Rd HASM GU27 198 D5
Peper Harow La
MFD/CHID GU8 158 F3
Peperharow Rd GODL GU7 159 M3
Peppard Rd CRAWE RH10 165 M6
Pepperbox La SHGR GU5 169 N12
Pepper Cl CTHM CR3 108 B7
Peppercorn Cl THHTH CR7 50 A2
Peppermint Cl CROY/NA CR0 49 H7
Peppers Yd HORS RH12 * 167 G6
Pepys Cl ASHTD KT21 83 K7
DTCH/LGLY SL3 12 E1
Pepys Rd RYNPK SW20 46 F2
Percheron Dr
WOKN/KNAP GU21 95 M1
Percival Rd FELT TW13 24 C3
MORT/ESHN SW14 18 F7
ORP BR6 71 L1
Percival Wy HOR/WEW KT19 63 M3
Percy Av ASHF TW15 23 K6
Percy Bryant Rd SUN TW16 24 B8
Percy Gdns WPK KT4 46 A8
Percy Rd GUW GU2 116 E6
HORS RH12 166 E6
HPTN TW12 25 K8
ISLW TW7 17 K6
MTCM CR4 48 D7
PGE/AN SE20 51 G1
SNWD SE25 50 C5
WHTN TW2 25 L2
Percy Wy WHTN TW2 25 M2
Peregrine Cl BRAK RG12 34 E5
CRAN GU6 186 D1
Peregrine Gdns CROY/NA CR0 69 H1
Peregrine Rd SUN TW16 42 B2
Peregrine Wy WIM/MER SW19 28 F8
Perifield DUL SE21 31 M2
Perimeter Rd East HORL RH6 160 E7
Perimeter Rd North
HORL RH6 160 A7
Perimeter Rd South
HORL RH6 175 Q12
Periwinkle Cl BOR GU35 180 B12
Perkin Cl HSLW TW3 16 E6
Perleybrooke La
WOKN/KNAP GU21 76 D7
Perowne St ALDT GU11 112 C7
Perran Rd BRXS/STRHM SW2 31 L3
Perrin Cl ASHF TW15 23 J6
Perrin Ct WOKN/KNAP GU21 11 K1
Perring Av FARN GU14 92 B1
Perring Rd FARN GU14 92 D8
Perrior Rd GODL GU7 168 B2
Perry Av EGRIN RH19 162 F2
Perry Cl GODL GU7 168 D4
Perryfield Rd CRAWW RH11 164 F5
Perryfield Wy
RCHPK/HAM TW10 26 E3
Perry Hl CAT SE6 33 J3
RGUW GU3 116 B2
Perry How WPK KT4 46 C8
Perrylands HORL RH6 175 J10
Perrylands La HORL RH6 161 J4
Perry Oak Dr HTHAIR TW6 13 L4
Perry Oaks BRAK RG12 35 H2
Perry Ri FSTH SE23 33 H4
Perry V FSTH SE23 32 F3
Perry Wy BOR GU35 196 E1
BRAK RG12 35 H2
FNM GU9 133 L2
LTWR GU18 74 C2
Persfield Ms EW KT17 * 64 C8
Persfield Rd EW KT17 64 D8
Pershore Gv CAR SM5 48 A6
Perth Cl CRAWW RH11 164 F1
RYNPK SW20 46 D2
Perth Rd BECK BR3 51 M2
Perth Wy HORS RH12 167 J5
Petauel Rd TEDD TW11 26 B6
Petavel Rd TEDD TW11 26 B7
Peter Av OXTED RH8 130 A3
Peterborough Rd CAR SM5 48 B6
CRAWE RH10 165 G8
GUW GU2 116 C6
Peterhouse Cl SHST GU47 52 C7
Petersfield Av STA TW18 22 F6
Petersfield Crs COUL/CHIP CR5 87 H5
Petersfield Ri PUT/ROE SW15 28 E2
Petersfield Rd STA TW18 22 E6
Petersham Av BF/WBF KT14 79 H2
Petersham Cl BF/WBF KT14 79 H2
RCHPK/HAM TW10 27 G3
SUT SM1 65 J4
Petersham Rd
RCHPK/HAM TW10 27 G4
Petersham Ter CROY/NA CR0 * 67 H2
Petersmead Cl
KWD/TDW/WH KT20 104 F5
Peterstow Cl WIM/MER SW19 29 H3
Peterwood Wy CROY/NA CR0 67 J1
Petley Rd HMSMTH W6 19 M1
Petridge Rd REDH RH1 148 C5
Petters Rd ASHTD KT21 83 J6
Pettiward Cl PUT/ROE SW15 19 M6
Petts La SHPTN TW17 41 K4
Petworth Cl COUL/CHIP CR5 106 F1
FRIM GU16 93 J1
Petworth Ct CRAWW RH11 164 B7
Petworth Dr HORS RH12 167 J2
Petworth Gdns RYNPK SW20 46 E3
Petworth Rd HASM GU27 198 E8
MFD/CHID GU8 183 N3
MFD/CHID GU8 199 R1
Pevensey Cl CRAWE RH10 165 L5
ISLW TW7 16 F2
Pevensey Rd FELT TW13 25 H2
TOOT SW17 30 A5
Pevensey Wy FRIM GU16 93 K1
Peverel Rd CRAWW RH11 164 A5
Peveril Dr TEDD TW11 26 A6
Pewley Bank GU GU1 7 K7
Pewley Hl GU GU1 7 H7
Pewley Point GU GU1 7 K8
Pewley Wy GU GU1 7 K7
Pewsey V BRAK RG12 35 J5
Pharaoh Cl MTCM CR4 48 C7
Pheasant Cl PUR/KEN CR8 87 L3
Philanthropic Rd REDH RH1 148 E2
Philip Gdns CROY/NA CR0 69 J1
Philip Rd STA TW18 23 G7
Philips Cl CAR SM5 48 D8
Philips Crs BOR GU35 180 E12
Phillips Cl BOR GU35 180 E12
CRAWE RH10 192 A12
GODL GU7 159 M7
RFNM GU10 135 H1
Phillips Hatch SHGR GU5 169 M1
Philpot La CHOB/PIR GU24 76 F2
Phipp's Bridge Rd MTCM CR4 48 A3
WIM/MER SW19 47 M2
Phoenix Cl WWKM BR4 70 A1
Phoenix Ct GU GU1 7 G7
Phoenix Dr HAYES BR2 71 G3
Phoenix La EGRIN RH19 163 M7
Phoenix Rd PGE/AN SE20 32 F7
Phoenix Wy HEST TW5 16 A1
Phyllis Av NWMAL KT3 46 E5
Pickering BRAK RG12 34 D5
Pickering Gdns CROY/NA CR0 50 C6
Pickering Pl GUW GU2 116 D6
Picket Post Cl BRAK RG12 35 J3
Pickets St BAL SW12 30 D1
Picketts Hl BOR GU35 180 B8
Picketts La REDH RH1 176 B1
Pickford St ALDT GU11 * 112 E7
Pickhurst Rd MFD/CHID GU8 199 R2
Pickins Piece DTCH/LGLY SL3 12 D4
Pickwick Cl HSLWW TW4 16 B7
Pickwick Gdns CBLY GU15 73 L5
Pickwick Rd DUL SE21 32 A1
Picquets Wy BNSTD SM7 85 H6
Picton Cl CBLY GU15 73 M2
Pierrefondes Av FARN GU14 92 E4
Pier Rd EBED/NFELT TW14 15 L7
Pigbush La BIL RH14 201 Q2
Pigeonhouse La
COUL/CHIP CR5 105 M7
Pigeon La HPTN TW12 25 K5
Pigeon Pass CRAWE RH10 193 P8
Pike Cl ALDT GU11 112 F7
Pikes Hl EW KT17 84 B3
Pikes La LING RH7 152 B8
Pilgrim Cl MRDN SM4 47 L7
Pilgrim Hl WNWD SE27 31 M5
Pilgrims Cl FNM GU9 4 F7
RDKG RH5 122 D6
SHGR GU5 141 K5
Pilgrims' La CTHM CR3 107 J8
OXTED RH8 110 F6
Pilgrims Pl ASHF TW15 * 23 J5
REIG RH2 125 K6
Pilgrims Vw ASHV GU12 135 M1
Pilgrims' Wy BH/WHM TN16 111 L5
BOR GU35 180 D12
CHOB/PIR GU24 75 K6
RDKG RH5 122 E5
REIG RH2 125 J6
RGUE GU4 139 H4
SAND/SEL CR2 68 C5
SHGR GU5 141 K5
Pilkington Rd ORP BR6 71 M2
Pilsden Cl WIM/MER SW19 * 29 G2
Pimms Cl RGUE GU4 117 K4
Pinckards MFD/CHID GU8 183 P12
Pincott La EHSLY KT24 119 L3
Pincott Rd WIM/MER SW19 29 M8
Pine Av CBLY GU15 73 G5
CHOB/PIR GU24 95 J3
WWKM BR4 51 L8
Pine Bank GSHT GU26 197 R1
Pine Cl ADL/WDHM KT15 78 E1
ASHV GU12 113 K3
CBLY GU15 72 B2
CRAWW RH11 164 E1
PGE/AN SE20 50 F1
PUR/KEN CR8 87 M7
WOKN/KNAP GU21 76 F7
Pine Coombe CROY/NA CR0 69 G3
Pinecote Dr ASC SL5 37 J7
Pine Ct FRIM GU16 * 93 K6
Pine Crs CAR SM5 86 A1
Pinecrest Gdns ORP BR6 71 L3
Pine Dean GT/LBKH KT23 101 L7
Pine Dr BLKW GU17 72 B6
Pinefields ADL/WDHM KT15 * 58 E3
Pine Gdns BRYLDS KT5 45 K6
HORL RH6 160 D4
Pine Gld ORP BR6 71 J3
Pine Gv BFOR GU20 55 G5
EDEN TN8 153 L7
EGRIN RH19 162 C2
RFNM GU10 156 B3
WEY KT13 59 L4
WIM/MER SW19 29 J6
Pine Grove Ms WEY KT13 * 59 M4
Pine Hl EPSOM KT18 84 A6
Pinehurst ASC SL5 37 G5
HORS RH12 166 F5
Pinehurst Av FARN GU14 92 E7
Pinehurst Cl
KWD/TDW/WH KT20 105 K4
Pinehurst Rd FARN GU14 92 D7
Pinel Cl VW GU25 39 H4
Pinelees Ct MORT/ESHN SW14 * 18 F6
Pine Mount Rd CBLY GU15 73 G5
Pine Pk RGUW GU3 * 115 K3
Pine Pl BNSTD SM7 85 G4
Pine Rdg CAR SM5 66 D7
Pine Ridge Dr RFNM GU10 155 L4
Pine Rd WOKS/MYFD GU22 96 F2
Pine Shaw CRAWE RH10 165 L3
Pines Rd LIPH GU30 196 D9
The Pines CBLY GU15 73 J2
HORS RH12 167 M4
NRWD SE19 * 31 L7
PUR/KEN CR8 87 L3
SUN TW16 42 D3
WOKN/KNAP GU21 77 J4
Pinetops HORS RH12 * 167 M5
Pine Tree Cl HEST TW5 15 L3
Pine Tree Hl WOKS/MYFD GU22 78 A6
Pine Trees STA TW18 * 22 B6
Pinetrees Cl CRAWE RH10 192 G2
Pine Vw BOR GU35 180 G11
Pine View Cl FNM GU9 134 D4
HASM GU27 198 D5
RGUE GU4 140 C6
Pine Wk BELMT SM2 66 A8
BNSTD SM7 86 C7
BRYLDS KT5 45 K6
COB KT11 81 G4
CTHM CR3 108 B4
EHSLY KT24 120 C2
GT/LBKH KT23 101 L7
Pine Wy EGH TW20 20 E7
Pine Way Cl EGRIN RH19 162 F6
Pine Wd SUN TW16 42 D1
Pinewood Av ADL/WDHM KT15 58 F7
Pinewood Cl CROY/NA CR0 69 H2
HORS RH12 166 A6
WOKN/KNAP GU21 11 G1
Pinewood Dr STA TW18 * 22 D6
Pinewood Gdns BAGS GU19 53 M6
Pinewood Gv ADL/WDHM KT15 58 E8
Pinewood Ms
STWL/WRAY TW19 14 A8
Pinewood Pk ADL/WDHM KT15 78 E1
FARN GU14 92 A2
Pinewood Rd ASHV GU12 114 A6
FELT TW13 24 E4
VW GU25 38 D3
Pinfold Rd STRHM/NOR SW16 31 H5
Pinglestone Cl WDR/YW UB7 14 B2
Pinkcoat Cl FELT TW13 24 E4
Pinkhurst La SWTR RH13 204 B7
Piper Rd KUT/HW KT1 9 J8
Pipers Cl COB KT11 81 G5
Pipers End SWTR RH13 203 R6
VW GU25 39 G3
Pipers Gdns CROY/NA CR0 51 H7
Pipers La PETW GU28 200 D10
Pipers Patch FARN GU14 92 E5
Pipewell Rd CAR SM5 48 B6
Pippbrook Gdns DORK RH4 144 E1
Pippin Cl CROY/NA CR0 51 J8
Pippins Ct ASHF TW15 23 L7
Piquet Rd PGE/AN SE20 50 F2
Pirbright Crs CROY/NA CR0 69 M5
Pirbright Rd FARN GU14 92 F6
RGUW GU3 114 C5
RGUW GU3 114 F3
WAND/EARL SW18 29 J2
Pirbright Ter CHOB/PIR GU24 * 95 J5
Pisley La RDKG RH5 172 B12
Pitcairn Rd MTCM CR4 30 C8
Pitchfont La OXTED RH8 110 D8
Pit Farm Rd GU GU1 117 K8
Pitfold Av HASM GU27 197 Q7
Pitfold Cl HASM GU27 197 R7
Pitlake CROY/NA CR0 2 B5
Pitland St RDKG RH5 171 P4
Pit La EDEN TN8 153 M5
Pitson Cl ADL/WDHM KT15 59 G3
Pitt Crs WIM/MER SW19 29 L5
Pitt La RFNM GU10 180 F3
Pitt Pl EW KT17 * 84 B4
Pitt Rd EW KT17 84 B4
ORP BR6 71 M3
THHTH CR7 49 M5
Pittville Gdns SNWD SE25 50 D3
Pitt Wy FARN GU14 92 C4
Pit Wood Gn
KWD/TDW/WH KT20 104 F2
Pixham La DORK RH4 122 F7
Pixholme Gv DORK RH4 122 F8
Pixton Wy CROY/NA CR0 69 J6

Place Farm Rd *REDH* RH1 **128** A4
Placehouse La *COUL/CHIP* CR5 **107** J1
Plaistow Rd *BIL* RH14 **201** L9
MFD/CHID GU8 **184** H10
MFD/CHID GU8 **200** A4
Plaistow St *LING* RH7 **178** D5
The Planes *CHERT* KT16 **40** F7
Plane St *SYD* SE26 **32** E4
Plane Tree Crs *FELT* TW13 **24** E4
Plantagenet Cl *WPK* KT4 **64** A3
Plantagenet Pk *BNFD* RG42 **35** J1
Plantain Crs *CRAWW* RH11 **164** C8
Plantation La *WARL* CR6 **109** H1
Plassy Rd *CAT* SE6 **33** L1
The Plat *HORS* RH12 **166** D7
Platt Meadow *RGUE* GU4 **118** A5
The Platt *LING* RH7 **178** H9
Plawsfield Rd *BECK* BR3 **51** G1
Plaws Hl *SHGR* GU5 **171** J3
Playgreen Wy *CAT* SE6 **33** K5
Playground Cl *BECK* BR3 **51** G2
Pleasance Rd *PUT/ROE* SW15 **19** L7
The Pleasance *PUT/ROE* SW15 **19** L6
Pleasant Gv *CROY/NA* CR0 **69** J2
Pleasant Pl *WOT/HER* KT12 **61** G5
Pleasant Vw *ORP* BR6 **71** M4
Pleasure Pit Rd *ASHTD* KT21 **83** L8
Plesman Wy *WLGTN* SM6 * **67** H7
Plevna Rd *HPTN* TW12 **43** L1
Pleydell Av *NRWD* SE19 **32** C8
Pleydell Gdns *NRWD* SE19 * **32** C7
Plough Cl *CRAWW* RH11 **164** B2
Ploughlands *BNFD* RG42 **34** C1
Plough La *COB* KT11 **80** D6
CRAN GU6 **187** L1
CROY/NA CR0 **67** H3
HORS RH12 **167** H4
PUR/KEN CR8 **67** J8
TEDD TW11 * **26** D6
WIM/MER SW19 **29** L6
Plough Lane Cl *WLGTN* SM6 **67** H4
Ploughmans End *ISLW* TW7 **17** G7
Plough Rd *HOR/WEW* KT19 **64** A6
HORL RH6 **161** M3
LING RH7 **178** H7
Plover Cl *CRAWW* RH11 **164** E2
STA TW18 **22** C4
Plovers Ri *CHOB/PIR* GU24 **95** H2
Plovers Rd *SWTR* RH13 **167** J6
Plum Cl *FELT* TW13 **24** D2
Plummer La *MTCM* CR4 **48** C1
Plumpton Wy *CAR* SM5 **66** B2
Pocket Cl *BRAK* RG12 * **34** A2
Pockford Rd *MFD/CHID* GU8 **184** A9
Pointers Hl *DORK* RH4 **143** M4
Pointers Rd *COB* KT11 **80** A7
The Pointers *ASHTD* KT21 **103** H2
Point Wharf La *BTFD* TW8 **18** A2
Polden Cl *FARN* GU14 **92** B2
Polecroft La *CAT* SE6 **33** J3
Polesden Gdns *RYNPK* SW20 **46** E3
Polesden La *RPLY/SEND* GU23 **98** C5
Polesden Rd *RDKG* RH5 **121** L3
Polesden Vw *GT/LBKH* KT23 **121** L1
Poles La *CRAWW* RH11 **191** M2
Polesteeple Hl *BH/WHM* TN16 **91** G7
Police Station Rd
WOT/HER KT12 **60** F5
Pollard Gv *CBLY* GU15 **73** M5
Pollard Rd *MRDN* SM4 **48** A5
WOKS/MYFD GU22 **11** K3
Pollardrow Av *BNFD* RG42 **34** C1
Pollards *CRAWW* RH11 **164** C5
Pollards Crs *STRHM/NOR* SW16 **49** H3
Pollards Dr *SWTR* RH13 **167** J7
Pollards Hl East
STRHM/NOR SW16 **49** J3
Pollards Hl North
STRHM/NOR SW16 **49** J3
Pollards Hl South
STRHM/NOR SW16 **49** H3
Pollards Hl West
STRHM/NOR SW16 **49** H3
Pollards Oak Crs *OXTED* RH8 **130** D6
Pollards Oak Rd *OXTED* RH8 **130** D6
Pollards Wood Hl *OXTED* RH8 **130** D4
Pollards Wood Rd *OXTED* RH8 **130** E5
STRHM/NOR SW16 **49** H2
Polsted La *RGUW* GU3 **137** M6
Polsted Rd *CAT* SE6 **33** J1
Poltimore Rd *GUW* GU2 **6** B7
Polworth Rd *STRHM/NOR* SW16 **31** H6
Pomeroy Cl *TWK* TW1 **17** L6
Pond Cl *BIL* RH14 **201** Q5
WOT/HER KT12 **60** D5
Pond Copse La *BIL* RH14 **201** Q4
Pond Cottage La *BECK* BR3 **51** K8
Pond Farm Cl
KWD/TDW/WH KT20 **104** E6
Pondfield Rd *GODL* GU7 **168** C3
HORS RH12 **203** J1
ORP BR6 **71** L2
PUR/KEN CR8 **87** L6
Pond Head La *RDKG* RH5 **171** R12
RDKG RH5 **187** Q2
Pond Hill Gdns *CHEAM* SM3 * **65** H5
Pond La *RFNM* GU10 **180** H5
SHGR GU5 **170** H2
Pond Meadow *GUW* GU2 **116** B8
Pond Moor Rd *BRAK* RG12 **34** E5
Pond Piece *LHD/OX* KT22 **81** L3
Pond Rd *BOR* GU35 **196** F1
EGH TW20 **21** M7
FARN GU14 **92** E7
WOKS/MYFD GU22 **96** D2
Pondside Cl *HYS/HAR* UB3 **15** G2
Ponds La *SHGR* GU5 **141** H8
The Ponds *WEY* KT13 **60** A5
Pondtail Cl *HORS* RH12 **167** G4
Pondtail Copse *HORS* RH12 **167** G3
Pondtail Dr *HORS* RH12 **167** G2
Pondtail Pk *HORS* RH12 **167** G3
Pondtail Rd *HORS* RH12 **166** F4
Pond Wy *EGRIN* RH19 **163** J4
TEDD TW11 **8** B1
Pond Wood Rd *CRAWE* RH10 **165** J2
Poneys Cl *BRAK* RG12 * **34** F4
Ponsonby Rd *PUT/ROE* SW15 **28** E1
Pony Cha *COB* KT11 **81** J3
Pook Hl *MFD/CHID* GU8 **199** M2
Pool Cl *BECK* BR3 **33** K6
E/WMO/HCT KT8 **43** J5
Pool Ct *CAT* SE6 **33** K3
Poole Court Rd *HSLWW* TW4 **16** B4
Pool End Cl *SHPTN* TW17 **41** K5
Poole Rd *HOR/WEW* KT19 **64** A5
WOKN/KNAP GU21 **10** C6
Pooley Av *EGH* TW20 **21** L6
Pooley Dr *MORT/ESHN* SW14 **18** F5
Pooley Green Rd *EGH* TW20 **21** M7
Pool Rd *ALDT* GU11 **134** F2
E/WMO/HCT KT8 **43** J5
Pope Cl *EBED/NFELT* TW14 **24** C2
WIM/MER SW19 * **30** A7
Pope's Av *WHTN* TW2 **26** B3
Popes Cl *DTCH/LGLY* SL3 **12** F2
Popes Gv *CROY/NA* CR0 **69** J2
WHTN TW2 **26** B3
Popes La *OXTED* RH8 **152** C1
Popes Md *HASM* GU27 **198** D6
Popeswood Rd *BNFD* RG42 **34** A1
Popham Cl *BRAK* RG12 **35** J6
FELT TW13 **25** H4
Popham Gdns *RCH/KEW* TW9 * **18** E5
Popinjays Rw *CHEAM* SM3 * **65** G4
Poplar Av *BFOR* GU20 **54** D3
LHD/OX KT22 **102** E4
MTCM CR4 **48** C1
ORP BR6 **71** L1
Poplar Cl *BRAK* RG12 **35** G3
CRAWW RH11 **164** E1
DTCH/LGLY SL3 **13** H3
FRIM GU16 **93** K6
Poplar Court Pde *TWK* TW1 * **17** M8
Poplar Crs *HOR/WEW* KT19 **63** M5
Poplar Dr *BNSTD* SM7 **85** G4
Poplar Farm Cl *HOR/WEW* KT19 **63** M5
Poplar Gdns *NWMAL* KT3 **46** A2
Poplar Gn *WOKS/MYFD* GU22 **10** D9
Poplar Gv *NWMAL* KT3 **46** A3
Poplar Rd *ASHF* TW15 **23** M6
CHEAM SM3 **47** J8
LHD/OX KT22 **102** E4
RGUE GU4 **139** H7
WIM/MER SW19 **47** K2
Poplar Rd South
WIM/MER SW19 **47** K3
The Poplars *ASC* SL5 **36** D5
SWTR RH13 **167** H6
Poplar Wk *CROY/NA* CR0 **2** C4
CTHM CR3 **108** B5
FNM GU9 **134** A2
Poplar Wy *FELT* TW13 **24** E4
Poppy Cl *HAYES* BR2 **70** F4
WLGTN SM6 **48** D8
Poppyhills Rd *CBLY* GU15 **73** J1
Poppy La *CROY/NA* CR0 **50** F7
Porchester *ASC* SL5 **36** D4
Porchester Md *BECK* BR3 **33** L7
Porchester Rd *KUT/HW* KT1 **9** L6
Porchfield Cl *BELMT* SM2 **65** L8
Porridge Pot Aly *GUW* GU2 **6** F8
Portal Cl *WNWD* SE27 **31** K4
Portesbery Rd *CBLY* GU15 **73** G3
Portesbery Hill Dr *CBLY* GU15 **73** G2
Porthcawe Rd *SYD* SE26 **33** H5
Portia Gv *BNFD* RG42 **35** H1
Portland Av *NWMAL* KT3 **46** C7
Portland Cl *WPK* KT4 **46** E7
Portland Crs *FELT* TW13 **24** A5
Portland Dr *REDH* RH1 **126** F3
Portland Pl *EW* KT17 **84** B2
SNWD SE25 **50** D4
Portland Place Flats *EW* KT17 * **84** B2
Portland Rd *ASHF* TW15 **23** H4
DORK RH4 **144** D1
EGRIN RH19 **162** F5
KUT/HW KT1 **8** F9
MTCM CR4 **48** B2
SNWD SE25 **50** E4
Portland Ter *FNM* GU9 * **134** A5
GU GU1 * **7** K6
RCH/KEW TW9 * **18** A6
Portley La *CTHM* CR3 **108** B3
Portley Wood Rd *CTHM* CR3 **108** C3
Portman Av *MORT/ESHN* SW14 **19** G5
Portman Cl *BNFD* RG42 **34** D1
Portman Rd *KUT/HW* KT1 **9** H7
Portmore Park Rd *WEY* KT13 **59** K2
Portmore Quays *WEY* KT13 **59** J3
Portmore Wy *WEY* KT13 * **59** K2
Portnall Dr *VW* GU25 **38** B6
Portnall Ri *VW* GU25 **38** C5
Portnall Rd *VW* GU25 **38** C5
Portnalls Cl *COUL/CHIP* CR5 **86** E6
Portnalls Ri *COUL/CHIP* CR5 **86** F6
Portnalls Rd *COUL/CHIP* CR5 **86** E7
Portsmouth Av *THDIT* KT7 **44** D7
Portsmouth Rd *CBLY* GU15 **73** K3
COB KT11 **80** D4
ESH/CLAY KT10 **61** K5
FRIM GU16 **73** H6
GSHT GU26 **198** B1
GUW GU2 **6** F9
LIPH GU30 **196** G12
MFD/CHID GU8 **182** E7
PUT/ROE SW15 **28** E2
RPLY/SEND GU23 **79** K8
RPLY/SEND GU23 **98** D6
Portugal Gdns *WHTN* TW2 * **25** M3
Portugal Rd *WOKN/KNAP* GU21 **10** F4
Port Wy *CHOB/PIR* GU24 **75** K7
Portway *EW* KT17 **64** D8
Portway Crs *EW* KT17 **64** D7
Postboys Rw *COB* KT11 * **80** D4
Post Horn La *FROW* RH18 **195** P12
Post House La *GT/LBKH* KT23 **101** K7
Post La *WHTN* TW2 **26** A2
Postmill Cl *CROY/NA* CR0 **68** F2
Potter Cl *MTCM* CR4 * **48** E2
Potteries La *FRIM* GU16 **93** J6
The Potteries *CHERT* KT16 **58** B5
FARN GU14 **92** A3
Potterne Cl *WIM/MER* SW19 **29** G1
Potters Cl *CROY/NA* CR0 **51** H8
MFD/CHID GU8 **159** J7
Potters Crs *ASHV* GU12 **113** L6
Potters Cft *SWTR* RH13 **167** H7
Potters Ga *FNM* GU9 **4** F3
Potters Gv *NWMAL* KT3 **45** M4
Potters Hl *MFD/CHID* GU8 **183** R5
Potters La *RPLY/SEND* GU23 **97** L7
STRHM/NOR SW16 * **31** G7
Potters Pl *HORS* RH12 **166** F7
Potters Wy *REIG* RH2 **147** M4
Pottery La *RFNM* GU10 **155** J3
Pottery Rd *BTFD* TW8 **18** B1
Poulcott *STWL/WRAY* TW19 **12** B8
Poulett Gdns *TWK* TW1 **26** C3
Poulter Pk *MRDN* SM4 * **48** B6
Poulters Wd *HAYES* BR2 **71** G4
Poulton Av *SUT* SM1 **66** A2
Pound Cl *BIL* RH14 **201** Q4
BOR GU35 **180** E12
GODL GU7 **168** B5
SURB KT6 **44** F8
Pound Ct *ASHTD* KT21 **83** J8
RGUW GU3 **115** L6
Pound Crs *LHD/OX* KT22 **102** A3
Pound Farm La *ASHV* GU12 **114** A8
ESH/CLAY KT10 **44** A8
Pound Fld *GU* GU1 **7** G2
Poundfield Gdns
WOKS/MYFD GU22 **97** M2
Poundfield La *BIL* RH14 **201** L6
Pound Hl *RGUW* GU3 **115** L7
Pound Hill Pl *CRAWE* RH10 **165** L4
Pound La *BFOR* GU20 **54** F5
GODL GU7 **168** B5
HOR/WEW KT19 **84** A1
RGUW GU3 **115** L7
SWTR RH13 **205** R11
Pound Pl *RGUE* GU4 **139** J7
Pound Place Cl *RGUE* GU4 **139** J6
Pound Rd *ASHV* GU12 **112** F8
BNSTD SM7 **85** K7
CHERT KT16 **40** E7
Pound St *CAR* SM5 **66** C4
Povey Cross Rd *HORL* RH6 **160** B5
Powderham Ct
WOKN/KNAP GU21 **76** A8
Powder Mill La *WHTN* TW2 **25** J2
Powell Cl *GUW* GU2 **138** C2
HORL RH6 **160** B2
Power Cl *GU* GU1 **6** F2
Powers Ct *TWK* TW1 **27** G1
Pownall Gdns *HSLW* TW3 **16** E6
Pownall Rd *HSLW* TW3 **16** E6
Poyle Gdns *BRAK* RG12 **35** G1
Poyle Pk *DTCH/LGLY* SL3 * **13** H5
Poyle Rd *DTCH/LGLY* SL3 **13** H5
GU GU1 **7** J8
RFNM GU10 **135** K2
Poynders Rd *CLAP* SW4 **30** F1
Poynes Rd *HORL* RH6 **160** B1
Poynings Rd *CRAWW* RH11 **190** G8
Prairie Cl *ADL/WDHM* KT15 **58** E2
Prairie Rd *ADL/WDHM* KT15 **58** E2
Pratts La *WOT/HER* KT12 **61** G3
The Precinct *CRAN* GU6 **186** D1
Premier Pde *HORL* RH6 * **160** E3
Prentice Cl *FARN* GU14 **92** E1
Prentis Rd *STRHM/NOR* SW16 **31** G5
Presburg Rd *NWMAL* KT3 **46** B5
Prescott *BRAK* RG12 **34** C7
Prescott Rd *DTCH/LGLY* SL3 **13** H4
Presentation Ms
BRXS/STRHM SW2 **31** J3
Prestbury Crs *BNSTD* SM7 **86** C6
Preston Cl *WHTN* TW2 **26** B4
Preston Ct *WOT/HER* KT12 **42** F8
Preston Dr *HOR/WEW* KT19 **64** B5
Preston Gv *ASHTD* KT21 **82** F7
Preston La
KWD/TDW/WH KT20 **104** F2
Preston Rd *NRWD* SE19 **31** L7
RYNPK SW20 **28** D8
SHPTN TW17 **41** K5
Prestons Rd *WWKM* BR4 **70** D2
Prestwick Cl *CRAWW* RH11 **190** G8
Prestwick La *HASM* GU27 **198** H3
MFD/CHID GU8 **199** M1
Prestwood Cl *CRAWW* RH11 **164** D1
Prestwood Gdns *CROY/NA* CR0 **2** D1
Prestwood La *CRAWW* RH11 **190** F3
Pretoria Rd *CHERT* KT16 **40** C8
STRHM/NOR SW16 **30** E7
Pretty La *COUL/CHIP* CR5 **106** F3
Prey Heath Cl
WOKS/MYFD GU22 **96** F6
Prey Heath Rd
WOKS/MYFD GU22 **96** E6
Price Cl *TOOT* SW17 **30** C4
Price Rd *CROY/NA* CR0 **67** L4
Prices La *REIG* RH2 **147** K3
Priddy's Yd *CROY/NA* CR0 **2** D6
Prideaux Gdns *RDKG* RH5 * **188** E1
Pridham Rd *THHTH* CR7 **50** A4
Priest Croft Cl *CRAWW* RH11 **164** C4
Priestfield Rd *FSTH* SE23 **33** H4
Priest Hl *OXTED* RH8 **130** E3
WDSR SL4 **20** F3
Priestlands Cl *HORL* RH6 **160** C2
Priest La *CHOB/PIR* GU24 **74** F5
Priestley Gdns
WOKS/MYFD GU22 **97** K2
Priestley Rd *GUW* GU2 **138** A1
MTCM CR4 **48** D2
Priestley Wy *CRAWE* RH10 **191** R3
Priests Br *MORT/ESHN* SW14 **19** H5
Priestwood Av *BNFD* RG42 **34** C1
Priestwood Court Rd
BNFD RG42 **34** C1
Priestwood Sq *BNFD* RG42 **34** C1
Priestwood Ter *BNFD* RG42 * **34** D1
Primrose Av *HORL* RH6 **160** E5
Primrose Cl *CAT* SE6 **33** M6
CRAWW RH11 **164** D7
WLGTN SM6 **48** E8
Primrose Copse *HORS* RH12 **167** G2
Primrose Dr *CHOB/PIR* GU24 **75** K5
Primrose Gdns *FARN* GU14 **92** B6
Primrose La *CROY/NA* CR0 **50** F8
FROW RH18 **195** P12
Primrose Pl *ISLW* TW7 **17** J4
Primrose Rdg *GODL* GU7 **159** L7
Primrose Rd *WOT/HER* KT12 **60** F4
Primrose Wk *BRAK* RG12 **34** F5
EW KT17 **64** C6
Primrose Wy *SHGR* GU5 **168** G4
Prince Albert Dr *ASC* SL5 **36** A4
Prince Albert Sq *REDH* RH1 **148** D5
Prince Andrew Wy *ASC* SL5 **36** A2
Prince Charles Crs *FARN* GU14 **92** E1
Prince Charles Wy *WLGTN* SM6 **66** E2
Prince Consort Dr *ASC* SL5 **36** A4
Prince George's Av
RYNPK SW20 **46** F2
Prince Georges Rd
WIM/MER SW19 **48** A1
Prince of Wales Rd *REDH* RH1 **149** K8
SUT SM1 **66** A1
Prince Regent Rd *HSLW* TW3 **16** F5
Prince Rd *SNWD* SE25 **50** B5
Prince's Av *ALDT* GU11 **112** F4
CAR SM5 **66** C6
GODL GU7 **159** M2
SAND/SEL CR2 **88** E5
SURB KT6 **63** K1
Princes Cl *BAGS* GU19 **54** B8
HPTN TW12 **26** A5
SAND/SEL CR2 **88** E5
Prince's Dr *LHD/OX* KT22 **82** B2
Princes Gdns *RGUW* GU3 * **116** B1
Princes Rd *ASHF* TW15 **23** J6
EGH TW20 **21** J7
FELT TW13 **24** C4
KUTN/CMB KT2 **9** J4
MORT/ESHN SW14 **19** G5
PGE/AN SE20 **33** G7
RCH/KEW TW9 **18** C3
RCHPK/HAM TW10 **18** C7
REDH RH1 **148** D3
TEDD TW11 **26** A5
WEY KT13 **59** L4
WIM/MER SW19 **29** K7
Princess Anne Rd *HORS* RH12 **203** J3
Princess Gdns
WOKS/MYFD GU22 **11** K3
Princess Margaret Rd
HORS RH12 **203** J2
Princess Mary Cl *GUW* GU2 **116** E4
Princess Mary's Rd
ADL/WDHM KT15 **58** F3
Princess Pde *ORP* BR6 * **71** K2
Princess Rd *CRAWW* RH11 **164** E4
CROY/NA CR0 **49** M6
WOKS/MYFD GU22 **11** K3
Prince's St *RCH/KEW* TW9 **18** B6
SUT SM1 **66** A3
Princess Wy *CBLY* GU15 **72** F4
REDH RH1 **126** D7
Princes Wy *CROY/NA* CR0 **67** J4
WIM/MER SW19 **29** H2
WWKM BR4 **70** C3
Princethorpe Rd *SYD* SE26 **33** G5
Pringle Gdns *PUR/KEN* CR8 **67** J8
STRHM/NOR SW16 **30** F5
Prior Av *BELMT* SM2 **66** B6
Prior Croft Cl *CBLY* GU15 **73** K5
Prior End *CBLY* GU15 **73** K4
Prioress Rd *WNWD* SE27 **31** L4
Prior Rd *CBLY* GU15 **73** L5
Priors Cl *FARN* GU14 **92** E1
GODL GU7 **137** K8
Priors Ct *WOKN/KNAP* GU21 **76** D8
Priors Cft *WOKS/MYFD* GU22 **97** K2
Priorsfield Rd *GODL* GU7 **159** K1
Priors Hatch La *GODL* GU7 **137** J8
Priors Md *GT/LBKH* KT23 **101** M7
The Priors *ASHTD* KT21 **103** G1
Priors Wk *CRAWE* RH10 **165** H4
Priors Wd *HASM* GU27 **198** A7
Priorswood *RGUW* GU3 **137** J7
Priory Av *CHEAM* SM3 **65** G3
Priory Cl *ASC* SL5 **37** K7
BECK BR3 **51** H3
DORK RH4 **144** D4
HORL RH6 **160** C2
HPTN TW12 **43** J1
SUN TW16 **24** D8
WIM/MER SW19 * **47** L1
WOKN/KNAP GU21 **78** A3
WOT/HER KT12 **60** D2
Priory Ct *CBLY* GU15 * **72** C4
DORK RH4 * **144** E4
Priory Crs *CHEAM* SM3 **65** G3
NRWD SE19 **31** M8
Priory Dr *REIG* RH2 **147** K2
Priory Gdns *ASHF* TW15 **24** A6
BARN SW13 **19** J5
HPTN TW12 **43** J1
SNWD SE25 **50** C4
Priory Gn *STA* TW18 **22** E6
Priory La *E/WMO/HCT* KT8 **43** K4
PUT/ROE SW15 **19** J7
RFNM GU10 **181** J1
Priory Ms *STA* TW18 **22** E6
Priory Rd *ASC* SL5 **35** L1
ASC SL5 **37** K7
CHEAM SM3 **65** G3
CHSGTN KT9 **63** H2
CROY/NA CR0 **49** K7
HPTN TW12 **25** J8
HSLW TW3 **16** F7
RCH/KEW TW9 **18** D1
REIG RH2 **147** K2
Priory St *FARN* GU14 **93** G5
The Priory *CROY/NA* CR0 * **67** K2
GDST RH9 **128** E5
Priory Wk *BRAK* RG12 **35** J4
Priory Wy *WDR/YW* UB7 **14** B1
Privet Rd *BOR* GU35 **180** B12
Probyn Rd *BRXS/STRHM* SW2 **31** L3
Proctor Cl *CRAWE* RH10 **165** L6
MTCM CR4 **48** D1
Proctor Gdns *GT/LBKH* KT23 **101** L7
Proctors Cl *EBED/NFELT* TW14 **24** D2
Profumo Rd *WOT/HER* KT12 **61** G4
Progress Wy *CROY/NA* CR0 **67** J1
Promenade Approach Rd
CHSWK W4 **19** H2
Promenade De Verdun
PUR/KEN CR8 **87** G1
The Promenade *CHSWK* W4 **19** H3
Propeller Rd *FARN* GU14 **92** E7
Prospect Av *FARN* GU14 **92** E3
Prospect Cl *HSLW* TW3 **16** C3
SYD SE26 **32** E5
Prospect Cots *WHTN* TW2 **16** F8
Prospect La *EGH* TW20 **20** D6
Prospect Pl *CRAWW* RH11 **164** E4
EW KT17 **84** B3
RYNPK SW20 **28** E8
STA TW18 **22** C6
Prospect Rd *ASHV* GU12 **113** K4
FARN GU14 **92** D5
RFNM GU10 **155** H6
SURB KT6 **44** F6
Prossers *KWD/TDW/WH* KT20 **105** G3
Providence La *HYS/HAR* UB3 **15** G2
Providence Pl
WOKS/MYFD GU22 * **78** D4
Providence Ter *CRAWE* RH10 * **193** M9
Provincial Ter *PGE/AN* SE20 * **33** G8
Prune Hl *EGH* TW20 **21** H8
Prunus Cl *CHOB/PIR* GU24 **75** H3
Puckridge Gate Rd *ALDT* GU11 **112** A3
Puckridge Hill Rd *ALDT* GU11 **112** B4
Puckshill *WOKN/KNAP* GU21 **76** A7
Puckshott Wy *HASM* GU27 **198** E5
Pudding La *HORL* RH6 **174** H9
Puffin Cl *BECK* BR3 **51** G5
Puffin Hl *CRAWE* RH10 **193** P8
Puffin Rd *CRAWW* RH11 * **190** G8
Pulborough Rd
WAND/EARL SW18 **29** J1
Pulborough Wy *HSLWW* TW4 **15** M6
Pullman Gdns *PUT/ROE* SW15 **19** M8
Pullman La *GODL* GU7 **159** M7
Pullmans Pl *STA* TW18 **22** D6
Pulteney Cl *ISLW* TW7 **17** K5
Pump Aly *BTFD* TW8 **18** A2
Pumping Station Rd
CHSWK W4 **19** H2
Pump La *ASC* SL5 **37** H1
Punchbowl La *RDKG* RH5 **145** G1
Punch Copse Rd *CRAWE* RH10 **165** H3
Purbeck Av *NWMAL* KT3 **46** C6
Purbeck Cl *REDH* RH1 **126** F3
Purbeck Dr *WOKN/KNAP* GU21 **77** J4
Purberry Gv *EW* KT17 **64** C8
Purberry Shot *EW* KT17 * **64** C8
Purbrook Ct *BRAK* RG12 **35** H6
Purcell Cl *PUR/KEN* CR8 **87** M4
Purcell Rd *CRAWW* RH11 **164** B7
Purley Bury Av *PUR/KEN* CR8 **87** M1
Purley Bury Cl *PUR/KEN* CR8 **87** M1
Purley Cl *CRAWE* RH10 **165** M7
Purley Downs Rd
SAND/SEL CR2 **67** M8
Purley Hl *PUR/KEN* CR8 **87** L2
Purley Knoll *PUR/KEN* CR8 **87** J1
Purley Oaks Rd *SAND/SEL* CR2 **68** A8
Purley Pde *PUR/KEN* CR8 * **87** K1
Purley Park Rd *PUR/KEN* CR8 **67** L8
Purley Ri *PUR/KEN* CR8 **87** J2
Purley Rd *SAND/SEL* CR2 **68** A6
Purley V *PUR/KEN* CR8 **87** L3
Purley Wy *CROY/NA* CR0 **49** J8
CROY/NA CR0 **67** K3
FRIM GU16 **93** H1
PUR/KEN CR8 **87** K1
Pursers Hollow *SHGR* GU5 **171** J2
Pursers La *SHGR* GU5 **142** A8
Purton Rd *HORS* RH12 **166** E5
Putney Common
PUT/ROE SW15 **19** M5
Putney Heath *PUT/ROE* SW15 **19** M8
Putney Hl *PUT/ROE* SW15 **29** G1
Putney Park Av *PUT/ROE* SW15 **19** K6
Putney Park La *PUT/ROE* SW15 **19** L6
Puttenham Heath Rd
RGUW GU3 **137** G5
Puttenham Hl *RGUW* GU3 **136** F4
Puttenham La *MFD/CHID* GU8 **136** F8
Puttenham Rd *RFNM* GU10 **135** M5
Puttocks Cl *HASM* GU27 **197** Q8
Pye Cl *CTHM* CR3 **108** A5
Pyecombe Ct *CRAWW* RH11 **164** B7
Pyegrove Cha *BRAK* RG12 **35** H7
Pylbrook Rd *SUT* SM1 **65** K2
Pyle Hl *WOKS/MYFD* GU22 **97** H7
Pymers Md *DUL* SE21 **31** M2
Pyne Rd *SURB* KT6 **45** K8
Pyrcroft La *WEY* KT13 **59** L4
Pyrcroft Rd *CHERT* KT16 **40** C7
Pyrford Common Rd
WOKS/MYFD GU22 **78** B6
Pyrford Heath
WOKS/MYFD GU22 **78** C6
Pyrford Rd *BF/WBF* KT14 **78** D4
WOKS/MYFD GU22 **78** E6
Pyrford Woods Cl
WOKS/MYFD GU22 **78** C5
Pyrford Woods Rd
WOKS/MYFD GU22 **78** C5
Pyrland Rd *RCHPK/HAM* TW10 **18** C8
Pyrmont Gv *WNWD* SE27 **31** L4
Pyrmont Rd *CHSWK* W4 **18** D1
Pytchley Crs *NRWD* SE19 **31** M7

Q

The Quadrangle *FRIM* GU16 * **92** F1
GUW GU2 **6** B6
Quadrant Ct *BRAK* RG12 **35** H3
Quadrant Rd *RCH/KEW* TW9 **18** A6
THHTH CR7 **49** L4
The Quadrant *ASHV* GU12 **113** K5
BELMT SM2 **65** M5
GU GU1 * **6** F6
RCH/KEW TW9 **18** B6
RYNPK SW20 **47** H1
Quadrant Wy *WEY* KT13 **59** J3
Quail Cl *HORS* RH12 **167** G2
Quail Gdns *SAND/SEL* CR2 **69** H8
Quakers Wy *RGUW* GU3 **115** M4
Qualitas *BRAK* RG12 **34** C8
Quality St *REDH* RH1 **126** E2
Quantock Cl *CRAWW* RH11 **164** D4
HYS/HAR UB3 **15** G2
Quarr Rd *CAR* SM5 **48** A6
Quarry Bank *LTWR* GU18 **74** C1
Quarry Cl *HORS* RH12 **167** J3
LHD/OX KT22 **103** G3
OXTED RH8 **130** B4
Quarry Gdns *LHD/OX* KT22 **103** G3
Quarry Hl *GODL* GU7 **159** L6
Quarry Hill Pk *REIG* RH2 **125** M5
Quarry Park Rd *SUT* SM1 **65** J5
Quarry Ri *EGRIN* RH19 **163** H2
SUT SM1 **65** J5

Quarry Rd GDST RH9 128 F2
GODL GU7 159 K2
OXTED RH8 130 B4
Quarry St GU GU1 7 G8
The Quarry BRKHM/BTCW RH3 124 A6
GU GU1 * 7 H5
Quarterbrass Farm Rd
HORS RH12 167 G2
Quartermaine Av
WOKS/MYFD GU22 97 J4
Quarter Mile Rd GODL GU7 168 B7
Quarters Rd FARN GU14 92 F7
Quebec Cl HORL RH6 161 K3
LIPH GU30 196 H10
Quebec Gdns BLKW GU17 72 A5
Queen Adelaide Rd
PGE/AN SE20 32 F7
Queen Alexandra's Wy
HOR/WEW KT19 83 K1
Queen Anne Dr ESH/CLAY KT10 62 B6
Queen Annes Cl WHTN TW2 26 A4
Queen Anne's Gdns
MTCM CR4 * 48 C3
Queen Anne's Ga FNM GU9 134 A2
Queen Annes Ms
LHD/OX KT22 * 102 E3
Queen Anne's Ter
LHD/OX KT22 * 102 E3
Queendale Ct
WOKN/KNAP GU21 76 C6
Queen Eleanor's Rd GUW GU2 138 C1
Queen Elizabeth Cl ASHV GU12 113 K7
Queen Elizabeth Dr
ALDT GU11 112 C7
Queen Elizabeth Gdns
MRDN SM4 47 K4
Queen Elizabeth Rd CBLY GU15 53 G8
HORS RH12 203 J2
KUTN/CMB KT2 9 G6
Queen Elizabeth's Dr
CROY/NA CR0 70 A8
Queen Elizabeth's Wk
WLGTN SM6 67 G3
Queen Elizabeth Wk
BARN SW13 19 K3
Queen Elizabeth Wy
WOKS/MYFD GU22 97 J1
Queenhill Rd SAND/SEL CR2 68 E8
Queenhythe Crs RGUE GU4 117 G2
Queenhythe Rd RGUE GU4 117 G2
Queen Mary Av CBLY GU15 72 D4
RYNPK SW20 47 G5
Queen Mary Cl SURB KT6 63 K2
WOKS/MYFD GU22 11 L3
Queen Mary Rd NRWD SE19 31 L7
SHPTN TW17 41 M2
Queen Mary's Av CAR SM5 66 C6
Queen Mary's Dr
ADL/WDHM KT15 58 C8
Queens Acre CHEAM SM3 65 G6
Queens Av ALDT GU11 112 F3
BF/WBF KT14 79 G2
FELT TW13 24 F5
Queensbridge Pk ISLW TW7 17 G7
Queens Cl CHOB/PIR GU24 75 K7
ESH/CLAY KT10 * 61 L3
FARN GU14 112 E1
KWD/TDW/WH KT20 104 D6
WLGTN SM6 66 E4
Queens Ct BELMT SM2 * 85 K1
FNM GU9 133 L2
WEY KT13 60 B4
WOKS/MYFD GU22 10 E8
Queens Court Ride COB KT11 80 D3
Queens Crs DORK RH4 * 144 D3
RCHPK/HAM TW10 18 C7
Queens Dr BRYLDS KT5 45 K7
GODL GU7 159 L2
GUW GU2 116 D5
LHD/OX KT22 81 M1
THDIT KT7 44 D6
Queen's Gdns HEST TW5 16 B3
Queens Garth FSTH SE23 * 32 F3
Queensgate COB KT11 81 G2
Queens Ga HORL RH6 160 D6
Queensgate Gdns
PUT/ROE SW15 19 L6
Queen's Gate Rd FARN GU14 112 E2
Queenshill Ldg ASC SL5 36 E3
Queens Hill Ri ASC SL5 36 F3
Queens Keep TWK TW1 * 17 M8
Queensland Av WIM/MER SW19 47 L1
Queens La FNM GU9 133 L2
Queensmead FARN GU14 92 E6
LHD/OX KT22 * 81 M1
Queen's Md MFD/CHID GU8 199 Q1
Queensmead Av EW KT17 64 E8
Queensmere Cl
WIM/MER SW19 29 G3
Queensmere Rd
WIM/MER SW19 29 G3
Queens Pde SWTR RH13 * 167 G8
Queens Park Gdns FELT TW13 24 C4
Queen's Park Rd CTHM CR3 108 B5
Queens Pine BRAK RG12 35 H6
Queen's Pl ASC SL5 36 D3
MRDN SM4 47 K4
WOT/HER KT12 60 B4
Queens Prom KUT/HW KT1 45 G4
Queen's Ride BARN SW13 19 L5
Queen's Ri RCHPK/HAM TW10 18 C8
Queens Rd ALDT GU11 112 C7
ASC SL5 37 G5
BECK BR3 51 H2
BELMT SM2 65 K8
CBLY GU15 72 E5
CHOB/PIR GU24 95 H2
CROY/NA CR0 49 L6
EGH TW20 21 J7
EGRIN RH19 162 F4
FARN GU14 113 G1
FELT TW13 24 E2
FNM GU9 133 M3
GU GU1 7 H4
HORL RH6 160 D3
HPTN TW12 25 L5
HSLW TW3 16 E5
KUTN/CMB KT2 9 K3
LIPH GU30 196 B10
MORT/ESHN SW14 19 G5
MRDN SM4 47 K4
MTCM CR4 48 A3
NWMAL KT3 46 C4
RCHPK/HAM TW10 18 C8
RCHPK/HAM TW10 27 J2
TEDD TW11 26 C7
THDIT KT7 44 C5
TWK TW1 26 C2
WEY KT13 60 B4
WIM/MER SW19 29 L6
WLGTN SM6 66 E4
WOKN/KNAP GU21 75 M8
WOT/HER KT12 60 C3
Queens Sq CRAWE RH10 164 F4
Queens Ter ISLW TW7 17 K6
THDIT KT7 * 44 D6
Queensthorpe Ms SYD SE26 * 33 G5
Queensthorpe Rd SYD SE26 33 G5
Queen St ASHV GU12 113 G7
CHERT KT16 40 D8
CROY/NA CR0 2 C9
GODL GU7 168 B5
SHGR GU5 141 M5
SWTR RH13 167 G8
Queensville Rd BAL SW12 31 G1
Queens Wk ASHF TW15 23 G5
Queens Wy FELT TW13 24 F5
Queensway CRAN GU6 186 E3
CRAWE RH10 165 G4
CROY/NA CR0 67 J5
EGRIN RH19 162 F4
FRIM GU16 93 K2
REDH RH1 126 C7
SUN TW16 42 E2
SWTR RH13 166 F8
WOT/HER KT12 60 E4
WWKM BR4 70 D3
Queensway North
WOT/HER KT12 60 F4
Queensway South
WOT/HER KT12 60 F4
Queenswood Av HPTN TW12 25 L7
HSLW TW3 16 C4
THHTH CR7 49 K5
WLGTN SM6 67 G3
Queenswood Rd FSTH SE23 33 H4
WOKN/KNAP GU21 96 A1
Quennell Cl ASHTD KT21 103 J1
Quennells Hl RFNM GU10 155 H3
Quentins Dr BH/WHM TN16 * 91 L6
Quentins Wk BH/WHM TN16 * 91 L6
Quentin Wy VW GU25 38 E4
Quicks Rd WIM/MER SW19 29 L8
Quiet Cl ADL/WDHM KT15 58 D3
Quiet Nook HAYES BR2 71 G2
The Quillot WOT/HER KT12 60 C4
Quince Cl ASC SL5 37 G4
Quince Dr CHOB/PIR GU24 75 L5
Quincy Rd EGH TW20 21 K6
Quintilis BRAK RG12 34 C8
Quintin Av RYNPK SW20 47 H1
Quinton Cl BECK BR3 51 M3
HEST TW5 15 L2
WLGTN SM6 66 E3
Quinton Rd THDIT KT7 44 D8
Quinton St WAND/EARL SW18 29 M3
Quintrell Cl WOKN/KNAP GU21 76 E7

R

Rabies Heath Rd REDH RH1 128 D8
Raby Rd NWMAL KT3 46 A4
Raccoon Wy HSLWW TW4 15 M4
Racecourse Rd LING RH7 178 G6
Racecourse Wy HORL RH6 160 C6
Rackfield HASM GU27 197 Q6
Rackham Cl CRAWW RH11 164 F6
Rackham Ms STRHM/NOR SW16 30 F7
Rackstraw Rd SHST GU47 52 A8
Racquets Court Hl GODL GU7 159 M3
Radar Rd FARN GU14 92 A8
Radbourne Rd BAL SW12 30 F1
Radcliffe Cl FRIM GU16 93 J2
Radcliffe Gdns CAR SM5 66 B6
Radcliffe Rd CROY/NA CR0 3 K6
Radcliffe Wy BNFD RG42 34 B1
Radford Cl FNM GU9 134 B4
Radford Rd CRAWE RH10 192 B1
Radius Pk EBED/NFELT TW14 * 15 J6
Rad La SHGR GU5 142 A8
Radlet Av SYD SE26 32 E4
Radley Cl EBED/NFELT TW14 24 C2
Radnor Cl MTCM CR4 49 H5
Radnor Ct REDH RH1 126 B8
Radnor Gdns TWK TW1 26 C3
Radnor La RDKG RH5 171 M2
Radnor Rd BRAK RG12 35 J3
SHGR GU5 171 J3
TWK TW1 26 C3
WEY KT13 59 K2
Radnor Wk CROY/NA CR0 51 H7
Radolphs KWD/TDW/WH KT20 105 G4
Radstock Wy REDH RH1 127 H3
Radstone Ct WOKS/MYFD GU22 10 E8
Raeburn Av BRYLDS KT5 45 L6
Raeburn Cl KUT/HW KT1 8 C3
Raeburn Ct WOKN/KNAP GU21 * 96 D1
Raeburn Wy SHST GU47 72 A3
Rae Rd FARN GU14 92 E8
RAF Gate Rd FARN GU14 92 E8
Rag Hill Rd BH/WHM TN16 111 G3
Raglan Cl ASHV GU12 112 F8
FRIM GU16 93 J1
HSLWW TW4 16 B7
REIG RH2 125 M6
Raglan Ct SAND/SEL CR2 67 L4
Raglan Rd REIG RH2 125 M6
WOKN/KNAP GU21 76 B8
Raikes La RDKG RH5 142 E8
Railey Rd CRAWE RH10 165 G4
Railshead Rd ISLW TW7 17 L6
Railton Rd GUW GU2 116 E4
Railway Ap CHERT KT16 * 40 C8
EGRIN RH19 162 E4
TWK TW1 26 D1
WLGTN SM6 * 66 E5
Railway Rd TEDD TW11 26 B5
Railway Side BARN SW13 19 H5
Railway Ter FELT TW13 24 D2
STA TW18 22 A6
Railway Vw DTCH/LGLY SL3 * 12 C5
Rainbow Ct WOKN/KNAP GU21 76 B6
Rainforest Wk BRAK RG12 34 E5
Rainville Rd HMSMTH W6 19 M1
Rake La MFD/CHID GU8 183 N2
Rakers Rdg HORS RH12 167 G4
Raleigh Av WLGTN SM6 67 G3
Raleigh Ct CRAWE RH10 * 191 R2
STA TW18 22 D5
Raleigh Dr BRYLDS KT5 45 M8
ESH/CLAY KT10 62 A4
HORL RH6 161 K3
Raleigh Gdns MTCM CR4 48 C3
Raleigh Rd FELT TW13 24 C3
PGE/AN SE20 33 G8
RCH/KEW TW9 18 C5
Raleigh Wk CRAWE RH10 165 G6
Raleigh Wy FELT TW13 24 F6
FRIM GU16 73 J6
Ralliwood Rd ASHTD KT21 103 K1
Ralph Perring Ct BECK BR3 51 K4
Ralphs Cross GT/LBKH KT23 * 101 M8
Ralphs Ride BRAK RG12 35 H3
Rama Cl STRHM/NOR SW16 31 H8
Rambler Cl STRHM/NOR SW16 30 F5
Ramblers Wy CRAWW RH11 191 L12
Rame Cl TOOT SW17 30 D6
Ramillies Cl ALDT GU11 113 H2
Ramones Ter MTCM CR4 * 48 F4
Ramornie Cl WOT/HER KT12 61 J3
Ram Pas KUT/HW KT1 8 D7
Ramsay Cl CBLY GU15 73 L1
Ramsay Rd BFOR GU20 55 H4
Ramsbury Cl BRAK RG12 34 B6
Ramsdale Rd TOOT SW17 30 D6
Ramsden Ga BAL SW12 * 30 E1
Ramsden Rd BAL SW12 30 D1
GODL GU7 168 A6
Ramsey Cl HORL RH6 160 C3
HORS RH12 167 G4
Ramsey Pl CTHM CR3 107 M4
Ramsey Rd THHTH CR7 49 J6
Ramslade Rd BRAK RG12 34 F5
Rams La MFD/CHID GU8 185 K11
Randal Crs REIG RH2 147 K2
Randalls Crs LHD/OX KT22 102 D2
Randalls Park Av LHD/OX KT22 102 D2
Randalls Park Dr LHD/OX KT22 102 D3
Randalls Rd LHD/OX KT22 102 B2
Randalls Wy LHD/OX KT22 102 D3
Randisbourne Gdns CAT SE6 * 33 L4
Randle Rd RCHPK/HAM TW10 26 F5
Randlesdown Rd CAT SE6 33 L4
Randolph Cl COB KT11 81 K5
KUTN/CMB KT2 * 27 M6
WOKN/KNAP GU21 76 B7
Randolph Rd EW KT17 84 C4
Ranelagh Av BARN SW13 19 K4
Ranelagh Crs ASC SL5 35 M1
Ranelagh Dr BRAK RG12 34 F3
TWK TW1 17 L6
Ranelagh Gdns CHSWK W4 18 F2
Ranelagh Pl NWMAL KT3 46 B5
Ranelagh Rd REDH RH1 126 B8
Ranfurly Rd SUT SM1 65 K1
Range Ride CBLY GU15 72 C2
Range Rd FARN GU14 92 A7
The Range SHGR GU5 169 K5
Range Vw SHST GU47 72 B1
Range Wy SHPTN TW17 41 K7
Rankine Cl FNM GU9 134 D3
Ranmere St BAL SW12 30 E2
Ranmore Av CROY/NA CR0 3 K8
Ranmore Cl REDH RH1 126 D5
Ranmore Common Rd
RDKG RH5 122 A7
Ranmore Pl WEY KT13 * 59 M4
Ranmore Rd BELMT SM2 65 G7
DORK RH4 144 D1
RDKG RH5 122 B8
Rannoch Rd HMSMTH W6 19 M1
Ransome Cl CRAWW RH11 190 G10
Ranyard Cl CHSGTN KT9 63 J2
Rapallo Cl FARN GU14 92 F5
Raphael Dr THDIT KT7 44 C8
Rapley Cl CBLY GU15 73 J1
Rapley Gn BRAK RG12 34 F6
Rapley's Fld CHOB/PIR GU24 95 H5
Rapsley La WOKN/KNAP GU21 75 L8
Rastell Av BRXS/STRHM SW2 31 G3
Ratcliffe Rd FARN GU14 92 C1
Rathbone Sq CROY/NA CR0 * 2 C9
Rathfern Rd CAT SE6 33 J2
Rathgar Cl REDH RH1 148 D5
Rathlin Rd CRAWW RH11 164 D7
Ravelin Cl RFNM GU10 132 C4
Raven Cl CRAWE RH10 193 P8
Ravendale Rd SUN TW16 42 C2
Ravenfield Rd TOOT SW17 30 C4
Raven La CRAWW RH11 164 E2
Ravens Ait SURB KT6 * 45 G5
Ravensbourne Av
STWL/WRAY TW19 23 H2
Ravensbourne Pk CAT SE6 33 K1
Ravensbourne Park Crs
CAT SE6 33 J1
Ravensbourne Rd CAT SE6 33 J1
TWK TW1 17 M8
Ravensbury Av MRDN SM4 47 M5
Ravensbury Gv MTCM CR4 48 A4
Ravensbury La MTCM CR4 48 A4
Ravensbury Rd
WAND/EARL SW18 29 L3
Ravensbury Ter
WAND/EARL SW18 29 L3
Ravenscar Rd SURB KT6 63 J1
Ravens Cl REDH RH1 126 C7
WOKN/KNAP GU21 75 M6
Ravenscourt SUN TW16 42 C1
Ravenscroft Cl ASHV GU12 113 M6
Ravenscroft Rd BECK BR3 50 F2
WEY KT13 79 M1
Ravensdale Gdns NRWD SE19 32 A8
Ravensdale Ms STA TW18 22 E7
Ravensdale Rd ASC SL5 36 D5
HSLWW TW4 16 B5
Ravensfield EGH TW20 20 E7
Ravensfield Gdns
HOR/WEW KT19 64 B4
Ravenshead Cl SAND/SEL CR2 88 F1
Ravenslea Rd BAL SW12 30 C1
Ravenstone Rd CBLY GU15 74 A4
Ravenstone St BAL SW12 30 D2
Ravens Wold PUR/KEN CR8 87 M5
Ravenswood Av SURB KT6 63 J1
WWKM BR4 51 M8
Ravenswood Cl COB KT11 81 G5
Ravenswood Ct
KUTN/CMB KT2 * 9 M1
WOKS/MYFD GU22 10 D7
Ravenswood Crs WWKM BR4 51 M8
Ravenswood Dr CBLY GU15 73 K4
Ravenswood Gdns ISLW TW7 17 H3
Ravenswood Rd BAL SW12 30 E1
CROY/NA CR0 2 A8
Rawlings Cl BECK BR3 51 M5
Rawlins Cl SAND/SEL CR2 69 J6
Rawlinson Rd ALDT GU11 112 F3
CBLY GU15 72 C3
Rawnsley Av MTCM CR4 48 A5
Raworth Cl CRAWE RH10 * 165 L6
Ray La LING RH7 178 B2
Rayleigh Av TEDD TW11 26 B7
Rayleigh Ct KUT/HW KT1 9 J6
Rayleigh Ri SAND/SEL CR2 68 B5
Rayleigh Rd WIM/MER SW19 47 J1
Raymead Av THHTH CR7 49 K5
Raymead Cl LHD/OX KT22 102 B4
Raymead Wy LHD/OX KT22 102 B4
Raymer Wk HORL RH6 160 F2
Raymond Cl DTCH/LGLY SL3 13 H3
SYD SE26 32 F6
Raymond Crs GUW GU2 138 C1
Raymond Rd BECK BR3 51 H4
WIM/MER SW19 29 H7
Raymond Wy ESH/CLAY KT10 * 62 D5
Rayners Cl DTCH/LGLY SL3 12 F2
Ray Rd E/WMO/HCT KT8 43 L5
Rays Rd WWKM BR4 51 M7
Raywood Cl HYS/HAR UB3 14 F2
Rdffye Ct HORS RH12 167 K5
The Readens BNSTD SM7 86 B6
Reading Arch Rd REDH RH1 126 C8
Reading Rd FARN GU14 92 F8
SUT SM1 65 M4
Read Rd ASHTD KT21 83 G7
Reads Rest La
KWD/TDW/WH KT20 105 J1
Reapers Cl HORS RH12 167 G4
Reapers Wy ISLW TW7 17 G7
Recovery St TOOT SW17 30 B6
Recreation Cl FARN GU14 72 C8
Recreation Rd GU GU1 6 F3
RFNM GU10 155 H6
SYD SE26 33 G5
Recreation Wy MTCM CR4 49 H3
Rectory Cl ASHTD KT21 103 J1
BF/WBF KT14 79 H3
BRAK RG12 34 F4
CRAN GU6 171 K11
GODL GU7 168 C7
RDKG RH5 188 D2
RGUE GU4 118 A6
RYNPK SW20 46 F2
SHGR GU5 169 J3
SHPTN TW17 41 K3
SURB KT6 44 F8
Rectory Gdn CRAN GU6 * 186 C2
Rectory Gdns BECK BR3 * 51 K1
Rectory Gn BECK BR3 51 J1
Rectory Gv CROY/NA CR0 2 A6
HPTN TW12 25 J5
Rectory La ASHTD KT21 83 J8
BF/WBF KT14 79 H3
BFOR GU20 54 F6
BH/WHM TN16 111 H5
BNSTD SM7 86 C5
BRAK RG12 34 E4
BRKHM/BTCW RH3 124 C6
CRAWW RH11 164 B2
GT/LBKH KT23 101 J8
HORL RH6 174 G10
LIPH GU30 197 J6
RFNM GU10 154 A5
SHGR GU5 141 J5
SURB KT6 44 F8
TOOT SW17 30 D6
WLGTN SM6 66 F3
Rectory Orch WIM/MER SW19 29 H5
Rectory Pk SAND/SEL CR2 88 B3
Rectory Pl GUW GU2 * 6 F9
Rectory Rd BARN SW13 19 K4
BECK BR3 51 K1
COUL/CHIP CR5 106 A7
FARN GU14 92 F5
HAYES BR2 71 G6
HSLWW TW4 15 L4
SUT SM1 65 K2
Rectory Rw BRAK RG12 34 E4
Red Admiral St HORS RH12 167 H4
Redan Gdns ASHV GU12 112 F7
Redan Hill Est ASHV GU12 * 112 F7
Redan Rd ASHV GU12 112 F7
Redbarn Cl PUR/KEN CR8 87 L1
Redberry Gv SYD SE26 32 F4
Redclose Av MRDN SM4 47 K5
Redcote Pl DORK RH4 123 G8
Redcourt WOKS/MYFD GU22 78 A5
Redcrest Gdns CBLY GU15 73 J4
Redcroft Wk CRAN GU6 186 D3
Red Deer Cl SWTR RH13 167 L6
Reddington Cl SAND/SEL CR2 68 A7
Redding Wy WOKN/KNAP GU21 75 M8
Redditch BRAK RG12 35 G7
Redditch Cl CRAWW RH11 164 A8
Reddons Rd BECK BR3 33 H8
Reddown Rd COUL/CHIP CR5 87 G8
Rede Ct WEY KT13 59 L2
Redehall Rd HORL RH6 161 L5
Redesdale Gdns ISLW TW7 17 K2
Redfern Av HSLWW TW4 25 K1
Redfern Rd CAT SE6 33 M1
Redford Av COUL/CHIP CR5 86 E5
HORS RH12 166 E5
THHTH CR7 49 J4
WLGTN SM6 67 H5
Redford Cl FELT TW13 24 C3
Redgarth Ct EGRIN RH19 162 C2
Redgate Dr HAYES BR2 70 E1
Redgrave Cl CROY/NA CR0 50 C6
Redgrave Dr CRAWE RH10 165 M5
Redhearne Flds RFNM GU10 181 K7
Redhill Rd COB KT11 79 L3
Red House La MFD/CHID GU8 157 M6
WOT/HER KT12 60 D1
Redhouse Rd BH/WHM TN16 110 F3
Red House Rd CROY/NA CR0 49 G6
Redkiln Cl SWTR RH13 167 J6
Redkiln Wy SWTR RH13 167 J6
Redland Gdns
E/WMO/HCT KT8 * 43 J4
Redlands COUL/CHIP CR5 87 H6
RDKG RH5 173 J3
Redlands La RDKG RH5 144 D8
RFNM GU10 132 D2
Redlands Wy BRXS/STRHM SW2 31 H1
Red La BOR GU35 180 G10
ESH/CLAY KT10 62 D5
OXTED RH8 130 E7
RDKG RH5 145 K7
Redleaves Av ASHF TW15 23 L7
Redlees Cl ISLW TW7 17 K6
Red Lion Ct HSLW TW3 * 16 E5
Red Lion La CHOB/PIR GU24 56 B7
FNM GU9 5 H6
Red Lion Rd CHOB/PIR GU24 56 B7
SURB KT6 63 J1
Red Lion St RCH/KEW TW9 18 A7
Red Lodge Rd WWKM BR4 51 M8
Redmayne CBLY GU15 73 M5
Red Oak Cl ORP BR6 71 L2
Red Oaks RFNM GU10 * 155 H6
Red River Ct HORS RH12 * 166 E4
Red Rd LTWR GU18 74 D2
Redroofs Cl BECK BR3 51 L1
Redstart Cl CROY/NA CR0 70 A8
Redstone Hl REDH RH1 126 D8
Redstone Hollow REDH RH1 148 D1
Redstone Mnr REDH RH1 126 D8
Redstone Pk REDH RH1 126 D8
Redstone Rd REDH RH1 148 D1
Redvers Buller Rd ALDT GU11 112 F2
Redvers Rd BRAK RG12 34 E5
WARL CR6 89 G8
Redway Dr WHTN TW2 25 M1
Redwing Av GODL GU7 138 A8
Redwing Cl SAND/SEL CR2 89 G1
SWTR RH13 167 J6
Redwing Gdns BF/WBF KT14 78 E2
Redwing Ri RGUE GU4 118 A6
Redwing Rd WLGTN SM6 67 H6
Redwood EGH TW20 40 B2
Redwood Cl CRAWE RH10 165 G2
PUR/KEN CR8 87 M4
Redwood Dr ASC SL5 37 L6
CBLY GU15 74 A5
Redwood Gv RGUE GU4 139 M6
Redwood Ms ASHF TW15 * 24 A8
Redwood Mt REIG RH2 125 K5
Redwoods ADL/WDHM KT15 58 D5
Reed Cl ALDT GU11 113 G3
Reed Dr REDH RH1 148 D3
Reedham Dr PUR/KEN CR8 87 J3
Reedham Park Av
PUR/KEN CR8 87 K6
Reedings CRAWW RH11 190 G9
Reed Pl BF/WBF KT14 78 B3
SHPTN TW17 41 J8
Reedsfield Cl ASHF TW15 23 L4
Reedsfield Rd ASHF TW15 23 L5
Reed's Hl BRAK RG12 34 E5
The Reeds Rd RFNM GU10 156 A8
Rees Gdns CROY/NA CR0 50 C6
Reeve Rd REIG RH2 147 M4
Reeves Cnr CROY/NA CR0 2 B6
Reeves Rd ASHV GU12 112 F8
Regal Ct MTCM CR4 48 C3
Regal Crs WLGTN SM6 66 E2
Regal Dr EGRIN RH19 163 G5
Regalfield Cl GUW GU2 116 D4
Regan Cl GUW GU2 116 E3
Regency Cl HPTN TW12 25 J6
Regency Ct ADL/WDHM KT15 * 59 G3
Regency Dr BF/WBF KT14 78 C3
Regency Gdns WOT/HER KT12 43 G8
Regency Ms BECK BR3 51 M1
Regency Wk CROY/NA CR0 51 H6
Regent Cl ADL/WDHM KT15 58 F7
HSLWW TW4 15 L3
REDH RH1 126 F3
Regent Ct BAGS GU19 54 C7
GUW GU2 * 116 E6
Regent Crs REDH RH1 126 C6
Regent Pde BELMT SM2 * 65 M5
Regent Pk LHD/OX KT22 * 82 D8
Regent Pl WIM/MER SW19 29 M6
Regent Rd BRYLDS KT5 45 J5
Regents Cl CRAWW RH11 164 E8
CTHM CR3 88 B8
SAND/SEL CR2 68 B5
Regents Dr HAYES BR2 71 G4
Regents Ms HORL RH6 160 D3
Regents Wk ASC SL5 36 F6
Regent Wy FRIM GU16 73 J8
Regina Rd SNWD SE25 50 D3
Reid Av CTHM CR3 108 A3
Reid Cl COUL/CHIP CR5 86 E6
Reigate Av SUT SM1 47 L8
Reigate Cl CRAWE RH10 165 M1
Reigate Hl REIG RH2 125 L4
Reigate Hill Cl REIG RH2 125 K5
Reigate Rd DORK RH4 123 H8
EW KT17 64 C8
HORL RH6 160 A4
KWD/TDW/WH KT20 85 G7
LHD/OX KT22 102 F5
LHD/OX KT22 103 H6
REDH RH1 148 C4
REIG RH2 125 M8
REIG RH2 175 M2
Reigate Wy WLGTN SM6 67 H4
Reindorp Cl GUW GU2 6 B5
Rembrandt Ct HOR/WEW KT19 64 C5
Rembrandt Wy WOT/HER KT12 60 E1
Rendle Cl CROY/NA CR0 50 C5
Renfree Wy SHPTN TW17 41 K7
Renfrew Rd HSLWW TW4 16 A4
KUTN/CMB KT2 9 M2
The Renmans ASHTD KT21 83 J6
Renmuir St TOOT SW17 30 C7
Rennie Cl ASHF TW15 23 G4
Rennie Ter REDH RH1 148 D1
Renown Cl CROY/NA CR0 2 B4

Replingham Rd
WAND/EARL SW18 29 J2
Repton Cl CAR SM5 66 B4
Repton Ct BECK BR3 51 L1
Reservoir Cl THHTH CR7 50 A3
Reservoir Rd FARN GU14 92 A8
Restmor Wy CAR SM5 66 D1
Restwell Av CRAN GU6 170 A11
Retreat Rd RCH/KEW TW9 18 A7
The Retreat BRYLDS KT5 45 J6
CRAN GU6 * 186 B1
EGH TW20 21 G7
MORT/ESHN SW14 19 H5
THHTH CR7 50 A4
WPK KT4 64 E2
Revell Cl LHD/OX KT22 101 L4
Revell Dr LHD/OX KT22 101 L4
Revell Rd KUT/HW KT1 9 M5
SUT SM1 65 J5
Revelstoke Av FARN GU14 92 E3
Revelstoke Rd
WAND/EARL SW18 29 K3
WIM/MER SW19 29 H5
WIM/MER SW19 29 M7
Revere Wy HOR/WEW KT19 64 B7
Revesby Cl CHOB/PIR GU24 75 G3
Revesby Rd CAR SM5 48 B6
Rewley Rd CAR SM5 48 A6
Rex Av ASHF TW15 23 K7
Reynard Cl HORS RH12 167 L4
Reynard Dr NRWD SE19 32 C8
Reynolds Av CHSGTN KT9 63 H6
Reynolds Cl CAR SM5 48 C6
WIM/MER SW19 48 A1
Reynolds Gn SHST GU47 72 A3
Reynolds Pl CRAWW RH11 164 E3
RCHPK/HAM TW10 18 C8
Reynolds Rd CRAWW RH11 164 E3
NWMAL KT3 46 A7
Reynolds Wy CROY/NA CR0 3 H9
Rheingold Wy WLGTN SM6 67 H7
Rhine Banks FARN GU14 92 A4
Rhodes Cl EGH TW20 21 M6
Rhodes Ct EGH TW20 * 21 M6
Rhodes Wy CRAWE RH10 165 H6
Rhododendron Ride EGH TW20 20 C6
Rhododendron Rd FRIM GU16 93 L1
Rhodrons Av CHSGTN KT9 63 H4
Rhyll Gdns ALDT GU11 112 C8
Rialto Rd MTCM CR4 48 D2
Ribble Pl FARN GU14 92 B3
Ribblesdale Rd
STRHM/NOR SW16 30 E6
Ricardo Ct SHGR GU5 169 J4
Ricards Rd WIM/MER SW19 29 J6
Rices Hl EGRIN RH19 162 F4
Richards Cl ASHV GU12 * 113 K4
HYS/HAR UB3 15 G1
Richards Fld HOR/WEW KT19 64 A7
Richards Rd COB KT11 81 L4
Richbell Cl ASHTD KT21 83 G8
Richborough Ct
CRAWW RH11 * 164 E4
Richens Cl HSLW TW3 17 G4
Richland Av COUL/CHIP CR5 86 D4
Richlands Av EW KT17 64 D3
Richmond Av
EBED/NFELT TW14 15 H8
RYNPK SW20 47 H1
Richmond Br TWK TW1 18 A7
Richmond Cl BH/WHM TN16 110 E1
EPSOM KT18 84 B4
FARN GU14 92 A6
FRIM GU16 73 J8
LHD/OX KT22 101 M6
Richmond Ct CRAWE RH10 165 C5
Richmond Crs STA TW18 * 22 C6
Richmond Dr SHPTN TW17 41 M6
Richmond Gn CROY/NA CR0 67 H2
Richmond Hl
RCHPK/HAM TW10 18 B8
Richmond Hill Ct
RCHPK/HAM TW10 18 B8
Richmond Pde TWK TW1 * 17 M8
Richmond Park Rd
KUTN/CMB KT2 8 F4
MORT/ESHN SW14 18 F7
Richmond Rd COUL/CHIP CR5 86 E5
CROY/NA CR0 67 H2
GODL GU7 168 A3
HORS RH12 166 F5
ISLW TW7 17 K6
KUTN/CMB KT2 27 G6
RYNPK SW20 46 E1
SHST GU47 72 B2
STA TW18 22 C6
THHTH CR7 49 L4
TWK TW1 26 E1
Richmond Wy EGRIN RH19 163 G5
GT/LBKH KT23 101 L6
Richmondwood ASC SL5 37 L8
Rickard Cl BRXS/STRHM SW2 31 K2
Rickards Cl SURB KT6 63 H1
Ricketts Hill Rd BH/WHM TN16 91 G8
Rickfield CRAWW RH11 164 C5
Rickford Hl RGUW GU3 96 A8
Rickman Cl BRAK RG12 34 F6
Rickman Crs ADL/WDHM KT15 58 E2
Rickman Hl COUL/CHIP CR5 86 E7
Rickman Hill Rd
COUL/CHIP CR5 86 E8
Rickman's La BIL RH14 201 J7
Ricksons La EHSLY KT24 119 L1
Rickwood HORL RH6 160 E2
Rickwood Pk RDKG RH5 * 173 L8
Rickyard GUW GU2 116 A8
The Riddings CTHM CR3 108 C7
Riddlesdown Av PUR/KEN CR8 87 M2
Riddlesdown Rd PUR/KEN CR8 67 M8
Ride La SHGR GU5 170 C2
Riders Wy GDST RH9 128 F5
The Ride BIL RH14 201 M7
Ride Wy CRAN GU6 170 G7
Rideway Cl CBLY GU15 72 E5
Ridge Cl BRKHM/BTCW RH3 145 L4
WOKS/MYFD GU22 96 E3
Ridgegate Cl REIG RH2 126 A6
Ridge Gn REDH RH1 149 H3
Ridge Green Cl REDH RH1 149 H3
Ridgehurst Dr HORS RH12 166 C8
Ridgelands LHD/OX KT22 102 A6
Ridge Langley SAND/SEL CR2 68 D8
Ridgemead Rd EGH TW20 20 E4
Ridge Moor Cl GSHT GU26 181 R12
Ridgemount GUW GU2 6 C5
WEY KT13 60 B1
Ridgemount Av
COUL/CHIP CR5 86 E7
CROY/NA CR0 69 G1
Ridge Mount Rd ASC SL5 37 K8
Ridgemount Wy REDH RH1 148 A2
Ridge Pk PUR/KEN CR8 67 G8
Ridge Rd CHEAM SM3 47 J8
MTCM CR4 30 E8
Ridgeside CRAWE RH10 165 H4
The Ridges RGUW GU3 138 F5
The Ridge ASC SL5 * 37 K7
BRYLDS KT5 45 K5
COUL/CHIP CR5 87 H4
CTHM CR3 110 B7
EPSOM KT18 83 M8
HORS RH12 203 K1
LHD/OX KT22 102 A6
PUR/KEN CR8 67 G8
WHTN TW2 26 A1
WOKS/MYFD GU22 11 J5
Ridge Wy EDEN TN8 153 M5
Ridgeway EGRIN RH19 162 F6
Ridge Wy FELT TW13 25 H4
Ridgeway HAYES BR2 70 D1
HOR/WEW KT19 83 M2
Ridgeway Rd VW GU25 39 H5
Ridgeway WOKN/KNAP GU21 10 B2
WOT/HER KT12 42 C8
Ridgeway Cl CRAN GU6 186 F2
DORK RH4 144 D4
LTWR GU18 74 D1
WOKN/KNAP GU21 10 A2
Ridgeway Ct REDH RH1 * 148 B1
Ridgeway Dr DORK RH4 144 D5
Ridgeway Gdns
WOKN/KNAP GU21 10 B2
Ridgeway Rd DORK RH4 144 D4
FNM GU9 5 K8
ISLW TW7 17 H2
REDH RH1 126 C8
Ridgeway Rd North ISLW TW7 17 H2
The Ridgeway BRAK RG12 34 F3
CHOB/PIR GU24 95 J2
CRAN GU6 186 E2
CROY/NA CR0 67 J2
HORL RH6 160 D5
HORS RH12 166 E5
LHD/OX KT22 81 M4
LHD/OX KT22 102 A5
LTWR GU18 54 E8
The Ridge Wy SAND/SEL CR2 68 B8
Ridgewell Cl SYD SE26 33 J5
Ridgewood Dr FRIM GU16 74 A6
Ridgley Rd MFD/CHID GU8 199 P1
Ridgway RCHPK/HAM TW10 * 18 B8
WIM/MER SW19 28 F8
WOKS/MYFD GU22 78 C5
Ridgway Gdns WIM/MER SW19 29 G8
Ridgway Hill Rd FNM GU9 5 J8
Ridgway Pde FNM GU9 * 5 K8
Ridgway Pl WIM/MER SW19 29 H7
Ridgway Rd FNM GU9 5 J9
WOKS/MYFD GU22 78 C5
The Ridgway BELMT SM2 66 A6
Riding Court Rd DTCH/LGLY SL3 12 B1
Riding Hl SAND/SEL CR2 88 D3
The Ridings ADL/WDHM KT15 58 B5
ASHTD KT21 83 G7
BH/WHM TN16 91 H7
BRYLDS KT5 45 K5
COB KT11 81 K2
CRAWE RH10 165 M3
EHSLY KT24 100 B7
EPSOM KT18 84 B5
EW KT17 64 C7
FRIM GU16 73 L6
KWD/TDW/WH KT20 105 J2
REIG RH2 126 A6
RPLY/SEND GU23 98 D5
SUN TW16 42 D1
The Riding CRAN GU6 186 D1
WOKN/KNAP GU21 77 L4
Ridlands Gv OXTED RH8 131 H4
Ridlands La OXTED RH8 131 H4
Ridlands Ri OXTED RH8 131 H4
Ridley Rd WARL CR6 88 F8
WIM/MER SW19 29 L8
Ridsdale Rd PGE/AN SE20 50 E1
WOKN/KNAP GU21 76 E7
Riesco Dr CROY/NA CR0 68 F5
Rigby Cl CROY/NA CR0 67 K2
Riggindale Rd
STRHM/NOR SW16 31 G6
Rillside CRAWE RH10 165 J7
Rill Wk EGRIN RH19 163 J4
Rimbault Cl ALDT GU11 113 G2
Rinaldo Rd BAL SW12 30 E1
Ringley Av HORL RH6 160 D3
Ringley Oak HORS RH12 167 J5
Ringley Park Av REIG RH2 148 A1
Ringley Park Rd REIG RH2 125 M8
Ringley Rd HORS RH12 167 H5
Ringmead BRAK RG12 34 B5
BRAK RG12 34 D8
Ringmore Dr RGUE GU4 117 M5
Ringmore Ri FSTH SE23 32 E1
Ringmore Rd WOT/HER KT12 60 F2
Ring Rd North HORL RH6 160 E6
Ring Rd South HORL RH6 160 F7
Ringstead Rd CAT SE6 33 L1
SUT SM1 66 A3
The Ring BRAK RG12 34 E1
Ringwold Cl BECK BR3 33 H8
Ringwood BRAK RG12 34 C7
Ringwood Av CROY/NA CR0 49 H7
REDH RH1 126 C5
Ringwood Cl ASC SL5 36 D4
CRAWE RH10 165 G6
Ringwood Gdns PUT/ROE SW15 28 D3
Ringwood Rd FARN GU14 92 F2
Ringwood Wy HPTN TW12 25 K5
Ripley Av EGH TW20 21 H7
Ripley By-Pass
RPLY/SEND GU23 98 B8
Ripley Cl CROY/NA CR0 69 M5
Ripley Gdns MORT/ESHN SW14 19 G5
Ripley La RPLY/SEND GU23 99 J6
Ripley Rd HPTN TW12 25 K8
RGUE GU4 119 G2
RPLY/SEND GU23 98 F8
Ripley Wy HOR/WEW KT19 83 K1
Ripon Cl CBLY GU15 74 A6
GUW GU2 116 C5
Ripon Gdns CHSGTN KT9 63 G4
Ripplesmere BRAK RG12 35 G5
Ripston Rd ASHF TW15 24 A6
Risborough Dr WPK KT4 46 D7
Rise Rd ASC SL5 37 H6
The Rise CRAWE RH10 165 L4
EGRIN RH19 162 F5
EHSLY KT24 100 B8
EW KT17 64 C8
KWD/TDW/WH KT20 104 F3
SAND/SEL CR2 68 F7
Ritchie Cl CRAWE RH10 165 L8
Ritchie Rd CROY/NA CR0 50 E6
Ritherdon Rd TOOT SW17 30 D3
River Av THDIT KT7 44 D7
Riverbank DORK RH4 * 143 L2
E/WMO/HCT KT8 44 B3
River Bank THDIT KT7 44 C5
Riverbank Wy BTFD TW8 17 M1
River Ct WOKN/KNAP GU21 77 M4
Riverdale RFNM GU10 155 H2
Riverdale Dr WAND/EARL SW18 29 L2
WOKS/MYFD GU22 97 J3
Riverdale Gdns TWK TW1 17 M7
Riverdale Rd FELT TW13 25 H5
TWK TW1 17 M8
Riverfield Rd STA TW18 22 C7
River Gdns CAR SM5 66 D1
EBED/NFELT TW14 15 L7
River Grove Pk BECK BR3 51 J1
Riverhead Dr BELMT SM2 65 L8
River Hl COB KT11 80 E5
Riverholme Dr HOR/WEW KT19 64 A7
River La COB KT11 81 H6
FNM GU9 4 B9
LHD/OX KT22 102 A3
RCHPK/HAM TW10 27 G2
Rivermead BF/WBF KT14 79 J3
River Md CRAWW RH11 164 C1
Rivermead E/WMO/HCT KT8 43 M3
River Md HORS RH12 166 E8
Rivermead KUT/HW KT1 * 45 G5
Rivermead Cl
ADL/WDHM KT15 * 58 F6
TEDD TW11 26 E6
Rivermead Rd CBLY GU15 72 E7
River Meads Av WHTN TW2 25 L4
River Mt WOT/HER KT12 42 C7
River Mount Gdns GUW GU2 138 F3
Rivernook Cl WOT/HER KT12 42 F5
River Park Av STA TW18 22 A5
River Reach TEDD TW11 26 F7
River Rd STA TW18 40 C1
River Rw FNM GU9 4 C8
Rivers Cl FARN GU14 93 H8
Riversdale Rd THDIT KT7 44 D5
Riversdell Cl CHERT KT16 40 D7
Riverside CHERT KT16 * 40 D2
DORK RH4 123 G8
EDEN TN8 153 M8
FROW RH18 195 M10
GU GU1 117 G6
HORL RH6 160 D5
HORS RH12 166 D7
RCH/KEW TW9 * 18 D1
SHPTN TW17 42 B7
STWL/WRAY TW19 20 F1
SUN TW16 * 43 G2
TWK TW1 26 E2
Riverside Av E/WMO/HCT KT8 44 A5
LTWR GU18 74 F1
Riverside Cl CHOB/PIR GU24 95 J2
FARN GU14 92 C4
KUT/HW KT1 45 G4
STA TW18 40 C1
WLGTN SM6 66 E2
Riverside Dr CHSWK W4 19 H2
ESH/CLAY KT10 61 K3
MTCM CR4 48 B5
RCHPK/HAM TW10 26 E4
SHGR GU5 169 K2
STA TW18 22 B6
Riverside Gdns
WOKS/MYFD GU22 97 L3
Riverside Ms CROY/NA CR0 * 67 H2
Riverside Pl STWL/WRAY TW19 14 A8
Riverside Rd STA TW18 22 C8
STWL/WRAY TW19 14 A7
TOOT SW17 29 L5
WOT/HER KT12 61 G3
The Riverside
E/WMO/HCT KT8 * 44 A3
Riverside Wk ISLW TW7 17 H5
KUT/HW KT1 8 C6
Riverside Wy CBLY GU15 72 D6
Riverside Yd TOOT SW17 29 L4
Riversmeet RFNM GU10 156 F5
River Vw ADL/WDHM KT15 * 58 F4
Riverview GU GU1 * 6 E3
Riverview Gdns BARN SW13 19 L1
COB KT11 80 D3
River View Gdns TWK TW1 26 C3
Riverview Pk CAT SE6 33 K3
Riverview Rd CHSWK W4 18 E2
HOR/WEW KT19 63 M3
River Wk SUN TW16 43 G2
WOT/HER KT12 42 D6
River Wy HOR/WEW KT19 64 A4
WHTN TW2 25 L3
Riverway STA TW18 40 E1
Rivett-Drake Cl GUW GU2 116 E4
Rivey Cl BF/WBF KT14 78 C4
Road House Est
WOKS/MYFD GU22 * 97 K2
Roakes Av ADL/WDHM KT15 58 E1
Robert Cl WOT/HER KT12 60 E4
Robertsbridge Rd CAR SM5 47 M7
Roberts Cl CHEAM SM3 65 G6
STWL/WRAY TW19 13 M8
THHTH CR7 50 A3
Roberts Ct CHSGTN KT9 * 63 G4
Robertson Wy ASHV GU12 113 J8
Roberts Rd ASHV GU12 113 G8
CBLY GU15 72 D3
Robert St CROY/NA CR0 2 D7
Roberts Wy EGH TW20 20 F8
Robert Wy FRIM GU16 93 J6
HORS RH12 167 J2
Robin Cl ADL/WDHM KT15 59 G4
ASHV GU12 113 J3
CRAWW RH11 164 E2
EGRIN RH19 162 F3
FELT TW13 25 H6
Robin Gdns REDH RH1 126 D6
Robin Gv BTFD TW8 17 M1
Robin Hl GODL GU7 168 A2
Robin Hill Dr CBLY GU15 73 K6
Robin Hood Cl FARN GU14 92 D2
Robinhood Cl MTCM CR4 48 F4
Robin Hood Cl
WOKN/KNAP GU21 76 C8
Robin Hood Crs
WOKN/KNAP GU21 76 B7
Robin Hood La HORS RH12 166 B4
PUT/ROE SW15 28 B4
RGUE GU4 97 J6
SUT SM1 65 K4
Robinhood La MTCM CR4 48 F3
Robin Hood Rd PUT/ROE SW15 28 B5
WOKN/KNAP GU21 76 C8
Robin Hood Wy PUT/ROE SW15 28 B5
Robinia Cl PGE/AN SE20 50 D1
Robin Rw CRAWE RH10 193 P8
Robins Dl WOKN/KNAP GU21 75 M7
Robins Gv WWKM BR4 70 D2
Robinson Cl WOKS/MYFD GU22 97 M2
Robinson Rd TOOT SW17 30 B7
Robinsway WOT/HER KT12 60 F3
Robinswood Ct HORS RH12 * 167 J5
Robin Wy GUW GU2 116 E4
STA TW18 22 C4
Robinwood Pl PUT/ROE SW15 28 A5
Robson Rd WNWD SE27 31 L4
Roby Dr BRAK RG12 35 G7
Roche Rd STRHM/NOR SW16 49 H1
Rochester Av FELT TW13 24 C3
Rochester Cl
STRHM/NOR SW16 * 31 H8
Rochester Gdns CROY/NA CR0 3 H7
CTHM CR3 108 B4
Rochester Pde FELT TW13 * 24 D4
Rochester Rd CAR SM5 66 C3
EGH TW20 22 A6
Roche Wk CAR SM5 48 A6
Rochford Wy CROY/NA CR0 49 H6
Rock Av MORT/ESHN SW14 19 G5
Rockbourne Rd FSTH SE23 33 G2
Rock Cl MTCM CR4 48 A2
Rockdale Dr GSHT GU26 197 Q2
The Rockery FARN GU14 92 A6
Rocket Rd FARN GU14 92 A8
Rockfield Cl OXTED RH8 130 C5
Rockfield Rd OXTED RH8 130 C4
Rockfield Wy SHST GU47 * 72 A1
Rock Gdns ALDT GU11 112 C8
Rockhampton Rd
SAND/SEL CR2 68 B5
STRHM/NOR SW16 31 K5
Rock Hl DUL SE21 32 C5
Rockingham Cl PUT/ROE SW15 19 J6
Rock La RFNM GU10 155 K4
Rockmount Rd NRWD SE19 32 A7
Rockshaw Rd REDH RH1 126 F1
Rocks La BARN SW13 19 K5
The Rocks EGRIN RH19 163 K7
Rockwell Gdns NRWD SE19 32 B5
Rockwood Pk EGRIN RH19 * 162 D8
Rocky La REDH RH1 126 D3
Rocombe Crs FSTH SE23 * 32 F1
Roden Gdns CROY/NA CR0 50 B6
Rodenhurst Rd CLAP SW4 30 F1
Rodgate La HASM GU27 199 M8
Rodmel Ct FARN GU14 93 H8
Rodmill La BRXS/STRHM SW2 31 H1
Rodney Cl NWMAL KT3 46 B5
WOT/HER KT12 * 42 F8
Rodney Gdns WWKM BR4 70 D3
Rodney Pl WIM/MER SW19 47 M1
Rodney Rd MTCM CR4 48 B2
NWMAL KT3 46 B5
WHTN TW2 25 K1
WOT/HER KT12 60 F1
Rodney Wy DTCH/LGLY SL3 13 H3
GU GU1 117 K7
Rodona Rd WEY KT13 80 A1
Rodway Rd PUT/ROE SW15 28 D1
Roebuck Cl ASHTD KT21 103 H2
FELT TW13 24 E5
REIG RH2 125 K8
SWTR RH13 167 L5
Roebuck Rd CHSGTN KT9 63 K4
Roedean Crs PUT/ROE SW15 19 H8
Roedeer Copse HASM GU27 197 R7
Roehampton Cl PUT/ROE SW15 19 K6
Roehampton Ga
PUT/ROE SW15 19 H8
Roehampton High St
PUT/ROE SW15 28 D1
Roehampton La
PUT/ROE SW15 19 K7
Roehampton V PUT/ROE SW15 28 C4
Roe Wy WLGTN SM6 67 H6
Roffes La CTHM CR3 108 A7
Roffey Cl HORL RH6 160 C3
PUR/KEN CR8 87 L6
Roffey's Cl CRAWE RH10 192 F1
Roffords WOKN/KNAP GU21 76 E7
Rogers Cl COUL/CHIP CR5 87 L8
Rogers La WARL CR6 89 J8
Rogers Md GDST RH9 128 E6
Rogers Rd TOOT SW17 30 A5
Rojack Rd FSTH SE23 33 G2
Rokeby Cl BRAK RG12 35 G2
Rokeby Pl RYNPK SW20 28 E8
Roke Cl MFD/CHID GU8 183 M4
PUR/KEN CR8 87 M4
Roke La MFD/CHID GU8 183 M4
Roke Lodge Rd PUR/KEN CR8 87 L3
Roke Rd PUR/KEN CR8 87 M5
Rokers La MFD/CHID GU8 159 G2
Roland Wy WPK KT4 64 C1
Rolinsden Wy HAYES BR2 71 G3
Rollesby Rd CHSGTN KT9 63 K5
Rolleston Rd SAND/SEL CR2 68 A6
Rollit Crs HSLW TW3 16 D7
Rolls Royce Cl WLGTN SM6 67 H6
Romana Ct STA TW18 * 22 D5
Roman Cl EBED/NFELT TW14 15 M7
Roman Farm Rd GUW GU2 116 A7
Roman Farm Wy GUW GU2 116 A7
Romanfield Rd
BRXS/STRHM SW2 31 J1
Roman Ri NRWD SE19 32 A7
Roman Rd DORK RH4 144 D4
Romans Wy WOKS/MYFD GU22 78 D5
Roman Wy BNFD RG42 35 J1
CROY/NA CR0 2 B5
FNM GU9 134 B5
Romany Gdns CHEAM SM3 47 K7
Romayne Cl FARN GU14 92 D4
Romberg Rd TOOT SW17 30 D4
Romeo Hl BNFD RG42 35 J1
Romeyn Rd STRHM/NOR SW16 31 J4
Rommany Rd WNWD SE27 32 A5
Romney Cl ASHF TW15 23 M6
CHSGTN KT9 63 H3
Romney Rd FARN GU14 92 B8
NWMAL KT3 46 A6
Romola Rd HNHL SE24 31 L2
Romsey Cl ALDT GU11 134 F3
ORP BR6 71 M3
Rona Cl CRAWW RH11 164 D7
Ronald Cl BECK BR3 51 J5
Ronelean Rd SURB KT6 63 J2
Ronneby Cl WEY KT13 60 B2
Ronson Wy LHD/OX KT22 102 D3
Rookeries Cl FELT TW13 24 E4
Rookery Cl LHD/OX KT22 102 B6
Rookery Dr DORK RH4 143 K4
Rookery Hl ASHTD KT21 83 K8
REDH RH1 176 G3
Rookery Md COUL/CHIP CR5 107 G4
Rookery Rd ORP BR6 71 J8
STA TW18 22 E6
The Rookery
STRHM/NOR SW16 * 31 J7
Rookery Wy
KWD/TDW/WH KT20 125 J1
Rook La CTHM CR3 107 K6
Rookley Cl BELMT SM2 65 L8
Rooks Hl SHGR GU5 169 M7
Rooksmead Rd SUN TW16 42 C2
Rookstone Rd TOOT SW17 30 C6
Rook Wy HORS RH12 167 H3
Rookwood Av NWMAL KT3 46 D4
SHST GU47 52 B8
WLGTN SM6 67 G3
Rookwood Cl REDH RH1 126 E3
Rookwood Ct GUW GU2 6 E9
Rookwood Pk HORS RH12 166 D6
Roothill La BRKHM/BTCW RH3 145 K6
Ropeland Wy HORS RH12 167 H2
Roper Wy MTCM CR4 48 D2
Rorkes Drift FRIM GU16 93 J5
Rosa Av ASHF TW15 23 K5
Rosalind Franklin Cl GUW GU2 138 B1
Rosamond St SYD SE26 32 E4
Rosamund Cl SAND/SEL CR2 68 A3
Rosamund Rd CRAWE RH10 165 K6
Rosary Cl HSLW TW3 16 B4
Rosary Gdns ASHF TW15 23 L5
Roseacre OXTED RH8 130 D7
Roseacre Cl SHPTN TW17 41 K5
Roseacre Gdns RGUE GU4 140 C6
Rose Av MRDN SM4 47 M5
MTCM CR4 48 C1
Rosebank EPSOM KT18 83 M4
PGE/AN SE20 32 E8
Rosebank Cl TEDD TW11 26 D7
Rosebery Av EW KT17 84 B4
NWMAL KT3 46 C2
THHTH CR7 49 M2
Rosebery Cl MRDN SM4 47 G6
Rosebery Crs
WOKS/MYFD GU22 97 J2
Rosebery Gdns SUT SM1 65 L3
Rosebery Pde EW KT17 * 64 C6
Rosebery Rd EPSOM KT18 104 A1
HSLW TW3 16 F7
KUT/HW KT1 9 L7
SUT SM1 65 J5
Rosebery Sq KUT/HW KT1 9 L7
Rosebine Av WHTN TW2 26 A1
Rosebriar Cl WOKS/MYFD GU22 78 D6
Rosebriars CTHM CR3 108 B2
ESH/CLAY KT10 61 M4
Rosebury Dr CHOB/PIR GU24 75 K5
Rose Bushes EW KT17 84 F6
Rosecourt Rd CROY/NA CR0 49 J6
Rosecroft Cl BH/WHM TN16 91 J8
Rosecroft Gdns WHTN TW2 26 A2
Rosedale ASHTD KT21 82 F8
ASHV GU12 112 F7
Rose Dl ORP BR6 71 L1
Rosedale Cl CRAWW RH11 164 C6
Rosedale Gdns BRAK RG12 34 D5
Rosedale Rd EW KT17 64 D4
RCH/KEW TW9 18 B6
Rosedene Av CROY/NA CR0 49 H7
MRDN SM4 47 K5
STRHM/NOR SW16 31 J4
Rosedene La SHST GU47 72 A2
Rose End WPK KT4 47 G8
Rosefield Cl CAR SM5 66 B4
Rosefield Gdns CHERT KT16 58 A5
Rosefield Rd STA TW18 22 D5
Rose Gdns FARN GU14 92 A6
FELT TW13 24 D3
STWL/WRAY TW19 23 G1
Roseheath Rd HSLWW TW4 16 C7
Rose Hl DORK RH4 144 D3
Rosehill ESH/CLAY KT10 62 D5
HPTN TW12 43 K1
Rose Hl SUT SM1 65 L1
Rose Hill Arch Ms DORK RH4 * 144 D2
Rosehill Av SUT SM1 47 M8
WOKN/KNAP GU21 76 F6
Rosehill Court Pde
MRDN SM4 * 47 M7
Rosehill Farm Meadow
BNSTD SM7 85 L5
Rosehill Gdns SUT SM1 65 L1
Rose Hill Pk West SUT SM1 47 M8
Rosehill Rd BH/WHM TN16 90 F7
Rose La RPLY/SEND GU23 99 G4
Roseleigh Cl TWK TW1 18 A8

Rosemary Av ASHV GU12 113 K1
E/WMO/HCT KT8 43 K3
HSLWW TW4 16 A4
Rosemary Cl CROY/NA CR0 49 H7
FARN GU14 92 A4
OXTED RH8 130 D7
Rosemary Ct HORL RH6 * 160 B2
Rosemary Crs RGUW GU3 116 C4
Rosemary Gdns CHSGTN KT9 63 H3
Rosemary La BLKW GU17 72 A5
CRAN GU6 201 N1
EGH TW20 39 L3
HORL RH6 160 E4
HORL RH6 174 H10
MORT/ESHN SW14 18 F5
RFNM GU10 155 H5
Rosemary Rd TOOT SW17 29 L4
Rosemead CHERT KT16 40 E7
Rosemead Av FELT TW13 24 C3
MTCM CR4 48 F3
Rosemead Cl REDH RH1 148 A2
Rose Meadow CHOB/PIR GU24 75 K3
Rosemont Rd NWMAL KT3 45 M3
RCHPK/HAM TW10 18 B8
Rosemount Av BF/WBF KT14 78 D3
Rosendale Rd HNHL SE24 31 M1
Roseneath Ct CTHM CR3 * 108 D7
Roseneath Dr MFD/CHID GU8 199 Q1
Roseneath Pl
STRHM/NOR SW16 31 K5
The Rosery CROY/NA CR0 51 G6
Rosethorn Cl BAL SW12 30 F1
Rosetrees GU GU1 139 K1
Rose Vw ADL/WDHM KT15 * 58 F4
Roseville Av HSLW TW3 16 D7
Rosevine Rd RYNPK SW20 46 F1
Rose Wk BRYLDS KT5 45 L5
CRAWW RH11 * 164 D6
WWKM BR4 69 M1
WWKM BR4 70 A1
Rosewarne Cl
WOKN/KNAP GU21 76 D8
Rosewell Cl PGE/AN SE20 32 E8
Rose Wd WOKS/MYFD GU22 11 G9
Rosewood Ct KUTN/CMB KT2 9 J3
Rosewood Dr SHPTN TW17 41 J5
Rosewood Gv SUT SM1 65 M1
Rosewood Rd BOR GU35 180 J12
Rosewood Ter PGE/AN SE20 * 32 F8
Rosewood Wy CHOB/PIR GU24 75 H3
Roslyn Cl MTCM CR4 48 A2
Ross Cl CRAWE RH10 165 H7
Rossdale SUT SM1 66 B4
Rossdale Rd PUT/ROE SW15 19 M6
Rosset Cl BRAK RG12 34 E4
Rossetti Gdns COUL/CHIP CR5 87 J7
Rossignol Gdns CAR SM5 66 D1
Rossindel Rd HSLW TW3 16 D7
Rossiter Rd BAL SW12 30 E2
Rosslea BFOR GU20 54 D3
Rosslyn Av BARN SW13 19 H5
EBED/NFELT TW14 15 K8
Rosslyn Cl SUN TW16 24 B7
WWKM BR4 70 C2
Rosslyn Pk WEY KT13 60 A3
Rosslyn Rd TWK TW1 17 M8
Rossmore Cl CRAWE RH10 192 C3
Ross Pde WLGTN SM6 66 E5
Ross Rd COB KT11 80 F1
SNWD SE25 50 B3
WHTN TW2 25 M2
WLGTN SM6 66 F5
Rosswood Gdns WLGTN SM6 66 E5
Rostella Rd TOOT SW17 30 A5
Rostrevor Rd WIM/MER SW19 29 K6
Rothbury Gdns ISLW TW7 17 K2
Rother Crs CRAWW RH11 164 B5
Rotherfield Rd CAR SM5 66 D3
Rotherhill Av
STRHM/NOR SW16 31 G7
Rothermere Rd CROY/NA CR0 67 J4
Rother Rd FARN GU14 92 B3
Rothervale HORL RH6 175 N4
Rotherwood Cl RYNPK SW20 47 H1
Rothesay Av RCHPK/HAM TW10 18 E6
RYNPK SW20 47 H2
Rothesay Rd SNWD SE25 50 A4
Rothes Rd DORK RH4 144 E1
Rothschild St WNWD SE27 31 L5
Rotunda Est ALDT GU11 * 112 E7
Rougemont Av MRDN SM4 47 K6
Roughets La REDH RH1 128 B3
Rough Fld EGRIN RH19 162 E1
Roughlands WOKS/MYFD GU22 78 B5
Rough Rew DORK RH4 144 E5
Rough Rd WOKS/MYFD GU22 95 M4
Rough Wy HORS RH12 167 J4
Rounce La CHOB/PIR GU24 75 G3
Roundals La MFD/CHID GU8 184 B6
Round Gv CROY/NA CR0 51 G7
Roundhay Cl FSTH SE23 33 G3
Round Hl SYD SE26 32 E3
Roundhill WOKS/MYFD GU22 11 K9
Roundhill Dr WOKS/MYFD GU22 11 K8
Roundhill Wy COB KT11 81 L1
GUW GU2 116 C8
Round Oak Rd WEY KT13 59 J3
Rounds Hl BNFD RG42 * 34 C1
Roundthorn Wy
WOKN/KNAP GU21 76 C6
Roundway CBLY GU15 73 M3
EGH TW20 21 M6
Roundway Cl CBLY GU15 73 M3
The Roundway ESH/CLAY KT10 62 C5
Roundwood Vw BNSTD SM7 85 G5
Roundwood Wy BNSTD SM7 85 G5
Roupell Rd BRXS/STRHM SW2 31 J2
Rouse Gdns DUL SE21 32 B5
Routh Rd WAND/EARL SW18 30 B1
Rowan Av EGH TW20 21 M6
Rowan Cha RFNM GU10 155 K4
Rowan Cl CBLY GU15 73 J1
CRAWE RH10 165 H4
GU GU1 116 E5
HORS RH12 167 L4
NWMAL KT3 46 B2
REIG RH2 147 M2
STRHM/NOR SW16 48 F1
Rowan Crs STRHM/NOR SW16 48 F1
Rowan Gdns CROY/NA CR0 3 K7
Rowan Gv COUL/CHIP CR5 106 E3
Rowan Md
KWD/TDW/WH KT20 104 E1
Rowan Rd BTFD TW8 17 L2
STRHM/NOR SW16 48 F2
Rowans Cl FARN GU14 72 B8
Rowanside Cl BOR GU35 196 H1
The Rowans GSHT GU26 197 Q3
SUN TW16 24 C6
WOKS/MYFD GU22 10 D8
Rowan Ter PGE/AN SE20 * 50 D1
WIM/MER SW19 * 29 H8
Rowan Wk HAYES BR2 71 J2
Rowan Wy HORS RH12 167 M4
Rowbarns Wy EHSLY KT24 120 C4
Rowbury GODL GU7 168 D2
Rowcroft Cl ASHV GU12 113 K3
Rowden Rd BECK BR3 51 H1
HOR/WEW KT19 63 M3
Rowdown Crs CROY/NA CR0 70 A7
Rowe La CHOB/PIR GU24 95 K6
Rowfant Cl CRAWE RH10 192 D7
Rowfant Rd TOOT SW17 30 D3
Row Hl ADL/WDHM KT15 58 C5
Rowhill Av ALDT GU11 134 C1
Rowhill Crs ALDT GU11 134 C1
Rowhills FNM GU9 134 A1
Rowhills Cl FNM GU9 134 C1
Rowhook Rd HORS RH12 188 A12
Rowhurst Av ADL/WDHM KT15 58 E5
Rowland Cl CRAWE RH10 177 K12
Rowland Gv SYD SE26 32 E4
Rowland Rd CRAN GU6 186 C2
Rowlands Rd HORS RH12 167 K3
Rowland Wy ASHF TW15 23 M8
WIM/MER SW19 47 L1
Row La SHGR GU5 170 D4
Rowley Cl BRAK RG12 35 H3
WOKS/MYFD GU22 78 D6
Rowley Ct CTHM CR3 107 M4
Rowlls Rd KUT/HW KT1 9 H8
Rowly Dr CRAN GU6 169 R12
Rowly Edge CRAN GU6 169 R11
Rowntree Rd WHTN TW2 26 B2
Rowplatt La EGRIN RH19 193 R2
The Row EDEN TN8 * 153 L5
Row Town ADL/WDHM KT15 58 C6
Roxborough Av ISLW TW7 17 J2
Roxburgh Cl CBLY GU15 73 M5
Roxburgh Rd WNWD SE27 31 L6
Roxford Cl SHPTN TW17 42 B5
Roxton Gdns CROY/NA CR0 69 J5
Royal Av WPK KT4 64 B1
Royal Botanic Gdns
RCH/KEW TW9 * 18 B2
Royal Circ WNWD SE27 31 K4
Royal Cl ORP BR6 71 L3
WIM/MER SW19 29 G3
WPK KT4 64 B1
Royal Dr EPSOM KT18 84 E8
Royal Earlswood Pk
REDH RH1 148 D4
Royale Cl ALDT GU11 134 F2
Royal Ms BAL SW12 30 E1
Royal Oak Ms TEDD TW11 26 D6
Royal Oak Rd
WOKN/KNAP GU21 76 F8
Royal Orchard Cl
WAND/EARL SW18 29 H1
Royal Rd TEDD TW11 26 A6
Royce Rd CRAWE RH10 191 R2
Roycroft Cl BRXS/STRHM SW2 * 31 K2
Roydon Ct WOT/HER KT12 60 D3
Roy Gv HPTN TW12 25 L7
Royston Av BF/WBF KT14 79 H2
SUT SM1 66 A2
WLGTN SM6 67 G3
Royston Cl CRAWE RH10 191 R3
HEST TW5 15 L3
WOT/HER KT12 42 D8
Royston Rd BF/WBF KT14 79 H2
PGE/AN SE20 51 G1
RCHPK/HAM TW10 18 B7
The Roystons BRYLDS KT5 45 L5
Rozeldene GSHT GU26 197 R2
Rubens St CAT SE6 33 J3
Rubus Cl CHOB/PIR GU24 75 H3
Ruckmans La RDKG RH5 188 C6
Rudd Hall Ri CBLY GU15 73 G6
Ruden Wy EW KT17 84 E5
Rudge Ri ADL/WDHM KT15 58 C4
Rudgwick Rd CRAWW RH11 164 B3
Rudloe Rd BAL SW12 30 F1
Rudsworth Cl DTCH/LGLY SL3 13 G3
Ruffetts Cl SAND/SEL CR2 68 E6
The Ruffetts SAND/SEL CR2 68 E6
Ruffetts Wy
KWD/TDW/WH KT20 85 H8
Rufwood CRAWE RH10 193 M5
Rugby Cl SHST GU47 52 B8
Rugby La BELMT SM2 65 G7
Rugby Rd TWK TW1 17 H8
Ruggles-Brise Rd ASHF TW15 23 G6
Rugosa Rd CHOB/PIR GU24 75 H3
Ruislip St TOOT SW17 30 C5
Rumsey Cl HPTN TW12 25 J7
Runcorn Cl CRAWW RH11 164 A8
Runes Cl MTCM CR4 48 A4
Runfold-St George
RFNM GU10 134 E4
Runnemede Rd EGH TW20 21 K6
Runnymede WIM/MER SW19 48 A1
Runnymede Cl WHTN TW2 16 E8
Runnymede Ct EGH TW20 21 K5
Runnymede Crs
STRHM/NOR SW16 49 G1
Runnymede Gdns HSLW TW3 16 E8
Runnymede Rd WHTN TW2 16 E8
Runtley Wood La RGUE GU4 97 J7
Runwick La RFNM GU10 4 A8
Rupert Ct E/WMO/HCT KT8 * 43 K4
Rupert Rd GUW GU2 6 D6
Rural Wy REDH RH1 126 D8
STRHM/NOR SW16 30 E8
Ruscoe Dr WOKS/MYFD GU22 11 H5
Ruscombe Wy
EBED/NFELT TW14 24 C1
Rusham Park Av EGH TW20 21 J7
Rusham Rd EGH TW20 21 J7
Rushams Rd HORS RH12 166 E7
Rush Common Ms
BRXS/STRHM SW2 31 H1
Rush Cft GODL GU7 168 D1
Rushden Cl NRWD SE19 32 A8
Rushdene Wk BH/WHM TN16 91 G7
Rushden Wy FNM GU9 134 A2
Rushett Cl THDIT KT7 44 E8
Rushett Dr DORK RH4 144 E5
Rushett La CHSGTN KT9 83 G2
Rushett Rd THDIT KT7 44 E7
Rushetts Pl CRAWW RH11 164 E1
Rushetts Rd CRAWW RH11 164 D1
REIG RH2 147 M4
Rushey Cl NWMAL KT3 46 A4
Rushey Gn CAT SE6 33 L1
Rushfords LING RH7 178 F3
Rushley Cl HAYES BR2 71 G3
Rushmead RCHPK/HAM TW10 26 E4
Rushmead Cl CROY/NA CR0 3 J9
Rushmere Ct WPK KT4 64 D1
Rushmere Pl EGH TW20 21 H6
WIM/MER SW19 29 G6
Rushmon Pl CHEAM SM3 * 65 H5
Rushmon Vls NWMAL KT3 * 46 C4
Rushmoor Cl GUW GU2 116 C5
Rushmoor Rd ALDT GU11 112 B6
Rusholme Gv NRWD SE19 32 B6
Rushton Av GDST RH9 150 F4
Rushworth Rd REIG RH2 125 K7
Rushy Meadow La CAR SM5 66 B1
Ruskin Av EBED/NFELT TW14 24 C1
RCH/KEW TW9 18 D2
Ruskin Cl CRAWE RH10 165 L1
Ruskin Dr WPK KT4 64 E1
Ruskin Rd CAR SM5 66 D4
CROY/NA CR0 2 B5
ISLW TW7 17 J5
STA TW18 22 C7
Ruskin Wy WIM/MER SW19 48 A2
Rusper Rd CRAWW RH11 164 B4
CRAWW RH11 190 D6
HORS RH12 167 J5
HORS RH12 190 A4
RDKG RH5 173 Q9
RDKG RH5 189 L2
Ruspers Keep CRAWW RH11 164 B3
Russel Cl BECK BR3 51 L3
Russel Cl BRAK RG12 35 G8
KWD/TDW/WH KT20 104 D7
WOKN/KNAP GU21 76 E5
Russell Ct BLKW GU17 72 A4
LHD/OX KT22 102 E4
Russell Dr STWL/WRAY TW19 14 A8
Russell Gdns RCHPK/HAM TW10 26 F3
Russell Green Cl PUR/KEN CR8 67 K8
Russell Hl PUR/KEN CR8 67 J8
Russell Hill Pl PUR/KEN CR8 87 K1
Russell Hill Rd PUR/KEN CR8 67 K8
Russell Kerr Cl CHSWK W4 * 18 F2
Russell Rd MTCM CR4 48 B3
SHPTN TW17 41 M7
WHTN TW2 17 J8
WIM/MER SW19 29 K8
WOKN/KNAP GU21 76 F5
WOT/HER KT12 42 D6
Russells KWD/TDW/WH KT20 105 G4
Russells Crs HORL RH6 160 D4
Russell Wy CRAWE RH10 165 J5
SUT SM1 65 L4
Russet Av SHPTN TW17 42 B3
Russet Cl HORL RH6 160 F3
RFNM GU10 135 H2
STWL/WRAY TW19 13 J8
WOT/HER KT12 61 G2
Russet Dr CROY/NA CR0 51 H8
Russet Gdns CBLY GU15 73 G6
Russet Gld ALDT GU11 134 A1
Russetts Cl WOKN/KNAP GU21 10 D2
Russet Wy RDKG RH5 145 G6
Russ Hl HORL RH6 190 D1
Russ Hill Rd HORL RH6 174 G11
Russington Rd SHPTN TW17 42 A6
Rusthall Cl CROY/NA CR0 50 F6
Rustic Av STRHM/NOR SW16 30 E8
Rustington Wk CHEAM SM3 47 J7
Ruston Av BRYLDS KT5 45 L7
Ruston Cl CRAWE RH10 165 L7
Ruston Wy ASC SL5 36 B2
Rutford Rd STRHM/NOR SW16 31 H6
Ruthen Cl EPSOM KT18 83 L4
Rutherford Cl BELMT SM2 66 A5
Rutherford Wy CRAWE RH10 191 R2
Rutherwick Cl HORL RH6 160 C3
Rutherwyke Cl EW KT17 64 D5
Rutherwyk Rd CHERT KT16 40 B7
Rutland Cl ALDT GU11 112 D6
ASHTD KT21 83 H7
HOR/WEW KT19 64 A8
MORT/ESHN SW14 18 E5
REDH RH1 126 C7
Rutland Dr MRDN SM4 47 K7
RCHPK/HAM TW10 27 G2
Rutland Gdns CROY/NA CR0 68 B3
Rutland Pk CAT SE6 33 J3
Rutland Rd WHTN TW2 26 A3
WIM/MER SW19 30 B8
Rutland Wk CAT SE6 33 J3
Rutlish Rd WIM/MER SW19 47 K1
Rutson Rd BF/WBF KT14 79 J4
Rutter Gdns MTCM CR4 48 A4
Rutton Hill Rd MFD/CHID GU8 182 F9
Ruxbury Rd CHERT KT16 40 A6
Ruxley Cl HOR/WEW KT19 63 L4
Ruxley Crs ESH/CLAY KT10 62 E6
Ruxley La HOR/WEW KT19 63 M4
Ruxley Ms HOR/WEW KT19 63 L4
Ruxley Rdg ESH/CLAY KT10 62 D6
Ruxton Cl COUL/CHIP CR5 86 F5
Ryan Dr BTFD TW8 17 K1
Rydal Cl CBLY GU15 74 A4
CRAWW RH11 190 G9
FARN GU14 92 A6
PUR/KEN CR8 88 A3
Rydal Dr WWKM BR4 70 B1
Rydal Gdns HSLW TW3 16 E8
PUT/ROE SW15 28 B6
Rydal Pl LTWR GU18 74 E1
Rydal Rd STRHM/NOR SW16 31 G6
Rydal Wy EGH TW20 21 L8
Ryde Cl RPLY/SEND GU23 98 F3
Ryde Heron WOKN/KNAP GU21 76 B7
Ryde Lands CRAN GU6 186 E1
Rydens Av WOT/HER KT12 60 F1
Rydens Cl WOT/HER KT12 60 F1
Rydens Gv WOT/HER KT12 61 G3
Rydens Pde
WOKS/MYFD GU22 * 97 L2
Rydens Pk WOT/HER KT12 61 G1
Rydens Rd WOT/HER KT12 60 E2
Rydens Wy WOKS/MYFD GU22 97 K2
Ryde Pl TWK TW1 17 M8
Ryders Wy HORS RH12 167 J2
Rydes Av GUW GU2 116 C5
Ryde's Hill Crs GUW GU2 116 C4
Ryde's Hill Rd GUW GU2 116 C6
The Ryde STA TW18 40 E1
Ryde Vale Rd BAL SW12 30 E3
Rydon's La COUL/CHIP CR5 107 M2
Rydon's Wood Cl
COUL/CHIP CR5 107 M2
Rye Ash CRAWE RH10 165 J3
Rye Brook Rd LHD/OX KT22 82 D8
Rye Cl FARN GU14 92 B3
GUW GU2 116 B7
Ryecotes Md DUL SE21 32 B2
Ryecroft Av WHTN TW2 25 L2
Ryecroft Dr HORS RH12 166 D6
Ryecroft Gdns BLKW GU17 72 B5
Ryecroft Meadow SWTR RH13 205 R11
Ryecroft Rd STRHM/NOR SW16 31 K7
Rye Fld ASHTD KT21 83 G7
Ryefield Rd NRWD SE19 31 M7
Rye Gv CRAN GU6 * 185 R2
LTWR GU18 55 H8
Ryelands CRAWW RH11 164 C5
HORL RH6 * 160 F2
Ryelands Cl CTHM CR3 108 B3
Ryelands Ct LHD/OX KT22 82 D8
Ryelands Pl WEY KT13 60 B2
Ryersh La RDKG RH5 173 K10
Ryfold Rd WIM/MER SW19 29 K4
Rykens La BRKHM/BTCW RH3 145 M5
Ryland Cl FELT TW13 24 C5
Rylandes Rd SAND/SEL CR2 68 E7
Ryle Rd FNM GU9 5 H7
Rymer Rd CROY/NA CR0 3 H2
Rysted La BH/WHM TN16 111 M8
Ryst Wood Rd FROW RH18 195 Q11
Rythe Cl CHSGTN KT9 62 F6
Rythe Ct THDIT KT7 44 D7
Rythe Rd ESH/CLAY KT10 62 A4
The Rythe ESH/CLAY KT10 61 L8

S

Sable Cl HSLWW TW4 15 M5
Sabre Ct ALDT GU11 112 B7
Sachel Court Rd CRAN GU6 185 N10
Sackville Cl EGRIN RH19 162 D2
Sackville Ct EGRIN RH19 * 163 G5
Sackville Est STRHM/NOR SW16 31 H4
Sackville La EGRIN RH19 162 C2
Sackville Rd BELMT SM2 65 K6
Saddleback Rd CBLY GU15 73 H1
Saddlebrook Pk SUN TW16 24 B8
Saddler Rw CRAWE RH10 164 F7
Saddlers Ms KUT/HW KT1 * 8 B5
Saddlers Scarp GSHT GU26 197 M1
Saddlers Wy EPSOM KT18 104 A1
Saddlewood CBLY GU15 72 F5
Sadler Cl MTCM CR4 48 C2
Sadlers Cl GU GU1 118 A7
Sadlers Gate Ms PUT/ROE SW15 19 M5
Sadlers Ride E/WMO/HCT KT8 43 M2
Saffron Cl CRAWW RH11 164 C7
CROY/NA CR0 49 H6
Saffron Platt GUW GU2 116 D4
Saffron Rd BRAK RG12 34 E4
Saffron Wy SURB KT6 45 G8
Sage Yd SURB KT6 * 45 J8
Sailors La MFD/CHID GU8 182 A7
Sainfoin Rd TOOT SW17 30 D3
Sainsbury Rd NRWD SE19 32 B6
St Agatha's Dr KUTN/CMB KT2 9 H1
St Agatha's Gv CAR SM5 48 C8
St Agnes Rd EGRIN RH19 162 F3
St Albans Av FELT TW13 25 G6
WEY KT13 59 K2
St Albans Cl RGUW GU3 115 L7
St Albans Farm
EBED/NFELT TW14 * 15 M7
St Alban's Gdns TEDD TW11 26 D6
St Alban's Gv CAR SM5 48 B7
St Albans Rd KUTN/CMB KT2 8 F1
REIG RH2 125 K6
SUT SM1 65 J3
St Amunds Cl CAT SE6 33 K5
St Andrew Av CHOB/PIR GU24 95 L3
St Andrews BRAK RG12 34 B6
CRAN GU6 * 186 A2
HORL RH6 * 160 E4
St Andrew's Cl REIG RH2 147 L1
SHPTN TW17 42 A4
STWL/WRAY TW19 12 B8
THDIT KT7 44 E8
WOKN/KNAP GU21 76 F7
St Andrew's Ct
WAND/EARL SW18 29 M3
St Andrews Gdns COB KT11 80 F3
St Andrews Ga
WOKS/MYFD GU22 10 E7
St Andrews Ms BAL SW12 31 G2
St Andrews Rd CAR SM5 66 B2
COUL/CHIP CR5 86 E6
CRAWW RH11 190 G8
CROY/NA CR0 2 C9
SURB KT6 45 G6
St Andrew's Sq SURB KT6 45 G6
St Andrew's Wk COB KT11 80 E5
St Andrew's Wy FRIM GU16 93 J2
OXTED RH8 131 H5
St Anne's Av STWL/WRAY TW19 23 G1
St Annes Bvd REDH RH1 126 D6
St Anne's Dr REDH RH1 126 D7
St Annes Gld BAGS GU19 54 A6
St Annes Mt REDH RH1 * 126 D7
St Annes Ri REDH RH1 126 D7
St Annes Rd CRAWE RH10 192 B3
GODL GU7 168 D4
St Annes Wy REDH RH1 * 126 D7
St Anns WOKS/MYFD GU22 * 10 C8
St Ann's Cl CHERT KT16 40 C5
St Ann's Hl WAND/EARL SW18 29 M1
St Ann's Hill Rd CHERT KT16 39 M6
St Anns Rd BARN SW13 * 19 J4
CHERT KT16 40 C6
St Anns Wy BH/WHM TN16 * 91 L6
CROY/NA CR0 67 L5
St Anthonys Cl BNFD RG42 34 D1
TOOT SW17 30 B3
St Anthony's Wy
EBED/NFELT TW14 15 J6
St Arvans Cl CROY/NA CR0 3 H7
St Aubin Cl CRAWW RH11 * 164 B8
St Aubyns DORK RH4 * 144 E4
St Aubyn's Av HSLW TW3 16 D7
WIM/MER SW19 29 J6
St Aubyn's Rd NRWD SE19 32 C7
St Augustine's Av
SAND/SEL CR2 67 M6
St Augustine's Cl ASHV GU12 113 G8
St Austins GSHT GU26 * 197 Q2
St Barnabas Av CHOB/PIR GU24 95 K4
St Barnabas Cl BECK BR3 51 M2
St Barnabas' Gdns
E/WMO/HCT KT8 43 K5
St Barnabas Rd MTCM CR4 30 D8
SUT SM1 66 A4
St Bartholomew's Cl SYD SE26 32 F5
St Bartholomew's Ct GU GU1 7 L7
St Benedict's Cl ALDT GU11 112 D8
St Benets Cl TOOT SW17 * 30 B3
St Benet's Gv CAR SM5 47 M7
St Bernards CROY/NA CR0 3 G8
St Bernards Cl WNWD SE27 32 A5
St Brelades Cl DORK RH4 144 D4
St Brelades Ct EDEN TN8 * 153 K6
St Brelades Rd CRAWW RH11 164 B8
St Catherines WEY KT13 * 59 L2
WOKS/MYFD GU22 96 F1
St Catherines Cl CHSGTN KT9 63 G5
TOOT SW17 * 30 B3
St Catherines Ct FELT TW13 24 D2
St Catherine's Cross
REDH RH1 128 B8
St Catherine's Dr GUW GU2 138 E4
St Catherine's Hl GUW GU2 138 F4
St Catherine's Pk GU GU1 7 L7
St Catherines Rd CRAWE RH10 165 L1
FRIM GU16 73 K8
St Chad Av WOKS/MYFD GU22 95 M4
St Chads Cl SURB KT6 44 F7
St Charles Pl WEY KT13 59 K4
St Christophers LING RH7 * 178 E5
St Christophers Cl
HASM GU27 * 198 B7
HORS RH12 166 F5
ISLW TW7 17 H3
St Christophers Gdns ASC SL5 36 A1
St Christopher's Ms
WLGTN SM6 66 F4
St Christophers Pl FARN GU14 92 C6
St Christopher's Rd FARN GU14 92 D6
HASM GU27 198 B7
St Clair Cl OXTED RH8 129 M4
REIG RH2 125 M8
St Clair Dr WPK KT4 64 E2
St Clair's Rd CROY/NA CR0 3 G6
St Clement Rd CRAWW RH11 164 B8
St Cloud Rd WNWD SE27 31 M5
St Crispins Wy CHERT KT16 57 M7
St Cross Rd FNM GU9 5 J2
FRIM GU16 93 K2
RFNM GU10 132 C4
St Cuthbert's Cl EGH TW20 21 G7
St Cyprian's St TOOT SW17 30 C5
St David's COUL/CHIP CR5 87 J7
St David's Cl FARN GU14 92 C1
FNM GU9 134 B2
REIG RH2 125 M7
WWKM BR4 51 L7
St David's Dr EGH TW20 20 F8
St Denis Rd WNWD SE27 32 A5
St Denys Cl PUR/KEN CR8 67 L8
WOKN/KNAP GU21 * 76 A8
St Dunstan's Hl SUT SM1 65 H3
St Dunstan's Rd FELT TW13 24 C4
HSLWW TW4 15 M4
SNWD SE25 50 C4
St Edmunds Cl CRAWW RH11 164 F1
TOOT SW17 30 B3
St Edmund's La WHTN TW2 25 L1
St Edmunds Sq BARN SW13 19 M1
St Edwards Cl CROY/NA CR0 90 A1
EGRIN RH19 162 D4
St Elizabeth Dr EPSOM KT18 83 M4
St Faith's Rd DUL SE21 31 L2
St Fillans WOKS/MYFD GU22 * 11 K4
St Fillans Rd CAT SE6 33 M2
St Francis Gdns CRAWE RH10 192 H1
St George Av
WOKS/MYFD GU22 95 L4
St Georges HORL RH6 * 160 E4
St George's Av WEY KT13 59 M5
St George's Cl FNM GU9 * 134 E3
HORL RH6 160 E3
WEY KT13 59 M4
St Georges Ct CRAWE RH10 164 F3
St George's Gdns EW KT17 84 C4
HORS RH12 167 H5
SURB KT6 63 L1
St George's Gv TOOT SW17 30 A4
St George's La ASC SL5 36 E3
St Georges Ms CHSWK W4 * 18 F1
FNM GU9 5 H2
St Georges Pde CAT SE6 * 33 J3
St Georges Rd ADL/WDHM KT15 58 F3
ASHV GU12 112 E8
BECK BR3 51 L1
CBLY GU15 73 G3
FELT TW13 25 G5
FNM GU9 5 L5
FNM GU9 134 E3
KUTN/CMB KT2 9 J3
MTCM CR4 48 E3
RCH/KEW TW9 18 C5
REDH RH1 149 G8
TWK TW1 17 L7
WEY KT13 60 A5
WIM/MER SW19 29 J7
WLGTN SM6 66 E4
St Georges Sq NWMAL KT3 * 46 B3
St George's Wk CROY/NA CR0 2 D6

St Georges Yd *FNM* GU9 5 H3
St German's Rd *FSTH* SE23 33 H2
St Gothard Rd *WNWD* SE27 32 A5
St Helena Ter *RCH/KEW* TW9 * 18 A7
St Helens *THDIT* KT7 * 44 B7
St Helen's Crs
STRHM/NOR SW16 49 J1
St Helen's Rd
STRHM/NOR SW16 49 J2
St Helier Av *MRDN* SM4 47 M7
St Helier Cl *CRAWW* RH11 164 C8
St Heliers Av *HSLWW* TW4 16 D7
St Hilda's Av *ASHF* TW15 23 H6
St Hilda's Cl *CRAWE* RH10 * 165 L1
HORL RH6 160 E3
TOOT SW17 30 B3
WOKN/KNAP GU21 76 A7
St Hilda's Rd *BARN* SW13 19 L1
Saint Hill Rd *EGRIN* RH19 162 C7
St Hughes Cl *TOOT* SW17 * 30 B3
St Hugh's Cl *CRAWE* RH10 165 L1
St Hugh's Rd *PGE/AN* SE20 * 32 E8
St Ives *CRAWE* RH10 * 165 L3
St James Av *EW* KT17 84 C1
FNM GU9 134 A5
SUT SM1 65 K4
St James Cl *EPSOM* KT18 84 B4
NWMAL KT3 46 C5
WOKN/KNAP GU21 76 D8
St James Ga *ASC* SL5 37 J7
CTHM CR3 * 108 D4
St James Ms *WEY* KT13 59 L3
St James Rd *CAR* SM5 66 B2
EGRIN RH19 162 E4
KUT/HW KT1 8 D7
MTCM CR4 30 D8
PUR/KEN CR8 87 L3
SURB KT6 45 G6
SUT SM1 65 K5
St James's Av *BECK* BR3 51 H3
HPTN TW12 25 M6
St James's Cl *TOOT* SW17 * 30 D6
St James's Ct *KUT/HW* KT1 * 8 E9
St James's Dr *BAL* SW12 30 C2
St James's Pk *CROY/NA* CR0 2 C1
St James's Pl *CRAN* GU6 186 B2
St James Sq *SURB* KT6 44 F7
St James's Rd *CROY/NA* CR0 2 B2
HPTN TW12 25 L6
St James's Rw *CHSGTN* KT9 * 63 G5
St James Ter *BAL* SW12 * 30 D2
FNM GU9 5 K1
St Joan Cl *CRAWW* RH11 164 F1
St John Cl *SWTR* RH13 167 H8
St John's *RDKG* RH5 144 F6
St Johns Av *EW* KT17 84 C2
LHD/OX KT22 102 E3
St Johns Church Rd *RDKG* RH5 143 J5
St Johns Cl *BH/WHM* TN16 * 91 L6
GUW GU2 6 A5
LHD/OX KT22 102 F3
St Johns Ct *EGH* TW20 21 K6
FARN GU14 * 92 A4
GDST RH9 * 151 J4
ISLW TW7 17 J4
St John's Crs *HORS* RH12 166 B6
St John's Dr *WAND/EARL* SW18 29 L2
WOT/HER KT12 42 F8
St John's Gv *BARN* SW13 * 19 J4
FNM GU9 5 H8
RCH/KEW TW9 * 18 B6
St John's Hl *COUL/CHIP* CR5 87 K7
St John's Hill Rd
WOKN/KNAP GU21 96 D1
St John's Lye (Festival Path)
WOKN/KNAP GU21 96 C1
St John's Meadow *LING* RH7 177 Q1
St Johns Ms *WOKN/KNAP* GU21 76 D8
St Johns Ri *BH/WHM* TN16 * 91 L6
WOKN/KNAP GU21 96 E1
St John's Rd *CAR* SM5 66 B2
CRAWW RH11 164 E4
CROY/NA CR0 2 B7
DORK RH4 143 M3
E/WMO/HCT KT8 44 A4
EGRIN RH19 162 F3
FARN GU14 92 B5
FELT TW13 25 J5
FNM GU9 5 H8
GUW GU2 138 C1
ISLW TW7 17 J4
KUT/HW KT1 8 B6
LHD/OX KT22 102 F3
NWMAL KT3 45 M3
PGE/AN SE20 32 F8
RCH/KEW TW9 18 B6
REDH RH1 148 C2
SUT SM1 65 K1
WIM/MER SW19 29 H8
WOKN/KNAP GU21 96 D1
St John's Road Rd
WOKN/KNAP GU21 76 E8
St John's St *GODL* GU7 168 C3
St John's Terrace Rd
REDH RH1 148 C2
St John's Wy *CHERT* KT16 58 D1
EDEN TN8 153 L6
St Joseph's Rd *ASHV* GU12 112 D8
St Jude's Cl *EGH* TW20 20 F6
St Jude's Rd *EGH* TW20 20 F5
St Julian's Cl
STRHM/NOR SW16 * 31 K5
St Julian's Farm Rd
WNWD SE27 31 K5
St Katharines Rd *CTHM* CR3 108 D7
St Kitts Ter *NRWD* SE19 32 B6
St Lawrence Wy *CTHM* CR3 108 A5
St Leonards Dr *CRAWE* RH10 165 J7
St Leonard's Gdns *HEST* TW5 16 B2
St Leonard's Rd *CROY/NA* CR0 2 A8
EPSOM KT18 104 F1
ESH/CLAY KT10 62 C5
MORT/ESHN SW14 18 F5
SURB KT6 45 G5
SWTR RH13 167 J8
THDIT KT7 44 D6
St Leonard's Wk
STRHM/NOR SW16 31 J8
St Louis Rd *WNWD* SE27 31 M5
St Luke's Cl *SNWD* SE25 50 E6
St Lukes Ct *WOKN/KNAP* GU21 * 77 M4
St Luke's Rd *CTHM* CR3 88 C8
St Luke's Sq *GU* GU1 7 L6
St Margaret's *GU* GU1 7 L2
KUTN/CMB KT2 * 27 M6
St Margarets Av *ASHF* TW15 23 L6
BH/WHM TN16 * 91 L6
CHEAM SM3 65 H2
EGRIN RH19 178 F11
St Margarets Ct
PUT/ROE SW15 * 19 L6
St Margaret's Crs
PUT/ROE SW15 * 19 L7
St Margarets Dr *EPSOM* KT18 84 A4
TWK TW1 17 L7
St Margaret's Gv *TWK* TW1 17 K8
St Margarets Ms
KUTN/CMB KT2 * 27 M6
St Margaret's Rd
COUL/CHIP CR5 106 E3
EGRIN RH19 163 G2
TWK TW1 17 L6
St Mark Av *CHOB/PIR* GU24 95 L5
St Marks Cl *FARN* GU14 92 F8
St Mark's Hl *SURB* KT6 45 H6
St Mark's La *HORS* RH12 167 H3
St Marks Pl *FNM* GU9 * 133 L2
WIM/MER SW19 * 29 J7
St Marks Rd *EPSOM* KT18 84 F8
MTCM CR4 48 C2
SNWD SE25 50 D4
TEDD TW11 26 E8
St Martha's Av
WOKS/MYFD GU22 97 J3
St Marthas Ct *RGUE* GU4 * 139 L6
St Martin's Av *EPSOM* KT18 84 B4
St Martins Cl *EHSLY* KT24 120 B3
EW KT17 * 84 C3
St Martin's Ct *ASHF* TW15 22 F6
St Martins Dr *WOT/HER* KT12 60 F2
St Martin's La *BECK* BR3 51 L5
St Martins Ms *DORK* RH4 144 D2
WOKS/MYFD GU22 78 D6
St Martin's Wy *TOOT* SW17 29 M4
St Mary Av *WLGTN* SM6 66 D2
St Marys *WEY* KT13 * 60 A2
St Mary's Av *STWL/WRAY* TW19 23 G1
TEDD TW11 * 26 C7
St Mary's Cl *CHSGTN* KT9 63 J6
EW KT17 64 C6
LHD/OX KT22 102 A5
OXTED RH8 130 B3
SUN TW16 42 D4
St Mary's Crs *ISLW* TW7 17 G2
STWL/WRAY TW19 23 G1
St Mary's Dr *CRAWE* RH10 165 K2
EBED/NFELT TW14 23 M1
St Mary's Gdns *BAGS* GU19 54 B6
HORS RH12 166 F8
St Mary's Gn *BH/WHM* TN16 90 F8
St Mary's Gv *BARN* SW13 19 L5
BH/WHM TN16 90 F8
RCH/KEW TW9 18 C6
St Mary's Hl *ASC* SL5 36 F5
St Mary's Mt *CTHM* CR3 108 C6
St Mary's Rd *ASC* SL5 36 E6
ASHV GU12 113 K4
CBLY GU15 72 F3
E/WMO/HCT KT8 44 A5
LHD/OX KT22 102 E4
REIG RH2 147 L1
SAND/SEL CR2 68 A8
SNWD SE25 50 B3
SURB KT6 44 F7
WEY KT13 60 A3
WIM/MER SW19 29 H6
WOKN/KNAP GU21 76 F7
WPK KT4 64 B1
St Marys Ter *GU* GU1 * 7 G7
St Marys Wy *GUW* GU2 116 B6
St Matthew's Av *SURB* KT6 45 H8
St Matthew's Rd *REDH* RH1 126 C7
St Michael's Av *RGUW* GU3 115 M3
St Michael's Cl *WOT/HER* KT12 60 F1
WPK KT4 64 C1
St Michaels Rd *ASHF* TW15 23 K6
ASHV GU12 112 E8
CBLY GU15 * 72 E4
CROY/NA CR0 2 D4
CTHM CR3 108 A4
EGRIN RH19 162 F3
FARN GU14 92 E3
WLGTN SM6 66 F5
WOKN/KNAP GU21 78 A4
St Mildred's Rd *GU* GU1 7 M1
St Monica's Rd
KWD/TDW/WH KT20 105 J3
St Nazaire Cl *EGH* TW20 * 21 M6
St Nicholas Av *GT/LBKH* KT23 101 L7
St Nicholas Crs
WOKS/MYFD GU22 78 D6
St Nicholas Dr *SHPTN* TW17 41 K7
St Nicholas Glebe *TOOT* SW17 30 D7
St Nicholas Hl *LHD/OX* KT22 102 E4
St Nicholas Rd *SUT* SM1 65 L4
THDIT KT7 44 C6
St Nicholas Wy *SUT* SM1 65 L3
St Nicolas Av *CRAN* GU6 186 D2
St Nicolas Cl *CRAN* GU6 186 D2
St Normans Wy *EW* KT17 64 D8
St Olave's Cl *STA* TW18 22 C8
St Olave's Wk
STRHM/NOR SW16 48 F2
St Omer Barracks *ALDT* GU11 113 G4
St Omer Rdg *GU* GU1 139 K1
St Omer Rd *GU* GU1 139 K1
St Oswald's Rd
STRHM/NOR SW16 49 L1
St Paul's Cl *ADL/WDHM* KT15 58 D3
ASHF TW15 23 M6
CAR SM5 48 B7
CHSGTN KT9 63 G3
HSLW TW3 16 C4
RFNM GU10 135 J2
St Pauls Ms *DORK* RH4 144 E3
St Pauls Rd *RCH/KEW* TW9 18 C5
STA TW18 22 A6
THHTH CR7 49 M3
WOKS/MYFD GU22 11 H5
St Paul's Rd East *DORK* RH4 144 E3
St Paul's Rd West *DORK* RH4 144 D3
St Peters *CHERT* KT16 * 57 M2
St Peters Av *BH/WHM* TN16 * 91 L6
St Peter's Cl *STA* TW18 22 C7
TOOT SW17 30 B3
WOKS/MYFD GU22 97 M2
St Peters Ct *E/WMO/HCT* KT8 43 K4
St Peter's Gdns *RFNM* GU10 155 J3
WNWD SE27 31 K4
St Peters Md *ASHV* GU12 113 L7
St Peter's Pk *ALDT* GU11 134 B1
St Peter's Rd *CRAWW* RH11 164 E4
CROY/NA CR0 2 E9
E/WMO/HCT KT8 43 K4
KUT/HW KT1 9 J7
TWK TW1 17 L7
WOKS/MYFD GU22 97 L3
St Peter's St *SAND/SEL* CR2 68 A4
St Peter's Wy *CHERT* KT16 58 B3
FRIM GU16 93 J2
St Philip's Av *WPK* KT4 64 E1
St Philip's Rd *SURB* KT6 45 G6
St Pier's La *LING* RH7 178 G6
St Pinnock Av *STA* TW18 40 D1
St Richards Ms *CRAWE* RH10 * 165 H4
St Sampson Rd *CRAWW* RH11 164 B8
St Saviour Av *CHOB/PIR* GU24 95 L3
St Saviours Pl *GU* GU1 * 6 F4
St Saviour's Rd *CROY/NA* CR0 2 C1
Saints Cl *WNWD* SE27 31 L5
St Simon's Av *PUT/ROE* SW15 19 M7
St Stephens Av *ASHTD* KT21 83 H7
St Stephens Cl *HASM* GU27 198 D6
St Stephens Cl *GDST* RH9 151 H4
St Stephen's Crs *THHTH* CR7 49 K3
St Stephen's Gdns *TWK* TW1 * 17 M8
St Stephen's Rd *HSLW* TW3 16 D8
St Swithun's Cl *EGRIN* RH19 * 163 G4
St Theresa Cl *EPSOM* KT18 83 M4
St Theresa's Rd
EBED/NFELT TW14 15 J6
St Thomas Cl *SURB* KT6 45 J8
WOKN/KNAP GU21 76 F7
St Thomas' Rd *CHSWK* W4 18 F2
St Thomas's Dr *RGUE* GU4 * 119 H5
St Thomas's Ms *GU* GU1 7 L7
St Thomas Wk *DTCH/LGLY* SL3 13 G2
St Vincent Cl *CRAWE* RH10 165 M5
WNWD SE27 31 L6
St Vincent Rd *WHTN* TW2 16 F8
WOT/HER KT12 60 E2
St Winifred's Rd *BH/WHM* TN16 91 J8
TEDD TW11 26 E7
Salamander Cl *KUTN/CMB* KT2 26 F6
Salamander Quay *KUT/HW* KT1 * 8 C5
Salbrook Rd *REDH* RH1 148 D8
Salcombe Dr *MRDN* SM4 47 G8
Salcombe Rd *ASHF* TW15 23 H5
Salcot Crs *CROY/NA* CR0 69 M8
Salcott Rd *CROY/NA* CR0 67 H2
Salehurst Rd *CRAWE* RH10 192 D7
Salem Pl *CROY/NA* CR0 2 B8
Salerno Cl *ALDT* GU11 112 D7
Salesian Vw *FARN* GU14 113 H1
Salford Rd *BRXS/STRHM* SW2 31 G2
Salisbury Av *SUT* SM1 65 J5
Salisbury Cl *WPK* KT4 64 C2
Salisbury Gdns
WIM/MER SW19 * 29 H8
Salisbury Gv *FRIM* GU16 93 K6
Salisbury Pl *BF/WBF* KT14 78 F1
Salisbury Rd *ASHV* GU12 113 K7
BNSTD SM7 85 L5
CAR SM5 66 C5
CRAWE RH10 165 H8
FARN GU14 92 F5
FELT TW13 24 F2
GDST RH9 128 F5
HSLWW TW4 15 M5
NWMAL KT3 46 A3
RCH/KEW TW9 18 B6
SNWD SE25 50 D6
WIM/MER SW19 29 H8
WOKS/MYFD GU22 97 H1
WPK KT4 64 A3
Salisbury Ter *FRIM* GU16 93 K6
Salix Cl *GT/LBKH* KT23 101 L5
SUN TW16 24 E8
Salmons La *CTHM* CR3 108 C2
Salmons La West *CTHM* CR3 108 B2
Salmons Rd *CHSGTN* KT9 63 H5
EHSLY KT24 120 F3
Saltash Cl *SUT* SM1 65 J3
Saltbox Hl *BH/WHM* TN16 90 E3
Salt Box Rd *RGUW* GU3 116 D3
Saltdean Cl *CRAWE* RH10 164 F7
Salterford Rd *TOOT* SW17 30 D7
Salterns Rd *CRAWE* RH10 165 L7
Salter's Hl *NRWD* SE19 32 A6
Saltire Gdns *BNFD* RG42 34 D1
Salt La *MFD/CHID* GU8 168 A11
Saltram Rd *FARN* GU14 93 H7
Salvador *TOOT* SW17 30 B6
Salvation Pl *LHD/OX* KT22 102 D6
Salvington Rd *CRAWW* RH11 164 B7
Salwey Cl *BRAK* RG12 34 E6
Samaritan Cl *CRAWW* RH11 164 A6
Samarkand Cl *CBLY* GU15 73 L5
Samos Rd *PGE/AN* SE20 50 E2
Samphire Cl *CRAWW* RH11 164 C7
Sampleoak La *RGUE* GU4 140 B7
Sampson Pk *BNFD* RG42 34 A1
Samuel Gray Gdns
KUTN/CMB KT2 8 D4
San Carlos Ap *ALDT* GU11 112 F7
Sanctuary Rd *HTHAIR* TW6 14 D8
Sandal Rd *NWMAL* KT3 46 B4
Sandalwood *GUW* GU2 6 C6
Sandalwood Av *CHERT* KT16 58 A2
Sandalwood Rd *FELT* TW13 24 E4
Sandbourne Av
WIM/MER SW19 47 L3
Sandcross La *REIG* RH2 147 J3
Sandell's Av *ASHF* TW15 23 M5
Sandeman Wy *SWTR* RH13 205 M9
Sanders Cl *HPTN* TW12 25 M6
Sandersfield Rd *BNSTD* SM7 85 K5
Sanders Pde
STRHM/NOR SW16 * 31 H7
Sanderstead Cl *BAL* SW12 30 F1
Sanderstead Court Av
SAND/SEL CR2 88 D3
Sanderstead Hl *SAND/SEL* CR2 88 B1
Sanderstead Rd *SAND/SEL* CR2 68 A6
Sandes Pl *LHD/OX* KT22 82 D8
Sandfield Ct *GU* GU1 7 G5
Sandfield Gdns *THHTH* CR7 49 L3
Sandfield Pl *THHTH* CR7 49 M3
Sandfield Rd *THHTH* CR7 49 L3
Sandfields *RPLY/SEND* GU23 98 A6
Sandfield Ter *GU* GU1 7 G5
Sandford Ct *ALDT* GU11 112 C8
Sandford Down *BRAK* RG12 35 J5
Sandford Rd *ALDT* GU11 112 C8
FNM GU9 133 L2
Sandgate La *WAND/EARL* SW18 30 B2
Sandhawes Hl *EGRIN* RH19 163 H1
Sandheath Rd *GSHT* GU26 181 P10
Sand Hl *FARN* GU14 92 E2
Sandhill La *CRAWE* RH10 193 N6
Sandhills *WLGTN* SM6 67 G3
Sandhills Ct *VW* GU25 39 H5
Sandhills La *VW* GU25 39 H5
Sandhills Rd *REIG* RH2 147 K2
Sandhurst Av *BRYLDS* KT5 45 L7
Sandhurst Cl *SAND/SEL* CR2 68 B7
Sandhurst Pde *CAT* SE6 * 33 M2
Sandhurst Wy *SAND/SEL* CR2 68 B6
Sandiford Rd *CHEAM* SM3 65 J1
Sandiland Crs *HAYES* BR2 70 C1
Sandilands *CROY/NA* CR0 3 L7
Sandlands Gv
KWD/TDW/WH KT20 104 D5
Sandlands Rd
KWD/TDW/WH KT20 104 D5
Sandmartin Wy *WLGTN* SM6 48 D8
Sandon Cl *ESH/CLAY* KT10 44 A7
Sandown Av *ESH/CLAY* KT10 61 M4
Sandown Cl *BLKW* GU17 72 A4
HEST TW5 15 K3
Sandown Ct *BELMT* SM2 * 65 L6
SYD SE26 * 32 E4
Sandown Crs *ALDT* GU11 134 E2
Sandown Dr *CAR* SM5 66 D7
FRIM GU16 73 G7
Sandown Ga *ESH/CLAY* KT10 62 A1
Sandown Rd *COUL/CHIP* CR5 86 D6
ESH/CLAY KT10 61 M3
SNWD SE25 50 E5
Sandpiper Cl *CRAWW* RH11 190 G9
Sandpiper Rd *SAND/SEL* CR2 89 G1
SUT SM1 65 J4
Sandpit Hall Rd *CHOB/PIR* GU24 76 D2
Sandpit Heath *RGUW* GU3 116 A4
Sandpit Rd *REDH* RH1 148 B1
Sandpits Rd *CROY/NA* CR0 69 G3
RCHPK/HAM TW10 27 G3
Sandra Cl *HSLW* TW3 16 E7
Sandringham Av *RYNPK* SW20 47 H1
Sandringham Cl
WIM/MER SW19 * 29 G2
WOKS/MYFD GU22 78 D6
Sandringham Dr *ASHF* TW15 23 G5
Sandringham Gdns
E/WMO/HCT KT8 43 K4
HEST TW5 15 K3
Sandringham Ms *HPTN* TW12 43 J1
Sandringham Pk *COB* KT11 81 J2
Sandringham Rd
CRAWW RH11 164 D8
HTHAIR TW6 14 B7
THHTH CR7 49 M5
WPK KT4 64 D2
Sandringham Wy *FRIM* GU16 93 J1
Sandrock *HASM* GU27 198 D7
Sandrock Hill Rd *RFNM* GU10 155 J3
Sandrock Pl *CROY/NA* CR0 69 G3
Sandrock Rd *DORK* RH4 143 L4
Sandroyd Wy *COB* KT11 81 K3
Sands Cl *RFNM* GU10 135 G7
Sands Rd *RFNM* GU10 134 F7
Sandy Cl *WOKS/MYFD* GU22 11 L6
Sandycombe Rd
EBED/NFELT TW14 24 D2
RCH/KEW TW9 18 D4
Sandycoombe Rd *TWK* TW1 17 M8
Sandy Ct *COB* KT11 81 J3
Sandy Cft *EW* KT17 64 F8
Sandy Dr *COB* KT11 81 K1
EBED/NFELT TW14 24 B2
Sandy Hill Rd *FNM* GU9 133 K2
WLGTN SM6 66 F7
Sandy Holt *COB* KT11 81 J3
Sandy La *ASC* SL5 35 M1
ASC SL5 37 K5
BELMT SM2 65 H7
BRAK RG12 34 F1
BRKHM/BTCW RH3 124 B8
CBLY GU15 73 H3
CHOB/PIR GU24 56 B7
COB KT11 81 J2
CRAWE RH10 193 M5
EGRIN RH19 162 F4
GODL GU7 168 A3
HASM GU27 197 P6
HASM GU27 198 F4
KWD/TDW/WH KT20 105 K5
MFD/CHID GU8 183 L1
MTCM CR4 48 D1
OXTED RH8 129 M3
OXTED RH8 130 E1
RCHPK/HAM TW10 26 F3
REDH RH1 127 H8
REDH RH1 127 L6
REDH RH1 149 G1
REIG RH2 146 E1
RFNM GU10 155 M8
RFNM GU10 181 M3
RGUW GU3 138 D5
RPLY/SEND GU23 97 M5
SHGR GU5 141 G7
TEDD TW11 26 D8
VW GU25 39 H5
WOKS/MYFD GU22 11 L6
WOKS/MYFD GU22 78 D6
WOT/HER KT12 42 E6
Sandy La North *WLGTN* SM6 67 G4
Sandy La South *WLGTN* SM6 66 F7
Sandy Md *HOR/WEW* KT19 63 K7
Sandy Rd *ADL/WDHM* KT15 58 D5
Sandy Wy *COB* KT11 81 K2
CROY/NA CR0 69 J2
WOKS/MYFD GU22 11 L6
WOT/HER KT12 42 C8
San Feliu Ct *EGRIN* RH19 163 J3
Sanger Av *CHSGTN* KT9 63 J4
Sanger Dr *RPLY/SEND* GU23 97 M4
Sangers Dr *HORL* RH6 160 C4
Sangley Rd *CAT* SE6 33 L2
SNWD SE25 50 B4
Santina Cl *FNM* GU9 134 A1
Sanway Cl *BF/WBF* KT14 79 H4
Sanway Rd *BF/WBF* KT14 79 H4
Sappho Ct *WOKN/KNAP* GU21 76 B6
Sapte Cl *CRAN* GU6 186 F2
Saracen Cl *CROY/NA* CR0 50 A6
Sarah Wy *FARN* GU14 92 E5
Sarel Wy *HORL* RH6 160 E1
Sargent Cl *CRAWE* RH10 165 H8
Sark Cl *CRAWW* RH11 164 C8
HEST TW5 16 D2
Sarsby Dr *STWL/WRAY* TW19 21 K3
Sarsen Av *HSLW* TW3 16 C4
Sarsfeld Rd *BAL* SW12 30 C2
Sarum *BRAK* RG12 34 B8
Sarum Gn *WEY* KT13 60 B2
Saturn Cl *CRAWW* RH11 164 A6
Saunders Cl *CRAWE* RH10 165 K4
Saunders Copse
WOKS/MYFD GU22 96 E4
Saunders La *WOKS/MYFD* GU22 96 C4
Saunton Av *HYS/HAR* UB3 15 J2
Saunton Gdns *FARN* GU14 92 D3
Savernake Wk *CRAWE* RH10 165 H7
Savernake Wy *BRAK* RG12 35 J6
Savery Dr *SURB* KT6 44 F7
Savile Cl *NWMAL* KT3 46 B5
THDIT KT7 44 C8
Savile Gdns *CROY/NA* CR0 3 K6
Saville Crs *ASHF* TW15 24 A7
Saville Gdns *CBLY* GU15 73 L4
Saville Rd *TWK* TW1 26 C2
Savill Gdns *RYNPK* SW20 46 D3
Savill Ms *EGH* TW20 21 G7
Savona Cl *WIM/MER* SW19 29 G8
Savoy Gv *BLKW* GU17 72 A6
Sawkins Cl *WIM/MER* SW19 29 G3
Sawtry Cl *CAR* SM5 48 A7
Sawyer's Hl *RCHPK/HAM* TW10 27 J1
Saxby Rd *BRXS/STRHM* SW2 31 H1
Saxby's La *LING* RH7 178 F4
Saxley *HORL* RH6 160 F2
Saxon Av *FELT* TW13 25 J3
Saxonbury Av *SUN* TW16 42 E3
Saxonbury Cl *MTCM* CR4 48 A3
Saxonbury Gdns *SURB* KT6 44 F8
Saxon Cl *SURB* KT6 45 G6
Saxon Crs *HORS* RH12 166 E5
Saxon Cft *FNM* GU9 5 J5
Saxon Dr *BNFD* RG42 35 J1
Saxonfield Cl *BRXS/STRHM* SW2 31 J1
Saxon Rd *ASHF* TW15 24 A7
CRAWE RH10 192 D8
KUTN/CMB KT2 8 E4
SNWD SE25 50 A5
WOT/HER KT12 61 G2
Saxons *KWD/TDW/WH* KT20 105 G3
Saxon Wy *REIG* RH2 125 J7
WDR/YW UB7 13 M1
Sayers Cl *FRIM* GU16 93 H2
LHD/OX KT22 101 M6
SWTR RH13 167 H7
The Sayers *EGRIN* RH19 162 D4
Sayes Ct *ADL/WDHM* KT15 58 E4
Sayes Court Farm Dr
ADL/WDHM KT15 58 E4
Sbac Tr *ALDT* GU11 112 B3
Scallows Cl *CRAWE* RH10 165 J3
Scallows Rd *CRAWE* RH10 165 J3
Scampton Rd
STWL/WRAY TW19 14 C8
Scarborough Cl *BELMT* SM2 85 J1
BH/WHM TN16 90 F8
Scarborough Rd *HTHAIR* TW6 14 F8
Scarbrook Rd *CROY/NA* CR0 2 C8
Scarlet Oaks *CBLY* GU15 73 H6
Scarlett Cl *WOKN/KNAP* GU21 76 C8
Scarlett's Rd *ALDT* GU11 112 D6
Scarth Rd *BARN* SW13 19 J5
Scawen Cl *CAR* SM5 66 D3
Scholars Rd *BAL* SW12 30 F2
Scholars Wk *GUW* GU2 6 D5
School Cl *CHOB/PIR* GU24 75 J5
GU GU1 117 G6
HORS RH12 167 K3
School Fld *EDEN* TN8 153 M7
School Hl *CWTH* RG45 52 A5
HORS RH12 166 C1
REDH RH1 126 F2
RFNM GU10 135 L5
RFNM GU10 155 J3
School House La *TEDD* TW11 26 E8
School La *ADL/WDHM* KT15 58 D3
ASC SL5 36 A1
BAGS GU19 54 A7
BFOR GU20 55 G5
CHOB/PIR GU24 95 H4
DORK RH4 144 A3
EGH TW20 21 K6
EGRIN RH19 163 L7
EHSLY KT24 119 L3
FROW RH18 195 N11
KUT/HW KT1 8 B5
LHD/OX KT22 102 A4
MFD/CHID GU8 159 H3
MFD/CHID GU8 199 Q1
RDKG RH5 122 F1
RFNM GU10 154 A4
RFNM GU10 156 A3
RGUE GU4 119 H5
RGUW GU3 114 C5
RGUW GU3 136 F5
RPLY/SEND GU23 99 L4
SHPTN TW17 41 L6
SURB KT6 45 K8
School Meadow *GUW* GU2 116 B7
School Pas *KUT/HW* KT1 9 H7
School Rd *ASC* SL5 37 G5
ASHF TW15 23 L7
BFOR GU20 54 E4
E/WMO/HCT KT8 44 A4
GSHT GU26 197 N2
HASM GU27 198 A8
HPTN TW12 25 M7
HSLW TW3 16 F5

KUT/HW KT1 8 B5
RFNM GU10 155 H6
WDR/YW UB7 14 A1
School Road Av HPTN TW12 25 M7
Schroder Ct EGH TW20 20 E6
Scillonian Rd GUW GU2 6 B7
Scizdons Climb GODL GU7 168 C5
Scoles Crs BRXS/STRHM SW2 31 K2
Scope Wy KUT/HW KT1 45 H4
Scory Cl CRAWW RH11 164 C7
Scotia Rd BRXS/STRHM SW2 31 K1
Scotland Bridge Rd
ADL/WDHM KT15 78 D1
Scotland Cl ASHV GU12 113 K4
Scotland Farm Rd ASHV GU12 113 K4
Scotland La HASM GU27 198 D8
Scotlands Cl HASM GU27 198 C8
Scotlands Dr HASM GU27 198 C8
Scotney Cl ORP BR6 71 K3
Scots Cl STWL/WRAY TW19 23 G2
Scotsdale Cl CHEAM SM3 65 H6
Scotshall La WARL CR6 89 M5
Scott Cl GUW GU2 116 D6
HOR/WEW KT19 63 M4
STRHM/NOR SW16 49 J1
Scott Farm Cl THDIT KT7 44 E8
Scott Gdns HEST TW5 16 A2
Scott Rd CRAWE RH10 165 H7
Scotts Av SUN TW16 24 B8
Scott's Ct FARN GU14 92 E2
Scotts Dr HPTN TW12 25 L8
Scotts Farm Rd
HOR/WEW KT19 63 M5
Scott's Grove Cl
CHOB/PIR GU24 76 A3
Scott's Grove Rd
CHOB/PIR GU24 75 L4
Scott's Hl HORL RH6 177 J5
Scotts Ms ASC SL5 35 L1
Scotts Wy SUN TW16 24 B8
Scott Ter BRAK RG12 35 H1
Scott Trimmer Wy HSLW TW3 16 B4
Scratchings La PETW GU28 200 D12
Scylla Crs HTHAIR TW6 23 L1
Scylla Pl WOKN/KNAP GU21 * 96 D1
Scylla Rd HTHAIR TW6 14 E8
Seabrook Dr WWKM BR4 70 B1
Seafire Wy ALDT GU11 112 B2
Seaford Rd CRAWW RH11 191 K12
HTHAIR TW6 14 A7
Seaforth Av NWMAL KT3 46 E5
Seaforth Gdns HOR/WEW KT19 64 C3
Sealand Rd HTHAIR TW6 14 D8
Seale La RFNM GU10 135 G5
RGUW GU3 136 C5
Seale Rd RFNM GU10 157 L1
Seaman's Gn RDKG RH5 173 L9
Searchwood Rd WARL CR6 88 E8
Searle Hl REIG RH2 147 K2
Searle Rd FNM GU9 5 J7
Searle's Vw HORS RH12 167 J4
Seaton Cl PUT/ROE SW15 28 E1
WHTN TW2 17 G8
Seaton Dr ASHF TW15 23 H3
Seaton Rd CBLY GU15 72 E4
MTCM CR4 48 B2
WHTN TW2 16 F8
Sebastopol Rd ALDT GU11 112 E7
MFD/CHID GU8 183 L9
Second Av ADL/WDHM KT15 58 E7
KWD/TDW/WH KT20 * 105 J8
MORT/ESHN SW14 19 H5
WOT/HER KT12 42 E6
Second Cl E/WMO/HCT KT8 43 L4
Second Cross Rd WHTN TW2 26 A3
Seddon Rd MRDN SM4 48 A5
Sedgefield Cl CRAWE RH10 192 D6
Sedgehill Rd CAT SE6 33 K6
Sedgemoor FARN GU14 92 E2
Sedgewick Cl CRAWE RH10 165 L4
Seebys Oak SHST GU47 72 A3
Seeley Dr DUL SE21 32 B5
Seely Rd TOOT SW17 30 D7
Seething Wells La SURB KT6 44 F6
Sefton Cl CHOB/PIR GU24 75 J3
Sefton Rd CROY/NA CR0 3 M4
HOR/WEW KT19 64 A8
Sefton St PUT/ROE SW15 19 M4
Segrave Cl WEY KT13 59 K6
Segsbury Gv BRAK RG12 35 H4
Sekhon Ter FELT TW13 25 K4
Selborne Av ALDT GU11 134 F2
Selborne Gdns FNM GU9 4 E9
Selborne Rd CROY/NA CR0 3 H8
NWMAL KT3 46 B2
Selbourne Av ADL/WDHM KT15 58 E8
SURB KT6 63 J1
Selbourne Cl ADL/WDHM KT15 58 E8
CRAWE RH10 192 C3
Selbourne Rd RGUE GU4 117 K5
Selbourne Sq GDST RH9 128 F4
Selby Cl CHSGTN KT9 63 H6
Selby Gn CAR SM5 48 B7
Selby Rd ASHF TW15 23 M7
CAR SM5 48 B7
PGE/AN SE20 50 D2
Selbys LING RH7 178 F4
Selby Wk WOKN/KNAP GU21 76 E8
Selcroft Rd PUR/KEN CR8 87 L2
Selham Cl CRAWW RH11 164 C3
Selhurst Cl WIM/MER SW19 29 G2
WOKN/KNAP GU21 10 F1
Selhurst New Rd SNWD SE25 50 B6
Selhurst Pl SNWD SE25 50 B6
Selhurst Rd SNWD SE25 50 B5
Selkirk Rd TOOT SW17 30 B5
WHTN TW2 25 M3
Sellar's Hl GODL GU7 168 A2
Sellincourt Rd TOOT SW17 30 B6
Sellindge Cl BECK BR3 33 J8
Sells Cl GU GU1 7 M7
Selsdon Av SAND/SEL CR2 68 A5
Selsdon Cl SURB KT6 45 H5
Selsdon Crs SAND/SEL CR2 68 F8
Selsdon Park Rd CROY/NA CR0 69 H7
Selsdon Rd ADL/WDHM KT15 78 D1
SAND/SEL CR2 68 A4
WNWD SE27 31 L4
Selsey Rd CRAWW RH11 164 C8
Selsfield Rd CRAWE RH10 193 M11
Seltops Cl CRAN GU6 186 E3
Selwood Cl STWL/WRAY TW19 * 13 M8
Selwood Gdns
STWL/WRAY TW19 13 M8
Selwood Rd CHEAM SM3 47 J8
CHSGTN KT9 63 G3
CROY/NA CR0 68 E1
WOKS/MYFD GU22 97 L2
Selworthy Rd CAT SE6 33 J4
Selwyn Av RCH/KEW TW9 18 C5
Selwyn Cl CRAWE RH10 165 L1
HSLWW TW4 16 B6
Selwyn Rd NWMAL KT3 46 A5
Semaphore Rd GU GU1 7 J8
Semley Rd STRHM/NOR SW16 49 H2
Semper Cl WOKN/KNAP GU21 76 B7
Send Barns La
RPLY/SEND GU23 98 B6
Send Cl RPLY/SEND GU23 97 M5
Send Hl RPLY/SEND GU23 97 M7
Send Marsh Rd
RPLY/SEND GU23 98 B5
Send Parade Cl
RPLY/SEND GU23 * 97 M5
Send Rd RPLY/SEND GU23 97 M5
Seneca Rd THHTH CR7 49 M4
Senga Rd WLGTN SM6 48 D8
Senhouse Rd CHEAM SM3 65 G2
Sentamu Cl HNHL SE24 31 L2
Sequoia Pk CRAWW RH11 164 F6
Serrin Wy HORS RH12 167 H4
Service Rd HORL RH6 160 D7
Setley Wy BRAK RG12 35 J3
Seven Acres CAR SM5 66 B1
Seven Arches Ap WEY KT13 59 J6
Seven Hills Cl WOT/HER KT12 60 B7
Seven Hills Rd (South)
COB KT11 80 B3
Seven Hills Rd WEY KT13 60 B6
Seven Kings Wy KUTN/CMB KT2 8 E4
Sevenoaks Cl BELMT SM2 65 K8
Seventh Av
KWD/TDW/WH KT20 * 105 J8
Severn Dr ESH/CLAY KT10 62 D1
WOT/HER KT12 61 G1
Severn Rd CRAWE RH10 165 L5
FARN GU14 92 B3
Seward Rd BECK BR3 51 G2
Sewer's Farm Rd RDKG RH5 172 A3
Sewill Cl HORL RH6 175 J10
Seymour Av CTHM CR3 107 M5
EW KT17 64 F7
MRDN SM4 47 G7
Seymour Cl E/WMO/HCT KT8 43 M5
Seymour Ct COB KT11 * 80 C3
Seymour Dr CBLY GU15 73 L1
Seymour Gdns BRYLDS KT5 45 J5
FELT TW13 24 E5
TWK TW1 26 E1
Seymour Ms EW KT17 64 D8
Seymour Pl SNWD SE25 50 E4
WOKS/MYFD GU22 96 E2
Seymour Rd BOR GU35 196 H1
CAR SM5 66 D4
CRAWW RH11 164 C8
E/WMO/HCT KT8 43 M5
GODL GU7 159 L6
HPTN TW12 25 M6
KUT/HW KT1 8 C4
MTCM CR4 48 D7
WAND/EARL SW18 29 J1
WIM/MER SW19 29 G4
Seymour Ter PGE/AN SE20 50 E1
Seymour Vls PGE/AN SE20 50 E1
Seymour Wy SUN TW16 24 B7
Shackleford Rd
MFD/CHID GU8 158 C6
MFD/CHID GU8 159 G2
WOKS/MYFD GU22 97 K2
Shacklegate La TEDD TW11 26 B5
Shackleton Cl ASHV GU12 113 J3
FSTH SE23 32 E3
Shackleton Rd CRAWE RH10 165 G7
Shackstead La GODL GU7 159 M6
Shadbolt Cl WPK KT4 64 C1
Shadyhanger GODL GU7 168 B3
Shady Nook FNM GU9 133 L3
Shaef Wy TEDD TW11 26 D8
Shaftesbury Av
EBED/NFELT TW14 15 K8
Shaftesbury Cl BRAK RG12 35 G5
Shaftesbury Crs STA TW18 23 G8
Shaftesbury Rd BECK BR3 51 J2
CAR SM5 48 A7
CHOB/PIR GU24 75 J6
CRAWE RH10 165 M6
RCH/KEW TW9 18 B5
WOKS/MYFD GU22 11 J6
Shaftesbury Wy WHTN TW2 26 A4
Shakespeare Av
EBED/NFELT TW14 15 K8
Shakespeare Gdns FARN GU14 92 A4
Shakespeare Rd
ADL/WDHM KT15 59 G3
Shakespeare Ter
RCH/KEW TW9 * 18 D5
Shakespeare Wy BNFD RG42 35 H1
FELT TW13 24 F5
Shalbourne Ri CBLY GU15 73 G4
Shalden Rd ASHV GU12 135 G1
Shaldon Dr MRDN SM4 47 H5
Shaldon Wy WOT/HER KT12 60 F2
Shalesbrook La FROW RH18 195 N12
Shalford Cl ORP BR6 71 M3
Shalford La RGUE GU4 139 H5
Shalford Rd GU GU1 139 G3
Shalstone Rd
MORT/ESHN SW14 18 E5
Shalston Vls SURB KT6 45 J6
The Shambles GU GU1 7 G7
Shamrock Cl FRIM GU16 93 G1
LHD/OX KT22 102 A3
Shamrock Rd CROY/NA CR0 49 J6
Shandys Cl HORS RH12 166 D8
Shanklin Ct ASHV GU12 112 F8
Shannon Wy BECK BR3 33 L7
Shap Crs CAR SM5 48 C8
Sharland Cl THHTH CR7 49 K6
Sharon Cl CRAWE RH10 165 J7
GT/LBKH KT23 101 K6
HOR/WEW KT19 83 M3
SURB KT6 44 F8
Sharpthorne Cl CRAWW RH11 164 B4
Shaw Cl CHERT KT16 57 M5
EW KT17 84 C1
SAND/SEL CR2 88 C2
Shaw Crs SAND/SEL CR2 88 B2
Shaw Dr WOT/HER KT12 42 F7
Shawfield La ASHV GU12 113 J7
Shawfield Rd ASHV GU12 113 J8
Shawford Rd HOR/WEW KT19 64 A5
Shaw Gv KWD/TDW/WH KT20 105 H6
Shawley Crs EPSOM KT18 84 F8
Shawley Wy EPSOM KT18 84 F8
Shaw Rd BH/WHM TN16 110 F2
Shaws Cottages FSTH SE23 33 H4
Shaws Rd CRAWE RH10 165 G3
Shaw Wy WLGTN SM6 67 H6
Shaxton Crs CROY/NA CR0 69 M7
Shearing Dr CAR SM5 47 M7
Shearwater Rd SUT SM1 65 J4
Sheath La LHD/OX KT22 81 L3
Sheen Common Dr
RCHPK/HAM TW10 18 D6
Sheen Court Rd
RCHPK/HAM TW10 18 D6
Sheendale Rd RCH/KEW TW9 18 C6
Sheenewood SYD SE26 32 E6
Sheen Gate Gdns
MORT/ESHN SW14 18 F6
Sheen La MORT/ESHN SW14 18 F6
Sheen Pk RCH/KEW TW9 18 C6
Sheen Rd RCH/KEW TW9 18 B6
Sheen Wy WLGTN SM6 67 J4
Sheen Wd MORT/ESHN SW14 18 F7
Sheepbarn La WARL CR6 90 D2
Sheepcote Cl HEST TW5 15 K2
Sheepfold Rd GUW GU2 116 C5
Sheephatch La RFNM GU10 156 E4
Sheephouse FNM GU9 5 J7
Sheephouse Gn RDKG RH5 143 J5
Sheephouse La RDKG RH5 143 J5
RDKG RH5 172 B2
Sheephouse Wy NWMAL KT3 46 B7
Sheeplands Av GU GU1 117 M6
Sheep Wk REIG RH2 125 J5
Sheepwalk SHPTN TW17 41 J6
Sheep Walk Ms WIM/MER SW19 29 G7
Sheerwater Av
ADL/WDHM KT15 78 C2
Sheerwater Rd
ADL/WDHM KT15 78 B2
Sheet's Heath La
CHOB/PIR GU24 95 K1
Sheffield Cl CRAWE RH10 165 K6
FARN GU14 92 C5
Sheffield Rd HTHAIR TW6 14 F8
Sheffield Wy HTHAIR TW6 15 G7
Shelburne Dr HSLWW TW4 16 D8
Sheldon Cl CRAWE RH10 165 M5
PGE/AN SE20 50 E1
REIG RH2 147 L1
Sheldon Ct GU GU1 7 L5
Sheldon St CROY/NA CR0 2 C8
Sheldrick Cl MTCM CR4 48 A2
Shelford Ri NRWD SE19 32 B8
Shelley Av BRAK RG12 35 H2
Shelley Cl BNSTD SM7 85 G5
COUL/CHIP CR5 87 J7
CRAWE RH10 165 L2
Shelley Ct CBLY GU15 72 F4
Shelley Crs HEST TW5 16 A3
Shelley Dr HORS RH12 204 D6
Shelley Rd EGRIN RH19 162 E4
HORS RH12 166 E6
Shelleys Ct SWTR RH13 * 167 K6
Shelley Wy WIM/MER SW19 30 A7
Shellfield Cl STWL/WRAY TW19 13 K7
Shellwood Dr RDKG RH5 144 F6
Shellwood Rd REIG RH2 146 A7
Shelly Ri FARN GU14 92 C3
Shellys Ct SWTR RH13 * 167 K6
Shelson Av FELT TW13 24 C5
Shelson Pde FELT TW13 * 24 C4
Shelton Av WARL CR6 88 F8
Shelton Cl GUW GU2 116 D3
WARL CR6 88 F7
Shelton Rd WIM/MER SW19 47 K1
Shelvers Gn
KWD/TDW/WH KT20 104 F3
Shelvers Hl
KWD/TDW/WH KT20 104 E3
Shelvers Sp
KWD/TDW/WH KT20 104 F3
Shelvers Wy
KWD/TDW/WH KT20 104 F3
Shenfield Cl COUL/CHIP CR5 106 E1
Shenley Rd HEST TW5 16 B3
Shenstone Pk ASC SL5 37 H4
Shepherd Cl CRAWE RH10 164 F7
FELT TW13 25 H5
Shepherd & Flock Rbt
FNM GU9 134 C5
Shepherds Cha BAGS GU19 54 B7
Shepherds Cl SHPTN TW17 41 L6
Shepherdsgrove La
EGRIN RH19 179 N12
Shepherds Hl BRAK RG12 34 F1
GUW GU2 116 D6
HASM GU27 198 D7
REDH RH1 106 F8
Shepherds La BFOR GU20 55 K4
GUW GU2 116 C5
Shepherds' Wk EPSOM KT18 103 L3
FARN GU14 92 B2
Shepherds Wy HORS RH12 167 K4
LIPH GU30 197 J10
RFNM GU10 156 F5
RGUE GU4 139 H5
SAND/SEL CR2 69 G6
Shepley Cl CAR SM5 66 D2
Shepley Dr ASC SL5 37 M5
Shepley End ASC SL5 37 M5
Sheppard Cl KUT/HW KT1 45 H4
Shepperton Court Dr
SHPTN TW17 41 L5
Shepperton Rd STA TW18 41 G4
Sheppey Cl CRAWW RH11 164 D8
Sheraton Cl BLKW GU17 72 B5
Sheraton Dr HOR/WEW KT19 83 M3
Sheraton Wk CRAWW RH11 * 191 L12
Sherborne Cl DTCH/LGLY SL3 13 H3
EPSOM KT18 84 F7
Sherborne Ct GUW GU2 * 6 F7
Sherborne Crs CAR SM5 48 B7
Sherborne Rd CHEAM SM3 65 K1
CHSGTN KT9 63 H4
EBED/NFELT TW14 24 A2
FARN GU14 113 G1
Sherbourne SHGR GU5 141 G5
Sherbourne Dr ASC SL5 38 A5
Sherbourne Gdns SHPTN TW17 42 B7
Sherbrooke Wy WPK KT4 46 E7
Shere Av BELMT SM2 64 F8
Shere Cl CHSGTN KT9 63 G4
RDKG RH5 144 F6
Shere La SHGR GU5 141 K5
Shere Rd CRAN GU6 171 J10
EHSLY KT24 119 M4
EHSLY KT24 141 M1
RGUE GU4 140 E2
SHGR GU5 141 H4
Sherfield Cl NWMAL KT3 45 L4
Sherfield Gdns PUT/ROE SW15 19 J8
Sheridan Cl ALDT GU11 134 D1
EGRIN RH19 162 D4
Sheridan Ct HSLWW TW4 16 B7
Sheridan Dr REIG RH2 125 L6
Sheridan Gra ASC SL5 37 K6
Sheridan Pl HPTN TW12 43 L1
Sheridan Rd FRIM GU16 93 G1
RCHPK/HAM TW10 26 F4
WIM/MER SW19 47 J1
Sheridans Rd GT/LBKH KT23 101 M8
Sheridan Wk CAR SM5 66 C4
Sheridan Wy BECK BR3 51 J1
Sheringham Av WHTN TW2 25 J2
Sheringham Rd PGE/AN SE20 50 E2
Sherington Cl FARN GU14 92 E3
Sherland Rd TWK TW1 26 C2
Shernden La EDEN TN8 179 R4
Sherriff Cl ESH/CLAY KT10 61 L1
Sherringham Av FELT TW13 24 D4
Sherrydon CRAN GU6 186 E1
Sherwin Crs FARN GU14 92 E1
Sherwood SURB KT6 63 G1
Sherwood Av
STRHM/NOR SW16 31 G8
Sherwood Cl BRAK RG12 35 K2
LHD/OX KT22 101 M5
WOKN/KNAP GU21 76 B7
Sherwood Crs REIG RH2 147 L4
Sherwood Park Rd MTCM CR4 48 F4
SUT SM1 65 K4
Sherwood Rd COUL/CHIP CR5 86 F6
CROY/NA CR0 50 E7
HPTN TW12 25 M6
WIM/MER SW19 29 J8
Sherwood Wk CRAWE RH10 165 H7
Sherwood Wy WWKM BR4 69 M1
Shetland Cl CRAWE RH10 192 D6
RGUE GU4 117 L3
Shewens Rd WEY KT13 60 A3
Shey Copse WOKS/MYFD GU22 11 L6
Shield Dr BTFD TW8 17 L1
Shield Rd ASHF TW15 23 M5
Shifford Pth FSTH SE23 33 G4
Shilburn Wy WOKN/KNAP GU21 76 D8
Shildon Cl CBLY GU15 74 A6
Shillinglee Rd BIL RH14 200 G6
MFD/CHID GU8 199 Q8
MFD/CHID GU8 200 B5
The Shimmings GU GU1 117 K7
Shinners Cl SNWD SE25 50 D5
Shinwell Wk CRAWW RH11 * 164 D8
Ship Aly FARN GU14 92 F3
Ship Field Cl BH/WHM TN16 110 F3
Ship Hl BH/WHM TN16 111 G3
Shipka Rd BAL SW12 30 E2
Ship La FARN GU14 92 F3
MORT/ESHN SW14 18 F5
Shipleybridge La HORL RH6 176 E12
Shipley Ct LIPH GU30 196 G10
Shipley Rd CRAWW RH11 164 C4
Shipman Rd FSTH SE23 33 G3
Ship St EGRIN RH19 162 F5
Ship Yd WEY KT13 59 K2
Shirburn Cl FSTH SE23 32 F1
Shire Cl BAGS GU19 54 B7
Shire Ct EW KT17 64 C6
Shire Horse Wy ISLW TW7 17 J5
Shire La ORP BR6 71 J6
Shire Pde CRAWE RH10 * 165 M3
Shire Pl CRAWE RH10 * 165 M3
REDH RH1 148 C2
Shires Cl ASHTD KT21 103 G1
The Shires RCHPK/HAM TW10 27 H5
Shirley Av BELMT SM2 65 J8
COUL/CHIP CR5 107 L1
CROY/NA CR0 50 F8
REDH RH1 148 C5
SUT SM1 66 B3
Shirley Church Rd
CROY/NA CR0 69 G2
Shirley Cl HSLW TW3 16 F7
Shirley Crs BECK BR3 51 H4
Shirley Dr HSLW TW3 16 F7
Shirley Hills Rd CROY/NA CR0 69 G4
Shirley Oaks Rd CROY/NA CR0 51 G8
Shirley Park Rd CROY/NA CR0 50 E8
Shirley Pl WOKN/KNAP GU21 75 M7
Shirley Rd CROY/NA CR0 50 E8
WLGTN SM6 66 F7
Shirley Rw SNWD SE25 * 50 D2
Shirley Wy CROY/NA CR0 69 J2
Shoe La ALDT GU11 112 D3
Shophouse La SHGR GU5 170 C2
Shord Hl PUR/KEN CR8 88 A6
Shore Cl EBED/NFELT TW14 24 D1
HPTN TW12 25 H6
Shore Gv FELT TW13 25 K3
Shoreham Cl CROY/NA CR0 50 F6
Shoreham Rd CRAWE RH10 165 L7
Shoreham Rd (East)
HTHAIR TW6 14 B7
Shoreham Rd (West)
HTHAIR TW6 14 B7
Shore's Rd WOKN/KNAP GU21 77 H4
Shorndean St CAT SE6 33 M2
Shortacres REDH RH1 127 J7
Short Cl CRAWW RH11 164 F2
Shortcroft Rd EW KT17 64 C6
Short Dale Rd ALDT GU11 134 F3
Shortfield Rd RFNM GU10 155 M8
Short Gallop CRAWE RH10 * 165 M3
Shortheath Crest FNM GU9 155 J3
Shortheath Rd FNM GU9 155 K3
Shortlands HYS/HAR UB3 15 G1
Shortlands Rd KUTN/CMB KT2 9 H3
Short La OXTED RH8 130 E6
STWL/WRAY TW19 23 J1
Short Rd CHSWK W4 19 H1
HTHAIR TW6 14 B8
Shortsfield Cl HORS RH12 166 F4
Shorts Rd CAR SM5 66 B3
Short St ALDT GU11 112 D7
Short Wy WHTN TW2 25 M1
Shortwood Av STA TW18 22 E4
Shotfield WLGTN SM6 66 E5
Shott Cl SUT SM1 65 M4
Shottermill HORS RH12 167 K2
Shottermill Pk HASM GU27 * 197 R6
Shottfield Av
MORT/ESHN SW14 19 H6
Shovelstrode La EGRIN RH19 163 L5
Shrewsbury Av
MORT/ESHN SW14 18 F6
Shrewsbury Cl SURB KT6 63 H1
Shrewsbury Rd BECK BR3 51 H3
CAR SM5 48 B7
HTHAIR TW6 14 F8
REDH RH1 126 B8
Shrewton Rd TOOT SW17 * 30 C8
Shrivenham Cl SHST GU47 72 A1
Shropshire Cl MTCM CR4 49 H4
Shrubbery Rd
STRHM/NOR SW16 31 H5
The Shrubbery FARN GU14 92 A6
SURB KT6 * 45 H8
Shrubbs Hl CHOB/PIR GU24 55 M7
Shrubbs Hill La ASC SL5 37 M6
Shrubbs La RFNM GU10 155 J5
Shrubland Gv WPK KT4 64 F2
Shrubland Rd BNSTD SM7 85 J6
Shrublands Av CROY/NA CR0 69 K3
Shrublands Cl SYD SE26 32 F4
Shrublands Dr LTWR GU18 74 E1
Shurlock Dr ORP BR6 71 M3
Sibthorp Rd MTCM CR4 * 48 C2
Sibton Rd CAR SM5 48 B7
Sickle Rd HASM GU27 198 A8
Sidbury Cl ASC SL5 37 K5
Siddeley Dr HSLWW TW4 16 B5
Siddons Rd CROY/NA CR0 67 K2
FSTH SE23 33 H3
Sidestrand Rd ALDT GU11 112 B2
Sideways La HORL RH6 175 M8
The Sidings ALDT GU11 112 F6
STA TW18 22 E5
Sidlaws Rd FARN GU14 92 A2
Sidmouth Av ISLW TW7 17 H4
Sidney Gdns BTFD TW8 18 A1
Sidney Rd BECK BR3 51 H2
SNWD SE25 50 D5
STA TW18 22 D5
TWK TW1 17 K8
WOT/HER KT12 60 E2
Signal Ct LING RH7 178 F4
Sigrist Sq KUTN/CMB KT2 8 F5
Silbury Av MTCM CR4 48 B1
Silchester Dr CRAWW RH11 164 C7
Silistria Cl WOKN/KNAP GU21 75 M8
Silkham Rd OXTED RH8 130 A1
Silkin Wk CRAWW RH11 * 191 L12
Silkmore La EHSLY KT24 99 K8
EHSLY KT24 119 L1
Silo Cl GODL GU7 168 C1
Silo Dr GODL GU7 168 C1
Silo Rd GODL GU7 168 C1
Silverbeck Wy
STWL/WRAY TW19 13 K7
Silver Birch Cl ADL/WDHM KT15 78 B2
CAT SE6 33 J4
Silver Birches Wy
MFD/CHID GU8 158 B6
Silver Cl KWD/TDW/WH KT20 105 H6
Silverdale SYD SE26 32 F5
Silverdale Av LHD/OX KT22 81 M4
WOT/HER KT12 60 C2
Silverdale Cl
BRKHM/BTCW RH3 145 L4
SUT SM1 65 J3
Silverdale Ct STA TW18 * 22 E6
Silverdale Dr SUN TW16 42 E2
Silver Dene PUT/ROE SW15 * 19 M7
Silver Dr FRIM GU16 73 M6
Silverglade CHSGTN KT9 82 F2
Silverhall St ISLW TW7 17 K5
Silver Hl SHST GU47 72 B1
Silverlands Cl CHERT KT16 * 58 A2
Silver La PUR/KEN CR8 87 G2
WWKM BR4 70 A1
Silverlea Gdns HORL RH6 160 F4
Silverleigh Rd THHTH CR7 49 J4
Silvermere Rw SNWD SE25 * 50 D2
Silversmiths Wy
WOKN/KNAP GU21 76 F8
Silverstone Cl REDH RH1 126 C6
Silver Tree Cl WOT/HER KT12 60 D3
Silverwood CRAWE RH10 * 193 L2
Silverwood Cl BECK BR3 33 K8
CROY/NA CR0 69 J7
Silverwood Dr CBLY GU15 73 K2
Silwood BRAK RG12 34 B8
Silwood Cl ASC SL5 37 G2
Silwood Pk ASC SL5 * 37 G2
ASC SL5 37 J3
Silwood Rd ASC SL5 37 J4
Simmil Rd ESH/CLAY KT10 62 B4
Simmonds Cl BNFD RG42 34 B1
Simmondstone La RFNM GU10 181 J7
Simmons Ga ESH/CLAY KT10 61 M4
Simmons Pl STA TW18 22 B6
Simms Cl CAR SM5 66 B1
Simone Dr PUR/KEN CR8 87 M6
Simons Cl CHERT KT16 57 M5
Simons Wk EGH TW20 20 F8
Simplemarsh Rd
ADL/WDHM KT15 58 D3
Simpson Rd HSLWW TW4 16 C8
RCHPK/HAM TW10 26 F5
Simpson Wy SURB KT6 44 F6
Sinclair Cl CRAWE RH10 165 L6
Sinclair Dr BELMT SM2 65 L7
Sincots Rd REDH RH1 126 C8

Sine Cl FARN GU14 92 E1
Single St BH/WHM TN16 91 L5
Singleton Cl CROY/NA CR0 2 C1
TOOT SW17 30 C8
Sinhurst Rd HORS RH12 166 A6
Sinhurst Rd CBLY GU15 72 E5
Sion Rd TWK TW1 26 E2
Sipson Cl WDR/YW UB7 14 D1
Sipson La HYS/HAR UB3 14 F1
Sipson Rd WDR/YW UB7 14 D2
Sipson Wy WDR/YW UB7 14 D2
Sir Cyril Black Wy
WIM/MER SW19 29 J8
Sirdar Rd MTCM CR4 30 D7
Siskin Av CRAWE RH10 193 P8
Siskin Cl HORS RH12 167 H4
Sissinghurst Cl CRAWE RH10 165 M3
Sissinghurst Rd CROY/NA CR0 3 M1
Sistova Rd BAL SW12 30 E2
Siward Rd TOOT SW17 29 M4
Six Acres SWTR RH13 203 Q7
Six Penny Cl EDEN TN8 179 R1
Sixteenth Av
KWD/TDW/WH KT20 * 105 J8
Sixth Av KWD/TDW/WH KT20 * 105 J8
Sixth Cross Rd WHTN TW2 25 M4
Skeena Hl WAND/EARL SW18 29 H1
Skelbrook St WAND/EARL SW18 29 L3
Skelwith Rd HMSMTH W6 19 M1
Skerne Rd KUTN/CMB KT2 8 D5
Skerne Wk KUTN/CMB KT2 8 D4
Skeynes Rd EDEN TN8 153 L8
Skid Hill La WARL CR6 90 C5
Skiffington Cl
BRXS/STRHM SW2 31 K2
Skiff La BIL RH14 201 Q11
Skimpedhill La BRAK RG12 34 D2
Skinners La ASHTD KT21 83 G8
HEST TW5 16 E3
MFD/CHID GU8 184 A8
Skipton Wy HORL RH6 160 E1
Skylark Vw HORS RH12 167 G2
Skyport Dr WDR/YW UB7 14 A2
Slade Ct CHERT KT16 58 A5
Slade Rd CHERT KT16 58 A5
CHOB/PIR GU24 95 G2
Slaidburn Gn BRAK RG12 35 H7
Slattery Rd FELT TW13 24 F2
Slaugham Ct CRAWW RH11 164 B7
Sleets Rd HORS RH12 166 B6
Slim Cl ALDT GU11 113 H2
Slim Rd CBLY GU15 72 F3
Slines New Rd CTHM CR3 109 G2
Slines Oak Rd WARL CR6 109 K1
Slinfold Wk CRAWW RH11 164 C3
Slip of Wd CRAN GU6 186 D1
Slipshatch Rd REIG RH2 147 J4
Slipshoe St REIG RH2 125 J8
The Slip BH/WHM TN16 111 M8
Sloane Gdns ORP BR6 71 M2
Sloane Wk CROY/NA CR0 51 J6
Slocock Hl WOKN/KNAP GU21 76 F7
Sloughbrook Cl HORS RH12 167 J3
Slough La BRKHM/BTCW RH3 124 D7
EPSOM KT18 103 M7
Slyfield Gn GU GU1 117 H4
Smallberry Av ISLW TW7 17 J4
Smallfield Rd HORL RH6 160 E3
Smallmead HORL RH6 160 E3
Smalls Hill Rd REIG RH2 174 F2
Smalls Md CRAWW RH11 164 E4
Smallwood Rd TOOT SW17 30 A5
Smart's Heath La
WOKS/MYFD GU22 96 D5
Smart's Heath Rd
WOKS/MYFD GU22 96 D5
Smeaton Rd WAND/EARL SW18 29 K1
Smeeds Cl EGRIN RH19 163 H2
Smitham Bottom La
PUR/KEN CR8 87 G2
Smitham Downs Rd
PUR/KEN CR8 87 H3
Smithbarn SWTR RH13 167 K6
Smithbarn Cl HORL RH6 160 E2
Smith Cl CRAWE RH10 164 F7
The Smithers
BRKHM/BTCW RH3 145 L2
Smithfield La RFNM GU10 180 F8
Smith Rd REIG RH2 147 J3
Smiths La EDEN TN8 131 M7
Smith Sq BRAK RG12 35 G1
Smith St BRYLDS KT5 45 J6
Smithwood Av CRAN GU6 170 A10
Smithwood Cl WIM/MER SW19 29 H3
Smithwood Common Rd
CRAN GU6 170 A9
Smithy Cl KWD/TDW/WH KT20 105 J8
Smithy La KWD/TDW/WH KT20 105 J8
RFNM GU10 180 D7
Smithy's Gn BFOR GU20 55 G5
Smoke La REIG RH2 147 L2
Smolletts EGRIN RH19 162 D5
Smugglers' La RDKG RH5 188 F6
Smugglers' Wy RFNM GU10 157 H1
Snailslynch FNM GU9 5 L3
Snakey La FELT TW13 24 D5
Snatts Hl OXTED RH8 130 C3
Snell Hatch CRAWW RH11 164 D4
Snellings Rd WOT/HER KT12 60 F4
Snipe La HASM GU27 198 B12
Snowdenham La SHGR GU5 168 H4
Snowdenham Links Rd
SHGR GU5 168 G3
Snowdon Rd FARN GU14 92 B2
Snowdon Rd West HTHAIR TW6 14 F8
Snowdown Cl PGE/AN SE20 50 F1
Snowdrop Cl CRAWW RH11 164 C8
HPTN TW12 25 K7
Snowdrop Wy CHOB/PIR GU24 75 K7
Snowerhill Rd
BRKHM/BTCW RH3 146 C4
Snow Hl CRAWE RH10 193 L2
Snowhill La CRAWE RH10 177 L12
Snows Paddock BFOR GU20 54 E2
Snows Ride BFOR GU20 54 E3
Snowy Fielder Waye ISLW TW7 17 L4
Snoxhall Fld CRAN GU6 186 C3
Soames Wk NWMAL KT3 46 B1
Soane Cl CRAWW RH11 164 A6
Solartron Rd FARN GU14 92 D6
Solecote GT/LBKH KT23 101 K7
Sole Farm Av GT/LBKH KT23 101 J7
Sole Farm Cl GT/LBKH KT23 101 J6
Sole Farm Rd GT/LBKH KT23 101 J7
Solna Av PUT/ROE SW15 19 M7
Soloms Court Rd BNSTD SM7 86 A7
Solway Cl HSLWW TW4 16 B5
Somerfield Cl
KWD/TDW/WH KT20 105 H1
Somergate HORS RH12 166 C7
Somersbury La CRAN GU6 187 L3
Somers Cl REIG RH2 125 K7
Somerset Av CHSGTN KT9 63 G3
RYNPK SW20 46 E2
Somerset Cl HOR/WEW KT19 64 B8
NWMAL KT3 46 B6
WOT/HER KT12 60 E4
Somerset Gdns
STRHM/NOR SW16 49 J3
TEDD TW11 26 B6
Somerset Rd BTFD TW8 17 M1
FARN GU14 92 F8
KUT/HW KT1 9 H7
REDH RH1 148 A2
TEDD TW11 26 B6
WIM/MER SW19 29 H5
Somerset Waye HEST TW5 16 B1
Somers Pl BRXS/STRHM SW2 31 J1
Somers Rd REIG RH2 125 K7
Somersweу RGUE GU4 139 H8
Somerton Av RCH/KEW TW9 18 E5
Somerton Cl PUR/KEN CR8 87 K6
Somertons Cl GUW GU2 116 D4
Somerville Av BARN SW13 19 M1
Somerville Dr CRAWE RH10 165 L1
Somerville Rd COB KT11 81 K4
PGE/AN SE20 33 G8
Sondes Farm DORK RH4 * 144 C2
Sondes Place Dr DORK RH4 144 C2
Songhurst Cl CROY/NA CR0 49 J6
Sonia Gdns HEST TW5 16 D2
Sonninge Cl SHST GU47 72 A1
Sonning Gdns HPTN TW12 25 H7
Sonning Rd SNWD SE25 50 D6
Soper Cl FSTH SE23 33 G2
Soper Dr CTHM CR3 108 A5
Sopwith Av CHSGTN KT9 63 H4
Sopwith Cl BH/WHM TN16 91 G6
KUTN/CMB KT2 27 J6
Sopwith Dr BF/WBF KT14 79 H1
Sopwith Rd HEST TW5 15 M2
Sopwith Wy KUTN/CMB KT2 8 E5
Sorbie Cl WEY KT13 59 M5
Sorrel Bank CROY/NA CR0 69 H8
Sorrel Cl CRAWW RH11 164 C8
Sorrel Dr LTWR GU18 74 C2
Sorrel Rd HORS RH12 167 H4
Sorrento Rd SUT SM1 65 L2
South Albert Rd REIG RH2 125 J7
Southampton Gdns MTCM CR4 49 H5
Southampton Rd HTHAIR TW6 14 C8
Southampton St FARN GU14 112 E1
South Atlantic Dr ALDT GU11 112 F6
South Av CAR SM5 66 D6
EGH TW20 21 M7
FNM GU9 134 A3
RCH/KEW TW9 * 18 D4
WOT/HER KT12 60 B8
South Bank SURB KT6 45 H6
Southbank THDIT KT7 44 E7
South Bank Ter SURB KT6 * 45 H6
South Beta Rd FARN GU14 92 E7
The South Border
PUR/KEN CR8 87 H1
Southborough Cl SURB KT6 45 G8
Southborough Rd (The Lane)
SURB KT6 * 45 H8
Southborough Rd SURB KT6 45 H8
Southbridge Pl CROY/NA CR0 2 C9
Southbridge Rd CROY/NA CR0 2 C9
Southbrook CRAWW RH11 191 M12
Southbrook Rd
STRHM/NOR SW16 49 H1
South Cl CRAWE RH10 165 H3
WHTN TW2 25 K4
WOKN/KNAP GU21 76 F6
South Close Gn REDH RH1 126 E3
Southcote WOKN/KNAP GU21 10 B2
Southcote Av BRYLDS KT5 45 L7
FELT TW13 24 D3
Southcote Dr CBLY GU15 73 K4
Southcote Rd REDH RH1 126 F4
SAND/SEL CR2 68 B8
SNWD SE25 50 E5
Southcroft EGH TW20 20 E6
Southcroft Av WWKM BR4 69 M1
Southcroft Rd
STRHM/NOR SW16 30 E7
South Croxted Rd DUL SE21 32 A4
Southdean Gdns
WIM/MER SW19 29 J3
Southdown Cl HORS RH12 167 K4
Southdown Dr RYNPK SW20 29 G8
Southdown Rd CAR SM5 66 D7
CTHM CR3 109 J4
RYNPK SW20 47 G1
WOT/HER KT12 61 H3
South Downs Wy RDKG RH5 122 F6
South Dr BELMT SM2 65 H8
BNSTD SM7 86 B3
CHOB/PIR GU24 94 F3
COUL/CHIP CR5 87 G5
RDKG RH5 144 F2
VW GU25 38 D7
South Eden Park Rd BECK BR3 51 L4
South End CROY/NA CR0 2 D9
GT/LBKH KT23 101 L8
SAND/SEL CR2 67 M4
Southend La CAT SE6 33 K5
Southend Rd BECK BR3 33 K8
Southerland Cl WEY KT13 59 M3
Southern Av EBED/NFELT TW14 24 D2
REDH RH1 148 D7
SNWD SE25 50 C3
Southern Down FELT TW13 * 24 F2
Southern Perimeter Rd
HTHAIR TW6 14 F7
STWL/WRAY TW19 13 M7
Southern Rd CBLY GU15 72 F3
Southerns La COUL/CHIP CR5 105 M6
Southern Wy FARN GU14 92 A6
FNM GU9 5 K5
Southey Rd WIM/MER SW19 29 K8
Southey St PGE/AN SE20 33 G8
South Farm La BAGS GU19 54 D7
Southfield Gdns TWK TW1 26 C5
Southfield Pl WEY KT13 59 L6
Southfields E/WMO/HCT KT8 44 B6
Southfields Av ASHF TW15 23 L7
Southfields Rd CTHM CR3 109 L7
South Gdns WIM/MER SW19 30 A8
Southgate Av CRAWE RH10 164 F7
South Gate Av FELT TW13 24 A5
Southgate Dr CRAWE RH10 164 F6
Southgate Pde CRAWE RH10 * 164 F6
Southgate Rd CRAWE RH10 164 F6
South Gv CHERT KT16 40 C6
SWTR RH13 167 G8
South Hl GODL GU7 168 C5
GU GU1 7 H7
South Hill Rd BRAK RG12 34 E6
Southholme Cl NRWD SE19 50 B1
South Holmes Rd SWTR RH13 167 L5
Southlands EGRIN RH19 162 F6
Southlands Av HORL RH6 160 D2
Southlands Cl ASHV GU12 113 K8
COUL/CHIP CR5 87 J7
Southlands Dr WIM/MER SW19 29 G3
Southlands La OXTED RH8 129 L8
Southlands Rd ASHV GU12 113 K8
Southland Wy HSLW TW3 17 G7
South La ASHV GU12 113 L8
KUT/HW KT1 8 D9
NWMAL KT3 46 A4
South La West NWMAL KT3 46 A4
South Lodge Av MTCM CR4 49 H4
South Lodge Rd WOT/HER KT12 60 D7
South Lynn Crs BRAK RG12 34 E5
South Md HOR/WEW KT19 64 C6
REDH RH1 126 C5
South Meadow CWTH RG45 52 A6
Southmead Rd ALDT GU11 134 E1
WIM/MER SW19 29 H2
Southmont Rd ESH/CLAY KT10 62 B1
South Munstead La
MFD/CHID GU8 168 E10
South Norwood Hl SNWD SE25 50 C3
South Oak Rd
STRHM/NOR SW16 31 J5
South Pde HORL RH6 * 160 C2
REDH RH1 * 126 F2
WLGTN SM6 * 66 F5
South Park Gv NWMAL KT3 45 M4
South Park Hill Rd
SAND/SEL CR2 68 A4
South Park La REDH RH1 150 D1
South Park Rd WIM/MER SW19 29 K7
South Pier Rd HORL RH6 160 D7
South Pl BRYLDS KT5 45 J7
South Rdg WEY KT13 59 L8
Southridge Pl RYNPK SW20 29 G8
South Ri CAR SM5 66 B7
South Rd ASHV GU12 113 J5
CHOB/PIR GU24 75 J6
CWTH RG45 52 B6
EGH TW20 20 F7
EWKG RG40 34 B8
FELT TW13 25 G6
FSTH SE23 33 G3
GUW GU2 116 E6
HPTN TW12 25 H7
LIPH GU30 196 H12
REIG RH2 147 L1
WEY KT13 59 L8
WHTN TW2 26 A4
WIM/MER SW19 30 A7
WOKN/KNAP GU21 76 F5
Southsea Rd KUT/HW KT1 45 H4
South Side RFNM GU10 135 J2
Southside Common
WIM/MER SW19 29 G7
South Station Ap REDH RH1 149 J2
South St DORK RH4 144 D3
EPSOM KT18 84 A3
FARN GU14 93 H8
FNM GU9 5 J3
GODL GU7 168 A5
HORS RH12 166 F7
ISLW TW7 17 K5
STA TW18 22 C6
South Ter DORK RH4 144 E3
SURB KT6 45 H6
South V NRWD SE19 32 B7
South Vale Rd SURB KT6 63 H1
South Vw BRAK RG12 34 A3
HOR/WEW KT19 63 K8
South View Cl CRAWE RH10 193 K2
Southview Cl TOOT SW17 30 D6
South View Ct NRWD SE19 * 31 M8
WOKS/MYFD GU22 10 D8
Southview Gdns WLGTN SM6 66 F6
South View Rd ASHTD KT21 103 G1
Southview Rd BOR GU35 180 G12
CTHM CR3 109 L6
WARL CR6 108 E2
Southviews SAND/SEL CR2 69 G7
Southville Cl EBED/NFELT TW14 24 B1
HOR/WEW KT19 64 A7
Southville Crs
EBED/NFELT TW14 24 B2
Southville Rd
EBED/NFELT TW14 24 B2
THDIT KT7 44 D7
South Wk ASHV GU12 113 G7
REIG RH2 * 125 L8
WWKM BR4 70 B2
Southwark Cl CRAWW RH11 164 D8
Southwater Cl BECK BR3 33 L8
CRAWW RH11 164 C4
South Wy CAR SM5 66 A8
CROY/NA CR0 69 H2
Southway CBLY GU15 72 E5
GUW GU2 6 A1
GUW GU2 116 C8
RYNPK SW20 47 G4
WLGTN SM6 66 F3
Southway Pk GUW GU2 * 116 D6
Southways Pk CRAWE RH10 * 191 N2
Southwell Park Rd CBLY GU15 72 E4
Southwell Rd CROY/NA CR0 49 K6
South Western Rd TWK TW1 17 K8
Southwick BAGS GU19 54 B8
Southwick Cl EGRIN RH19 162 E3
Southwick Ct BRAK RG12 35 H6
Southwold BRAK RG12 34 B8
Southwood Av CHERT KT16 57 M6
COUL/CHIP CR5 86 F5
KUTN/CMB KT2 45 M1
WOKN/KNAP GU21 76 A8
Southwood Cha CRAN GU6 186 E4
Southwood Cl WPK KT4 47 G8
Southwood Crs FARN GU14 92 A6
Southwood Dr BRYLDS KT5 45 M7
Southwood Gdns
ESH/CLAY KT10 62 D2
Southwood La FARN GU14 92 A6
Southwood Rd FARN GU14 92 B5
South Worple Wy
MORT/ESHN SW14 19 G5
Sovereign Cl PUR/KEN CR8 67 J8
Sovereign Ct E/WMO/HCT KT8 43 J4
Sovereign Dr CBLY GU15 73 M2
Sovereign Hts DTCH/LGLY SL3 12 D1
Space Waye EBED/NFELT TW14 15 L7
Spa Cl SNWD SE25 50 B1
Spa Dr EPSOM KT18 83 K4
Spa Hl NRWD SE19 50 A1
Spalding Rd TOOT SW17 30 E6
Sparks Cl HPTN TW12 25 H7
Sparrow Cl HPTN TW12 25 H7
Sparrow Farm Dr
EBED/NFELT TW14 24 F1
Sparrow Farm Rd EW KT17 64 D3
Sparrowhawk Cl RFNM GU10 133 G1
Sparrow Rw CHOB/PIR GU24 55 L5
Sparrows Md REDH RH1 126 D5
Spartan Cl WLGTN SM6 67 H6
Sparvell Rd WOKN/KNAP GU21 95 L1
Spats La BOR GU35 180 E9
Speakers Ct CROY/NA CR0 * 2 E3
Speart La HEST TW5 16 B2
Speedbird Wy WDR/YW UB7 13 L2
Speedwell Cl RGUE GU4 117 M5
Speedwell Wy HORS RH12 167 H4
Speer Rd THDIT KT7 44 C6
Speirs Cl NWMAL KT3 46 C6
Speke Rd THHTH CR7 50 A2
Spelthorne Gv SUN TW16 24 C8
Spelthorne La ASHF TW15 23 M8
Spence Av BF/WBF KT14 79 H4
Spencer Cl EPSOM KT18 104 B1
FRIM GU16 93 H3
WOKN/KNAP GU21 77 M4
Spencer Gdns EGH TW20 21 G6
MORT/ESHN SW14 18 F7
Spencer Hl WIM/MER SW19 29 H7
Spencer Hill Rd
WIM/MER SW19 29 H8
Spencer Pl CROY/NA CR0 2 F1
Spencer Rd BNFD RG42 34 C1
CHSWK W4 18 F2
COB KT11 80 E5
CTHM CR3 108 A3
E/WMO/HCT KT8 43 M4
ISLW TW7 17 G3
MTCM CR4 48 C7
MTCM CR4 48 D3
RYNPK SW20 46 E1
SAND/SEL CR2 68 B4
WHTN TW2 26 B4
Spencers La HORL RH6 175 J8
Spencers Pl HORS RH12 166 E5
Spencers Rd CRAWW RH11 164 E5
HORS RH12 166 E6
Spencer Wy REDH RH1 148 D5
Spenser Av WEY KT13 59 K7
Spenser Ms DUL SE21 32 A2
Spiceall RGUW GU3 137 L6
Spicer Cl WOT/HER KT12 42 F6
Spicers Fld LHD/OX KT22 82 A3
Spices Yd CROY/NA CR0 2 D9
Spiers Wy HORL RH6 160 E5
Spindle Wy CRAWE RH10 165 H5
Spindlewood Gdns
CROY/NA CR0 2 F9
Spindlewoods
KWD/TDW/WH KT20 104 E4
Spinis BRAK RG12 34 B8
Spinner Gn BRAK RG12 34 D5
Spinney Cl BECK BR3 51 L4
COB KT11 81 K1
CRAWE RH10 193 P5
HORS RH12 167 L3
NWMAL KT3 46 B5
WPK KT4 64 C2
Spinneycroft LHD/OX KT22 82 A5
Spinney Dr EBED/NFELT TW14 23 M1
Spinney Gdns NRWD SE19 32 C6
Spinney Hl ADL/WDHM KT15 58 C4
Spinney Oak CHERT KT16 58 A5
The Spinney ASC SL5 37 H5
BARN SW13 * 19 L1
CBLY GU15 73 M3
CHEAM SM3 64 F3
CRAWW RH11 164 D6
EPSOM KT18 104 E1
GSHT GU26 197 M1
GT/LBKH KT23 101 L6
HASM GU27 * 197 Q8
HASM GU27 198 D5
HORL RH6 160 D1
LHD/OX KT22 81 M2
PUR/KEN CR8 87 L1
RPLY/SEND GU23 118 F1
STRHM/NOR SW16 30 F4
SUN TW16 42 D1
The Spinning Wk SHGR GU5 141 K5
Spital Heath DORK RH4 144 F1
Spitfire Wy FARN GU14 112 B1
Spoil La RFNM GU10 135 J2
Spokane Cl ALDT GU11 134 C1
Spook Hl RDKG RH5 144 E7
Spooners Rd HORS RH12 167 K5
Spooner Wk WLGTN SM6 67 G4
Sportsbank St CAT SE6 33 M1
Spout Hl CROY/NA CR0 69 K4
Spout La EDEN TN8 131 M8
STWL/WRAY TW19 13 K7
Spout La North
STWL/WRAY TW19 13 L6
Spratts La CHERT KT16 58 B5
Spreighton Rd
E/WMO/HCT KT8 43 L4
Spring Av EGH TW20 21 H7
Spring Bottom La REDH RH1 127 M1
Springbourne Ct BECK BR3 51 M1
Springclose La CHEAM SM3 65 H5
Spring Copse CRAWE RH10 192 H2
Springcopse Rd REIG RH2 147 M1
Spring Cnr FELT TW13 * 24 D4
Springcross Av BLKW GU17 72 A6
Springfarm Rd HASM GU27 197 R8
Springfield EGRIN RH19 162 E1
LTWR GU18 74 F1
OXTED RH8 130 A4
Springfield Av HPTN TW12 25 L7
RYNPK SW20 47 J3
Springfield Cl
WOKN/KNAP GU21 76 A8
Springfield Crs HORS RH12 166 E7
Springfield Dr LHD/OX KT22 102 B1
Springfield Gdns WWKM BR4 69 L1
Springfield Gv SUN TW16 42 D1
Springfield La WEY KT13 59 L3
Springfield Mdw WEY KT13 59 L3
Springfield Pk HORS RH12 * 166 F6
Springfield Park Rd
HORS RH12 166 E7
Springfield Pl NWMAL KT3 45 M4
Springfield Ri SYD SE26 32 E5
Springfield Rd ASHF TW15 23 J6
ASHV GU12 113 K4
CBLY GU15 73 K4
CRAWW RH11 164 E5
DORK RH4 143 L3
DTCH/LGLY SL3 12 E2
EDEN TN8 153 L8
EW KT17 64 F8
GU GU1 7 J5
HORS RH12 166 F7
KUT/HW KT1 45 H4
SYD SE26 32 E6
TEDD TW11 26 D6
THHTH CR7 49 M1
WHTN TW2 25 K2
WIM/MER SW19 29 J6
WLGTN SM6 66 E4
Springfields Cl CHERT KT16 40 E8
Springfield Wy MFD/CHID GU8 158 B6
Spring Gdns ASC SL5 36 E4
BH/WHM TN16 90 F8
CBLY GU15 73 K4
CRAWE RH10 192 H2
E/WMO/HCT KT8 43 M5
FARN GU14 92 D2
WLGTN SM6 66 F4
Spring Gv GODL GU7 168 B1
HPTN TW12 43 L1
LHD/OX KT22 101 L5
MTCM CR4 48 D1
Spring Grove Crs HSLW TW3 16 F3
Spring Grove Rd HSLW TW3 16 F3
RCHPK/HAM TW10 18 C7
Springhaven Cl GU GU1 117 K8
Springhill MFD/CHID GU8 158 B6
Spring Hl SYD SE26 32 F5
Springholm Cl BH/WHM TN16 90 F8
Springhurst Cl CROY/NA CR0 69 J3
Springlakes Est ASHV GU12 * 113 H6
Spring La FNM GU9 133 K2
OXTED RH8 130 A5
SNWD SE25 50 E6
SWTR RH13 203 P6
Spring La West FNM GU9 133 K3
Spring Meadow BRAK RG12 35 G1
FROW RH18 195 N12
Spring Park Av CROY/NA CR0 69 G1
Springpark Dr BECK BR3 51 M3
Spring Park Rd CROY/NA CR0 69 G1
Spring Plat CRAWE RH10 165 L4
Spring Plat Ct CRAWE RH10 * 165 L4
Spring Ri EGH TW20 21 H7
Spring Rd FELT TW13 24 C4
Spring St EW KT17 64 C7
Springvale Cl GT/LBKH KT23 101 L8
Spring Wy EGRIN RH19 163 H1
Springwell Rd HEST TW5 16 A3
RDKG RH5 173 L6
STRHM/NOR SW16 31 K5
Springwood MFD/CHID GU8 159 K8
Spring Woods VW GU25 38 E4
Sprucedale Gdns CROY/NA CR0 69 G3
WLGTN SM6 67 H7
Spruce Dr LTWR GU18 74 D2
Spruce Rd BH/WHM TN16 91 G6
Spur Dr KWD/TDW/WH KT20 105 L3
Spurfield E/WMO/HCT KT8 43 L3
Spurgeon Av NRWD SE19 50 A1
Spurgeon Cl CRAWW RH11 * 164 E3
Spurgeon Rd NRWD SE19 32 A8
Spur Rd EBED/NFELT TW14 15 L7
ISLW TW7 17 K2
Spurs Ct ALDT GU11 112 B7
The Spur WOKN/KNAP GU21 75 L8
Spy La BIL RH14 201 R5
Square Dr HASM GU27 198 D12
The Square BH/WHM TN16 110 F2
BRAK RG12 35 H4
CAR SM5 66 D4
CRAWE RH10 164 F4
GUW GU2 138 C2
LING RH7 178 D5
LIPH GU30 196 G9
RCH/KEW TW9 18 B7
WDR/YW UB7 13 L3
Squarey St TOOT SW17 29 M4
Squerryes Mede
BH/WHM TN16 * 131 M1
The Squerryes CTHM CR3 108 B3
Squire's Bridge Rd
SHPTN TW17 41 J4
Squires Cl CRAWE RH10 193 M5
Squires Ct WIM/MER SW19 29 K5
Squires Hill La RFNM GU10 156 F4
Squire's Rd SHPTN TW17 41 J4
Squires Wk ASHF TW15 24 A8
Squirrel Cl CRAWW RH11 164 D1
HSLWW TW4 15 M5
Squirrel La FARN GU14 92 D4
Squirrel Rdg CRAWE RH10 * 193 N6
Squirrels Cl GODL GU7 138 A8
Squirrels Gn GT/LBKH KT23 101 K5
WPK KT4 64 C1
Squirrel's Wy EPSOM KT18 84 A5
Squirrel Wd BF/WBF KT14 78 E2

Stable Cl CRAWE RH10 165 M7
EPSOM KT18 104 B1
KUTN/CMB KT2 27 J7
Stable Cft BAGS GU19 54 A7
Stable Ms REIG RH2 125 K8
WNWD SE27 31 M6
Stables End ORP BR6 71 M2
The Stables COB KT11 81 J4
Stacey's Farm Rd
MFD/CHID GU8 158 A6
Stacey's Meadow
MFD/CHID GU8 157 M5
Stackfield Rd CRAWW RH11 164 A5
Staddon Cl BECK BR3 51 H4
Staddon Ct BECK BR3 51 H4
Staff College Rd CBLY GU15 72 E3
Staffhurst Wood Rd
OXTED RH8 152 F3
Stafford Cl CHEAM SM3 65 H5
CTHM CR3 108 C5
Stafford Gdns CROY/NA CR0 67 J4
Stafford Lake
WOKN/KNAP GU21 75 K8
Stafford Pl RCHPK/HAM TW10 27 J1
Stafford Rd CRAWW RH11 164 C1
CROY/NA CR0 67 K3
CTHM CR3 108 C5
NWMAL KT3 45 M3
WLGTN SM6 66 F5
Staffords Pl HORL RH6 160 E4
Staff Rd ASHV GU12 112 F7
Stagbury Av COUL/CHIP CR5 86 B8
Stagbury Cl COUL/CHIP CR5 106 B1
Stagbury House
COUL/CHIP CR5 106 B1
Stagelands CRAWW RH11 164 D2
Stag Hl GUW GU2 6 B5
Stag La PUT/ROE SW15 28 C4
Stag Leys ASHTD KT21 103 H2
Stag Leys Cl BNSTD SM7 86 B5
Stags Wy ISLW TW7 17 J1
Stainash Crs STA TW18 22 E6
Stainash Pde STA TW18 * 22 E6
Stainbank Rd MTCM CR4 48 E3
Staines Av CHEAM SM3 65 G1
Staines By-Pass STA TW18 22 B4
Staines La CHERT KT16 40 D6
Staines Lane Cl CHERT KT16 40 C5
Staines Rd CHERT KT16 40 B6
EBED/NFELT TW14 24 B1
STA TW18 40 E1
STWL/WRAY TW19 21 J2
WHTN TW2 25 M4
Staines Rd East SUN TW16 24 D8
Staines Rd West ASHF TW15 23 M8
SUN TW16 24 C8
Stainford Cl ASHF TW15 24 A6
Stainton Wk
WOKN/KNAP GU21 * 76 F8
Staiths Wy
KWD/TDW/WH KT20 104 E2
Stake La FARN GU14 92 D5
Stakescorner Rd RGUW GU3 138 D8
Stambourne Wy NRWD SE19 32 B8
WWKM BR4 69 M2
Stamford Av FRIM GU16 73 J8
Stamford Green Rd
EPSOM KT18 83 L3
Stamford Rd WOT/HER KT12 61 G2
Stanborough Cl HPTN TW12 25 J7
Stanborough Rd HSLW TW3 17 G5
Stanbridge Cl CRAWW RH11 164 A5
Stanbridge Rd EDEN TN8 153 L7
PUT/ROE SW15 19 M5
Standard Rd HSLWW TW4 16 B5
ORP BR6 71 K8
Standen Cl EGRIN RH19 162 B2
Standen Pl HORS RH12 167 K2
Standen Rd WAND/EARL SW18 29 K1
Standford Hl BOR GU35 196 B4
Standford La BOR GU35 196 B2
Standinghall La CRAWE RH10 192 F11
Standon La RDKG RH5 187 R3
Stane Cl WIM/MER SW19 29 L8
Stane St BIL RH14 203 M10
RDKG RH5 172 E11
RDKG RH5 188 D3
Stane Wy EW KT17 64 D8
Stanford Cl HPTN TW12 25 J7
Stanford Orch HORS RH12 166 C2
Stanford Rd STRHM/NOR SW16 49 H2
Stanfords Pl LING RH7 178 E6
The Stanfords EW KT17 84 C2
Stanford Wy HORS RH12 166 A6
STRHM/NOR SW16 49 G2
Stanger Rd SNWD SE25 50 D4
Stangrove Rd EDEN TN8 153 M8
Stan Hl HORL RH6 174 F9
Stanhope Gv BECK BR3 51 J5
Stanhope Heath
STWL/WRAY TW19 13 M8
Stanhope Rd CAR SM5 66 D6
CBLY GU15 72 D4
CROY/NA CR0 3 G8
Stanhopes OXTED RH8 130 E2
Stanhope Ter WHTN TW2 * 26 C1
Stanhope Wy
STWL/WRAY TW19 13 M8
Stanier Cl CRAWE RH10 165 K5
Staniland Dr WEY KT13 79 J1
Stanley Av BECK BR3 51 M3
NWMAL KT3 46 D5
Stanley Cl COUL/CHIP CR5 87 J7
CRAWE RH10 165 G6
Stanleycroft Cl ISLW TW7 17 H3
Stanley Gdns MTCM CR4 * 30 D7
SAND/SEL CR2 88 D2
WLGTN SM6 66 F5
WOT/HER KT12 60 F4
Stanley Gardens Rd
TEDD TW11 26 B6
Stanley Gv CROY/NA CR0 49 K6
Stanley Hl CHOB/PIR GU24 94 F4
Stanley Park Rd CAR SM5 66 C6
Stanley Rd ASHF TW15 23 J6
BELMT SM2 65 L5
CAR SM5 66 D6
CROY/NA CR0 49 K7
HSLW TW3 16 F6
MORT/ESHN SW14 18 E6
MRDN SM4 47 K4
MTCM CR4 30 D8
WHTN TW2 26 A4
WIM/MER SW19 29 K8
WOKN/KNAP GU21 10 F4
Stanley Sq CAR SM5 66 C7
Stanley St CTHM CR3 107 M4
Stanley Wk BRAK RG12 34 F2
SWTR RH13 167 G7
Stanley Wy SWTR RH13 167 G7
Stanmore Cl ASC SL5 36 D4
Stanmore Gdns RCH/KEW TW9 18 C5
SUT SM1 65 M2
Stanmore Rd RCH/KEW TW9 18 C5
Stanmore Ter BECK BR3 51 K2
Stannet Wy WLGTN SM6 66 F3
Stansfield Rd HSLWW TW4 15 L4
Stanstead Gv CAT SE6 33 J2
Stanstead Rd CTHM CR3 108 B6
FSTH SE23 33 H2
Stansted Rd HTHAIR TW6 14 C8
Stanthorpe Cl
STRHM/NOR SW16 * 31 H6
Stanthorpe Rd
STRHM/NOR SW16 31 H6
Stanton Av TEDD TW11 26 B7
Stanton Cl CRAN GU6 186 A2
HOR/WEW KT19 63 L4
WPK KT4 47 G8
Stanton Rd BARN SW13 19 J4
CROY/NA CR0 2 C2
RYNPK SW20 47 G2
Stantons Whf SHGR GU5 169 K2
Stanton Wy SYD SE26 33 J5
Stanwell Cl STWL/WRAY TW19 14 A8
Stanwell Gdns
STWL/WRAY TW19 14 A8
Stanwell Moor Rd STA TW18 22 E3
WDR/YW UB7 13 L3
Stanwell New Rd STA TW18 22 E5
Stanwell Pl STWL/WRAY TW19 * 13 M8
Stanwell Rd ASHF TW15 23 H4
DTCH/LGLY SL3 12 E5
EBED/NFELT TW14 23 M1
Staplecross Ct CRAWW RH11 164 B8
Staplefield Cl
BRXS/STRHM SW2 * 31 H2
Stapleford Cl KUT/HW KT1 9 K7
WIM/MER SW19 29 H1
Staple Hl CHOB/PIR GU24 56 A5
Staplehurst BRAK RG12 34 B7
Staplehurst Cl REIG RH2 147 M4
Staplehurst Rd CAR SM5 66 B6
REIG RH2 147 M4
Staple La RGUE GU4 119 H7
SHGR GU5 141 J1
Stapleton Gdns CROY/NA CR0 67 K4
Stapleton Rd TOOT SW17 30 D4
Star And Garter Hl
RCHPK/HAM TW10 27 H2
Starborough Rd EDEN TN8 179 M5
Star Cl SWTR RH13 167 K5
Star Hl RFNM GU10 181 J7
Star Hill Dr RFNM GU10 181 J6
Star La ASHV GU12 113 J7
COUL/CHIP CR5 106 D4
Starling Rd CROY/NA CR0 51 H6
Star Post Rd CBLY GU15 73 H1
Star Rd ISLW TW7 17 G4
Starrock La COUL/CHIP CR5 106 D2
Starrock Rd COUL/CHIP CR5 106 E1
Starts Cl ORP BR6 71 K2
Starts Hill Av ORP BR6 71 L4
Starts Hill Rd ORP BR6 71 L2
Starwood Cl BF/WBF KT14 78 F1
State Farm Av ORP BR6 71 L3
Staten Gdns TWK TW1 26 C2
Statham Ct BNFD RG42 34 B1
Station Ap ASHV GU12 113 K2
BECK BR3 51 H1
BELMT SM2 65 H6
BELMT SM2 65 L8
BF/WBF KT14 78 D2
BLKW GU17 72 B5
COUL/CHIP CR5 86 C8
COUL/CHIP CR5 87 G6
CROY/NA CR0 2 F6
CTHM CR3 88 D7
DORK RH4 122 F8
EDEN TN8 153 M8
EHSLY KT24 100 B8
ESH/CLAY KT10 62 B5
EW KT17 64 E8
GODL GU7 168 A5
GU GU1 6 E6
GU GU1 7 J5
HOR/WEW KT19 64 C4
HOR/WEW KT19 84 A3
HORL RH6 160 E3
HORS RH12 190 C12
HPTN TW12 43 K1
KUT/HW KT1 9 K5
LHD/OX KT22 102 D3
MFD/CHID GU8 183 N9
OXTED RH8 130 B3
PUR/KEN CR8 * 87 K1
RCH/KEW TW9 18 D3
RDKG RH5 173 J12
SAND/SEL CR2 68 A7
SHPTN TW17 * 41 M6
STA TW18 22 D6
STRHM/NOR SW16 31 G6
SUN TW16 42 D1
SYD SE26 33 G5
VW GU25 39 G4
WEY KT13 59 K5
WOKS/MYFD GU22 10 E6
Station Ap East REDH RH1 148 C2
Station Approach Rd
CHSWK W4 18 F2
COUL/CHIP CR5 87 G5
HORL RH6 * 160 E6
KWD/TDW/WH KT20 104 F4
Station Ap West REDH RH1 148 C2
Station Av CTHM CR3 108 D6
HOR/WEW KT19 64 B7
NWMAL KT3 46 B3
WOT/HER KT12 60 D3
Station Cl HPTN TW12 43 L1
SWTR RH13 167 G7
Station Crs ASHF TW15 23 G5
Station Est BECK BR3 51 G4
Station Estate Rd
EBED/NFELT TW14 24 E2
Station Garage Ms
STRHM/NOR SW16 * 31 G7
Station Gdns CHSWK W4 18 F2
Station Hl ASC SL5 36 D3
CRAWE RH10 165 K3
FNM GU9 5 K4
HAYES BR2 70 D1
Station La MFD/CHID GU8 183 M9
MFD/CHID GU8 183 Q3
Station Pde BAL SW12 * 30 D2
BECK BR3 * 51 G4
BELMT SM2 * 65 M5
EBED/NFELT TW14 * 24 E1
EHSLY KT24 * 100 B8
RCH/KEW TW9 18 D3
VW GU25 39 G5
Station Ri WNWD SE27 31 L3
Station Rd ADL/WDHM KT15 58 F3
ADL/WDHM KT15 59 G3
ALDT GU11 112 E7
ASC SL5 37 K6
ASHF TW15 23 J5
BAGS GU19 54 B5
BARN SW13 19 K5
BELMT SM2 65 K8
BF/WBF KT14 78 D2
BIL RH14 201 Q6
BRAK RG12 34 E3
BRKHM/BTCW RH3 124 A7
CAR SM5 66 C3
CHERT KT16 40 C8
CHOB/PIR GU24 76 C2
CHSGTN KT9 63 H4
COB KT11 81 H7
CRAWE RH10 164 F5
CRAWE RH10 193 N5
CROY/NA CR0 2 C4
CTHM CR3 88 C8
CTHM CR3 109 H4
DORK RH4 144 D2
EDEN TN8 153 M6
EGH TW20 21 K6
EGRIN RH19 162 E4
ESH/CLAY KT10 62 A1
FARN GU14 92 E5
FRIM GU16 72 F8
FROW RH18 195 N10
GDST RH9 151 H4
GODL GU7 168 A5
GODL GU7 168 C2
HORL RH6 160 E3
HORS RH12 166 E1
HORS RH12 186 G11
HORS RH12 203 J2
HPTN TW12 43 L1
HSLW TW3 16 E6
KUT/HW KT1 8 C4
KUTN/CMB KT2 9 J5
LHD/OX KT22 102 D3
LING RH7 178 F4
LIPH GU30 196 G11
NRWD SE19 32 D7
NWMAL KT3 46 E5
PGE/AN SE20 32 F7
PUR/KEN CR8 87 M4
REDH RH1 126 C7
REDH RH1 126 F2
RGUE GU4 139 H6
SHGR GU5 169 J2
SHPTN TW17 41 M5
SNWD SE25 50 C4
STWL/WRAY TW19 12 C8
SUN TW16 24 D8
SWTR RH13 167 H7
SWTR RH13 204 E10
TEDD TW11 26 D7
THDIT KT7 44 C7
TWK TW1 26 C2
WIM/MER SW19 47 M1
WOKS/MYFD GU22 10 D7
WWKM BR4 51 M8
Station Rd East ASHV GU12 113 J2
OXTED RH8 130 B3
Station Rd North REDH RH1 126 F2
Station Rd South REDH RH1 126 F2
Station Rd West OXTED RH8 130 B3
Station Rw RGUE GU4 139 H6
Station Vw ASHV GU12 113 K1
GU GU1 6 E5
Station Wy BRAK RG12 34 F2
CHEAM SM3 65 H5
CRAWE RH10 164 F5
Station Yd ASHF TW15 * 23 J5
KWD/TDW/WH KT20 * 105 J3
PUR/KEN CR8 * 87 L2
TWK TW1 26 D1
Staunton Rd KUTN/CMB KT2 8 F1
Staveley Gdns CHSWK W4 19 G3
Staveley Rd ASHF TW15 24 A7
CHSWK W4 18 F1
Staveley Wy WOKN/KNAP GU21 76 B7
Stavordale Rd CAR SM5 47 M7
Stayne End VW GU25 38 D4
Stayton Rd SUT SM1 65 K2
Steadfast Rd KUT/HW KT1 8 D5
Steam Farm La
EBED/NFELT TW14 15 J6
Steele Rd ISLW TW7 17 K6
Steeles Rd ALDT GU11 112 E5
Steel's La LHD/OX KT22 81 M4
Steep Hl CHOB/PIR GU24 55 M6
CROY/NA CR0 3 G9
STRHM/NOR SW16 31 G4
Steeple Cl WIM/MER SW19 29 H5
Steeple Heights Dr
BH/WHM TN16 91 G7
Steeple Point ASC SL5 36 E3
Steepways GSHT GU26 181 N11
Steeres Hl HORS RH12 189 R6
Steerforth Copse SHST GU47 52 B7
Steerforth St
WAND/EARL SW18 29 L3
Steers La CRAWE RH10 192 B1
Steers Md MTCM CR4 48 C1
Stella Rd TOOT SW17 30 C7
Stembridge Rd PGE/AN SE20 50 E2
The Stennings EGRIN RH19 162 D2
Stepbridge Pth
WOKN/KNAP GU21 10 B6
Stepgates CHERT KT16 40 E7
Stepgates Cl CHERT KT16 * 40 E7
Stephen Cl CRAWW RH11 164 F1
EGH TW20 21 M7
Stephendale Rd FNM GU9 134 A5
Stephenson Dr EGRIN RH19 163 G7
Stephenson Pl CRAWE RH10 165 K4
Stephenson Rd WHTN TW2 25 K1
Stephenson Wy CRAWE RH10 165 K4
Stepney Cl CRAWE RH10 165 L6
Stepney Wy MTCM CR4 48 D1
The Steps EHSLY KT24 * 121 G1
Sterling Buildings
HORS RH12 * 166 F7
Sterling Centre BRAK RG12 35 G3
Sterling Pk CRAWE RH10 * 192 A2
Sternhold Av BRXS/STRHM SW2 31 H3
Sterry Dr HOR/WEW KT19 64 B3
THDIT KT7 44 B6
Steucers La FSTH SE23 33 H2
Steve Biko La CAT SE6 33 K5
Steve Biko Wy HSLW TW3 16 D5
Stevenage Rd CRAWW RH11 164 A8
Stevens Cl BECK BR3 33 K7
EW KT17 84 B2
HPTN TW12 25 J7
Stevens' La ESH/CLAY KT10 62 D6
Stevens Pl PUR/KEN CR8 87 L5
Stewards Ri RFNM GU10 155 J2
Stewart KWD/TDW/WH KT20 105 G3
Stewart Av SHPTN TW17 41 K4
Stewart Cl HPTN TW12 25 H7
WOKN/KNAP GU21 76 C7
Steyning Cl CRAWE RH10 165 G2
PUR/KEN CR8 87 L6
Steyning Wy HSLWW TW4 15 M6
Stickle Down FRIM GU16 94 A1
Stile Gdns HASM GU27 198 A7
Stile Pth SUN TW16 42 D3
Stillers MFD/CHID GU8 * 199 Q1
Stillingfleet Rd BARN SW13 19 K2
Stirling Av SHPTN TW17 42 B3
WLGTN SM6 67 H6
Stirling Cl ASHV GU12 113 J4
BNSTD SM7 85 J7
CRAWE RH10 165 K5
FARN GU14 92 D6
FRIM GU16 73 H7
STRHM/NOR SW16 48 F1
Stirling Dr CTHM CR3 107 M3
Stirling Gv HSLW TW3 16 F4
Stirling Rd GUW GU2 116 A8
WHTN TW2 25 K1
Stirling Wk BRYLDS KT5 45 L6
Stirling Wy ALDT GU11 112 A2
EGRIN RH19 163 J2
SWTR RH13 167 H7
Stirrup Wy CRAWE RH10 165 M3
Stites Hill Rd COUL/CHIP CR5 107 L2
Stoatley Hollow HASM GU27 198 B5
Stoatley Ri HASM GU27 198 B5
Stoatley River HASM GU27 198 B5
Stoats Nest Rd COUL/CHIP CR5 87 H5
Stockbridge Dr ALDT GU11 134 F3
Stockbury Rd CROY/NA CR0 50 F6
Stockers La WOKS/MYFD GU22 97 J2
Stockfield HORL RH6 * 160 E2
Stockfield Rd ESH/CLAY KT10 62 B4
STRHM/NOR SW16 31 J4
Stockhams Cl SAND/SEL CR2 68 A8
Stock Hl BH/WHM TN16 91 G6
Stockhurst Cl PUT/ROE SW15 19 M4
Stockport Rd
STRHM/NOR SW16 49 G1
Stocks Cl HORL RH6 160 E4
Stockton Rd REIG RH2 147 K3
Stockwell Rd EGRIN RH19 162 F7
Stockwood Ri CBLY GU15 73 J4
Stockwood Wy FNM GU9 134 C2
Stocton Cl GU GU1 6 F2
Stocton Rd GU GU1 7 G2
Stodart Rd PGE/AN SE20 50 F1
Stoford Cl WIM/MER SW19 29 H2
Stoke Cl COB KT11 81 J6
Stoke Flds GU GU1 7 H4
Stokeford Cl BRAK RG12 35 J5
Stoke Gv GU GU1 7 H4
Stoke Hills FNM GU9 5 L1
Stoke Ms GU GU1 7 H4
Stoke Mill Cl GU GU1 117 G6
Stoke Park Ct GU GU1 * 7 H4
Stoke Ridings
KWD/TDW/WH KT20 * 105 G5
Stoke Rd COB KT11 81 H6
GU GU1 7 H1
KUTN/CMB KT2 27 M8
WOT/HER KT12 60 F2
Stokesby Rd CHSGTN KT9 63 J5
Stokes Cl CRAWE RH10 165 L7
Stokesheath Rd LHD/OX KT22 81 M1
Stokes Ridings
KWD/TDW/WH KT20 105 G5
Stokes Rd CROY/NA CR0 51 G6
Stompond La WOT/HER KT12 60 D1
Stonards Brow SHGR GU5 169 N5
Stonebanks WOT/HER KT12 42 D7
Stonebridge Ct HORS RH12 * 166 D7
Stonebridge Flds RGUE GU4 139 G7
Stonebridge Whf RGUE GU4 139 G7
Stonecot Cl CHEAM SM3 47 H8
Stonecot Hl CHEAM SM3 47 H8
Stonecourt Cl HORL RH6 160 F3
Stone Crs EBED/NFELT TW14 24 C1
Stonecroft Wy CROY/NA CR0 49 H7
Stonecrop Cl CRAWW RH11 164 C7
Stonecrop Rd RGUE GU4 117 M6
Stonedene Cl BOR GU35 196 G1
FROW RH18 195 Q11
Stonefield Cl CRAWE RH10 164 F5
Stonegate CBLY GU15 73 M3
Stone Hatch CRAN GU6 185 R10
Stonehill Cl GT/LBKH KT23 101 K7
MORT/ESHN SW14 19 G7
Stonehill Crs CHERT KT16 57 H5
Stonehill Ga ASC SL5 * 37 G6
Stonehill Pk BOR GU35 196 G1
Stonehill Rd BOR GU35 196 H1
CHERT KT16 57 H5
LTWR GU18 54 D8
MORT/ESHN SW14 18 F7
Stonehills Ct DUL SE21 32 B4
Stone House Gdns CTHM CR3 108 B7
Stonehouse Ri FRIM GU16 73 H8
Stonehouse Rd LIPH GU30 197 J9
Stoneleigh Av WPK KT4 64 D2
Stoneleigh Broadway EW KT17 64 D4
Stoneleigh Cl EGRIN RH19 163 G3
Stoneleigh Ct FRIM GU16 73 J8
Stoneleigh Crs HOR/WEW KT19 64 D4
Stoneleigh Pk WEY KT13 59 M5
Stoneleigh Park Av
CROY/NA CR0 51 G6
Stoneleigh Park Rd
HOR/WEW KT19 64 C5
Stoneleigh Rd CAR SM5 48 B7
OXTED RH8 131 H4
Stonell's Rd TOOT SW17 29 M4
Stone Park Av BECK BR3 51 K4
Stonepark Dr FROW RH18 195 P11
Stonepit Cl GODL GU7 159 L5
Stone Pl WPK KT4 64 D1
Stoners Cl HORL RH6 160 A6
Stones La DORK RH4 143 M3
Stone's Rd EW KT17 84 B1
Stone St ASHV GU12 135 G1
Stoneswood Rd OXTED RH8 130 E5
Stoney Bottom GSHT GU26 197 P2
Stoney Brook GUW GU2 116 B7
Stoneybrook HORS RH12 166 C8
Stoney Cft COUL/CHIP CR5 106 F4
Stoneyfield Rd COUL/CHIP CR5 87 J7
Stoneyfields FNM GU9 134 B8
Stoneyland Ct EGH TW20 21 J6
Stoneylands Rd EGH TW20 21 J6
Stoney La NRWD SE19 32 C7
Stoney Rd BNFD RG42 34 D1
Stonny Cft ASHTD KT21 83 J7
Stony Hl ESH/CLAY KT10 61 J6
Stopham Rd CRAWE RH10 165 L7
Stormont Wy CHSGTN KT9 62 F4
Storrington Rd CROY/NA CR0 3 K3
Storr's La RGUW GU3 95 M6
Stoughton Av CHEAM SM3 65 G4
Stoughton Cl PUT/ROE SW15 28 D2
Stoughton Rd GUW GU2 116 D5
Stour Cl HAYES BR2 70 F3
Stourhead Cl FARN GU14 93 G5
WIM/MER SW19 29 G1
Stourhead Gdns RYNPK SW20 46 D3
Stourton Av FELT TW13 25 J5
Stovolds Hl CRAN GU6 185 N4
Stovold's Wy ALDT GU11 134 C1
Stowell Av CROY/NA CR0 70 A8
Strachan Pl RYNPK SW20 28 F7
Strafford Rd HSLW TW3 16 C5
TWK TW1 26 D1
Strand Cl CRAWE RH10 165 M6
EPSOM KT18 104 A1
Strand Dr RCH/KEW TW9 18 E2
Strand-on-the-Green
CHSWK W4 18 D1
Stratfield BRAK RG12 34 B8
Stratford Ct NWMAL KT3 46 A4
Stratford Rd ASHV GU12 113 J1
HTHAIR TW6 14 E8
THHTH CR7 49 K4
Strathavon Cl CRAN GU6 170 A10
Strathbrook Rd
STRHM/NOR SW16 31 J5
Strathcona Av GT/LBKH KT23 121 H2
Strathcona Gdns
WOKN/KNAP GU21 95 M1
Strathdale STRHM/NOR SW16 31 J6
Strathdon Dr TOOT SW17 30 A4
Strathearn Av HYS/HAR UB3 15 J2
WHTN TW2 25 M2
Strathearn Rd SUT SM1 65 K4
WIM/MER SW19 29 K6
Strathmore Cl CTHM CR3 108 B3
Strathmore Rd CRAWW RH11 164 C1
CROY/NA CR0 2 D2
TEDD TW11 26 B5
WIM/MER SW19 29 K4
Strathville Rd
WAND/EARL SW18 29 L3
Strathyre Av STRHM/NOR SW16 49 K3
Stratton Av WLGTN SM6 67 G7
Stratton Cl HSLW TW3 16 C3
WIM/MER SW19 47 J2
WOT/HER KT12 * 42 F8
Stratton Rd SUN TW16 42 C2
WIM/MER SW19 47 K2
Stratton Ter BH/WHM TN16 131 M1
Stratton Wk FARN GU14 92 D2
Strawberry Cl CHOB/PIR GU24 95 G3
Strawberry Ct FRIM GU16 94 A1
Strawberry Flds
CHOB/PIR GU24 75 K5
ORP BR6 71 L4
Strawberry Hill Rd TWK TW1 26 C4
Strawberry La CAR SM5 66 C2
Strawberry Ri CHOB/PIR GU24 75 K5
Strawberry V TWK TW1 26 C4
Straw Cl CTHM CR3 107 M5
Strawson Ct HORL RH6 160 C2
Stream Cl BF/WBF KT14 79 H2
Stream Farm Cl RFNM GU10 156 A2
Streamline Ms EDUL SE22 32 E2
Stream Pk EGRIN RH19 162 B2
Stream Valley Rd RFNM GU10 155 M3
Streatham Cl
STRHM/NOR SW16 * 31 H3
Streatham Common
STRHM/NOR SW16 * 31 G8
Streatham Common North
STRHM/NOR SW16 31 J6
Streatham Common South
STRHM/NOR SW16 31 H7
Streatham Ct
STRHM/NOR SW16 31 H4
Streatham Gn
STRHM/NOR SW16 * 31 H5
Streatham High Rd
STRHM/NOR SW16 31 H5
Streatham Hl
BRXS/STRHM SW2 31 H2
Streatham Pl
BRXS/STRHM SW2 31 H1
Streatham Rd MTCM CR4 48 D1
Streatham V
STRHM/NOR SW16 30 F8
Streathbourne Rd TOOT SW17 30 D3

Streatleigh Pde
STRHM/NOR SW16 * 31 H3
Streel's La PETW GU28 200 C12
Streeters Cl GODL GU7 168 D3
Streeters La WLGTN SM6 67 G2
Streetfield Rd SWTR RH13 203 Q6
Street Hl CRAWE RH10 192 D8
Streets Heath CHOB/PIR GU24 75 J2
The Street ASHTD KT21 83 J8
BIL RH14 200 H7
BRKHM/BTCW RH3 124 A8
CRAN GU6 171 K11
EHSLY KT24 119 L2
EHSLY KT24 121 G1
HORL RH6 174 H10
LHD/OX KT22 102 A4
MFD/CHID GU8 159 G2
MFD/CHID GU8 182 D5
MFD/CHID GU8 184 H1
RDKG RH5 173 L11
RFNM GU10 135 J4
RFNM GU10 155 H3
RFNM GU10 180 D3
RGUE GU4 118 D4
RGUE GU4 119 G5
RGUE GU4 139 H5
RGUW GU3 136 E5
RGUW GU3 137 L7
SHGR GU5 169 K2
SWTR RH13 203 Q5
Stretton Rd CROY/NA CR0 3 H1
RCHPK/HAM TW10 26 F3
Strickland Cl CRAWW RH11 164 A5
Strickland Rw
WAND/EARL SW18 30 A1
Stringer's Av RGUE GU4 117 G2
Stringhams Copse
RPLY/SEND GU23 98 C6
Strodes College La EGH TW20 21 J6
Strode St EGH TW20 21 K5
Strond Green Gdns
CROY/NA CR0 50 F7
Strond Green Wy
CROY/NA CR0 50 F7
Strood La HORS RH12 204 D2
Stroud Crs PUT/ROE SW15 28 C4
Stroude Rd EGH TW20 21 K7
VW GU25 39 H4
Stroudes Cl WPK KT4 46 C7
Stroud Green Wy CROY/NA CR0 50 F6
Stroud La SHGR GU5 169 R7
Stroudley Cl CRAWE RH10 165 K5
Stroud Rd SNWD SE25 50 D6
WIM/MER SW19 29 K4
Stroudwater Pk WEY KT13 59 L5
Stroud Wy ASHF TW15 23 L7
Strudgate Cl CRAWE RH10 165 K6
Strudwicks Fld CRAN GU6 186 E1
Stuart Av WOT/HER KT12 42 F8
Stuart Cl CRAWE RH10 165 L5
FARN GU14 92 D4
Stuart Crs CROY/NA CR0 69 J2
REIG RH2 147 K3
Stuart Gv TEDD TW11 26 B6
Stuart Pl MTCM CR4 48 C1
Stuart Rd RCHPK/HAM TW10 26 E3
REIG RH2 147 K3
THHTH CR7 49 M4
WARL CR6 108 E2
WIM/MER SW19 29 K4
Stuart Wy EGRIN RH19 163 G6
STA TW18 22 E7
VW GU25 38 D4
Stubbs Folly SHST GU47 72 A2
Stubbs La KWD/TDW/WH KT20 125 J2
Stubbs Moor Rd FARN GU14 92 C4
Stubbs Wy WIM/MER SW19 48 A1
Stubfield HORS RH12 166 D6
Stubpond La LING RH7 177 Q10
Stubs Cl DORK RH4 144 F4
Stubs Hl DORK RH4 144 F4
Stucley Rd HEST TW5 16 F2
Studios Rd SHPTN TW17 41 J3
Studland Rd BF/WBF KT14 79 J3
KUTN/CMB KT2 8 F1
SYD SE26 33 G6
Stumblets CRAWE RH10 165 L3
Stumps Hill La BECK BR3 33 K7
Sturdee Cl FRIM GU16 73 H8
Sturt Av HASM GU27 198 A8
Sturt Ct RGUE GU4 117 L6
Sturt Rd FNM GU9 133 L2
FRIM GU16 93 J4
Sturt's La KWD/TDW/WH KT20 124 C1
Stychens Cl REDH RH1 127 M7
Stychens La REDH RH1 127 M7
Styles End GT/LBKH KT23 121 L1
Styles Wy BECK BR3 51 M4
Styventon Pl CHERT KT16 40 C7
Subrosa Dr REDH RH1 126 E4
Subrosa Pk REDH RH1 * 126 E4
Succomb's Hl CTHM CR3 108 E2
Succombs Pl WARL CR6 108 E2
Sudbrook Gdns
RCHPK/HAM TW10 27 H4
Sudbrook La
RCHPK/HAM TW10 27 H2
Sudbury Gdns CROY/NA CR0 3 H9
Suffield Cl SAND/SEL CR2 89 G2
Suffield La RGUW GU3 158 C1
Suffield Rd PGE/AN SE20 50 F2
Suffolk Cl BAGS GU19 54 B7
HORL RH6 160 D4
Suffolk Ct FRIM GU16 94 A1
Suffolk Dr RGUE GU4 117 L3
Suffolk Rd BARN SW13 19 J2
SNWD SE25 50 C4
WPK KT4 64 C1
Suffolk Vls WAND/EARL SW18 * 29 K1
Sugden Rd THDIT KT7 44 D8
Sulina Rd BRXS/STRHM SW2 31 H1
Sullington Hl CRAWW RH11 164 F6
Sullington Md HORS RH12 166 B6
Sullivan Cl E/WMO/HCT KT8 43 L3
FARN GU14 92 D5
Sullivan Dr CRAWW RH11 164 A8
Sullivan Rd CBLY GU15 72 D4
Sullivans Reach WOT/HER KT12 42 D7
Sultan St BECK BR3 51 G2
Summer Av E/WMO/HCT KT8 44 B5
Summer Crossing THDIT KT7 44 C5
Summerene Cl
STRHM/NOR SW16 30 F8
Summerfield ASHTD KT21 103 G1
Summerfield La RFNM GU10 155 K7
SURB KT6 63 G1
Summerfield Pl CHERT KT16 * 58 A5
Summerfields Cl
ADL/WDHM KT15 58 C4
Summer Gdns CBLY GU15 73 M4
E/WMO/HCT KT8 44 B5
Summerhayes Cl
WOKN/KNAP GU21 77 H4
Summerhays COB KT11 81 G3
Summerhill GODL GU7 168 A3
Summerhill Wy MTCM CR4 48 D1
Summerhouse Av HEST TW5 16 B3
Summerhouse Cl GODL GU7 168 A6
Summerhouse La
WDR/YW UB7 14 A1
Summerhouse Rd GODL GU7 168 A6
Summerlands CRAN GU6 186 D1
Summerlay Cl
KWD/TDW/WH KT20 105 H3
Summerleigh WEY KT13 * 60 A5
Summerley St
WAND/EARL SW18 29 L3
Summerly Av REIG RH2 125 K7
Summer Rd E/WMO/HCT KT8 44 B5
Summersbury Dr RGUE GU4 139 H8
Summersbury Hall
RGUE GU4 * 139 H8
Summers Cl BELMT SM2 65 K6
WEY KT13 79 K1
Summers La GODL GU7 159 K1
Summer's Rd GODL GU7 168 D1
Summerstown TOOT SW17 29 M4
Summersvere Cl CRAWE RH10 165 J1
Summerswood Cl
PUR/KEN CR8 88 A6
Summer Trees SUN TW16 42 E1
Summerville Gdns SUT SM1 65 J5
Summerwood Rd TWK TW1 17 J8
Summit Wy NRWD SE19 32 B8
Sumner Cl LHD/OX KT22 102 A6
ORP BR6 71 M3
Sumner Gdns CROY/NA CR0 49 K8
Sumner Pl ADL/WDHM KT15 58 D4
Sumner Rd CROY/NA CR0 2 A3
FNM GU9 5 K1
Sumner Rd South
CROY/NA CR0 49 K8
Summit Pl WEY KT13 59 K6
Sun Brow HASM GU27 198 A8
Sunbury Av MORT/ESHN SW14 19 G6
Sunbury Cl WOT/HER KT12 42 D6
Sunbury Ct SUN TW16 43 G2
Sunbury Court Rd SUN TW16 42 F2
Sunbury La WOT/HER KT12 42 D6
Sunbury Rd CHEAM SM3 65 G2
FELT TW13 24 C4
Sunbury Wy FELT TW13 24 F6
Suncroft Pl SYD SE26 32 F4
Sundale Av SAND/SEL CR2 68 F8
Sunderland Mt FSTH SE23 * 33 G3
Sunderland Rd FSTH SE23 33 G3
Sundew Cl CRAWW RH11 164 C8
LTWR GU18 75 G1
Sundial Av SNWD SE25 50 C2
Sundon Crs VW GU25 38 E5
Sundown Av SAND/SEL CR2 88 C1
Sundown Rd ASHF TW15 23 M6
Sundridge Rd CROY/NA CR0 3 K1
WOKS/MYFD GU22 97 K1
Sun Hl WOKS/MYFD GU22 96 E3
Sun Inn Rd MFD/CHID GU8 185 J8
Sunken Rd CROY/NA CR0 68 F4
Sunkist Wy WLGTN SM6 67 H7
Sunlight Cl WIM/MER SW19 * 29 M7
Sunmead Cl LHD/OX KT22 102 C4
Sunmead Pde LHD/OX KT22 * 102 D4
Sunmead Rd SUN TW16 42 D3
Sunna Gdns SUN TW16 42 E2
Sunning Av ASC SL5 37 H7
Sunningdale Av FELT TW13 25 H3
Sunningdale Cl SURB KT6 63 H1
Sunningdale Ct CRAWE RH10 164 F6
Sunningdale Pk ASC SL5 * 37 J5
Sunningdale Rd SUT SM1 65 J2
Sunninghill Cl ASC SL5 37 G4
Sunninghill Pk ASC SL5 * 37 G2
Sunninghill Rd ASC SL5 37 G5
BFOR GU20 54 D2
Sunningvale Av BH/WHM TN16 90 F5
Sunningvale Cl BH/WHM TN16 91 G6
Sunny Av CRAWE RH10 193 M5
Sunnybank ASC SL5 36 D4
Sunny Bank EPSOM KT18 83 M6
SNWD SE25 50 D4
WARL CR6 89 H7
Sunnybank Ms ASHV GU12 * 113 L6
Sunnybank Rd FARN GU14 92 A3
Sunnycroft Rd HSLW TW3 16 E4
SNWD SE25 50 D4
Sunnydale ORP BR6 71 K1
Sunnydell La FNM GU9 155 K3
Sunnydene Rd PUR/KEN CR8 87 L3
Sunnydene St SYD SE26 33 H5
Sunny Down MFD/CHID GU8 183 M4
Sunny Hl MFD/CHID GU8 183 M4
Sunnyhill Cl CRAWE RH10 193 M5
Sunny Hill Rd ALDT GU11 112 A7
Sunnyhill Rd STRHM/NOR SW16 31 H5
Sunnyhurst Cl SUT SM1 65 K2
Sunnymead CRAWE RH10 * 193 N5
CRAWW RH11 164 F4
Sunnymead Av MTCM CR4 49 G3
Sunnymead Rd PUT/ROE SW15 19 L7
Sunnymede Av CAR SM5 86 A1
HOR/WEW KT19 64 B7
Sunny Nook Gdns
SAND/SEL CR2 68 A5
Sunny Ri CTHM CR3 108 A6
Sunnyside CAT SE6 * 33 J1
WIM/MER SW19 29 H7
WOKN/KNAP GU21 * 95 L1
WOT/HER KT12 42 F5
Sunnyside Rd BOR GU35 196 H1
TEDD TW11 26 A5
Sunnyview Cl ASHV GU12 112 F8
Sunray Av BRYLDS KT5 63 L1
Sunrise Cl FELT TW13 25 J4
Sunset Gdns SNWD SE25 50 B2
Sunset Rd WIM/MER SW19 28 E6
Sunshine Wy MTCM CR4 48 C2
Sunvale Av HASM GU27 197 Q7
Sunvale Cl HASM GU27 197 Q7
Surbiton Ct SURB KT6 44 F6
Surbiton Crs KUT/HW KT1 45 H4
Surbiton Hall Cl KUT/HW KT1 45 H4
Surbiton Hill Pk BRYLDS KT5 45 J5
Surbiton Hill Rd SURB KT6 45 H4
Surbiton Rd CBLY GU15 53 K8
KUT/HW KT1 45 G4
Surrey Av CBLY GU15 72 D5
Surrey Gdns EHSLY KT24 100 C5
Surrey Gv SUT SM1 66 A2
Surrey Hills Av
KWD/TDW/WH KT20 123 M5
Surrey Ms WNWD SE27 32 B5
Surrey Rd WWKM BR4 51 L8
Surrey St CROY/NA CR0 2 C6
Surrey Wy GUW GU2 6 C2
Surridge Ct BAGS GU19 54 B7
Surridge Gdns NRWD SE19 32 A7
Sury Basin KUTN/CMB KT2 8 D4
Sussex Av ISLW TW7 17 H5
Sussex Border Pth
CRAWE RH10 193 J3
EDEN TN8 179 R9
EGRIN RH19 163 H4
EGRIN RH19 179 L12
HASM GU27 198 G12
HORL RH6 161 H6
HORL RH6 175 M9
HORS RH12 189 R6
HORS RH12 202 B1
LIPH GU30 196 H12
MFD/CHID GU8 200 H3
RDKG RH5 187 R8
RDKG RH5 189 J5
Sussex Cl NWMAL KT3 46 B4
REIG RH2 148 A1
TWK TW1 17 L8
WOKN/KNAP GU21 75 M8
Sussex Ct WOKN/KNAP GU21 75 M7
Sussex Gdns CHSGTN KT9 63 G5
Sussex Pl NWMAL KT3 46 B4
Sussex Rd CAR SM5 66 C5
MTCM CR4 * 49 H5
NWMAL KT3 46 B4
SAND/SEL CR2 68 A5
WOKN/KNAP GU21 75 M8
WWKM BR4 51 L8
Sussex Ter PGE/AN SE20 * 32 F8
Sutherland Av BH/WHM TN16 91 G7
RGUE GU4 117 H2
SUN TW16 42 D2
Sutherland Cha ASC SL5 36 B2
Sutherland Dr RGUE GU4 117 K5
WIM/MER SW19 48 A1
Sutherland Gdns
MORT/ESHN SW14 19 H5
SUN TW16 42 C2
WPK KT4 46 E8
Sutherland Gv TEDD TW11 26 B6
WAND/EARL SW18 29 J1
Sutherland Rd CHSWK W4 19 G1
CROY/NA CR0 49 K7
Sutton Av WOKN/KNAP GU21 96 B1
Sutton Cl BECK BR3 51 L1
CHSWK W4 * 18 F1
Sutton Common Rd
CHEAM SM3 47 J7
Sutton Ct BELMT SM2 65 M6
CHSWK W4 * 18 F1
Sutton Court Rd CHSWK W4 18 F1
SUT SM1 65 M5
Sutton Dene HSLW TW3 16 E3
Sutton Gdns CROY/NA CR0 50 C5
REDH RH1 127 G3
Sutton Green Rd RGUE GU4 97 H8
Sutton Gv SUT SM1 66 A4
Sutton Hall HEST TW5 16 D2
Sutton Hl RGUE GU4 117 M3
Sutton La BNSTD SM7 85 L2
DTCH/LGLY SL3 12 E1
HSLW TW3 16 C4
RDKG RH5 171 N1
Sutton La South CHSWK W4 18 F1
Sutton Park Rd SUT SM1 65 L5
Sutton Pl DTCH/LGLY SL3 12 E1
RDKG RH5 171 L1
Sutton Rd CBLY GU15 53 K8
HEST TW5 16 D3
Sutton Sq HEST TW5 16 C3
Sutton Wy HEST TW5 16 C3
Swaby Rd WAND/EARL SW18 29 M3
Swaffield Rd WAND/EARL SW18 29 M1
Swain Cl STRHM/NOR SW16 30 E7
Swain Rd THHTH CR7 49 M5
Swains Rd MTCM CR4 30 C8
Swaledale BRAK RG12 34 D5
Swaledale Cl CRAWW RH11 164 E7
Swale Rd FARN GU14 92 A3
Swallands Rd CAT SE6 33 K4
Swallow Cl MFD/CHID GU8 183 M2
STA TW18 22 C5
Swallowdale SAND/SEL CR2 69 G7
Swallowfield EGH TW20 20 E7
LING RH7 178 H7
Swallowfield Cl SWTR RH13 205 R12
Swallow Gdns
STRHM/NOR SW16 31 G6
Swallow La RDKG RH5 144 E8
Swallow Ri WOKN/KNAP GU21 75 M7
Swallow Rd CRAWW RH11 164 E2
Swallow St CRAWE RH10 193 P8
Swallowtail Rd HORS RH12 167 H3
Swan Barn Rd HASM GU27 198 E7
Swan Cl CROY/NA CR0 3 G1
FELT TW13 25 H5
Swancote Gn BRAK RG12 34 E5
Swan Ct GU GU1 117 G6
Swan Island TWK TW1 * 26 D4
Swan La EDEN TN8 153 M5
GU GU1 7 G6
HORL RH6 175 J10
Swan Mill Gdns DORK RH4 122 F8
Swanns Meadow
GT/LBKH KT23 101 K8
Swann Wy HORS RH12 166 B6
Swan Pl BARN SW13 19 J4
Swan Rd FELT TW13 25 H5
Swansea Rd HTHAIR TW6 14 F8
Swans Ghyll FROW RH18 195 M10
Swan St ISLW TW7 17 L5
The Swansway WEY KT13 * 59 K2
Swanton Gdns WIM/MER SW19 29 G2
Swan Wk HORS RH12 * 166 F7
SHPTN TW17 42 B7
Swanwick Cl PUT/ROE SW15 28 C1
Swanworth La RDKG RH5 122 E2
Swaynesland Rd EDEN TN8 131 J8
Swayne's La GU GU1 118 B8
Sweeps Ditch Cl STA TW18 40 E1
Sweeps La EGH TW20 21 J6
Sweet La SHGR GU5 171 J1
Sweetwater Cl SHGR GU5 169 N5
Sweetwater La
MFD/CHID GU8 183 P6
SHGR GU5 169 N5
Swievelands Rd
BH/WHM TN16 110 E1
Swift La BAGS GU19 54 C6
CRAWW RH11 164 F2
Swift Rd FELT TW13 25 H4
FNM GU9 133 L2
Swift's Cl RFNM GU10 134 E8
Swinburne Crs CROY/NA CR0 50 F6
Swinburne Rd PUT/ROE SW15 19 K6
Swindon Rd HORS RH12 166 E5
HTHAIR TW6 14 F8
Swinfield Cl FELT TW13 25 H5
Swingate Rd FNM GU9 5 L8
Swinley Rd ASC SL5 35 M4
Swires Shaw HAYES BR2 71 G3
Swiss Cl RFNM GU10 155 J5
Swissland Hl EGRIN RH19 178 F11
Switchback La RFNM GU10 155 K6
Swordfish Wy FARN GU14 112 B2
Swordsman's Rd FRIM GU16 94 A1
Sycamore Av HORS RH12 167 M4
Sycamore Cl CAR SM5 66 C3
CRAWW RH11 164 E1
FELT TW13 24 D4
FRIM GU16 73 H8
LHD/OX KT22 102 C4
SAND/SEL CR2 68 B4
Sycamore Ct WEY KT13 60 C2
Sycamore Dr ASHV GU12 113 J2
EGRIN RH19 163 H4
FRIM GU16 73 H7
RFNM GU10 155 K3
Sycamore Gdns MTCM CR4 48 A2
Sycamore Gv NWMAL KT3 46 B3
PGE/AN SE20 50 D1
Sycamore Ri BNSTD SM7 85 G4
BRAK RG12 35 G3
Sycamore Rd FARN GU14 93 G7
GU GU1 7 G3
WIM/MER SW19 28 F7
The Sycamores FARN GU14 93 G6
GT/LBKH KT23 101 M6
Sycamore Wk EGH TW20 20 E7
REIG RH2 147 M3
Sycamore Wy TEDD TW11 26 F7
Sydcote DUL SE21 * 31 M3
Sydenham Av SYD SE26 32 E6
Sydenham Hl FSTH SE23 32 E3
Sydenham Pk SYD SE26 32 F4
Sydenham Park Rd SYD SE26 32 F4
Sydenham Ri FSTH SE23 32 E3
Sydenham Rd CROY/NA CR0 2 E4
GU GU1 7 H7
SYD SE26 33 G6
Sydenham Station Ap
SYD SE26 32 F5
Sydmons Ct FSTH SE23 * 32 F1
Sydney Av PUR/KEN CR8 87 J2
Sydney Crs ASHF TW15 23 L7
Sydney Pl GU GU1 7 L6
Sydney Rd EBED/NFELT TW14 24 D2
GU GU1 7 L6
RCH/KEW TW9 18 B6
RYNPK SW20 47 G2
SUT SM1 65 K3
TEDD TW11 26 C6
Sydney Smith Av FARN GU14 92 E8
Sydney Ter ESH/CLAY KT10 * 62 C5
Sykes Dr STA TW18 22 E6
Sylvan Cl OXTED RH8 130 E3
SAND/SEL CR2 68 E8
WOKS/MYFD GU22 11 K7
Sylvan Gdns SURB KT6 45 G7
Sylvan Hl NRWD SE19 50 B1
Sylvan Rd CRAWE RH10 165 J6
NRWD SE19 50 C1
Sylvanus BRAK RG12 34 C7
Sylvan Wy REDH RH1 148 E1
WWKM BR4 70 B3
Sylvaways Cl CRAN GU6 186 F2
Sylverdale Rd CROY/NA CR0 2 A7
PUR/KEN CR8 87 L3
Sylvia Ct CHOB/PIR GU24 75 K5
Syon Gate Wy BTFD TW8 17 L2
Syon La ISLW TW7 17 J1
Syon Pk ISLW TW7 * 17 L5
Syon Park Gdns ISLW TW7 17 J2
Syon Pl FARN GU14 93 G5
Sythwood WOKN/KNAP GU21 76 E7
Szabo Crs RGUW GU3 114 E8

T

Tabarin Wy EW KT17 84 F6
Tabor Gdns CHEAM SM3 65 J5
Tabor Gv WIM/MER SW19 29 H8
Tachbrook Rd
EBED/NFELT TW14 24 C1
Tadmor Cl SUN TW16 42 C4
Tadorne Rd
KWD/TDW/WH KT20 104 F3
Tadworth Av NWMAL KT3 46 C4
Tadworth Cl
KWD/TDW/WH KT20 105 G4
Tadworth St
KWD/TDW/WH KT20 104 F5
Taffy's How MTCM CR4 48 B3
Tait Rd CROY/NA CR0 3 G1
Talbot Cl FRIM GU16 93 K5
REIG RH2 147 L1
Talbot La HORS RH12 166 F8
Talbot Pl BAGS GU19 54 B6
Talbot Rd ASHF TW15 23 G6
CAR SM5 66 D4
FNM GU9 5 G7
ISLW TW7 17 K6
LING RH7 178 E6
THHTH CR7 50 A4
WHTN TW2 26 B2
Talcott Pth BRXS/STRHM SW2 * 31 K2
Taleworth Cl ASHTD KT21 103 G2
Taleworth Pk ASHTD KT21 103 G2
Taleworth Rd ASHTD KT21 103 G1
Talfourd Wy REDH RH1 148 C3
Talgarth Dr FARN GU14 93 G7
Talisman Sq SYD SE26 32 D5
Talisman Wy EW KT17 84 F6
Tallis Cl CRAWW RH11 164 B7
Tallow Rd BTFD TW8 17 M2
Tall Trees DTCH/LGLY SL3 13 H3
EGRIN RH19 * 163 G5
STRHM/NOR SW16 49 J3
Tally Rd OXTED RH8 131 H5
Talma Gdns WHTN TW2 26 B1
Talmage Cl FSTH SE23 32 F1
Talman Cl CRAWW RH11 * 164 A5
Tamar Cl CRAWE RH10 165 L5
Tamarind Cl GUW GU2 116 D3
Tamerton Sq
WOKS/MYFD GU22 10 C9
Tamesis Gdns WPK KT4 64 B1
Tamian Wy HSLWW TW4 15 M6
Tamworth BRAK RG12 35 G7
Tamworth La MTCM CR4 48 E3
Tamworth Pk MTCM CR4 48 E4
Tamworth Pl CROY/NA CR0 2 C6
Tamworth Rd CROY/NA CR0 2 C6
Tanbridge Pk HORS RH12 166 D8
Tanbridge Pl HORS RH12 166 E8
Tandridge Gdns SAND/SEL CR2 88 C3
Tandridgehill La GDST RH9 129 J2
Tandridge La LING RH7 178 A1
OXTED RH8 129 K5
Tandridge Rd WARL CR6 109 G1
Tanfield Rd CROY/NA CR0 2 C9
Tangier Rd GU GU1 139 K1
RCHPK/HAM TW10 18 E5
Tangier Wy
KWD/TDW/WH KT20 85 H7
Tangier Wd
KWD/TDW/WH KT20 85 H8
Tangle Oak EGRIN RH19 193 R1
Tanglewood Cl CHERT KT16 56 E2
CROY/NA CR0 68 F2
WOKS/MYFD GU22 78 A6
Tanglewood Ride
CHOB/PIR GU24 75 G2
Tanglewood Wy FELT TW13 24 E4
Tangley Gv PUT/ROE SW15 28 C1
Tangley La RGUW GU3 116 C4
Tangley Park Rd HPTN TW12 * 25 J6
Tanglyn Av SHPTN TW17 41 K5
Tangmere Gv KUTN/CMB KT2 27 G6
Tangmere Rd CRAWW RH11 164 B4
Tanhouse Rd OXTED RH8 130 A6
Tanhurst La RDKG RH5 172 A7
Tanker Rd FARN GU14 92 E8
Tankerton Rd SURB KT6 63 J1
Tankerton Ter CROY/NA CR0 * 49 J7
Tankerville Rd
STRHM/NOR SW16 31 G8
Tank Rd CBLY GU15 72 C4
Tanners Cl WOT/HER KT12 42 E6
Tanners Dean LHD/OX KT22 103 G4
Tannersfield RGUE GU4 139 H8
Tanner's Hl BRKHM/BTCW RH3 145 L2
Tanners La HASM GU27 198 D6
Tanners Md EDEN TN8 153 M8
Tanners Meadow
BRKHM/BTCW RH3 145 L4
Tanners Yd BAGS GU19 * 54 B6
Tannery Cl CROY/NA CR0 51 G5
SWTR RH13 203 P6
Tannery La RPLY/SEND GU23 98 B4
SHGR GU5 168 H1
The Tannery REDH RH1 126 B8
Tannsfeld Rd SYD SE26 33 G6
Tansy Cl RGUE GU4 117 M6
Tantallon Rd BAL SW12 30 D2
Tanyard Av EGRIN RH19 163 H5
Tanyard Cl CRAWE RH10 165 L7
SWTR RH13 167 H8
Tanyard Wy HORL RH6 160 E2
Tapestry Cl BELMT SM2 65 L6
Taplow Ct MTCM CR4 48 B4
Tapner's Rd
BRKHM/BTCW RH3 146 C6
Tapping Cl KUTN/CMB KT2 9 J3
Tara Pk COUL/CHIP CR5 106 C2
Tarbat Ct SHST GU47 72 A1
Target Cl EBED/NFELT TW14 15 H8
Tarham Cl HORL RH6 160 B1
Tarleton Gdns FSTH SE23 32 E2
Tarmac Wy WDR/YW UB7 13 L2
Tarnbrook Wy BRAK RG12 35 H7
Tarn Cl FARN GU14 92 B7
Tarn Rd GSHT GU26 197 Q2
Tarragon Dr GUW GU2 116 D3
Tarragon Gv SYD SE26 33 G7
Tarrant Pl BF/WBF KT14 * 78 C3
Tarrington Cl
STRHM/NOR SW16 * 31 G5
Tartar Hl COB KT11 80 E3
Tartar Rd COB KT11 80 F3
Tasker Cl HYS/HAR UB3 14 F2
Tate Cl LHD/OX KT22 102 F5
Tate Rd SUT SM1 65 K4
Tates Wy HORS RH12 203 J2
Tatsfield La BH/WHM TN16 111 J3
Tattenham Corner Rd
EPSOM KT18 84 C7
Tattenham Crs EPSOM KT18 84 D8
Tattenham Gv EPSOM KT18 84 E8
Tattenham Wy
KWD/TDW/WH KT20 85 H7
Taunton Av CTHM CR3 108 C5
HSLW TW3 16 F4
RYNPK SW20 46 E2
Taunton Cl CHEAM SM3 47 K8
Taunton La COUL/CHIP CR5 107 K1
Tavern Cl CAR SM5 48 B7

Tavistock Cl STA TW18 23 G8
Tavistock Crs MTCM CR4 49 H4
Tavistock Gdns FARN GU14 92 E2
Tavistock Gv CROY/NA CR0 2 E2
Tavistock Rd CAR SM5 48 A8
CROY/NA CR0 2 E3
Tawfield BRAK RG12 34 B7
Tawny Cl FELT TW13 24 D4
Tawny Rw SHST GU47 * 72 A1
Tayben Av WHTN TW2 17 H8
Tay Cl FARN GU14 92 B3
Tayles Hill Dr EW KT17 64 C8
Taylor Av RCH/KEW TW9 18 E4
Taylor Cl HOR/WEW KT19 83 K1
HPTN TW12 25 M6
HSLW TW3 16 F3
Taylor Rd ASHTD KT21 83 G7
MTCM CR4 30 B8
WLGTN SM6 66 E4
Taylors Cl BOR GU35 180 A12
Taylors Ct FELT TW13 24 D3
Taylors Crs CRAN GU6 186 E2
Taylors La BOR GU35 180 A12
SYD SE26 32 E5
Taylor Wk CRAWW RH11 164 E4
Taymount Ri FSTH SE23 32 F3
Taynton Dr REDH RH1 127 G4
Teal Cl HORS RH12 166 F4
SAND/SEL CR2 89 G1
Teal Ct DORK RH4 * 144 D1
Tealing Dr HOR/WEW KT19 64 A3
Teasel Cl CRAWW RH11 164 D7
CROY/NA CR0 51 G8
Teazlewood Pk LHD/OX KT22 82 D7
Tebbit Cl BRAK RG12 35 G2
Teck Cl ISLW TW7 17 K4
Tedder Cl CHSGTN KT9 62 F4
Tedder Rd SAND/SEL CR2 69 G6
Teddington Cl HOR/WEW KT19 64 A8
Teddington Pk TEDD TW11 26 C6
Teddington Park Rd
TEDD TW11 26 C5
Tedham La GDST RH9 177 N2
Tees Cl FARN GU14 92 B3
Teesdale CRAWW RH11 164 E7
Teesdale Av ISLW TW7 17 K3
Teesdale Gdns ISLW TW7 17 K3
SNWD SE25 50 B2
Teevan Cl CROY/NA CR0 3 M1
Teevan Rd CROY/NA CR0 3 M2
Tegg's La WOKS/MYFD GU22 78 C6
Tekels Av CBLY GU15 73 H4
Tekels Wy CBLY GU15 73 J6
Telconia Cl BOR GU35 196 H1
Telegraph La ESH/CLAY KT10 62 C3
Telegraph Pas
BRXS/STRHM SW2 31 H1
Telegraph Rd PUT/ROE SW15 28 F1
Telegraph Tr WLGTN SM6 86 D1
Telferscot Rd BAL SW12 31 G2
Telford Av BRXS/STRHM SW2 31 H2
Telford Cl NRWD SE19 32 C7
Telford Ct GU GU1 7 L5
Telford Dr WOT/HER KT12 42 F7
Telford Pl CRAWE RH10 165 G5
Telford Rd WHTN TW2 25 K1
Telham Ct CRAWW RH11 * 164 B7
Tellisford ESH/CLAY KT10 61 L3
Temperley Rd BAL SW12 30 D1
Tempest Rd EGH TW20 21 M7
Templar Pl HPTN TW12 25 K8
Temple Av CROY/NA CR0 69 J2
Temple Bar Rd
WOKN/KNAP GU21 96 C1
Temple Cl CRAWE RH10 165 M5
Templecombe Ms
WOKS/MYFD GU22 11 H4
Templecombe Wy MRDN SM4 47 H5
Templedene Av STA TW18 22 E8
Temple Field Cl
ADL/WDHM KT15 58 E5
Temple Gdns STA TW18 40 C1
Temple La RDKG RH5 173 M11
Templeman Cl PUR/KEN CR8 87 K6
Templer Av FARN GU14 92 D8
Temple Rd CROY/NA CR0 2 E9
HOR/WEW KT19 84 A2
HSLW TW3 16 E6
RCH/KEW TW9 18 C4
Temple's Cl RFNM GU10 134 F8
Temple Sheen Rd
MORT/ESHN SW14 18 F6
Templeton Cl NRWD SE19 50 A1
Temple Wy BNFD RG42 34 B1
SUT SM1 66 A2
Temple Wood Dr REDH RH1 * 126 C5
Ten Acre WOKN/KNAP GU21 76 D8
Ten Acre La EGH TW20 39 M2
Ten Acres Cl LHD/OX KT22 102 A6
Tenbury Ct BAL SW12 31 G2
Tenby Dr ASC SL5 37 G5
Tenby Rd FRIM GU16 93 K1
Tenchley's La OXTED RH8 131 G5
OXTED RH8 131 H7
Tenham Av BRXS/STRHM SW2 31 G3
Tenniel Cl GUW GU2 116 E6
Tennison Cl COUL/CHIP CR5 107 L2
Tennison Rd SNWD SE25 50 C4
Tennyson Av NWMAL KT3 46 E5
TWK TW1 26 C2
Tennyson Cl CRAWE RH10 165 K2
EBED/NFELT TW14 15 K8
HORS RH12 167 H3
Tennyson Ri EGRIN RH19 162 D4
Tennyson Rd ADL/WDHM KT15 59 H3
ASHF TW15 23 H6
HSLW TW3 16 F4
PGE/AN SE20 33 G8
WIM/MER SW19 29 M7
Tennyson's La HASM GU27 198 F9
Tenterden Gdns CROY/NA CR0 3 M1
Tenterden Rd CROY/NA CR0 3 M1
Tenth Av
KWD/TDW/WH KT20 * 105 J8
Tern Rd CRAWW RH11 190 G8
Terrace Gdns BARN SW13 19 J4
Terrace La RCHPK/HAM TW10 18 B8
Terrace Rd WOT/HER KT12 42 E7
The Terrace ADL/WDHM KT15 59 H4
ASC SL5 37 G5
BARN SW13 19 H4
CBLY GU15 72 C4
CWTH RG45 52 A4
FARN GU14 * 93 G6
FSTH SE23 * 33 H1
WOKS/MYFD GU22 * 97 K3
Terra Cotta Rd GDST RH9 150 F4
Terrac St RCH/KEW TW9 18 C6
Terrapin Rd TOOT SW17 30 E4
Terry Rd CRAWW RH11 191 L12
Testard Rd GUW GU2 6 E7
Testers Cl OXTED RH8 130 E5
Teviot Cl GUW GU2 116 D5
Tewkesbury Av FSTH SE23 32 E2
Tewkesbury Cl BF/WBF KT14 79 G1
Tewkesbury Rd CAR SM5 48 A8
Thackeray Cl ISLW TW7 17 K4
WIM/MER SW19 29 G8
Thakeham Cl SYD SE26 32 E6
Thames Av CHERT KT16 40 D3
Thames Bank
MORT/ESHN SW14 18 F4
Thames Cl CHERT KT16 40 E7
FARN GU14 92 B3
HPTN TW12 43 L2
Thames Down Link ASHTD KT21 83 K2
HOR/WEW KT19 63 M3
WPK KT4 64 A2
Thames Eyot TWK TW1 * 26 D3
Thamesfield Ct SHPTN TW17 41 M7
Thamesfield Ms SHPTN TW17 * 41 M7
Thamesgate STA TW18 40 E2
Thamesgate Cl
RCHPK/HAM TW10 26 E5
Thameside TEDD TW11 8 C2
Thames Md WOT/HER KT12 42 D7
Thames Meadow
E/WMO/HCT KT8 43 K3
SHPTN TW17 42 A8
Thames Pth BARN SW13 19 J3
ISLW TW7 17 M4
STA TW18 22 B4
STA TW18 22 C8
STWL/WRAY TW19 21 H3
WEY KT13 59 L1
WOT/HER KT12 42 D5
Thamespoint TEDD TW11 * 8 C2
Thames Reach KUT/HW KT1 * 8 D4
Thames Rd CHSWK W4 18 E1
Thames Side KUT/HW KT1 8 D5
STA TW18 40 F5
THDIT KT7 44 E6
Thames St HPTN TW12 43 L2
KUT/HW KT1 8 D6
STA TW18 22 C6
SUN TW16 42 E3
WEY KT13 59 L1
WOT/HER KT12 42 C7
Thamesvale Cl HSLW TW3 16 D4
Thames Village CHSWK W4 18 F3
Thanescroft Gdns CROY/NA CR0 3 H8
Thanet Dr HAYES BR2 71 G2
Thanet Pl CROY/NA CR0 2 D9
Tharp Rd WLGTN SM6 67 G4
Thatcher Cl CRAWE RH10 164 F7
Thatchers Cl HORL RH6 160 E1
HORS RH12 167 H5
Thatchers La RGUW GU3 116 A1
Thatchers Wy ISLW TW7 17 G7
Thaxted Pl RYNPK SW20 29 G8
Thayers Farm Rd BECK BR3 51 H1
Theal Cl SHST GU47 72 A1
Theatre Rd FARN GU14 112 E1
The Beverly MRDN SM4 47 G6
The Courtyard HAYES BR2 71 H5
The Farriers EDEN TN8 153 L6
The Green WIM/MER SW19 29 G6
Thelma Gv TEDD TW11 26 D7
Thelton Av HORS RH12 166 A6
Theobald Rd CROY/NA CR0 2 A5
Theobalds Wy FRIM GU16 73 M6
Thepps Cl REDH RH1 149 J3
Therapia La CROY/NA CR0 49 H7
Theresa's Wk SAND/SEL CR2 68 A7
Thesiger Rd PGE/AN SE20 33 G8
Thetford Rd ASHF TW15 23 H5
NWMAL KT3 46 B5
Theydon Cl CRAWE RH10 165 J6
Thicket Crs SUT SM1 65 M3
Thicket Gv PGE/AN SE20 32 D8
Thicket Rd PGE/AN SE20 32 E8
SUT SM1 65 M3
Thicket Ter PGE/AN SE20 * 32 D8
Thickthorne La STA TW18 22 D8
Third Av KWD/TDW/WH KT20 * 105 J8
Third Cl E/WMO/HCT KT8 43 L4
Third Cross Rd WHTN TW2 26 A3
Thirlmere Cl EGH TW20 21 L8
FARN GU14 92 B5
Thirlmere Rd CRAWW RH11 190 G9
STRHM/NOR SW16 31 G5
Thirsk Ct ASHV GU12 113 G7
Thirsk Rd MTCM CR4 30 D8
SNWD SE25 50 A4
Thirteenth Av
KWD/TDW/WH KT20 * 105 J8
Thistlecroft Rd WOT/HER KT12 60 F3
Thistledene BF/WBF KT14 78 C3
THDIT KT7 44 B6
Thistledown V BIL RH14 * 201 N5
The Thistles LHD/OX KT22 102 F4
Thistle Wy HORL RH6 161 M2
Thistlewood Crs CROY/NA CR0 90 A2
Thistleworth Cl ISLW TW7 17 G2
Thistley Cl COUL/CHIP CR5 107 G4
Thistley La CRAN GU6 186 D1
Thistledown V BIL RH14 201 N5
Thomas Av CTHM CR3 107 M3
Thomas Dean Rd SYD SE26 * 33 J5
Thomas' La CAT SE6 33 L1
Thomas Wall Cl SUT SM1 65 L4
Thompson Av RCH/KEW TW9 18 E5
Thompson Cl CHEAM SM3 47 K8
Thompson Rd HSLW TW3 16 E6
Thompsons Cl CHOB/PIR GU24 95 G5
Thompson's La CHOB/PIR GU24 56 A7
Thomson Crs CROY/NA CR0 49 K8
Thorburn Cha SHST GU47 72 B3
Thorburn Wy WIM/MER SW19 * 48 A1
Thorkhill Gdns THDIT KT7 44 D8
Thorkhill Rd THDIT KT7 44 E8
Thorley Cl BF/WBF KT14 78 D4
Thorley Gdns
WOKS/MYFD GU22 78 D4
Thornash Cl WOKN/KNAP GU21 76 F5
Thornash Rd WOKN/KNAP GU21 76 F6
Thornash Wy
WOKN/KNAP GU21 76 F5
Thorn Bank GUW GU2 6 A8
Thornberry Wy GU GU1 117 J4
Thornbury Av ISLW TW7 17 G2
Thornbury Rd ISLW TW7 17 G2
Thorn Cl RFNM GU10 155 J5
Thorncombe St SHGR GU5 168 G6
Thorn Ct BELMT SM2 * 65 L6
Thorncroft EGH TW20 20 F8
Thorncroft Cl COUL/CHIP CR5 107 K1
Thorncroft Rd SUT SM1 65 L3
Thorndean St
WAND/EARL SW18 29 M3
Thorndon Gdns
HOR/WEW KT19 64 B3
Thorndown La BFOR GU20 55 G6
Thorndyke Cl CRAWE RH10 165 M5
Thorne Cl ASHF TW15 23 M8
ESH/CLAY KT10 62 D6
Thorneloe Gdns CROY/NA CR0 67 L4
Thorne's Cl BECK BR3 51 M3
Thorne St BARN SW13 19 H5
Thorneycroft Cl WOT/HER KT12 42 F6
Thornfield Gn BLKW GU17 72 C6
Thornhill BRAK RG12 35 H4
Thornhill Av SURB KT6 63 H1
Thornhill Rd ALDT GU11 113 G5
CROY/NA CR0 2 D1
SURB KT6 63 H1
Thornhill Vw GSHT GU26 * 197 Q2
Thornhill Wy SHPTN TW17 41 K5
Thornlaw Rd WNWD SE27 31 K5
Thornleas Pl EHSLY KT24 100 B7
Thorn Rd RFNM GU10 155 J5
Thornsbeach Rd CAT SE6 33 M2
Thornsett Pl PGE/AN SE20 50 E2
Thornsett Rd PGE/AN SE20 50 E2
WAND/EARL SW18 29 L3
Thornsett Ter PGE/AN SE20 * 50 E2
Thornton Av BRXS/STRHM SW2 31 G2
CROY/NA CR0 49 J6
Thornton Cl GUW GU2 116 D5
HORL RH6 160 B3
Thornton Crs COUL/CHIP CR5 107 K1
Thornton Dene BECK BR3 51 K2
Thornton Gdns BAL SW12 31 G2
Thornton Hl WIM/MER SW19 29 H8
Thornton Pl HORL RH6 160 B3
Thornton Rd BAL SW12 31 G1
CAR SM5 48 B7
MORT/ESHN SW14 19 G5
THHTH CR7 49 K5
WIM/MER SW19 29 G7
Thornton Rw THHTH CR7 49 K5
Thornville Gv MTCM CR4 47 M2
Thornyhurst Rd FRIM GU16 93 K5
Thorold Cl SAND/SEL CR2 69 G8
Thorold Rd FNM GU9 5 J2
Thorpe By-Pass EGH TW20 39 K3
Thorpe Cl CROY/NA CR0 89 M1
SYD SE26 * 33 G5
Thorpe Ct TOOT SW17 30 B5
Thorpe Lea Rd EGH TW20 39 L1
Thorpe Pk CHERT KT16 * 40 C3
Thorpe Rd CHERT KT16 40 A5
KUTN/CMB KT2 8 F2
STA TW18 22 A6
Thorpes Cl GUW GU2 116 D5
Thorpeside Cl STA TW18 40 B2
Thorpewood Av SYD SE26 32 E3
Thorsden Cl WOKS/MYFD GU22 10 D9
Thorsden Ct WOKS/MYFD GU22 10 D8
Thorsden Wy NRWD SE19 * 32 B6
Thrale Rd STRHM/NOR SW16 30 F6
Three Acres HORS RH12 166 D8
Three Acres Pk REDH RH1 * 148 C4
Three Arch Rd REDH RH1 148 D4
Three Bridges Rd
CRAWE RH10 165 H4
Three Castles Pth ASC SL5 35 M3
Three Gates GU GU1 117 M7
Three Gates La HASM GU27 198 E6
Three Mile Rd RDKG RH5 171 M7
Three Pears Rd GU GU1 118 B8
Threestile Rd HORS RH12 188 G12
Three Stiles Rd FNM GU9 4 D2
Threshfield BRAK RG12 34 D5
Thriffwood SYD SE26 32 F4
Thrift V RGUE GU4 118 A5
Thrigby Rd CHSGTN KT9 63 J5
Throwley Rd SUT SM1 65 L4
Throwley Wy SUT SM1 65 L3
Thrupp Cl MTCM CR4 48 E2
Thrupps Av WOT/HER KT12 61 G4
Thrupps La WOT/HER KT12 61 G4
Thundery Hl RFNM GU10 135 J5
Thurbans Rd FNM GU9 155 K2
Thurbarn Rd CAT SE6 33 L6
Thurbarns Hl RDKG RH5 173 M8
Thurlby Rd WNWD SE27 31 K5
Thurleston Av MRDN SM4 47 H5
Thurlestone Cl SHPTN TW17 * 41 M6
Thurlestone Pde SHPTN TW17 * 41 M6
Thurlestone Rd WNWD SE27 31 K4
Thurlow Hl DUL SE21 31 M2
Thurlow Park Rd DUL SE21 31 L3
Thurlow Wk CRAN GU6 186 D4
Thurlton Ct WOKN/KNAP GU21 10 D3
Thurne Wy HORS RH12 203 J2
Thurnham Wy
KWD/TDW/WH KT20 105 G2
Thursby Rd WOKN/KNAP GU21 76 D8
Thursley Crs CROY/NA CR0 70 A6
Thursley Gdns WIM/MER SW19 29 G3
Thursley Rd MFD/CHID GU8 182 C4
RFNM GU10 181 P6
Thurso St TOOT SW17 30 A5
Thurstan Rd RYNPK SW20 28 E8
Thyer Cl ORP BR6 71 M3
Thyme Ct RGUE GU4 117 L5
Tibbenham Pl CAT SE6 33 L2
Tibbets Cl WIM/MER SW19 29 G2
Tibbet's Ride PUT/ROE SW15 29 G1
Ticehurst Cl CRAWE RH10 192 D7
Ticehurst Rd FSTH SE23 33 H3
Tichborne Cl BLKW GU17 72 A4
Tichborne Pl ASHV GU12 135 G1
Tichbourne Cl FRIM GU16 73 J6
Tichmarsh HOR/WEW KT19 63 M8
Tidenham Gdns CROY/NA CR0 3 H7
Tideswell Rd CROY/NA CR0 69 K2
PUT/ROE SW15 19 M6
Tideway Cl RCHPK/HAM TW10 26 E5
Tidwells Lea BNFD RG42 35 H1
Tiepigs La WWKM BR4 70 B1
Tierney Rd BRXS/STRHM SW2 31 H2
Tierney Ter BRXS/STRHM SW2 * 31 H2
Tilburstow Hill Rd GDST RH9 128 F6
Tildesley Rd PUT/ROE SW15 19 M8
Tile Barn Cl FARN GU14 92 D3
Tilehouse Rd RGUE GU4 139 H5
Tilehurst La RDKG RH5 145 H3
Tilehurst Rd CHEAM SM3 65 H4
WAND/EARL SW18 30 A2
Tilers Cl REDH RH1 126 F5
Tiler's Wy REIG RH2 147 M4
Tilford Av CROY/NA CR0 69 M6
Tilford Gdns WIM/MER SW19 29 G2
Tilford Rd FNM GU9 5 L5
GSHT GU26 182 A12
RFNM GU10 156 F6
RFNM GU10 181 P4
Tilford St RFNM GU10 156 F6
Tilgate Common REDH RH1 127 M7
Tilgate Dr CRAWE RH10 191 P12
Tilgate Pde CRAWE RH10 165 G7
Tilgate Pl CRAWE RH10 165 G7
Tilgate Wy CRAWE RH10 165 G7
Tilia Cl SUT SM1 65 J4
Tilletts La HORS RH12 166 B1
Tilley La EPSOM KT18 103 M5
Tilley Rd FELT TW13 24 D2
Tillingbourne Rd RGUE GU4 139 H6
Tillingdown Hl CTHM CR3 108 E4
Tillingdown La CTHM CR3 108 E7
Tillotson Cl CRAWE RH10 165 M5
Tilson Gdns BRXS/STRHM SW2 31 H1
Tilt Cl COB KT11 81 H6
Tilthams Corner Rd GODL GU7 168 E1
Tilthams Gn GODL GU7 168 E2
Tilt Meadow COB KT11 81 H6
Tilt Rd COB KT11 81 G6
Tilt Vw COB KT11 * 80 F5
Tiltwood Dr CRAWE RH10 193 P4
Timber Bank FRIM GU16 93 K4
Timber Cl FNM GU9 * 5 G3
GT/LBKH KT23 121 M1
WOKS/MYFD GU22 78 C5
Timbercroft HOR/WEW KT19 64 B3
Timberham Farm Rd
HORL RH6 160 A6
Timber Hl ASHTD KT21 103 H1
Timber Hill Rd CTHM CR3 108 D6
Timberlands CRAWW RH11 191 L12
Timberling Gdns SAND/SEL CR2 68 A8
Timbermill Ct HASM GU27 198 A7
Timberslip Dr WLGTN SM6 67 G7
The Timbers CHEAM SM3 * 65 H5
SWTR RH13 205 R11
Timbertop Rd BH/WHM TN16 90 F8
Time Sq BRAK RG12 34 E2
Times Sq SUT SM1 * 65 L4
Timline Gn BRAK RG12 35 J2
Timperley Gdns REDH RH1 126 B6
Timsway STA TW18 22 C6
Tindale Cl SAND/SEL CR2 88 A1
Tinmans Rw COB KT11 * 80 F8
Tinsey Cl EGH TW20 21 L6
Tinsley Cl CRAWE RH10 165 J1
SNWD SE25 50 E3
Tinsley Gn CRAWE RH10 192 A2
Tinsley La CRAWE RH10 165 J1
Tinsley La North CRAWE RH10 192 J2
Tinsley La South CRAWE RH10 165 J2
Tintagel Cl EW KT17 84 C4
Tintagel Dr FRIM GU16 73 J8
Tintagel Wy WOKS/MYFD GU22 11 H4
Tintells La EHSLY KT24 119 L2
Tintern Cl WIM/MER SW19 29 M8
Tintern Rd CAR SM5 48 A8
CRAWW RH11 164 C6
Tippits Md BNFD RG42 34 A2
Tipton Dr CROY/NA CR0 3 H9
Tirlemont Rd SAND/SEL CR2 67 M6
Tirrell Rd CROY/NA CR0 49 M6
Tisbury Rd STRHM/NOR SW16 49 H2
Titchfield Rd CAR SM5 48 A8
Titchfield Wk CAR SM5 48 A7
Titchwell Rd WAND/EARL SW18 30 A2
Tite Hl EGH TW20 21 G6
Tithe Barn Cl KUTN/CMB KT2 9 G5
Tithe Cl VW GU25 39 G6
WOT/HER KT12 42 E6
Tithe La STWL/WRAY TW19 12 C8
Tithe Orch EGRIN RH19 193 R1
Tithepit Shaw La WARL CR6 88 E7
Titlarks Hill Rd ASC SL5 37 L8
Titmus Dr CRAWE RH10 165 H7
Titness Pk ASC SL5 * 37 K3
Titsey Hl WARL CR6 110 C6
Titsey Rd OXTED RH8 130 E1
Tiverton Cl CROY/NA CR0 3 J1
Tiverton Rd HSLW TW3 16 F4
Tiverton Wy CHSGTN KT9 62 F4
Tivoli Rd HSLWW TW4 16 B6
WNWD SE27 31 M6
Toad La BLKW GU17 72 B5
HSLWW TW4 16 C6
Tobin Cl HOR/WEW KT19 83 L1
Toby Wy SURB KT6 63 L1
Todds Cl HORL RH6 160 B1
Toftwood Cl CRAWE RH10 165 L5
Toland Sq PUT/ROE SW15 19 K7
Tolldene Cl WOKN/KNAP GU21 76 B7
Tollers La COUL/CHIP CR5 107 J1
Toll Gdns BRAK RG12 35 H3
Tollgate GU GU1 118 A7
Tollgate Av REDH RH1 148 C5
Tollgate Dr DUL SE21 32 B3
Tollgate Rd DORK RH4 144 E5
Tollhouse La WLGTN SM6 66 F7
Tolson Rd ISLW TW7 17 K5
Tolvaddon WOKN/KNAP GU21 76 D7
Tolverne Rd RYNPK SW20 46 F1
Tolworth Broadway SURB KT6 45 L8
Tolworth Cl SURB KT6 45 L8
Tolworth Park Rd SURB KT6 63 J1
Tolworth Ri North BRYLDS KT5 45 M7
Tolworth Ri South BRYLDS KT5 45 M8
Tolworth Rd SURB KT6 63 H1
Tolworth Underpass
(Kingston By-Pass)
BRYLDS KT5 63 L1
Tomlin Cl HOR/WEW KT19 84 A1
Tomlins Av FRIM GU16 73 J7
Tomlinscote Wy FRIM GU16 73 K7
Tomtit Crs CRAWE RH10 193 P8
Tomtits La FROW RH18 195 M12
Tonbridge Cl BNSTD SM7 86 C4
Tonbridge Rd E/WMO/HCT KT8 43 H4
Tonfield Rd CHEAM SM3 47 J8
Tongham Mdw RFNM GU10 135 H2
Tongham Rd ALDT GU11 135 G4
ASHV GU12 135 G2
RFNM GU10 134 F5
Tonstall Rd HOR/WEW KT19 64 A8
MTCM CR4 48 D2
Tooting Bec Gdns
STRHM/NOR SW16 31 G5
Tooting Bec Rd TOOT SW17 30 D4
Tooting Gv TOOT SW17 30 B6
Tooting High St TOOT SW17 30 B7
Topiary Sq RCH/KEW TW9 18 C5
The Topiary ASHTD KT21 103 H2
FARN GU14 92 B6
Topladly Pl FNM GU9 133 M2
Topsham Rd TOOT SW17 30 C4
Top Terrace Rd FARN GU14 112 D1
Torcross Dr FSTH SE23 32 F3
Torin Ct EGH TW20 20 F6
Torland Dr LHD/OX KT22 82 A4
Tor La WEY KT13 80 A1
Tormead Cl SUT SM1 65 K5
Tormead Rd GU GU1 7 M3
Toronto Dr HORL RH6 161 K3
Torridge Rd DTCH/LGLY SL3 12 E1
THHTH CR7 49 L5
Torridon Cl WOKN/KNAP GU21 76 E7
Torrington Cl BOR GU35 * 180 B12
ESH/CLAY KT10 62 B5
Torrington Rd ESH/CLAY KT10 62 B5
Torrington Sq CROY/NA CR0 2 E2
Torrington Wy MRDN SM4 47 K7
Tor Rd FNM GU9 4 D4
Torr Rd PGE/AN SE20 33 G8
Torwood La CTHM CR3 108 C2
Torwood Rd PUT/ROE SW15 19 K7
Totford La RFNM GU10 136 B6
Totland Cl FARN GU14 92 D3
Tottenham Rd GODL GU7 168 B3
Tottenham Wk SHST GU47 52 A8
Totterdown St TOOT SW17 30 C5
Totton Rd THHTH CR7 49 K3
Tournai Cl ALDT GU11 113 H2
Tovil Cl PGE/AN SE20 50 D2
Tower Cl EGRIN RH19 162 D7
HORL RH6 160 C3
PGE/AN SE20 32 E8
WOKN/KNAP GU21 10 A5
Tower Ct EGRIN RH19 * 162 F3
Tower Gdns ESH/CLAY KT10 62 E6
Tower Gv WEY KT13 60 B1
Tower Hl DORK RH4 144 E4
FARN GU14 92 D6
SWTR RH13 204 H9
Towerhill SHGR GU5 141 M6
Tower Hill Ri SHGR GU5 141 M6
Tower Hill Rd DORK RH4 144 E4
Tower Ri RCH/KEW TW9 18 B5
Tower Rd GSHT GU26 197 R1
KWD/TDW/WH KT20 104 F5
LIPH GU30 196 G9
WHTN TW2 26 B4
Towers Pl RCH/KEW TW9 18 B7
The Towers PUR/KEN CR8 87 M5
Towers Wk WEY KT13 59 L5
Tower Vw CROY/NA CR0 51 H8
Towfield Rd FELT TW13 25 J3
Town Barn Rd CRAWW RH11 164 E4
Townend CTHM CR3 108 B4
Town End Cl CTHM CR3 108 B4
GODL GU7 168 B5
Town End Pde KUT/HW KT1 * 8 D8
Town End St GODL GU7 168 B5
Town Farm Wy
STWL/WRAY TW19 * 23 G1
Townfield Rd DORK RH4 144 D3
Town Field Wy ISLW TW7 17 K4
Towngate COB KT11 81 H5
Town Hl LING RH7 178 F5
Town La STWL/WRAY TW19 23 G1
Town Md CRAWW RH11 164 F3
REDH RH1 128 A7
Town Meadow BTFD TW8 18 A2
Townmead Rd RCH/KEW TW9 18 E4
Town Quay STA TW18 * 40 F3
Townsend Cl BRAK RG12 35 H5
Townsend La
WOKS/MYFD GU22 97 L3
Townsend Ms
WAND/EARL SW18 29 M3
Townsend Rd ASHF TW15 23 H6
Townshend Rd RCH/KEW TW9 18 C6
Townshend Ter RCH/KEW TW9 18 C6
Townshott Cl GT/LBKH KT23 101 K8
Townside Pl CBLY GU15 73 G3
Town Sq BRAK RG12 34 F2
Town Tree Rd ASHF TW15 23 K6
Town Whf ISLW TW7 * 17 L5
Towpath SHPTN TW17 41 J8
Towpath Wy CROY/NA CR0 50 C6
Towton Rd WNWD SE27 31 M3
Toynbee Rd RYNPK SW20 47 H1
The Tracery BNSTD SM7 85 L5
Tracious Cl WOKN/KNAP GU21 76 E6
Trafalgar Av WPK KT4 47 G8
Trafalgar Ct COB KT11 80 D3
FNM GU9 5 J5
Trafalgar Dr WOT/HER KT12 60 E2
Trafalgar Rd HORS RH12 166 F5
WHTN TW2 26 A3
WIM/MER SW19 29 L8
Trafalgar Wy CBLY GU15 72 C5
CROY/NA CR0 67 J1
Trafford Rd FRIM GU16 93 G1
THHTH CR7 49 J5
Tramway Pth MTCM CR4 48 B4
Tranmere Rd WAND/EARL SW18 29 M3

WHTN TW2 25 L1
Tranquil Dl BRKHM/BTCW RH3 124 C6
Transport Av BTFD TW8 17 L1
Transport Rd FARN GU14 92 E8
Trap La RDKG RH5 188 A3
Traps La NWMAL KT3 46 B2
Trasher Md DORK RH4 144 F5
Travellers Wy HSLWW TW4 15 M4
Travis La SHST GU47 72 A2
Treadcroft Dr HORS RH12 167 H4
Treadwell Rd EPSOM KT18 84 C5
Trebor Av FNM GU9 5 L6
Tredenham Cl FARN GU14 112 F1
Tredown Rd SYD SE26 32 F6
Tredwell Rd WNWD SE27 31 L5
Tree Av HASM GU27 198 A5
Treebourne Rd BH/WHM TN16 90 F7
Treebys Av RGUE GU4 117 G2
Tree Cl RCHPK/HAM TW10 27 G2
Treelands RDKG RH5 144 F5
Treen Av BARN SW13 19 H5
Treeside Dr FNM GU9 134 B2
Tree Tops CTHM CR3 88 D8
Treetops GDST RH9 151 H3
Tree Tops Av CBLY GU15 73 K1
Treeview CRAWW RH11 191 M12
Tree View Cl NRWD SE19 50 B1
Tree View Ct REIG RH2 * 126 A8
Treeway REIG RH2 125 L5
Trefoil Cl HORS RH12 167 H4
Trefoil Crs CRAWW RH11 164 C8
Tregaron Gdns NWMAL KT3 46 B4
Tregarthen Pl LHD/OX KT22 102 F3
Tregarth Pl WOKN/KNAP GU21 76 C7
Tregolls Dr FARN GU14 92 F6
Trehaven Pde REIG RH2 147 L3
Trehern Rd MORT/ESHN SW14 19 G5
Trelawn Cl CHERT KT16 57 M6
Trelawne Dr CRAN GU6 186 D3
Trelawney Gv WEY KT13 59 K5
Treloar Gdns NRWD SE19 32 A7
Tremaine Rd PGE/AN SE20 50 E2
Tremayne Wk CBLY GU15 73 M5
Trenance WOKN/KNAP GU21 76 D7
Trenchard Cl WOT/HER KT12 60 F4
Trenear Cl SWTR RH13 167 H7
Trenham Dr WARL CR6 88 F6
Trenholme Rd PGE/AN SE20 32 E8
Trenholme Ter PGE/AN SE20 32 E8
Trent Cl CRAWW RH11 164 B6
FARN GU14 92 B3
Trentham Crs
WOKS/MYFD GU22 97 K3
Trentham Rd REDH RH1 148 C2
Trentham St WAND/EARL SW18 29 K2
Trenton Cl FRIM GU16 73 K7
Trent Rd DTCH/LGLY SL3 12 E1
Trent Wy WPK KT4 64 F2
Treport St WAND/EARL SW18 29 L1
Tresillian Wy WOKN/KNAP GU21 76 D7
Tresta Wk WOKN/KNAP GU21 76 D5
Trevanne Plat CRAWE RH10 165 M3
Trevelyan BRAK RG12 34 B7
Trevelyan Rd TOOT SW17 30 C7
Trevereux Hl OXTED RH8 131 K6
Treville St PUT/ROE SW15 28 E1
Treviso Rd FSTH SE23 33 G3
Trevithick Cl EBED/NFELT TW14 24 C2
Trevor Cl ISLW TW7 17 J7
Trevor Rd WIM/MER SW19 29 H8
Trevose Av BF/WBF KT14 78 C4
Trewenna Dr CHSGTN KT9 63 G4
Trewince Rd RYNPK SW20 46 F1
Trewint St WAND/EARL SW18 29 M3
Trewsbury Rd SYD SE26 33 G6
Treyford Cl CRAWW RH11 164 B4
The Triangle KUT/HW KT1 45 M2
WOKN/KNAP GU21 76 F8
Trigg's Cl WOKS/MYFD GU22 10 A9
Trigg's La WOKN/KNAP GU21 76 F8
WOKS/MYFD GU22 96 F1
Trig St RDKG RH5 173 M9
Trilby Rd FSTH SE23 33 G3
Trimmers Cl FNM GU9 133 L2
Trimmers Fld FNM GU9 134 B8
Trimmers Wd GSHT GU26 181 Q11
Trindles Rd REDH RH1 149 J2
Tringham Cl CHERT KT16 57 L4
WOKN/KNAP GU21 75 M8
Trinity SHST GU47 52 B7
Trinity Church Rd BARN SW13 19 L1
Trinity Churchyard GU GU1 * 7 H7
Trinity Cl CRAWE RH10 165 L2
HSLWW TW4 16 B6
SAND/SEL CR2 68 B7
STWL/WRAY TW19 13 M8
Trinity Ct BNFD RG42 * 34 C1
Trinity Crs ASC SL5 37 K5
TOOT SW17 30 C3
Trinity Flds FNM GU9 133 K3
Trinity Hl FNM GU9 133 K3
Trinity Ms PGE/AN SE20 * 50 F1
Trinity Pde HSLW TW3 * 16 E5
Trinity Ri BRXS/STRHM SW2 31 L1
Trinity Rd RCH/KEW TW9 * 18 C5
TOOT SW17 30 C3
WIM/MER SW19 29 K7
WOKN/KNAP GU21 75 L8
Tritton Av CROY/NA CR0 67 H3
Tritton Rd DUL SE21 32 A4
Trittons KWD/TDW/WH KT20 104 F3
Triumph Cl HYS/HAR UB3 14 F3
Trodd's La RGUE GU4 140 C1
Trojan Wy CROY/NA CR0 67 J2
Troon Cl CRAWW RH11 190 G8
Trotsworth Av VW GU25 39 H4
Trotters La CHOB/PIR GU24 76 E2
Trotter Wy HOR/WEW KT19 83 K2
Trotton Cl CRAWE RH10 165 L7
Trotts La BH/WHM TN16 131 M1
Trotwood Cl SHST GU47 52 B7
Trout Rd HASM GU27 197 R7
Trowers Wy REDH RH1 126 E5
Trowlock Av TEDD TW11 26 F7
Trowlock Wy TEDD TW11 8 C1
Troy La EDEN TN8 153 J5
Troy Rd NRWD SE19 32 A7
Trumpetshill Rd
BRKHM/BTCW RH3 146 D1
Trumpsgreen Av VW GU25 39 G6
Trumps Green Cl VW GU25 39 H5
Trumpsgreen Rd VW GU25 38 F8
Trumps Mill La VW GU25 39 J6
Trundle Md HORS RH12 166 F4
Trunley Heath Rd SHGR GU5 161 F1
Truslove Rd WNWD SE27 31 K6
Truss Hill Rd ASC SL5 36 F5
Trys Hill Longcross Rd
CHERT KT16 57 H2
Trystings Cl ESH/CLAY KT10 62 D5
Tucker Rd CHERT KT16 58 A5
Tuckers Dr CRAN GU6 186 A2
Tuckey Gv RPLY/SEND GU23 98 C6
Tudor Av HPTN TW12 25 K7
WPK KT4 64 E2
Tudor Cir GODL GU7 168 B2
Tudor Cl ASHF TW15 23 G5
BNSTD SM7 85 H5
CHEAM SM3 65 G4
CHSGTN KT9 63 H4
COB KT11 81 J3
COUL/CHIP CR5 87 K8
CRAWE RH10 165 M5
EGRIN RH19 163 G6
GSHT GU26 197 Q3
GT/LBKH KT23 101 J6
HORL RH6 161 L3
HPTN TW12 25 M6
SAND/SEL CR2 88 E5
WLGTN SM6 66 F6
WOKS/MYFD GU22 11 G5
Tudor Dr KUTN/CMB KT2 27 H6
MRDN SM4 47 G6
WOT/HER KT12 43 G8
Tudor Gdns BARN SW13 19 H5
TWK TW1 26 C2
WWKM BR4 69 M2
Tudor La WDSR SL4 20 F1
Tudor Pl MTCM CR4 30 B8
NRWD SE19 * 32 C8
Tudor Rd ASHF TW15 24 A7
BECK BR3 51 M3
GODL GU7 168 B2
HPTN TW12 25 K8
HSLW TW3 17 G6
KUTN/CMB KT2 9 J3
NRWD SE19 32 C8
SNWD SE25 50 E5
The Tudors REIG RH2 * 125 M5
Tudor Wk LHD/OX KT22 102 D2
Tudor Wy WOKN/KNAP GU21 75 M8
Tuesley Cnr GODL GU7 168 A6
Tuesley La GODL GU7 168 A6
Tufton Gdns E/WMO/HCT KT8 43 L2
Tugela Rd CROY/NA CR0 50 A6
Tugela St CAT SE6 33 J3
Tuggles Plat HORS RH12 166 B2
Tugmutton Cl ORP BR6 71 L3
Tugwood Cl COUL/CHIP CR5 107 G3
Tulip Cl CROY/NA CR0 51 G8
HPTN TW12 25 J7
Tulip Ct HORS RH12 * 166 F5
Tullett Rd CRAWE RH10 165 K8
Tulls La BOR GU35 196 C3
Tull St CAR SM5 48 C7
Tulse Cl BECK BR3 51 M3
Tulse Hl BRXS/STRHM SW2 31 L2
Tulsemere Rd WNWD SE27 31 M3
Tulyar Cl KWD/TDW/WH KT20 104 E1
Tumber St EPSOM KT18 103 M7
Tumblewood Rd BNSTD SM7 85 H6
Tumbling Bay WOT/HER KT12 42 D6
Tummons Gdns SNWD SE25 50 B2
Tunbridge Crs LIPH GU30 196 G8
Tunbridge La LIPH GU30 196 G7
Tunley Rd TOOT SW17 30 D3
Tunnel Link Rd HTHAIR TW6 14 D7
Tunnel Rd FARN GU14 92 B8
Tunnel Rd East WDR/YW UB7 14 E2
Tunnel Rd West WDR/YW UB7 14 D3
Tunnmeade CRAWW RH11 164 A5
Tunsgate GU GU1 7 H7
Tunsgate Sq GU GU1 * 7 G7
Tunstall Rd CROY/NA CR0 3 H4
Tunworth Crs PUT/ROE SW15 19 J8
Tupwood La CTHM CR3 108 D8
Tupwood Scrubbs Rd
CTHM CR3 * 108 D2
CTHM CR3 128 D2
Turf Hill Rd CBLY GU15 73 J1
Turfhouse La CHOB/PIR GU24 56 B7
Turing Dr BRAK RG12 34 D5
Turkey Oak Cl NRWD SE19 50 B1
Turle Rd STRHM/NOR SW16 49 H2
Turnberry BRAK RG12 34 B6
Turner Av MTCM CR4 48 C1
WHTN TW2 25 M4
Turner Cl RGUE GU4 117 J5
Turner Ct EGRIN RH19 163 H2
Turner Ms BELMT SM2 65 L6
Turner Pl SHST GU47 72 A3
Turner Rd BH/WHM TN16 90 F2
NWMAL KT3 46 A7
Turners Cl STA TW18 22 E6
Turners Hill Rd CRAWE RH10 192 D7
CRAWE RH10 193 L3
EGRIN RH19 162 B8
Turners La WOT/HER KT12 60 E5
Turners Md MFD/CHID GU8 199 R2
Turners Meadow Wy BECK BR3 51 J1
Turners Wy CROY/NA CR0 67 K1
Turney Rd DUL SE21 31 M1
Turnham Cl GUW GU2 138 F4
Turnoak Av WOKS/MYFD GU22 97 H2
Turnoak La WOKS/MYFD GU22 97 H2
Turnpike La SUT SM1 65 M4
Turnpike Link CROY/NA CR0 3 H6
Turnpike Pl CRAWW RH11 164 F2
Turnpike Rd BNFD RG42 34 A2
Turnpike Wy ISLW TW7 17 K3
Turnstone Cl SAND/SEL CR2 69 H8
Turnville Cl LTWR GU18 54 D8
Turpin Rd EBED/NFELT TW14 15 J8
Turpins Ri BFOR GU20 54 E3
Turpin Wy WLGTN SM6 66 E6
Turtledove Av CRAWE RH10 193 P8
Tuscany Gdns CRAWE RH10 165 G2
Tushmore Av CRAWE RH10 165 G1
Tushmore Ct CRAWE RH10 * 165 G2
Tushmore Crs CRAWE RH10 165 G1
Tushmore La CRAWE RH10 165 G2
Tussock Cl CRAWW RH11 164 C6
Tuxford Cl CRAWE RH10 165 L6
Tweed Cl FARN GU14 92 B3
Tweeddale Rd CAR SM5 48 A8
Tweed La BRKHM/BTCW RH3 145 L5
CRAWW RH11 164 B1
Tweed Rd DTCH/LGLY SL3 12 E1
Tweedsmuir Cl FARN GU14 92 A6
Twelve Acre Cl GT/LBKH KT23 101 J6
Twelve Acre Crs FARN GU14 92 A4
Twelve Av
KWD/TDW/WH KT20 * 105 J8
Twickenham Br TWK TW1 17 M7
Twickenham Cl CROY/NA CR0 67 J2
Twickenham Rd FELT TW13 25 J4
ISLW TW7 17 K6
RCH/KEW TW9 17 M7
TEDD TW11 26 D6
Twilley St WAND/EARL SW18 29 L1
Twining Av WHTN TW2 25 M4
Twinoaks COB KT11 81 K3
Twitten La EGRIN RH19 193 R1
The Twitten CRAWW RH11 164 E4
LING RH7 * 178 E5
Two Ways BIL RH14 201 R5
Twycross Rd GODL GU7 168 A2
Twyford La RFNM GU10 155 L3
Twyford Rd CAR SM5 48 A8
Twyhurst Ct EGRIN RH19 162 E2
Twyne Cl CRAWW RH11 164 B6
Twyne Cl HORL RH6 160 F2
Twynersh Av CHERT KT16 40 C6
Tybenham Rd WIM/MER SW19 47 K3
Tychbourne Dr RGUE GU4 117 M5
Tydcombe Rd WARL CR6 108 F1
Tye La ORP BR6 71 M4
Tylden Wy HORS RH12 167 J3
Tylecroft Rd STRHM/NOR SW16 49 H2
Tylehost GUW GU2 116 D4
Tyler Gdns ADL/WDHM KT15 58 F3
Tyler Rd CRAWE RH10 164 F7
Tylers Cl GDST RH9 128 E4
Tylers Ct CRAN GU6 * 186 C2
Tylney Av NRWD SE19 32 C6
Tylston Meadow LIPH GU30 196 G8
Tynan Cl EBED/NFELT TW14 24 D2
Tyndalls GSHT GU26 198 A1
Tyne Cl CRAWE RH10 165 L5
FARN GU14 92 B3
Tynedale Rd
BRKHM/BTCW RH3 145 L4
Tynemouth Rd MTCM CR4 30 D8
Tynley Gv RGUE GU4 117 G2
Tyson Gdns FSTH SE23 * 32 F1
Tyson Rd FSTH SE23 32 F1
Tythebarn Cl RGUE GU4 117 L3
Tythebarns La
RPLY/SEND GU23 98 D8
Tytherton BRAK RG12 34 F2

U

Uckfield Gv MTCM CR4 48 D1
Udney Park Rd TEDD TW11 26 D6
Uffington Dr BRAK RG12 35 H4
Uffington Rd WNWD SE27 31 K5
Ullathorne Rd
STRHM/NOR SW16 30 F5
Ullswater BRAK RG12 34 B7
Ullswater Av FARN GU14 92 B6
Ullswater Cl FNM GU9 133 K3
LTWR GU18 54 E8
PUT/ROE SW15 * 28 A5
Ullswater Ct ASHV GU12 * 113 J4
Ullswater Crs COUL/CHIP CR5 87 H6
PUT/ROE SW15 28 A5
Ullswater Rd BARN SW13 19 K2
LTWR GU18 54 E8
WNWD SE27 31 L4
Ulstan Cl CTHM CR3 109 K5
Ulwyn Av BF/WBF KT14 79 H3
Umberstone VW GU25 39 G6
Umbria St PUT/ROE SW15 19 K8
Underhill Cl GODL GU7 168 B6
Underhill La FNM GU9 155 L2
Underhill Park Rd REIG RH2 125 K5
Underhill Rd EDUL SE22 32 E2
RDKG RH5 173 Q8
Underwood BRAK RG12 34 B6
CROY/NA CR0 69 M5
Underwood Av ASHV GU12 113 H8
Underwood Cl CRAWE RH10 193 N5
Underwood Ct CTHM CR3 108 C6
Underwood Rd CTHM CR3 108 B7
HASM GU27 198 A6
Undine St TOOT SW17 30 C6
Union Cl SHST GU47 52 B7
Union Rd CROY/NA CR0 2 D1
FNM GU9 5 J4
FRIM GU16 94 A1
Union St ALDT GU11 112 D7
CHOB/PIR GU24 94 D3
FARN GU14 92 D5
KUT/HW KT1 8 D6
Unity Cl CROY/NA CR0 69 L7
NRWD SE19 31 M6
University Rd WIM/MER SW19 30 A7
Unstead La SHGR GU5 168 F2
Unwin Av EBED/NFELT TW14 15 G7
Unwin Rd ISLW TW7 17 H5
Upavon Gdns BRAK RG12 35 J5
Updown Hl BFOR GU20 55 G5
Upfield CROY/NA CR0 68 E1
HORL RH6 160 D5
Upfield Cl HORL RH6 160 D5
Upfold Cl CRAN GU6 170 A11
Upfold La CRAN GU6 170 B12
Upfolds Gn RGUE GU4 117 M4
Upland Rd BELMT SM2 66 A6
CBLY GU15 73 G2
CTHM CR3 109 K2
EDUL SE22 32 D1
SAND/SEL CR2 68 A4
Uplands ASHTD KT21 103 G2
BECK BR3 51 K2
Uplands Cl HASM GU27 198 E5
MORT/ESHN SW14 18 E7
Uplands Dr LHD/OX KT22 82 A4
Uplands Rd FNM GU9 134 B8
PUR/KEN CR8 87 M7
Upland Wy EPSOM KT18 84 F8
Uppark Gdns HORS RH12 167 J3
Upper Beulah Hl NRWD SE19 50 B1
Upper Bourne La RFNM GU10 155 K4
Upper Bourne V RFNM GU10 155 K4
Upper Bridge Rd REDH RH1 126 B8
Upper Brighton Rd SURB KT6 45 H7
Upper Broadmoor Rd
CWTH RG45 52 A4
Upper Butts BTFD TW8 17 M1
Upper Charles St CBLY GU15 72 F3
Upper Chobham Rd CBLY GU15 73 K6
Upper Church La FNM GU9 5 H4
Upper Cl FROW RH18 195 N11
Upper College Ride CBLY GU15 73 H1
Upper Court Rd CTHM CR3 109 K5
HOR/WEW KT19 83 M1
Upper Dr BH/WHM TN16 90 F8
Upper Dunnymans BNSTD SM7 85 J4
Upper Edgeborough Rd GU GU1 7 M6
Upper Elmers End Rd
BECK BR3 51 H4
Upper Elms Rd ALDT GU11 112 D8
Upper Fairfield Rd
LHD/OX KT22 102 E3
Upper Farm Rd
E/WMO/HCT KT8 43 J4
Upper Forecourt HORL RH6 160 E7
Upper Gordon Rd CBLY GU15 73 G4
Upper Gn East MTCM CR4 48 C2
Upper Gn West MTCM CR4 48 C2
Upper Grotto Rd TWK TW1 26 C3
Upper Gv SNWD SE25 50 B4
Upper Guildown Rd GUW GU2 138 E3
Upper Hale Rd FNM GU9 133 L2
Upper Halliford Rd
SHPTN TW17 42 B2
SHPTN TW17 42 B4
Upper Ham Rd
RCHPK/HAM TW10 27 G5
Upper Harestone CTHM CR3 128 D1
Upper High St EW KT17 84 B3
Upper House La SHGR GU5 169 Q8
Upper Kiln DORK RH4 * 144 F4
Upper Lodge Wy
COUL/CHIP CR5 107 G4
Upper Manor Rd GODL GU7 168 B2
MFD/CHID GU8 159 H8
Upper Mt HASM GU27 198 G4
Upper Mulgrave Rd
BELMT SM2 65 H6
Upper Old Park La FNM GU9 133 J4
Upper Park Rd CBLY GU15 73 G4
KUTN/CMB KT2 9 J1
Upper Pth DORK RH4 * 144 F4
Upper Pillory Down CAR SM5 86 D3
Upper Pines BNSTD SM7 86 C7
Upper Pinewood Rd
ASHV GU12 113 M6
Upper Queen St GODL GU7 168 B5
Upper Richmond Rd
PUT/ROE SW15 19 L6
Upper Richmond Rd West
RCHPK/HAM TW10 18 D6
Upper Rd WLGTN SM6 67 G4
Upper Rose Hl DORK RH4 144 E3
Upper St Michael's Rd
ALDT GU11 134 E1
Upper Sawleywood
BNSTD SM7 85 J4
Upper School Dr HASM GU27 198 A8
Upper Selsdon Rd
SAND/SEL CR2 68 C7
Upper Shirley Rd CROY/NA CR0 68 F2
Upper South Vw FNM GU9 5 J2
Upper Springfield
MFD/CHID GU8 158 A5
Upper Sq ISLW TW7 17 K5
Upper Stanford Rd
CHOB/PIR GU24 95 J7
Upper St SHGR GU5 141 J4
Upper Sunbury Rd HPTN TW12 43 J1
Upper Sutton La HEST TW5 16 D3
Upper Teddington Rd
TEDD TW11 8 A3
Upper Terrace Rd FARN GU14 112 D1
Upperton Rd GUW GU2 6 E7
Upper Tooting Pk TOOT SW17 30 C3
Upper Tooting Rd TOOT SW17 30 C5
Upper Tulse Hl
BRXS/STRHM SW2 31 J1
Upper Union St ALDT GU11 112 C7
Upper Union Ter ALDT GU11 * 112 D7
Upper Vann La MFD/CHID GU8 184 D4
Upper Vernon Rd SUT SM1 66 A4
Upper Verran Rd CBLY GU15 73 G6
Upper Village Rd ASC SL5 36 F5
Upper Wk VW GU25 39 H4
Upper Wy FNM GU9 4 F8
Upper West St REIG RH2 125 J8
Upper Weybourne La
FNM GU9 134 A1
Upper Woodcote Village
PUR/KEN CR8 87 G3
Upshire Gdns BRAK RG12 35 J4
Upshot La WOKS/MYFD GU22 78 C7
Upton WOKN/KNAP GU21 76 E7
Upton Cl FARN GU14 93 G6
Upton Dene BELMT SM2 65 L6
Upton Rd HSLW TW3 16 D5
THHTH CR7 50 A2
Upwood Rd STRHM/NOR SW16 49 H1
Urmston Dr WIM/MER SW19 29 H2
Usherwood Cl
KWD/TDW/WH KT20 123 M5
Uvedale Cl CROY/NA CR0 90 A1
Uvedale Crs CROY/NA CR0 90 A1
Uvedale Rd OXTED RH8 130 C3
Uxbridge Rd FELT TW13 25 G3
HPTN TW12 25 L6
KUT/HW KT1 45 G4

V

Vachery La CRAN GU6 186 E5
Vaillant Rd WEY KT13 59 M3
Vale Cl COUL/CHIP CR5 87 H4
ORP BR6 71 K3
RFNM GU10 155 M5
TWK TW1 * 26 D4
WEY KT13 60 A2
WOKN/KNAP GU21 10 C3
Vale Ct WEY KT13 60 A2
Vale Crs PUT/ROE SW15 28 B5
Vale Cft ESH/CLAY KT10 62 C6
Vale Dr HORS RH12 166 E7
Vale Farm Rd
WOKN/KNAP GU21 10 C6
Valentyne Cl CROY/NA CR0 90 B1
Vale Rd ASHV GU12 113 K2
ASHV GU12 113 K5
CBLY GU15 72 D5
ESH/CLAY KT10 62 B7
MTCM CR4 49 G3
SUT SM1 65 L3
WEY KT13 60 A2
WPK KT4 64 C2
Vale Rd North SURB KT6 63 H1
Vale St DUL SE21 32 A4
The Vale COUL/CHIP CR5 87 H4
CROY/NA CR0 69 G1
EBED/NFELT TW14 15 L8
HEST TW5 16 B1
SUN TW16 * 24 D7
Vale Wood Dr RFNM GU10 156 A5
Vale Wood La GSHT GU26 197 P1
Valewood Rd HASM GU27 198 D9
Valiant Wy FARN GU14 112 A1
Valley End Rd CHOB/PIR GU24 55 L5
Valleyfield Rd
STRHM/NOR SW16 31 J6
Valley Gdns WIM/MER SW19 30 A8
Valley La RFNM GU10 155 M2
Valley Rd FRIM GU16 93 M1
PUR/KEN CR8 88 A5
STRHM/NOR SW16 31 J5
Valley Side LIPH GU30 196 G8
Valley Vw BH/WHM TN16 90 F8
GODL GU7 168 A5
Valley View Gdns PUR/KEN CR8 88 B5
Valley Wk CROY/NA CR0 68 F1
Vallis Wy CHSGTN KT9 63 G3
Valnay St TOOT SW17 30 C6
Valroy Cl CBLY GU15 73 G3
Vampire Wy FARN GU14 112 B1
Vanbrugh Cl CRAWW RH11 164 A7
Vanbrugh Dr WOT/HER KT12 42 F7
Vancouver Cl HOR/WEW KT19 83 M1
Vancouver Ct HORL RH6 161 K3
Vancouver Dr CRAWW RH11 164 F1
Vancouver Rd FSTH SE23 33 H3
RCHPK/HAM TW10 26 F5
Vanderbilt Rd
WAND/EARL SW18 29 L2
Van Dyck Av NWMAL KT3 46 A7
Vandyke BRAK RG12 34 B6
Vandyke Cl REDH RH1 126 C6
Vanguard Cl CROY/NA CR0 2 A4
THHTH CR7 49 L4
Vanguard Wy CROY/NA CR0 3 J9
EDEN TN8 179 M3
EGRIN RH19 195 P2
HTHAIR TW6 15 H4
OXTED RH8 110 D8
WARL CR6 89 J3
WLGTN SM6 67 H6
Vanneck Sq PUT/ROE SW15 * 19 K7
Vanners CRAWE RH10 165 G3
Vanners Pde BF/WBF KT14 * 79 H3
Vann Farm Rd RDKG RH5 188 F1
Vann Lake RDKG RH5 188 G1
Vann Lake Rd RDKG RH5 188 G2
Vann La MFD/CHID GU8 184 A4
Vant Rd TOOT SW17 30 C6
Vapery La CHOB/PIR GU24 95 G3
Varley Dr TWK TW1 17 L6
Varley Wy MTCM CR4 48 A2
Varna Rd HPTN TW12 * 43 L1
Varney Cl FARN GU14 92 B4
Varsity Dr TWK TW1 17 J7
Varsity Rw MORT/ESHN SW14 18 F4
Vaughan Rd THDIT KT7 44 E7
Vaughan Wy DORK RH4 144 D2
Vaux Crs WOT/HER KT12 60 E5
Vauxhall Gdns SAND/SEL CR2 67 M5
Veals Md MTCM CR4 48 B1
Vectis Gdns TOOT SW17 30 E7
Vectis Rd TOOT SW17 30 E7
Vegal Crs EGH TW20 20 F6
Vellum Dr CAR SM5 66 D2
Venner Rd SYD SE26 32 F7
Ventnor Rd BELMT SM2 65 L6
Ventnor Ter ASHV GU12 112 F8
Venton Cl WOKN/KNAP GU21 76 E7
Venus Ms MTCM CR4 48 B3
Verbania Wy EGRIN RH19 163 J4
Verdayne Av CROY/NA CR0 51 G8
Verdayne Gdns WARL CR6 88 F6
Verdun Rd BARN SW13 19 K2
Vereker Dr SUN TW16 42 D3
Verge Wk ALDT GU11 134 D2
Vermont Rd NRWD SE19 32 A7
SUT SM1 65 L2
Verner Cl BOR GU35 196 D1
Vernon Av RYNPK SW20 47 G2
Vernon Cl CHERT KT16 58 A5
HOR/WEW KT19 63 M5
HORS RH12 167 K4
STWL/WRAY TW19 23 H2
Vernon Dr ASC SL5 36 A2
CTHM CR3 107 M4
Vernon Rd FELT TW13 24 C3
MORT/ESHN SW14 19 G5
SUT SM1 65 M4
Vernon Wk
KWD/TDW/WH KT20 105 G2
Vernon Wy GUW GU2 116 C7
Vern Pl BH/WHM TN16 110 F3
Verona Dr SURB KT6 63 H1
Veronica Gdns
STRHM/NOR SW16 48 F1
Veronica Rd TOOT SW17 31 E4
Verralls WOKS/MYFD GU22 11 K5
Verran Rd BAL SW12 * 30 E1
CBLY GU15 73 G7
Versailles Rd PGE/AN SE20 32 D8
Verulam Av PUR/KEN CR8 86 F2
Veryan WOKN/KNAP GU21 76 D7
Vesey Cl FARN GU14 92 D4
Vestris Rd FSTH SE23 33 G3

Vevers Rd REIG RH2 147 L3
Vevey St CAT SE6 33 J3
Vibart Gdns BRXS/STRHM SW2 31 J1
Vibia Cl STWL/WRAY TW19 23 G1
Viburnum Ct CHOB/PIR GU24 75 H3
Vicarage Av EGH TW20 21 L7
Vicarage Cl FNM GU9 5 M9
GT/LBKH KT23 101 K7
KWD/TDW/WH KT20 105 H6
LING RH7 178 E5
WPK KT4 46 B8
Vicarage Ct BECK BR3 * 51 H3
EGH TW20 21 L7
Vicarage Crs EGH TW20 21 L6
Vicarage Dr BECK BR3 51 K1
MORT/ESHN SW14 19 G7
Vicarage Farm Rd HEST TW5 16 B3
Vicarage Flds WOT/HER KT12 42 F6
Vicarage Gdns ASC SL5 36 D5
GSHT GU26 197 P2
MTCM CR4 48 B3
Vicarage Ga GUW GU2 6 A8
Vicarage Gate Ms
KWD/TDW/WH KT20 * 105 H6
Vicarage Hl FNM GU9 5 M9
Vicarage La FNM GU9 5 H4
FNM GU9 5 M9
FNM GU9 133 M2
HASM GU27 198 A7
HORL RH6 160 C2
LHD/OX KT22 102 E4
RDKG RH5 173 L11
RPLY/SEND GU23 97 M8
STA TW18 40 E3
STWL/WRAY TW19 21 J2
Vicarage Ms CHSWK W4 * 19 H1
Vicarage Rd BAGS GU19 53 M6
BLKW GU17 72 B5
CHOB/PIR GU24 76 A1
CRAWE RH10 193 M6
CROY/NA CR0 67 K2
EGH TW20 21 L6
KUT/HW KT1 8 A4
KUT/HW KT1 8 D6
LING RH7 178 E5
MORT/ESHN SW14 18 F7
STA TW18 22 B5
SUN TW16 24 C7
SUT SM1 65 K3
TEDD TW11 26 D6
WHTN TW2 16 F8
WHTN TW2 26 B3
WOKS/MYFD GU22 97 J3
Vicarage Wy DTCH/LGLY SL3 13 G2
Vicars Oak Rd NRWD SE19 32 B7
Vickers Cl WLGTN SM6 67 J6
Vickers Dr North WEY KT13 59 H8
Vickers Dr South WEY KT13 79 H1
Vickers Rd ASHV GU12 113 J4
Victoria Av CBLY GU15 72 D4
E/WMO/HCT KT8 43 L3
HSLW TW3 16 D7
SAND/SEL CR2 67 M8
SURB KT6 45 G6
WLGTN SM6 66 D2
Victoria Cl E/WMO/HCT KT8 43 K3
HORL RH6 160 D3
WEY KT13 60 A2
Victoria Cottages
RCH/KEW TW9 18 C3
Victoria Ct BAGS GU19 54 B8
RGUE GU4 * 139 H6
Victoria Crs NRWD SE19 32 B7
WIM/MER SW19 * 29 J8
Victoria Dr WIM/MER SW19 29 G2
Victoria Gdns BH/WHM TN16 90 F5
HEST TW5 16 B3
Victoria Ms WAND/EARL SW18 29 M2
Victoria Pde RCH/KEW TW9 * 18 D3
Victoria Pl EW KT17 84 B2
RCH/KEW TW9 18 A7
Victoria Rd ADL/WDHM KT15 59 G3
ALDT GU11 112 D7
ASC SL5 36 E5
COUL/CHIP CR5 87 G5
CRAN GU6 186 C2
CRAWW RH11 164 E4
EDEN TN8 179 R1
FARN GU14 92 E5
FELT TW13 24 E2
FNM GU9 5 J4
GODL GU7 168 B5
GU GU1 7 J5
HORL RH6 160 D3
KUT/HW KT1 9 H7
MORT/ESHN SW14 19 G5
MTCM CR4 30 B8
REDH RH1 148 D1
SHST GU47 52 B8
STA TW18 22 B4
SURB KT6 45 G6
SUT SM1 66 A4
TEDD TW11 26 D7
TWK TW1 26 E1
WEY KT13 60 A2
WOKN/KNAP GU21 76 A7
WOKS/MYFD GU22 10 D6
Victoria St EGH TW20 20 F7
SWTR RH13 167 G7
Victoria Ter DORK RH4 * 144 D2
Victoria Tr ALDT GU11 112 A2
Victoria Vls RCH/KEW TW9 18 C5
Victoria Wy EGRIN RH19 163 G6
LIPH GU30 196 G9
WEY KT13 60 A2
WOKN/KNAP GU21 10 D6
Victor Rd PGE/AN SE20 33 G8
TEDD TW11 26 B6
Victors Dr HPTN TW12 * 25 H7
Victory Av MRDN SM4 47 M5
Victory Cl STWL/WRAY TW19 23 H2
Victory Park Rd
ADL/WDHM KT15 58 F3
Victory Pl NRWD SE19 * 32 B7
Victory Rd CHERT KT16 40 D8
HORS RH12 166 E6
WIM/MER SW19 29 M8
View Cl BH/WHM TN16 90 F6
Viggory La WOKN/KNAP GU21 76 E5
Vigilant Cl SYD SE26 32 D5
Viking BRAK RG12 34 B5
Village Cl WEY KT13 60 A2
Village Gdns EW KT17 64 C8
Village Green Av
BH/WHM TN16 91 H7
Village Green Wy
BH/WHM TN16 91 H7
Village Rd EGH TW20 39 M3
Village Rw BELMT SM2 65 K6
Village St RDKG RH5 173 Q8
Village Wy ASHF TW15 23 J5
BECK BR3 51 K4
SAND/SEL CR2 88 D3
Villiers Av BRYLDS KT5 45 J5
WHTN TW2 25 J2
Villiers Cl BRYLDS KT5 45 J4
Villiers Gv BELMT SM2 65 G7
Villiers Rd BECK BR3 51 G2
ISLW TW7 17 H4
KUT/HW KT1 9 G9
The Villiers WEY KT13 * 60 A5
Vinall Gdns HORS RH12 166 A5
Vincam Cl WHTN TW2 25 K1
Vincennes Est WNWD SE27 32 A5
Vincent Av BRYLDS KT5 45 L8
CAR SM5 86 A1
Vincent Cl CHERT KT16 40 B7
ESH/CLAY KT10 61 L2
LHD/OX KT22 101 L5
SWTR RH13 167 H7
WDR/YW UB7 14 D1
Vincent Dr DORK RH4 144 D3
SHPTN TW17 42 B3
Vincent La DORK RH4 144 D2
Vincent Ri BRAK RG12 35 H3
Vincent Rd CHERT KT16 40 B7
COB KT11 81 H6
COUL/CHIP CR5 86 F6
CROY/NA CR0 3 H2
DORK RH4 144 D2
HSLWW TW4 16 A5
ISLW TW7 17 G3
KUT/HW KT1 9 K8
Vincent Rw HPTN TW12 25 M7
Vincents Cl COUL/CHIP CR5 106 C2
Vincent Sq BH/WHM TN16 90 F3
Vincents Wk DORK RH4 144 D2
Vincent Wk DORK RH4 * 144 D2
Vine Cl ALDT GU11 112 D3
BRYLDS KT5 45 J6
RFNM GU10 155 K5
RGUW GU3 96 A8
STWL/WRAY TW19 13 K7
SUT SM1 65 M2
Vine House Cl FRIM GU16 93 K6
Vine Pl HSLW TW3 16 E6
Vineries Cl WDR/YW UB7 14 D1
The Vineries CAT SE6 * 33 K2
Vine Rd BARN SW13 19 J5
E/WMO/HCT KT8 43 M4
Vine Rw RCHPK/HAM TW10 * 18 B7
Viners Cl WOT/HER KT12 42 F6
Vine St ALDT GU11 112 D8
Vine Wy RFNM GU10 155 K4
Vineyard Cl CAT SE6 33 K2
KUT/HW KT1 9 G8
Vineyard Hill Rd
WIM/MER SW19 29 K5
Vineyard Pth
MORT/ESHN SW14 19 G5
Vineyard Rd FELT TW13 24 D4
Vineyard Rw KUT/HW KT1 8 A4
The Vineyard
RCHPK/HAM TW10 18 A7
SUN TW16 * 42 D3
Viney Bank CROY/NA CR0 69 J7
Viola Av EBED/NFELT TW14 15 M8
STWL/WRAY TW19 23 H3
Viola Cft BNFD RG42 35 J1
Violet Cl CHEAM SM3 47 H8
WLGTN SM6 48 D8
Violet Gdns CROY/NA CR0 67 L4
Violet La SAND/SEL CR2 67 L4
Virginia Av VW GU25 38 F5
Virginia Cl ASHTD KT21 83 G8
NWMAL KT3 45 M4
STA TW18 40 F3
WEY KT13 59 M5
Virginia Dr VW GU25 38 F5
Virginia Gdns FARN GU14 92 F7
Virginia Pk VW GU25 * 39 H4
Virginia Pl COB KT11 80 D4
Virginia Rd THHTH CR7 49 M1
Viscount Cl ASHV GU12 113 J4
Viscount Gdns BF/WBF KT14 79 H2
Viscount Rd STWL/WRAY TW19 23 G1
Viscount Wy HTHAIR TW6 15 H6
Vivien Cl CHSGTN KT9 63 H6
Vivienne Cl CRAWW RH11 164 F1
TWK TW1 18 A8
Voewood Cl NWMAL KT3 46 C6
Vogan Cl REIG RH2 147 L3
Volta Wy CROY/NA CR0 49 J8
Voss Ct STRHM/NOR SW16 31 H7
Vowels La EGRIN RH19 193 Q11
Vulcan Cl CRAWW RH11 164 E8
Vulcan Wy CROY/NA CR0 70 B8
WLGTN SM6 67 H7

W

Wadbrook St KUT/HW KT1 8 D7
Waddington Av
COUL/CHIP CR5 107 K1
Waddington Cl
COUL/CHIP CR5 107 L1
CRAWW RH11 164 C7
Waddington Wy NRWD SE19 49 M1
Waddon Cl CROY/NA CR0 67 K2
Waddon Court Rd
CROY/NA CR0 67 K3
Waddon Marsh Wy
CROY/NA CR0 49 J8
Waddon New Rd CROY/NA CR0 2 A7
Waddon Park Av CROY/NA CR0 67 K3
Waddon Rd CROY/NA CR0 67 K2
Waddon Wy CROY/NA CR0 67 K5
Wade's La TEDD TW11 26 D6
Wadham SHST GU47 52 C8
Wadham Cl CRAWE RH10 165 L1
SHPTN TW17 41 M7
Wadhurst Cl PGE/AN SE20 50 E2
Wadlands Brook Rd
EGRIN RH19 178 E12
Wagbullock Ri BRAK RG12 34 F6
Wagg Cl EGRIN RH19 163 H4
Waggon Cl GUW GU2 116 B7
Waggoners Hollow BAGS GU19 54 B7
Waggoners Wy GSHT GU26 197 M2
Waggoners Wells Rd
GSHT GU26 197 M3
Wagtail Cl HORS RH12 166 F2
Wagtail Gdns SAND/SEL CR2 69 G8
Wagtail Wk BECK BR3 51 M5
Waights Ct KUTN/CMB KT2 8 F4
Wain End HORS RH12 167 G4
Wainford Cl WIM/MER SW19 29 G2
Wainwright Gv ISLW TW7 17 G6
Wainwrights CRAWE RH10 164 F7
Wake Cl GUW GU2 116 E3
Wakefield Cl BF/WBF KT14 79 H2
Wakefield Gdns NRWD SE19 32 B8
Wakefield Rd
RCHPK/HAM TW10 18 A7
Wakehams Green Dr
CRAWE RH10 165 M1
Wakehurst Dr CRAWE RH10 164 F7
Wakehurst Ms HORS RH12 166 C8
Wakely Cl BH/WHM TN16 90 F8
Walburton Rd PUR/KEN CR8 86 F3
Walbury BRAK RG12 35 H4
Waldeck Gv WNWD SE27 31 L4
Waldeck Rd MORT/ESHN SW14 18 F5
Waldegrave Gdns TWK TW1 26 C3
Waldegrave Pk TWK TW1 26 C5
Waldegrave Rd NRWD SE19 32 C8
TWK TW1 26 C5
Waldegrove CROY/NA CR0 3 J8
Waldemar Rd WIM/MER SW19 29 K6
Walden Cottages RGUW GU3 114 D6
Walden Gdns THHTH CR7 49 J4
Waldenshaw Rd FSTH SE23 32 F2
Waldens Park Rd
WOKN/KNAP GU21 76 F7
Waldens Rd WOKN/KNAP GU21 10 A5
Waldo Pl MTCM CR4 30 B8
Waldorf Cl SAND/SEL CR2 67 L7
Waldorf Hts BLKW GU17 72 A5
Waldram Crs FSTH SE23 32 F2
Waldram Park Rd FSTH SE23 33 G2
Waldron Hl BRAK RG12 35 J1
Waldronhyrst CROY/NA CR0 67 L3
Waldron Rd WAND/EARL SW18 29 M4
The Waldrons CROY/NA CR0 2 C9
OXTED RH8 130 C5
Waldy Ri CRAN GU6 186 D1
Wales Av CAR SM5 66 C4
Walesbeech CRAWE RH10 165 J5
Waleton Acres WLGTN SM6 * 66 F5
Waley's La RDKG RH5 188 E4
Walford Rd RDKG RH5 144 E6
Walham Ri WIM/MER SW19 29 H7
Walhatch Cl FROW RH18 195 N11
Walker Cl EBED/NFELT TW14 24 C1
HPTN TW12 25 J7
Walker Rd CRAWE RH10 165 K6
Walkerscroft Md CAT SE6 33 L3
DUL SE21 31 M2
Walker's Rdg CBLY GU15 73 H4
Walkfield Dr EPSOM KT18 84 E7
Walking Bottom SHGR GU5 170 H3
The Walk OXTED RH8 129 K7
Wallace Cl RGUW GU3 115 M4
SHPTN TW17 42 A4
Wallace Crs CAR SM5 66 C4
Wallace Flds EW KT17 84 C2
Wallace Sq COUL/CHIP CR5 107 G4
Wallace Wk ADL/WDHM KT15 58 F3
Wallace Wy ALDT GU11 112 C6
Wallage La CRAWE RH10 193 J7
The Walled Gdn BIL RH14 201 Q2
BRKHM/BTCW RH3 146 A1
KWD/TDW/WH KT20 105 G4
Waller La CTHM CR3 108 C5
Wall Hill Rd EGRIN RH19 163 L8
Wallingford Cl BRAK RG12 35 H4
Wallington Rd CBLY GU15 53 K8
Wallis Ct CRAWE RH10 * 191 Q3
Wallis Ms LHD/OX KT22 * 102 D4
Wallis Wy SWTR RH13 167 K5
Wallorton Gdns
MORT/ESHN SW14 19 G6
Walmer Cl FRIM GU16 93 J2
Walnut Cl ALDT GU11 134 D1
CAR SM5 66 C4
EPSOM KT18 84 C5
Walnut Dr
KWD/TDW/WH KT20 105 H6
Walnut Gv BNSTD SM7 85 G4
Walnut La CRAWW RH11 164 D1
Walnut Ms BELMT SM2 65 M6
The Walnuts HORS RH12 * 166 F5
Walnut Tree Av MTCM CR4 * 48 B3
Walnut Tree Cl BARN SW13 19 J3
BNSTD SM7 85 H2
GU GU1 6 E5
Walnut Tree Gdns GODL GU7 168 B2
Walnut Tree La BF/WBF KT14 79 G2
Walnut Tree Pk GU GU1 * 6 E3
Walnut Tree Pl
RPLY/SEND GU23 98 A5
Walnut Tree Rd BTFD TW8 18 B1
HEST TW5 * 16 C1
SHPTN TW17 41 M3
Walpole Av COUL/CHIP CR5 87 G6
COUL/CHIP CR5 106 C1
RCH/KEW TW9 18 C4
Walpole Crs TEDD TW11 26 C6
Walpole Gdns WHTN TW2 26 B3
Walpole Pl TEDD TW11 26 C6
Walpole Rd CROY/NA CR0 2 E5
SURB KT6 45 H7
TEDD TW11 26 C6
WDSR SL4 20 E1
WHTN TW2 26 B3
WIM/MER SW19 30 A7
Walrus Rd FARN GU14 112 A1
Walsham Rd EBED/NFELT TW14 24 E1
Walsh Crs CROY/NA CR0 90 B2
Walsingham Gdns
HOR/WEW KT19 64 B3
Walsingham Rd CROY/NA CR0 69 M8
MTCM CR4 48 C5
Walter's Md ASHTD KT21 83 H7
Walter's Rd SNWD SE25 50 B4
Walter St KUTN/CMB KT2 8 E5
Waltham Av GUW GU2 116 E5
Waltham Cl SHST GU47 52 A8
Waltham Rd CAR SM5 48 A8
CTHM CR3 108 E4
Walton Av CHEAM SM3 65 J2
NWMAL KT3 46 C4
Walton Bridge Rd SHPTN TW17 42 B7
Walton Ct WOKN/KNAP GU21 11 H2
Walton Dr ASC SL5 36 C1
SWTR RH13 167 M5
Walton Gdns FELT TW13 24 C5
Walton Gn CROY/NA CR0 69 L7
Walton Heath CRAWE RH10 165 M2
Walton La SHPTN TW17 42 A7
WEY KT13 59 M1
WOT/HER KT12 41 M8
Walton Pk WOT/HER KT12 61 G1
Walton Park La WOT/HER KT12 61 H1
Walton Rd EPSOM KT18 103 M3
WOKN/KNAP GU21 11 G4
WOT/HER KT12 43 G5
Walton St KWD/TDW/WH KT20 104 D6
Walton Ter WOKN/KNAP GU21 11 J2
Walton Wy MTCM CR4 48 F4
Wanborough Dr
PUT/ROE SW15 28 E2
Wanborough Hl RGUW GU3 136 F3
Wanborough La CRAN GU6 186 F1
Wandle Bank CROY/NA CR0 67 H2
WIM/MER SW19 30 A7
Wandle Cl ASHV GU12 113 K8
CRAWE RH10 165 L5
Wandle Ct HOR/WEW KT19 63 M3
Wandle Court Gdns
CROY/NA CR0 67 H2
Wandle Rd CROY/NA CR0 2 C8
CROY/NA CR0 67 H2
MRDN SM4 48 A5
TOOT SW17 30 B3
WLGTN SM6 66 E1
Wandle Side CROY/NA CR0 67 J2
WLGTN SM6 66 E2
Wandle Wy MTCM CR4 48 C5
WAND/EARL SW18 29 L2
Wandsdyke Cl FRIM GU16 93 J1
Wanmer Ct REIG RH2 * 125 K7
Wansford Gn
WOKN/KNAP GU21 76 C7
Wanstraw Gv BRAK RG12 35 H7
Wantage Cl BRAK RG12 35 H5
CRAWE RH10 165 L7
Wantage Rd SHST GU47 72 A1
Wapiti Wy FARN GU14 112 A1
The Waplings
KWD/TDW/WH KT20 * 104 E6
Wapshott Rd STA TW18 22 B7
Warbank Cl CROY/NA CR0 70 B8
Warbank Crs CROY/NA CR0 70 B8
Warbank La KUTN/CMB KT2 28 C8
Warblers Gn COB KT11 81 J4
Warboys Ap KUTN/CMB KT2 27 L7
Warboys Rd KUTN/CMB KT2 27 L7
Warburton Cl EGRIN RH19 163 H4
Warburton Rd WHTN TW2 25 L2
Warbury La WOKN/KNAP GU21 75 M6
War Coppice Rd CTHM CR3 128 A1
Ward Cl SAND/SEL CR2 68 B4
Ward La WARL CR6 88 F6
Wardle Cl BAGS GU19 54 B6
Wardley St WAND/EARL SW18 29 L1
The Wardrobe RCH/KEW TW9 * 18 A6
Wards Pl EGH TW20 21 M7
Wards Stone Pk BRAK RG12 35 H7
Ward St GU GU1 7 H6
Wareham Cl HSLW TW3 16 E6
Wareham Rd BRAK RG12 35 J5
Warenne Hts REDH RH1 148 A2
Warenne Rd LHD/OX KT22 101 M4
Warfield Rd BRAK RG12 34 F1
EBED/NFELT TW14 24 B1
HPTN TW12 43 L1
Wargrove Dr SHST GU47 72 A1
Warham Rd SAND/SEL CR2 * 67 M4
Waring St WNWD SE27 31 M5
Warkworth Gdns ISLW TW7 17 K2
Warlingham Rd THHTH CR7 49 L4
Warltersville Wy HORL RH6 160 F5
Warminster Rd SNWD SE25 50 D2
Warminster Sq SNWD SE25 50 D2
Warminster Wy MTCM CR4 48 E1
Warner Av CHEAM SM3 65 H1
Warner Cl CRAWE RH10 165 L8
HPTN TW12 25 J6
HYS/HAR UB3 15 G2
Warners La SHGR GU5 141 H7
Warnham Court Ms
HORS RH12 * 187 R9
Warnham Court Rd CAR SM5 66 C6
Warnham Rd CRAWE RH10 165 J6
HORS RH12 166 A5
Warpole Pk WEY KT13 59 K6
Warramill Rd GODL GU7 168 D4
Warren Av BELMT SM2 65 J8
RCHPK/HAM TW10 18 E6
SAND/SEL CR2 69 G6
Warren Cl EGRIN RH19 193 R2
ESH/CLAY KT10 61 M3
Warren Cnr RFNM GU10 132 F2
Warren Cutting KUTN/CMB KT2 28 A8
Warren Down BNFD RG42 34 B1
Warren Dr CRAWW RH11 164 C3
KWD/TDW/WH KT20 105 J4
Warren Dr North BRYLDS KT5 45 L8
Warren Dr South BRYLDS KT5 45 M8
Warreners La WEY KT13 60 A7
Warren Hl EPSOM KT18 84 A6
Warren La LHD/OX KT22 81 M2
OXTED RH8 130 D8
WOKS/MYFD GU22 78 D8
Warren Lodge Dr
KWD/TDW/WH KT20 105 H6
Warren Md BNSTD SM7 84 F5
Warrenne Rd
BRKHM/BTCW RH3 145 M2
Warrenne Wy REIG RH2 125 K8
Warren Pk KUTN/CMB KT2 27 M7
KWD/TDW/WH KT20 * 123 M5
WARL CR6 89 G8
Warren Park Rd SUT SM1 66 A5
Warren Ri FRIM GU16 73 H6
KUTN/CMB KT2 46 A1
Warren Rd ADL/WDHM KT15 58 D8
ASHF TW15 24 B8
BNSTD SM7 84 F4
CROY/NA CR0 3 H3
GODL GU7 168 B2
GU GU1 7 L6
HAYES BR2 70 D1
KUTN/CMB KT2 27 M7
PUR/KEN CR8 87 L2
REIG RH2 125 L7
WHTN TW2 17 G8
WIM/MER SW19 30 B7
Warren Rw ASC SL5 36 A2
The Warren ALDT GU11 112 C8
ASHTD KT21 103 J2
BELMT SM2 66 A7
BRAK RG12 * 35 J4
EHSLY KT24 120 C4
FNM GU9 134 B1
HEST TW5 16 C2
KWD/TDW/WH KT20 105 H5
LHD/OX KT22 81 M2
WPK KT4 64 A3
Warren Wy WEY KT13 59 M5
Warren Wood Cl HAYES BR2 70 D1
Warrington Cl CRAWW RH11 164 A8
Warrington Ms ALDT GU11 134 B1
Warrington Rd CROY/NA CR0 2 A8
RCHPK/HAM TW10 18 A7
Warrington Sp WDSR SL4 20 E1
Warwick BRAK RG12 35 H7
Warwick Av EGH TW20 39 M1
STA TW18 22 F7
Warwick Cl ALDT GU11 134 F1
CBLY GU15 73 L6
HPTN TW12 25 M8
RDKG RH5 173 J2
Warwick Deeping CHERT KT16 57 M4
Warwick Dr PUT/ROE SW15 19 L5
Warwick Gdns ASHTD KT21 82 F7
THDIT KT7 44 C5
THHTH CR7 * 49 K4
Warwick Gv BRYLDS KT5 45 J7
Warwick La WOKN/KNAP GU21 96 D1
Warwick Pl THDIT KT7 * 44 D6
Warwick Rd ASHF TW15 23 H6
ASHV GU12 93 J8
COUL/CHIP CR5 86 F4
FARN GU14 112 A1
HSLWW TW4 15 L5
KUT/HW KT1 8 B4
NWMAL KT3 45 M3
PGE/AN SE20 50 E3
RDKG RH5 173 K3
REDH RH1 126 C7
SUT SM1 65 M4
THDIT KT7 44 C5
THHTH CR7 49 K3
WHTN TW2 26 B2
Warwicks Bench GU GU1 7 H8
Warwick's Bench Rd GU GU1 7 J9
Warwick Wold Rd REDH RH1 127 K3
Wasdale Cl SHST GU47 52 A7
Washford La BOR GU35 180 A12
Washington Cl REIG RH2 125 K6
Washington Rd BARN SW13 19 K2
CRAWW RH11 164 A7
KUT/HW KT1 9 J7
WPK KT4 64 E1
Washpond La WARL CR6 89 M8
Wasp Green La REDH RH1 176 G1
Wassand Cl CRAWE RH10 165 J4
Wastdale Rd FSTH SE23 33 G2
Watchetts Dr CBLY GU15 72 F7
Watchetts Lake Cl CBLY GU15 73 G6
Watchetts Rd CBLY GU15 72 E6
Watchmoor Point CBLY GU15 * 72 E5
Watchmoor Rd CBLY GU15 72 D6
Watcombe Rd SNWD SE25 50 E5
Waterbank Rd CAT SE6 33 L4
Watercress Wy
WOKN/KNAP GU21 76 E7
Waterden Rd GU GU1 7 K5
Waterer Gdns
KWD/TDW/WH KT20 85 H8
Waterer Ri WLGTN SM6 67 G5
Waterers Ri WOKN/KNAP GU21 76 A7
Waterfall Cl VW GU25 38 C3
Waterfall Cottages
WIM/MER SW19 30 A7
Waterfall Rd WIM/MER SW19 30 A7
Waterfall Ter TOOT SW17 30 B7
Waterfield
KWD/TDW/WH KT20 104 E2
Waterfield Cl SWTR RH13 167 H6
Waterfield Dr WARL CR6 108 E1
Waterfield Gdns CRAWW RH11 164 A6
SNWD SE25 50 B4
Waterfield Gn
KWD/TDW/WH KT20 104 E2
Waterfields LHD/OX KT22 102 E1
Waterford Cl COB KT11 81 H1
Waterham Rd BRAK RG12 34 E6
Waterhouse La
KWD/TDW/WH KT20 105 J3
PUR/KEN CR8 107 M1
REDH RH1 128 C6
Waterhouse Md SHST GU47 72 A2
Waterlakes EDEN TN8 179 R1
Waterlands La HORS RH12 203 R1
Water La CHOB/PIR GU24 95 H1
COB KT11 81 J4
EDEN TN8 179 L2
FARN GU14 92 D2
FNM GU9 134 C5
GDST RH9 151 G4
GT/LBKH KT23 101 H8
KUT/HW KT1 8 D5
MFD/CHID GU8 183 Q5
OXTED RH8 110 D8
RCH/KEW TW9 18 A7
RDKG RH5 171 N1
SHGR GU5 140 E4
TWK TW1 26 D2
Water Lea CRAWE RH10 165 J5
Waterloo Cl CBLY GU15 73 L2

EBED/NFELT TW14 24 C2
Waterloo Pl CAR SM5 * 66 C2
RCH/KEW TW9 18 D1
Waterloo Rd ASHV GU12 112 F8
HOR/WEW KT19 84 A3
SUT SM1 66 A4
Waterloo Ter WEY KT13 * 59 K3
Waterlow Rd REIG RH2 147 M1
Waterman Cl BOR GU35 196 A3
Watermans Cl KUTN/CMB KT2 * 8 E3
Waterman Sq PGE/AN SE20 32 F8
Water Md COUL/CHIP CR5 86 C7
Watermead EBED/NFELT TW14 24 B2
KWD/TDW/WH KT20 104 E3
WOKN/KNAP GU21 76 C6
Watermead La CAR SM5 48 C6
Watermead Rd CAT SE6 33 M5
Watermens Sq PGE/AN SE20 * 32 F8
Watermill Cl RCHPK/HAM TW10 26 F4
Water Mill Wy FELT TW13 25 J3
Watermill Wy WIM/MER SW19 47 M1
Waterperry La CHOB/PIR GU24 56 C8
Waters Dr STA TW18 22 C5
Watersedge HOR/WEW KT19 63 M3
Waterside EGRIN RH19 163 J4
HORL RH6 160 D1
Waterside Av BECK BR3 51 L5
Waterside Cl CRAWW RH11 164 A6
GODL GU7 168 D4
SURB KT6 63 H1
Waterside Dr WOT/HER KT12 42 E5
Waterside La GODL GU7 159 M6
Waterside Ms GU GU1 116 F6
Waterside Rd GU GU1 117 H5
Waterside Wy TOOT SW17 29 M5
WOKN/KNAP GU21 76 E8
Waterslade REDH RH1 126 B8
Watersmeet Cl RGUE GU4 117 K3
Watersplash Cl KUT/HW KT1 8 E8
Water Splash La ASC SL5 37 H1
Watersplash Rd SHPTN TW17 41 K4
Waters Rd KUT/HW KT1 9 L7
Waters Sq KUT/HW KT1 9 L8
Water Tower Hl CROY/NA CR0 2 F9
Waterway Rd LHD/OX KT22 102 D4
Waterworks Cl FROW RH18 195 N9
Watery La CHOB/PIR GU24 56 A8
RYNPK SW20 47 J2
Wates Wy MTCM CR4 48 C6
Watford Cl GU GU1 7 M4
Wathen Rd DORK RH4 144 E1
Watlings Cl CROY/NA CR0 51 H6
Watlington Gv SYD SE26 33 H6
Watney Cl PUR/KEN CR8 87 J3
Watney Rd MORT/ESHN SW14 18 F5
Watneys Rd CROY/NA CR0 49 G5
Watson Av CHEAM SM3 65 H1
Watson Cl CRAWE RH10 165 L7
WIM/MER SW19 30 B7
Watson Rd DORK RH4 143 M3
Wattendon Rd PUR/KEN CR8 87 L6
Watts Cl KWD/TDW/WH KT20 * 105 G4
Watts Common Rd ALDT GU11 112 B2
Watt's La KWD/TDW/WH KT20 105 G4
TEDD TW11 26 D6
Watts La WOKN/KNAP GU21 76 D5
Watt's Md KWD/TDW/WH KT20 105 G4
Watts Rd FARN GU14 92 C4
THDIT KT7 44 D7
Wavel Pl SYD SE26 32 C5
Wavendene Av EGH TW20 21 M8
Waveney Wk CRAWE RH10 165 K6
Waverleigh Rd CRAN GU6 186 D4
Waverley BRAK RG12 34 B5
Waverley Av BRYLDS KT5 45 L6
PUR/KEN CR8 88 B6
SUT SM1 65 L1
WHTN TW2 25 J2
Waverley Cl CBLY GU15 73 J5
E/WMO/HCT KT8 43 K5
FNM GU9 * 5 L4
Waverley Ct HORS RH12 * 166 E7
WOKS/MYFD GU22 10 D7
Waverley Dr ASHV GU12 113 K3
CBLY GU15 73 H4
CHERT KT16 58 A2
VW GU25 38 D4
Waverley Gdns ASHV GU12 113 K3
Waverley La FNM GU9 5 M4
Waverley Pl LHD/OX KT22 * 102 E4
Waverley Rd BAGS GU19 54 B6
COB KT11 81 L4
EW KT17 64 E4
FARN GU14 93 G6
SNWD SE25 50 E4
WEY KT13 59 K4
Waverley Wy CAR SM5 66 B5
Waverton Rd
WAND/EARL SW18 29 M1
Wavertree Rd
BRXS/STRHM SW2 31 J2
Waye Av HEST TW5 15 K3
Wayland Cl BRAK RG12 35 J4
Waylands STWL/WRAY TW19 12 B8
Waylett Pl WNWD SE27 31 L4
Wayman Rd FARN GU14 92 B1
Wayneflete Tower Av
ESH/CLAY KT10 61 K2
Waynflete Av CROY/NA CR0 2 A8
Waynflete La FNM GU9 4 D4
Waynflete St WAND/EARL SW18 29 M3
Ways End CBLY GU15 73 H5
Wayside CRAWW RH11 164 A6
CROY/NA CR0 * 69 L5
MORT/ESHN SW14 18 F6
RDKG RH5 * 173 L11
Wayside Ct TWK TW1 17 M8
The Way REIG RH2 126 A7
Weald Cl HAYES BR2 71 H1
RGUE GU4 139 H6
SWTR RH13 205 M9
Weald Dr CRAWE RH10 165 J5
Wealdstone Rd CHEAM SM3 65 J1
The Weald EGRIN RH19 163 G2
Weald Wy CTHM CR3 128 B2
REIG RH2 147 M4
Weare St RDKG RH5 188 D6
Weasdale Ct WOKN/KNAP GU21 76 C6
Weatherall Cl ADL/WDHM KT15 58 E4
Weatherhill Cl HORL RH6 161 J3
Weatherhill Rd HORL RH6 161 K3
Weather Wy BRAK RG12 34 F2
Weaver Cl CRAWW RH11 * 164 A5
Weavers Cl ISLW TW7 17 J6
Weavers Down LIPH GU30 * 196 C10
Weavers Gdns FNM GU9 155 J2
Weaver Wk WNWD SE27 31 L5
Webb Cl BAGS GU19 54 B8
CRAWW RH11 191 L12
Webb Rd MFD/CHID GU8 183 K2
Webster Cl LHD/OX KT22 81 L4
Websters Cl WOKS/MYFD GU22 96 D2
Weddell Rd CRAWE RH10 165 H7
The Wedges SWTR RH13 203 Q12
Wedgwoods BH/WHM TN16 * 110 F3
Wedgwood Wy NRWD SE19 31 M8
Weighbridge Rd
ADL/WDHM KT15 58 E7
Weighton Rd PGE/AN SE20 50 E2
Weihurst Gdns SUT SM1 66 A4
Weir Av FARN GU14 92 D6
Weirbrook CRAWE RH10 165 J7
Weir Cl FARN GU14 92 D6
Weir Pl STA TW18 40 B1
Weir Rd BAL SW12 30 F2
CHERT KT16 40 E7
WIM/MER SW19 29 L4
WOT/HER KT12 42 D6
Welbeck BRAK RG12 34 B5
Welbeck Cl EW KT17 64 D6
FARN GU14 92 C5
NWMAL KT3 46 C5
Welbeck Rd CAR SM5 48 B8
SUT SM1 66 A1
Welcomes Rd PUR/KEN CR8 87 M5
Weldon Dr E/WMO/HCT KT8 43 J4
Weldon Wy REDH RH1 127 G3
Welford Pl WIM/MER SW19 29 H5
Welham Rd TOOT SW17 30 D6
Welhouse Rd CAR SM5 48 B8
Welland Cl DTCH/LGLY SL3 12 D1
Wellbrook Rd ORP BR6 71 K3
Well Cl CBLY GU15 72 E5
STRHM/NOR SW16 31 J5
WOKN/KNAP GU21 76 F7
Weller Cl CRAWE RH10 165 M5
Weller Dr CBLY GU15 72 F6
Weller Pl ORP BR6 * 91 K1
Wellers Cl BH/WHM TN16 131 M1
Wellesford Cl BNSTD SM7 85 J7
Wellesley Cl ASHV GU12 113 J2
BAGS GU19 53 M6
Wellesley Court Rd
CROY/NA CR0 * 2 E6
Wellesley Crs WHTN TW2 26 B3
Wellesley Gdn FNM GU9 133 M2
Wellesley Ga ASHV GU12 * 112 E8
Wellesley Gv CROY/NA CR0 2 E5
Wellesley Pde WHTN TW2 * 26 B4
Wellesley Rd ALDT GU11 112 A6
BELMT SM2 65 M5
CROY/NA CR0 2 D3
RFNM GU10 181 N3
WHTN TW2 26 A4
Welley Av STWL/WRAY TW19 12 B6
Welley Rd STWL/WRAY TW19 12 B7
Well Farm Rd CTHM CR3 108 D1
Wellfield EGRIN RH19 163 K6
Wellfield Gdns CAR SM5 66 B8
Wellfield Rd STRHM/NOR SW16 31 H5
Wellhouse La
BRKHM/BTCW RH3 146 A3
Wellhouse Rd BECK BR3 51 J4
BRKHM/BTCW RH3 146 B3
Wellingham Wy HORS RH12 190 F11
Wellington Av ALDT GU11 112 C7
HSLW TW3 16 D7
VW GU25 38 E6
WPK KT4 64 F2
Wellington Cl CRAWE RH10 192 D4
WOT/HER KT12 42 C8
Wellington Crs NWMAL KT3 45 M3
Wellington Dr BRAK RG12 35 G5
PUR/KEN CR8 67 J8
Wellington Gdns ALDT GU11 * 112 C8
WHTN TW2 26 A5
Wellingtonia Wy EDEN TN8 153 M7
Wellington La FNM GU9 134 A2
Wellington Pl ASHV GU12 113 J5
COB KT11 81 K2
GODL GU7 * 168 B2
Wellington Rd ASHF TW15 23 H6
CROY/NA CR0 2 B2
CTHM CR3 107 M4
EBED/NFELT TW14 15 H7
HORS RH12 167 G7
HPTN TW12 26 A5
WIM/MER SW19 29 K3
Wellington Rd North
HSLWW TW4 16 C5
Wellington Rd South
HSLWW TW4 16 C6
Wellington St ALDT GU11 112 D7
Wellington Ter
WOKN/KNAP GU21 * 76 B8
Wellington Town Rd
EGRIN RH19 162 E2
Wellington Wy FARN GU14 112 A2
HORL RH6 160 C1
WEY KT13 59 K8
Well La HASM GU27 198 E7
MFD/CHID GU8 * 183 L9
MORT/ESHN SW14 18 F7
WOKN/KNAP GU21 76 F7
Well Pth WOKN/KNAP GU21 76 F7
Well Rd RFNM GU10 132 B3
Wells Cl BH/WHM TN16 131 M1
GT/LBKH KT23 101 L6
HORS RH12 166 C7
SAND/SEL CR2 68 B4
Wells Cottages FNM GU9 155 K2
Wellside Gdns
MORT/ESHN SW14 18 F6
Wells La ASC SL5 36 E4
RGUW GU3 114 F5
Wells Lea EGRIN RH19 162 E2
Wells Meadow EGRIN RH19 162 E2
Wells Park Rd SYD SE26 32 D4
Wells Pl REDH RH1 126 E4
WAND/EARL SW18 29 M1
Wells Rd CRAWE RH10 * 165 G8
EPSOM KT18 83 L5
RGUE GU4 117 M5
Well Wy EPSOM KT18 83 K5
Wellwood Cl COUL/CHIP CR5 87 H4
SWTR RH13 167 L5
Wellwynds Rd CRAN GU6 186 D3
Welwyn Av EBED/NFELT TW14 15 J8
Welwyn Cl CRAWW RH11 164 A7
Wembley Rd HPTN TW12 43 K1
Wembury Pk LING RH7 177 R9
Wendela Cl WOKS/MYFD GU22 10 F8
Wendley Dr ADL/WDHM KT15 58 C8
Wendling Rd SUT SM1 48 A8
Wendover Dr FRIM GU16 73 M6
NWMAL KT3 46 C6
Wendover Pl STA TW18 22 A6
Wendover Rd STA TW18 22 A6
Wendron Cl WOKN/KNAP GU21 76 D8
The Wend COUL/CHIP CR5 87 G4
Wendy Crs GUW GU2 116 D6
Wenlock Cl CRAWW RH11 164 C6
Wenlock Edge DORK RH4 * 144 F4
Wensleydale CRAWW RH11 164 E7
Wensleydale Dr CBLY GU15 74 A4
Wensleydale Gdns HPTN TW12 25 L8
Wensleydale Rd HPTN TW12 25 K8
Wentworth Av ASC SL5 35 M2
Wentworth Cl ASHF TW15 23 L5
ASHV GU12 113 K2
FNM GU9 134 C3
HAYES BR2 * 70 D1
MRDN SM4 47 K7
RPLY/SEND GU23 98 E3
SURB KT6 63 G1
Wentworth Crs ASHV GU12 113 K3
Wentworth Dene WEY KT13 59 L4
Wentworth Dr CRAWE RH10 165 M3
VW GU25 38 C4
Wentworth Rd CROY/NA CR0 49 K7
Wentworth Wy ASC SL5 35 M2
SAND/SEL CR2 88 D5
Werndee Rd SNWD SE25 50 D4
Wesley Av HSLW TW3 16 B4
Wesley Cl CRAWW RH11 164 A7
HORL RH6 160 D1
REIG RH2 147 J1
Wesley Dr EGH TW20 21 K7
Wessels KWD/TDW/WH KT20 105 G3
Wessex Av WIM/MER SW19 47 K2
Wessex Cl KUT/HW KT1 9 L5
THDIT KT7 62 C1
Wessex Ct BECK BR3 * 51 H1
Wessex Pl FNM GU9 5 K5
Wessex Ter MTCM CR4 * 48 B5
Westacres ESH/CLAY KT10 61 J6
West Av CRAWE RH10 165 H2
FNM GU9 134 A3
REDH RH1 148 C6
WLGTN SM6 67 H4
WOT/HER KT12 60 B8
West Bank DORK RH4 144 C3
Westbank Rd HPTN TW12 25 M7
West Barnes La NWMAL KT3 46 E5
RYNPK SW20 46 E3
Westbourne Av CHEAM SM3 65 H1
Westbourne Dr FSTH SE23 33 G2
Westbourne Rd CROY/NA CR0 50 C6
FELT TW13 24 C4
SHST GU47 72 B2
STA TW18 22 E8
SYD SE26 33 G7
Westbrook FROW RH18 * 195 M10
Westbrook Av HPTN TW12 25 J8
Westbrook Gdns BRAK RG12 34 F1
Westbrook Hl MFD/CHID GU8 157 M5
Westbrook Rd GODL GU7 159 M4
HEST TW5 16 C2
STA TW18 22 C6
THHTH CR7 50 A1
Westbury Av ESH/CLAY KT10 62 C5
Westbury Cl CTHM CR3 * 88 C8
SHPTN TW17 * 41 L6
Westbury Gdns FNM GU9 134 B5
Westbury Pl BTFD TW8 18 A1
Westbury Rd BECK BR3 51 H3
CROY/NA CR0 50 A6
FELT TW13 25 G2
NWMAL KT3 46 A4
PGE/AN SE20 51 G1
Westbury Ter BH/WHM TN16 111 M8
BH/WHM TN16 131 M1
Westbury Wy ASHV GU12 113 G7
Westcar La WOT/HER KT12 60 E5
West Chiltington La
SWTR RH13 203 R11
West Cl ASHF TW15 23 H5
FNM GU9 134 A2
Westcombe Av CROY/NA CR0 49 H6
Westcombe Cl BRAK RG12 35 G7
West Common Rd HAYES BR2 70 D1
Westcoombe Av RYNPK SW20 46 C1
Westcote Rd
STRHM/NOR SW16 30 F6
Westcott Cl CROY/NA CR0 69 L7
Westcott Rd DORK RH4 144 C2
Westcott St DORK RH4 143 L3
Westcott Wy BELMT SM2 64 F8
Westcroft Gdns MRDN SM4 47 J3
Westcroft Rd CAR SM5 66 D3
West Cross Wy BTFD TW8 17 L1
Westdene WOT/HER KT12 60 E4
Westdene Mdw CRAN GU6 185 R2
Westdene Wy WEY KT13 60 B2
West Down GT/LBKH KT23 121 L1
Westdown Rd CAT SE6 33 K1
West Dr ADL/WDHM KT15 58 E8
ASC SL5 38 A6
BELMT SM2 65 G7
CAR SM5 66 A8
KWD/TDW/WH KT20 85 G8
STRHM/NOR SW16 30 E5
West End Gdns ESH/CLAY KT10 61 J4
West End Gv FNM GU9 4 E4
West End La ESH/CLAY KT10 61 J4
HASM GU27 199 L5
HYS/HAR UB3 14 F2
RFNM GU10 155 H8
Westerdale Dr FRIM GU16 73 L6
Westerfolds Cl
WOKS/MYFD GU22 11 L4
Westerham Cl ADL/WDHM KT15 58 F5
BELMT SM2 * 65 K8
Westerham Hl BH/WHM TN16 111 L4
Westerham Rd HAYES BR2 71 G5
OXTED RH8 130 D3
Westerley Crs SYD SE26 * 33 J6
Westermain ADL/WDHM KT15 58 F8
Western Av CHERT KT16 40 D3
CHOB/PIR GU24 95 K3
EGH TW20 39 L3
Western Cl CHERT KT16 40 D3
Western Dr SHPTN TW17 42 A5
Western La BAL SW12 30 D1
Western Perimeter Rd
HTHAIR TW6 13 L5
Western Pl DORK RH4 * 144 D2
Western Rd ALDT GU11 112 B8
BNFD RG42 34 B1
MTCM CR4 48 B1
SUT SM1 65 K4
West Farm Av ASHTD KT21 82 F8
West Farm Cl ASHTD KT21 102 F1
West Farm Dr ASHTD KT21 103 G1
Westfield RDKG RH5 171 K1
REIG RH2 125 L5
Westfield Av SAND/SEL CR2 88 A3
WOKS/MYFD GU22 97 H3
Westfield Cl SUT SM1 65 J3
Westfield Common
WOKS/MYFD GU22 97 H4
Westfield Dr GT/LBKH KT23 101 L4
Westfield Gv WOKS/MYFD GU22 97 H2
Westfield La RFNM GU10 155 H3
Westfield Pde
ADL/WDHM KT15 * 59 G8
Westfield Rd BECK BR3 51 J2
CBLY GU15 72 E7
CRAWW RH11 164 D4
CROY/NA CR0 2 A5
GU GU1 117 H4
MTCM CR4 48 B2
SURB KT6 45 G5
SUT SM1 65 J3
WOKS/MYFD GU22 97 H4
WOT/HER KT12 43 H7
Westfields BARN SW13 19 J5
Westfields Av BARN SW13 19 H5
Westfield Wy
WOKS/MYFD GU22 97 H4
West Flexford La RGUW GU3 137 H1
West Gdns EW KT17 64 B8
TOOT SW17 30 B7
Westgate Est
EBED/NFELT TW14 * 23 L2
Westgate Rd BECK BR3 51 M1
SNWD SE25 50 E4
Westglade FARN GU14 92 A5
West Green Dr CRAWW RH11 164 E4
West Gv WOT/HER KT12 60 E3
West Gun Copse Rd
SWTR RH13 204 E12
West Hall BF/WBF KT14 * 78 F4
Westhall Pk WARL CR6 108 F1
Westhall Rd WARL CR6 88 D8
Westhay Gdns
MORT/ESHN SW14 18 E7
West Heath CHOB/PIR GU24 95 G5
West Heath Rd FARN GU14 92 C5
West Hl EGRIN RH19 162 E5
EGRIN RH19 178 F11
HOR/WEW KT19 83 M3
MFD/CHID GU8 157 M6
ORP BR6 91 J2
OXTED RH8 130 A4
SAND/SEL CR2 68 B7
WIM/MER SW19 29 G1
West Hill Av HOR/WEW KT19 83 M2
West Hill Bank OXTED RH8 130 A4
West Hill Cl CHOB/PIR GU24 95 L2
MFD/CHID GU8 157 M6
West Hill Rd WOKS/MYFD GU22 10 B9
West Hoathly Rd EGRIN RH19 194 D10
Westhorpe Rd PUT/ROE SW15 19 M5
West House Cl WIM/MER SW19 29 H2
Westhumble St RDKG RH5 122 E5
Westland Cl
STWL/WRAY TW19 * 14 B8
Westland Dr HAYES BR2 70 C1
Westlands Ct EPSOM KT18 83 M5
Westlands Wy OXTED RH8 130 A1
West La EGRIN RH19 162 E5
RDKG RH5 143 G5
Westleas HORL RH6 160 B1
Westlees Cl RDKG RH5 144 F5
Westleigh Av COUL/CHIP CR5 86 D6
PUT/ROE SW15 19 M7
Westmacott Dr
EBED/NFELT TW14 24 D2
Westmead FARN GU14 92 E6
West Md FNM GU9 * 5 G3
HOR/WEW KT19 64 B5
Westmead PUT/ROE SW15 28 E1
WOKN/KNAP GU21 76 E8
Westmead Dr REDH RH1 148 D8
Westmead Rd SUT SM1 66 A3
West Meads GUW GU2 138 C1
HORL RH6 160 F3
Westminster Av THHTH CR7 49 L2
Westminster Cl
EBED/NFELT TW14 24 D2
TEDD TW11 26 D6
Westminster Ct
WOKS/MYFD GU22 * 97 L3
Westminster Rd CRAWE RH10 165 L5
SUT SM1 66 A1
Westmoat Cl BECK BR3 33 M8
Westmont Rd ESH/CLAY KT10 62 B1
Westmoreland Dr BELMT SM2 65 L7
Westmoreland Rd BARN SW13 19 J3
Westmoreland Ter
PGE/AN SE20 * 32 E8
Westmore Rd BH/WHM TN16 110 F3
Westmorland Cl
HOR/WEW KT19 64 B8
TWK TW1 17 L8
Westmorland Dr CBLY GU15 73 L6
Westmorland Wy MTCM CR4 49 G4
West Mt GUW GU2 * 6 E8
Weston Av ADL/WDHM KT15 58 D3
E/WMO/HCT KT8 43 H4
THDIT KT7 44 B7
Weston Cl COUL/CHIP CR5 107 J2
Weston Ct GODL GU7 168 B3
Weston Dr CTHM CR3 107 M3
CTHM CR3 108 D6
Weston Flds SHGR GU5 140 F5
Weston Gdns ISLW TW7 17 G3
WOKS/MYFD GU22 78 B6
Weston Gn THDIT KT7 44 B8
Weston Green Rd
ESH/CLAY KT10 44 A8
Weston Gv BAGS GU19 54 C7
Weston Lea EHSLY KT24 100 A7
Weston Pk KUT/HW KT1 8 E6
THDIT KT7 44 B8
Weston Park Cl THDIT KT7 * 44 B8
Weston Rd EW KT17 84 B1
GUW GU2 6 A1
THDIT KT7 44 B8
Westons Hl SWTR RH13 204 C12
Weston Wy WOKS/MYFD GU22 78 B6
Westover Cl BELMT SM2 65 L7
Westow Hl NRWD SE19 32 B7
Westow St NRWD SE19 32 B7
West Pde HORS RH12 166 F5
West Park Av RCH/KEW TW9 18 D3
West Park Cl HEST TW5 16 C1
West Park Rd CRAWE RH10 193 L2
HOR/WEW KT19 83 J2
LING RH7 177 P9
RCH/KEW TW9 18 D3
West Parkside WARL CR6 89 K5
West Pl WIM/MER SW19 28 F6
West Rp HTHAIR TW6 14 D3
West Rdg RFNM GU10 * 135 J4
West Ring RFNM GU10 135 J2
West Rd CBLY GU15 73 G4
CHSGTN KT9 82 F1
EBED/NFELT TW14 24 A1
FARN GU14 92 D1
GU GU1 7 K5
KUTN/CMB KT2 45 M1
REIG RH2 147 L1
WEY KT13 59 L7
West Sheen V RCH/KEW TW9 18 C6
West Side Common
WIM/MER SW19 28 F7
Westside Ct CHOB/PIR GU24 * 75 H3
West St CAR SM5 66 C3
CRAWW RH11 164 F5
CROY/NA CR0 2 D9
DORK RH4 144 D2
EGRIN RH19 162 F5
EPSOM KT18 83 M3
EW KT17 64 B8
FNM GU9 4 F4
HASM GU27 198 D7
HOR/WEW KT19 83 M3
HORS RH12 166 F7
LING RH7 178 H8
REIG RH2 125 J8
SUT SM1 65 L4
WOKN/KNAP GU21 10 E5
West Street La CAR SM5 66 C3
West Street Pl CROY/NA CR0 2 D9
West Temple Sheen
MORT/ESHN SW14 18 E7
West Vw EBED/NFELT TW14 23 M2
West View Av CTHM CR3 88 C8
Westview Cl REDH RH1 148 B3
West View Gdns EGRIN RH19 162 F5
West View Rd BOR GU35 196 H1
WARL CR6 108 E1
Westville Rd THDIT KT7 44 D7
Westward Ho GU GU1 117 J6
Westwates Cl BRAK RG12 35 G1
West Wy CAR SM5 66 A8
CRAWE RH10 165 J3
CROY/NA CR0 69 H1
HEST TW5 16 C3
SHPTN TW17 42 A6
SWTR RH13 203 Q6
Westway CRAWE RH10 192 F2
CTHM CR3 108 A4
GUW GU2 116 C6
HORL RH6 160 E7
RYNPK SW20 46 E4
Westway Cl RYNPK SW20 46 E3
West Way Gdns CROY/NA CR0 69 G4
Westway Gdns REDH RH1 126 D5
Westways BH/WHM TN16 111 M8
EDEN TN8 153 M7
HOR/WEW KT19 64 C3
Westwell Rd
STRHM/NOR SW16 31 H7
Westwell Road Ap
STRHM/NOR SW16 31 H7
Westwick Gdns HSLWW TW4 15 L4
Westwood Av ADL/WDHM KT15 78 C2
NRWD SE19 49 M1
Westwood Cl ESH/CLAY KT10 61 M2
Westwood Gdns BARN SW13 19 J5
Westwood Hl SYD SE26 32 D6
Westwood La RGUW GU3 114 D6
Westwood Pk FSTH SE23 32 E1
Westwood Pl SYD SE26 * 32 D6
Westwood Rd BARN SW13 19 J5
BFOR GU20 55 G4
COUL/CHIP CR5 87 G8
Wetherby Gdns FARN GU14 112 F1
Wetherby Wy CHSGTN KT9 63 H6
Wettern Cl SAND/SEL CR2 68 B8
Wetton Pl EGH TW20 21 J6
Wexfenne Gdns
WOKS/MYFD GU22 78 E6
Wexford Rd BAL SW12 30 C1
Wey Av CHERT KT16 40 D3
Wey Bank RFNM GU10 154 B6
Weybank RPLY/SEND GU23 79 H6
Weybank Cl FNM GU9 5 K2
Weybarton BF/WBF KT14 79 J3
Weybourne Pl SAND/SEL CR2 68 A8
Weybourne Rd FNM GU9 134 B4
Weybourne St
WAND/EARL SW18 29 M3
Weybridge Pk WEY KT13 59 L4
Weybridge Rd
ADL/WDHM KT15 59 J3
THHTH CR7 49 K4
Weybrook Dr RGUE GU4 117 L3
Wey Cl ASHV GU12 113 K8
BF/WBF KT14 78 E3
CBLY GU15 72 E4
Weycombe Rd HASM GU27 198 D5

Wey Ct ADL/WDHM KT15 59 G7
GODL GU7 168 D3
HOR/WEW KT19 63 M3
Weydon Farm La FNM GU9 5 G6
Weydon Hill Cl FNM GU9 5 H7
Weydon Hill Rd FNM GU9 5 H7
Weydon La FNM GU9 4 D9
Weydon Mill La FNM GU9 5 G6
Weydown Cl RGUW GU3 116 C3
WIM/MER SW19 29 H2
Weydown La RGUW GU3 116 D3
Weydown Rd HASM GU27 198 C6
Wey Hl HASM GU27 198 B7
Weyland Cl LIPH GU30 196 H8
Weylands Pk WEY KT13 60 A5
Weylea Av RGUE GU4 117 K5
Wey Lodge Cl LIPH GU30 * 197 J9
Wey Manor Rd
ADL/WDHM KT15 59 G7
Weymead Cl CHERT KT16 40 F8
Weymouth Ct BELMT SM2 * 65 L6
Wey Rd GODL GU7 168 D4
WEY KT13 59 J2
Weyside Cl BF/WBF KT14 79 J2
Weyside Gdns GU GU1 116 E6
Wey South Pth CRAN GU6 185 M11
Wey - South Pth GUW GU2 7 G8
RGUE GU4 139 H8
SHGR GU5 169 P9
Weysprings HASM GU27 198 A6
Weyview Cl GU GU1 116 F6
Wey View Ct GU GU1 6 E5
Weywood Cl FNM GU9 134 C2
Weywood La FNM GU9 134 B2
Wharf Bridge Rd ISLW TW7 17 L5
Wharfedale Gdns THHTH CR7 49 J4
Wharfenden Wy FRIM GU16 93 J3
Wharf La RPLY/SEND GU23 97 M5
TWK TW1 26 D2
Wharf Rd ASHV GU12 113 K5
FRIM GU16 93 J3
GU GU1 6 F4
STWL/WRAY TW19 20 F1
Wharf St GODL GU7 168 B5
Wharf Wy FRIM GU16 93 J3
Wharncliffe Gdns SNWD SE25 50 B2
Wharncliffe Rd SNWD SE25 50 A2
Whateley Cl GUW GU2 116 E3
Whateley Rd PGE/AN SE20 33 G8
Whatley Av RYNPK SW20 47 G3
Whatley Gn BRAK RG12 * 34 E6
Whatman Rd FSTH SE23 33 G1
Whatmore Cl
STWL/WRAY TW19 13 K8
Wheatash Rd ADL/WDHM KT15 58 E1
Wheatfield Wy HORL RH6 160 E2
KUT/HW KT1 8 E8
Wheathill Rd PGE/AN SE20 50 E2
Wheat Knoll PUR/KEN CR8 87 M6
Wheatlands HEST TW5 16 D1
Wheatlands Rd TOOT SW17 30 D4
Wheatley BRAK RG12 34 B5
Wheatley Rd ALDT GU11 112 C7
ISLW TW7 17 J5
Wheatsheaf Cl CHERT KT16 58 A5
HORS RH12 167 H4
WOKN/KNAP GU21 10 E2
Wheatsheaf La FUL/PGN SW6 19 M2
STA TW18 22 C8
Wheatstone Cl CRAWE RH10 192 A2
WIM/MER SW19 48 A1
Wheeler Av OXTED RH8 130 A3
Wheeler La MFD/CHID GU8 183 M3
Wheeler Rd CRAWE RH10 165 K6
Wheelers La
BRKHM/BTCW RH3 145 M2
EPSOM KT18 83 M4
HORL RH6 161 K3
Wheelers Wy EGRIN RH19 193 R2
Wheelwrights La GSHT GU26 197 M1
Wheelwrights Pl
DTCH/LGLY SL3 * 12 F2
Whelan Wy WLGTN SM6 67 G2
Wherwell Rd GUW GU2 6 E7
Whetstone Rd FARN GU14 92 A4
Whimbrel Cl SAND/SEL CR2 88 A1
Whinfell Cl STRHM/NOR SW16 31 G6
Whins Cl CBLY GU15 72 E5
Whins Dr CBLY GU15 72 E5
Whinshill Ct ASC SL5 37 K8
Whipley Cl RGUE GU4 117 L5
Whistler Cl CRAWE RH10 165 H7
Whistler Gv SHST GU47 72 A3
Whistley Cl BRAK RG12 35 H3
Whitby Cl BH/WHM TN16 110 E1
FARN GU14 93 H8
Whitby Gdns SUT SM1 66 A1
Whitby Rd SUT SM1 66 A1
Whitchurch Cl ALDT GU11 135 G3
Whitcome Ms RCH/KEW TW9 18 E3
White Acres Rd FRIM GU16 93 J5
Whitebeam Dr REIG RH2 147 L3
White Beam Wy
KWD/TDW/WH KT20 104 D3
Whiteberry Rd RDKG RH5 172 C2
White Bridge Av MTCM CR4 48 A4
White Bridge Cl
EBED/NFELT TW14 15 J8
White Bushes REDH RH1 148 D5
White City CWTH RG45 52 A4
White Cottage Cl FNM GU9 134 A3
Whitecroft Wy BECK BR3 51 M4
Whitefield Av PUR/KEN CR8 86 F8
Whitegates WOKS/MYFD GU22 97 J2
Whitegate Wy
KWD/TDW/WH KT20 104 E2
Whitehall Crs CHSGTN KT9 63 G4
Whitehall Dr CRAWW RH11 164 A4
Whitehall Farm La VW GU25 39 H3
Whitehall Gdns CHSWK W4 18 E1
Whitehall La EGH TW20 21 J8
REIG RH2 147 J4
STWL/WRAY TW19 12 D8
VW GU25 39 J1
Whitehall Pde EGRIN RH19 * 162 F4
Whitehall Park Rd CHSWK W4 18 E1
Whitehall Pl WLGTN SM6 66 E3
Whitehall Rd THHTH CR7 49 K5
White Hart Ct HORS RH12 166 F5
White Hart La BARN SW13 19 H4
RGUW GU3 115 K7
White Hart Mdw
RPLY/SEND GU23 98 F3
White Hart Rw CHERT KT16 * 40 D7
Whitehead Cl
WAND/EARL SW18 29 M1
White Heron Ms TEDD TW11 * 26 C7
White Hl BFOR GU20 54 E3
COUL/CHIP CR5 106 A5
SAND/SEL CR2 68 A8
Whitehill Cl CBLY GU15 73 G2
Whitehill La REDH RH1 128 A1
RPLY/SEND GU23 99 M5
Whitehill Pl VW GU25 39 H5
Whitehill Rd BOR GU35 196 B4
White Horse Dr EPSOM KT18 83 M5
White Horse La
RPLY/SEND GU23 98 F3
Whitehorse La SNWD SE25 50 B4
Whitehorse Rd CROY/NA CR0 2 E1
HORS RH12 167 L3
Whitehouse Cl FARN GU14 92 E3
Whitehouse Dr GU GU1 117 L8
White House La RGUE GU4 117 G3
White House Wk FNM GU9 134 A2
White Knights Rd WEY KT13 59 M6
White Knobs Wy CTHM CR3 108 D7
Whitelands Crs
WAND/EARL SW18 29 H1
Whitelands Dr ASC SL5 36 A1
White La ASHV GU12 113 M8
OXTED RH8 110 E5
RFNM GU10 135 M2
RGUE GU4 139 M2
Whiteley Rd NRWD SE19 32 A6
Whiteleys Wy FELT TW13 25 K4
White Lion Wk GU GU1 7 G7
White Ldg NRWD SE19 31 L8
White Lodge Cl BELMT SM2 65 M6
ISLW TW7 17 K4
White Lodge Gdns REDH RH1 148 D8
Whitely Hl CRAWE RH10 192 E12
Whitemore Rd GU GU1 117 G4
White Oak Dr BECK BR3 51 M2
Whiteoaks BNSTD SM7 85 L3
White Pillars WOKS/MYFD GU22 96 F2
Whitepost Hl REDH RH1 126 B8
White Post La RFNM GU10 155 K5
White Rd CBLY GU15 72 C3
White Rose La FNM GU9 155 L2
WOKS/MYFD GU22 10 F7
Whites Rd FARN GU14 93 H8
Whitethorn Av COUL/CHIP CR5 86 D5
Whitethorn Cl ASHV GU12 113 L8
Whitethorn Gdns CROY/NA CR0 68 E1
White Wy GT/LBKH KT23 101 L8
Whitewood Cottages
BH/WHM TN16 110 F2
Whitewood La GDST RH9 177 N3
Whitfield Cl GUW GU2 116 D5
HASM GU27 198 D4
Whitfield Rd HASM GU27 198 D5
Whitford Gdns MTCM CR4 48 C3
Whitgift Av SAND/SEL CR2 67 M4
Whitgift St CROY/NA CR0 2 C8
Whitland Rd CAR SM5 48 A8
Whitlet Cl FNM GU9 5 G5
Whitley Cl STWL/WRAY TW19 14 B8
Whitley Wy FARN GU14 92 B8
Whitlock Dr WIM/MER SW19 29 H1
Whitmead Cl SAND/SEL CR2 68 A5
Whitmead La RFNM GU10 157 H4
Whitmoor La RGUE GU4 97 G8
Whitmoor Rd BAGS GU19 54 C8
Whitmoor Vale Rd GSHT GU26 181 L10
Whitmore Cl SHST GU47 72 A1
Whitmore Gn FNM GU9 134 B3
Whitmore La ASC SL5 37 K5
Whitmore Rd BECK BR3 51 J3
Whitmores Cl EPSOM KT18 * 83 M5
Whitmore V GSHT GU26 181 L11
Whitmore Vale Rd GSHT GU26 197 N1
Whitmore Wy HORL RH6 160 A2
Whitnell Wy PUT/ROE SW15 * 19 M7
Whitstable Cl BECK BR3 51 J1
Whitstable Pl CROY/NA CR0 67 M3
Whitstone La BECK BR3 51 L5
Whittaker Av RCH/KEW TW9 * 18 A7
Whittaker Rd CHEAM SM3 65 J2
Whittell Gdns SYD SE26 32 F4
Whittington College
EGRIN RH19 * 162 B1
Whittington Rd CRAWE RH10 164 F7
Whittlebury Cl CAR SM5 66 C6
Whittle Cl ASHV GU12 113 J4
Whittle Crs FARN GU14 92 C2
Whittle Rd HEST TW5 15 M2
Whittle Wy CRAWE RH10 191 R1
Whitton Dene HSLW TW3 16 E7
ISLW TW7 17 G7
Whitton Manor Rd WHTN TW2 16 F8
Whitton Rd BRAK RG12 35 J3
HSLW TW3 16 E7
WHTN TW2 17 H8
Whitton Waye HSLW TW3 16 D8
Whitworth Rd CRAWW RH11 191 N2
SNWD SE25 50 B3
Whopshott Av
WOKN/KNAP GU21 76 F6
Whopshott Cl
WOKN/KNAP GU21 76 E6
Whopshott Dr
WOKN/KNAP GU21 76 F6
Whynstones Rd ASC SL5 36 D5
Whyte Av ASHV GU12 135 G2
Whytebeam Vw CTHM CR3 88 C8
Whytecliffe Rd North
PUR/KEN CR8 87 L1
Whytecliffe Rd South
PUR/KEN CR8 87 K2
Whytecroft HEST TW5 16 A2
Whyteleafe Hl CTHM CR3 108 B1
Whyteleafe Rd CTHM CR3 108 B3
Whytings SWTR RH13 205 R11
Wickers Oake NRWD SE19 * 32 C5
Wicket Hl RFNM GU10 155 K3
The Wickets ASHF TW15 23 H5
The Wicket CROY/NA CR0 69 K4
Wickham Av CHEAM SM3 64 F4
CROY/NA CR0 69 H1
Wickham Cl HORL RH6 160 C2
NWMAL KT3 46 C5
Wickham Ct WWKM BR4 * 70 A3
Wickham Court Rd WWKM BR4 69 M1
Wickham Crs WWKM BR4 69 M1
Wickham La EGH TW20 21 K8
Wickham Rd BECK BR3 51 L3
CBLY GU15 73 H1
CROY/NA CR0 51 J8
CROY/NA CR0 68 F1
Wickham V BRAK RG12 34 B6
Wickham Wy BECK BR3 51 M4
Wickhurst La HORS RH12 166 B7
Wick La EGH TW20 20 C7
Wick Rd EGH TW20 20 E8
TEDD TW11 26 E8
Wide Wy MTCM CR4 49 G3
Widgeon Wy HORS RH12 166 F4
Wigan Rd FARN GU14 112 A1
Wiggie La REDH RH1 126 D6
Wiggins La RCHPK/HAM TW10 26 F3
Wigley Rd FELT TW13 25 G3
Wigmore La RDKG RH5 173 K8
Wigmore Rd CAR SM5 66 A1
Wilberforce Wy BRAK RG12 35 G5
WIM/MER SW19 29 G7
Wilbury Av BELMT SM2 65 J8
Wilbury Rd WOKN/KNAP GU21 10 B6
Wilcot Cl CHOB/PIR GU24 75 K6
Wilcot Gdns CHOB/PIR GU24 75 J6
Wilcox Gdns SHPTN TW17 41 H3
Wilcox Rd SUT SM1 * 65 L3
TEDD TW11 26 A5
Wildacre Cl BIL RH14 201 N6
Wild Acres BF/WBF KT14 78 F1
Wildcroft Dr RDKG RH5 145 G5
Wildcroft Rd PUT/ROE SW15 28 F1
Wildcroft Wd MFD/CHID GU8 183 L3
Wilderness Ri EGRIN RH19 178 H12
Wilderness Rd FRIM GU16 73 H7
GUW GU2 138 C2
OXTED RH8 130 B4
The Wilderness
E/WMO/HCT KT8 43 M5
HPTN TW12 * 25 L5
Wilders Cl FRIM GU16 73 G6
WOKN/KNAP GU21 76 F8
Wilderwick Rd EGRIN RH19 178 H12
Wildfell Rd CAT SE6 33 L1
Wildfield Cl RGUW GU3 115 L7
Wildgoose Dr HORS RH12 166 C6
Wildridings Rd BRAK RG12 34 D5
Wild Ridings Sq BRAK RG12 34 D4
Wildwood Cl CRAN GU6 * 186 E4
EHSLY KT24 100 C7
WOKS/MYFD GU22 78 C5
Wildwood Ct PUR/KEN CR8 88 A5
Wildwood La CRAN GU6 185 R8
Wilford Rd CROY/NA CR0 * 2 D1
Wilfred St WOKN/KNAP GU21 10 A6
Wilhelmina Av COUL/CHIP CR5 106 F1
Wilkes Rd BTFD TW8 18 B1
Wilkins Cl MTCM CR4 48 B1
Wilkinson Gdns SNWD SE25 50 B1
Wilks Gdns CROY/NA CR0 51 H8
Willats Cl CHERT KT16 * 40 C6
Willcocks Cl CHSGTN KT9 63 H2
Willems Av ALDT GU11 112 C7
Willett Rd THHTH CR7 49 K5
Willetts Wy BIL RH14 201 Q6
Willey Broom La CTHM CR3 107 K7
Willey Farm La CTHM CR3 107 M8
Willey La CTHM CR3 108 A7
William Booth Rd PGE/AN SE20 50 D1
William Evans Rd
HOR/WEW KT19 83 K1
William Evelyn Ct RDKG RH5 * 143 J5
William Farthing Cl
ALDT GU11 * 112 D7
William Gdns PUT/ROE SW15 19 L7
William Rd CTHM CR3 108 A4
GU GU1 6 F4
SUT SM1 65 M4
WIM/MER SW19 29 H8
Williams Dr HSLW TW3 16 D6
Williams Gv SURB KT6 44 F6
Williams La MORT/ESHN SW14 18 F5
MRDN SM4 47 M6
Williamson Cl HASM GU27 198 G4
Williams Pl CRAN GU6 171 K12
Williams Ter CROY/NA CR0 67 K5
William St CAR SM5 66 B2
Williams Wy CRAWE RH10 165 K4
Willingham Wy KUT/HW KT1 9 J7
Willington Cl CBLY GU15 72 E3
Willis Av BELMT SM2 66 B5
Willis Cl EPSOM KT18 83 L3
Willis Rd CROY/NA CR0 2 D1
Willmore End WIM/MER SW19 47 L1
Willoughby Av CROY/NA CR0 67 J3
Willoughby Rd BRAK RG12 34 C3
KUTN/CMB KT2 9 H4
TWK TW1 17 M7
Willow Av BARN SW13 19 J4
Willow Bank WOKS/MYFD GU22 97 H4
Willowbank Gdns
KWD/TDW/WH KT20 104 E4
Willow Brean HORL RH6 160 B2
Willowbrook HPTN TW12 * 25 L6
Willowbrook Rd
STWL/WRAY TW19 23 H2
The Willow Centre MTCM CR4 48 C5
Willow Cl ADL/WDHM KT15 78 C1
BTFD TW8 17 M1
CRAWE RH10 165 G2
DTCH/LGLY SL3 12 F2
EGRIN RH19 162 E2
FRIM GU16 93 H5
LIPH GU30 197 J10
RDKG RH5 173 K5
Willow Cnr HORL RH6 175 J10
Willow Ct FRIM GU16 73 G8
HORL RH6 * 176 A3
Willow Crs FARN GU14 92 E2
Willowdene Cl WHTN TW2 25 M1
Willow Dr BRAK RG12 34 F1
RGUW GU3 114 F8
RPLY/SEND GU23 98 D6
Willow Flds ASHV GU12 113 L8
Willow Gdns HSLW TW3 * 16 D3
LIPH GU30 197 J10
Willow Gn CHOB/PIR GU24 75 K3
Willowhayne Dr WOT/HER KT12 42 E7
Willowhayne Gdns WPK KT4 64 F3
Willow La BLKW GU17 72 A5
GU GU1 117 K7
MTCM CR4 48 C5
Willow Md DORK RH4 144 D1
EGRIN RH19 163 G5
MFD/CHID GU8 183 M4
Willowmead STA TW18 40 E1
Willowmead Cl
WOKN/KNAP GU21 76 D6
Willowmere ESH/CLAY KT10 61 M3
Willow Mt CROY/NA CR0 * 3 H8
Willow Pk ASHV GU12 113 J7
Willow Rdg CRAWE RH10 193 M10
Willow Rd DTCH/LGLY SL3 13 H4
GODL GU7 168 C1
HORS RH12 167 L4
NWMAL KT3 45 M4
REDH RH1 147 M3
WLGTN SM6 66 E6
Willows Av MRDN SM4 47 L5
Willows Pth EPSOM KT18 83 L4
The Willows BECK BR3 * 51 K1
BF/WBF KT14 79 H3
ESH/CLAY KT10 62 B5
LTWR GU18 74 F1
MFD/CHID GU8 199 P1
RFNM GU10 134 F5
RGUE GU4 * 118 A6
RGUW GU3 * 116 C3
WEY KT13 59 K2
Willow Ter PGE/AN SE20 * 50 E1
Willow Tree Cl
WAND/EARL SW18 29 L2
Willowtree Wy THHTH CR7 49 K1
Willow V LHD/OX KT22 101 L5
Willow Vw WIM/MER SW19 48 A1
Willow Wk CHEAM SM3 65 J2
EGH TW20 20 F6
KWD/TDW/WH KT20 123 L4
ORP BR6 71 L2
REDH RH1 148 E2
SHGR GU5 141 K5
Willow Wy ASHV GU12 135 H1
BF/WBF KT14 78 F1
FNM GU9 134 A3
GDST RH9 128 E6
GU GU1 116 E4
HOR/WEW KT19 64 A5
SUN TW16 42 D4
SYD SE26 32 E4
WHTN TW2 25 L3
WOKS/MYFD GU22 97 H2
Willow Wood Crs SNWD SE25 50 B6
Wills Crs HSLW TW3 16 E8
Willson Rd EGH TW20 20 E6
Wilmar Gdns WWKM BR4 51 L8
Wilmer Cl KUTN/CMB KT2 27 J6
Wilmer Crs KUTN/CMB KT2 27 J6
Wilmerhatch La EPSOM KT18 83 M6
Wilmington Av CHSWK W4 19 G2
Wilmot Rd CAR SM5 * 66 C4
PUR/KEN CR8 87 K2
Wilmots Cl REIG RH2 125 M7
Wilmot's La REDH RH1 177 J2
Wilmot Wy BNSTD SM7 85 K5
CBLY GU15 73 J6
Wilna Rd WAND/EARL SW18 29 M1
Wilson Av MTCM CR4 30 B8
Wilson Cl CRAWE RH10 165 M7
SAND/SEL CR2 68 A4
Wilson Dr CHERT KT16 57 L4
Wilson Rd ASHV GU12 113 G8
CHSGTN KT9 63 J5
FARN GU14 92 C6
Wilsons KWD/TDW/WH KT20 105 G3
Wilsons Rd BOR GU35 180 G12
Wilson Wy WOKN/KNAP GU21 10 A4
Wilton Cl WDR/YW UB7 14 A1
Wilton Ct FARN GU14 93 G6
Wilton Crs WIM/MER SW19 47 J1
Wilton Gdns E/WMO/HCT KT8 43 K3
WOT/HER KT12 43 G8
Wilton Gv NWMAL KT3 46 C6
WIM/MER SW19 29 J8
Wilton Pl ADL/WDHM KT15 59 G7
Wilton Rd CBLY GU15 72 E6
HSLWW TW4 16 A5
REDH RH1 148 C1
WIM/MER SW19 30 B8
Wilton Wk FELT TW13 * 24 E3
Wiltshire Gdns WHTN TW2 25 M2
Wiltshire Rd THHTH CR7 49 K3
Wilverley Crs NWMAL KT3 46 B6
Wilwood Rd BNFD RG42 34 B1
Wimbart Rd
BRXS/STRHM SW2 * 31 J1
Wimbeldon Park Side
PUT/ROE SW15 28 E1
Wimbledon Br WIM/MER SW19 29 J7
Wimbledon Cl CBLY GU15 53 J8
Wimbledon Hill Rd
WIM/MER SW19 29 H7
Wimbledon Park Rd
WIM/MER SW19 29 H4
Wimbledon Park Side
WIM/MER SW19 29 G3
Wimbledon Rd CBLY GU15 53 J8
TOOT SW17 29 M5
Wimblehurst Rd HORS RH12 166 F5
Wimborne Av REDH RH1 148 C5
Wimborne Cl EW KT17 84 B3
WPK KT4 46 F8
Wimborne Wy BECK BR3 51 G3
Wimland Hl HORS RH12 190 A11
Wimland Rd HORS RH12 189 R9
Wimlands La HORS RH12 190 A10
Wimpole Cl KUT/HW KT1 9 H7
Wimshurst Cl CROY/NA CR0 49 H8
Wincanton Cl CRAWE RH10 165 M4
Wincanton Rd
WAND/EARL SW18 29 J1
Winchcombe Rd CAR SM5 48 A7
Winchelsey Ri SAND/SEL CR2 68 C5
Winchendon Rd TEDD TW11 26 A5
Winchester Av HEST TW5 16 C1
Winchester Cl DTCH/LGLY SL3 13 H3
ESH/CLAY KT10 61 K3
KUTN/CMB KT2 9 M2
Winchester Ms WPK KT4 65 G1
Winchester Rd ASHV GU12 113 K6
CRAWE RH10 165 G8
FELT TW13 25 J4
HYS/HAR UB3 15 H2
RFNM GU10 181 N2
TWK TW1 17 L8
WOT/HER KT12 42 D8
Winchester St FARN GU14 112 F1
Winchfield Rd SYD SE26 33 H6
Winchilsea Crs
E/WMO/HCT KT8 43 M2
Winchstone Cl SHPTN TW17 41 J4
Windall Cl NRWD SE19 50 D1
Windborough Rd CAR SM5 66 D6
Windermere Av
WIM/MER SW19 47 L3
Windermere Cl
EBED/NFELT TW14 24 B2
EGH TW20 21 L8
FARN GU14 92 B6
ORP BR6 71 L2
STWL/WRAY TW19 23 G3
Windermere Ct ASHV GU12 * 113 J5
Windermere Rd
COUL/CHIP CR5 87 H5
CROY/NA CR0 3 K3
LTWR GU18 54 E8
PUT/ROE SW15 28 B5
STRHM/NOR SW16 48 F1
WWKM BR4 70 B1
Windermere Wy FNM GU9 133 K3
REIG RH2 126 B7
Windfield Cl SYD SE26 33 G5
Windgates RGUE GU4 117 M5
Windham Av CROY/NA CR0 70 A8
Windham Rd RCH/KEW TW9 18 C5
The Windings SAND/SEL CR2 88 C1
Winding Wood Dr CBLY GU15 73 L5
Windlebrook Gn BNFD RG42 34 D1
Windle Cl BFOR GU20 55 G5
Windlesham Ct BFOR GU20 54 F3
Windlesham Gv
WIM/MER SW19 29 G2
Windlesham Rd BNFD RG42 34 C1
CHOB/PIR GU24 75 H1
Windley Cl FSTH SE23 32 F3
Windmill Av EW KT17 84 C1
Windmill Cl CTHM CR3 107 M3
EW KT17 84 C2
HORL RH6 160 E3
SUN TW16 24 B8
SURB KT6 44 F8
SWTR RH13 167 K6
Windmill Ct CRAWE RH10 164 F2
Windmill Dr BOR GU35 180 G11
HAYES BR2 70 F3
LHD/OX KT22 102 E5
REIG RH2 126 A6
Windmill End EW KT17 84 C2
Windmill Fld BFOR GU20 55 G5
Windmill Gv CROY/NA CR0 2 C1
Windmill La EGRIN RH19 162 E2
EGRIN RH19 163 K6
EW KT17 84 C2
SURB KT6 44 E7
Windmill Ri KUTN/CMB KT2 9 L2
Windmill Rd ASHV GU12 112 F8
BNFD RG42 34 C1
CROY/NA CR0 2 D1
HPTN TW12 25 L6
MTCM CR4 48 F5
SUN TW16 42 B1
WIM/MER SW19 28 E6
Windmill Rd West SUN TW16 42 B2
Windmill Shott EGH TW20 21 J7
Windmill Ter SHPTN TW17 * 42 B7
Windmill Wy REIG RH2 126 A6
Windrum Cl HORS RH12 204 G9
Windrush NWMAL KT3 45 L4
Windrush Cl CHSWK W4 * 18 F2
CRAWW RH11 164 B6
SHGR GU5 169 J3
Windrush La FSTH SE23 33 G4
Windsor Av CHEAM SM3 65 H2
E/WMO/HCT KT8 43 K3
NWMAL KT3 45 M5
WIM/MER SW19 47 M1
Windsor Cl CRAWW RH11 164 E8
FARN GU14 92 E5
GUW GU2 138 C2
WNWD SE27 31 M5
Windsor Court Rd
CHOB/PIR GU24 56 B7
Windsor Crs FNM GU9 133 L3
Windsor Dr ASHF TW15 23 G5
Windsor Gdns ASHV GU12 113 J8
CROY/NA CR0 67 H2
Windsor Gv WNWD SE27 31 M5
Windsor Ms CAT SE6 33 M2
Windsor Park Rd HYS/HAR UB3 15 J2
Windsor Pl CHERT KT16 * 40 D6
EGRIN RH19 163 H5
Windsor Ride ASC SL5 35 L5
BRAK RG12 35 H8
CBLY GU15 72 D1
Windsor Rd ASC SL5 36 C2
BOR GU35 180 A12
CHOB/PIR GU24 56 B7
FARN GU14 93 G8
FARN GU14 112 A1
HSLWW TW4 15 L4
KUTN/CMB KT2 8 E3
RCH/KEW TW9 18 C4
STWL/WRAY TW19 12 B8
SUN TW16 24 D8
TEDD TW11 26 A6
THHTH CR7 49 L2
WDSR SL4 21 G2
WPK KT4 64 D1
Windsor St CHERT KT16 40 D6
Windsor Wk BOR GU35 180 A12
WEY KT13 59 L4
Windsor Wy ALDT GU11 112 E7
FRIM GU16 93 J1
WOKS/MYFD GU22 11 M4
Winds Rdg RPLY/SEND GU23 97 M7
Windways MFD/CHID GU8 185 J6
Windycroft Cl PUR/KEN CR8 87 G3
Windyridge CRAWW RH11 164 C5
Windy Ridge Cl
WIM/MER SW19 29 G6
Windy Wd GODL GU7 159 M6

Winern Glebe BF/WBF KT14 79 G3
Winery La KUT/HW KT1 9 G8
Winey Cl CHSGTN KT9 62 F6
Winfield Gv RDKG RH5 173 Q8
Winfrith Rd WAND/EARL SW18 29 M1
Wingate Ct ALDT GU11 112 C7
Wingate Crs CROY/NA CR0 49 H6
Wingfield Cl ADL/WDHM KT15 58 E8
Wingfield Gdns FRIM GU16 74 A6
Wingfield Rd KUTN/CMB KT2 27 J7
Wingrave Rd HMSMTH W6 19 M1
Wings Cl FNM GU9 133 L3
SUT SM1 65 K3
Wings Rd FNM GU9 133 L3
Winifred Rd COUL/CHIP CR5 86 D6
HPTN TW12 25 K5
WIM/MER SW19 47 K1
Winkfield Rd ASC SL5 36 D1
Winkworth Pl BNSTD SM7 85 J4
Winkworth Rd BNSTD SM7 85 K4
Winnington Wy
WOKN/KNAP GU21 76 E8
Winnipeg Cl LIPH GU30 196 H10
Winscombe BRAK RG12 34 B5
Winsford Rd CAT SE6 33 J4
Winslow Rd HMSMTH W6 19 M1
Winslow Wy FELT TW13 25 G4
WOT/HER KT12 60 F2
Winstanley Cl COB KT11 80 E4
Winston Cl FRIM GU16 93 J3
Winston Dr COB KT11 81 H6
Winston Wk RFNM GU10 155 M3
Winston Wy WOKS/MYFD GU22 97 L2
Winterbourne HORS RH12 167 J2
Winterbourne Gv WEY KT13 59 M5
Winterbourne Rd CAT SE6 33 J2
THHTH CR7 49 K4
Winter Box Wk
RCHPK/HAM TW10 18 C7
Winterdown Gdns
ESH/CLAY KT10 61 J5
Winterdown Rd ESH/CLAY KT10 61 H5
Winterfold CRAWE RH10 165 J7
Winterfold Cl WIM/MER SW19 29 H3
Winter Gdns CRAWW RH11 164 E5
Winterhill Wy RGUE GU4 117 L4
Wintersells Rd BF/WBF KT14 59 G8
Winters Rd THDIT KT7 44 E7
Winterstoke Rd FSTH SE23 33 J2
Winterton Ct SWTR RH13 167 G7
Winton Rd ALDT GU11 112 D8
FNM GU9 5 L1
ORP BR6 71 L3
Winton Wy STRHM/NOR SW16 31 K6
Wireless Rd BH/WHM TN16 91 G5
Wire Mill La LING RH7 177 R9
Wisbeach Rd CROY/NA CR0 50 A5
Wisborough Ct CRAWW RH11 164 B7
Wisborough Rd SAND/SEL CR2 68 C7
Wiseton Rd TOOT SW17 30 B2
Wishanger La RFNM GU10 180 G7
Wishbone Wy
WOKN/KNAP GU21 76 C6
Wishmoor Cl CBLY GU15 73 H1
Wishmoor Rd CBLY GU15 73 H1
Wisley Gdns FARN GU14 92 A7
Wisley La RPLY/SEND GU23 79 H6
Wistaria Cl ORP BR6 71 L1
Wiston Ct CRAWW RH11 164 B7
Witham Rd ISLW TW7 17 G3
PGE/AN SE20 50 F3
Witherby Cl CROY/NA CR0 68 B4
Wither Dl HORL RH6 160 B2
Witherslack Cl BOR GU35 196 G1
Withey Brook HORL RH6 160 A6
Witheygate Av STA TW18 22 E7
Withey Mdw HORL RH6 160 A5
Withies La RGUW GU3 137 M7
The Withies LHD/OX KT22 102 E2
WOKN/KNAP GU21 76 B7
Withybed Cnr
KWD/TDW/WH KT20 104 E5
Withy Cl LTWR GU18 54 F8
Withypitts CRAWE RH10 193 M10
Withypitts East CRAWE RH10 193 M10
Witley Crs CROY/NA CR0 69 M5
Witney Pth FSTH SE23 33 G4
Wittenham Rd BRAK RG12 35 J1
Wittering Cl KUTN/CMB KT2 27 G6
Wittmead Rd FRIM GU16 93 J5
Wivenhoe Ct HSLW TW3 16 C6
Wiverton Rd SYD SE26 32 F7
Wix Hl EHSLY KT24 119 L4
Woburn Av FARN GU14 93 G5
PUR/KEN CR8 87 K1
Woburn Cl FRIM GU16 73 K8
WIM/MER SW19 29 M7
Woburn Hl ADL/WDHM KT15 58 F1
Woburn Pk ADL/WDHM KT15 * 59 G1
Woburn Rd CAR SM5 48 B8
CRAWW RH11 164 C6
CROY/NA CR0 2 D3
Wodeland Av GUW GU2 6 D8
Woffington Cl TEDD TW11 8 A4
Woking Cl PUT/ROE SW15 19 J6
Wokingham Rd BNFD RG42 34 C1
Woking Rd GU GU1 7 H1
Wold Cl CRAWW RH11 164 B6
Woldhurstlea Cl CRAWW RH11 164 C6
Woldingham Rd WARL CR6 108 E2
Wolds Dr ORP BR6 71 K3
The Wold CTHM CR3 109 K4
Wolfe Rd ASHV GU12 112 F8
Wolfington Rd WNWD SE27 31 L5
Wolf's Hl OXTED RH8 130 D5
Wolf's Rd OXTED RH8 130 E4
Wolfs Wd OXTED RH8 130 D6
Wolseley Av WAND/EARL SW18 29 K3
Wolseley Gdns CHSWK W4 18 E1
Wolseley Rd ALDT GU11 112 D8
GODL GU7 168 B3
MTCM CR4 48 D7
Wolsey Cl HSLW TW3 16 F6
KUTN/CMB KT2 9 M5
RYNPK SW20 28 E8
WPK KT4 64 D3
Wolsey Crs CROY/NA CR0 69 M7
MRDN SM4 47 J7
Wolsey Dr KUTN/CMB KT2 27 H6
WOT/HER KT12 43 G8
Wolsey Gv ESH/CLAY KT10 61 L3
Wolsey Rd ASHF TW15 23 H5
E/WMO/HCT KT8 44 A4
ESH/CLAY KT10 61 L3
HPTN TW12 25 L7
SUN TW16 24 C8
Wolsey Wk WOKN/KNAP GU21 10 D5
Wolsey Wy CHSGTN KT9 63 K4
Wolstonbury Cl CRAWW RH11 164 E6
Wolvens La RDKG RH5 143 K6
RDKG RH5 172 F4
Wolverton Av KUTN/CMB KT2 9 K4
Wolverton Cl HORL RH6 160 C5
Wolverton Gdns HORL RH6 160 C4
Wolves Hl RDKG RH5 189 K1
Wonersh Common Rd
SHGR GU5 169 L2
Wonersh Wy BELMT SM2 65 G7
Wonford Cl KUTN/CMB KT2 46 B1
KWD/TDW/WH KT20 104 D8
Wonham La
BRKHM/BTCW RH3 146 C1
Wonham Wy SHGR GU5 142 A6
Wontford Rd PUR/KEN CR8 87 K5
Wontner Rd BAL SW12 30 C3
Woodall Cl CHSGTN KT9 62 F6
The Woodbarn FNM GU9 * 5 K5
Woodbastwick Rd SYD SE26 33 G7
Woodberry Cl MFD/CHID GU8 183 P12
SUN TW16 24 D7
Woodbine Cl WHTN TW2 26 A3
Woodbine Gv PGE/AN SE20 32 E8
Woodbine La WPK KT4 64 E2
Woodbines Av KUT/HW KT1 8 D9
Woodborough Rd
PUT/ROE SW15 19 L6
Woodbourne FNM GU9 134 B2
Woodbourne Av
STRHM/NOR SW16 31 G4
Woodbourne Dr
ESH/CLAY KT10 62 C5
Woodbourne Gdns WLGTN SM6 66 E6
Woodbridge Av LHD/OX KT22 82 D8
Woodbridge Ct HORS RH12 * 167 K4
Woodbridge Dr CBLY GU15 73 G2
Woodbridge Gv LHD/OX KT22 82 D8
Woodbridge Hl GUW GU2 6 C1
Woodbridge Hill Gdns GUW GU2 6 B1
Woodbridge Mdw GU GU1 6 E2
Woodbridge Rd GU GU1 6 D1
Woodbury Av EGRIN RH19 163 H5
Woodbury Cl BH/WHM TN16 91 J8
CROY/NA CR0 3 K6
EGRIN RH19 163 H5
Woodbury Dr BELMT SM2 65 M8
Woodbury St TOOT SW17 30 B6
Woodby Dr ASC SL5 37 J7
Wood Cl REDH RH1 175 R1
Woodcock Dr CHOB/PIR GU24 55 M6
Woodcock Hl EGRIN RH19 178 A11
Woodcock La CHOB/PIR GU24 55 L6
Woodcombe Crs FSTH SE23 32 F2
Woodcote CRAN GU6 186 A1
GUW GU2 138 E4
HORL RH6 160 E2
Woodcote Av THHTH CR7 49 L4
WLGTN SM6 66 E7
Woodcote Cl EPSOM KT18 84 A4
KUTN/CMB KT2 27 J6
Woodcote End EPSOM KT18 84 A5
Woodcote Gn WLGTN SM6 66 F7
Woodcote Green Rd
EPSOM KT18 83 M6
Woodcote Grove Rd
COUL/CHIP CR5 87 G5
Woodcote House Ct
EPSOM KT18 * 84 A5
Woodcote Hurst EPSOM KT18 83 M6
Woodcote La PUR/KEN CR8 87 G1
Woodcote Ms WLGTN SM6 66 E5
Woodcote Pk COUL/CHIP CR5 * 86 E3
Woodcote Park Av
PUR/KEN CR8 86 F1
Woodcote Park Rd
EPSOM KT18 83 M6
Woodcote Pl ASC SL5 36 C1
WNWD SE27 * 31 L6
Woodcote Rd FROW RH18 195 M11
WLGTN SM6 66 E5
Woodcote Side EPSOM KT18 83 M6
Woodcote Valley Rd
PUR/KEN CR8 87 G3
Woodcot Gdns FARN GU14 92 A5
Woodcott Ter ASHV GU12 135 G1
Woodcourt CRAWW RH11 191 M12
Wood Crest BELMT SM2 * 65 M6
Woodcrest Rd PUR/KEN CR8 87 H3
Woodcrest Wk REIG RH2 126 B6
Woodcroft Rd CRAWW RH11 190 G9
THHTH CR7 49 L5
Woodcut Rd RFNM GU10 155 J4
Wooden Bridge Ter
WNWD SE27 * 31 L4
Woodend ESH/CLAY KT10 61 M1
FARN GU14 93 G6
Wood End HORS RH12 167 M4
Woodend LHD/OX KT22 102 F7
NRWD SE19 31 M7
SUT SM1 65 M1
Woodend Cl CRAWE RH10 165 J2
WOKN/KNAP GU21 96 D1
Wood End Cl WOKS/MYFD GU22 78 C6
Woodend Dr ASC SL5 36 E5
Woodend Pk COB KT11 81 G5
Woodend Rd FRIM GU16 93 M2
The Wood End WLGTN SM6 66 E7
Woodenhill BRAK RG12 34 B7
Wooderson Cl SNWD SE25 50 B4
Woodfield ASHTD KT21 83 G7
Woodfield Av CAR SM5 66 D5
STRHM/NOR SW16 31 G4
Woodfield Cl ASHTD KT21 83 G7
COUL/CHIP CR5 106 F1
CRAWE RH10 165 G3
NRWD SE19 31 M8
REDH RH1 126 B7
Woodfield Gdns NWMAL KT3 46 C5
Woodfield Gv
STRHM/NOR SW16 31 G4
Woodfield Hl COUL/CHIP CR5 106 E1
Woodfield La ASHTD KT21 83 H7
Woodfield Rd ASHTD KT21 83 G7
CRAWE RH10 165 H2
HORS RH12 203 J2
HSLWW TW4 15 L4
THDIT KT7 62 C1
The Woodfields SAND/SEL CR2 88 C1
Woodfield Wy REDH RH1 126 B7
Woodford Gn BRAK RG12 35 J4
Woodgate Av CHSGTN KT9 63 G4
Woodgate Dr
STRHM/NOR SW16 31 G8
Woodgates Cl SWTR RH13 167 J6
Woodgavil BNSTD SM7 85 J6
Woodger Cl RGUE GU4 117 M6
Woodhall Av DUL SE21 32 C4
Woodhall Dr DUL SE21 32 C4
Woodhall La ASC SL5 55 H1
Woodham La ADL/WDHM KT15 78 B2
WOKN/KNAP GU21 77 L3
Woodham Park Rd
ADL/WDHM KT15 58 C8
Woodham Park Wy
ADL/WDHM KT15 78 C1
Woodham Ri
WOKN/KNAP GU21 11 G1
Woodham Rd CAT SE6 33 M4
WOKN/KNAP GU21 10 D1
Woodham Waye
WOKN/KNAP GU21 77 L4
Woodhatch Rd REIG RH2 148 A4
Woodhatch Spinney
COUL/CHIP CR5 87 H6
Woodhaven Ms
WOT/HER KT12 * 60 D3
Woodhaw EGH TW20 21 L5
Woodhayes HORL RH6 160 E2
Woodhayes Rd
WIM/MER SW19 28 F8
Woodhill RPLY/SEND GU23 98 A8
Woodhill Ct RPLY/SEND GU23 98 A7
Woodhill La SHGR GU5 169 P5
Woodhouse La RDKG RH5 171 M1
Woodhouse St BNFD RG42 * 34 B1
Woodhurst La OXTED RH8 130 B5
Woodhurst Pk OXTED RH8 130 B4
Woodhyrst Gdns PUR/KEN CR8 87 L5
Wooding Gv CRAWW RH11 191 L12
Woodland Av CRAN GU6 186 E2
Woodland Cl BIL RH14 203 K11
EHSLY KT24 120 C1
HOR/WEW KT19 * 64 B5
NRWD SE19 32 B7
SWTR RH13 167 L5
Woodland Ct OXTED RH8 130 A2
Woodland Crs FARN GU14 92 F3
Woodland Dr CRAWE RH10 193 N5
EHSLY KT24 120 C1
RDKG RH5 172 H12
RFNM GU10 155 L3
Woodland Gdns ISLW TW7 17 H5
SAND/SEL CR2 88 F1
Woodland Gv CROY/NA CR0 67 K6
WEY KT13 60 A3
Woodland Hl NRWD SE19 32 B7
Woodland Ms
STRHM/NOR SW16 31 H4
Woodland Ri OXTED RH8 130 B4
Woodland Rd NRWD SE19 32 B6
THHTH CR7 49 K4
Woodlands ADL/WDHM KT15 59 H2
ASHTD KT21 * 83 J8
CRAWE RH10 165 M2
RPLY/SEND GU23 98 C7
RYNPK SW20 46 F4
WOKS/MYFD GU22 10 D8
Woodlands Av BF/WBF KT14 78 D2
FNM GU9 134 B2
NWMAL KT3 46 A1
REDH RH1 148 C1
WPK KT4 64 C1
Woodlands Cl ASC SL5 36 C6
ASHV GU12 113 K4
BIL RH14 * 203 K11
BLKW GU17 72 B8
CHERT KT16 57 L8
CRAN GU6 186 E2
CRAWE RH10 193 N6
ESH/CLAY KT10 62 C6
Woodlands Copse ASHTD KT21 83 G6
Woodlands Ct REDH RH1 * 148 C2
SHST GU47 52 C8
WOKS/MYFD GU22 10 D9
Woodlands Dr GDST RH9 151 H3
SUN TW16 42 F2
Woodlands Gdns EPSOM KT18 84 E4
Woodlands Gv COUL/CHIP CR5 86 E7
ISLW TW7 17 H4
Woodlands La BFOR GU20 55 J6
COB KT11 81 K7
HASM GU27 198 A6
Woodlands Pde ASHF TW15 23 M7
Woodlands Pk
ADL/WDHM KT15 58 C4
GU GU1 117 L7
KWD/TDW/WH KT20 123 L5
WOKN/KNAP GU21 77 M3
Woodlands Ride ASC SL5 36 D6
Woodlands Rd BARN SW13 19 J5
BF/WBF KT14 78 C4
CBLY GU15 72 E4
EGRIN RH19 163 H1
EPSOM KT18 83 K5
FARN GU14 92 A3
GT/LBKH KT23 121 J2
GU GU1 117 G4
ISLW TW7 17 H5
LHD/OX KT22 82 A8
MFD/CHID GU8 184 A4
REDH RH1 148 C2
SURB KT6 45 G7
Woodlands Rd East VW GU25 38 F4
Woodlands Rd West VW GU25 38 F4
The Woodlands ESH/CLAY KT10 61 M1
HORL RH6 161 L3
ISLW TW7 17 J4
NRWD SE19 31 M8
WLGTN SM6 66 E7
Woodlands Wk BLKW GU17 72 B8
SWTR RH13 205 R12
Woodlands Wy ASHTD KT21 83 K6
KWD/TDW/WH KT20 123 M4
Woodland Vw GODL GU7 138 B8
Woodland Wk ASHV GU12 113 G6
HOR/WEW KT19 63 K5
Woodland Wy BRYLDS KT5 63 L1
CROY/NA CR0 51 H8
CTHM CR3 128 B2
KWD/TDW/WH KT20 105 H4
MRDN SM4 47 J4
MTCM CR4 30 D8
PUR/KEN CR8 87 K3
SWTR RH13 167 K5
WEY KT13 60 A4
WWKM BR4 69 M2
Wood La CTHM CR3 108 A6
FARN GU14 92 D6
ISLW TW7 17 H1
KWD/TDW/WH KT20 85 J7
RFNM GU10 135 M4
WEY KT13 59 M7
WOKN/KNAP GU21 76 A8
Woodlark Gld CBLY GU15 73 G2
Woodlawn Crs WHTN TW2 25 L3
Woodlawn Dr FELT TW13 25 G3
Woodlawn Gv
WOKN/KNAP GU21 10 F1
Woodleigh Gdns
STRHM/NOR SW16 31 H4
Woodley Cl TOOT SW17 30 C8
Woodley La SUT SM1 66 B2
Wood Lodge La WWKM BR4 69 M2
Woodmancote Gdns
BF/WBF KT14 78 D3
Woodmancott Cl BRAK RG12 35 J5
Woodmancourt GODL GU7 159 M1
Woodman Ms RCH/KEW TW9 18 E3
Woodman Rd COUL/CHIP CR5 86 F5
Woodmans Hl CRAWW RH11 191 M12
Woodmansterne La
BNSTD SM7 85 L5
Woodmansterne Rd CAR SM5 66 B8
COUL/CHIP CR5 86 F5
STRHM/NOR SW16 30 F8
Woodmansterne St BNSTD SM7 86 B5
Woodmere BRAK RG12 35 H4
Woodmere Av CROY/NA CR0 51 G7
Woodmere Cl CROY/NA CR0 51 G7
Woodmere Gdns CROY/NA CR0 51 G7
Woodnook Rd
STRHM/NOR SW16 30 E6
Woodpecker Cl COB KT11 81 H2
RFNM GU10 133 G1
Woodpecker La RDKG RH5 173 R7
Woodpecker Mt CROY/NA CR0 69 H7
Woodpeckers MFD/CHID GU8 183 M2
Woodpecker Wy CRAWE RH10 193 P7
WOKS/MYFD GU22 97 G5
Woodplace Cl COUL/CHIP CR5 106 F1
Woodplace La COUL/CHIP CR5 106 F2
Woodridge Cl BRAK RG12 34 F3
Wood Riding
WOKS/MYFD GU22 78 B5
Wood Ridings WEY KT13 * 59 K5
Wood Ri GUW GU2 116 B6
Wood Rd BH/WHM TN16 90 F8
CBLY GU15 72 E8
FNM GU9 133 M2
GODL GU7 168 C2
GSHT GU26 181 Q11
SHPTN TW17 41 K4
Woodrough Copse SHGR GU5 169 K4
Woodroyd Av HORL RH6 160 C4
Woodroyd Gdns HORL RH6 160 C5
Woodruff Av GU GU1 117 K5
Woods Hill Cl EGRIN RH19 163 L7
Woods Hill La EGRIN RH19 163 L7
Woodshore Cl VW GU25 38 E6
Woodside CBLY GU15 72 C2
EHSLY KT24 99 M8
KWD/TDW/WH KT20 125 J2
LHD/OX KT22 101 L4
SWTR RH13 167 L5
WIM/MER SW19 29 J6
WOT/HER KT12 42 D8
Woodside Av ESH/CLAY KT10 44 B7
SNWD SE25 50 E6
WOT/HER KT12 60 E3
Woodside Cl BRYLDS KT5 45 M7
CTHM CR3 108 B6
WOKN/KNAP GU21 76 A7
Woodside Court Rd
CROY/NA CR0 3 M2
Woodside Crs HORL RH6 161 K3
Woodside Gn SNWD SE25 50 E6
Woodside Pk SNWD SE25 50 D6
Woodside Rd COB KT11 81 K3
CRAWE RH10 165 H2
FARN GU14 112 C2
FNM GU9 134 B2
GUW GU2 116 C7
KUTN/CMB KT2 8 E3
MFD/CHID GU8 199 P1
NWMAL KT3 46 A2
PUR/KEN CR8 87 H3
RDKG RH5 173 L6
SNWD SE25 50 E6
SUT SM1 65 M2
Woodside Wy CROY/NA CR0 50 F6
MTCM CR4 48 E1
REDH RH1 148 D1
REDH RH1 148 D6
VW GU25 38 E3
Woodslands HORL RH6 161 G2
Woodsome Ldg WEY KT13 59 M5
Woodspring Rd
WIM/MER SW19 29 H3
Woodstock EGRIN RH19 162 D3
RGUE GU4 118 E2
Woodstock Av CHEAM SM3 47 J7
ISLW TW7 17 K7
Woodstock Cl CRAN GU6 186 E4
HORS RH12 167 G4
WOKN/KNAP GU21 10 C4
Woodstock Gdns BECK BR3 51 L1
Woodstock Gv GODL GU7 168 B2
Woodstock La North SURB KT6 62 F1
Woodstock La South
ESH/CLAY KT10 62 E4
Woodstock Ri CHEAM SM3 47 J8
Woodstock Rd CAR SM5 66 D4
COUL/CHIP CR5 86 E6
CROY/NA CR0 2 E8
Woodstocks FARN GU14 92 F3
Woodstock Wy MTCM CR4 48 F2
Woodstone Av EW KT17 64 D4
Wood St ASHV GU12 113 K3
EGRIN RH19 162 E4
KUT/HW KT1 8 E5
MTCM CR4 48 D7
REDH RH1 126 F3
Woodsway LHD/OX KT22 82 B4
Woodsyre SYD SE26 32 C5
Woodthorpe Rd ASHF TW15 23 G6
PUT/ROE SW15 19 L6
Wood V FSTH SE23 32 E2
Woodvale Av SNWD SE25 50 C3
Woodview CHSGTN KT9 82 F1
Woodview Cl ASHTD KT21 83 K6
ORP BR6 71 M1
PUT/ROE SW15 28 A5
SAND/SEL CR2 88 E4
Woodville Cl TEDD TW11 26 D5
Woodville Gdns SURB KT6 * 45 G7
Woodville Rd LHD/OX KT22 102 E2
MRDN SM4 47 K4
RCHPK/HAM TW10 26 E4
THHTH CR7 50 A3
Woodward Cl ESH/CLAY KT10 62 C5
Woodwards CRAWW RH11 191 L12
Woodway CBLY GU15 72 E4
GU GU1 117 L7
Wood Wy ORP BR6 71 K1
Woodyard La DUL SE21 32 B1
Woodyers Cl SHGR GU5 169 L2
Woolborough Cl CRAWE RH10 165 G3
Woolborough La CRAWE RH10 165 J2
REDH RH1 176 E1
Woolborough Rd
CRAWE RH10 164 F3
Woolfords La MFD/CHID GU8 157 L8
Woolhampton Wy BRAK RG12 35 G5
Woolhams CTHM CR3 108 C8
Woollards Rd ASHV GU12 113 K5
Woolmead Rd FNM GU9 5 J2
The Woolmead FNM GU9 5 J3
Woolmer Hill Rd HASM GU27 197 P6
Woolmer La LIPH GU30 196 H5
Wool Rd RYNPK SW20 28 E7
Woolsack Wy GODL GU7 168 C5
Woolstone Rd FSTH SE23 33 H3
Wootton Cl EPSOM KT18 84 B6
Worbeck Rd PGE/AN SE20 50 E2
Worcester Cl CROY/NA CR0 69 J1
FARN GU14 92 E2
MTCM CR4 48 D2
Worcester Ct WOT/HER KT12 60 F1
Worcester Dr ASHF TW15 23 L7
Worcester Gdns WPK KT4 64 B2
Worcester Park Rd WPK KT4 63 M2
Worcester Rd BELMT SM2 65 K6
CRAWE RH10 165 G8
GUW GU2 116 C6
REIG RH2 125 K7
WIM/MER SW19 29 J6
Wordsworth BRAK RG12 34 C5
Wordsworth Av PUR/KEN CR8 88 A5
Wordsworth Cl CRAWE RH10 165 K2
Wordsworth Dr CHEAM SM3 64 F3
Wordsworth Md REDH RH1 126 E6
Wordsworth Pl HORS RH12 167 H2
Wordsworth Ri EGRIN RH19 162 D4
Wordsworth Rd
ADL/WDHM KT15 59 G3
HPTN TW12 25 J5
PGE/AN SE20 33 G8
WLGTN SM6 66 F5
Works Rd ADL/WDHM KT15 58 E7
World's End COB KT11 80 D4
EPSOM KT18 * 84 A6
Worlds End Hl BRAK RG12 35 J6
Wormley La MFD/CHID GU8 183 P8
Worple Av ISLW TW7 17 K7
STA TW18 22 E7
WIM/MER SW19 29 G8
Worple Rd EPSOM KT18 84 B4
ISLW TW7 17 K6
LHD/OX KT22 102 E5
RYNPK SW20 46 F2
STA TW18 22 E8
WIM/MER SW19 29 H8
Worple Road Ms
WIM/MER SW19 29 J7
Worplesdon Hl
WOKS/MYFD GU22 95 M4
Worplesdon Rd RGUW GU3 116 C3
Worple St MORT/ESHN SW14 19 G5
The Worple STWL/WRAY TW19 12 C8
Worple Wy RCHPK/HAM TW10 18 B7
Worsfold Cl RPLY/SEND GU23 97 L5
Worslade Rd TOOT SW17 30 A5
Worsley Bridge Rd SYD SE26 33 J6
Worsley Rd FRIM GU16 93 J2
Worsted Gn REDH RH1 127 G3
Worsted La EGRIN RH19 163 J6
Worthfield Cl HOR/WEW KT19 64 A6
Worthing Rd HEST TW5 16 C1
HORS RH12 166 E8
SWTR RH13 204 H11
Worthing Road Picts Hl
SWTR RH13 205 J9
Worthington Cl MTCM CR4 48 E4
Worthington Rd SURB KT6 45 J8
Worth Park Av CRAWE RH10 165 L3
Worth Rd CRAWE RH10 165 L4
Worth Wy CRAWE RH10 165 M5
CRAWE RH10 192 D8
Wortley Rd CROY/NA CR0 49 K7
Worton Gdns ISLW TW7 17 G4
Worton Rd ISLW TW7 17 J5
Worton Wy ISLW TW7 17 G4
Wotton Dr RDKG RH5 143 H6
Wotton Wy BELMT SM2 64 F8
Wrabness Wy STA TW18 40 E1
Wray Cl EGRIN RH19 163 L7
Wray Common Rd REIG RH2 125 M7
Wrayfield Av REIG RH2 125 M7
Wrayfield Rd CHEAM SM3 65 G2
Wraylands Dr REIG RH2 126 A6
Wray La REIG RH2 125 M4
Wraymead Pl REIG RH2 * 125 L7
Wray Mill Pk REIG RH2 126 A6
Wray Park Rd REIG RH2 125 L7
Wray Rd BELMT SM2 65 J7
Wraysbury Cl HSLWW TW4 16 B7

Wraysbury Gdns *STA* TW18 ... 22 B5
Wraysbury Rd *STA* TW18 ... 21 M4
Wrecclesham Hl *RFNM* GU10 ... 155 H4
Wrecclesham Rd *FNM* GU9 ... 4 C9
The Wrekin *FARN* GU14 ... 93 H8
Wren Cl *HORS* RH12 ... 167 G2
SAND/SEL CR2 ... 69 G8
Wren Ct *ASHV* GU12 ... 113 L6
CRAWE RH10 * ... 165 G7
Wren Crs *ADL/WDHM* KT15 ... 59 G4
Wren's Av *ASHF* TW15 ... 23 M6
Wren's Hl *LHD/OX* KT22 ... 81 M5
Wren St *CRAWE* RH10 ... 193 P8
Wren Wy *FARN* GU14 ... 92 C2
Wright Cl *CRAWE* RH10 * ... 165 K8
Wright Gdns *SHPTN* TW17 ... 41 K5
Wright Rd *HEST* TW5 ... 15 M2
Wrights Rd *SNWD* SE25 ... 50 B3
Wright's Rw *WLGTN* SM6 ... 66 E3
Wrotham Hl *MFD/CHID* GU8 ... 184 H10
Wroxham *BRAK* RG12 ... 34 C5
Wroxham Wk *CRAWE* RH10 ... 165 K6
Wrythe Gn *CAR* SM5 ... 66 C2
Wrythe Green Rd *CAR* SM5 ... 66 C2
Wrythe La *CAR* SM5 ... 48 A8
Wyatt Cl *FELT* TW13 ... 25 G2
Wyatt Dr *BARN* SW13 ... 19 L1
Wyatt Park Rd
BRXS/STRHM SW2 ... 31 J3
Wyatt Rd *STA* TW18 ... 22 D6
Wyatt's Cl *GODL* GU7 ... 168 D3
Wyche Gv *SAND/SEL* CR2 ... 67 M6
Wych Elm Ri *GU* GU1 ... 7 K9
Wychelm Rd *LTWR* GU18 ... 74 F1
Wych Hl *WOKS/MYFD* GU22 ... 96 F1
Wych Hill La *WOKS/MYFD* GU22 ... 97 H1
Wych Hill Pk *WOKS/MYFD* GU22 ... 10 A9
Wych Hill Ri *WOKS/MYFD* GU22 ... 96 F1
Wychwood *BIL* RH14 ... 201 N6
Wychwood Av *BRAK* RG12 ... 35 J4
THHTH CR7 ... 49 M3
Wychwood Cl *ASHV* GU12 ... 113 J7
SUN TW16 ... 24 D7
Wychwood Pl *CBLY* GU15 ... 53 L8
Wycliffe Rd *WIM/MER* SW19 ... 29 L7
Wydell Cl *MRDN* SM4 ... 46 F6
Wydenhurst Rd *CROY/NA* CR0 ... 3 M1
Wyecliffe Gdns *REDH* RH1 ... 126 F4
Wye Cl *ASHF* TW15 ... 23 L5
Wyeths Ms *EW* KT17 * ... 84 C3
Wyeth's Rd *EW* KT17 ... 84 C3
Wyke Av *ASHV* GU12 ... 114 A6
Wyke Cl *ISLW* TW7 ... 17 J1
Wykeham Cl *WDR/YW* UB7 ... 14 D1
Wykeham Rd *FNM* GU9 ... 5 J1
GU GU1 ... 118 A7
Wyke La *ASHV* GU12 ... 114 A6
Wyke Rd *RYNPK* SW20 ... 46 F2
Wykwood *LIPH* GU30 ... 197 J9
Wylam *BRAK* RG12 ... 34 C5
Wyldewood *ASC* SL5 ... 37 G6
Wyleu St *FSTH* SE23 ... 33 H1
Wymering Ct *FARN* GU14 ... 93 G6
Wymond St *PUT/ROE* SW15 ... 19 M5
Wyncote Wy *SAND/SEL* CR2 ... 69 G7
Wyndham Av *COB* KT11 ... 80 D3
Wyndham Cl *BELMT* SM2 ... 65 K6
Wyndham Crs *CRAN* GU6 ... 185 R2
HSLWW TW4 ... 16 C8
Wyndham Rd *KUTN/CMB* KT2 ... 9 H2
WOKN/KNAP GU21 ... 76 E8
Wyndham St *ASHV* GU12 ... 112 F8
Wyndhurst Cl *SAND/SEL* CR2 ... 67 L6
Wynell Rd *FSTH* SE23 ... 33 G4
Wynfields *FRIM* GU16 ... 93 J6
Wynlea Cl *CRAWE* RH10 ... 193 M5
Wynnstow Pk *OXTED* RH8 ... 130 C5
Wynsham Wy *BFOR* GU20 ... 54 E4
Wynton Gdns *SNWD* SE25 ... 50 B5
Wynton Gv *WOT/HER* KT12 ... 60 D2
Wyphurst Rd *CRAN* GU6 ... 186 C1
Wyresdale *BRAK* RG12 ... 35 H7
Wysemead *HORL* RH6 ... 160 F2
Wyvern Cl *ASHV* GU12 * ... 113 J4
BRAK RG12 ... 34 D4
Wyvern Est *NWMAL* KT3 * ... 46 D3
Wyvern Pl *ADL/WDHM* KT15 * ... 58 E3
Wyvern Rd *PUR/KEN* CR8 ... 67 K8

Y

Yaffle Rd *WEY* KT13 ... 59 M8
Yale Cl *HSLWW* TW4 ... 16 C7
SHST GU47 ... 52 C7
Yarborough Rd
WIM/MER SW19 ... 48 A1
Yarbridge Cl *BELMT* SM2 * ... 65 L8
Yardley *BRAK* RG12 ... 34 C5
Yardley Cl *REIG* RH2 ... 125 L6
Yard Md *EGH* TW20 ... 21 K4
Yarm Cl *LHD/OX* KT22 ... 102 F5
Yarm Court Rd *LHD/OX* KT22 ... 102 F5
Yarmouth Cl *CRAWE* RH10 ... 165 J6
Yarm Wy *LHD/OX* KT22 ... 102 F5
Yarrow Cl *HORS* RH12 ... 167 H4
Yatesbury Cl *FNM* GU9 ... 4 C9
Yattendon Rd *HORL* RH6 ... 160 E3
Yaverland Dr *BAGS* GU19 ... 54 A7
Yeats Cl *REDH* RH1 ... 147 M3
Yeend Cl *E/WMO/HCT* KT8 ... 43 K4
Yellowcress Dr *CHOB/PIR* GU24 ... 75 K6
Yenston Cl *MRDN* SM4 ... 47 K6
Yeoman Dr *STWL/WRAY* TW19 ... 23 H2
Yeomanry Cl *EW* KT17 ... 84 C2
Yeomans Cl *FARN* GU14 ... 92 D4
RFNM GU10 ... 135 J1
Yeomans La *LIPH* GU30 ... 196 F9
Yeomans Pl *BOR* GU35 ... 180 D12
Yeomans Ter
WOKN/KNAP GU21 * ... 75 M6
Yeomans Wy *CBLY* GU15 ... 73 H4
Yeoman Wy *REDH* RH1 ... 148 E5
Yeoveney Cl *STWL/WRAY* TW19 ... 22 A3
Yeovil Cl *FARN* GU14 ... 93 G8
Yeovil Rd *SHST* GU47 ... 52 B8
Yeovilton Pl *KUTN/CMB* KT2 ... 27 G6
Yetminster Rd *FARN* GU14 ... 93 G8
Yewbank Cl *PUR/KEN* CR8 ... 88 A5
Yew Cnr *BRAK* RG12 ... 34 F3
Yewens *MFD/CHID* GU8 ... 183 Q12
Yewlands Cl *BNSTD* SM7 ... 85 L5
Yew La *EGRIN* RH19 ... 162 C2
Yew Pl *WEY* KT13 * ... 60 C2
The Yews *ASHF* TW15 * ... 23 L5
BF/WBF KT14 * ... 79 H2
Yew Tree Bottom Rd *EW* KT17 ... 84 E7
Yew Tree Cl *COUL/CHIP* CR5 ... 106 C1
HORL RH6 ... 160 D1
WPK KT4 ... 46 B8
Yew Tree Dr *CTHM* CR3 ... 108 C7
GU GU1 ... 116 E3
Yew Tree Gdns *EPSOM* KT18 ... 83 M5
Yew Tree La *REIG* RH2 ... 125 L5
Yewtree Rd *BECK* BR3 ... 51 J3
Yew Tree Rd *DORK* RH4 ... 122 D8
HORL RH6 ... 174 H10
MFD/CHID GU8 ... 183 L3
Yewtrees *EGH* TW20 ... 39 M3
Yew Trees *SHPTN* TW17 ... 41 J4
Yew Tree Wk *EHSLY* KT24 ... 121 G1
FRIM GU16 ... 73 H8
HSLWW TW4 ... 16 C7
PUR/KEN CR8 ... 67 M8
Yockley Cl *CBLY* GU15 ... 74 A6
Yolland Cl *FNM* GU9 ... 133 M2
York Av *EGRIN* RH19 ... 163 G5
MORT/ESHN SW14 ... 18 F7
York Cl *BF/WBF* KT14 ... 79 H2
MRDN SM4 ... 47 L4
SWTR RH13 ... 167 J6
York Crs *ALDT* GU11 ... 112 C8
Yorke Gdns *REIG* RH2 ... 125 K7
Yorke Ga *CTHM* CR3 ... 108 A4
Yorke Rd *REIG* RH2 ... 125 K7
York Gdns *WOT/HER* KT12 ... 61 G1
York Hl *WNWD* SE27 ... 31 L4
York Pl *CBLY* GU15 ... 73 G2
York Rd *ALDT* GU11 ... 112 C8
ASHV GU12 ... 113 K6
BELMT SM2 ... 65 K5
BF/WBF KT14 ... 79 G2
BH/WHM TN16 ... 110 E1
CBLY GU15 ... 73 G2
CRAWE RH10 ... 165 G8
CROY/NA CR0 ... 49 K7
FARN GU14 ... 92 C8
FARN GU14 ... 112 B1
FNM GU9 ... 5 K7
GU GU1 ... 7 H5
HSLW TW3 ... 16 E5
KUTN/CMB KT2 ... 9 H3
RCHPK/HAM TW10 ... 18 C7
SAND/SEL CR2 ... 69 G8
TEDD TW11 ... 26 B5
WEY KT13 ... 59 M4
WIM/MER SW19 ... 29 L7
WOKS/MYFD GU22 ... 10 B8
Yorkshire Rd *MTCM* CR4 ... 49 H5
York St *MTCM* CR4 ... 48 D7
TWK TW1 ... 26 D2
York Terrace La *CBLY* GU15 * ... 72 D4
Yorktown Rd *SHST* GU47 ... 72 B2
York Wy *CHSGTN* KT9 ... 63 H6
FELT TW13 ... 25 J4
Youlden Cl *CBLY* GU15 ... 73 K4
Youlden Dr *CBLY* GU15 ... 73 K4
Youngs Dr *ASHV* GU12 ... 113 J7
Young St *LHD/OX* KT22 ... 102 C6
Youngstroat La
CHOB/PIR GU24 ... 57 H8
Yukon Rd *BAL* SW12 ... 30 E1

Z

Zealand Av *WDR/YW* UB7 ... 14 A2
Zennor Rd *BAL* SW12 ... 30 F2
Zermatt Rd *THHTH* CR7 ... 49 M4
Zig Zag Rd *PUR/KEN* CR8 ... 87 M6
RDKG RH5 ... 122 F4
Zinnia Dr *CHOB/PIR* GU24 ... 75 K6
Zion Pl *THHTH* CR7 ... 50 A4
Zion Rd *THHTH* CR7 ... 50 A4

Index - featured places

Abbey Business Park
FNM GU9 ... 156 C1
Abbey Industrial Estate
MTCM CR4 ... 48 C5
Abbeylands School
ADL/WDHM KT15 ... 58 D4
Abbey Mill Business Park
RGODL GU7 ... 159 H5
Abbey Mills
WIM/MER SW19 ... 47 M1
Abbey Primary School
MRDN SM4 ... 47 K7
The Abbey School
FNM GU9 ... 5 M6
Abbey Trading Estate
SYD SE26 ... 33 H6
Abbotsbury Primary School
MRDN SM4 ... 47 K5
Abbots Hospital
GU GU1 ... 7 H6
Aberdour School
KWD/TDW/WH KT20 ... 85 J8
Abinger Common First School
RDKG RH5 ... 143 G8
Abro Industrial Estate
ALDT GU11 ... 113 G6
Acorn Medical Centre
TWK TW1 ... 26 D2
Acorns CE School
REIG RH2 ... 146 D6
The Acorns First School
BRKHM/BTCW RH3 ... 124 A8
Acre Road Health Clinic
KUTN/CMB KT2 ... 9 G3
ACS Egham International School
EGH TW20 ... 38 F1
Acting School
GUW GU2 ... 6 F8
Acumen (Anglo School)
NRWD SE19 ... 50 B1
Adamsrill Primary School
SYD SE26 ... 33 H4
Addington Business Centre
CROY/NA CR0 ... 70 B8
Addington Court Golf Club
CROY/NA CR0 ... 69 J7
Addington Golf Club
CROY/NA CR0 ... 69 J3
Addington High School
CROY/NA CR0 ... 90 B2
Addington Palace Golf Club
CROY/NA CR0 ... 69 H5
Addiscombe CC
CROY/NA CR0 ... 3 L8
Addlestone Cemetery
ADL/WDHM KT15 ... 58 D1
Adult Education Centre
CBLY GU15 ... 72 E4
FNM GU9 ... 5 G4
GU GU1 ... 7 J6
GODL GU7 ... 168 B4
Aerodrome Hotel
CROY/NA CR0 ... 67 K5
Airborne Forces Museum
ALDT GU11 ... 112 D4
Airbus Coach Station
HTHAIR TW6 ... 14 C5
Airport Gate Business Centre
WDR/YW UB7 ... 14 C2
Airport Industrial Estate
BH/WHM TN16 ... 91 G5
Albany Clinic
WIM/MER SW19 ... 29 L8
Albany Park Canoe & Sailing Centre
TEDD TW11 ... 8 C1
Albany Park Industrial Estate
FRIM GU16 ... 72 E8
Albemarle Primary School
WIM/MER SW19 ... 29 H3
Alderbrook Primary School
BAL SW12 ... 30 E1
Aldershot & Farnham County Court
ALDT GU11 ... 112 E7
Aldershot Health Centre
ALDT GU11 ... 112 C7
Aldershot Military Museum
ALDT GU11 ... 112 F2
Aldershot Military Stadium
ALDT GU11 ... 112 F3
Aldershot Outpatients
ALDT GU11 ... 112 E6
Aldershot Town FC
ALDT GU11 ... 112 F7
Aldro School
MFD/CHID GU8 ... 158 F2
Alexander Barracks
CHOB/PIR GU24 ... 94 E3
Alexander House Hotel
CRAWE RH10 ... 193 P8
Alexandra Infant School
KUTN/CMB KT2 ... 9 J3
PGE/AN SE20 ... 33 G8
Alexandra Junior School
HSLW TW3 ... 16 E4
SYD SE26 ... 33 G7
The All England Lawn Tennis & Croquet Club
WIM/MER SW19 ... 29 G4
All Hallows Catholic School
FNM GU9 ... 134 C2
All Saints Benhilton CE Primary School
SUT SM1 ... 65 L2
All Saints CE Infant School
LHD/OX KT22 ... 102 D1
RFNM GU10 ... 156 F6
All Saints CE Junior School
NRWD SE19 ... 50 B1
All Saints CE Primary School
CAR SM5 ... 66 D4
HORS RH12 ... 167 J3
PUT/ROE SW15 ... 19 M5
WIM/MER SW19 ... 29 M8
Alpine Snowsports Dry Ski Slope
ALDT GU11 ... 112 F5
The Alton School
PUT/ROE SW15 ... 28 C1
Ambleside Junior School
WOT/HER KT12 ... 42 F8
Amen Corner Business Park
BRAK RG12 ... 34 A2
The American Community School
COB KT11 ... 61 G8
Amesbury School
GSHT GU26 ... 197 R4
AMF Bowling
CRAWW RH11 ... 164 F4
Amida Golf
FELT TW13 ... 25 K4
The Andrew Ewing Primary School
HEST TW5 ... 16 C2
Anerley School
NRWD SE19 ... 50 D1
The Angel Posting House & Livery Hotel
GU GU1 ... 7 G6
Animal Care College
ASC SL5 ... 36 D3
Apex Retail Park
FELT TW13 ... 25 J4
Apostolic Nuncio
WIM/MER SW19 ... 28 F4
Applegarth Primary School
CROY/NA CR0 ... 69 L5
Apple Orchard School
SHGR GU5 ... 169 L6
Aragon Primary School
MRDN SM4 ... 47 H7
The Archbishop Lanfranc School
CROY/NA CR0 ... 49 H6
Archbishop Tenisons CE School
CROY/NA CR0 ... 3 J8
Archdeacon Cambridge's CE Primary School
WHTN TW2 ... 26 B3
Archway Theatre
HORL RH6 ... 160 D4
Arena Leisure Centre
CBLY GU15 ... 72 F3
Arlington Business Park
BRAK RG12 ... 34 D2
Army Golf Club
ALDT GU11 ... 112 B3
Army Medical Services Museum
ASHV GU12 ... 93 L8
Army Training Regiment
CHOB/PIR GU24 ... 94 F3
Arnhem Barracks
ALDT GU11 ... 112 D6
Arrow Industrial Estate
FARN GU14 ... 92 C7
Art School
BECK BR3 ... 51 H5
Arts Link Theatre Cinema
CBLY GU15 ... 73 G3
Arun House
HORS RH12 ... 167 G6
Arunside Primary School
HORS RH12 ... 166 D7
Ascot Racecourse
ASC SL5 ... 36 C3
Ashburton Community School
CROY/NA CR0 ... 50 E7
Ashburton Primary School
CROY/NA CR0 ... 50 E6
The Ashcombe School
DORK RH4 ... 122 E8
Ashdown Forest Golf Club
FROW RH18 ... 195 N12
Ashdown Forest Health Centre
FROW RH18 ... 195 M10
Ashford CE Primary School
ASHF TW15 ... 23 L7
Ashford Clinic
ASHF TW15 ... 23 H4
Ashford High School
ASHF TW15 ... 23 H4
Ashford Industrial Estate
ASHF TW15 ... 23 M5
Ashford Manor Golf Club
ASHF TW15 ... 23 J7
Ashford Park Primary School
ASHF TW15 ... 22 F5
The Ashford & St Peters Hospital
CHERT KT16 ... 58 A2
STWL/WRAY TW19 ... 23 H3
Ashford Sports Club
ASHF TW15 ... 23 G5
STWL/WRAY TW19 ... 23 J2
Ash Grange CP School
ASHV GU12 ... 113 L7
Ashley Centre Shopping Precinct
EPSOM KT18 ... 84 A3
Ashley Primary School
WOT/HER KT12 ... 42 D8
Ash Manor School
ASHV GU12 ... 135 J1
Ashtead Clinic
ASHTD KT21 ... 83 H7
Ashtead CC
ASHTD KT21 ... 83 H7
Ashtead Hospital
ASHTD KT21 ... 103 H2
Ashton House School
ISLW TW7 ... 17 G3
Ashurst Wood Primary School
EGRIN RH19 ... 163 M7
Ash Vale Health Centre
ASHV GU12 ... 113 L5
Aspen House Secondary & Primary School
BRXS/STRHM SW2 ... 31 H2
Asquith Court School
HPTN TW12 ... 43 L1
Assembly Rooms
SURB KT6 ... 45 H4
The Astolat Industrial Estate
RGUW GU3 ... 138 F8
Aston Clinic
NWMAL KT3 ... 46 B4
Astra Business Centre
REDH RH1 ... 175 R2
Athelney Primary School
CAT SE6 ... 33 K4
Athelstan House School
HPTN TW12 ... 43 K1
Atkinson Morley Hospital
RYNPK SW20 ... 28 E8
Atlas Medical Centre
HORL RH6 ... 160 D7
Atwood Primary School
SAND/SEL CR2 ... 88 D4
Audley Primary School
CTHM CR3 ... 108 B3
Auriol Junior School
HOR/WEW KT19 ... 64 C3
The Avenue Primary School
BELMT SM2 ... 65 K8
BAA Heathrow Visitor Centre
HTHAIR TW6 ... 14 E3
Back Care Clinic
WPK KT4 ... 46 D8
Badshot Lea Village Infant School
FNM GU9 ... 134 D3
Bagshot School
BAGS GU19 ... 54 B6
Baldwins Hill Primary School
EGRIN RH19 ... 162 D2
Balgowan Primary School
BECK BR3 ... 51 H2
Balham Boys Preparatory Secondary School
BAL SW12 ... 30 E2
Balham Girls Preparatory Secondary School
TOOT SW17 ... 30 C4
Balham Health Centre
BAL SW12 ... 30 E3
Balham Leisure Centre
TOOT SW17 ... 30 D3
Bandon Hill Cemetery
WLGTN SM6 ... 67 G4
Bandon Hill Primary School
WLGTN SM6 ... 67 G5
Banstead Athletic FC
KWD/TDW/WH KT20 ... 104 F2
Banstead Clinic
BNSTD SM7 ... 85 K5
Banstead County Junior School
BNSTD SM7 ... 85 J5
Banstead Downs Golf Club
BELMT SM2 ... 85 K1
Banstead Infant School
BNSTD SM7 ... 85 J5
Banstead Sports Centre
KWD/TDW/WH KT20 ... 104 F2
Banstead Village Clinic
BNSTD SM7 ... 85 L5
Barfield School
RFNM GU10 ... 134 E6
Barn Elms Athletics Track
BARN SW13 ... 19 L4
Barn Elms Water Sports Centre
PUT/ROE SW15 ... 19 M4
Barnes Hospital
MORT/ESHN SW14 ... 19 H5
Barnes Primary School
BARN SW13 ... 19 H5
Barnes Sports Club
BARN SW13 ... 19 J3
Barnett Wood Infant School
ASHTD KT21 ... 83 G7
Barnsbury Junior School
WOKS/MYFD GU22 ... 97 G3
Barnwood County First School
GUW GU2 ... 116 A7
Barrow Hedges Primary School
CAR SM5 ... 66 B6
Barrow Hills School
MFD/CHID GU8 ... 183 M5
Barwell Business Park
CHSGTN KT9 ... 63 G6
Baston School
HAYES BR2 ... 70 E1
Battersea Tutorial College
TOOT SW17 ... 30 D3
Beacon Hill County Primary School
GSHT GU26 ... 181 P11
Beacon School
BNSTD SM7 ... 85 H7
Beatrix Potter Primary School
WAND/EARL SW18 ... 29 M2
Beauclerc Infant School
SUN TW16 ... 42 F3
Beaufort Primary School
WOKN/KNAP GU21 ... 76 C6
Beaumont Junior School
ALDT GU11 ... 112 B7
Beaumont Primary School
PUR/KEN CR8 ... 87 J4
Beaver Industrial Estate
LIPH GU30 ... 196 H11
The Beavers Community Primary School
HSLWW TW4 ... 15 M5
Beckenham Business Centre
BECK BR3 ... 33 H7
Beckenham Crematorium
BECK BR3 ... 50 F3
Beckenham CC
BECK BR3 ... 33 L8
Beckenham Hospital
BECK BR3 ... 51 J2
Beckenham Leisure Centre
BECK BR3 ... 51 H1
Beckenham Place Park Golf Course
BECK BR3 ... 33 L7
Beckenham RFC
BECK BR3 ... 51 H4
Beckenham Town FC
BECK BR3 ... 51 K5
Beckmead School
BECK BR3 ... 51 K8
Beddington Infants School
WLGTN SM6 ... 66 F2
Beddington Medical Centre
CROY/NA CR0 ... 67 H3
Beddington Park Primary School
CROY/NA CR0 ... 67 G2
Beddington Trading Estate
CROY/NA CR0 ... 49 H8
Bedelsford Special School
KUT/HW KT1 ... 8 E9
Bedfont Health Clinic
EBED/NFELT TW14 ... 24 B1
Bedfont Industrial Park
ASHF TW15 ... 24 A4
Bedfont J & I School
EBED/NFELT TW14 ... 15 H8

Bedfont Lakes Country Park
EBED/NFELT TW14 .... 23 M3
Bedford Lakes Office Park
EBED/NFELT TW14 .... 23 M2
Bedington Infant School
WLGTN SM6 .... 66 F3
Beech House School
SAND/SEL CR2 .... 68 C8
Beechnut Industrial Estate
ASHV GU12 .... 112 E8
Beecholme Primary School
MTCM CR4 .... 48 E1
Beechwood School
STRHM/NOR SW16 .... 31 H4
Belfry Shopping Centre
REDH RH1 .... 126 C6
Bellerby Theatre
GU GU1 .... 7 G5
Belle Vue Infant School
ASHV GU12 .... 113 F3
Bell Farm Junior School
WOT/HER KT12 .... 60 F3
Bellingham Trading Estate
CAT SE6 .... 33 L4
Belmont Preparatory School
RDKG RH5 .... 171 P3
Benedict Primary School
MTCM CR4 .... 48 A2
Bensham Manor School
THHTH CR7 .... 49 M5
Benson Primary School
CROY/NA CR0 .... 69 H2
The Bentall Shopping Centre
KUT/HW KT1 .... 8 D6
Bentley CE Primary School
RFNM GU10 .... 154 A4
Bentley Trimmings Business Park
RFNM GU10 .... 154 A4
Berkeley Primary School
HEST TW5 .... 16 A1
The Berkshire Golf Club
ASC SL5 .... 53 M1
Bertram House School
TOOT SW17 .... 30 D3
Best Western Master Robert Hotel
HEST TW5 .... 16 C3
Betchworth Park Golf Club
DORK RH4 .... 145 H1
Bethlem Royal Hospital
BECK BR3 .... 51 K7
Beulah Infant School
THHTH CR7 .... 49 M2
Beverley School
NWMAL KT3 .... 46 D5
Beverley Trading Estate
MRDN SM4 .... 47 G7
Bewbush Community Primary School
CRAWW RH11 .... 164 A7
Bewbush Leisure Centre
CRAWW RH11 .... 164 B8
Bewbush Medical Centre
CRAWW RH11 .... 164 A7
Bewhurst County First School
CRAWW RH11 .... 164 B7
Biggin Hill Airport
BH/WHM TN16 .... 90 F2
Biggin Hill Business Park
BH/WHM TN16 .... 91 G5
Biggin Hill Primary School
BH/WHM TN16 .... 91 H6
Bilton Industrial Estate
BRAK RG12 .... 34 B4
Bingham Hotel
TWK TW1 .... 18 A8
Binscombe Medical Centre
RCODL GU7 .... 168 A1
Birches Industrial Estate
EGRIN RH19 .... 162 B2
Birch Hill Medical Centre
BRAK RG12 .... 34 E7
Birch Hill Primary School
BRAK RG12 .... 34 F8
Birdworld & Underwaterworld
RFNM GU10 .... 154 F6
Bishop David Brown School
WOKN/KNAP GU21 .... 78 A3
Bishop Gilpin Primary School
WIM/MER SW19 .... 29 J6
Bishop Perrin CE Primary School
WHTN TW2 .... 25 L1
Bishopsgate School
EGH TW20 .... 20 D4
Bishop's Table Hotel
FNM GU9 .... 5 G3
Bishop Thomas Grant School
STRHM/NOR SW16 .... 31 J6
Bishop Wand CE Secondary School
SUN TW16 .... 42 C2
Bisley CE Primary School
CHOB/PIR GU24 .... 75 K6
Blackburn Trading Estate
STWL/WRAY TW19 .... 14 C8
Blackdown Barracks
FRIM GU16 .... 94 A3
Black Down (NT)
HASM GU27 .... 199 J11
Blackwater & Hawley Leisure Centre
BLKW GU17 .... 72 A6
Blackwater Industrial Estate
BLKW GU17 .... 72 B4
Blackwater Trading Estate
ASHV GU12 .... 135 G1
Blackwell Primary School
EGRIN RH19 .... 162 F2
Bleach's Yard Industrial Estate
LIPH GU30 .... 196 H11
Blenheim Business Centre
MTCM CR4 .... 48 C1
Blenheim High School
HOR/WEW KT19 .... 64 A8
Blenheim Shopping Centre
PGE/AN SE20 .... 32 F8
Bletchingley Golf Club
REDH RH1 .... 128 A7
Blossom House School
RYNPK SW20 .... 28 F8

Bluebell Railway
EGRIN RH19 .... 194 B11
The Blue School
ISLW TW7 .... 17 K5
Bocketts Farm Park
LHD/OX KT22 .... 102 C7
Bohunt Manor
LIPH GU30 .... 196 G10
Bohunt School
LIPH GU30 .... 196 G9
Bond First School
MTCM CR4 .... 48 C2
Bond Primary School
MTCM CR4 .... 48 C2
Bookham Grange Hotel
GT/LBKH KT23 .... 101 H5
Bookham Industrial Estate
GT/LBKH KT23 .... 101 J5
Borers Business Park
CRAWE RH10 .... 192 H2
Borough Hall
RCODL GU7 .... 168 B4
Boundary Business Centre
WOKN/KNAP GU21 .... 11 H2
Boundary Business Park
MTCM CR4 .... 48 A2
Bourne Business Park
ADL/WDHM KT15 .... 58 F1
Bourne Hall Health Centre
EW KT17 .... 64 C7
Bourne Hall Museum
EW KT17 .... 64 C7
Bourne Mill Industrial Estate
FNM GU9 .... 134 B6
The Bourne School
RFNM GU10 .... 156 A2
Bourne Tennis Club
FNM GU9 .... 5 K8
Boxgrove Primary School
GU GU1 .... 117 L7
Box Hill Country Park
KWD/TDW/WH KT20 .... 123 H6
Box Hill School
RDKG RH5 .... 122 E1
Bracknell Business Centre
BRAK RG12 .... 34 C2
Bracknell RFC
BRAK RG12 .... 35 H1
Bracknell Sports Centre
BRAK RG12 .... 34 F5
Bracknell Town FC
BRAK RG12 .... 34 F2
Bracknell & Wokingham College
BRAK RG12 .... 34 F2
Brakenhale School
BRAK RG12 .... 34 E4
Brambletye Junior School
REDH RH1 .... 148 D2
Brambletye School
EGRIN RH19 .... 163 K8
The Bramley Business Centre
SHGR GU5 .... 169 J2
Bramley CE Infant School
SHGR GU5 .... 169 K3
Bramley Golf Club
SHGR GU5 .... 168 H2
Bramley School
KWD/TDW/WH KT20 .... 104 D7
Brentford Business Centre
BTFD TW8 .... 17 M2
Brentford County Court
BTFD TW8 .... 18 A2
Brentford FC London Broncos RLFC (Griffin Park)
BTFD TW8 .... 18 A1
Brentford Health Centre
BTFD TW8 .... 17 M1
Brentford School for Girls
BTFD TW8 .... 18 A1
Brent Knoll School
FSTH SE23 .... 33 G4
Brentwaters Business Park
BTFD TW8 .... 17 M2
Brewery Mews Business Centre
ISLW TW7 .... 17 J5
Brickfields Industrial Park
BRAK RG12 .... 34 D2
Bridge Industrial Estate
HORL RH6 .... 160 E3
The Bridge Leisure Centre
SYD SE26 .... 33 J6
Bridge Medical Centre
CRAWE RH10 .... 165 J3
Brigstock Medical Centre
THHTH CR7 .... 49 L5
Bristow Infant & Nursery School
CBLY GU15 .... 72 E7
Britannia Industrial Estate
DTCH/LGLY SL3 .... 13 H4
British Transport Police
GU GU1 .... 6 E5
BRIT School for Performing Arts
CROY/NA CR0 .... 50 A6
Broadbridge Heath Retail Park
HORS RH12 .... 166 B6
Broadbridge Heath Stadium
HORS RH12 .... 166 B7
Broadfield East First School
CRAWW RH11 .... 164 E8
Broadfield Health Centre
CRAWW RH11 .... 164 D8
Broadford Park Business Centre
RGUE GU4 .... 139 G7
Broadlands Business Campus
HORS RH12 .... 189 K9
Broadmead Primary School
CROY/NA CR0 .... 50 A6
The Broadmere Primary School
WOKN/KNAP GU21 .... 78 A3
Broadmoor CP School
CWTH RG45 .... 52 A5
Broadmoor Hospital
CWTH RG45 .... 52 B4
Broadwater Park Golf Club
RCODL GU7 .... 168 D2
Broadwater Park Golf Club & Driving Range
RCODL GU7 .... 168 E1

Broadwater Primary School
TOOT SW17 .... 30 A5
Broadwater School
RCODL GU7 .... 168 D1
Brockenhurst Hotel
ASC SL5 .... 36 E6
Brockham School
BRKHM/BTCW RH3 .... 145 L2
Brocklebank Health Centre
WAND/EARL SW18 .... 29 L1
Bromley Road Infant School
BECK BR3 .... 51 L1
Bromley Road Retail Park
CAT SE6 .... 33 L3
Brookfield Primary School
CHEAM SM3 .... 47 H8
Brookham School
LIPH GU30 .... 197 K11
Brooklands Airfield (disused)
WEY KT13 .... 59 J8
Brooklands Business Park
WEY KT13 .... 59 K8
Brooklands College
WEY KT13 .... 59 K5
Brooklands Industrial Estate
WEY KT13 .... 59 H8
Brooklands Museum
WEY KT13 .... 59 K7
Brookmead Industrial Estate
REIG RH2 .... 125 L6
The Brook School
CRAWE RH10 .... 165 L7
The Brook Trading Estate
ASHV GU12 .... 113 H6
Brookwood Cemetery
CHOB/PIR GU24 .... 95 L4
Brookwood County Primary School
CHOB/PIR GU24 .... 95 K2
Broomfield House School
RCH/KEW TW9 .... 18 C3
Broomsleigh Business Park
SYD SE26 .... 33 J6
Broomwood Hall Lower School
BAL SW12 .... 30 D1
Browning Barracks
ALDT GU11 .... 112 D4
Broxhead Trading Estate
BOR GU35 .... 180 A11
Brunel University
ISLW TW7 .... 17 H2
TWK TW1 .... 17 L6
Brunel University (Runnymede Campus)
EGH TW20 .... 21 G4
Brunel University Track (Osterley Campus)
ISLW TW7 .... 17 H2
Buchan Country Park
CRAWW RH11 .... 190 H12
Buckingham Primary School
HPTN TW12 .... 25 J6
Buckland Infant School
CHSGTN KT9 .... 63 J4
Buckland Primary School
STA TW18 .... 22 F8
Burghwood Clinic
BNSTD SM7 .... 85 J6
Burhill Golf Club
WOT/HER KT12 .... 60 D7
Burhill Infant School
WOT/HER KT12 .... 61 G5
Burleigh Infant School
CRAWE RH10 .... 193 N5
Burlington Infant School
NWMAL KT3 .... 46 C4
Burnhill Business Centre
BECK BR3 .... 51 K2
Burntwood School
TOOT SW17 .... 30 A3
Burpham Foundation Primary School
RGUE GU4 .... 117 K4
Burstow Business Centre
HORL RH6 .... 161 L1
Burstow Lodge Business Centre
HORL RH6 .... 160 E5
Burstow Primary School
HORL RH6 .... 161 K3
Burvale Cemetery
WOT/HER KT12 .... 60 D5
Burwood Park School & College
WOT/HER KT12 .... 60 C5
Burys Court School
REIG RH2 .... 146 F6
Busbridge CE Junior School
RCODL GU7 .... 168 C6
Busbridge Infant School
RCODL GU7 .... 168 C7
Bushy Hill Junior School
GU GU1 .... 118 A6
Business Aviation Centre
FARN GU14 .... 112 C2
Butterfly House
ISLW TW7 .... 17 L3
Byfleet Business Centre
BF/WBF KT14 .... 79 G1
Byfleet CP School
BF/WBF KT14 .... 79 G1
Byfleet Industrial Estate
BF/WBF KT14 .... 79 G1
Byron Primary School
COUL/CHIP CR5 .... 87 H7
Calvi House Pre-preparatory School
COB KT11 .... 80 B3
Camberley CC
CBLY GU15 .... 73 G6
Camberley County Infant School
CBLY GU15 .... 72 E4
Camberley Health Centre
CBLY GU15 .... 72 E6
Camberley Heath Golf Club
CBLY GU15 .... 73 K5
Camberley Magistrates Court
CBLY GU15 .... 73 G3
Camberley RFC
CBLY GU15 .... 72 F6

Camberley Town FC
CBLY GU15 .... 72 E6
Cambridge Park Bowling & Sports Club
TWK TW1 .... 17 M8
Camden Junior School
CAR SM5 .... 66 C3
Camelsdale County First School
HASM GU27 .... 198 A8
Campana Finishing School
RFNM GU10 .... 134 D8
Camphill Industrial Estate
BF/WBF KT14 .... 78 E1
Camphill Road First School
BF/WBF KT14 .... 78 E2
Campion House College
ISLW TW7 .... 17 J2
Camp Road Industrial Estate
FARN GU14 .... 112 F1
Canbury 2000 Business Park
KUTN/CMB KT2 .... 8 F5
Canbury Business Centre
KUTN/CMB KT2 .... 8 F5
Canbury Medical Centre
KUTN/CMB KT2 .... 9 G1
Canbury School
KUTN/CMB KT2 .... 27 L1
The Canons Leisure Centre
MTCM CR4 .... 48 C4
Capital Business Centre
MTCM CR4 .... 48 C5
SAND/SEL CR2 .... 68 A5
Caplan Estate
MTCM CR4 .... 48 F1
Cardinal Newman Catholic Primary School
WOT/HER KT12 .... 61 G2
Cardinal Road Infant School
FELT TW13 .... 24 E2
Carew Manor School
WLGTN SM6 .... 67 G2
Carlisle Infant School
HPTN TW12 .... 25 L7
The Carlton Mitre Hotel
E/WMO/HCT KT8 .... 44 B3
Carlyle Business Centre
CHERT KT16 .... 40 D7
Carrier Business Park
CRAWE RH10 .... 165 K3
Carshalton AFC
SUT SM1 .... 66 B2
Carshalton College of Further Education
CAR SM5 .... 66 C2
Carshalton High School for Boys
CAR SM5 .... 66 A1
Carshalton High School for Girls
CAR SM5 .... 66 B2
Carshalton War Memorial Hospital
CAR SM5 .... 66 C4
Carwarden House School
CBLY GU15 .... 73 K6
The Cassel Hospital
RCHPK/HAM TW10 .... 27 G5
Castle Hill Primary School
CROY/NA CR0 .... 69 M5
The Caterham Dene Hospital
CTHM CR3 .... 108 C5
Caterham Preparatory School
CTHM CR3 .... 108 C8
Caterham School
CTHM CR3 .... 108 C8
Catford Cricket & Sports Club
CAT SE6 .... 33 L2
Catford Cyphers CC
CAT SE6 .... 33 J3
Catford Trading Estate
CAT SE6 .... 33 L3
Catford Wanderers Sports Club
CAT SE6 .... 33 M5
Cathedral Hill Industrial Estate
GUW GU2 .... 6 B2
Cator Park School for Girls
BECK BR3 .... 33 K4
Cavendish Primary School
CHSWK W4 .... 19 H2
The Cedars Primary School
HEST TW5 .... 15 K2
Centaurs Business Centre
ISLW TW7 .... 17 K1
Centaurs RFC
ISLW TW7 .... 17 J1
Centrale Shopping Centre
CROY/NA CR0 .... 2 C5
Central Estate
ALDT GU11 .... 112 E8
Central Medical Centre
MRDN SM4 .... 47 M4
Central London Golf Club
TOOT SW17 .... 30 A3
Central Sussex College
CRAWE RH10 .... 165 G4
Central Sussex College (East Grinstead Campus)
EGRIN RH19 .... 162 F4
Centre Court Shopping Centre
WIM/MER SW19 .... 29 J7
Chaffinch Business Park
BECK BR3 .... 51 G3
Chalk Lane Hotel
EPSOM KT18 .... 84 A5
Chambers Business Park
WDR/YW UB7 .... 14 D1
Chandler Junior School
MFD/CHID GU8 .... 183 M4
Chandlers Field Primary School
E/WMO/HCT KT8 .... 43 K5
Chandos Business Centre
WLGTN SM6 .... 66 F7
Charles Darwin School
BH/WHM TN16 .... 91 J5
Charlwood Place
HORL RH6 .... 174 H9
Charlwoods Industrial Estate
EGRIN RH19 .... 162 F2
Charlwood Village Infant School
HORL RH6 .... 175 J10

Charrington Bowl
SURB KT6 .... 63 L1
Charterhouse
RCODL GU7 .... 159 M3
Charterhouse School Students Residences
RCODL GU7 .... 159 L2
Charters School
ASC SL5 .... 37 G7
Chartfield School
PUT/ROE SW15 .... 19 L7
Chartham Park Golf Club
EGRIN RH19 .... 178 D11
Chase Bridge Primary School
WHTN TW2 .... 17 H8
Chatsworth J & I School
HSLW TW3 .... 16 F6
Cheam Common J & I School
WPK KT4 .... 64 E1
Cheam Fields Primary School
CHEAM SM3 .... 65 H4
Cheam High School
CHEAM SM3 .... 65 H3
Cheam Leisure Centre
CHEAM SM3 .... 65 G3
Cheam Park Farm Junior School
CHEAM SM3 .... 65 H2
Cheam Sports Club
CHEAM SM3 .... 65 H6
Cheapside CE Primary School
ASC SL5 .... 37 H1
Chelsea Fields Industrial Estate
WIM/MER SW19 .... 48 A1
Chennestone Community School
SUN TW16 .... 42 E2
Cherry Lodge Golf Club
BH/WHM TN16 .... 91 K7
Cherry Wood Primary School
FARN GU14 .... 92 D3
Chertsey Business Centre
CHERT KT16 .... 40 D7
Chertsey Cemetery
CHERT KT16 .... 58 D1
Chertsey Hall
CHERT KT16 .... 40 D7
Chertsey Museum
CHERT KT16 .... 40 D6
Chertsey Recreation Centre
CHERT KT16 .... 40 B8
Chertsey Town FC
CHERT KT16 .... 40 C6
Chessington CC
CHSGTN KT9 .... 62 F6
Chessington Community College & Sports Centre
CHSGTN KT9 .... 63 G6
Chessington Golf Club
CHSGTN KT9 .... 63 G6
Chessington World of Adventures
CHSGTN KT9 .... 62 F8
Chestnut Grove School
BAL SW12 .... 30 D2
Chesworth Junior School
SWTR RH13 .... 167 H6
Chiddingfold Golf Club
MFD/CHID GU8 .... 199 Q4
Chilworth CE Infant School
RGUE GU4 .... 140 A6
Chinthurst School
KWD/TDW/WH KT20 .... 104 F5
Chipstead Golf Club
COUL/CHIP CR5 .... 86 C8
Chipstead RFC
COUL/CHIP CR5 .... 106 C3
Chipstead Valley Primary School
COUL/CHIP CR5 .... 86 D6
Chiswick Community School
CHSWK W4 .... 19 G2
Chiswick House
CHSWK W4 .... 19 G1
Chobham Common National Nature Reserve
CHOB/PIR GU24 .... 55 M2
Chobham FC
CHOB/PIR GU24 .... 76 C2
Chobham Golf Club
WOKN/KNAP GU21 .... 76 A5
Chobham RFC
CHOB/PIR GU24 .... 56 B8
Chobham St Lawrence CE Primary School
CHOB/PIR GU24 .... 76 B1
Christ Church CE Infant School
NWMAL KT3 .... 46 B3
Christchurch CE Infant School
VW GU25 .... 38 D3
Christ Church CE Junior School
NWMAL KT3 .... 46 A3
Christ Church CE Primary School
BRXS/STRHM SW2 .... 31 J2
BRYLDS KT5 .... 45 K6
FSTH SE23 .... 33 G3
Christchurch Junior School
CHERT KT16 .... 58 A5
Christ Church Primary School
PUR/KEN CR8 .... 67 L8
Christian Meeting Hall
BECK BR3 .... 51 K1
Christ's College Guildford
GU GU1 .... 116 F5
Christ's College Ski Club
GU GU1 .... 116 F5
Christ's Hospital Infirmary
SWTR RH13 .... 204 F11
Christ's Hospital School
SWTR RH13 .... 204 E12
The Christ's Hospital Sports Centre
SWTR RH13 .... 204 E11
Christs School
RCH/KEW TW9 .... 18 C7
Christ the King RC First School
STWL/WRAY TW19 .... 14 A8
Chrysalis Theatre
BAL SW12 .... 30 D2
Chrysanthemum Clinic
CHSWK W4 .... 18 F2

Churchfields Primary School
BECK BR3 .... 51 G3
Church Hill House Hospital
BRAK RG12 .... 34 D5
Churchill CE Primary School
BH/WHM TN16 .... 111 M7
Churchill College
RYNPK SW20 .... 46 F2
The Churchill Medical Centre
KUTN/CMB KT2 .... 9 H5
Cineworld Cinema
FELT TW13 .... 24 E3
City Business Centre
SWTR RH13 .... 167 G8
The City Business Centre
CRAWW RH11 .... 191 N3
City of London Freemens School
ASHTD KT21 .... 103 L1
Civil Service College
ASC SL5 .... 37 J5
Clandon CE Infant School
RGUE GU4 .... 118 D5
Clandon Park (NT)
RGUE GU4 .... 118 D6
Clandon Regis Golf Club
RGUE GU4 .... 118 C5
Clare House Primary School
BECK BR3 .... 51 M2
Claremont Fan Court School
ESH/CLAY KT10 .... 61 L5
Claremont Landscape Garden (NT)
ESH/CLAY KT10 .... 61 K6
Clarence Road School
SWTR RH13 .... 167 G8
Clarendon Primary School
ASHF TW15 .... 23 J4
Clarendon Special School
HPTN TW12 .... 25 L7
Claygate Primary School
ESH/CLAY KT10 .... 62 B6
Clayton Barracks
ALDT GU11 .... 113 G5
Cleves Junior School
WEY KT13 .... 60 C3
Clewborough House School at Cheswycks
FRIM GU16 .... 93 L4
Clifton Hill School
CTHM CR3 .... 108 A6
Clockhouse Industrial Estate
EBED/NFELT TW14 .... 23 L2
Cobham Bus Museum
COB KT11 .... 79 M2
The Cobham Health Centre
COB KT11 .... 80 E3
Cobham RFC
COB KT11 .... 81 G2
Coliseum Business Centre
CBLY GU15 .... 72 D6
College Fields Business Centre
WIM/MER SW19 .... 48 B1
The College of Law
RGUW GU3 .... 138 F4
The College of Richard Collyer
HORS RH12 .... 167 G5
The College of St Barnabas
LING RH7 .... 178 G9
College Town Infant School
SHST GU47 .... 72 B1
College Town Junior School
SHST GU47 .... 72 B1
Collingwood College
CBLY GU15 .... 73 K1
Collingwood Preparatory School
WLGTN SM6 .... 66 E4
Collis Primary School
TEDD TW11 .... 26 E7
Colnbrook CE Primary School
DTCH/LGLY SL3 .... 13 G3
Colnbrook Sports Club
DTCH/LGLY SL3 .... 13 J3
Coln Industrial Estate
DTCH/LGLY SL3 .... 13 J2
Coloma Convent Girls School
CROY/NA CR0 .... 69 J4
Colonnades Leisure Park
CROY/NA CR0 .... 67 K5
Colours Sports Club
SUT SM1 .... 65 M4
Coltwood Business Centre
ALDT GU11 .... 112 E7
Compton Place Business Centre
CBLY GU15 .... 72 D5
Concorde Business Park
BH/WHM TN16 .... 91 G5
Coney Hill School
HAYES BR2 .... 70 C1
Connaught Business Centre
CROY/NA CR0 .... 67 J5
MTCM CR4 .... 48 C5
Connaught County Junior School
BAGS GU19 .... 54 B7
The Connaught School
ASHV GU12 .... 135 H2
Coombe Girls School
NWMAL KT3 .... 46 A2
Coombe Hill Golf Club
KUTN/CMB KT2 .... 28 A8
Coombe Hill J & I School
NWMAL KT3 .... 46 A1
Coombe Wood Golf Club
KUTN/CMB KT2 .... 9 M3
The Copthorne Business Centre
CRAWE RH10 .... 192 G1
Copthorne CE Junior School
CRAWE RH10 .... 192 G2
Copthorne Fairway Infant School
CRAWE RH10 .... 192 G2
Copthorne Golf Club
CRAWE RH10 .... 192 H2
Copthorne Hotel
CRAWE RH10 .... 192 F3
Copthorne Hotel & Resort Effingham Park
CRAWE RH10 .... 193 L1

Copthorne Junior School
CRAWE RH10 .... 192 G1
Copthorne Preparatory School
CRAWE RH10 .... 193 K2
Copthorne Squash Club
CRAWE RH10 .... 192 F3
Cordwalles Junior School
CBLY GU15 .... 73 J1
Corinthian Casuals FC
SURB KT6 .... 63 K2
Cornfield School
REDH RH1 .... 148 C5
Cosmic Cycle
HORS RH12 .... 166 E7
Coulsdon CE Primary School
COUL/CHIP CR5 .... 87 J8
The Coulsdon Eye Clinic
COUL/CHIP CR5 .... 86 F5
Coulsdon High School
COUL/CHIP CR5 .... 107 L2
Coulsdon Manor Golf Club
COUL/CHIP CR5 .... 87 J6
Coulsdon Sixth Form College
COUL/CHIP CR5 .... 107 K1
Country Gardens Estate
BFOR GU20 .... 54 F1
County Mall Shopping Centre
CRAWE RH10 .... 165 G4
County Oak Retail Park
CRAWW RH11 .... 191 N3
Court Farm Industrial Estate
STWL/WRAY TW19 .... 14 C8
Courtwood Primary School
CROY/NA CR0 .... 69 J8
Cove CC
FARN GU14 .... 92 B5
Cove Infant School
FARN GU14 .... 92 B3
Cove Junior School
FARN GU14 .... 92 B4
Cove School
FARN GU14 .... 92 B4
Coworth Flexlands School
CHOB/PIR GU24 .... 76 C1
Craggy Island Climbing Centre
GU GU1 .... 117 H4
Cranford Community College
HEST TW5 .... 15 L1
Cranford Infant School
HSLWW TW4 .... 15 K4
Cranford Junior School
HSLWW TW4 .... 15 L4
Cranleigh Golf and Leisure Club
CRAN GU6 .... 170 E11
Cranleigh Health Centre
CRAN GU6 .... 186 C3
Cranleigh Infant School
CRAN GU6 .... 186 D2
Cranleigh Leisure Centre
CRAN GU6 .... 186 C3
Cranleigh Preparatory School
CRAN GU6 .... 186 C1
Cranleigh School
CRAN GU6 .... 170 B12
Cranleigh Village Hospital
CRAN GU6 .... 186 C2
Cranmer Primary School
MTCM CR4 .... 48 C4
Cranmore School
EHSLY KT24 .... 119 M3
Crawley College Annexe
CRAWW RH11 .... 164 E3
Crawley Down CE School
CRAWE RH10 .... 193 N5
Crawley Down Health Centre
CRAWE RH10 .... 193 M5
Crawley Health Clinic
CRAWE RH10 .... 165 G4
Crawley Hospital
CRAWW RH11 .... 164 E4
The Crawley Lawn Tennis Club
CRAWE RH10 .... 165 K2
Crawley Leisure Centre Athletics Arena
CRAWE RH10 .... 165 H5
Crawley Museum (Goffs Park House)
CRAWW RH11 .... 164 D5
Crawley RFC
CRAWW RH11 .... 191 K3
Crawley Ridge Infant School
CBLY GU15 .... 73 J2
Crawley Swimming Pool
CRAWE RH10 .... 165 H5
Crawley Town FC
CRAWW RH11 .... 164 E8
Cricket Green School
MTCM CR4 .... 48 B3
Crockham Hill CE Primary School
EDEN TN8 .... 131 M7
Croham Hurst Golf Club
SAND/SEL CR2 .... 68 C5
Crondall Primary School
RFNM GU10 .... 132 C3
Cross Farm Infant School
FRIM GU16 .... 93 H3
Crouch Industrial Estate
LHD/OX KT22 .... 102 D1
Crown Lane Primary School
WNWD SE27 .... 31 M1
Crown Wood Primary School
BRAK RG12 .... 35 G6
Croydon Airport Industrial Estate
CROY/NA CR0 .... 67 K6
Croydon Bowling Club
SAND/SEL CR2 .... 67 M4
Croydon Cemetery
CROY/NA CR0 .... 49 J5
Croydon Clocktower Cinema
CROY/NA CR0 .... 2 D7
Croydon College
CROY/NA CR0 .... 2 E6
Croydon Crematorium
THHTH CR7 .... 49 H5
Croydon Fairfield Halls Cinema
CROY/NA CR0 .... 2 E7
Croydon FC
SNWD SE25 .... 50 F5

Croydon High Junior School GDST
SAND/SEL CR2 .... 88 E1
Croydon Mosque & Islamic Centre
THHTH CR7 .... 49 K6
Croydon Road Industrial Estate
CROY/NA CR0 .... 50 F4
Croydon Sports Arena
SNWD SE25 .... 50 F5
Crystal Palace FC (Selhurst Park)
SNWD SE25 .... 50 B4
Crystal Palace Museum
NRWD SE19 .... 32 C7
Cuaco Sports Ground
BECK BR3 .... 33 K7
Cuddington Cemetery
WPK KT4 .... 64 E1
Cuddington CP School
WPK KT4 .... 64 C2
Cuddington Croft Primary School
BELMT SM2 .... 65 G7
Cuddington Golf Club
BNSTD SM7 .... 85 H3
Cudham CE Primary School
BH/WHM TN16 .... 91 K6
Culvers House Primary School
MTCM CR4 .... 48 D8
Cumnor House School
SAND/SEL CR2 .... 67 L7
Cypress Infant School
SNWD SE25 .... 50 B2
Cypress Junior School
SNWD SE25 .... 50 B2
Cyprus College of Art
WNWD SE27 .... 31 L5
D'Albiac House
HTHAIR TW6 .... 14 D4
Dalmain Primary School
FSTH SE23 .... 33 H2
Danesfield Manor School
WOT/HER KT12 .... 60 E1
Danes Hill Pre-preparatory School
LHD/OX KT22 .... 81 M3
Danes Hill School
LHD/OX KT22 .... 82 A4
Danetree School
HOR/WEW KT19 .... 63 M6
Dapdune Wharf (NT)
GU GU1 .... 6 E3
Darell Primary School
RCH/KEW TW9 .... 18 D5
Darley Dene Infant School
ADL/WDHM KT15 .... 58 F4
Darrick Wood Primary School
ORP BR6 .... 71 L3
Darrick Wood School
ORP BR6 .... 71 L2
Darrick Wood Sports Centre
ORP BR6 .... 71 M2
Darrick Wood Swimming Pool
ORP BR6 .... 71 L2
Darwin Centre
BH/WHM TN16 .... 91 J6
David Livingstone Primary School
THHTH CR7 .... 49 M1
Davidson Primary School
CROY/NA CR0 .... 3 J1
Dawnay County Primary School
GT/LBKH KT23 .... 101 K7
Denbies Wine Estate
RDKG RH5 .... 122 E6
Denmead School
HPTN TW12 .... 25 K8
Desmond Anderson Primary School
CRAWE RH10 .... 164 F8
De Stafford College
CTHM CR3 .... 108 C3
Deutsche Schule
RCHPK/HAM TW10 .... 27 G2
Devonshire Primary School
BELMT SM2 .... 65 M6
Diana Fountain
E/WMO/HCT KT8 .... 44 C2
Dockwell's Industrial Estate
EBED/NFELT TW14 .... 15 L7
Donhead (Wimbledon College Preparatory School)
WIM/MER SW19 .... 29 G8
Donyngs Recreation Centre
REDH RH1 .... 126 B7
Doods Brow School
REDH RH1 .... 127 J7
Dorchester Primary School
WPK KT4 .... 46 F8
The Dorking Business Park
DORK RH4 .... 144 D1
Dorking Cemetery
DORK RH4 .... 122 F8
Dorking FC (Meadowbank)
DORK RH4 .... 144 D1
Dorking General Hospital
DORK RH4 .... 144 D3
Dorking Golf Club
RDKG RH5 .... 144 F3
Dorking Halls
DORK RH4 .... 144 F1
Dorking Lawn Tennis & Squash Club
DORK RH4 .... 144 D4
Dorking Museum
DORK RH4 .... 144 D2
Dorking RFC
BRKHM/BTCW RH3 .... 123 L8
Dorking Swimming & Sports Centre
DORK RH4 .... 144 F1
Dormansland Primary School
LING RH7 .... 179 J8
Douglas Bader Foundation
PUT/ROE SW15 .... 19 K8
Dovers Green School
REIG RH2 .... 147 M4
Downe Primary School
ORP BR6 .... 91 K1

Down House
ORP BR6 .... 91 K2
Downsend School -Ashtead Lodge
ASHTD KT21 .... 83 H8
Downsend School Epsom Lodge
EW KT17 .... 84 C3
Downsend School Leatherhead Lodge
LHD/OX KT22 .... 102 F2
Downshire Golf Complex
EWKG RG40 .... 34 A7
Downsview Primary School
NRWD SE19 .... 31 M8
Downs Way County Primary School
OXTED RH8 .... 130 B1
Drayton House School
GU GU1 .... 7 M6
Drift Golf Club
EHSLY KT24 .... 100 B5
Driving Test Centre
CRAWW RH11 .... 164 F5
Ducks Infant School
DUL SE21 .... 32 C4
Duke of Kent School
CRAN GU6 .... 171 J1
Dulwich College
DUL SE21 .... 32 B2
Dulwich College Preparatory School
DUL SE21 .... 32 B4
Dulwich College Track
DUL SE21 .... 32 B3
Dulwich Picture Gallery
DUL SE21 .... 32 A1
Dulwich & Sydenham Hill Golf Club
DUL SE21 .... 32 D3
Dundonald Primary School
WIM/MER SW19 .... 29 J8
Dunnings Squash Club
EGRIN RH19 .... 162 F7
Dunottar School
REIG RH2 .... 148 A1
Dunraven School & Upper School
STRHM/NOR SW16 .... 31 J4
Dunsfold Aerodrome
CRAN GU6 .... 185 N8
Duppas Junior School
CROY/NA CR0 .... 67 L4
Dysart School
KUTN/CMB KT2 .... 27 G5
SURB KT6 .... 45 H7
Eagle Trading Estate
MTCM CR4 .... 48 C6
Eardley Primary School
STRHM/NOR SW16 .... 30 F7
Earlsfield Primary School
WAND/EARL SW18 .... 29 M3
Earlswood Infant School
REDH RH1 .... 148 D1
East Court
EGRIN RH19 .... 163 G3
Eastern Business Centre
BRAK RG12 .... 35 G2
Eastern Business Park
HTHAIR TW6 .... 15 J4
East Grinstead Health Clinic
EGRIN RH19 .... 162 F3
East Grinstead Sports Club
EGRIN RH19 .... 162 D8
Easthampstead Park Crematorium
EWKG RG40 .... 34 A8
Easthampstead Park School
BRAK RG12 .... 34 A6
East Horsley Camping & Caravan Club
EHSLY KT24 .... 99 J3
East Molesey CC
E/WMO/HCT KT8 .... 43 M3
East Sheen Cemetery
RCHPK/HAM TW10 .... 18 D7
East Sheen Primary School
MORT/ESHN SW14 .... 19 H4
East Surrey College
REDH RH1 .... 126 D4
East Surrey Hospital
REDH RH1 .... 148 E4
East Surrey Museum
CTHM CR3 .... 108 C6
Eastwick Infant School
GT/LBKH KT23 .... 101 L6
Eastwick Junior School
GT/LBKH KT23 .... 101 L6
Ebbisham County Infants School
EPSOM KT18 .... 83 M4
Ebbisham Sports Club
HOR/WEW KT19 .... 83 M2
Ecclesbourne Primary School
THHTH CR7 .... 49 N5
Echelford Primary School
ASHF TW15 .... 23 L6
Eclipse Estate
HOR/WEW KT19 .... 83 M3
Edenbridge & District War Memorial Hospital
EDEN TN8 .... 179 R2
Edenbridge Golf & Country Club
EDEN TN8 .... 153 K7
Edenbridge Leisure Centre
EDEN TN8 .... 153 M7
The Edenbridge Medical Centre
EDEN TN8 .... 153 M7
Edenbridge Primary School
EDEN TN8 .... 153 M8
Edenham High School
CROY/NA CR0 .... 51 N7
Edenvale Child Health Clinic
MTCM CR4 .... 30 D8
Eden Walk Shopping Centre
KUT/HW KT1 .... 8 E7
Edes Business Park
WLGTN SM6 .... 66 D1
Edgeborough School
RFNM GU10 .... 155 M6

The Edge Sports Centre
HASM GU27 .... 197 Q5
Edward Pauling School
FELT TW13 .... 24 B3
Eelmoor Road Depot Trading Estate
FARN GU14 .... 92 D7
Effingham Community Sports Centre
EHSLY KT24 .... 121 H1
Effingham CC
EHSLY KT24 .... 100 E6
Effingham Golf Club
EHSLY KT24 .... 121 G2
Effingham Park Golf Club
CRAWE RH10 .... 193 L1
Egham Business Village
EGH TW20 .... 39 M2
Egham CC
EGH TW20 .... 21 L7
Egham Sports Centre
EGH TW20 .... 21 L7
Egham Town FC
EGH TW20 .... 21 M7
Electrical Trades Union College
ESH/CLAY KT10 .... 61 K3
The Electric Theatre
GU GU1 .... 6 F6
Elfrida Primary School
CAT SE6 .... 33 L5
Eliot Bank Primary School
FSTH SE23 .... 32 E3
Elizabeth Barracks
CHOB/PIR GU24 .... 94 D3
The Elizabeth Johnson Organisation
LIPH GU30 .... 196 C5
Ellingham Primary School
CHSGTN KT9 .... 63 G6
Elliott Industrial Park
ASHV GU12 .... 113 H7
Elliott School
PUT/ROE SW15 .... 19 M8
Elmbridge Leisure Centre
WOT/HER KT12 .... 42 E5
Elmbridge Museum
WEY KT13 .... 59 K3
Elm Court School
WNWD SE27 .... 31 L3
Elm House Business Centre
MFD/CHID GU8 .... 158 C5
Elmhurst School
SAND/SEL CR2 .... 68 A3
The Elmsleigh Centre Shopping Precinct
STA TW18 .... 22 C5
Elmwood J & I School
CROY/NA CR0 .... 2 B1
Elm Wood Primary School
DUL SE21 .... 32 A4
Embassy of the Holy See
WIM/MER SW19 .... 28 F4
Emberhurst School
ESH/CLAY KT10 .... 44 A7
Ember Sports Club
ESH/CLAY KT10 .... 43 M8
Emerson College
FROW RH18 .... 195 Q10
Englefield Green Infant School
EGH TW20 .... 20 F6
Ensham Secondary School
TOOT SW17 .... 30 C6
Enterprise Industrial Estate
ASHV GU12 .... 113 J2
Epsom Bowls
EPSOM KT18 .... 84 B4
Epsom Business Park
EW KT17 .... 84 B1
Epsom Cemetery
EPSOM KT18 .... 84 B6
Epsom College
EW KT17 .... 84 D4
Epsom County & Magistrates Court
EPSOM KT18 .... 84 A3
Epsom Downs Racecourse
EPSOM KT18 .... 84 C7
Epsom & Ewell High School
HOR/WEW KT19 .... 63 M5
Epsom General Hospital
EPSOM KT18 .... 83 M5
Epsom Golf Club
EW KT17 .... 84 D5
Epsom Health Clinic
EPSOM KT18 .... 84 B3
Epsom Primary School
HOR/WEW KT19 .... 84 A1
Epsom Sports Club
EPSOM KT18 .... 84 A5
Ernest Bevin College
TOOT SW17 .... 30 B4
Esher CE High School
ESH/CLAY KT10 .... 61 K2
Esher Church Primary School
ESH/CLAY KT10 .... 61 M5
Esher College
THDIT KT7 .... 44 B7
Esher RFC
WOT/HER KT12 .... 61 H1
Essendene Lodge School
CTHM CR3 .... 108 C4
Estcots County Primary School
EGRIN RH19 .... 163 H4
Eversley Medical Centre
CROY/NA CR0 .... 49 K6
Evolution House
RCH/KEW TW9 .... 18 B4
Ewell Athletics Track
HOR/WEW KT19 .... 64 A5
Ewell Castle Junior School
EW KT17 .... 64 C7
Ewell Castle School
EW KT17 .... 64 D7
Ewell Grove Infant School
EW KT17 .... 64 C7
Ewhurst CE Infant School
CRAN GU6 .... 171 J12
Express by Holiday Inn
CROY/NA CR0 .... 2 C6
Fairchildes Primary School
CROY/NA CR0 .... 90 B2

Fairfax Industrial Estate
ASHV GU12 .... 113 H1
Fairfield Medical Centre
GT/LBKH KT23 .... 101 L8
Fairfield Trade Park
KUT/HW KT1 .... 9 H9
Fairholme Primary School
EBED/NFELT TW14 .... 24 A2
Fairlawn Primary School
FSTH SE23 .... 32 F1
Fairoaks Airport
CHOB/PIR GU24 .... 77 J1
Fairview Industrial Estate
OXTED RH8 .... 130 D7
Fairview Medical Centre
STRHM/NOR SW16 .... 49 H1
Falcon Hotel
FARN GU14 .... 92 F8
Farleigh Court Golf Club
WARL CR6 .... 89 L7
Farleigh Primary School
WARL CR6 .... 89 G7
Farleigh Rovers FC
WARL CR6 .... 89 J6
Farlington School
HORS RH12 .... 204 C3
Farnborough Aerospace
Centre
FARN GU14 .... 112 C1
Farnborough Airport
FARN GU14 .... 92 C8
Farnborough Business Centre
FARN GU14 .... 92 C7
Farnborough College of
Technology
FARN GU14 .... 92 F7
FARN GU14 .... 112 E1
Farnborough Gate Retail Park
FARN GU14 .... 92 F2
Farnborough Grange Infants
School
FARN GU14 .... 92 D1
Farnborough Hill School
FARN GU14 .... 92 F3
Farnborough Recreation Centre
FARN GU14 .... 92 E6
Farnborough RFC
FARN GU14 .... 92 D3
Farnborough Town FC
FARN GU14 .... 92 D1
Farncombe CC
RGODL GU7 .... 168 C2
Farncombe CE Infant School
RGODL GU7 .... 168 B2
Farnell House Medical Centre
HSLW TW3 .... 16 E3
Farnham Business Centre
FNM GU9 .... 5 K2
Farnham Business Park
FNM GU9 .... 4 F7
Farnham Castle Keep
FNM GU9 .... 5 G1
Farnham College
FNM GU9 .... 5 K6
Farnham Golf Club
RFNM GU10 .... 135 G7
Farnham Health Centre
FNM GU9 .... 5 J2
Farnham Heath End School
FNM GU9 .... 134 B3
Farnham Hospital
FNM GU9 .... 134 B6
Farnham House Hotel
RFNM GU10 .... 154 F1
Farnham Museum
FNM GU9 .... 5 G4
Farnham Park Golf Club
FNM GU9 .... 133 L5
Farnham Retail Park
FNM GU9 .... 134 B6
Farnham Road Hospital
GUW GU2 .... 6 D7
Farnham Sports Centre
FNM GU9 .... 5 K3
Farnham Trading Estate
FNM GU9 .... 134 C2
Faygate Business Centre
HORS RH12 .... 190 C12
Felbridge Primary School
EGRIN RH19 .... 162 A1
Felnex Trading Estate
WLGTN SM6 .... 66 B1
Feltham Airparcs Leisure Centre
FELT TW13 .... 25 G3
Feltham Athletics Arena
EBED/NFELT TW14 .... 24 D1
Felthambrook Industrial Estate
FELT TW13 .... 24 E4
Feltham Community College
FELT TW13 .... 24 F3
Feltham Hill Infant School
FELT TW13 .... 24 C4
Feltham Hill Junior School
FELT TW13 .... 24 C4
Feltham & Hounslow
Borough FC
EBED/NFELT TW14 .... 24 D1
Feltham Superbowl
FELT TW13 .... 24 E3
Feltonfleet School
COB KT11 .... 80 B3
Fenstanton J & I School
BRXS/STRHM SW2 .... 31 K2
Fernhill Primary School
FARN GU14 .... 72 C8
Fernhill School
FARN GU14 .... 72 C8
Fetcham Social & Sports Club
LHD/OX KT22 .... 102 B3
Fetcham Village Infant School
LHD/OX KT22 .... 102 A4
Film House Cinema
RCH/KEW TW9 .... 18 A7
Finton House School
TOOT SW17 .... 30 C3
Fircroft Primary School
TOOT SW17 .... 30 C3
First Quarter Business Park
HOR/WEW KT19 .... 84 B1
Fishing Club House
FROW RH18 .... 195 J10

Five Ways Business Centre
FELT TW13 .... 24 E4
Folly Hill Infant School
FNM GU9 .... 133 K3
Follys End Christian High School
SNWD SE25 .... 50 B6
Fonthill Lodge School
EGRIN RH19 .... 162 D7
Fontigarry Farm Business Park
REIG RH2 .... 175 M1
The Foot Clinic
WIM/MER SW19 .... 29 H7
The Foot Health Centre
COUL/CHIP CR5 .... 87 G5
Fordbridge Medical Centre
ASHF TW15 .... 23 J5
Fordwater Trading Estate
CHERT KT16 .... 40 F8
Forestdale Primary School
CROY/NA CR0 .... 69 H7
Forest End Medical Centre
BRAK RG12 .... 34 E6
Foresters Primary School
WLGTN SM6 .... 67 G5
Forest Hill Business Centre
FSTH SE23 .... 32 F3
Forest Hill Industrial Estate
FSTH SE23 .... 32 F3
Forest Hill Pools
SYD SE26 .... 32 F3
Forest Hill School
FSTH SE23 .... 33 G4
Forest Row Business Park
FROW RH18 .... 195 N10
Forest Row CE Infant School
FROW RH18 .... 195 N11
Forest Row CE Primary School
FROW RH18 .... 195 N11
The Forest School
SWTR RH13 .... 167 J8
Forge Lane Primary School
FELT TW13 .... 25 H7
Forge Wood Industrial Estate
CRAWE RH10 .... 192 A3
Foxbridge Golf Club
BIL RH14 .... 201 M8
Fox Hill Primary School
BRAK RG12 .... 34 E5
Foxhills Club & Resort
CHERT KT16 .... 57 J3
Franciscan Primary School
TOOT SW17 .... 30 D5
Franklin Industrial Estate
PGE/AN SE20 .... 50 F1
Freehold Industrial Estate
HSLWW TW4 .... 15 M7
Freemantles School
REIG RH2 .... 40 B7
Frensham Common &
Country Park
RFNM GU10 .... 181 K3
Frensham Heights School
RFNM GU10 .... 155 K7
Frensham Pond Hotel
RFNM GU10 .... 180 H5
Frensham Pond Sailing Club
RFNM GU10 .... 180 H4
The Friary Centre
GU GU1 .... 6 F6
Frimley Business Park
FARN GU14 .... 92 E1
Frimley CE Junior School
FRIM GU16 .... 93 H2
Frimley Green Medical Centre
FRIM GU16 .... 93 J3
Frimley Park Hospital
CBLY GU15 .... 73 G7
Fulham FC (Craven Cottage)
PUT/ROE SW15 .... 19 M3
Fullbrook School
ADL/WDHM KT15 .... 78 D1
Fuller Smith & Turner Sports
Club
CHSWK W4 .... 19 H3
Fulwell Golf Club
HPTN TW12 .... 26 A5
Furzedown Primary School
TOOT SW17 .... 30 E7
Furzefield Primary School
REDH RH1 .... 127 G2
Gaflac Sports Ground Pavilion
SUN TW16 .... 42 D1
Gardener Industrial Estate
SYD SE26 .... 33 H6
Garden Primary School
MTCM CR4 .... 49 G3
Garfield Primary School
WIM/MER SW19 .... 29 M7
Garratt Park Secondary
Special School
WAND/EARL SW18 .... 29 L4
Garth Hill College
BNFD RG42 .... 34 F1
Garth Primary School
MRDN SM4 .... 48 A5
The Garth Road Industrial
Centre
MRDN SM4 .... 46 F7
Gateway Business Centre
SYD SE26 .... 33 H7
Gatton Manor Hotel Golf &
Country Club
RDKG RH5 .... 188 A3
Gatton Park Business Centre
REDH RH1 .... 126 E4
Gatton School
TOOT SW17 .... 30 B5
Gatwick Airport
HORL RH6 .... 160 C7
Gatwick Gate Industrial Estate
HORL RH6 .... 175 P12
Gatwick Industrial Estate
HORL RH6 .... 175 J11
Gatwick Manor Golf Club
CRAWE RH10 .... 191 P2
Gatwick Medical Centre
HORL RH6 .... 160 E7
Gatwick Moat House Hotel
HORL RH6 .... 160 B5
Gatwick Park Hospital
HORL RH6 .... 160 B4

Gatwick Worth Hotel
HORL RH10 .... 192 E6
Genesis Business Centre
SUT SM1 .... 167 J6
Genesis Business Park
WOKN/KNAP GU21 .... 11 L1
George Abbot School
GU GU1 .... 117 K6
Georgian House Hotel
HORS RH12 .... 198 E6
Gilbert Scott Primary School
SAND/SEL CR2 .... 69 H6
Glebelands School
CRAN GU6 .... 186 C2
Glenesk School
EHSLY KT24 .... 100 A7
Glenlyn Medical Centre
E/WMO/HCT KT8 .... 43 M5
Glenthorne High School
CHEAM SM3 .... 47 K8
Glyn Technology School
EW KT17 .... 84 C1
Goal Farm Golf Club
CHOB/PIR GU24 .... 95 G3
The Godalming Badminton Club
RGODL GU7 .... 168 A7
Godalming Business Centre
RGODL GU7 .... 168 C5
Godalming College
RGODL GU7 .... 168 A7
Godalming County Junior
School
RGODL GU7 .... 168 C4
Godalming & Guildford FC
RGODL GU7 .... 168 D3
Godalming Leisure Centre
RGODL GU7 .... 168 D2
Godalming Museum
RGODL GU7 .... 168 A5
Godstone Farm
GDST RH9 .... 128 F7
Godstone Village School
GDST RH9 .... 128 E6
Goldsworth CP School
WOKN/KNAP GU21 .... 76 F8
Goldsworth Park Health Centre
WOKN/KNAP GU21 .... 76 D7
Goldsworth Park Trading Estate
WOKN/KNAP GU21 .... 76 D6
Goldsworth Road Industrial
Estate
WOKN/KNAP GU21 .... 10 A6
Golf Driving Range
REDH RH1 .... 148 D3
Gonville Primary School
THHTH CR7 .... 49 J5
Good Shepherd RC Primary
School
CROY/NA CR0 .... 69 L6
Gordons School
CHOB/PIR GU24 .... 75 H2
Gorringe Park Primary School
MTCM CR4 .... 48 D1
Gosbury Hill Health Centre
CHSGTN KT9 .... 63 H3
Gosden House School
SHGR GU5 .... 168 H1
Gossops Green Clinic
CRAWW RH11 .... 164 B6
Gossops Green Community
Primary School
CRAWW RH11 .... 164 C5
Grace Business Centre
MTCM CR4 .... 48 C6
Grafham Grange School
SHGR GU5 .... 169 L9
Granard Primary School
PUT/ROE SW15 .... 19 L8
Grand Avenue Primary School
BRYLDS KT5 .... 45 M7
The Grange Community Infant
School
ADL/WDHM KT15 .... 58 C8
Grange Community Junior
School
FARN GU14 .... 92 C1
The Grange Hotel
BRAK RG12 .... 34 F2
Granton Primary School
STRHM/NOR SW16 .... 30 F8
Grasshoppers RFC
ISLW TW7 .... 17 J1
Grassroots School
HPTN TW12 .... 43 K1
Graveney School
TOOT SW17 .... 30 E7
Grayshott CE Primary School
GSHT GU26 .... 197 N2
Grayshott Clinic
GSHT GU26 .... 197 N1
Grayswood CE Aided Infant
School
HASM GU27 .... 198 G3
Great Bookham County
Infant School
GT/LBKH KT23 .... 101 K8
Great Hollands Health Centre
BRAK RG12 .... 34 C6
Great Hollands Primary School
BRAK RG12 .... 34 B5
Great Hollands Recreation
Centre
EWKG RG40 .... 34 B8
Great West Trading Estate
BTFD TW8 .... 17 L1
Greenacre School for Girls
BNSTD SM7 .... 85 M3
Green Business Centre
ECH TW20 .... 21 M5
Green Field Effective Education
EGRIN RH19 .... 162 E4
Greenfield School
WOKS/MYFD GU22 .... 10 C9
Greenfields School
FROW RH18 .... 195 K12
Green Lane Primary School
WPK KT4 .... 46 E7
Greenmead Primary School
PUT/ROE SW15 .... 19 L7
The Green School for Girls
ISLW TW7 .... 17 K2

Greenshaw High School
SUT SM1 .... 65 M1
Greenvale Primary School
SAND/SEL CR2 .... 89 G1
Greenvale School
FSTH SE23 .... 33 H4
Greenway School
HORS RH12 .... 166 E6
Green Wrythe Primary School
CAR SM5 .... 48 A6
Gresham Industrial Estate
ASHV GU12 .... 113 H7
Gresham Primary School
SAND/SEL CR2 .... 88 C2
Gresham Way Industrial Estate
WIM/MER SW19 .... 29 L4
Greville Primary School
ASHTD KT21 .... 83 J7
Grey Court School
RCHPK/HAM TW10 .... 27 G4
Grist Memorial Sports Club
E/WMO/HCT KT8 .... 44 B5
Grovebell Industrial Estate
FNM GU9 .... 4 C9
Grove County Primary School
FRIM GU16 .... 73 H7
Grove House (Froebel College)
PUT/ROE SW15 .... 19 J8
Grove House Primary School
for Deaf Children
WNWD SE27 .... 31 L3
Grovelands School
WOT/HER KT12 .... 42 E6
Grove Park Primary School
CHSWK W4 .... 18 F1
Grove Road Primary School
HSLW TW3 .... 16 D6
The Groves Medical Centre
NWMAL KT3 .... 46 B3
Grove Village Medical Centre
EBED/NFELT TW14 .... 24 B2
Guards Polo Club
EGH TW20 .... 38 A1
Guildford Business Park
GUW GU2 .... 6 C2
Guildford Castle
GU GU1 .... 7 H7
Guildford Cathedral
GUW GU2 .... 6 C4
Guildford College
(Merrist Wood Campus)
RGUW GU3 .... 115 M2
Guildford College
(Stoke Park Campus)
GU GU1 .... 7 H2
Guildford County School
GU GU1 .... 6 D7
Guildford Crematorium
RGODL GU7 .... 168 E1
Guildford Cricket Ground
(Surrey CCC)
GU GU1 .... 6 F3
Guildford Discovery
GU GU1 .... 7 H6
Guildford Golf Club
GU GU1 .... 117 M8
Guildford Grove Primary School
GUW GU2 .... 116 B8
Guildford High School
GU GU1 .... 7 J4
Guildford Hockey & CC
GU GU1 .... 6 F4
Guildford House Gallery
GU GU1 .... 7 H7
Guildford Industrial Estate
GUW GU2 .... 6 A2
Guildford Lido
GU GU1 .... 7 H1
Guildford Museum
GU GU1 .... 7 G7
Guildford Natural Health
Centre
GU GU1 .... 7 G7
The Guildford Nuffield
Hospital
GUW GU2 .... 116 B8
Guildford Road Industrial
Estate
FNM GU9 .... 5 M1
Guildford Rowing Club
GU GU1 .... 7 G9
Guildford Spectrum
GU GU1 .... 7 K1
Guildford Spectrum Athletics
Stadium
GU GU1 .... 117 H6
Gumley House Convent School
ISLW TW7 .... 17 K5
Hackbridge Primary School
WLGTN SM6 .... 48 D8
Hale Primary School
FNM GU9 .... 133 L2
Haling Manor High School
SAND/SEL CR2 .... 67 L6
Hall Grove Farm Industrial
Estate
BAGS GU19 .... 54 C4
Hall Grove School
BAGS GU19 .... 54 D4
Halliford Health Clinic
SHPTN TW17 .... 42 B4
Halliford School
SHPTN TW17 .... 41 M7
Hall South Wimbledon
RYNPK SW20 .... 47 G1
Hall South Wimbledon Junior
Department
PUT/ROE SW15 .... 28 D4
Halsford Park Primary School
EGRIN RH19 .... 162 C4
Halstead Preparatory School
WOKN/KNAP GU21 .... 11 G1
Ham Health Clinic
RCHPK/HAM TW10 .... 26 F4
Ham House (NT)
RCHPK/HAM TW10 .... 26 F2
Hamilton Road Industrial
Estate
WNWD SE27 .... 32 A5
Hammersmith Industrial Estate
HMSMTH W6 .... 19 M1

Hammersmith New Cemetery
RCH/KEW TW9 .... 18 E4
Hammerwood Park
EGRIN RH19 .... 195 R3
Hammond Junior School
LTWR GU18 .... 54 D8
Ham & Petersham CC
RCHPK/HAM TW10 .... 27 G5
Hampton Cemetery
HPTN TW12 .... 25 K8
Hampton Community College
HPTN TW12 .... 25 K6
Hampton Court House School
E/WMO/HCT KT8 .... 44 B2
Hampton Court Palace
E/WMO/HCT KT8 .... 44 C3
Hampton Court Palace Golf Club
SURB KT6 .... 44 F5
Hampton Farm Industrial Estate
FELT TW13 .... 25 H4
Hampton FC
HPTN TW12 .... 43 L1
Hampton Hill Junior School
HPTN TW12 .... 25 M6
Hampton Infant School
HPTN TW12 .... 25 J8
Hampton Junior School
HPTN TW12 .... 43 K1
The Hampton Medical Centre
HPTN TW12 .... 25 K8
Hampton Open Air Pool
HPTN TW12 .... 25 M8
Hampton Road Industrial Park
CROY/NA CR0 .... 49 M6
Hampton School
HPTN TW12 .... 25 K6
Hampton Wick Infant School
KUT/HW KT1 .... 8 B3
Hamsey Green Infant School
WARL CR6 .... 88 E6
Hamsey Green Junior School
WARL CR6 .... 88 E6
Hankley Common Golf Club
RFNM GU10 .... 157 G8
Hanworth Business Park
CHERT KT16 .... 40 C8
Hanworth Trading Estate
FELT TW13 .... 25 H4
Harmans Water J & I School
BRAK RG12 .... 35 H5
Harris City Technology College
NRWD SE19 .... 50 C1
Harrodian School
BARN SW13 .... 19 J2
Harven School of English
WOKS/MYFD GU22 .... 11 G6
Haseltine Primary School
SYD SE26 .... 33 J5
Haslemere Hall
HASM GU27 .... 198 D6
Haslemere Hospital & Health
Centre
HASM GU27 .... 198 E6
Haslemere Industrial Estate
EBED/NFELT TW14 .... 15 K7
WAND/EARL SW18 .... 29 L3
Haslemere Museum
HASM GU27 .... 198 E6
Haslemere Primary School
MTCM CR4 .... 48 A2
Hatchlands Park (NT)
RGUE GU4 .... 119 J4
Hatfield Primary School
MRDN SM4 .... 47 H6
Havenbury Industrial Estate
DORK RH4 .... 144 D1
Hawes Down Clinic
WWKM BR4 .... 70 A1
Hawkedale GM School
SUN TW16 .... 42 C3
The Hawker Centre
KUTN/CMB KT2 .... 27 G6
Hawkins Clinic
EW KT17 .... 84 F5
RYNPK SW20 .... 46 C1
Hawley CP School
BLKW GU17 .... 72 B6
Hawley Lane Industrial Estate
FARN GU14 .... 92 E1
Hawley Place School
BLKW GU17 .... 72 B8
The Hawthorns School
REDH RH1 .... 127 L5
The Hawth Theatre, Cinema &
Conference Complex
CRAWE RH10 .... 165 H5
Hayes Grove Priory Hospital
HAYES BR2 .... 70 D1
The Hayes Primary School
PUR/KEN CR8 .... 87 L6
Hayes School
HAYES BR2 .... 70 E1
Haysbridge Business Centre
GDST RH9 .... 177 P3
Hazelwick School
CRAWE RH10 .... 165 J2
Hazelwood School
OXTED RH8 .... 130 D5
Headley Park Country Club
BOR GU35 .... 180 C8
Headstart Montessori School
TOOT SW17 .... 29 M4
Heath Business Centre
HSLW TW3 .... 16 F6
REDH RH1 .... 176 A2
Heathcote Medical Centre
KWD/TDW/WH KT20 .... 105 G4
Heathermount the Learning
Centre
ASC SL5 .... 37 G6
Heather Ridge County Infant
School
CBLY GU15 .... 74 A5
Heatherwood Hospital
ASC SL5 .... 36 B3
Heathfield College
HAYES BR2 .... 70 F5
Heathfield Primary School
WHTN TW2 .... 25 K2
Heathfield School
ASC SL5 .... 35 L2

The Heathland School
HSLWW TW4 .... 16 C8
Heathmere Primary School
PUT/ROE SW15 .... 28 D2
Heathrow Airport
HTHAIR TW6 .... 14 E4
Heathrow Airport Central Bus
& Coach Station
HTHAIR TW6 .... 14 D5
Heathrow International
Trading Estate
HSLWW TW4 .... 15 D3
Heathrow Primary School
WDR/YW UB7 .... 14 C1
Heathrow Terminal 5
(under construction)
HTHAIR TW6 .... 13 M5
Heathrow World Cargo Centre
HTHAIR TW6 .... 14 C7
Heathside School
WEY KT13 .... 59 J4
Heavers Farm Primary School
SNWD SE25 .... 50 C5
Helix Business Park
CBLY GU15 .... 72 E6
Helston Court Business Centre
WIM/MER SW19 .... 28 E6
Henderson Hospital
BELMT SM2 .... 65 K7
Henry Cavendish Primary School
BAL SW12 .... 30 F2
Henry Tyndale School
FARN GU14 .... 92 F3
Hermitage County First School
WOKN/KNAP GU21 .... 96 B1
The Hermitage School
WOKN/KNAP GU21 .... 96 B1
The Herons Swimming &
Fitness Centre
HASM GU27 .... 198 A6
Heron Way Primary School
SWTR RH13 .... 167 K8
Hersham Trading Estate
WOT/HER KT12 .... 61 H1
Heston Community School
HEST TW5 .... 16 D2
Heston Community Sports Hall
HEST TW5 .... 16 D2
Heston Industrial Mall
HEST TW5 .... 16 C2
Heston Infant School
HEST TW5 .... 16 D2
Heston Junior School
HEST TW5 .... 16 D1
Heston Park CC
HEST TW5 .... 16 C1
Heston Swimming Baths
HEST TW5 .... 16 C1
Hewitts Industrial Estate
CRAN GU6 .... 186 A2
Highclere Hotel
ASC SL5 .... 37 C5
High Elms Country Park
ORP BR6 .... 71 M6
High Elms Golf Club
ORP BR6 .... 71 M6
Highfield School
LIPH GU30 .... 197 K11
WAND/EARL SW18 .... 30 B1
Highview Primary School
WLCTN SM6 .... 67 H4
Hillbrook Primary School
TOOT SW17 .... 30 C5
Hillcrest School
SWTR RH13 .... 203 P5
Hillcroft College
SURB KT6 .... 45 H6
Hillcroft Primary School
CTHM CR3 .... 108 B5
Hillcross Primary School
MRDN SM4 .... 47 J4
Hill's Cemetery
HORS RH12 .... 166 C7
Hill School
BH/WHM TN16 .... 111 L5
Hilltop Primary School
CRAWW RH11 .... 164 E6
Hinchley Wood Primary School
ESH/CLAY KT10 .... 62 D1
Hinchley Wood School &
Sixth Form Centre
ESH/CLAY KT10 .... 62 D1
The Hindhead Golf Club
GSHT GU26 .... 181 N11
Hitherfield Primary School
STRHM/NOR SW16 .... 31 K3
HM Customs
HTHAIR TW6 .... 14 E4
HM Prison
CHOB/PIR GU24 .... 75 J7
RPLY/SEND GU23 .... 118 F1
WAND/EARL SW18 .... 30 A1
BELMT SM2 .... 85 M2
HM Young Offender
Institution
FELT TW13 .... 24 K4
Hobbs Industrial Estate
LING RH7 .... 177 Q10
Hockley Industrial Centre
REDH RH1 .... 148 C1
Hoebridge Golf Centre
WOKS/MYFD GU22 .... 11 L9
Hoe Bridge Pre Preparatory
School
WOKS/MYFD GU22 .... 97 L1
Hogan Business Centre
WOKN/KNAP GU21 .... 10 C6
Hogarth Business Park
CHSWK W4 .... 19 H1
Hogarth's House
CHSWK W4 .... 19 G1
Hogs Back Brewery
RFNM GU10 .... 135 J4
Holbeach Primary School
CAT SE6 .... 33 K1
Holbrook Primary School
HORS RH12 .... 167 G2
Holbrook Recreation Centre
HORS RH12 .... 167 H2
Hollybush Business Centre
HORL RH6 .... 192 E1

Hollybush Industrial Park
ALDT GU11 .... 113 H4
The Hollyfield School
SURB KT6 .... 45 H5
Holly Lodge Primary School
ASHV GU12 .... 113 J1
Hollymount Primary School
RYNPK SW20 .... 46 F1
Holly Spring Infant School
BRAK RG12 .... 35 H2
Hollywood Bowl
CRAWE RH10 .... 164 F3
The Holme Primary School
BOR GU35 .... 180 C11
Holmesdale School
REIG RH2 .... 125 L6
Holmethorpe Industrial
Estate
REDH RH1 .... 126 E5
Holy Cross Hospital
HASM GU27 .... 198 A6
Holy Cross Preparatory School
KUTN/CMB KT2 .... 27 M8
Holy Cross RC Convent School
NWMAL KT3 .... 46 A4
Holy Cross RC Primary School
CAT SE6 .... 33 M2
Holy Family RC Primary School
ADL/WDHM KT15 .... 58 D4
Holy Ghost RC Primary School
BAL SW12 .... 30 C1
Holy Trinity CE Junior School
GU GU1 .... 7 M7
WLGTN SM6 .... 66 F3
Holy Trinity CE Primary School
ASC SL5 .... 37 K6
BRXS/STRHM SW2 .... 31 J1
CHOB/PIR GU24 .... 75 K2
RCHPK/HAM TW10 .... 18 D6
SYD SE26 .... 32 F3
The Holy Trinity CE School
CRAWW RH11 .... 164 C6
Holy Trinity Primary School
WIM/MER SW19 .... 29 K7
Homefield Preparatory School
SUT SM1 .... 65 K4
Hones Yard Business Park
FNM GU9 .... 5 L4
Hook Rise South Industrial Park
CHSGTN KT9 .... 63 J2
The Hop Kiln
FNM GU9 .... 5 H6
Horley Anderson Centre
HORL RH6 .... 160 B3
Horley Health Centre
HORL RH6 .... 160 D3
Horley Infant School
HORL RH6 .... 160 D3
The Horniman Museum
& Gardens
FSTH SE23 .... 32 E2
Horniman Primary School
FSTH SE23 .... 32 E2
Hornsby House School
BAL SW12 .... 30 D2
Horsell CE Junior School
WOKN/KNAP GU21 .... 76 F6
Horsell Village County
Infant School
WOKN/KNAP GU21 .... 10 A4
Horsham Arts Centre
HORS RH12 .... 166 F7
Horsham CC & Sports Club
HORS RH12 .... 166 E8
Horsham FC
SWTR RH13 .... 167 G8
Horsham Golf & Fitness Club
SWTR RH13 .... 204 H11
Horsham Hospital
HORS RH12 .... 166 F6
Horsham Museum
HORS RH12 .... 166 F8
Horsham Trading Estate
SWTR RH13 .... 167 H5
Horsham YMCA FC
SWTR RH13 .... 167 G8
Horsley Sports Club
EHSLY KT24 .... 120 C1
Horton Country Park
HOR/WEW KT19 .... 63 K7
Horton Hospital
HOR/WEW KT19 .... 83 M1
Horton Park Golf & Country Club
HOR/WEW KT19 .... 63 M6
Horton Trading Estate
DTCH/LGLY SL3 .... 12 E5
Hoskins Place Industrial Estate
CBLY GU15 .... 72 E6
Hotel Ibis
CRAWE RH10 .... 191 P2
HYS/HAR UB3 .... 15 H3
Hounslow Business Park
HSLW TW3 .... 16 D6
Hounslow CC
HSLW TW3 .... 16 C4
Hounslow Cemetery
HSLWW TW4 .... 25 J1
Hounslow College
Independent School
FELT TW13 .... 25 G5
Hounslow Heath Golf Club
HSLWW TW4 .... 16 A7
Hounslow Heath Infant School
HSLWW TW4 .... 16 B5
Hounslow Heath Junior School
HSLWW TW4 .... 16 B5
Hounslow Manor School
HSLW TW3 .... 16 E5
Hounslow Manor Sports Hall
HSLW TW3 .... 16 E5
Hounslow Town Primary
School
HSLW TW3 .... 16 F5
Howard of Effingham School
EHSLY KT24 .... 121 G1
Howard Primary School
CROY/NA CR0 .... 67 M3
HSBC Sports Club
BECK BR3 .... 33 H7
Hubbard School
EGRIN RH19 .... 162 F4

Humphries Industrial Estate
BRAK RG12 .... 34 E4
Hurlands Business Centre
FNM GU9 .... 134 C5
Hurst Green School
OXTED RH8 .... 130 D6
Hurst Lodge School
ASC SL5 .... 36 E8
Hurst Park Primary School
E/WMO/HCT KT8 .... 43 K3
Hurtmore Golf Club
RGODL GU7 .... 159 J2
Hurtwood House
RDKG RH5 .... 171 M7
Hurtwood Inn Hotel
SHGR GU5 .... 170 H3
Hyland Business Centre
REDH RH1 .... 126 C8
Hythe First & Middle School
STA TW18 .... 22 A6
Ibstock Place School
PUT/ROE SW15 .... 19 H8
Ifield Golf & Country Club
CRAWW RH11 .... 190 G7
IKEA Store Croydon
CROY/NA CR0 .... 49 J8
Imber Court Trading Estate
E/WMO/HCT KT8 .... 44 A6
Imberhorne Business Centre
EGRIN RH19 .... 162 C2
Imberhorne School
EGRIN RH19 .... 162 C3
The Imber Sports Centre
EGRIN RH19 .... 162 E2
Immanuel CE Primary School
STRHM/NOR SW16 .... 31 H7
Imperial College Athletic
Ground
HYS/HAR UB3 .... 14 F1
Imperial College of Science
Technology & Medicine
ASC SL5 .... 37 J3
Independent Business Park
EGRIN RH19 .... 162 B2
The Industrial Estate
EDEN TN8 .... 153 L6
Ingfield Manor School
BIL RH14 .... 203 K11
Innkeeper's Lodge
BECK BR3 .... 51 K6
CBLY GU15 .... 73 J5
GODL SU7 .... 159 M6
REDH RH1 .... 126 D8
SAND/SEL CR2 .... 67 M7
WEY KT13 .... 60 B2
WOKN/KNAP GU21 .... 10 D4
WOT/HER KT12 .... 60 D2
Inwood Business Centre
HSLW TW3 .... 16 E6
The Islamic Grammar School
WAND/EARL SW18 .... 29 J1
Isleworth Cemetery
ISLW TW7 .... 17 K4
Isleworth Recreation Centre
ISLW TW7 .... 17 J6
Isleworth & Syon School for Boys
ISLW TW7 .... 17 H2
Isleworth Town Primary School
ISLW TW7 .... 17 J4
Itchingfield Primary School
SWTR RH13 .... 204 B11
Ivybridge Primary School
TWK TW1 .... 17 J8
Ivybridge Retail Park
ISLW TW7 .... 17 J7
Ivydene Industrial Estate
EGRIN RH19 .... 163 L6
Jack & Jill School
HPTN TW12 .... 25 K7
WHTN TW2 .... 26 A3
James Dixon Primary School
PGE/AN SE20 .... 50 D1
James Searle Industrial Estate
HORS RH12 .... 167 H5
Jenner Health Centre
FSTH SE23 .... 33 H2
The Jigsaw School
FRIM GU16 .... 93 H6
John Nightingale School
E/WMO/HCT KT8 .... 43 J3
John Nike Athletics Stadium
BRAK RG12 .... 34 F5
John Paul II RC School
WIM/MER SW19 .... 29 G1
John Ruskin College
SAND/SEL CR2 .... 69 H6
Joseph Hood Primary School
RYNPK SW20 .... 47 H2
Jubilee Hall Clinic
CRAWE RH10 .... 165 J4
Julians Primary School
STRHM/NOR SW16 .... 31 K5
Jurys Inn Hotel
CROY/NA CR0 .... 2 D5
HTHAIR TW6 .... 15 J5
Kangley Business Centre
SYD SE26 .... 33 J4
Kelsey Park School
BECK BR3 .... 51 K3
Kelvin Business Centre
CRAWE RH10 .... 165 H1
Kempton Park Racecourse
SUN TW16 .... 24 E8
Kendall Court Business Centre
CBLY GU15 .... 72 C5
Kenley Primary School
PUR/KEN CR8 .... 88 B6
Kenley Sports Club
PUR/KEN CR8 .... 87 M4
Kensington Avenue Primary
School
THHTH CR7 .... 49 K1
Kenyngton Manor Primary
School
SUN TW16 .... 24 D6
Keston CE Primary School
HAYES BR2 .... 71 G4
Keston Primary School
COUL/CHIP CR5 .... 107 K1
Kew College
RCH/KEW TW9 .... 18 D2

Kew Gardens
(Royal Botanic Gardens)
BTFD TW8 .... 18 B3
Kew Palace
RCH/KEW TW9 .... 18 C2
Kew Retail Park
RCH/KEW TW9 .... 18 E3
Kew Riverside Primary School
RCH/KEW TW9 .... 18 E4
Kilmorie Primary School
FSTH SE23 .... 33 H3
Kiln Park Business Centre
EW KT17 .... 84 D1
Kimpton Industrial Estate
CHEAM SM3 .... 65 J1
King Athelstan Primary School
KUT/HW KT1 .... 9 G8
King Edwards School
MFD/CHID GU8 .... 183 N8
Kingfield School
WOKS/MYFD GU22 .... 97 K2
The Kingfisher Sports Centre
KUT/HW KT1 .... 8 F7
The Kings Centre
ALDT GU11 .... 112 D7
Kings College School
WIM/MER SW19 .... 28 F7
Kings College for the Arts &
Technology
GUW GU2 .... 116 B8
Kings Court First School
WDSR SL4 .... 20 D1
Kingscroft School
STA TW18 .... 22 D7
Kingsdale School
DUL SE21 .... 32 B4
Kingsfield Business Centre
REDH RH1 .... 148 D1
Kingsgate Business Centre
KUTN/CMB KT2 .... 8 E4
Kingsgrove Industrial Estate
FARN GU14 .... 92 D6
Kings House School
RCHPK/HAM TW10 .... 18 C7
Kings International College
for Business and the Arts
CBLY GU15 .... 72 F7
Kingsley Primary School
CROY/NA CR0 .... 49 J8
Kingsmeadow Athletics Centre
KUT/HW KT1 .... 9 K9
Kingsmead Shopping Centre
FARN GU14 .... 92 E6
Kings Road Industrial Estate
HASM GU27 .... 198 B7
Kings School of English
BECK BR3 .... 51 J2
Kingston Business Centre
CHSGTN KT9 .... 63 H2
Kingston Cemetery
KUT/HW KT1 .... 9 J8
Kingston College of Further
Education
KUT/HW KT1 .... 8 D8
Kingston College Theatre
KUT/HW KT1 .... 8 D8
Kingston Crematorium
KUT/HW KT1 .... 9 J9
Kingston Crown Court
KUT/HW KT1 .... 8 D8
Kingston Grammar School
KUTN/CMB KT2 .... 9 G6
Kingston Hospital
KUTN/CMB KT2 .... 9 L4
Kingstonian FC
KUT/HW KT1 .... 9 L9
Kingstons Industrial Estate
ASHV GU12 .... 113 H7
Kingston University
BRYLDS KT5 .... 45 K5
KUT/HW KT1 .... 8 F9
KUTN/CMB KT2 .... 28 A6
KUTN/CMB KT2 .... 28 A8
PUT/ROE SW15 .... 28 C3
Kingsway Business Park
HPTN TW12 .... 43 J1
Kingswey Business Park
WOKN/KNAP GU21 .... 77 M4
Kingswood Golf Club
KWD/TDW/WH KT20 ...... 105 K6
Kingswood House School
HOR/WEW KT19 .... 83 L3
Kingswood Primary School
KWD/TDW/WH KT20 ...... 125 J2
WNWD SE27 .... 32 A5
Knaphill Junior School
WOKN/KNAP GU21 .... 75 M8
Knaphill Lower School
WOKN/KNAP GU21 .... 75 L8
Knollmead Primary School
BRYLDS KT5 .... 63 M1
Knowle Park Infant School
STA TW18 .... 22 D6
Knowl Hill School
CHOB/PIR GU24 .... 95 H4
Ladycross Business Park
LING RH7 .... 179 K10
The Lady Eleanor Holles School
HPTN TW12 .... 25 L6
Ladymead Retail Centre
GU GU1 .... 6 C1
Laine Theatre Arts
EW KT17 .... 84 B3
Laker Industrial Estate
BECK BR3 .... 33 J6
Lakeside Country Club
FRIM GU16 .... 93 K3
Lakeside Industrial Estate
DTCH/LGLY SL3 .... 13 H2
DTCH/LGLY SL3 .... 13 K1
Lakeside International Hotel
FRIM GU16 .... 93 K3
Lakeside Primary School
FRIM GU16 .... 73 J2
Laleham CE Primary School
STA TW18 .... 40 F2
Laleham Golf Club
CHERT KT16 .... 40 A7
Laleham Lea Preparatory
School
PUR/KEN CR8 .... 67 H8

Lambeth Cemetery
TOOT SW17 .... 29 M6
Lambeth College
STRHM/NOR SW16 .... 31 H3
Lambeth Crematorium
TOOT SW17 .... 29 M5
Lambs Business Park
GDST RH9 .... 150 E4
Lamont Business Centre
CROY/NA CR0 .... 49 H7
Lampton School
HSLW TW3 .... 16 D3
Langbourne Primary School
DUL SE21 .... 32 B4
Langley Green Primary School
CRAWW RH11 .... 164 E2
Langley Park Girls School
& Sports Centre
BECK BR3 .... 51 L5
Langley Park School for Boys
BECK BR3 .... 51 L6
Langshott County Infant School
HORL RH6 .... 160 F3
Langshott Manor Hotel
HORL RH6 .... 161 G1
The Lansbury Estate
WOKN/KNAP GU21 .... 76 A8
La Retraite RC Girls' School
BAL SW12 .... 30 F1
Latchmere Primary School
KUTN/CMB KT2 .... 9 G1
Lavender Park Golf Club
ASC SL5 .... 35 M3
Lawson Hunt Industrial Park
HORS RH12 .... 166 A5
Lazards Sports Club
SUN TW16 .... 42 E1
Leatherhead Business Park
LHD/OX KT22 .... 102 E1
Leatherhead Clinic
LHD/OX KT22 .... 102 F3
Leatherhead CC
LHD/OX KT22 .... 102 D4
Leatherhead FC
LHD/OX KT22 .... 102 D4
Leatherhead Golf Club
LHD/OX KT22 .... 82 D6
Leatherhead Hospital
LHD/OX KT22 .... 102 F4
Leatherhead Industrial Estate
LHD/OX KT22 .... 102 D3
Leatherhead Institute
LHD/OX KT22 .... 102 E3
Leatherhead Leisure Centre
& Water Park
LHD/OX KT22 .... 102 D5
Leatherhead Museum
LHD/OX KT22 .... 102 E4
Leechpool Lane Primary School
SWTR RH13 .... 167 K5
Leigh Close Industrial Estate
NWMAL KT3 .... 46 A4
Leith Hill Tower (NT)
RDKG RH5 .... 172 C6
Lewin Mead Community
Mental Health Centre
STRHM/NOR SW16 .... 31 G7
Lewis Clinic
CAR SM5 .... 66 D3
Liberty Middle School
MTCM CR4 .... 48 B2
The Licensed Victuallers School
ASC SL5 .... 35 M2
Lightwater Country Park
LTWR GU18 .... 54 C8
Lightwater Village School
LTWR GU18 .... 54 D8
Limes Business Centre
HORL RH6 .... 175 J11
Limpsfield CE Infant School
OXTED RH8 .... 130 D4
Limpsfield Chart Golf Club
OXTED RH8 .... 130 F3
Limpsfield Grange School
OXTED RH8 .... 130 D1
Limpsfield Lawn Tennis Club
OXTED RH8 .... 130 D2
Linden Bridge School
WPK KT4 .... 64 D2
Linden Lodge School
WIM/MER SW19 .... 29 H2
Lindon Bennett School
FELT TW13 .... 25 G6
Lingfield Notre Dame School
LING RH7 .... 178 G6
Lingfield Park Golf Club
LING RH7 .... 178 G7
Lingfield Park Racecourse
LING RH7 .... 178 G6
Lingfield Primary School
LING RH7 .... 178 E5
Lingfield Squash & Leisure Club
LING RH7 .... 178 G6
The Link Day Primary School
CROY/NA CR0 .... 67 H3
The Link Secondary School
CROY/NA CR0 .... 67 J3
Links Primary School
TOOT SW17 .... 30 D7
Linley House School
BRYLDS KT5 .... 45 J6
Linsford Business Park
FRIM GU16 .... 93 J6
Liongate Hotel
E/WMO/HCT KT8 .... 44 C3
Lion & Lamb Yard Shopping
Centre
FNM GU9 .... 5 G2
Lion Retail Park
WOKS/MYFD GU22 .... 11 J3
Liphook CE Junior School
LIPH GU30 .... 196 F9
Liphook Infant School
LIPH GU30 .... 196 F9
Little Eden & Eden High
School
FELT TW13 .... 25 G5
Littlehaven Infant School
HORS RH12 .... 167 J4
Little Mead Industrial Estate
CRAN GU6 .... 186 A2

Littleton CE Infant School SHPTN TW17 ...41 K3
Little Wandsworth School TOOT SW17 ...30 D3
Lloyds Register CC DUL SE21 ...32 A2
Lodge School PUR/KEN CR8 ...87 G2
Lombard Business Park CROY/NA CR0 ...49 J7
WIM/MER SW19 ...47 M2
London Cornish RFC PUT/ROE SW15 ...28 C4
London Irish RFC SUN TW16 ...42 D1
London Ladies & Girls FC CAT SE6 ...33 L6
London Living Theatre SYD SE26 ...33 G5
London Road Medical Centre CROY/NA CR0 ...49 K6
London Scottish Golf Club WIM/MER SW19 ...28 E4
London Temple Visitors Centre LING RH7 ...177 J10
London Welsh FC RCH/KEW TW9 ...18 B5
London Wetland Centre BARN SW13 ...19 L3
Lonesome Primary School MTCM CR4 ...48 E2
Longacre School SHGR GU5 ...169 N5
The Longcroft Clinic BNSTD SM7 ...85 M4
Long Ditton County Infant School SURB KT6 ...44 F8
Longford Community School EBED/NFELT TW14 ...24 C1
Longford Industrial Estate HPTN TW12 ...25 L7
Longley Trading Estate CRAWE RH10 ...165 J1
Longmead Business Centre HOR/WEW KT19 ...84 A3
Longmead Industrial Estate HOR/WEW KT19 ...84 A1
Longshot Industrial Estate BRAK RG12 ...34 B3
Longwood Business Park SUN TW16 ...42 C5
The Look Out Discovery Centre BRAK RG12 ...35 G8
Lorraine Infant School CBLY GU15 ...53 K8
Loseley Fields Primary School RGODL GU7 ...138 B8
Loseley Park RGUW GU3 ...138 C6
Lovelace Primary School CHSGTN KT9 ...62 F4
Lower Sydenham Industrial Estate SYD SE26 ...33 J6
Lowfield Heath Industrial Estate HORL RH6 ...175 P12
Lowther Primary School BARN SW13 ...19 K1
Loxwood Primary School BIL RH14 ...201 R5
LSE Sports Club NWMAL KT3 ...46 A6
Ludshott Common (NT) GSHT GU26 ...197 N2
Lyndhurst School CBLY GU15 ...72 E4
Lyne & Longcross CE Infant School CHERT KT16 ...57 L1
Lynton Preparatory School EW KT17 ...84 C1
Lyons Farm Estate SWTR RH13 ...204 B3
Lyon Way Industrial Estate FRIM GU16 ...72 F8
Lythe Hill Hotel & Spa HASM GU27 ...199 J8
Macdonald Bush Hotel FNM GU9 ...5 J3
Macdonald Hotel ASC SL5 ...36 F6
CBLY GU15 ...73 J3
DORK RH4 ...144 E2
RDKG RH5 ...122 F5
Macdonald Thames Lodge STA TW18 ...22 B6
The Magna Carta School EGH TW20 ...22 A7
Maidenbower First & Middle School CRAWE RH10 ...165 M6
Maidenbower Junior School CRAWE RH10 ...165 M6
Main Square Shopping Centre CBLY GU15 ...72 F3
Malcolm Primary School PGE/AN SE20 ...32 F8
The Malden Centre NWMAL KT3 ...46 C4
Malden Golf Club NWMAL KT3 ...46 B7
Malden Manor Primary School NWMAL KT3 ...46 B7
Malden Parochial Primary School WPK KT4 ...46 B8
Malden Road Baths CHEAM SM3 ...65 G3
Malham Road Industrial Estate FSTH SE23 ...33 G2
The Mall School WHTN TW2 ...26 A4
Malmesbury Primary School MRDN SM4 ...47 M7
Manby Lodge Infant School WEY KT13 ...59 L3
Manorcroft Primary School EGH TW20 ...21 K7
Manor Drive Health Centre WPK KT4 ...46 C8

Manor Farm Business Centre RFNM GU10 ...135 J3
Manorfield Primary School HORL RH6 ...160 C3
Manor Green College CRAWW RH11 ...164 C2
Manor Green Primary School CRAWW RH11 ...191 N3
Manor House Hotel ALDT GU11 ...140 E1
Manor House School GT/LBKH KT23 ...121 H1
Manor Infant School FARN GU14 ...92 C3
Manor Mead School SHPTN TW17 ...41 L5
Manor Park Industrial Estate ASHV GU12 ...112 F8
Manor Park Primary School SUT SM1 ...65 M4
The Manor School BF/WBF KT14 ...79 H4
Maple Grove Business Centre HSLWW TW4 ...15 M6
Maple House School THHTH CR7 ...49 M6
Maple Industrial Estate FELT TW13 ...24 D3
Maple Infant School SURB KT6 ...45 G5
Marble Hill House TWK TW1 ...26 F1
Marden Lodge Primary School CTHM CR3 ...108 E2
Margaret Roper Catholic Primary School PUR/KEN CR8 ...67 K8
Mariner Business Centre CROY/NA CR0 ...67 J4
Marion Vian Primary School BECK BR3 ...51 G5
The Marist Preparatory School ASC SL5 ...37 G5
The Marist RC Primary School BF/WBF KT14 ...78 C3
Marist Senior School ASC SL5 ...37 G4
The Marjory Kinnon School EBED/NFELT TW14 ...15 H7
Marlborough County Infant School ALDT GU11 ...112 F2
Marlborough CC DUL SE21 ...32 D2
Marlborough Primary School ISLW TW7 ...17 K3
Marlborough Trading Estate RCH/KEW TW9 ...18 E3
Marshfields CE School CHERT KT16 ...58 B5
Marshgate Primary School RCHPK/HAM TW10 ...18 C7
Marymount International School KUTN/CMB KT2 ...27 M8
Mary Wallace Theatre TWK TW1 ...26 D2
Maswell Park Health Centre HSLW TW3 ...16 F7
The Matthew Arnold School STA TW18 ...22 F7
Maybury Business Centre WOKS/MYFD GU22 ...11 J5
Maybury Infant School WOKN/KNAP GU21 ...10 F4
Mayday University Hospital THHTH CR7 ...49 L6
McKay Trading Estate DTCH/LGLY SL3 ...13 H4
The Mead Infant School WPK KT4 ...64 C2
Meadlands Primary School RCHPK/HAM TW10 ...26 F5
Meadowbrook Industrial Centre CRAWE RH10 ...165 J1
Meadowcroft County Infant School CHERT KT16 ...58 C2
The Meadow School BOR GU35 ...196 B1
The Meadows (Superstores) SHST GU47 ...72 B4
Meadow Vale Primary School BNFD RG42 ...34 C1
The Meads Primary School EGRIN RH19 ...162 F6
Meath Green Infant School HORL RH6 ...160 C1
Meath Green Junior School HORL RH6 ...160 C1
Meath School CHERT KT16 ...58 A6
Megabowl KUT/HW KT1 ...8 F6
Melrose Special School MTCM CR4 ...48 B3
Merland Rise Primary School EPSOM KT18 ...104 C1
Merrist Wood Golf Club RGUW GU3 ...115 M3
Merrow Business Centre RGUE GU4 ...118 A5
Merrow CE Infant School RGUE GU4 ...118 A6
Merstham Primary School REDH RH1 ...126 F2
Merton Abbey Primary School WIM/MER SW19 ...47 L1
Merton Adult College RYNPK SW20 ...47 H3
Merton College SMER SM4 ...47 J6
Merton Industrial Park WIM/MER SW19 ...47 M1
Merton Park Primary School WIM/MER SW19 ...47 J2
Merton Road Industrial Estate WAND/EARL SW18 ...29 K1
Metro Business Centre SYD SE26 ...33 J7

Metro Industrial Centre ISLW TW7 ...17 H4
Metropolitan Police FC E/WMO/HCT KT8 ...44 A6
Metropolitan Police Hayes Sports Club HAYES BR2 ...70 C1
Michael Hall School FROW RH18 ...195 L12
Middle Hill Health Clinic ALDT GU11 ...112 D6
Midleton Industrial Estate GUW GU2 ...6 C2
Milbourne Lodge Junior School ESH/CLAY KT10 ...61 M4
Milbourne Lodge School ESH/CLAY KT10 ...62 A5
Milford Golf Club MFD/CHID GU8 ...159 K8
Milford Hospital RGODL GU7 ...183 R1
Milford School MFD/CHID GU8 ...159 J8
Military Cemetery CHOB/PIR GU24 ...95 J3
Millais School SWTR RH13 ...167 J7
Mill Chase Community School BOR GU35 ...196 A2
Mill Farm Business Park HSLWW TW4 ...25 H1
Mill Green Business Park MTCM CR4 ...48 C7
Mill Lane Trading Estate CROY/NA CR0 ...67 J2
The Mill Primary School CRAWW RH11 ...164 C4
Mill Ride Golf Club ASC SL5 ...36 A1
Milton Mount Primary School CRAWE RH10 ...165 K2
Mitcham CC MTCM CR4 ...48 B4
Mitcham Golf Club MTCM CR4 ...48 D5
Mitcham Industrial Estate MTCM CR4 ...48 D1
Mitcham Vale High School MTCM CR4 ...48 E2
Mole Business Park LHD/OX KT22 ...102 D3
Molesey Hospital E/WMO/HCT KT8 ...43 K5
Mollison Drive Health Centre WLGTN SM6 ...67 H6
Monks Hill Sports Centre SAND/SEL CR2 ...69 G6
Monks Orchard Primary School CROY/NA CR0 ...51 C5
Monument Bridge East Industrial Estate WOKN/KNAP GU21 ...11 J2
Moore Place Golf Club ESH/CLAY KT10 ...61 K4
Moor House School OXTED RH8 ...130 C6
Moor Lane Junior School CHSGTN KT9 ...63 J4
Morden Cemetery MRDN SM4 ...46 F6
Morden First School MRDN SM4 ...47 K5
Morden Hall Medical Centre WIM/MER SW19 ...47 L3
Morden Hall Park (NT) MRDN SM4 ...47 M4
Morden Park Pool MRDN SM4 ...47 J5
Morden Road Clinic WIM/MER SW19 ...47 L3
More House School RFNM GU10 ...155 M7
Mortimer School STRHM/NOR SW16 ...31 G3
Mortlake Cemetery MORT/ESHN SW14 ...19 H5
Mortlake Crematorium RCH/KEW TW9 ...18 E4
Moss Lane School RGODL GU7 ...168 A5
Mount Alvernia Hospital GU GU1 ...7 K7
Mount Medical Centre FELT TW13 ...25 H3
The Mount Primary School NWMAL KT3 ...9 M8
Murky Puddle Theatre NWMAL KT3 ...46 C3
Muschamp Primary School CAR SM5 ...66 B1
Museum of Richmond TWK TW1 ...18 A7
Museum of Rugby & Twickenham Stadium Tours WHTN TW2 ...17 H8
Musical Museum BTFD TW8 ...18 B1
Mytchett Primary School FRIM GU16 ...93 J5
Nash College of Further Education WWKM BR4 ...70 C2
The National Archives RCH/KEW TW9 ...18 E2
The National Centre for Young People with Epilepsy LING RH7 ...178 H5
National Physical Laboratory TEDD TW11 ...26 B7
National Sports Centre NRWD SE19 ...32 D7
Natural Therapy Clinic TOOT SW17 ...30 E6
Natwest Sports Club BECK BR3 ...33 J7
NEC Harlequins RFC (Twickenham Stoop Stadium) WHTN TW2 ...26 B1
Nelson Hospital RYNPK SW20 ...47 J2

Nelson Primary School WHTN TW2 ...16 E8
Nelson Trading Estate WIM/MER SW19 ...47 L1
NE Surrey College of Technology EW KT17 ...84 D1
New Addington Pools & Fitness Centre CROY/NA CR0 ...69 M8
New Brentford Cemetery HSLW TW3 ...16 C4
New Chiswick Pool CHSWK W4 ...19 H2
Newdigate Endowed CE Infant School RDKG RH5 ...173 Q8
New Haw Therapy Clinic ADL/WDHM KT15 ...58 E8
Newhouse Farm Business Centre HORS RH12 ...167 M2
Newland House School TWK TW1 ...26 C5
New Life School EGRIN RH19 ...162 E3
New Lodge School DORK RH4 ...122 E7
New Monument School WOKS/MYFD GU22 ...11 M2
Newport Junior School ASHV GU12 ...113 G8
New Victoria Hospital KUTN/CMB KT2 ...46 B1
New Victoria Theatre WOKN/KNAP GU21 ...10 D5
New Zealand Golf Club ADL/WDHM KT15 ...78 B2
Nightingale Industrial Estate HORS RH12 ...167 G6
Nightingale School TOOT SW17 ...30 B1
Nomad Theatre EHSLY KT24 ...120 C2
Nonsuch High School for Girls CHEAM SM3 ...65 G6
Nonsuch Industrial Estate HOR/WEW KT19 ...84 B1
Nonsuch Primary School EW KT17 ...64 E4
Norbury Complementary Therapy Clinic STRHM/NOR SW16 ...49 J1
Norbury Health Centre STRHM/NOR SW16 ...49 J2
Norbury Manor Primary School STRHM/NOR SW16 ...49 H1
Norbury Manor Secondary Girls School STRHM/NOR SW16 ...49 K1
Norbury Trading Estate STRHM/NOR SW16 ...49 J2
North Croydon Medical Centre THHTH CR7 ...49 L6
North Downs Golf Club CTHM CR3 ...109 K7
North East Surrey Crematorium NWMAL KT3 ...46 F6
North Farnborough County Infant School FARN GU14 ...93 G4
North Feltham Trading Estate EBED/NFELT TW14 ...15 L6
Northgate Primary School CRAWE RH10 ...165 G2
North Heath Lane Industrial Estate HORS RH12 ...167 G3
North Heath Primary School HORS RH12 ...167 G4
North Holmwood CC RDKG RH5 ...144 F7
Northlands Business Park HORS RH12 ...188 D9
Northolmes Junior School HORS RH12 ...167 K4
Northtown Trading Estate ASHV GU12 ...113 H8
North Weylands Industrial Estate WOT/HER KT12 ...61 H1
The Norwegian School WIM/MER SW19 ...28 F8
Norwood Heights Shopping Centre NRWD SE19 ...32 B7
Norwood School NRWD SE19 ...31 M6
Notre Dame Preparatory School COB KT11 ...80 C1
Novello Theatre ASC SL5 ...37 G5
Nutfield Cemetery REDH RH1 ...127 G7
Nutfield Church CE Primary School REDH RH1 ...149 J1
Nutfield Priory Hotel REDH RH1 ...126 F8
Nutley Dean Business Park HORL RH6 ...174 H3
Oak Farm Community School FARN GU14 ...92 D3
Oakfield Junior School LHD/OX KT22 ...101 M5
Oakfield Preparatory School DUL SE21 ...32 A3
Oakfield Road Industrial Estate PGE/AN SE20 ...32 F8
Oakfield School WOKS/MYFD GU22 ...78 C5
Oak Hill Health Centre SURB KT6 ...45 H6
Oakhyrst Grange School CTHM CR3 ...108 A8
Oaklands Infant School BH/WHM TN16 ...90 F6
Oaklands Junior School BH/WHM TN16 ...90 F6

Oaklands School ISLW TW7 ...17 G5
Oak Lane Cemetery TWK TW1 ...26 D1
Oak Lane Medical Centre TWK TW1 ...26 E1
Oak Lodge JMI School WWKM BR4 ...51 L7
Oak Lodge School BAL SW12 ...30 C1
Oak Park Golf Club RFNM GU10 ...132 D3
The Oaks Primary School CRAWE RH10 ...165 H7
Oaks Sports Centre CAR SM5 ...86 C1
Oak Tree Clinic WOKN/KNAP GU21 ...76 A8
Oakview Business Park MFD/CHID GU8 ...183 Q7
Oakwood Independent School PUR/KEN CR8 ...87 L3
Oakwood Industrial Park CRAWE RH10 ...165 J1
Oakwood School HORL RH6 ...160 E3
Oakwood Sports Centre HORL RH6 ...160 F3
Oast House Centre STA TW18 ...22 C5
Oatlands Park Hotel WEY KT13 ...59 M2
Oatlands School WEY KT13 ...60 A3
Occupational Health Centre CROY/NA CR0 ...2 E8
Odeon Cinema BECK BR3 ...51 K2
ESH/CLAY KT10 ...61 L3
EW KT17 ...84 B3
KUT/HW KT1 ...8 F6
RCH/KEW TW9 ...18 A7
STRHM/NOR SW16 ...31 H4
WIM/MER SW19 ...29 K8
Odeon Multiplex GU GU1 ...6 F6
Old Barnes Cemetery BARN SW13 ...19 L4
Old Barn Theatre CRAWW RH11 ...164 B2
Old Beckenhamian RFC WWKM BR4 ...70 A2
The Old Cottage Hospital EW KT17 ...84 C1
Oldfield House Special School HPTN TW12 ...43 J1
Oldfields Trading Estate SUT SM1 ...65 K2
Old Guildfordians RFC GU GU1 ...7 M1
Old Palace School CROY/NA CR0 ...2 B7
Old Thorns Hotel, Golf & Country Club LIPH GU30 ...196 C10
Old Tiffinians Sports Ground E/WMO/HCT KT8 ...44 B5
Old Town Hall CHERT KT16 ...40 D7
HORS RH12 ...166 F8
RGODL GU7 ...168 A8
Old Vicarage School RCHPK/HAM TW10 ...18 B8
Ongar Place Infant School ADL/WDHM KT15 ...58 D5
Onslow Infant School GUW GU2 ...138 C2
Open University EGRIN RH19 ...162 F4
Orange Tree Theatre RCH/KEW TW9 ...18 B6
Orchard Business Centre BECK BR3 ...33 J6
REDH RH1 ...175 R1
Orchard Hill College WLGTN SM6 ...66 E5
The Orchard Junior School HSLWW TW4 ...16 D6
The Orchard School E/WMO/HCT KT8 ...44 A5
Orchards Community Infant School REIG RH2 ...147 K3
Orchard Way Primary School CROY/NA CR0 ...51 H7
Oriel High School CRAWE RH10 ...164 F4
Oriel Primary School FELT TW13 ...25 H4
Orleans House Gallery TWK TW1 ...26 E2
Orleans Infant School TWK TW1 ...26 E1
Osteopathic Clinic HOR/WEW KT19 ...64 A4
Osterley Park & House (NT) ISLW TW7 ...16 F1
Our Lady Immaculate RC Primary School BRYLDS KT5 ...45 L8
Our Lady of the Rosary RC Primary School STA TW18 ...22 D7
Our Lady Queen of Heaven County Primary School CRAWW RH11 ...164 D2
Our Lady Queen of Heaven RC Primary School WIM/MER SW19 ...29 G1
Our Lady & St Philip Neri RC Infants School FSTH SE23 ...33 G4
Our Lady & St Philip Neri RC Primary School SYD SE26 ...33 H5
Outwood Windmill REDH RH1 ...177 J1
Oval Primary School CROY/NA CR0 ...3 G4
Overton Grange School BELMT SM2 ...65 L7

Owlsmoor Primary School
SHST GU47 .... 52 B8
Oxshott Village Sports Club
LHD/OX KT22 .... 81 M4
Oxted Health Centre
OXTED RH8 .... 130 C3
Oxted & Limpsfield Hospital
OXTED RH8 .... 130 A2
Oxted School
OXTED RH8 .... 130 C3
Pachesham Park Golf Centre
LHD/OX KT22 .... 82 B8
Paddock School
PUT/ROE SW15 .... 19 J6
Painshill Park
COB KT11 .... 80 D4
Palmerston Business Centre
SUT SM1 .... 65 M4
Palm House
RCH/KEW TW9 .... 18 C3
Papplewick School
ASC SL5 .... 36 C1
Parchmore Medical Centre
THHTH CR7 .... 49 M3
Parish Church CE Primary
School
CROY/NA CR0 .... 2 A8
Park Crematorium
ASHV GU12 .... 135 C3
Park Farm Industrial Estate
FRIM GU16 .... 72 F8
Park Hall Trading Estate
WNWD SE27 .... 31 M4
Park Hill Junior School
CROY/NA CR0 .... 3 G8
Park Hill School
KUTN/CMB KT2 .... 9 K3
Park House RFC
HAYES BR2 .... 70 F1
The Park Inn Heathrow
WDR/YW UB7 .... 14 E2
Park Mead Primary School
CRAN GU6 .... 186 E1
Park Primary School
ALDT GU11 .... 134 F2
Park Recreation Centre
HORS RH12 .... 166 F7
Park School
WOKS/MYFD GU22 .... 11 G6
Parkside Hospital
WIM/MER SW19 .... 29 G4
Parkside School
COB KT11 .... 81 K8
Parkway Trading Estate
HEST TW5 .... 15 M1
Park Wood Golf Club
BH/WHM TN16 .... 111 H4
Parsonage Business Park
HORS RH12 .... 167 H5
Parsons Mead School
ASHTD KT21 .... 103 H1
Passfield Mill Business Park
LIPH GU30 .... 196 C4
The Patrick Doody Clinic &
Health Centre
WIM/MER SW19 .... 29 K8
Pattinson Clinic
RCH/KEW TW9 .... 18 A7
The Paul Robeson Theatre
HSLW TW3 .... 16 E5
Pavilion Restaurant
RCH/KEW TW9 .... 18 B4
Pavilions in the Park
HORS RH12 .... 166 F6
Paxton Primary School
NRWD SE19 .... 32 C7
Payne Clinic
EW KT17 .... 84 D3
Peacock Cinema
WOKN/KNAP GU21 .... 10 C5
The Peacocks Shopping Centre
WOKN/KNAP GU21 .... 10 C5
Peall Road Industrial Estate
CROY/NA CR0 .... 49 J6
Peaslake School
SHGR GU5 .... 171 K2
The Peel Centre
BRAK RG12 .... 34 E2
Pelham Court Business Centre
CRAWW RH11 .... 164 D8
Pelham Primary School
WIM/MER SW19 .... 29 K8
Pennthorpe School
HORS RH12 .... 202 H2
Pennyhill Park Hotel & the Spa
BAGS GU19 .... 53 L7
Penwortham Primary School
STRHM/NOR SW16 .... 30 E7
Perrymount Primary School
FSTH SE23 .... 33 G3
Perrywood Business Park
REDH RH1 .... 148 E8
The Petersham Hotel
RCHPK/HAM TW10 .... 27 H1
Pewley Down Infant School
GU GU1 .... 7 J7
Phoenix College
MRDN SM4 .... 47 L5
Phoenix Leisure Centre
CAT SE6 .... 33 L1
Pierreponte School
RFNM GU10 .... 156 B8
The Pilgrims Way Primary
School
FNM GU9 .... 5 G7
Pilton Estate
CROY/NA CR0 .... 2 B5
Pine Ridge Golf Club
FRIM GU16 .... 74 A7
Pine Ridge Infant School
CBLY GU15 .... 53 K8
The Pines Primary School
BRAK RG12 .... 34 D7
The Pines Trading Estate
RGUW GU3 .... 116 B6
Pine Trees Business Park
STA TW18 .... 22 B6
Pinewood Infant School
FARN GU14 .... 92 A2
Pinnacles Cricket & Squash Club
SUT SM1 .... 65 K5

Pioneers Industrial Park
CROY/NA CR0 .... 49 H8
Pippins School
ASHF TW15 .... 23 J5
DTCH/LGLY SL3 .... 13 J5
Pirbright Camp
CHOB/PIR GU24 .... 94 E2
Pirbright Primary School
CHOB/PIR GU24 .... 95 H4
Piries Place
HORS RH12 .... 166 F7
Pitfarm Lawn Tennis Club
GU GU1 .... 117 K8
Pitwood Park Industrial
Estate
KWD/TDW/WH KT20 .... 105 G2
Pixham School
DORK RH4 .... 122 F8
Plaistow & Kirdford Primary
School
BIL RH14 .... 201 J6
Playhouse Cinema
EPSOM KT18 .... 84 A4
Playhouse Theatre
EPSOM KT18 .... 83 M3
Plaza Cinema
OXTED RH8 .... 130 B3
Plough Industrial Estate
LHD/OX KT22 .... 102 D2
The Point (UCI Cinema &
Hollywood Bowl)
BRAK RG12 .... 34 E2
Polesden Lacey (NT)
RDKG RH5 .... 121 K4
Polka Theatre for Children
WIM/MER SW19 .... 29 L7
Polygon Business Centre
DTCH/LGLY SL3 .... 13 J4
Pond Meadow School
GUW GU2 .... 116 B7
Pools in the Park
RCH/KEW TW9 .... 18 A6
Poplar Primary School
WIM/MER SW19 .... 47 K3
Portesbery School
CBLY GU15 .... 73 G3
Portland Medical Centre
SNWD SE25 .... 50 E5
Potters Gate CE Primary
School
FNM GU9 .... 4 F3
Potters International Hotel
ALDT GU11 .... 112 C5
Pound Hill Infant School
CRAWE RH10 .... 165 L3
Pound Hill Junior School
CRAWE RH10 .... 165 L3
The Pountney Clinic
HSLW TW3 .... 16 D5
Powell Corderoy Primary
School
DORK RH4 .... 144 C3
Premier Cinema
DORK RH4 .... 144 F1
Premier Travel Inn
ALDT GU11 .... 112 B7
BAGS GU19 .... 54 B4
BH/WHM TN16 .... 111 H8
BRAK RG12 .... 34 E2
BTFD TW8 .... 18 B1
CHSGTN KT9 .... 62 F8
COB KT11 .... 80 F2
CRAWE RH10 .... 191 P2
CRAWE RH10 .... 192 C1
CRAWW RH11 .... 164 D5
CRAWW RH11 .... 164 E6
CROY/NA CR0 .... 67 K5
CROY/NA CR0 .... 68 D4
EGRIN RH19 .... 162 B1
EPSOM KT18 .... 83 M4
FARN GU14 .... 92 B6
GU GU1 .... 7 H1
HOR/WEW KT19 .... 64 B4
HORL RH6 .... 160 C5
HORS RH12 .... 167 G6
HSLW TW3 .... 16 D5
HTHAIR TW6 .... 15 H3
KWD/TDW/WH KT20 .... 105 H1
REDH RH1 .... 148 B2
SHST GU47 .... 72 A2
WHTN TW2 .... 25 M2
WIM/MER SW19 .... 47 M1
WOKN/KNAP GU21 .... 76 F7
Preymead Industrial Estate
FNM GU9 .... 134 E2
Prince Consort's Library
ALDT GU11 .... 112 C6
Princes Hall
ALDT GU11 .... 112 D7
Princes Mead Shopping Centre
FARN GU14 .... 92 E6
Princess of Wales
Conservatory
RCH/KEW TW9 .... 18 C2
The Princess Royal Barracks
FRIM GU16 .... 94 A2
The Princess Royal University
Hospital
ORP BR6 .... 71 K2
Princess Square Shopping
Centre
BRAK RG12 .... 34 E2
Prins Willem-alexander School
WOKS/MYFD GU22 .... 11 L5
Prior Heath Infant School
CBLY GU15 .... 73 K4
Priors Field School
RGODL GU7 .... 137 J8
Priory CE Primary School
WIM/MER SW19 .... 29 L6
The Priory CE Voluntary
Aided School
DORK RH4 .... 144 C3
Priory Retail Park
WIM/MER SW19 .... 30 A8
Priory School
BNSTD SM7 .... 85 K5
Priory Special School
SNWD SE25 .... 50 C4
Progress Business Park
CROY/NA CR0 .... 67 J1

Prospect House School
PUT/ROE SW15 .... 29 G1
Purley Community Health Clinic
PUR/KEN CR8 .... 87 K1
Purley & District War Memorial
Hospital
PUR/KEN CR8 .... 87 K1
Purley Downs Golf Club
SAND/SEL CR2 .... 88 A1
Purley John Fisher RFC
COUL/CHIP CR5 .... 107 K2
Purley Oaks Primary School
SAND/SEL CR2 .... 68 A6
Purley Secretarial & Language
College
PUR/KEN CR8 .... 87 K1
Purley Sports Club
PUR/KEN CR8 .... 67 G8
Putney Leisure Centre
PUT/ROE SW15 .... 19 M6
Putney Lower Common
Cemetery
BARN SW13 .... 19 L4
Putneymead Medical Centre
PUT/ROE SW15 .... 19 M6
Putney Park School
PUT/ROE SW15 .... 19 L6
Putney Vale Cemetery
PUT/ROE SW15 .... 28 D3
Putney Vale Crematorium
PUT/ROE SW15 .... 28 D3
Puttenham CE Infant School
RGUW GU3 .... 136 E5
Puttenham Golf Club
RGUW GU3 .... 137 G5
Pyrcroft Primary School
CHERT KT16 .... 40 B6
Pyrford Golf Club
WOKS/MYFD GU22 .... 78 E7
Pyrford Primary School
WOKS/MYFD GU22 .... 78 C6
Quality Hotel
DTCH/LGLY SL3 .... 12 E1
Quarryside Business Park
REDH RH1 .... 126 E4
Queen Charlotte's Cottage
RCH/KEW TW9 .... 18 A4
Queen Eleanor's CE Junior School
GUW GU2 .... 6 A6
Queen Elizabeth Hospital
BNSTD SM7 .... 85 M8
Queen Elizabeth II Silver
Jubilee School
SWTR RH13 .... 167 J8
Queen Elizabeth's Foundation
Training College
LHD/OX KT22 .... 82 A7
Queen Mary's Hospital for
Children
SUT SM1 .... 47 M8
Queen Mary's University
Hospital
PUT/ROE SW15 .... 19 K8
Queen's Building
HTHAIR TW6 .... 14 E1
The Queens CE Primary School
RCH/KEW TW9 .... 18 C2
Queens Manor Primary School
FUL/PGN SW6 .... 19 M2
Queens Medical Centre
RCHPK/HAM TW10 .... 18 C7
Queen's Road Cemetery
CROY/NA CR0 .... 49 M6
Queens Sports Centre
RGODL GU7 .... 159 L2
Queen Victoria Hospital
EGRIN RH19 .... 163 G2
Radisson Edwardian Hotel
HYS/HAR UB3 .... 14 F2
Rainbow Industrial Estate
RYNPK SW20 .... 46 F2
Rainbow Leisure Centre
EW KT17 .... 84 B2
Rainbow Natural Health Centre
REDH RH1 .... 148 C1
The Raleigh School
EHSLY KT24 .... 99 M1
Ramada Hotel
CRAWE RH10 .... 165 J2
EHSLY KT24 .... 120 C3
RFNM GU10 .... 135 K4
Randalls Park Crematorium
LHD/OX KT22 .... 102 B2
Ranelagh School
BRAK RG12 .... 34 F3
Rathfern Primary School
FSTH SE23 .... 33 J2
Ravenstone Primary School
BAL SW12 .... 30 D2
Ravens Wood School
HAYES BR2 .... 71 G2
Raynes Park High School
RYNPK SW20 .... 46 E3
Raynes Park Sports Ground
RYNPK SW20 .... 46 D2
Raynes Park Vale FC
RYNPK SW20 .... 47 G5
Red Gates School
CROY/NA CR0 .... 67 K4
Redhill Aerodrome
REDH RH1 .... 149 H5
Redhill Business Centre
REDH RH1 .... 126 C7
Redhill College
REDH RH1 .... 148 E1
Redhill FC
REDH RH1 .... 148 C4
Redhill & Reigate Golf Club
REDH RH1 .... 148 A3
The Redlands Primary School
DORK RH4 .... 144 E5
Red Lion Business Park
SURB KT6 .... 63 J1
Redstone Cemetery
REDH RH1 .... 148 E1
Reedham Park School
PUR/KEN CR8 .... 87 K4
Reed Place Business Park
SHPTN TW17 .... 41 J8
Reeds School
COB KT11 .... 81 K2

Regal Cinema
CRAN GU6 .... 186 B2
Regina Coeli RC Primary
School
SAND/SEL CR2 .... 67 L6
Reigate College
REIG RH2 .... 125 L7
Reigate Day Hospital
REDH RH1 .... 126 A8
Reigate Grammar School
REIG RH2 .... 125 M8
Reigate Heath Golf Club
REIG RH2 .... 124 F8
Reigate Hill Golf Club
REIG RH2 .... 126 D2
Reigate Manor Hotel
REIG RH2 .... 125 L5
Reigate Parish Infant School
REIG RH2 .... 125 M8
Reigate Priory Junior School
REIG RH2 .... 125 K8
Reigate Priory & Museum
REIG RH2 .... 125 L8
Reigate St Marys Preparatory
& Choir School
REIG RH2 .... 125 L8
Reigate School
REIG RH2 .... 147 M3
The Renaissance Hotel
HTHAIR TW6 .... 14 F3
The Retail Business Centre
EW KT17 .... 64 C5
Rewards Centre
HSLW TW3 .... 16 F5
Rhoda McGaw Theatre & Cinema
WOKN/KNAP GU21 .... 10 D5
RHS Garden Wisley
RPLY/SEND GU23 .... 79 M8
Ricards Lodge High School
WIM/MER SW19 .... 29 J5
Richard Atkins Primary School
BRXS/STRHM SW2 .... 31 H1
Richmond Adult & Community
College
RCH/KEW TW9 .... 18 A6
Richmond American
International University
RCHPK/HAM TW10 .... 18 B4
The Richmond Clinic
RCH/KEW TW9 .... 18 C6
Richmond Community College
TWK TW1 .... 26 C7
Richmond FC
RCH/KEW TW9 .... 18 A6
The Richmond Gate Hotel
RCHPK/HAM TW10 .... 27 H1
The Richmond Golf Club
RCHPK/HAM TW10 .... 27 H2
The Richmond Green Medical
Centre
RCH/KEW TW9 .... 18 A7
The Richmond Hill Hotel
RCHPK/HAM TW10 .... 27 H1
Richmond House School
HPTN TW12 .... 25 J6
Richmond Magistrates Court
RCH/KEW TW9 .... 18 A6
Richmond Park Golf Club
PUT/ROE SW15 .... 28 B1
Richmond Road Medical Centre
KUTN/CMB KT2 .... 8 C2
Richmond Theatre
RCH/KEW TW9 .... 18 A6
Richmond upon Thames
College
WHTN TW2 .... 26 B1
Riddlesdown High School
PUR/KEN CR8 .... 88 B4
The Ridgeway Community
School
FNM GU9 .... 5 K9
Ridgeway Primary School
SAND/SEL CR2 .... 68 B7
Rikkyo School in England
HORS RH12 .... 202 C1
Ripley CC
RPLY/SEND GU23 .... 98 F3
Ripley CE Infant School
RPLY/SEND GU23 .... 98 E3
Ripley Court School
RPLY/SEND GU23 .... 98 F3
Ritz Cinema
HORS RH12 .... 167 G7
Riverdene Industrial Estate
WOT/HER KT12 .... 61 G4
River Gardens Business Centre
EBED/NFELT TW14 .... 15 L6
River Mole Business Park
ESH/CLAY KT10 .... 43 K8
Riversdale Primary School
WAND/EARL SW18 .... 29 K2
Riverside Business Centre
WAND/EARL SW18 .... 29 L2
The Riverside Business Centre
GU GU1 .... 6 E4
Riverside Business Park
WIM/MER SW19 .... 47 M1
Riverside Park Industrial
Estate
FNM GU9 .... 5 L2
Riverside Wandle Trading
Estate
MTCM CR4 .... 48 C7
Riverview CE Primary School
HOR/WEW KT19 .... 63 M3
Riverway Industrial Estate
RGUW GU3 .... 168 F1
Roan Industrial Estate
MTCM CR4 .... 48 B1
Robin Hood Infant School
SUT SM1 .... 65 K4
Robin Hood Junior School
SUT SM1 .... 65 L4
Robin Hood Lane Health Centre
SUT SM1 .... 65 K4
Robin Hood Primary School
KUTN/CMB KT2 .... 28 A6
Rock & Bowl Bowling Alley
EGRIN RH19 .... 162 F4
Rockmount Primary School
NRWD SE19 .... 31 M7

Rodborough Technology
College
MFD/CHID GU8 .... 183 N2
Rodd Estate
SHPTN TW17 .... 41 M5
Roehampton Church School
PUT/ROE SW15 .... 28 E1
The Roehampton Priory
Hospital
PUT/ROE SW15 .... 19 J6
Roehampton Recreation Centre
PUT/ROE SW15 .... 28 C1
Roehampton University
(Digby Stuart College)
PUT/ROE SW15 .... 19 J7
Roehampton University
(Froebel College)
PUT/ROE SW15 .... 19 J8
Roehampton University
(Southlands College)
PUT/ROE SW15 .... 19 J7
Roffey Social & Sports Club
HORS RH12 .... 167 K4
Rokeby School
KUTN/CMB KT2 .... 27 M8
Roke Primary School
PUR/KEN CR8 .... 87 M4
Roker Park Golf Club
RGUW GU3 .... 116 A3
Roman Industrial Estate
CROY/NA CR0 .... 3 G1
Romans Business Park
FNM GU9 .... 5 L1
Ronald Rose Primary School
PUT/ROE SW15 .... 29 G1
Rosary RC Infant School
HEST TW5 .... 16 C1
Rosebery School
EPSOM KT18 .... 83 M4
Roselands Clinic
NWMAL KT3 .... 45 M4
Rosemead Preparatory School
DUL SE21 .... 31 M3
Rosendale Primary School
DUL SE21 .... 31 M1
Rose of Kingston
(Kingston Theatre)
KUT/HW KT1 .... 8 C7
Rosslyn Park RFC
PUT/ROE SW15 .... 19 J4
The Rotunda
KUT/HW KT1 .... 8 F6
Roundshaw J & I School
WLGTN SM6 .... 67 H6
Rowan Preparatory School
ESH/CLAY KT10 .... 62 C6
Rowans School
RYNPK SW20 .... 28 D8
Rowfant Business Centre
CRAWE RH10 .... 193 K7
Rowledge CE (Controlled)
Primary School
RFNM GU10 .... 155 G6
The Royal Alexandra & Albert
School
REIG RH2 .... 126 B3
Royal Army Medical Corps
ALDT GU11 .... 113 G5
Royal Ascot Golf Club
ASC SL5 .... 36 D2
Royal Ashdown Forest Golf
Club
FROW RH18 .... 195 P12
The Royal Ballet School
RCHPK/HAM TW10 .... 28 A2
The Royal Berkshire Ramada
Plaza Hotel
ASC SL5 .... 37 K3
Royal Botanic Gardens Kew
School
RCH/KEW TW9 .... 18 C2
Royal Grammar School
GU GU1 .... 7 H5
Royal Holloway University
of London
EGH TW20 .... 21 G7
EGH TW20 .... 39 G1
Royal Holloway University of
London (Hall of Residence)
EGH TW20 .... 21 G5
Royal Hospital
RCH/KEW TW9 .... 18 B5
Royal Hospital & Home
PUT/ROE SW15 .... 28 E1
The Royal Junior School
GSHT GU26 .... 197 Q4
The Royal Kent CE Primary
School
LHD/OX KT22 .... 81 M4
Royal Logistic Corps
Museum
FRIM GU16 .... 94 A1
Royal Marsden Hospital
BELMT SM2 .... 65 M8
Royal Mid-surrey Golf Club
RCH/KEW TW9 .... 18 A5
Royal Military Academy
CBLY GU15 .... 72 D2
Royal Military School of Music
WHTN TW2 .... 17 G8
Royal Russell School
CROY/NA CR0 .... 68 E5
The Royal School
HASM GU27 .... 198 C3
Royal & Sun Alliance Sports
Club
HORS RH12 .... 167 H3
Royal Surrey County Hospital
GUW GU2 .... 116 B8
Royal Wimbledon Golf Club
WIM/MER SW19 .... 28 E6
Royston Primary School
PGE/AN SE20 .... 51 G1
RSPCA HQ
HORS RH12 .... 166 F8
Rudgwick Medical Centre
HORS RH12 .... 202 H2
Rudgwick Primary School
HORS RH12 .... 203 J2
Rufus Business Centre
WIM/MER SW19 .... 29 L3

Runnymede Hospital
CHERT KT16 58 A2
Runnymede Hotel & Spa
EGH TW20 21 L4
Runnymede (NT)
EGH TW20 21 H4
Rural Life Centre
RFNM GU10 156 C6
Rushey Green Primary School
CAT SE6 33 L2
Rusper Golf Club
RDKG RH5 189 R1
Rusper Primary School
HORS RH12 189 R6
The Russell JMI School
RCHPK/HAM TW10 27 G3
The Russell School
RCHPK/HAM TW10 27 G2
Rutherford Way Industrial Estate
CRAWE RH10 191 R2
Rutlish School
RYNPK SW20 47 J2
Rydens School
WOT/HER KT12 60 F2
Rydes Hill Preparatory School
RGUW GU3 116 C6
Rydon Business Centre
LHD/OX KT22 102 D2
Ryebrook Business Park
LHD/OX KT22 102 D2
Ryelands Primary School
SNWD SE25 50 E5
Sackville Community College
EGRIN RH19 163 H4
Sacred Heart Catholic Primary School
PUT/ROE SW15 19 K7
Sacred Heart RC Primary School
NWMAL KT3 46 D4
TEDD TW11 26 E8
Safari Cinema
CROY/NA CR0 2 B2
St Agathas RC Primary School
KUTN/CMB KT2 9 H1
St Albans RC Aided Primary School
E/WMO/HCT KT8 43 L5
St Andrews Catholic School
LHD/OX KT22 102 F2
St Andrews CE First & Middle School
CRAWE RH10 165 J5
St Andrews CE Infant School
FNM GU9 5 H4
St Andrews CE School
CROY/NA CR0 2 B8
St Andrews Primary School
COB KT11 80 F3
St Andrew's School
WOKN/KNAP GU21 10 A3
St Annes Catholic Primary School
BNSTD SM7 85 K6
CHERT KT16 40 D8
St Annes County Primary School
STWL/WRAY TW19 23 H1
St Anne's Special School
MRDN SM4 47 K5
St Anns Heath Junior School
VW GU25 39 J5
St Anslems RC Primary School
TOOT SW17 30 D4
St Anthonys Hospital
WPK KT4 47 G8
St Anthonys RC Primary School
PGE/AN SE20 50 E1
St Augustines Primary School
FRIM GU16 73 J7
St Augustines RC Primary School
CAT SE6 33 L6
St Bartholomews CE Primary School
SYD SE26 32 F5
St Bartholomews Primary School
HASM GU27 198 D5
St Bedes CE Junior School
RPLY/SEND GU23 98 A6
St Bedes RC Infant School
BAL SW12 31 G2
St Bedes School
REDH RH1 126 B5
St Bernadette Catholic Junior School
BAL SW12 30 F1
St Bernadettes County Primary School
FARN GU14 92 D4
St Boniface RC Primary School
TOOT SW17 30 C6
St Catherine's Hospice
CRAWE RH10 164 F6
St Catherine's Primary School
REDH RH1 128 A7
St Catherines School
SHGR GU5 169 J2
TWK TW1 26 C3
St Cecilia's CE Primary School
WAND/EARL SW18 29 H1
St Cecilias RC Primary School
WPK KT4 65 G1
St Chads RC Primary School
SNWD SE25 50 B5
St Charles Borromeo RCP School
WEY KT13 59 K2
St Christophers School
BECK BR3 51 M2
EPSOM KT18 84 B4
St Clare Business Park
HPTN TW12 25 M7
St Clements Primary School
EW KT17 64 C7
St Cuthbert Mayne RC Primary School
CRAN GU6 186 D2
St Cuthberts CE Primary School
EGH TW20 20 F8
St Cyprians Greek Orthodox Primary School
THHTH CR7 49 M2
St Davids College
WWKM BR4 51 L7
St Davids Health Centre
STWL/WRAY TW19 23 G1
St Davids School
ASHF TW15 23 J4
PUR/KEN CR8 87 J1
St Dominics School
MFD/CHID GU8 183 R8
St Dunstans Catholic Primary School
WOKS/MYFD GU22 11 G5
St Dunstans CE Primary School
CHEAM SM3 65 H5
St Dunstans College
CAT SE6 33 J2
St Ebba's Hospital
HOR/WEW KT19 63 M7
St Edmunds RC Primary School
RGODL GU7 168 C6
WHTN TW2 25 L1
St Edmunds School
GSHT GU26 197 Q2
St Elizabeths RC Primary School
RCHPK/HAM TW10 18 C8
St Elpheges RC Primary School
WLGTN SM6 67 H5
St Francis Catholic School
CTHM CR3 108 C3
St Francis of Assisi Primary School
CRAWE RH10 165 G5
St Francis RC Primary School
ASC SL5 36 D6
St Francis; Westborough Primary School
GUW GU2 116 C7
St Georges Business Park
WEY KT13 59 K7
St Georges College
ADL/WDHM KT15 59 G2
St George's College Track
ADL/WDHM KT15 59 G1
St George's Hill Golf Club
WEY KT13 79 M1
St Georges Hospital
TOOT SW17 30 B6
St Georges Industrial Estate
CBLY GU15 72 E6
KUTN/CMB KT2 27 G6
St Georges School
ASC SL5 36 E4
St Giles CE (Aided) Infant School
ASHTD KT21 83 J8
St Giles School
SAND/SEL CR2 67 L5
St Helier Hospital
CAR SM5 47 M8
St Hilarys School
RGODL GU7 168 A6
Saint Hill Manor
EGRIN RH19 194 D9
St Hugh of Lincoln RCP School
WOKN/KNAP GU21 96 A1
St Ignatius RC Primary School
SUN TW16 42 D1
St Ives School
HASM GU27 198 F5
St James CE Primary School
MFD/CHID GU8 157 M6
WEY KT13 59 M2
St James Independent School
TWK TW1 26 D3
St James Medical Centre
CROY/NA CR0 2 F2
St James RC Primary School
WHTN TW2 26 B4
St James the Great RC Primary School
THHTH CR7 49 L2
St John Fisher RC Primary School
RYNPK SW20 46 F5
St Johns Beaumont School
WDSR SL4 20 E3
St Johns Catholic Primary School
HORS RH12 166 D8
St Johns CE Infant School
RFNM GU10 181 K8
St Johns CE Primary School
CROY/NA CR0 69 G2
CTHM CR3 108 E8
KUT/HW KT1 8 F9
PGE/AN SE20 32 F8
St Johns CP School
WOKN/KNAP GU21 76 B8
St Johns Primary School
REDH RH1 148 B2
St Johns School
LHD/OX KT22 102 E3
St John the Baptist CE Junior School
KUT/HW KT1 8 C3
St John the Baptist CE Primary School
BMLY BR1 33 M5
St John the Baptist School
WOKS/MYFD GU22 97 K1
St Josephs Catholic Primary School
ALDT GU11 134 D1
EPSOM KT18 83 M4
St Joseph's Catholic Primary School
GUW GU2 116 C6
St Josephs Catholic Primary School
REDH RH1 126 B7
St Josephs College
STRHM/NOR SW16 31 L7
St Josephs RC Infant School
NRWD SE19 31 M7
St Josephs RC Junior School
NRWD SE19 31 M7
St Josephs RC Primary School
BRAK RG12 35 G2
DORK RH4 144 D2
KUT/HW KT1 9 G7
St Josephs School
CRAN GU6 170 E11
St Judes CE Junior School
EGH TW20 20 F7
St Lawrence Business Centre
FELT TW13 24 E3
St Lawrence Catholic School
FELT TW13 24 E3
St Lawrence Junior School
E/WMO/HCT KT8 44 A3
St Lawrence Primary School
EHSLY KT24 121 G1
St Leonards CE Primary School
STRHM/NOR SW16 31 G6
St Leonards Community nfant School
SWTR RH13 167 H7
St Lukes CE Primary School
KUTN/CMB KT2 9 G4
WNWD SE27 31 M6
St Lukes School
THHTH CR7 49 K4
St Margaret Clitherow RC Primary School
BRAK RG12 34 C7
St Margarets Business Centre
TWK TW1 26 D1
St Margarets CE Primary School
CRAWW RH11 164 D3
St Margaret's School
KWD/TDW/WH KT20 105 G3
St Marks Catholic School
HSLW TW3 16 C5
St Marks CE Aided Primary School
RGODL GU7 159 L6
St Marks CE Primary School
FARN GU14 113 G1
SNWD SE25 50 D4
St Marks Primary School
MTCM CR4 48 C2
St Martin in the Fields High School
BRXS/STRHM SW2 31 L2
St Martins CE Junior School
EPSOM KT18 84 A5
St Martins CE Primary School
DORK RH4 144 C1
St Martins House Business Centre
EHSLY KT24 120 B3
St Martins Walk Shopping Centre
DORK RH4 144 E1
St Mary Magdalens Catholic Primary School
MORT/ESHN SW14 19 G5
St Mary & St Peters CE Primary School
TEDD TW11 26 B6
St Marys Catholic Infant School
CROY/NA CR0 2 E4
St Marys CE Aided Infant School
RFNM GU10 181 J2
St Marys CE First School
MFD/CHID GU8 159 H3
St Marys CE Infant School
LHD/OX KT22 102 F4
St Marys CE Junior School
OXTED RH8 130 B2
STWL/WRAY TW19 14 B8
THDIT KT7 44 E8
St Mary's Cemetery
HORS RH12 166 F8
St Marys CE Primary School
BF/WBF KT14 79 H3
CHSGTN KT9 63 H5
EGRIN RH19 162 E3
HORS RH12 166 E8
MFD/CHID GU8 199 Q2
TWK TW1 26 D1
St Mary's College University of Surrey
TWK TW1 26 C4
St Mary's High School
CROY/NA CR0 2 D3
St Marys Infant School
CAR SM5 66 B3
St Mary's Junior School
TWK TW1 26 E1
St Marys RC Infant School
CAR SM5 66 C4
St Marys RC Primary School
BECK BR3 33 M8
ISLW TW7 17 K5
WIM/MER SW19 29 K8
St Marys School Ascot
ASC SL5 36 E7
St Marys Tutorial College
GUW GU2 6 F9
St Matthews CE (Aided) Infant School
COB KT11 80 E8
St Matthews CE Primary School
REDH RH1 126 C6
RYNPK SW20 46 D1
SURB KT6 45 H7
St Michaels Abbey
FARN GU14 92 F4
St Michaels CE First School
RDKG RH5 122 F1
St Michaels CE Infant School
ALDT GU11 134 E1
St Michaels CE Junior School
ALDT GU11 134 E1
St Michaels CE Primary School
ASC SL5 37 G5
BRAK RG12 34 D5
WAND/EARL SW18 29 J1
St Michaels RC School
ASHF TW15 23 K6
St Michaels & St Martins RC Primary School
HSLWW TW4 16 C5
St Michaels Sydenham CE Primary School
SYD SE26 33 H5
St Nicholas Centre
SUT SM1 65 L4
St Nicholas CE Primary School
SHPTN TW17 41 L6
St Nicholas School
CRAN GU6 186 C2
PUR/KEN CR8 87 K3
REDH RH1 127 G3
St Nicolas CE Infant School
GUW GU2 6 E8
St Omer Barracks
ALDT GU11 113 G5
St Patricks Catholic Primary School
FARN GU14 93 G5
St Pauls Catholic College
SUN TW16 42 D1
St Pauls CE Aided Primary School
DORK RH4 144 E2
St Pauls CE Infant School
RFNM GU10 135 K2
St Pauls CE Junior School
KUTN/CMB KT2 9 K3
St Pauls CE Primary School
ADL/WDHM KT15 58 D3
BTFD TW8 18 A1
CHSGTN KT9 63 H3
St Pauls RC Primary School
THDIT KT7 44 B7
St Peter & Paul CE Infant School
CTHM CR3 107 K7
St Peters Catholic Comprehensive School
GU GU1 117 M7
St Peters Catholic Primary School
EGRIN RH19 162 D3
St Peters CE (Aided) Primary School
FNM GU9 155 J2
St Peters CE Junior School
FARN GU14 92 F5
St Peters CE Primary School
OXTED RH8 129 K7
St Peters Primary School
SAND/SEL CR2 68 A5
St Peters RC Primary School
LHD/OX KT22 102 F2
St Philips School
CHSGTN KT9 63 G5
St Phillips Infant School
SYD SE26 32 E5
St Philomenas Catholic High School
CAR SM5 66 B4
St Piers Further Education College (NCYPE)
LING RH7 178 H6
St Piers School (NCYPE)
LING RH7 178 H5
St Polycarps Catholic Primary School
FNM GU9 5 L5
St Raphaels Hospice
WPK KT4 65 G1
St Richards with St Andrews CE Primary School
RCHPK/HAM TW10 26 E4
St Robert Southwell Primary School
HORS RH12 167 K3
St Stephens CE Junior School
TWK TW1 17 K8
St Stephens CE Primary School
GDST RH9 151 J3
St Teresas Preparatory School
EHSLY KT24 121 G2
St Teresas School
RDKG RH5 121 G6
St Thomas Becket RC Primary School
SNWD SE25 50 D6
St Thomas of Canterbury Catholic Primary School
GU GU1 117 L8
St Thomas of Canterbury Primary School
MTCM CR4 48 D3
St Walter & St John Sports Ground
TOOT SW17 30 B2
St Wilfrids RC School
CRAWW RH11 164 D5
St William of York Primary School
FSTH SE23 33 H1
Salesian College
CHERT KT16 40 D8
FARN GU14 93 G8
Salesian RC School
CHERT KT16 58 B1
Salfords Industrial Estate
REDH RH1 148 D8
REDH RH1 175 R1
Salfords Primary School
REDH RH1 148 D6
Sampson Business Park
CBLY GU15 72 E6
The Samuel Cody School
FARN GU14 112 E2
Sandcross Junior School
REIG RH2 147 J3
Sanderstead Junior School
SAND/SEL CR2 68 A7
Sandfield CP School
GU GU1 7 G5
Sandhurst School
SHST GU47 52 A8
Sandown Industrial Park
ESH/CLAY KT10 61 K1
Sandown Park Racecourse
ESH/CLAY KT10 61 L2
Sandown Sports Club & Ski Centre
ESH/CLAY KT10 61 L2
Sandringham Infant School
FRIM GU16 93 J2
Sandy Lane Primary School
BNFD RG42 34 F1
Satellite Business Village
CRAWE RH10 191 P3
Savill Garden (Windsor Great Park)
EGH TW20 20 B7
Saxon Business Centre
WIM/MER SW19 47 M2
Saxon CP School
SHPTN TW17 41 J5
Sayer Clinic
CROY/NA CR0 67 J3
Sayes Court Junior School
ADL/WDHM KT15 58 E4
Scott Broadwood CE Infant School
RDKG RH5 173 L11
Scott Broadwood School
RDKG RH5 188 D1
The Screen at Reigate
REIG RH2 125 K8
Screen Cinema
WOT/HER KT12 42 D8
Seaton House School
BELMT SM2 66 A8
Secombe Centre
SUT SM1 65 L5
Sedgehill School
CAT SE6 33 L6
Selhurst High School for Boys
CROY/NA CR0 50 A6
The Selhurst Medical Centre
SNWD SE25 50 B6
Sellincourt School
TOOT SW17 30 B7
Selsdon Community Centre
SAND/SEL CR2 68 E8
Selsdon High School
SAND/SEL CR2 69 G6
Selsdon Park Hotel & Golf Course
SAND/SEL CR2 88 F1
Selsdon Primary School
SAND/SEL CR2 68 F7
Selsdon Road Industrial Estate
SAND/SEL CR2 68 A6
Semaphore Tower
COB KT11 80 A7
Send CC
RPLY/SEND GU23 97 L6
Send CE Infant School
RPLY/SEND GU23 98 A6
Seymour First & Middle School
CRAWW RH11 164 D8
Shalford Infant School
RGUE GU4 139 H6
Shalford Mill (NT)
RGUE GU4 139 H5
Shannon Corner Retail Park
NWMAL KT3 46 D4
Shawfield Primary School
ASHV GU12 113 K6
Shawley Primary School
EPSOM KT18 84 F8
Sheen International School
MORT/ESHN SW14 19 H6
Sheen Lane Health Centre
MORT/ESHN SW14 18 F5
Sheen Lawn Tennis & Squash Club
MORT/ESHN SW14 18 F7
Sheen Mount Primary School
RCHPK/HAM TW10 18 E7
Sheen Sports Centre
MORT/ESHN SW14 19 H6
Shelley Primary School
HORS RH12 166 A6
Shepperton Business Park
SHPTN TW17 41 M5
Shepperton Health Centre
SHPTN TW17 41 L5
Shepperton Studios
SHPTN TW17 41 J3
Sheraton Skyline Hotel
HYS/HAR UB3 15 G2
Shere CE Infant School
SHGR GU5 141 K5
Sheringdale Primary School
WAND/EARL SW18 29 J2
Sherwood Park School
WLGTN SM6 67 G2
Sherwood School
MTCM CR4 48 F4
The Ship Hotel
WEY KT13 59 L2
Shirley Clinic
CROY/NA CR0 50 F8
Shirley High School
CROY/NA CR0 69 G2
Shirley Oaks Hospital
CROY/NA CR0 50 F7
Shirley Park Golf Club
CROY/NA CR0 68 E1
Shirley Wanderers RFC
WWKM BR4 69 M3
Shooting Star House (Childrens Hospice)
HPTN TW12 25 J7
Shortwood Infant School
STA TW18 22 E4
Shotfield Health Clinic
WLGTN SM6 66 E5
Shottermill Infant School
HASM GU27 198 A6
Shrewsbury House School
SURB KT6 63 G1
Silverglade Business Park
CHSGTN KT9 82 F2
Silvermere Golf Club
COB KT11 79 L3
Silver Wing Industrial Estate
CROY/NA CR0 67 J5

Singlegate Primary School
WIM/MER SW19 .... 30 A8
Sir Greville Sprat Stadium
RGODL GU7 .... 159 L3
Sir William Perkins School
CHERT KT16 .... 40 B8
The Sixth Form College
FARN GU14 .... 92 E2
Skimped Hill Health Centre
BRAK RG12 .... 34 E2
Sky Business Park
EGH TW20 .... 39 M2
Slinfold CE Primary School
SWTR RH13 .... 203 Q5
Slinfold Park Golf & Country
Club
SWTR RH13 .... 203 N7
Slyfield Industrial Estate
GU GU1 .... 117 G3
Smallberry Green Primary
School
ISLW TW7 .... 17 K4
Smallwood Primary School
TOOT SW17 .... 30 A5
Smitham Primary School
COUL/CHIP CR5 .... 86 F6
Smithbrook Clinic
CRAN GU6 .... 185 N2
Snowhill Business Centre
CRAWE RH10 .... 193 N1
Sofitel
HORL RH6 .... 160 C6
South Bookham School
GT/LBKH KT23 .... 121 M1
Southborough School
SURB KT6 .... 63 G6
South Croydon Medical Centre
SAND/SEL CR2 .... 67 M6
South Croydon Sports Club
CROY/NA CR0 .... 68 B4
Southern Clinic
REIG RH2 .... 147 M1
South Farnborough County
Junior School
FARN GU14 .... 93 G7
South Farnborough Infant
School
FARN GU14 .... 113 G1
South Farnham School
FNM GU9 .... 134 B8
Southfields Community
College
WAND/EARL SW18 .... 29 K2
Southfields Park Primary School
HOR/WEW KT19 .... 63 L8
Southgate Primary School
CRAWE RH10 .... 164 F6
South Hill Park Arts Centre
BRAK RG12 .... 34 C4
South Lewisham Health Centre
CAT SE6 .... 33 M5
South London Crematorium
MTCM CR4 .... 48 F2
South London Tamil School
CROY/NA CR0 .... 2 D1
South London Theatre
WNWD SE27 .... 31 M4
Southmead Primary School
WIM/MER SW19 .... 29 G7
South Norwood Country Park
SNWD SE25 .... 50 F4
South Norwood Hill Medical
Centre
SNWD SE25 .... 50 B2
South Norwood Medical
Centre
SNWD SE25 .... 50 B4
South Norwood Pools &
Fitness Centre
SNWD SE25 .... 50 D5
South Norwood Primary
School
SNWD SE25 .... 50 D4
South Nutfield CC
REDH RH1 .... 149 J2
South Park Hotel
SAND/SEL CR2 .... 68 B3
South Thames College
PUT/ROE SW15 .... 19 J8
TOOT SW17 .... 30 B6
Southville Community School
EBED/NFELT TW14 .... 24 C2
Southwark Sports Ground
DUL SE21 .... 32 C2
South West Middlesex
Crematorium
FELT TW13 .... 25 H2
South West Surrey Business
Centre
GU GU1 .... 7 H5
Southwood Golf Club
FARN GU14 .... 92 B7
Southwood Infant School
FARN GU14 .... 92 A6
Sparrow Farm Community
Junior School
EW KT17 .... 64 E4
Sparrow Farm Infant School
EBED/NFELT TW14 .... 24 F1
Sparrow Farm Junior School
EBED/NFELT TW14 .... 24 F1
Spelthorne Clinic
ASHF TW15 .... 24 A7
Spelthorne Infant School
ASHF TW15 .... 24 A7
Spelthorne Leisure Centre
STA TW18 .... 22 D6
Spelthorne Sixth Form College
ASHF TW15 .... 23 J5
Spelthorne Sports Club
ASHF TW15 .... 24 A8
Spitfire Business Park
CROY/NA CR0 .... 67 K5
Spring Copse Business Park
SWTR RH13 .... 203 N6
Springfield Christian School
CAT SE6 .... 33 J4
Springfield Hospital
TOOT SW17 .... 30 B4
Springfield Primary School
SUN TW16 .... 42 B1

Spring Grove Primary School
ISLW TW7 .... 17 G4
Springlake Country Club
ALDT GU11 .... 113 H5
Spring Park Primary School
CROY/NA CR0 .... 69 K2
Springwell Infant School
HEST TW5 .... 16 B2
Springwell Junior School
HEST TW5 .... 16 B2
Sprint Industrial Estate
BF/WBF KT14 .... 79 G1
Spurgeon's College
SNWD SE25 .... 50 B2
Squerrys Court Manor House
& Gardens
BH/WHM TN16 .... 131 M2
SS Peter & Paul RC Primary
School
MTCM CR4 .... 48 C4
Stafford Cross Business Park
CROY/NA CR0 .... 67 J4
Staines County Court
STA TW18 .... 22 D6
Staines Preparatory School
STA TW18 .... 22 D6
Staines RFC
FELT TW13 .... 24 D6
Staines Town FC
STA TW18 .... 22 D8
Stamford Green County
Primary School
HOR/WEW KT19 .... 83 L2
Stammerham Business
Centre
HORS RH12 .... 189 M6
Standen (NT)
EGRIN RH19 .... 194 E9
Stanford Primary School
STRHM/NOR SW16 .... 49 G1
Stanhill Court Hotel
HORL RH6 .... 174 F8
Stanley J & I School
TEDD TW11 .... 26 B5
Stanley Park High School
CAR SM5 .... 66 D5
Stanley Park Primary School
CAR SM5 .... 66 C6
Stanley Technical High School
SNWD SE25 .... 50 C3
Stanton Square Industrial
Estate
SYD SE26 .... 33 J5
Starborough Castle
EDEN TN8 .... 179 N4
Starhurst School
RDKG RH5 .... 144 F4
Stepgates Community School
CHERT KT16 .... 40 E7
The Stepping Stone School
GSHT GU26 .... 198 A2
Stewart Fleming Primary
School
PGE/AN SE20 .... 50 F3
Stirling Way Industrial Estates
CROY/NA CR0 .... 49 H7
Stoke Hill CP School
GU GU1 .... 116 F5
Stompond Lane Track
WOT/HER KT12 .... 60 D1
Stoneleigh First School
EW KT17 .... 64 E3
Stoughton County Junior
School
GUW GU2 .... 116 E5
Stowford College
BELMT SM2 .... 65 M6
Strand on the Green J & I
School
CHSWK W4 .... 18 D1
Strathmore School
RCHPK/HAM TW10 .... 27 G2
Strawberry Hill Golf Club
WHTN TW2 .... 26 B4
Streatham Cemetery
TOOT SW17 .... 30 B4
Streatham & Clapham High
School (Junior Department)
BRXS/STRHM SW2 .... 31 J2
Streatham & Clapham High
School (Senior Department)
STRHM/NOR SW16 .... 30 F4
Streatham & Croydon RFC
THHTH CR7 .... 49 K5
Streatham Ice Rink
STRHM/NOR SW16 .... 31 H6
Streatham Leisure Centre
STRHM/NOR SW16 .... 31 H3
Streatham Modern School
STRHM/NOR SW16 .... 31 H7
Streatham Park Cemetery
MTCM CR4 .... 48 F2
Streatham Swimming Pool
STRHM/NOR SW16 .... 31 H6
Streatham Vale Sports Club
STRHM/NOR SW16 .... 30 F8
Streatham Wells Primary
School
BRXS/STRHM SW2 .... 31 J3
Streete Court School
GDST RH9 .... 129 H4
Strodes College
EGH TW20 .... 21 J6
Stubbs Industrial Estate
ALDT GU11 .... 113 H4
Studholme Medical Centre
ASHF TW15 .... 23 J5
The Study Preparatory School
WIM/MER SW19 .... 29 G6
The Study School
NWMAL KT3 .... 46 B5
Sturt Priory Hospital
KWD/TDW/WH KT20 .... 104 D8
Summit Business Park
SUN TW16 .... 24 D8
Sunbury Business Centre
SUN TW16 .... 42 B1

Sunbury Health Centre
SUN TW16 .... 42 D2
Sunbury Leisure Centre
SUN TW16 .... 42 C1
Sunbury Manor School
SUN TW16 .... 42 C1
Sun Life Trading Estate
EBED/NFELT TW14 .... 15 K5
Sunningdale Golf Club
ASC SL5 .... 37 K8
Sunningdale Ladies Golf Club
ASC SL5 .... 37 J8
Sunningdale School
ASC SL5 .... 37 H6
Sunnydown School
CTHM CR3 .... 108 C3
Sunnyhill Primary School
STRHM/NOR SW16 .... 31 J5
Surbiton Business Centre
SURB KT6 .... 45 G6
Surbiton Cemetery
KUT/HW KT1 .... 45 K4
Surbiton Golf Club
CHSGTN KT9 .... 62 E3
Surbiton High School
KUT/HW KT1 .... 45 H4
Surbiton Hospital
SURB KT6 .... 45 H6
Surbiton Natural Health Centre
SURB KT6 .... 45 H6
Surex Swimming Pools
BH/WHM TN16 .... 91 G5
Surrey Business Park
EW KT17 .... 84 B1
Surrey County Hall
KUT/HW KT1 .... 8 D9
Surrey Downs Golf Club
KWD/TDW/WH KT20 .... 105 M4
Surrey Heath Museum
CBLY GU15 .... 73 G3
Surrey History Centre
WOKN/KNAP GU21 .... 10 A7
Surrey Institute of Art & Design
FNM GU9 .... 5 G3
HOR/WEW KT19 .... 84 B2
Surrey National Golf Club
CTHM CR3 .... 107 L5
Surrey Probation Service
GU GU1 .... 6 F5
The Surrey & Sussex
Crematorium
CRAWE RH10 .... 192 C2
Surrey Welfare Court Service
GU GU1 .... 6 F6
Sussex Manor Business Park
CRAWE RH10 .... 191 R3
Sutton Alternative Health
Centre
SUT SM1 .... 65 L4
Sutton Arena
CAR SM5 .... 48 A7
Sutton Bowling Club
BELMT SM2 .... 65 K7
Sutton Cemetery
CHEAM SM3 .... 65 J1
Sutton Civic Centre
SUT SM1 .... 65 L4
Sutton College of Learning
for Adults
SUT SM1 .... 65 L4
Sutton General Hospital
BELMT SM2 .... 65 L8
Sutton Grammar School
for Boys
SUT SM1 .... 65 M4
Sutton Green Golf Club
WOKS/MYFD GU22 .... 97 H4
Sutton High Junior School
SUT SM1 .... 65 L5
Sutton High School for Girls
GDST
SUT SM1 .... 65 K5
Sutton Superbowl
SUT SM1 .... 65 L4
Sutton United FC
SUT SM1 .... 65 K3
Sutton West Centre
SUT SM1 .... 65 K4
The Swan Centre
LHD/OX KT22 .... 102 E3
The Swan Inn Hotel
MFD/CHID GU8 .... 199 R2
Swansmere School
WOT/HER KT12 .... 42 F8
Swan Walk Shopping Centre
HORS RH12 .... 166 F7
Swedish School
BARN SW13 .... 19 K1
Swinley CP School
CRAWE RH10 .... 165 H6
Swinley Forest Golf Club
ASC SL5 .... 36 D5
Sydenham Girls School
ASC SL5 .... 36 C7
Sydenham Girls School
SYD SE26 .... 32 E4
Sydenham High Junior School
SYD SE26 .... 32 E5
Sydenham High Senior School
SYD SE26 .... 32 E6
Sydenham High School Sports
Ground
CAT SE6 .... 33 K6
Syon House
BTFD TW8 .... 17 M3
Syon Park
BTFD TW8 .... 17 M4
Syon Park School
ISLW TW7 .... 17 L3
Sythwood Primary School
WOKN/KNAP GU21 .... 76 E6
Taberner House
CROY/NA CR0 .... 2 D7
TA Centre
CHERT KT16 .... 40 D7
HORS RH12 .... 166 F7
Tadworth Primary School
KWD/TDW/WH KT20 .... 105 G4
Tait Road Industrial Estate
CROY/NA CR0 .... 3 G1
Talavera Junior School
ALDT GU11 .... 112 D6

Tamian Industrial Estate
HSLWW TW4 .... 15 M6
Tamworth Manor High School
STRHM/NOR SW16 .... 49 G3
Tanbridge House School
HORS RH12 .... 166 C7
Tanbridge Retail Park
HORS RH12 .... 166 E7
Tandem Centre
WIM/MER SW19 .... 48 A1
Tandridge Golf Club
OXTED RH8 .... 129 M5
Tasis the American School
in England
EGH TW20 .... 39 M7
Tatsfield Primary School
BH/WHM TN16 .... 111 G3
Tattenham Health Centre
EPSOM KT18 .... 84 C8
TAVR Centre
KUT/HW KT1 .... 45 G2
Teddington Business Park
TEDD TW11 .... 26 C6
Teddington Cemetery
TEDD TW11 .... 26 B7
Teddington Clinic
TEDD TW11 .... 26 B7
Teddington Lock
TEDD TW11 .... 26 E5
Teddington Memorial Hospital
TEDD TW11 .... 26 B7
Teddington Pool & Fitness
Centre
TEDD TW11 .... 26 D6
Teddington School
TEDD TW11 .... 8 C1
The Teddington Theatre Club
E/WMO/HCT KT8 .... 44 A5
Telferscot Primary School
BAL SW12 .... 30 F2
Temperate House
RCH/KEW TW9 .... 18 C4
Thames Ditton & Esher Golf Club
ESH/CLAY KT10 .... 61 G2
Thames Ditton Infant School
THDIT KT7 .... 44 C6
Thames Ditton Junior School
THDIT KT7 .... 44 C7
Thamesmead School
SHPTN TW17 .... 42 M4
Thatched House Hotel
SUT SM1 .... 65 J5
Theatre Centre
BECK BR3 .... 51 L2
Theatre Magenta
LHD/OX KT22 .... 102 D1
Theatre of the Dispossessed
WIM/MER SW19 .... 29 G2
The Theatre on the Hill
CTHM CR3 .... 108 B4
Therapia Trading Estate
CROY/NA CR0 .... 49 G7
Therfield School
LHD/OX KT22 .... 102 D1
Thistle Hotel
HORL RH6 .... 160 D1
WDR/YW UB7 .... 13 M3
Thomas Bennett Community
College
CRAWE RH10 .... 164 F7
Thomas More Catholic School
PUR/KEN CR8 .... 67 J8
Thornchace School
GU GU1 .... 117 M8
Thorncroft Manor
LHD/OX KT22 .... 102 D5
Thornton Heath Health Centre
THHTH CR7 .... 49 M4
Thornton Heath Pools &
Fitness Centre
THHTH CR7 .... 49 M4
Thornton Road Industrial Estate
CROY/NA CR0 .... 49 H6
Thorpe CC
EGH TW20 .... 39 L4
Thorpe CE Infant School
EGH TW20 .... 39 M3
Thorpe Industrial Park
EGH TW20 .... 40 A1
Thorpe Lea Primary School
EGH TW20 .... 22 A7
Thorpe Park
CHERT KT16 .... 40 B4
Three Bridges Community
Centre
CRAWE RH10 .... 165 J4
Three Bridges CC
CRAWE RH10 .... 165 J4
Three Bridges FC
CRAWE RH10 .... 165 J4
Three Bridges First School
CRAWE RH10 .... 165 J3
Three Bridges Junior School
CRAWE RH10 .... 165 J4
Three Counties Education Trust
RFNM GU10 .... 156 A3
Tiffin Girls School
KUTN/CMB KT2 .... 27 H7
Tiffin School & Sports Centre
KUTN/CMB KT2 .... 9 G6
Tilgate Forest Business
Centre
CRAWW RH11 .... 191 N12
Tilgate Forest Golf Centre
CRAWE RH10 .... 165 J8
Tilgate Park
CRAWE RH10 .... 191 Q12
Tillingbourne Junior School
RGUE GU4 .... 139 L7
Times Square Shopping Centre
SUT SM1 .... 65 L4
Tobias School of Art
EGRIN RH19 .... 162 D7
Tollgate Primary School
CROY/NA CR0 .... 50 F6
Tolworth CP School
SURB KT6 .... 45 J8
Tolworth Girls School
SURB KT6 .... 63 J2
Tolworth Recreation Centre
SURB KT6 .... 63 J2

Tomlinscote School &
Sixth Form College
FRIM GU16 .... 73 J7
Tooting Bec Athletics Track
TOOT SW17 .... 30 E5
Tooting Leisure Centre
TOOT SW17 .... 30 A5
Tooting & Mitcham United
Football Club
MTCM CR4 .... 48 D1
Tormead School
GU GU1 .... 7 M3
Tower Hill Primary School
FARN GU14 .... 92 C6
Tower House School
MORT/ESHN SW14 .... 18 F6
Tower Industrial Estate
SNWD SE25 .... 50 D4
Town Farm Primary School
STWL/WRAY TW19 .... 23 G1
Toyhorse International
Stud Farm
BIL RH14 .... 202 H5
Traditions Golf Club
WOKS/MYFD GU22 .... 78 D5
Trafalgar Community Infant
School
HORS RH12 .... 166 E5
Trafalgar Primary & Infant
School
WHTN TW2 .... 26 A3
Travelodge
BRAK RG12 .... 34 A1
BTFD TW8 .... 18 B1
DORK RH4 .... 144 F1
GU GU1 .... 6 E2
HEST TW5 .... 15 M1
HEST TW5 .... 16 B1
HORL RH6 .... 175 P12
KUTN/CMB KT2 .... 9 F6
LHD/OX KT22 .... 102 D4
LIPH GU30 .... 196 E8
STA TW18 .... 22 B5
The Treaty Centre
HSLW TW3 .... 16 E5
Trefoil Montessori School
of Arts
LING RH7 .... 177 Q1
Trident Business Centre
TOOT SW17 .... 30 C6
Trident Industrial Estate
DTCH/LGLY SL3 .... 13 H5
Trinity St Marys Primary School
BAL SW12 .... 30 D2
Trinity School
CROY/NA CR0 .... 68 F1
Trumps Green Infant School
VW GU25 .... 39 G6
Tudor Lodge
PUR/KEN CR8 .... 67 H8
Tudor Lodge Health Centre
WIM/MER SW19 .... 29 G1
Tudors Business Centre
KWD/TDW/WH KT20 .... 105 J4
Turners Hill CE Primary School
CRAWE RH10 .... 193 M10
Turney School
DUL SE21 .... 31 M1
Tweeddale Primary School
CAR SM5 .... 48 A7
Twickenham Cemetery
WHTN TW2 .... 25 L2
Twickenham Park Health
Centre
TWK TW1 .... 17 M8
Twickenham Preparatory
School
HPTN TW12 .... 43 L1
Twickenham Stadium
ISLW TW7 .... 17 H8
Twickenham Trading Estate
TWK TW1 .... 17 J8
Two Bridges Business Park
SAND/SEL CR2 .... 68 A5
Two Rivers Retail Park
STA TW18 .... 22 B5
Tyrrells Wood Golf Club
LHD/OX KT22 .... 103 J6
UCI Cinema
SUT SM1 .... 65 L4
UGC Cinema
CRAWE RH10 .... 164 F3
The Ullswater Business Park
COUL/CHIP CR5 .... 87 H6
Ullswater Trading Estate
COUL/CHIP CR5 .... 87 H6
Unicorn Primary School
BECK BR3 .... 51 L5
Unicorn School
RCH/KEW TW9 .... 18 C3
Unicorn Trading Estate
HASM GU27 .... 198 C6
United Services Sports Ground
CHSWK W4 .... 19 H3
University College for the
Creative Arts at Epsom
EPSOM KT18 .... 84 A4
University of London Athletics
Ground
NWMAL KT3 .... 46 D5
The University of Surrey
GUW GU2 .... 6 B3
University of Westminster
CHSWK W4 .... 18 F3
University Vandals RFC
SHPTN TW17 .... 41 M7
Upper Tooting Independent
High School
TOOT SW17 .... 30 B3
Ursuline High School
RYNPK SW20 .... 29 G8
Ursuline Preparatory School
RYNPK SW20 .... 29 G8
The Vale Medical Centre
FSTH SE23 .... 33 H3
Vale Primary School
EPSOM KT18 .... 104 A1
Valley End CC
CHOB/PIR GU24 .... 55 K6
Valley End CE Infant School
CHOB/PIR GU24 .... 55 K5

The Valley Gardens
ECH TW20 .... 38 C2

Vestry Hall
MTCM CR4 .... 48 C3

Vicarage Lane Clinic
HASM GU27 .... 198 A7

Victoria Clinic
WOKN/KNAP GU21 .... 10 E4

Victoria Junior School
FELT TW13 .... 24 E2

Victor Seymour Infant School
CAR SM5 .... 66 C2

Victory Business Centre
ISLW TW7 .... 17 J6

The Vine Clinic
KUTN/CMB KT2 .... 8 E1

Vine Medical Centre
E/WMO/HCT KT8 .... 43 M3

The Vineyard Primary School
RCHPK/HAM TW10 .... 18 B8

Virgo Fidelis Convent Schools
NRWD SE19 .... 31 M7

Viscount Industrial Estate
DTCH/LGLY SL3 .... 13 H5

VUE Cinema
CROY/NA CR0 .... 67 J1
STA TW18 .... 22 C5

Vulcan Business Centre
CROY/NA CR0 .... 70 B7

Waddon Clinic
CROY/NA CR0 .... 67 K4

Waddon Infant School
CROY/NA CR0 .... 67 K4

The Waldegrave Clinic
TEDD TW11 .... 26 C6

Waldegrave Girls School
WHTN TW2 .... 26 A4

Waldorf School of SW London
STRHM/NOR SW16 .... 30 F3

Wallace Fields County Infant School
EW KT17 .... 84 D3

Wallace Fields Junior School
EW KT17 .... 84 D2

Wallbrook Business Centre
HSLWW TW4 .... 15 L5

Wallington County Grammar School
WLGTN SM6 .... 66 E2

Wallington High School for Girls
WLGTN SM6 .... 66 E7

Walsh Memorial CE Infant School
ASHV GU12 .... 113 J8

Walton Business Centre
WOT/HER KT12 .... 42 E7

Walton Casuals FC
WOT/HER KT12 .... 42 E5

Walton Community Hospital
WOT/HER KT12 .... 60 E1

Walton Heath Golf Club Shop
KWD/TDW/WH KT20 .... 104 E2

Walton & Hersham FC
WOT/HER KT12 .... 60 D1

Walton Leigh School
WOT/HER KT12 .... 60 B3

Walton-on-thames CC
WOT/HER KT12 .... 42 C8

Walton on the Hill CE Junior School
KWD/TDW/WH KT20 .... 104 D7

Walton on the Hill Primary School
KWD/TDW/WH KT20 .... 104 E6

Walton Swimming Pool
WOT/HER KT12 .... 42 E8

Wandle Trading Estate
MTCM CR4 .... 48 C8

Wandle Valley School
CAR SM5 .... 48 B7

Wandsworth Adult College
TOOT SW17 .... 30 B3

Wandsworth Cemetery
WAND/EARL SW18 .... 29 M2

Wandsworth Trading Estate
WAND/EARL SW18 .... 29 L1

Warehouse Theatre
CROY/NA CR0 .... 2 E6

Warlingham Park School
WARL CR6 .... 89 K6

Warlingham RFC & John Fisher Sports Club
WARL CR6 .... 88 E6

Warlingham School
WARL CR6 .... 88 E6

Warlingham Sports Club
WARL CR6 .... 89 G7

War Memorial Sports Ground
SUT SM1 .... 66 B3

Warnham CE Primary School
HORS RH12 .... 166 C1

Warren Mead Infant School
BNSTD SM7 .... 84 F5

Warren Mead Junior School
BNSTD SM7 .... 85 G5

Warwick Quadrant & Harlequin Theatre, Cinema & Library
REDH RH1 .... 126 D7

The Warwick School
REDH RH1 .... 126 E7

The Watchetts Junior School
CBLY GU15 .... 72 F7

Waterfield First School
CRAWW RH11 .... 164 A6

Watergate School
CAT SE6 .... 33 L6

Watermans Arts, Cinema & Theatre Centre
BTFD TW8 .... 18 B1

Watermans Business Park
STA TW18 .... 22 B5

Watermeads High School
MRDN SM4 .... 48 A6

Watermill Museum
EDEN TN8 .... 179 L1

Waterside Business Centre
ISLW TW7 .... 17 L6

Waterside Trading Estate
ADL/WDHM KT15 .... 59 H3

Wattenden Primary School
PUR/KEN CR8 .... 87 L7

Wattlehurst Farm
HORS RH12 .... 188 H6

The Watts Gallery
RGUW GU3 .... 137 L6

The Wavell School
ALDT GU11 .... 112 E2

Waverley Abbey CE School
RFNM GU10 .... 156 F4

Waverley Abbey House
FNM GU9 .... 156 E1

The Weald CE Primary School
RDKG RH5 .... 173 L6

Wellington Primary School
HSLW TW3 .... 16 C4

Wellington Shopping Centre
ALDT GU11 .... 112 D7

Wentworth Golf Club
VW GU25 .... 38 D5

West Ashtead Primary School
ASHTD KT21 .... 103 G2

Westbourne Primary School
SUT SM1 .... 65 K2

West Byfleet Golf Club
BF/WBF KT14 .... 78 C3

West Byfleet Health Centre
BF/WBF KT14 .... 78 D3

West Byfleet Physiotherapy Clinic
BF/WBF KT14 .... 78 D2

West Byfleet Primary School
BF/WBF KT14 .... 78 E2

Westcott CE First School
DORK RH4 .... 143 M3

Westcroft Leisure Centre
CAR SM5 .... 66 D3

West Dene School
PUR/KEN CR8 .... 87 J3

Westend County Infant School
ALDT GU11 .... 112 C8

West End Sports & Social Club
ESH/CLAY KT10 .... 61 J5

West Ewell Infant School
HOR/WEW KT19 .... 64 A4

Westfield Primary School
WOKS/MYFD GU22 .... 97 H3

Westfields Primary School
BARN SW13 .... 19 J4

West Green First School
CRAWW RH11 .... 164 E4

West Hill Golf Club
CHOB/PIR GU24 .... 95 L3

West Hill School
LHD/OX KT22 .... 82 D8

West Kent Golf Club
ORP BR6 .... 91 H2

West Middlesex University Hospital
ISLW TW7 .... 17 K4

Westmoor Community Clinic
PUT/ROE SW15 .... 28 D1

West Norwood Clinic
WNWD SE27 .... 31 M3

West Norwood Crematorium
WNWD SE27 .... 31 M4

Weston Green School
THDIT KT7 .... 44 B8

West Park Hospital
EPSOM KT18 .... 83 H2

West Ramp Coach Park
HTHAIR TW6 .... 14 D3

West Surrey Golf Club
MFD/CHID GU8 .... 183 Q3

West Thames College
ISLW TW7 .... 17 H3

West Thornton Primary School
CROY/NA CR0 .... 49 J7

Westward Preparatory School
WOT/HER KT12 .... 60 E1

The Westway Clinic
REDH RH1 .... 126 B7

West Wickham Swimming Baths
WWKM BR4 .... 51 M8

West Wimbledon Primary School
RYNPK SW20 .... 46 E3

Westwood Language College for Girls
NRWD SE19 .... 31 M8

Weybourne County Infant School
FNM GU9 .... 134 B3

Weybridge Business Park
ADL/WDHM KT15 .... 59 H3

Weybridge CC
WEY KT13 .... 60 B1

Weybridge Hospital & Primary Care Centre
WEY KT13 .... 59 K3

Weydon County Secondary School
RFNM GU10 .... 4 D9

Weydown Industrial Estate
HASM GU27 .... 198 D6

Weyfield Primary School
GU GU1 .... 117 G5

Weyford Infant School
BOR GU35 .... 196 A1

Weyford Junior School
BOR GU35 .... 196 A1

Wey House School
SHGR GU5 .... 168 H1

Wey Retail Park
BF/WBF KT14 .... 79 H2

The Wheatsheaf Hotel
VW GU25 .... 38 C3

White Hart Industrial Estate
BLKW GU17 .... 72 B4

Whitehill Cemetery
BOR GU35 .... 196 B2

Whitehorse Manor Primary School
THHTH CR7 .... 50 A5

The White House Preparatory School
BAL SW12 .... 31 G2

Whitelands College
PUT/ROE SW15 .... 28 C1

Whitgift School
SAND/SEL CR2 .... 67 M4

Whitgift Shopping Centre
CROY/NA CR0 .... 2 D5

Whitton Health Centre
WHTN TW2 .... 25 M2

Whitton Health Clinic
WHTN TW2 .... 25 L2

Whitton School
WHTN TW2 .... 25 L3

Whitton Sports & Fitness Centre
WHTN TW2 .... 25 L3

Whyteleafe Business Village
CTHM CR3 .... 88 C7

Whyteleafe FC
CTHM CR3 .... 108 C1

Whyteleafe School
CTHM CR3 .... 88 C8

Wickham Court School
WWKM BR4 .... 70 A3

Wickham Theatre
WWKM BR4 .... 70 A2

Wide Way Health Clinic
MTCM CR4 .... 49 G3

Wildridings CP School
BRAK RG12 .... 34 D4

The Wildwood Golf Club
CRAN GU6 .... 185 R11

William Byrd School
HYS/HAR UB3 .... 14 F1

William Cobbett Junior School
FNM GU9 .... 134 B3

William Hogarth School
CHSWK W4 .... 19 H1

William Morris Primary School
MTCM CR4 .... 49 G3

Willington School
WIM/MER SW19 .... 29 J7

Willow Business Centre
MTCM CR4 .... 48 C5

Willow Business Park
SYD SE26 .... 32 F4

Wilson's School
WLGTN SM6 .... 67 H5

Wimbledon Chase Primary School
RYNPK SW20 .... 47 H1

Wimbledon Common Golf Club
WIM/MER SW19 .... 28 E6

Wimbledon Common Pre-preparatory School
WIM/MER SW19 .... 28 F7

Wimbledon (Gap Road) Cemetery
WIM/MER SW19 .... 29 L5

Wimbledon High School
WIM/MER SW19 .... 29 H7

Wimbledon House School
WIM/MER SW19 .... 47 H1

Wimbledon Lawn Tennis Museum
WIM/MER SW19 .... 29 H4

Wimbledon Magistrates Court
WIM/MER SW19 .... 29 K7

Wimbledon Park Athletics Track
WIM/MER SW19 .... 29 J3

Wimbledon Park Golf Club
WIM/MER SW19 .... 29 J4

Wimbledon Park Primary School
WIM/MER SW19 .... 29 K3

Wimbledon Recreation Centre
WIM/MER SW19 .... 29 L7

Wimbledon RFC
RYNPK SW20 .... 28 C8

Wimbledon School of Art
WIM/MER SW19 .... 29 K8
WIM/MER SW19 .... 47 H1

Wimbledon Squash & Badminton Club
WIM/MER SW19 .... 29 H8

Wimbledon Stadium
WIM/MER SW19 .... 29 L5

Wimbledon Stadium Business Centre
WIM/MER SW19 .... 29 L4

Wimbledon Theatre
WIM/MER SW19 .... 29 K8

Windlemere Golf Club
CHOB/PIR GU24 .... 75 H1

Windlesham Golf Club
BAGS GU19 .... 54 C5

Windlesham Village Infant School
BFOR GU20 .... 54 D3

Windmill Trading Estate
MTCM CR4 .... 48 F5
SUN TW16 .... 42 A1

Winkworth Arboretum (NT)
MFD/CHID GU8 .... 168 F11

The Winston Churchill School
WOKN/KNAP GU21 .... 76 B8

Winterbourne Infant School
THHTH CR7 .... 49 K4

Wishmore Cross School
CHOB/PIR GU24 .... 56 B8

Wispers School
HASM GU27 .... 198 D4

Witley CE Controlled Infant School
MFD/CHID GU8 .... 183 N5

Witley Common (NT)
MFD/CHID GU8 .... 183 K3

Woking Athletics Track
WOKN/KNAP GU21 .... 77 M3

Woking Business Park
WOKN/KNAP GU21 .... 11 K2

Woking College
WOKS/MYFD GU22 .... 97 K2

Woking Community Hospital
WOKS/MYFD GU22 .... 10 E7

Woking FC
WOKS/MYFD GU22 .... 97 J2

Woking Golf Club
WOKS/MYFD GU22 .... 96 D2

Woking High School
WOKN/KNAP GU21 .... 10 A1

Woking & Horsell CC
WOKN/KNAP GU21 .... 10 A5

Woking Hospice
WOKS/MYFD GU22 .... 10 E7

Woking Leisure Centre
WOKS/MYFD GU22 .... 10 E9

Woking Nuffield Hospital
WOKN/KNAP GU21 .... 77 H4

Woking St John's Crematorium
WOKN/KNAP GU21 .... 96 B1

Woldingham Golf Club
CTHM CR3 .... 109 G2

Woldingham School
CTHM CR3 .... 109 H7

Wolfson Medical Centre
RYNPK SW20 .... 28 D8

Wolsey Junior School
CROY/NA CR0 .... 70 A6

Wolsey Place Shopping Centre
WOKN/KNAP GU21 .... 10 D5

Wonersh & Shamley Green CE Infant School
SHGR GU5 .... 169 N4

Woodbridge Business Park
GU GU1 .... 6 E2

Woodbrook School
BECK BR3 .... 51 J1

Woodcote High School
PUR/KEN CR8 .... 87 G3

Woodcote House School
BFOR GU20 .... 54 E4

Woodcote Park Golf Club
COUL/CHIP CR5 .... 86 F4

Woodcotes Primary School
COUL/CHIP CR5 .... 87 G4

Wooden Hill Primary School
BRAK RG12 .... 34 B7

Woodfield School
REDH RH1 .... 127 H3

Woodlands Park Hotel
COB KT11 .... 81 M7

Woodlands School
LHD/OX KT22 .... 102 F4

Woodlea Primary School
CTHM CR3 .... 109 J4

Woodmansterne Primary School
BNSTD SM7 .... 86 C4
STRHM/NOR SW16 .... 49 G1

Woodmansterne Sports Club
BNSTD SM7 .... 86 B5

Woodside Health Centre
SNWD SE25 .... 50 E5

Woodside Infants School
CROY/NA CR0 .... 3 L1

Wood Street County Infant School
RGUW GU3 .... 115 M6

Woodville Junior School
LHD/OX KT22 .... 102 E2

Woolmer Hill Athletics Track
HASM GU27 .... 197 Q5

Woolmer Hill Technology College
HASM GU27 .... 197 Q6

World Business Centre Heathrow
HTHAIR TW6 .... 14 F3

Worple Primary School
ISLW TW7 .... 17 K6

Worplesdon CP School
RGUW GU3 .... 116 A4

Worplesdon Golf Club
WOKS/MYFD GU22 .... 96 B4

Worsley Bridge Junior School
BECK BR3 .... 33 K8

Worth School
CRAWE RH10 .... 192 G12

Worton Hall Industrial Estate
ISLW TW7 .... 17 H6

Wray Common County Middle School
REIG RH2 .... 126 A7

Wray Common Primary School
REIG RH2 .... 126 A7

Wraysbury Medical Centre
STWL/WRAY TW19 .... 12 C8

Wraysbury Primary School
STWL/WRAY TW19 .... 12 B8

Wrencote
CROY/NA CR0 .... 2 D8

Wyke CP School
RGUW GU3 .... 114 C5

Wyke Green Golf Club
ISLW TW7 .... 17 J1

Yattendon School
HORL RH6 .... 160 D2

Yehudi Menuhin School
COB KT11 .... 101 K1

YMCA Community & Sports Centre
REDH RH1 .... 148 D3

York Clinic
WOKN/KNAP GU21 .... 10 D6

York House Medical Centre
WOKS/MYFD GU22 .... 10 E7

York Town Industrial Estate
CBLY GU15 .... 72 D4

Yvonne Arnaud Theatre
GU GU1 .... 7 G8

Zennor Road Industrial Estate
BAL SW12 .... 30 F2

Acknowledgements

Schools address data provided by Education Direct.

Petrol station information supplied by Johnsons

One-way street data provided by © Tele Atlas N.V. Tele Atlas

Garden centre information provided by

Garden Centre Association  Britains best garden centres

Wyevale Garden Centres

The statement on the front cover of this atlas is sourced, selected and quoted from a reader comment and feedback form received in 2004